The Routledge Handbook of Vocabulary Studies

The Routledge Handbook of Vocabulary Studies provides a cutting-edge survey of current scholarship in this area. Divided into four sections, which cover understanding vocabulary; approaches to teaching and learning vocabulary; measuring knowledge of vocabulary; and key issues in teaching, researching, and measuring vocabulary, this *Handbook*:

- brings together a wide range of approaches to learning words to provide clarity on how best vocabulary might be taught and learned;
- provides a comprehensive discussion of the key issues and challenges in vocabulary studies, with research taken from the past 40 years;
- includes chapters on both formulaic language as well as single-word items;
- features original contributions from a range of internationally renowned scholars as well as academics at the forefront of innovative research.

The Routledge Handbook of Vocabulary Studies is an essential text for those interested in teaching, learning, and researching vocabulary.

Stuart Webb is Professor of Applied Linguistics at the University of Western Ontario, Canada. His research interests include vocabulary studies, extensive reading and listening, and language learning through watching television.

Routledge Handbooks in Linguistics

Routledge Handbooks in Linguistics provide overviews of a whole subject area or sub-discipline in linguistics, and survey the state of the discipline including emerging and cutting-edge areas. Edited by leading scholars, these volumes include contributions from key academics from around the world and are essential reading for both advanced under-graduate and postgraduate students.

The Routledge Handbook of Language and Humor
Edited by Salvatore Attardo

The Routledge Handbook of Language and Dialogue
Edited by Edda Weigand

The Routledge Handbook of Language and Politics
Edited by Ruth Wodak and Bernhard Forchtner

The Routledge Handbook of Language and Media
Edited by Daniel Perrin and Colleen Cotter

The Routledge Handbook of Ecolinguistics
Edited by Alwin F. Fill and Hermine Penz

The Routledge Handbook of Lexicography
Edited by Pedro A. Fuertes-Olivera

The Routledge Handbook of Discourse Processes, Second Edition
Edited by Michael F. Schober, David N. Rapp, and M. Anne Britt

The Routledge Handbook of Phonetics
Edited by William F. Katz and Peter F. Assmann

The Routledge Handbook of Vocabulary Studies
Edited by Stuart Webb

Further titles in this series can be found online at www.routledge.com/series/RHIL

The Routledge Handbook of Vocabulary Studies

Edited by Stuart Webb

Routledge
Taylor & Francis Group

LONDON AND NEW YORK

First published 2020
by Routledge
2 Park Square, Milton Park, Abingdon, Oxon OX14 4RN

and by Routledge
605 Third Avenue, New York, NY 10017

First issued in paperback 2022

Routledge is an imprint of the Taylor & Francis Group, an informa business

Publisher's Note
The publisher has gone to great lengths to ensure the quality of this reprint but points out that some imperfections in the original copies may be apparent.

British Library Cataloguing-in-Publication Data
A catalogue record for this book is available from the British Library

Library of Congress Cataloging-in-Publication Data
A catalog record for this book has been requested

ISBN: 978-1-03-240127-0 (pbk)
ISBN: 978-1-138-73572-9 (hbk)
ISBN: 978-0-429-29158-6 (ebk)

DOI: 10.4324/9780429291586

Typeset in Times New Roman
by Apex CoVantage, LLC

For Machiko, without whose support this volume would not have been possible.

Contents

Contents

Contents

Figures

Tables

Tables

Contributors

Laurence Anthony is Professor of Applied Linguistics at the Faculty of Science and Engineering, Waseda University, Japan. He is a former director and current program coordinator of the Center for English Language Education in Science and Engineering (CELESE). His main interests are in corpus linguistics, educational technology, and English for Specific Purposes (ESP) program design and teaching methodologies.

Oliver Ballance is a teacher-researcher working on English for Specific Purposes programs at Victoria University of Wellington, New Zealand. Oliver's academic work explores how language technologies can be used to support second language acquisition and development in professional and academic contexts.

Joe Barcroft is Professor of Spanish and Second Language Acquisition and Affiliate Professor of Psychological & Brain Sciences at Washington University in St Louis, USA. His research focuses on second language vocabulary learning, input processing, the bilingual mental lexicon, and psycholinguistic approaches to issues in second language acquisition.

Frank Boers is Professor at the University of Western Ontario, Canada. His early publications were in the field of lexicology, with a focus on polysemy and metaphor. His more recent interests, however, stem from his extensive experience as an EFL teacher. He now publishes mostly about L2 instructional methods.

Tom Cobb pioneered language learning technologies for reading and vocabulary development in many ESL lands in the 1980s and 1990s. He now lives and works in Montreal, Canada, teaching courses at a French-speaking university and conducting research in technology development and applied linguistics. Tom's Compleat Lexical Tutor website (www.lextutor.ca) provides teachers with tools to support language instruction.

Kathy Conklin is Full Professor in Psycholinguistics at the University of Nottingham, UK. A major focus of her research is on the application of psycholinguistic methods to the exploration of lexical and formulaic language processing in a first and second language. Her work has appeared in *Applied Linguistics*, *Brain and Language*, *Bilingualism: Language and Cognition*, and *Second Language Research*.

Averil Coxhead teaches undergraduate and postgraduate courses in applied linguistics and TESOL in the School of Linguistics and Applied Language Studies, Victoria University of

Wellington, Aotearoa/New Zealand. She is the author of *Vocabulary and English for Specific Purposes Research* (2018; Routledge). Her current research includes specialized vocabulary in spoken and written English and other languages.

Thi Ngoc Yen Dang is Lecturer at the University of Leeds, UK. She obtained her PhD from Victoria University of Wellington, New Zealand. Her research interests include vocabulary studies and corpus linguistics. Her articles have been published in *Language Learning*, *English for Specific Purposes*, *Journal of English for Academic Purposes*, and *ITL – International Journal of Applied Linguistics*.

Brigitta Dóczi teaches at the Department of English Applied Linguistics of Eötvös Loránd University in Budapest, Hungary, where she offers courses in vocabulary research, business English, pedagogical grammar, and pedagogical phonology. Her research interests are second language vocabulary development as well as task-based teaching. Recently, she has been doing research comparing the mental lexicon of teacher trainees and translator trainees.

Aline Godfroid is Associate Professor in Second Language Studies at Michigan State University, USA. Her primary research interests are in second language psycholinguistics, the teaching and learning of vocabulary, and quantitative research methodology. She co-directs the Second Language Studies Eye-Tracking Lab at Michigan State University.

Peter Yongqi Gu is Associate Professor at the School of Linguistics and Applied Language Studies, Victoria University of Wellington, New Zealand. His main research interests fall under learner autonomy and learning strategies, vocabulary acquisition, and language assessment.

Henrik Gyllstad is Associate Professor of English Linguistics at the Centre for Languages and Literature, Lund University, Sweden. His research interests include language testing, second language acquisition, and multilingualism, especially to do with vocabulary, phraseology, and lexical processing. His work has appeared in journals such as *Applied Linguistics*, *Language Learning*, and *Studies in Second Language Acquisition*.

Judit Kormos is Professor of Second Language Acquisition at Lancaster University, UK. She has published widely on the topics of individual differences in language learning and the cognitive processes of using and acquiring additional languages. She is also renowned for her research and teacher education activities for teaching languages to students with specific learning differences.

Benjamin Kremmel is a researcher and lecturer at the University of Innsbruck, Austria, where he is heading the Language Testing Research Group Innsbruck. His research interests are in language testing, particularly in the areas of vocabulary assessment, L2 reading assessment, and language assessment literacy. He has published his work in *Language Testing*, *Language Assessment Quarterly*, *Applied Linguistics*, and *TESOL Quarterly*.

Kristopher Kyle is Assistant Professor of Linguistics at the University of Oregon, USA. His research interests include second language acquisition, second language writing, corpus linguistics, computational linguistics, and second language assessment. He is particularly interested in developing natural language processing tools to test/build theories related to vocabulary development, second language acquisition, and second language writing development (usually using learner corpora).

Batia Laufer is Professor (Emerita) of Applied Linguistics at the University of Haifa, Israel. She has lectured, supervised research, and published widely on several areas of vocabulary acquisition: effective teaching, contribution to reading, testing, cross-linguistic influence, ease and difficulty in learning, dictionary use, and attrition.

Lei Lei is Professor in the School of Foreign Languages, Huazhong University of Science and Technology, China. His research interests are corpus-based studies on vocabulary and academic English. His publications have appeared in *Applied Linguistics*, *International Journal of Corpus Linguistics*, *Journal of English for Academic English*, *Journal of Quantitative Linguistics*, and *RELC Journal*, among others.

Linda H. F. Lin holds a PhD in applied linguistics. She works for the English Language Centre of the Hong Kong Polytechnic University. Her research interests include vocabulary studies, corpus analysis, and applications of concordancing in teaching and learning.

Seth Lindstromberg trained as a secondary school teacher in Canada. However, from 1977 to 2016, he was an EFL teacher in Japan and then the UK, where he also worked as an EFL teacher trainer. His main research interests are pedagogical applications of cognitive linguistics, the semantics of English prepositions, methods for teaching L2 vocabulary, and language teaching methods generally.

Dilin Liu is Professor/Coordinator of Applied Linguistics/TESOL in the English Department at the University of Alabama, USA. His research focuses on corpus-based description/teaching of lexis/grammar. He has published extensively, including numerous articles in many different journals, such as *Applied Linguistics*, *Cognitive Linguistics*, *ESP*, *Journal of English for Academic Purposes*, *Modern Language Journal*, *Studies in the Second Language Acquisition*, and *TESOL Quarterly*.

Fanny Meunier is Professor of English Language, Linguistics, and Didactics at the University of Louvain (UCLouvain), Belgium. She has been involved in learner corpus research for more than 20 years and her main research interest is the link between second language acquisition (SLA) studies and pedagogical applications. She is also actively involved in pre- and in-service teacher training and is collaborating with several international research projects on, among other aspects, bi- and multi-literacies and digital literacies.

Imma Miralpeix obtained her PhD from the University of Barcelona, Spain, where she is a lecturer and researcher. Her main research interests include second language vocabulary acquisition, especially lexical development and assessment, and multilingualism. She is the author of several publications in these areas and has taken part in different funded projects on second language learning and teaching.

Tatsuya Nakata is Associate Professor at Faculty of Letters, Hosei University, Japan. His research interests include second language acquisition and computer-assisted language learning. His research has appeared in publications such as *Studies in Second Language*

Acquisition, Language Teaching Research, International Review of Applied Linguistics in Language Teaching, and *The Modern Language Journal.*

Paul Nation is Emeritus Professor of Applied Linguistics in the School of Linguistics and Applied Language Studies at Victoria University of Wellington, New Zealand. He is the author of several books and articles on vocabulary and the methodology of language teaching. His website contains numerous free resources for learners, teachers, and researchers.

Jonathan Newton is Associate Professor in the School of Linguistics and Applied Language Studies (LALS), Victoria University of Wellington, New Zealand. His research and scholarship focus on vocabulary teaching and learning, task-based language teaching, and intercultural dimensions of language education. He is passionate about working alongside language teachers to address classroom teaching and learning challenges.

Taha Omidian is a PhD student at Victoria University of Wellington, New Zealand. Taha's research interests include the acquisition, processing, and use of vocabulary and phraseology, academic writing, and learner corpora.

Ana Pellicer-Sánchez is Associate Professor of Applied Linguistics and TESOL at the UCL Institute of Education, UK. Her research centers around the teaching and learning of vocabulary in a second or foreign language, with a particular focus on learning from reading. Her recent research has made use of eye tracking to explore the cognitive processes involved in vocabulary learning.

Elke Peters is Associate Professor at KU Leuven, Belgium. Her research interests involve incidental and deliberate learning of single words and multiword units in a foreign language. She is interested in how different types of input can contribute to vocabulary learning. She has published her research in journals such as *Language Learning, Studies in Second Language Acquisition, Language Teaching Research,* and the *Modern Language Journal.*

David D. Qian is Professor of Applied Linguistics at the Hong Kong Polytechnic University. He is interested in multifaceted research in applied linguistics, including language assessment, vocabulary studies, and analysis of academic and professional corpora. He co-founded the Asian Association for Language Assessment (AALA) and served as its co-president (2014–2015) and president (2016–2017).

John Read is Professor of Applied Language Studies at the University of Auckland, New Zealand. His research and scholarship have focused on the assessment of second language vocabulary knowledge and the testing of English for academic and occupational purposes.

Yosuke Sasao is Associate Professor of Applied Linguistics at Kyoto University, Japan. His research interests include vocabulary acquisition, language assessment, pedagogical grammar, and academic writing. His articles have been published in journals such as *ITL – International Journal of Applied Linguistics, Language Teaching Research, Language Testing,* and *RELC Journal.*

Norbert Schmitt is Professor of Applied Linguistics at the University of Nottingham, UK. He is interested in all aspects of second language vocabulary acquisition, use, and assessment, and has published and presented widely on these topics. He is currently writing a book on language issues for the general public.

Rob Schoonen is Chair Professor of Applied Linguistics at Radboud University, the Netherlands, and Senior Researcher at the Centre of Language Studies, Nijmegen. His research interests are language proficiency, vocabulary knowledge, language assessment, and research methodology.

Anna Siyanova-Chanturia is Senior Lecturer in Applied Linguistics at Victoria University of Wellington, New Zealand. Anna's research interests include psychological aspects of second language acquisition, bilingualism, usage-based approaches to language acquisition, processing and use, vocabulary and multiword items, and quantitative research methods (corpora, eye movements, EEG/ERPs).

Tessa Spätgens completed a PhD at the University of Amsterdam, the Netherlands, on the semantic network and reading comprehension in monolingual and bilingual children. Her linguistic interests include language acquisition, multilingualism, and language teaching.

Laura Vilkaitė-Lozdienė is Assistant Professor at Vilnius University, Lithuania. Her current research focuses on vocabulary acquisition in a second language as well as on identification and processing of formulaic language.

Stuart Webb is Professor of Applied Linguistics at the University of Western Ontario, Canada. His research interests include vocabulary studies, extensive reading and listening, and language learning through watching television. His articles have been published in journals such as *Applied Linguistics* and *Language Learning*.

Brent Wolter is Professor at Ocean University of China and at Idaho State University, USA. His main research area is second language vocabulary acquisition, with a particular interest in how psycholinguistic and cognitive factors affect lexical acquisition and activation. His work has been published in a number of leading journals in the field.

David Wood is Professor of Applied Linguistics at Carleton University in Ottawa, Canada, with a long career in language teaching and applied linguistics research and teaching. He has published and presented extensively on formulaic language in speech fluency and in academic discourse, and also has authored/edited several volumes on formulaic language.

Akifumi Yanagisawa is working on a PhD in applied linguistics at the University of Western Ontario, Canada. His PhD research involves meta-analytic studies of the Involvement Load Hypothesis and Technique Feature Analysis. His research interests focus on second language vocabulary learning and the psychological conditions that contribute to language learning.

Acknowledgments

I am grateful to everyone who contributed to this volume. I know that each person had many commitments, so making the time to write a chapter meant extra work on weekends and nights. However, it is the work of the group as a whole that makes the volume meaningful and worthwhile. Perhaps the best thing about doing research on vocabulary is the opportunity to meet and spend time with the people who work in this area. Not only are the many contributors to this volume great researchers but their kindness, generosity, and spirit make working in this area motivating, interesting, and enjoyable. I believe that the positive culture within the field of vocabulary is the result of the leadership of those who have defined our field for so many years: Paul Nation, Batia Laufer, and Paul Meara. They have been kind, supportive, and generous to so many of us that their influence continues with the next generations of researchers.

I have been very fortunate to have had the chance to learn from and work with a lot of exceptional people. These opportunities have made my contribution to this volume possible. I am most grateful to Paul Nation. Not only is Paul an outstanding scholar, but it is his wisdom, kindness, generosity, and friendship that I find to be most outstanding. I have little doubt that working with Paul was the key to everything good that I have done as an academic. I am also indebted to Frank Boers, whose advice has helped to shape my work and this volume for the better. I would also like to thank my students. Having great students is a joy and I have been very lucky to work with and learn from Thi Ngoc Yen Dang, Yosuke Sasao, Tatsuya Nakata, Michael Rodgers, Akifumi Yanagisawa, Takumi Uchihara, Su Kyung Kim, Zhouhan Jin, and many others. I am also grateful to the many researchers of vocabulary who I have been lucky enough to meet, have a beer or glass of wine with, and consider to be my friends.

Finally, I would like to thank the team at Routledge for their work on the *Handbook* and making its publication a very positive process. I would also like to thank Frank Boers, Ana Pellicer-Sánchez, Elke Peters, Paul Nation, and Takumi Uchihara for their valuable comments and suggestions.

1

Introduction

Stuart Webb

Introduction

In 1980, Paul Meara's article "Vocabulary Acquisition: A Neglected Aspect of Language Learning" was published. Indeed, at that time there were relatively few studies being published that were focused on the construct of vocabulary, or the teaching and learning of words, and research on second language (L2) vocabulary was particularly scarce. However, perhaps fueled by the influential work of Paul Nation, Batia Laufer, and Paul Meara, there is now much greater interest in studies of vocabulary.

Today, there is a great deal of research conducted on vocabulary, and an increased range in topics relating to words. There are now a number of excellent books that provide a comprehensive review of lexical studies. Nation (2001, 2013) and Schmitt (2010) have provided the widest ranging overviews of vocabulary research in general, while Read's (2000) *Assessing Vocabulary* has been the key book devoted to measuring vocabulary knowledge. More recently, interest in learning sequences of words has generated great interest with Schmitt's (2004) *Formulaic Sequences: Acquisition, Processing, and Use*; Wray's (2002) *Formulaic Language and the Lexicon*; and Boers and Lindstromberg's (2009) *Optimizing a Lexical Approach to Instructed Second Language Acquisition* being among the key texts in this area. Moreover, with the development of new approaches to researching vocabulary, there has also been the publication of books providing guidance to help graduate students and researchers with their research. There are now books on how to develop word lists (Nation, 2016) and how to use eye tracking for data collection (Conklin, Pellicer-Sánchez, & Carrol, 2018; Godfroid, 2019), as well as texts devoted to issues related to researching vocabulary (Nation & Webb, 2011; Schmitt, 2010). Surprisingly, there have been few collective volumes focused on vocabulary. Schmitt and McCarthy's (1997) *Vocabulary: Description, Acquisition and Pedagogy* and Bogaards and Laufer's (2004) *Vocabulary in a Second Language: Selection, Acquisition, and Testing* are the best collections on vocabulary, because each covered a variety of important topics that were written by notable researchers. Recently, there have also been several special issues of journals devoted to vocabulary, including the April 2010 issue of *Reading in a Foreign Language* edited by Averil Coxhead, the May 2012 issue of the *RELC Journal* edited by Paul Nation, the January 2017 issue of *Language Teaching*

Research edited by Batia Laufer, the May 2017 issue of *Language Teaching Research* on multiword units edited by Anna Siyanova-Chanturia, and the April 2018 issue of *ITL – International Journal of Applied Linguistics* edited by Stuart Webb.

The aim of this volume was to build on these earlier texts by providing a comprehensive coverage of vocabulary studies from key researchers in the field today. What makes this volume unique is the wide range of themes on lexis, and the many different perspectives of the researchers. The diversity of issues and foci of the researchers should make it a useful reference text, help to expand on the discussions of vocabulary, and highlight important areas for future research.

Who Is Currently Researching Vocabulary?

One of the goals of the volume was to try to bring different views to some of the subjects. While vocabulary researchers agree on many things, each person brings a different perspective to the research literature. Sometimes these differences are quite small. For example, I believe that many of us (e.g., Averil Coxhead, Jonathan Newton, Irina Elgort, Stuart Webb) who have studied and worked with Paul Nation at Victoria University of Wellington may echo much of what he has written about. There is good reason for this, the biggest being that Paul has written about so many different topics, and even if it takes us a while to recognize it, in the end we usually find that his suggestions are correct. Although we might have differences in our views, these views may often have developed from his earlier work, and so are often similar to his. Moreover, we might consider that there are other schools of thought such as from those who have studied and worked with Paul Meara at Swansea University, and those who have learned from Norbert Schmitt at the University of Nottingham. Paul Meara's influence likely extends to his colleagues, Tess Fitzpatrick and Jim Milton, and the many students who have learned about vocabulary research from them (e.g., Rob Waring, Brent Wolter, Dale Brown, Jeff Stewart). Norbert Schmitt's viewpoint on research has also likely impacted the work of his many students (e.g., Ana Pellicer-Sánchez, Anna Siyanova-Chanturia, Benjamin Kremmel, Laura Vilkaitė-Lozdienė, Beatriz González Fernández) and colleagues (Kathy Conklin, Zoltan Dornyei). Of course all of these researchers have also had a large impact on the wider research community.

With the increase in research on vocabulary there has also been an increase in the number of people investigating it, and these researchers are certainly not limited to those just mentioned. Perhaps nobody has contributed as many seminal studies of L2 vocabulary as Batia Laufer (University of Haifa, Israel). The breadth and influence of her research continues to grow today. Her research initially focused on issues related to lexical difficulty. However, it has touched on a large number of areas related to lexis, such as the development of tests, lexical coverage, formulaic language, and incidental and intentional vocabulary learning. Her work with Jan Hulstijn on the development of the Involvement Load Hypothesis should be considered to be one of the key contributions to vocabulary acquisition research in the last 20 years. While Batia Laufer has focused on a wide range of themes, the impact of John Read in the area of vocabulary testing has had great influence. His book *Assessing Vocabulary* must be considered the essential work in this area, and the continued development and validation of the Word Associates Test should be considered as an important landmark in the development of tests of vocabulary knowledge.

If we think about the different places where people are researching vocabulary, then we can see that there are researchers in a diverse range of countries. With the large body of work completed by Paul Meara, Norbert Schmitt, Ron Carter, and Michael McCarthy in the United Kingdom, not surprisingly there is still a large number of researchers focused on lexis there, such as Judit Kormos, Dana Gablasova, and Vaclav Brezina (University of Lancaster), Thi Ngoc Yen Dang (University of Leeds), Seth Lindstromberg, Philip Durrant (University of Exeter), and Ana Pellicer-Sánchez (University College London). Elsewhere in Europe, researchers are a little more isolated, with Henrik Gyllstad (Lund University) and Fanny Forsberg Lundell (Stockholm University) in Sweden, Benjamin Kremmel (University of Innsbruck) in Austria, Laura Vilkaitė-Lozdienė (Vilnius University) in Lithuania, Rob Schoonen (Radboud University) and Tessa Spätgens (University of Amsterdam) in the Netherlands, Imma Miralpeix and Raquel Serrano (University of Barcelona) in Spain, and Brigitta Dóczi (Eötvös Loránd University) in Hungary. There is also a lot of interest in vocabulary research in Asia with researchers such as Rob Waring (Notre Dame Seishin University), Atsushi Mizumoto, Tatsuya Nakata, and Alan Hunt (Kansai University), David Beglar (Temple University Japan), Laurence Anthony (Waseda University), Junko Yamashita (Nagoya University), and Yosuke Sasao (Kyoto University) all conducting lexical studies in Japan, whereas, David D. Qian (Hong Kong Polytechnic University) and Anna Chang (Hsing-Wu University) are based in Hong Kong and Taiwan, respectively.

Vocabulary has also been a popular topic among researchers in Belgium, led by the work of Frank Boers. His cognitive linguistics studies on the teaching and learning of single and multi-word items have fueled many useful articles by his former colleagues and students: June Eyckmans (Ghent University), Hélène Stengers and Julie Deconinck (Vrije Universiteit Brussel), and Aline Godfroid (now at Michigan State University). Sylviane Granger and her colleagues Fanny Meunier and Magali Paquot at Université Catholique de Louvain have made an impact on research of formulaic language by conducting a large number of corpus-based studies with a particular focus on learner language use. More recently, Elke Peters and Maribel Montero Perez and their students at KU Leuven University have made important contributions to research on vocabulary, perhaps most notably with their research on multimodal learning of words.

In North America, researchers tend to be more scattered. In the US, Joe Barcroft (Washington University in St. Louis), Brent Wolter (Idaho State University), Dilin Liu (University of Alabama), Kristopher Kyle (University of Hawai'i at Manoa), Scott Crossley (Georgia State University), Scott Jarvis (University of Utah), and Dee Gardner and Mark Davies (Brigham Young University) have emerged as key vocabulary researchers. In Canada, Tom Cobb (Université du Québec à Montréal), Marlise Horst (Concordia University), Sima Paribakht (University of Ottawa), David Wood and Michael Rodgers (Carleton University), and the team at the University of Western Ontario (Frank Boers, myself, and students such as Akifumi Yanagisawa, Takumi Uchihara, Zhouhan Jin, Su Kyung Kim) have been frequent contributors to the literature on teaching and learning single and multiword items.

How Might We Classify the Many Investigations of Vocabulary?

With so many lexical studies being conducted, it is perhaps useful to classify research into distinct categories to reveal potential gaps in the literature, as well as to highlight areas that receive more or less attention. There are many different ways in which we might classify research on vocabulary. The following sections are a few of the possibilities.

Description, Pedagogy, and Assessment

This volume is loosely structured around these three categories, as they are at the heart of understanding much of what is written about vocabulary. Description entails understanding what is involved in knowing a word or sequence of words, the factors that influence learning, how vocabulary learning is related to other components of language development, how we might classify vocabulary, and how vocabulary fits into existing theories of language learning. Description is central to understanding and evaluating research on vocabulary. Nation's (2001, 2013) description of vocabulary knowledge is the most important work on the subject to date, which is why this volume begins with this topic (see Nation, this volume).

Much of the research on vocabulary has focused on pedagogy. Research has examined the efficacy of different vocabulary learning activities (e.g., Laufer & Shmueli, 1997), learners' strategies in vocabulary learning (e.g., Gu & Johnson, 1996), and the tools (e.g., word lists, flash cards, dictionaries) that can be used for teaching and learning words (e.g., Dang, Coxhead, & Webb, 2017; Laufer & Hadar, 1997; Nakata, 2011). A key contribution in this area was Laufer and Hulstijn's (2001) Involvement Load Hypothesis, which sought to identify factors present in text-based activities that contribute to vocabulary learning and provide a testable framework that could predict the relative efficacy of such activities. Before the Involvement Load Hypothesis, the rationale for why more words might be learned through completing one activity rather than another was that in the former the words may have been processed more deeply than in the latter. While this might well be true, it is also a very unsatisfactory statement because there is no means to determine what constitutes deep processing. Although the Involvement Load Hypothesis may also be in need of refinement (e.g., Folse, 2006), it raised awareness of the need to look at the psychological conditions within activities that contribute to learning. Moreover, it also motivated the development of other frameworks such as Barcroft's (2002) TOPRA model and Nation and Webb's (2011) Technique Feature Analysis that shed further light on the relative efficacy of activities (see chapters by Laufer and Lindstromberg, this volume).

Assessment of vocabulary knowledge plays a large role in both pedagogy and research. In the classroom, tests of vocabulary knowledge can motivate study, raise awareness of different aspects of vocabulary knowledge (see Yanagisawa and Webb, this volume), indicate the extent of lexical development within a course (see Kremmel, this volume), and reveal which words students know and which words they need to learn (see chapters by Gyllstad and Kyle, this volume). In research, the quality and focus of tests of vocabulary knowledge may affect whether or not vocabulary learning is found to occur, as well as the number of words participants are found to "know" (see Read, this volume). More sensitive test formats, such as those employing a meaning recognition format, are likely to reveal greater learning or knowledge, while more demanding formats, such as form recall, are likely to show less learning or knowledge (see Laufer & Goldstein, 2004; Godfroid, this volume). Moreover, a mismatch between what is learned (e.g., written form) and what is measured (e.g., form-meaning connection) may provide misleading results (Webb & Piasecki, 2018). There is much that needs to be considered when selecting or designing tests of vocabulary knowledge, and of particular importance is the need to carefully consider the multidimensionality of vocabulary knowledge and assess the aspects of knowledge that are most likely to be learned or known (Nation & Webb, 2011).

Single-Word Items vs. Multiword Items

Although researchers have long been aware of the importance of learning sequences of words as well as individual words (e.g., Palmer, 1933), until recently the vast majority of studies had focused on single-word items. However, with advances in technology, it is now much easier to identify and research multiword items (see chapters by Meunier and Wood, this volume). Indeed, in the last 30 years, more and more has been written about formulaic language, to the point that there are many of the same lines of research for multiword items as single-word items. For example, there are studies looking at the factors that affect learning multiword items (see Boers, this volume), how formulaic language is processed (see Conklin, this volume), how tests can be created to measure knowledge of multiword items (see Gyllstad, this volume), and the resources that are available for learning formulaic language (see Meunier, this volume).

Although research on multiword items is still in its infancy, there are also some questions that we might hope would be answered by now. What might be the most important question to answer is whether it is more effective to learn words as individual items or as sequences of items, as this may help to optimize instruction. For example, is it better to learn the form and meaning of *take* and encounter it in context, or is it more effective to learn the forms and meanings of the most frequent sequences in which it occurs (*take care, take place, take advantage*) and encounter each of these in several sentences?

Despite the long history of research on individual words, there are still some very important practical questions that remain unanswered. Perhaps the most important of these questions is how many words can students learn in different periods of time? This is a particularly important question because answering it would allow teachers, learners, and program developers to set meaningful goals for courses, programs, and study periods. If we aim for our students to understand most forms of speech, research suggests that they need to know the 3,000 most frequent word families. A word family is made up of a headword (e.g., *approach*), its inflections (*approaches, approaching, approached*), and its derivations (*approachable, unapproachable*). If the goal is for students to understand written text, then the objective should be that they know the most frequent 8,000 word families, and if we expect them to reach the vocabulary size of an educated L1 user, then they should learn 15,000 word families. Without understanding how many words that students can learn in courses and over different durations, it is unlikely that language learning programs will be highly effective.

Intentional vs. Incidental Word Learning

Intentional and incidental vocabulary learning often seem to be discussed as the only two approaches to learning words. Exercises and activities that are designed to explicitly focus students on learning words are labeled as examples of intentional vocabulary learning, whereas activities that involve learning words through encounters in meaning-focused input are labeled as examples of incidental vocabulary learning (see chapters by Lindstromberg and Webb, this volume). This distinction makes some sense because there are many activities, such as flash cards, fill in the blanks, and matching exercises, that are designed to make students focus on learning words to develop lexical knowledge. There are also many other situations that involve encountering input through reading and listening in which there may be no intention to learn words, and yet through these experiences words are in fact learned.

The advantage of labeling vocabulary learning as intentional and incidental is that it allows us to see the similarities between different learning conditions, as well as their strengths and weaknesses. For example, we might note that vocabulary learning is relatively effective when we learn words intentionally through using flash cards, filling in blanks, and writing words in sentences in comparison to encountering unknown words when reading, listening, or viewing television. The disadvantage of categorizing vocabulary learning as an intentional-incidental dichotomy is that we may lose sight of the many differences among the different intentional learning activities, as well as the differences among the incidental learning activities. Moreover, as with most dichotomies, there may also be the urge to state that one is good or effective and the other is bad or less effective. However, we should not think of intentional and incidental vocabulary learning as being in competition with each other but rather as useful complements to each other.

Processing vs. Learning Words

Another distinction that is made in research is studies focused on rates of processing words and those that look at the amounts of vocabulary learning (see chapters by Conklin, Godfroid, and Pellicer-Sánchez, this volume). Most studies of vocabulary have focused on word learning perhaps in part because of the ease with which we can assess vocabulary gains using paper and pencil tests. Studies of lexical processing are becoming much more common because improved technology has provided new tools for measuring lexical processing such as reaction time tasks and eye tracking.

Processing speed is sometimes viewed as indicating the strength of links within the mental lexicon, as well as the strength of knowledge that someone has for a word or sequence of words; words that are more closely linked or are better known should be processed more quickly than those that are less closely linked or less well known. In fact, processing speed can also be considered a measure of vocabulary learning because it provides a very sensitive measure of vocabulary knowledge that may be difficult to reveal through more traditional paper and pencil tests. It is probably easiest to see processing speed as a measure of lexical fluency; the faster that we can process a word, the more fluent our access to that word (see chapters by Conklin and Godfroid, this volume).

Depth of Vocabulary Knowledge vs. Breadth of Vocabulary Knowledge

Breadth of vocabulary knowledge refers to the number of words known. In studies of breadth, knowing a word is typically indicated by whether students know the form-meaning connections of words. Depth of vocabulary knowledge refers to how well a word is known, and this is usually indicated by whether students know aspects of knowledge, such as collocation, multiple meanings of words, and derivations, rather than only knowing form-meaning connection. Generally, it is only in the last 20 years that research has started to focus on depth of knowledge. Before that, knowing a word was pretty much always indicated by whether or not students knew form-meaning connection.

Although there has been quite a lot written about depth of vocabulary knowledge, most new studies of words still equate vocabulary learning with gaining knowledge of form-meaning connection. There is good reason to measure knowledge of form-meaning connection. Knowledge of form-meaning connection is essential for comprehension; the more words we understand in a text, the more likely we are to understand that text (Hu & Nation, 2000; Laufer, 1989; Schmitt, Jiang, & Grabe, 2011). Moreover, this is true for not only reading comprehension but also for listening comprehension (van Zeeland & Schmitt, 2013). However, it is also extremely important to recognize the multidimensional nature of vocabulary knowledge; there are many different aspects of word knowledge and so measuring any one aspect of knowledge is only providing a partial evaluation of what might be known. Therefore, while measuring knowledge of form-meaning connection may provide a useful measurement of vocabulary knowledge, it is also a very limited evaluation of what might have been learned (see chapters by Godfroid, Nation, Webb, Yanagisawa and Webb, this volume).

More research on depth of vocabulary knowledge is also needed. Perhaps of greatest benefit would be the development and validation of new measures of vocabulary depth (see chapters by Godfroid, Gyllstad, Read, Yanagisawa and Webb, this volume). The development of earlier tests, such as the Vocabulary Knowledge Scale (Wesche & Paribakht, 1996) and the Word Associates Test (Read, 1993, 1998), were very important innovations in lexical assessment. However, there is a need to keep improving and expanding on these earlier measures. In particular, it would be useful to have measures of different aspects of vocabulary knowledge such as derivation and collocation with test items selected according to word frequency levels. This would allow teachers and researchers to measure knowledge of the most useful words for different components of depth. Moreover, this would also allow us to compare knowledge of these aspects with the results of established tests that use a similar format such as the Vocabulary Levels Test (Webb, Sasao, & Ballance, 2017).

Quantitative vs. Qualitative Studies of Vocabulary

Within applied linguistics and other research disciplines, studies are often classified by design with the most common classification being quantitative and qualitative studies. Within lexical studies this categorization does not really apply, however, because there are very few qualitative studies of vocabulary (notable exceptions include Gu, 2003; Haastrup & Henriksen, 2000). This is a major limitation of the research on vocabulary. Although we can learn much through quantitative studies of words, there is also a great deal that is unaccounted for that deserves attention. For example, when we look for differences in the amount of word learning through different conditions, we might find that Condition X was more effective than Condition Y. This is useful because it provides some indication of the relative efficacy of the two conditions. However, within each condition, it is likely that there was some variation in the amount of learning; most students may have learned the most through Condition X, but a few may have learned very little. Moreover, a few students may have learned more through Condition Y than through Condition X. Qualitative and mixed methods studies (e.g., Godfroid & Schmidtke, 2013) can help to shed more light on inconsistencies within data sets and expand upon earlier quantitative studies.

Vocabulary and the Four Skills

Another way that we might categorize studies of vocabulary is around the four skills: reading, writing, listening, and speaking. Unfortunately, this would lead to an extremely long section on reading, followed by shorter and shorter sections on writing, listening, and speaking in that order. Most research on vocabulary has looked at the words in written text. For example, we can analyze the vocabulary in corpora of written text to determine word and multiword frequencies and the strength of the relationships between words. We can also look at how reading different types of text contributes to vocabulary learning and how the factors within these texts and the characteristics of the learners affect gains. The reason why most studies have focused on written text is that it is easiest to collect this text type to create corpora, or modify written text to suit research purposes. This has allowed us to learn much about the vocabulary in written text (e.g., Nation, 2006), and the extent to which words can be learned through reading (e.g., Webb, 2008).

There has also been a fair amount of research on vocabulary and writing, with many studies focusing on the lexical richness or lexical variation of learner writing (e.g., Kyle, this volume; Laufer & Nation, 1995). With much improved software, such as TAALES (Kyle, Crossley, & Berger, 2018), AntWordProfiler (Anthony, 2014), and AntConc (Anthony, 2018), that indicates the lexical frequency, formulaic language, and lexical relationships between words in text, there is a large amount of information that can be revealed about the words used in writing (see chapters by Anthony and Kyle, this volume). One challenge with conducting these studies is that while researchers can analyze the words that participants use in their writing, there is a lack of clarity about the words that are not used. For example, if we are interested in the proportion of lower frequency words that are used in student writing, we cannot know if the figures accurately reflect productive knowledge of words. Instead, the figures reflect the choices that students made about which words to use; some students may choose to focus on accuracy and use more of the higher frequency words that they are most familiar with, others may choose to take more risks and use lower frequency words that they are less familiar with, while others may have written their text according to the frequencies of the words that they knew. Studies of lexical richness in writing do, however, provide very useful indications of the vocabulary that is used between L1 and L2 students (e.g., Crossley & McNamara, 2009).

In contrast to studies of reading and writing, there is relatively little research on vocabulary learning through listening and speaking, or the words and sequences of words encountered in spoken discourse. It is likely that the reason for this is that these are more challenging skills to investigate. For example, it is quite easy to create a corpus of written text that is tens of millions of words in size, because there are billions of words of written text freely available online. However, there is relatively little transcribed spoken text freely available, and so analysis of the vocabulary found in speech is less common. Examining vocabulary learning through speaking and listening is particularly difficult in the classroom, because of the unpredictability of interaction, the large number of variables involved, as well as the challenges of accurately recording the interaction. Despite these challenges, the number of studies investigating the vocabulary of spoken language (e.g., Dang & Webb, 2014), and learning words through speaking (e.g., Newton, 2013; Nguyen & Boers, 2018) and listening (e.g., Peters & Webb, 2018; Vidal, 2003, 2011), appears to be increasing. There would be great value in examining vocabulary learning through speaking and listening in new studies. Hopefully recent studies in this area will reveal useful methodological approaches that can be incorporated into new studies.

Vocabulary and the Four Strands

Nation (2007) introduced the four strands as an approach to L2 curriculum development that would provide diverse opportunities for learning. Although the four strands was initially focused on course or curriculum development, its principles also apply to opportunities for lexical development. The four strands are meaning-focused input, meaning-focused output, language-focused learning, and fluency development. Nation suggests that each strand has similar importance, and that a balance in learning between the four strands should provide the greatest benefit to students.

Meaning-focused input involves learning words incidentally through repeated encounters during reading and listening. Meaning-focused input tasks, such as extensive reading and viewing, focus learners on comprehension rather than vocabulary learning. Through encountering words in meaning-focused tasks, students may learn not only the form-meaning connections of words but also learn how they can be used in context. A large number of studies have investigated incidental vocabulary learning with meaning-focused written input (see Webb, this volume). The greatest potential for further research in this area may be through investigating incidental learning with meaning-focused spoken input.

Meaning-focused output involves developing productive vocabulary knowledge through using words in speech and writing in tasks that focus on communication rather than intentional word learning. Although there are a reasonable number of studies devoted to vocabulary learning through meaning-focused writing (e.g., Crossley & McNamara, 2009; Laufer & Nation, 1995), there are few studies that have looked at vocabulary learning through meaning-focused speaking. This is an area where further research is clearly needed.

Language-focused learning involves the intentional learning of words through exercises and activities such as sentence production and flash cards. Language-focused learning might be what most students and teachers consider to be at the heart of lexical development, because it involves the deliberate teaching and learning of words. However, when we consider that native speakers know as many as 15,000 to 20,000 word families (Goulden, Nation, & Read, 1990) and that you need to know 8,000 to 9,000 word families to understand English novels and newspapers (Nation, 2006), it should be evident that intentional vocabulary learning on its own will not be successful in helping students reach these targets. There are a large number of studies investigating language-focused vocabulary learning activities (e.g., Webb, 2007, 2009; see also chapters by Laufer and Lindstromberg, this volume). However, the research tends to be limited to examining a relatively small number of different activities (Webb, Yanagisawa, & Uchihara, under review). It would be useful for new studies to look at the extent to which common learning conditions, such as matching exercises, true/false questions, cloze activities, and crosswords, contribute to vocabulary learning.

Fluency development involves processing and using vocabulary at a faster rate. Gains in the rate of processing and using words should be viewed as an indication of vocabulary learning (see Godfroid, this volume). Speed reading, 4/3/2 activity, and repeated reading and viewing are examples of activities designed to promote fluency development. Fluency development has tended to receive less attention than the other three strands, both in the classroom and in research. In recent years there has been increased focus on lexical fluency (e.g., Pellicer-Sánchez, 2015). However, with relatively few studies of fluency development, more research is clearly warranted.

The Organization of This *Handbook*

This volume is organized into four parts: Part I, Understanding Vocabulary; Part II, Approaches to Teaching and Learning Vocabulary; Part III, Measuring Knowledge of Vocabulary; and Part IV, Key Issues in Teaching, Researching, and Measuring Vocabulary. The first part is composed of chapters that are at the heart of researching, learning, teaching, and testing words. These chapters explore what it means to know a word, what affects vocabulary learning, explanation of the different types of words (e.g., academic, technical, high-, mid-, and low-frequency words, formulaic language), lexical processing, vocabulary size, and how vocabulary fits into language learning theories. In order to research, teach, and test words, it is necessary to have a grasp of these topics. The second part is devoted to issues related to teaching and learning words. It begins with the broader areas of incidental and intentional learning and then moves to narrower topics, such as vocabulary learning strategies, word lists, and resources for learning words. All of the chapters in this part are linked with both pedagogy and research; there is typically a large amount of research in each area, and each subject should be considered when developing a program of vocabulary learning.

The third part, Measuring Knowledge of Vocabulary, begins with chapters focused on measuring depth of knowledge of single-word items and measuring knowledge of multiword items. It then moves on to discussion of the different approaches to measuring vocabulary knowledge. A goal of this section was to include an explanation of newer approaches to measuring vocabulary knowledge, such as eye tracking, response times, Coh-Metrix, and

TAALES software, as well as tests that have become recently available, such as the Word Part Levels Test (Sasao & Webb, 2017) and the Guessing from Context Test (Sasao & Webb, 2018). Thus, it should provide a useful update on older books that have focused on the topic of measuring vocabulary, such as Read's (2000) excellent *Assessing Vocabulary*.

The final part, Key Issues in Teaching, Researching, and Measuring Vocabulary, was designed to look at issues that might not have been covered in significant depth in earlier chapters, as well as to provide an overview of important themes from the perspective of other experts in the field. Two chapters focus on research issues related to investigating single-word items and formulaic language. These chapters were included because they are likely to be of interest to graduate students and researchers who are planning to start working in this area. Similarly, two chapters focus on key issues in teaching and learning vocabulary (single-word items are the focus of one chapter, while formulaic language is the focus of the other). These chapters may be starting points for teachers looking to help their students do a better job of vocabulary learning. The final two chapters deal with key issues related to measuring vocabulary knowledge and resources for researching vocabulary. While it is likely that all six of the key issues chapters will touch on some of the topics in the other sections, the overlap should hopefully guide readers to explore different parts of the book in more detail.

When first reading the chapters in this volume, I was often struck by the thought that I would have written things very differently. This variation in discussion of subjects is what I believe to be the greatest value of the *Handbook*. Topics that I felt that I knew quite well were described from different perspectives, and this originality in explanation was informative, interesting, and useful. I was thrilled to have read such a great collection of contributions and I know that this book will be an essential resource for myself. I hope that you will find it equally useful.

References

Anthony, L. (2014). *AntWordProfiler* (Version 1.4.1) [Computer Software]. Tokyo, Japan: Waseda University. Retrieved from www.laurenceanthony.net/software

Anthony, L. (2018). *AntConc* (Version 3.5.7) [Computer Software]. Tokyo, Japan: Waseda University. Retrieved from www.laurenceanthony.net/software

Barcroft, J. (2002). Semantic and structural elaboration in L2 lexical acquisition. *Language Learning, 52*, 323–363.

Boers, F., & Lindstromberg, S. (2009). *Optimizing a lexical approach to instructed second language acquisition*. Basingstoke, UK: Palgrave Macmillan.

Bogaards, P., & Laufer, B. (Eds.). (2004). *Vocabulary in a second language: Selection, acquisition, and testing*. Amsterdam: John Benjamins Publishing.

Conklin, K., Pellicer-Sánchez, A., & Carrol, G. (2018). *Eye-tracking: A guide for applied linguistics research*. Cambridge, UK: Cambridge University Press.

Crossley, S. A., & McNamara, D. S. (2009). Computational assessment of lexical differences in L1 and L2 writing. *Journal of Second Language Writing, 18*(2), 119–135.

Dang, T. N. Y., Coxhead, A., & Webb, S. (2017). The academic spoken word list. *Language Learning, 67*(4), 959–997.

Dang, T. N. Y., & Webb, S. (2014). The lexical profile of academic spoken English. *English for Specific Purposes, 33*, 66–76.

Folse, K. S. (2006). The effect of type of written exercise on L2 vocabulary retention. *TESOL Quarterly, 40*(2), 273–293.

Godfroid, A. (2019). *Eye tracking in second language acquisition and bilingualism: A research synthesis and methodological guide*. New York: Routledge.

Godfroid, A., & Schmidtke, J. (2013). What do eye movements tell us about awareness? A triangulation of eye-movement data, verbal reports and vocabulary learning scores. In J. M. Bergsleithner,

S. N. Frota, & J. K. Yoshioka (Eds.), *Noticing and second language acquisition: Studies in honor of Richard Schmidt* (pp. 183–205). Honolulu, HI: University of Hawai'i, National Foreign Language Resource Center.

Goulden, R., Nation, P., & Read, J. (1990). How large can a receptive vocabulary be? *Applied Linguistics*, *11*(4), 341–363.

Gu, P. Y. (2003). Fine Brush and Freehand 1: The vocabulary-learning art of two successful Chinese EFL learners. *TESOL Quarterly*, *37*(1), 73–104.

Gu, P. Y., & Johnson, R. K. (1996). Vocabulary learning strategies and language learning outcomes. *Language Learning*, *46*(4), 643–679.

Haastrup, K., & Henriksen, B. (2000). Vocabulary acquisition: Acquiring depth of knowledge through network building. *International Journal of Applied Linguistics*, *10*(2), 221–240.

Hu, M., & Nation, I. S. P. (2000). Vocabulary density and reading comprehension. *Reading in a Foreign Language*, *13*(1), 403–430.

Kyle, K., Crossley, S. A., & Berger, C. M. (2018). The tool for the automatic analysis of lexical sophistication (TAALES): Version 2.0. *Behavior Research Methods*, *50*(3), 1030–1046. https://doi.org/10.3758/s13428-017-0924-4

Laufer, B. (1989). What percentage of text lexis is essential for comprehension? In C. Lauren & M. Nordman (Eds.), *Special language: From humans thinking to thinking machines* (pp. 316–323). Clevedon, UK: Multilingual Matters.

Laufer, B., & Goldstein, Z. (2004). Testing vocabulary knowledge: Size, strength, and computer adaptiveness. *Language Learning*, *54*(3), 399–436.

Laufer, B., & Hadar, L. (1997). Assessing the effectiveness of monolingual, bilingual, and "bilingualised" dictionaries in the comprehension and production of new words. *The Modern Language Journal*, *81*(2), 189–196.

Laufer, B., & Hulstijn, J. (2001). Incidental vocabulary acquisition in a second language: The construct of task-induced involvement. *Applied Linguistics*, *22*(1), 1–26.

Laufer, B., & Nation, P. (1995). Vocabulary size and use: Lexical richness in L2 written production. *Applied Linguistics*, *16*(3), 307–322.

Laufer, B., & Shmueli, K. (1997). Memorizing new words: Does teaching have anything to do with it? *RELC Journal*, *28*(1), 89–108.

Nakata, T. (2011). Computer-assisted second language vocabulary learning in a paired-associate paradigm: A critical investigation of flashcard software. *Computer Assisted Language Learning*, *24*(1), 17–38.

Nation, I. S. P. (2001). *Learning vocabulary in another language*. Cambridge, UK: Cambridge University Press.

Nation, I. S. P. (2006). How large a vocabulary is needed for reading and listening? *The Canadian Modern Language Review*, *63*, 59–82.

Nation, I. S. P. (2007). The four strands. *Innovation in Language Learning and Teaching*, *1*(1), 1–12.

Nation, I. S. P. (2013). *Learning vocabulary in another language* (2nd ed.). Cambridge, UK: Cambridge University Press.

Nation, I. S. P. (2016). *Making and using word lists for language learning and testing*. Amsterdam: John Benjamins.

Nation, I. S. P., & Webb, S. (2011). *Researching and analyzing vocabulary*. Boston, MA: Heinle Cengage Learning.

Newton, J. (2013). Incidental vocabulary learning in classroom communication tasks. *Language Teaching Research*, *17*(2), 164–187.

Nguyen, C. D., & Boers, F. (2018). The effect of content retelling on vocabulary uptake from a TED Talk. *TESOL Quarterly*. Early view online version available at https://doi.org/10.1002/tesq.441

Palmer, H. E. (1933). *Second interim report on English collocations*. Tokyo, Japan: Kaitakusha.

Pellicer-Sánchez, A. (2015). Developing automaticity and speed of lexical access: The effects of incidental and explicit teaching approaches. *Journal of Spanish Language Teaching*, *2*(2), 112–126.

Peters, E., & Webb, S. (2018). Incidental vocabulary acquisition through watching a single episode of L2 television. *Studies in Second Language Acquisition*, *40*(3), 551–577.

Read, J. (1993). The development of a new measure of L2 vocabulary knowledge. *Language Testing, 10*(3), 355–371. https://doi.org/10.1177/026553229301000308

Read, J. (1998). Validating a test to measure depth of vocabulary knowledge. In A. Kunnan (Ed.), *Validation in language assessment* (pp. 41–60). Mahwah, NJ: Erlbaum.

Read, J. (2000). *Assessing vocabulary*. Cambridge, UK: Cambridge University Press.

Sasao, Y., & Webb, S. (2017). The word part levels test. *Language Teaching Research, 21*(1), 12–30.

Sasao, Y., & Webb, S. (2018). The guessing from context test. *ITL – International Journal of Applied Linguistics, 169*(1), 115–141.

Schmitt, N. (Ed.). (2004). *Formulaic sequences: Acquisition, processing, and use*. Amsterdam: John Benjamins.

Schmitt, N. (2010). *Researching vocabulary: A vocabulary research manual*. Basingstoke, UK: Palgrave Macmillan.

Schmitt, N., Jiang, X., & Grabe, W. (2011). The percentage of words known in a text and reading comprehension. *The Modern Language Journal, 95*(1), 26–43.

Schmitt, N., & McCarthy, M. (Eds.). (1997). *Vocabulary: Description, acquisition and pedagogy*. Cambridge, UK: Cambridge University Press.

van Zeeland, H., & Schmitt, N. (2013). Lexical coverage in L1 and L2 listening comprehension: The same or different from reading comprehension? *Applied Linguistics, 34*(4), 457–479.

Vidal, K. (2003). Academic listening: A source of vocabulary acquisition? *Applied Linguistics, 24*(1), 56–89.

Vidal, K. (2011). A comparison of the effects of reading and listening on incidental vocabulary acquisition. *Language Learning, 61*(1), 219–258.

Webb, S. (2007). Learning word pairs and glossed sentences: The effects of a single sentence on vocabulary knowledge. *Language Teaching Research, 11*(1), 63–81.

Webb, S. (2008). The effects of context on incidental vocabulary learning. *Reading in a Foreign Language, 20*, 232–245.

Webb, S. (2009). The effects of receptive and productive learning of word pairs on vocabulary knowledge. *RELC Journal, 40*(3), 360–376.

Webb, S., & Piasecki, A. (2018). Re-examining the effects of word writing on vocabulary learning. *ITL – International Journal of Applied Linguistics, 169*(1), 72–93.

Webb, S., Sasao, Y., & Ballance, O. (2017). The updated Vocabulary Levels Test: Developing and validating two new forms of the VLT. *ITL – International Journal of Applied Linguistics, 168*(1), 34–70.

Webb, S., Yanagisawa, A., & Uchihara, T. (under review). How effective are intentional vocabulary learning activities? A meta-analysis.

Wesche, M., & Paribakht, T. S. (1996). Assessing second language vocabulary knowledge: Depth versus Breadth. *Canadian Modern Language Review, 53*(1), 13–40.

Wray, A. (2002). *Formulaic language and the lexicon*. Cambridge, UK: Cambridge University Press.

Part I
Understanding Vocabulary

2

The Different Aspects of Vocabulary Knowledge

Paul Nation

Introduction

Knowing a word involves knowledge of a variety of different aspects of knowledge, and these aspects of knowledge can be known to different levels of strength and detail, and to different levels of fluency. The main reason for a teacher to be interested in what is involved in knowing a word is so that the focus and balance of a language course ensures the development of well-rounded, usable vocabulary knowledge. Thus, this chapter focuses on how the various aspects of knowing a word relate to learning, teaching, and testing.

There are several principles that relate to knowing a word.

1 Not all aspects of word knowledge are equally important.
2 Word knowledge can be described in terms of breadth (aspects), depth (strength), and fluency.
3 Word knowledge develops over a period of time.
4 Some knowledge is limited to individual words, while other knowledge is systematic.
5 Some knowledge needs to be learned, while other knowledge is constructed through common sense and knowledge of the world.
6 The difficulty of acquiring knowledge (learning burden) is affected by a variety of factors including regularity of patterning, the learner's L1, other known languages, opportunity and experience, personal commitment, the quality of teaching, and the quality of course design.
7 Vocabulary knowledge is most likely to develop if there is a balance of incidental and deliberate appropriate opportunities for learning.
8 Learned aspects of word knowledge are affected by a small number of psychological learning conditions.
9 Fluency of word knowledge can be a useful learning focus.
10 Testing word knowledge requires careful thought about the purpose of testing, the aspects and strength of knowledge to be tested, the effects of test item type, and the people being tested.

Teachers and course designers need to be aware of the various aspects of knowing a word and need to know how to observe and support their development.

Critical Issues and Topics

The most widely known description of what is involved in knowing a word comes from Nation (2013a, p. 49) as shown in Table 2.1.

The receptive-productive distinction runs through each of the nine aspects in this table. Receptive knowledge is the kind of knowledge needed for listening and reading. At its most basic, it involves being able to recall a meaning when meeting a word form. Productive knowledge is the kind of knowledge needed for speaking and writing. At its most basic it involves being able to recall a word form in order to express a meaning. Receptive knowledge is easier to gain than productive knowledge. However, the kind of learning that is done should match the kind of knowledge needed. So, if a learner's goal is to read the language, then the most effective kinds of learning will involve incidental learning while reading and deliberate receptive learning using flash cards. If however a learner needs to use all the four skills of listening, speaking, reading, and writing, then there needs to be incidental learning through all four skills and both receptive and productive deliberate learning (Griffin & Harley, 1996; Waring, 1997; Webb, 2009). The two principles that lie behind these research findings is that we learn what we focus on, and we should focus on what we need.

Let us now look at each of the parts of Table 2.1 to see the kind of knowledge involved, and how it might be learned.

Table 2.1 What is involved in knowing a word

Form	Spoken	R	What does the word sound like?
		P	How is the word pronounced?
	Written	R	What does the word look like?
		P	How is the word written and spelled?
	Word parts	R	What parts are recognizable in this word?
		P	What word parts are needed to express the meaning?
Meaning	Form and meaning	R	What meaning does this word form signal?
		P	What word form can be used to express this meaning?
	Concept and referents	R	What is included in the concept?
		P	What items can the concept refer to?
	Associations	R	What other words does this make us think of?
		P	What other words could we use instead of this one?
Use	Grammatical functions	R	In what patterns does the word occur?
		P	In what patterns must we use this word?
	Collocations	R	What words or types of words occur with this one?
		P	What words or types of words must we use with this one?
	Constraints on use (register, frequency, . . .)	R	Where, when, and how often would we expect to meet this word?
		P	Where, when, and how often can we use this word?

Note: In column 3, R = receptive knowledge, P = productive knowledge.

Source: Adapted from Nation, 2013a

Knowing the Spoken Form of Words

One of the early stages in learning the spoken form of a word involves learning any new sounds that are not in the L1, and at a more general level developing awareness of how sounds can fit together, for example in consonant clusters and consonant vowel combinations. Each language has its own collection of sounds and permitted sound combinations, and even young native speakers have a feeling for what combinations are normal and what are not. Some languages have a variety of consonant clusters while others have few or none. For a native speaker, the learning of sounds is largely systematic, with highly contrasting open and closed sounds being learned early (this partly explains why children's words for mother and father are very similar in different unrelated languages), and with a roughly predictable order of learning sound features. With foreign language learners the first language sound system has major positive and negative influences. Age of learning is strongly related to the likelihood of second language learners acquiring a native-like pronunciation, with younger learners more likely to be successful. There are several explanations for this, each emphasizing maturational, cognitive, or affective factors. The maturational explanation suggests around a certain age that there are physical changes in the brain that make the learning of a new sound system difficult. The cognitive explanation suggests that as the first language sound system becomes more strongly established, it becomes a kind of filter that influences a learner's view of a different sound system (Flege, 1981). The affective explanation says that our pronunciation is an important part of our identity and taking on a new pronunciation, even for a different language, is seen as having to change an important part of who we are (Stevick, 1978). Each of these explanations requires a different approach to learning, with some experimental ways of dealing with the affective explanation involving the consumption of alcohol or the use of chemical relaxants (Guiora, Beit-Hallami, Brannon, Dull, & Scovel, 1972; Brannon, & Dull, 1972).

Acquiring a stable pronunciation of words is important for vocabulary learning, especially for young learners (Service & Kohonen, 1995), because one way that words can enter long-term memory is through the phonological loop, and a stable pronunciation is needed for a word to enter the phonological loop. Older learners however can draw on a wider range of memory strategies beyond formal repetition.

Developing knowledge of the spoken forms of words occurs across the four strands of learning through meaning-focused listening to input, learning through having to engage in spoken communication (meaning-focused output), deliberate learning and teaching, and spoken fluency development. Some adult learners of foreign languages stress the importance of knowledge of articulatory phonetics in improving their pronunciation.

Knowing the Written Form of Words

It is possible to learn another language without learning to read or write it, but especially for learners of English as a foreign language, being able to read allows access to a very large amount of graded reading material, which can provide an enormous boost in developing language proficiency.

Learning to read has a strong phonological basis (Perfetti & Lesgold, 1979) and this is especially true in languages whose writing system is systematically related to the spoken language through an alphabetic or syllabic writing system. An early requirement for learning to read an alphabetic language like English is phonological awareness. In essence this is the realization that words can be broken into separate sounds, and separate sounds can combine to make words. Some children are not ready to deal with this before the age of six while others are ready much earlier. A very useful activity to develop phonological awareness in a young child is to play games like this – What word is this /p/ – /e/ – /t/? (The separate sounds are not the names of the letters as when saying the alphabet, but are the sounds). When the child gets good at doing this, then the child can take the role of breaking the word into sounds to test the listener. After phonological awareness, the next important piece of knowledge in learning to read is the alphabetic principle, that is, that sounds can be represented by letters. In some languages this representation is very regular and predictable. In English, there are many variants and exceptions, but there is still a core of regularity.

Learning the written form of words needs to occur across the four strands of meaning-focused input (learning by reading texts at the right level), meaning-focused output (having to write words and sentences), language-focused learning (deliberately learning letter shapes, sound-spelling correspondences, and word attack skills, and memorizing irregular words), and fluency development (doing plenty of very easy reading).

Knowing Word Parts

For English, knowledge of word parts primarily involves being able to use the inflectional system of the language, with the next step involving the more gradual growth of knowledge of the derivational affixes. Mochizuki and Aizawa (2000) tested Japanese learners' knowledge of English affixes, finding that affix knowledge increased with vocabulary size, and that there were notable gaps in their knowledge. Schmitt and Meara (1997) and McLean (2017) also found a relationship between vocabulary size and affix knowledge. Sasao and Webb (2017) developed a comprehensive Word Part Levels Test which was used with a variety of learners to propose levels of affix knowledge. The better-known affixes tended to be those that occurred more frequently. There were also high correlations between item difficulty estimates for learners with the same L1 and the total participants' item difficulty estimates. This showed that the first language did not play a strong role in knowledge of English affixes, and learning opportunity through input was likely to have had the greatest effect.

Knowledge of word stems (Wei, 2015), such as *pos* (put), *vers* (turn), and *cept* (take), is best not considered as an aspect of knowing a word, as this knowledge is largely meta-cognitive and not obvious to most native speakers. Word stem knowledge is most usefully developed as a mnemonic device for linking form and meaning.

Connecting Form and Meaning

Being able to recognize or produce the spoken or written form of a word is not much use unless the form has a connection with a meaning. In terms of language use, the most important aspects of vocabulary knowledge for a learner of English as a foreign language are knowledge of the word form and the form-meaning connection. This is because in order to start to read and listen, a learner needs to be able to recognize the form of useful words and be able to attach a meaning to them. For beginners this meaning will be an L1 word. The form-meaning connection is simply attaching a known form to a known meaning.

It is possible to know the form of a word and to know a meaning for a word and yet not realize that the two are connected. This is a bit like the common enough phenomenon of being familiar with someone's name through having heard about them and not realizing that you have already met that person but did not know that that was their name. This phenomenon is common enough in learning a foreign language because in the early and intermediate

stages of foreign language learning, first language concepts, usually in the form of translations, are used as the initial meanings for foreign language words. Thus for many foreign language words, initial learning involves learning a word form and making the form-meaning
connection with the first language concept.

It is worthwhile separating out the form-meaning connection as an aspect of knowing a
word because there are very helpful learning conditions, such as receptive and productive
retrieval, varied retrieval and elaboration, which can strengthen this aspect of knowledge.
The very well-researched keyword technique (Pressley, 1977) is a mnemonic technique specifically designed to make the form-meaning connection. Research by Deconinck, Boers,
and Eyckmans (2017) shows that getting learners to consider whether the form of a newly
met L2 word fits its meaning has very positive effects on establishing the form-meaning connection. This technique is somewhat like the etymological analysis that Boers and colleagues
(see, e,g., Boers and Lindstromberg, 2009) advocate for learning multiword figuratives.

The form-meaning connection is usually easy to make for cognates and loanwords. This
is because of the closely similar forms; for example, *revolusi* (in Indonesian) and *revolution*
(in English) share a roughly similar meaning.

Learning the Concept and Referents

Most words have a core meaning that runs through all or most of their uses. For example,
the word *green* has many listed senses in dictionaries referring to color, vegetables, lack of
ripeness, inexperience, and so on, but when we look at them, they all seem to share a common core meaning. This should not be surprising because they are all signaled by the same
word form. As we might expect, it is easier to learn a new sense for a word than it is to learn
a completely new word, especially if the new sense and the known senses have a common
underlying meaning (Bogaards, 2001). Thus, it is a useful teaching and learning strategy
to draw attention to core meanings and to consider how newly met senses relate to known
senses. When using a dictionary for example, it is worth looking at all senses of a word to
see what is common, rather than just focusing on the relevant contextual sense.

Some words have completely unrelated meanings for the same spoken or written form.
Usually these unrelated meanings have different histories and it is an accident that they share
the same word form. Table 2.2 provides the technical terms for the types of relationships
with some examples.

The most frequent 2,000 words of English (West, 1953) contains seven homographs
(*close, lead, minute, present, row, wind,* and *wound*), 55 homonyms, and 147 homophones
(Parent, 2012). The *Academic Word List* (Coxhead, 2000) contains 60 homonyms and homographs, but in only five cases would both words meet the criteria for inclusion in the list –
issue, volume, objective, abstract, and *attribute* (Wang & Nation, 2004).

A feature of homonyms and homographs is that it is very unusual for two words like
bear (to carry) and *bear* (the animal) to have roughly similar frequencies of occurrence.

Table 2.2 Homonyms, homographs, and homophones

	Spoken form	Written form	Meaning	Examples
Homonyms	The same	The same	Different	band (group) – (hoop/ring)
Homographs	Different	The same	Different	minute (time) – (very small)
Homophones	The same	Different	Different	peace – piece

Typically one word makes up well over 70% of the total occurrences. *Bear* (the verb) for example accounts for 92% of the occurrences of the form and *bear* (the animal) 8%. In the most frequent 2,000 words of English only six homonyms (*bowl, ring, rest, net, yard, miss*) have roughly similar frequencies (see Nation, 2016, Chapter 3 for more detail).

Where possible, homonyms, homographs, and homophones should not be taught together, and the most frequent items should be taught first.

Developing Associations With Words

Associations between words (Miller & Fellbaum, 1991) are largely developed incidentally through receptive and productive language use. There are also associations which occur through knowledge of the world and through common sense. There are some conventional associations, such as opposites, synonyms, and hyponyms, that can be established through deliberate learning, but there is likely to be little value in teaching them.

There are numerous activities that involve classifying words into groups and arranging them into semantic maps which can be seen as a form of elaboration which may help strengthen learning.

Learning the Grammar of Words

Part of word knowledge involves being able to use words. Some of this knowledge relates to language systems and some relates to particular words. Let us look at systematic knowledge first. English nouns may be countable or uncountable and this affects whether they can have singular and plural forms, whether they can be used with numerals, articles, and determiners like *much, many, each*, and *every*, and subject-verb agreement. English verbs can be transitive and intransitive, which affects the use of the passive and what can occur after the verb. Some adjectives can be modified for degree, some taking *–er* and *–est*, and others *more* and *most*.

For many learners of English as a foreign language, learning this kind of systematic knowledge involves profound conceptual development, particularly if the particular knowledge is not similar to first language use. Learning the singular plural distinction, for example, is much more difficult than learning to add *–s* for plurals and so on. It involves developing the concepts of countability and uncountability and applying this view of nouns to their classification and use. It is not surprising that even very advanced learners of English as a foreign language often struggle with singular and plural.

There is some value in giving deliberate attention to grammar, especially for consciousness raising and for self-monitoring of language production. However it is likely that the systematic knowledge of grammatical features which underlies normal language use is ultimately the result of incidental learning from large amounts of meaningful comprehensible input. It is thus useful to see the learning of grammar occurring across the four strands of meaning-focused input, meaning-focused output, language-focused learning, and fluency development. Three of these strands involve incidental learning and one involves deliberate learning. This is probably about the right balance for learning grammar. Ellis (2005) describes an excellent set of principles for the learning of grammar which largely fits with the four strands.

Some grammar knowledge is word-based. That is, it relates to particular words. It is at this point that grammatical knowledge and collocational knowledge overlap. Knowing the word *agree* involves knowing that it is used as a verb, that it is intransitive but it can occur in sentences such as *We are all agreed that . . .* , that when it is not a simple sentence (*I agree*) it is typically followed by a preposition group beginning with *with*, or an object clause beginning with *that*. No other verb takes the same set of patterns. When beginning to learn the word *agree*, it makes sense to memorize one or two of its most frequent uses in example sentences. This memorization should include analysis and understanding of the parts of the example sentences, rather than simply memorizing them as unanalyzed wholes. This can also be done through the use of substitution tables.

Concordance analysis can be a useful way of gathering information for such teaching and for intermediate and advanced learners the use of concordances can support learning (Cobb, 1997).

Dealing With Collocations

Sinclair (2004) puts the case most strongly for giving attention to collocations: "The lexical unit is best described maximally, not minimally" (p. 81). However, this should be taken to mean that in addition to giving attention to words as units we should also see how they behave in larger units. This is because the vast majority of multiword units are made up of parts where the meanings of the parts make an obvious contribution to the meaning of the whole, and where the parts behave grammatically and semantically in ways that are consistent with their use in other places (Liu, 2010). That is, collocations are not arbitrary groupings of words but are typically regular predictable combinations.

The biggest problem in dealing with research on collocation is coming up with a definition of what can be considered a collocation and then following that consistently. For the purposes of language learning, it is useful to classify collocations into core idioms, figuratives, and literals (Grant & Nation, 2006). Core idioms make up a small number of collocations in English, probably around 100. In core idioms, the meanings of the parts do not clearly relate to the meaning of the whole. It is likely that early in their history there was a connection but this is now not known. The most common core idioms include *as well (as)*, *by and large*, *out of hand*, *serve someone right*, and *take someone to task*.

Figuratives have two related meanings – a literal meaning and a figurative meaning. Here are some examples – *saved by the bell*, *give someone the green light*, *walking on air*, *between a rock and a hard place*. Many figuratives are related to a particular topic area – *out for the count* relates to boxing, *toe the line* relates to military drill, and *threw in his hand* relates to card playing. Gaining awareness of the origin of a figurative helps learning (Boers & Lindstromberg, 2009).

The meaning of literals is closely connected to the meanings of the parts, although it is possible to set up a scale of transparency from those very clearly connected (*like ice cream*) to those containing elements of opaqueness (*put up with*, *about time*). Martinez and Schmitt (2012) have a very carefully made lists of the most useful of these semi-opaque collocations.

These three meaning-transparency-based categories of collocations each have their different language-focused learning approaches (Grant & Nation, 2006). Core idioms need to be memorized as complete units. Because most of them are not frozen but can have different forms (*you're pulling my leg*; *your leg's being pulled*; *pull the other one, it's got bells on it*), it is worth giving some attention to the parts. The learning of some core idioms may be helped by creating false etymologies, such as *cats and dogs* in the expression *raining cats and dogs*. Figuratives need to be dealt with using the obvious strategy of relating the literal meaning to the figurative meaning, and where possible finding out the topic area of the literal meaning. Literals can be largely learned incidentally, although in the early stages of learning a language it is well worth memorizing very useful expressions (*How much does that cost?*, *Thanks very much, I'd like* . . .) in order to quickly develop spoken fluency (Nation & Crabbe, 1991). Semi-opaque literals require a mixture of analysis and memorization.

The fluency development strand of a course sets up good conditions for collocational knowledge to grow and strengthen. There are several reasons for this. Firstly, receptive fluency development activities (listening and reading) should involve large amounts of input and this can increase noticing and repetition. Secondly, fluency activities often involve some pressure to go faster, and this pressure can encourage learners to restructure their knowledge to work with larger units of language, with words rather than letters, and with phrases rather than words (McLaughlin, 1990). Thirdly, repetition in input usually involves varied repetition rather than verbatim repetition (Webb & Nation, 2017), and varied retrieval is a very effective learning condition (Joe, 1998). The fluency development strand and the other incidental learning strands of meaning-focused input and meaning-focused output are important for all aspects of vocabulary knowledge. Language-focused learning, of which teaching is only a part, needs to be accompanied by learning through use.

A lot of work on collocations has focused on formulaic sequences (Schmitt, 2004; Wray, 2008). Formulaic sequences are units of language that are most likely stored as whole units for the purposes of language use. The motivations for such storage are frequency of occurrence (If a phrase or sentence is used or met often, it is more efficiently stored as a whole unit) and irregularity (If a phrase or sentence cannot be easily reconstructed or analyzed, then it needs to be treated as a unit). Such storage contributes to fluency.

Managing Constraints on Use

A rather small number of words and phrases are marked by restrictions on their use, and being aware of these restrictions is one aspect of knowing a word. Swear words are the most striking examples of such restrictions. There are numerous situations where they cannot be appropriately used. Other restrictions on use include politeness restrictions (words like *fat, old, stupid* need to be avoided when talking to the person they apply to), geographical restrictions (dialects such as US English vs. UK English), age restrictions (language used to talk to children), datedness restrictions in that some words are old-fashioned, and frequency restrictions in that some words are so rare that they sound strange when they are used for common situations.

A very wide ranging restriction in English comes from the very important contrast between spoken and written language (Biber & Conrad, 2009). In formal writing the use of colloquial spoken expressions seems inappropriate. In friendly spoken language and in friendly letters and emails, formal written language sounds unfriendly. In English, this contrast comes partly from the Germanic vs. Latinate vocabulary contrast, with Latinate vocabulary being more formal. Learning about restrictions on use can occur through feedback on use, and through informed observation of proficient users of the language. A few words, like swear words, need to come with a health warning when they are first learned.

The Conditions for Learning

Listing the aspects of what is involved in knowing a word makes vocabulary learning and vocabulary teaching seem like formidable tasks. This is of course partly true. Learners need to know a lot of words and there is a lot to know about each word. However, let us now look at how these formidable tasks are made manageable, but before that it is useful to briefly

Table 2.3 Conditions affecting vocabulary learning

Number of meetings	Initial occurrence/repetition	
Quality of attention	Incidental attention	Deliberate attention
Noticing		
Receptive or productive retrieval		
Varied receptive meetings or productive use		
Elaboration		

Source: Adapted from Webb & Nation, 2017

consider the psychological conditions that favor learning. Table 2.3 summarizes these conditions (Webb & Nation, 2017).

The two major conditions in Table 2.3 are *Number of meetings* and *Quality of attention*. Essentially, vocabulary learning depends on how often words are met and the quality or depth of the mental processing at each meeting (Nakata, 2011). The major contrast regarding quality of processing is between incidental attention and deliberate attention, with deliberate attention typically resulting in stronger learning. Both incidental and deliberate attention can occur with different degrees of quality. Noticing is the most superficial but nonetheless still useful level of attention. For incidental learning this could involve simply noticing an unknown word during reading or listening. For deliberate learning this could involve looking up the word in a dictionary or making a word card containing the word and its meaning. The next level of attention involves retrieval and depends on previous noticing. Receptive retrieval occurs when a learner sees or hears a word and has to recall its meaning. This can occur incidentally while reading or deliberately when working with flash cards. Productive retrieval occurs when a learner wants to express a meaning and has to recall the appropriate spoken or written word form. Receptive and productive retrieval are more effective for learning if they involve some degree of difference from previous retrievals or previous noticings, that is, varied meetings or use (Joe, 1998). Fortunately, when words are met again incidentally during listening and reading, they typically occur in different contexts. Elaboration involves some enrichment during the meeting with a word. In incidental learning, this enrichment can come from meeting or having to produce a word in a memorable communicative situation. During reading, a memorable picture may result in elaboration by enriching knowledge of the word, or reading the word on a sign or label may make its occurrence memorable. In deliberate learning, elaboration can occur through the use of a mnemonic technique such as the keyword technique, through word part analysis, or through the analysis of core meaning in a dictionary entry.

The receptive-productive distinction runs through all the learning conditions in Table 2.3, including number of meetings. In general, productive meetings are more demanding and more likely to result in stronger learning than receptive meetings (Griffin & Harley, 1996). The ranking of the levels of quality of attention is largely for explanatory purposes and is definitely not to suggest that ideally all meetings should involve deliberate productive elaboration. However, there are small but effective ways of increasing the quality of attention that learners and teachers could use. Here are some of the most useful ways.

1   Before looking up a word in a dictionary try to guess or recall its meaning. This replaces noticing with retrieval or elaboration.

2   Use flash cards rather than vocabulary notebooks. Notebooks typically present the form and meaning together (noticing) rather than encouraging retrieval of the form or meaning (Nakata, 2011).
3   Encourage extensive reading of graded readers (Day & Bamford, 1998). This provides large amounts of repetition of vocabulary and involves varied receptive retrieval. Talking about what has been read provides an opportunity for productive varied retrieval.
4   Use linked skills activities (Nation, 2013b, Chapter 15) where learners deal with the same material across three different skills, for example, they may read a text, talk about it, and then write about it. This encourages repetition, retrieval, and varied meetings and use.
5   At the beginning and end of a class, get the learners to recall what they covered in previous classes or in the present class session. This encourages deliberate attention, retrieval, and perhaps elaboration. It can also help move receptive learning to productive use.

Although we have mainly looked at learning word form and the form-meaning connection in the preceding examples, the conditions for learning apply to all aspects of knowing a word. Let us now look at how the aspects of knowing a word are likely to be learned.

Developing Word Knowledge

As has been noted several times in this chapter, learning is not solely dependent upon teaching, but it occurs across the four strands of meaning-focused input, meaning-focused output, language-focused learning, and fluency development. Teaching makes up part of the language-focused learning strand, sharing time with deliberate study. If there is plenty of input and the chance to produce language under both easy and slightly demanding conditions, then a lot of incidental vocabulary learning will occur.

Vocabulary learning is a cumulative process, both in increasing the number of words known and in increasing depth of knowledge of words (Read, 2004). Each word needs to be met several times in a variety of ways and we should expect knowledge of each word to grow and strengthen over time rather than expect each word to be fully learned on the first meeting. A teacher's concern should not be with how a word should be introduced to the learners, but with how it can be met multiple times in a variety of contexts.

The learning burden of a word is the amount of effort needed to learn it. Words differ in their learning burden, with some words being very easy to learn because they are like L1 words, and others requiring various degrees of effort. The learning burden of a word depends on its relationship with L1 words or with words in other languages that the learner knows, and on its regularity with regard to the systems of form, meaning, and use within the L2. Speakers of European languages which are related to English may find that they already know a lot about English vocabulary because the same words occur within their first language. For example, around 80% of the words in the Academic Word List (Coxhead, 2000) have roughly similar forms and meanings in Spanish. Now, with lots of borrowings of English words into languages such as Japanese (Daulton, 2008), Thai, and Indonesian, learners will already know some English vocabulary even before they begin to learn English.

Some words in a foreign language may have a regular predictable spelling while others have an unusual spelling. The senses of some words stay close to their core meaning. The grammar of some words is largely predictable from their part of speech. Research by De Groot (2006) suggests that words that are easy to learn because they fit into regular systems are not only easier to learn but are also well retained. That is, high levels of learning effort are not essential for good retention, if what is being learned fits into known patterns.

If teachers have knowledge of the learners' L1 and are familiar with the writing system, morphology, and grammar of the L2, they can readily work out the learning burden of L2 words and direct deliberate attention to the aspects of knowledge that most strongly affect the learning burden of a particular word. For example, words like *one*, *yacht*, and *receive* need attention to spelling. Words like *fork*, *sweet*, and *agree* need attention to core meaning. Words like *discuss*, *enjoy*, and *police* need attention to grammar.

The various aspects of word knowledge are not equally important. For initial learning we would expect spoken word form and the form-meaning connection to be the first aspects that would be learned for most words. This knowledge allows the beginnings of comprehension. For a survival vocabulary (Nation & Crabbe, 1991) intended for productive use, spoken word form, the form-meaning connection, and some very basic grammatical knowledge would be important. Other aspects of knowledge can become focuses of attention as proficiency develops.

Future Directions

The model of word knowledge used in this chapter is not at all sophisticated. It is static and treats the various aspects as unrelated parts. It is a convenient way of covering a range of kinds of knowledge but it does not represent vocabulary in use. It also does not represent how a vocabulary develops. A model more focused on use and growth is likely to provide insights that can enrich learning and research. The work of Paul Meara (2006) has gone a long way towards doing this, and this work needs to be continued.

Knowledge of vocabulary develops in many ways, as a result of deliberate learning, direct teaching, incidental learning, transfer from the L1, knowledge of language systems, and the integration of language knowledge with real-world knowledge. There is a lack of longitudinal studies that consider learning from a variety of sources and examine how word knowledge develops over time and under what conditions. Such studies need not all be long-term but can look at what happens to word knowledge over short periods of time. For example, Barcroft's (2007) study of opportunities for word retrieval while reading has useful implications for glossaries and dictionary use. Similarly, studies of what happens to particular words during extensive reading (Horst, 2005; Pigada & Schmitt, 2006; Pellicer-Sánchez & Schmitt, 2010) have useful messages for the use and design of graded readers. Pellicer-Sánchez's (2016) eye-tracking study provided a fascinating view into what can happen to previously unknown words while reading. We need more process-focused studies of this kind and quality.

Research on morphological knowledge (McLean, 2017; Mochizuki & Aizawa, 2000) shows that some groups of learners have very poor knowledge of the derivational affixes of English. This knowledge is way below what learners should know at their current proficiency level. This has a major effect on their vocabulary size and their ability to cope with vocabulary while reading. There is virtually no research which shows how this knowledge can be quickly developed through deliberate learning. There is also a need to examine the role of extensive reading and extensive listening in supporting the development of this knowledge, as Sasao and Webb (2017) found a relationship between frequency and knowledge. Morphological knowledge is at the intersection of breadth and depth of vocabulary knowledge and needs to be an important learning focus in the beginning and intermediate levels of language learning.

The quality of research on collocation continues to improve, in part helped by the increasing power of computers and the increasing availability of spoken and written corpora of various kinds. A largely neglected area in collocation involves the transparency of collocations, namely how easy is it to get the meaning of the collocation from the meaning of its parts. This is also called compositionality. As argued earlier in this chapter, the transparency of collocations is directly related to how they are comprehended and learned. The categories of core idioms, figuratives, and literals relate to transparency, but within each of these categories there are degrees of transparency. Studies looking at both frequency and transparency could provide data on the size of the learning task for collocations and further refine our understanding of how they might be learned. This could lead to studies of how learners actually cope with them in context.

Testing Control of Aspects of Word Knowledge

There is now a growing number of tests examining learners' knowledge of the written form and the form-meaning connection, and some of these are available in bilingual versions. These include the Vocabulary Size Test (Nation & Beglar, 2007) and the Updated Vocabulary Levels Test (Webb, Sasao, & Ballance, 2017). The Picture Vocabulary Size Test (Anthony & Nation, 2017) uses both spoken and written cues to test knowledge of the most frequent 6,000 words of English and is intended for use with young children. There has been vigorous and very helpful debate and research on the unit of counting, the item format and the role of guessing (including the use of *I don't know*), and the interpretation of such tests. This debate and research will undoubtedly improve the nature and use of such tests and will provide useful guidelines for future tests of different aspects of word knowledge.

Webb and Sasao (2013) have developed carefully constructed tests of word part knowledge. Read's (1995) work on the Word Associates Test combined collocational knowledge and knowledge of associations and encouraged research on the relationship between breadth and depth of vocabulary knowledge (Qian, 1999), with the finding that as vocabulary size (breadth) grows, so does depth of knowledge.

There is a need for tests that look for systematic aspects of word knowledge, such as control of the spelling system, dealing with related senses of words, and the ability to understand figuratives. Some of the measures used with young native speakers, such as the running record (Clay, 2013) where a learner is scored on the ability to read a text aloud, and reading comprehension tests may be adapted to become useful diagnostic tools when working with learners of English as a foreign language.

There is also a need for diagnostic tests of strategies for dealing with aspects of word knowledge that are relevant for foreign language learners. Sasao and Webb (2018) have developed a test to measure skill in guessing from context, which is a strategy for dealing with word meaning. Dictionary use is another such strategy for accessing word meaning, and flash card use is a strategy for learning form-meaning connections. There are form, meaning, and use strategies which can all contribute to knowing words.

There are three important messages to take from this chapter. Firstly, there is more to knowing a word than knowing what it means. Secondly, depth of word knowledge gradually develops in a variety of ways and teaching is only one of the contributors to this knowledge, although not the only one where teachers can have a positive influence. Thirdly, it is possible to monitor the development of many aspects of knowledge through tests and observational procedures, and both teachers and learners should make use of these.

Further Reading

Nation, I. S. P. (2013). Knowing a word. In I. S. P. Nation (Ed.), *Learning vocabulary in another language* (2nd ed.). Cambridge: Cambridge University Press, Chapter 2, pages 44–91.

This chapter focuses on knowing a word, with an extended discussion of the receptive-productive distinction and the nine aspects involved in knowing a word. There is a substantial list of references for the chapter and these can be updated by referring to the regularly updated vocabulary bibliography that appears on Nation's website, particularly those articles followed by the reference number [2].

Nation, I. S. P. (2013). Finding and learning multiword units. In I. S. P. Nation (Ed.), *Learning vocabulary in another language* (2nd ed.). Cambridge: Cambridge University Press, Chapter 12, pages 479–513.

This chapter looks critically at research on collocation and multiword units and suggests ways of searching for them in corpora and in classifying them.

Webb, S., & Nation, I. S. P. (2017). Learning burden. In S. Webb & I. S. P. Nation (Eds.), *How vocabulary is learned*. Oxford: Oxford University Press, pages 25–42.

This chapter has a detailed discussion of learning burden and how it can be applied.

Sasao, Y., & Webb, S. (2017). The word part levels test. *Language Teaching Research, 21*(1), 12–30.

This comprehensive study of knowledge of English affixes provides tests of three kinds of affix knowledge plus results that can be used to guide teaching.

Related Topics

The mental lexicon, the relationship between vocabulary knowledge and proficiency, L1 and L2 vocabulary size and growth, how vocabulary fits into theories of L2 learning, incidental vocabulary learning, measuring depth of vocabulary knowledge

References

Anthony, L., & Nation, I. S. P. (2017). *Picture Vocabulary Size Test* (Version 1.0.0) [Computer Software]. Tokyo, Japan: Waseda University. Retrieved from www.laurenceanthony.net/software/pvst

Barcroft, J. (2007). Effects of opportunities for word retrieval during second language vocabulary learning. *Language Learning, 57*(1), 35–56.

Biber, D., & Conrad, S. (2009). *Register, genre, and style*. Cambridge, UK: Cambridge University Press.

Boers, F., & Lindstromberg, S. (2009). *Optimizing a lexical approach to instructed second language acquisition*. Basingstoke, UK: Palgrave Macmillan.

Bogaards, P. (2001). Lexical units and the learning of foreign language vocabulary. *Studies in Second Language Acquisition, 23*, 321–343.

Clay, M. (2013). *An observation survey of early literacy achievement* (3rd ed.). Portsmouth, NH: Heinemann Publishing.

Cobb, T. (1997). Is there any measurable learning from hands-on concordancing? *System, 25*(3), 301–315.

Coxhead, A. (2000). A new academic word list. *TESOL Quarterly, 34*(2), 213–238.

Daulton, F. E. (2008). *Japan's built-in lexicon of English-based loanwords*. Clevedon, UK: Multilingual Matters.

Day, R. R., & Bamford, J. (1998). *Extensive reading in the second language classroom*. Cambridge, UK: Cambridge University Press.

de Groot, A. (2006). Effects of stimulus characteristics and background music on foreign language vocabulary learning and forgetting. *Language Learning, 56*(3), 463–506.

Deconinck, J., Boers, F., & Eyckmans, J. (2017). "Does the form of this word fit its meaning?" The effect of learner-generated mappings on L2 word recall. *Language Teaching Research, 21*(1), 31–53.

Ellis, R. (2005). Principles of instructed language learning. *System, 33*, 209–224.

Flege, J. E. (1981). The phonological basis of foreign accent: A hypothesis. *TESOL Quarterly, 15*(4), 443–455.

Grant, L., & Nation, I. S. P. (2006). How many idioms are there in English? *ITL – International Journal of Applied Linguistics, 151*, 1–14.

Griffin, G. F., & Harley, T. A. (1996). List learning of second language vocabulary. *Applied Psycholinguistics, 17*, 443–460.

Guiora, A. Z., Beit-Hallami, B., Brannon, R. C. L., Dull, C. Y., & Scovel, T. (1972). The effects of experimentally induced changes in ego states on pronunciation ability in a second language: An exploratory study. *Comprehensive Psychiatry, 13*, 421–428.

Guiora, A. Z., Brannon, R. C. L., & Dull, C. Y. (1972). Empathy and second language learning. *Language Learning, 22*(1), 111–130.

Horst, M. (2005). Learning L2 vocabulary through extensive reading: A measurement study. *Canadian Modern Language Review, 61*(3), 355–382.

Joe, A. (1998). What effects do text-based tasks promoting generation have on incidental vocabulary acquisition? *Applied Linguistics, 19*(3), 357–377.

Liu, D. (2010). Going beyond patterns: Involving cognitive analysis in the learning of collocations. *TESOL Quarterly, 44*(1), 4–30.

Martinez, R., & Schmitt, N. (2012). A phrasal expressions list. *Applied Linguistics, 33*(3), 299–320.

McLaughlin, B. (1990). Restructuring. *Applied Linguistics, 11*(2), 113–128.

McLean, S. (2017). Evidence for the adoption of the flemma as an appropriate word counting unit. *Applied Linguistics*, 1–24. https://doi.org/10.1093/applin/amw050

Meara, P. (2006). Emergent properties of multilingual lexicons. *Applied Linguistics, 27*(4), 620–644.

Miller, G. A., & Fellbaum, C. (1991). Semantic networks in English. *Cognition, 41*, 197–229.

Mochizuki, M., & Aizawa, K. (2000). An affix acquisition order for EFL learners: An exploratory study. *System, 28*, 291–304.

Nakata, T. (2011). Computer-assisted second language vocabulary learning in a paired-associate paradigm: A critical investigation of flashcard software. *Computer Assisted Language Learning, 24*(1), 17–38.

Nation, I. S. P. (2013a). *Learning vocabulary in another language* (2nd ed.). Cambridge, UK: Cambridge University Press.

Nation, I. S. P. (2013b). *What should every EFL teacher know*. Seoul: Compass Publishing (available free from Paul Nation's web site).

Nation, I. S. P. (2016). *Making and using word lists for language learning and teaching*. Amsterdam: John Benjamins.

Nation, I. S. P., & Beglar, D. (2007). A vocabulary size test. *The Language Teacher, 31*(7), 9–13.

Nation, I. S. P., & Crabbe, D. (1991). A survival language learning syllabus for foreign travel. *System, 19*(3), 191–201.

Parent, K. (2012). The most frequent English homonyms. *RELC Journal, 43*(1), 69–81.

Pellicer-Sánchez, A. (2016). Incidental L2 vocabulary acquisition from and while reading: An eye-tracking study. *Studies in Second Language Acquisition, 38*(1), 97–130.

Pellicer-Sánchez, A., & Schmitt, N. (2010). Incidental vocabulary acquisition from an authentic novel: Do *Things Fall Apart*? *Reading in a Foreign Language, 22*(1), 31–55.

Perfetti, C. A., & Lesgold, A. M. (1979). Coding and comprehension in skilled reading and implications for reading instruction. In L. B. Resnick et al. (Eds.), *Theory and practice of early reading* (pp. 57–84). Hillsdale, NJ: Lawrence Erlbaum Associates.

Pigada, M., & Schmitt, N. (2006). Vocabulary acquisition from extensive reading: A case study. *Reading in a Foreign Language, 18*(1), 1–28.

Pressley, M. (1977). Children's use of the keyword method to learn simple Spanish vocabulary words. *Journal of Educational Psychology, 69*(5), 465–472.

Qian, D. (1999). Assessing the roles of depth and breadth of vocabulary knowledge in reading comprehension. *Canadian Modern Language Review, 56*(2), 282–307.

Read, J. (1995). Refining the word associates format as a measure of depth of vocabulary knowledge. *New Zealand Studies in Applied Linguistics, 1*, 1–17.

Read, J. (2004). Plumbing the depths: How should the construct of vocabulary knowledge be defined? In P. Bogaards & B. Laufer (Eds.), *Vocabulary in a second language: Selection, acquisition and testing* (pp. 209–227). Amsterdam: John Benjamins.

Sasao, Y., & Webb, S. (2017). The word part levels test. *Language Teaching Research, 21*(1), 12–30.

Sasao, Y., & Webb, S. (2018). The guessing from context test. *ITL – International Journal of Applied Linguistics, 169*(1), 115–141.

Schmitt, N. (Ed.). (2004). *Formulaic sequences*. Amsterdam: John Benjamins.

Schmitt, N., & Meara, P. (1997). Researching vocabulary through a word knowledge framework: Word associations and verbal suffixes. *Studies in Second Language Acquisition, 19*, 17–36.

Service, E., & Kohonen, V. (1995). Is the relation between phonological memory and foreign language learning accounted for by vocabulary acquisition? *Applied Psycholinguistics, 16*, 155–172.

Sinclair, J. (2004). New evidence, new priorities, new attitudes. In J. Sinclair (Ed.), *How to use corpora in language teaching* (pp. 271–299). Amsterdam: John Benjamins.

Stevick, E. W. (1978). Toward a practical philosophy of pronunciation: Another view. *TESOL Quarterly, 12*(2), 145–150.

Wang, M.-T. K., & Nation, P. (2004). Word meaning in academic English: Homography in the Academic Word List. *Applied Linguistics, 25*(3), 291–314.

Waring, R. (1997). A study of receptive and productive learning from word cards. *Studies in Foreign Languages and Literature (Notre Dame Seishin University, Okayama), 21*(1), 94–114.

Webb, S. (2009). The effects of receptive and productive learning of word pairs on vocabulary knowledge. *RELC Journal, 40*(3), 360–376.

Webb, S., & Nation, I. S. P. (2017). *How vocabulary is learned*. Oxford, UK: Oxford University Press.

Webb, S., & Sasao, Y. (2013). New directions in vocabulary testing. *RELC Journal, 44*(3), 263–277.

Webb, S., Sasao, Y., & Ballance, O. (2017). The updated Vocabulary Levels Test: Developing and validating two new forms of the VLT. *ITL – International Journal of Applied Linguistics, 168*(1), 34–70.

Wei, Z. (2015). Does teaching mnemonics for vocabulary learning make a difference? Putting the keyword method and the word part technique to the test. *Language Teaching Research, 19*(1), 43–69.

West, M. (1953). *A general service list of English words*. London, UK: Longman, Green & Co.

Wray, A. (2008). *Formulaic language: Pushing the boundaries*. Oxford, UK: Oxford University Press.

3

Classifying and Identifying Formulaic Language

David Wood

Introduction

Formulaic language (FL) is generally defined as multiword language phenomena which holistically represent a single meaning or function, and are likely mentally stored and used as unanalyzed wholes, as are single words. The phenomenon itself is generally called formulaic language, and items themselves are referred to as formulaic sequences. FL is a rather enigmatic and elusive element of language, in itself it is a relatively recent subject of focus in linguistics and applied linguistics even though key categories and types have been subjects of scrutiny since the early to mid 1900s.

Over a long period of time the multiword units we now call formulaic language were examined more or less in isolation. This is largely due to the fact that researchers were looking at different and relatively discrete categories of multiword units, often working in quite separate areas of linguistics or other fields, including social anthropology and neurology. Over time, the existing research was examined and reinterpreted as a whole body of knowledge, but it was the late 1990s when the term FL came into common use, largely as a result of the work of Wray (e.g., 1999). The term is now standard, and a great deal of important work has been conducted into many aspects of FL and its use.

Critical Issues and Topics

There is a surprising range and scope of types of formulaic language, as seen in detail later. The categories, when examined, show quite a bit of overlap and imprecision, and are subject to interpretation. For example, determining whether a given sequence is a collocation or an idiom is sometimes a challenge. Some items do not fit comfortably in any specific category, or fall into cracks, for example sequences like *and then* or *sooner or later* are really difficult to categorize. Advances in corpus analysis technology and techniques have helped uncover new types of formulaic sequences, but all the same a sort of orthodoxy has been established over time, which can be puzzling. It is unclear, for example, how significant it is to determine a lexical bundle by means of frequency only, as compared to a sequence identified using frequency in combination with other statistical measures. As well, some categories overlap, and, perhaps most alarmingly, there is no firm consensus that all the categories are similarly processed semantically or psycholinguistically. It is also logical to question whether the categorizations are useful to researchers or teachers. Is it possible that the classifications are really just leftovers from early studies in phraseology, and that they are largely irrelevant to concerns particular to applied research or language teaching?

The identification of formulaic language in spoken or written texts is a challenging enterprise. Formulaic sequences may be identified in corpora by frequency, and the ways in which formulaic sequences are produced also gives us clues as to what multiword combinations might be formulaic. A potentially valuable means of determining formulaicity involves expert or native speaker judgment, especially useful when applied to small or very specific data sets. Although it is often best to try to use a combination of measures, in many cases absolute certainty in identification can be elusive. Even using combinations of corpus frequency and statistical measures of co-occurrence, along with acoustical features and judges, it is common to hedge one's claims about formulaicity. We can hope that new and more reliable or valid means of identifying formulaic language will come along in time.

Classifications

FL has been labeled in many different ways, and nearly 20 years ago it was Wray and Perkins (2000, p. 3) who identified 40 terms. The main categories of FL are collocations, idioms, lexical phrases, lexical bundles, metaphors, proverbs, phrasal verbs, n-grams, concgrams, and compounds. Some of the sequences are characterized mainly by their structural/semantic/syntactic properties, some by their pragmatic utility, and some by their distribution in particular corpora.

Sequences Distinguished by Structural, Semantic, or Syntactic Properties

Collocations

The term collocation has been around for many years, and research has been inspired by the pioneering work of Firth in the 1950s. Collocations likely come into use because of repeated context-dependent use. Such terms as *senior management*, *single parent*, and *plastic surgery* are examples of collocated pairs of words. Collocation basically refers to a syntagmatic relationship among words which co-occur. The relationship may be restricted to relationships which conform to certain syntactic and/or semantic criteria. Collocations can be in a syntactic relationship such as verb + object for example *make a decision*. Two approaches to collocation research have dominated: frequency-based and phraseological (see Granger & Paquot, 2008, for an overview of these). The frequency-based approach is in the tradition of the work of Firth (1951, 1957) and deals with the statistical probabilities of words appearing together, while the phraseological approach, dating back to very early work in Soviet phraseology, is much more concerned with restrictive descriptions of multiword units, and takes quite narrow views of what constitutes a collocation. To add to the complexity of the use of the term collocation, researchers have used it more creatively, sometimes as an umbrella term for multiword units in general. Frequency-based work on collocation was developed by Halliday, Mitchell and Greenbaum, Sinclair, and Kjellmer. These researchers extended and refined the definition to specify that a collocation is a function of the frequency of a word appearing in a certain lexical context as compared to its frequency in language as a whole.

They included syntactic and semantic aspects in descriptions of collocations, and explored the issue of what span of words to consider a collocation. Jones and Sinclair (1974) found that the span of words which is optimal for a collocation is four words to the right or left of a node, or core word. Kjellmer worked on the *Dictionary of English Collocations* (1994) defining a collocation as a continuous and recurring sequence of two or more words which are grammatically well formed. This led to the development of computer-based frequency driven study of collocations.

Unlike the frequency-focused researchers, phraseologists tend to see collocations as multi-word units whose component relations are variable and whose meaning is somewhat transparent (Nesselhauf, 2005). For example, Cowie (1994) placed collocations along a scale from composites, combinations below the sentence level with lexical or syntactic functions (e.g., *red herring*), and formulae, often sentence-length and having pragmatic functions (e.g., *how are you?*). Composites can be fully opaque and/or invariable, as in "pure idioms" (e.g., *kick the bucket*). "Figurative idioms" can have both a literal and figurative meaning (e.g., *to play a part*), and restricted collocations in which at least one element is literal and the other figurative (e.g., *explode a myth*). Cowie gives no restrictions on the number of words or the span of words in a collocation.

Idioms

Idioms are perhaps the archetypal formulaic sequence. Unfortunately, they are as ambiguous as collocations, and share with them a sort of dual personality, with idiom referring both to a specific type of FL, and some researchers using the term more broadly, with definitions encompassing proverbs, slang expressions, and so on. In general, however, the term is used to refer to word combinations which are, in the words of Moon (1998, p. 4), "fixed and semantically opaque or metaphorical", for example, *kick the bucket* or *spill the beans*.

A key quality of an idiom is its semantic non-compositionality and non-productive form. Wood (1981) noted that the meaning of an idiom is not the sum of the meanings of its component parts, that is, it is not compositional, and its structure must not be transformable, that is, it is non-productive, or frozen. Examples of items which meet these two criteria are *kick the bucket* and *by and large*, which cannot be understood by means of their constituent parts, nor can they be grammatically manipulated. In fact, many types of formulaic sequences display idiomaticity to greater or lesser degrees.

The modern scholar with the most useful definitions and categories of idioms is Moon (1998), who defined idioms as "semi-transparent and opaque metaphorical expressions such as *spill the beans* and *burn one's candle at both ends*" (p. 5). She differentiated idioms from fixed expressions such as routine expressions, sayings, similes, and so on (Moon, 1998, p. 2). Somewhat later, Grant and Bauer (2004) added the stipulation that an idiom is also non-figurative, meaning that its meaning must not be interpretable from the component words. Applying the criteria of Grant and Bauer, *kill two birds with one stone* is not an idiom because its meaning may be seen as nonliteral, and then interpreted again through examining its pragmatic intent. In contrast, applying the criteria of Grant and Bauer, *by and large* is an idiom, because it is both nonliteral and provides no indication of its figurative meaning.

In sum, there are five basic defining criteria of an idiom (see Skandera, 2004; Wood, 2015):

1   An idiom is two or more words in length.
2   Semantically opaque (the meaning of the whole is not the sum of the meanings of individual component words) – examples might be *spic and span* and *to and fro*

in which the component words are also opaque, *spic*, *span*, or *fro* are never used outside of these contexts (see Allerton, 1984). Many instances of opaque idioms have historical roots, for example *kick the bucket* (die), relates to the slaughtering of pigs.

3 Noncompositionality – the words that make up an idiom cannot be analyzed for meaning or function. This is akin to/linked to semantic opacity.

4 Mutual expectancy – this can also be termed *lexicality*, and refers to the fact that the component words of an idiom co-occur in a fixed manner, giving the idiom a unitary form to accompany its holistic meaning or function. It is, in essence, operating as a single lexical item.

5 Lexicogrammatical invariablity/frozenness/fixedness – the component words in an idiom are fixed and cannot be substituted by synonyms. In fact, some idioms do not even allow syntactic or morphological variation. Examples include *hook line and sinker* or *beat around the bush*; we cannot, for example, pluralize any of the nouns in these sequences, nor, for example, passivize the voice to render another appropriate idiom such as *the bush is beaten around.*

Metaphors

A metaphor is a sequence based on an unconventional reference in which words are used to describe something ordinarily far from its normal scope of denotation, producing a discord between a literal interpretation and a metaphoric interpretation. Metaphors have a common structure: the *vehicle* is the term used in an unusual manner, and the *topic* is the referent of the vehicle. The shared semantic content between the vehicle and topic are the *grounds*. An example might be *time is a healer*, in which *healer* is the vehicle, used in an unconventional sense, and *time* is the topic. In this case the grounds is the view of time acting like a physical remedy or medical practitioner, healing spiritual or emotional injuries and wounds in the same way as physical illnesses and injuries are healed by medicine or nurses. A metaphor can also be a simile, using *is like* or *kind of*. An example would be *life is like a box of chocolates*. The power of metaphor is linked to the semantic distance between vehicle and topic, and the relative explicitness of the vehicle.

Proverbs

Proverbs are generally sentence-length sequences which display an opaque relationship between literal and figurative meanings. Proverbs provide advice and warning (*a stitch in time saves nine*), instruction and explaining (*early to bed and early to rise*), and communicate common experience and observations (*like death and taxes*). They are taken from a store of proverbs shared by a cultural group or community. They are generally brief, direct, have simple syntax, contain elements of metaphor and sometimes dated or archaic structure or words.

Compounds

A compound is a sequence of two words (see ten Hacken, 2004), the second of which usually functions as the *head* or *core* of the compound – for example *desk computer* describes a type of computer and *computer desk* describes a type of desk (see Williams, 1981). The head represents a type and the nonhead serves to classify the head. There are three forms of compounds:

1 **Closed form**, in which the words are written as one, such as *hardcore* or *laptop*
2 **Hyphenated form**, in which the lexical items are separated by hyphens, such as *brother-in-law* or *open-handed*
3 **Open form**, in which the two words are written separately, such as *grocery store* or *real estate*

Compounds are sometimes written as single words if the unit is strongly lexicalized. The words may be linked by a hyphen and over time become blended orthographically into a single word. Words modified by adjectives, for example, *a metal table*, are different from a compound word, for example, *a coffee table*, in the degree to which the non-headword changes the essential character of the head, or the degree to which the modifier and the noun are inseparable. In the example of *coffee table*, the compound represents a single entity, a particular type of table which is always identified in the same way, whereas the *metal table* is simply a table being described by means of the material from which it is made. The adjective slot in the sequence can be filled by any number of choices.

Phrasal Verbs

Phrasal verbs are distinguished largely by their distinctive structural makeup, lexical verbs combined with a preposition, particle, or both, with often nonliteral meanings, or both literal and figurative interpretations, like idioms. Three structural categories exist:

1 **Verb + preposition (prepositional phrasal verbs)**

   She quickly *picked up* some Portuguese on her Brazilian vacation.
   I happened to *bump into* my former boss on the street.

2 **Verb + particle (particle phrasal verbs)**

   You can *show* that *off* at the next party.
   I tried not to *cave in* under the stress of the divorce.

3 **Verb + particle + preposition (particle-prepositional phrasal verbs)**

   He is always *going on about* something or other.
   Jane *looks up to* her older brother.

According to Liu (2008, p. 22) there are three fundamental criteria for determining whether an item is a phrasal verb:

1 No adverb between the lexical verb and preposition or particle; for example, we cannot say *The kids loaded slowly up on chocolates before we got there.*
2 The particle cannot be at the front of a sentence; for example, we cannot say *Up with I am not putting any more outbursts.*
3 It cannot exist as only literal in meaning, but needs to have a figurative meaning, as in the preceding examples.

Sequences Distinguished by Pragmatic Utility

Lexical Phrases

Lexical phrases are a pragmatically specialized subset of formulaic sequences first described by Nattinger and DeCarrico (1992). The phrases fall into two structural categories: **strings of specific lexical items**, mostly unitary and grammatically canonical, and **generalized frames**, category symbols and specific lexical items. The phrases display four characteristics: length and grammatical status; canonical or noncanonical shape; variability or fixedness; continuousness or discontinuousness, the latter allowing lexical insertions (Nattinger and DeCarrico, 1992, pp. 37, 38). There are four broad categories of lexical phrases: *polywords*, which function as single words, without variability or lexical insertions (e.g., "for the most part", "so far so good"); *institutionalized expressions*, sentence-length, invariable, and usually continuous (e.g., "a watched pot never boils", "nice meeting you", "long time no see"); *phrasal constraints*, which have variations of lexical and phrase categories, and are generally continuous (e.g., "a ___ ago", "the ___er the ___er"); and *sentence builders*, which contribute to the construction of full sentences with fillable slots (e.g., "I think that X", "not only X but Y") (pp. 38–45). It is clear that this particular taxonomy exhibits considerable overlap with other categories of formulaic language, such as proverbs, idioms, and collocations. The distinguishing feature of lexical phrases is that Nattinger and DeCarrico used pragmatic function as their common characteristic.

Pragmatic Formulas

In pragmatics, *formula* is used to refer to formulaic sequences employed for specific pragmatic purposes (Bardovi-Harlig, 2012). Various terms have been used for the types of sequences which have pragmatic functions in spoken interaction, including conversational routines, pragmatic idioms, speech formulas, routine formulas, situation formulas, and situation-bound utterances. These formulas are pragmalinguistic resources in spoken language and serve as the most socially appropriate means of accomplishing particular pragmatic functions. These include greetings (*how are you, what's going on, how are things*) and turn-taking (*let me add . . . , I also think . . . , not only that, but . . .*).

Sequences Distinguished by Their Distribution in Corpora

Lexical Bundles

Lexical bundles (see Biber, Johansson, Leech, Conrad, & Finegan, 1999) are formulaic sequences distinguished by the procedures by which they are identified in corpora, and the fact that they are linked purely to functions in discourse, and are not meaning units. Lexical bundles may be considered more a type of multiword unit than strictly formulaic sequences, since there is no indication in the literature that they are stored or retrieved as wholes. They are researched using particular methods which focus exclusively on frequency and function. Research on lexical bundles tends to overwhelmingly focus on academic language, particularly written text.

Lexical bundles can be briefly defined as "combinations of three or more words which are identified in a corpus of natural language by means of corpus analysis software programs" (Wood, 2015, p. 45). Lexical bundles appear in a range of texts in a corpus. They have been shown to be essential to the construction of academic writing, with particular bundles used more in specific disciplines (Cortes, Jones, & Stoller, 2002).

The pioneer of lexical bundles research is Biber (2006), who discovered that academic disciplines use specific lexical bundles, and created a categorization of functions of bundles – *referential bundles* – which refer to real or abstract entities or to textual content or attributes, for example, "the size of the . . .", "one of the things"; *stance bundles*, which express attitudes or assessments of certainty, for example, ". . . are likely to be . . .", "what do you think . . ."; *discourse organizers*, which indicate connections between previous and subsequent discourse, for example, "on the other hand", "as well as . . .".

Concgrams

A concgram is a combination of two or more words, but is distinctive in that it is a noncontinuous sequence, with the constituent words separated by others. The COBUILD team at the University of Birmingham in the 1980s were the first to use computer software to search corpora for noncontiguous word sequences. According to Sinclair (2005), it is likely that researchers will similarly uncover new patterns of word sequences, with "intercollocability" and "interparaphrasability", already entering the picture.

Clearly there is a surprising range and scope of types of formulaic language. The phenomenon is not a unitary construct, and classifications overlap and require considerable interpretation. Looking at a sequence and determining whether it is, for example, a collocation or an idiom, one may experience quite a bit of indecision. Some items may appear to fit with no particular category, for example, sequences like *and then* or *sooner or later* seem to defy labeling. Thanks to corpus analysis technology and techniques we have discovered new types of formulaic sequences.

In any case, formulaic sequences fall into various categories based on their features or usage. The descriptions of categories have evolved over time, and the classifications are somewhat fluid, with plenty of overlap and outliers.

Identification

It is useful to have a definition of formulaic language, and a sense of what the major categories are, because this takes us one step toward being able to handle it in research and in education. However, sooner or later any researcher or educator will come up against an obstacle which is tough to deal with: how can one go about identifying formulaic sequences in texts, spoken or written?

To understand the challenge of identification, examine the first two sentences in this section, and attempt to identify the formulaic sequences. Issues crop up immediately. Several multiword sequences stand out as more or less idiomatic, for example, *one step toward, handle it, tough to deal with, sooner or later*. How confident can one be with these decisions, and what features of the sequences lead us to decide they are formulaic or idiomatic? More importantly, what other elements of the sentences are formulaic but are not readily accessible to our intuitions and perceptions? How can they be uncovered? This question has been a preoccupation in the study of formulaic language. Perhaps one might decide that some sequences are more formulaic than others, but even then, what can guide the decisions? How frequently they are used in a given register? Prosodic features of the production of the sequence? Their frequency in a large corpus?

Fortunately, there are a number of reliable and well-developed means of identifying formulaic sequences. Some are more reliable than others, and they lend themselves to particular purposes and texts.

Frequency and Statistical Measures

It is axiomatic that particular formulaic sequences are generally recurring in a particular register, and a word sequence which sees frequent use is probably formulaic, provided it is also a more or less unitary meaning or function unit. Maybe they will also be mentally stored and retrieved as a single unit.

A distributional or frequency-based approach to identifying formulaic sequences is quite common in research (Durrant & Mathews-Aydınlı, 2011). Statistical identification of formulaic language is a very productive method. In this type of identification procedure a set of parameters is established, marked by minimum lengths of sequences, minimum criteria for frequency, usually expressed as occurrences per million words in a corpus. The corpus is scanned for word combinations that fit within the parameters. Frequency cutoffs can range from 10 to 40 occurrences per million words (Biber et al., 1999; Simpson-Vlach & Ellis, 2010). The sequences which are uncovered by this type of corpus-based, statistically driven procedure are often not complete structural units (Cortes, 2004), and the majority of research of this type has uncovered units labeled *lexical bundles* (e.g., Biber et al., 1999) or *multiword constructions* (Liu, 2012; Wood & Appel, 2014). In some cases, researchers have used these parameters as part of a more elaborate process of identification, and have employed the term *formulaic sequences* (e.g., Simpson-Vlach & Ellis, 2010).

Logically, this statistical approach is used mostly with large corpora of hundreds of thousands, if not millions, of words. These corpora are created to be representative of specific registers of language. A purely frequency-based approach has some serious limitations if used with smaller data sets, particularly because minimum frequency cutoffs may be very difficult to set. For example, in a corpus of a million words, a frequency cutoff of 40 occurrences per million words would mean a given sequence would need to occur 40 times in order to be considered formulaic or a lexical bundle. But if a corpus has, say, 100,000 words, the sequence would only need to occur four times. This makes it challenging to identify sequences as formulaic using frequency-based methods alone when working with small corpora. A further limitation of using frequency alone as a criterion for formulaicity is that additional steps are also required to eliminate meaningless combinations of words – some content-specific word combinations can easily pass the frequency test and yet not be formulaic, for example, proper names such as *Ford Motor Company* or verbal tics or nonlexical fillers such as so, so, so. . . . Furthermore, it would be difficult to rely wholly on frequency for identifying formulaicity transcribed conversations on a range of topics. Many sequences which are formulaic might appear only once or twice in such a diverse and small set of data. A very important drawback of using frequency-based analysis is the fact that frequency gives us absolutely no real indication of the holistic processing, which is often an important concern in some types of research – there is no way to rely on frequency measures to identify formulaic sequences in individual idiolects unless extra means of analysis are used. A good example of this is evident in a study by Schmitt, Grandage, and Adolphs (2004) in which formulaic sequences were identified in a corpus by means of statistical measures. The sequences were then integrated into spoken dictation tasks in which dictated texts were designed to overload the participants' short-term memory capacities. Evidence of holistic storage of the sequences in the participants' reconstructions of the dictations varied greatly from participant to participant (Schmitt, Grandage, and Adolphs, 2004).

Some word sequences which appear to be formulaic in terms of saliency and unitary meaning or function may not actually appear at particularly high frequency in a given corpus. For example, *in spite of* or *how are you* may not be frequent in any particular corpus or genre, but we would probably agree that they show formulaicity, because they contain words which very commonly occur in this order, and they have a particular unitary meaning or function. The probability that words will co-occur like this can be measured statistically using measures of association such as Mutual Information (MI). MI is a measure of how likely a given set of words are to occur together in a set sequence in comparison to chance. MI does not have a particular statistical significance cutoff, but many researchers have used an MI of 3.0 or higher as an indication of statistical strength of co-occurrence (e.g., Church and Hanks, 1990; Hunston, 2002). A higher MI represents a stronger probability of co-occurrence, and is quite a strong objective measure of formulaicity, if used in combination with other frequency measures. Other similar measures of strength of association of words are used in corpus linguistics. For example, Gries (2008, 2012) uses a measure called the Fisher-Yates exact probability test in examining the strength of the relationships between a given word and a construction in which it occurs. Some studies combine data of various types such as corpus measures of association, eye tracking, and response latency. These types of measures are generally called *psycholinguistic measures*.

When frequency measures are not feasible for analysis of a small or very specific corpus, it is possible to look at a large general corpus, such as the British National Corpus (BNC) or the Corpus of Contemporary American English (COCA). These huge sets of language data can provide a wealth of information about particular word combinations in real-life language use. An example of this is in a study by Wood and Namba (2013) in which they identified useful formulaic sequences to help individual Japanese university students improve their oral presentations. The researchers first identified useful sequences by means of native speaker/ proficient speaker intuition, and then turned to the COCA to check their frequencies and statistical strength of co-occurrence. The researchers looked for the sequences in the spoken language subcorpus of the COCA, using a frequency cutoff of at least ten occurrences per million words and with a Mutual Information score (MI) of at least 3.0. In this way, they could be certain that the identified sequences were frequent in speech and that they consisted of words with a high frequency of co-occurrence. A novel means of determining formulaicity is the use of online search engines such as Google. Shei (2008) pointed out that there are really no readily available corpora which are large enough to give full coverage of language use for many types of investigation. Shei presents a strong case for researchers and educators to use the internet as an enormous corpus, readily exploited by means of a search engine such as Google to identify and retrieve word sequences for research and language teaching and learning support. It is a simple matter of Googling a given sequence and examining the resulting hits, which may contain extremely valuable information about its frequency, form, variability, and functions.

Psycholinguistic Measures

Studies in which identification of formulaic language is a focus have used measures of processing speed. These measures may include reaction times (e.g., Conklin & Schmitt, 2012), eye movement (e.g., Underwood, Schmitt, & Galpin, 2004), and electrophysiological (ERP) measures (e.g., Tremblay & Baayen, 2010).

Measures such as eye tracking or response latencies require that participants read, making them unsuitable for research involving children or nonliterate individuals. It is obvious that these psycholinguistic measures are useful in identifying sequences psycholinguistically stored by any one individual, but they are much less helpful in showing how commonly used a formulaic sequence may be in a broader speech community. These measures may reveal formulaic sequences which are rare, unusual, or one-off, used idiosyncratically by a speaker.

Acoustic Analysis

A common criterion for identification of formulaic sequences in speech is *phonological coherence*, a term coined by Peters (1983). Phonological coherence is a characteristic of formulaic production in which a word sequence is uttered fluently, with no hesitations and an unbroken intonation Peters (1983, p. 8). Formulaic sequences exhibit certain prosodic characteristics, such as alignment with pauses and intonation units, resistance to internal dysfluency, no internal hesitations, fast speech rhythm, and stress placement restrictions (see Lin, 2010, 2012). It is important to bear in mind that phonological coherence characterizes formulaic sequences in a given individual's idiolect, and that analysis of this type is restricted by the quantity of data which can be processed by an individual and the technological tools used to record and analyze speech data.

Criteria Checklists and Native-Speaker Intuition

Researchers sometimes discover that frequency, psycholinguistic processing, or acoustic analysis measures are insufficient to identify formulaic sequences in various types of data, especially spoken data. This is often resolved by means of criteria checklists that blend specific features associated with formulaicity.

A proponent of the use of such checklists has been Wray (2002), who reviewed methods of detecting formulaic sequences in many data types. She notes that use of corpus analysis computer software is one possible method of identification, but points out some shortcomings of reliance on frequency in particular:

> It seems, on the surface, entirely reasonable to use computer searches to identify common strings of words, and to establish a certain frequency threshold as the criterion for calling a string "formulaic" . . . (however) problems regarding the procedures of frequency counts can be identified. Firstly, corpora are probably unable to capture the true distribution of certain kinds of formulaic sequences. . . . The second serious problem is that the tools used in corpus analysis are no more able to help decide where the boundaries between formulaic sequences fall than native speaker judges are.
>
> *(pp. 25, 27, 28)*

It is obvious that small data sets composed of spoken discourse present challenges for computer corpus analysis software. For one thing, the discourse or topic-specific speech in such data sets, combined with the small total word count, make it very difficult to rely on frequency alone, since some sequences might occur only once or be used very idiosyncratically. It is also often the case that formulaic sequences blend into surrounding language; many also have large fillable slots, presenting a great challenge for corpus analysis software. Research involving second language learners often produces data with large numbers of nonstandard or idiosyncratic sequences. In the end, a researcher can turn to one quite daunting measure in identifying formulaicity in language, what Wray terms "the application of common sense" (p. 28).

Native-Speaker Judgment

Fortunately, it is readily possible to apply common sense to the task of identifying formulaic sequences, especially that of second language speakers, by examining language performance and comparing it to native-speaker use of formulaic sequences. This involves the use of native-speaker judgment and a checklist of criteria. Wray (2002, p. 23) points out five challenges inherent in this type of procedure:

1   It has to be restricted to smaller data sets.
2   Inconsistent judgment may occur due to fatigue or alterations in judgment thresholds over time.
3   There may be variation between judges.
4   There may not be a single answer as to what to search for.
5   Application of intuition in such a way may occur at the expense of knowledge we do not have at the surface level of awareness.

Recall how challenging it was at the beginning of this chapter to isolate formulaic sequences without any guiding criteria. This challenge can be at least partially overcome by use of a **checklist** of specific criteria. The standard procedure for this involves judges studying the criteria which inform a checklist, and examining a corpus to apply the criteria and identify sequences which appear to be formulaic. A high degree of interrater reliability among judgments is a good general measure of the strength of a given judgment.

A number of checklists have been used in such research; some checklists developed for specific populations, others more general. Following are descriptions of three such checklists which have been used in various studies: an early checklist elaborated by Coulmas (1979); a checklist applicable to a range of child and adult native or non-native speakers (Wray & Namba, 2003); a checklist used to identify formulaicity in second language acquisition of speech fluency (Wood, 2006, 2009, 2010).

Coulmas, 1979

Coulmas (1979, p. 32) lays out nine specific criteria for formulaicity:

1   At least two morphemes long (i.e., two words)
2   Coheres phonologically
3   Individual elements are not used concurrently in the same form separately or in other environments
4   Grammatically advanced compared to other language
5   Community-wide formula
6   Idiosyncratic chunk
7   Repeatedly used in the same form
8   Situationally dependent
9   May be used inappropriately

Wray and Namba, 2003

Wray and Namba (2003) presented a very flexible and comprehensive checklist, originally used in a study of speech of bilingual children. The checklist is applicable to many types of data and consists of 11 criteria, rated on a Likert Scale of 1 to 5. This is quite refined in that it deals with the issue of gradience or ranges of formulaicity:

1 By my judgment, there is something grammatically unusual about this wordstring.
2 By my judgment, part or all of the wordstring lacks semantic transparency.
3 By my judgment, this wordstring is associated with a specific situation and/or register.
4 By my judgment, the wordstring as a whole performs a function in communication or discourse other than, or in addition to, conveying the meaning of the words themselves.
5 By my judgment, this precise formulation is the one most commonly used by this speaker/writer when conveying this idea.
6 By my judgment, the speaker/writer has accompanied this wordstring with an action, use of punctuation, or phonological pattern that gives it special status as a unit, and/or is repeating something s/he has just heard or read.
7 By my judgment, the speaker/writer, or someone else has marked this wordstring grammatically or lexically in a way that gives it special status as a unit.
8 By my judgment, based on direct evidence or my intuition, there is a greater than-chance-level probability that the speaker/writer will have encountered this precise formulation before, from other people.
9 By my judgment, although this wordstring is novel, it is a clear derivation, deliberate or otherwise, of something that can be demonstrated to be formulaic in its own right.
10 By my judgment, this wordstring is formulaic, but it has been unintentionally applied inappropriately.
11 By my judgment, this wordstring contains linguistic material that is too sophisticated, or not sophisticated enough, to match the speaker's general grammatical and lexical competence.

Native-Speaker Judgment: Wood, 2010

Wood (2010) published a study examining the possible effect of use of formulaic language on speech fluency in second language learners of English. Identifying formulaic sequences was central to the methods used in the research.

Five criteria were integrated into the checklist. They were used as guides for native-speaker judges, and no one criterion or combination of criteria was required in order for a sequence to be labeled as formulaic.

1 **Phonological coherence and reduction**. Formulaic sequences may be produced with phonological coherence (Coulmas, 1979; Wray, 2002), lacking internal pausing and exhibiting a continuous intonation contour. Phonological reduction is also possible, involving phonological fusion, reduction of syllables, deletion of schwa, all of which are characteristic of the most frequent phrases in English (Bybee, 2002).
2 **The taxonomy used by Nattinger and DeCarrico (1992)**. This taxonomy was described above, and is not required in every case, but as a potential guide to determining formulaicity. If a sequence matched a category in the taxonomy it might be flagged as formulaic.

3   **Greater length/complexity than other output**. This is a typical feature of formulaic language in second language speech. For example, a participant might say *I would like . . .* or *I don't understand*, using these structures only in these particular sequences and never successfully using *would* or negatives using *do* in other contexts.

4   **Semantic irregularity, as in idioms and metaphors**. Sequences which meet this criterion are usually standard phrases and expressions.

5   **Syntactic irregularity**. Formulaic sequences can be syntactically irregular, especially idioms.

In Wood's (2010) study, non-native-like sequences were accepted as formulaic. A sequence could have been misperceived and stored as an idiosyncratic string, as in *what's happened* instead of *what happened*, or *thanks god* instead of *thank god*. The need to produce second language speech under the pressure of recording also might have caused utterances to contain irregular features, articulatory slips, or gaps and inaccuracies. Therefore, a sequence could match the checklist criteria and still be idiosyncratic, misperceived, stored with errors, or misarticulated.

The three checklists described here are organized so that none of the criteria are necessary; nor must all be met in order for a sequence to be labeled formulaic. Wray and Namba (2003) use a 5-point Likert scale for each criterion, from *strongly agree* to *don't know* to *strongly disagree*. All three checklists are quite different from the distributional, psycholinguistic, and acoustic measures described earlier, since they place primary importance on informed judgments based on a range of criteria. The checklists show considerable agreement on the characteristics of formulaicity, all making reference to phonological characteristics and complexity.

Future Directions

Formulaic language is certainly not a unitary or monolithic construct. The categories overlap, display imprecision, and are subject to considerable interpretation. Judging whether a sequence is a collocation or an idiom is tricky, despite the fact that a number of researchers have attempted to assign specific characteristics to particular types. Many multiword items defy strict or ready classification; for example, sequences like *and then* or *sooner or later* are difficult to categorize. The advent of corpus analysis technology and methods have enabled the discovery of new types of formulaic sequences. It is difficult to see the importance of the distinction between, for example, identifying a sequence identified using frequency alone and identifying one using a combination of frequency and other statistical measures such as Mutual Information.

In general, it has been established that one can determine possible formulaicity in a number of ways. One way is by using frequency statistics, applying criteria to a specific corpus, or checking the frequency or mutual information of individual items in very large corpora such as the BNC, COCA, or even internet search engines. Formulaicity may be determined in whole or in part by psycholinguistic or acoustical features of a sequence and its processing. Expert or native-speaker judgment about formulaicity is a good way to gauge formulaicity with spoken data or smaller or quite specific data sets. In this type of procedure, a checklist of characteristics of formulaicity provides a guide for judges. Formulaic language can be challenging to identify, and it may be best to employ various means or a combination of measures, and even then absolute certainty is likely to be elusive. Whether one uses corpus frequency, statistical measures of co-occurrence acoustical features, or judges and checklists, decisions are likely to be expressed with some hedging. Presumably future developments in research will yield more exact means of determining formulaicity.

Further Reading

Wood, D. (2015). *Fundamentals of formulaic language: An introduction.* London, UK and New York, NY: Bloomsbury.

> This volume represents the only existing overview of formulaic language for researchers and students. It contains chapters which summarize current knowledge on a full range of topics, including categorization, identification, mental processing, corpus-based research, spoken and written language, and teaching.

Wray, A. (2002). *Formulaic language and the lexicon.* Cambridge: Cambridge University Press.

> This is a classic work on formulaic language in which Wray lays a strong theoretical and research foundation for studies of formulaic language. It includes essential perspectives on processing, acquisition, and research methods.

Schmitt, N. (Ed.). (2004). *Formulaic sequences: Acquisition, processing and use.* Philadelphia, PA: John Benjamins.

> This volume represents one of the first compilations of original research on formulaic language from a range of perspectives. Many of the studies are excellent models of research in corpus and psycholinguistic explorations of formulaic language.

Related Topics

Phraseology, formulaic language in language teaching, lexical approach, lexical bundles, construction grammar, multiword units

References

Allerton, D. J. (1984). Three (or four) levels of word cooccurrence restriction. *Lingua, 63*(1), 17–40.

Bardovi-Harlig, K. (2012). Formulas, routines, and conventional expressions in pragmatics research. *Annual Review of Applied Linguistics, 32,* 206–227.

Biber, D. (2006). *University language: A corpus-based study of spoken and written registers.* Philadelphia, PA: John Benjamins.

Biber, D., Johansson, S., Leech, G., Conrad, S., & Finegan, E. (1999). *Longman grammar of spoken and written English.* Harlow, UK: Pearson.

Bybee, J. (2002). Phonological evidence for exemplar storage of multiword sequences. *Studies in Second Language Acquisition, 24,* 215–221.

Church, K. W., & Hanks, P. (1990). Word association norms, mutual information, and lexicography. *Computational Linguistics, 16,* 22–29.

Conklin, K., & Schmitt, N. (2012). The processing of formulaic language. *Annual Review of Applied Linguistics, 32,* 45–61.

Cortes, V. (2004). Lexical bundles in published and student disciplinary writing: Examples from history and biology. *English for Specific Purposes, 23,* 397–423.

Cortes, V., Jones, J., & Stoller, F. (2002, April). *Lexical bundles in ESP reading and writing.* Paper presented at TESOL Conference, Salt Lake City, UT.

Coulmas, F. (1979). On the sociolinguistic relevance of routine formulae. *Journal of Pragmatics, 3*(3/4), 239–266.

Cowie, A. P. (1994). Phraseology. In R. E. Asher (Ed.), *The encyclopedia of language and linguistics* (pp. 3168–3171). Oxford, UK: Pergamon.

Durrant, P., & Mathews-Aydınlı, J. (2011). A function-first approach to identifying formulaic language in academic writing. *English for Specific Purposes, 30*(1), 58–72.

Firth, J. R. (1951). Modes of meaning. In J. R. Firth (Ed.), *Essays and studies* (pp. 118–149). London, UK: Oxford University Press.

Firth, J. R. (Ed.). (1957). *Papers in linguistics 1934–1951*. Oxford, UK: Oxford University Press.

Granger, S., & Paquot, M. (2008). Disentangling the phraseological web. In S. Granger & F. Meunier (Eds.), *Phraseology: An interdisciplinary perspective* (pp. 27–50). Philadelphia, PA: John Benjamins.

Grant, I. E., & Bauer, L. (2004). Criteria for redefining idioms: Are we barking up the wrong tree? *Applied Linguistics, 25*, 38–61.

Gries, S. T. (2008). Corpus-based methods in analyses of SLA data. In P. Robinson & N. C. Ellis (Eds.), *Handbook of cognitive linguistics and second language acquisition* (pp. 406–431). New York, NY: Routledge, Taylor & Francis.

Gries, S. T. (2012). Frequencies, probabilities, association measures in usage-/exemplar-based linguistics: Some necessary clarifications. *Studies in Language, 36*(3), 477–510.

Hunston, S. (2002). *Corpora in applied linguistics*. Cambridge, UK: Cambridge University Press.

Jones, S., & Sinclair, J. (1974). English lexical collocations. *Cahiers de lexicologie, 24*, 15–61.

Kjellmer, G. (1994). *A dictionary of English collocations: Based on the Brown Corpus*. Oxford, UK: Clarendon Press.

Lin, P. (2010). The phonology of formulaic sequences: A review. In D. Wood (Ed.), *Perspectives on formulaic language: Acquisition and communication* (pp. 174–193). New York, NY and London, UK: Continuum.

Lin, P. (2012). Sound evidence: The missing piece of the jigsaw in formulaic language research. *Applied Linguistics, 33*(3), 342–347.

Liu, D. (2008). *Idioms: Description, comprehension, acquisition, and pedagogy*. New York, NY and London, UK: Routledge.

Liu, D. (2012). The most frequent multiword constructions in academic written English: A multi-corpus study. *English for Specific Purposes, 31*(1), 25–35.

Moon, R. (1998). Frequencies and forms of phrasal lexemes in English. In A. P. Cowie (Ed.), *Phraseology: Theory, analysis, and applications* (pp. 79–100). Oxford, UK: Clarendon Press.

Nattinger, J. R., & DeCarrico, J. S. (1992). *Lexical phrases and language teaching*. Oxford, UK: Oxford University Press.

Nesselhauf, N. (2005). *Collocations in a learner corpus*. Philadelphia, PA: John Benjamins.

Peters, A. M. (1983). *Units of language acquisition*. Cambridge, UK: Cambridge University Press.

Schmitt, N., Grandage, S., & Adolphs, S. (2004). Are corpus-derived recurrent clusters psycholinguistically valid? In N. Schmitt (Ed.), *Formulaic sequences: Acquisition, processing, and use* (pp. 127–151). Philadelphia, PA: John Benjamins.

Shei, C. C. (2008). Discovering the hidden treasure on the internet: Using Google to uncover the veil of phraseology. *Computer Assisted Language Learning, 21*(1), 67–85.

Simpson-Vlach, R., & Ellis, N. (2010). An academic formulas list: New methods in phraseology research. *Applied Linguistics, 31*, 487–512.

Sinclair, J. (2005). Corpus and text – Basic principles. In M. Wynne (Ed.), *Developing linguistic corpora: A guide to good practice* (pp. 1–16). Oxford, UK: Oxbow Books.

Skandera, P. (2004). What are idioms? In D. J. Allerton, N. Nesselhauf, & P. Skandera (Eds.), *Phraseological units: Basic concepts and their applications* (pp. 23–36). Basel: Schwabe AG.

ten Hacken, P. (2004). What are compounds? In D. J. Allerton, N. Nesselhauf, & P. Skandera (Eds.), *Phraseological units: Basic concepts and their applications* (pp. 53–66). Basel: Schwabe AG.

Tremblay, A., & Baayen, H. (2010). Holistic processing of regular four-word sequences: A behavioural and ERP study of the effects of structure, frequency, and probability on immediate free recall. In D. Wood (Ed.), *Perspectives on formulaic language: Acquisition and communication* (pp. 151–172). New York, NY and London, UK: Continuum.

Underwood, G., Schmitt, N., & Galpin, A. (2004). The eyes have it: An eye-movement study into the processing of formulaic sequences. In N. Schmitt (Ed.), *Formulaic sequences: Acquisition, processing, and use* (pp. 153–172). Philadelphia, PA: John Benjamins.

Williams, E. (1981). On the notions lexically related and head of a word. *Linguistic Inquiry, 12*, 245–274.

Wood, D. (2006). Uses and functions of formulaic sequences in second language speech: An exploration of the foundations of fluency. *Canadian Modern Language Review, 63*(1), 13–33.

Wood, D. (2009). Effects of focused instruction of formulaic sequences on fluent expression in second language narratives: A case study. *Canadian Journal of Applied Linguistics, 12*(1), 39–57.

Wood, D. (2010). *Formulaic language and second language speech fluency: Background, evidence, and classroom applications*. London and New York, NY: Continuum.

Wood, D. (2015). *Fundamentals of formulaic language: An introduction*. London and New York, NY: Bloomsbury.

Wood, D., & Appel, R. (2014). Multiword constructions in first year university textbooks and in EAP textbooks. *Journal of English for Academic Purposes, 15*, 1–13.

Wood, D., & Namba, K. (2013). *Focused instruction of formulaic language: Use and awareness in a Japanese university class*. The Asian Conference on Language Learning Official Conference Proceedings 2013, Osaka, Japan, pp. 203–212.

Wood, M. M. (1981). *A definition of idiom*. Bloomington, IN: University of Indiana Linguistics Club.

Wray, A. (1999). Formulaic language in learners and native speakers. *Language Teaching, 32*(4), 213–231.

Wray, A. (2002). *Formulaic language and the lexicon*. Cambridge, UK: Cambridge University Press.

Wray, A., & Namba, K. (2003). Use of formulaic language by a Japanese-English bilingual child: A practical approach to data analysis. *Japanese Journal for Multilingualism and Multiculturalism, 9*(1), 24–51.

Wray, A., & Perkins, M. R. (2000). The functions of formulaic language: An integrated model. *Language and Communication, 20*, 1–28.

4

An Overview of Conceptual Models and Theories of Lexical Representation in the Mental Lexicon

Brigitta Dóczi

Introduction

The literature has been abundant with theories and studies on vocabulary acquisition. One of the most intriguing questions raised by researchers has been concerned with how and where words might be stored and represented in the mind, where the center of lexical storage is assumed to be the *mental lexicon*. At first glance, the concept of the mental lexicon might seem straightforward, as suggested by the commonly used *dictionary metaphor* (Fay & Cutler, 1977), which emphasizes the analogy of pairing word meanings with their sound representations. However, as pointed out by Jarema and Libben (2007), providing a precise and concise definition of the mental lexicon poses a challenge. The reason for this stems from the fact that most psycholinguistic research aims to go beyond what is stored in the lexicon and concentrates on lexical access and how we retrieve words in order to gather information on lexical representation.

Aitchison (2012) argued that there are two underlying reasons that justify the necessity for the mental lexicon to be structured in a logical way. Firstly, the fact that there are a vast number of words calls for some sort of logical ordering, because, in her reasoning, psychologists have indicated that the human memory is "flexible and extendable" as long as "the information is structured" (p. 5). Secondly, the impossible speed with which words are searched, found, and recalled from tens (or maybe hundreds) of thousands of words implies a logical organization. Word searches and slips of the tongue, aphasic research, and psycholinguistic experiments have all been valuable sources of evidence; furthermore, our understanding of the lexical processes in the mind has also been supported by the conclusions of theoretical research. In Aitchison's view, the closest and simplest analogy for modeling the mental lexicon is that of a map, and she provides the example of the London Underground, where the stations are connected by rails of different lengths and there are several possible ways of getting from one point to another. Even though it is easy to understand and accept this metaphor, the author warns us that, unfortunately, the links in the mental lexicon are mostly hypothetical and so far invisible, not to mention the difficulty of establishing what exactly is stored in the lexicon, all of which means that it takes "inspired guesswork" (p. 41) to convey the sheer complexity of this storage system.

In light of this argumentation, *the present chapter aims to give an up-to-date overview of the theories and models of the first language mental lexicon, followed by a similar analysis of the bilingual lexicon.* Following the definition of key concepts, an argument is developed for a view of vocabulary knowledge that encompasses both mental representations encoded in memory as well as ability and control in the usage of this knowledge in producing and comprehending language. As far as research methods are concerned, we will see an abundance and diversity of techniques applied: word associations, cross-language semantic and translation priming experiments, picture-naming tasks, as well as studies on aphasia. These different approaches have all yielded ample empirical data for exploring lexical organization and access. The chapter points out that while the mental lexicon might not have a specific modular localization in the human brain, it can serve as a useful metaphor in modeling and understanding how words are stored, organized, and accessed in the different languages one speaks.

Critical Issues and Topics

The Conceptual Organization of the L1 Mental Lexicon

For the conceptualization of the mental lexicon, we need to look into the origins of this construct. In early theories of language acquisition, language was viewed as a system of grammatical rules, where words were assumed to fill the gaps in sentences, which were produced by means of the necessary morphological and syntactic transformations (Chomsky, 1965). In this view, the mental lexicon was regarded as no more than a repository of lexical, phonological, and morphological information pertaining to words. However, as the boundaries between lexis and grammar seem to diminish, "many linguists have come to see words not simply as flesh that gives life to grammatical structures, but as bones that are themselves grammatical rich entities" (Elman, 2009, p. 548). As opposed to the views held by Chomsky (1965) and other linguists, usage-based approaches assume a functional or semantic dimension of language production and comprehension as well as child language development, whereby syntactic encoding is driven by words (e.g., Tomasello, 2003). Both Bresnan's (1982) lexical theory of syntax and Levelt's (1989) model of speech production highlight the relevance of the syntactic features of words in triggering syntactic encoding when speakers produce sentences. These developments have had important consequences for how knowledge might be organized and represented in the mind, because syntactic regularities of language, traditionally seen as "rules", are now seen as indistinguishable from linguistic construction units (e.g., words, phrases, formulaic expressions, and chunks). Thus, the shift from rule-based theories to usage-based models has changed the conceptualization of the mental lexicon, extending the types of knowledge that it needs to be capable of storing.

Other advances in cognitive psychology have also contributed to a more pragmatic and complex view of the mental lexicon. For one, the incorporation of Dynamic Systems Theory (van Geert, 1994) in the language acquisition process gives an account of the dynamicity of language development and emergentist theoreticians have also indicated that language acquisition is a non-modular, nonlinear process (e.g., de Bot, Lowie, Thorne, & Verspoor, 2013; Thomas & Karmiloff-Smith, 2002). In Dynamic Systems Theory, language is viewed as a structure that contains a set of interconnected subsystems, such as a lexical system, a phonological system and a syntactic system, which interact with and influence each other (for a detailed discussion, see Larsen-Freeman & Cameron, 2008). In light of this, the mental lexicon might be identified as a lexical system but at the same time the boundaries with other systems are blurred. Connectionist theories also reject the idea of distinct language modules, such as the mental lexicon and a separate lexical encoding system. They claim that language storage, comprehension, and production take place with the help of a dynamic network of interrelated components stored and circulated in this vast interactive system (Elman, 1990). Cognitive Linguistic Theory further argues that language processing occurs along a "continuum of construction at all levels" (de Bot et al., 2013, p. 209), from morphemes to whole discourse level utterances. The development of such an interconnected dynamic linguistic system is simply due to repetitive language use, where observed patterns are followed and thus more and more complex structures can emerge over time. Furthermore, the developmental process is dependent on external factors (such as human cognition and processing abilities) and is subject to constant change, affecting the whole system.

These findings pose the question whether a mental lexicon actually exists and if the concept is necessary at all (Elman, 2009). Lexical processing and conceptualization might be explained without referring to a mental lexicon as a single system accountable for storing lexical and semantic information (Dilkina, McClelland, & Plaut, 2008). That being said, there is no doubt that lexical knowledge must somehow be organized even if there is no isolated area of the brain responsible for it. There may not exist a separate linguistic module, but the mental lexicon as a metaphor might help us in understanding lexical storage, retrieval, and acquisition.

In Jarema and Libben's interpretation (2007) the mental lexicon is defined as "the cognitive system that constitutes the capacity for conscious and unconscious lexical activity" (p. 2). This definition of the lexicon seems the most adequate for the following reasons. On the one hand, incorporating a systematic view conveys the complexity of lexical organization and highlights the various processes that take place related to lexical retrieval. On the other hand, the definition of the mental lexicon as a capacity enables us to take all the aspects of language into consideration: including the possession, acquisition, conceptualization, use, and loss of lexical knowledge. Even if we are often unaware of the phenomenon, what is subject to the greatest change and development in our lifetime among all the aspects of language is our lexical knowledge. This indicates that the mental lexicon is in constant flux. Therefore, we adopt this characterization of the mental lexicon as a system with capacity because it draws our attention to all the processes that can be achieved.

As for the organization of concepts in the lexicon, several models have been put forward. In the following section the earliest and most fundamental models of the lexical organization are outlined, followed by the problematic issues related to them, as well as how these are viewed in the most recent literature.

Early Models of Lexical Organization

One of the first theoretical models was Collins and Quillian's *hierarchical network model* (1969, 1970, 1972), which assumes that information in our memory is stored in categories linked to one another in a hierarchical fashion and organized as "pyramids" with superordinate categories (e.g., *animal*) at the top, more specific ones in the middle (*bird* or *fish*), and subordinate ones (e.g., *penguin* or *salmon*) at the bottom of the hierarchy (Collins & Quillian, 1969, p. 242).

The *hierarchical network model* claims that single words with their typical features are only linked to the closest concepts (Figure 4.1). This results in what is referred to as cognitive

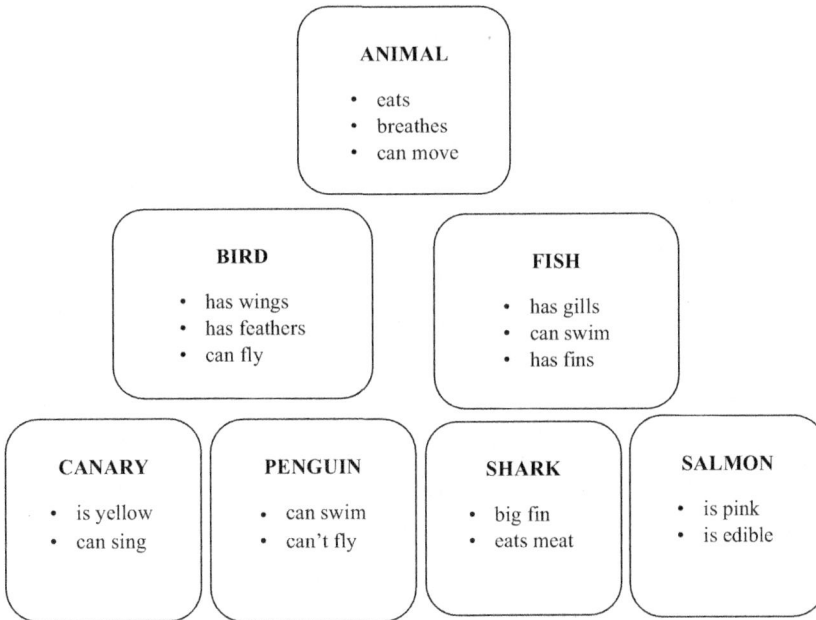

Figure 4.1 The hierarchical network model
Source: Adapted from Collins & Quillian, 1969

economy, which implies that one type of information only appears at one level of the hierarchy: the highest one possible. For example, the feature that birds can move is stored at the highest level *animal*. Another characteristic of the model is category size effect, which refers to the phenomenon that when faced with two sentences, such as *Robin is a bird* and *Robin is an animal*, less time is needed to verify the sentence *Robin is a bird*, as it is a subcategory of the term *animal*. The justification for this lies in the fact that as the category becomes larger, it becomes more abstract, therefore, the number of defining features decrease and the retrieval process takes longer because the brain needs more scanning to verify the information (Collins & Quillian, 1969, 1970).

However, it is important to note that the *hierarchical network model* has raised several concerns over the years. One is the so-called typicality effect, meaning that not all the instances of a concept are equally good examples of it; for example, a shark or a guppy might be more of a typical fish than a blue ray. The "familiarity effect" is also problematic: experiments have indicated that the retrieval process is shorter for familiar characteristics (e.g., *sharks are predators*) than for unfamiliar ones (*sharks' skeletons are made of cartilage and connective tissue*). Thirdly, cognitive economy seems to be violated as features might belong to more or sometimes all the categories of the hierarchy and not necessarily only the closest one. For instance, in the case of a penguin, it might be categorized as an *animal* even before the category *bird*, triggering the activation of a higher category first.

The other feature-oriented model constructed is the *semantic feature* or *feature comparison model* (Smith, Shoben, & Rips, 1974), which is based on the premise that concepts are stored as sets of attributes in our memory. For example, a bird might be considered to have characteristics like having feathers and wings, being able to fly, and lay eggs, while a robin

DEFINING FEATURES

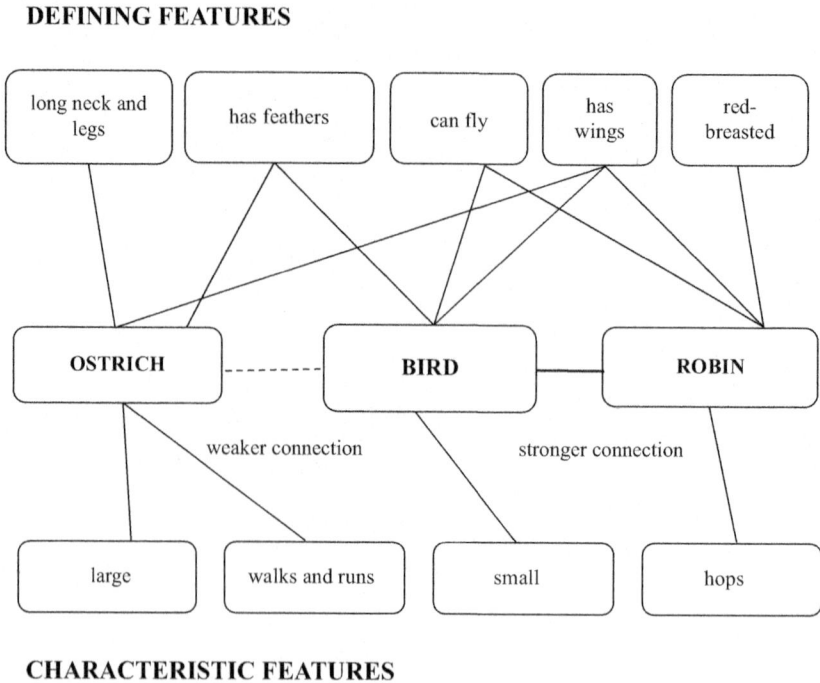

Figure 4.2   The semantic feature model

Source: Adapted from Smith et al., 1974

has feathers and wings, can fly, lays eggs, can be red-breasted, is small, and hops. As the features might vary in the extent to which they are central to the description of the given concept, the basic tenet of this theory is that there are two distinctive sets of attributes stored in the mental lexicon: defining and characteristic features (Figure 4.2). The main difference between these two categories arises from the fact that, whereas defining features are fundamental to the definition of the concept, characteristic features are typical but not salient.

Certain aspects of the *semantic feature model* provide an explanation for what the *hierarchical network model* cannot. First, as the concept *robin* shares more defining features with the notion of *bird* than with that of *ostrich*, a *robin* can be seen as a more typical bird than an *ostrich*. The problem of the typicality effect is resolved and we can explain why a sentence like *A robin is a bird* might be verified faster than *An ostrich is a bird*. The *semantic feature model* also justifies the rejection of false sentences, such as *An ostrich is a fish*, as these two concepts would share very few categories, which points to the fact that category size effect is overcome. Finally, the *semantic feature model* accounts for hedges like *Whales are sort of fish*. The rationale behind this phenomenon is that although they do not belong to the same category, they share certain characteristic features with them (e.g., the fact that they live in water).

Unfortunately, in spite of all the perceivable positive features of the two models just mentioned, it was shown that both the *hierarchical model* and the *semantic feature model* failed to predict reaction times, and were also influenced by other factors, such as the form of a word and the order in which participants encountered them. Finally, some ambiguous concepts, such as *game*, might have vague defining features or they may fall into categories that are too large (e.g., *plant* or *animal*), making the processing longer (Housel & Acker, 1977).

Similar to the previously mentioned *hierarchical* and *semantic feature models*, the *spreading activation model* also assumes that it is concepts, rather than words, that are activated in the mental lexicon. However, in the *spreading activation model* (Collins & Quillian, 1969, 1970) concepts are viewed as connected nodes where the distance between concepts depends on the degree of their association (see Figure 4.3). Collins and Loftus (1975) hypothesized that there are two separate networks for storing data in the mental lexicon: one for lexical information such as orthography and phonology, while the other is strictly semantic and stores information about concepts. Nevertheless, the two network systems are seen to be in close relation to each other (Collins & Loftus, as cited in Ferrand & New, 2004).

There are two reasons why the *spreading activation model* has come to be accepted as the most well-established out of the three theories. Because the mental lexicon has recently been pictured as a network of associations, instead of a rigidly hierarchical structure, this implies that each word might be related to several others. Furthermore, the fact that some links are stronger obviates the need to differentiate between defining and characteristic features. The *spreading activation model* also explains why positive priming tasks work: when participants are given a closely associated word (a prime) before a target word, they perform better in the process of retrieval, which indicates that there is a stronger link between certain notions (Reisberg, 2007).

However, one of the problematic issues with the *spreading activation model* is the fact that it assumes that every person possesses an entirely different mental lexicon. This leads to difficulties in finding emerging patterns with regard to lexical access or production. Moreover, as the model is based on concepts, it fails to take into consideration other aspects of word knowledge, such as phonology, orthography, or syntax (Bock & Levelt, 1994). This problem was solved in Bock and Levelt's *revised spreading activation model* (1994), where, apart from the conceptual connections, various levels of a lexical entry are marked, accounting for

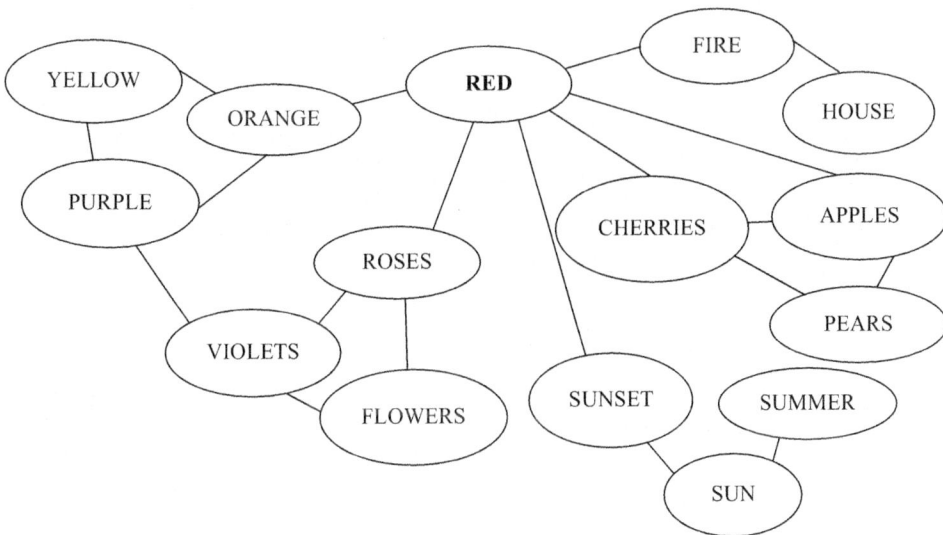

Figure 4.3 The spreading activation model

Source: Adapted from Collins & Loftus, 1975

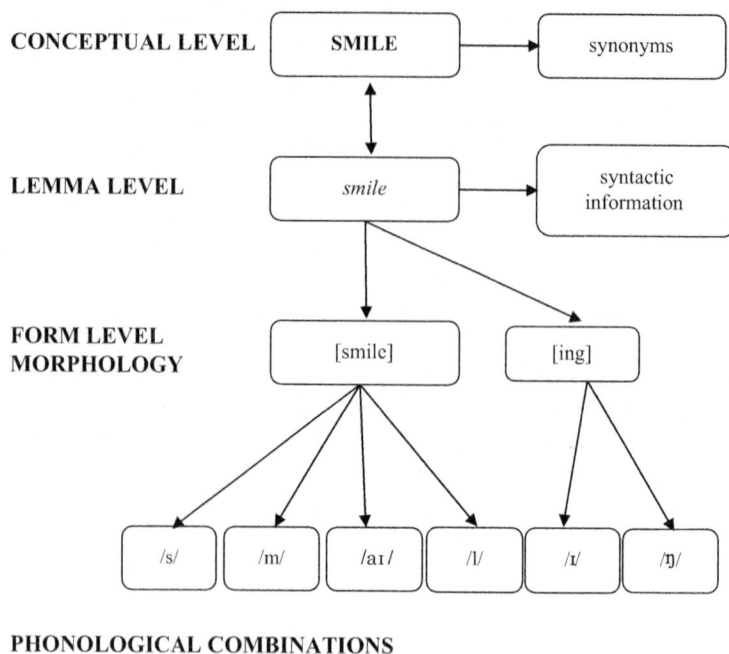

PHONOLOGICAL COMBINATIONS

Figure 4.4   The revised spreading activation model

Source: Adapted from Bock & Levelt, 1994

syntax as well as phonology (Figure 4.4). There is a similarity between the *revised spreading activation model* and Aitchison's *cobweb theory* (2012) because they both argue that lexical items might be linked to others according to phonology, orthography, syntax, or semantics.

Storage, Lexical Selection, and Retrieval in the Mental Lexicon

As we turn our attention to more current views on the structure and organization of the mental lexicon, it is important to clarify what types of information it may contain: conceptual (the ideas to be expressed), morphological (lemmas or word forms), and semantic (word meanings). In psycholinguistics the construct of vocabulary entails the storage and retrieval of words from the language processing system and the entity of *lemma* is regarded as the basic unit of lexical storage and representation in the mental lexicon. According to Levelt's (1989) model of speech production (see Figure 4.5), lexical encoding involves three steps: first, depending on the speaker's intention, the relevant concept is selected, and this is followed by the retrieval of the corresponding lemma, which contains information about the syntactic and morphological characteristics of the lexical unit in question. Last, the phonological form of the lemma, the so-called lexeme, is extracted and the word is pronounced. It is still a question of debate in psycholinguistic studies of lexical access whether the lemma contains semantic as well as syntactic information. Neurological research suggests that a lemma contains only syntactic information and the word meaning is stored at the conceptual level (Levelt, Roelofs, & Meyer, 1999).

However, as researchers have pointed out (Jarvis, 2009; Kormos, 2006; Pavlenko, 1999, 2009), the term *concept* had been applied inconsistently and thus the definitions of *conceptual*

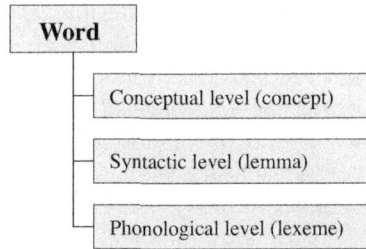

Figure 4.5   The process of lexical selection
Source: Adapted from Levelt et al., 1999

knowledge and *semantic knowledge* were not precisely defined or differentiated in the field of psycholinguistics. While the former notion refers to concepts and ideas stemming from thought processes, experience, various schemas, and mental images, which are "organized into structured categories of thought and categories of meaning" (Jarvis, 2009, p. 101), the latter construct represents word meaning, that is, the mental links between lemmas and concepts as well as lemmas and other lemmas. The significance of this distinction becomes all the more apparent in regard to the conceptualization of the bilingual lexicon, which will be discussed in the second part of this chapter.

The philosophical question that arises from this is whether conceptual and semantic representations should be distinguished, which has been a point of contention in the literature. Some researchers, such as de Groot and Keijzer (2000) and Francis (2005), have argued for the interrelationship of conceptual and semantic information. Founded on the work of Hintzman (1986), their argument claims that abstract knowledge, such as that of word meanings, should not be separated from knowledge of concepts, because both are part of an exemplar made up of all the memory traces that originate from previous experiences. This way both the concept and the meaning of a word comprise a complete set of these traces and when a specific word, such as "happiness" is accessed, it results in the activation of all the memory traces that contain significant information in relation to this particular concept. The implication of this view is that these traces are culture-bound and may vary, depending on the language and the culture. By contrast, other researchers (e.g., Paradis, 2000; Pavlenko, 1999, 2009) argue that concepts can exist independent of word meanings as they are "multisensory units of meaning independent of whether a corresponding word exists" (Paradis, 2000, p. 22) and "language is only one way to access concepts" (ibid.).

The dichotomy between the separatist and integrated perspectives has led to an ongoing debate and two opposing views with regard to the theoretical representation of conceptual and semantic knowledge in the mental lexicon. The one-level view proposes that the two types of knowledge should be viewed as indistinguishable. In Roelofs' (1992) and Levelt et al.'s (1999) models of lexical access, concepts and word meanings are undivided units that are stored and activated together. Concepts can be either lexical (i.e., there is a single-word representation for them) or non-lexical (i.e., they can be expressed with a multiword phrase or sentence) and they are manifested by independent nodes that are linked to each other (for a detailed discussion, see Roelofs, 2000). In this sense, lexical representations (word meanings) are viewed as a subset of all conceptual representations. Culture and language specificity allow speakers of different languages to have a distinct conceptual representation of a single concept; for example, the English word "summer" might entail completely different associations in various languages. Additionally, lexical representations are also built upon and linked to imagery and background information. When accessing a lexical entry, concepts are activated and they spread activation to lemmas, which comprise syntactic and morphological (but not semantic) knowledge. Lemmas are also incorporated into an integrated network, where activation can also spread item by item. Roelofs (2000) justifies aphasic patients' failure to access semantic representations, even though they were aware of the concepts and were able to describe them, by referring to the damage in the links between the conceptual and lemma levels. Another source of evidence that lexical and semantic knowledge are part of a common cognitive system has been produced by semantic dementia patients (see Dilkina, McClelland, & Plaut, 2010).

The two-level view advocated by Paradis (1997, 2000) and Pavlenko (1999, 2009) makes a distinction between conceptual and semantic knowledge. Similar to the integrated theory, concepts are also seen as interconnected networks of features that receive various degrees of activation based on the given communicative context. However, Paradis (2000) argues that semantic knowledge is not a component of the concept itself but of the language system, and conceptual and lexical characteristics "map onto each other, but are distinct entities" (p. 24). His observations originate from research on aphasia, which reported aphasic patients' failure to retrieve lexical entries despite the fact that they were able to access the conceptual features of the given word. Pavlenko (1999, 2009) believes that it is also necessary to distinguish between conceptual and semantic representations due to the cultural differences between various languages.

With regard to lexical representation, another question is that of stability (or instability). De Bot and Lowie (2010) criticized previous research and models, most of which was based on word associations, translation, and picture recognition tasks, for assuming that lexical representations are stable and invariant. In fact, they contend that, similar to all other aspects of language processing, lexical representations need to be viewed as "dynamic, episodic and therefore inherently unstable" (p. 117). They also highlight the relevance of time, context-sensitivity, and prior use. They suggest that the stability of lexical representation may also be dependent on lexical subsets, which are determined and influenced by factors such as context, frequency, register, recency, and language variety. Since a particular lexical item may belong to several subsets at the same time with varying degrees of connections, there is considerable variation in terms of ease of access and retrieval in this dynamic network.

The Bilingual Lexicon: An Interactive Network System

As we have seen in the previous sections, defining the mental lexicon poses a challenge, so when a speaker starts to use a second or third language, conceptualizing the mental lexicon is even more difficult. In the field of psycholinguistics, opposing views have emerged as to whether the lexical items of the different languages one speaks are stored separately or in a common lexicon with interrelated concepts (Pavlenko, 1999, 2009; Kormos, 2006; Singleton, 2007). The aim of the next section is to address this ongoing debate and look at the available evidence.

In support of the separatist perspective, Meara's (1982, 1984 as cited in Wolter, 2001) findings based on word association tests, revealed that in comparison to the L1 lexicon, there are less stable connections for words in the L2 lexicon and semantic links are also qualitatively different. Furthermore, he also found that phonology may have a significant organizing role in the L2 lexicon. Singleton (2007) also presented evidence in favor of separate mental lexicons. One of his arguments posited that since languages are based on highly divergent morpho-syntactic and phonological structures, bilingual and multilingual speakers need to refer to analogies based on the newly acquired language system. This implies separate routes for lexical access and activation. Additional support for separation was provided by aphasic patients and extreme cases of L1 attriters, who only experienced loss in one of their languages (Paradis & Goldblum, 1989; Schmid, 2002).

Currently, there is a more widely accepted view that there is a shared lexicon manifested as an interactive network system. However, the degree of interaction within the system is still in debate. The idea of a common storage system was first supported by reaction time experiments with cognates, which demonstrated that lexical units of both languages are activated and compete for selection (Colomé & Miozzo, 2010). Later studies also addressed the role of frequency and word length, while recent research has turned attention to lexical availability and the role of various semantic categories. For example, a recent study investigated how more abstract prompts, such as emotion words, might affect lexical access (see Catalan & Dewaele, 2017). Another determining factor has been the level of proficiency. For instance, in the case of advanced L2 speakers, both languages have been found to receive activation (Shook & Marian, 2012) and lexical access through translation happens faster, whereas less fluent bilinguals are slower at accessing lexical and conceptual connections (Dufour & Kroll, 1995). Thirdly, if the morphological systems of the two languages are similar, it triggers faster translation (for an overview see Kroll & Tokowitz, 2009). More recently the attention has shifted from the notion of commonality to the extent of this interconnectedness. In an attempt to investigate the bilingual network system, Wolter (2001) and Zareva and Wolter (2012) both indicated that in the case of well-known words there are differences in the types of connections between L1 and L2 words, while conversely, for less well-known words the links were found to be more similar. These findings are also supported by Wilks and Meara (2002), who claim that there is a higher number of connections at the core of the lexicon than at the periphery, and they postulate that the network structures of L1 and L2 lexicons might differ, because the links between L1 lexical items are stronger and more salient than the connections between L2 words. They claim that there is a higher number of links at the core of the lexicon than at the periphery with weightier links between L1 lexical items. In Wolter's view, depth of word knowledge might have a significant role in determining how well lexical items are integrated into the bilingual lexicon (Wolter, 2001). Since dimensions of lexical knowledge appear to be acquired incrementally (see Dóczi & Kormos, 2016), this results in various strengths of connectivity and susceptibility to constant change in the lexicon. The strength in links is also influenced by cross-linguistic factors which may determine the level of interconnectedness (Pavlenko, 2009; Singleton, 2007). Pavlenko (2009) illustrated this with cross-linguistic semantic priming and picture naming experiments and stated that morphological and phonological representations might be stored at separate levels, whereas words meanings and concepts are mostly shared.

As reported by Pavlenko (2014), recent research has also indicated that bilinguals and multilinguals experience a substantial amount of interaction between their languages in both directions, referred to as *bidirectional transfer* or *cross-linguistic influence*. In other words, since the two languages exert a continuous effect on each other, L1 and L2 lexical representations might be modified at any time, causing changes in the connection weights (strength of links) between concepts and their lexical representations in both languages. There is growing evidence that these cross-connections might also impact L1 connections, challenging the assumption of a stable L1 (Malt, Li, Pavlenko, Zhu, & Ameel, 2015).

Lexical Access in the Bilingual Mental Lexicon

Although the models used for lexical organization in the mother tongue have also been justified for bilinguals, they have been revised slightly for lexical access in the second language. In their theoretical overview, French and Jacquet (2004) outlined four types of hierarchical models of lexical organization for bilinguals: the *word association, concept-mediation, mixed,* and *revised hierarchical* models. Founded on the *hierarchical model* of Potter, So, Von Eckhardt, and Feldman (1984), which differentiates between concepts and word meanings, each of the models is characterized by a separate set of lexis for each language, as well as a common conceptual base. However, it is "the location and weighting of the links" (French & Jacquet, 2004, p. 88) that differentiates the models from each other, as detailed in the next section.

The basic tenet of the *word-association model* is that L2 lexical items are directly connected only to their L1 equivalents, but not to their corresponding concepts, which renders the recall of a concept unnecessary when an L1 word is translated into L2 (Figure 4.6). Researchers like French and Jacquet (2004) as well as Kormos (2006) have pointed out the fact that this model is the most suitable for modeling L2 lexical knowledge in the case of lower level speakers, as studies have shown that their reactions were faster to L2 translations than images of words, and they were also faster at translating cognates than noncognates (Kroll & Curley, 1988; Chen & Leung, 1989).

In the *concept-mediation model*, both L1 and L2 words are linked to the same concept but not to each other (Figure 4.7). Contrary to the previous alternative, this theory is applicable in the case of higher-level L2 proficiency speakers who do not need to rely any more on L1 translations to access concepts. Potter et al.'s study (1984) can serve as support for this model, as they found that proficient L2 speakers were faster at naming pictures than providing L1 equivalents for the same words.

The *mixed model*, as suggested by its name, is a combination of the former theories and assumes that L1 and L2 words are linked to each other, as well as to a shared concept (Figure 4.8). The rationale behind this is that even as learners' level of proficiency increases, the link between L1 and L2 words does not necessarily disappear: there may be different routes of activation for different word types, and several factors, such as the level of abstractness and similarity in word form, might also influence lexical access. For example, a study

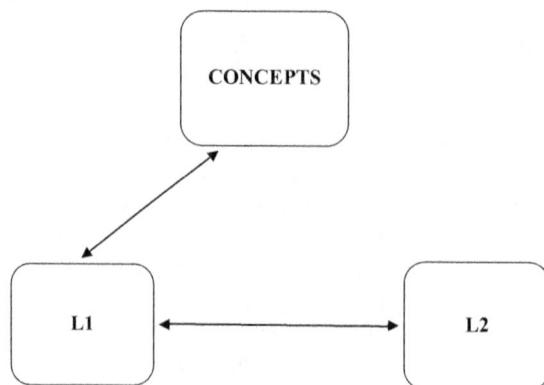

Figure 4.6 The word-association model

Source: Adapted from French & Jacquet, 2004

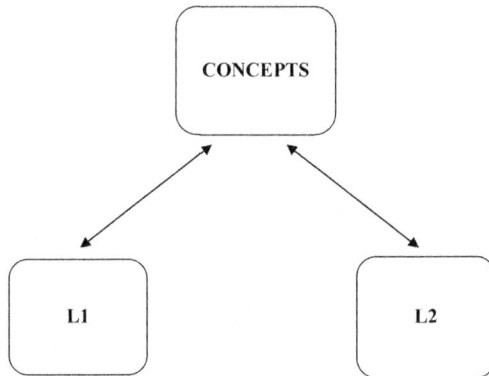

Figure 4.7   The concept-mediation model
Source: Adapted from French & Jacquet, 2004

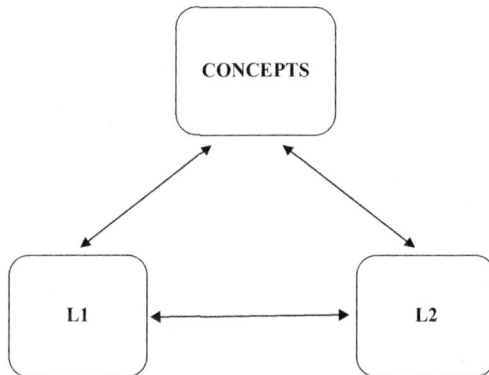

Figure 4.8   The mixed model
Source: Adapted from French & Jacquet, 2004

by Talamas, Kroll, and Dufour (1995) revealed that advanced L2 learners rejected L1–L2 word pairs more slowly if they were semantically related, and accepted them faster if they were cognates.

The fourth model to be presented here is the *revised hierarchical model* of Kroll and Stewart (1990, 1994), which also features one shared concept and links between L1 and L2 equivalents. However, the novelty of the model comes from the difference in the strength of the links, which depend on the direction (Dóczi & Kormos, 2016). As indicated in Figure 4.9, there is a stronger link between a concept and its semantic representation in L1 and we can suppose weaker links between the translation equivalents in the direction of L1 to L2 than from L2 to L1. A number of studies found evidence to support this as participants needed less time to recognize L1 words than images of concepts (see Kormos, 2006). The model has also been praised for showing the developmental progress and changes in the direction of links between conceptual and semantic representation, illustrating the dynamic nature of the bilingual lexicon (Altarriba & Basnight-Brown, 2009). From the perspective of language development, the revised hierarchical model successfully accounts for the importance of

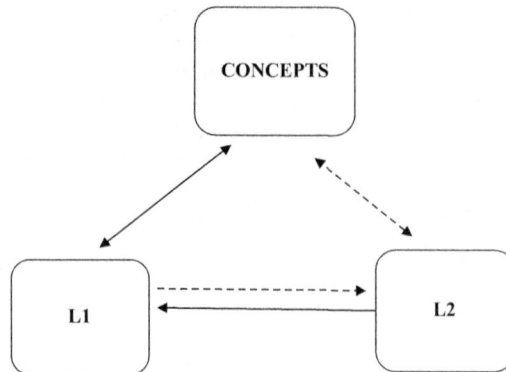

Figure 4.9   The revised hierarchical model
Source: Adapted from French & Jacquet, 2004

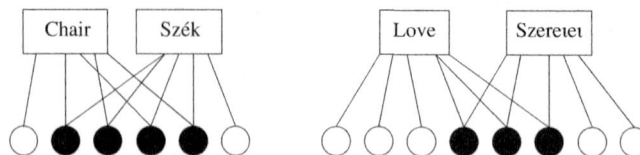

Figure 4.10   The conceptual feature model
Source: Adapted from de Groot, 1992

L1–L2 connectivity in the case of lower level learners, because they need L1 translation equivalents to access L2 words. However, as they become more proficient, the formation and strengthening of links between L2 words and concepts makes the L1 translation redundant. Nevertheless, the model has been challenged on the grounds that concepts might be culture or language-bound and they might not have overlapping conceptual representations (Pavlenko, 2009).

In contrast to the previous theories, de Groot's *conceptual feature model*, or *distributed feature model* (1992), is based on the assumption that although words are connected to concepts, a given word might have a similar or a different representation in the two languages (see Figure 4.10). In fact, certain words (such as a concrete word like *chair*) might share their conceptual representation in both languages, others may be partially overlapping, and in the case of some words, the conceptual representations might have very little or nothing in common. An example of partial overlap might be the conceptual representation of *love* in English and Hungarian, because while the concept covers both human and romantic feelings in English, these are represented by two different concepts in Hungarian. This framework successfully accounts for cross-linguistic differences, as demonstrated by de Groot (1992) and van Hell and de Groot (1998). The researchers found that cognates and concrete words were translated faster by bilinguals than noncognates and abstract words. Nevertheless, Pavlenko (2009) challenged the model for a number of reasons. On the one hand, it fails to take into account the context of words, and contrary to the revised hierarchical model, it does not reflect language and vocabulary development. Pavlenko's concern also derives from the fact that although concrete words and cognates were used to support the framework, it may not necessarily imply that they have completely overlapping conceptual representations.

The dynamic nature of lexical development is reflected in Dong's *shared asymmetrical model* (as cited in Pavlenko, 2009). In this model the L1 and L2 lexicons are linked, with connections to a common repository of shared conceptual elements (see Figure 4.11). In Pavlenko's view, even though the concepts are vaguely represented in the model, both the differences across the two languages and the developmental process are accounted for.

In one of the most recent models, Pavlenko (2009) aimed to incorporate the positive aspects of earlier frameworks. Similar to the *revised hierarchical model*, the *modified hierarchical model* (Figure 4.12) emphasizes the "developmental progression from lexical to

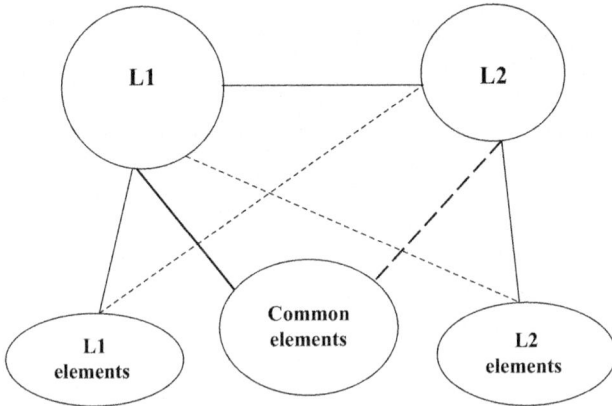

Figure 4.11 The shared asymmetrical model
Source: Dong et al., 2005, adapted from Pavlenko, 2009, p. 146

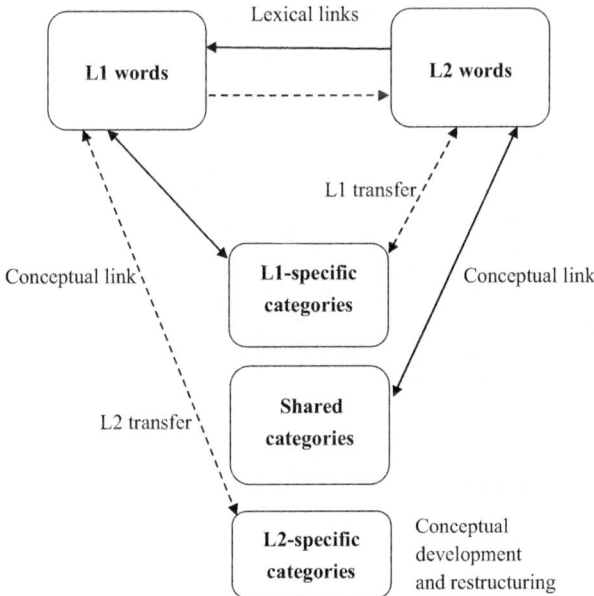

Figure 4.12 The modified hierarchical model
Source: Adapted from Pavlenko, 2009, p. 147

conceptual mediation" (p. 146), while also accounting for cross-linguistic and cross-cultural differences between languages. These features were present in the *distributed feature* and *shared asymmetrical models*. The uniqueness of the model is due to the distinction between language-specific, partially shared, and completely overlapping conceptual features. As an example of a language-specific concept, Pavlenko provided the examples of *privacy* and *frustration*, two concepts that might not be understood in certain cultures. She addressed the difficulty of formulation in the case of such words and provided examples from earlier studies, where participants overcame this by relying on "code-switching, lexical borrowing or loan translation" (p. 147). Pavlenko also stressed the relevance of context-dependence and task-performance, which are both reflected in her framework. Most importantly, the *modified hierarchical model* accounts for all the continuous implicit restructuring of the mental lexicon that might occur when encountering unknown L2 concepts. The model suggests that if there is no L1 concept available, links between concepts and lexical items can be restructured or inhibited when necessary, depending on the linguistic and social context. This also solves the problem of having two concepts for one lexical item (as the concepts "tongue" and "language" only have one lexical representation "nyelv" in Hungarian) for the process of semantic transfer. The greatest strengths of the model come from the assumption that conceptual and lexical categorizations can be clearly defined and separated, and the fact that the process of activation "becomes a two-way interaction between the mind and the environment" (p. 147).

Future Directions

While the lexical decision task was most frequently used in earlier research on the mental lexicon, recently, other, more varied research methods have been applied in the field (Libben, 2017). Libben postulated that several aspects of psycholinguistic research on the mental lexicon make it comparable to research on quantum physics, and he also pointed to the impossibility of concrete physical conceptualization in the brain. In his view, we have yet to actually see a word in the mind, and words should rather be conceptualized "as encapsulating a set of possibilities that may or may not be manifested by individual speakers of a language" (p. 54). This change in perspective and incorporating notions of quantum physics might provide an exciting avenue for further research.

Another emerging area is the utilization of network science to quantitatively observe complex network structures in lexical processing (see Castro & Stella, 2018; Stella & Brede, 2015). For example, Stella, Beckage, and Brede (2017) and Stella, Beckage, Brede, and De Domenico (2018) propose a multiplex lexical framework for modeling early language acquisition, where connectivity is based on relationships such as free association, co-occurence of words, similarity of features, or phonological representation. To further test their hypothesis, the authors call for more longitudinal investigations as well as the inclusion of different age groups.

There is also further research potential in the use of both word association data and text-corpus data in modeling lexical knowledge in order to explore developmental changes. According to De Deyne and his colleagues (2016), while the former type of analytical tool is able to provide a more direct view into the mental lexicon, the latter one is more adept at demonstrating how language might shape the processes and dynamics of its structure.

On another front, there seems to be a lot of potential in exploring the organization of the second language mental lexicon with the help of computational tools as well. In a recent study by Borodkin, Kenett, Faust, and Mashal (2016), the authors found that even highly proficient second language learners displayed less modular and more local connections in their second language compared to their mother tongue. In an attempt to deepen our knowledge of bilingual lexical processing, it may be interesting to examine to what extent other factors, such as age, level, and language-learning background might affect the structural links and their characteristics in the second (or perhaps third) language lexicon.

Conclusion

The present chapter has reviewed both theoretical and empirical evidence regarding the construct and systematic organization of the mental lexicon. In contrast to earlier theories, using vocabulary is no longer viewed as filling the slots in a sentence with the help of various transformations. Instead, it is viewed as linguistic construction units (e.g., words, lexical phrases, and formulaic expressions) in their own right, which cannot be separated from their syntactic regularities. This has led to a paramount shift in our view of the mental lexicon, which is now regarded as a complex and dynamic subsystem responsible for both conscious and unconscious lexical processes. The mental lexicon is now conceptualized as an integrated network of lexical items. This flexible network view of the lexicon is in line with Dynamic Systems Theory, as well as other connectionist theories that suppose a single-system view, where there are no lexicons per se, but the underlying representation of lexical knowledge is based on features, exemplars, and associations rather than concepts.

In the earliest, feature-oriented models of the mental lexicon the emphasis was on lexical organization rather than how lexical items are accessed or retrieved. Bock and Levelt's (1994) *revised spreading activation model* appears to have overcome this issue, because apart from the conceptual layer, syntax and phonology are also accounted for. Lexical selection is divided into three consecutive stages: (1) concepts are selected and activated, (2) the corresponding lemma is retrieved, and (3) the corresponding lexeme is assigned and triggered using the relevant morphological and phonological information. Psycholinguistic research has also addressed the interrelationship of conceptual and semantic knowledge and it is still a debated question whether the lemma contains syntactic information relating to a particular lexical entry.

From the perspective of the bilingual lexicon, researchers have focused on the issue of language specificity and there is growing evidence that the L2 network is less well-organized than its L1 equivalent. What we know now is that L1 and L2 lexical items are connected with each other, as well as with elements of the conceptual layer to varying degrees. Moreover, it is also clear that their influence on each other is continuous and bi-directional. Models for the organization of the bilingual lexicon are founded on L1 models but they have been slightly revised in an attempt to reflect its complexity. The most recent and detailed model of Pavlenko (2009) is characterized by aspects such as the strength of the links and associations between L1 and L2 words, conceptual representation and cross-cultural differences, and developmental progress.

Although there are still a lot of questions and considerable debate among researchers with regard to lexical organization, access, selection, and which research methods are most suitable for investigation, it is unquestionable that the mental lexicon is susceptible to constant adjustment and restructuring, depending on several factors. These factors include context, frequency, and recency of use, which results in a lot of variation and variability rather than stability.

Further Reading

Aitchison, J. (2012). *Words in the mind: An introduction to the mental lexicon.* Malden, MA: Wiley-Blackwell.

This classic reflects upon our basic knowledge of the mental lexicon and its structure in order to demonstrate how we learn, store, and retrieve words. Aitchison's *Words in the Mind* presents the results of a growing body of research to a wider audience interested in the conceptualization of the mental lexicon. The newest (4th) edition has been expanded, contains a new chapter on meaning change, and includes new references.

Jarema, G., & Libben, G. (Eds.). (2007). *The mental lexicon: Core perspectives.* Oxford, UK: Elsevier Press.

This edited volume gives insight into concepts related to human cognition and the mental lexicon by focusing on lexical representation and processing in the mind. It provides a thorough overview of concepts, issues, and research findings in the field.

Pavlenko, A. (Ed.). (2009). *The bilingual mental lexicon: Interdisciplinary approaches* (pp. 125–160). Clevedon, UK: Multilingual Matters.

This thematic volume bring together key perspectives related to the bilingual mental lexicon, including the nature of conceptual representation and semantic processing. It covers a wide range of views on the investigative techniques applied in psycholinguistics and also develops new models of lexical processing in the second language.

Related Topics

Single-word items, multiword items, lexical processing, theories of second language learning

References

Aitchison, J. (2003). *Words in the mind: An introduction to the mental lexicon.* Malden, Basil, UK: Wiley-Blackwell.

Aitchison, J. (2012). *Words in the mind: An introduction to the mental lexicon.* Malden, MA: Wiley-Blackwell.

Altarriba, J., & Basnight-Brown, D. M. (2009). An overview of semantic processing in bilinguals: Method and findings. In A. Pavlenko (Ed.), *The bilingual mental lexicon: Interdisciplinary approaches* (pp. 79–98). Clevedon, UK: Multilingual Matters.

Bock, K., & Levelt, W. (1994). Language production: Grammatical encoding. In M. A. Gernsbacher (Ed.), *Handbook of psycholinguistics* (pp. 945–984). San Diego, CA: Academic Press.

Borodkin, K., Kenett, Y. N., Faust, M., & Mashal, N. (2016). When pumpkin is closer to onion than to squash: The structure of the second language lexicon. *Cognition, 156,* 60–70.

Bresnan, J. (1982). *The mental representation of grammatical relations.* Cambridge, MA: MIT Press.

Castro, N., & Stella, M. (2018). The multiplex structure of the mental lexicon influences picture naming in people with aphasia. *Applied Network Science, 3*(13), 1–18.

Catalan, J. R., & Dewaele, J. M. (2017). Lexical availability of young Spanish EFL learners: Concrete and emotion words. *Language, Culture and Curriculum* (in print).

Chen, H.-C., & Leung, Y.-S. (1989). Patterns of lexical processing in a nonnative language. *Journal of Experimental Psychology: Learning, Memory and Cognition, 15,* 316–325.

Chomsky, N. (1965). *Aspects of the theory of syntax.* Cambridge, MA: MIT Press.

Collins, A. M., & Loftus, E. F. (1975). A spreading activation theory of semantic processing. *Psychological Review, 82,* 407–428.

Collins, A. M., & Quillian, M. R. (1969). Retrieval time from semantic memory. *Journal of Verbal Learning and Verbal Behavior, 8,* 240–247.

Collins, A. M., & Quillian, M. R. (1970). Does category size affect categorization time? *Journal of Verbal Learning and Verbal Behavior, 9*(4), 432–438.

Collins, A. M., & Quillian, M. R. (1972). How to make a language user. In E. Tulving & W. Donaldson (Eds.), *Organization of memory* (pp. 309–351). New York, NY: Academic Press.

Colomé, À., & Miozzo, M. (2010). Which words are activated during bilingual word production? *Journal of Experimental Psychology: Learning, Memory, and Cognition, 36*, 96–109. https://doi.org/10.1037/a0017677

de Bot, K., & Lowie, W. M. (2010). On the stability of representations in the multilingual lexicon. In M. Pütz & L. Sicola (Eds.), *Cognitive processing in second language acquisition* (pp. 117–134). (Converging evidence in language and communication research). Amsterdam: John Benjamins Publishers.

de Bot, K., Lowie, W. M., Thorne, S. L., & Verspoor, M. (2013). Dynamic Systems Theory as a theory of second language development. In M. Mayo, Gutierrez-Mangado, & M. Adrián (Eds.), *Contemporary approaches to second language acquisition* (pp. 199–220). Amsterdam: John Benjamins.

De Deyne, S., Kenett, Y. N., Anaki, D., Faust, M., & Navarro, D. J. (2016). Large-scale network representations of semantics in the mental lexicon. In *Big data in cognitive science: From methods to insights* (pp. 174–202). London: Psychology Press/Taylor & Francis.

de Groot, A. M. B. (1992). Bilingual lexical representation: A closer look at conceptual representations. In R. Frost & L. Katz (Eds.), *Orthography, phonology, morphology, and meaning* (pp. 389–412). Amsterdam: Elsevier.

de Groot, A. M. B., & Keijzer, R. (2000). What is hard to learn is easy to forget: The roles of word concreteness, cognate status, and word frequency in foreign-language vocabulary learning and forgetting. *Language Learning, 50*, 1–56.

Dilkina, K., McClelland, J. L., & Plaut, D. C. (2008). A single-system account of semantic and lexical deficits in five semantic dementia patients. *Cognitive Neuropsychology, 25*, 136–164.

Dilkina, K., McClelland, J. L., & Plaut, D. C. (2010). Are there mental lexicons? The role of semantics in lexical decision. *Brain Research, 1365*, 66–81.

Dóczi, B., & Kormos, J. (2016). *Longitudinal developments in vocabulary knowledge and lexical organization.* New York, NY: Oxford University Press.

Dong, Y., Gui, S., & MacWhinney, B. (2005). Shared and separate meanings in the bilingual mental lexicon. *Language and Cognition, 8*, 221–238.

Dufour, R., & Kroll, J. F. (1995). Matching words to concepts in two languages: A test of the concept mediation model of bilingual representation. *Memory & Cognition, 23*(2), 166–180.

Elman, J. L. (1990). Finding structure in time. *Cognitive Science, 14*, 179–211.

Elman, J. L. (2009). On the meaning of words and dinosaur bones: Lexical knowledge without a lexicon. *Cognitive Science, 33*, 547–582.

Fay, D., & Cutler, A. (1977). Malapropisms and the structure of the mental lexicon. *Linguistic Inquiry, 8*, 505–520. Retrieved from www.jstor.org/stable/4177997

Ferrand, L., & New, B. (2004). Semantic and associative priming in the mental lexicon. In P. Bonin (Ed.), *The mental lexicon: Some words to talk about words* (pp. 25–44). New York, NY: Nova Science Publishers.

Francis, W. S. (2005). Bilingual semantic and conceptual representation. In J. Kroll & A. M. B. DeGroot (Eds.), *Handbook of bilingualism: Psycholinguistic perspectives* (pp. 251–267). New York, NY: Oxford University Press.

French, R. M., & Jacquet, M. (2004). Understanding bilingual memory: Models and data. *Trends in Cognitive Sciences, 8*(2), 87–93. Retrieved from http://leadserv.ubourgogne.fr/people/french/bilingual_memory.TICS.french_jacquet.pdf

Hintzman, D. (1986). "Schema abstraction" in a multiple-trace memory model. *Psychological Review, 93*, 411–428.

Housel, T. J., & Acker, S. R. (1977, December). *A critical comparison of the network and feature comparison models of semantic memory.* Paper presented at the Annual Meeting of the Speech Communication Association, Washington, DC.

Jarema, G., & Libben, G. (2007). Introduction: Matters of definition and *core perspectives.* In G. Jarema & G. Libben (Eds.), *The mental lexicon: Core perspectives* (pp. 1–5). Oxford, UK: Elsevier Press.

Jarvis, S. (2009). Lexical transfer. In A. Pavlenko (Ed.), *The bilingual mental lexicon: Interdisciplinary approaches* (pp. 99–124). Clevedon, UK: Multilingual Matters.

Kormos, J. (2006). *Speech production and second language acquisition.* Mahwah, NJ: Lawrence Erlbaum Associates.

Kroll, J. F., & Curley, J. (1988). Lexical memory in novice bilinguals: Evidence from sentence priming. In M. Gruneberg, P. Morris, & R. Sykes (Eds.), *Practical aspects of memory* (Vol. 2, pp. 389–395). London, UK: John Wiley.

Kroll, J. F., & Stewart, E. (1990, November). *Concept mediation in bilingual translation.* Paper presented at the 31st Annual Meeting of the Psychonomic Society, New Orleans, LA.

Kroll, J. F., & Stewart, E. (1994). Category interference in translation and picture naming: Evidence for asymmetric connections between bilingual memory representations. *Journal of Memory & Language, 33,* 149–174.

Kroll, J. F., & Tokowitz, N. (2009). Models of bilingual representation and processing: Looking back and to the future. In J. Kroll & A. M. B. de Groot (Eds.), *Handbook of bilingualism: Psycholinguistic perspectives* (pp. 531–554). New York, NY: Oxford University Press.

Larsen-Freeman, D., & Cameron, L. (2008). *Complex systems and applied linguistics.* Oxford, UK: Oxford University Press.

Levelt, W. J. M. (1989). *Speaking: From intention to articulation.* Cambridge, MA: MIT Press.

Levelt, W. J. M., Roelofs, A., & Meyer, A. S. (1999). A theory of lexical access in speech production. *Behavioural and Brain Science, 22,* 1–38.

Libben, G. (2017). The quantum metaphor and the organization of words in the mind. *Cultural Cognitive Science, 1,* 49–55.

Malt, B., Li, P., Pavlenko, A., Zhu, H., & Ameel, E. (2015). Bidirectional lexical interaction in late immersed Mandarin-English bilinguals. *Journal of Memory and Language, 82,* 86–104.

Meara, P. M. (1982). Word associations in a foreign language. *Nottingham Linguistic Circular, 11*(2), 29–38.

Meara, P. (1984). The study of lexis in interlanguage. In A. Davies & C. Criper & A. P. R. Howatt (Eds.), *Interlanguage* (pp. 225–235). Edinburgh: Edinburgh University Press.

Paradis, M. (1997). The cognitive neuropsychology of bilingualism. In A. De Groot & J. Kroll (Eds.), *Tutorials in bilingualism: Psycholinguistic perspectives* (pp 331–354). Mahwah, NJ: Lawrence Erlbaum.

Paradis, M. (2000). Cerebral representation of bilingual concepts. *Bilingualism: Language and Cognition, 3,* 22–24.

Paradis, M., & Goldblum, M. C. (1989). Selective crossed aphasia in a trilingual aphasic patient followed by reciprocal antagonism. *Brain and Language, 36,* 62–75.

Pavlenko, A. (1999). New approaches to concepts in bilingual memory. *Bilingualism: Language and Cognition, 2,* 209–230.

Pavlenko, A. (2009). Conceptual representation in the bilingual lexicon and second language vocabulary learning. In A. Pavlenko (Ed.), *The bilingual mental lexicon: Interdisciplinary approaches* (pp. 125–160). Clevedon, UK: Multilingual Matters.

Pavlenko, A. (2014). *The bilingual mind and what it tells us about language and thought.* Cambridge, UK: Cambridge University Press.

Potter, M. C., So, K. F., Von Eckhardt, B., & Feldman, L. B. (1984). Lexical and conceptual representation in beginning and more proficient bilinguals. *Journal of Verbal Learning and Verbal Behaviour, 23,* 23–38.

Reisberg, D. (2007). *Cognition: Exploring the science of the mind.* New York, NY: Norton.

Roelofs, A. (1992). A spreading-activation theory of lemma retrieval in speaking. *Cognition, 42,* 107–142.

Roelofs, A. (2000). Word meanings and concepts: What do the findings from aphasia and language specificity really say? *Bilingualism: Language and Cognition, 3,* 19–21.

Schmid, M. S. (2002). *First language attrition, use and maintenance: The case of German Jews in anglophone countries.* Amsterdam, Holland: John Benjamins.

Shook, A., & Marian, V. (2012). Bimodal bilinguals co-activate both languages during spoken comprehension. *Cognition, 124*(3), 314–324.

Singleton, D. (2007). How integrated is the integrated mental lexicon? In Zs. Lengyel & J. Navracsics (Eds.), *Second language lexical processes: Applied linguistic and psycholinguistic perspectives* (pp. 3–16). Clevedon, UK: Multilingual Matters.

Smith, E. E., Shoben, E. J., & Rips, L. J. (1974). Structure and process in semantic memory: A featural model for semantic decisions. *Psychological Review, 1*, 214–241.

Stella, M., Beckage, N. M., & Brede, M. (2017). Multiplex lexical networks reveal patterns in early word acquisition in children. *Scientific Reports, 7*, 46730.

Stella, M., Beckage, N. M., Brede, M., & De Domenico, M. (2018). Multiplex model of mental lexicon reveals explosive learning in humans (under review).

Stella, M., & Brede, M. (2015). Patterns in the English language: Phonological networks, percolation and assembly models. *Journal of Statistical Mechanics: Theory and Experiment, 5*, P05006.

Talamas, A., Kroll, J. F., & Dufour, R. (1995). *Form-related errors in second language learning: A preliminary stage in the acquisition of L2 vocabulary*. Unpublished manuscript, Pennsylvania State University, University Park.

Thomas, M. S. C., & Karmiloff-Smith, A. (2002). Are developmental disorders like cases of adult brain damage? Implications from connectionist modelling. *Behavioural and Brain Sciences, 25*, 727–788.

Tomasello, M. (2003). *Constructing a language: A usage-based theory of language acquisition*. Cambridge, MA: Harvard University Press.

Van Geert, P. (1994). *Dynamic systems of development: Change between complexity and chaos*. New York, NY: Prentice-Hall.

van Hell, J. G., & de Groot, A. M. B. (1998). Conceptual representation in bilingual memory: Effects of concreteness and cognate status in word association. *Language and Cognition, 1*(3), 193–211.

Wilks, C., & Meara, P. M. (2002). Untangling word webs: Graph theory and the notion of density in second language word association networks. *Second Language Research, 18*, 303–324.

Wolter, B. (2001). Comparing the L1 and L2 mental lexicon. A depth of individual word knowledge model. *Studies in Second Language Acquisition, 23*, 41–69.

Zareva, A., & B. Wolter. (2012). The "promise" of three methods of word association analysis to L2 lexical research. *Second Language Research, 28*, 41–67.

5

The Relationship Between Vocabulary Knowledge and Language Proficiency

David D. Qian and Linda H. F. Lin

Introduction

The relationship between vocabulary knowledge and language proficiency is multifaceted. Vocabulary knowledge is "fundamental to all language use" (Schmitt, Cobb, Horst, & Schmitt, 2015) and thus is a crucial part of language learning. Achieving certain levels and qualities of lexical knowledge is one of the important prerequisites for successful language learning. This makes lexical knowledge a powerful predictor of learners' language proficiency and even their academic achievement (Lin & Morrison, 2010). Meanwhile, learners' lexical competence tends to improve as their language proficiency develops (Zareva, Schwanenflugel, & Nikolova, 2005) since the process of applying the four macro language skills (i.e., reading, listening, speaking, and writing) in communication is most conducive to imprinting newly learned words into memory (Laufer, 2013).

Grounds for the Prominent Role of Vocabulary Knowledge in Language Learning

One of the reasons for the widely recognized importance of lexical knowledge in language learning is the inextricably intertwined relationship between lexis and grammar. The strong association between the two language forms has led to the appearance of lexicogrammar (Halliday & Matthiessen, 2013), a linguistic view that focuses on the integration rather than the disparity between grammar and vocabulary. Nevertheless, when the two language forms are compared, in particular in the process of second language (L2) acquisition, lexical competence is often considered more important than syntactic knowledge in achieving effective communication. The critical role of lexical knowledge in L2 learning is further confirmed by studies investigating factors that affect learners' communication. Lexical errors have been found to be the most numerous type of error in L2 learners' language production, and were identified as a major factor hindering L2 learners' communication (Llach, 2011). A notable example is Santos (1998), who elicited responses from tertiary teachers in reaction to mistakes made by their L2 students in academic writing. The study reveals that lexical errors were the most severe obstruction to the understanding of the students' texts. This finding was in line with Djokic's (1999) investigation, which reports that vocabulary errors "cause momentary confusion" and "bring about misunderstanding" (p. 128). This misunderstanding not only interrupts the flow of communication but may also cause a communication breakdown (Llach, 2011). Difficulties in lexical use have also been deeply felt by many L2 students who believe that, of all the error types in their language production, the ones pertaining to vocabulary use are most damaging. Some types of lexical errors such as those in word collocation and word choice are persistent in the language production of some learners. They not only frequently appear in the language production of L2 beginners but also in that of high-proficiency learners (Gass & Selinker, 2008).

Vocabulary Knowledge of L1 and L2 Learners

Although an adequate knowledge of words is important for both first language (L1) and L2 learners, researchers (e.g., Jiang, 2000) believe that inappropriate lexical use causes more communication problems in the language production of L2 learners than of L1 learners, largely due to different lexical development processes of the two types of learners.

The lexical development of an L1 child is relatively fast due to his/her extensive and highly contextual exposure to the language, which makes it possible for the child to develop the semantic, syntactic, and morphological knowledge of a word. These three types of information about the word form an integrated part of the lexical entry in the child's lexicon, which is automatically activated when the word is used. This automatic and simultaneous activation of all three types of information is crucial for the learners' appropriate and efficient contextual use of the word.

The lexical development of L2 learners, on the other hand, is much more onerous. When L2 learners, in particular those who learn the target language in classroom settings, learn a word, they face two practical constraints. The first constraint is a lack of input opportunities in terms of both quantity and quality. In other words, there is a shortage of opportunities for learners to have sufficient and highly contextual exposure to the target language. This restriction causes significant difficulties in the learners' extraction of the semantic, syntactic, and morphological knowledge about a word. The second constraint, which is likely to have a more serious impact on L2 learning, is the existence of an established conceptual/semantic system in the learners' lexicon. The presence of the established L1 lexical system can greatly facilitate the acquisition of L2 words by providing a source for learners to draw on, but, meanwhile, it could also cause L2 learners, in particular adult learners, to over-depend on the L1 semantic and syntactic knowledge about a word while learning new words (Ellis & Shintani, 2013).

Quality and Quantity of Vocabulary Knowledge

The quantitative aspect of lexical knowledge refers to the number of words existing in a learner lexicon. This comprises the learner's knowledge of the form and meaning of a word which can be simply recalled. The qualitative aspect of vocabulary knowledge, on the other hand, refers to a learner's deep and extensive lexical knowledge and ability to use the word appropriately and efficiently. Having learned a word does not only mean the learner can recall the form and retrieve the meaning of the word in a vocabulary test, but it also implies the effective use of the word for authentic communication purposes, such as reading a newspaper article or writing an email message.

Researchers also divide word knowledge into two facets: receptive vocabulary and productive vocabulary. The receptive vocabulary forms the *size*, or *breadth*, of a learner's vocabulary in the mental lexicon. This part of the vocabulary knowledge needs to be further developed into productive knowledge in order to be used in a communication context. The development from receptive to productive vocabulary can be seen on a continuum, starting from superficial familiarity with the word and ending with an ability to use the word correctly in free production. The process of progressing on this continuum is the development of qualities or depth of one's lexical knowledge, also known as vocabulary depth (Henriksen, 1999; Qian, 1999, 2002, 2005; Read, 2007).

Despite the importance of mastering depth of vocabulary knowledge in language learning, investigations into L2 vocabulary acquisition have mostly focused on the size rather than depth of vocabulary knowledge, probably due to the difficulty in developing quality measures for assessing the depth dimension. On the other hand, the straightforward construct of vocabulary size tests, which normally measure only one superficial dimension of a learner's lexical knowledge, results in a variety of measures for assessing breadth of vocabulary knowledge. In research, vocabulary size tests reportedly play an important role in predicting success in learners' proficiency. Zareva et al. (2005), for example, found that vocabulary size was one of the strongest discriminating factors of L2 learners' proficiency level. Vocabulary size measures were also found to correlate well with scores on proficiency tests such as the International English Language Testing System (IELTS) and the Test of English as a Foreign Language (TOEFL). Stæhr (2008), for example, compared the vocabulary size of 88 lower secondary EFL students in Denmark with their examination grades on listening, reading, and writing skills. Results of the study show a strong positive association of their vocabulary size with their reading and writing abilities and a moderate positive association with their listening comprehension.

The construct of the quality dimension of a learner's lexical knowledge, on the other hand, is complex and multifaceted. It is not only unquantifiable but also difficult to conceptualize. Schmitt (2014) regards it as "the wooliest, least definable, and least operationalisable construct in the entirety of cognitive science" (p. 920). Consequently, Daller, Milton, and Treffers-Daller (2007) subdivided the quality aspect of lexical knowledge into *depth* and *fluency*. This division has created a three-dimensional space to view a learner's vocabulary knowledge, namely, *breadth*, *depth*, and *fluency*. Here, fluency is defined as the ease, or speed and accuracy, with which words are used in language production. This division is important because it "moves the conceptualisation of lexical proficiency onward from simple knowledge to the ability to use that knowledge" (Schmitt, 2014, p. 920). To improve learners' vocabulary fluency is to increase the automaticity (Qian, 2002) of their lexical use and should be the ultimate goal of most language learners.

Notwithstanding the complexity in conceptualizing the construct of depth of lexical knowledge, vocabulary depth has also been found to be closely associated to learners' language skills, in particular productive skills (i.e., speaking and writing). For example, Zareva et al. (2005) found L2 learners' knowledge in word associations was one of the strongest indictors of their proficiency level. Crossley, Salsbury, and McNamara (2014) analyzed spoken and written texts produced by L2 learners and found that a very important component in the depth construct, collocation accuracy, accounted for 84% of the variance in the writing scores and explained 89% of the holistic speaking scores. This finding underscores the importance of knowledge of lexical collocation in speaking and writing proficiency. Achieving a high collocation accuracy demands both syntagmatic and paradigmatic information of the involved words. Acquiring such knowledge requires extensive exposure to a context which can provide sufficient and meaningful target language input and enable activities leading to quality output in the target language. For this purpose, Qian and Schedl (2004) even explored the possibility of developing such a measure in the reading comprehension part of a new TOEFL test.

Reading, listening, speaking, and writing are the four main language modalities. The former two, reading and listening, mainly require learners' receptive language skills in comprehending written and aural texts, respectively, while the latter two require learners' productive skills in producing written and oral texts, respectively. The productive skills are thus more demanding. The four language skills will be examined separately in their association with vocabulary knowledge in the next two sections.

Critical Issues and Topics

Vocabulary Knowledge and Receptive Language Skills

Vocabulary knowledge is at the heart of the two receptive skills. Vocabulary size is found to be closely associated with the two receptive skills (Laufer & Ravenhorst-Kalovski, 2010; Qian, 1999, 2002) and vocabulary depth has been identified to be a better predictor of these two skills than vocabulary size (Han, 2017; Qian, 2002). The nature of these two modalities has made it possible for scholarly work to investigate the percentage of words a learner needs to know in order to comprehend a stretch of written and spoken discourse, known as *lexical coverage* (Nation, 2006). The establishment of lexical coverage allows researchers to determine the number of words learners need to know to achieve a required comprehension level, or *vocabulary size*.

Reading

Reading has attracted much research attention. Qian (1999, 2002) and Qian and Schedl (2004) conducted a series of studies with samples ranging from 74 to 217 young adult English-as-a-second-language (ESL) learners in Canada to examine the role of lexical knowledge in reading comprehension. Findings from these investigations indicated that both breadth and depth of vocabulary knowledge play a major role in ESL learners' reading processes since the scores on tests measuring depth and breadth of vocabulary knowledge correlated significantly and positively with readings scores. More importantly, the studies also revealed that the depth dimension is not only an effective predictor of reading comprehension but can also provide additional prediction of reading comprehension over and above the prediction already made by the size dimension. Additional studies have also been conducted to explore the role of depth of vocabulary knowledge in determining ESL learners' success in lexical inferencing (Nassaji, 2006; Qian, 2005). Results from these studies indicated that depth of vocabulary knowledge also plays a critical role in lexical inferencing, as it accounts for a significant portion of variance in learners' ability to successfully infer the meanings of unknown words. These findings have since been supported empirically by a number of recent studies (e.g., Laufer & Ravenhorst-Kalovski, 2010; Prior, Goldina, Shany, Geva, & Katzir, 2014).

Given the centrality of lexical knowledge in reading comprehension, researchers looked into a possible lexical coverage *threshold* that learners should reach in order to achieve adequate comprehension of written texts. The earliest research pertaining to lexical coverage suggested a need for 95% lexical coverage (Laufer, 1989). Accepting this figure, however, means that there are over 15 unknown words on every page, which could hinder the reading comprehension of some learners. A follow-up study by Hu and Nation (2000) recommended a 98% coverage as the standard for unassisted L2 reading. To make the concept more practical for L2 teaching and learning, Laufer and Ravenhorst-Kalovski (2010) suggested two lexical coverage figures based on their findings: a minimal coverage of 95% for basic comprehension and an optimal coverage of 98% for a better comprehension. A linear relationship between lexical coverage and reading comprehension suggests that the establishment of a lexical threshold should depend on the level of comprehension that is aimed for (Schmitt, Jiang, & Grabe, 2011). The higher the requirement for the comprehension level, the larger the coverage necessary, and in turn the vocabulary size that is required. The 95% coverage figure requires a vocabulary size of the 4,000 to 5,000 word families and the 98% coverage 8,000 word families for written text. This finding is in line with Nation's (2006) study, which posits that a vocabulary size of around 8,000 to 9,000 families plus proper nouns is needed to reach the 98% coverage necessary for adequate reading comprehension.

Listening

The process of listening comprehension differs from that of reading comprehension, and vocabulary knowledge plays different roles in these two processes (van Zeeland & Schmitt, 2013). Compared with the robust research initiatives on the relationship between vocabulary knowledge and reading proficiency, the number of studies on the association between lexical knowledge and listening proficiency is rather limited. Unlike reading processes which can be either bottom-up, top-down, or integrative, depending on the reader's proficiency level, listening is more a top-down process due to the nature of the input. While similar factors are at work in the process of reading and listening, such as lexical knowledge, genre knowledge, topic familiarity, text organization, and world/subject knowledge, the fleeting nature of spoken language, which demands the activation of a short-term working memory, requires a different role of vocabulary knowledge in the listening process. When reading, learners can refer back to lexical items in the text to facilitate their comprehension, but this is not possible during the fast-moving process of listening, which can be onerous to many learners. This could explain the considerable variation identified in the listening comprehension scores awarded to learners with a similar vocabulary size (e.g., Stæhr, 2009; van Zeeland & Schmitt, 2013) since their general language proficiency levels can be different. However, a counterargument holds that spoken language is usually not as lexically dense as written language. This feature, coupled with the assistance of nonverbal communicative devices, such as tone, gesture, and facial expression, can alleviate the difficulty in lexical processing, and such facilitation is nonexistent in a typical reading process.

Stæhr (2008) explored the relationship between vocabulary size and three language modalities – reading, writing, and listening – with a sample of 88 lower secondary EFL students in Denmark. Results of the study indicated that the size dimension of the participants' vocabulary was significantly, but variously, correlated with the three language skills (reading at $r = 0.83$, $p < .01$; writing at $r = 0.73$, $p < .01$; listening at $r = 0.69$, $p < .01$). A later study (Stæhr, 2009) with 115 advanced EFL learners in Denmark probed the relationship between both vocabulary breadth and depth and listening comprehension, and detected a correlation similar to that of his previous study (Stæhr, 2008) between vocabulary size and listening comprehension. As regards vocabulary depth, Stæhr (2009) reported a positive correlation of 0.65 ($p < .01$) with listening comprehension. A follow-up stepwise multiple regression analysis showed that the variable of vocabulary size was a better predictor of listening comprehension than vocabulary depth, which led Stæhr to claim that vocabulary size is the fundamental dimension of vocabulary knowledge in listening comprehension.

Somewhat conflicting results have also been reported in a number of very recent studies (e.g., Dabbagh, 2016; Han, 2017; Wang & Treffers-Daller, 2017). Examining the listening comprehension performance of 151 EFL university students in China, Wang and Treffers-Daller (2017) found that vocabulary size was a strong predictor of listening comprehension. Dabbagh (2016), when investigating the listening comprehension performance of 73 university EFL students in Iran, found that only depth of vocabulary knowledge could provide significant prediction of learners' listening comprehension; vocabulary size, on the other hand, was not a strong predictor of the learner's listening success. Han (2017) furthered this line of research by developing audio forms of the Vocabulary Levels Test and the Word Associates Test, to represent depth and size of vocabulary knowledge respectively. Han administered the newly developed aural tests together with the traditional written forms of the same measures to 718 EFL learners from four universities in Mainland China, and confirmed that scores on written and aural vocabulary knowledge measures were both positively and significantly correlated with listening scores to different degrees: (1) the vocabulary depth score from the written-form Word Associates Test and the vocabulary size score from the audio-form Vocabulary Levels Test were highly predictive of listening performance, (2) scores on written vocabulary depth were found to be more predictive than scores on written vocabulary size, and (3) aural vocabulary size scores were more predictive than written vocabulary size scores. Furthermore, (4) both written and aural vocabulary depth scores provided a better prediction of listening performance of EFL advanced learners than written and aural vocabulary size scores, which interestingly provided a better prediction of listening performance of low proficiency learners than vocabulary depth scores. The comprehensive results of the study suggest that the relationship between vocabulary knowledge and listening proficiency can change along with the development of a learner's proficiency level. As these results somewhat differ from previous research findings, replication studies are desirable so that a more profound understanding of these issues can be achieved.

Another noteworthy finding from Stæhr's (2009) study was that a vocabulary size of 5,000 word families could enable adequate listening comprehension of academic text. This contrasts with the suggestions of 6,000 to 7,000 word families made by Nation (2006) and that of 3,000 to 4,000 word families from Nation and Webb (2011) for an adequate comprehension of spoken texts. The figure, nonetheless, is rather distant from the size of 2,000 to 3,000 word families suggested by van Zeeland and Schmitt (2013). Further investigation is highly desirable to either confirm or disconfirm these claims.

Vocabulary Knowledge and Productive Language Skills

Corpora and Lexical Analysis

Compared with the scholarly work pertaining to the relationship between vocabulary knowledge and the two receptive language skills, research on the relationship between vocabulary knowledge and the two productive language skills, namely, speaking and writing, has been rather insufficient (Saito, Webb, Trofimovich, & Isaacs, 2016). This paucity is possibly owing to the complication of measuring the quality of learner output; it is more challenging to assess the relationship between vocabulary knowledge and writing and speaking proficiency than between vocabulary knowledge and reading and listening proficiency. However, with the availability of various corpora and computer programs specifically designed for analyzing corpus data, there has been an increasing amount of research examining the relationship between vocabulary knowledge and productive language skills. The availability of such electronic data and tools have made possible large-scale investigations into lexical features and patterns, such as "word collocations, formulaic language in different registers, and lexical bundles in spoken and written English" (Paribakht & Webb, 2016, p. 121).

Corpora that have been used for lexical analysis include the British National Corpus (BNC), COCA (Corpus of Contemporary American English), and American National Corpus (ANC). Learner corpora, such as International Corpus of Learner English (ICLE), appear to be more useful in this area of research as they enable comparative interlanguage analysis between learner language and native speakers' output. Results from such analysis can reveal patterns and problems that are typical in the learner language, such as overuse, underuse, or misuse of a lexical item. Further, with the large amount of data available, corpus-driven comparative analysis may possibly help teachers and researchers trace the cause of problems in learners' language use.

Computer programs, such as RANGE (www.victoria.ac.nz/lals/about/staff/paul-nation# vocab-programs), AntWordProfiler (www.laurenceanthony.net/software/antwordprofiler/), VocabProfile (www.lextutor.ca/vp/), and P_Lex (Meara & Bell, 2001), enable researchers to explore lexical richness in learners' language production, both in written and spoken forms, although the number of studies on written texts is much higher than that of spoken texts, probably due to the relative ease in collecting and processing written data. Some of these programs are freely available on Tom Cobb's website, *Compleat Lexical Tutor*. These programs can measure lexical features that are considered dimensions of lexical richness, including *lexical frequency*, or "words from different frequency levels" (Laufer & Nation, 1995, p. 311); *lexical variation*, or the variety of activated words in language production; and *lexical sophistication*, or the proportion of infrequent words in a text. Information on lexical richness has been found to relate closely to learners' language proficiency (Daller & Phelan, 2007; Laufer & Nation, 1995; Lin & Morrison, 2010).

Vocabulary knowledge is a crucial component of the two productive language skills. For L2 learners, vocabulary use is one of the most important factors that determine their writing quality (Leki & Carson, 1994). Effective speaking also depends heavily on word knowledge, particularly so with L2 learners (de Jong, Steinel, Florijn, Schoonen, & Hulstijn, 2012). Compared with receptive language skills, productive language skills exert a high demand on the quality dimension of learners' lexical knowledge. This is evident in Crossley et al.'s (2014) study which demonstrated that collocation accuracy, a crucial component in the depth dimension of vocabulary knowledge, explained 84% of the variance in evaluations of writing and 89% of the variance in evaluations of speaking. These findings underscore the importance of collocation accuracy in learner production and suggest that superficial knowledge of words primarily learned in isolation, for example from decontextualized word lists, may not lead to successful language production, be it in written or spoken form. On the other hand, lexical fluency, or the ease (speed and accuracy) with which words are used in language production, plays a more determining role (Schmitt, 2014). Improving learners' lexical fluency is to increase the automaticity of their lexical use, which requires "intensive exposure to meaningful L2 input and interaction" (Saito et al., 2016, p. 697). The importance of exposure to contextualized vocabulary learning therefore rests in the complex organization of the multidimensional aspects of vocabulary knowledge in a learner's mental lexicon (Milton, 2009; Schmitt, 2010, 2014). Factors such as the number of nodes, or links, a word has with other words, the way these nodes are organized and the level of strength between them, could all have an impact on the learner's language production.

Many of the above aspects of vocabulary knowledge (e.g., collocation, connotation, and register constraints) are implicit in character. Their acquisition thus requires extensive and highly contextual exposure to the target language. Some aspects of a learner's word knowledge, such as polysemous senses, may have been well developed because these parts of vocabulary knowledge are more amenable to intentional learning. Other aspects, such as word association and word collocation, which require much exposure to diverse contexts, however, may have not been acquired by the learner in the same stage and thus links between these aspects may have not been fully developed.

Meara (1982) argues that words are connected very differently in the mental lexicon of an L2 learner and a native speaker of the language. A native speaker's lexis is primarily organized in paradigmatic associations while that of an L2 learner is largely in syntagmatic associations. This disparity in organizing word knowledge components could affect the appropriateness and effectiveness of L2 learners in the use of the target language. Another factor is that some learners partially develop their L2 vocabulary links in the lexicon by transferring their existing L1 lexical knowledge to newly learned L2 words (Webb, 2007). This may mean that many L2 learners develop their vocabulary networks in the lexicon according to their existing L1 lexical links (Milton, 2009). These L1-related networks could lead to further differences in L2 learners' language performance.

Some types of vocabulary depth knowledge such as word association and connotation are intuitive and difficult to explain and thus demand extensive exposure to diverse contexts. Insufficiency in either frequency or duration in the exposure could affect the strength of knowledge in some parts. This lack of strength could weaken the learner's ability to effectively employ many words in the lexicon.

Theories of working memory also lend explanation for the higher demand on lexical competency in L2 speaking and writing. Language production is a complex process for L2 learners. This complexity can be manifested in the writing process. One of the most influential models in this regard (Kellogg, 1996) divides writing into three, albeit recursive, processes: formulation, execution, and monitoring. The first process involves writers' formulating and organizing ideas, which demands their cognitive and metacognitive resources. The second process involves the execution of the formulated plans, i.e., to translate ideas into linguistic forms. This stage requires writers' cognitive and linguistic knowledge, including retrieving related lexical items, encoding clauses and sentences syntactically, and establishing cohesive relationships in the written text. The last process is to monitor the quality of the created text, to ascertain whether the composed text effectively expresses the writer's intention. If not, revision needs to be undertaken. This stage requires the use of writers' linguistic, cognitive, and metacognitive resources. Kellogg's model indicates a writing task requires different facets of the writer's knowledge, some at lower-order (linguistic) and some at higher-order (cognitive and metacognitive) levels. Studies have provided empirical evidence showing that cognitive and metacognitive knowledge is a major discriminating factor in the performance of an L1 writer (Victori, 1999) whereas linguistic knowledge is more instrumental in predicting the writing proficiency of L2 learners (Sasaki & Hirose, 1996). This difference can be explained by the theory of working memory capacity.

Working memory refers to a person's mental capacity to store and orchestrate resources connected to a task (Baddeley, 2003). The role of working memory is described as "a bottleneck for learning" (Gathercole & Alloway, 2008, p. 12). During the process of composing a spoken or written text, for example, a learner's linguistic, cognitive, and metacognitive knowledge stored in long-term memory, has to be processed by working memory at the same time. If a learner has obtained automatized linguistic knowledge, as is often the case in L1 writing, the learner can attend more closely to the cognitive aspects of the task such as organizing ideas and enhancing the persuasiveness of the text. However, many L2 learners are found to be "tied up with word- or sentence-level processes" (Sasaki & Hirose, 1996, p. 158). When this lower-order processing load increases, the working memory capacity available for the higher-order (cognitive) aspects of writing/speaking, which are required in all the three processes in Kellogg's model, is reduced. The consequence of this insufficient activation of cognitive knowledge is very likely reduced quality of the written/spoken product.

The preceding working memory theories point to the importance of automatization of L2 learners' lexical and syntactic knowledge. Of these two language domains, lexical knowledge deserves more attention from advanced L2 learners. At this proficiency level, most of these learners have gained a sufficient understanding of syntactic rules (You, 2010). Their level of automaticity in lexical use has thus become more instrumental in composing a spoken or written text.

Speaking

The demanding nature of lexical automaticity in the productive skills has resulted in challenges to some learners who aim at sophisticated communication, for example, speaking in an academic context in the target language. However, if learners only need to engage in "a simple conversation", knowing the 2,000 most frequent words could be "adequate" (Laufer & Nation, 2012, p. 169). This figure is possibly derived from a large-scale investigation (Schonell, 1956) which examined the spoken interaction of Australian workers and found that 99% of the words used in their conversations were from the most frequent 2,000 word families. This figure, however, was challenged by Adolphs and Schmitt (2003). By analyzing the *Cambridge and Nottingham Corpus of Discourse in English* (CANCODE) and spoken component of the *British National Corpus* (BNC), Adolphs and Schmitt contend that conducting everyday conversation competently would require more than what is available at the 2,000-word level, which can only allow learners to engage in simple conversations. They suggest that sophisticated oral communication requires a much larger vocabulary.

The demanding nature of lexical automaticity is evident in Saito et al. (2016), which examined the lexical factors that determined the comprehensibility (ease of understanding) of oral narratives delivered by 40 French learners of English. The results indicate that lexical appropriateness, fluency and diversity are the main discriminating factors of the learners' comprehensibility. The study also found that comprehensibility for beginner-to-intermediate learners was closely associated with their fluent and correct use of L2 words, whereas in the case of intermediate-to-advanced learners, comprehensibility was more related to their level of sophistication in using L2 lexis, meaning "morphologically accurate use of complex, less familiar, and polysemous words" (Saito et al., 2016, p. 678). These results were in line with findings from Crossley et al. (2014), which found collocation accuracy (a fundamental element in lexical appropriateness) critically important in their learners' speaking performance.

Lu (2012) corroborates Saito et al. (2016) and in addition argues that lexical variation can be a strong predictor of learners' speaking ability. By analyzing the *Spoken English Corpus of Chinese Learners* (Wen, Wang, & Liang, 2005), Lu explored the relationship between lexical richness (lexical diversity, density and sophistication) and the speaking performance of Chinese learners of English in mainland China. Results showed that lexical variation (diversity) correlated strongly with learners' scores on evaluations of speaking performance. Lexical density was found to have no impact and lexical sophistication (words beyond the 2,000 frequency level in BNC) "a very small" impact on learners speaking performance (p. 14). Lexical sophistication has long been regarded as an effective indicator of learners' language proficiency (Daller & Phelan, 2007; Laufer & Nation, 1995). This very small impact made by lexical sophistication on the learners' speaking ability was possibly a consequence of learners' lack of exposure to contextual language learning activities in mainland China (Lin, 2015).

Writing

The demand on lexical competence in writing is as high as that in speaking if not more. Writing, defined as the production of an original meaningful written text (Laufer, 2013), is a highly complex task due to the conventions required by a large variety of genres. Tasks such as filling in blanks and correcting lexical or grammatical errors in a passage, connecting two simple sentences to make a complex sentence, or copying a written text, are not considered "writing" in this chapter, although some of these task formats have appeared in the writing component of some high-stakes English proficiency tests such as *the National Matriculation English Test* in China (Lin, 2015; Qi, 2007; You, 2010).

Vocabulary knowledge has been found to correlate significantly with learners' writing performance (Lin, 2015; Shi & Qian, 2012; Stæhr, 2008). Lin analyzed the performance of 67 Hong Kong university students on three language measures: Vocabulary Level's Test, Word Associates Test, and a writing test. Results showed that scores on the two vocabulary tests representing learners' lexical knowledge could predict a quarter (25%) of their writing scores. The study also found that scores on vocabulary depth added 11% variance over and above the variance explained by vocabulary size, thus contributing an additional unique prediction of the participants' writing scores. Results of Shi and Qian (2012) and Stæhr (2008) also confirm that vocabulary knowledge makes an important contribution to L2 learners' writing proficiency.

Research on lexical richness in L2 learners' writing draws from the notion that high-frequency words are learned at the beginning of their L2 acquisition. As the learners become more proficient, new properties of words and polysemous words start to be gathered in their mental lexicon. This allows for sophistication in their lexical use, for example, employing lower frequency words, having more diversity in word choice and achieving more appropriate word collocation. This notion is empirically supported by Laufer and Nation (1995), who found that the higher the proficiency level, the more likely the learner was able to deploy low-frequency words in writing. Two later studies, Daller and Phelan (2007) and Lerenzo-Dus (2007), provide further empirical evidence for this notion, confirming that lexical sophistication serves as an effective indicator of a learner's writing. A recent study (Bestgen, 2017) also found that both lexical diversity and lexical sophistication are significant predictors of ESL learners' writing quality, and competence in using formulaic language is the best predictor of their writing ability. However, it is worth noting that measures of lexical richness may produce different results when applied to different genres. For example, Olinghouse and Wilson (2013) report that vocabulary diversity has a unique predicating power for the quality of learners' story texts, whereas sophisticated use of content words is a strong predictor of the writing quality of persuasive and informative texts.

Future Directions

Many topics related to the examination of the relationship between vocabulary knowledge and language proficiency are under-researched, in particular those pertaining to the two productive language skills. The area with perhaps the greatest value for further research is examining the extent to which learners are able to use memorized words appropriately in speaking and writing. Learners may occasionally have to rely on dictionaries and vocabulary lists in association with preparation for high-stakes examinations (Lin, 2015; Qi, 2007; You, 2010). Words learned through such channels often cannot be used fluently in their language production. Many of these learners finally have a relatively large vocabulary size but do not know much about the words that they have studied and are unable to use them effectively (Schmitt, 2014). Milton (2009) suggests that they have a large number of words stored in the mental lexicon but these words are poorly organized for retrieval. This issue emerged in Lin's (2015) study which explored the relationship between learners' lexical knowledge and their writing proficiency. The participants in this study included two groups of first year university students. One group was from mainland China where there is a shortage of L2 input and output opportunities. The other group was from Hong Kong where there are abundant L2 input and output opportunities and an increasing demand for advanced English language proficiency learners to fill prestigious jobs in the territory. The mainland partici-pants reported that their vocabulary knowledge was derived mainly from vocabulary lists. Some of the participants reportedly memorized as many as 200 new words per day. Their Hong Kong counterparts, however, relied much less on vocabulary lists. A large proportion of their vocabulary knowledge was acquired from reading and listening. This supports the notion that vocabulary size is the basic dimension of learners' vocabulary knowledge and vocabulary depth serves to further refine their word knowledge and facilitates automaticity in retrieving words for language production (Qian, 2002; Qian & Schedl, 2004; Schmitt, 2008; Stæhr, 2009).

Lu (2012) also found that lexical sophistication only had "a very small" impact on the speaking proficiency of the English learners in mainland China (p. 14). Results of these two studies, however, deviate from other studies on the relationship between learners' lexical knowledge and their ability in language production (e.g., Laufer, 1994; Laufer & Nation, 1995). This deviation is very likely a consequence of the unconducive English learning con-text in mainland China (Lin, 2015). More research is desirable to gain a better understanding of the impact of language learning context on learners' ability to use the target language.

Furthermore, there is still a paucity of research on automaticity of vocabulary knowledge and its role in language performance. While investigation into automaticity has been chal-lenging due to its difficulty in operationalization, the advancement of modern technology, in particular eye tracking and brain imaging techniques (e.g., EEG and fMRI) makes it possible to research this dimension of vocabulary knowledge in relation to language processing and proficiency levels.

The second area that requires further investigation is the contribution depth of vocabulary knowledge can make to explaining the variance in learners' speaking production. The contri-butions of depth of vocabulary knowledge that go beyond vocabulary size have ranged from 5% for listening comprehension (Stæhr, 2009) to 13% for reading comprehension (Qian, 2002) and 11% for writing performance (Lin, 2015). It would be interesting to see if the construct of depth of vocabulary knowledge can also make a unique and significant contribu-tion to the prediction of learners' speaking ability. In addition, the figures derived from Han (2017), Qian (1999, 2002), Stæhr (2008, 2009), and Lin (2015) varied concerning the predic-tive power of vocabulary depth relative to that of vocabulary size. Even though explanations may have been provided for the discrepancies between these figures in the context of indi-vidual studies, replicated studies, and meta-analysis would be useful to clarify the findings.

Another area that needs scholarly attention is the role of the first 3,000 word families in predicting the language proficiency of advanced L2 learners. Laufer and Ravenhorst-Kalovski (2010) studied 745 Israeli students in an academic college, and both teachers and learners informally reported that students with a vocabulary size of 3,000 families still could not manage required reading assigned to them even after having completed three semesters of mandatory English support classes. Lin (2015) analyzed the writing performance of 150 university students in Hong Kong. The learners' lexical knowledge at the 3,000-word level was weakly associated with their writing scores. When a regression analysis was performed to identify the contribution that the learners' word knowledge at the 3,000 and 5,000 frequency levels could make to their writing performance, the 3,000 level was forced out from the equation, indicating its insignificant role in predicting the learners' writing scores. A recent paper by Dabbagh (2016), which examined the listening comprehension of 73 EFL students in an Iranian university, found only a weak correlation between the students' vocabulary knowledge of the 3,000 word families and their listening comprehension. Results from these and other similar studies indicate that word knowledge at the 3,000-word-family level has a rather limited role in predicting learners' language proficiency. Therefore, more investigations should be conducted to determine which word frequency levels can effectively predict L2 learners' language proficiency for various purposes. Findings from such investigations will possibly provide significant pedagogical implications. A further reason for conducting such investigations is that there is an increasing agreement in the literature that the 5,000-word level constitutes the minimum threshold required for undertaking academic studies in an English-medium university (Roche & Harrington, 2013). Based on this threshold, the 3,000-word level is far below the required level. Given these findings, it is not surprising to see a suggested new boundary of high-frequency English words (see Schmitt & Schmitt, 2014). Following this suggestion, the level of 3,000 word families should be included in the high-frequency vocabulary. This may mean the first 3,000 word families play a very limited role in predicting the language proficiency of advanced L2 learners.

Further Readings

Qian, D. D. (2002). Investigating the relationship between vocabulary knowledge and academic reading performance: An assessment perspective. *Language Learning, 52*, 553–536.

Based on a synthesis of related conceptual and empirical studies, this paper was among the first to recognize the importance of depth of vocabulary knowledge in second language reading comprehension. It provides an in-depth empirical analysis of the complex relationships between the size and depth of vocabulary knowledge in a learner's lexicon.

Schmitt, N. (2014). Size and depth of vocabulary knowledge: What the research shows. *Language Learning, 64*(4), 913–951.

This article critically reviews recent empirical studies on the relationship between size and depth of vocabulary knowledge. The article evaluates the merits of such conceptualization but also points out issues arising from this line of research.

Related Topics

The different aspects of vocabulary knowledge, L1 and L2 vocabulary size and growth, measuring depth of vocabulary knowledge, measuring lexical richness, key issues in measuring vocabulary knowledge

References

Adolphs, S., & Schmitt, N. (2003). Lexical coverage of spoken discourse. *Applied Linguistics, 24*(4), 425–438.

Baddeley, A. D. (2003). Working memory: Looking back and looking forward. *Nature Reviews Neuroscience, 4*, 829–839.

Bestgen, Y. (2017). Beyond single-word measures: L2 writing assessment, lexical richness and formulaic competence. *System, 69*, 65–78.

Crossley, S. A., Salsbury, T., & McNamara, D. S. (2014). Assessing lexical proficiency using analytic ratings: A case for collocation accuracy. *Applied Linguistics, 36*(5), 570–590.

Dabbagh, A. (2016). The predictive role of vocabulary knowledge in listening comprehension: Depth or breadth? *International Journal of English Language and Translation Studies, 3*, 1–13.

Daller, H., Milton, J., & Treffers-Daller, J. (2007). Editor's introduction. In H. Daller, J. Milton, & J. Treffers-Daller (Eds.), *Modelling and assessing vocabulary knowledge* (pp. 133–149). Cambridge, UK: Cambridge University Press.

Daller, H., & Phelan, D. (2007). What is in a teacher mind? Teacher ratings of EFL essays and different aspects of lexical richness. In H. Daller, J. Milton, & J. Treffers-Daller (Eds.), *Modelling and assessing vocabulary knowledge* (pp. 133–149). Cambridge, UK: Cambridge University Press.

de Jong, N. H., Steinel, M. P., Florijn, A. F., Schoonen, R., & Hulstijn, J. H. (2012). Facets of speaking proficiency. *Studies in Second Language Acquisition, 34*, 5–34.

Djokic, D. (1999). Lexical Errors in L2 learning and communication. *Rassegna Italina di Lingustistica Aplicata, 1*, 123–135.

Ellis, R., & Shintani, N. (2013). *Exploring language pedagogy through second language acquisition research*. Florence, KY: Routledge.

Gass, S., & Selinker, L. (2008). *Second language acquisition: An introductory course* (3rd ed.). New York, NY: Taylor & Francis.

Gathercole, S. E., & Alloway, T. P. (2008). Working memory and classroom learning. In K. Thurman & K. Fiorello (Eds.), *Cognitive development in K-3 classroom learning: Research applications*. Mahwah, NJ: Lawrence Erlbaum.

Halliday, M. A. K., & Matthiessen, C. M. (2013). *Halliday's introduction to functional grammar* (4th ed.). New York, NY: Routledge.

Han, D. (2017). *Evaluating the relationship between vocabulary knowledge and listening comprehension in English as a foreign language*. Unpublished doctoral thesis, Hong Kong Polytechnic University, Hong Kong.

Henriksen, B. (1999). Three dimensions of vocabulary development. *Studies in Second Language Acquisition, 21*, 303–317.

Hu, M., & Nation, I. S. P. (2000). Unknown vocabulary density and reading comprehension. *Reading in a Foreign Language, 13*(1), 403–430.

Jiang, N. (2000). Lexical representation and development in a second language. *Applied Linguistics, 21*(1), 47–77.

Kellogg, R. T. (1996). A model of working memory in writing. In C. M. Levy & S. Ransdell (Eds.), *The science of writing: Theories, methods, individual differences and applications* (pp. 57–71). Mahwah, NJ: Lawrence Erlbaum.

Laufer, B. (1989). What percentage of text lexis is essential for comprehension? In C. Lauren & M. Nordman (Eds.), *Special language: From humans thinking to thinking machines* (pp. 316–323). Clevedon, UK: Multilingual Matters.

Laufer, B. (1994). The lexical profile of second language writing: Does it change over time? *RELC Journal, 25*(2), 21–33.

Laufer, B. (2013). Vocabulary and writing. In C. A. Chapelle (Ed.), *The encyclopedia of applied linguistics*. Boston, MA: Wiley-Blackwell.

Laufer, B., & Nation, I. S. P. (1995). Vocabulary size and use: Lexical richness in written production. *Applied Linguistics, 16*, 307–331.

Laufer, B., & Nation, I. S. P. (2012). Vocabulary. In S. M. Gass & A. Mackey (Eds.), *The Routledge handbook of second language acquisition* (pp. 163–176). New York, NY: Routledge.

Laufer, B., & Ravenhorst-Kalovski, G. C. (2010). Lexical threshold revisited: Lexical text coverage, learners' vocabulary size and reading comprehension. *Reading in a Foreign Language, 22*(1), 15.

Leki, I., & Carson, J. G. (1994). Students' perceptions of EAP writing instruction and writing needs across the disciplines. *TESOL Quarterly, 28*, 81–101.

Lerenzo-Dus, N. (2007). The best of both worlds? Combined methodological approaches to the assessment of vocabulary in oral proficiency interviews. In H. Daller, J. Milton, & J. Treffers-Daller (Eds.), *Modelling and assessing vocabulary knowledge* (pp. 133–149). Cambridge, UK: Cambridge University Press.

Lin, L. H. F. (2015). *Role of depth of vocabulary knowledge in EFL Learners' writing proficiency.* Unpublished doctoral thesis, Hong Kong Polytechnic University, Hong Kong.

Lin, L. H. F., & Morrison, B. (2010). The impact of the medium of instruction in Hong Kong secondary schools on tertiary students' vocabulary. *Journal of English for Academic Purposes, 9*, 255–266.

Llach, M. P. (2011). *Lexical errors and accuracy in foreign language writing.* Bristol, UK: Multilingual Matters.

Lu, X. (2012). The relationship of lexical richness to the quality of ESL learners' oral narratives. *The Modern Language Journal, 96*(2), 190–208.

Meara, P. M. (1982). Word association in a foreign language: A report from the Birkbeck vocabulary project. *Nottingham Linguistic Circular, 11*, 29–37.

Meara, P. M., & Bell, H. (2001). P_Lex: A simple and effective way of describing the lexical characteristics of short L2 texts. *Prospect, 16*(3), 323–337.

Milton, J. (2009). *Measuring second language vocabulary acquisition.* Bristol, UK: Multilingual Matters.

Nassaji, H. (2006). The relationship between depth of vocabulary knowledge and L2 learners' lexical inferencing strategy use and success. *The Modern Language Journal, 90*(3), 387–401.

Nation, I. S. P. (2006). How large a vocabulary is needed for reading and listening? *Canadian Modern Language Review, 63*, 59–82.

Nation, I. S. P., & Webb, S. (2011). *Researching and analyzing vocabulary.* Boston, MA: Heinle.

Olinghouse, N. G., & Wilson, J. (2013). The relationship between vocabulary and writing quality in three genres. *Reading and Writing, 26*(1), 45.

Paribakht, T. S., & Webb, S. (2016). The relationship between academic vocabulary coverage and scores on a standardized English proficiency test. *Journal of English for Academic Purposes, 21*, 121–132.

Prior, A., Goldina, A., Shany, M., Geva, E., & Katzir, T. (2014). Lexical inference in L2: Predictive roles of vocabulary knowledge and reading skill beyond reading comprehension. *Reading and Writing, 27*(8), 1467–1484.

Qi, L. (2007). Is testing an efficient agent for pedagogical change? Examining the intended washback of the writing task in a high-stakes English test in China. *Assessment in Education: Principles, Policy & Practice, 14*(1), 51–74.

Qian, D. D. (1999). Assessing the roles of depth and breadth of vocabulary knowledge. *Canadian Modern Language Review, 56*(2), 282–307.

Qian, D. D. (2002). Investigating the relationship between vocabulary knowledge and academic reading performance: An assessment perspective. *Language Learning, 52*, 53–536.

Qian, D. D. (2005). Demystifying lexical inferencing: The role of aspects of vocabulary knowledge. *TESL Canada Journal, 22*(2), 34–54.

Qian, D. D., & Schedl, M. (2004). Evaluation of an in-depth vocabulary knowledge measure for assessing reading performance. *Language Testing, 21*(1), 28–52.

Read, J. (2007). Second language vocabulary assessment: Current practices and new directions. *International Journal of English Studies, 7*(2), 105–126.

Roche, T., & Harrington, M. (2013). Recognition vocabulary knowledge as a predictor of academic performance in an English as a foreign language setting. *Language Testing in Asia, 3*(1), 1–13.

Saito, K., Webb, S., Trofimovich, P., & Isaacs, T. (2016). Lexical profiles of comprehensible second language speech: The role of appropriateness, fluency, variation, sophistication, abstractness, and sense relations. *Studies in Second Language Acquisition, 38*(4), 677–701.

Santos, T. (1998). Professor's reactions to the academic writing to non-native speaking students. *TESOL Quarterly, 22*, 69–90.

Sasaki, M., & Hirose, K. (1996). Explanatory variables for EFL students' expository writing. *Language Learning, 46*(1), 137–174.

Schmitt, N. (2008). Instructed second language vocabulary learning. *Language Teaching Research, 12,* 329–363.

Schmitt, N. (2010). *Researching vocabulary: A vocabulary research manual.* Houndmills, Basingstoke, Hampshire and New York, NY: Palgrave Macmillan.

Schmitt, N. (2014). Size and depth of vocabulary knowledge: What the research shows. *Language Learning, 64*(4), 913–951.

Schmitt, N., Cobb, T., Horst, M., & Schmitt, D. (2015). How much vocabulary is needed to use English? Replication of van Zeeland & Schmitt (2012), Nation (2006) and Cobb (2007). *Language Teaching, 50*(2), 212–226.

Schmitt, N., Jiang, X., & Grabe, W. (2011). The percentage of words known in a text and reading comprehension. *Modern Language Journal, 95*(1), 26–43.

Schmitt, N., & Schmitt, D. (2014). A reassessment of frequency and vocabulary size in L2 vocabulary teaching1. *Language Teaching, 47*(4), 484–503.

Schonell, F. J. (1956). *A study of the oral vocabulary of adults: An investigation into the spoken vocabulary of the Australian worker* (No. 1). Brisbane: University of Queensland Press.

Shi, L., & Qian, D. (2012). How does vocabulary knowledge affect Chinese EFL learners' writing quality in web-based settings? Evaluating the relationships among three dimensions of vocabulary knowledge and writing quality. *Chinese Journal of Applied Linguistics, 35*(1), 117–127.

Stæhr, L. S. (2008). Vocabulary size and the skills of listening, reading and writing. *Language Learning Journal, 36*(2), 139–152.

Stæhr, L. S. (2009). Vocabulary knowledge and advanced listening comprehension in English as a foreign language. *Studies in Second Language Acquisition, 31*(4), 577–607.

van Zeeland, H., & Schmitt, N. (2013). Lexical coverage in L1 and L2 listening comprehension: The same or different from reading comprehension? *Applied Linguistics, 34*(4), 457–479.

Victori, M. (1999). An analysis of writing knowledge in EFL composing: A case study of two effective and two less effective writers. *System, 27,* 537–555.

Wang, Y., & Treffers-Daller, J. (2017). Explaining listening comprehension among L2 learners of English: The contribution of general language proficiency, vocabulary knowledge and metacognitive awareness. *System, 65,* 139–150.

Webb, S. (2007). The effects of synonymy on vocabulary learning. *Reading in a Foreign Language, 19*(2), 120–136.

Wen, Q., Wang, L., & Liang, M. (2005). *Spoken and written English corpus of Chinese learners.* Beijing: Foreign Language Teaching and Research Press.

You, X. (2010). *Writing in the devil's tongue: A history of English composition in China.* Carbondale, IL: Southern Illinois University Press.

Zareva, A., Schwanenflugel, P., & Nikolova, Y. (2005). Relationship between lexical competence and language proficiency: Variable sensitivity. *Studies in Second Language Acquisition, 27*(4), 567–595.

6

Frequency as a Guide for Vocabulary Usefulness

High-, Mid-, and Low-Frequency Words

Laura Vilkaitė-Lozdienė and Norbert Schmitt

Introduction

If a person wants to acquire a second language, learning its vocabulary is definitely an important task. However, we cannot teach or learn all the words in a language, as there are simply too many of them. Therefore, some decisions need to be made, and some words have to be prioritized. The best way of choosing which words to teach or to learn depends on the purpose of learning. For example, if a person wants to become proficient in a specialized area (e.g., medicine), teaching a list of vocabulary items specific to that area might be the most useful approach (assuming a foundation of general English is already in place). If an academic tone in writing is desired, then working with words and phrases drawn from academic corpora might help the learner achieve this goal. But if the learning purpose is more general (e.g., to be able to read an article online or to be able to converse while traveling in a foreign country), then a way of selecting the most useful non-specialist vocabulary is necessary. For these "general" purposes, frequency has proven a very useful tool.

There are a number of reasons why frequency is important. First of all, the idea of the importance of frequency can be explained by the Zipf's law: "[w]ords occur according to a famously systematic frequency distribution such that there are few very high-frequency words that account for most of the tokens in text . . . and many low-frequency words" (Piantadosi, 2014). To put it another way, we can focus on a limited number of high-frequency words and achieve comprehension of most of the running words in any text. Therefore, unsurprisingly, frequency has a proven history in aiding language pedagogy: frequency lists have been used for decades for teaching the most useful general words (since West, 1953 and before), and lexical coverage studies have tried to establish how many words students need to understand in order to cope with English. Psycholinguistics studies also show that the frequency of words predicts their reading difficulty both in L1 and in L2 (van Heuven, Mandera, Keuleers, & Brysbaert, 2014). So frequency is not only a textual phenomenon which can be observed when analyzing corpora but it also has psychological validity. Finally, usage-based theories of language acquisition emphasize the effect of frequency when acquiring both individual words and tendencies of use of word sequences (Bybee,

2006, 1998; Ellis, 2002). Overall, frequency seems to have an effect on word processing and its acquisition.

For language pedagogy, there are two aspects regarding frequency to take into account:

- Frequent words are more important, as they are encountered more often than less frequent words (lexical coverage studies, Zipf's law).
- Words that are encountered more often have better chances of being learned.

In this chapter, we will only consider the first claim: high-frequency words are the most useful ones and they give learners the best value for their study effort. Thus, they need special attention in a language classroom.

Frequency is a good guiding criterion for word selection as it is very straightforward and objective. While knowing word frequency itself does not help much to decide on whether to teach a particular word or not, it can be used to divide words into groups (e.g., high-frequency, low-frequency) and to select a reasonable number of words to teach. An important question then remains where the best and the most meaningful cut-points for frequency bands should be, and what we should do with words labeled as high-frequency, mid-frequency, and low-frequency. In this chapter, we discuss these questions, as well as some limitations in the current frequency framework. Finally, we will offer some initial suggestions of where to move next.

Critical Issues and Topics

We will start by looking at the usefulness of frequency as a guiding criterion for choosing which vocabulary to teach, beginning with a brief discussion of the historical development of the idea of frequency in language pedagogy. We will then move on to the current understanding of high-, mid-, and low-frequency vocabulary.

Historical Development of Frequency in Pedagogy

While teaching and learning foreign languages has been relevant for thousands of years, there used to be no principled way to handle foreign language vocabulary, other than focusing on whatever words happened to occur in a text of interest. Furthermore, grammar has received the lion's share of attention in most traditional classrooms. Vocabulary started to be systematically approached only in the early 20th century, with a strand of lexical research attempting to make vocabulary easier by limiting it to some degree. This was known as the *Vocabulary Control Movement*.

In the early 1930s, K. Ogden and I.A. Richards developed a *Basic English*: a vocabulary of 850 words. It was supposed to be quickly learned and express any meaning that could be communicated in regular English. But the 850 words were so polysemous (with an estimated 12,000 meaning senses) that it was not really that much of a simplification, and so Basic English did not end up having much of an impact. Another approach in the Vocabulary Control Movement was to use systematic criteria to select the most useful words for language learning, developing principles of presenting common vocabulary first, and limiting the number of new words in any text. This approach was much more successful, and culminated in the *General Service List of English Words* (*GSL*) (West, 1953). The GSL was a list of about 2,000 words based on word frequency but also on structural value, universality, subject range, definition words, word-building capacity, and style (Howatt, 1984). The GSL had the advantage of listing different parts of speech and different meaning senses, which made it much more useful than a simple frequency count.

With generative grammar and Chomskian ideas (e.g., Chomsky, 1986), the focus on vocabulary faded for a time. But in the later 20th century, computerized corpora became available which allowed the quick and reliable calculation of frequencies, and also the identification of patterns of vocabulary occurrence. Before the introduction of computerized corpora in the 1960s, the majority of linguistic studies were based on a small number of examples, quite commonly invented by a researcher (Hunston, 2012). The development of computers and the ability to collect, store, and analyze millions of word occurrences had a large influence on linguistics. The importance of frequency also became established with corpus research: linguists' attention has shifted from what is possible in language towards what is typical and used frequently (Barlow, 2011). Word counts have provided some very useful insights into the way the vocabulary of English works, and helped to rejuvenate interest in vocabulary issues.

Around the same time, Paul Nation led the way in focusing attention on vocabulary from the pedagogical perspective. He designed a program called RANGE (available on his website[1]) for analyzing the vocabulary of any text. The program divided vocabulary into 1,000, 2,000, and off-list items, so essentially it set in place a high-frequency/low-frequency dichotomy. In Nation's research (e.g., 2001a) high-frequency words were considered to be the first 2,000 most frequent word families, then there were academic words (initially the *University Word List*, and later the *Academic Word List* (Coxhead, 2000)). Other words that were not included in these established categories were labeled as low-frequency.

In 2014, Schmitt and Schmitt introduced an idea that had been floating around the vocabulary community for a while: the words beyond the 2,000 frequency band are important and should not be considered just off-list items. They suggested moving the boundary for high-frequency vocabulary to 3,000 word families, and introduced the term *mid-frequency vocabulary*.[2] The most commonly used current frequency framework revolves around Schmitt and Schmitt's high/mid/low-frequency categories. Therefore we will look at it in more detail in later sections.

Related Concepts

In order to talk about the current understanding of high-, mid-, and low-frequency words, two important related concepts need to be introduced and discussed. First, it is important to consider how a **word** is defined and what is counted as a word in any frequency count. We will discuss the differences between two commonly used counting units – **word families** and **lemmas**. Second, figures cited as thresholds for high- or low-frequency words are often adopted from **coverage** research. Therefore, it is important to briefly discuss this research as well.

Word Family and Lemma

It seems to be intuitively clear that researchers should agree on a unit of counting if they want to have reliable frequency counts across different studies (Bauer & Nation, 1993). At the moment, most coverage research and frequency lists are based on *word family* as a counting unit. Word family is a unit that includes both the base form of the word (such as, *work*) and its inflections (e.g., *worked*, *works*), as well as its main derivations (e.g., *worker*). The idea of the word family was introduced in order to systematically approach vocabulary in language pedagogy (Bauer & Nation, 1993). The assumption is that once learners know a meaning of a base word (such as *work*) and have some knowledge of morphology and meanings of the main affixes, they do not need to learn each single word in a language but instead can derive the meanings of word family members (such as *worker*) from the base form. Hence using word families in a way reduces learning burden for L2 learners because they can systematically infer the meaning of the word family members. Especially for the receptive language use (reading or listening) this idea seems to be reasonable. Also, word families seem to have psychological validity and to be represented in the mental lexicon (Nagy, Anderson, Schommer, Scott, & Stallman, 1989). Hence there is an additional argument (apart from lowering the learning load for the learners) to use them as counting units.

However, Bauer and Nation (1993) have claimed that "[a]s a learner's knowledge of affixation develops, the size of the word family increases" (p. 253). While this idea makes sense when considering individual learners, in practice researchers need to pre-set a list of tokens constituting a word family and use it for coverage research, frequency lists, or vocabulary testing. Hence, the common assumption becomes the following: once a base word is known, the whole word family is known. Because of this, the word family approach is problematic. As Nation (2001b) has pointed out, the main problem with using word families is deciding which word forms should be included in a word family. Some affixes, and consequently some word family members, are transparent and thus easy to decipher, but others may not be. Also, what seems transparent for one learner can be beyond the level of comprehension for a different learner (Nation, 2001b). So it is not easy to clearly define a word family that would apply to all language users. Schmitt and Zimmerman (2002) have shown that learners do not necessarily have productive knowledge of all the members of a word family. Kremmel (2016) has also suggested that if a base word is known, it does not mean that all of its word family members are known. Derivation seems not to be easily acquired (at least productively). For example, González Fernández and Schmitt (2019) have asked learners to provide derivational forms of all four word classes (nouns, verbs, adjective, and adverbs) for each of their target words and they have found that learners typically can recognize forms of two to three word classes in a word family, but not all the derivatives. Regarding the ability to produce the word forms, their participants could typically only produce two out of the four forms. Gardner and Davies (2014) have also pointed out that the word family does not take into account part of speech information, and that some members of a word family can be quite distant from each other in terms of their meaning (e.g., *process*, *proceeding*). Overall, it might be that the concept of word family is more problematic for productive rather than for receptive knowledge, but even receptively it may not work reliably. If the learners do not understand/know the members of the word family, then the assumption underlying word families fails.

There are also two more issues with word families. The first one is technical: lists based on word families are more difficult to compute automatically than lists based on lemmas or word forms. The second one is more pedagogical. Teachers and learners (and even researchers) might misinterpret figures based on word families when using research outputs (e.g., lists of words, targets for learning), and simply understand them as "individual words". This could lead to a misleading sense of the vocabulary learning required. Because of all these issues, word families seem to be useful counting units when we are dealing with receptive knowledge and with advanced learners or even native speakers. But they do not reliably work in all the situations with all the different language learners.

Therefore, recently there have been suggestions to move from word families to lemmas as counting units (Kremmel, 2016). Lemmas can be defined as "words with a common stem, related by inflection only and coming from the same part of speech" (Gardner & Davies, 2014, p. 4). As such, the lemma is a much more straightforward unit: no arbitrary decisions about what to classify as the same lemma need to be made. Because of that, it is much easier to operationalize lemmas computationally as well. Also, it easier and safer to make assumptions about learners' knowledge as inflectional affixes tend to be regular and learners do not need to reach an advanced level to recognize and understand them.

To date, most coverage research has been based on word families. Considering the problems with the word family approach, there has been some discussion of using lemmas instead. However, a lemma-based approach also has limitations. Lemmas might be too restricted for counting, as some derivational affixes are usually transparent (such as –er to indicate an agent noun) and do not cause difficulties for learners. On the other hand, lemmas can be used with different inflections, so further research would be needed to establish whether lemmas are not problematic receptively, at least for beginner learners. Finally, it seems that the members of a word family also follow the Zipfian distribution (the most frequent member is much more frequent that the others). So it remains an empirical question if moving from word families to lemmas would actually change much in our understanding of high/mid/low-frequency vocabulary. Overall, it is obvious that both lemmas and word families have limitations, so at the moment there is no way to strongly favor one or the other. Further research on the validity of those two counting units would be very useful to make more informed decisions in the future.

As most of the currently available research is based on word families, most of the calculations in this chapter will be presented in that unit. We will also introduce some suggestions about how the thresholds for high- and low-frequency vocabulary might change if we moved to lemmas instead of word families.

Lexical Coverage

Lexical coverage studies mostly can be divided into two groups:

- Studies focusing on how many words of a text/listening passage one needs to know in order to gain adequate comprehension: coverage as a "percentage of known words in a piece of discourse" (van Zeeland & Schmitt, 2013, p. 457).
- Studies focusing on the frequency profile of certain texts: "Coverage refers to the percentage of tokens in a text which are accounted for (covered by) particular word lists" (Nation, 2004, p. 7).

These two approaches complement each other. For pedagogical purposes, we must first determine the percentage of words in a text a learner needs to know in order to understand it, and then we must establish how many lexical items one needs to learn to reach that percentage.

The lexical thresholds for comprehension have been estimated both for written and for spoken texts. In 1989, Laufer suggested that one needs to comprehend about 95% of a text in order to be able to understand that text. Later she suggested that 3,000 word families constitute a lexical threshold required for reading comprehension (Laufer, 1992). This number has been refined, and now two thresholds for comprehension have been suggested: an optimal one, which is the knowledge of 8,000 word families yielding the coverage of 98% (including proper nouns), and a minimal one of 4,000 to 5,000 word families resulting in the coverage 95% of texts (Laufer & Ravenhorst-Kalovski, 2010). Hsueh-Chao and Nation (2000) have also suggested that we need to understand 98% of written texts in order to comprehend them, while Schmitt, Jiang, and Grabe (2011) have concluded that there is no clear threshold: comprehension increases almost linearly as coverage increases. However, they suggested that 98% seems to be a reasonable threshold. For listening, on the other hand, it seems that a somewhat lower threshold can work. For example, van Zeeland and Schmitt (2013) have shown that even at 90% coverage levels most of their participants showed adequate comprehension, but at the 95% level, there was less individual variation.

Once the required lexical coverage for comprehension is established, the next question is how many words (lemmas/word families) one needs to acquire to achieve this percentage. This number will depend on what type of texts one wants to read or listen to. For spoken language, corpus research examining the CANCODE corpus seems to show that 2,000 word families are enough for almost 95% coverage (2,000 word families provide 94.76% coverage while 3,000 provide 95.91% coverage) (Adolphs & Schmitt, 2003). For written language, the numbers are higher. For example, Hirsh and Nation (1992) analyzed three novels and calculated that about 5,000 word families are needed to achieve 97% to 98% coverage. For more challenging material, such as academic texts, this number might be even higher.

Nation (2006) summarized the relationship between coverage and frequency bands as illustrated in Figure 6.1. From this figure, it becomes clear that the first thousand words provide by far the highest coverage – about 80% of all texts. But this is partly because of the extremely high frequency of function words, which are almost solely in this frequency band. For example, the first 100 most frequent words in English (virtually all function words) cover about 49% of the running words in texts (Nation, 2001b). The coverage of following frequency bands consistently becomes smaller, and all the words less frequent than the 14K level actually cover only about 1% of English.

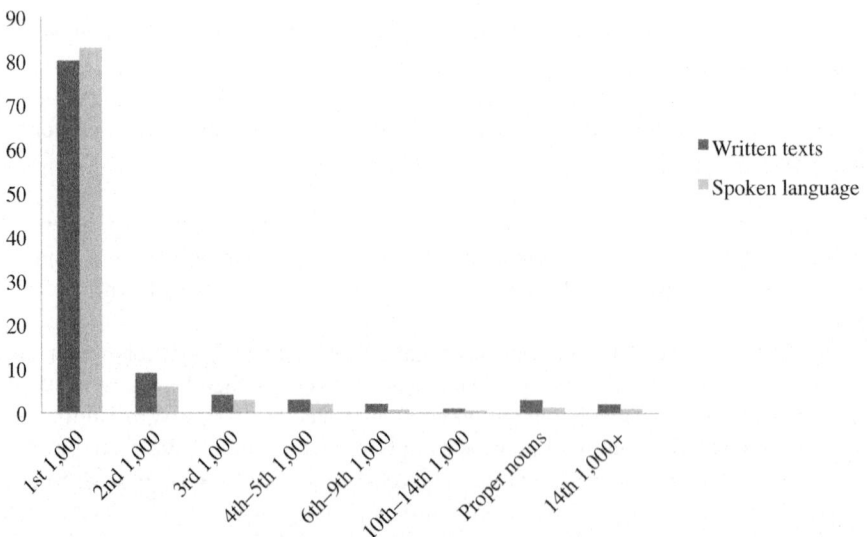

Figure 6.1 Vocabulary size and text coverage

It is important to notice that if one needs, for example, 3,000 word families to reach 95% coverage of a written text, these families are not simply any words in a language, but specifically the most frequent 3,000 ones. This emphasizes the importance of high-frequency words even more. Learners should aim to know enough words to achieve the required coverage of a text/listening passage in order to understand it adequately. Therefore, the thresholds for high-, mid-, and low-frequency words are usually calculated with coverage in mind, so that the resulting figures can indicate what learners knowing this vocabulary can do.

High-, Low-, and Mid-Frequency Words

High-Frequency Words

High-frequency vocabulary consists of words that are the most frequent in language and consequently provide the highest coverage. Therefore, teachers should prioritize high-frequency words because they are the most useful (Nation, 2001a; Read, 2004). The importance of the high-frequency words is not a new idea. As already noted, a very influential list of the most important words (*GSL*) was created in 1950s (West, 1953). While frequency was not the only criterion for creating this list, it was one of the main ones. The need for a list that can be used for pedagogical purposes has not disappeared. New versions of the lists of general vocabulary are continuously being created, such as the *New General Service List* (Brezina & Gablasova, 2015), which lists about 2,000 words occurring across various corpora, and making up core high-frequency vocabulary. While the original GSL is now rather out-dated, in general, the most frequent words tend to remain relatively stable across both time periods and corpora. For example, Nation (2004) compared the GSL with the most frequent word lists compiled based on the BNC and showed that they contain much of the same vocabulary. Hence, it seems the most frequent words in the language are relatively stable, no matter which corpus you use, and do not change quickly over time (Kilgarriff, 2007; Nation, 2004).

There is a general understanding that high-frequency words are important. However, the question of where to draw the line defining high-frequency remains. Different criteria for identifying high-frequency words have been considered, such as relying on coverage research and reaching the 95% lexical threshold, the range of words in different texts and frequency lists, feasibility of teaching these words in a language course, a cost-benefit analysis, etc. (Nation, 2001a). Nation (2001a) suggested that 2,000 most frequent word families should be labeled as high-frequency vocabulary. This figure of 2,000 has been widely cited in teacher guidebooks and research publications (e.g., Nation, 1990; Read, 2000; Schmitt, 2000; Thornbury, 2002). Nation has also set this frequency level for his text coverage analysis tool (*VocabProfiler*, www.lextutor.ca) and his Vocabulary Levels Test (Nation, 1983; Schmitt, Schmitt, & Clapham, 2001), effectively establishing this threshold for high-frequency vocabulary. However, Nation (2001a) himself has clearly stated that this decision is open to debate. Setting the threshold to 3,000 words has also been suggested (e.g., Schmitt & Schmitt, 2014; Waring & Nation, 1997). After Schmitt and Schmitt's (2014) paper, the boundary of 3,000 word families for high-frequency words is becoming more accepted, because the learners who reach this level are able to communicate in a range of situations. Also, the 3,000 most frequent word families often approach the 95% coverage level for many texts (see Figure 6.1).

However, it has to be noted that there are also some studies that suggest lowering the threshold for high-frequency words rather than increasing it. They show that students fail to learn 2,000 most frequent words so potentially this goal is too ambitious and a more realistic goal of 1,000 words should be used for defining high-frequency vocabulary (Dang & Webb, 2017). However, a better way of thinking about this is probably that the 2,000 to 3,000 most frequent words are necessary to engage with English in useful ways, and so they should be considered high-frequency vocabulary (see Figure 6.1). But in terms of *learning goals*, 1,000 words may well be a suitable *initial* goal. Dang and Webb (2017) also note that the cumulative coverage of the frequency bands beyond the first 1,000 drops considerably, suggesting that the first 1,000 most frequent words are clearly the most useful ones. But this disregards the fact that the drop is mainly caused by the function words occurring in the first 1,000 words. If function words are taken out of the frequency profile (as makes pedagogic sense because function words are not typically taught as vocabulary items, but rather as grammar items), then the drop in coverage of *content words* is much more gradual (see Kremmel, 2016 for an illustration of this). Still, we must always take account of how students learn, and so it may often be useful pedagogically to sequence high-frequency items into the essential vocabulary (be it 1,000 words (Dang & Webb, 2017) or 800 lemmas (Dang & Webb, 2016)) to start with at the beginner level, and then move onto the other high-frequency words (up to 3,000 words) required to use English in many contexts.

If we set the threshold for high frequency vocabulary at the 3,000 most frequent word families, we must decide how to best approach this vocabulary in a language classroom. Nation (2001a) has suggested that teachers should directly teach high-frequency words, and students should deliberately learn them using word cards or dictionaries as necessary. Explicit direct teaching seems to be important because even these high-frequency words may not be frequent enough for the learners to get enough exposure to learn them incidentally from reading (Cobb, 2007). Therefore, these words should be the focus of the language syllabus. They can be addressed in various vocabulary exercises, used in graded readers, or even provided as target lists for learning for language learners. Teachers should probably start focusing on the 1,000 most frequent content words first as they are will have the most value for their learners.

However, while high-frequency words are essential, this does not mean that teachers should be completely driven by frequency information. Nation (1990) has noted that many words important for classroom context and classroom management (e.g., *pencil, blackboard*) are not necessarily frequent in general English, but will definitely be important in a classroom setting. Also, depending on learners' age, some of the high-frequency words might be not be useful for them. Hence, frequency lists should be seen more as a useful indication rather than a prescription.

The figure of 3,000 cited earlier is based on word families. If the field moved to lemmas as counting units, how would the high-frequency threshold change? It might seem that we need many more lemmas than word families, as a word family on average contains from one and a half to four derivations depending on how inclusive the definition of a family is (Nation, 2001b). Hence, one word family could translate to even more than four lemmas (e.g., nation, nationalize, national, nationally, international, internationalization, and so on). Consequently, the borderlines for high-frequency and mid-frequency vocabulary should increase if we moved from word families to lemmas. However, this increase might be not as large as might be supposed. Some current research shows that around the 3,000 most frequent lemmas are enough to reach 98% coverage in conversations (based on BNC data, Schmitt et al., under review). If this is the case, then we might actually be able to leave the definition of the high-frequency lemmas same as we had for high-frequency word families – 3,000 – as this amount would still be enough for learners. Furthermore, counting in lemmas would not entail assumptions of knowledge of any lower frequency word family

Cumulative text coverage

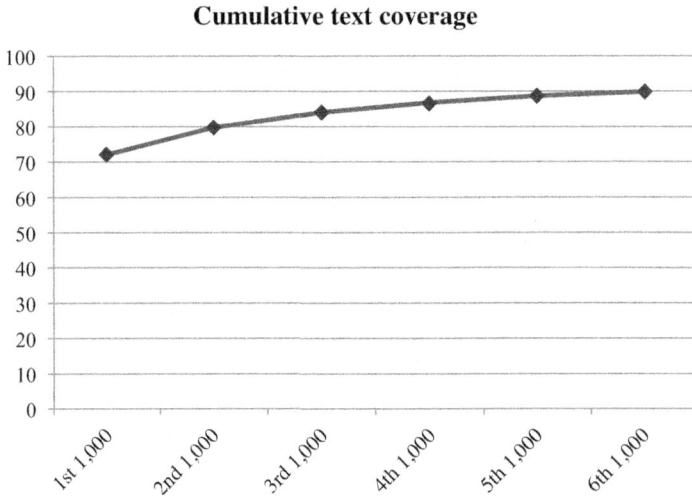

Figure 6.2 Vocabulary size (in lemmas) and cumulative text coverage in the Brown corpus

members. However, regarding reading, a larger threshold might be needed. For example, Schmitt et al. (under review) have calculated that about 6,000 lemmas are needed to reach the 95% threshold for reading adult fiction. Waring and Nation (1997) have also provided figures based on lemmas derived from the Brown corpus (see Figure 6.2 for a summary). In their study, the 3,000 most frequent lemmas give coverage of about 84% of the corpus. It is less than word families would, but not massively so. The actual threshold for high-frequency words based on lemmas is yet to be established, but it does not seem to change dramatically from the one we have for word families.

Low-Frequency Words

Let's now look at the other extreme of the frequency continuum – low-frequency words. What to consider low-frequency is not so well-established. Nation (2001b), for example, has divided vocabulary into high-frequency vocabulary, academic words, technical words, and low-frequency vocabulary, but does not clearly indicate where the low-frequency words begin. Schmitt and Schmitt (2014) have suggested that 9,000+ word families should be labeled as low-frequency words. However, they admitted that a clear boundary is difficult to establish because each different 1000-word level from around 9,000 words does not add much to the coverage. Hence, they have based their threshold on the fact that the 9,000 most frequent word families in the Nation's BNC frequency lists cover 95.5% of the Corpus of Contemporary American English (COCA). As COCA is a huge collection of language, they concluded that reaching an adequate coverage of such a vast variety of texts is a good criterion to define everything beyond that as low-frequency vocabulary.

Nation (2001b) has noted that low-frequency vocabulary consists of some words that are moderately frequent but do not make it to high-frequency, and also includes proper names that are usually quite easy to identify and understand. There are also some words that in general language are infrequent, but actually belong to a specific field. For some people these words will be important and widely used, while for others they will be low-frequency vocabulary. After that, there are a lot of words that are simply very rare in a language. This distinction is important, as specialist vocabulary will definitely be useful for people learning English for specific purposes, while words that are simply very infrequent for everybody do not require much pedagogical attention. For example, *scalpel* is low frequency in general, but important specialist vocabulary for surgeons. Conversely, *umbrage* is a low-frequency word that is unlikely to be particularly useful for anyone. As the benefits of learning low-frequency words in terms of added coverage are rather limited, and there are so many them, it is not very useful to dedicate a lot of classroom attention to low-frequency words. Rather, Nation (2001b) advocates focusing on learning strategies, such as guessing their meaning, drawing on word part knowledge, or using dictionaries to deal with these words.

If we move towards lemmas as counting units, where should we draw the line for low-frequency vocabulary? We could follow the criterion of Schmitt and Schmitt (2014) and ask how much vocabulary we need to reach the 95% to 98% coverage of a broad range of texts, as illustrated in a large corpus. Based on the recent corpus study (Schmitt et al., under review) a not overly large number of lemmas are needed to reach this coverage: e.g., around 9,000 lemmas are enough for understanding academic writing, and 11,000 for comprehension of adult fiction. Spoken language requires much less: about 3,000 lemmas to reach 95% coverage of conversations, and around 6,000 lemmas to reach this level of coverage of TV shows. Magazines seem to need the largest number of lemmas – about 14,000 lemmas. So, if we took the largest figure as a threshold between mid-frequency and low-frequency vocabulary, it would be around 14,000 lemmas. If, on the other hand, we sought some kind of average of words needed for understanding various kind of texts, it would seem to be around 10,000 to 11,000 lemmas. This figure is larger than the before-mentioned 9,000 word families, but using lemmas as counting units would not push it unrealistically too far. While more research is needed to be able to reliably draw the threshold for low-frequency words in lemmas, this number seems to be a couple of thousands rather than several times larger than for word families. This is probably the case because most of the coverage of the typical word family is usually provided by its most frequent member(s).

Mid-Frequency Words

Schmitt and Schmitt (2014) labeled the vocabulary between high-frequency words (3,000) and low-frequency words (9,000+) as *mid-frequency vocabulary*. Mid-frequency vocabulary is a relatively new term. This frequency range includes words that were traditionally labeled as academic vocabulary and technical vocabulary, but also some of the other words that are more frequent than in the 9,000 frequency band. Nation (2001b) noted that beyond the high-frequency level, one's vocabulary grows depending on one's interests, jobs, professions, and therefore is more idiosyncratic. Gardner (2013) has also noted that beyond the very highest frequency bands, words start becoming increasingly more domain-dependent and frequency lists drawn from different corpora could differ considerably at each thousand frequency band. Because of that, it is not that easy to provide mid-frequency lists useful for the majority of learners. Therefore, after the high-frequency words are acquired, the words to teach depend on the specific interests and needs of the learners (Read, 2004).

Mid-frequency vocabulary is essentially a gap learners need to fill in order to move on to reading authentic texts, especially in academic contexts. For instance, Nation's (2006) and Schmitt et al.'s (under review) research has indicated that learners need to know many thousands of items beyond high-frequency vocabulary to read virtually any kind of authentic text in English. So these mid-frequency words might not be relevant for all the L2 learners: for those who have less ambitious goals in a second language (e.g., just casual conversation), high-frequency words might suffice. But for those that have more ambitious goals in learning an L2, such as studying or working in an L2 environment, these words will be very important.

Schmitt and Schmitt (2014) reviewed a number of studies and have shown that mid-frequency vocabulary is not addressed well in classrooms at the moment: textbooks do not typically cover it systematically, and teachers do not focus on it or use it enough in their classroom talk. We do not have conclusive research on this band of vocabulary to give very specific advice on how to deal with it and more studies are needed.

Mid-frequency words can be acquired incidentally, but the research suggests leaving them all to be picked up in this manner is problematic. To start with, studies on incidental word acquisition from reading (e.g., Day et al., 1991; Horst, 2005; Horst, Cobb, & Meara, 1998; Pellicer-Sánchez & Schmitt, 2010; Pigada & Schmitt, 2006) show that incidental word acquisition is possible, but rather slow and a number of encounters is needed for the acquisition to occur. This does not mean that incidental acquisition is not useful: different aspects of word knowledge seem to be enhanced and the depth of vocabulary knowledge is increased. However, for acquiring a form-meaning link of new words, incidental learning is not very effective and its gains are modest (Read, 2004). This is partially the case because words beyond high-frequency level are simply not encountered frequently enough (Cobb, 2007).

One way of addressing mid-frequency words is focusing on lists of specific words for specific purposes, such as academic vocabulary (Coxhead, 2000) or Engineering English (Hsu, 2014). Another approach is to promote increased exposure, e.g., through extensive reading and graded readers. There are now suggestions to write mid-frequency readers that focus on recycling mid-frequency vocabulary (Nation & Anthony, 2013; see also Paul Nation's website[3] for a number of these readers free of charge). Computerized programs for learning vocabulary can also be a way to give students exposure and enough recycling of new vocabulary (Cobb, 2010). This seems to be a viable potential way forward, as nowadays computers/personal notebooks/smartphones are owned by most schools and learners.

Final Remarks

If one wants to learn a second language for general purposes, frequency seems to be an objective and useful criterion to prioritize words to focus on. It does not require any subjective judgment and frequency lists can be easily obtained for many languages. For English, there seem to be around 3,000 most frequent word families that deserve explicit direct attention, in order to give learners the best chances to be able to comprehend the majority of the words in a wide range of texts. If learners want to be able to use English in a variety of contexts, engaging in conversations and reaching an optimal understanding of written texts, knowledge of the 9,000 most frequent word families (i.e., mid-frequency vocabulary) is necessary. Above this threshold, low-frequency vocabulary becomes relatively rare, and it is of little pedagogical relevance unless the words are domain-specific. Dividing vocabulary based on frequency is not the only way to choose what to teach/learn first. Especially after high-frequency words are mastered, the needs of individual learners might differ considerably. However, at least the high-frequency end of the continuum is definitely worth attention in any classroom, as it provides a platform for all language use.

So far we have only focused on high-, mid-, and low-frequency words for choosing how many words and which words to teach. However, it is worth briefly mentioning that frequency bands are important for other applications as well. One of them can be language assessment. For example, Laufer and Nation (1995) suggested calculating learners' lexical profiles in order to measure their lexical knowledge in L2 writing. According to these scholars, the amount of high-frequency words one uses in their writing is an indication of their overall L2 command, and discriminates between learners of different proficiencies. Most vocabulary size tests are also based on the idea of frequency as a sampling rationale, e.g., Meara (1992), Nation and Beglar (2007), Schmitt et al. (2001), and Webb, Sasao, and Ballance (2017) sample words from frequency bands in order to estimate vocabulary size.

Future Directions

We would like to propose three potential directions for future research: incorporating formulaic sequences in our understanding of high-frequency vocabulary, triangulating research findings, and reconsidering the idea of word family. We will discuss these in turn.

The first suggestion is moving away from only individual words, and incorporating formulaic sequences into our vocabulary lists, coverage studies, and subsequently into our understanding of what high-, mid-, and low-frequency vocabulary consists of. Formulaic language is made up of "combinations of at least two words favored by native speakers in preference to an alternative combination which could have been equivalent had there been no conventionalization" (Erman & Warren, 2000, p. 31). There are a number of reasons why taking formulaic language into consideration is important. First, it seems to make up from one-third to one-half of discourse (Conklin & Schmitt, 2012) which means it is very widespread in language use. Second, if individual words are known, but the meaning of a figurative sequence is not, it hinders understanding (Martinez & Murphy, 2011). Hence, we can calculate a lexical threshold needed for an adequate comprehension of a text, but if it contains idiomatic formulaic sequences, the vocabulary figures will tell us little of the actual comprehension a learner will achieve.

Ideally, we would like to have a frequency list that incorporates both words and formulaic sequences; then we could recalculate the coverage figures and divide vocabulary based on frequency of lexical items instead of the frequency of single words. The idea is not new. Waring and Nation (1997) also mentioned that some idioms and expressions behave like high-frequency words, while Schmitt and Schmitt (2014) have discussed the limitation of looking only at individual words. However, so far, we have no list that includes both words and longer lexical items.

Second, replication of reported studies and triangulation of the methods employed would be extremely useful. So far the research on high-, mid-, and low-frequency vocabulary is based mostly on corpus data or on studies of lexical coverage. Coverage figures are mostly drawn from studies where participants read texts with certain percentages of words missing. However, more empirical evidence from quasi-experimental classroom studies would be useful to see what learners can actually do in real-world teaching contexts. Questions like the following would be interesting to ask:

- What can learners actually do if they know only high-frequency words?
- Do typical learners actually learn mid-frequency vocabulary, or can they survive perfectly well without it in various contexts?
- What strategies do learners use to cope with texts if they do not know low-frequency words? Or do they merely skip over them without problems?

We believe integrating corpus results with empirical research on actual learner performance would go some way in determining the amount of vocabulary learners need to get things done in language.

Finally, we feel the idea of word family has to be critically reconsidered. The assumption underlying word family is that learners can recognize the members of a word family, so it is a meaningful unit to use for calculations of receptive knowledge. This assumption has been challenged: learners typically recognize some but not all members of a word family and perform even worse on a productive level. This suggests moving to lemmas as a more pedagogically sound counting unit. But this might not be the optimal solution either. We have to admit that learners can typically use some very frequent and consistent affixes, e.g., *-er* (*learn/learner*). Therefore, the lemma might actually be too small a counting unit. Ideally then, we could like to use lemma +, that is a lemma with a few transparent affixes that learners can consistently and reliably comprehend/produce. The problem at the moment is that we do not know what these affixes are and it remains an empirical question.

So for the moment, it is probably best to use the lemma until the research has been carried out to establish the best pedagogical unit that learners can actually use. This means we would need to reconsider the thresholds for high- and mid-frequency vocabulary with lemmas in mind. Some research is now being done to establish the size targets necessary to use English in lemma terms (e.g., Schmitt et al., under review), and some of the suggested numbers are already discussed in this chapter. More research is needed until these numbers can be reliably reported. However, initial evidence suggests that moving from word families to lemmas would not change the thresholds for high-, mid-, and low-frequency vocabulary drastically. At the same time, they could be based on fewer assumptions and may be easier to interpret.

Further Reading

Schmitt, N., & Schmitt, D. (2014). A reassessment of frequency and vocabulary size in L2 vocabulary teaching. *Language Teaching, 47*(4), 484–503. https://doi.org/org/10.1017/S0261444812000018

This is the original article that has suggested moving the threshold of high-frequency words to 3,000 word families and lowering the boundary of low frequency words to 9,000 word families. It also labeled the vocabulary in between as "mid-frequency" vocabulary. The paper gives research-based reasons for these boundaries and addresses the pedagogical challenges with mid-frequency vocabulary.

Nation, I. S. P. (2001). How many high frequency words are there in English. *Language, Learning and Literature: Studies Presented to Hakan Ringbom.* Abo Akademi University, Abo: English Department Publications, *4*, 167–181.

This paper explains why the distinction between high-frequency and low-frequency words is critical and gives pedagogical advice on how to treat those words differently.

Nation, I. S. P. (2006). How large a vocabulary is needed for reading and listening? *Canadian Modern Language Review/La Revue Canadienne Des Langues Vivantes, 63*(1), 59–82. https://doi.org/10.3138/cmlr.63.1.59

This article reports on coverage research that sets out to answer a question how many word families one needs to read a novel, a newspaper, a graded reader, to watch a children's movie, or to understand unscripted spoken English. This paper suggests that 8,000 to 9,000 words families are needed for dealing with written texts and 6,000 to 7,000 word families for dealing with spoken discourse.

Laufer, B., & Ravenhorst-Kalovski, G. C. (2010). Lexical threshold revisited: Lexical text coverage, learners' vocabulary size and reading comprehension. *Reading in a Foreign Language, 22*(1), 15–30.

The paper looks at lexical coverage and tries to estimate more accurately how many words one needs to understand in a text in order to achieve comprehension. The authors suggest 98% for optimal and 95% coverage for adequate comprehension.

Laura Vilkaitė-Lozdienė and Norbert Schmitt

Related Topics

Academic vocabulary, technical vocabulary, L1 and L2 vocabulary size and growth, word lists

Notes

1 *Range* program online: www.victoria.ac.nz/lals/about/staff/paul-nation#publications
2 Although the idea of frequency as a pedagogical tool presumably is useful for all languages, the vast majority of frequency-based research has been done on the English language. Thus, the figures reported in this chapter are for English, and may differ for other languages.
3 Freely available graded readers: www.victoria.ac.nz/lals/about/staff/paul-nation#free-graded-readers

References

Adolphs, S., & Schmitt, N. (2003). Lexical coverage of spoken discourse. *Applied Linguistics*, *24*(4), 425–438. https://doi.org/10.1093/applin/24.4.425

Barlow, M. (2011). Corpus linguistics and theoretical linguistics. *International Journal of Corpus Linguistics*, *16*(1), 3–44. https://doi.org/10.1075/ijcl.16.1.02bar

Bauer, L., & Nation, P. (1993). Word families. *International Journal of Lexicography*, *6*(4), 253–279. https://doi.org/10.1093/ijl/6.4.253

Brezina, V., & Gablasova, D. (2015). Is there a core general vocabulary? Introducing the new general service list. *Applied Linguistics*, *36*(1), 1–22. https://doi.org/10.1093/applin/amt018

Bybee, J. (1998). The emergent lexicon. *Chicago Linguistic Society*, *34*(2), 421–435.

Bybee, J. (2006). From usage to grammar: The mind's response to repetition. *Language*, *82*(4), 711–733. https://doi.org/10.1353/lan.2006.0186

Chomsky, N. (1986). *Knowledge of language: Its nature, origin, and use*. London: Greenwood Publishing Group.

Cobb, T. (2007). Computing the vocabulary demands of L2 reading. *Language Learning & Technology*, *11*(3), 38–63.

Cobb, T. (2010). Learning about language and learners from computer programs. *Reading in a Foreign Language*, *22*(1), 181–200.

Conklin, K., & Schmitt, N. (2012). The processing of formulaic language. *Annual Review of Applied Linguistics*, *32*, 45–61. https://doi.org/10.1017/S0267190512000074

Coxhead, A. (2000). A new academic word list. *TESOL Quarterly*, *34*(2), 213–238. https://doi.org/10.2307/3587951

Dang, T. N. Y., & Webb, S. (2016). Making an essential word list for beginners. In I. S. P. Nation (Ed.), *Making and using word lists for language learning and testing* (pp. 153–167). Amsterdam: John Benjamins.

Dang, T. N. Y., & Webb, S. (2017). Evaluating lists of high-frequency words. *ITL-International Journal of Applied Linguistics*, *167*(2), 132–158. https://doi.org/10.1075/itl.167.2.02dan

Day, R., Omura, C., & Hiramatsu, M. (1991). Incidental EFL vocabulary learning and reading. *Reading in a Foreign Language*, *7*(2), 541–551.

Ellis, N. C. (2002). Frequency effects in language processing. *Studies in Second Language Acquisition*, *24*(2), 143–188. https://doi.org/10.1017/S0272263102002024

Erman, B., & Warren, B. (2000). The idiom principle and the open choice principle. *Text – Interdisciplinary Journal for the Study of Discourse*, *20*(1), 29–62.

Gardner, D. (2013). *Exploring vocabulary: Language in action*. London, UK: Routledge.

Gardner, D., & Davies, M. (2014). A new academic vocabulary list. *Applied Linguistics*, *35*(3), 305–327. https://doi.org/10.1093/applin/amt015

González Fernández, B., & Schmitt, N. (2019). Word knowledge: Exploring the relationships and order of acquisition of vocabulary knowledge components. *Applied Linguistics*, amy057, https://doi.org/10.1093/applin/amy057

Hirsh, D., & Nation, P. (1992). What vocabulary size is needed to read unsimplified texts for pleasure? *Reading in a Foreign Language, 8*, 689–689.

Horst, M. (2005). Learning L2 vocabulary through extensive reading: A measurement study. *Canadian Modern Language Review, 61*(3), 355–382. https://doi.org/10.3138/cmlr.61.3.355

Horst, M., Cobb, T., & Meara, P. (1998). Beyond a Clockwork Orange: Acquiring second language vocabulary through reading. *Reading in a Foreign Language, 11*(2), 207–223.

Howatt, A. P. R. (1984). *A history of English language teaching*. Oxford, UK: Oxford University Press.

Hsu, W. (2014). Measuring the vocabulary load of engineering textbooks for EFL undergraduates. *English for Specific Purposes, 33*, 54–65.

Hsueh-Chao, M. H., & Nation, P. (2000). Unknown vocabulary density and reading comprehension. *Reading in a Foreign Language, 13*(1), 403–430.

Hunston, S. (2012). Corpus linguistics: Historical development. In *The encyclopaedia of applied linguistics*. John Wiley & Sons, Inc. Retrieved from http://onlinelibrary.wiley.com/doi/10.1002/9781405198431.wbeal0257/abstract

Kilgarriff, A. (2007). Googleology is bad science. *Computational Linguistics, 33*(1), 147–151. https://doi.org/10.1162/coli.2007.33.1.147

Kremmel, B. (2016). Word families and frequency bands in vocabulary tests: Challenging conventions. *TESOL Quarterly, 50*(4), 976–987. https://doi.org/10.1002/tesq.329

Laufer, B. (1989). What percentage of text-lexis is essential for comprehension. In C. Lauren & M. Nordman (Eds.), *Special language: From humans thinking to thinking machines* (pp. 316–323). Philadelphia: Multilingual Maters.

Laufer, B. (1992). How much lexis is necessary for reading comprehension? In H. Bejoint & P. Arnaud (Eds.), *Vocabulary and applied linguistics* (pp. 126–132). London: Macmillan.

Laufer, B., & Nation, P. (1995). Vocabulary size and use: Lexical richness in L2 written production. *Applied Linguistics, 16*(3), 307–322.

Laufer, B., & Ravenhorst-Kalovski, G. C. (2010). Lexical threshold revisited: Lexical text coverage, learners' vocabulary size and reading comprehension. *Reading in a Foreign Language, 22*(1), 15–30.

Martinez, R., & Murphy, V. A. (2011). Effect of frequency and idiomaticity on second language reading comprehension. *TESOL Quarterly, 45*(2), 267–290. https://doi.org/10.5054/tq.2011.247708

Meara, P. (1992). *EFL vocabulary tests*. ERIC Clearinghouse. Retrieved from www.lognostics.co.uk/vlibrary/meara1992z.pdf

Nagy, W., Anderson, R. C., Schommer, M., Scott, J. A., & Stallman, A. C. (1989). Morphological families in the internal lexicon. *Reading Research Quarterly*, 262–282.

Nation, I. S. P. (1983). Testing and teaching vocabulary. *Guidelines, 5*(1), 12–25.

Nation, I. S. P. (1990). *Teaching and learning vocabulary*. New York: Heinle & Heinle Publishers.

Nation, I. S. P. (2001a). How many high frequency words are there in English. *Language, Learning and Literature: Studies Presented to Hakan Ringbom. Abo Akademi University, Abo: English Department Publications, 4*, 167–181.

Nation, I. S. P. (2001b). *Learning vocabulary in another language*. Cambridge, UK: Cambridge University Press.

Nation, I. S. P. (2004). A study of the most frequent word families in the British National Corpus. *Vocabulary in a Second Language: Selection, Acquisition, and Testing*, 3–13.

Nation, I. S. P. (2006). How large a vocabulary is needed for reading and listening? *Canadian Modern Language Review/La Revue Canadienne Des Langues Vivantes, 63*(1), 59–82. https://doi.org/10.3138/cmlr.63.1.59

Nation, I. S. P., & Anthony, L. (2013). Mid-frequency readers. *Journal of Extensive Reading, 1*, 5–16.

Nation, I. S. P., & Beglar, D. (2007). A vocabulary size test. *The Language Teacher, 31*(7), 9–13.

Pellicer-Sánchez, A., & Schmitt, N. (2010). Incidental vocabulary acquisition from an authentic novel: Do things fall apart? *Reading in a Foreign Language, 22*(1), 31–55.

Piantadosi, S. T. (2014). Zipf's word frequency law in natural language: A critical review and future directions. *Psychonomic Bulletin & Review, 21*(5), 1112–1130.

Pigada, M., & Schmitt, N. (2006). Vocabulary acquisition from extensive reading: A case study. *Reading in a Foreign Language, 18*(1), 1–28.

Read, J. (2000). *Assessing vocabulary.* Cambridge and New York, NY: Cambridge University Press.

Read, J. (2004). Research in teaching vocabulary. *Annual Review of Applied Linguistics, 24*, 146–161. https://doi.org/10.1017/S0267190504000078

Schmitt, N. (2000). *Vocabulary in language teaching.* Cambridge, UK: Cambridge University Press.

Schmitt, N. et al. (under review). How much vocabulary is required for listening and reading in English?

Schmitt, N., Jiang, X., & Grabe, W. (2011). The percentage of words known in a text and reading comprehension. *The Modern Language Journal, 95*(1), 26–43. https://doi.org/10.1111/j.1540-4781.2011.01146.x

Schmitt, N., & Schmitt, D. (2014). A reassessment of frequency and vocabulary size in L2 vocabulary teaching. *Language Teaching, 47*(4), 484–503. https://doi.org/org/10.1017/S0261444812000018

Schmitt, N., Schmitt, D., & Clapham, C. (2001). Developing and exploring the behaviour of two new versions of the Vocabulary Levels Test. *Language Testing, 18*(1), 55–88. https://doi.org/10.1177/026553220101800103

Schmitt, N., & Zimmerman, C. B. (2002). Derivative word forms: What do learners know? *TESOL Quarterly, 36*(2), 145–171. https://doi.org/10.2307/3588328

Thornbury, S. (2002). *How to teach vocabulary.* Harlow: Pearson Education.

van Heuven, W. J. B., Mandera, P., Keuleers, E., & Brysbaert, M. (2014). SUBTLEX-UK: A new and improved word frequency database for British English. *The Quarterly Journal of Experimental Psychology, 67*(6), 1176–1190. https://doi.org/10.1080/17470218.2013.850521

van Zeeland, H., & Schmitt, N. (2013). Lexical coverage in L1 and L2 listening comprehension: The same or different from reading comprehension? *Applied Linguistics, 34*(4), 457–479. https://doi.org/10.1093/applin/ams074

Waring, R., & Nation, I. S. P. (1997). Vocabulary size, text coverage, and word lists. In N. Schmitt & M. McCarthy (Eds.), *Vocabulary: Description, acquisition and pedagogy* (pp. 6–19). Cambridge, UK: Cambridge University Press.

Webb, S., Sasao, Y., & Ballance, O. (2017). The updated Vocabulary Levels Test. *ITL – International Journal of Applied Linguistics, 168*(1), 33–69. https://doi.org/10.1075/itl.168.1.02web

West, M. (1953). *A general service list of English words.* London, UK: Longman, Green and Co.

7

Academic Vocabulary

Averil Coxhead

Introduction

Research investigating academic vocabulary has been largely driven by the needs of English as a second or foreign language learners preparing to study in English in higher education contexts. This field of research is growing rapidly along with English for Academic Purposes (EAP). Academic vocabulary sits between "conversational words" and "subject-specific words" in Beck, McKeown, & Kucan's (2013) well-known three-tiered model of vocabulary. In this chapter, we will look at critical topics relating to academic vocabulary and consider options for future research.

Critical Issues and Topics

This section looks at several key issues and topics relating to academic vocabulary in research, beginning with a short section on why academic vocabulary is important. The next topic looks at definitions of academic vocabulary, followed by the identification of single words as academic vocabulary and then academic multiword units such as collocations, lexical bundles, and formulas in written academic texts. The nature of vocabulary in spoken academic texts is the focus of the following section. Academic spoken vocabulary is a fairly new area of research. It is followed by a short discussion of academic vocabulary in secondary school/middle school contexts. The final topic is academic vocabulary in learning and teaching programs.

Why Is Academic Vocabulary Important?

Research suggests that academic vocabulary is important for several reasons. Firstly, it is a key element of written academic texts. Word list research has found that academic vocabulary can represent anywhere from 10% (Coxhead, 2000) to 14% (Gardner & Davies, 2014) of the words in such texts. These figures suggest that one word in ten or one word in seven in a line of written academic text might be an academic word. Academic study in English-medium institutions requires a large amount of reading, and vocabulary load research suggests that students need to know a substantial number of words to cope with understanding academic texts. According to Nation (2006), learners need 8,000 to 9,000 word families plus proper nouns to reach 98% coverage of academic written texts. This level of lexical coverage has been found to be sufficient to understand written text (Hu & Nation, 2000; Schmitt, Jiang, & Grabe, 2011). Academic spoken texts also require substantial vocabulary knowledge. Students need to know 4,000 word families plus proper nouns and marginal words to reach 95% coverage of lectures, and up to 8,000 word families plus proper nouns and marginal words to reach 98% coverage (Dang & Webb, 2014). Research suggests that lexical coverage of 95% is sufficient to understand spoken discourse (van Zeeland & Schmitt, 2013). However, increased coverage is likely to increase the number of listeners who can adequately understand speech. Academic word lists are important because they might provide a shortcut to learning the kinds of words that students may often encounter in their academic reading and listening. For example, learning the 1,741 words of the Academic Spoken Word List (Dang, Coxhead, & Webb, 2017) may allow learners to recognize 92% to 93% of the words in academic speech, which is higher than the coverage they may achieve from learning the most frequent 2,000 words of general vocabulary (91%).

Vocabulary testing research suggests that many second language learners of English have low levels of vocabulary knowledge and slow rates of vocabulary growth in a range of contexts, including Denmark (Henriksen & Danelund, 2015) and Taiwan (Webb & Chang, 2012). Learners studying in English-medium institutions need help with vocabulary in general, and they need more help with academic vocabulary in particular because academic vocabulary is found in higher proportions in academic texts than in other kinds of texts, which is an indication of specialization. For example, academic lexis does not occur with the same frequency in general English texts such as fiction (Coxhead, 2000; Gardner & Davies, 2014) and newspapers (Gardner & Davies, 2014) as it does in academic texts. Another important point is that understanding academic texts may be challenging for certain groups of learners. Maxwell (2013) puts this point succinctly by writing, "Nobody is a native speaker of Academic English". Corson (1995) points out that the social background of learners may have an impact on exposure to academic vocabulary. He coined the term "lexical bar", and explains that it

> represents a gulf between the everyday meaning systems and the high status meaning systems created by the introduction of an academic culture of literacy. This is a barrier that everyone has to cross at some stage in their lives, if they are to become "successful candidates" in the "conventional forms of education".
>
> *(Corson, 1995, pp. 180–181)*

Coxhead (2000) found that over 80% of her Academic Word List had Greek and Latin roots. It almost goes without saying that learners with first language backgrounds or knowledge of Romance languages will have an advantage over learners who come from languages which do not draw on Graeco-Latin vocabulary. This means learners need to know about word parts in academic vocabulary. See Sasao and Webb (2017) and Sasao (this volume) for more information on word parts and testing this aspect of vocabulary knowledge.

Vocabulary is an important element of university discourse, as Basturkmen and Shackleford (2015) found in their study of first-year accountancy lectures at a university in New Zealand. Explaining and talking about vocabulary was the most frequent language-related episode that occurred among participants in that study. This focus on vocabulary can be seen throughout many areas of teaching and learning in English for Academic Purposes, which demonstrates that there is raised awareness of academic vocabulary in pedagogy as well as research. Academic word lists, for example, can be found as integrated sections of English for Academic Purposes (EAP) programs in many places in the world. They can also be found in learner dictionaries, on websites, in learning materials, and vocabulary tests (see Nation, 2016). A practical tool like an academic word list can be immediately useful as a guide for deciding which words to focus on in EAP classes or for independent learning (see Dang, this volume for more on word lists; see also Nation, 2016). Recent research into academic vocabulary research has ranged from large-scale corpus-based studies of written academic vocabulary such as Gardner and Davies (2014) and Browne, Culligan, and Phillips (2013); spoken academic vocabulary (Dang et al., 2017); middle school vocabulary (Greene & Coxhead, 2015); and specialized vocabulary in areas such as discipline-specific vocabulary, for example, business studies (Nelson, n.d.), chemistry (Valipouri & Nassaji, 2013), medicine (Wang, Liang, & Ge, 2008), and chemistry and engineering (Ward, 2009) (see Liu & Lei, this volume for more on technical vocabulary; see also Coxhead, 2018). Academic vocabulary is also a part of corpus-based websites that allow learners and teachers to investigate academic vocabulary in use, for example, the 425-million-word Corpus of Contemporary American English (COCA) (available at http://corpus.byu.edu/coca/) includes academic word lists from which it was derived, and these are now readily available online.

Defining Academic Vocabulary

An important discussion point about academic vocabulary is how it is defined, because definitions drive how it is identified in research. There is a dilemma here (Hyland, 2016), as there are multiple perspectives on academic vocabulary. One way to think about academic vocabulary is that it fits between general vocabulary and technical vocabulary. Indeed, the organization of this volume situates this chapter on academic vocabulary between a chapter on high-, mid-, and low-frequency words and technical vocabulary. This middle ground approach, in turn, identifies academic vocabulary as "items which are widespread in academic discourse, but not very frequent in general English ([for example] *establish*, *evidence*)" (Charles & Pecorari, 2016, p. 110). In English for Academic Purposes, this approach is termed "English for General Academic Purposes (EGAP)". In the EGAP approach, as Hyland (2016, p. 18) points out, "teachers attempt to isolate the skills, language forms, and study activities thought to be common to all disciplines". Examples of general academic word lists include Coxhead's (2000) Academic Word List (AWL), Gardner & Davies (2014) Academic Vocabulary List, Browne et al.'s (2013) New Academic Word List, and Dang et al.'s (2017) Spoken Academic Word List. The main idea of these studies was to identify academic vocabulary which all learners in EAP will encounter in their academic texts, no matter what subject area they are studying (Coxhead, 2000; Charles & Pecorari, 2016). A feature of general academic vocabulary, according to Coxhead (2000, p. 124) is that, "Academic words (e.g., *substitute*, *underlie*, *establish*, *inherent*) are not highly salient in academic texts, as they are supportive of but not central to the topics of the texts in which they occur".

Gardner and Davies (2014) (see also Nation, 2016) point out that academic vocabulary is actually spread across all frequency levels in English from high- to mid- to low-frequency words. This definition means that words can be academic vocabulary in some contexts and general vocabulary in others, depending on the discipline or context. An example of such vocabulary is *area*, which is used in everyday English and in mathematics. Some studies have focused on the usefulness of general academic lists in particular subject areas, such as the Academic Word List in agriculture texts (9.06% coverage) (Martínez, Beck, & Panza,

2009) and applied linguistics texts (11.17% coverage) (Vongpumivitch, Huang, & Chang, 2009). For a synthesis of such studies, see Coxhead (2011, 2016).

English for Specific Academic Purposes (ESAP) is based on research into specific domains of study, which Hyland (2016, p. 19) argues is preferable to general academic English because, "In many situations, . . . EAP is most successful when it is tailored to meet the needs of the specific circumstances of the students". Hyland & Tse (2007) and Durrant (2014) argue against general academic word lists on the grounds that the needs of all EAP students cannot be met by one such list. Durrant (2016) has picked up this same issue with Gardner and Davies' (2014) AVL, drawing on corpora of student writing. See Gardner and Davies (2016) for a response to that article. Hyland and Tse (2007) provide analysis and examples of discipline-specific academic vocabulary meanings and use to make their case against general academic vocabulary. One example is *issue*, which occurs fairly evenly across science, engineering, and social science with the meaning of *topic*, but with lower levels of occurrence across the disciplines with the meaning *flow out*. Wang and Nation (2004) investigated homography in Coxhead's AWL and found that if the homographs they found in the list were separated, all but three word families would still meet the selection criteria for the AWL. These words are *intelligence*, *panel*, and *offset*. Specialized word lists such as Valipouri and Nassaji (2013) in chemistry, and Ward's (2009) basic engineering word list, are examples of subject-driven identification of specialized academic vocabulary. Another approach to ESAP vocabulary is to look at a wider discipline such as science, and develop a word list that identifies lexis that occurs across subjects in that area, as Coxhead and Hirsh's (2007) Science Word List does. This approach adds a layer of specialization for EAP students who might take a range of science-based courses in their first year of university and then choose to continue their studies in a particular area such as biology or chemistry. For more on technical vocabulary, see the chapter by Liu and Lei in this volume.

Nation, Coxhead, Chung, and Quero (2016, p. 150) suggest that the general vs. discipline-specific debate needs a compromise, arguing that "Working on the core meaning and uses of an academic word enables rather than disables current or later learning in more discipline-specific texts". Hyland (2016, p. 17) also suggests some common ground by envisaging academic vocabulary as being in "a continuum rather than a dichotomy". Moreover, Dang et al. (2017) point out that both approaches to identifying academic vocabulary practically ignore the fact that EAP learners are not one homogenous group; they have different levels of vocabulary knowledge. This suggests that academic words that are useful for one learner may not necessarily be useful for another.

Identifying Single Words as Academic Vocabulary

Early studies focused on identifying academic vocabulary relied on hand counts of lexis in contexts such as student annotations on textbooks, for example Lynn (1973) and Ghadessy (1979). As technology has developed in the last few decades, more recent studies of academic vocabulary have adopted a corpus-based approach. In this section, we will look at different ways to identify academic words in corpora, including common core, corpus comparison, and keyword methodologies, drawing on examples from English for Academic Purposes research. The definitions of academic vocabulary above play out in the identification of academic vocabulary in these studies because whatever definition a researcher adopts will affect the outcome of studies which aim to identify academic vocabulary.

A common core approach is based on the idea that there is a "general pool of language of high frequency items that predominates all uses of language" (Basturkmen, 2006, p. 16).

A feature of the common core approach is an assumption that learners who are focused on academic vocabulary will already have some knowledge of these high-frequency words in English. Coxhead's (2000) AWL is an example of a common core approach, because it used West's (1953) *General Service List of Words* (GSL) to represent high frequency words. This approach did not take into account that some high-frequency words are also academic words (Nation, 2016). As mentioned already, recent research on vocabulary knowledge of second and foreign language learners of English suggests that vocabulary knowledge of high-frequency vocabulary can be patchy, at best (see, for example, Webb & Chang, 2012; Henriksen & Danelund, 2015; Coxhead & Boutorwick, 2018). Basing the AWL, for example, on an existing general service word list means that decisions made for selecting items for West's (1953) GSL have an impact on the selection of items for the AWL. See Nation (2016), Gardner & Davies (2014), and Hyland & Tse (2007), for example, for critical discussions of the AWL. Browne et al.'s New Academic Word List (2013) is built on a new general service list, developed by the same researchers, and is another example of a common core approach to academic vocabulary.

Other examples of common core approaches to academic vocabulary include Coxhead & Hirsh's (2007) Science Word List. The focus of this research was lexical items that occurred outside West's General Service List (GSL) (1953) and Coxhead's (2000) AWL, and met selection principles from an analysis of a corpus of study guides, laboratory manuals, and textbook chapters from first year university courses in 14 subjects in the sciences.

A corpus comparison approach uses two corpora: a specialized academic corpus and (usually) a general English corpus. This approach allows investigators to identify words which occur more frequently in academic English than in general English. Gardner and Davies (2014) developed the Academic Vocabulary List (AVL) using corpus comparison. This list is based on lemmas rather than word families (see Dang's chapter, this volume, for more on units of counting in word list development). The academic corpus used by Gardner and Davies (2014) is the 120-million-word academic subsection of the Corpus of Contemporary American English (COCA). This subsection contains nine disciplines, including business and finance; education; humanities; history; law and political science; medicine and health; philosophy, religion, psychology; science and technology; and social science. The academic corpus is made up of journal articles, newspapers, and magazines, and the non-academic corpus contains texts such as magazines and fiction. Table 7.1 shows the top 50 items in the Academic Vocabulary List (Gardner & Davies, 2014).

Nation (2016) highlights a problem with this corpus comparison for academic vocabulary by Gardner and Davies (2014), which is that words such as *history*, *low*, and *both* are included in the list. While the methodology which was used might well select such items, they do not seem to be especially academic in nature.

Identifying academic words by their keyness is also a corpus comparison approach. Keyness studies focus on word frequencies in different corpora, and higher frequency in a specialized corpus is seen as a marker of academic vocabulary. Paquot (2010) developed an Academic Keyword List (AKL) using two academic written corpora (professional writing and student writing by native speakers of English). She drew on principles of keyness, range, and distribution of vocabulary. The AKL includes single and multiword items, and includes high-frequency vocabulary. Some AKL examples are *according to*, *relation to*, *second*, *scope*, *requirement*, and *late*. The AKL can be found at www.uclouvain.be/en-372126.html.

Studies into single academic words illustrate the importance of this lexis. Let's turn now to academic multiword units.

Table 7.1 Top 50 items of the Academic Vocabulary List

Items 1–25	Part of speech	Items 26–50	Part of speech
study	n	history	n
group	n	develop	v
system	n	suggest	v
social	j	economic	j
provide	v	low	j
however	r	relationship	n
research	n	both	r
level	n	value	n
result	n	require	v
include	v	role	n
important	j	difference	n
process	n	analysis	n
use	n	practice	n
development	n	society	n
data	n	thus	r
information	n	control	n
effect	n	form	n
change	n	report	v
table	n	rate	n
policy	n	significant	j
university	n	figure	n
model	n	factor	n
experience	n	interest	n
activity	n	culture	n
human	j	need	n

Note: The parts of speech noted in Table 7.1 are n = noun, v = verb, j = adjective, and r = adverb.

Source: Gardner and Davies, 2014, p. 317

Identifying Academic Multiword Units

This section begins with the smallest multiword unit, academic collocations (made up of two words), and then moves on to lexical bundles and academic formulas which contain three or more words in strings. Several studies have investigated two-word combinations with a statistical relationship in academic corpora. Coxhead and Byrd (2012) report on patterns in collocations of items from the AWL. They find examples of AWL words occurring in noun phrases which are long and fairly complex, a feature of academic written texts noted by Biber, Johansson, Leech, Conrad, and Finegan (1999; see also Biber, 2006). They also find AWL words that occur together, as in *analysis and assessment* and *analysis and interpretation*. Coxhead and Byrd (2012) analyzed the collocations of the AWL word *concept* and found two main uses. One involved the description and evaluation of a concept (for example, *basic, central, dangerous,* and *different*) and the second type referred to the origin of the concept or its specific area of use (as in *economic, ideological, legal,* and *Anglo-American*) (p. 13). Another example is *assessment*, whereby collocates before the word provide information about types of assessment (e.g., *brief; appropriate*) and collocates after the word provide some sort of characterization of the item which is being assessed (e.g., *assessment of success*; *assessment of change*) (Byrd & Coxhead, 2012, p. 12).

Durrant's (2009) study of academic collocations involved a 25-million-word academic written corpus that contained the following disciplines: arts and humanities; engineering; law and education; medicine and health sciences; science; and social sciences. He used a keyword analysis to compare the occurrences of collocations in the academic corpus with a non-academic corpus. Durrant (2009) identified 1,000 collocations, and found that 763 of them were grammatical, in that they contained one non-lexical word (for example, *assume that*, *associated with*, and *based on*). This finding is a reminder of the importance of high-frequency vocabulary in academic texts (actually, in all texts, see Dang et al., 2017), and highlights the problem with the exclusion of high frequency words in Coxhead's AWL (Durrant, 2009).

Another study of academic collocations resulted in Ackermann and Chen's Academic Collocation List (ACL) (2013), which was developed using a common core approach by analyzing the Pearson International Corpus of Academic English (PICAE). PICAE contains journal articles and textbooks from 28 disciplines and contains over 25 million running words. PICAE has four disciplines: applied sciences and professions, humanities, social sciences, and natural/formal sciences. The collocations were identified in the corpus using a computer program, and the data was then refined using expert ratings until the final list of 2,468 items was reached (downloadable from http://pearsonpte.com/research/academic-collocation-list/). Ackermann and Chen (2013) categorized their Academic Collocation List according to grammatical patterns. Almost three-quarters of the Academic Collocations List were in a noun combination category (for example, *assessment process* and *classic example*).

The studies highlighted here illustrate that corpus-based studies into academic collocations result in a great deal of data, and it is no mean feat to work through the data sets to decide what might be worth investigating further, what meets selection criteria, and what might be the most useful items for teachers and learners. Note that both studies which have been discussed here present large numbers of academic collocations which would be quite daunting to take into English for Academic Purposes classrooms.

Moving beyond two-word combinations takes us to lexical bundles, which are words in a string of three or more words which occur frequently (Biber et al., 1999). Examples of lexical bundles include *on the basis of*, *on the other hand*, and *at the same time*. Biber, Conrad, and Cortes (2004) found that lexical bundles in academic texts occur more often in spoken classroom language than in textbooks or academic written prose. An explanation for this finding is that the lexical bundles in classroom discourse are "useful for instructors who need to organise and structure discourse which is at the same time informational, involved, and produced with real-time production constraints" (Biber, 2006, p. 148). Biber (2006) found more lexical bundles in natural science than in business, engineering, humanities, and social science, which he associates with the heavier technical content of natural science.

Differences in frequency and lexical bundles in disciplines have also been noted by Hyland (2008), Pickering and Byrd (2008), and Byrd and Coxhead (2010). Like Biber, Conrad, and Cortes (2004), Pickering and Byrd (2008) found more lexical bundles in spoken than written academic texts. Byrd and Coxhead (2010) found that arts, commerce, law and science shared 73 four-word lexical bundles. One example of a shared bundle is *on the other hand*. It had a total frequency of 353 in Coxhead's academic written corpus from the AWL study, and occurred most often in the law subsection of the corpus (35%), followed by commerce (27%), arts (27%), and then science (15%). Law contained the highest number of lexical bundles at 5.44%, followed by commerce at 2.65%. Arts and science both had lower levels of lexical bundles at around 1.45%. Hyland (2008) also found low levels of lexical bundles in applied linguistics.

Another study of multiword units containing strings of more than three words was carried out by Simpson-Vlach and Ellis (2010), who were in search of pedagogically useful academic formulas. Simpson-Vlach and Ellis (2010) used a quantitative analysis of corpora to identify academic formulas (the Academic Formulas List – AFL) in academic written English and academic spoken English, drawing on statistical analyses and comparisons with non-academic written and spoken corpora. They then asked experienced language teachers and language testers to rate a sample of formulas based on whether they were a formulaic expression, were cohesive, and worth teaching. Three lists were developed from this process. One list is the core AFL list, which contains both written and spoken formulas (for example, *in terms of, at the same time, from the point of view, in order to,* and *as well as*). The second list contains 200 spoken academic formulas (for example, *be able to, blah blah blah, this is the, you know what I mean,* and *you can see*), and the third list contains 200 written academic formulas (for example, *even though the, a wide range of, was based on, take into account the,* and *as can be seen*). The formulas were also categorized according to their functions in texts, such as ability and possibility (*allows us to; are able to*) and evaluation (*an important role in; is consistent with*). Note that the formulas are made up of high frequency words in strings. This point is important when we think about the nature of academic vocabulary and multiword units: high frequency and non-content words predominate in these patterns (Durrant, 2009).

A more wide-ranging study of academic multiword units comes from Liu (2012) who investigated the occurrences of lexical bundles, phrasal verbs, and idioms, drawing from studies such as Biber et al. (1999), Carter and McCarthy (2006), Simpson-Vlach and Ellis (2010), Gardner and Davies (2007), and also from dictionaries. Liu (2012) used the academic sections of the Corpus of Contemporary American English (COCA) and British National Corpus to look for these multiword units in the corpora and he ranked the resulting list of 228 frequent multiword units into three frequency bands. The first band has 77 units which occur 100 times or more in the corpora; the second bank contains 85 units which occur between 50 and 99 times in the corpora, and the final band contains 67 units which occurred between 20 and 49 times. Some examples from the first band include *according to* (det + N), *as well as* (det + N), and NP *suggest that*.

All of these studies into multiword units in academic written English suggest that there are many such units, in many patterns. Byrd and Coxhead (2007) point out that bringing such patterns into classrooms can be quite tricky, and learners tend to use fewer lexical bundles in their academic writing than professional writers (see Cortes, 2004).

Academic Vocabulary in Spoken Academic English

Spoken academic vocabulary in English is a much less-researched topic than written academic vocabulary. Until the advent of large scale academic spoken corpora, such as the British Academic Spoken Corpus (BASE) (see Thompson & Nesi, 2001) and the Michigan Corpus of Academic Spoken English (MICASE) (Simpson, Briggs, Ovens, & Swales, 2002), it was much more difficult and expensive to obtain spoken academic texts for analysis. The lectures in the BASE and MICASE corpora have featured in an analysis of lexical bundles in academic speaking (Nesi & Basturkmen, 2006), who focused on the cohesive discourse in the lectures and the use of referential bundles and discourse organizers, such as *at the same* time and *if you want to*.

The vocabulary needed for listening to academic speech was explored in Dang and Webb's (2014) analysis of the BASE corpus. This study found that the most frequent 4,000-word families plus proper nouns and marginal words provided 95% coverage of the corpus, and the most frequent 8,000-word families plus proper nouns and marginal words provided 98% coverage. Dang and Webb (2014) also noted that learners can reach 95% coverage of academic spoken texts if they know the 3,000 most frequent word families in English and Coxhead's (2000) AWL. This study suggests that spoken academic texts require fewer general academic words than written academic texts. Dang and Webb (2014) found that the AWL accounted for 4% of spoken academic texts. A study by Thompson (2006) reported that the AWL covered 4.9% of a corpus of lectures. For more on academic vocabulary and listening to lectures, see Rodgers and Webb (2016).

Research has also looked into the vocabulary of listening assessments. Webb and Paribakht (2015) analyzed texts used in a Canadian university admission test called CanTEST and found that the most frequent 4,000-word families covered 95% of these texts but that the most frequent 10,000-word families were needed to reach 98% coverage. In another study, Paribakht and Webb (2016) found variation of AWL coverage of reading and listening passages in a university admission test, with higher coverage in reading (6.31%) than listening.

A more recent study by Dang, Coxhead, and Webb (2017) on vocabulary in academic spoken texts has resulted in an Academic Spoken Word List (ASWL) of 1,741-word families. The ASWL was developed from a corpus of 13 million running words from lectures, seminars, labs, and tutorials. This word list took a core academic vocabulary approach and as well as corpus-based measures, and it included teacher and student-based data. A key feature of the ASWL is it can be adapted according to the vocabulary knowledge of different learners. Dang et al. (2017) found that knowledge of ASWL can help learners reach between 92% and 96% coverage of academic spoken English.

Academic Vocabulary in Secondary School/Middle School Contexts

Much research on academic vocabulary has been situated in higher education contexts, and yet it is also important to secondary school or middle school education (Crossman & Pinchbeck, 2012; Greene & Coxhead, 2015; Roessingh, 2016). One study that looks into academic vocabulary in middle school textbooks in the US is based on Jennifer Greene's 18 million running word middle school corpus of 109 textbooks from grades 6 to 8 in the subjects English grammar and writing, health, mathematics, science, and social sciences and history (Greene & Coxhead, 2015). West's GSL (1953) accounted for nearly 80% of the words in the corpus, and Coxhead's AWL covers nearly 5.4%. The middle school vocabulary lists from each of the five subject areas contained items which only occurred outside the GSL. Selection criteria for the middle school lists include frequency and range from within each subject area, leading to words in the science list such as *energy, organism, element, and react*; and *equation, graph, fraction,* and *data* in the mathematics list. Each middle school vocabulary list contains between 600 to 800 word types, and coverage of their respective subject-based corpora range from the lowest at 5.83% in social studies and history through to 10.17% in science (Greene & Coxhead, 2015, p. 23).

Several studies have looked into coverage of Coxhead's AWL (2000) in secondary school texts. Roessingh (2016) found higher proportions of the AWL in expository texts (9.86%) than literary texts (5.5%). In a study of academic vocabulary in the teacher talk of three teachers (maths, science, and English as an additional language) in an international school in Germany for grade 6 students (aged 10–11 years), Coxhead (2017) found that the coverage of the AWL on average was 1.92%. This figure is around half the coverage reported by Dang and Webb (2014) of the AWL in university-level spoken texts. The percentage of AWL words in the teacher talk increased in all three subjects over the course of a year, from around 1% in each subject to 2.05% in science, 2.45% in English as an additional language, and 2.78% in mathematics. Coxhead, Stevens, and Tinkle (2010) examined the occurrence of Coxhead's AWL in a corpus of secondary school science textbooks and found the list covered 7.05%. This coverage was 2% lower than the AWL coverage in the science subcorpus from the original AWL study which was made up of university-level texts. Coxhead et al. (2010) also investigated the coverage of Coxhead and Hirsh's (2007) Science Word List (317 word families) and found that it covered 5.90% of their corpus of secondary school science textbooks, which is higher than the coverage reported by Coxhead and Hirsh in university-level science texts (3.79%). These figures suggest that the Science Word List is potentially more useful for secondary school learners than students preparing for university studies. For more on coverage of the Science Word List in specialized texts, see Coxhead and Quero (2015).

Academic Vocabulary in Learning Programs

The final topic in this section concerns research into academic vocabulary in programs of study. There is a growing interest in this research, because identifying academic vocabulary to support EAP learners and their teachers is one thing, but putting the results of such studies into practice and evaluating the effectiveness of approaches to teaching and learning is quite another. Storch and Tapper (2009) report on increased and appropriate use of AWL words in EAP student writing over time in an Australian context, while Crossman and Pinchbeck (2012) report on increased sophistication in academic vocabulary use in writing by seven Generation 1.5 learners in a university preparation course in Canada. Luxton, Fry, and Coxhead (2017) report on gains in academic vocabulary knowledge over a six-month period. Their study involved 2,642 students in 35 secondary schools in Aotearoa/New Zealand, and was based on responses on the academic section of Schmitt, Schmitt, and Clapham's (2001) Vocabulary Levels Test. The participants were roughly divided between monolingual speakers of English and bilingual/and or multilingual English-language speakers, and participants studied a range of subjects in secondary school, including English literature, English as a second language, physical education, religious education, technology, and science. Teachers were provided with suggestions for focusing on academic vocabulary development in classes and were supported in their attempts to focus on this lexis. Statistically significant gains in test results were reported by Pasifka students, Māori-medium (kura kaupapa) students, students who spoke languages other than English at home, second language speakers of English who had spent between three to five years in New Zealand, and those who had attended English language support classes. Luxton et al. (2017, p. 14) also found high coverage figures (19%) for Coxhead's AWL in assessment texts at the secondary school level. The importance of academic vocabulary in assessment texts was highlighted in interviews with secondary school teachers (Coxhead, 2018).

There is value in finding out more about how learners develop their understanding and use of academic multiword units. Jones and Haywood (2004) reported on an attempt to include 80 lexical bundles (such as *there were no significant differences* and *studies have shown that*) selected from work by Biber et al. (1999) into EAP coursework, and to measure student use of these multiword units in their writing. Jones and Haywood (2004) found that the classroom activities helped raise the learners' awareness of the lexical bundles, but this awareness was not accompanied by much evidence of actual use in writing. Another example of such research is

Li and Schmitt's (2009) study of a Chinese first language MA student's use of multiword units (lexical phrases) in writing over an academic year in a British university.

Future Directions

This chapter has demonstrated that while there is a growing literature on academic vocabulary, the majority of this research has focused on the identification of this lexis. Moreover, these studies have tended to employ a range of corpus-based methodologies and predominantly target undergraduate-level education. More research is needed to examine academic vocabulary in secondary school and postgraduate education in different contexts, and draw on both written and spoken data. Both single-word and multiword unit analyses are needed for these contexts. It is also important that corpus-based research is complemented by qualitative approaches, as can be seen in the work by Simpson-Vlach and Ellis (2010) and Dang et al. (2017). More studies are also needed into academic spoken events other than lectures. There is also a need to find out more about how academic vocabulary is learned and how this vocabulary develops over time.

Another important area for future research is replication studies. Miller and Biber (2015) examine approaches to validation of word lists, including academic word lists, and draw attention to the need to find out more about how different corpora can have an impact on the selection of items and whether the same results would or could be found using different corpora. Replication is also important in academic vocabulary learning and teaching studies.

Another direction for future research is to investigate the extent to which academic vocabulary occurs in languages other than English. A couple of studies are already underway in this area, including, for example, Danish at the University of Copenhagen by Anne Sofie Jakobsen (see Jakobsen, Coxhead, & Henriksen, 2018) and Welsh as part of the CorCenCC (Corpws Cenedlaethol Cymraeg Cyfoes – The National Corpus of Contemporary Welsh) project, led by Dr. Dawn Knight at Cardiff University (go to www.corcencc.org/). The predominance of research in this chapter is based on English for Academic Purposes, but this work needs to be balanced by ground-breaking research in other languages and in different levels of education.

Further Reading

Hyland, K., & Shaw, P. (Eds.). *Routledge handbook of English for Academic Purposes*. London: Routledge.

This volume contains chapters which relate to or directly discuss aspects of academic vocabulary.

Nation, I. S. P. (2016). *Making and using word lists for language learning and testing*. Amsterdam: John Benjamins.

This book contains a chapter on specialized vocabulary and word lists.

Coxhead, A. (2018). *Vocabulary and English for specific purposes research: Quantitative and qualitative perspectives*. London: Routledge.

This book has chapters on academic vocabulary in secondary school contexts and university in English-medium contexts.

Related Topics

Classifying and identifying formulaic language; frequency as a guide for vocabulary usefulness; high-, mid-, and low-frequency words; technical vocabulary; word list; and key issues in researching multiword items

References

Ackermann, K., & Chen, Y.-H. (2013). Developing the Academic Collocation List (ACL) – A corpus-driven and expert-judged approach. *Journal of English for Academic Purposes, 12*(4), 235–247.

Basturkmen, H. (2006). *Ideas and options in English for specific purposes.* Mahwah, NJ: Lawrence Erlbaum.

Basturkmen, H., & Shackleford, N. (2015). How content lecturers help students with language: An observational study of language-related episodes in interaction in first year accounting classrooms. *English for Specific Purposes, 37,* 87–97.

Beck, I., McKeown, M., & Kucan, L. (2013). *Bringing words to life: Robust vocabulary instruction* (2nd ed.). New York, NY: Guildford Press.

Biber, D. (2006). *University language.* Amsterdam: John Benjamins.

Biber, D., Conrad, S., & Cortes, V. (2004). If you look at . . . : Lexical bundles in university teaching and textbooks. *Applied Linguistics, 25*(3), 371–405.

Biber, D., Johansson, S., Leech, G., Conrad, S., & Finegan, E. (1999). *Longman grammar of spoken and written English.* Harlow, UK: Pearson Education.

Browne, C., Culligan, B., & Phillips, J. (2013). *A new academic word list.* Retrieved from www.newacademicwordlist.org/.

Byrd, P., & Coxhead, A. (2010). *On the other hand*: Lexical bundles in academic writing and in the teaching of EAP. *University of Sydney Papers in TESOL, 5,* 31–64.

Carter, R., & McCarthy, M. (2006). *Cambridge grammar of English.* Cambridge, UK: Cambridge University Press.

Charles, M., & Pecorari, D. (2016). *Introducing English for academic purposes.* London, UK: Routledge.

Corson, D. (1995). *Using English words.* Boston, MA: Kluwer Academic.

Cortes, V. (2004). Lexical bundles in published and student disciplinary writing: Examples from history and biology. *English for Specific Purposes, 23,* 397–423.

Coxhead, A. (2000). A new academic word list. *TESOL Quarterly, 34*(2), 213–238.

Coxhead, A. (2011). The Academic Word List ten years on: Research and teaching implications. *TESOL Quarterly, 45*(2), 355–362.

Coxhead, A. (2016). Reflecting on Coxhead (2000) A New Academic Word List. *TESOL Quarterly, 50*(1), 181–185.

Coxhead, A. (2017). The lexical demands of teacher talk: An international school study of EAL, Maths and Science. *Oslo Studies in Language, 9*(3), 29–44.

Coxhead, A. (2018). *Vocabulary and English for specific purposes research: Quantitative and qualitative perspectives.* London, UK: Routledge.

Coxhead, A. & Boutorwick, T. J. (2018). Longitudinal vocabulary development in an EMI international school context: Learners and texts in EAL, Maths and Science. *TESOL Quarterly, 52*(3), 588–610.

Coxhead, A., & Byrd, P. (2007). Preparing writing teachers to teach the vocabulary and grammar of academic prose. *Journal of Second Language Writing, 16,* 129–147.

Coxhead, A., & Byrd, P. (2012). Collocations and Academic Word List: The strong, the weak and the lonely. In I. Moskowich & B. Crespo (Eds.), *Encoding the past, decoding the future: Corpora in the 21st century* (pp. 1–20). Newcastle upon Tyne, UK: Cambridge Scholars Publishing.

Coxhead, A., & Hirsh, D. (2007). A pilot science word list for EAP. *Revue Francaise de Linguistique Appliqueé, 7*(2), 65–78.

Coxhead, A., & Quero, B. (2015). Investigating a science vocabulary list in university medical textbooks. *TESOLANZ Journal, 23,* 55–65.

Coxhead, A., Stevens, L., & Tinkle, J. (2010). Why might secondary science textbooks be difficult to read? *New Zealand Studies in Applied Linguistics, 16*(2), 35–52.

Crossman, K., & Pinchbeck, G. (2012). An intensive Academic English course for Generation 1.5 ELLs bound for post-secondary studies: Curriculum design, development and implementation. *TESL Canada Journal, 6,* 231–245.

Dang, T. N. Y., Coxhead, A., & Webb, S. (2017). The academic spoken word list. *Language Learning*, *67*(3), 959–997.

Dang, T. N. Y., & Webb, S. (2014). The lexical profile of academic spoken English. *English for Specific Purposes*, *33*, 66–76.

Durrant, P. (2009). Investigating the viability of a collocation list for students of English for academic purposes. *English for Specific Purposes*, *28*, 157–169.

Durrant, P. (2014). Discipline- and level-specificity in university students' written vocabulary. *Applied Linguistics*, *35*(3), 328–356.

Durrant, P. (2016). To what extent is the Academic Vocabulary List relevant to university student writing? *English for Specific Purposes*, *43*, 49–61.

Gardner, D., & Davies, M. (2007). Pointing out frequent phrasal verbs: A corpus-based analysis. *TESOL* Quarterly, *41*(2), 339–359.

Gardner, D., & Davies, M. (2014). A new academic vocabulary list. *Applied Linguistics*, *35*(3), 305–327.

Gardner, D., & Davies, M. (2016). A response to "to what extent is the Academic Vocabulary List relevant to university student writing?". *English for Specific Purposes*, *43*, 62–68.

Ghadessy, M. (1979). Frequency counts, word lists, and material preparation: A new approach. *English Teaching Forum*, *17*(1), 24–27.

Greene, J., & Coxhead, A. (2015). *Academic vocabulary for middle school students: Research-based lists and strategies for key content areas*. Baltimore, MD: Brookes.

Henriksen, B., & Danelund, L. (2015). Studies of Danish L2 learners' vocabulary knowledge and the lexical richness of their written production in English. In P. Pietilä, K. Doró, & R. Pipalová (Eds.), *Lexical issues in L2 writing* (pp. 1–27). Newcastle upon Tyne, UK: Cambridge Scholars Publishing.

Hu, M., & Nation, I. S. P. (2000). Vocabulary density and reading comprehension. *Reading in a Foreign Language*, *23*, 403–430.

Hyland, K. (2008). As can be seen: Lexical bundles and disciplinary variation. *English for Specific Purposes*, *27*, 4–21.

Hyland, K. (2016). General and specific EAP. In K. Hyland & P. Shaw (Eds.), *The Routledge handbook of English for academic purposes* (pp. 17–29). Abingdon, Oxon, UK: Routledge.

Hyland, K., & Tse, P. (2007). Is there an "academic vocabulary"? *TESOL Quarterly*, *41*(2), 235–253.

Jakobsen, A. S., Coxhead, A., & Henriksen, B. (2018). General and academic high frequency vocabulary in Danish. *Nordand*, *13*(1), 64–89.

Jones, M., & Haywood, S. (2004). Facilitating the acquisition of formulaic sequences: An exploratory study in an EAP context. In N. Schmitt (Ed.), *Formulaic sequences* (pp. 269–291). Amsterdam: John Benjamins.

Li, J., & Schmitt, N. (2009). The acquisition of lexical phrases in academic writing: A longitudinal case study. *Journal of Second Language Writing*, *18*, 85–102.

Liu, D. (2012). The most frequently-used multi-word constructions in academic written English: A multi-corpus study. *English for Specific Purposes*, *31*, 25–35.

Luxton, J., Fry, J., & Coxhead, A. (2017). Exploring the knowledge and development of academic English vocabulary of students in NZ secondary schools. *SET*, *17*(1), 12–22.

Lynn, R. W. (1973). Preparing word lists: A suggested method. *RELC Journal*, *4*(1), 25–32.

Martínez, I., Beck, S., & Panza, C. (2009). Academic vocabulary in agriculture research articles. *English for Specific Purposes*, *28*, 183–198.

Maxwell, L. (2013, October 28). Common core ratchets up language demands for English learners. *Education Week*. Retrieved from www.edweek.org/ew/articles/2013/10/30/10cc-academiclanguage.h33.html

Miller, D., & Biber, D. (2015). Evaluating reliability in quantitative vocabulary studies: The influence of corpus design and composition. *International Journal of Corpus Linguistics*, *20*(1), 30–53.

Nation, I. S. P. (2006). How large a vocabulary is needed for reading and listening? *Canadian Modern Language Review*, *63*(1), 59–82.

Nation, I. S. P. (2016). *Making and using word lists for language learning and testing*. Amsterdam: John Benjamins.

Nation, I. S. P., & Coxhead, A., Chung, M., & Quero, B. (2016). Specialized word lists. In I. S. P. Nation (Ed.), *Making and using word lists for language learning and testing* (pp. 145–151). Amsterdam: John Benjamins.

Nelson, M. (n.d.). *Mike Nelson's business English lexis site*. Retrieved from http://users.utu.fi/micnel/business_english_lexis_site.htm

Nesi, H., & Basturkmen, H. (2006). Lexical bundles and discourse signalling in academic lectures. *International Journal of Corpus Linguistics, 11*(3), 283–304.

Paquot, M. (2010). *Academic vocabulary in learner writing*. London, UK: Continuum.

Paribakht, T. S., & Webb, S. (2016). The relationship between academic vocabulary coverage and scores on a standardized English proficiency test. *English for Academic Purposes, 21*, 121–132.

Pickering, L., & Byrd, P. (2008). Investigating connections between spoken and written academic English: Lexical bundles in the AWL and in MICASE. In D. Belcher & A. Hirvela (Eds.), *The oral/literate connection: Perspectives on L2 speaking, writing and other media interactions* (pp. 110–132). Ann Arbor, MI: University of Michigan Press.

Rodgers, M., & Webb, S. (2016). Listening to lectures. In K. Hyland & P. Shaw (Eds.), *The Routledge handbook of English for academic purposes* (pp. 165–176). Abingdon, Oxon, UK: Routledge.

Roessingh, H. (2016). Academic language in K-12: What is it, how is it learned, and how can we measure it? *BC TEAL Journal, 1*(1), 67–81.

Sasao, Y., & Webb, S. (2017). The word part levels test. *Language Teaching Research, 21*(1), 12–30.

Schmitt, N., Jiang, X., & Grabe, W. (2011). The percentage of words known in a text and reading comprehension. *The Modern Language Journal, 95*(1), 26–43.

Schmitt, N., Schmitt, D., & Clapham, C. (2001). Developing and exploring the behaviour of two new versions of the Vocabulary Levels Test. *Language Testing, 18*(1), 55–88.

Simpson-Vlach, R., Briggs, S., Ovens, J., & Swales, J. (2002). *The Michigan Corpus of academic spoken English*. Ann Arbor, MI: The Regents of the University of Michigan.

Simpson-Vlach, R., & Ellis, N. (2010). An academic formulas list: New methods in phraseology research. *Applied Linguistics, 31*(4), 487–512.

Storch, N., & Tapper, J. (2009). The impact of an EAP course on postgraduate writing. *Journal of English for Academic Purposes, 8*(3), 207–223.

Thompson, P. (2006). A corpus perspective on the lexis of lectures, with a focus on economics lectures. In K. Hyland & M. Bondi (Eds.), *Academic discourse across disciplines* (pp. 253–270). New York, NY: Peter Lang.

Thompson, P., & Nesi, H. (2001). The British Academic Spoken English (BASE) Corpus Project. *Language Teaching Research, 5*(3), 263–264.

Valipouri, L., & Nassaji, H. (2013). A corpus-based study of academic vocabulary in chemistry research articles. *Journal of English for Academic Purposes, 12*, 248–263.

van Zeeland, H., & Schmitt, N. (2013). Lexical coverage in L1 and L2 listening comprehension: The same or different from reading comprehension? *Applied Linguistics, 34*(4), 457–479.

Vongpumivitch, V., Huang, J., & Chang, Y.-C. (2009). Frequency analysis of the words in the Academic Word List (AWL) and non-AWL content words in applied linguistics research papers. *English for Specific Purposes, 28*(1), 33–41.

Wang, J., Liang, S., & Ge, G. (2008). Establishment of a medical academic word list. *English for Specific Purposes, 27*(4), 442–458.

Wang, K., & Nation, I. S. P. (2004). Word meaning in academic English: Homography in the Academic Word List. *Applied Linguistics, 25*(3), 291–314.

Ward, J. (2009). A basic engineering English word list for less proficient foundation engineering undergraduates. *English for Specific Purposes, 28*, 170–182.

Webb, S., & Chang, A. (2012). Second language vocabulary growth. *RELC Journal, 43*(1), 113–126.

Webb, S., & Paribakht, T. (2015). What is the relationship between the lexical profile of test items and performance on a standardized English proficiency test? *English for Specific Purposes, 38*, 34–43.

West, M. (1953). *A general service list of English words*. London, UK: Longman, Green and Co.

8

Technical Vocabulary

Dilin Liu and Lei Lei

Introduction

Technical vocabulary generally refers to words and phrases that are used and known mainly in a specific profession, trade, or, for simplicity purposes, subject area (henceforth, "subject area" or simply "subject" will be used as a generic term to refer to both "profession" and "trade"). Because of its subject-specific nature, technical vocabulary varies significantly from one subject area to another. Furthermore, technical words are ubiquitous and highly frequent in professional language. As such, technical vocabulary constitutes a very important and required knowledge for those who work directly or indirectly in a subject area as well as for students studying the subject. This chapter attempts to explore the key issues and topics related to technical vocabulary. Future directions in the work on technical vocabulary will also be briefly discussed.

Critical Issues and Topics

In this section, the following critical issues related to technical vocabulary will be addressed: (1) its definition, (2) its identification, (3) its role and importance in language use and learning, and (4) strategies and methods for learning and teaching technical vocabulary. However, the issue of the identification of technical vocabulary will be explored in much greater length due to its central importance in the study of technical vocabulary and its technical complexity.

Definition of Technical Vocabulary

On the surface, technical vocabulary seems to be a straightforward term referring to lexical items used with specialized meanings in a subject known mainly to a particular community of users. Yet, a close examination of the research on the topic reveals a lack of true consensus on not only how to define but also how label technical vocabulary. Regarding its labels, technical vocabulary has been referred to variously as "discipline specific vocabulary" (Woodward-Kron, 2008); "domain-specific glossaries" (Periñán-Pascual, 2015);

"scientific/technical terms" (Yang, 1986); "specialised lexis" (Baker, 1988); "specialist terms" (Woodward-Kron, 2008, p. 239); "specialized vocabulary" (Robinson, 1980); "terminological words", "terms", or simply "terminology" (Bečka, 1972, pp. 47–48; Kit & Liu, 2008; Peruzzo, 2014); and "terminological units" (Cabré, 1999). However, more recently, as will be explained later in the section, "technical vocabulary" has become an established term in applied linguistics to refer to a specific category of specialized words different from academic vocabulary, another group of specialized words (Nation, 2013; Nation & Coxhead, 2012).

As for the variations in the definition of technical vocabulary, first, there appear to be two views on the scope of subject areas that may be considered technical: a broader view and a narrower view. The broader view holds that technical words may occur in any subject (be it an art, science, or engineering) and they include words of various types, ranging from those that are used almost exclusively in a subject area (e.g., *arthrodesis* and *laparoscopy* in surgery medicine) to those that boast a high-frequency in general language but are used with a subject-specific meaning (e.g., *balance* and *interest* in banking business) or are important concepts in a subject without a separate subject-specific meaning (e.g., *neck* and *nose* in anatomy). In short, in this broader view, "Technical vocabulary is subject related, occurs in a specialist domain, and is part of a system of subject knowledge" (Chung & Nation, 2004, p. 252).

In contrast, the narrower view assumes that technical vocabulary is confined to specialized words in hard science, engineering, medicine, or trades only, as is evidenced by the following quote on technical vocabulary learning from the webpage of the Applied Linguistics Program at the University of Warwick (Technical Vocabulary, 2017):

> technical vocabulary is . . . often [found] in the fields of Science, Engineering and Medicine. . . . In Arts, Humanities and Social science disciplines, there will also be a requirement to use what may be termed "specialised" vocabulary, though this will not usually be deemed to be "technical".

Based on this quote, words with specialized meanings in arts, humanities, and social science are simply specialized vocabulary, not technical vocabulary. This restricted view of technical vocabulary can also be seen in Brieger and Pohl's (2002) textbook on technical vocabulary and Ardasheva and Tretter's (2017) research on the teaching of technical vocabulary to high school ESL students because both studies focused exclusively on vocabulary in engineering, sciences, and trades.

This restricted view has several problems. First, in today's world, the distinction between disciplines is not always clear-cut thanks to the increased interdisciplinary work across many different fields and also to the increased use of technology and scientific research methods in arts, humanities, and social sciences. Second, the use of the term "specialized vocabulary" to refer to technical terms in arts, humanities, and social sciences only adds to the confusion of the terms used in the discussion of technical vocabulary, because, as noted earlier, "specialized vocabulary" has actually often been used to refer to technical vocabulary. Furthermore, more recently, the term "specialized vocabulary" has been used as a generic term that covers both "academic vocabulary" and "technical vocabulary" (Nation, 2013; Nation & Coxhead, 2012). Although both academic and technical words are specialized vocabulary, they differ in that while academic vocabulary consists of words that occur across a wide range of subjects, technical vocabulary is composed of words with a specialized meaning used usually in one specific subject. Such a distinction is not really new, however, as it can be traced to

Bečka's (1972, p. 48) classification of specialized terminology into "notional terms" and "descriptive and technical terms": "Notional terms form the actual core of the terminology of scientific disciplines whilst descriptive and technical terms form the nomenclature of the respective branches of science". By defining "notional terms" as "core of the terminology of scientific disciples" and "descriptive and technical terms" as words of "specific branches of science", Bećka appears to consider the former to be general academic vocabulary and the latter to be discipline-specific technical vocabulary.

However, it is worth noting that whereas the distinction between academic and technical vocabularies is clear and sensible, there are some overlapping items between the two groups thanks largely to the fact that sometimes a word may have different specialized meanings in different subjects. For example, the word *tension* may refer to *electricity tension* in physics, *mental tension* in psychology, and *muscle tension* in physiology (Bečka, 1972, p. 49). Because of its high dispersion across disciplines, *tension* is on Coxhead's (2000) Academic Word List (AWL), but it could also be a technical word for physiology, physics, and psychology, respectively, due to its specialized meaning in each of the fields.

Another difference concerning the definition of technical vocabulary is that not all scholars agree that those high-frequency technical words used with or without a specialized meaning in a subject are technical terms. For example, while Ha and Hyland (2017) do not consider those without a specialized meaning technical words, Baker (1988) and Yang (1986) consider all high-frequency ones (with or without a specialized meaning) to be only "sub-/semi-technical words/terms". To the latter scholars, only words that have an exclusive technical meaning, such as *arthrodesis*, deserve the label of technical vocabulary. However, such a view and the attempt to differentiate the two types of technical words may be problematic if examined closely. First the technical and semi-/sub-technical differentiation is arguably not particularly meaningful, especially for language learning and teaching purposes. In fact, the so-called sub-technical words are actually more difficult to learn due to their polysemous meanings and the fact that their technical meanings are often "opaque" according to Watson Todd (2017). Second, the differentiation may not always be easy to make because, as noted in the previous paragraph, many technical words actually have more than one specialized meaning and some may appear across several different subject areas. Such technical words are labeled as sub-technical by some scholars (Baker, 1988, pp. 96–97; Yang, 1986, p. 95) and many of them, such as *accuracy* and *normal*, are on Coxhead's (2000) AWL.

As for the differentiation between those technical words with a specialized meaning and those without one, the problem is that such differentiation is sometimes gradable rather than binary, as shown in the Ha and Hyland (2017) study to be discussed later. Take for example the aforementioned words in the two categories (*neck* and *nose* as technical words in anatomy without a specialized meaning vs. *balance* and *interest* in banking business with a specialized meaning). Whereas it is fairly safe to say that *neck* and *nose* have no specialized meanings in anatomy and that *interest* has a specialized meaning in banking, we cannot really say for certain whether *balance* has a truly specialized meaning. This is because we can argue that the special meaning of *balance* in banking is actually a metaphorical extension of its common meaning. In fact, as contemporary cognitive linguistics has shown, the different meanings of a polysemous word are generally related, with most of its meanings being metaphorical extensions of its core meaning (Tyler, 2012).

If we agree that the two differentiations just mentioned are not particularly meaningful and feasible in the definition of technical vocabulary, then, technical vocabulary may indeed come not only from general common high-frequency words (as in the case of the aforementioned words *balance* and *interest*) but also from academic words (as in the case of *tension*).

In fact, a large majority of technical words are high-frequency and academic words. As reported in Nation (2013, p. 20), an analysis of the composition of the words in an academic textbook reveals that 68.5% of the words in the textbook belong to the first 2,000 words (i.e., those in the General Service List [GSL]), 6.9% are academic words (i.e., those in the AWL), 20.6% are technical words, and 4% are other words. Of the 20.6% technical words, 9.2% are those in the GSL, 6.2% are those in the AWL, and only 5.2% are not from the first two categories. This means that when the technical words are treated as a separate group with a 100% value, 45% of them are common high-frequency words used with a specialized meaning, 30% are AWL words, and only 25% are low-/lower-frequency technical words.

In short, technical vocabulary is subject-bound, referring to words used in a specific subject for communicating subject-specific knowledge. It includes both high-frequency and academic words that are used with a specialized meaning in a specific subject as well as those low/lower-frequency words that appear almost exclusively in a subject. Together with academic words, technical words help form specialized vocabulary. Finally, before we move onto the next section, it is necessary to note that technical vocabulary is not limited to individual words. It includes multiword units and their acronyms, such as *Acquired Immunodeficiency Syndrome* (*AIDS*), *flux theorem*, and *static electric field* (Brieger & Pohl, 2002; Yang, 1986). In fact, multiword technical units are common and many studies on technical vocabulary have included multiword terms (e.g., Nazar, 2016; Periñán-Pascual, 2015; Yang, 1986).

Identification of Technical Vocabulary

Existing methods used for identifying technical vocabulary can be categorized into two major groups: (1) judgment-based (e.g., Brieger & Pohl, 2002; Chung & Nation, 2003) and (2) corpus-based (e.g., Bernier-Colborne & Drouin, 2014; Chung, 2003), although it is important to note that many studies have now incorporated both types of methods (e.g., Ha & Hyland, 2017; Kwary, 2011; Watson Todd, 2017). Judgment-based methods require subjective decisions made based on subject-domain knowledge and they may involve the use of a rating scale, a technical dictionary, and/or contextual clues of words in the text in which they appear, as illustrated in Chung and Nation (2004). The use of a dictionary is considered a judgment-based method because many traditional dictionaries have been compiled based on the compilers' intuitive decisions. In contrast, corpus-based methods typically employ computerized search, analysis, and comparison of various frequency and dispersion (the number of occurrence of a word across texts/corpora) measures and linguistic features of lexical items for automatic or semi-automatic identification of technical terms (e.g., Bernier-Colborne & Drouin, 2014; Chung, 2003; Kit & Liu, 2008; Nazar, 2016; Periñán-Pascual, 2015). Although corpus-based methods still involve some judgment decisions, such as the selection of the features to consider and statistical formulas to use, such approaches, being largely quantitative in nature, are generally more objective and reliable. More importantly, thanks to the rapid advancements in computer technology and corpus linguistics, corpus-based methods have become increasingly more sophisticated and effective and are now widely used. Later, we describe the two groups of methods and their procedures and discuss their respective strengths and weaknesses where appropriate.

Before we proceed to the discussion of these methods, it is necessary to clarify the issue involving the use of "word family", "lemma", or "word type (form)" as the counting unit in the identification and reporting of technical vocabulary. As we know, in the development of word lists, some scholars (e.g., Coxhead in her 2000 AWL) use word family, others (e.g., Gardner and Davies in their 2014 Academic Vocabulary List) use lemma. In technical vocabulary research, "word type" has also been used (e.g., Baker, 1988; Chung, 2003; Ha & Hyland, 2017). It seems that "word family" is not a very good option because often not all members of a word family are technical words (Chung & Nation, 2003) and a word-family-based selection threshold may miss a technical word in the family (Ha & Hyland, 2017).

Concerning judgment-based methods, as noted previously, such methods require experts in the subject area (sometimes researchers, material writers, and/or teachers) to determine, based on their knowledge of the subject domain, whether and/or to what extent a word is related to and has specific technical meaning in the subject in question. The reason for using experts in this method is that, as discussed earlier, technical vocabulary is subject-related; making sound judgment decisions regarding technical vocabulary, therefore, requires a solid knowledge of the subject domain in question. Furthermore, while some technical words – mainly those of Latin or Greek origin (e.g., *pectora* and *vertebrae* in anatomy or medicine in general) – are easy to identify with a good accuracy, most other technical words are actually often difficult to determine, especially those that are high-frequency words used with or without a specialized meaning in a subject, a problem that researchers have long noted (e.g., Bečka, 1972). Thus, as already mentioned, judgment decisions on technical vocabulary are largely intuition-based and may not have good reliability. Therefore, researchers (e.g., Chung & Nation, 2003; Watson Todd, 2017) have used rating scales to help make the judgment more valid and reliable. Chung and Nation (2003) used a four-step rating scale (shown in Table 8.1) to identify technical words in an anatomy textbook and an applied linguistics textbook.[1]

Based on this rating scale, words belonging to Step 3 or 4 are considered technical terms while those in Step 1 or 2 are deemed nontechnical. The rating scale was found to be highly reliable with an inter-rater reliability of 0.95. By applying the rating scale, Chung and Nation (2004) identified 4,270 technical word types (37.6% of a total 11,305 word types) in the anatomy textbook and 835 technical word types (16.3% of total of 5,137 word types) in the applied

Table 8.1 A rating scale for finding technical words (as applied to the anatomy text)

Step 1
Words such as function words that have a meaning that has no particular relationship with the field of anatomy, that is, words independent of the subject matter. Examples include *the, is, between, adjacent, amounts.*

Step 2
Words that have a meaning that is minimally related to the field of anatomy in that they describe the position, movements, or features of the body. Examples include *superior, part, forms, pairs, structures.*

Step 3
Words that have a meaning that is closely related to the field of anatomy. They refer to parts, structures, or functions of the body, such as the regions of the body and systems of the body. The words may have some restrictions of usage depending on the subject field. Examples include *chest, trunk, neck, abdomen, breast.* Words in this category may be technical terms in a special field like anatomy and yet may occur with the same meaning in other fields and not be technical terms in those fields.

Step 4
Words that have a meaning specific to the field of anatomy and are not likely to be known in general language. They refer to structures and functions of the body. These words have clear restrictions of usage depending on the subject field. Examples include *thorax, sternum, costal, vertebrae, pectora.*

Source: Chung and Nation, 2003, p. 105, but with some examples omitted. Reprinted by permission of *Reading in a Foreign Language*

linguistics textbook. Their finding indicates that the percentage of technical words in a specialized text varies substantially across subject areas with those texts in sciences/engineering/trades boasting a much higher percentage than those in arts/humanities/social sciences.

Now, let us have a brief look at the other two judgment methods: using dictionaries and using contextual information. In the dictionary method, the first step is to choose a good, highly reputable technical dictionary. Usually the more widely and the longer a dictionary has been in use, the higher its quality will be. In terms of how to use a dictionary to identify technical words in a text, usually, for a word to be a technical item in the subject, it needs to be listed as a main or subentry in the dictionary (Chung & Nation, 2004). Regarding the use of contextual clues in a text to identify technical vocabulary, generally, there are three main types of clues provided by the authors of the text: "(i) definitions, (ii) typographical clues like bolding, italics, and brackets, and (iii) labels in diagrams or illustrations" (Chung & Nation, 2004, p. 256). As for the effectiveness and accuracy of the two methods, Chung and Nation's (2004) comparison of the two methods against the use of a rating scale indicates that using a technical dictionary has a higher accuracy rate than using contextual clues. Ha and Hyland (2017) made the best use of dictionaries and contextual information (in the form of examining concordance lines), but their study used a combined approach involving both corpus analysis and judgment decisions, so it will be discussed later in the section on combined methods.

Regarding corpus-based methods, as already explained, they typically examine and compare the frequency and dispersion measures of words and use computer programs to process such information to automatically or semi-automatically identify technical words of interest. The automatic process so used has been known as "automatic term extraction/recognition", among others (Kageura & Umino, 1996; Kit & Liu, 2008; Periñán-Pascual, 2015). Depending on the aspects of the information searched and analyzed and on the procedures used, corpus-based term extractions can be grouped into two approaches: "linguistically oriented" and "statistically oriented" although most studies employ both approaches simultaneously (Kageura & Umino, 1996, p. 271). Linguistically oriented approaches focus first on the formal features of words, such as parts of speech and grammatical structures (e.g., noun-noun or adjective-noun structure), and/or the semantic features, such as the semantic role of a lexical unit, semantic relationships, and semantic similarities. Earlier linguistically oriented approaches focused mostly on the formal aspects of words as reported in Kageura and Umino (1996), but the recent decade has seen studies focused on semantic features (e.g., Bertels & Speelman, 2014; Peruzzo, 2014). Usually, after the analysis and tagging of linguistic and/or semantic features, linguistically oriented approaches submit the features to various frequency statistical analysis. In some cases, after terms have been automatically extracted, they are then checked and verified by the researcher based on the relevant semantic features already specified.

In contrast, statistically oriented approaches take a straightforward frequency approach by simply and directly computing and comparing the frequency and dispersion measures of lexical items in a technical corpus of interest against a large general language corpus. This is because technical terms almost always occur much more frequently in a technical corpus than in a general corpus given that both corpora are large and representative enough of the type of language they each represent. This fact of technical terms occurring significantly more frequently in a technical corpus forms the basis of the statistical formulas or procedures used to identify and select technical terms. The most basic and straightforward formulas simply compute and compare the differences in the raw frequency and dispersion numbers of the words between the technical corpus and the general language corpus used in a study (e.g., Baker, 1988). More sophisticated formulas involve the comparison of more complex measures, such as the ratio between the frequency or the percentage of frequency of a lexical item in a specialized corpus and its frequency or percentage of frequency in a large general language corpus (Ahmad, Davies, Fulford, & Rogers, 1994) and the "rank difference" of a word in the two comparison corpora (Kit & Liu, 2008). Other sophisticated formulas include even more complex measures, such as Nazar's (2016) comparative "distributional analysis" of the characteristics of the co-occurrence patterns of words in a technical and a general corpus and Periñán-Pascual's (2015) "composite measure" that combines well-weighted values of a lexical item's "salience", "relevance", and "cohesion".

Furthermore, the computer programs used in corpus-based approaches often include some facilitating components to enhance their extraction accuracy and efficiency, such as the inclusion of a "stop list" of words to automatically exclude nontechnical words, such as function words. Finally, it is important to reiterate that in corpus-based comparison approaches, the general corpus should be very large, usually much larger than the technical corpus and it should not include any texts from the latter (Nation & Coxhead, 2012). Below, we offer a brief chronological overview of the development of the corpus-based approaches and a basic description of the procedures used in the studies reviewed.

Bečka (1972) and Yang (1986) were among the earliest corpus-based studies on technical vocabulary, although Bečka's main focus was the examination of vocabulary composition in technical texts, not technical vocabulary identification. Bečka's (1972) compared the frequencies and dispersions (what he called "disponibility") of three types of words in a balanced Czech technical corpus: grammatical (i.e., function), nontechnical, and technical. It was found that the words with the highest frequencies and dispersions were all function words, words with high to moderate frequencies and dispersions were mainly nontechnical words, and words with the lowest frequencies (one or two occurrences) and dispersions were mainly technical terms. It is important to note that, being among the earliest corpus-based work, Bečka's study did not employ any true statistical analysis, nor did it seem to have been done using a computer program because some of the results were reported as "estimation" numbers (Bečka, 1972, p. 51). Also, the study failed to include a general language corpus for comparison purposes. In this sense, the study is not a true linguistically or statistically oriented corpus-based study

Yang (1986) used computer programs to investigate the possibility of identifying technical vocabulary in a science/engineering corpus of nine texts plus a general language text (a novel) for comparison purposes. Via various frequency and distribution analysis, Yang demonstrated that it was possible to use corpus analysis to automatically identify what he labeled as "sub-technical words" and "technical terms". Like Bečka's results, Yang's also showed that words with both a high frequency and dispersion tend to include many function words while words with a relatively low frequency but a high dispersion consist of many subtechnical words (such as *accuracy, conclusion,* and *feature* (many of which, as noted earlier, are actually AWL words). In comparison, words that exhibit a very low dispersion include many technical terms (such as *bandwidth, carboxyl,* and *electrolysis*). Yang also showed the possibility to identify multiword technical terms by tagging the parts of speech of the words in the corpus and by using a computerized program with a stop list. However, Yang did not give any definitive cutoff frequency and dispersion measures for identifying sub-technical and technical terms. Hence, although Yang employed both linguistic and statistical analyses, his study is not a true linguistically or statistically oriented study, either.

Baker (1988) and Chung (2003) were among the early studies that might be said to have used a true statistically oriented corpus approach. Using a medical and two comparison corpora – a smaller medical corpus and the 7.3 million-word COBUILD Corpus of General English, Baker (1988) first identified the 218 most frequent words in the medical corpus and then compared the frequencies of the words in the medical corpus with their frequencies in the two comparison corpora. Due to a significant size difference among the corpora, Baker (1988, p. 95) used frequency percentage (number of occurrence divided by total number of words in the corpus) and "ratio of frequency percentages (RFP)" in her comparison. Words with a low RFP (defined as 5 or below) between the medical and General English corpora were considered general lexis items, such as *the*, whose RFP was 1.3 (5.57 FP in medical corpus/4.23 FP in general English corpus). In contrast, words with a very high RFP ratio (defined as 300 or above, i.e., an occurrence of 300 times more in the medical corpus than in the general corpus) and a similar ratio between the medical and small medical corpus were identified as technical terms. Of the 218 words, 92 were general lexis items, 65 were sub-technical terms, and 61 were technical terms.

To identify technical words in anatomy, Chung used an anatomy corpus (the same one with 425,192 tokens used in Chung and Nation (2003) mentioned earlier) and a comparison corpus of general language, three times larger, made up of approximately 1,892,000 tokens from the LOB and Wellington corpora (with all the texts in natural sciences in them excluded). Using the computer program RANGE, Chung identified a total of 66,223 word types in the two corpora. Then, she excluded the 54,867 types that appeared only in the general corpus and used the normalized frequencies of the remaining words and their frequency ratios in the two corpora to rank and group them. Using a frequency ratio of 300 (i.e., an occurrence of 300 times or more in the anatomy corpus than in the general corpus) as the cutoff, Chung identified 4,598 technical words in anatomy.

As an example of the more recent studies that used more sophisticated statistical measures, Periñán-Pascual (2015) proposed and tested an SRC "composite measure" formula that combines three statistical measures: "salience", "relevance", and "cohesion" in identifying technical terms. In simple words, "salience" assesses how prevalent a word is in a subject domain by measuring its frequency in a given text (known as term frequency or TF) in a specialized corpus compared with the inverse proportion of the word in the entire corpus (known as inversed document frequency or IDF). "Relevance" measures how likely the word may actually appear in the specialized domain by comparing its frequency in the specialized corpus with its frequency in a large comparison general corpus. "Cohesion" is used for assessing multiword terms as it measures the degree of association between the words in a multiword unit, i.e., how likely the words in the unit do co-occur. Periñán-Pascual tested the accuracy rate of the SRC composite measure formula coded in DEXTER (Discovering and Extracting TERminology) against the accuracy rate of the S, R, and C individual measures in two experiments. The first experiment involved an English electronics corpus of 520,383 tokens and the second one used a Spanish medical corpus of 197,812 tokens. The results from both experiments showed that the accuracy rate of the SRC composite measure was much higher than that of each of the single measures.

Finally, let us turn to studies that have combined judgment-based methods with corpus-based methods, a practice found in several recent studies (Ha & Hyland, 2017; Kwary, 2011; Peruzzo, 2014; Watson Todd, 2017). Of these studies, Ha and Hyland (2017), Kwary (2011), and Watson Todd (2017) were similar in that they all employed a corpus-based keyword analysis and a judgment rating. Because of their similarity, we look only at Ha and Hyland (2017). In examining technical vocabulary in finance, the two authors employed arguably the most sophisticated rating system so far labeled "Technicality Analysis Model" (TAM), which classifies words into five levels of technicality: "least technical" (words with no specialized meaning in finance, e.g., *comparable*), "slightly technical" (words that have specialized finance meaning that is related to its general meanings, e.g., *capital*), "moderately technical" (words that have a specialized sense that may be remotely related or not related to its general senses, e.g., *exposure*), "very technical", words that have "a specialised sense that is not related to any of its general senses", e.g., *facility* used in the sense of a money borrowing arrangement), and "most technical" (words that have only a special sense without a general meaning, e.g., *escrow*) (Ha & Hyland, 2017, pp. 44–46). To trial this system, they first conducted a keyword analysis using a 6.7-million-word finance corpus with texts from four finance sectors and the academic subcorpus of the BNC Baby as a comparison corpus. It generated a list of 837 keywords that were each "specific to one or two financial sectors" (Ha & Hyland, 2017, p. 40).

Then, the two authors and several graduate students individually rated these keywords by using the TAM and checking the meanings of the words in a general English dictionary and a business English dictionary and, when necessary, reading concordance lines involving the words using WordSmith tools and WordBanks. Because they followed a rigorous level-by-level procedure to decide the technical level of a word by starting from the least to the most technical level, they attained a 95% inter-rater reliability on 100 words randomly from the 837 keywords. Based on their TAM rating, of the 837 words, 672 (82.29%) are lest technical, 42 (5.09%) are slightly technical, 88 (10.51%) are moderately technical, 26 (3.11%) are very technical, and 9 (1.08%) are most technical (Ha & Hyland, 2017, pp. 44–45). Based on their finding "that a word specific to a financial sector is not necessarily technical", Ha and Hyland (2017, p. 44) argue that "technicality and specificity are distinct concepts". However, it is very important to note that while the use of a sophisticated rating scale helps make the identification decisions more valid and reliable, the decisions so made are still subjective and susceptible to errors as admitted by Ha and Hyland (2017, p. 45). Finally, a brief mention of Peruzzo (2014) is in order because her study did not use a rating scale in her combined method, but she incorporated the use of a semi-automatic term extraction with the use of "an event template" she developed based on a frame-based terminology model with the assistance of experts. The template covers all aspects related to a crime event, such as *victim*, *offender*, and *harm*.

The Role and Importance of Technical Vocabulary in Language Use and Learning

Corpus studies on vocabulary use in specialized texts have shown that a significant portion (between 20% and 30%) of the vocabulary in such writing is composed of technical vocabulary (Nation, 2013). Besides being shown in the studies already mentioned earlier (e.g., Chung & Nation, 2004), such a finding has also been reported in many other studies, including Lei and Liu's (2016) study on the vocabulary use in a medical research article corpus and a medical textbook corpus. The results in Lei and Liu (2016, p. 49) reveal that medicine-specific vocabulary (including both high-frequency words with special medical meanings and low-frequency technical medical vocabulary) accounts for 31.75% of the tokens in the medical research article corpus and 30.44% in the medical textbook corpus. Given such a high percentage of technical words in specialized language, such as EAP and ESP, it is necessary for learners of such language to grasp these words, considering especially that research has shown that to fully understand a text, particularly an academic text, a reader needs to know about 98% of the running words in a text (Hu & Nation, 2000; Schmitt, Jiang, & Grabe, 2011).

Furthermore, research has also demonstrated that knowing technical vocabulary is indispensable for developing subject knowledge. For example, Woodward-Kron's (2008) longitudinal study of undergraduate education majors' learning and use of subject knowledge in education reveals the high importance of understanding technical vocabulary. The subject knowledge Woodward examined was related to child development and theories about thinking and learning in children. The major source of data were six students' writing assignments on the aforementioned topics. Via a close analysis of the students' writing, including their definitions and use of technical terms, such as *egocentric, scaffolding, ZPD* (Zone of Proximal Development), and *Triarchic theory of intelligence*, Woodward finds that understanding technical terms is imperative in students' learning of specialist knowledge. She makes the point clear by stating that "learning specialist knowledge in pre-service teacher education involves adopting technical terms as well as coming to terms with the abstract dimension of the discourse" (Woodward-Kron, 2008, p. 234).

A good grasp of technical vocabulary is also essential in professional communication (e.g., Knoch, 2014). In a study on ESL aviation test takers' technical English skills, Knoch (2014) had ten experienced native-English-speaking pilots listen and assess the recorded performance (speech samples) of nine non-native aviation test takers. The assessment included a writing and speaking component (a written questionnaire and a group oral interview). The results indicate that the understanding and use of technical vocabulary was considered by the rating pilots to be extremely important in aviation communication, as can be evidenced by the following quotes from two of the pilots in their assessment of the performance of the test takers being evaluated: "*they* [test takers] *understood what they were talking about . . . and all the relevant aviation type terms were there* [comment by #8 pilot-rater; underline added]. . . . *I could understand him and he put enough* [technical] *information out to give me confidence . . .* [comment by #3 pilot-rater]" (Knoch, 2014, p. 84).

Finally, there are two additional reasons that technical vocabulary deserves special attention in language learning. First, L2 learners often experience great difficulty in grasping such vocabulary due to, among other reasons, the low overall frequency of many technical words in general language and the specialized meanings of those polysemous technical words with a high-frequency use in nontechnical senses (Coxhead, Demecheleer, & McLaughlin, 2016; Watson Todd, 2017; Woodward-Kron, 2008). The latter technical words are especially challenging because learners often find their technical meanings opaque (Watson Todd, 2017). The other additional reason that technical vocabulary deserves special attention is the fact that with rapid advancements in various fields and technology in general, new technical words emerge constantly. In other words, learners and professionals alike have to learn technical words continuously. In fact, the study of technical terms is so important that "[t]erminology is [now] part of the programs of several university degrees and postgraduate courses (Translating and Interpreting, Applied Languages, Information Science)" (Alcina, 2009/2011, p. 1).

Strategies and Methods for Learning and Teaching Technical Vocabulary

Historically, some language educators (e.g., Cowan, 1974) did not think that it was a language teacher's job and/or it was within his/her ability to teach technical vocabulary due to their lack of knowledge in the technical subject. However, today, with better understandings of technical vocabulary and its importance as well as more effective methods to teach such words, most experts and teachers believe that specialized words can and "should be taught and studied in a variety of complementary ways" and language teachers "may be able to make a useful contribution" in this regard (Nation, 2013, pp. 32, 305; see also Fernández, Flórez de la Colina, & Peters, 2009). Through proper training and/or self-study, language teachers may be able to develop adequate knowledge in a technical field and can learn strategies and methods to help learners more effectively acquire technical vocabulary (Alcina, 2009/2011). In fact, there has been an increased interest in the teaching of technical vocabulary as evidenced by quite a few recent studies that explore effective ways for teaching technical vocabulary (Ardasheva & Tretter, 2017; Fernández et al., 2009; Gablasova, 2015) and a special issue of the journal *Terminology* devoted to the topic (Alcina, 2009/2011).

Based on recent research (Alcina, 2009; Fernández et al., 2009), the most useful strategy in teaching technical vocabulary is to engage learners in active meaningful learning activities, such as having learners identify technical terms and build term banks in their field on their own. The teacher only serves as a facilitator. Meaningful learning also calls for studying technical words in context, rather than in isolation (although the latter can be helpful in some ways and with some technical words). This is because contextual information may often enable learners to figure out and better understand the meanings of technical words (Nation, 2013). Also, studying technical words in context enables learners to learn the typical collocates of such words, which is very important because, like words in general, technical words often have their typical collocates (Nazar, 2016). Technical corpora and online technical data sources including terminology banks/bases have been found especially useful for context-based learning of the meanings and typical collocates of technical words (Alcina, 2009; Fernández et al., 2009). These tools can provide learners with the opportunity and resources to identify and compile their own technical word lists or banks (Fernández et al., 2009).

As another example of active learning, it will be very effective to explore and understand the connections between the technical meanings of polysemous technical words and their core meanings, connections that often exist in this group of technical words (Nation, 2013). For instance, the medical stoppage/cessation meaning of the word *arrest* in *cardiac arrest* and *respiratory arrest* is a metaphorical extension of its more commonly known meaning of seizing and putting a person in custody because when a person is arrested, his/her normal life activities come to a stop or are stopped. Teachers can have students examine and compare corpus examples of the two uses of such a word and then discuss and uncover the semantic connection between the two meanings. In the case of *arrest*, such a comparison should enable learners to see how the medical meaning of the word is a metaphorical extension of its more commonly known meaning. In fact, research on cognitive linguistics theory-inspired teaching has shown that a focus on the metaphorical extensions in the use of words can make vocabulary teaching significantly more effective (Boers & Demecheleer, 1998; Tyler, 2012). In their respective empirical studies on the teaching of prepositions, Boers and Demecheleer (1998) and Tyler (2012) found that exploring the metaphorical extensions in the use of prepositions significantly enhanced the participating students' correct understanding and use of the prepositions they were learning. Similar positive results should be expected for using such an approach in teaching the meanings of many technical words.

There are also some tested or proven useful practices for learning and teaching technical terms. For example, the teaching of affixes of terms of Latin or Greek origin, such as the teaching of the prefixes *inter* vs. *intra* in terms like *internet* and *intranet* and teaching of the suffixes *cide* and *logy* in *herbicide* and *physiology* (Brieger & Pohl, 2002). One other long-time useful practice is the use of technical dictionaries and now technical word lists thanks to the recent publication of many new rigorously developed and pedagogically focused technical word lists in a variety of subjects, including Lei and Liu's (2016) in medicine and Watson Todd's (2017) in engineering. However, with limited study time, learners often need to prioritize words on a list and focus on the most useful items, rather than covering all the items (Watson Todd, 2017). Another reason for doing so is that research has shown that a "deeper focus on fewer words" is much more effective than a general coverage of more words (Ardasheva & Tretter, 2017, p. 256).

Finally, recent research (Ardasheva & Tretter, 2017; Fernández et al., 2009; Gablasova, 2015) has shown the importance of using learner L1 or using a bilingual approach in L2 learning of technical vocabulary. Gablasova (2015) compared two groups of Slovak students learning technical terms: one group was instructed in their L1 and the other was taught in English. The results revealed a clear advantage for the L1 instructed group, as they made fewer errors and showed more complete understanding of the target words on the post-instruction test. The findings seem to suggest that when possible, in L2 learning of technical vocabulary, students may benefit from learning and checking the meanings of the target technical words in their L1.

Future Directions

It can be seen in the preceding discussion that while scholars may continue debating on what technical vocabulary is and exploring its role in language, future work on technical vocabulary will likely focus mostly on how to accurately and efficiently identify technical words and how to effectively learn and teach such words. Next, we discuss some likely future developments related to the latter two issues.

First, regarding the issue of technical vocabulary identification, researchers will continue their effort to develop and find more rigorous, sophisticated, and effective methods of detection and extraction by applying new methods and technology developed in computational and corpus linguistics. There will also be more efforts to incorporate or combine computerized quantitative methods with new theories and tools emerging from qualitative research work, as has been done by Peruzzo (2014). In other words, there will likely be more use of combined methods to identify technical vocabulary. Furthermore, there may be continued work on identifying bilingual technical words using parallel corpora as was done by Macken, Lefever, and Hoste (2013). Also, there will likely be more effort to identify non-nominal technical words, especially technical verbs because, as Faber and L'Homme (2014) pointed out in their study on verbs in technical texts, verbs frame technical concepts (nouns) and are indispensable in our understanding of technical terms.

Concerning the learning and teaching of technical words, first, there surely will be continued endeavor to find more effective teaching strategies and methods, especially those that make use of new technology, corpora, and/or learners' L1. Second, there will be more work in the development of pedagogy-oriented, discipline-specific technical word lists, including sub-discipline lists. This is because research (e.g., Bertels & Speelman, 2014; Grabowski, 2015) has shown that vocabulary use varies significantly even across different sub-field corpora of the same discipline (machining and pharmaceutical respectively in the two cited studies). Also, as bilingual lists have been found particularly useful for L2 learners (Fernández et al., 2009), many of the new word lists will likely be bilingual.

Further Reading

Alcina, A. (Ed.). (2009/2011). Teaching and learning terminology: New strategies and methods. *(special issue)*. *Terminology, 15*. Republished as an anthology (2011). Amsterdam: Benjamins.

This special issue consists of seven articles that introduce new theories and practices in the teaching and learning of terminology or technical terms. It covers the learning of technical terms in several disciplines or areas of study, including architect and construction, law, and translation studies.

Coxhead, A. (2018). *Vocabulary and English for specific purposes research: Quantitative and qualitative perspectives*. London: Routledge.

This recently published book provides a comprehensive coverage of research on the identification and categorization of specialized vocabulary (i.e., academic and technical vocabulary) for ESP as well as the value of specialized vocabulary lists for learning. Particularly worth mentioning is that it has a chapter (Chapter 8) devoted to technical vocabulary in the trades. While technical vocabulary abounds in the trades area, the topic has not received much attention until recently.

Related Topics

Academic vocabulary, high-, mid-, and low-frequency words, measuring depth of vocabulary knowledge, word lists

Note

1 This same rating scale was also employed in identifying technical words in the same anatomy text in Chung (2003), but it was included only for the purpose of evaluating a corpus comparison approach, the focus of this Chung study. In contrast, the use of the scale was the main focus of the Chung and Nation (2003) study. This is the reason that Chung and Nation (2003) is cited in this chapter as an example of a judgment-based method using a scale while Chung (2003) is given as an example of corpus-based method.

References

Ahmad, K., Davies, A., Fulford, H., & Rogers, M. (1994). What is a term? The semi-automatic extraction of terms from text. In M. Snell-Hornby, F. Pochhacker, & K. Kaindl (Eds.), *Translation studies: An interdiscipline* (pp. 267–278). Amsterdam: Benjamins.

Alcina, A. (Ed.). (2009/2011). Teaching and learning terminology: New strategies and methods (special issue). *Terminology, 15*(1). Republished as an anthology (2011). Amsterdam: Benjamins.

Ardasheva, Y., & Tretter, T. R. (2017). Developing science-specific, technical vocabulary of high school newcomer English learners. *International Journal of Bilingual Education and Bilingualism, 20*, 252–271.

Baker, M. (1988). Sub-technical vocabulary and the ESP teacher: An analysis of some rhetorical terms in medical journal articles. *Reading in a Foreign Language, 4*, 91–105.

Bečka, J. V. (1972). The lexical composition of specialised texts and its quantitative aspect. *Prague Studies in Mathematical Linguistics, 4*, 47–64.

Bernier-Colborne, G., & Drouin, P. (2014). Creating a test corpus for term extractors through term annotation. *Terminology, 20*, 50–73.

Bertels, A., & Speelman, D. (2014). Clustering for semantic purposes: Exploration of semantic similarity in a technical corpus. *Terminology, 20*, 279–303.

Boers, F., & Demecheleer, M. (1998). A cognitive semantic approach to teaching prepositions. *ELT Journal, 52*(3), 197–204.

Brieger, N., & Pohl, A. (2002). *Technical English: Vocabulary and grammar*. Andover, UK: Heinle Cengage Learning.

Cabré, M. (1999). *Terminology: Theory, methods, and applications*. Amsterdam: John Benjamins.

Chung, T. M. (2003). A corpus comparison approach for extracting terminology. *Terminology, 9*, 221–245.

Chung, T. M., & Nation, P. (2003). Technical vocabulary in specialised texts. *Reading in a Foreign Language, 15*, 103–116.

Chung, T. M., & Nation, P. (2004). Identifying technical vocabulary. *System, 32*, 251–263.

Cowan, J. R. (1974). Lexical and syntactic research for the design of EFL reading materials. *TESOL Quarterly, 8*(4), 389–400.

Coxhead, A. (2000). A new academic word list. *TESOL Quarterly, 34*(2), 213–238.

Coxhead, A., Demecheleer, M, & McLaughlin, E. (2016). The technical vocabulary of Carpentry: Loads, lists and bearings. *The TESOLANZ Journal, 24*, 38–71.

Faber, P., & L'Homme, P. (2014). Lexical semantic approaches to terminology: An introduction. *Terminology, 20*, 143–150.

Fernández, T., Flórez de la Colina, M. A., & Peters, P. (2009). Terminology and terminography for architecture and building construction. *Terminology, 15*, 10–36.

Gablasova, D. (2015). Learning technical words through L1 and L2: Completeness and accuracy of word meanings. *English for Specific Purposes, 39*, 62–74.

Grabowski, L. (2015). Keywords and lexical bundles within English pharmaceutical discourse: An attempt at a corpus-driven description. *English for Specific Purposes, 28*, 23–33.

Ha, A., & Hyland, K. (2017). What is technicality? A technicality analysis model for EAP vocabulary. *Journal of English for Academic Purposes, 28*, 35–49.

Hu, M., & Nation, P. (2000). Vocabulary density and reading comprehension. *Reading in a Foreign Language, 13*, 403–430.

Kageura, K., & Umino, B. (1996). Methods of automatic term recognition: A review. *Terminology, 3*, 259–289.

Kit, C., & Liu, X. (2008). Measuring mono-word termhood by rank difference via corpus comparison. *Terminology, 14*, 204–229.

Knoch, U. (2014). Using subject specialists to validate an ESP rating scale: The case of the International Civil Aviation Organisation (ICAO) rating scale. *English for Specific Purposes, 33*, 77–86.

Kwary, D. A. (2011). A hybrid method for determining technical vocabulary. *System, 39*, 175–185.

Lei, L., & Liu, D. (2016). A new medical academic word list: A corpus-based study with enhanced methodology. *Journal of English for Academic Purposes, 22*, 42–53.

Macken, L., Lefever, E., & Hoste, V. (2013). TExSIS: Bilingual terminology extraction from parallel corpora using chunk-based alignment. *Terminology, 19*, 1–30.

Nation, I. S. P. (2013). *Learning vocabulary in another language.* Cambridge, UK: Cambridge University.

Nation, I. S. P., & Coxhead, A. (2012). Special purposes vocabulary. In C. A. Chapelle (Ed.), *Encyclopedia of applied linguistics.* Hoboken, NJ: Wiley Blackwell.

Nazar, R. (2016). Distributional analysis applied to terminology extraction: First results in the domain of psychiatry in Spanish. *Terminology, 22*, 141–170.

Periñán-Pascual, C. (2015). The underpinnings of a composite measure for automatic term extraction: The case of SRC. *Terminology, 21*, 151–179.

Peruzzo, K. (2014). Term extraction and management based on event templates: An empirical study on an EU corpus. *Terminology, 20*, 151–170.

Robinson, P. (1980). *ESP (English for specific purposes).* Oxford, UK: Pergamon Press.

Schmitt, N., Jiang, X., & Grabe, W. (2011). The percentage of words known in a text and reading comprehension. *Modern Language Journal, 95*, 26–43.

Simpson-Vlach, R., & Ellis, N. C. (2010). An academic formulas list: New methods in phraseology research. *Applied Linguistics, 31*, 487–512.

Technical Vocabulary (from the webpage of Applied Linguistics Program, University of Warwick). (2017). Retrieved from https://www2.warwick.ac.uk/fac/soc/al/globalpad/openhouse/academicenglishskills/vocabulary/tech/

Tyler, A. (2012). *Cognitive linguistics and second language learning: Theoretical basics and experimental evidence.* London, UK and New York, NY: Routledge.

Watson Todd, R. W. (2017). An opaque engineering word list: Which words should a teacher focus on? *English for Specific Purposes, 45*, 31–39.

Woodward-Kron, R. (2008). More than just jargon: The nature and role of specialist language in learning disciplinary knowledge. *Journal of English for Academic Purposes, 7*, 234–249.

Yang, H. (1986). A new technique for identifying scientific/technical terms and describing science texts. *Literary and Linguistic Computing, 1*, 93–103.

9

Factors Affecting the Learning of Single-Word Items[1]

Elke Peters

Introduction

An important topic in vocabulary research is focused on why some words are more difficult to learn than other words and why some learners are better than others at learning new words. Research has looked to answer questions such as: Is it more difficult for Dutch-speaking learners of English to learn the word *dog* than the word *cat*? Is it easier to learn the more concrete word *house* than the more abstract word *health*? Is a word that occurs more than once in a text easier to learn? Is word learning affected by learners' vocabulary size or working memory?

This chapter discusses factors that affect the learning of single words in a foreign language (FL). Those factors can be related to (1) word properties (*word-related factors*), (2) the use of words in context (*contextual factors*), or (3) individual learner differences (*learner-related factors*). Factors which affect learning multiword units are discussed in the following chapter.

Critical Issues and Topics

Word-Related Factors That Affect the Learning of Single Words

Twenty years ago, Batia Laufer (1997) published the chapter "What's in a Word That Makes It Hard or Easy? Intra-Lexical Factors Affecting Vocabulary Acquisition", in which she discussed the factors that could affect the learning difficulty of a word. Since the publication of that chapter, more studies have explicitly addressed the question of which word-related factors affect the learnability, processing, and use of words. Research in this area looks at the extent to which the learning of FL words is affected by orthographic, phonological, and/ or semantic factors in the L1 or the L2.

Cognates

Cognates have traditionally been defined as words that are phonologically or orthographically, semantically and historically related across languages. In the field of second language acquisition, however, cognates are commonly defined as words with a high form and meaning overlap regardless of the etymology. Such a definition allows for the inclusion of loanwords (Rogers, Webb, & Nakata, 2015). Genetically related languages, such as Germanic languages or Romance languages, share more cognates than non-genetically related languages. An example of a cognate item would be the Dutch word *huis*, the German word *Haus*, and the English word *house*. False cognates or false friends, on the other hand, have a high form overlap, but do not share the same meaning. An example would be the English word *actual* and the Dutch word *actueel* (*current* in English). A cognate is considered easier to learn than a noncognate because the word in the foreign language is similar in form and meaning to the word in the L1. A false cognate, however, is more difficult to learn, because learners may often assume that the L2 word carries the same meaning as the similar L1 form (Bensoussan & Laufer, 1984).

The majority of studies investigating the role of cognates in vocabulary learning have been carried out in psycholinguistic studies focusing on cross-linguistic effects on language *processing* (see Otwinowska, 2016; van Hell & Tanner, 2012). These studies, which have used a wide array of implicit and explicit measures, have shown facilitatory processing for cognates, meaning that cognates are read, recognized, or processed faster and with fewer errors than noncognates (e.g., Van Assche, Duyck, & Brysbaert, 2013).

A handful of studies have compared the *learning* of cognates and noncognates (de Groot & Keijzer, 2000; Lotto & de Groot, 1998; Rogers et al., 2015; Tonzar, Lotto, & Job, 2009). These studies, using paired-associate learning (PAL), in which learners had to learn a list of cognates and a list of noncognates, showed that form recall was better overall for cognates than for noncognates (de Groot & Keijzer, 2000; Lotto & de Groot, 1998; Rogers et al., 2015; Tonzar et al., 2009); meaning recall was higher for cognates than for noncognates (de Groot & Keijzer, 2000), and retrieval times were faster for cognates than for noncognates (de Groot & Keijzer, 2000; Lotto & de Groot, 1998). Findings also suggest that knowledge of cognates might be more durable than that of noncognates (Rogers et al., 2015). However, Tonzar et al.'s (2009) study indicated that the cognate facilitation effect might level off with more exposure. In spite of the limited number of studies investigating the learnability of cognates and noncognates, the beneficial effect of cognates seems to be relatively uniform across age groups and languages.

The number of studies investigating the effect of cognateness on incidental vocabulary acquisition from different modes of input (written, aural, or audio-visual input) is very limited. Vidal (2003, 2011) studied the role of cognateness in incidental vocabulary learning through reading and listening to academic texts. She showed that in reading, as well as in listening, learners are more likely to learn words that are similar to words in their L1. At the same time, her findings indicated that the effect of cognates might be larger in spoken than in written texts. Vidal (2011) stated that cognates have a "a clearer facilitative effect for listeners" than for readers (p. 246). In a study focusing on incidental vocabulary acquisition through viewing TV, Peters and Webb (2018) explored whether word learning would be mediated by cognateness. Their findings showed that the odds of picking up a cognate were higher than the odds of learning a noncognate, although the magnitude of the effect depended on the word knowledge aspect tested. Together, those three studies suggest that the beneficial effect of cognates holds for written, spoken, and audio-visual input, albeit with a larger impact in spoken modalities. Perhaps learners rely more on cognates when processing spoken input because they cannot go back to a previous word to derive its meaning as they can with written input.

Less is known about learners' spontaneous *use* of cognates in speech or writing. One study investigating young ESL learners' use of cognates in written production (Horst &

Collins, 2006) found a decrease in the number of cognates used over time (i.e., after 400 hours of instruction). The findings showed that learners relied more on cognate lower-frequency words than on noncognate high-frequency words (i.e., words belonging to the 1,000 most frequent words) at the beginning of a course, but that was no longer true at the end of the course. Likewise, Bardel and Lindqvist (2011) found that less advanced learners used a considerable number of low-frequency cognates. Finally, *false* cognates have been shown to be a frequent source of errors in FL production (Ringbom, 1982, as cited in Laufer, 1991).

It should also be pointed out here that a cognate facilitation effect has been attested in vocabulary tests (Cobb, 2000; Elgort, 2012; Laufer & McLean, 2016; Puimège & Peters, 2019b; Willis & Ohashi, 2012). Generally, the number of correct responses for test items is higher for those that are cognates than noncognates. Cobb (2000) demonstrated that French-speaking test takers were able to answer English-French cognate test items correctly without having been exposed to those items in English before. Additionally, the cognate effect seems to be stronger for low-proficiency learners than high-proficiency learners (Laufer & McLean, 2016) and for low-frequency-items compared to high-frequency items (Elgort, 2012). However, Laufer and Levitzky-Aviad (2018) recently showed that the inclusion of cognates makes a negligible difference in test scores overall.

The studies reviewed above provide robust evidence for the facilitative effect of cognates on the processing and learning of new words, although its effect might be modulated by other factors, such as type of input and learners' proficiency level.

Words That Are Similar in Form or Meaning

Words can have a similar form (spelling, sound), or meaning in the L1 or L2. Synforms are words that are similar in form, e.g., *adopt/adapt, economic/economical, capable/capacious,* or *considerable/considerate.* It was Laufer (1988, 1991) who first coined the term *synform* to refer to different types of form similarity, such as synphones (similar sounding words), syngraphs (script similarity) and synmorphs (similar morphological structure). Laufer (1991, 1997) distinguished between general synformic similarity and specific synformic similarity. The former refers to the characteristics shared by all synforms (e.g., the identical number of syllables of the words, the identical stress patterns and part of speech), whereas the latter was classified into ten types of synforms, each representing a different type of similarity between two words. Laufer argues that form similarity can cause problems in reading comprehension as well as in production. The most difficult synforms are those that only differ in their suffix (e.g., *economic/economical, industrial/industrious*) and in their vowels (e.g., *adopt/adapt, proceed/precede*). Laufer proposes that similar words should not be taught together because their similarity in form might lead to cross-association and prevent learners from establishing a strong form-meaning link. At the same time, synforms deserve explicit teaching time, because learners might not notice the formal differences between them. The distinction between similar words is thus best taught at a later stage after the words have been learned separately.

Another issue that should be addressed here is what Laufer (1997) calls deceptive transparency. She argued that English morphemes can be deceptive because words sometimes look as if they consist of meaningful morphemes, whereas the different parts of the word are not real morphemes. For instance, the verb *retreat* can be misinterpreted as *treat again.* Learners assume that the verb form consists of the prefix *re-* meaning *again* and of the verb *treat* meaning *try to cure* and thus fail to recognize the word *retreat* as an unfamiliar word. Similarly, the adjective *consensual* might be divided into the morphemes *con-* (*with, together*) and *sensual* (*related to feelings or physical pleasure*) instead of being linked to the verb *consent*, from which it is derived.

The learning difficulty of a word is also determined by its pronounceability, i.e., similarity (or not) in spoken form. Foreign language learners are faced with FL phonemes that are not used in their L1, e.g., the English dental fricatives /q/ and /ð/ for <th> are absent in Dutch. As a result, words such as *thane*, *thank*, and *these* will be harder to learn than words that accord with the phonotactic patterns in Dutch. Similarly, it might be difficult for Dutch-speaking learners of English to learn the difference in pronunciation between *bed* /bed/ and *bad* /bæd/, because the latter vowel sound is not used in Dutch. FL learners should thus recognize those phonemes that are not found in their L1, distinguish them from other phonemes, and learn how to pronounce them. Perhaps the most influential study in this area was by Ellis and Beaton (1993a) who found that the ease of productive learning (learning the L2 word form) is determined by the degree to which phonotactic patterns of the L2 words match those of the L1. The more the pronunciation of the L2 word is in line with the learner's expectations of the phonotactic sequences in their L1, the easier the word will be to learn. In addition, phonological clustering (phonological similarity across L2 words) does not seem to hinder word learning (Wilcox & Medina, 2013), because the repetition of phonemes is argued to reduce learners' cognitive load.

Words can also be similar to other L2 words in terms of meaning or be semantically related to other L2 words. Webb (2007b) found that it was easier to learn synonyms (words with approximately the same meaning) of known words than to learn new words without a known synonym. However, synonymy did not facilitate learning of all word knowledge aspects. Further, the facilitative effect of synonymy does not entail that semantically related words should be taught together at the same time. Research has shown that grouping new words in semantic clusters (e.g., *oak*, *maple*, *birch*) tends to hinder word learning (Tinkham, 1993; Waring, 1997; Wilcox & Medina, 2013) because of interference effects; the presentation of words that are too similar might result in competing memory traces (Higa, 1963). Yet, in a recent study, Nakata and Suzuki (2018) did not find support for the fact that semantically related words are more difficult to learn, although they did find more interference errors in the learning phase of the semantically related words.

Word Length

Word length has received less attention in vocabulary research. One well-known study that investigated word length was Ellis and Beaton (1993a), who found a negative correlation between word length (number of letters) and word learning, but more so in productive learning than in receptive learning. In a more recent study (Barclay, 2017), word length (number of letters) was shown to affect the extent as well as the speed of learning. However, word length only affected meaning recall and not meaning recognition. Barcroft and Rott (2010) found that after a learning session, learners were able to produce more two-syllable words than three-syllable words. However, looking at incidental vocabulary acquisition from audio-visual input, Puimège and Peters (2019a) found that longer words (number of syllables) are more likely to be learned (form recall) than shorter words. This might seem counterintuitive at first sight, but given that it is more difficult to segment spoken input than written input, longer words might be more salient and noticeable than shorter words or one-syllable words. Finally, Willis and Ohashi (2012) investigated which factors could explain Japanese learners' knowledge of English words. To the best of our knowledge, this is the only study that operationalized word length in three ways: as the number of letters, syllables, and phonemes. All three measures correlated negatively with word knowledge, meaning that test takers knew more short words than long words, but word length operationalized as the number of phonemes was the best predictor of the three.

One explanation why longer words might be more difficult is that they allow for more phonotactic and orthographic variation (Ellis & Beaton, 1993a). However, longer words can be morphologically transparent, making a word such as *interdisciplinary* not intrinsically more difficult than *bun*, as argued by Laufer (1997). A further complicating factor is that at least in English, frequent words tend to be short(er) words, making it difficult to separate the two variables. It is clear that more research in which word length is properly isolated is needed if we want to draw firm conclusions on the effect of word length in different learning settings, such as list learning or incidental vocabulary acquisition.

Part of Speech

There are a number of reasons why learning foreign language nouns, verbs, or adjectives might not be the same. One reason is that verbs appear in more different forms than nouns and adjectives because verbs can be marked for number (e.g., *is – are*), person (e.g., *walk – walks*), or tense (e.g., *walk – walked, sing – sang*). Secondly, nouns differ from verbs in lexical properties, such as hypernymy, concreteness, imageability, meaningfulness, and polysemy (Crossley, Subtirelu, & Salsbury, 2013). In general, nouns refer to entities and as such are more specific, concrete, imageable, meaningful, and unambiguous. Verbs, on the other hand, are inherently relational – barring some exceptions (*to rain*), and as a consequence are more abstract, polysemous, less imageable, less meaningful, and less concrete. To understand and learn the meaning of a verb, learners thus need to rely on contextual clues (syntagmatic relationship), indicating that verb meaning is probably established at the clause level. "To know the verb properly, the learner needs to know its collocations too" (Nissen & Henriksen, 2006, p. 402). Like verbs, adjectives are relational categories, which obtain their specific meaning from the noun they modify. Adjectives are "semantically underspecified if isolated" (Nissen & Henriksen, 2006, p. 402), making their learning potentially more difficult.

The research evidence for a part of speech effect on word learning, however, is limited. Ellis and Beaton (1993a) found that nouns are easier to learn than verbs regardless of the learning method (keyword, free learning, with or without imagery mediation), but they also found that nouns are more imageable than verbs. The facilitative effect of nouns could thus be an imageability effect (Ellis & Beaton, 1993b). In a study that controlled for concreteness of the target items, Barclay (2017) did not find an effect of part of speech, neither in the posttests nor in the attrition of word knowledge, which could indicate that it is not part of speech, but concreteness or imageability that affects the learning ease of words.

Few studies have looked at the effect of part of speech on incidental vocabulary acquisition. In a study using a comic book, Horst and Meara (1999) found a clear learning advantage for nouns compared to verbs, adjectives, and adverbs, which may be explained by the visual support of the book illustrations in their reading treatment. They argue that the comic book functioned as a picture dictionary for many items. However, it seems reasonable to assume that the reported effect of word class might also stem from the items' concreteness because concrete words in particular will benefit from visually supported input. Although it did not specifically target different grammatical classes, the case study by Pigada and Schmitt (2006) could be considered relevant because they reported the learning gains for nouns and verbs in an extensive reading experiment. Their findings showed better learning gains for verbs where spelling and meaning recall were concerned, but not where grammatical knowledge was concerned (i.e., giving the article *le/la* for nouns and the correct preposition for verbs). Compared to verbs, nouns also needed more encounters for learning of meaning to occur. However, care should be taken not to overgeneralize these findings because only one learner participated in the case study. Van Zeeland and Schmitt (2013) showed that part of speech had an effect on incidental vocabulary acquisition through listening. Nouns were easier to learn than verbs and adjectives in the three tests used (form recognition, grammar recognition, and meaning recall).

Taken together, the evidence for a word class effect on the learnability of words is still inconclusive. This may in part be explained by the methodological differences between the studies, but also by other confounding variables, such as concreteness or imageability.

Concreteness and Imageability

Concreteness was already hinted at in the previous section as a potentially confounding variable with part of speech. In this chapter, we will not distinguish between concreteness and imageability because both variables are highly correlated (Crossley, Kyle, & Salsbury, 2016; de Groot, 2006). Concrete words (words referring to concrete entities) tend to be words that are easy to imagine, whereas abstract words (words referring to abstract entities) are words that are often difficult to imagine.

Concreteness has been investigated in intervention studies and corpus studies. Studies using paired-associate learning (PAL) have shown that concrete words are more readily recalled than abstract words (Ellis & Beaton, 1993b; Lawson & Hogben, 1998). de Groot and Keijzer (2000) extended these findings in a highly controlled list learning experiment focusing on the effect of concrete and abstract words on several measures: receptive as well as productive learning, reaction times, and forgetting. They found that concrete words were easier to learn than abstract words (i.e., they needed fewer retrievals or practice). Secondly, higher recall scores were revealed for concrete words than abstract words, both in terms of receptive and in terms of productive learning. Also, more forgetting occurred for abstract words than for concrete words. Finally, concrete words were retrieved faster than abstract words. This means that concreteness affected the speed of learning, the speed of processing and the breadth of learning. The facilitative effect of concreteness was corroborated in a later list learning study (de Groot, 2006).

Concrete words have also been shown to be easier to learn in incidental vocabulary learning studies. The facilitative effect of nouns in Horst and Meara's (1999) study could be attributed to these words' concreteness rather than their grammatical class. Comparing the effectiveness of sentence reading and writing, Pichette, de Serres, and Lafontaine (2012) found that concrete words were better recalled than abstract words in an immediate post-test, regardless of the treatment. However, in a delayed posttest, higher scores were only found for concrete words in the writing activity. Elgort and Warren (2014) demonstrated that concreteness also affected word learning (meaning recall) when learners had read several chapters from a nonfiction book. Additionally, concreteness had an effect on learners' tacit lexical knowledge, as measured in a lexical decision task. In a large-scale study with young learners that explored incidental vocabulary learning from out-of-school exposure, Puimège and Peters (2019b) found that concreteness was a significant predictor of learning at the level of meaning recognition. Recently, three studies using aural input found a positive effect of concreteness on word learning and word use (Crossley et al., 2016; Puimège & Peters, 2019a; van Zeeland & Schmitt, 2013). Van Zeeland and Schmitt (2013), using four listening passages, found an advantage for concrete words over abstract words at three levels of word learning: form recognition, grammar recognition, and meaning recall. Similarly, Puimège and Peters (2019a) found a positive relationship between concreteness and incidental word learning from audio-visual input (form recall). Finally, analyzing naturalistic data, Crossley et al. (2016) argued that concreteness was an important predictor of lexical acquisition, which was measured as learners' spontaneous use of words in speech. As learners progressed over time, they used fewer concrete words and more abstract words. Finally, changes in the use of concrete words also correlated with an increase in overall proficiency, indicating that concreteness could be considered an aspect of L2 lexical proficiency. Taken together, the studies reviewed here point to a learning advantage of concrete words over abstract words.

Polysemy and Homonymy

In addition to learning new words, FL learners are also faced with the challenge of learning new meanings of known word forms. Such word forms can be either polysemous words or homonyms. Polysemous words are words with multiple, related meanings, whereas homonyms are words with distinct, unrelated meanings. An example of the former would be *mouth*, which can refer to (1) the part of your face, (2) the entrance of a cave, (3) place where a river meets the ocean/sea, or (4) the top part of a bottle. *Bank* (*river bank* vs. *money bank*) would be an example of a homonym. High-frequency words tend to be more polysemous than low-frequency words (Crossley, Salsbury, & McNamara, 2010).

Research findings suggest that polysemous words might be difficult to learn. Saemen (1970, as cited in Nation, 2013) found that polysemy might be a difficulty-inducing factor in guessing the meaning from context. Learners had more difficulty guessing the meaning of a polysemous item when the real word was used than when a non-word was used because learners tended to adhere to the meaning(s) they were familiar with. Similarly, Bensoussan and Laufer (1984) showed that learners performed worse at guessing the meanings of polysemes than of other words because they applied "preconceived notions" instead of using the context to infer the meaning. Moreover, polysemy was the most frequent cause of incorrect guessing, which illustrates that learning a new meaning of a familiar word does not come automatically. To decrease the likelihood of incorrect guessing, learners could be offered the core meaning of unfamiliar polysemous words (Verspoor & Lowie, 2003) when they have to infer the figurative meaning. Verspoor and Lowie (2003) report that guessing the figurative meaning through knowledge of a core sense allows for more precise elaboration and hence, a stronger form-meaning link between the new, figurative meaning and the known word form.

Two longitudinal studies, albeit with different methodologies examined how polysemy is related to lexical development. Schmitt (1998) tested three participants' lexical growth at regular intervals over the course of a year. The findings showed how difficult it is to make progress in knowledge of the meanings of a word. Despite considerable learning gains at the beginning, hardly any new meanings were learned during the 12 months of the study. This might be related to the difficulties learners experience in discovering more peripheral and figurative meanings of the words whose core meanings they already know. Crossley et al.'s (2010) findings seem to partially parallel those of Schmitt (1998). At the initial stages of learning, learners were able to use new, frequent and polysemous words in spoken interaction, but only in their core meanings. They did not produce multiple meanings of those words. It was only after four months that word meaning expansion in learners' spontaneous speech could be noticed. Even though we do not know whether at the beginning learners knew the other meanings of the words analyzed, the study does show that learners first used words' core meanings before extending their use to new meanings for those words. This finding differs from Schmitt (1998), who did not find many gains in multiple word meanings over the course of one year. However, given the different methodologies used in the two studies (assessing vocabulary *knowledge* by means of vocabulary tests vs. analyzing learners' *use* of words in spontaneous speech), care should be taken when directly comparing the findings of the two studies, as knowledge and use are different word knowledge aspects

Conclusion

Twenty years after Laufer's (1997) chapter on word difficulty, research has added to our understanding of word-related factors that affect the learning, processing, and use of words. Table 9.1 summarizes the main findings of the studies reviewed.

Contextual Factors That Affect the Learning of Single Words

The learning of single words can also be affected by the way words are used in context. For instance, the informativeness of the context in which a word is used has been found to positively affect word learning (Webb, 2008). A considerable amount of research has focused on the effect of multiple occurrences of words in input (frequency of occurrence). Additionally, research has explored how L2 frequency and to a lesser extent L1 frequency of words might facilitate or hinder word learning.

Frequency of Occurrence

There is robust evidence that repeated encounters with unknown words in written input, and in written input followed by vocabulary-focused activities contribute to vocabulary learning (Godfroid et al., 2018; Horst, Cobb, & Meara, 1998; Laufer & Rozovski-Roitblat, 2011; Pellicer-Sánchez & Schmitt, 2010; Peters, Hulstijn, Sercu, & Lutjeharms, 2009; Rott, 1999; Webb, 2007a). Most reading studies indicate that considerable learning gains can occur after eight to ten encounters. However, different aspects of knowledge might need different numbers of encounters. For example, Webb (2007a) found that to gain productive knowledge of words a greater number of encounters were needed than to gain receptive knowledge. Recent evidence from eye-tracking studies (Elgort, Brysbaert, Stevens, & Van Assche, 2018; Godfroid et al., 2018; Mohamed, 2018; Pellicer-Sánchez, 2016) has shown that repeated

Table 9.1 Facilitative and difficulty-inducing factors for word learning, processing, and use

Facilitative factors	Difficulty-inducing factors	Inconclusive
Cognates	False cognates	
Phonotactic regularity	No phonotactic regularity	
	Synformy	
		Word length
		Part of speech
Morphological transparency	Deceptive morphological transparency	
Concrete words	Abstract words	
One form, one meaning	Polysemy/homonymy	

encounters also result in faster reading times of new words. In contrast to the findings of the aforementioned studies, Webb and Chang (2015a) did not find a relationship between frequency of occurrence and learning gains in an extensive reading-while-listening setting (13 weeks), possibly because of the larger time gap between learners' encountering words in the input and the test.

Research investigating the effect of frequency in listening studies is far more limited. Vidal (2003) found that frequency of occurrence in spoken text predicted word learning, but other word-related factors explained more variance. In a follow-up study (Vidal, 2011), this finding was corroborated, but this time it was also revealed that the effect of frequency of occurrence was much smaller in listening compared to reading. Finally, van Zeeland and Schmitt (2013) showed that frequency of occurrence (3, 7, 11, or 15 occurrences) did not affect all aspects of word knowledge (form recognition, grammar, meaning recall) in the same way. Further, they only found a weak frequency effect in the immediate posttests.

The effect of frequency of occurrence has also been investigated in three TV viewing studies. In his longitudinal study, Rodgers and Webb (in press) found a small correlation between frequency and word learning when a tough test was used (multiple choice test with distractors sharing aspects of the form and meaning with the correct answer), but not in a sensitive test (a multiple choice test with distractors not semantically related to the correct answer). In a study comparing the effect of L1 subtitles and captions, Peters, Heynen, and Puimège (2016) found that frequency of occurrence contributed positively to the learning gains made through viewing a video clip, but its effect was related to learners' prior vocabulary knowledge. Finally, the positive effect of frequency of occurrence on vocabulary learning from audio-visual input was also found in a study by Peters and Webb (2018).

Frequency of occurrence has also been addressed in deliberate vocabulary learning studies in which learners were given the opportunity to retrieve new words (Barcroft, 2007) or were asked to retrieve and use new words in vocabulary-focused activities during one learning session (Nakata, 2017; Peters, 2014). In line with the incidental vocabulary acquisition studies, frequency of occurrence (or retrieval) has been shown to facilitate vocabulary learning gains in the short term (Folse, 2006) as well as in the long term (Nakata, 2017; Peters, 2012, 2014). Both Nakata and Peters found that five retrievals resulted in significantly higher learning gains than one or three retrievals. The studies discussed here all focused on the effect of frequency of occurrence within one learning session. Although some research has looked at spacing or frequency of occurrence over time, research into the effect of spacing in deliberate vocabulary learning has yielded mixed findings. In a number of studies, Nakata and colleagues (Nakata, 2015; Nakata & Suzuki, 2018; Nakata & Webb, 2016) found that expanding spacing resulted in slightly higher learning gains than equal spacing, especially if the words are semantically unrelated. Yet, Schuetze (2015) only found an effect on short-term gains and more so for content words compared to function words. It seems that more research is warranted into how word features interact with spacing effects.

L1 Frequency

An underinvestigated factor that could affect the learning difficulty of a FL word is the frequency of the corresponding L1 word. De Groot and her colleagues investigated L1 frequency in a number of studies, all using paired-associate learning (de Groot, 2006; de Groot & Keijzer, 2000; Lotto & de Groot, 1998). They found that L1 frequency had a small effect on word learning, but its effect diminished with more retrieval practice (more learning occurrences). Further, it was shown that target words paired with infrequent L1 words were more easily forgotten than target words paired with frequent words. The facilitative effect of L1 frequency is explained in terms of concept familiarity, i.e., familiar concepts will be encountered more frequently than less familiar concepts. As a result, these concepts are more firmly entrenched in the mental lexicon, making it easier to link a new FL word form to a familiar, well-stored concept. The influence of L1 frequency on learners' use of L2 words has not received much attention yet. An exception is Paquot's (2017) corpus study that showed how learners' use of lexical bundles was influenced by the L1 frequency of the lexical bundles. Learners preferred to use lexical bundles in English that had a frequent L1 equivalent. Whether this finding also holds for single words is still an open question.

L2 Frequency

Vocabulary researchers have placed great emphasis on word frequency in the language (L2), as a model for vocabulary learning and vocabulary development. L2 frequency is mostly operationalized as corpus-derived frequency, whereby corpus frequency is considered a proxy for learners' exposure to L2 input. The frequency-based account of vocabulary learning holds that high-frequency words are normally learned before low-frequency words (Ellis, 2002). Further, Puimège and Peters (2019b) showed that the relationship between word knowledge and frequency became stronger with age. It seems that learners get more sensitive to frequency patterns as they have more contact with English-language input. The frequency-based pattern of acquisition is also the rationale behind the development of frequency-based vocabulary tests, which sample items from different frequency bands of 1,000 words. The two most well-known examples (for English) are probably the Vocabulary Levels Test (Nation, 1990, Schmitt, Schmitt, & Clapham, 2001) and the Vocabulary Size Test (Nation & Beglar, 2007). Such tests tend to show an implicational scale in the test sections that correspond to different 1,000-word frequency bands, which means that test takers commonly obtain lower scores on sections testing low-frequency words than on sections targeting high-frequency words (see Batista & Horst, 2016, for a French frequency-based test and Schmitt et al., 2001, for an English frequency-based test). This implicational scale in test results is often seen as evidence for the frequency-based model of vocabulary learning. Of course, deviations from this frequency pattern are possible in contexts where learners are rarely exposed to authentic FL input and where learners' main source of input is the teacher and the textbook (Milton, 2007). Corpus analyses of English textbooks have shown that textbooks contain a large proportion of low-frequency words (Bardel et al., 2012; Milton & Vassiliu, 2000, as cited in Milton, 2007), which could explain why some learners might know more words from a lower frequency band (e.g., the 5,000 most frequent words) than words from a higher frequency band (e.g., the 3,000 most frequent words).

Corpus studies have also investigated whether a frequency pattern is attested in learners' spontaneous *use* of words. The findings suggest that more proficient writers tend to use fewer words from the first 1,000 words in English than less proficient writers (Laufer & Nation, 1995). Further, the use of low-frequency words in writing texts is often considered a feature of proficiency. For instance, FL learners' essays that contain more low-frequency words tend to receive higher scores than essays with more high-frequency words (Crossley, Salsbury, McNamara, & Jarvis, 2011). However, a word of caution is in order here because not *using* a word in writing or speech does not entail that learners do not *know* the word, as productive vocabulary use has been shown to develop at a slower rate than productive vocabulary knowledge (Laufer & Paribakht, 1998).

Learner-Related Factors That Affect the Learning of Single Words

Although several learner-related factors, such as learners' topic familiarity or background knowledge (Pulido, 2004, 2007), inferencing skills (Hulstijn, 1993), or language aptitude (Li, 2016), have been investigated in relation to the learning of single words, this section will focus only on the role of learners' prior vocabulary knowledge and working memory for reasons of space.

Learners' Prior Vocabulary Knowledge

Learners with a larger vocabulary size tend to understand reading and listening texts better than learners with a smaller vocabulary size (Laufer & Ravenhorst-Kalovski, 2010; Noreillie, Kestemont, Heylen, Desmet, & Peters, 2018; Stæhr, 2009; Schmitt, Jiang, & Grabe, 2011). Similarly, it has been shown that prior vocabulary knowledge also plays a role in incidental vocabulary acquisition from reading. Horst et al. (1998) revealed that there was a positive correlation between prior knowledge and learning gains, albeit not a strong one. Webb and Chang (2015b) carried out a longitudinal study which focused on vocabulary learning through extensive reading. They also found an effect of prior vocabulary knowledge on incidental vocabulary acquisition, as higher-level participants learned significantly more words than lower-level participants.

The role of prior vocabulary knowledge has been addressed in a limited number of TV viewing studies, but its effect seems to be less consistent than in reading studies. Studies on vocabulary learning from watching short subtitled (L1 or L2 subtitles) video clips (Montero Perez, Peters, Clarebout, & Desmet, 2014; Montero Perez, Peters, & Desmet, 2018; Peters et al., 2016; Puimège & Peters, 2019a) showed a positive correlation between prior vocabulary knowledge and vocabulary learning for most but not all word knowledge aspects. Using a full-length one-hour TV documentary, Peters and Webb (2018) found that learners with more prior vocabulary knowledge picked up more words incidentally at the level of meaning recall as well as at the level of meaning recognition. In contrast, Rodgers (2013) did not find that learners with greater vocabulary knowledge learned more words through extensive TV viewing than learners with less vocabulary knowledge.

Working Memory

Researchers have been interested in the relationship between learners' working memory and vocabulary learning in order to explain why some learners are better than others at learning new words. Working memory entails storage (phonological short-term memory, or PSTM) as well as storage and manipulation of information (complex working memory, or WM). The former is commonly measured by non-word repetition or forward digit span tasks, whereas the latter is typically measured by a backward digit span, or a reading or listening span task (Kormos & Sáfár, 2008). One of the most well-known models of working memory is Baddeley's (2003) model, which consists of the central executive, the audio-visual sketchpad, and the phonological loop. The latter in particular has been argued to be important for vocabulary learning (Juffs & Harrington, 2011). For instance, a strong relationship has been found between phonological short-term memory (non-word repetition) and L1 vocabulary knowledge (Gathercole, 2006).

Although most research into the role of PSTM and/or WM in L2 vocabulary point to a positive relationship between PSTM and/or WM on the one hand and vocabulary learning on the other, it should be noted that data in these studies were collected in very different ways: in learners' test performance (Kormos & Sáfár, 2008; Speciale, Ellis, & Bywater, 2004), in learners' deliberate learning of new words (Elgort, Candry, Boutorwick, Eyckmans, & Brysbaert, 2016; Martin & Ellis, 2012), and in learners' incidental learning of new words (Montero Perez, 2018). Second, different measures have been used to tap into PSTM and WM (e.g., a listening span task in Speciale, Ellis, & Bywater, 2004, a backward digit span task in Montero Perez, 2018) (see Juffs & Harrington, 2011, for an overview of different WM measures).

Even though there is generally a positive link with vocabulary learning, the effects of PSTM or WM might differ depending on the proficiency level of the learners, as was shown in the study by Kormos and Sáfár (2008), who found no link between PSTM and vocabulary use, as measured in a standardized test, in the case of beginners. Further, the effects of PSTM or WM might be different depending on the word knowledge aspect tested (comprehension or production of vocabulary) (Martin & Ellis, 2012; Speciale et al., 2004). In a study with intermediate and high-intermediate EFL learners, Elgort et al. (2016) found that learners with a larger WM (measured in an operation span task) did not only learn more words, but also had faster reaction times to newly learned words. A recent study by Montero Perez (2018) showed that WM (backward digit span task) is also related to French-as-a-foreign-language learners' incidental learning of new words from audio-visual input. Yet, PSTM (forward digit span task) did not predict vocabulary learning. Despite the methodological differences, the findings emerging from these studies show that learners with a larger WM tend to learn more words.

Future Directions

Although there has been a considerable amount of research into the factors affecting the learning of single words and some findings seem quite robust (cognates, frequency, concreteness), the studies reviewed differ in their focus (learning, processing, use of single words), type of input under investigation (written, spoken, audio-visual), the learning conditions (incidental and deliberate learning [with or without context]), and word knowledge aspects tested (recall, recognition, spontaneous use, receptive, productive). So, some questions remain. Is productive learning of single words affected by the same factors as receptive learning, given that productive learning is considered more difficult than receptive learning (Nation, 2013). How does receptive vocabulary development differ from productive vocabulary development and (spontaneous) productive use? How can we better link the findings from intervention studies, which typically focus on a limited number of word knowledge aspects (e.g., meaning recall or recognition, form recall or recognition), with those from corpus studies, which analyze learners' use of words in speech or writing? In addition, little is still known about how learners pick up vocabulary from inside the classroom (teacher talk and textbook) and from out-of-school exposure to FL input (computer games, internet, social media, chatting) (see Puimège & Peters, 2019b, for an exception). Further, vocabulary research has put great emphasis on frequency in explaining vocabulary learning and development, but the picture emerging from the studies reviewed is more complex and nuanced (see also Puimège & Peters, 2019b). So, is a frequency-based approach to vocabulary learning comprehensive and nuanced enough to account for the sheer complexity of factors that could play a role in the learning of single words? Finally, it should be pointed out that in the bulk of studies discussed in this chapter data were collected with university learners learning English, raising questions about the generalizability of at least some of the findings. What follows are some suggestions for further research.

One avenue to pursue in future research seems to be a triangulation of methods. The use of different methodological approaches (intervention studies, processing studies, corpus studies) would allow us to study word learning from different perspectives and to gain a deeper understanding of word learning.

Second, relatively few longitudinal studies have been carried out to investigate the learning of single words. The fact that frequency of occurrence was found to foster vocabulary learning in one-off learning sessions but not in extensive reading or extensive viewing conditions indicates that we need more longitudinal research to obtain a full and nuanced picture of word learning.

Third, vocabulary learning can take place inside and outside the FL classroom. Our understanding of vocabulary learning would increase if we also investigated how different factors affect vocabulary learning from classroom-based input (textbooks, teacher talk, peer interaction) as well as from out-of-school exposure to the FL.

At a more theoretical level, it might be useful to study vocabulary learning within a framework that provides a more comprehensive account of word learning than frequency-based accounts. Such a theory could be a usage-based approach to language because it links frequency (tokens as well as type frequency) to other determinants of learning, such as form (salience), prototypicality, redundancy, and mechanisms of selective attention, blocking and overshadowing (Ellis, 2006; Ellis, Donnell, & Römer, 2015). Several researchers (Crossley et al., 2011, 2016; Paquot, 2017) have already pointed to the explanatory potential of usage-based accounts of language for vocabulary learning.

A final avenue to explore is how learner characteristics and the languages under investigation affect word learning. If we want to truly generalize findings about factors affecting the learning of single words, we need research into a wider variety of participant profiles (e.g., young learners, adolescents, low educated and low-literate learners) and into a wider variety of first and second/foreign languages.

Further Reading

Laufer, B. (1997). What's in a word that makes it hard or easy? Intralexical factors affecting vocabulary acquisition. In N. Schmitt & M. McCarthy (Eds.), *Vocabulary: Description, acquisition, and pedagogy* (pp. 140–155). Cambridge: Cambridge University Press.

Even though Laufer's chapter was published more than 20 years ago, it is still very relevant because it nicely illustrates how word-related factors might affect the learning of new words.

Nation, I. S. P. (2013). *Learning vocabulary in another language*. Cambridge, UK: Cambridge University Press.

Paul Nation's all-encompassing book on vocabulary learning provides the reader with a comprehensive overview of vocabulary research and its pedagogic implications. By zooming in on, among others, what is involved in knowing a word and factors that relate to vocabulary learning from different modalities, the book shows which factors can affect the learning burden of words.

Otwinowska, A. (2016). *Cognate vocabulary in language acquisition and use: Attitudes, awareness, activation*. Bristol, UK: Multilingual Matters.

This book brings together research into the learning, processing, and use of cognates. It also highlights how cognate awareness can be used in the classroom.

Related Topics

The different aspects of vocabulary knowledge, factors affecting the learning of multiword items, processing single-word and multiword items, incidental vocabulary learning, intentional vocabulary learning

Note

1 I would like to thank my colleagues Maribel Montero Perez, Paul Pauwels, and Eva Puimège for their comments on earlier drafts of this chapter.

References

Baddeley, A. (2003). Working memory and language: An overview. *Journal of Communication Disorders, 36*(3), 189–208.

Barclay (2017, March). *The effect of word class and word length on the decay of lexical knowledge.* Paper presented at AAAL 2017, Portland.

Barcroft, J. (2007). Effects of opportunities for word retrieval during second language vocabulary learning. *Language Learning, 57*(1), 35–56.

Barcroft, J., & Rott, S. (2010). Partial word form learning in the written mode in L2 German and Spanish. *Applied Linguistics, 31*(5), 623–650.

Bardel, C., Gudmundson, A., & Lindqvist, C. (2012). Aspects of lexical sophistication in advanced learners' oral production. *Studies in Second Language Acquisition, 34*(2), 269–290.

Bardel, C., & Lindqvist, C. (2011). Developing a lexical profiler for spoken French and Italian L2: The role of frequency, cognates and thematic vocabulary. In L. Robers, G. Pallotti, & C. Bettoni (Eds.), *EUROSLA yearbook 11* (pp. 75–93). Amsterdam: Benjamins.

Batista, R., & Horst, M. (2016). A new receptive vocabulary size test for French. *Canadian Modern Language Review, 72*(2), 211–233.

Bensoussan, M., & Laufer, B. (1984). Lexical guessing in context in EFL reading comprehension. *Journal of Research in Reading, 7*(1), 15–32.

Cobb, T. (2000). One size fits all? Francophone learners and English vocabulary tests. *Canadian Modern Language Review, 57*(2), 295–324.

Crossley, S. A., Kyle, K., & Salsbury, T. (2016). A usage-based investigation of L2 lexical acquisition: The role of input and output. *The Modern Language Journal, 100*(3), 702–715.

Crossley, S. A., Salsbury, T., & Mcnamara, D. (2010). The development of polysemy and frequency use in English second language speakers. *Language Learning, 60*(3), 573–605.

Crossley, S. A., Salsbury, T., McNamara, D. S., & Jarvis, S. (2011). Predicting lexical proficiency in language learner texts using computational indices. *Language Testing, 28*(4), 561–580.

Crossley, S. A., Subtirelu, N., & Salsbury, T. (2013). Frequency effects or context effects in second language word learning. What predicts early lexical production? *Studies in Second Language Acquisition, 35*(4), 727–755.

de Groot, A. (2006). Effects of stimulus characteristics and background music on foreign language vocabulary learning and forgetting. *Language Learning, 56*(3), 463–506.

de Groot, A., & Keijzer, R. (2000). What is hard to learn is easy to forget: The roles of word concreteness, cognate status, and word frequency in foreign-language vocabulary learning and forgetting. *Language Learning, 50*(1), 1–56.

Elgort, I. (2012). Effects of L1 definitions and cognate status of test items on the Vocabulary Size Test. *Language Testing, 30*(2), 253–272.

Elgort, I., Brysbaert, M., Stevens, M., & Van Assche, E. (2018). Contextual word learning during reading in a second language. *Studies in Second Language Acquisition, 40*(2), 341–366.

Elgort, I., Candry, S., Boutorwick, T. J., Eyckmans, J., & Brysbaert, M. (2016). Contextual word learning with form-focused and meaning-focused elaboration. *Applied Linguistics, 39*(5), 646–667.

Elgort, I., & Warren, P. (2014). L2 vocabulary learning from reading: Explicit and tacit lexical knowledge and the role of learner and item variables. *Language Learning, 64*(2), 365–414.

Ellis, N. C. (2002). Frequency effects in language processing. A review with implications for implicit and explicit language acquisition. *Studies in Second Language Acquisition, 24,* 143–188.

Ellis, N. C. (2006). Selective attention and transfer phenomena in L2 acquisition: Contingency, cue competition, salience, interference, overshadowing, blocking, and perceptual learning. *Applied Linguistics*, *27*(2), 164–194.

Ellis, N. C., & Beaton, A. (1993a). Psycholinguistic determinants of foreign language vocabulary learning. *Language Learning*, *43*(4), 559–617.

Ellis, N. C., & Beaton, A. (1993b). Factors affecting the learning of foreign language vocabulary: Imagery keyword mediators and phonological short-term memory. *The Quarterly Journal of Experimental Psychology*, *46*(3), 533–558.

Ellis, N. C., Donnell, M. B. O., & Römer, U. (2015). Usage-Based language learning. In B. MacWhinney & W. O'Grady (Eds.), *The handbook of language emergence* (pp. 163–180). Chichester: John Wiley & Sons.

Folse, K. S. (2006). The effect of type of written exercise on L2 vocabulary retention. *TESOL Quarterly*, *40*(2), 273–293.

Gathercole, S. E. (2006). Non-word repetition and word learning: The nature of the relationship. *Applied Psycholinguistics*, *27*(4), 513–543.

Godfroid, A., Ahn, J., Choi, I., Ballard, L., Cui, Y., Johnston, S., Lee, S., Sarkar, A., & Yoo, H. (2018). Incremental vocabulary learning in a natural reading context: An eye-tracking study. *Bilingualism: Language & Cognition*, *21*(3), 563–584.

Higa, M. (1963). Interference effects of intralist word relationships in verbal learning. *Journal of Verbal Learning and Verbal Behavior*, *2*(2), 170–175.

Horst, M., Cobb, T., & Meara, P. (1998). Beyond a Clockwork Orange: Acquiring second language vocabulary through reading. *Reading in a Foreign Language*, *11*(2), 207–223.

Horst, M., & Collins, L. (2006). From faible to strong: How does their vocabulary grow? *The Canadian Modern Language Review/La Revue Canadienne Des Langues Vivantes*, *63*(1), 83–106.

Horst, M., & Meara, P. (1999). Test of a model for predicting second language lexical growth through reading. *Canadian Modern Language Review*, *56*(2), 308–328.

Hulstijn, J. H. (1993). When do foreign-language readers look up the meaning of unfamiliar words? The influence of task and learner variables. *The Modern Language Journal*, *77*(2), 139–147.

Juffs, A., & Harrington, M. (2011). Aspects of working memory in L2 learning. *Language Teaching*, *44*(2), 137–166.

Kormos, J., & Sáfár, A. (2008). Phonological short-term memory, working memory and foreign language performance in intensive language learning. *Bilingualism: Language and Cognition*, *11*(2), 261–271.

Laufer, B. (1988). The concept of "synforms" (similar lexical forms) in vocabulary acquisition. *Language and Education*, *2*(2), 113–132.

Laufer, B. (1991). *Similar lexical forms in interlanguage*. Tübingen: Gunter Narr.

Laufer, B. (1997). What's in a word that makes it hard or easy? Intralexical factors affecting vocabulary acquisition. In N. Schmitt & M. McCarthy (Eds.), *Vocabulary: Description, acquisition, and pedagogy* (pp. 140–155). Cambridge, UK: Cambridge University Press.

Laufer, B., & Levitzky-aviad, T. (2018). Loanword proportion in vocabulary size tests. Does it make a difference? *ITL – International Journal of Applied Linguistics*, *169*(1), 95–114.

Laufer, B., & McLean, S. (2016). Loanwords and vocabulary size test scores: A case of different estimates for different L1 learners. *Language Assessment Quarterly*, *13*(3), 202–217.

Laufer, B., & Nation, I. S. P. (1995). Vocabulary size and use: Lexical richness in L2 written production. *Applied Linguistics*, *16*(3), 307–322.

Laufer, B., & Paribakht, T. (1998). The relationship between passive and active vocabularies: Effects of language learning context. *Language Learning*, *48*(3), 365–391.

Laufer, B., & Ravenhorst-Kalovski, G. (2010). Lexical threshold revisited: Lexical text coverage, learners' vocabulary size and reading comprehension. *Reading in a Foreign Language*, *22*(1), 15–30.

Laufer, B., & Rozovski-Roitblat, B. (2011). Incidental vocabulary acquisition: The effects of task type, word occurrence and their combination. *Language Teaching Research*, *15*(4), 391–411.

Lawson, M. J., & Hogben, D. (1998). Learning and recall of foreign-language vocabulary: Effects of a keyword strategy for immediate and delayed recall. *Learning and Instruction, 8*(2), 179–194.

Li, S. (2016). The construct validity of language aptitude: A meta-analysis. *Studies in Second Language Acquisition, 38*(4), 801–842.

Lotto, L., & de Groot, A. (1998). Effects of learning method and word type on acquiring vocabulary in an unfamiliar language. *Language Learning, 48*(1), 31–69.

Martin, K. I., & Ellis, N. C. (2012). The roles of phonological short-term memory and working memory in L2 grammar and vocabulary learning. *Studies in Second Language Acquisition, 34*(3), 379–413.

Milton, J. (2007). Lexical profiles, learning styles and the construct validity of lexical size tests. In J. Daller, J. Milton, & J. Treffers-Daller (Eds.), *Modelling and assessing vocabulary* (pp. 47–58). Cambridge, UK: Cambridge University Press.

Milton, J. and Vassiliu, P. (2000). Frequency and the lexis of low-level EFL texts. In K. Nicolaidis & M. Mattheoudakis Eds.) *Proceedings of the 13th Symposium in Theoretical and Applied Linguistics* (pp. 444–455). Thessaloniki: Aristotle, University of Thessaloniki.

Mohamed, A. A. (2018). Exposure frequency in L2 reading: An eye-movement perspective of incidental vocabulary acquisition. *Studies in Second Language Acquisition, 40*(2), 269–293.

Montero Perez, M. (2018 September). *Incidental vocabulary learning from viewing: The role of working memory and vocabulary knowledge.* Paper presented at the EuroSLA Conference, Münster.

Montero Perez, M., Peters, E., Clarebout, G., & Desmet, P. (2014). Effects of captioning on video comprehension and incidental vocabulary learning. *Language Learning & Technology, 18*(1), 118–141.

Montero Perez, M., Peters, E., & Desmet, P. (2018). Vocabulary learning through viewing video: The effect of two enhancement techniques. *Computer Assisted Language Learning, 31*(1–2), 1–26.

Nakata, T. (2015). Effects of expanding and equal spacing on second language vocabulary learning: Does gradually increasing spacing increase vocabulary learning. *Studies in Second Language Acquisition, 37*(4), 677–711.

Nakata, T. (2017). Does repeated practice make perfect? The effects of within-session repeated retrieval on second language vocabulary learning. *Studies in Second Language Acquisition, 39*(4), 653–679.

Nakata, T., & Suzuki, Y. (2018). Effects of massing and spacing on the learning of semantically related and unrelated words. *Studies in Second Language Acquisition,* 1–25.

Nakata, T., & Webb, S. (2016). Does studying vocabulary in smaller sets increase learning? *Studies in Second Language Acquisition, 38*(3), 523–552.

Nation, I. S. P. (1990). *Teaching and learning vocabulary.* Boston, MA: Heinle and Heinle.

Nation, I. S. P. (2013). *Learning vocabulary in another language.* Cambridge, UK: Cambridge University Press.

Nation, I. S. P., & Beglar, D. (2007). A vocabulary size test. *The Language Teacher, 31*(7), 9–13.

Nissen, H. B., & Henriksen, B. (2006). Word class influence on word association test results. *International Journal of Applied Linguistics, 16*(3), 389–408.

Noreillie, A., Kestemont, B., Heylen, K., Desmet, P., & Peters, E. (2018). Vocabulary knowledge and listening comprehension at an intermediate level in English and French as foreign languages An approximate replication study of Stæhr (2009). *ITL – International Journal of Applied Linguistics, 169*(1), 212–231.

Otwinowska, A. (2016). *Cognate vocabulary in language acquisition and use. Attitudes, awareness, activation.* Bristol, UK: Multilingual Matters.

Paquot, M. (2017). L1 frequency in foreign language acquisition: Recurrent word combinations in French and Spanish EFL learner writing. *Second Language Research, 33*(1), 13–32.

Pellicer-Sánchez, A. (2016). Incidental L2 vocabulary acquisition from and while reading. *Studies in Second Language Acquisition, 38*(1), 97–130.

Pellicer-Sánchez, A., & Schmitt, N. (2010). Incidental vocabulary acquisition from an authentic novel: Do things fall apart? *Reading in a Foreign Language, 22*(1), 31–55.

Peters, E. (2012). The differential effects of two vocabulary instruction methods on EFL word learning: A study into task effectiveness. *International Review of Applied Linguistics in Language Teaching, 50*(3), 213–238.

Peters, E. (2014). The effects of repetition and time of posttest administration on EFL learners' form recall of single words and collocations. *Language Teaching Research*, *18*(1), 75–94.

Peters, E., Heynen, E., & Puimège, E. (2016). Learning vocabulary through audiovisual input: The differential effect of L1 subtitles and captions. *System*, *63*, 134–148.

Peters, E., Hulstijn, J. H., Sercu, L., & Lutjeharms, M. (2009). Learning L2 German vocabulary through reading: The effect of three enhancement techniques compared. *Language Learning*, *59*(1), 113–151.

Peters, E., & Webb, S. (2018). Incidental vocabulary acquisition through viewing L2 television and factors that affect learning. *Studies in Second Language Acquisition*, *40*(3), 551–577.

Pichette, F., Serres, de L., & Lafontaine, M. (2012). Sentence reading and writing for second language vocabulary acquisition. *Applied Linguistics*, *33*(1), 66–82.

Pigada, M., & Schmitt, N. (2006). Vocabulary acquisition from extensive reading: A case study. *Reading in a Foreign Language*, *18*(1), 1–28.

Puimège, E., & Peters, E. (2019a). Learning L2 vocabulary from audiovisual input: An exploratory study into incidental learning of single words and formulaic sequences. *Language Learning Journal*.

Puimège, E., & Peters, E. (2019b). Learners' English vocabulary knowledge prior to formal instruction: The role of learner-related and word-related variables. *Language Learning*.

Pulido, D. (2004). The relationship between text comprehension and second language incidental vocabulary acquisition: A matter of topic familiarity? *Language Learning*, *54*(3), 469–523.

Pulido, D. (2007). The effects of topic familiarity and passage sight vocabulary on L2 lexical inferencing and retention through reading. *Applied Linguistics*, *28*(1), 66–86.

Ringbom, H. (1982). The influence of other languages on the vocabulary of foreign language learners. *IRAL*, 85–96.

Rodgers, M. P. H. (2013). *English language learning through viewing television: An investigation of comprehension, incidental vocabulary acquisition, lexical coverage, attitudes, and captions*. Unpublished PhD thesis, Victoria University, Wellington, New Zealand.

Rodgers, M. P. H., & Webb, S. (in press). Incidental vocabulary learning through viewing television. *ITL-International Journal of Applied Linguistics*.

Rogers, J., Webb, S., & Nakata, T. (2015). Do the cognacy characteristics of loanwords make them more easily learned than noncognates? *Language Teaching Research*, *19*(1), 9–27.

Rott, S. (1999). The effect of exposure frequency on intermediate language learners' incidental vocabulary acquisition through reading. *Studies in Second Language Acquisition*, *21*, 589–619.

Schmitt, N. (1998). Tracking the incremental acquisition of second language vocabulary: A longitudinal study. *Language Learning*, *48*(2), 281–317.

Schmitt, N., Jiang, X., & Grabe, W. (2011). The percentage of words known in a text and reading comprehension. *The Modern Language Journal*, *95*(1), 26–43.

Schmitt, N., Schmitt, D., & Clapham, C. (2001). Developing and exploring the behaviour of two new versions of the Vocabulary Levels Test. *Language Testing*, *18*(1), 55–88.

Schuetze, U. (2015). Spacing techniques in second language vocabulary acquisition: Short-term gains vs. long-term memory. *Language Teaching Research*, *19*(1), 28–42.

Speciale, G., Ellis, N. C., & Bywater, T. (2004). Phonological sequence learning and short-term store capacity determine second language vocabulary acquisition. *Applied Psycholinguistics*, *25*(2), 293–321.

Stæhr, L. S. (2009). Vocabulary knowledge and advanced listening comprehension in English as a foreign language. *Studies in Second Language Acquisition*, *31*(4), 577–607.

Tinkham, T. (1993). The effect of semantic clustering on the learning of second language vocabulary. *System*, *21*(3), 371–380.

Tonzar, C., Lotto, L., & Job, R. (2009). L2 Vocabulary acquisition in children: Effects of learning method and cognate status. *Language Learning*, *59*(3), 623–646.

Van Assche, E., Duyck, W., & Brysbaert, M. (2013). Verb processing by bilinguals in sentence contexts. *Studies in Second Language Acquisition*, *35*(2), 237–259.

van Hell, J. G., & Tanner, D. (2012). Second language proficiency and cross-language lexical activation. *Language Learning*, *62*(Suppl. 2), 148–171.

van Zeeland, H., & Schmitt, N. (2013). Incidental vocabulary acquisition through L2 listening: A dimensions approach. *System, 41*(3), 609–624.

Verspoor, M., & Lowie, W. (2003). Making sense of polysemous words. *Language Learning, 53*(3), 547–586.

Vidal, K. (2003). Academic listening: A source of vocabulary acquisition? *Applied Linguistics, 24*(1), 56–89.

Vidal, K. (2011). A comparison of the effects of reading and listening on incidental vocabulary acquisition. *Language Learning, 61*(1), 219–258.

Waring, R. (1997). The negative effects of learning words in semantic sets: A replication. *System, 25*(2), 261–274.

Webb, S. (2007a). The effects of repetition on vocabulary knowledge. *Applied Linguistics, 28*(1), 46–65.

Webb, S. (2007b). The effects of synonymy on second-language vocabulary learning. *Reading in Foreign Language, 19*(2), 120–136.

Webb, S. (2008). The effects of context on incidental vocabulary learning. *Reading in a Foreign Language, 20*(2), 232–245.

Webb, S., & Chang, A. C.-S. (2015a). Second language vocabulary learning through extensive reading with audio support: How do frequency and distribution of occurrence affect learning? *Language Teaching Research, 19*(6), 667–686.

Webb, S., & Chang, A. C.-S. (2015b). How does prior word knowledge affect vocabulary learning progress in an extensive reading program? *Studies in Second Language Acquisition, 37*(4), 651–675.

Wilcox, A., & Medina, A. (2013). Effects of semantic and phonological clustering on L2 vocabulary acquisition among novice learners. *System, 41*(4), 1056–1069.

Willis, M., & Ohashi, Y. (2012). A model of L2 vocabulary learning and retention. *Language Learning Journal, 40*(1), 125–137.

10

Factors Affecting the Learning of Multiword Items

Frank Boers

Introduction

There is now a broad consensus in applied linguistics that second or foreign language learners (henceforth L2 learners) stand to gain a lot from acquiring considerable numbers of multiword items (henceforth MWIs). MWI is used in this chapter as an umbrella term for a wide range of expressions comprising more than a single word, which have in the literature received various labels, including "lexical phrase", "multiword unit", "phrasal expression", "chunk", "prefab", "phraseme", "collocation", "idiom", "lexical bundle", and "formulaic sequence". Research has demonstrated that familiarity with MWIs aids receptive as well as productive fluency (e.g., see Conklin, this volume). It aids receptive fluency because knowledge of MWIs makes discourse relatively predictable. For example, on hearing or reading *last but not*, a proficient language learner will be able to anticipate *least*. Similarly, reading a wordstring such as *the difference was not statistically* is likely to prime *significant* in a reader who is familiar with the genre of quantitative research reports. Knowledge of MWIs aids productive fluency because well-mastered MWIs can be retrieved from memory as prefabricated units rather than being assembled at the time of speaking. Such "holistic" retrieval of MWIs is particularly plausible in the case of fixed expressions that show no morphological or syntactic variability (e.g., *on the other hand*; *happy birthday*; *no strings attached*; *at the end of the day*; and so on).

Broad knowledge of MWIs is also indispensable for comprehension of reading and listening texts (Kremmel, Brunfaut, & Alderson, 2017; Yeldham, 2018), because the meaning of many MWIs (e.g., *cut corners* – "not following regulations to save money or effort") transcends that of the individual words of which they are made up. Learners whose own language use exhibits good mastery of MWIs tend to be perceived as proficient language users as well (Bestgen, 2017; Crossley, Salsbury, & McNamara, 2015; Stengers, Boers, Housen, & Eyckmans, 2011).

Given that L2 learners stand to gain so much from learning MWIs, it is worth investigating the factors that are likely to facilitate or hinder this learning. For one thing, it may help to estimate whether particular MWIs stand a good chance of being acquired relatively fast and without much effort on the part of a language learner. For another, it may inform the nature of instructional intervention where intervention is deemed necessary. A major challenge in discerning the factors that play a part in the acquisition of L2 MWIs, however, is that the class of MWIs is very large and made up of very diverse (types of) items, and so the factors affecting their learning are bound to differ from one (type of) MWI to the next. Another challenge is to take account of individual learner profiles, because an MWI that poses few problems to one learner (for example because it has a close equivalent in that learner's L1) may be quite elusive to another.

The multifarious nature of MWIs is also reflected in the different procedures that researchers apply to identify MWIs in language (see Wood, this volume). Such identification procedures have in recent times become increasingly informed by corpus data. One procedure is to screen a corpus for highly frequent uninterrupted wordstrings (or so-called n-grams). Wordstrings that meet a certain frequency criterion stipulated by researchers are customarily labeled "lexical bundles" (e.g., Biber & Barbieri, 2007; Biber, Conrad, & Cortes, 2004). For example, strings such as *for instance*, *as if*, *as soon as*, and *one of the* will qualify as lexical bundles depending on the frequency threshold stipulated. Another corpus-based procedure is to look for strong word partnerships, i.e., frequent co-occurrences of (content) words regardless of whether they are immediately adjacent to one another. The above-chance co-occurrence of words is commonly called "collocation" (Sinclair, 1991). The strength of the word partnership is often determined on the basis of a "mutual information score" (MI score), which reflects the extent to which two words seek each other's company rather than the company of other words. A combination such as *tell + joke* is a case in point, because it is *tell* rather than another linguistic action verb that collocates with *joke*. The fact that native speakers are unlikely to make lexical substitutions in such expressions (e.g., *say a joke*) illustrates that frequency distributions in a representative corpus can serve as a reliable proxy of how strongly particular words are associated with one another in language users' mental lexicons (Hoey, 2005; Taylor, 2012). It is worth noting that word partnerships of low frequency words (e.g., *wreak havoc*) can also yield very high MI scores. Endeavors to create lists of MWIs to be prioritized in learning will therefore typically consider frequency thresholds as well as collocational strength among the criteria for inclusion (e.g., Martinez & Schmitt, 2012; Simpson-Vlach & Ellis, 2010).

Yet another identification procedure, in use already long before the advent of corpus linguistics, is to evaluate whether the meaning of a given wordstring can or cannot be inferred straightforwardly by adding up the meanings of the constituent words. If not, then the wordstring is considered to be "non-compositional", i.e., its meaning transcends that of the individual words combined. The traditional label for MWIs identified on such semantic grounds is "idiom". The class of idioms itself is also diverse, however, because some (e.g., *pull strings*) may be interpretable thanks to cultural background knowledge (e.g., familiarity with the image of a puppeteer manipulating the strings attached to his puppets), while others (e.g., *by and large*) are truly opaque (Grant & Bauer, 2004). Figurative phrasal and prepositional verbs (e.g., *turn up*) can also be considered idioms by virtue of their non-compositionality (e.g., Kövecses & Szabó, 1996), but also within this class of MWIs we find gradation in transparency. The universally shared association of "more" with "up" (Kövecses, 2005) may help a learner appreciate the use of *up* in *turn up (the sound)*, but its use in an expression such as *(we'll have to) put up with (her)* is likely to elude this kind of reasoned interpretation.

Apart from their semantic non-compositionality, idioms are of course also characterized by a high degree of fixedness at the level of form. For example, one does not normally substitute "pull" in *pull strings* by another verb or use "string" as a singular noun – if one wishes to preserve the figurative meaning of the idiom. Neither does *by and large* lend itself to adaptations such as "by and quite large". Given their fixed lexical makeup, it is not surprising that many word combinations which were identified as idioms in the pre-corpus-linguistics era also meet the corpus-based criterion of above-chance co-occurrence (and thus reflect the phenomenon of "collocation"; e.g., Macis & Schmitt, 2017). What has become increasingly apparent thanks to corpus linguistics, though, is that phraseology (or what Sinclair [1991] called the "Idiom Principle" as opposed to the "Open Choice Principle") encompasses much more than "idioms" in the traditional sense.

At the same time, the observation that MWIs vary in their semantic compositionality is undeniably relevant to the subject of the present chapter, because compositionality is associated with transparency of meaning, and transparency of meaning is naturally one of the factors likely to influence the learnability of a given MWI. Other likely factors include the frequency of occurrence of the MWI in the samples of the target language that a learner is exposed to (e.g., *play a part* will be encountered more often than *rule the roost*), because this can be expected to affect the pace at which a given word association is established in the learner's mental lexicon. Whether learning an MWI is "just" a matter of remembering a combination of familiar words (e.g., *do + damage*) or remembering a combination involving new words (e.g., *seek + solace*) is another likely factor, because recalling new word forms is challenging in its own right. Several more characteristics of MWIs likely to influence learning will be discussed further below.

Apart from characteristics of the MWIs proper, the chances of MWI learning will inevitably also depend on the circumstances and the activities through which a learner engages with the target language. To give just one example for now, more encounters with a given MWI in samples of the target language may be needed in conditions where the learner is not focusing specifically on the MWI than in conditions where the MWI is made the object of intentional study (provided the study procedure is an efficient one). In what follows, we will therefore distinguish different opportunities or scenarios for MWI learning, moving from the uptake of MWIs from content-focused reading to deliberate MWI-focused learning.

Critical Issues and Topics

Estimating the Chances of MWI Acquisition From Texts, Without Instructional Intervention

When language learning happens as a by-product of message-focused activities, this is usually called "incidental" learning, as opposed to deliberate efforts to commit language items or features to memory (see Webb, this volume, and Lindstromberg, this volume, for more in-depth discussions of incidental and intentional vocabulary learning, respectively). Many studies of incidental learning have concerned the incremental acquisition of words from reading, but only relatively recently have MWIs attracted interest in this strand of research as well. Reminiscent of the work on incidental word learning (e.g., Rott, 1999; also see Peters, this volume), the role of frequency of encounters with the same MWIs has figured high on the research agenda. What the evidence to date suggests is that it will typically take multiple encounters with an MWI for measurable learning outcomes to emerge. A study which illustrates this is Webb, Newton, and Chang (2013), where EFL learners read short stories containing 18 preselected verb + noun expressions (e.g., *raise + question*). The texts were accompanied by an audio-recording of the stories for the learners to silently read along with. The duration of the reading-while-listening activity was slightly over 30 minutes. Different versions of the texts were created such that learners encountered the same MWIs just once, five times, or more than five times. Immediate post-reading tests confirmed the expectation that frequency of encounters positively influences the chances of acquisition. However, they also revealed that meeting the MWIs five times still generated only modest outcomes, with a success rate of just 12% on a test where the learners were presented with the verb of the expression and were asked to supply the missing noun (e.g., *raise* _____). A conceptual replication of Webb et al. (2013) was conducted by Pellicer-Sánchez (2017), who invented six adjective + pseudo-noun combinations and incorporated these in a text (of about 2,300 words). In one version of the text, they were incorporated four times each. On a post-reading test (administered one week later) where the participants who had read this text were asked to recall the adjective that preceded each pseudo-noun, the success rate was just 7%.

Findings such as these demonstrate that MWIs can be acquired through reading, but they also give reason to believe that the pace of incidental uptake of most MWIs will be slow when learners read authentic (i.e., non-manipulated) texts. This is because, although MWIs *as a class* are omnipresent, very few individual members of that class will occur repeatedly in the same stretch of text. For example, Boers and Lindstromberg (2009, pp. 42–43) found only one instance of *tell + truth* in 100 pages of a police story (a genre where use of this expression might be expected). In settings where a learner is not regularly exposed to substantial amounts of input, it is not difficult to imagine that the interval between two encounters with the same MWI may be too long for the learner to recognize it as a recurring word combination. The recognition of recurrent word combinations may also be hindered by morphological and syntactic variability. For example, if a learner were to meet an utterance such as *because of a criminal offence he was believed to have committed years ago*, the syntagmatic distance between *offence* and *commit* may obscure their collocational bond. In addition, word partnerships need not be totally exclusive. For instance, learners will meet the noun *research* not only in the company of *conduct* but also of *do* and *carry out*, and so it may take many encounters with this noun for them to discern its collocational scope.

MWIs are perhaps especially likely to escape a learner's attention during content-focused reading (or listening) if they consist of familiar words (e.g., *do your homework*; *have a dream*) and when their meaning is (perceived to be) transparent. Studies that make use of eye tracking have indeed shown that short and highly familiar words (e.g., *do* and *have*) attract little attention during reading (e.g., Rayner, Slattery, Drieghe, & Liversedge, 2011; Williams & Morris, 2004). If, in addition, the semantic contribution of one part of an MWI is negligible, it is understandable that learners give precedence during processing to the part that carries the most meaning (e.g., *homework* and *dream* rather than *do* and *have*). If that suffices for the learner to make sense of the message, then the collocational patterning may go unnoticed. That content words but not their phraseological patterning tend to be prioritized by learners was illustrated in a study by Hoang and Boers (2016), where learners were asked to retell a story they had read and listened to twice. The original text contained a high number of MWIs, but the learners were found to reproduce hardly any of these in their own rendering of the story. They did extract content words from the original text, including ones featuring in the MWIs, but stripped bare of the phraseological patterning in which these had been met.

If it is true that high-frequency words in transparent MWIs attract little attention, then this also offers an explanation for the persistent interference of L1 in learners' use of these kinds of MWIs (e.g., Laufer & Waldman, 2011; Nesselhauf, 2003; Yamashita & Jiang, 2010). For example, if *do* in *do homework* or *have* in *have a dream* attract little attention, then it is not so surprising to find cases of L1 transfer (e.g., "make your homework" from L1 Dutch; "make a dream" from L1 French) (also see Nguyen & Webb, 2017; Wolter & Gyllstad, 2011).

In comparison, one might expect nontransparent MWIs (e.g., idioms) to attract more attention during reading, because learners may be puzzled by them. This is not necessarily so, however. Martinez and Murphy (2011), for instance, demonstrated that learners may not realize a given wordstring (e.g., *over the hill* – "growing too old for certain activities") is actually an idiom in cases where the available context does not preclude a literal reading of them ("on the other side of the hill"). Littlemore, Chen, Koester, and Barnden (2011) found that international students at a British university not only failed to grasp the intended meaning behind many of their lecturers' idioms, but also that they were seldom aware of their misunderstanding. The misinterpretations were typically due to transfer from deceptive counterpart expressions in the students' L1. When idioms do attract attention because they are experienced as puzzling, the next obstacle on the path to learning them, of course, is their very nature – their lack of transparency. Research suggests that contextual clues (if available at all) will not always help (Boers, Eyckmans, & Stengers, 2007). In addition to seeking contextual clues, learners may try to infer the figurative meaning of an idiom through a literal reading of the expression. In fact, experiments by Cieślicka (2006, 2010) have revealed that second language learners tend to be more inclined than L1 speakers to activate a literal reading of the content words of an idiom, despite knowledge of the "idiomatic" meaning of the expression. When it comes to interpreting new idioms, however, it is an inclination which can easily put a learner on the wrong track. This is because the first meaning of a constituent word that springs to mind may not be the meaning which is at the origin of the expression. For example, if they mistake *the wings* in *waiting in the wings* for the wings of a bird (rather than the wings on the side of a theater stage), then this is highly unlikely to lead them to a correct interpretation of this idiom. In other words, cases of homonymy (or polysemy) make this strategy error-prone. Additional interpretation difficulties arise from cross-cultural differences. An idiom may have its roots in a culture-specific domain which the learner is simply not familiar with (Boers, 2003), or it may have a content word whose symbolic nature prompts different associations in the learner's culture (Hu & Fong, 2010). The most obvious case where an idiom will resist interpretation, of course, is when a key constituent word is totally new to the learner. For example, an intermediate learner is unlikely to know the word *keel* (the lower part of a boat), and so will not be able to draw on such knowledge in an attempt to infer the meaning of *on an even keel* ("making steady progress").

When reviewing the study by Webb et al. (2013) above, I mentioned that the reading texts were accompanied by an audio-recording of the stories. This is relevant, because mode of input may be yet another factor that influences the rate of MWI uptake from texts. On the one hand, listening input may be helpful because the availability of prosodic cues can make it easier to discern MWIs (Lin, 2012). For example, pauses normally occur at the boundaries of fixed expressions, not inside them, and so pauses can signal that a particular wordstring functions as a unit. On the other hand, a possible downside is that MWIs tend to be produced relatively fast in speech and with phonetic reduction of function words (e.g., articles and prepositions) (Bybee, 2002). As a result, learners may find it hard to "catch" the precise composition of MWIs during real-time listening. However, when a written text is also available, being able to see the words may compensate for this downside.

Enhancing the Chances of MWI Uptake From Texts

Several types of text manipulation may help to accelerate MWI learning from reading. One is to embed multiple instances of the same MWIs in texts. The effect of such "seeding" or "flooding" of texts with pre-selected MWIs was actually investigated in the aforementioned

Frank Boers

studies by Webb et al. (2013) and Pellicer-Sánchez (2017). In one version of the stories used by Webb et al., readers encountered no fewer than 15 instances of each of the 18 target verb + noun expressions. The immediate post-reading tests showed significantly better uptake in comparison to the reading conditions where the MWIs were incorporated fewer times. It is thus undeniable that seeding texts with recurring instances of MWIs can foster incidental acquisition. It is worth mentioning, though, that as many as 15 encounters still offered no guarantee of productive knowledge. For example, the mean success rate on the test where the learners were prompted to supply the missing noun (e.g., *raise* _____) was 55%. One of the text versions used by Pellicer-Sánchez in her experiment was seeded with eight instances of six target adjective + pseudo-noun expressions. Again, this appeared to positively influence learning in comparison with a text version containing only four instances, but the success rate on the test which asked the participants to recall the adjectives that went with the given pseudo-nouns nonetheless remained low – 15%. It is of course conceivable that further encounters with the same MWIs would eventually result in robust knowledge, because incidental learning is known to be a gradual, incremental process, driven by continued exposure.

Skeptics may argue that seeding a text with MWIs requires considerable creativity and resourcefulness on the part of the materials writer. An alternative or complementary type of text manipulation is to increase the salience of MWIs in a text. This can be done by means of "typographic enhancement" (i.e., highlighting the presence of MWIs through underlining, using bold typeface, etc.). The rationale for this type of intervention rests on the notion that attention is vital for learning and that steps which direct learners' attention to features which they might otherwise not pay attention to are therefore useful (Sharwood-Smith, 1993). As discussed earlier, lack of spontaneous attention to MWIs is one of the explanations for their relatively slow uptake, and so typographic enhancement seems a promising way of addressing this problem. This promise, of course, rests on the assumption that learners' attention is effectively drawn to typographically enhanced MWIs in a text. This assumption was confirmed in an eye-tracking study by Choi (2017). In that study, learners who read a text where MWIs were enhanced (by means of bold typeface) tended to look at these more and for longer than learners who read the same text without any enhancement. Post-reading tests also showed a positive effect of enhancement on memory, thus lending support to the pedagogic implementation of this technique. Additional evidence for the usefulness of typographic enhancement for MWI learning is reported by Sonbul and Schmitt (2013), Szudarski and Carter (2016) and Boers et al. (2017). What the findings appear to suggest is that the increased awareness effected by enhancement can reduce the number of encounters with an MWI that would otherwise be necessary to obtain robust learning outcomes. It would be interesting to find out (through a combination of eye tracking and posttest measures) whether typographic enhancement of an early instance of a given MWI might suffice to increase learners' intake of subsequent instances even if these are not enhanced.

There are some limitations to typographic enhancement, however. One is that it can only be applied in moderation, because enhancing too much of a text defeats the purpose of making selected items stand out. Another is that learners' increased attention to the enhanced segments of a text may come at the expense of attention they would otherwise give to the unenhanced segments of the text. Evidence of this side-effect or trade-off effect is reported in the aforementioned eye-tracking study by Choi (2017). A third and perhaps the greatest limitation of enhancement is that, while it can orient a reader's attention to language forms, it cannot ensure on its own that the learner will grasp the meaning of those forms. In the case of transparent MWIs, this is of course not an issue, but in the case of nontransparent ones it certainly is (unless clarifying context is available).

On a more positive note, however, learners have been found more likely to look up the meaning of enhanced MWIs than unenhanced ones (Bishop, 2004; Peters, 2012). Whether or not learners manage to actually find the desired information in resources such as dictionaries will inevitably depend on the quality and functionality of those resources and on the learners' skills to navigate them (Chen, 2016; Dziemianko, 2014; Laufer, 2011; also see Meunier, this volume). The learner's curiosity about the meaning of a given MWI can of course also be satisfied readily by supplying glosses or annotations with the text. This has indeed been done in some investigations of MWI uptake from reading (e.g., Peters, 2012), but the effect of providing these glosses was not the focus of interest (i.e., not an "independent variable") in these studies. Again, it might be useful to know how explaining the meaning of an MWI on an early encounter in a text affects learners' engagement with the MWI on subsequent re-encounters.

Looking back at the learning conditions discussed in this section, it is debatable whether the learning gains accrued from them should be labeled "incidental", since deliberate efforts are obviously made here to orient learners' attention to language items, even though the primary interest supposedly lies with the content of texts. Such conditions are perhaps more aptly labeled "semi-incidental" instead. In the following section, we turn to activities in which it must be clear for the learner that the intention is to learn MWIs.

Before doing so, one more observation worth making about the body of research on "incidental" MWI learning is that few of these studies include an exploration of whether a given input condition fosters learning of some (types of) MWIs better than others. It is true that most of the studies selected a set of target MWIs that were alike in broadly structural terms (e.g., verb + noun, or adjective + noun combinations), but little attention seems to have been paid, for example, to differences in semantic characteristics of these items, such as their (non-)transparency.

Factors Likely to Affect the Deliberate Learning of MWIs

In the realm of deliberate, MWI-focused learning activities, there appears to be a greater inclination to select types of targets on the basis of semantic criteria. For example, McCarthy and O'Dell's resources for independent study distinguish between "collocations" (2005) and "idioms" (2002), where "collocations" refers to relatively transparent MWIs and "idioms" to relatively opaque ones. (However, see Boers and Webb [2015] for a discussion of the intricacies involved in determining which MWIs are transparent and which are not – for a given language learner.)

Let's first consider activities that mostly concern "collocations". As these are generally deemed to be semantically transparent, such activities tend to be oriented towards accurate production of the MWIs. A well-recognized factor affecting the success of MWI learning is that of congruency with counterpart MWIs in the learner's L1: When counterpart expressions in the learner's L1 are non-congruent (e.g., in Dutch "do a suggestion" instead of *make a suggestion*, and "with other words" instead of *in other words*), this will hinder learning. This type of hindrance is a case of "inter-lexical" interference. A study illustrating its impact is Peters (2016), where learners were given a list of 18 MWIs and their L1 translations and practiced these in exercises (e.g., fill-in-the-blank). Half of the MWIs were congruent with the counterpart expression in the learners' L1 while the other half were not. Congruency emerged as a strong predictor of accurate responses in a productive recall test. Because L1 interference appears so persistent in learners' renderings of L2 MWIs, Laufer and Girsai (2008) make a strong case (supported by findings from a quasi-experimental classroom study) for instruction that explicitly draws students' attention to L1 – L2 contrasts, for example through translation exercises.

Another factor affecting learning success is the phenomenon of "intra-lexical" interference, where an MWI constituent is erroneously substituted by another L2 word which bears a resemblance to it. This may be due to a formal resemblance, for example, when *in* competes for selection with *on* ("in purpose" instead of *on purpose*) or when *make* competes with *take* ("make a picture" instead of *take a picture*). Or it may be due to a semantic resemblance, such as when *say* competes with *tell* ("say the truth" instead of *tell the truth*). Confusability appears particularly high when words competing for lexical selection lack semantic distinctiveness (e.g., *do* and *make*). Many authors of MWI-focused instructional materials are clearly aware of this problem, because they design exercises where learners are presented with sets of such confusable items and required to sort them out (Boers, Dang, & Strong, 2017). Whether this is actually a judicious approach is a matter of some debate, however. Webb and Kagimoto (2011), for example, found that presenting learners with adjective + noun expressions where the adjectives bear semantic resemblance (e.g., *narrow escape* and *slim chance*; *tall order* and *high spirits*) resulted in poorer learning than when the co-presentation of such items was avoided. Boers, Demecheleer, Coxhead, and Webb (2014) tested the effectiveness of various exercise formats for practicing verb + noun expressions (e.g., *make a suggestion*; *do business*) used in commercially available EFL textbooks, and found generally very poor learning outcomes. Many of the participants' wrong responses in the posttests were attributable to interference from the other lexical items they had been presented with in the exercises. This happened particularly often when the exercises were of a matching format, where the MWIs were broken up and the learners were required to reassemble them (e.g., by choosing the appropriate noun to go with a given verb). Although vocabulary exercises are evaluated more extensively in a different chapter (Laufer, this volume), it is worth mentioning a few ways in which the risk of intra-lexical interference of the kind discussed here can be reduced. One is to design exercises where the MWIs are kept intact from the very start. For example, Boers et al. (2017) compared fill-in-the-blank exercises where learners were required either to choose appropriate verbs from a list (*make, take, pay*, etc.) to complete verb + noun expressions (e.g., *a ceremony to* _____ *tribute to soldiers who died in the war*) or to choose from a list of intact expressions (*make a contribution, take a toll, pay tribute*, etc.) to complete blanks (e.g., *a ceremony to* _____ *to soldiers who died in the war*). Delayed posttests revealed the latter exercise type to be significantly more effective. Another way is to minimize error at the exercise stage by providing sufficient opportunities for learning the target MWIs prior to the exercise, such that the exercise serves the purpose of (successful) retrieval practice (see Lindstromberg, this volume, Nakata, this volume) rather than as an introduction of new language through a trial-and-error experience. Since these suggestions seem uncontroversial and even commonsensical, it is surprising to find that about half of the MWI-focused exercises in a large sample of EFL course books analyzed by Boers et al. (2017) are *not* preceded by exemplars of the MWIs needed in the exercise and that about half of these trial-and-error exercises require learners to assemble broken-up MWIs, thus potentially increasing the risk of intra-lexical interference. Also noteworthy is that MWIs are typically practiced just once, i.e., in only one exercise, in most course books. And yet, research also shows that during deliberate work repeated engagement with the same MWIs makes a big difference (Peters, 2014; Zhang, 2017).

When it comes to the intentional learning of idioms, the challenge is not only to remember their lexical composition but also the meanings of these items, since idioms, by definition, have meanings that do not follow straightforwardly from adding up the basic meanings of their constituent words. As already mentioned, however, not all idioms are equally non-transparent. It is to be expected that learners will find the meaning of an idiom which they experience as transparent (e.g., *to keep a straight face*) easier to remember than that of an idiom whose literal meaning looks unrelated to the figurative meaning (e.g., *to paint the town red*). This expectation was borne out in an experiment conducted by Steinel, Hulstijn, and Steinel (2007), where learners studied a series of L2 idioms paired with L1 explanations. Interestingly, a factor that was found to be an even stronger predictor of posttest recall successes in the same experiment was the degree of imageability of the idioms, i.e., how readily an expression calls up a mental picture of a concrete scene. For example, *to be/get off the hook* was rated as much more imageable by the participants than *to hang fire*. Imageability is strongly associated with concreteness of meaning (Paivio, 1986; also see Peters, this volume, and Lindstromberg, this volume), and so it is not surprising that the meaning of highly imageable idioms is easier to remember than that of idioms which evoke no imagery – all else being equal. The imageability of an idiom derives from a literal reading of the expression, as long as this literal reading can be made sense of. A literal reading of *off the hook* can readily evoke the image of a fish that has managed to wriggle free of a fisherman's hook. *Hang fire*, on the other hand, would seem less easy to "picture".

If imageability is an influential factor in (intentional) idiom learning, then it is worth investigating if particular target idioms can be made more imageable, and thus more memorable, through instructional intervention. A tried and tested way of doing this is to briefly clarify the (plausible) literal underpinning of an idiom where this underpinning is not already obvious (see Boers & Lindstromberg, 2009, for a review). Clarifying the theater origin of *waiting in the wings* and the sailing origin of *on an even keel* could be examples of this approach. It is noteworthy in this context that recent editions of several idiom dictionaries also provide information about the (plausible) literal underpinnings of idioms – where such knowledge is available. An alternative or complementary way of enhancing the imageability of a figurative idiom, of course, is to provide a visual illustration of its literal meaning (Szczepaniak & Lew, 2011).

The above discussion about idioms concerned first and foremost the learning of their meanings. With regard to learning the lexical makeup of idioms there is another feature exhibited by many idioms that merits mention – inter-word phonological repetition, as in the case of rhyme (e.g., *be left high and dry*) and alliteration (e.g., *set the scene*). In English phraseology, it is the incidence of alliteration that is particularly conspicuous (Boers & Lindstromberg, 2009), especially among idioms (e.g., *turn the tables*), aphorisms (e.g., *it takes two to tango*), similes (e.g., *good as gold*), and binomials (e.g., *part and parcel*) (Lindstromberg, 2018). It appears that such a sound pattern has the potential to give wordstrings (e.g., *time will tell*; *a slippery slope*) an advantage over near-synonymous ones (e.g., *time will say*, *a slippery track*) in the "competition" to attain MWI status in the language. Research indicates that a structural pattern such as alliteration and (near-) rhyme (e.g., *go with the flow*, *cook the books*) can also render L2 expressions relatively memorable (see Eyckmans & Lindstromberg, 2017, for a review), at least when learners' attention is directed to the presence of the pattern (e.g., Eyckmans, Boers, & Lindstromberg, 2016). The evidence for a comparative advantage of alliterative and/or rhyming MWIs in learning conditions *without* attention-directing has been mixed and less compelling. (e.g., Boers, Lindstromberg, & Eyckmans, 2014). It may nonetheless be worth taking such structural patterns into consideration also when examining and comparing the rate of uptake of MWIs during incidental learning activities such as reading-while-listening, in case they do facilitate uptake (Boers, Lindstromberg, & Webb, 2014). An unexplored possibility to date appears to be the use of typographic enhancement to direct learners' attention to patterns such as alliteration during reading.

Looking at a Particular Case: Phrasal and Prepositional Verbs

The class of MWIs known as phrasal and prepositional verbs (e.g., *look it up*, *make up a story*, *look up to someone*) helps to illustrate several of the factors discussed earlier, but also to illustrate two extra ones. One of these extra factors is the typological proximity vs. distance between the learner's L1 and the target language. Although there are no grounds for believing that languages differ in their overall degree of "formulaicity" or "idiomaticity" (Stengers et al., 2011), there may be a class of MWIs in the target language that is absent from (or rare in) the learner's L1. For many learners of English this holds true for phrasal and prepositional verbs (henceforth PVs). The absence of a structurally similar category of phrasal units in these learners' L1 (e.g., in the case of romance languages) is one explanation for their poor knowledge of English PVs as attested, for example, in Garnier and Schmitt (2016). It also helps to explain why such learners tend to avoid using them when single-word alternatives (e.g., *refuse* instead of *turn down*) are available (Dagut & Laufer, 1985; Liao & Fukuya, 2004; Siyanova & Schmitt, 2007). For learners whose L1 does have structural equivalents, learning English PVs has been shown to be less troublesome (Hulstijn & Marchena, 1989; Laufer & Eliasson, 1993). In short, the case of PVs demonstrates another level of L1 influence than the sort of inter-lexical interference we discussed above in connection with collocational partnerships, because – depending on the learners' L1 background – it can concern a whole class of MWIs.

Many English PVs occur frequently in natural discourse and, given the positive association between frequent encounters and uptake, this can be expected to aid acquisition. This, however, leads us to the second factor which PVs help to illustrate – their highly polysemous nature (Gardner & Davies, 2007). The same verb + particle combination can have various uses (e.g., *make up a story* vs. *make up after an argument* vs. *make up one's face* vs. *make up the difference* vs. *make up a bed* vs. *make up for something*). Learning to discriminate between these various functions as they occur in input texts is likely to require many encounters with the same verb + particle combination, and learning PVs deliberately must be intricate as well, because it requires establishing different meaning correspondences for a single form.

Add to this some of the factors discussed earlier, and the complexity of mastering PVs becomes even more apparent. For example, the words which make up PVs – short (high-frequency) verbs and prepositions – tend not to be particularly distinctive, and so (1) they are not likely to attract much spontaneous attention and (2) they are susceptible to the kind of intra-lexical interference already mentioned in connection with verb-noun collocations (Strong & Boers, 2019). Another factor is the non-compositionality (and thus likely non-transparency) of many PVs. In that regard, PVs pose interpretation problems akin to (other) idioms. In some cases, the form-meaning correspondence of a figuratively used PV can be made more memorable if a plausible explanation for this correspondence is available. For example, the use of *out* in PVs such as *find out* and *figure out* may be explained as follows: (1) people associate understanding/knowing something with seeing it (hence expressions such as *I see*, meaning "I understand"); (2) if something is inside a closed container one cannot see it, and thus not "know" it; (3) if it is brought out of the container, it becomes visible and thus "known". Classroom experiments have yielded some support for such interventions (see Boers, 2013, for a review). There are limits to this, however, because (1) finding explanations such as these is certainly not always easy for teachers (but see Lindstromberg, 2010, for a helpful resource) and (2) not all such explanations may be perceived by learners as plausible, especially if the language manifests apparent contradictions (e.g., given the preceding seeing-is-knowing explanation for *out* in *find out*, why then do we say *look it up* and not "look it out"?). When we discussed the learning of idioms, we mentioned how catchy sound patterns such as alliteration and rhyme can render the lexical composition of a fair number of those MWIs comparatively memorable. Unfortunately, the class of PVs has very few members that are amenable to this.

On a more positive note, although many PVs are polysemous, not all their uses are equally common. Once the frequent uses have been identified through corpus research (Garnier & Schmitt, 2015), these may then be given priority in instructional materials, in the same spirit as giving priority to high-utility words over lower-utility ones in language programs (Nation, 2013).

Future Directions

While considerable advances have been made in identifying factors that affect the learning of MWIs, several questions remain. One set of questions concerns the profile of the learners. For example, age may matter. If it is true that adult learners' familiarity with written language leads them to treat words rather than larger units as the building blocks of language (Wray, 2002), then one may wonder if young L2 learners are more inclined than (literate) adults to pick up "chunks" from L2 discourse (e.g., Myles, Hooper, & Mitchel, 1998). Another learner characteristic is (phonological) short-term memory, which has already been shown to play an important part in other domains of language learning (e.g., Martin & Ellis, 2012; Speciale, Ellis, & Bywater, 2004), and which seems very likely to matter also here, given the polyword nature of MWIs. A third factor inviting further research is the nature of learners' prior L2 learning experience. Of particular pedagogic relevance here is the extent to which instructional programs with a regular focus on MWIs (e.g., Boers, Eyckmans, Kappel, Stengers, & Demecheleer, 2006; Jones & Haywood, 2004; Peters & Pauwels, 2015) foster a long-term appreciation of phraseology, such that learners will autonomously notice and learn MWIs long after completing the instructional program.

Another question is to what extent the factors discussed in this chapter affect the learning of MWIs in various language types (e.g., Durrant, 2013). The research on MWI learning to date is no different from the larger body of research on second or foreign language learning in that the vast majority of the publications focus on English as the target language.

A final point worth reiterating is that it would be helpful if future investigations of the rates of MWI learning observed under particular input conditions or pedagogic interventions could also examine differential effects at the item level. Owing to the great diversity of MWIs as well as the multifaceted nature of MWI knowledge, it is very likely that instructional choices that work well for some MWIs and for some purposes will not work as well for others. Horses for courses, so to speak. In this regard, we have mentioned potential factors such as compositionality, congruency with L1, frequency of occurrence, collocational strength, collocational proximity, length of the expression, morpho-syntactic fixedness, and catchiness of intra-lexical phonological patterns. All these concern MWIs as whole units, however. Meriting further research as well is how features of the building blocks of MWIs, i.e., their constituent words, influence their learnability and can inform pedagogic intervention.

Further Reading

Heredia, R., & Cieślicka, A. (Eds.) (2015). *Bilingual figurative language processing*. Cambridge, UK: Cambridge University Press.

This edited volume provides much greater coverage of the research on the processing and acquisition of L2 figurative expressions, such as idioms, than could be offered in the present chapter.

Siyanova-Chanturia, A., & Pellicer-Sánchez, A. (Eds.). (2018). *Understanding formulaic language: A second language acquisition perspective*. London, UK: Routledge.

This edited volume offers state-of-the-art reviews of research on the nature, processing, and acquisition of formulaic language (an umbrella term for a range of multiword items). Five of the reviews are pedagogy oriented.

Related Topics

Defining multiword items/types of multiword items, learning single-word items vs. multiword items, processing single and multiword items, incidental vocabulary learning, deliberate vocabulary learning, resources for learning multiword items, evaluating exercises for learning vocabulary, measuring knowledge of multiword items, key issues in teaching multiword items, key issues in researching multiword items

References

Bestgen, Y. (2017). Beyond single-word measures: L2 writing assessment, lexical richness and formulaic competence. *System, 69*, 65–78.

Biber, D., & Barbieri, F. (2007). Lexical bundles in university spoken and written registers. *English for Specific Purposes, 26*, 263–286.

Biber, D., Conrad, S., & Cortes, V. (2004). If you look at . . . : Lexical bundles in university teaching and textbooks. *Applied Linguistics, 25*, 371–405.

Bishop, H. (2004). The effect of typographic salience on the look up and comprehension of unknown formulaic sequences. In N. Schmitt (Ed.), *Formulaic sequences* (pp. 227–248). Amsterdam: John Benjamins.

Boers, F. (2003). Applied linguistics perspectives on cross-cultural variation in conceptual metaphor. *Metaphor and Symbol, 18*, 231–238.

Boers, F. (2013). Cognitive Linguistic approaches to second language vocabulary: Assessment and integration. *Language Teaching, 46*, 208–224.

Boers, F., Dang, C. T., & Strong, B. (2017). Comparing the effectiveness of phrase-focused exercises. A partial replication of Boers, Demecheleer, Coxhead, and Webb (2014). *Language Teaching Research, 21*, 362–280.

Boers, F., Demecheleer, M., Coxhead, A., & Webb, S. (2014). Gauging the effects of exercises on verb – noun collocations. *Language Teaching Research, 18*, 54–74.

Boers, F., Demecheleer, M., He, L., Deconinck, J., Stengers, H., & Eyckmans, J. (2017). Typographic enhancement of multiword units in second language text. *International Journal of Applied Linguistics, 27*, 448–469.

Boers, F., Eyckmans, J., Kappel, J., Stengers, H., & Demecheleer, M. (2006). Formulaic sequences and perceived oral proficiency: Putting a lexical approach to the test. *Language Teaching Research, 10*, 245–261.

Boers, F., Eyckmans, J., & Stengers, H. (2007). Presenting figurative idioms with a touch of etymology: More than mere mnemonics? *Language Teaching Research, 11*, 43–62.

Boers, F., & Lindstromberg, S. (2009). *Optimizing a lexical approach to instructed second language acquisition*. Basingstoke, UK: Palgrave Macmillan.

Boers, F., Lindstromberg, S., & Eyckmans, J. (2014). Is alliteration mnemonic without awareness-raising? *Language Awareness, 23*, 291–303.

Boers, F., Lindstromberg, S., & Webb, S. (2014). Further evidence of the comparative memorability of alliterative expressions in second language learning. *RELC Journal*, *45*, 85–99.

Boers, F., & Webb, S. (2015). Gauging the semantic transparency of idioms: Do natives and learners see eye to eye? In R. Heredia & A. Cieślicka (Eds.), *Bilingual figurative language processing* (pp. 368–392). Cambridge, UK: Cambridge University Press.

Bybee, J. (2002). Phonological evidence for exemplar storage of multiword sequences. *Studies in Second Language Acquisition*, *24*, 215–221.

Chen, Y. (2016). Dictionary use for collocation production and retention: A CALL-based study. *International Journal of Lexicography*, *30*, 225–251.

Choi, S. (2017). Processing and learning of enhanced English collocations: An eye-movement study. *Language Teaching Research*, *21*, 403–426.

Cieślicka, A. (2006). Literal salience in on-line processing of idiomatic expressions by second language learners. *Second Language Research*, *22*, 115–144.

Cieślicka, A. (2010). Formulaic Language in L2: Storage, retrieval and production of idioms by second language learners. In M. Putz & L. Sicola (Eds.), *Cognitive processing in second language acquisition* (pp. 149–168). Amsterdam: John Benjamins.

Crossley, A. S., Salsbury, T., & McNamara, D. S. (2015). Assessing lexical proficiency using analytic ratings: A case for collocation accuracy. *Applied Linguistics*, *36*, 570–590.

Dagut, M., & Laufer, B. (1985). Avoidance of phrasal verbs – A case for contrastive analysis. *Studies in Second Language Acquisition*, *7*, 73–79.

Durrant, P. (2013). Formulaicity in an agglunating language: The case of Turkish. *Corpus Linguistics and Linguistic Theory*, *9*, 1–38.

Dziemianko, A. (2014). On the presentation and placement of collocations in monolingual English learners' dictionaries: Insights into encoding and retention. *International Journal of Lexicography*, *27*, 259–279.

Eyckmans, J., Boers, F., & Lindstromberg, S. (2016). The impact of imposing processing strategies on L2 learners' deliberate study of lexical phrases. *System*, 56, 127–139.

Eyckmans, J., & Lindstromberg, S. (2017). The power of sound in L2 idiom learning. *Language Teaching Research*, *21*, 341–361.

Gardner, D., & Davies, M. (2007). Pointing out frequent phrasal verbs: A corpus-based analysis. *TESOL Quarterly*, *41*, 339–359.

Garnier, M., & Schmitt, N. (2015). The PHaVE List: A pedagogical list of phrasal verbs and their most frequent meaning senses. *Language Teaching Research*, *19*, 645–666.

Garnier, M., & Schmitt, N. (2016). Picking up polysemous phrasal verbs: How many do learners know and what facilitates this knowledge? *System*, *59*, 29–44.

Grant, L., & Bauer, L. (2004). Criteria for redefining idioms: Are we barking up the wrong tree? *Applied Linguistics*, *25*, 38–61.

Hoang, H., & Boers, F. (2016). Re-telling a story in a second language: How well do adult learners mine an input text for multiword expressions? *Studies in Second Language Learning and Teaching*, *6*, 513–535.

Hoey, M. (2005). *Lexical priming: A new theory of words and language*. London, UK: Routledge.

Hu, Y-H., & Fong, Y-Y. (2010). Obstacles to conceptual-metaphor guided L2 idiom interpretation. In S. De Knop, F. Boers, & A. De Rycker (Eds.), *Fostering language teaching efficiency through cognitive linguistics* (pp. 293–317). Berlin: Mouton de Gruyter.

Hulstijn, J. H., & Marchena, E. (1989). Avoidance: Grammatical or semantic causes? *Studies in Second Language Acquisition*, *11*, 241–255.

Jones, M., & Haywood, S. (2004). Facilitating the acquisition of formulaic sequences: An exploratory study. In N. Schmitt (Ed.), *Formulaic sequences* (pp. 269–300). Amsterdam: John Benjamins.

Kövecses, Z. (2005). *Metaphor in culture: Universality and variation*. Cambridge, UK: Cambridge University Press.

Kövecses, Z., & Szabó, P. (1996). Idioms: A view from cognitive semantics. *Applied Linguistics*, *17*, 326–355.

Kremmel, B., Brunfaut, T., & Alderson, J. C. (2017). Exploring the role of phraseological knowledge in foreign language reading. *Applied Linguistics, 38*, 848–870.

Laufer, B. (2011). The contribution of dictionary use to the production and retention of collocations in a second language. *International Journal of Lexicography, 24*, 29–49.

Laufer, B., & Eliasson, S., (1993). What causes avoidance in L2 learning: L1–L2 difference, L1–L2 similarity, or L2 complexity? *Studies in Second Language Acquisition, 15*, 35–48.

Laufer, B., & Girsai, N. (2008). Form-focused instruction in second language vocabulary learning: A case for contrastive analysis and translation. *Applied Linguistics, 29*, 694–716.

Laufer, B., & Waldman, T. (2011). Verb-noun collocations in second language writing: A corpus analysis of learners' English. *Language Learning, 61*, 647–672.

Liao, Y., & Fukuya, Y. J. (2004). Avoidance of phrasal verbs: The case of Chinese learners of English. *Language Learning, 54*, 193–226.

Lin, P. M. (2012). Sound evidence: The missing piece of the jigsaw in formulaic language research. *Applied Linguistics, 33*, 342–347.

Lindstromberg, S. (2010). *English prepositions explained* (2nd ed.). Amsterdam: John Benjamins.

Lindstromberg, S. (2018). Surplus interword phonological similarity in English multiword units. *Corpus Linguistics and Linguistic Theory*. Ahead of print: https://doi.org/10.1515/cllt-2017-0013.

Littlemore, J., Chen, P. T., Koester, A., & Barnden, J. (2011). Difficulties in metaphor comprehension faced by international students whose first language is not English. *Applied Linguistics, 32*, 408–429.

Macis, M., & Schmitt, N. (2017). Not just "small potatoes": Knowledge of the idiomatic meanings of collocations. *Language Teaching Research, 21*, 321–340.

Martin, K. I., & Ellis, N. C. (2012). The roles of phonological STM and working memory in L2 grammar and vocabulary learning. *Studies in Second Language Acquisition, 34*, 379–413.

Martinez, R., & Murphy, V. A. (2011). Effect of frequency and idiomaticity on second language reading comprehension. *TESOL Quarterly, 45*, 267–290.

Martinez, R., & Schmitt, N. (2012). A phrasal expressions list. *Applied Linguistics, 33*, 299–320.

McCarthy, M., & O'Dell, F. (2002). *English idioms in use*. Cambridge, UK: Cambridge University Press.

McCarthy, M., & O'Dell, F. (2005). *English collocations in use*. Cambridge, UK: Cambridge University Press.

Myles, F., Hooper, J., & Mitchel, R. (1998). Rote or rule? Exploring the role of formulaic language in classroom foreign language learning. *Language Learning, 48*, 323–364.

Nation, I. S. P. (2013). *Learning vocabulary in another language* (2nd ed.). Cambridge, UK: Cambridge University Press.

Nesselhauf, N. (2003). The use of collocations by advanced learners of English and some implications for teaching. *Applied Linguistics, 24*, 223–242.

Nguyen, T. M. H., & Webb, S. (2017). Examining second language receptive knowledge of collocation and factors that affect learning. *Language Teaching Research, 21*, 298–320.

Paivio, A. (1986). *Mental representations: A dual coding approach*. New York, NY: Oxford University Press.

Pellicer-Sánchez, A. (2017). Learning L2 collocations incidentally from reading. *Language Teaching Research, 21*, 381–402.

Peters, E. (2012). Learning German formulaic sequences: The effect of two attention-drawing techniques. *Language Learning Journal, 40*, 65–79.

Peters, E. (2014). The effects of repetition and time of post-test administration on EFL learners' form recall of single words and collocations. *Language Teaching Research, 18*, 75–94.

Peters, E. (2016). The learning burden of collocations: The role of interlexical and intralexical factors. *Language Teaching Research, 20*, 113–138.

Peters, E., & Pauwels, P. (2015). Learning academic formulaic sequences. *Journal of English for Academic Purposes, 20*, 28–39.

Rayner, K., Slattery, T. J., Drieghe, D., & Liversedge, S. P. (2011). Eye movements and word skipping during reading: Effects of word length and predictability. *Journal of Experimental Psychology. Human Perception and Performance, 37*, 514–528.

Rott, S. (1999). The effect of exposure frequency on intermediate language learners' incidental vocabulary acquisition and retention through reading. *Studies in Second Language Acquisition, 21,* 589–619.

Sharwood-Smith, M. (1993). Input enhancement and instructed SLA: Theoretical bases. *Studies in Second Language Acquisition, 15,* 165–179.

Simpson-Vlach, R., & Ellis, N. C. (2010). An academic formulas list: New methods in phraseology research. *Applied Linguistics, 31,* 487–512.

Sinclair, J. (1991). *Corpus, concordance, collocation.* Oxford, UK: Oxford University Press.

Siyanova, A., & Schmitt, N. (2007). Native and nonnative use of multi-word vs. one-word verbs. *International Review of Applied Linguistics, 45,* 119–139.

Sonbul, S., & Schmitt, N. (2013). Explicit and implicit lexical knowledge: Acquisition of collocations under different input conditions. *Language Learning, 63,* 121–159.

Speciale, G., Ellis, N. C., & Bywater, T. (2004). Phonological sequence learning and short-term store capacity determine second language vocabulary acquisition. *Applied Psycholinguistics, 25,* 293–321.

Steinel, M. P., Hulstijn, J. H., & Steinel, W. (2007). Second language idiom learning in a paired-associate paradigm: Effects of direction of learning, direction of testing, idiom imageability, and idiom transparency. *Studies in Second Language Acquisition, 29,* 449–484.

Stengers, H., Boers, F., Housen, A., & Eyckmans, J. (2011). Formulaic sequences and L2 oral proficiency: Does the type of target language influence the association? *International Review of Applied Linguistics in Language Teaching, 49,* 321–343.

Strong, B., & Boers, F. (2019). The error in trial and error: Exercises on phrasal verbs. *TESOL Quarterly, 53,* 289–319.

Szczepaniak, R., & Lew, R. (2011). The role of imagery in dictionaries of idioms. *Applied Linguistics, 32,* 323–347.

Szudarski, P., & Carter, R. (2016). The role of input flood and input enhancement in EFL learners' acquisition of collocations. *International Journal of Applied Linguistics, 26,* 245–265.

Taylor, J. R. (2012). *The mental corpus: How language in represented in the mind.* Oxford, UK: Oxford University Press.

Webb, S., & Kagimoto, E. (2011). Learning collocations: Do the number of collocates, position of the node word, and synonymy affect learning? *Applied Linguistics, 32,* 259–276.

Webb, S., Newton, J., & Chang, A. (2013). Incidental learning of collocation. *Language Learning, 63,* 91–120.

Williams, R. S., & Morris, R. K. (2004). Eye movements, word familiarity, and vocabulary acquisition. *European Journal of Cognitive Psychology, 16,* 312–339.

Wolter, B., & Gyllstad, H. (2011). Collocational links in the L2 mental lexicon and the influence of L1 intralexical knowledge. *Applied Linguistics, 32,* 430–449.

Wray, A. (2002). *Formulaic language and the lexicon.* Cambridge, UK: Cambridge University Press.

Yamashita, J., & Jiang, N. (2010). L1 influence on the acquisition of L2 collocations: Japanese ESL users and EFL learners acquiring English collocations. *TESOL Quarterly, 44,* 647–668.

Yeldham, M. (2018). The influence of formulaic language on L2 listener decoding in extended discourse. *Innovation in Language Learning and Teaching, 12,* 105–119.

Zhang, X. (2017). Effects of receptive-productive integration tasks and prior knowledge of component words on L2 collocation development. *System, 66,* 156–167.

11

Learning Single Words vs. Multiword Items

Ana Pellicer-Sánchez

Introduction

Although vocabulary learning research has traditionally been characterized by a single-word-centered conceptualization of lexical knowledge, examining the acquisition of items beyond the single word has recently gained a more prominent role in vocabulary research. It is now widely agreed that multiword units[1] should also be a component of the vocabulary learning curriculum and that they should be taught alongside single-word items.

Single words and multiword units evidently differ in their form and in the form-meaning connections they bear with them. Multiword units have a more complex and usually longer form; they are subject to different levels of compositionality; and are commonly associated with more opaque, figurative meanings. Laufer (1997) claims that factors such as idiomaticity and complexity negatively affect the learning of lexical items, suggesting that idiomatic expressions are more difficult to learn than their non-idiomatic single-word equivalents. As Peters (2014) argues, "It is not unlikely that the learning burden of collocations is higher because it is more difficult to allocate attentional resources to the formal properties of two (or more) words compared to one" (p. 90). We might therefore expect that the distinctive features of single words and multiword units lead to sizable differences in their learning. The remarkable increase in the number of studies investigating the acquisition of multiword units has brought about a better understanding of the conditions leading to their learning. Nevertheless, the potentially differential learning patterns that single words and multiword units exhibit is yet to be empirically proven.

The aim of this chapter is thus to shed light into the learning of single words and multiword units and of the conditions that affect these processes. The present discussion is framed around three themes that are crucial in creating the conditions for successful vocabulary intake: the relative effectiveness of different modes of exposure; the need for repeated exposures; and the degree of noticing and attention to unknown vocabulary. The best account of the learning of these two types of lexical items is provided by those studies that have included both single words and multiword units in their experimental design. Thus, the present discussion and conclusions draw heavily from such studies (e.g., Alali & Schmitt, 2012; Laufer & Girsai, 2008; Peters, 2009, 2014). The paucity of this type of research makes us also resort in this discussion to empirical studies that have examined the learning of single words *or* multiword expressions. In spite of the myriad of methodological differences across these studies, it seems possible to identify some converging results from those earlier investigations.

Critical Issues and Topics

Successful vocabulary intake occurs "because certain conditions are established which facilitate learning", namely repetition, noticing, retrieval, varied encounters and varied use, and elaboration (Webb & Nation, 2017, p. 61). According to Webb and Nation (2017), two key factors underpin these conditions: repetition and the quality of attention at each encounter. This quality of attention to target items when they are encountered is determined, among other factors, by the learning approach chosen, as different teaching methods and input modes will make learners attend to lexical items in different ways and will result in different levels of engagement with the target vocabulary. Repetition and learning approach are two crucial issues in the teaching and learning of vocabulary and are therefore chosen to frame the discussion provided in this chapter. In addition to these two factors, the quality of attention to unknown vocabulary also depends on learners' noticing of the lexical items. Therefore, the third key issue discussed in this section is the examination of methods that have been used to increase learners' noticing of the target vocabulary in an attempt to foster their learning. The present section aims at shedding some light into our understanding of the learning of single words and multiword units in relation to these three main topics.

Effectiveness of Learning Approaches

The manner in which lexical items are learned affects their learning burden (Nation, 1990), and it is one of the factors determining the quantity and quality of attention that learners are likely to pay to lexical items. In the discussion of approaches to vocabulary learning, a main distinction is usually made between *incidental* and *deliberate* or *intentional learning* approaches. The main difference between these two complementary approaches is the intentionality (or lack of) to learn new lexical items and commit them to memory. Incidental learning is defined as "learning which accrues as a by-product of language usage, without the intended purpose of learning a particular linguistic feature" (Schmitt, 2010, p. 29), whereas in deliberate learning approaches learners have the specific goal to learn vocabulary (Schmitt, 2008). One of the key questions in the examination of the learning of single words and multiword units is whether the same approaches can be used to learn both types of items and whether they would have a similar effect on learning gains. In fact, the few available studies empirically comparing the learning of single words and multiword sequences have focused on exploring the relative effectiveness of different learning methods.

Deliberate Learning

The use of vocabulary activities that explicitly direct learners' attention to unknown lexical items creates the conditions for deliberate learning to occur. This happens for example when learners memorize a set of words from word lists, translation pairs, or flash cards. Investigations of the effect of explicit vocabulary activities on the acquisition of single words abound. Previous research has shown that a variety of explicit exercises and task types are effective for the acquisition of single words, with learning rates that go up to 70% in some studies (e.g., Laufer, 2005). Some of the methods investigated include memorization and mnemonic techniques such as the keyword method (e.g., Barcroft, 2009; Brown & Perry, 1991; Ellis & Beaton, 1993; Jones, 1995); written vocabulary activities, such as fill in the blanks and original sentence writing (e.g., Barcroft & Rott, 2010; Folse, 2006; Zou, 2016); and first language (L1) translation (e.g., Joyce, 2015), just to name a few. Empirical evidence has also shown that new vocabulary can be learned from pushed-output activities that make learners produce language orally (e.g., De la Fuente, 2002; Ellis & He, 1999; Ellis, Tanaka, & Yamazaki, 1994), and that these activities support learners in the challenging transition from receptive to productive knowledge. Deliberate learning of single words does not only lead to the acquisition of declarative knowledge of vocabulary (at the receptive and productive level) but also to the development of the automaticity and fluency with which newly learned words are processed (Elgort, 2011; Pellicer-Sánchez, 2015), triggering the acquisition of both representational and functional aspects of vocabulary knowledge (Elgort, 2011). As Schmitt (2008) notes, deciding which activity or explicit approach is best for vocabulary learning is problematic, because of the many methodological and contextual differences among the existing studies. A less problematic assumption though, is that the effectiveness of a particular task depends on the degree of involvement and engagement with the unknown vocabulary. As proposed by Laufer and Hulstijn (2001), the task's involvement load, i.e., the amount of need, search, and evaluation that it leads learners to do, affects word learning and retention. Research has shown that explicit activities with differing levels of involvement lead to different learning rates (e.g., Keating, 2008).

Luckily, studies examining the effect of explicit activities on the learning of multiword units is no longer an anomaly in vocabulary research. Recent research has provided evidence that multiword items can be deliberately learned from a range of activities that present items both in context and in a decontextualized manner (Le, Rodgers, & Pellicer-Sánchez, 2017). Multiword sequences can be learned from receptive activities, such as presenting multiword units in sentences with translations (e.g., Webb & Kagimoto, 2011) and from productive tasks that require learners to produce the multiword sequences in gapped sentences (e.g., Webb & Kagimoto, 2009) and in free sentence writing (e.g., Zhang, 2017). Among the different explicit approaches to the learning of multiword units, gap-filling exercises seem to be the most commonly used in EFL textbooks. Boers, Demecheleer, Coxhead, and Webb (2014) found that one of the most frequent formats involved matching exercises in which learners had to provide the missing components of the target units in the form of a gap-filling exercise, sometimes from a set of options provided. They found that this type of exercises actually led to very poor gains, which they interpreted as a consequence of learners making the wrong choices. Interestingly, Boers, Dang, and Strong (2017) found that most activities in EFL textbooks did not provide exemplars of the target multiword units before the focused exercise, which was identified as a possible source for the incorrect guesses and wrong choices that learners often make in gap-filling exercises. The use of concordancers might help to address this problem and a few studies have indeed shown that explicit activities that require learners to work with a concordancer help to build learners' formulaic knowledge (e.g., Chan & Liou, 2005; Sun & Wang, 2003). These studies have shown that focused instruction can lead to the improvement of learners' receptive and productive knowledge of multiword units, with productive knowledge usually measured in cued production tasks. Learning multiword units over an extended period of time can also promote the integration of the acquired knowledge in learners' writing (e.g., Alhassan & Wood, 2015; Peters & Pauwels, 2015). Sustained deliberate learning of multiword units can also be an effective awareness-raising technique. Jones and Haywood (2004) showed that the deliberate study of formulaic sequences over a ten-week period through reading and writing activities was successful in raising students' awareness of formulaic sequences and had a positive effect on learners' written productions. The relative effectiveness of the focused exercises examined depends on a range of factors such as the language proficiency of learners (Webb & Kagimoto, 2009), previous knowledge of multiword units, and the specific type of sequence examined (Chan & Liou, 2005).

Most of the explicit activities mentioned above have been used for the learning of both single words and multiword units. There are other activities, however, that seem to be especially (or even exclusively) relevant for the learning of multiword units, as they focus on exploiting a feature that is particularly salient in multiword sequences. Deliberate learning through activities that attempt to engage learners with salient features of multiword units, such as through building connections between idiomatic and literal meanings (e.g., Boers, Demecheleer, & Eyckmans, 2004) and through focusing on sound patterns (e.g., Boers, Lindstromberg, & Eyckmans, 2014; Eyckmans, Boers, & Lindstromberg, 2016) have been shown to lead to gains on learners' knowledge of multiword units. These approaches are likely to be more effective for the teaching of multiword units than single words (Alali & Schmitt, 2012).

The studies reviewed in this section suggest that the type of focused exercises that lead to the successful deliberate learning of single words, can also be effective for the acquisition of multiword units. Nevertheless, an important question is whether the same deliberate learning approach would result in similar gains for both types of lexical items. One of the few studies comparing the learning gains of single words and multiword units from explicit activities was conducted by Peters (2014). The EFL learners in this study were exposed to the target items in non-communicative, decontextualized vocabulary exercises. The two experimental groups differed in the time of the first posttest: Group 1 was tested immediately after the treatment; and Group 2 was tested one week after the treatment. Both groups were tested again two weeks after the treatment. Results showed that the explicit treatment led to the acquisition of vocabulary and that after only one session (approximately 100 minutes) learners could recall the form of both single words and collocations. Importantly, the recall of single words in the first posttest was significantly higher than that of collocations (Group 1: 8.10 vs. 6.81; Group 2: 5.00 vs. 3.57, out of 12), but the effect size was moderate for both groups. The significance of this difference disappeared in the second posttest (Group 1: 3.71 vs. 3.76; Group 2: 6.29 vs. 4.79).

The difference in learning gains for single words and multiword units seems to be modulated by the level of lexical mastery measured. Alali and Schmitt (2012) explored the learning of single words and idioms from three different deliberate learning conditions: (1) presentation of target items and translation equivalents; (2) presentation of target items and translations + oral repetition of target items; (3) presentation of target items and translations + fill in the gaps activities. They measured receptive and productive knowledge of the single words and idioms on immediate and delayed posttests (12 days after presentation). Results showed that the three learning conditions led to gains in knowledge of both single words and idioms, which led them to conclude that "the generally parallel results between idioms and words hint that other methodologies may also produce learning gains for formulaic sequences that are similar to the gains for words" (p. 165). Crucially, results showed that there were no significant differences between the learning of single words and multiword units from the three conditions at the level of recognition but significant differences emerged when looking at recall scores. Results of this study suggest that both single words and idioms can be taught using the same approaches and that they are learned at a similar rate when looking at receptive scores but interesting differences among the various learning conditions appear when recall scores are considered.

A different picture emerged from the results of the study by Laufer and Girsai (2008). They examined the effectiveness of three different learning conditions on the acquisition of single words and collocations: (1) a meaning-focused communicative approach that involved reading a text and a group discussion; (2) vocabulary activities including multiple-choice and fill-in the gaps; and (3) and a translation task with brief contrastive instruction. In the immediate test, the explicit contrastive analysis and translation group outperformed the other two groups in all measures of active and passive recall and this advantage was the same for single words and collocations. Importantly, although this was not the focus of the study, the descriptive statistics showed that the scores for collocations were higher than single words in all measures at both immediate and delayed testing points. These findings might suggest that the learning conditions investigated here, which were different from those examined by Alali and Schmitt (2012), had a stronger effect on the learning of collocations or that the multiword expressions in this study were easier to learn. Higher gains for collocations than for single words were also found in the studies by Kasahara (2010, 2011). Japanese university students in Kasahara (2011) were asked to remember a set of target items (either unknown single words or known-and-unknown word combinations) presented in a list alongside their definitions. Results of both immediate and delayed meaning recall tests showed that collocations allowed significantly better retention and retrieval of the meanings than the single words.

The studies comparing the learning of single words and multiword units seem to suggest that, provided that other factors and conditions remain constant, knowledge of both types of lexical items accrue in a similar way, and that "at least some of the teaching methodologies we use for individual words can be effective in teaching formulaic sequences" (Alali & Schmitt, 2012, p. 153). With the exception of Alali and Schmitt (2012) who suggested differences in learning gains at the recall level, the other studies do not seem to support the claim that multiword units are more difficult to learn than single words, with some studies even suggesting that certain multiword combinations might be easier to learn than single words (e.g., Kasahara, 2010, 2011). Even when an initial difference between gains for single words and multiword units was observed (Peters, 2014), it disappeared after a short period of time.

Incidental Learning

Meaning-focused activities with which learners engage for communicative purposes, without a specific intention to learn new vocabulary, create the conditions for incidental learning to occur. This happens, for example, when learners read a text or watch a movie for general comprehension. It is worth noting that this does not mean that there cannot be deliberate or intentional learning in these cases. We could easily imagine a situation where a learner is reading a text for comprehension, encounters an unknown word, and makes a deliberate and intentional effort to guess it from context and commit it to memory. We would then argue that there is intentionality and deliberate learning in this case, even though the condition was not intended to lead to deliberate learning. Distinguishing between incidental and deliberate approaches is difficult, but we can distinguish between the learning conditions that are intended to engage learners in intentional or incidental learning (Pellicer-Sánchez & Boers, 2019). Thus, the discussion presented in this section refers to those conditions that engage learners in a communicative activity without a particular focus on vocabulary, and where vocabulary learning happens as a by-product of the main communicative task.

Investigations on the incidental acquisition of single words are abundant and have mainly focused on learning from reading. The benefits of reading for the incidental acquisition of vocabulary have been demonstrated both for L1 speakers (e.g., Saragi, Nation, & Meister, 1978) and L2 learners (e.g., Day, Omura, & Hiramatsu, 1991; Zahar, Cobb, & Spada, 2001; Pigada & Schmitt, 2006; Pellicer-Sánchez & Schmitt, 2010; Webb, 2007). Studies exploring extensive reading treatments have generally revealed larger gains than those examining the effect of shorter reading tasks (e.g., Horst, 2005; Pigada & Schmitt, 2006; Pellicer-Sánchez & Schmitt, 2010; Webb & Chang, 2015a). Learning new words incidentally from listening is also possible, but the added difficulty in noticing unknown words in the auditory input has led to smaller gains (e.g., Brown, Waring, & Donkaewbua, 2008; van Zeeland & Schmitt, 2013; Vidal, 2011). The simultaneous presentation of written and aural input in reading-while-listening conditions has also afforded the incidental acquisition of single words (Webb & Chang, 2015b), with some evidence suggesting that this bimodal input condition might be superior to listening-only (Brown et al., 2008) and reading-only (Webb & Chang, 2012) conditions. Multimodal exposure that combines both verbal and visual information has also been shown to create the conditions for incidental vocabulary learning to occur. Single words can be learned from watching television programs (e.g., Rodgers, 2013; Peters & Webb, 2018) and captioned videos (e.g., Montero, Peters, & Desmet, 2018; Muñoz, 2017; Neuman & Koskinen, 1992; Winke, Gass, & Sydorenko, 2010), and the benefits seem to be higher than reading-only conditions (e.g., Neuman & Koskinen, 1992).

By contrast, very few studies have investigated the incidental learning of multiword items and the focus has long been on the acquisition of collocations. The available studies have shown that collocations can be successfully learned from reading (Pellicer-Sánchez, 2017) and reading-while-listening conditions (Webb, Newton, & Chang, 2013). The relative effectiveness of different input modes has recently been compared by Webb and Chang (under review) and results point at an advantage of the reading-while-listening mode over reading-only and listening-only. Importantly, Webb and Chang found that listening led to higher gains than reading, suggesting that listening might play a more prominent role in the acquisition of two-word combinations than of single words. The presence of intonation contours and prosodic form of multiword units may help learners identify them as chunks and might support their learning.

A direct comparison of the incidental learning of single words and multiword units has only been carried out by Laufer and Girsai (2008). The gains of the meaning-focused instruction group in their study, who completed only communicative tasks (i.e., reading comprehension and pair/group discussion), indicted that collocations were better learned from incidental exposure than single words, and this was the case both for the immediate and delayed posttests. However, the gains were in general quite low, leading them to conclude that the group that did not receive focused instruction showed very little learning. The combination of reading with focused activities led to better gains for both single words and collocations.

Overall, the same type of input modes that are beneficial for the incidental acquisition of single words seem to lead to the learning of multiword units (particularly collocations). Incidental learning gains for both types of items seem to be boosted when written and auditory input are combined in reading-while-listening conditions. Although listening has led to the smallest gains in single-word learning, initial evidence suggests that it may play a greater role in the learning of multiword units, pointing at a differential effect of input modes on the learning of collocations and single words.

Rate of Decay

It is evident from the discussion provided thus far that vocabulary learning studies have had a clear focus on examining *learning gains*. Nonetheless a common finding from the vocabulary learning literature is that part of that acquired knowledge decays (Schmitt, 2007). There has recently been a call for more research on the rate at which accrued lexical knowledge is forgotten, since a better understanding of the conditions that contribute to lexical decay, as well as of the factors affecting this process, will help to inform pedagogical practices. Recent investigations have shown that part of the lexical knowledge acquired from deliberate learning is lost after as little as one month and that the factors that affect the learning of words do not have the same effect on the process of decay (Barclay, 2017). Frequency of exposure is one of the factors that plays a role in the process of lexical decay and more exposures during the learning phase seems to lead to better retention of the learned vocabulary (Barclay, 2017). A pertinent issue to the present discussion concerns the durability of learning gains of single words and multiword units. Would newly acquired knowledge of multiword units be retained at the same rate as knowledge of single words or are any of these lexical items prone to a more rapid decay? A tentative answer to this question can be formulated by exploring the learning gains of those studies that have included both an immediate and a delayed posttest in their design.

One of such studies was conducted by Alali and Schmitt (2012). They measured knowledge of single-word items and idioms immediately after the treatment and on delayed tests (12 days after the presentation of items). The authors reported that the results of the immediate and delayed tests were very similar and that there was some expected decline. Although this was not the aim of the study, a comparison of the knowledge "lost", i.e., immediate scores minus delayed scores, of single words and idioms provides useful insights about their rate of decay. The reported descriptive statistics show that the amount of single-word and multiword knowledge that decayed from the immediate to the delayed test was very similar, with a loss of three points in both cases and both tests (form recall: 3.6 [single words], 2.9 [idioms]; meaning recall: 3.37 [single words], 3.87 [idioms]). These similar descriptive figures suggest that the newly acquired knowledge of single words and multiword units (at least of the type explored in this study) might be retained at a similar level.

A similar pattern was observed in the results of the study by Peters (2014). All participants were tested in two testing sessions, but participant groups differed in the time of those sessions (Group 1: one and two weeks after treatment; Group 2: immediate test and two weeks after treatment). A large and significant effect of time was found on the learning gains. Results of Group 1 showed that recall scores were lower in the second test, providing evidence that some of the lexical knowledge shown in the first test was lost one week later. Looking at the means of items in all repetition groups across the two testing sessions, we observe that there were more single words forgotten than collocations (1.46 vs. 1.02, max = 4). However, the interaction between test time and item type was only small. Unexpectedly, scores of Group 2 were actually higher in the second test than in the immediate test, which was attributed to the possibility of participants verifying their responses after the first test. Importantly for this discussion, the difference between the immediate and delayed tests for single words and for collocations did not reach statistical significance. Similarly, Laufer and Girsai (2008) observed that some of the scores in the one-week delayed test were higher than in the immediate test, which they also explain as the effect of learners' checking some of the items in the dictionary or with their peers after the first testing session. Interestingly, the collocation scores in the delayed test were always higher than those in the immediate test, whereas in the case of single words they were mostly the same or slightly lower. Although this was not empirically tested in their study and is based on observations of the mean scores, it might indicate interesting differences about the retention of knowledge of single words and multiword units. It is important to note though that the higher scores in delayed tests than in immediate tests could also be attributed to a testing effect, as has been suggested for both the retention of single words (e.g., Peters & Webb, 2018) and multiword combinations (e.g., Webb, Newton, & Chang, 2013).

Taken together, compelling evidence for any difference between single words and multiword items in the rate of decay is yet to be explicitly examined. Existing evidence points towards the similarity in the rate at which knowledge of single words and multiword units is not only learned but also forgotten.

Quantity of Encounters

Exposure to repeated encounters is a key factor in the learning of single words and multiword units (Wood, 2002). Research has furnished evidence that repeated exposure to new and partially known vocabulary is crucial in achieving lexical mastery. Studies exploring the role of frequency of exposure have mainly been conducted in the context of incidental learning from reading with far fewer studies examining frequency effects during vocabulary-focused instruction (Peters, 2014).

Earlier investigations of the role of frequency in the incidental learning of single words showed that repeated exposures to new vocabulary determined learning gains and suggested that the threshold for considerable vocabulary learning was around eight to ten encounters (e.g., Pigada & Schmitt, 2006; Pellicer-Sánchez & Schmitt, 2010; Webb, 2007). This number of exposures also seems to be sufficient for learning vocabulary from reading-while-listening conditions (Brown et al., 2008), but more encounters seem to be necessary if words are learned from listening-only conditions (van Zeeland & Schmitt, 2013). Although the specific frequency threshold suggested has varied, the majority of studies demonstrated the significance of the effect. Less conclusive evidence comes from studies looking at the effect of frequency of exposure on the acquisition of multiword units. In the context of incidental learning from reading, Pellicer-Sánchez (2017) and Szudarski and Carter (2016) showed that a higher number of encounters with new collocations was not necessarily better. Nevertheless, these studies compared only two frequency groups (4 vs. 8 in Pellicer-Sánchez, 2017; 6 vs. 12 in Szudarski & Carter, 2016). When increasing the number of frequency groups and the overall number of exposures to target collocations, a stronger and significant effect of frequency seems to emerge. The study by Webb, Newton, and Chang (2013) showed a significant effect of frequency of exposure, with an advantage of the 10 and 15 repetitions groups. This suggests that the frequency threshold for the learning of multiword sequences might be similar to that of single words. Through repeated exposures in written input learners do not only acquire knowledge of the form and meaning of words but they also improve the fluency with which single-word items (e.g., Godfroid et al., 2017; Mohamed, 2018; Pellicer-Sánchez, 2016) and multiword items (e.g., Pellicer-Sánchez & Siyanova-Chanturia, under review) are processed in context.

Repeated exposures to lexical items also play a major role in the deliberate learning of new vocabulary. Studies on single-word learning have shown that increased retrievals lead to significantly higher vocabulary gains in various deliberate learning conditions such as learning from word pairs (e.g., Nakata, 2017) and fill-in-the-blanks and sentence writing exercises (e.g., Folse, 2006). Very few studies have examined the role of repeated exposures on the learning of both single words and multiword combinations. Peters (2014) examined the effect of repetition (1, 3, or 5 exposures) on the deliberate learning of both single words and collocations from explicit vocabulary activities and found a large, significant effect of repetition on the scores of both types of lexical items. In general, words and collocations appearing five times were significantly better learned than those appearing only once. In the study by Alali and Schmitt (2012), the comparison of the learning conditions that received only one exposure to the target items and the two conditions that involved one extra exposure revealed an advantage of repetition for both single words and idioms, providing further evidence for the similar role of frequency for the two types of lexical items investigated. Crucially, findings showed that it was not just the amount but also the type of exposure that made a difference. Recall of both single words and multiword units was better achieved when the repetition was through written activities than through oral repetition of the target items, suggesting an interesting interaction between the number of exposures and the mode in which the items are repeated.

Frequency of exposure it is not the only factor affecting the learning process and its effect is certainly modulated by multiple factors. More recent investigations have rightly noted the complexity of this factor and the need to consider its interaction with other factors such as relevance, saliency, and distribution of the encounters, both for single words (Laufer & Rozovski-Roitblat, 2015; Webb & Chang, 2015a) and multiword units (Szudarski & Carter, 2016), abandoning the earlier, more simplistic view of the role of frequency of exposure. As Chen and Truscott (2010) argued, "the goal of research should not be to identify a definitive number of exposures needed but rather to understand a complex process involving multiple, interacting variables" (p. 694).

In spite of the very few studies examining the role of frequency of exposure on the learning of multiword units and of the scarcer evidence comparing its effect on single words and formulaic sequences, current research seems to suggest that both types of lexical items are very similarly affected by this factor, both in terms of the size of the effect and the number of encounters needed for sizeable gains to be accrued. Initial evidence also suggests that certain input modalities might modulate the effect of frequency of exposure, further demonstrating the need to look at the interactions between frequency and other influential factors.

Noticing of Unknown Vocabulary

Providing various and varied encounters with target lexical items does not guarantee their successful acquisition. For the input to turn into intake, learners need to notice those unknown items (Schmidt, 1990, 1992) and unfortunately this is not always the case. As Peters (2012) argues, "In order to learn new words, FL [foreign language] learners need to notice new words, allocate attentional resources to them and process their lexical information elaborately to establish a form-meaning link" (p. 66). In the case of formulaic language, not noticing the form of a multiword unit should have an effect on its processing and its learning as a lexical unit (Bishop, 2004). It could be argued that noticing is particularly important for the learning of multiword units, as certain types of sequences often consist of components that are known to learners and they might fail to notice their association with other (adjacent or nonadjacent) words. In deliberate learning through explicit vocabulary activities, the learning condition created ensures (or aims to ensure) to some extent learners' noticing of the target items as their attention is explicitly directed to the lexical items to be learned. However, a lack of noticing is particularly critical in incidental learning conditions, as "the mental elaboration which is claimed to affect retention may not necessarily take place" (Laufer & Shmueli, 1997, p. 89). Thus, an important concern in vocabulary learning research has been to explore ways to make target vocabulary more salient, increasing the chances of it being noticed by learners. These conditions characterized by steps to increase learners' attention to particular lexical items while maintaining the communicative goal of the activity have been described in the literature as being between the realms of intentional and incidental learning and have been referred to as *semi-incidental learning* approaches (Pellicer-Sánchez & Boers, 2019).

Two commonly used attention-drawing techniques include typographical enhancement (e.g., bolding, italicizing, and underlining) and instructions given to learners. Studies conducted with single words have shown that several types of attention-drawing techniques influence learners' look up behavior. Peters et al. (2009), for example, showed that a task-induced word relevance technique (i.e., making learners pay attention to unfamiliar words in the text via comprehension questions) affected not only learner's dictionary look up behavior but also promoted vocabulary knowledge. In the context of formulaic language learning, studies have shown that making multiword units more salient through typographical salience affects learners' look up behavior (Bishop, 2004), and that these changes in processing behavior lead to larger gains, with effects that are comparable to those of deliberate learning through explicit activities (Sonbul & Schmitt, 2013). Choi (2016), taking advantage of the benefits of eye tracking, provided empirical evidence that the benefits found in enhanced conditions were indeed due to an increase in the processing time on enhanced forms.

The really interesting question for the present discussion is whether a given attention-drawing technique would have a similar effect on the acquisition of multiword units and single words. Some evidence comes from a study by De Ridder (2002) who investigated the effect of typographic salience on clicking behavior on a text with highlighted hyperlinks. Results showed that learners were more likely to consult glosses which had highlighted hyperlinks, and that consulting glosses did not have a significant effect on text comprehension. De Ridder included both single words and multiword units in the study, which suggests that this technique could be used to increase learners' attention to both types of items. Unfortunately, no distinction was made between the two item types in the analysis.

The effect of typographical enhancement could be further increased by explicit instructions provided to learners. Peters (2009) examined the effect of combining textual enhancement and instructions on recall of individual words and collocations. The EFL learners in this study read a text with words and collocations underlined and glossed in the margin with L1 translation. Two treatment conditions were explored: Learners in Group 1 were told to read the text paying attention to unfamiliar vocabulary (general task); while learners in Group 2 were told to pay attention to unknown individual words and collocations that they encountered in the text. Results of an immediate, recall posttest showed that both treatments led to vocabulary gains but no significant differences between the two treatment groups emerged. Analysis of the interview data revealed that learners in both treatment groups exhibited the same strategies and attentional priorities. Results did not reveal a significant interaction between treatment conditions (i.e., general vs. specific task) and the type of item (single words vs. collocations), suggesting that the two attention-drawing techniques used had the same effect on both types of items.

In a follow-up study, Peters (2012) compared the effect of these two attention-raising techniques (instruction methods and typographical salience) on the learning of single words and multiword items. Results showed that asking learners to pay attention to formulaic sequences while reading was not an effective method, and that typographical salience (bold typeface and underlining) seemed to be a more effective technique, particularly in the case of multiword units. Learners recalled more formulaic sequences that were presented in the typographical salient condition than those that were not salient, however this was not the case for single-word items. These results came from a small number of participants and should therefore be treated with caution, but they indicate the need to further explore the differential effect that enhancement and attention-drawing techniques might have on formulaic sequences and single words.

Future Directions

The discussion provided in this chapter has identified some interesting trends that advance our understanding of the conditions contributing to the successful learning of single words and multiword units. The existing empirical evidence is scant and limited to a few contexts and types of items. Any conclusions drawn need to be taken as a tentative evaluation of the research that has been conducted thus far and need to be contested and corroborated in future research.

With the exception of those deliberate approaches that are specifically suitable for the teaching of certain types of multiword units (e.g., Boers et al., 2014), it seems that single words and multiword units can be learned from the same type of exposure and learning approaches. When other potentially confounding factors are controlled for (e.g., length of treatment, contextual factors, etc.), deliberate and incidental learning approaches lead to the acquisition of both single words and multiword units. Existing evidence suggests that different deliberate approaches cause similar gains in single-word and multiword learning, particularly at the level of recognition. Differences in the learning of individual words and sequences might emerge at the recall level, but further evidence is needed to confirm this conclusion. In the context of incidental learning, single words and multiword units exhibit a similar learning pattern, with studies suggesting that bimodal exposure in reading-while-listening conditions might lead to the highest gains. Recent evidence has pointed at the possibility of a differential effect of input modes on the two types of lexical items investigated, with listening possibly having a stronger effect on the learning of multiword sequences (Webb & Chang, under review). This differential effect of input modalities on the acquisition of single words and multiword units should be addressed in future investigations. Initial observations suggest that single words and multiword units are not only similarly learned but their knowledge also decays in a comparable way.

Concerning the role of the quantity of encounters with unknown vocabulary, research has shown that it is equally important for the deliberate and incidental learning of single words and multiword items. Nonetheless the effect of frequency is bound to interact with many other factors and future research should aim at gaining a better understanding of such complex interactions. As demonstrated in this chapter, studies on the learning of formulaic language have almost exclusively looked at the acquisition of collocations. Future research should look at other types of multiword units and compare the effectiveness of different learning approaches on the acquisition of sequences of distinct characteristics. It is remarkable that scarcely any studies have examined the effect of individual differences on the learning of single words and multiword items (e.g., Muñoz, 2017). This would clearly improve our understanding of the effectiveness of different learning approaches and would help to explain some of the conflicting findings.

In sum, the quality and quantity of exposures seem to be able to override the effect of the intrinsic properties of multiword units that have been claimed to make them particularly challenging for learners. The struggle with formulaic sequences may stem from the lack of sufficient and adequate exposure to unknown sequences and from the fact that, even when learners get appropriate exposure, they may fail to notice the sequences in the input (Bishop, 2004; Pawley & Syder, 1983). Fortunately, attention-drawing techniques such as typographical enhancement can help to solve this insufficient noticing. Future research endeavors should investigate the optimum combination of factors (i.e., repeated encounters, learning approach, level of attention, etc.) to maximize the learning of various types of words and multiword units.

Further Reading

Pellicer-Sanchez, A., & Boers, F. (2019). Pedagogical approaches to the teaching and learning of formulaic sequences. In A. Siyanova-Chanturia and A. Pellicer-Sánchez (Eds.), *Understanding formulaic language: A second language acquisition perspective* (pp. 153–173). New York, NY: Routledge.

This chapter provides a comprehensive review of empirical work that has examined the effects of different procedures for teaching and learning multiword units. The chapter is framed around two main approaches to vocabulary learning: incidental learning from meaning-focused input and intentional learning from explicit vocabulary activities.

Schmitt, N. (2008). Instructed second language vocabulary learning. *Language Teaching Research,* *12*(3), 329–363.

This review article provides an overview of second language vocabulary research and of the factors facilitating vocabulary learning, with a particular focus on single words. It discusses approaches for maximizing vocabulary learning in teaching programs.

Webb, S. & Nation, P. (2017). *How vocabulary is learned.* Oxford, UK: Oxford University Press.

This book provides an introduction to the main ideas behind the teaching and learning of vocabulary, covering both the learning of single words and multiword units. It provides a comprehensive overview of the factors and conditions contributing to vocabulary learning and discusses how to apply them to the design of a vocabulary teaching program.

Related Topics

Factors affecting the learning of single-word items, factors affecting the learning of multiword items, processing single-word and multiword items, incidental vocabulary learning, deliberate vocabulary learning

Note

1 The terms *multiword units* and *formulaic sequences/language* are used interchangeably in this chapter as the umbrella terms to refer to the different types of multiword combinations that have the tendency to occur together in written and spoken discourse.

References

Alali, F. A., & Schmitt, N. (2012). Teaching formulaic sequences: The same as or different from teaching single words? *TESOL Journal, 3*(2), 153–180.

Alhassan, L., & Wood, D. (2015). The effectiveness of focused instruction of formulaic sequences in augmenting L2 learners' academic writing skills: A quantitative research study. *Journal of English for Academic Purposes, 17,* 51–62.

Barclay, S. (2017). *The effect of word class and word length on the decay of lexical knowledge.* Paper presented at the Annual Conference of the American Association of Applied Linguistics, 18–21 March 2017, Portland, USA.

Barcroft, J. (2009). Strategies and performance in intentional L2 vocabulary learning. *Language Awareness*, *18*(1), 74–89.

Barcroft, J., & Rott, S. (2010). Partial word form learning in the written mode in L2 German and Spanish. *Applied Linguistics*, *31*(5), 623–650.

Bishop, H. (2004). The effect of typographic salience on the look up and comprehension of unknown formulaic sequences. In N. Schmitt (Ed.), *Formulaic sequences: Acquisition, processing, and use* (pp. 228–248). Amsterdam: John Benjamins.

Boers, F., Dang, C. T., & Strong, B. (2017). Comparing the effectiveness of phrase-focused exercises. A partial replication of Boers, Demecheleer, Coxhead, and Webb (2014). *Language Teaching Research*, *21*, 362–280.

Boers, F., Demecheleer, M., Coxhead, A., & Webb, S. (2014). Gauging the effects of exercises on verb–noun collocations. *Language Teaching Research*, *18*, 54–74.

Boers, F., Demecheleer, M., & Eyckmans, J. (2004). Etymological elaboration as a strategy for learning figurative idioms. In P. Bogaards & B. Laufer. (Eds.), *Vocabulary in a second language: Selection, acquisition and testing* (pp. 53–78). Amsterdam and Philadelphia, PA: John Benjamins.

Boers, F., Lindstromberg, S., & Eyckmans, J. (2014). Is alliteration mnemonic without awareness-raising? *Language Awareness*, *23*, 291–303.

Brown, R., Waring, R., & Donkaewbua, S. (2008). Incidental vocabulary acquisition from reading, reading-while-listening, and listening. *Reading in a Foreign Language*, *20*, 136–163.

Brown, T., & Perry, F. (1991). A comparison of three learning strategies vocabulary acquisition. *TESOL Quarterly*, *25*, 655–670.

Chan, T. P., & Liou, H. C. (2005). Effects of web-based concordancing instruction on EFL students' learning of verb–noun collocations. *Computer Assisted Language Learning*, *18*, 231–251.

Chen, C., & Truscott, J. (2010). The effects of repetition and L1 lexicalization on incidental vocabulary acquisition. *Applied Linguistics*, *31*(5), 693–713.

Choi, S. (2016). Processing and learning of enhanced English collocations: An eye-movement study. *Language Teaching Research*, *21*(3), 403–426.

Day, R. R., Omura, C., & Hiramatsu, M. (1991). Incidental EFL vocabulary learning and reading. *Reading in a Foreign Language*, *7*, 541–551.

De La Fuente, M. J. (2002). Negotiation and oral acquisition of Spanish L2 vocabulary: The roles of input and output in the receptive and productive acquisition of words. *Studies in Second Language Acquisition*, *24*(1), 81–112.

De Ridder, I. (2002). Visible or invisible links: Does the highlighting of hyperlinks affect incidental vocabulary learning, text comprehension, and the reading process? *Language Learning and Technology*, *6*(1), 123–146.

Elgort, I. (2011). Deliberate learning and vocabulary acquisition in a second language. *Language Learning*, *61*(2), 367–413.

Ellis, N. C., & Beaton, A. (1993). Factors affecting the learning of foreign language vocabulary: Imagery keyword mediators and phonological short-term memory. *Quarterly Journal of Experimental Psychology*, *46A*, 533–558.

Ellis, R., & He, X. (1999). The roles of modified input and output in the incidental acquisition of word meanings. *Studies in Second Language Acquisition*, *21*(2), 285–301.

Ellis, R., Tanaka, Y., & Yamazaki, A. (1994). Classroom interaction, comprehension, and the acquisition of L2 word meanings. *Language Learning*, *44*(3), 449–491.

Eyckmans, J., Boers, F., & Lindstromberg, S. (2016). The impact of imposing processing strategies on L2 learners' deliberate study of lexical phrases. *System*, *56*, 127–139.

Folse, K. (2006). The effect of type of written exercise on L2 vocabulary retention. *TESOL Quarterly*, *40*(2), 273–293.

Godfroid, A., Ahn, J., Choi, I., Ballard, L., Cui, Y., Johnston, S., . . . Yoon, H. (2017). Incidental vocabulary learning in a natural reading context: An eye-tracking study. *Bilingualism: Language and Cognition*, 1–22. Advance online view. https://doi.org/10.1017/S1366728917000219.

Horst, M. (2005). Learning L2 vocabulary through extensive reading: A measurement study. *The Canadian Modern Language Review, 61*, 355–382.

Jones, F. (1995). Learning an alien lexicon: A teach-yourself case. *Second Language Research, 12*(2), 95–111.

Jones, M., & Haywood, S. (2004). Facilitating the acquisition of formulaic sequences: An exploratory study in an EAP context. In N. Schmitt (Ed.), *Formulaic sequences: Acquisition, processing, and use* (pp. 269–300). Amsterdam: John Benjamins.

Joyce, P. (2015). L2 vocabulary learning and testing: The use of L1 translation versus L2 definition. *The Language Learning Journal, 46*(3), 217–227. https://doi.org/10.1080/09571736.2015.1028088

Kasahara, K. (2010). Are two words better than one for intentional vocabulary learning? *Annual Review of English Language Education in Japan, 21*, 91–100.

Kasahara, K. (2011). The effect of known-and-unknown word combinations on intentional vocabulary learning. *System, 39*, 491–499.

Keating, G. D. (2008). Task effectiveness and word learning in a second language: The involvement load hypothesis on trial. *Language Teaching Research, 12*(3), 365–386.

Laufer, B. (1997). What's in a word that makes it hard or easy? Intralexical factors affecting the difficulty of vocabulary acquisition. In N. Schmitt & M. McCarthhy (Eds.), *Vocabulary: Description, acquisition, and pedagogy* (pp. 140–155). Cambridge, UK: Cambridge University Press.

Laufer, B. (2005). Focus on form in second language vocabulary acquisition. In S. H. Foster-Cohen, M. P. Garcia-Mayo, & J. Cenoz (Eds.), *EUROSLA yearbook 5* (pp. 223–250). Amsterdam: John Benjamins.

Laufer, B., & Girsai, N. (2008). Form-focused instruction in second language vocabulary learning: A case for contrastive analysis and translation. *Applied Linguistics, 29*(4), 694–716.

Laufer, B., & Hulstijn, J. (2001). Incidental vocabulary acquisition in a second language: The construct of task-induced involvement. *Applied Linguistics, 22*, 1–26.

Laufer, B., & Rozovski-Roitblat, B. (2015). Retention of new words: Quantity of encounters, quality of task, and degree of knowledge. *Language Teaching Research, 19*(6), 687–711.

Laufer, B., & Shmueli, K. (1997). Memorizing new words: Does teaching have anything to do with it? *RELC Journal, 28*(1), 89–108.

Le, D. T., Rodgers, M. P. H., & Pellicer-Sánchez, A. (2017). Teaching formulaic sequences in an English-language class: The effects of explicit instruction versus coursebook instruction. *TESL Canada Journal, 34*(3), 11–139.

Mohamed, A. A. (2018). Exposure frequency in L2 reading: An eye-movement perspective of incidental vocabulary learning. *Studies in Second Language Acquisition, 40*(2), 269–293.

Montero Perez, M., Peters, E., & Desmet, P. (2018). Vocabulary learning through viewing video: The effect of two enhancement techniques. *Computer Assisted Language Learning, 31*(1–2), 1–26.

Muñoz, C. (2017). The role of age and proficiency in subtitle reading. An eye-tracking study. *System, 67*, 77–86.

Nakata, K. (2017). Does repeated practice make perfect? The effects of within-session repeated retrieval on second language vocabulary learning. *Studies in Second Language Acquisition, 39*, 653–679.

Nation, I. S. P. (1990). *Teaching and learning vocabulary*. New York, NY: Newbury House.

Neuman, S., & Koskinen, P. (1992). Captioned television as comprehensible input: Effects of incidental word learning in context for language minority students. *Reading Research Quarterly, 27*, 94–106.

Pawley, A., & Syder, F. H. (1983). Two puzzles for linguistic theory: Nativelike selection and nativelike fluency. In J. C. Richards & R. W. Schmidt (Eds.), *Language and Communication* (pp. 191–225). London, UK: Longman.

Pellicer-Sánchez, A. (2015). Developing automaticity and speed of lexical access: The effects of incidental and explicit teaching approaches. *Journal of Spanish Language Teaching, 2*(2), 112–126.

Pellicer-Sánchez, A. (2016). Incidental L2 vocabulary acquisition from and while reading: An eye tracking study. *Studies in Second Language Acquisition, 38*, 97–130.

Pellicer-Sánchez, A. (2017). Learning L2 collocations incidentally from reading. *Language Teaching Research*, *21*(3), 381–402.

Pellicer-Sánchez, A., & Boers, F. (2019). Pedagogical approaches to the teaching and learning of formulaic language. In A. Siyanova-Chanturia & A. Pellicer-Sánchez (Eds.), *Understanding formulaic language: A second language acquisition perspective* (pp. 153–173). New York, NY: Routledge.

Pellicer-Sánchez, A., & Schmitt, N. (2010). Incidental vocabulary acquisition from an authentic novel: Do things fall apart? *Reading in a Foreign Language*, *22*, 31–55.

Pellicer-Sánchez, A., & Siyanova-Chanturia, A. (under review). Learning collocations incidentally from reading: A comparison of eye movements in a first and second language.

Peters, E. (2009). Learning collocations through attention-drawing techniques: A qualitative and quantitative analysis. In A. Barfield & H. Gyllstad (Eds.), *Researching collocations in another language: Multiple interpretations* (pp. 194–207). Basingstoke, UK: Palgrave MacMillan.

Peters, E. (2012). Learning German formulaic sequences: The effect of two attention-drawing techniques. *The Language Learning Journal*, *40*(1), 65–79.

Peters, E. (2014). The effects of repetition and time of post-test administration on EFL learners' form recall of single words and collocations. *Language Teaching Research*, *18*(1), 75–94.

Peters, E., Hulstijn, J. H., Sercu, L., & Lutjeharms, M. (2009). Learning L2 German vocabulary through reading: The effect of three enhancement techniques compared. *Language Learning*, *59*(1), 113–151.

Peters, E., & Pauwels, P. (2015). Learning academic formulaic sequences. *Journal of English for Academic Purposes*, *20*, 28–39.

Peters, E., & Webb, S. (2018). Incidental vocabulary acquisition through viewing L2 television and factors that affect learning. *Studies in Second Language Acquisition*. Advance online publication. https://doi.org/10.1017/S0272263117000407

Pigada, M., & Schmitt, N. (2006). Vocabulary acquisition from extensive reading: A case study. *Reading in a Foreign Language*, *18*, 1–28.

Rodgers, M. P. H. (2013). *English language learning through viewing television: An investigation of comprehension, incidental vocabulary acquisition, lexical coverage, attitudes, and captions*. Unpublished doctoral dissertation, Victoria University, Wellington, New Zealand.

Saragi, T., Nation, I. S. P., & Meister, G. F. (1978). Vocabulary learning and reading. *System*, *6*(2), 72–78.

Schmidt, R. (1990). The role of consciousness in second language learning. *Applied Linguistics*, *11*, 129–158.

Schmidt, R. (1992). Awareness and second language acquisition. *Annual Review of Applied Linguistics*, *13*, 206–226.

Schmitt, N. (2007). Current trends in vocabulary learning and teaching. In J. Cummins & C. Davison (Eds.), *The international handbook of English language teaching* (Vol. 2, pp. 746–759). New York, NY: Springer.

Schmitt, N. (2008). Instructed second language vocabulary learning. *Language Teaching Research*, *12*(3), 329–363.

Schmitt, N. (2010). *Researching vocabulary: A vocabulary research manual*. Basingstoke, UK: Palgrave Macmillan.

Sonbul, S., & Schmitt, N. (2013). Explicit and Implicit lexical knowledge: Acquisition of collocations under different input conditions. *Language Learning*, *63*, 121–159.

Sun, Y. C., & Wang, L. Y. (2003). Concordancers in the EFL classroom: Cognitive approaches and collocation difficulty. *Computer Assisted Language Learning*, *16*, 83–94.

Szudarski, P., & Carter, R. (2016). The role of input flood and input enhancement in EFL learners' acquisition of collocations. *International Journal of Applied Linguistics*, *26*, 245–265.

van Zeeland, H., & Schmitt, N. (2013). Incidental vocabulary acquisition through L2 listening: A dimensions approach. *System*, *41*, 609–624.

Vidal, K. (2011). A comparison of the effects of reading and listening on incidental vocabulary acquisition. *Language Learning*, *61*(1), 219–258.

Webb, S. (2007). The effects of repetition on vocabulary knowledge. *Applied Linguistics, 28*, 46–65.

Webb, S., & Chang, A. (2012). Vocabulary learning through assisted and unassisted repeated reading. *Canadian Modern Language Review, 68*(3), 267–290.

Webb, S., & Chang, A. (2015a). Second language vocabulary learning through extensive reading with audio support: How do frequency and distribution of occurrence affect learning? *Language Teaching Research, 19*, 667–686.

Webb, S., & Chang, A. (2015b). How does prior word knowledge affect vocabulary learning progress in an extensive reading program? *Studies in Second Language Studies, 37*, 651–675.

Webb, S., & Chang, A. (under review). How does mode of input affect the incidental learning of multiword combinations?

Webb, S., & Kagimoto, E. (2009). The effects of vocabulary learning on collocation and meaning. *TESOL Quarterly, 43*, 55–77.

Webb, S., & Kagimoto, E. (2011). Learning collocations: Do the number of collocates, position of the node word, and synonymy affect learning? *Applied Linguistics, 32*, 259–276.

Webb, S., & Nation, P. (2017). *How vocabulary is learned.* Oxford, UK: Oxford University Press.

Webb, S., Newton, J., & Chang, A. (2013). Incidental learning of collocation. *Language Learning, 63*, 91–120.

Winke, P., Gass, S., & Sydorenko, T. (2010). The effects of captioning videos for foreign language listening activities. *Language Learning & Technology, 14*(1), 65–86.

Wood, D. (2002). Formulaic language in acquisition and production: Implications for teaching. *TESL Canada Journal, 20*, 1–15.

Zahar, R., Cobb, T., & Spada, N. (2001). Acquiring vocabulary through reading: Effect of frequency and contextual richness. *Canadian Modern Language Review, 57*, 541–572.

Zhang, X. (2017). Effects of receptive-productive integration tasks and prior knowledge of component words on L2 collocation development. *System, 66*, 156–167.

Zou, D. (2016). Vocabulary acquisition through cloze exercises, sentence-writing and composition-writing: Extending the evaluation component of the involvement load hypothesis. *Language Teaching Research, 21*(1), 54–75.

12

Processing Single-Word and Multiword Items

Kathy Conklin

Introduction

There are a number of "emergentist-type" models that hold that experience with language plays an important role in the creation, entrenchment, and processing of linguistic patterns: usage-based approaches, connectionist models, and exemplar models of linguistic knowledge. In these models, *frequency effects* reflect implicit learning, such that words' representations are strengthened each time they are encountered (Ellis, 2002). Crucially, this fundamental assumption should apply equally to single words, phrases, and constructions. However, an important question arises from views that maintain that linguistic representation and processing is underpinned by experience with language: what is the impact of learning, knowing and using more than one language?

Firstly, learning, knowing, and using more than one language means that language use is by necessity divided. In other words, second language speakers use both of their languages, including their L1, less frequently than monolinguals use their one language. This gives rise to reduced lexical entrenchment, which can be accounted for in different ways. One explanation holds that the connections between an item's orthographic form, phonological form, and its meaning are strengthened as a function of exposure. When there is less use, this results in weaker ties between an item's form (phonology, orthography) and concepts (e.g., Weaker Links Hypothesis: Gollan, Montoya, Cera, & Sandoval, 2008). Another potential explanation is that using more than one language leads to reduced baseline activation for L2 words and potentially for L1 words (e.g., Bilingual Interactive Activation Plus Model, BIA+: Dijkstra & van Heuven, 2002). The consequence of the "weaker links" and/or reduced baseline activation is slower processing. More precisely, single-word and multiword items should be processed more quickly by monolinguals, whose entire language experience is with one language, than by speakers of more than one language, whose language use is divided. Further, for speakers of more than one language, processing generally should be faster in their L1 than L2, as experience with the L1 is usually greater. If, on the other hand, language experience is fairly equivalent in the L1 and L2, processing speed should be correspondingly fast in the two, although slower than for a monolingual whose experience is not divided. Finally, if a speaker has greater exposure to the L2 than the L1, then processing in the L2 should be faster than the L1.

Emergentist and usage-based models predict that the frequency effects outlined earlier should be apparent for both single-word and multiword items. As will be discussed in more detail in the following section, native and non-native speakers by and large have a processing advantage for frequent words over infrequent ones. Native speakers have a well-documented processing advantage for multiword items, while the evidence for non-native speakers is somewhat mixed. One explanation for this is that non-native speakers have not encountered multiword items a sufficient number of times for an advantage to emerge. With increased proficiency, they should show a native-like pattern, presumably due to ample exposure/frequency. An additional possibility is that non-native speakers actually do have a processing advantage – it is simply that they have been tested on the "wrong" items. In other words, the language that learners encounter in textbooks and classrooms does not align well with native-speaker language – or at least not with language that is represented in large corpora which are often used to identify items for a study. Thus, it may be that L2 learners have a processing advantage for multiword items that appear in their textbooks, but not for matched items that are frequent in native-speaker language but that do not occur in their texts. In other words, non-native speakers may exhibit a sensitivity to the frequency of multiword units that they have encountered – it is just that they are not encountering the same ones as native speakers do. Such a finding would underscore the importance of the input textbooks and classrooms provide to learners.

A second consequence of knowing and using more than one language is that knowledge of one language can influence the processing of the other. That is, multiple languages can be activated simultaneously and this cross-language activation influences processing (e.g., Odlin, 1989). In general, effects of cross-language activation are seen where there are instances of cross-language overlap – and non-native speakers will have a repertoire of single- and multiword items that overlap in the L1/L2 in a variety of ways. For example, a French learner of English will have single-word items that overlap in the two languages in different respects: semantics only in *dog/chien*; orthography and somewhat in phonology but not semantics in *coin*-'money'/*coin*-'corner'; phonology but not orthography and semantics in *pool*-'place for swimming'/*poule*-'chicken'; and semantics, phonology, and orthography in *piano/piano*. Similarly, there will be multiword items that overlap in various ways, some of which are illustrated by the following idioms: *throw money out the window/jeter l'argent par les fenêtres*, which literally is "to throw money through the windows"; *to cost an arm and a leg/coûter les yeux de la tête*, which literally is "to costs the eyes in your head"; *to feel blue/avoir le cafard*, which literally is "to have the cockroach"; and "to have a hangover" has no idiomatic expression in English, but in French is *avoir la gueule de bois*, which literally is "to have the wooden face". An important question in the literature has been how these different types of overlap influence processing.

In the following section, we will look at the evidence for frequency effects for single- and multiword items in the L1 and L2. We will then look in more detail at the input that non-native speakers receive from their textbooks and how this might relate to the presence or absence of frequency effects. Finally, we will explore how cross-language overlap influences processing.

Critical Issues and Topics

Frequency Effects

As Monsell says, frequency of occurrence should be given "its rightful place as a fundamental shaper of a lexical system always dynamically responsive to experience" (1991, p. 150). This should be true for individual words and sequences of words that occur together (binomials *bride and groom*; collocations *abject poverty*; phrasal verbs *pick up*; idioms *kick the bucket*; lexical bundles *you know what*, etc.). Accordingly, in emergentist and usage-based theories, the frequency of the input – in both an L1 and L2 – underpins the development of linguistic knowledge and its organization, as well as having a profound effect on processing (e.g., Bybee & Hopper, 2001; Ellis, 2002). Items that are encountered more frequently, be that in an L1 or L2, are processed more quickly. Generally, speakers have more exposure to linguistic input in their L1 than L2, and monolinguals have more input in their single language than non-native speakers do to either language. This situation is depicted in Figure 12.1A, where the number of occurrences (frequency) for single-word and multiword items is greater going from the L2 to L1 and then to the single language of monolinguals. As frequency increases, processing is faster, which means that responses should be faster for monolinguals and then for non-natives in their L1, as well as for non-natives in their L1

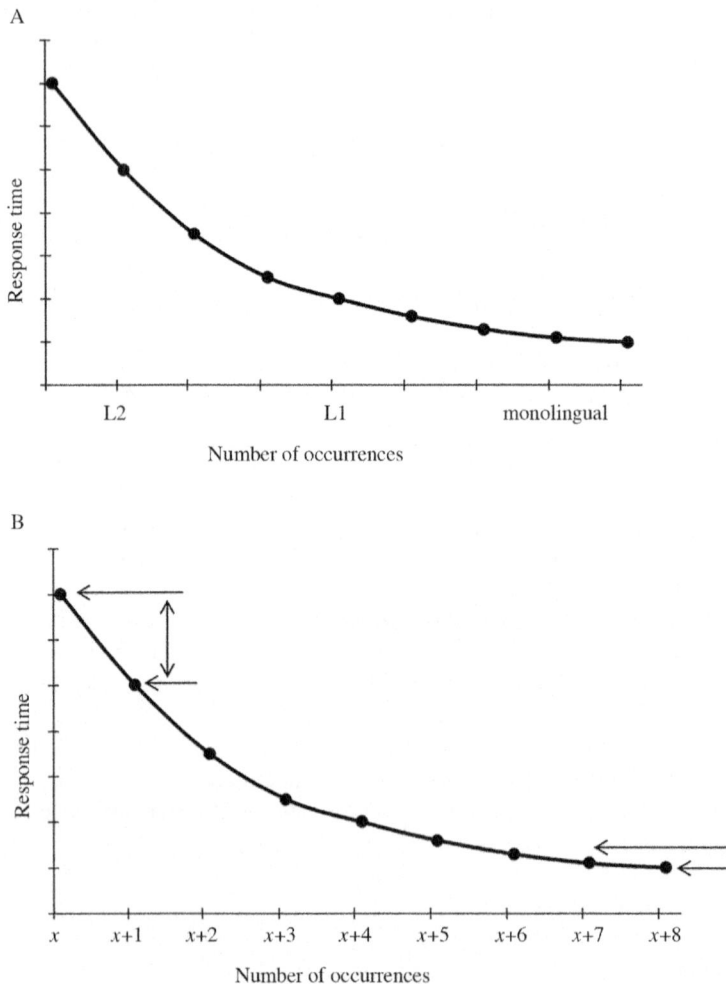

Figure 12.1 Panel A demonstrates that the number of occurrences (frequency) to linguistic input generally increases from L2 to L1 for bilinguals and then to monolinguals in their single language. Panel B illustrates asymptotic word processing and demonstrates that low frequency items benefit more from additional occurrences (*x* to *x* + 1) than high frequency items (*x* + 7 to *x* + 8).

compared to their L2. Alongside this, there are limits on how fast the processing system can get, and therefore word processing is thought to be asymptotic. This is illustrated in Figure 12.1B, which shows that with each occurrence of an item, progressively less speed-up occurs. Thus, low frequency words, which are farther to the left on the *x*-axis, benefit more from repeated exposures (become faster), while repeated exposures to high frequency words provides little gain. More precisely, going from *x* to *x* + 1 yields more of a processing advantage than going from *x* + 7 to *x* + 8. This has important consequences in the L2, where items have been encountered less, and therefore, should benefit more from increased exposure. In what follows, we will look at the evidence for these kinds of frequency effects for single-word and multiword items in the L1 and L2.

In the L1, there is plentiful evidence that frequently used words are easier to recognize and are responded to more quickly than less frequently used ones (e.g., *cat* vs. *gnat*), and that speakers are sensitive to fairly subtle frequency differences (for an overview see Harley, 2014). This has been substantiated across a diverse range of tasks that vary in their naturalness. On the less natural end of the spectrum, frequency effects have been found in tasks that present single words on a computer screen and measure decision/response times. For example, in a lexical decision task (deciding whether a string of letters is a word or not), frequent words elicit faster "yes" responses than less frequent ones. In eye tracking, where more natural stimuli such as sentences and longer stretches of text can be presented, a frequency effect has also been found: readers' eyes fixate less on high-frequency words than low-frequency ones. Taken together, there is robust and converging evidence that frequency influences the amount of processing effort for single-word items in the L1.

As is illustrated in Figure 12.1A, second language speakers generally have less exposure to their L2. In other words, items in the L2 have a reduced frequency. The implication of this is that they should activate words more slowly in the L2 than L1, and both more slowly than monolinguals. While there is a much smaller literature on L2 frequency effects (for a discussion see Diependaele, Lemhöfer, & Brysbaert, 2013), in studies that present single words and measure decision/response times (e.g., lexical decision task), the general finding mirrors what is depicted in Figure 12.1A – higher-frequency words are processed faster. Additionally, it has been found that second language speakers have larger "frequency effects" in their L2 than L1, as well as having larger frequency effects in their L1 than monolinguals do in their single language (see Whitford, Pivneva, & Titone, 2016).

We can understand these kinds of results in terms of Figure 12.1, and more concretely by considering bilinguals (who in this example have L1-English and L2-French) and monolingual English speakers. The bilinguals will have encountered L2/French words (e.g., *chien*) less than L1-English ones (e.g., *dog*), meaning that they are operating more towards the left-hand side of the figure. This is where differences from an additional exposure are greatest, thus yielding larger frequency effects in the L2. Further, the second language speakers will have encountered words in their L1 – because their language use is divided – less than monolinguals. Thus, their L1 is operating more to the left-hand side of the figure than monolinguals, which again means that small changes in frequency lead to larger effects. While eye-tracking findings are somewhat mixed, studies such as those by Diependaele et al. (2013) and Whitford and Titone (2012) largely bear out the patterns depicted in Figure 12.1. Notably, Whitford and Titone observed larger L2 than L1 frequency effects in L1-dominant speakers, and found that this effect was modulated by individual differences in current L2 exposure. Thus, in addition to mirroring what we have discussed thus far, they found that as L2 use increased, or in other words moved rightwards on Figure 12.1, less of a frequency effect was evident. The implication of increased L2 use is that less language use is dedicated to the L1, thereby pushing it leftwards on the figure, where frequency effects will be greater – which was the case in Whitford and Titone's study. Crucially, such evidence convincingly demonstrates that L1 and L2 word frequency effects are driven by an individual's experience with language.

Do multiword items demonstrate frequency effects akin to those that are found for single-word items? If they do, this would suggest that similar to individual words, each and every occurrence of a multiword item contributes to its entrenchment memory. To address this, studies generally compare decision/response times (e.g., responding to whether a string is a phrase or not) or eye tracking of more natural texts containing multiword items and matched novel language. For example, Carrol and Conklin (2014, 2017) compared the processing of the idiom *spill the beans* to a novel phrase *spill the chips* (frequency of 23 vs. 0 in the British National Corpus (BNC)). The processing advantage for the idiom compared to the control phrase was taken as an indication that the former is entrenched in memory. Thus, evidence for a frequency effect can come from comparing the processing of frequent and infrequent (or non-existing) multiwords items. Additionally, many studies look for an explicit effect of frequency, which is generally done by exploring whether frequency (established from a corpus) or a measure of familiarity (generally established in a rating task) can at least partially account for response times, often using mixed-effects or regression analyses.

There is a growing body of work showing that both children and adults in the L1 have a processing advantage for multiword items of various types (binomials, collocations, phrasal verbs, idioms, lexical bundles, etc.), and often such studies explicitly demonstrate frequency effects for multiword items (e.g., Arnon & Snider, 2010; Arnon & Cohen Priva, 2013; Bannard & Matthews, 2008; Carrol & Conklin, 2017; Durrant & Doherty, 2010; Jacobs, Dell, Benjamin, & Bannard, 2016; Siyanova-Chanturia, Conklin, & van Heuven, 2011; Tremblay, Derwing, Libben, & Westbury, 2011; Vilkaité, 2016). Taken together, research on the L1 demonstrates that reading, listening, and recognizing multiword items is influenced by frequency. In other words, multiword items are processed more quickly than novel language controls, and more frequent multiword items are processed more quickly than less frequent ones.

In the L2 literature, a similar processing advantage is not always observed for multiword items. In particular, idioms do not seem to exhibit the processing advantage in the L2 that they do in the L1 (e.g., Conklin & Schmitt, 2008; Siyanova-Chanturia, Conklin, & Schmitt, 2011). This has led to the claim that non-native speakers process multiword items more compositionally, which makes the properties of the individual words that make them up, as well as their meanings, more salient than phrase-level features such as frequency and meaning (Cieślicka, Heredia, & Olivares, 2014). In contrast, a usage-based approach would hold that non-natives simply have not encountered the idioms a sufficient number of times in the L2 for a processing advantage to emerge. A set of studies by Carrol and Conklin (2014, 2017) explored this question. They presented English monolinguals and Chinese/L1-English/L2 speakers with English idioms and controls (*spill the beans/chips*) and translated Chinese idioms and controls that did not exist in English, or in other words that had a frequency of zero in English (e.g., *draw a snake and add feet/hair*). In line with previous research, their results demonstrated faster processing of English idioms by monolinguals but not by the non-native speakers. Crucially, the Chinese-L1 speakers had a processing advantage for the translated idioms compared to their controls. This was explained by these multiword items being frequent, albeit in their L1. Thus, when idioms are frequent, they do demonstrate a processing advantage – even in the L2.

Work on more compositional multiword items demonstrates that non-native speakers are sensitive to L2 frequency (e.g., Hernández, Costa, & Arnon, 2016; Jiang & Nekrasova, 2007; Siyanova-Chanturia et al., 2011; Sonbul, 2015; Wolter & Gyllstad, 2013). For example, in an eye-tracking experiment, Siyanova-Chanturia et al. (2011) presented native and non-native speakers with English binomials (sequences of *x* and *y*, where *x* and *y* are from the same lexical class and often have a preferred word order, e.g., *church and state* vs. *state and church*). They found faster reading times for the binomials compared to their corresponding less frequent reversed forms. This was the case for native speakers, as well as for more proficient non-native speakers but not less proficient ones. Thus, non-natives who have higher L2 proficiency, and arguably more exposure to the L2, show the typical frequency advantage for the multiword items. This finding points to the importance of the amount of exposure, and therefore the input that non-native speakers receive.

Another body of research shows that processing time is not only dependent on the frequency of an individual word, but also on its predictability from the previous (and sometimes following) context (McDonald & Shillcock, 2003). In such research, predictability is generally conceived of in two ways. It can be a word-to-word contingency (often referred to as "transitional probability") that is established using a corpus. For example, the BNC can be used to determine how likely *on* is following *rely*. Alternatively, predictability can be established more subjectively and can be assessed relative to a particular discourse, sentence, or phrase context. This is generally done via a cloze task. For both types of predictability, more predictable words have decreased processing times, and in reading tasks, highly predictable words are often skipped altogether (Ehrlich & Rayner, 1981; McDonald & Shillcock, 2003). This has important implications for the processing of multiword items. For example, the word *abject* predicts a very limited set of upcoming words (*poverty, failure, misery, horror, terror, apology*), some of which could be considered frequent multiword items (e.g., the collocation *abject poverty*). Crucially, the predictability of these upcoming words will (largely) be predicated on language exposure – in other words frequency. For a word to become predictable, it will need to have occurred in the same/similar context a sufficient number of times.

Before turning to the next section, it is important to note a caveat about frequency. Frequency measures from corpora are often viewed as an index of linguistic experience. Thus, if word *y* is frequent in a large, representative corpus, it is assumed that speakers have encountered it more than word *z* that is less frequent in the corpus. Often the corpora that are used provide measures of printed word frequency, which we know intuitively do not provide a metric of all of a speakers' wide and varied experience with language. As Gernsbacher (1984) notes, corpora *only* provide an approximation of actual exposure, which may be particularly problematic for low frequency words. For instance, the word *recasts* only has a frequency of five in the BNC, making it very low frequency. However, in the SLA community the term is likely fairly familiar. Therefore, if we carried out a processing study on applied linguists, the word *recasts* would likely demonstrate faster processing than is predicted by its corpus frequency due to our exposure to the word. As this demonstrates, corpus frequency does not necessarily align with actual experience with a language. This will be particularly true for L2 speakers, especially in foreign language learning contexts. Because of this, subjective familiarity ratings may provide a more reliable measure of exposure to single-word and multiword items. The role of input on frequency effects will be explored in more detail next.

The Actual Input and Multiword Item Processing

What we have seen thus far is that, unlike native speakers, non-native speakers do not always demonstrate a processing advantage for multiword items. In particular, idioms do not seem to elicit a processing advantage. Idioms may be particularly problematic for non-native speakers because computing the meaning of the individual words does not generally yield the figurative meaning (e.g., *kick + the + bucket* = "die"). If we know that links between an item's form and meaning are strengthened by exposure, it may simply be the case that non-native speakers have not encountered idioms a sufficient number of times to strengthen the connections between the form (*kick the bucket*) and meaning ("die"). In fact, amongst the various types of multiword items, idioms tend to be fairly low frequency. Therefore, on an emergentist or usage-based approach, the lack of evidence for a processing advantage for idioms is not very surprising. Other types of multiword items, like binomials, tend to be higher frequency, and consequently we would expect a processing advantage for them. As we saw earlier, Siyanova-Chanturia, Conklin, and van Heuven (2011) found a processing advantage for binomials in more proficient non-natives but not in less proficient ones. This suggests that lower proficiency participants have not encountered the items a sufficient number of times – in other words are lacking in input – for them to be entrenched in memory, and as a result for an advantage to emerge.

One way to more specifically address the roll of input is to ascertain what multiword items are frequent in L2 input and then determine whether these items are processed more quickly than matched items that do not occur in the input. In a recent study, Northbrook and Conklin (2018) extracted three-word lexical bundles from the English textbooks of Japanese junior high school students. They compared the processing of these to matched control phrases that were not present in the textbooks, but which were much more common in a native-speaker reference corpus (e.g., lexical bundle *do you play*, 16 occurrences in textbooks and 136 in SUBTLEXus vs. control *do you hear*, 0 occurrences in textbooks and 1,183 in SUBTLEXus). The students performed a yes/no decision on whether a phrase was possible. Responses were more accurate and faster for lexical bundles that appeared in their textbooks. Further, more frequent textbook lexical bundles were responded to more quickly and accurately than less frequent ones.

This study is important because it indicates that not only are EFL learners sensitive to whether or not items occurred in their texts, but also to the frequency of occurrence of a given item in them. These findings support emergentist and usage-based approaches whereby every exposure to an item influences its entrentchment and processing. Crucially, these results underscore the importance of the input given to students. More precisely, their processing advantage was *not* for items that are frequent in the large native-speaker corpus (*do you hear*) but for ones that occur repeatedly in their textbook (*do you play*). It is important to note that the items in the study were not explicity taught, which highlights the importance of *all* of the input – even that which is only intended to provide supporting context in demonstrating a particular word, item or gramatical construction. These findings emphasize the need to carefully think through the input students are given. Further we need to consider the possibility that non-native speakers do not demonstrate a processing advantage for multiword items simply because they are not receiving enough of the "right" input and/or they are being tested on the "wrong" items. Finally, the Northbrook and Conklin study demonstrates that even beginning learners in an EFL context show a very native-like formulaic processing benefit for multiword items. More precisely, they are exhibiting a phenomenon that is evident in native speakers and advanced non-natives. Unfortunately, it appears that this advantage is for genre specific textbook language that is not reflective of actual native-speaker English.

Most of the literature exploring frequency effects in multiword items has focused on speakers who have had a considerable amount of input – even the junior high school learners in the Northbrook and Conklin study had been exposed to English for a few years. This leaves open the question of how much input is needed for a processing advantage to arise. This question is primarily being explored in the L2 literature (Pellicer-Sánchez, 2017; Sonbul & Schmitt, 2013; Szudarski, 2012; Webb, Newton, & Chang, 2013). These studies have either presented non-native speakers with (1) existing multiword items, however, even with pretests to assess knowledge, we cannot be certain that the items had never been encountered before, or (2) non-words, which may unduly draw attention to the items. A recent study by Conklin and Carrol (submitted) addresses these concerns, by monitoring monolingual readers' eye movements when they were presented with short stories containing existing patterns (*time and money*) and novel ones (*wires and pipes*). In line with the wider literature, they found a processing advantage for the multiword item (*time and money*) compared to a matched control (*money and time*). Crucially, at the beginning of the story there was no processing advantage for the novel item *wires and pipes* over *pipes and wires*. After encountering the former four to five times, an item-specific preference emerged, such that the former was processed more quickly than the latter. Remarkably, this happened during the course of reading a story, demonstrating that sensitivity to lexical patterns arises rapidly in a natural context.

These results support the view that multiword items are learned automatically. It is thought that when a person attends to a particular input that some of its attributes, such as frequency, which require little or no intentional processing, are automatically encoded in memory (Hasher & Zacks, 1984). Thus, when readers attend to a story, the frequency of lexical patterns is encoded. It is exactly this frequency of occurrence that allows for new multiwords items to become entrenched in memory and to elicit a processing advantage. An open question is how long-lasting this effect is: will the processing advantage that emerges after four to five occurrences of a novel pattern be evident a day later, a week later, etc.? Research looking at training on multiword items show that effects are apparent for up to two weeks (Sonbul & Schmitt, 2013) but decline after six (Szudarski & Conklin, 2014).

The Effect of Cross-Language Activation

A prominent factor affecting single-word recognition in an L1 is lexical ambiguity, or the number of meanings that a word has (e.g., *bank* "a place where you keep money", "the side of a river"). The frequency of meanings for an ambiguous word can be balanced (relatively equal) or unbalanced (one meaning is more frequent). The frequency of the two meanings *and* the strength of the (biasing) context in which the word appears both influence processing patterns and leads to what has been termed the *subordinate-bias effect* (Duffy, Morris, & Rayner, 1988). The basic finding is that when frequency-balanced ambiguous words occur in neutral contexts, readers spend more time processing them than unambiguous control words matched on length and frequency. However, if they occur in a context biased towards one of their meanings, there is no difference in processing times for the frequency-balanced ambiguous words and their matched controls. In contrast, there is no difference in processing for frequency-imbalanced ambiguous and matched control words in a neutral context. If a context biases a less-frequent meaning, processing times are longer for the ambiguous word than the control. The effect on response times resulting from having multiple meanings seems to be true of words that share orthography and phonology (*bank*), share orthography but differ in phonology (*tear*), and share phonology but differ in orthography (e.g., *boar/bore*; Folk, 1999). If the ambiguous words have different parts of speech (e.g., *duck* as a noun verb), and the subordinate meaning is the only syntactically permissible continuation of a sentence, then there appears to be no subordinate meaning "cost" on fixations (Folk & Morris, 2003).

Words can also share lexical properties across languages. Thus, just as *bank* has two meanings, the word *pain* has two meanings for someone who speaks English ("hurt") and French ("bread"). Words like *pain* are referred to as interlingual homographs, and share orthography (and often have similar phonologies) but have distinct meanings. Interlingual homophones share their phonology, but not their orthography and semantics. These are words like *pool/poule* in English and French, respectively. Words can also have the same/similar form in terms of phonology and/or orthography, as well as meaning across languages. These are words like *table* in English, *table* in French, and テーブル ("teburu") in Japanese and are referred to as cognates.[1] Interlingual homographs and homophones, as well as cognates, have been used extensively to investigate whether speakers of two languages selectively activate a single language or non-selectively activate both when processing in one language. A large body of evidence demonstrates that word activation occurs in a language non-selective way, even when the social and linguistic context calls for the use of only one language (for a review, see van Hell & Tanner, 2012).

In a study by Chambers and Cooke (2009) English/L1-French/L2 speakers were presented with a computer screen containing static images of a swimming pool, a chicken (*la poule* is a near homophone of *pool*) and two distractor objects (a strawberry and a boot). Participants listened to sentences that either biased or not the meaning of the homophone (e.g., *Marie va décrire/nourir la poule* "Marie will describe/feed the chicken"). Participants' eye-movements were monitored time-locked to the noun *poule* to determine whether they considered both the chicken and swimming pool to be referents of the homophone. In the unbiased context ("describe the chicken"), Chambers and Cooke found increased looks to the picture of the pool that were all but eliminated in the biased context ("feed the chicken"). Thus, much like monolinguals, the non-native speakers activated all the words that corresponded to the auditory input, even when they came from the language that was not currently being used. Similar to native speakers, this activation was mediated by the biasing context.

Most of the research in this area has looked at how cross-language overlap influences processing speed (for an overview see van Hell & Tanner, 2012). In general, cognates are processed more quickly and accurately than matched noncognates across a wide variety of comprehension and production tasks, languages, and non-native-speaker proficiencies. By and large, research demonstrates a processing difference for interlingual homographs and homophones relative to matched control words. However, whether they are processed faster or slower depends on factors such as task demands and stimulus list composition (the proportion of homographs or homophones relative to controls words and filler items) and proficiency. Importantly, effects of cross-language overlap are modulated by the amount of phonological, orthographic, and semantic overlap between the words in the two languages (Allen & Conklin, 2013; Dijkstra, Miwa, Brummelhuis, Sappelli, & Baayen, 2010; although see Allen & Conklin, 2017 for natural text reading in different-script languages) and can be influenced by the biasing strength of the sentence context (Whitford et al., 2016).

As we saw in the Introduction, multiword items can be the same/similar across languages (often referred to as "congruent"), as well as differing in various ways (referred to as "incongruent"). In recent years, a number of studies have investigated how L1-L2 congruency in multiword items influences processing, although this research has primarily investigated idioms and collocations.[2] Overall the literature in this area points to a cross-language effect, such that L1-L2 overlap aids online processing, or at least some aspects of it (Carrol, Conklin, & Gyllstad, 2016; Titone, Columbus, Whitford, Mercier, & Libben, 2015; Yamashita & Jiang, 2010; Wolter & Gyllstad, 2011, 2013; Wolter & Yamashita, 2015). This is demonstrated in an eye tracking by Carrol, Conklin, and Gyllstad (2016) who presented Swedish/ L1-English/L2 speakers with idioms that were congruent in Swedish and English, English only idioms, and Swedish only idioms that were translated into English. Processing of the idioms was compared to that of matched control phrases, both of which were presented in single sentences that were designed such that what preceded the phrase gave no clues as to the intended meaning, but the sentences were completed in such a way that they made sense (e.g., *It was hard to break the ice at the party* vs. *It was hard to crack the ice when the windows froze*). English native speakers showed a consistent advantage for idioms that existed in English (English only and congruent idioms). However, translated Swedish items were read much more slowly, indicating that encountering unknown idioms causes disruption for readers. Swedish native speakers showed no real difference in their reading times for English-only idioms and control phrases. In contrast, for the Swedish-only and congruent idioms, there was a clear advantage for idioms over controls. Interestingly, there was *no* difference between the two item types, meaning that there was no "added" advantage for congruent idioms that are assumed to be represented in both languages.

When looking at congruency, Titone et al. (2015) highlighted the importance of distinguishing between formal, semantic or conceptual, and pragmatic levels of overlap. Thus, congruency at these different levels may influence processing in different ways and/or have a different time course. What we do know from the literature is that while form congruency may benefit processing, when a task requires the activation of a figurative meaning the situation is likely more complex. In the case of idioms, it may be that recognition of their form is in general faster than for literal phrases. However, when participants are required to make explicit semantic judgments, their figurative nature may mean that greater processing effort is required – especially if the link between their form and meaning is not strong (which may be particularly true for low-proficiency non-natives). Further, it is important to point out that the discussion in this section simply highlights the overall pattern of results that can be found in the literature. These generalizations do not always hold, and reconciling differences across studies is challenging for a number of reasons: effects attributable to task differences; differences in the participants (beginner/intermediate/high proficiency, early/late bilinguals, early/late learners, EFL/ESL contexts, etc.); and differences in how terms like congruent/ incongruent and collocation/idiom are applied (e.g., *thick skin* is a collocation that is also idiomatic). Much more research is needed to disentangle the many factors at play and how these interact with cross-language overlap.

Future Directions

As we have seen, increased exposure leads to stronger connections between a word's form (orthographic and/or phonological) and meaning, while less exposure gives rise to weaker connections – which has a profound impact on processing speed. This is a fundamental principle of emergentist and usage-based approaches and underpins the frequency effects that we have discussed. In the L1 literature, a number of other factors have been shown to influence single-word processing: word length; age of acquisition (AoA); and neighborhood size (both number and frequency),[3] as well as the regularity of neighbours' grapheme-to-phoneme correspondence (for an overview, see Harley, 2014). The impact of such factors has been well documented in the L1 and some work has been done in the L2; however more research is needed in the L2.

We see clear frequency effects for multiword items, which are most evident in an L1. However, more research is needed to ascertain how findings from single words – such as the ones illustrated by Figure 12.1 – align with multiword items. Low frequency single words benefit more from additional exposures (have more of a speed up) than high frequency items. It is unclear whether this is true of multiword items as well. Further, there is considerable work to be done on the processing of multiword items in the L2, exploring how processing is influenced by a range of item-based factors (e.g., meaning transparency), participant variables, and the linguistic context in which an item appears (clause, sentence, type of discourse).

Questions also remain about the input needed for frequency effects to develop for multiword items. The study by Conklin and Carrol (submitted) showed that a processing advantage emerged for binomials (*wires and pipes* vs. *pipes and wires*) after four to five occurrences. However, is this true for other types of multiword items (collocations, phrasal verbs, idioms, lexical bundles, etc.), or might more/less input be needed? Similarly, does the type of input matter? Their study presented a "naturalistic" story. What happens when the context approximates a classroom situation and the input is enhanced and/or explicitly taught? If frequency requires little or no intentional processing and is automatically encoded in memory (Hasher & Zacks, 1984), what is the impact of drawing more attention to it? Enhancement or explicit teaching could add an extra burden to memory and attention, which might actually constrain statistical learning (Kareev, 1995; Turk-Browne, Junge, & Scholl, 2005). Finally, as was pointed out earlier, we know little about how durable such learning is and how it is affected by a range of participant variables such as proficiency.

Lastly, there is considerable evidence that non-native speakers activate input from both of their languages, even when the task, as well as the linguistic and social context only necessitates the use of one language. This cross-language activation is mediated by the immediate linguistic context (e.g., how biasing a sentence is to a particular meaning), as well as the amount of cross-language overlap (e.g., *piano/piano* are identical cognates vs. *vocabulary/vocabulaire* are non-identical cognates) and proficiency. However, the full impact of these variables, and crucially how they interact, has only begun to be explored.

As a final thought, proficiency and learning context (EFL/ESL) have been mentioned throughout as a variable that needs further study. However, the issue is much more complex. We need to consider other variables such as age of acquisition (AoA) and language use. For example in a recent study, López and Vaid (2018) investigated idiom processing by "language brokers", which refers to "informal translators" like children for their parents in immigrant communities. They found that brokers showed greater activation of idioms in both the L1 and L2, compared to non-brokers. This study only highlights one non-native speaking population. Broad group differences and individual speaker variation are important variables that remain to be explored in further detail.

Further Reading

Schwieter, J. W. (Ed.). (2015). *The Cambridge handbook of bilingual processing*. Cambridge, UK: Cambridge University Press.

This book provides an excellent overview of processing in the L2 – looking at acquisition, comprehension, and production, as well as the cognitive consequences of learning, knowing, and using more than one language.

Siyanova-Chanturia, A., & Van Lancker Sidtis, D. (2018). What on-line processing tells us about for-mulaic language. In A. Siyanova-Chanturia & A. Pellicer-Sanchez (Eds.), *Understanding formulaic language: A second language acquisition perspective.* London: Routledge.

The chapter reviews psycholinguistic and neurolinguistic investigations of multiword items across a range of tasks and paradigms and explores key issues like frequency and entrenchment.

Conklin, K., & Carrol, G. (2018). First language influence on the processing of formulaic language in a second language. In A. Siyanova-Chanturia & A. Pellicer-Sánchez (Eds.), *Understanding formu-laic language: A second language acquisition perspective.* London: Routledge.

This chapter provides a detailed overview of the influence of cross-language overlap (congruency) on the processing of multiword items, in particular on idioms, collocations, and translated formu-laic language.

Heredia, R. R., & Cieślicka, A. B. (Eds.). (2015). *Bilingual figurative language processing.* Cam-bridge, UK: Cambridge University Press.

This book explores how non-native speakers acquire, represent, and process figurative language like idioms, irony, and metaphors.

Whitford, V., Pivneva, I., & Titone, D. (2016). Eye Movement Methods to Investigate Bilingual Reading. In: R. R. Heredia, J. Altarriba, & A. B. Cieślicka (Eds.), *Methods in bilingual reading comprehension research.* New York, NY: Springer Science+ Business Media LLC, pp. 183–211.

Although the title of this chapter indicates it is about eye tracking (which it is), the authors provide an excellent summary of processing effects arising from cross-language activation and reduced lexical entrenchment in non-native speakers.

Related Topics

Mental lexicon; high-, mid-, and low-frequency words; learning single-word items vs. multiword items; incidental vocabulary learning; key issues in researching multiword items

Notes

1 In linguistic terms, Japanese words like *table*/テーブル' ("teburu") are in fact "loanwords" because they have been borrowed into the language. However, it is the overlap in form and meaning that underpins the processing advantage for cognates and not their linguistic origins. Because loanwords share form and meaning, they are treated as cognates in the processing literature.

2 In many of the studies what are referred to as collocations could easily be seen to be at least partially figurative or idiomatic (e.g., *thick skin* is a collocation meaning "ability to ignore verbal attacks and criticism"). This is further problematized by the fact that a literal/figurative distinction is often confounded with the congruent/incongruent classification.

3 Orthographic or phonological neighbors are words that differ from one another by only one letter or sound, respectively. For example, the word "hint" has the neighbors "hilt", "hind", "hunt", "mint", "tint", "flint", "lint", "pint", etc.

References

Allen, D., & Conklin, K. (2013). Cross-linguistic similarity and task demands in Japanese-English bilingual processing. *PLOS One, 8*(8), 1–14.

Allen, D., & Conklin, K. (2017). Naturalistic reading in the L2 and the impact of word frequency and cross-linguistic similarity. *Journal of the Ochanomizu University English Society, 7,* 41–57.

Arnon, I., & Cohen Priva, U. (2013). More than words: The effect of multiword frequency and con-stituency on phonetic duration. *Language and Speech, 56*(3), 349–371.

Arnon, I., & Snider, N. (2010). More than words: Frequency effects for multiword phrases. *Journal of Memory and Language, 62*(1), 67–82.

Bannard, C., & Matthews, D. (2008). Stored word sequences in language learning: The effect of familiarity on children's repetition of four-word combinations. *Psychological Science, 19*(3), 241–248.

Bybee, J., & Hopper, P. (2001). *Frequency and the emergence of linguistic structure*. Amsterdam: Benjamins.

Carrol, G., & Conklin, K. (2014). Getting your wires crossed: Evidence for fast processing of L1 idioms in an L2. *Bilingualism: Language and Cognition, 17*(4), 784–797.

Carrol, G., & Conklin, K. (2017). Cross language priming extends to formulaic units: Evidence from eye-tracking suggests that this idea "has legs". *Bilingualism: Language and Cognition, 20*(2), 299–317.

Carrol, G., Conklin, K., & Gyllstad, H. (2016). Found in translation: The influence of L1 on the processing of idioms in L2. *Studies in Second Language Acquisition, 38*(3), 403–443.

Chambers, C. G., & Cooke, H. (2009). Lexical competition during second-language listening: Sentence context, but not proficiency, constrains interference from the native lexicon. *Journal of Experimental Psychology: Learning, Memory, and Cognition, 35*(4), 1029–1040.

Cieślicka, A. B., Heredia, R. R., & Olivares, M. (2014). It's all in the eyes: How language dominance, salience, and context affect eye movements during idiomatic language processing. In M. Pawlak & L. Aronin (Eds.), *Essential topics in applied linguistics and multilingualism* (pp. 21–41). New York: Springer International Publishing.

Conklin, K., & Carrol, G. (submitted). Words go together like "bread and butter": The rapid, automatic learning of lexical patterns.

Conklin, K., & Schmitt, N. (2008). Formulaic sequences: Are they processed more quickly than non-formulaic language by native and nonnative speakers? *Applied Linguistics, 29*(1), 72–89.

Diependaele, K., Lemhöfer, K., & Brysbaert, M. (2013). The word frequency effect in first and second language word recognition: A lexical entrenchment account. *Quarterly Journal of Experimental Psychology, 66*(5), 843–863.

Dijkstra, T., Miwa, K., Brummelhuis, B., Sappelli, M., & Baayen, H. (2010). How cross-language similarity and task demands affect cognate recognition. *Journal of Memory and Language, 62*(3), 284–301.

Dijkstra, T., & van Heuven, W. J. B. (2002). The architecture of the bilingual word recognition system: From identification to decision. *Bilingualism: Language and Cognition, 5*(3), 175–197.

Duffy, S. A., Morris, R. K., & Rayner, K. (1988). Lexical ambiguity and fixation times in reading. *Journal of Memory and Language, 27*(4), 429–446.

Durrant, P., & Doherty, A. (2010). Are high-frequency collocations psychologically real? Investigating the thesis of collocational priming. *Corpus Linguistics and Linguistic Theory, 6*(2), 125–155.

Ehrlich, S. F., & Rayner, K. (1981). Contextual effects on word perception and eye movements during reading. *Journal of Verbal Learning and Verbal Behavior, 20*(6), 641–655.

Ellis, N. C. (2002). Frequency effects in language processing: A review with implications for theories of implicit and explicit language acquisition. *Studies in Second Language Acquisition, 24*(2), 143–188.

Folk, J. R. (1999). Phonological codes are used to access the lexicon during silent reading. *Journal of Experimental Psychology: Learning, Memory, and Cognition, 25*(4), 892–906.

Folk, J. R., & Morris, R. K. (2003). Effects of syntactic category assignment on lexical ambiguity resolution in reading: An eye movement analysis. *Memory and Cognition, 31*(1), 87–99.

Gernsbacher, M. A. (1984). Resolving 20 years of inconsistent interactions between lexical familiarity and orthography, concreteness, and polysemy. *Journal of Experimental Psychology: General, 113*(2), 256–281.

Gollan, T. H., Montoya, R. I., Cera, C., & Sandoval, T. C. (2008). More use almost always means a smaller frequency effect: Aging, bilingualism, and the weaker links hypothesis. *Journal of Memory and Language, 58*(3), 787–814.

Harley, T. A. (2014). *The psychology of language: From data to theory* (4th ed.). London, UK: Psychology Press.

Hasher, L., & Zacks, R. T. (1984). Automatic processing of fundamental information: The case of frequency of occurrence. *American Psychologist, 39*(12), 1372–1388.

Hernández, M., Costa, A., & Arnon, I. (2016). More than words: Multiword frequency effects in non-native speakers. *Language, Cognition and Neuroscience, 31*(6), 785–800.

Jacobs, C. L., Dell, G. S., Benjamin, A. S., & Bannard, C. (2016). Part and whole linguistic experience affect recognition memory for multiword sequences. *Journal of Memory and Language, 87*, 38–58.

Jiang, N. A., & Nekrasova, T. M. (2007). The processing of formulaic sequences by second language speakers. *The Modern Language Journal, 91*(3), 433–445.

Kareev, Y. (1995). Through a narrow window: Working memory capacity and the detection of covariation. *Cognition, 56*(3), 263–269.

López, B., & Vaid, J. (2018). Fácil or A piece of cake: Does variability in bilingual language brokering experience affect idiom comprehension? *Bilingualism: Language and Cognition, 21*(2), 340–354. https://doi.org/10.1017/S1366728917000086

McDonald, S. A., & Shillcock, R. C. (2003). Eye movements reveal the on-line computation of lexical probabilities during reading. *Psychological Science, 14*(6), 648–652.

Monsell, S. (1991). The nature and locus of word frequency effects in reading. In D. Besner & G. W. Humphreys (Eds.), *Basic processes in reading: Visual word recognition* (pp. 148–197). Hillsdale, NJ: Erlbaum.

Northbrook, J. & Conklin, K. (2018). Is what you put in what you get out? – Textbook-derived lexical bundle processing in beginner English learners. *Applied Linguistics*, Online First, 1–19.

Odlin, T. (1989). *Language transfer: Cross-linguistic influence in language learning*. Cambridge, UK: Cambridge University Press.

Pellicer-Sánchez, A. (2017). Learning L2 collocations incidentally from reading. *Language Teaching Research, 21*(3), 381–402.

Siyanova-Chanturia, A., Conklin, K., & Schmitt, N. (2011). Adding more fuel to the fire: An eye-tracking study of idiom processing by native and nonnative speakers. *Second Language Research, 27*(2), 251–272.

Siyanova-Chanturia, A., Conklin, K., & van Heuven, W. J. B. (2011). Seeing a phrase "time and again" matters: The role of phrasal frequency in the processing of multiword sequences. *Journal of Experimental Psychology: Learning, Memory and Cognition, 37*(3), 776–784.

Sonbul, S. (2015). Fatal mistake, awful mistake, or extreme mistake? Frequency effects on off-line/on-line collocational processing. *Bilingualism: Language and Cognition, 18*(3), 419–437.

Sonbul, S., & Schmitt, N. (2013). Explicit and implicit lexical knowledge: Acquisition of collocations under different input conditions. *Language Learning, 63*(1), 121–159.

Szudarski, P. (2012). Effects of meaning- and formed-focused instruction on the acquisition of verb–noun collocations in L2 English. *Journal of Second Language Teaching and Research, 1*(2), 3–37.

Szudarski, P., & Conklin, K. (2014). Short- and long-term effects of rote rehearsal on ESL learners processing of L2 collocations. *TESOL Quarterly, 48*(4), 833–842.

Titone, D., Columbus, G., Whitford, V., Mercier, J., & Libben, M. (2015). Contrasting bilingual and monolingual idiom processing. In R. Heredia & A. Cieślicka (Eds.), *Bilingual figurative language processing* (pp. 171–207). Cambridge, UK: Cambridge University Press.

Tremblay, A., Derwing, B., Libben, G., & Westbury, G. (2011). Processing advantages of lexical bundles: Evidence from self-paced reading and sentence recall tasks. *Language Learning, 61*(2), 569–613.

Turk-Browne, N. B., Junge, J., & Scholl, B. J. (2005). The automaticity of visual statistical learning. *Journal of Experimental Psychology: General, 134*(4), 552–564.

Van Hell, J. G., & Tanner, D. (2012). Second language proficiency and cross-language lexical activation. *Language Learning, 62*(s2), 148–171.

Vilkaité, L. (2016). Are nonadjacent collocations processed faster? *Journal of Experimental Psychology: Learning, Memory, and Cognition, 42*(10), 1632–1642.

Webb, S., Newton, J., & Chang, A. (2013). Incidental learning of collocation. *Language Learning, 63*(1), 91–120.

Whitford, V., Pivneva, I., & Titone, D. (2016). Eye movement methods to investigate bilingual reading. In R. R. Heredia, J. Altarriba, & A. B. Cieślicka (Eds.), *Methods in bilingual reading comprehension research* (pp. 183–211). New York, NY: Springer Science+ Business Media LLC.

Whitford, V., & Titone, D. (2012). Second-language experience modulates first- and second-language word frequency effects: Evidence from eye movement measures of natural paragraph reading. *Psychonomic Bulletin and Review, 19*(1), 73–80.

Wolter, B., & Gyllstad, H. (2011). Collocational Links in the L2 mental lexicon and the influence of L1 intralexical knowledge. *Applied Linguistics, 32*(4), 430–449.

Wolter, B., & Gyllstad, H. (2013). Frequency of input and L2 collocational processing: A comparison of congruent and incongruent collocations. *Studies in Second Language Acquisition, 35*(3), 451–482.

Wolter, B., & Yamashita, J. (2015). Processing collocations in a second language: A case of first language activation? *Applied Psycholinguistics, 36*(5), 1193–1221.

Yamashita, J., & Jiang, N. (2010). L1 influence on the acquisition of L2 collocations: Japanese ESL users and EFL learners acquiring English collocations. *TESOL Quarterly, 44*(4), 647–668.

13

L1 and L2 Vocabulary Size and Growth

Imma Miralpeix

Introduction

Vocabulary size is a dimension of lexical knowledge that has been studied for a long time and has aroused the interest of many researchers, because knowing how many words we know and how our vocabularies grow is essential for different purposes. For example, at a theoretical level, this information can help us to chart native (NS) vs. non-native (NNS) speaker lexical development and see whether there are patterns of vocabulary growth. At a practical level, it can assist in determining how much vocabulary we need to know in order to use another language.

Knowing a certain number of words, in either L1 or L2, is crucial for effective communication. Initially, learners' skill in using the language is heavily dependent on the number of words they know because "without words to express a wide range of meanings, communication in an L2 just cannot happen in a meaningful way" (McCarthy, 1990, p. viii). Nation (1993a, p. 131) has also pointed out that "an emphasis on vocabulary size . . . [is] an essential prerequisite to the development of skill in language use". Different studies have shown that vocabulary size is closely related to proficiency; the bigger one's vocabulary is, the more proficient s/he is in a language. In English, for example, there is a close relationship between vocabulary size and how well one understands, reads, writes, and performs on other formal linguistic tasks (Staehr, 2008; Miralpeix & Muñoz, 2018), and size has also been related to academic achievement (Saville-Troike, 1984; Milton & Treffers-Daller, 2013). In brief:

> Tests of vocabulary size have been shown to predict success in reading, writing, and general language proficiency as well as academic achievement . . . , whereas other types of vocabulary tests as yet have not.
>
> *(Laufer & Goldstein, 2004, pp. 401–402)*

Critical Issues and Topics

In this chapter, we mainly address three critical issues in L1 and L2 vocabulary size and growth. First of all, we present similarities and differences between learning words in L1 and L2. Secondly, we summarize what research has found so far in relation to vocabulary size in

L1 and L2. Thirdly, we focus on measuring vocabulary size. Finally, the chapter closes with several suggestions on areas that need further investigation.

Vocabulary Learning in L1 and L2: Same or Different?

There are some similarities between L1 and L2 vocabulary learning: both children and L2 learners are faced with the enormous challenge of having to learn thousands of words. They have to isolate meaningful units, retain their forms, and learn and store their meanings (Meara, 1988; Singleton, 1999). All these difficulties are common to both L1 and L2 learners irrespective of the languages they learn or the ages at which they learn them.

We also have some signs that the relationship between L1 vocabulary and L2 vocabulary development might be quite close. For example, Skehan (1989) finds that social class, vocabulary development and parental education have a significant strong relationship with foreign language (FL) achievement, and that L1 vocabulary size in young learners can help to predict FL skills almost ten years later. Furthermore, although there are many individual differences regarding our capacity to learn vocabulary, if a learner is good at learning words in his/her L1, he/she may also be successful doing so in other languages, and vice versa: those who have problems at picking up words will have them in any language (Meara, 1996).

However, L2 lexical development differs from L1 lexical development: the way we learn words in our L1 is different from how we do it in L2, and the differences are basically related to three elements: the learner himself/herself, the context in which the language is learned, and the type of languages involved in the learning process.

First of all, compared to L1 learners, L2 learners are cognitively more mature and probably have already acquired a range of strategies that children do not yet have. In addition, L2 learning takes place in the presence of an already acquired lexicon (Meara, 1988). Exposure also is essential for vocabulary acquisition, and the difference between the amount of exposure learners get when learning the L1 or an L2 in formal settings is quite considerable (e.g., see Nagy & Anderson, 1984). Children tend to learn L1 vocabulary incidentally, as massive oral and written input is readily available to them, although deliberate learning can also enhance the lexical growth of L1 learners during their school years. However, when learning an L2 in formal contexts, incidental learning does not often occur because the amount of input available is very low, and students do not encounter the same words a sufficient number of times to learn them. Consequently, vocabulary is usually learned deliberately, and the percentage of words learned incidentally tends to be very low (e.g., see Waring & Nation, 2004 on the amount of vocabulary learned incidentally from reading). In order to maximize learning, formal instruction is often complemented with additional exposure (e.g., Hannibal, 2017 finds that greater gaming with English input is significantly related to larger vocabulary sizes in young Swedish English learners). Therefore, all of this suggests that "there is not a lot to be gained in trying to find points of contact between studies of early vocabulary acquisition in an L1 and an L2" and that we should focus instead on the points of contact that may exist between L2 vocabulary acquisition and vocabulary acquisition in older L1 speakers, especially adolescents (Meara, 1988). Finally, the type of languages involved in the learning process is also a factor that has an effect on lexical growth rates. For example, learners' L1 can help determine whether the L2 words are initially easy or difficult, depending on the likelihood of finding them in the mother tongue as well (Nation, 1990).

How Many Words Do We Know in L1 and L2?

When trying to answer the question of how many words we know in a language, either in L1 or at the different stages of learning an L2, there are actually two questions which must first be addressed, namely: "What constitutes a word?" and "What does it mean to know a word?" This will help us make better sense of the studies determining the number of different words we know or need to learn. After all, the count will obviously vary depending on what is taken as a word. Likewise, we should be aware that a word can be "known" in different ways, and that studies on vocabulary size may differ in what they consider a "known word". Consequently, vocabulary size estimates may also vary depending on the study. Therefore, the following subsections briefly deal with these two issues and how they can affect lexical assessment, so that later we can concentrate on the empirical results provided by research into vocabulary size.

What Is a Word?

It is rather difficult to define what a word is. Some people even disagree with the use of the term "word". Carter (1987), for instance, states that the variable orthographic, phonological, grammatical, and semantic properties of words are best captured by the use of the term "lexical item". Likewise, Sinclair (2004, p. 281), who believes that meaning is related to word patterns and not to individual words, uses the term "lexical item" to refer to "one or more words that together make up a unit of meaning".

Nation (1990) highlights the fact that the criteria used to establish boundaries between words have an important effect on learning to distinguish words. They can be distinguished entirely on their form (e.g., *wish* and *wishes* are different words), on their meaning (e.g., the *foot* of a person and the *foot* of a bed might be considered one or two words), or with reference to either the learners' mother tongue or the L2 (e.g., a *steamboat* is one word in English but *barco de vapor* may be thought to have three words in Spanish). It can thus be asserted that there are many different kinds of vocabulary items or words, and this is especially true when NNS learners "eye their target language as linguistic outsiders" (Folse, 2004, p. 1).

Although we know that writing imposes word breaks that do not always have much psychological reality (Wray, 2015), a "word" is usually considered to be the linguistic unit which has a space on either side when written. Strictly speaking, this definition would correspond to what is known as a "token". When counting "words" in a text, the number of tokens or "individual words" is normally related to the number of types (or the number of different words) that the text has. However, in language acquisition, when talking about "words", we usually mean "lemmas". A lemma consists of the base (defined as the simplest form of a word) and inflected forms of a word (e.g., *waste*, *wasted*, and *wasting* are one lemma). Another widely used term is "word family", which is formed by the base word, all of its inflections and its common derivatives (e.g., *light*, *lights*, *lighting*, *lighten*, and *enlightenment* constitute a word family). In most studies of vocabulary size, the term "word" usually refers to "word families" or "lemmas". Additionally, word frequency lists, which are used for estimates, are made of word families or are often lemmatized. Obviously, tallies of vocabulary size using word families are lower than tallies using lemmas.

Studies on vocabulary size have often used word families (Webb & Nation, 2017, p. 44). It should be acknowledged, though, that we cannot always automatically assume that learners knowing the most basic inflections or derivatives of a word will also know all the other members of the word family (Gardner, 2007; Nagy et al., 2006). There have also been attempts to establish a correspondence between quantities of different units, but this equivalence should just be taken as a very rough indication (e.g., a typical English word family is thought to have seven "closely related members", and multiplying the number of word families by 1.6 gives an approximation of the number of lemmas).

What Does It Mean to Know a Word?

What we mean by word knowledge is not easy to describe, as vocabulary knowledge is thought to have many facets. One of the most comprehensive frameworks on what knowing a word entails was provided by Nation (2001, p. 27), and it includes knowledge of form, meaning, and use. A well-known distinction between receptive and productive vocabulary knowledge is also often made when talking about learners' knowledge.

Although Melka (1997) states that it is almost impossible to find a clear and adequate definition of what is meant by reception and production (i.e., passive and active vocabularies), we usually assume that receptive vocabulary involves being able to recognize and understand a word when it is encountered in listening or reading, while productive vocabulary means being able to use it in speech or writing. From the standpoint of receptive knowledge, knowing a word receptively implies knowing what the word means in a particular context, being able to recognize its collocations or being able to identify its written form so that it is recognized when reading. From the standpoint of productive knowledge, knowing a word entails being able to use it in order to adapt the degree of formality to any given situation or being able to pronounce it correctly, among other aspects (Nation, 1990, 2001). Receptive vocabularies are also thought to be bigger than productive vocabularies (as reception precedes production); however, trying to quantify both has been shown to be problematic.

The picture is further complicated by the fact that words can be just partially known (actually, partial knowledge is very common, especially for words that are not very frequent in a language): lexical knowledge is not uniform across the receptive-productive distinction. Moreover, there may be an imbalance between oral and written vocabulary sizes; low-proficiency learners may have more imbalanced vocabularies, while more advanced learners have usually developed written and spoken vocabularies of similar sizes (Schmitt, 2014).

As Meara (1999) states, this widely accepted view of the lexicon, including the distinction between receptive and productive vocabulary, is clearly an "oversimplification", as pointed out by Ellegard back in 1960. However, even today it is not clear what sort of model could possibly replace it, and estimates of vocabulary size are usually given in terms of receptive or productive knowledge. In the meantime, this perspective (as well as what we take as "a word") has undoubtedly influenced the way vocabulary size has been tested.

Very often, frequency lists have been taken as the basis for designing tests, as learners are more likely to know the vocabulary which is very frequent in a language, while it is more difficult for them to encounter and learn words that are used less often. Most of the tests available nowadays assess receptive vocabulary and aim to tap learning based on the link between form and meaning; that is, learners are presented with words from different frequency levels and asked if they know the most basic meaning of the word, as in Yes/No tests (Meara & Buxton, 1987), or they are asked to match each word with its correct meaning among those provided, as in the Vocabulary Levels Test (VLT: Nation, 1990; Schmitt, Schmitt, & Clapham, 2001; Webb, Sasao, & Ballance, 2017) or Vocabulary Size Test (VST: Nation & Beglar, 2007; Coxhead, Nation, & Sim, 2014). Productive vocabulary is believed to be more difficult to estimate, and reliable tools to assess it are very scarce. The Lexical

Frequency Profile (LFP, Laufer & Nation, 1995) can give the percentage of words in a text belonging to different frequency bands, although it cannot provide an estimate of vocabulary size. Furthermore, the productive version of the VLT (Laufer & Nation, 1999) is actually considered to measure "controlled productive vocabulary", as the first letters of a written word are given in a context so the learner can supply the rest of the word. This support calls into question whether it is really tapping into "productive knowledge".

How Many Words Do We Know in L1?

Bearing in mind the reflections in the previous sections, we will now present what vocabulary studies have found in relation to the number of words known in our first language. There is some normative data on L1 English, mostly from parental diaries and experimental studies. For example, there is a whole range of studies using the monolingually normed standardized *MacArthur-Bates Communicative Development Inventories* (Fenson et al., 2007) to study lexical development in children up to 36 months of age in English and other languages. However, as Meara (1999) highlights, the data so far consists in very general estimates for early infancy and adulthood. It is generally assumed that, as a rule of thumb, children's vocabulary in English L1 grows at a rate of about 1,000 word families per year (Biemiller & Slonim, 2001; Goulden, Nation, & Read, 1990). Nation and Waring (1997) have offered indications on the size of children's vocabulary in English as an L1, and they state that a five-year-old knows between 4,000 and 5,000 word families, 2,000 to 3,000 of which are also known productively. This means that children can acquire quite a lot of vocabulary from oral input before they go to school and learn how to read. Incidental learning by reading will become crucial to lexical development in the school years, as children start engage in contact with written input and may read about a million words per year (Nagy, Herman, & Anderson, 1985). Oral input will also contribute to further lexical development (Webb & Nation, 2017) and, therefore, vocabulary growth will be considerable in this period.

There are also several studies estimating the vocabulary size of adult native speakers. Seashore (1933) posited that a junior college student knows about 15,000 nontechnical English root words, about 52,000 derivatives of roots, and 3,000 special terms, as he found with a four-choice recognition test with words sampled from a dictionary. More recent studies like Goulden et al. (1990) suggest that average-educated native speakers know about 17,000 base words, excluding proper nouns, compound words, abbreviations, and foreign words. These results were obtained using a sample from Webster's dictionary and were similar to estimates of college students by D'Anna, Zechmeister, and Hall (1991): about 16,785 different words. However, as Brysbaert, Stevens, Mandera, and Keuleers (2016) have shown, there is a great deal of variation. According to their study, an average 20-year-old student knows about 42,000 lemmas and 4,200 multiword expressions, derived from 11,100 word families. They observed that these numbers could range from 27,000 to 52,000 lemmas, depending on factors like how much the person reads and watches media with verbal content. They also highlighted that from ages 20 to 60, vocabulary size can increase by 6,000 lemmas (for a summary of studies estimating the number of English words known by native speakers, see Table 3 in Brysbaert et al., 2016, p. 1116).

It should be noted that although there is quite a lot of research on the early acquisition of L1 vocabulary in children, there is very little research on young L1 learners at school, and "literature in this field is instead dominated by studies of learners of additional languages" (Sealey, 2009, p. 39). This is an area that should deserve more attention because, as stated earlier, it has been suggested that there may be points of contact between L1 and L2 vocabulary acquisition, especially in adolescents (Meara, 1988).

How Many Words Do We Know in L2?

Studies on L2 vocabulary growth are available, although there is still a lot of research yet to be done. First of all, we do not actually have normative data on vocabulary growth in L2 speakers, which makes comparisons with L1 learners impossible (Meara, 1996). Furthermore, due to the different measures used in the studies and the varying characteristics of the groups studied, it is also often difficult to establish comparisons among L2 learners' vocabulary sizes. In this area, most research consists of one-off studies that do not track development over long periods of time; different studies make use of different units (lemmas, word families, etc.), and quite often the units used in the counts are not specified.

We know, however, that L2 growth is unlikely to reach the rate of 1,000 word families, as expected with L1 learners (Webb & Nation, 2017). These authors suggest that learning 500 word families per year should be an "attainable target" provided that learners have adequate monitoring and support. If we take into account that West (1953) suggests that a minimally adequate vocabulary must consist of 2,000 words for communication, and that Liu and Nation (1985) consider 3,000 receptive word families a crucial threshold, then with an average of 500 word families learned per year, five to six years should be enough time to master about 3,000 words. Nevertheless, some L2 learners never reach these targets. One of the reasons for this lack of success is the amount of input learners are exposed to.

A distinction is often made in L2 learning between learning the language in a natural setting, an environment in which the target language is encountered outside the classroom, and in a formal setting, where the amount of exposure is limited to the time the language is learned in class.

Vocabulary Size and Growth in Natural Settings

Several studies have been conducted with students learning the language in immersion settings; examples include Qian (2002) and Mochida and Harrington (2006). Qian (2002) used an older version of the VLT to estimate the receptive vocabulary of 217 university students and undergraduates learning English in Canada. As the maximum score of the test was 90 (18 points per each of the five bands he used), he operationalized the estimate as "VS" ("Vocabulary Size" Measure) in percentages, yielding a mean result of 59.99%, which is not straightforward to interpret and compare. In an immersion context as well, Mochida and Harrington (2006) used a Yes/No test and VLT to infer the receptive vocabulary of 36 undergraduate and postgraduate students with different L1s learning English in Australia. The study compares the scores from both tests and addresses issues of reliability. The results are provided not as a general estimate but as words known at different frequency levels (2k, 3k, 5k, 10k words and words from the Academic Word List; Coxhead, 2000). In the US, Zimmerman (2004) investigated whether there was a difference between the vocabulary size scores of newly placed students (new arrivals) and continuing students at three different proficiency levels. Using a productive version of the VLT, it was unexpectedly found that new arrivals at any given level had larger vocabularies than continuing students at the same levels, with a difference of at least 377 word families. However, this might also be caused by the adaptation of the VLT test used in the study.

There is also research comparing the receptive vocabulary sizes of students in two contexts (natural vs. formal). One example is the study by Laufer and Nation (1995), which examines the vocabulary sizes of a group of learners in Israel (formal setting) and New Zealand (immersion). Results from the LFPs cannot be given as general estimates (as one figure, e.g., 6,000 words) but as percentages of words known in each of the frequency bands; thus, a collection of figures is necessary (e.g., 70% at 1k, 40% at 2k . . .). A more recent example is Dóczi and Kormos (2016), who used the VST to compare the vocabulary growth of non-native international students at a British university with those attending an intensive language teaching program in a bilingual secondary school in Hungary over the course of a year: again, results are given in terms of mastery of each frequency band. The findings of these studies are not always easy to relate to others and are often difficult to work with. Some authors have considered the possibility of assembling all the figures coming from a profile or frequency bands into one figure. Laufer (1995) suggested that the results for each band of the profile could be grouped into two figures (bands 1k and 2k on the one hand and 3k and 4k on the other), yielding a condensed profile. The "beyond 2,000" measure she proposes is then the percentage of words belonging to bands 3 and 4, although not many researchers have followed this recommendation.

Finally, Zareva, Schwanenflugel, and Nikolova (2005) examine a group of learners at two proficiency levels in an instructional setting (learning English in Bulgaria) and compared their vocabulary sizes to a group of native speakers in the US, which were taken as a baseline. Significant differences in vocabulary sizes were found among native speakers, L2 advanced, and intermediate learners. The authors used in this case a specific vocabulary size measure derived from a scale devised for their particular study.

Vocabulary Size and Growth in Formal Settings

There are quite a lot of studies on vocabulary size estimations for learners of English in instructional settings. Table 13.1 presents a selection of 20 studies carried out in different countries since the 1980s when the number of publications related to vocabulary learning started to increase. The last column of the table summarizes the results obtained on learners' vocabulary sizes (information on the proficiency levels and tests used can be found in the previous columns for each study). It should be acknowledged that estimating vocabulary size is not the ultimate or sole aim in some of these studies. For example, Nurweini and Read (1999) have two main objectives, the first being estimating vocabulary size and the second analyzing vocabulary depth. In these cases, only the information on vocabulary size is presented; that is, following the example of Nurweini and Read's study, we indicate the results of the estimate and not the word association tests and the interview that they conducted to fulfill the second objective, which was related to analyzing vocabulary depth.

Out of the 20 studies included in the table, many involve the use of the VLT, either the receptive or productive version. Nevertheless, only at low levels is it common for some of the sections of the receptive test to be used (as in Jiménez, Ruiz de Zarobe, & Cenoz, 2006), and in some recent studies, learners took the revised versions by Schmitt, Schmitt, & Clapham (2001) instead of the original VLT versions. Other authors adapted this test for their own purposes, such as Fan (2000), who created nine different versions similar to the VLT to assess productive vocabulary at different levels. Webb and Chang (2012) used a bilingual version of the VLT in Taiwan (with high school learners). Apart from the VLT, there are also studies measuring receptive vocabulary size with Yes/No tests. For example, Milton (2009) found out that in private EFL schools in Greece learners gained about 500 words per year.

Table 13.1 Studies estimating vocabulary size in EFL learners from different countries since the 1980s

Author and year	Country	Participants	Receptive/ productive	Test	Estimate vocabulary size
Gui (1982)	China	Secondary school and university	Receptive	Multiple-choice vocabulary test in Chinese	1,200 words at secondary school and up to 6,000 at university
Takala (1985)	Finland	Primary school (450 hours instruction): N = 2,415	Receptive and productive	Translation test • Receptive: L2–L1 • Productive: L1–L2	About 1,000 words receptively and productively (range 450–1,500)
Jaatinen and Mankkinen (1993)	Finland	Graduate and undergraduate: N = 89 (52 first-year, 37 advanced)	Receptive	Two multiple-choice vocabulary tests	18,100 words. Advanced students knew 2,400 words more than their peers (19,500 vs. 17,100)
Waring (1997)	Japan	Elementary to upper intermediate: N = 76	Receptive and productive	VLT: Receptive and productive versions (1k, 2k, 3k, 5k)	• Receptive: 49.72%–60.84% • Productive: 17.04%–31.48%
Laufer (1998)	Israel	Secondary school: N = 26 (Grade 10) N = 22 (Grade 11)	Receptive and productive	• VLT: Receptive and productive versions (2k, 3k, 5k, AWL) • LFP	• Receptive: 1,900–3,500 words • Productive: 1,700–2,550 words (controlled), 7% approx. >2k (free)
Nurweini and Read (1999)	Indonesia	University (1st year): N = 324	Receptive	Translation task (based on GSL-first 2,000 words- and AWL)	1,226 words
Cobb and Horst (1999)	China	University: N = 21 (1st year) N = 28 (2nd year)	Receptive	VLT (2k, 3k, 5k, AWL)	• Virtually all 2k • 91.7%–91% (3k) • 64.4%–73.4% (5k) • 72.2%–72% (AWL)
Ishihara, Okada, and Matsui (1999)	Japan	University (2nd year): N = 362	Receptive and productive	• Recognition test (supply Japanese equivalents for English words) • Production test: write English words for six semantic contexts	• Receptive: 2,000–2,500 words • Productive: scores approx. 30 (out of 80)
Fan (2000)	China	University (1st year): N = 138	Receptive and productive	• Receptive: VLT (2k, 3k, AWL) • Productive: nine different versions, similar to productive VLT	• Receptive: 62.12% (2k), 48.16% (3k), 45.72% (AWL) • Productive: 53%–81.3% words recognized also recalled

Author and year	Country	Participants	Receptive/ productive	Test	Estimate vocabulary size
Cobb (2000)	Canada	University (after nine years of instruction): N = More than 1,000	Receptive	VLT (2k, AWL)	74% (2k), 68% (AWL)
Tschirner (2004)	Germany	University (1st year): N = 142	Receptive and productive	VLT: Receptive and productive versions (2k, 3k, 5k, 10k, AWL)	72% of the students do not have a receptive vocabulary of 3,000 words and 79% fail the productive 2,000 level
Jiménez et al. (2006)	Spain	Primary education (Grade 6): N = More than 130	Receptive	VLT (1k and 2k)	Estimates lower than 1,000 words
Miralpeix (2007)	Spain	University: N = 64 (intermediate) N = 93 (advanced)	Receptive	X_Lex and Y_Lex (up to 10k)	• 3,950 words (intermediate) • 5,954 words (advanced)
Webb (2008)	Japan	University: N = 83	Receptive and productive	Translation test (180 words) • 90 words L2–L1 (Receptive) • 90 words L1–L2 (Productive)	• Receptive: 73.52% • Productive: 68.69%
Milton (2009)	Greece	Beginner to FCE (Private EFL schools): N = 227	Receptive	X_Lex (up to 5k)	500 words (Junior) to 3,500 (FCE), average gain 500 words/year
Orosz (2009)	Hungary	Primary-secondary schools (Grades 3 to 12): N = 726	Receptive	X_Lex (up to 5k)	500 words (Grade 3) to 3,500 (Grade 12), average gain 300–400 words/year
Webb and Chang (2012)	Taiwan	Secondary school and university (longitudinal): N = 166	Receptive	VLT (bilingual version, 1k and 2k)	47% of students mastered 1k and 16% 2k at university
Zhang and Lu (2014)	China	University (1st-2nd year), longitudinal: N = 360	Receptive	VLT (2k, 3k, 5k, AWL, 10k)	Good mastery of 2k, massive improvement in 5k, moderate improvement in other bands

(Continued)

Table 13.1 (Continued)

Author and year	Country	Participants	Receptive/ productive	Test	Estimate vocabulary size
Roghani and Milton (2017)	Iran	Beginner to advanced (Foreign language teaching institutes): N = 92	Receptive and productive	• Receptive: X_Lex (up to 5k) • Productive: 4 category generation tasks and VLT	• Receptive: 3,000 words approx. • Productive: 1,000 words approx.
Miralpeix and Muñoz (2018)	Spain	University (upper intermediate/ advanced): N = 42	Receptive	X_Lex and Y_Lex (up to 10k)	5,127 words (range: 2,500–7,200)

Orosz (2009) saw in Hungary that while grade 3 learners had a mean of 500 words, at grade 12 it was of more than 3,000. Miralpeix and Muñoz (2018) also used a Yes/No test (assessing up to 10,000 words) to measure vocabulary sizes of more advanced university EFL learners in Spain, who knew receptively a mean of 5,100 words (although the range varied from 2,500 to 7,200).

In order to create the vocabulary size tests, some of the studies in Table 13.1 use standard frequency counts different from Nation's lists on which the VLT is based. Examples include Nurweini and Read (1999), who created their tests based on the General Service List (GSL, West, 1953), and Miralpeix (2007) and Miralpeix & Muñoz (2018), who use the JACET list (Ishikawa et al., 2003). Jaatinen and Mankkinen (1993) use 100-word samples from the Collins COBUILD Dictionary to design their multiple-choice tests, and the same procedure is applied by Zareva et al. (2005), who selected words by sampling from a dictionary to test receptive vocabulary knowledge.

Indeed, receptive vocabulary is more commonly estimated in the literature. Of the studies presented here, 12 estimate receptive vocabulary (such as Gui, 1982; Cobb & Horst, 1999; Zhang & Lu, 2014) and eight estimate both receptive and productive vocabularies (such as Laufer, 1998; Tschirner, 2004; and Webb, 2008). Concerning receptive vocabulary, though, estimates made from data obtained when supplying L1 equivalents or synonyms for the words tested (Ishihara, Okada, & Matsui, 1999) can be different from those obtained when matching words with their definitions or synonyms (as in the VLT used in some studies). Likewise, the productive vocabulary estimated in these studies can also be different in nature: firstly, there are instances of what might be called "controlled productive vocabulary", that is, where the subject has a clue on how to produce the word, such as in the productive version of the VLT, where the first letters of a written word are given in context so the learner can supply the rest of the word. Another example is Takala (1985), who uses translations to estimate productive vocabulary. Ishihara et al. (1999) and Roghani and Milton (2017) estimate what might be called "free productive vocabulary". In both studies, learners are asked to produce words belonging to a particular semantic field without further support.

There are some studies also worth mentioning that are not included in Table 13.1. For instance, some present tests devised to estimate vocabulary size, either receptive like the Eurocentres Vocabulary Size Test (EVST: Meara & Jones, 1988), productive like Lex30 (Fitzpatrick & Meara, 2004) or both, like the Computer Adaptive Test of Size and Strength

(CATSS, Laufer & Goldstein, 2004). Others, like Cameron (2002), compare the results of different receptive vocabulary size tests on the same learners.

Measuring Vocabulary Size and Growth in L1 and L2

It is evident that for a long time researchers have been confronted with problems on assessment that still persist nowadays. Although some authors state that the differences between subjective estimates (how many words we think we know) and objective results (in vocabulary size tests) are not considerable (Ringeling, 1984), consistent deviation between subjective and objective data has usually been found. Zechmeister et al. (1993) also suggest that our metacognitive knowledge about how many words we know or how many words we aim at learning in the target language is very limited. This superficial knowledge may also be applied to teachers' perceptions of students' vocabulary. Riley and Whistler (2000) report a study where teachers' subjective estimates were compared with results obtained in a levels test taken by Japanese learners of English; there was noticeable disagreement between teachers' judgments along with an underestimate of students' vocabulary.

In addition, as we have seen in the previous sections, widely varying estimates tend to be the norm rather than the exception, and there are a number of aspects that are a hindrance when trying to obtain vocabulary size estimates. Apart from the aforementioned problems defining what a word is and what constitutes word knowledge, the methodology used to test vocabulary size also raises a number of concerns in both L1 and L2 testing. The first has to do with sampling: the words to be tested have often been selected from dictionaries or frequency lists, but not always using suitable criteria (Nation, 1993b). This is one of the reasons why Nation and Webb (2011, p. 196) claim that "well over 100 years of research on the measurement of the VS of NS has resulted in little useful data". Melka (1997) adds several other linguistic and extra-linguistic factors that can account for the discrepancy in estimates: results are often affected by test context, test grading, the role of cognates and the notion of avoidance. The amount of context can be very important in generating or recognizing a word. Therefore, in tests where linguistic context is provided (e.g., a multiple-choice test with the word embedded in a sentence), learners may earn higher scores than in others where the word appears on its own. Likewise, the way tests are graded (i.e., when an item is considered "correct" or "incorrect") has a direct effect on the final score: marking a test leniently or strictly will provide different vocabulary size estimates (Webb & Chang, 2012). Furthermore, cognates can initially help recognition, although realizing that equivalences between languages are limited may cause confusion in word recognition at later stages. Finally, testees may voluntarily avoid using certain words (e.g., they may have doubts on their spelling, pronunciation, usage, etc.), so researchers cannot actually be sure of what words are unknown or avoided.

All these methodological issues are compounded by the difficulties in the estimation process itself, that is, how we infer learners' total vocabulary sizes from a reliable sample of words they know. Receptive vocabulary size tests usually assume that if a high percentage of the words in a sample from a specific frequency band is known, all the words in that frequency band will also be known. This seems a reasonable assumption provided we consider that the frequency of words in learners' input resembles that of the word lists from which the testing words are extracted. However, it might be problematic when the input to which learners are exposed differs from the type of language used to make corpora and word lists (e.g., low-level learners in formal settings are usually exposed to words that can only be found in lower frequency bands such as *firefly* or *fairy*). A similar problem can be found if we estimate productive vocabulary from oral or written samples produced by students; not only are we unsure of the words they may be avoiding, it is also difficult to extrapolate a figure unless we use sophisticated mathematical procedures. The other alternative, namely describing the output in terms of the bands to which the most words produced belong, is not very helpful; apart from having a collection of different figures (as many as there are frequency bands), the measure may not be sensitive enough to gauge small increases in vocabulary.

Future Directions

Further research on vocabulary size and growth will necessarily have to look for new assessment methods, focus on languages other than English, and concentrate more on the role of individual differences in L1/L2 lexical development.

New Assessment Methods and Computer Modeling

Even as we are striving to overcome some of the obstacles to measuring receptive vocabulary size (e.g., using more reliable sampling methods), productive vocabulary size has been largely unexplored. It is difficult to use production to extrapolate how big vocabularies are, and it may be more suitable to compare relative vocabulary sizes, such as the vocabulary someone uses for a particular task compared to what others (e.g., NS or learners at different proficiency levels) use when performing the same tasks. A range of different tasks, such as cartoon storytelling or picture description, may be needed for this purpose, and tools using different estimation methods can help researchers obtain reliable estimates. Two of these tools are V_Capture and V_Size (Meara & Miralpeix, 2017).

V_Capture is based on the idea developed by biologists interested in counting the number of species in a particular area by capturing and then recapturing animals in traps on a number of different occasions. This process is similar to comparing the words produced in a particular task over several performances. Mathematics uses the proportion of animals captured (in the case of vocabulary that would equal words used) on both occasions to estimate the number of animals or species being studied (Meara & Olmos, 2010). Estimates by V_Size are based on the Power Law, a ranked distribution found not just in language but also in other physical and biological phenomena like earthquake size or social network connectivity. The program assumes that certain words in language (in high-frequency bands) are more frequent than others (in low-frequency bands) and that there is a direct relationship between the number of times a word occurs in a corpus and its rank in a frequency list generated by the corpus. Therefore, it allows researchers to go beyond the mere shape of the frequency profile generated by a text and enquires into what the profile tells us about the size of the productive vocabulary of the person who produced the text.

While these two programs are instances of workable solutions to the problems of measuring productive vocabulary size, computer modeling of vocabulary growth is another promising avenue. Simulation work can help us explore this phenomenon by testing different models and seeing if the data generated by the models confirms or refutes our hypotheses. Models usually rely on a number of parameters which can have different values, and running the model with different combinations of parameter values helps us see if we can make sense of the data that the model generates. DevLex and Mezzofanti illustrate this line of research.

Ping, Farkas, and MacWhinney (2004, p. 1357) define DevLex as "a cognitively plausible, linguistically scalable model to account for lexical development in children". The results obtained from the simulations they performed with this model match up with hypotheses from empirical research on vocabulary development related to category emergence and reorganization, lexical confusion, and age-of-acquisition effects. Therefore, the model captures a number of important issues occurring in early lexical acquisition. Mezzofanti (Meara & Miralpeix, 2017) is a very basic simulator that tests the predictions of vocabulary growth proposed by Riegel (1968). He argued that a tentative approach to modeling vocabulary acquisition was to assume that it was governed by three basic factors: the number of words available in the learning environment, the rate at which the words are adopted by learners and the amount of time learners spend learning the language. By working with the simulator using these parameter sets, a number of interesting issues appear which are worth studying in detail, such as the effects of L2 immersion on vocabulary size and lexical growth in late bilinguals.

Languages Other Than English

Most research on vocabulary size and development has been conducted with English L1 speakers or L2 learners, although other typologically different languages should be investigated if we want to reach reliable conclusions on how vocabularies grow. There is just some research on vocabulary size estimates in students learning languages other than English (e.g., Eyckmans, 2004, with Dutch, and Batista & Horst, 2016, with French). Furthermore, only a few studies have analyzed learners from different L1s learning the same L2. For example, Milton (2009) measured the English vocabulary sizes of L1 Arabic, Farsi, and Greek learners to check for possible L1 effects in formal L2 learning, and Milton and Alexiou (2009) used vocabulary size tests results in different languages from different L1 learner groups to relate scores with the CEFR levels. There are also no studies comparing lexical growth in learners who share the same L1 but are learning different L2s (or studies assessing vocabulary growth rates in different languages in the same multilingual individuals).

This dearth of studies is also partly due to the need for new assessment methods, as discussed earlier, and the weaknesses of the ones we use. Cobb (2000) shows that standardized tests do not take into account what the learner already knows through his or her L1, and this may give rise to misleading results on L2 vocabulary size tests. In a series of studies he conducted with French learners of English, it was evident that scores on the vocabulary-size tests depended on how well the students answered with cognates. However, a study by Laufer and Levitzky- Aviad (2018) with Hebrew learners of English indicated that, overall, the proportion of loanwords in the vocabulary size test did not significantly affect the results. Still, this may not happen with other languages. Knowing more about how L1 (or any previously learned languages) affects the acquisition of L2 words would be useful not just to test vocabulary size but also to deepen our knowledge of lexical access and organization.

Individual Differences

The role of individual differences in L1 and L2 lexical development should also be brought back on the agenda for future research. As pointed out by Dale and Goodman (2004), if we want to describe growth patterns and assess how prototypical they truly are, the rate and shape of specific individual growth trajectories should be studied, as group means very often mask individual differences.

Suggestions by Takala (1985) encompassed more research on young populations to include lower stages of vocabulary development and end-of-secondary school students with different ability levels. His studies on the English vocabulary of Finnish schoolchildren after seven years of studying the language (about 450 hours of exposure) provide estimates of vocabulary knowledge ranging from 450 words in slow learners to 1,500 in fast learners. More recently, Webb and Chang (2015) found out that small differences in vocabulary knowledge between learners led to large differences in the amount of words learned through an extensive reading program (even if all participants in the study were Taiwanese learners of English at the same proficiency level, with the same age and with the same amount of exposure to the target language).

Research has shown that there are both genetic and environmental contributions to individual differences. When trying to disentangle these two in L1 lexical acquisition, Dionne, Dale, Boivin, and Plonin (2003) indicate that even if environmental factors outweigh genetic factors in early vocabulary development, the latter can explain up to 20% and 12% of lexical knowledge at age two and three, respectively. Setting aside the debate on whether certain variables are actually predetermined or subject to change, what happens later on in L1 learners at school? As we have pointed out, there is not enough research on that. And if this occurs in L1 lexical development, what happens in L2 or additional language learning? If environmental conditions are similar (i.e., learning context, type of input, amount of exposure, etc.), how does vocabulary growth vary in different language learners?

Data on variation ranges taking into account individual differences such as aptitude, self-confidence or intelligence will undoubtedly be useful to help learners with different profiles expand their vocabularies. As stated at the beginning of the chapter, vocabulary size is a crucial dimension in the development of L2 proficiency, and therefore helping learners expand their lexical repertoires will always be worth the effort.

Further Reading

Jackson, C. W., Schatschneider, C., & Leacox, L. (2014). Longitudinal analysis of receptive vocabulary growth in young Spanish English-Speaking children from migrant families. *Language, Speech, and Hearing Services in Schools*, *40*(1), 40–51.

This longitudinal study describes trajectories of development of receptive vocabulary in a group of young Latino/a English language learners from socioeconomically disadvantaged migrant families, it also examines predictors of lexical performance and growth rate.

Meara, P. M. (2007). Growing a vocabulary. In L. Roberts, A. Gürel, S. Tatar, & L. Marti (Eds.), *EUROSLA yearbook, 7* (pp. 49–65). Amsterdam: John Benjamins.

This article shows how computer modeling can help us study vocabulary growth. By using models with very few parameters, the author explores how lexical networks expand and the possibilities that Boolean networks modeling offers to vocabulary researchers.

Williams, J., Segalowitz, N., & Leday, T. (2014). Estimating second language productive vocabulary: A capture-recapture approach. *The Mental Lexicon*, *9*(1), 23–47.

This paper investigates the extent to which a capture-recapture method can provide a reliable indication of productive vocabulary size by assessing a group of English/French bilinguals using this new technique, as well as another word-association productive test.

Related Topics

Lexical knowledge, vocabulary testing, L1 and L2 learning, word lists, language development

References

Batista, R., & Horst, M. (2016). A new receptive vocabulary size test for French. *Canadian Modern Language Review*, *72*(2), 211–233.

Biemiller, A., & Slonim, N. (2001). Estimating root word vocabulary growth in normative and advantaged population: Evidence for a common sequence of vocabulary acquisition. *Journal of Educational Psychology, 93*(3), 498–520.

Brysbaert, M., Stevens, M., Mandera, P., & Keuleers, E. (2016). How many words do we know? Practical estimates of vocabulary size dependent of word definition, the degree of language input and the participant's age. *Frontiers in Psychology, 7*(7), 1–11.

Cameron, L. (2002). Measuring vocabulary size in English as an additional language. *Language Teaching Research, 6*(2),145–173.

Carter, R. (1987). *Vocabulary. Applied linguistic perspectives.* London, UK: Allen & Unwin.

Cobb, T. (2000). One size fits all? Francophone learners and English vocabulary. *The Canadian Modern Language Review, 57*(2), 295–324.

Cobb, T., & Horst, M. (1999). Vocabulary sizes of some city university students. *Journal of the Division of Language Studies of the City University of Hong Kong, 1*(1), 59–68.

Coxhead, A. (2000). A new academic word list. *TESOL Quarterly, 34*(2), 213–238.

Coxhead, A., Nation, P., & Sim, D. (2014). Creating and trialling six forms of the Vocabulary Size Test. *TESOLANZ Journal, 22*, 13–26.

Dale, P. S., & Goodman, J. C. (2004). Commonality and individual differences in vocabulary growth'. In M. Tomasello & D. I. Slobin (Eds.), *Beyond nature-nurture: Essays in honor of Elizabeth Bates* (pp. 41–78). Mahwah, NJ: Lawrence Erlbaum.

D'Anna, C. A., Zechmeister, E. B., & Hall, J. W. (1991). Toward a meaningful definition of vocabulary size. *Journal of Reading Behaviour, 23*(1), 109–122.

Dionne, G., Dale, P. S., Boivin, M., & Plonin, R. (2003). Genetic evidence for bidirectional effects of early lexical and grammatical development. *Child Development, 74*(2), 394–412.

Dóczi, B., & Kormos, J. (2016). *Longitudinal developments in vocabulary knowledge and lexical organization.* Oxford, UK: Oxford University Press.

Ellegard, A. (1960). Estimating vocabulary size. *Word, 16*(2), 219–244.

Eyckmans, J. (2004). *Measuring receptive vocabulary size. Reliability and validity of the Yes/No vocabulary test for French-speaking learners of Dutch.* Unpublished doctoral dissertation, Catholic University of Nijmegen, The Netherlands.

Fan, M. (2000). How big is the gap and how to narrow it? An investigation into the active and passive vocabulary knowledge of L2 learners. *RELC Journal, 31*(2), 105–119.

Fenson, L., Marchman, V. A., Thal, J. D., Dale, P. S., Reznick, J. S., & Bates, E. (2007). *MacArthur-Bates communicative development inventories: User's guide and technical manual.* Baltimore, MD: Brookes Publishing.

Fitzpatrick, T., & Meara, P. M. (2004). Exploring the validity of a test of productive vocabulary Vigo. *Vigo International Journal of Applied Linguistics, 1*, 55–73.

Folse, K. S. (2004). *Vocabulary myths: Applying second language research to classroom teaching.* Ann Arbor, MI: The University of Michigan Press.

Gardner, D. (2007). Validating the construct of *Word* in applied corpus-based vocabulary research: A critical survey. *Applied Linguistics, 28*(2), 241–265.

Goulden, R., Nation, P., & Read, J. (1990). How large can a receptive vocabulary be? *Applied Linguistics, 11*(4), 341–363.

Gui, S. (1982). A survey of the size of vocabulary knowledge of Chinese students. *Language Learning and Communication, 1*(2), 163–178.

Hannibal, S. (2017). Gaming as English language learning resource among young children in Denmark. *CALICO Journal, 34*(1), 1–19.

Ishihara, K., Okada, T., & Matsui, S. (1999). English vocabulary recognition and production: A preliminary survey report. *Doshisha Studies in Language and Culture, 2*(1), 143–175.

Ishikawa, S., Uemura, T., Kaneda, M., Shimizu, S., Sugimori, N., & Tono, Y. (2003). *JACET list of 8000 basic words.* Tokyo: JACET.

Jaatinen, S., & Mankkinen, T. (1993). The size of vocabulary of university students of English. In *Finns as learners of English: Three studies.* Jyväskylä: University of Jyväskylä, 147–211.

Jiménez, RM., Ruiz de Zarobe, Y., & Cenoz, J. (2006). Vocabulary profiles of English foreign language learners in English as a subject and as a vehicular language. *Views, 15*(3), 23–27.

Laufer, B. (1995). Beyond 2000. A measure of productive lexicon in a second language. In L. Eubank, L. Selinker, & M. Sharwood Smith (Eds.), *The current state of interlanguage. Studies in honour of William E. Rutherford* (pp. 265–272). Amsterdam: John Benjamins.

Laufer, B. (1998). The development of passive and active vocabulary in a second language: Same or different? *Applied Linguistics, 19*(2), 255–271.

Laufer, B., & Goldstein, Z. (2004). Testing vocabulary knowledge: Size, strength, and computer adaptiveness. *Language Learning, 54*(3), 399–436.

Laufer, B., & Levitzky-Aviad, T. (2018). Loanword proportion in vocabulary size tests. *ITL Review of Applied Linguistics, 169*(1), 95–114.

Laufer, B., & Nation, P. (1995). Vocabulary size and use: Lexical richness in L2 written production. *Applied Linguistics, 16*(3), 307–323.

Laufer, B., & Nation, P. (1999). A vocabulary size test of controlled productive ability. *Language Testing, 16*(1), 33–51.

Liu, N., & Nation, P. (1985). Factors affecting guessing vocabulary in context. *RELC Journal, 16*(1), 33–42.

McCarthy, M. J. (1990). *Vocabulary*. Oxford, UK: Oxford University Press.

Meara, P. M. (1988). Learning words in an L1 and an L2. *Polyglot, 9*(3), D1–E14.

Meara, P. M. (1996). The dimensions of lexical competence. In G. Brown, K. Malmkjagr, & J. Williams (Eds.), *Performance and competence in second language acquisition* (pp. 33–51). Cambridge, UK: Cambridge University Press.

Meara, P. M. (1999). Lexis: Acquisition. In B. Spolsky (Ed.), *Concise encyclopedia of educational linguistics* (pp. 565–567). New York, NY: Elsevier.

Meara, P. M., & Buxton, B. (1987). An alternative to multiple choice vocabulary tests. *Language Testing, 4*(2), 142–154.

Meara, P. M., & Jones, G. (1988). Vocabulary size as a placement indicator. In P. Grunwell (Ed.), *Applied linguistics in society* (pp. 80–87). London, UK: CILT.

Meara, P. M., & Miralpeix, I. (2017). *Tools for researching vocabulary*. Bristol, UK: Multilingual Matters.

Meara, P. M., & Olmos, J. C. (2010). Words as species: An alternative approach to estimating productive vocabulary size. *Reading in a Foreign Language, 22*(1), 222–236.

Melka, F. (1997). Receptive vs. productive aspects of vocabulary. In N. Schmitt & M. McCarthy (Eds.), *Vocabulary: Description, acquisition and pedagogy* (pp. 84–102). Cambridge, UK: Cambridge University Press.

Milton, J. (2009). *Measuring second language vocabulary acquisition*. Bristol, UK: Multilingual Matters.

Milton, J., & Alexiou, T. (2009). Vocabulary size and the common European framework of reference for languages. In B. Richards, M. Daller, D. Malvern, P. Meara, J. Milton, & J. Treffers-Daller (Eds.), *Vocabulary studies in first and second language acquisition* (pp. 194–211). Basingstoke: Palgrave.

Milton, J., & Treffers-Daller, J. (2013). Vocabulary size revisited: The link between vocabulary size and academic achievement. *Applied Linguistics Review, 4*(1), 151–172.

Miralpeix, I. (2007). *Testing receptive vocabulary size: X_Lex and Y_Lex*. Paper presented at the 29th Language Testing Research Colloquium, Barcelona.

Miralpeix, I., & Muñoz, C. (2018). Receptive vocabulary size and its relationship to EFL language skills. *IRAL, 56*(1), 1–24.

Mochida, A., & Harrington, M. (2006). The Yes/No Test as a measure of receptive vocabulary knowledge. *Language Testing, 23*(1), 73–98.

Nagy, W. E., & Anderson, R. C. (1984). How many words are there in printed school English? *Reading Research Quarterly, 19*(3), 304–330.

Nagy, W. E., Berninger, V. W., & Abbott, R. D. (2006). Contributions of morphology beyond phonology to literacy outcomes of upper elementary and middle-school students. *Journal of Educational Psychology, 98*(1), 134–147.

Nagy, W. E., Herman, P. A., & Anderson, R. C. (1985). Learning words from context. *Reading Research Quarterly*, *20*(2), 233–253.

Nation, P. (1990). *Teaching and learning vocabulary*. New York, NY: Newbury House.

Nation, P. (1993a). Vocabulary size, growth and use. In R. Schreuder & B. Weltens (Eds.), *The bilingual lexicon* (pp. 115–134). Amsterdam: John Benjamins.

Nation, P. (1993b). Using dictionaries to estimate vocabulary size: Essential, but rarely followed, procedures. *Language Testing*, *10*(1), 27–40.

Nation, P. (2001). *Learning vocabulary in another language*. Cambridge, UK: Cambridge University Press.

Nation, P., & Beglar, D. (2007). A vocabulary size test. *The Language Teacher*, *31*(1), 9–13.

Nation, P., & Waring, R. (1997). Vocabulary size, text coverage and word lists. In N. Schmitt & M. McCarthy (Eds.), *Vocabulary: Description, acquisition and pedagogy* (pp. 6–19). Cambridge, UK: Cambridge University Press.

Nation, P., & Webb, S. (2011). *Researching and analyzing vocabulary*. Boston, MA: Heinle Cengage Learning.

Nurweini, A., & Read, J. (1999). The English vocabulary knowledge of Indonesian university students. *English for Specific Purposes*, *18*(2), 161–175.

Orosz, A. (2009). The growth of young learners' English vocabulary size. In M. Nikolov (Ed.), *Early learning of foreign languages* (pp. 181–195). Bristol, UK: Multilingual Matters.

Ping, L., Farkas, I., & MacWhinney, B. (2004). Early lexical development in a self-organizing neural network. *Neural Networks*, *17*, 1345–1362.

Qian, D. D. (2002). Investigating the relationship between vocabulary knowledge and academic reading performance: An assessment perspective. *Language Learning*, *52*(3), 513–536.

Riegel, K. (1968). Some theoretical considerations of bilingual development. *Psychological Bulletin*, *70*(6), 647–670.

Riley, P., & Whistler, B. (2000). Teacher perceptions of student vocabulary. In D. Brooks, R. Long, & J. Robbins (Eds.), *Teacher belief, teacher action: Connecting research and the classroom* (pp. 153–159). Tokyo: JALT.

Ringeling, T. (1984). Subjective estimations as a useful alternative to word frequency counts. *Interlanguage Studies Bulletin – Utrecht*, *8*(1), 59–69.

Roghani, S., & Milton, J. (2017). Using category generation tasks to estimate productive vocabulary size in a foreign language. *TESOL International Journal*, *12*(1), 128–142.

Saville-Troike, M. (1984). What really matters in second language learning for academic achievement? *TESOL Quarterly*, *18*(2), 199–219.

Schmitt, N. (2014). Size and depth of vocabulary knowledge: What the research shows. *Language Learning*, *64*(4), 913–951.

Schmitt, N., Schmitt, D., & Clapham, C. (2001). Developing and exploring the behaviour of two new versions of the Vocabulary Levels Test. *Language Testing*, *18*(1), 55–88.

Sealey, A. (2009). Exploring vocabulary with young L1 learners: the contribution of a corpus. In B. Richards, M. Daller, D. Malvern, P. Meara, J. Milton, & J. Treffers-Daller (Eds.), *Vocabulary studies in first and second language acquisition* (pp. 39–58). Basingstoke: Palgrave.

Seashore, R. H. (1933). The measurement and analysis of extent of vocabulary. *Psychological Bulletin*, *30*, 709–710.

Sinclair, J. (2004). New evidence, new priorities, new attitudes. In J. Sinclair (Ed.), *How to use corpora in language teaching* (pp. 271–299). Amsterdam: John Benjamins.

Singleton, D. (1999). *Exploring the second language mental lexicon*. Cambridge, UK: Cambridge University Press.

Skehan, P. (1989). *Individual differences in second language learning*. London, UK: Arnold.

Staehr, L. S. (2008). Vocabulary size and the skills of listening, reading and writing. *The Language Learning Journal*, *36*(2), 139–152.

Takala, S. (1985). Estimating students' vocabulary sizes in foreign language teaching. In V. Kohonen, H. Von Hessen, & C. Klein-Braley (Eds.), *Practice and problems in language testing* (pp. 157–165). Tampere: AfinLa.

Tschirner, E. (2004). Breadth of vocabulary and advanced English study: An empirical investigation. *Electronic Journal of Foreign Language Teaching, 1*(1), 27–39.

Waring, R. (1997). A comparison of the receptive and productive vocabulary sizes of some second language learners. *Immaculata, The Occasional Papers at Notre Dame Seishin University, 1*, 53–68.

Waring, R., & Nation, P. (2004). Second language reading and incidental vocabulary learning. In D. Albrechtsen, K. Haastrup, & B. Henriksen (Eds.), *Angles on the English speaking world. Writing and vocabulary in foreign language acquisition* (pp. 97–110). Copenhagen: Museum Tusculanum Press.

Webb, S. (2008). Receptive and productive vocabulary sizes of L2 learners. *Studies in Second Language Acquisition, 30*(1), 79–95.

Webb, S., & Chang, A. (2012). Second language vocabulary growth. *RELC Journal, 43*(1), 113–126.

Webb, S., & Chang, A. (2015). How does prior word knowledge affect vocabulary learning progress in an extensive reading program? *Studies in Second Language Acquisition, 37*(4), 651–675.

Webb, S., & Nation, P. (2017). *How vocabulary is learned.* Oxford, UK: Oxford University Press.

Webb, S., Sasao, Y., & Ballance, O. (2017). The updated Vocabulary Levels Test: Developing and validating two new forms of the VLT. *ITL – International Journal of Applied Linguistics, 168*(1), 34–70.

West, M. (1953). *A general service list of English words.* London, UK: Longman.

Wray, A. (2015). Why are we so sure we know what a word is? In J. R. Taylor (Ed.), *The Oxford handbook of the word* (pp. 725–750). Oxford, UK: Oxford University Press.

Zareva, A., Schwanenflugel, P., & Nikolova, Y. (2005). Relationship between lexical competence and language proficiency. *Studies in Second Language Acquisition, 27*(4), 567–595.

Zechmeister, E. B., D'Anna, C. A., Hall, J. W., Paus, C. H., & Smith, J. A. (1993). Metacognitive and other knowledge about mental lexicon: Do we know how many words we know? *Applied Linguistics, 14*(2), 188–206.

Zhang, X., & Lu, X. (2014). A longitudinal study of receptive vocabulary breadth knowledge growth and vocabulary fluency development. *Applied Linguistics, 35*(3), 283–304.

Zimmerman, K. J. (2004). *The role of vocabulary size in assessing second language proficiency.* Unpublished master's thesis, Brigham Young University, Provo, UT.

14

How Does Vocabulary Fit Into Theories of Second Language Learning?

Judit Kormos

Introduction

For a long time, second language acquisition research has been primarily concerned with how second language (L2) learners' grammatical system develops. Although L2 vocabulary research has grown substantially in the past 30 years, Schmitt's (2010) observation that we lack a comprehensive theory of vocabulary acquisition still holds today. Nevertheless, several important lines of research and theorizing can be identified that help us develop a better understanding of how lexical development forms an integral part of second language learning processes.

In this chapter, I will discuss what kind of input can promote vocabulary acquisition and how the expansion of vocabulary knowledge can be influenced by language comprehension and attentional processes. I will describe the features of input that can promote or hinder the noticing of novel lexical forms, meanings, and other aspects of lexical knowledge. This will be followed by an elaboration of how psycholinguistic theories account for the encoding of lexical knowledge in long-term memory. The chapter will highlight that vocabulary development is a complex process in which various input and learning conditions interact with factors that influence the allocation of learners' attention to lexical items and the integration of new knowledge into an existing lexical system. The chapter will conclude with suggestions for future directions for a closer integration of vocabulary research and second language acquisition theories.

Critical Issues and Topics

The Role of Input in Vocabulary Learning

It is unquestionable that some kind of input is necessary to acquire previously unknown lexical items and to expand and enrich lexical knowledge (Gass, 1997). Nevertheless, language input, which can be any "potentially processable language data which are made available by chance or by design, to the language learner" (Sharwood Smith, 1993, p. 167), is no guarantee of L2 development because not every novel piece of information one is exposed to is attended to and subsequently learned. Therefore, one critical issue for vocabulary research is what type of input enhances lexical development. L2 learners are exposed to many different types of input, including authentic and instructionally designed written and spoken texts, spoken interactions in and outside classrooms, traditional paper-based and computer mediated vocabulary learning and practice tasks, and contextualized and decontextualized word lists. These can all be beneficial for lexical development, but their effectiveness can vary depending on the target vocabulary, students' level of proficiency, existing lexical knowledge, and the instructional context.

Intentional Learning in Explicit Instructional Contexts

In the beginning stages of L2 learning, particularly up to the point of acquiring the first 2,000 to 3,000 words in the target language, the intentional learning of vocabulary is necessary (Coady, 1997). Intentional learning involves "cognitive processes that have learning as a goal rather than an incidental outcome" (Bereiter & Scardamalia, 1989, p. 363) and is associated with high levels of attentional focus and consciousness. Intentional learning is goal-oriented and its success strongly depends on the individual's motivation to learn and the effective use of self-regulation strategies (Tseng, Dörnyei, & Schmitt, 2006). Intentional learning is usually supported by means of explicit, language-focused instruction (Nation, 2008). This type of instruction directs learners' attention to various aspects of lexical knowledge (e.g., meaning, collocations, syntactic information associated with lexical items). Explicit instructional conditions tend to engage students in explicit learning processes, which are associated with a high level of attention control, targeted and sustained attentional focus, and assist in discovering patterns of relationships in the input (Ellis, 1994). The primary outcome of explicit learning is explicit knowledge, which can be defined as "facts that speakers of a language have learned" (R. Ellis, 2006, p. 95). Explicit learning can, however, also result in the development of implicit knowledge (McLaughlin, Osterhout, & Kim, 2004), which can be characterized as "abstract, unconscious and rule-like representations" (Ellis, 2007, p. 19).

One common type of highly explicit and intentional learning activity is when students are asked to memorize word lists. These word lists can be decontextualized and consist of lists of isolated words with either their definitions or meaning equivalents in the students' first language (L1), or contextualized and embedded in sentences. Decontextualized word lists can be highly effective in enlarging L2 learners' vocabulary size in the short and long term (for a review see Laufer, 2006) because students' attention is focused on establishing a form-meaning link (Webb, 2007). In the early stages of L2 learning, the need to process the context in which novel words occur explains why the retention rate for contextualized word lists is lower than for decontextualized ones (Qian, 1999). It is, however, questionable whether depth of word knowledge, such as syntactic information, collocations, and associations, can be acquired if L2 learners encounter words devoid of context. Interestingly, Webb's (2007) study found no significant difference in learning gains in semantic, syntactic, orthographic, and associative knowledge of words between contextualized and decontextualized contexts. He argued that as they lack context, L2 learners can rely on their L1 vocabulary knowledge and make successful inferences about the syntactic and semantic characteristics of L2 words.

A recently developed way of offering rich context for intentional vocabulary learning is data-driven learning (DDL), which uses corpus linguistic tools to present authentic situations of lexical usage to learners (Johns, 1990). Data-driven learning is based on usage-based theories of second language acquisition, which argue that learning happens through the probabilistic extraction of regularities from the input rather than rule-based learning

(Ellis, 2014). Usage-based theories postulate no clear separation between grammar and lexis and argue that the grammatical system emerges as a result of logically organized vocabulary, and patterns of language use are acquired through repeated encounters with words (Hoey, 2005). This assumption is particularly important for the acquisition of multiword lexical units and DDL approaches have been applied to teaching these elements of the lexico-grammatical system. DDL exposes learners to sentences or longer stretches of phrases which contain examples of target lexical items. They are a form of input enhancement, whereby the salience of a lexical item is increased by both providing several examples and highlighting them in some way. These enhancement techniques help learners to focus their attention on target items and analyze patterns of lexical use such as syntactic, stylistic, and pragmatic features and collocations (Flowerdew, 2015). DDL approaches were found to be more efficient than traditional word-list teaching approaches in Cobb and Boulton's (2015) meta-analysis of previous research with learners of English and were shown to be an effective teaching tool for lower-level learners in Vyatkina's (2016) study with students of German. These results provide evidence for the significance of enriched input and guided discovery in developing not only form-meaning links but also depth of lexical knowledge.

Vocabulary Development in Incidental Learning Contexts

In the previous section, I presented the role of explicit input through which learners acquire lexical knowledge intentionally. The analysis of incidental learning of vocabulary by means of different types of input is, however, less straightforward because in incidental learning lack of intentionality is more difficult to establish. One of the issues surrounding the distinction of intentional vs. incidental learning is that intentionality can be perceived as a continuum (Barcroft, 2004). The focus and level of attention and the concomitant learning effort can vary while students engage in vocabulary learning tasks. Students might make conscious attempts to discover form-meaning associations while being exposed to extensive and intensive reading as well as listening texts, but they might lack intentionality to commit them to long-term memory (Ender, 2014). Therefore, it is important to recognize that both explicit and implicit learning processes can operate in incidental learning contexts. Furthermore, L2 learners might approach tasks and input differently, and even though researchers or teachers create conditions in which learners are not meant to learn words intentionally, they might still engage consciously with novel words.

In incidental learning contexts students can take several courses of action to deal with unknown lexical items. First of all, they can decide to ignore them. Second, they can choose to discover the meanings of unknown words or phrases and apply lexical processing strategies (Fraser, 1999). Third, at higher levels of proficiency, L2 learners can "implicitly absorb the meaning of an unknown lexical item and map it onto a given form" (Ender, 2014, p. 556). Ender points out, however, that this implicit learning mechanism usually occurs after the word or phrase has already been repeatedly encountered.

A number of arguments support the significance of exposure to large quantities of reading and listening texts for promoting vocabulary development through incidental learning. One of them is based on studies of L1 acquisition that demonstrate that extensive reading and listening to input such as stories is highly beneficial for enriching children's vocabulary size and depth (Nagy, Herman, & Anderson, 1985). Moreover, the development of vocabulary knowledge beyond the first 2,000 to 3,000 words mostly happens through incidental learning by means of reading or listening (Coady, 1997). Additionally, certain aspects of lexical knowledge, such as grammatical knowledge related to lexical items, collocations, or constraints on use, are primarily acquired implicitly (Ellis, 1994), and for implicit learning to result in measurable gains a substantial amount of input is necessary (Ellis, 2002).

Nonetheless, there are a number of constraints on how efficient incidental learning can be through extensive and intensive reading and listening. As mentioned earlier, students often ignore unknown words, especially if they are non-salient and if a sufficient level of understanding can be achieved without them (Vidal, 2011). Even if students decide to make a conscious attempt to discover the meaning of words, they might not have a sufficient level of existing vocabulary knowledge to allow them to understand a text and apply successful lexical inferencing strategies (Elgort & Warren, 2014). Another frequent obstacle to incidental vocabulary learning can be a lack of contextual clues (Huckin & Coady, 1999; Webb, 2008) to support learners in analyzing the meaning of unfamiliar words. Furthermore, for certain types of words, such as verbs, it is not only important that learners encounter them frequently but that they meet them in diverse contexts (Crossley, Subtirelu, & Salsbury, 2013). Varied contexts also help learners to develop rich semantic representations and depth in other types of word knowledge (Ellis & Ferreira, 2009).

Another reason for the relatively modest learning gains made through extensive reading and listening (e.g., Horst, Cobb, & Meara, 1998; Waring & Takaki, 2003) is that a large number of encounters are necessary for learners to acquire depth of word knowledge. In order to develop a rich and accurate lexical representation, learners might need between 5 and 16 repetitions of an item in the input (Nation, 1990; Pellicer-Sánchez & Schmitt, 2010; Webb, 2007). These repetitions also need to be phased so that forgetting does not occur before a new encounter occurs (Baddeley, 2003). Therefore, the frequency of words above the 2,000 level in "naturally occurring" and instructionally unmodified texts might not be high enough to allow for repeated encounters. Nation's (2014) corpus linguistic analysis of authentic novels suggests, however, that it is likely that manageable amounts of extensive reading provide enough repeated encounters of words for vocabulary learning to occur for words up to the 9,000-word frequency level.

Effect of the Modality of Input on Lexical Development

Vocabulary learning outcomes might also differ depending on whether students encounter novel words through listening or reading, or in both modalities. The written mode is more permanent and allows the reader to revisit the text and unfamiliar words, whereas the spoken mode is momentary and language processing usually takes place under time pressure. The comprehension of spoken and written as well as multimodal discourse is influenced not only by the features of a text, but also the characteristics of readers or listeners. One important cognitive individual difference that affects language comprehension and vocabulary learning is working memory capacity. Working memory is a multi-component memory system consisting of the central executive, which coordinates two modality-specific subsystems, the phonological loop and the visuo-spatial sketchpad. The phonological loop is responsible for the manipulation and retention of speech, and the visuo-spatial sketchpad processes visual and spatial information (Baddeley, 2003). The central executive controls the focus and maintenance of attention and regulates the flow of information through the system (Gathercole, 1999). The acquisition of words through listening is more strongly constrained by working memory limitations, and consequently tends to be less successful than the learning of words through reading (see, e.g., Nelson, Balass, & Perfetti, 2005 on L1 vocabulary learning and Brown, Waring, & Donkaewbua, 2008 on L2 word learning). The acquisition of words through listening requires higher numbers of repeated encounters than the learning of words through reading (Brown et al., 2008), although similarity to L1 and whether a word is relevant for the comprehension of key ideas in the listening text are also significant determiners of successful vocabulary learning (Vidal, 2011). The question is, however, whether these observations regarding the advantage of the reading mode persist with the development of L2 proficiency.

Vidal's (2011) study revealed that, overall, students were able to retain more novel words that they encountered in academic reading texts than unfamiliar vocabulary they heard in lectures. Interestingly, however, the benefits of reading written texts decreased for high proficiency learners. This change can be explained with reference to the psycholinguistic mechanisms involved in spoken language comprehension. These comprise the perception of sounds in the stream of speech, the segmentation of the speech signal into words, the retrieval of the meaning of recognized words, and syntactic analysis. In a quick sequence of parallel processing, this linguistic analysis results in the establishment of the meaning of an utterance which is aided by relevant background knowledge and the discourse context (Anderson, 1995). As low proficiency L2 learners' phonological and attentional system is still strongly attuned to their L1, and they might lack sufficient level of automaticity in processing, these learners might experience particular difficulties in recognizing unfamiliar words during listening. They might also find it challenging to apply lexical inferencing strategies under time pressure and to hold relevant information in working memory that would aid them in the successful establishment of an accurate form-meaning link (Goh, 2000). In comparison, high-proficiency learners can carry out low-level linguistic processing of spoken information automatically and efficiently, and might have sufficient attentional resources not only for comprehending the meaning of a text, but the ability to apply lexical inferencing strategies and encode new word meanings in long-term memory. Vidal's study also showed that in a delayed posttest for advanced level participants, the difference between spoken and written modes disappeared. She argued that high proficiency participants benefit from hearing unknown words because it allows them to process verbal information directly in phonological short-term memory, which operates with sub-vocally rehearsed material (Baddeley, 2003). When words are presented in the written mode, they first need to be processed orthographically, i.e., the letters need to be recognized. This is followed by phonological processing, which involves the conversion of letters into sounds, the combination of sounds into syllables, and finally phonological activation of the word form. In this process of written word recognition, several problems can occur, which might result in inaccurate decoding of the phonological form of a word. Vidal (2011) concludes that "direct – in some cases repeated – access to the phonological storage might result in more stable, distinct and durable memory traces" (p. 244).

Another question worth asking is what benefits multimodal input, such as listening to a text while reading, brings for the development of lexical knowledge. The access to read-aloud technology and video subtitling makes this type of input easily available to an increasingly large group of language learners. Brown et al.'s (2008) study suggests that vocabulary gains through reading while listening are commensurate with reading only, and significantly higher than through listening only (for similar results see also Webb & Chang, 2012). They argue that listening to a text that is being read out with appropriate sentence intonation assists low-proficiency learners in processing the meaning of larger semantic units. Furthermore, when a text is read as well as listened to, it is processed in both visual and auditory working memory, which assists in retaining information and building connections between them (Moreno & Mayer, 2002). This explains findings in educational psychology that have shown that multimodal presentation can enhance the comprehension and recall of information (for a recent review see Wood, Moxley, Tighe, & Wagner, 2018).

In the discussion so far, the role of comprehended and comprehensible input has been considered. At the same time, however, a certain proportion of the input also needs to contain unfamiliar or incomprehensible elements, otherwise it only serves to reinforce existing knowledge and does not contribute to the acquisition of previously unknown lexical items. Previous research suggests that between 95% (Laufer, 1989) and 98% (Hu & Nation, 2000) of words in a written text need to be familiar to learners so that they gain a sufficient understanding of the text and this understanding supports vocabulary development. A key process that assists learners in transforming incomprehensible input into new forms of lexical knowledge has been traditionally called "noticing the gap" (Schmidt, 1990) in the field of second language acquisition. The role of attention, noticing, and engagement will be discussed in the next section.

The Role of Attention and Engagement in Vocabulary Development

One of the major factors that determines whether or not input will become intake is the attention paid to it (Schmidt, 1990). Although attention is a key concept in the field of SLA research, as well as in cognitive psychology, there is still no consensus as to what attention actually is (Shinn-Cunningham, 2008). Two characteristics of attentional processing, however, seem to be key to all conceptualizations of attention, namely that attention is subject to intentional control and is selective (e.g., Smith & Kosslyn, 2006; Styles, 2006). The term consciousness is often used interchangeably with attention. It is, however, important to distinguish consciousness, which is the understanding of one's experiences (Max Velmans, 2009), from attention. Consciousness assists in summarizing information that "pertains to the current state of the organism and its environment and ensuring this compact summary is accessible to the planning areas of the brain" (Koch & Tsuchiya, 2006, p. 17). While attentional processing might take place without consciousness, attention, with consciousness, is necessary for the registration of stimuli in working memory, and thus people can distinguish between stimuli and provide a full report of them (Koch & Tsuchiya, 2006). The ability to offer a report on consciously perceived information that has been processed by the attentional system is regarded as awareness (Lamme, 2003).

The definition of attention in SLA research is ambiguous, as different studies interpret it in different ways. Some consider attention as a cognitive mechanism that involves conscious awareness (e.g., Schmidt, 1990), whereas others make a distinction between awareness and attention (e.g., Godfroid, Boers, & Housen, 2013; Robinson, 1995; Tomlin & Villa, 1994). Noticing, according to Schmidt (1995), is an attentional process that involves both consciousness and awareness. Schmidt (1990) also highlights that noticing is a "private experience, although noticing can be operationally defined as availability for verbal report, subject to certain conditions" (p. 132). According to the definitions in cognitive psychology just cited, awareness involves the possibility of offering verbal reports, and therefore what Schmidt calls "noticing" can be equated with "awareness". In a more recent discussion, Godfroid et al. (2013) separate awareness and attention and view them as two sides of the same coin. They argue that a certain level of attention is sufficient for registering new stimuli in long-term memory. This is similar to the views of both Tomlin and Villa (1994) and Robinson (1995), who argue that awareness is not a necessary condition for the development of new linguistic knowledge. In line with Robinson (1995), Godfroid et al. (2013) define noticing as "a cognitive process in which the amount of attention paid to a new language element in the input exceeds a critical threshold, which causes the language element to enter WM and become the object for further processing" (p. 493). Nevertheless, the question remains of how to determine the threshold beyond which a stimulus enters WM. Indrarathne and Kormos (2017) suggest that given these theoretical problems and the fact that the concept of noticing is not present in the psychological literature, it might be expedient to use the construct of attention instead of noticing in investigating how L2 learners process input.

The investigation of attentional processing of lexical items in the input has received a major boost with the availability of eye-tracking technology that allows researchers to establish where learners focus their attentional resources while they read. For example, Godfroid et al.'s (2013) eye-tracking study revealed that "for every second longer that a participant looked at a novel word while reading, she was 8% more likely to identify that word correctly on the subsequent vocabulary test" (p. 507). Strong associations were also found between total fixation duration, i.e., the length of time spent gazing at a word, and the ability to recall the meaning of target words in Pellicer-Sánchez's (2016) study, and between total fixation duration and meaning recall and recognition in Godfroid et al.'s (2018) research. These studies provide strong support for the important role of attentional processing in the acquisition of L2 word form-meaning associations. They indicate that lexical items that come into L2 learners' attentional focus are further processed in working memory. These working memory processes can involve sub-vocal rehearsal in phonological short-term memory, which assists learners to keep verbal material active before it can be encoded in long-term memory (Baddeley, 2003). Additionally, rehearsal might also help the elaboration of material in working memory, which can help L2 learners acquire additional meanings of words and collocations, patterns of spelling and pronunciation or grammatical information related to lexical items (Dóczi & Kormos, 2016). Recent eye-tracking research by Elgort, Brysbaert, Stevens, and Assche (2018) and Godfroid et al. (2018) also offers insights into how many exposures might be necessary for the reliable establishment of meaning representations and the elaboration of semantic information. The eye-movement patterns of L2 learners in both of these studies indicate that the first five to ten encounters with novel words serve to strengthen the knowledge of the form of a word, and only after the seventh to tenth encounters do learners start linking the form of words with their meaning.

Attention also forms a key part of Craik and Lockhart's (1972) depth of processing model, on which Laufer and Hulstijn's (2001) Involvement Load Hypothesis (ILH) is based. In this hypothesis, involvement is assumed to consist of three components: *need* (to learn a given word), *search*, which refers to how the meaning of a word is discovered, and *evaluation*, which

> entails the comparison of the word's meaning with other words, a specific meaning of a word with its other meanings, or comparing the word with other words in order to assess whether a word does or does not fit its context.
>
> *(p. 544)*

These three factors can form a continuum and can be present in vocabulary learning contexts to different degrees. Hulstijn and Laufer (2001) found empirical support that the higher the involvement, the more successful is lexical learning (for a meta-analysis see Huang, Eslami, & Wilson, 2012). In addition to noticing, Schmitt's (2008) concept of engagement also includes features of involvement and attributes an important role to "increased attention focused on the lexical item, increased noticing of the lexical item; increased intention to learn the lexical item and increased amount of time spent engaging with the lexical item" (p. 339). Engagement in a broader sense has also become a focus of recent research in the field of second language acquisition. Engagement is a "heightened state of attention and involvement in which participation is reflected not only in the cognitive dimension but in social, behavioural and affective dimensions" (Philp & Duchesne, 2016, p. 3). Therefore, self-regulated vocabulary learning, which is a joint behavioral and affective realization of engagement, also influences how L2 learners allocate their attention to lexical items and what effort they exert in learning them (e.g., Tseng et al., 2006; Elgort & Warren, 2014). Nation and Webb's (2011) Technique Feature Analysis (TFA) has recently expanded Laufer and Hulstijn's (2001) ILH and Schmitt's concept of vocabulary engagement. In their extended framework five factors determine the depth of processing in vocabulary learning tasks: motivation, noticing, retrieval, generation, and retention. In a comparative study, Hu and Nassaji (2016) found that TFA provided better estimates of the success of vocabulary learning through different types of tasks than ILH.

It is also important to consider what features of a lexical item are likely to attract learners' attention in the input. In addition to the role of frequency, which was discussed earlier, other factors, such as salience, similarity with L1 and predictability, also play a role in determining what learners pay attention to. The adaptation of Wickens' (Wickens, 2007) model of attention to the context of vocabulary learning can offer useful insights into features that draw learners' attention to a word. According to the model, four factors determine what aspects of the input receive attention: Salience, Effort, Expectancy, and Value (SEEV). The model predicts that when different pieces of information enter into a competition for attentional resources, individuals pay attention to stimuli that are salient, require less effort to process, are expected in the given situation and have high value in terms of the task to be undertaken. This model can explain why learners might ignore unknown L2 words that are not relevant for an acceptable level of understanding of a listening or reading text, or that do not fit with the students' schemata of co-text and context. Vidal's (2011) study showed that a significant factor in drawing students' attention to unknown words was whether they were technical words necessary for comprehension of a lecture. Similar results were obtained by Elgort and Warren (2014), who found that key content words in a reading text were remembered better than words that had lower key content value.

In the field of second language acquisition, in addition to frequency, perceptual salience, morphological regularity, and semantic complexity have been found to determine overall salience (Goldschneider & DeKeyser, 2001). These factors can also explain attentional processing of vocabulary in the input. For example, predictability from word form and word parts was found to be a better indicator of the learnability of words through listening than frequency of occurrence in the input in Vidal's (2011) study.

The characteristics of L1 are also an important factor in what lexical items L2 learners consider salient in the input. The concept of learned attention can explain that L2 learners' attention tends to be tuned to features in the input that are consistent with their L1 system (N. Ellis, 2006). L2 learners often ignore cues in the input that are not in line with their L1 at different levels of language, such as phonology, morphology, and semantics. In other words, these cues might not attract sufficient attention because they are unexpected (see Wickens' 2007 model, explained earlier). This might be one of the reasons why cognate words, i.e., words similar in phonological and/or orthographical form in L1 and L2, are noticed and learned more successfully than noncognate ones (de Groot & Keijzer, 2000; Ellis & Beaton, 1993; Vidal, 2011). Learned attention can also influence the processing of false cognates ("false friends"), which are words that are similar in phonological and/or orthographic form in L1 and L2 but have different meanings in the two languages. These words have been found to cause difficulties in acquisition because the difference in meaning or form in the two languages might not be salient for learners (Laufer, 1990). In addition, learned attention can be an obstacle to acquiring other aspects of vocabulary knowledge, such as syntactic, phonological, orthographic, sociolinguistic and collocational characteristics of words that are potentially similar in the learners' L1 and L2.

Encoding Lexical Knowledge in Long-Term Memory

In the previous sections I discussed how the input L2 learners are exposed to is processed and how it can become intake for lexical development. In this section I will describe theories that can account for how long-term memory traces of lexical knowledge are created. Many models of L2 vocabulary acquisition are built on Aitchison's (1994) conceptualization of the processes of lexical development in children. The first step in Aitchison's theory is called *labeling*, which is the stage when children associate an initial semantic meaning with the form of a lexical item. In the next *packaging* phase, this initial semantic meaning is fine-tuned. Fine-tuning involves an analysis of how far the semantic field associated with a particular phonological form can be extended and to what extent it can be further specified. For example, in the initial stages of word learning, children might call any animal that has four legs and whiskers a cat, and they need to gain sufficient experience to establish which animals are in fact cats and not lions or pumas. The final process of vocabulary learning involves linking the newly acquired lexical item with other words in the existing lexical system. More recent models of adult vocabulary learning in L1 also assume that new word learning involves the establishment of memory traces of the formal characteristics (e.g., spelling, pronunciation) of a word and its meaning, and then building up strong associations between form and meaning (Tamminen & Gaskell, 2013). These connections between form and meaning are reinforced by each encounter with the word, which also create memory traces of the context in which the word was seen or heard (Bolger, Balass, Landen, & Perfetti, 2008). Repeated exposure to novel lexical items also assists in refining the various meanings of words and developing rich lexical representations so that word recognition and recall can proceed quickly and without effort (Perfetti, 2007).

In both monolingual and bilingual child language acquisition, vocabulary learning might take place quickly, which is called *fast mapping* (Hu, 2012). In this fast-mapping process, children can connect a new L2 word form with the relevant concept without reference to its L1 equivalent although, as Hu's findings suggest, the memory traces for these words might not be long-lasting. Adults' vocabulary learning, however, is assumed to be a two-stage process (Davis & Gaskell, 2009). First, an episodic memory trace of the new word is established quickly, which is then followed by consolidation processes, "such as stabilization (strengthening of a memory trace), generalization (extraction of gist/rules), and *integration* (formation of new relations between novel and old knowledge)" (van der Ven, Takashima, Segers & Verhoeven, 2015, p. 1). These consolidation processes require time and might be better supported by a written than a spoken context (van der Ven et al., 2015).

Truscott and Sharwood-Smith's (2004) Acquisition by Processing Theory (APT) offers a similar account of vocabulary learning in L2, and it also describes how syntactic information related to words is encoded. Truscott and Sharwood-Smith propose that upon the first encounter with an unfamiliar word, an empty syntactic structure that corresponds to the phonological form of the word is created. Next, the grammatical category for the syntactic structure of the word is identified based on the context. For example, if the learner hears the word "selfie" for the first time in the sentence "He took a selfie", they will construct a syntactic structure for a noun because "selfie" is preceded by an article. The following steps in Truscott and Sharwood-Smith's (2004) theory are similar to the previously described models of L1 vocabulary learning and involve the establishment and consolidation of the meaning of a word.

In L2 vocabulary learning, it is important to consider that most L2 learners already have a well-developed mental L1 lexicon (see Dóczi, this volume). The different aspects of lexical information represented in the L1 mental lexicon are strongly interlinked and are activated simultaneously or with very brief intervals (Levelt, 1989). In L2 learning, however, all these aspects of knowledge need to be developed and are intertwined with the existing L1 system (for a review of these relationships see Kormos, 2006). In many L2 learning contexts, the first step in word learning often involves nothing more than the establishment of the phonological and/or orthographic form of the L2 word, which is the creation of an episodic memory trace that lacks semantic or syntactic elaboration (Jiang, 2000). In the following consolidation phase, an association between the form and meaning of the word is established, and semantic, morphological and syntactic information of a corresponding L1 word might also be transferred. Jiang (2000) postulates that in the final stage of development, which learners might not always reach, a rich lexical representation of the L2 word is established and inaccurately transferred L1 features are weakened.

Vocabulary Development From the Perspective of Dynamic Systems Theory

Vocabulary development is a complex process in which various input conditions and characteristics interact with factors influencing the allocation of learners' attention to lexical items. The establishment of rich memory traces in long-term memory and their integration into the learners' mental lexicon is also a dynamic and interactive process. Therefore, Dynamic Systems Theory (DST) (Larsen-Freeman & Cameron, 2008) can prove useful for elucidating some of the complexities of lexical development.

An important assumption of DST is that initial conditions, such as learners' existing knowledge system, resources and characteristics, and the context, have a strong influence on developmental patterns (Verspoor, de Bot, & Lowie, 2011). With regard to vocabulary development, this means that learners' existing L1 mental lexicon interacts with newly acquired L2 lexical items and the conditions and context in which these words are learned. The dynamic interaction of these factors can make development unpredictable and changes in vocabulary growth might not take place along a smooth incremental path (see e.g., Dóczi & Kormos, 2016).

DST also helps us explain that there are periods when the lexical system expands and is enriched, but there are also phases of stabilization, i.e., plateaus when no observable development takes place. For example, Spoelman and Verspoor's research indicates (2010) that phases of lexical and syntactic development might alternate. As explained earlier, usage-based theories of second language acquisition postulate that lexical and syntactic systems are strongly interrelated (Ellis, 2014). Therefore, development in the areas of lexis and syntax can be mutually supportive, as indicated by Spoelman and Verspoor's (2010) results. On other occasions, lexical and syntactic processes were found to be interdependent. This was demonstrated in Verspoor, Schmid, and Xu's (2012) study, where lexical change was a precursor to syntactic development. DST can also offer an explanation for negative developmental changes, such as periods of "backslide" in L2 lexical knowledge, which is being particularly prone to forgetting if knowledge is not used regularly and over long periods of time (de Bot & Weltens, 1995). In Dóczi and Kormos' (2016) longitudinal study conducted in an EAP context in the UK, some learners, instead of increasing their vocabulary size, demonstrated a lower level of vocabulary knowledge at the end of the academic year than at the beginning. Finally, from a dynamic view of development, it follows that there is no final stage or end state that a learner can or needs to reach; as de Bot, Lowie, Thorne, and Verspoor (2013) point out, "some changes caused by internal reorganization may not be externally visible or may appear to be stable but the underlying processes may have changed. There will always be some degree of variability in a system" (p. 212).

Future Directions

Existing research in the field of vocabulary learning has mostly focused on the interrelationship of the cognitive processes involved in acquiring L2 lexical knowledge and L2 development. Although we have a fairly detailed understanding of how students learn new form-meaning associations from input intentionally and incidentally, less is known about how other aspects of vocabulary knowledge, such as syntactic, collocational, stylistic, and orthographic knowledge related to lexical items, develop. Further studies on how lexical knowledge can influence syntactic development would also assist in a closer integration of vocabulary and second language acquisition research. Future investigations using eye-tracking and introspective methods could shed light on how the context in which a lexical item occurs affects the development of various types of lexical knowledge.

It is also important to extend the line of studies on vocabulary learning to interactive contexts. L2 learning is rarely a solitary activity, and second language acquisition often takes place in interaction with others. Interactions foster L2 learning by allowing language users to test their hypotheses, gain feedback and receive support, and as a result consolidate and expand their lexical knowledge (Doughty & Pica, 1986). There is a scarcity of studies that have investigated how negotiation of meaning and feedback in interactive situations can contribute to L2 development (for exceptions, see Ellis & He, 1999; Newton, 2013). Further research that focuses on the micro- and macro-social context of learning would yield new insights into how sociocultural factors affect lexical development.

Further Reading

Dóczi, B., & Kormos, J. (2016). *Longitudinal developments in vocabulary knowledge and lexical organization.* Oxford, UK: Oxford University Press. Chapter 5

This chapter discusses vocabulary learning in various theories of second language acquisition in depth. It also gives a detailed account of how learners process input for learning new words, and how interaction and output opportunities contribute to lexical development.

Schmitt, N. (2010). *Researching vocabulary: A vocabulary research manual.* Basingstoke, UK: Palgrave Macmillan.

This book offers a comprehensive overview of the development of different types of vocabulary knowledge. It also includes a wide array of research instruments applied in investigating the breadth and depth of vocabulary knowledge.

Vidal, K. (2011). A comparison of the effects of reading and listening on incidental vocabulary acquisition. *Language Learning, 61*(2), 219–258.

This article presents an important piece of research on the differential effect of reading and listening to academic texts on incidental vocabulary acquisition. Vidal also investigates how features of unknown words in the input influence incidental learning in written and spoken modes and how proficiency differences affect the uptake of words in these two modes.

Ender, A. (2014). Implicit and explicit cognitive processes in incidental vocabulary acquisition. *Applied Linguistics, 37*(4), 536–560.

Ender's research offers detailed insights into the psycholinguistic mechanisms of implicit and explicit vocabulary learning. Her study relates the use of lexical inferencing strategies to the development of implicit and explicit knowledge. Based on her findings, she proposes a multilevel model of factors that influence incidental vocabulary acquisition.

Related Topics

Incidental vocabulary learning, deliberate vocabulary learning, factors affecting the learning of single-word and multiword items, mental lexicon

References

Aitchison, J. (1994). *Words in the mind. An introduction to the mental lexicon.* Malden, Basil: Blackwell.

Anderson, J. R. (1995). *Cognitive psychology and its implications* (4th ed). New York, NY: Freeman.

Baddeley, A. (2003). Working memory: Looking back and looking forward. *Nature Reviews, Neuroscience, 4*(10), 829–839.

Barcroft, J. (2004). Second language vocabulary acquisition: A lexical input approach. *Foreign Language Annals, 37*(2), 200–208.

Bereiter, C., & Scardamalia, M. (1989). Intentional learning as a goal of instruction. In B. Resnick (Ed.), *Knowing, learning, and instruction: Essays in honor of Robert Glaser* (pp. 361–392). New York, NY: Routledge.

Bolger, D. J., Balass, M., Landen, E., & Perfetti, C. A. (2008). Context variation and definitions in learning the meanings of words: An instance-based learning approach. *Discourse Processes, 45*(2), 122–159.

Brown, R., Waring, R., & Donkaewbua, S. (2008). Incidental vocabulary acquisition from reading, reading-while listening, and listening to stories. *Reading in a Foreign Language, 20*(1), 136–163.

Coady, J. (1997). L2 vocabulary acquisition through extensive reading. In J. Coady & T. Huckin (Eds.), *Second language vocabulary acquisition: A rationale for pedagogy* (pp. 225–237). Cambridge, UK: Cambridge University Press.

Cobb, T., & Boulton, A. (2015). Classroom applications of corpus analysis. In D. Biber & R. Reppen (Eds.), *The Cambridge handbook of English corpus linguistics* (pp. 460–477). Cambridge, UK: Cambridge University Press.

Craik, F. I. M., & Lockhart, R. S. (1972). Levels of processing: A framework for memory research. *Journal of Verbal Learning and Verbal Behavior, 11*(4), 671–684.

Crossley, S. A., Subtirelu, N., & Salsbury, T. (2013). Frequency effects or context effects in second language word learning: What predicts early lexical production? *Studies in Second Language Acquisition, 35*(4), 727–755.

Davis, M. H., & Gaskell, M. G. (2009). A complementary systems account of word learning: Neural and behavioural evidence. *Philosophical Transactions of the Royal Society of London B: Biological Sciences, 364*(1536), 3773–3800.

de Bot, K., Lowie, W., Thorne, S. L., & Verspoor, M. (2013). Dynamic systems theory as a theory of second language development. In M. Mayo, K. Gutierrez-Mangado, & M. Adrián (Eds.), *Contemporary approaches to second language acquisition* (pp. 199–220). Amsterdam: John Benjamins.

de Bot, K., & Weltens, B. (1995). Foreign language attrition. *Annual Review of Applied Linguistics, 15*(1), 151–164.

De Groot, A. M. B., & Keijzer, R. (2000). What is hard to learn is easy to forget: The roles of word concreteness, cognate status, and word frequency in foreign-language vocabulary learning and forgetting. *Language Learning, 50*(1), 1–56.

Dóczi, B., & Kormos, J. (2016). *Longitudinal developments in vocabulary knowledge and lexical organization.* Oxford, UK: Oxford University Press.

Doughty, C., & Pica, T. (1986). Information-gap tasks: Do they facilitate second language acquisition? *TESOL Quarterly, 20*, 305–326.

Elgort, I., Brysbaert, M., Stevens, M., & Van Assche, E. (2018). Contextual word learning during reading in a second language: An eye-movement study. *Studies in Second Language Acquisition, 40*(2), 341–366.

Elgort, I., & Warren, P. (2014). L2 vocabulary learning from reading: Explicit and tacit lexical knowledge and the role of learner and item variables. *Language Learning, 64*(2), 365–414.

Ellis, N. C. (1994). Introduction: Implicit and explicit language learning: An overview. In N. Ellis (Ed.), *Implicit and explicit learning of languages* (pp. 1–31). London, UK: Academic Press.

Ellis, N. C. (2002). Frequency effects in language acquisition: A review with implications for theories of implicit and explicit language acquisition. *Studies in Second Language Acquisition, 24*(1), 143–188.

Ellis, N. C. (2006). Selective attention and transfer phenomena in L2 acquisition: Contingency, cue competition, salience, interference, overshadowing, blocking and perceptual learning. *Applied Linguistics, 27*(1), 164–194.

Ellis, N. C. (2007). The weak interface, consciousness, and form-focused instruction: Mind the doors. In S. Fotos & H. Nassaji (Eds.), *Form-focused instruction and teacher education: Studies in honour of Rod Ellis* (pp. 17–33). Oxford, UK: Oxford University Press.

Ellis, N. C. (2014). Cognitive and social language usage. *Studies in Second Language Acquisition, 36*(3), 397–402.

Ellis, N., C., & Beaton, A. (1993). Psycholinguistic determinants of foreign language vocabulary learning. *Language Learning, 43*(4), 559–617.

Ellis, N. C., & Ferreira-Junior, F. (2009). Construction learning as a function of frequency, frequency distribution, and function' *The Modern Language Journal, 93*(3), 370–385.

Ellis, R. (2006). Current issues in the teaching of grammar: An SLA perspective. *TESOL Quarterly, 40*(1), 83–107.

Ellis, R., & He, X. (1999). The roles of modified input and output in the incidental acquisition of word meanings. *Studies in Second Language Acquisition, 21*, 285–301.

Ender, A. (2014). Implicit and explicit cognitive processes in incidental vocabulary acquisition. *Applied Linguistics, 37*(4), 536–560.

Flowerdew, L. (2015). Data-driven learning and language learning theories. In B. Lenko-Szymanska & A. Boulton (Eds.), *Multiple affordances in language corpora for data-driven learning* (pp. 15–36). Amsterdam: John Benjamins.

Fraser, C. A. (1999). Lexical processing strategy use and vocabulary learning through reading. *Studies in Second Language Acquisition, 21*(2), 225–241.

Gass, S. (1997). *Input, interaction, and the second language learner*. Mahwah, NJ: Lawrence Erlbaum.

Gathercole, S. E. (1999). Cognitive approaches to the development of short-term memory. *Trends in Cognitive Sciences, 3*(3), 410–419.

Godfroid, A., Ahn, J., Choi, I., Ballard, L., Cui, Y., Johnston, S., . . . Yoon, H. (2018). Incidental vocabulary learning in a natural reading context: An eye-tracking study. *Bilingualism: Language and Cognition, 21*(3), 563–584.

Godfroid, A., Boers, F., & Housen, A. (2013). An eye for word: Gauging the role of attention in incidental L2 vocabulary acquisition by means of eye-tracking. *Studies in Second Language Acquisition, 35*(4), 483–517.

Goh, C. C. M. (2000). Cognitive perspective on language learners' listening comprehension problems. *System, 28*(1), 55–75.

Goldschneider, J. M., & DeKeyser, R. M. (2001). Explaining the "natural order of L2 morpheme acquisition" in English: A meta-analysis of multiple determinants. *Language Learning, 51*(1), 1–50.

Hoey, M. P. (2005). *Lexical priming: A new theory of words and language*. London, UK: Routledge.

Horst, M., Cobb, T., & Meara, P. (1998). Beyond a Clockwork Orange: Acquiring second language vocabulary through reading. *Reading in a Foreign Language, 11*, 207–223.

Hu, C. F. (2012). Fast-mapping and deliberate word-learning by EFL children. *The Modern Language Journal, 96*(4), 439–453.

Hu, H. C. M., & Nassaji, H. (2016). Effective vocabulary learning tasks: Involvement load hypothesis versus technique feature analysis. *System, 56*, 28–39.

Hu, M., & Nation, I. S. P. (2000). Vocabulary density and reading comprehension. *Reading in a Foreign Language, 23*(4), 403–430.

Huang, S., Eslami, Z. R., & Wilson, V. (2012). The effects of task-involvement load on L2 incidental vocabulary learning: A meta-analytic study. *The Modern Language Journal, 96*(4), 544–557.

Huckin, T., & Coady, J. (1999). Incidental vocabulary acquisition in a second language: A review. *Studies in Second Language Acquisition, 21*(2), 181–193.

Hulstijn, J. H., & Laufer, B. (2001). Some empirical evidence for the involvement load hypothesis in vocabulary acquisition. *Language Learning, 51*(4), 539–558.

Indrarathne, B., & Kormos, J. (2017). Attentional processing of input in explicit and implicit learning conditions: An eye-tracking study. *Studies in Second Language Acquisition, 37*(3), 401–430.

Jiang, N. (2000). Lexical representation and development in a second language. *Applied Linguistics, 21*(1), 47–77.

Johns, T. (1990). From printout to handout: Grammar and vocabulary teaching in the context of data driven learning. *CALL Austria, 10*(1), 14–34.

Koch, C., & Tsuchiya, N. (2006). Attention and consciousness: Two distinct brain processes. *Trends in Cognitive Sciences, 11*(1),16–22.

Kormos, J. (2006). *Speech production and second language acquisition.* Mahwah, NJ: Lawrence Erlbaum Associates.

Lamme, V. A. F. (2003). Why visual attention and awareness are different. *Trends in Cognitive Sciences, 7*, 12–18.

Larsen-Freeman, D., & Cameron, L. (2008). *Complex systems and applied linguistics.* Oxford, UK: Oxford University Press.

Laufer, B. (1989). What percentage of text-lexis is essential for comprehension? In C. Lauren & M. Nordman (Eds.), *Special language: From humans to thinking machines* (pp. 316–323). Clevedon, UK: Multilingual Matters.

Laufer, B. (1990). Why are some words more difficult than others? Some intralexical factors that affect the learning of words. *International Review of Applied Linguistics, 28*(2), 293–307.

Laufer, B. (2006). Comparing focus on form and focus on FormS in second language vocabulary learning. *Canadian Modern Language Review, 63*(1), 149–166.

Laufer, B., & Hulstijn, J. (2001). Incidental vocabulary acquisition in a second language. *Applied Linguistics, 22*(1), 1–26.

Levelt, W. J. M. (1989). *Speaking: From intention to articulation.* Cambridge, MA: MIT Press.

Max Velmans, G. (2009). How to define consciousness – and how not to define consciousness. *Journal of Consciousness Studies, 16*(5), 139–156.

McLaughlin, J., Osterhout, L., & Kim, A. (2004). Neural correlates of second-language word learning: Minimal instruction produces rapid change. *Nature Neuroscience, 7*(7), 703–704.

Moreno, R., & Mayer, R. E. (2002). Verbal redundancy in multimedia learning: When reading helps listening. *Journal of Educational Psychology, 94*(1), 156–163.

Nagy, W. E., Herman, P. A & Anderson, R. C. (1985). Learning words from context. *Reading Research Quarterly, 20*(2), 233–253.

Nation, I. S. P. (1990). *Teaching and learning vocabulary.* New York, NY: Heinle and Heinle.

Nation, I. S. P. (2008). *Teaching vocabulary: Techniques and strategies.* Boston, MA: Heinle.

Nation, I. S. P. (2014). How much input do you need to learn the most frequent 9,000 words?. *Reading in a Foreign Language, 26*(2), 1–16.

Nation, I. S. P., & Webb, S. (2011). *Researching and analyzing vocabulary.* Boston, MA: Heinle.

Nelson, J. R., Balass, M., & Perfetti, C. A. (2005). Differences between spoken and written input in learning new words. *Written Language and Literacy, 8*(2), 25–44.

Newton, J. (2013). Incidental vocabulary learning in classroom communication tasks. *Language Teaching Research, 17*(2), 164–187.

Pellicer-Sánchez, A. (2016). Incidental L2 vocabulary acquisition from and while reading: An eye tracking study. *Studies in Second Language Acquisition, 38*, 97–130.

Pellicer-Sánchez, A, & Schmitt, N. (2010). Incidental vocabulary acquisition from an authentic novel: Do "things fall apart?". *Reading in a Foreign Language*, *22*(1), 31–55.

Perfetti, C. (2007). Reading ability: Lexical quality to comprehension. *Scientific Studies of Reading*, *8*(2), 293–304.

Philp, J., & Duchesne, S. (2016). Exploring engagement in tasks in the language classroom. *Annual Review of Applied Linguistics.*, *36*, 50–72.

Qian, D. D. (1999). Assessing the role of depth and breadth of vocabulary knowledge in reading comprehension. *The Canadian Modern Language Review*, *56*(2), 282–308.

Robinson, P. (1995). Attention, memory, and the "*Noticing*" hypothesis. *Language Learning*, *45*(2), 283–331.

Schmidt, R. W. (1990). The role of consciousness in second language learning. *Applied Linguistics*, *11*(1), 129–158.

Schmidt, R. W. (1995). Consciousness and foreign language learning: A tutorial on the role of attention and awareness in learning. In R. W. Schmidt (Ed.), *Attention and awareness in foreign language learning* (pp. 1–63). Honolulu, HI: University of Hawai'i Press.

Schmitt, N. (2010). *Researching vocabulary: A vocabulary research manual*. Basingstoke, UK: Palgrave Macmillan.

Schmitt, N. (2008). Instructed second language vocabulary learning. *Language Teaching Research*, *12*(3), 329–363.

Sharwood Smith, M. (1993). Input enhancement in instructed SLA. *Studies in Second Language Acquisition*, *15*(2), 165–179.

Shinn-Cunningham, B. G. (2008). Object-based auditory and visual attention. *Trends in Cognitive Science*, *12*(1), 182–186.

Smith, E. E., & Kosslyn, S. M. (2006). *Cognitive psychology: Mind and brain*. Upper Saddle River, NJ: Prentice Hall.

Spoelman, M., & Verspoor, M. (2010). Dynamic patterns in development of accuracy and complexity: A longitudinal case study in the acquisition of Finnish' *Applied Linguistics*, *31*(4), 532–553.

Styles, E. A. (2006). *The psychology of attention* (2nd ed.). Hove, NJ: Psychology Press.

Tamminen, J., & Gaskell, M. G. (2013). Novel word integration in the mental lexicon: Evidence from unmasked and masked semantic priming. *The Quarterly Journal of Experimental Psychology*, *66*(5), 1001–1025.

Tomlin, R. S., & Villa, V. (1994). Attention in cognitive science and SLA. *Studies in Second Language Acquisition*, *16*(2), 185–204.

Truscott, J., & Sharwood-Smith, M. (2004). Acquisition by processing: A modular perspective on language development. *Bilingualism: Language and Cognition*, *7*(1), 1–20.

Tseng, T., Dörnyei, Z., & Schmitt, N. (2006). A new approach to assessing strategic learning: The case of self-regulation in vocabulary acquisition. *Applied Linguistics*, *27*(1), 78–102.

van der Ven, F., Takashima, A., Segers, E., & Verhoeven, L., (2015). Learning word meanings: Overnight integration and study modality effects' *PLOS One*, *10*(5), e0124926.

Verspoor, M., De Bot, K., & Lowie, W. (Eds.). (2011). *A dynamic approach to second language development: Methods and techniques* (Vol. 29). John Benjamins Publishing.

Verspoor, M., Schmid, M. S., & Xu, X. (2012). A dynamic usage based perspective on L2 writing development. *Journal of Second Language Writing*, *21*(2), 239–263.

Vidal, K., (2011). A comparison of the effects of reading and listening on incidental vocabulary acquisition. *Language Learning*, *61*(2), 219–258.

Vyatkina, N. (2016). Data-driven learning for beginners: The case of German verb-preposition collocations. *ReCALL*, *28*(1), 207–226.

Waring, R., & Takaki, M. (2003). At what rate do learners learn and retain new vocabulary from reading a graded reader? *Reading in a Foreign Language*, *15*(1), 130–163.

Webb, S. A. (2007). The effect of repetition on vocabulary knowledge. *Applied Linguistics*, *28*(1), 46–65.

Webb, S. A. (2008). The effect of context on incidental vocabulary learning. *Reading in a Foreign Language, 20*(2), 232–245.

Webb, S. A., & Chang, A, C-S. (2012). Vocabulary learning through assisted and unassisted repeated reading. *Canadian Modern Language Review, 68*(3), 267–290.

Wickens, C. D., (2007). Attention to second language. *International Review of Applied Linguistics, 45*(2), 177–191.

Wood, S. G., Moxley, J. H., Tighe, E. L., & Wagner, R. K. (2018). Does use of text-to-speech and related read-aloud tools improve reading comprehension for students with reading disabilities? A meta-analysis. *Journal of Learning Disabilities, 51*(1), 73–84.

Part II
Approaches to Teaching and Learning Vocabulary

15

Incidental Vocabulary Learning

Stuart Webb

Introduction

Defining Incidental Vocabulary Learning

Despite much being written about incidental vocabulary learning, definitions of the construct still vary. Two definitions predominate in the literature. The first has been used widely in the field of psychology since early in the 20th century and operationalizes incidental vocabulary learning as occurring when learners are not forewarned that a vocabulary test will follow (Hulstijn, 2001). The second is more commonly used within applied linguistics and defines incidental word learning as occurring as the by-product of a meaning-focused task (e.g., Chen & Truscott, 2010; Ellis, 1999; Wesche & Paribakht, 1999). Variation in definitions may occur in part because incidental learning is often contrasted with intentional learning, and in this comparison it is easy to see some degree of intention within the incidental learning construct. For example, when we encounter an unknown word in meaning-focused input, we may often pause and think about what that word might mean. Indeed eye-tracking studies investigating incidental vocabulary learning clearly show that during reading, learners spend more time (have longer fixation durations) focused on novel vocabulary than known vocabulary, and that this increased attention to unknown words contributes to learning (Godfroid et al., 2018; Pellicer-Sánchez, 2016). Intention to learn vocabulary might also depend on what is encountered in input. For example, if we encounter an unknown word in spoken and written input, we might shift our focus between understanding the input and inferring the meaning of the unknown word. Moreover, different learners are likely to have different intentions when engaging with input which may include obtaining information, understanding the message, learning language features (grammar and vocabulary), or simply finishing (or appearing to finish) an assigned task. The degree of intention to learn unfamiliar words may also depend on interest, need, and importance.

Awareness that there may be degrees of intention within the incidental learning paradigm leads to questions of whether different variations of reading, listening to, and viewing meaning-focused input meet the conditions necessary for incidental learning to occur. Consider the following scenarios:

1 Reading a text that can be easily understood (only 2% of the words are unknown) in the classroom.
2 Reading the same text at home with access to a dictionary to support comprehension.
3 Reading the same text at home, but in this case the unknown words are typographically enhanced.
4 Reading a text that can be easily understood (only 2% of the words are unknown) at home.

In the first scenario, despite it being a meaning-focused task, an argument might be made that because it occurs in the classroom, the students' intention is to learn language rather than comprehending the L2 input. In the second scenario, a similar argument might be made that because learners can access a dictionary to look up unknown words, their intention is to learn those unknown words rather than to support comprehension. In the third scenario, it might be suggested that the typographical enhancement included in the text may lead learners to focus on learning the unknown words. In the final scenario, there appears to be less of an argument that there is intention to learn vocabulary. However, if this is true, it implies that only when learners engage with meaning-focused input outside of the classroom is there a focus on understanding the meaning of a text rather than learning any language features within the text. This seems unrealistic; learners may frequently focus on understanding input in the classroom for the purpose of enjoyment and interest, after all many activities are designed to be interesting and enjoyable. Similarly, learners may frequently choose to engage with meaning-focused input outside of the classroom for the purpose of learning language; their primary purpose of engaging with meaning-focused input may be to improve their language proficiency. Thus, when we consider students engaging with meaning-focused L2 input, it may not be possible to rule out that there is some intention to learn language.

If we consider incidental vocabulary learning from a pedagogical perspective (rather than degrees of intention) then the definition of learning words as a by-product of meaning-focused activities or tasks works well. From a teaching and learning perspective, it is the purpose of the activity that carries weight rather than where intention and attention is placed during the activity. Thus, any meaning-focused tasks such as those in the preceding four scenarios, as well as reading, listening, and viewing for the purpose of interest, information, and enjoyment, would contribute to incidental word learning. The inclusion of glosses, textual enhancement, the context of learning (classroom vs. at home), and the availability of dictionaries to support comprehension would not affect the definition. In contrast, word-focused activities in which the purpose is to learn vocabulary in exercises such as cloze, matching, sentence production, and flash cards would be classified as intentional learning. Another way to look at it, which would help to eliminate the research issues related to definitions of intentional and incidental learning is to simply agree that the terms are problematic. Using the labels "meaning-focused learning" and "language-focused learning" two terms included in Nation's (2007) four strands of learning is more transparent and avoids the issues of attention and intention. I propose that we follow this course.

Studies of Incidental Learning

In their seminal study of incidental vocabulary learning, Nagy, Herman, and Anderson (1985) proposed that "Incidental learning from context during free reading is the major mode of vocabulary acquisition during the school years, and the volume of experience with written language, interacting with reading comprehension ability, is the major determinant of vocabulary growth (p. 234)". Their hypothesis that knowledge of words is gained in small increments through repeated encounters in text has stimulated a large number of studies with research findings and discussion providing strong support. There have since been a great deal of studies indicating that incidental vocabulary learning through reading has the potential to fuel lexical development. Research has shown that L1 (Jenkins, Stein, & Wysocki, 1984; Nagy, Anderson, & Herman, 1987; Nagy et al., 1985) and L2 words (Day, Omura, & Hiramatsu, 1991; Pitts, White, & Krashen, 1989; Waring & Takaki, 2003), and L2 collocations (Pellicer-Sánchez, 2017; Webb, Newton, & Chang, 2013) are learned incidentally through reading. There are relatively few studies of incidental learning through other modes of input. However, these studies also show that words are learned incidentally through listening (van Zeeland & Schmitt, 2013a; Vidal, 2003, 2011) and viewing (Montero Perez, Peters, Clarebout, & Desmet, 2014; Peters & Webb, 2018).

A primary focus of research on incidental vocabulary learning has been the role that frequency of occurrence plays in learning. Studies have demonstrated that the more that unknown words are encountered in context, the more likely they are to be learned (e.g., Chen & Truscott, 2010; Horst, Cobb, & Meara, 1998; Jenkins et al., 1984; Pigada & Schmitt, 2006; Rott, 1999; Saragi, Nation, & Meister, 1978; Waring & Takaki, 2003). Although more encounters with words in context increases the potential that they will be learned, there does not appear to be a threshold that ensures learning. This was perhaps best demonstrated by Saragi et al.'s (1978) study which showed that 70% of participants learned one target word that was encountered once in a story, while another word that was encountered 96 times was only learned by 40% of the participants.

The reason why there is not a threshold of encounters that ensures that incidental learning occurs is that there are many factors besides frequency that affect learning words in meaning-focused input (see chapters by Peters and Boers, this volume). For example, having background knowledge increases the potential for vocabulary learning to occur through reading (Pulido, 2004). Also having a larger vocabulary size (Webb & Chang, 2015a; Webb & Paribakht, 2015) and being more proficient in the L2 (Zahar, Cobb, & Spada, 2001) have a positive effect on learning words incidentally, perhaps because learners may know more of the words they encounter and thus have greater lexical coverage of the input (Schmitt, Jiang, & Grabe, 2011; van Zeeland & Schmitt, 2013b). Moreover, some words are simply easier to learn than others because they share similar forms and meanings to items in the learners' L1 (Peters & Webb, 2018; Rogers, Webb, & Nakata, 2015). Another factor that influences incidental learning is the amount of information provided in the input (Webb, 2008). Sometimes there may be a great deal of information about the words that are encountered in context making it easier to learn those items. However, sometimes input includes little or misleading information about the meanings of words that are presented making it very challenging to infer the meaning of an unknown word. Thus, while frequency of occurrence increases the potential to learn words encountered in input, encountering a word a certain number of times may not guarantee learning.

Critical Issues and Topics

What Is Learned Through Encountering Words When Reading and Listening?

Perhaps what is most important about incidental vocabulary learning is the contribution that it makes to the development of lexical knowledge. Encountering words repeatedly in input contributes to all aspects of vocabulary knowledge. When learners see the same words again and again in written text, they will learn the spellings of the words, as well as the spellings of their inflections and derivations. They may also gain at least partial knowledge of the spoken forms of the word. Similarly, when words are repeatedly encountered in aural input, learners are likely to learn their different spoken forms, and gain at least partial knowledge of their written forms. It is important to note, however, that the knowledge gained incidentally through encountering words in spoken and written input is most likely to be receptive rather than productive. Receptive knowledge refers to the knowledge necessary to understand words when they are encountered, whereas productive knowledge refers to the knowledge needed to use words. This means that while learners may be able to recognize the spoken and written forms of unknown words through encountering words in input, they may not necessarily be able to produce their different derivations (Schmitt & Zimmerman, 2002).

The different meanings a word conveys are also likely to be gradually learned incidentally as it is encountered repeatedly over time. The most frequent meaning is likely to be acquired first, but as secondary and peripheral meanings of a word are encountered multiple times, they are also likely to be learned. For example, learners may initially learn that a common meaning of *run* is for someone to move quickly on their feet from one place to another. However, they may later learn that this meaning can be extended. For example, *run for your life* and *go for a run* are related but different in meaning. Moreover, encountering run in *run a business* and *run for office* extend knowledge of the concept of the word further. Through repeated encounters in input knowledge of the different meanings of polysemous words is likely to be gained. The same argument applies to both the semantic and syntagmatic associations of words. The more that a word is encountered in context, the more likely we are to learn what is associated with that word. For example, as we encounter the word (ice) *hockey* more and more, we may learn words with related meanings such as its superordinate association (sport) and its coordinate associations (skiing, football, basketball). We may also learn its syntagmatic associates or collocations such as *player*, *game*, *score*, and *Toronto Maple Leafs* if we live in Canada. Of course, some of this knowledge may also be gained by applying/transferring our L1 knowledge to a new L2 word (Webb, 2007a). For example, a dog in Japan or France is still going to have semantic associates such as *pet*, *cat*, and *beagle*, and syntagmatic associates such as *walk*, *collar*, and *leash*. However, these L2 forms still need to be learned initially, and there will often be differences. For example, in English we turn a light on or off, whereas in Chinese we open and close a light. Through encountering words in input, learners are able to develop and refine their L2 knowledge of novel words.

What is particularly important to remember when considering what is gained through incidental vocabulary learning, is how these gains might be different through intentional learning approaches. Although everything that is gained through incidental learning can certainly be learned intentionally, this is likely to be the exception rather than the norm. Most intentional learning activities such as learning with flash cards, matching activities, and multiple-choice activities focus on linking L2 form to meaning. While there are certainly intentional learning activities such as sentence production and cloze activities that may include focus on learning other aspects of knowledge such as semantic association, collocation, and word parts, the extent to which knowledge is gained is limited. Typically, it should be assumed that at best a small fraction of word knowledge can be gained through completing an intentional learning activity (as well as encountering a word a small number of times in meaning-focused input). Of course, the amount of vocabulary knowledge gained through intentional learning can be increased through rich instruction involving the completion of multiple activities designed to develop word knowledge. However, the knowledge gained through these activities will still likely be relatively small; at best only a few of the different derivations, meanings, associations, and collocations are likely to be learned. This does not mean that intentional vocabulary learning does not have value. Intentional learning leads to effective and efficient gains in vocabulary knowledge that may provide the foundation necessary for incidental learning to occur; L2 learners are unlikely to learn words incidentally from input if they do not know many of the words in that input (Liu & Nation, 1985). Moreover, intentional learning of words can be used to focus on developing the knowledge that is most needed. For example, it may be useful for advanced learners to intentionally learn some formulaic language to reduce the number of odd word combinations that they produce.

Because there is value in both incidental and intentional learning, they should not be viewed as being in competition with each other. Instead, it is important to understand that both forms of learning are useful and likely necessary. Therefore, incidental and intentional learning should be seen as complementary approaches to learning.

The Dichotomy of Known and Unknown in Applied Linguistics Is Problematic

The previous section highlighted the fact that there is much to learn about each word (see also Nation, this volume). Although this is widely accepted in the literature on vocabulary knowledge, it is not always reflected in research, and it is rarely reflected in pedagogy. This is problematic, because when research on incidental and intentional vocabulary learning is discussed, the process of learning words gradually over time through repeated encounters is often forgotten. Instead, there may be a conclusion that words have been learned and are now known or that they remain unknown. This dichotomy of known and unknown is misleading, because in all likelihood, in research and pedagogy, only a small fraction of knowledge about words has been learned, and the words are at best partially known. Perhaps the reason for this is that people often think in terms of dichotomies: good vs. evil, right vs. wrong, comprehensible vs. incomprehensible, and known vs. unknown. Working with dichotomies is imprecise. For example, people are unlikely to be 100% good nor 100% evil, and language input presented to learners is likely to be understood to different degrees rather than being perfectly understood or incomprehensible. Similarly, words studied intentionally in an activity or encountered in a book or television program are unlikely to be known and unknown. Instead, they are most likely to be partially known. In contrast, most test formats do work in dichotomies and tests are an important feature of teaching, learning, and researching language. Test results may thus mislead teachers, researchers, and learners about what has been learned. Positive test results may suggest that words have been learned, when in fact they have only been partially learned. Negative test results suggest that no knowledge has been gained about a word, which may or may not be true. In some cases, knowledge may have been gained but it simply was not sufficient to answer a question. In other cases, knowledge may be gained (e.g., collocation), but the test (e.g., meaning recall) did not measure the type of knowledge gained. In addition, knowledge may be gained but the question was not designed very well, and the test taker was unable to demonstrate their knowledge. In all cases, it is important to note that a test is unlikely to measure comprehensive knowledge of a word; it will not reveal whether learners know all of the different forms (spoken and written) of a word. Nor will it indicate if all meanings, associations, and collocations are known. Instead, most tests are simply assessing a particular feature of word knowledge, and often are measuring a fraction of the knowledge of that feature.

It is also important to be aware that tests measure knowledge of a word at a particular instance. This creates the false assumption that if a word is known, that it will continue to be known, and that there is no need for vocabulary knowledge to further develop. Because we know that knowledge of words tends to be gained in small increments over time, a test may provide a useful indication of some of the knowledge that may have been gained at that time. Thus, teachers, learners, and researchers need to be aware that there is likely much more to be learned about that word, and that this knowledge is likely to be gained over time through further encounters with it in input, and through using it in output. Moreover, it is also necessary to be aware that vocabulary knowledge may also decay. For example, although tests may have indicated that words are learned (incidentally or intentionally), if they are not encountered or used, that knowledge is likely to be forgotten. This is one of the challenges for teachers when using a topic-based syllabus. Words that are encountered and learned in a unit on climate, are unlikely to be recycled with knowledge retained or developed further when completing units on food, health, and the solar system.

There may also be an assumption that if words are found to be known on a test, and then unknown on a subsequent delayed test, that knowledge of the word has completely gone. Whether this is true remains to be determined. However, it may well be that the decay in knowledge is simply insufficient to score correctly on the test. How knowledge will subsequently be affected by further opportunities for learning in the event of encountering the word in input or in intentional learning also remains to be explored. However, if we consider our own learning experience, we may forget words, and then subsequently remember them when they are encountered at a later date. How knowledge of words moves backwards and forwards deserves investigation.

Is Incidental Vocabulary Learning Affected by the Mode of Input?

Research indicates that learners are more likely to encounter L2 spoken input than written input outside of the classroom (Kuppens, 2010; Lindgren & Muñoz, 2013; Peters, 2018). Lindgren and Muñoz (2013) investigated the different types of input that foreign language learners were exposed to outside of the classroom. They found that young learners listened to English language songs and watched films in English with L1 subtitles more often than reading L2 books. Similarly, Peters (2018) found that more than 40% of EFL learners surveyed watched English language television programs and movies in their free time several times a week, while only 1% of the learners responded that they read L2 books as often as that. Together these studies suggest that L2 television, movies, and songs may be the most common sources of L2 input outside of the classroom, and that learners are becoming less engaged with reading L2 books on their own.

The wealth of research showing that incidental vocabulary learning occurs through reading reveals the potential value of written text to lexical development (e.g., Godfroid et al., 2018; Pellicer-Sánchez, 2016). However, studies that have been conducted on other modes of input have consistently revealed that vocabulary is also learned incidentally through reading while listening (Webb & Chang, 2012, 2015a, 2015b), listening (van Zeeland & Schmitt, 2013a; Vidal, 2003, 2011), and viewing (Montero Perez et al., 2014; Peters & Webb, 2018). Moreover, these studies tend to suggest that many of the factors, such as frequency (Peters & Webb, 2018; van Zeeland & Schmitt, 2013a; Vidal, 2003, 2011), cognacy (Peters & Webb, 2018), and prior vocabulary knowledge (Montero Perez et al., 2014; Webb & Chang, 2015a), that affect incidental vocabulary learning through reading also affect learning words in other modes.

Webb and Nation (2017) suggest that the value of spoken input to lexical development has been understated. This may have occurred because earlier research suggested that written discourse provided greater opportunities to learn lower frequency words (Hayes, 1988). However, more recent studies suggest that the proportion of low-frequency words found in spoken input is not that different from that of written input. For example, although Webb and Macalister (2013) reported that 1.76% of the words in the Wellington Written Corpus were beyond the 10,000-word frequency level, Rodgers and Webb (2011) found that 1.22% of the words in 288 television programs were at this level, and Webb and Rodgers (2009) found that 1.12% of the words in a corpus of 312 movies were beyond the 10,000-word frequency level. Because research suggests that both L1 and L2 learners tend to encounter much more input through watching television than through reading (L1: Statistics Canada, 1998; United States Bureau of Labor, 2006; L2: Lindgren & Muñoz, 2013; Peters, 2018), the potential for learning vocabulary through spoken input may be at least as great as it is for learning through written input.

If so Few Words Are Learned Incidentally Through Reading, Listening, or Viewing, Wouldn't It Be More Effective to Learn Words Intentionally?

Studies of incidental vocabulary learning reveal small gains after a relatively large amount of study time. For example, Horst et al. (1998) found that EFL students learned on average 4.6/23 unknown target words through reading while listening to a graded reader over six hours. In another study that involved reading a graded reader, Waring and Takaki (2003) reported that 10.6 and 4.6 of 25 words were found to be known on meaning recognition and meaning recall immediate posttests, and three months later only 6.1 and 0.9 of these words were scored as correct on those tests, respectively. Similarly, Rodgers (2013) found that after seven hours of viewing episodes of a television show, EFL students learned 6.4/28 unknown target words on average. Peters and Webb (2018) found that after viewing a one-hour television program EFL students learned 3.86/48 and 3.73/33 unknown target words on meaning recall and meaning recognition tests, respectively. Moreover, Pavia, Webb, and Faez (in press) found that the largest gains made by beginner EFL learners through listening to songs several times were 2.19/13 unknown target words on a test of form recognition and 1.34/5 unknown target collocations on a test of collocation recognition.

Together the preceding studies show that incidental vocabulary learning gains are typically small. The few words that are learned in such studies often lead to questions of whether the gains are meaningful; it could be argued that the time spent learning words incidentally could be better used to learn words intentionally and generate a greater number of words learned. It is true that in a short amount of time, intentional learning is likely to lead to a greater number of words learned than incidental learning. However, there are several reasons why incidental vocabulary learning gains are not only meaningful but central to L2 lexical development.

First and most importantly, there are too many words to learn through deliberate study. Goulden, Nation, and Read (1990) found that educated L1 users of English know approximately 15,000 to 20,000 word families. In informal surveys I have conducted on how many English words EFL students have been taught in the classroom over a six- to nine-year program of study, the most common responses of advanced EFL learners studying in MA TESOL and applied linguistics programs have been 2,000 or 3,000 words. Knowing the most frequent 3,000 word families may allow learners to understand most forms of spoken input (Webb & Nation, 2017). However, it would be far below an L1 adult vocabulary size. Moreover, it is also less than the 8,000 to 9,000 word families necessary to understand written text without support (Nation, 2006), and the 4,000 word families needed to understand academic spoken text (Dang & Webb, 2014). Although independent study is an important part of language learning, it would seem unlikely that students would be able to intentionally learn enough words to understand written text without support, and certainly not develop an L1 adult vocabulary size.

The second reason why incidental vocabulary learning is central to lexical development is that a recent meta-analysis of studies of intentional vocabulary learning indicated that the efficacy of intentional vocabulary learning is likely overstated. Webb, Yanagisawa, and Uchihara (under review) found that although the percentage learning gains made through intentional vocabulary learning have tended to be high on immediate form and meaning recall posttests (58.5% to 60.1%), the gains are relatively small on delayed form and meaning recall posttests (25.1% to 39.4%). The results of the meta-analysis indicated that intentional vocabulary learning in most activities is far from guaranteed. If we use the larger estimate of 3,000 words that learners are taught in the classroom over many years, together with the higher delayed percentage learning gains from the meta-analysis (39.4%), this would only lead to 1,089 words learned intentionally over six to nine years. Thus, to reach the lexical goals necessary to understand most forms of spoken input (knowledge of the most frequent 3,000 word families) and written input (the most frequent 8,000 to 9,000 word families), intentional learning needs to be supplemented with incidental learning.

Third, studies of incidental vocabulary learning are likely to underestimate learning. There are six reasons for this:

1   Tests used to measure learning may not be sensitive enough to reveal small incremental gains in vocabulary knowledge (Nagy et al., 1985).
2   Most studies operationalize learning as gains in knowledge of form-meaning connection, but other aspects of vocabulary knowledge are also likely to be gained through encountering unknown or partially known words in input (Webb, 2007b).
3   Knowledge of non-target words may also be gained through encountering unknown words in meaning-focused input (Horst et al., 1998). These may be mid- and low-frequency words. However, it is likely that knowledge of many higher frequency words also increases through exposure to meaning-focused input. Gains for higher frequency words are most likely to occur in the areas of faster processing speeds, and increased knowledge of derivations and collocations.
4   In most studies of incidental vocabulary learning students do not have access to the resources to support learning (peers, teachers, parents, dictionaries) that they may typically have in the classroom and at home. It may be that it is how learners respond to incidental gains in vocabulary knowledge (e.g., discussing words with peers, teachers, parents; writing words in notes or compositions) that is the key to whether or not knowledge is retained.
5   Most studies have investigated learning from a single text, which leads to relatively small gains. However, studies that have looked at learning from multiple texts tend to show a larger percentage of learning gains than those that have looked at learning from a single text (Webb & Chang, 2015b).
6   There may often be the assumption that the gains made through exposure to one text, will double through the exposure to two texts, and triple through exposure to three texts, and so on. However, this is incorrect, because as input doubles and triples the number of words with ten or more encounters increases at a much higher rate. This is particularly true for high- and mid-frequency words which are common to many spoken and written texts.

The final reason why incidental vocabulary learning gains have value is that as noted earlier, much can be learned about a word through repeatedly encountering it in input. Through repeated encounters in input, detailed knowledge of the form, meaning, and use of a word can gradually be gained. For example, consider the word *take*. A search for collocates within a span of two words to the right in Mark Davies' Corpus of Contemporary American English (Davies, 2008–) lists the following as the 50 most frequent items: *care, look, place, off, advantage, away, break, long, action, responsibility, account, seriously, steps, control, risks, short, pictures, step, chance, stand, deep, longer, picture, easy, quick, chances, risk, effect, turns, charge, lead, granted, note, credit, pride, closer, notes, notice, listen, shape, seat, shower, measures, anymore, breath, consideration, nap, root, classes, precautions.* Although there may be an argument that some of these collocations are less important than others, it is easy to see the value in knowing all of them. Moreover, this argument continues to apply to items much further down the list (i.e., 99. take [a] cab; 100. take [a] hint), as well as the many items that occur to the left of *take* (e.g., should, must, willing, decided, ready). It is hard to imagine that the many collocations of high frequency words can be learned in any other way than through repeated encounters in meaning-focused input. However, it is important to note that while research does show that collocations can be learned incidentally (Pellicer-Sánchez, 2017; Webb et al., 2013), as well as other aspects of vocabulary knowledge (e.g., Webb, 2007b), gaining such comprehensive knowledge of words incidentally is dependent on encountering massive amounts of input. Thus, although much can be learned about words through repeated encounters in input, if learners do not encounter much input then relatively little will be learned about words and few words will be learned incidentally. This means that perhaps the key to L2 lexical development may be to develop an approach to learning that ensures that learners encounter huge amounts of input.

Are the Incidental Vocabulary Learning Gains Made Through Reading, Listening, or Viewing a Single Text Representative of the Amount of Learning That Occurs Through Encountering Multiple Texts?

Most studies of incidental vocabulary learning have looked at the question of how many words are learned through reading, listening, or viewing a single text (e.g., Day, Omura, & Hiramatsu, 1991; Horst et al., 1998; Peters & Webb, 2018; Saragi et al., 1978; Waring & Takaki, 2003; Zahar, Cobb, & Spada, 2001). There is good reason to examine learning from a single text; more variables can be controlled to ensure that any learning gains can be attributed to encountering the words in that text. Although these studies clearly show that incidental vocabulary learning occurs, there is reason to question whether these studies are representative of the number of words that might be learned incidentally through encountering input. The reason for this is that incidental learning theory suggests that words are learned gradually with knowledge gained in small increments through repeated encounters in input (Nagy et al., 1985). Although there are repeated encounters with words in a single text, it is unlikely that what is gained through exposure to one text is the same as what is gained through exposure to multiple texts. The reason for this is that the factors that affect learning may change.

There are many factors that may change with exposure to different numbers of texts. For example, the learning environment, motivation at the time of exposure, the learning support that is present, and a learner's interest in the text are all likely to affect whether words are learned incidentally from exposure to input. Spacing is one factor that will change to a large degree with exposure to different numbers of texts. Research tends to show that greater spacing between encounters with words has a positive effect on learning gains (e.g., Nakata, 2015). There is little research on how spacing affects incidental vocabulary learning. However, spacing of target words in single and multiple texts is likely to be very different as the interval between encounters may change from seconds and minutes to days and weeks. Because the factors that affect learning are likely to be different, researchers should be cautious about generalizing learning gains that occur through exposure to a single text to learning from a greater number of texts.

In fact, research does suggest that the percentage learning gains are different when learning through single and multiple texts. For example, in studies investigating incidental vocabulary learning through reading a single text, gains have ranged from 6.5% to 8.6% (Pitts, White, & Krashen, 1989), 7.2% (Zahar, Cobb, & Spada, 2001), and 18% to 42% (Waring & Takaki, 2003). In contrast, the few studies that have investigated incidental vocabulary learning through reading multiple texts have found consistently large gains ranging from 28% to 63% (Webb & Chang, 2015a), 43% to 80% (Cho & Krashen, 1994), 44% (Webb & Chang, 2015b), 51% (Horst, 2005), and 65% (Pigada & Schmitt, 2006). Taken together, the difference in findings between studies investigating learning from single and multiple texts suggests that researchers should be careful not to generalize gains made through a single text to gains made through exposure to multiple texts. Moreover, the difference in findings suggests that perhaps research on incidental learning should begin to focus more on longitudinal studies of incidental vocabulary learning through exposure to multiple texts.

Future Directions

There are five areas where research on incidental vocabulary learning is needed. The first of these is research focused on determining the extent to which learning occurs through encountering different types of input. In the last 30 years, the development of new technologies has strongly impacted the ways in which learners may encounter language. More traditional forms of input such as books and magazines may not account for as much input with learners as other forms of input such as television, movies, websites, YouTube, video games, email, electronic texts, twitter, and VOIP applications such as FaceTime and Skype. This does not mean that a focus on learning with traditional types of input should be abandoned; there will be many learners who are engaged with learning from these sources. However, there is a need to investigate the degree to which other sources of input can contribute to lexical development. Research on the contributions of other types of input to incidental vocabulary learning would raise awareness of their value for learning. Education on the benefits of different sources of input is likely the key to their inclusion in learning programs, and providing more choices to students and training with these sources of input may help more learners to engage with meaning-focused input outside of the classroom.

Ecologically valid studies of incidental vocabulary learning is a second area of research that is needed. The vast majority of studies on learning words incidentally have looked at learning from a single text. There has been good reason to conduct such studies; they allow the careful control of variables and thus ensure that learning can be attributed to encountering the target input. However, a limitation of these studies is that they may not reflect vocabulary learning from meaning-focused input inside and outside of the classroom, where variables beyond the source of input may affect learning. It may well be that studies of incidental vocabulary learning lack ecological validity to a certain degree, because learners' behavior when encountering unknown words in meaning-focused input varies. For example, sometimes learners may simply ignore unknown words. Perhaps at other times they may consult with students, teachers, or parents about the meaning of a word, collocation, sentence, or passage. While on other occasions they may write vocabulary in a notebook, consult a dictionary, say it out loud, or try to use it in their speech or writing. There is likely great variation in how learners approach unknown vocabulary that is encountered in meaning-focused input, and research has yet to examine much of this variation.

Similarly, it is not clear to what extent many of the factors noted above such as consultation with peers, teachers, and dictionaries, and using words in speech and writing contribute to incidental vocabulary learning gains. Frequency of occurrence is the one factor that has received the bulk of attention with cross-sectional studies suggesting it has a moderate impact on learning (e.g., Horst et al., 1998; Vidal, 2003) and longitudinal studies indicating it has a smaller impact on learning (Rodgers, 2013; Webb & Chang, 2015b). This might suggest that perhaps within a single text frequency of occurrence is an important factor for short-term retention. However, perhaps it is other factors such as the use of words in speech or writing that are key to long-term retention. Further research examining how different factors expand on incidental learning gains may shed more light on how words are learned and retained.

A fourth area of research that is needed is investigation of the individual differences in vocabulary learning gains that occur through exposure to meaning-focused input. Because studies of incidental vocabulary learning summarize the vocabulary learning gains in descriptive statistics tables, it is not clear to what extent individuals vary in their learning. Research suggests that more proficient learners and those with greater vocabulary knowledge tend to learn the most words incidentally (Webb & Chang, 2015a; Zahar, Cobb, & Spada, 2001). Webb and Chang (2015a) suggest that differences in incidental vocabulary learning gains are likely to lead to Matthew effects where the weakest students continue to learn less and become further and further behind the strongest students. Further research investigating individual differences in vocabulary learning gains would help to determine the extent to which this happens. This in turn may lead to studies focused on helping improve the vocabulary learning outcomes of the students who need the most help with their learning.

Finally, perhaps the most important area for research on incidental vocabulary learning is on the development of approaches designed to vastly increase the amount of input that L2 learners receive. As mentioned earlier, incidental vocabulary learning is dependent on encountering words repeatedly. This is essential because lexical development involves learning the different spoken and written inflectional and derivational forms, meanings, collocations, associations, and constraints on use of words. If input is limited, few words will be learned and relatively little will be learned about them. Therefore, perhaps key to the lexical development of L2 learners is finding ways to ensure that a great deal of input is encountered.

Extensive reading has the potential to provide large amounts of input to learners (Day & Bamford, 1998). However, not everyone loves to read, and most programs involve reading one book a week, which is not enough input for much vocabulary learning. Webb (2015) proposed extensive viewing (of L2 television) together with extensive reading as a way to increase the amount of L2 input that learners engage with inside and outside of the classroom. However, the more types of input that language learning programs provide support for their learners to engage with, the greater the potential that students will find a source of input that they are motivated to learn with on their own. Thus, perhaps it should be extensive learning with different types of meaning-focused input that is the goal.

As noted by Webb (2015), there are challenges to learning with different types of meaning-focused input in the classroom. Perhaps the biggest of which is getting everyone (teachers, students, parents, program directors) to buy into the value of students quietly reading, viewing television and movies, watching YouTube videos, or reading and sending emails for large amounts of classroom time. The goal of extensive learning in the classroom is to get learners to engage with the L2 outside of the classroom. If that occurs, the potential gains are huge and may provide the solution to students reaching advanced and native-like vocabulary sizes. However, more research is first needed to reveal the value of engaging with different types of L2 input. Research should raise awareness of the benefits of learning with meaning-focused input, and teachers, learners, parents, and program directors are then more likely to be encouraged to spend time on incidental vocabulary (and language) learning inside and outside of the classroom.

Further Reading

Nagy, W. E., Herman, P., & Anderson, R. C. (1985). Learning words from context. *Reading Research Quarterly, 20*(2), 233–253.

This article provides insight into the challenges of measuring incidental word learning gains, and explains the importance of incidental vocabulary learning for L1 lexical development. It is the study that motivated much of the research on the topic of incidental vocabulary learning.

Nation, I. S. P. (2013). *Learning vocabulary in another language* (2nd ed.). Cambridge, UK: Cambridge University Press.

Nation's *Learning Vocabulary in Another Language* has been the essential reference related to teaching and learning vocabulary for almost 20 years. The discussion of incidental vocabulary learning is comprehensive and insightful.

Webb, S., & Nation, I.S.P. (2017). *How vocabulary is learned*. Oxford, UK: Oxford University Press.

This book expands on many of the topics in this chapter. It includes discussion of incidental and intentional vocabulary learning, as well as approaches to helping learners to engage with meaning-focused input outside of the classroom.

Related Topics

The different aspects of vocabulary knowledge, factors affecting the learning of single-word items, factors affecting the learning of multiword items, intentional L2 vocabulary learning, sensitive measures of vocabulary knowledge and processing: expanding Nation's framework

References

Chen, C., & Truscott, J. (2010). The effects of repetition and L1 lexicalization on incidental vocabulary acquisition. *Applied Linguistics, 31*, 693–713.

Cho, K., & Krashen, S. (1994). Acquisition of vocabulary from the Sweet Valley Kids series: Adult ESL acquisition. *Journal of Reading, 37*(8), 662–667.

Dang, T. N. Y., & Webb, S. (2014). The lexical profile of academic spoken English. *English for Specific Purposes, 33*, 66–76.

Davies, M. (2008–). *The corpus of contemporary American English (COCA): 560 million words, 1990-present*. Retrieved from https://corpus.byu.edu/coca/.

Day, R. R., & Bamford, J. (1998). *Extensive reading in the second language classroom*. Cambridge, UK: Cambridge University Press.

Day, R. R., Omura, C., & Hiramatsu, M. (1991). Incidental EFL vocabulary learning and reading. *Reading in a Foreign Language, 7*, 541–551.

Ellis, R. (1999). *Learning a second language through interaction*. Amsterdam: John Benjamins.

Godfroid, A., Ahn, J., Choi, I., Ballard, L., Cui, Y., Johnston, S., . . . Yoon, H. J. (2018). Incidental vocabulary learning in a natural reading context: An eye-tracking study. *Bilingualism: Language and Cognition, 21*(3), 563–584.

Goulden, R., Nation, P., & Read, J. (1990). How large can a receptive vocabulary be? *Applied Linguistics, 11*, 341–363.

Hayes, D. P. (1988). Speaking and writing: Distinct patterns of wordchoice. *Journal of Memory and Language, 27*(5), 572–585.

Horst, M. (2005). Learning L2 vocabulary through extensive reading: A measurement study. *Canadian Modern Language Review, 61*(3), 355–382.

Horst, M., Cobb, T., & Meara, P. (1998). Beyond a Clockwork Orange: Acquiring second language vocabulary through reading. *Reading in a Foreign Language, 11*(2), 207–223.

Hulstijn, J. (2001). Intentional and incidental second-language vocabulary learning: A reappraisal of elaboration, rehearsal and automaticity. In P. Robinson (Ed.), *Cognition and second language instructions* (pp. 258–286). Cambridge, UK: Cambridge University Press.

Jenkins, J. R., Stein, M. L., & Wysocki, K. (1984). Learning vocabulary through reading. *American Educational Research Journal, 21*, 767–787.

Kuppens, A. H. (2010). Incidental foreign language acquisition from media exposure. *Learning, Media and Technology, 35*(1), 65–85.

Lindgren, E., & Muñoz, C. (2013). The influence of exposure, parents, and linguistic distance on young European learners' foreign language comprehension. *International Journal of Multilingualism, 10*(1), 105–129. https://doi.org/10.1080/14790718.2012.679275

Liu, N., & Nation, I. S. P. (1985). Factors affecting guessing vocabulary in context. *RELC Journal, 16*(1), 33–42.

Montero Perez, M., Peters, E., Clarebout, G., & Desmet, P. (2014). Effects of captioning on video comprehension and incidental vocabulary learning. *Language Learning & Technology, 18*(1), 118–141.

Nagy, W. E., Anderson, R. C., & Herman, P. A. (1987). Learning word meanings from context during normal reading. *American Educational Research Journal, 24*(2), 237–270.

Nagy, W. E., Herman, P., & Anderson, R. C. (1985). Learning words from context. *Reading Research Quarterly, 20*(2), 233–253.

Nakata, T. (2015). Effects of expanding and equal spacing on second language vocabulary learning: Does gradually increasing spacing increase vocabulary learning? *Studies in Second Language Acquisition, 37*(4), 677–711.

Nation, I. S. P. (2006). How large a vocabulary is needed for reading and listening? *The Canadian Modern Language Review, 63*, 59–82.

Nation, I. S. P. (2007). The four strands. *Innovation in Language Learning and Teaching, 1*(1), 1–12.

Pavia, N., Webb, S., & Faez, F. (in press). Incidental vocabulary learning from listening to L2 songs. *Studies in Second Language Acquisition.*

Pellicer-Sánchez, A. (2016). Incidental L2 vocabulary acquisition from and while reading. *Studies in Second Language Acquisition, 38*(1), 97–130.

Pellicer-Sánchez, A. (2017). Incidental learning of L2 collocations: A classroom study. *Language Teaching Research, 21*(3), 381–402. https://doi.org/10.1177/1362168815618428.

Peters, E. (2018). The effect of out-of-class exposure to English language media on learners' vocabulary knowledge. *ITL International Journal of Applied Linguistics, 169*(1), 142–168.

Peters, E., & Webb, S. (2018). Incidental vocabulary acquisition through watching a single episode of L2 television. *Studies in Second Language Acquisition, 40*(3), 551–557. https://doi.org/10.1017/S0272263117000407

Pigada, M., & Schmitt, N. (2006). Vocabulary acquisition from extensive reading: A case study. *Reading in a Foreign Language, 18*(1), 1–28.

Pitts, M., White, H., & Krashen, S. (1989). Acquiring second language vocabulary through reading: A replication of the Clockwork Orange study using second language acquirers. *Reading in a Foreign Language, 5*(2), 271–275.

Pulido, D. (2004). The relationship between text comprehension and second language incidental vocabulary acquisition: A matter of topic familiarity? *Language Learning, 54*(3), 469–523.

Rodgers, M. P. H. (2013). *English language learning through viewing television: An investigation of comprehension, incidental vocabulary acquisition, lexical coverage, attitudes, and captions.* Unpublished PhD thesis, Victoria University, Wellington, New Zealand.

Rodgers, M. P. H., & Webb, S. (2011). Narrow viewing: The vocabulary in related television programs. *TESOL Quarterly, 45*(4), 689–717.

Rogers, J., Webb, S., & Nakata, T. (2015). Do the cognacy characteristics of loanwords make them more easily learned than noncognates? *Language Teaching Research, 19*(1), 9–27.

Rott, S. (1999). The effect of exposure frequency on intermediate language learners' incidental vocabulary acquisition through reading. *Studies in Second Language Acquisition, 21,* 589–619.

Saragi, T., Nation, I. S. P., & Meister, G. F. (1978). Vocabulary learning and reading. *System, 6,* 72–78.

Schmitt, N., Jiang, X., & Grabe, W. (2011). The percentage of words known in a text and reading comprehension. *Modern Language Journal, 95*(1), 26–43.

Schmitt, N., & Zimmerman, C. (2002). Derivative word forms: What do learners know? *TESOL Quarterly, 36*(2), 145–171.

Statistics Canada. (1998). *Average time spent on activities, by sex.* Ottawa, ON: Author. Retrieved October 21, 2007 from http://www40.statcan.ca/l01/cst01/famil36a.htm

United States Bureau of Labor. (2006). *American time use survey summary.* Washington, DC: Author. Retrieved October 21, 2007 from www.bls.gov/news.release/atus.nr0.htm

van Zeeland, H., & Schmitt, N. (2013a). Incidental vocabulary acquisition through L2 listening: A dimensions approach. *System, 41*(3), 609–624.

van Zeeland, H., & Schmitt, N. (2013b). Lexical coverage in L1 and L2 listening comprehension: The same or different from reading comprehension? *Applied Linguistics, 34*(4), 457–479.

Vidal, K. (2003). Academic listening: A source of vocabulary acquisition? *Applied Linguistics, 24*(1), 56–89. https://doi.org/10.1093/applin/24.1.56

Vidal, K. (2011). A comparison of the effects of reading and listening on incidental vocabulary acquisition. *Language Learning, 61*(1), 219–258.

Waring, R., & Takaki, M. (2003). At what rate do learners learn and retain new vocabulary from reading a graded reader? *Reading in a Foreign Language, 15*(2), 130–163.

Webb, S. (2007a). The effects of synonymy on vocabulary learning. *Reading in a Foreign Language, 19*(2), 120–136.

Webb, S. (2007b). The effects of repetition on vocabulary knowledge. *Applied Linguistics, 28*(1), 46–65.

Webb, S. (2008). The effects of context on incidental vocabulary learning. *Reading in a Foreign Language, 20,* 232–245.

Webb, S. (2015). Extensive viewing: Language learning through watching television. In D. Nunan & J.C. Richards (Eds.), *Language learning beyond the classroom* (pp. 159–168). New York, NY: Routledge.

Webb, S., & Chang, A, C-S. (2012). Vocabulary learning through assisted and unassisted repeated reading. *Canadian Modern Language Review, 68*(3), 267–290.

Webb, S., & Chang, A. C. S. (2015a). How does prior word knowledge affect vocabulary learning progress in an extensive reading program? *Studies in Second Language Acquisition, 37*(4), 651–675. https://doi.org/10.1017/S0272263114000606

Webb, S., & Chang, A. C. S. (2015b). Second language vocabulary learning through extensive reading: How does frequency and distribution of occurrence affect learning? *Language Teaching Research, 19*(6), 667–686.

Webb, S., & Macalister, J. (2013). Is text written for children appropriate for L2 extensive reading? *TESOL Quarterly, 47*(2), 300–322.

Webb, S., & Nation, I. S. P. (2017). *How vocabulary is learned.* Oxford, UK: Oxford University Press.

Webb, S., Newton, J., & Chang, A. C. S. (2013). Incidental learning of collocation. *Language Learning, 63*(1), 91–120.

Webb, S., & Paribakht, T. S. (2015). What is the relationship between the lexical profile of test items and performance on a standardized English proficiency test? *English for Specific Purposes, 38,* 34–43.

Webb, S., & Rodgers, M. P. H. (2009). The lexical coverage of movies. *Applied Linguistics, 30*(3), 407–427.

Webb, S., Yanagisawa, A., & Uchihara, T. (under review). How effective are intentional vocabulary learning activities? A meta-analysis.

Wesche, M., & Paribakht, T. (1999). Introduction. *Studies in Second Language Acquisition, 21*, 175–180.

Zahar, R., Cobb, T., & Spada, N, (2001). Acquiring vocabulary through reading: Effects of frequency and contextual richness. *The Canadian Modern Language Review, 57*, 541–572.

16

Intentional L2 Vocabulary Learning

Seth Lindstromberg

Introduction

A Practical Outline of Intentional Learning

It is generally possible, over a given period of time, for post-early-childhood learners to acquire more L2 vocabulary intentionally than incidentally (Barcroft, 2015; Hulstijn, 2003; Laufer, 2005). Thus, one might expect there to be numerous pertinent, in-depth discussions about what intentional learning is and about how it differs from incidental learning. However, such discussions are scarce and their portrayals of intentional learning are indistinct. Indeed, it seems that in cognitive science there is no current theory of learning that includes the presence or absence of an intention to learn as a construct or a critical element (cf., Hulstijn, 2003, p. 356). That said, few if any modern authorities doubt that people can make decisions about what to try to learn, how to try, when to start, and when to quit (e.g., Bjork, Dunlosky, & Kornell, 2013). This must be one reason why, theory or no theory, the notion of intentional learning is one that L2 researchers can hardly do without.

Going by how intentional learning is referred to in the literature on L2 vocabulary learning, it falls under the heading of *language-focused learning*, one of Nation's (2013) "four strands" of a well-balanced program for learning an additional language. Authorities on memory such as Roediger (2008) see intentional learning as separable into intentional encoding and intentional retrieval. In experimental psychology as a whole, it is operationalized as learning that happens when those who learn are aware that there will be a test of retention, whereas *incidental* learning is deemed to occur when those who learn are not aware that a retention test is coming (Baddeley, Eysenck, & Anderson, 2009). However, this sharp distinction poorly reflects the full range of situations in which intentional learning in some sense evidently occurs (Barcroft, 2015; Hulstijn, 2001, 2003; McLaughlin, 1965; Postman, 1964). One fact left out of account by the operational definition of intentional learning is that in a school setting or in the context of an experiment, learners may well suppose that a test will follow an episode of vocabulary study even when no forewarning of a retrieval test is given. (Thus, researchers aiming to maintain conditions of incidental learning sometimes try to forestall such suppositions by feeding participants a cover story.) More fundamentally, the operational definition takes no account of the likelihood that individuals can have intentions to learn that are independent of any belief on their part that a researcher, teacher, or other authority is going to test them (e.g., Barcroft, 2015). Another difficulty for anyone seeking to sharply delineate intentional learning is the evidence that a practice that is ordinarily associated with intentional learning – namely, using word cards to memorize L2 forms and form-meaning mappings – can result in a level of fluent accessibility in memory which is typical of what results from long-term incidental learning (Elgort, 2011). I should mention that there is evidence from a study involving electro-encephalogram recordings that incidental and intentional learning of L1 words result in different modifications of functional brain networks associated with verbal episodic memory (Kuhnert et al., 2013), but it is not clear what this might imply for learning L2 words or for being able to retrieve their meanings and forms from a memory store which supports everyday language use. Moreover, weighing against speculation that incidental and intentional learning may be qualitatively different activities, there is a wide range of evidence that, in terms of behavior, the difference between intentional and incidental learning is a matter of degree (Postman, 1964; McLaughlin, 1965). Importantly, there are circumstances in which learning appears to be wholly unaffected by the level of an individual's intention to learn; and the same can be said of levels of desire and of motivation. Rather than being crucial factors in learning these are factors that may influence learning indirectly, if at all (Baddeley et al., 2009). What *is* crucial is how information is processed (Baddeley et al., 2009). For the time being, then, it seems best to think of intentional learning not as a type or even a mode of learning *per se* but to think of intention as a possible condition on learning (cf., Roediger, 2008) that may be absent or present to a greater or lesser degree. Finally, it has been remarked (Laufer, 2005) that the idea of intentional learning of vocabulary assumes that one can learn vocabulary essentially as one can learn nonlinguistic skills and bodies of knowledge in the sense that (1) lexical items that have been learned can be part of one's declarative knowledge, (2) knowledge of these items can also become proceduralized, whereby they can be used and understood without conscious attention and control, and (3), ultimately their forms may become automatically and instantaneously available when needed.

Viewing intentional learning now from the standpoint of someone who reads articles reporting quantitative investigations of L2 vocabulary learning, it is noteworthy that one can decide whether or not they have to do with *intentional* learning with widely varying degrees of confidence. While it seems reasonable to assume that the clearest cases of intentional learning do in fact feature forewarning of a retrieval test, additional indicators are needed.[1] An especially useful one is whether participants in a study were asked to learn a specified set of items (Barcroft, 2015; McLaughlin, 1965; Postman, 1964).[2] Two other indicators are whether learners received explicit instructions about how to engage with, or process, the to-be-learned items (e.g., McLaughlin, 1965; Postman, 1964) and whether learners followed the instructions with signs of awareness that the main goal was to learn vocabulary rather than, say, just to read and understand a story. In other words, a situation of intentional learning tends to differ from a situation of incidental learning in that the former involves a high degree of focus on vocabulary learning, rather than "on other possible tasks or other possible stimuli in the learner's environment" (Barcroft, 2015, p. 51). To be more specific here, an instruction to count the number of syllables in specified items is likely to lead to intentional processing of the items' *forms*, while the instruction to use each targeted item in a meaningful written sentence is likely to result primarily in the intentional processing of *meanings* (Barcroft, 2015). To continue, the presentation of targeted items in a situation of intentional learning tends to follow a pattern such that the items appear a predetermined number of times and for predetermined durations (Barcroft, 2015). Finally, to come at the matter from two other directions, intentional and incidental learning have been found to show differences of degree with respect to certain variables. For example, whereas the objective, real world frequency of (partly) unfamiliar lexical items is a key variable in incidental vocabulary learning, it is apparently of minor or even negligible importance in intentional vocabulary learning (de Groot & Keijzer, 2000; Lindstromberg & Eyckmans, 2019). Also, the superiority of intentional over incidental vocabulary learning that is seen in tests of retrieval may disappear or even be reversed in a test of recognition (Eagle & Leiter, 1964). It seems relevant to add that the replicability of many common findings in the experimental study of intentional learning may depend on what type of test or experimental design is used (Roediger, 2008). For example, it is commonly found that "generation" (or production) of to-be-learned information promotes learning better than just "receiving" (e.g., reading) it; however, a design change can cause the generation effect to disappear or even reverse (Roediger, 2008).

The Scope and Aims of Discussion

Because various practicalities of intentional L2 vocabulary learning are dealt with in other chapters of this book, the main aims of this chapter are few in number. Indeed, the main aim of describing intentional learning has already been partly accomplished. The additional principal aims are to elaborate on certain crucial matters of background and then to call attention to a few of the complexities in carrying out and making sense of relevant empirical studies. These studies are ones that involve what Laufer (2005, p. 223) has called "*pure* focus on forms" (my emphasis), and they have to do with vocabulary learning in planned episodes occurring neither within nor in close relation to a communicative task of the sort advocated by recent proponents of task-based learning (e.g., Ellis, Basturkmen, & Loewen, 2002).[3] This category of studies overlaps considerably with Barcroft's category of studies concerning "intentional learning and direct instruction", which he places at the most intentional end of the "incidental-intentional continuum" (2015, p. 48). It is this end of the continuum that we focus on in this chapter. (For discussion of pedagogical techniques which evidently fall nearer to the middle of the continuum, e.g., provision of input enhancement and textual glosses (Barcroft, 2015), see Pellicer-Sánchez, this volume.)

Critical Issues and Topics

Although matters important for understanding a discussion of intentional learning L2 vocabulary have been touched on in other chapters, it may be helpful to take a longer look at several of them.[4]

Retrieval Practice and the Testing Effect

In an authoritative appraisal of ten much-studied and often-recommended practices and techniques for the intentional learning of information of various kinds, Dunlosky, Rawson, Marsh, Nathan, & Willingham (2013) concluded that only two are of high utility. One of these, *distributed practice*, is discussed in Chapter 20 (see Nakata, this volume). The other is *retrieval practice* (aka practice testing), which Dunlosky et al. (2013, p. 6) define as "self-testing or taking practice tests over to-be-learned material". The rationale for retrieval practice is based on the testing effect, which is the strong and consistent finding that information that is actively recalled becomes more retrievable subsequently than would be the case without a test or if the test were replaced by an equally long session of restudying (e.g., Karpicke & Roediger, 2008; Roediger & Butler, 2011; Karpicke, 2017). An important qualification here is that although a retrieval test generally turns out to be more beneficial in the long-term than an equally long-lasting session of restudying, restudying tends to appear most beneficial in the short term. A partial explanation for this common finding is that a test of retrieval strengthens relevant memory traces more durably than restudying does because it is more focused.

To say more about retrieval, a recent hypothesis (Kornell, Klein, & Rawson, 2015) sees it as a two-stage process. First, an individual becomes aware of a "retrieval cue", such as a question or a gap in a sentence, and the cue triggers a mental search for an appropriate response. Second, the individual either retrieves the response or does not retrieve it but luckily *is given* the response "from the outside" (perhaps in the form of feedback). Either way, appropriate connections in memory are strengthened; and, in some cases, inappropriate connections are weakened. The key conclusion is that what matters is not retrieval in and of itself but rather the processing that goes on during the search for the response and the processing that goes on after the response becomes available. To elaborate, it is during the first episode of processing that the memory traces of related information are activated and it is during the second episode that connections among the memory traces for the cue, for the related information, and for the response become stronger. Because difficult retrieval entails more processing, tests which make retrieval easy tend to be less effective in the long term than tests that make retrieval effortful. For example, tests that require retrieval from working memory, as opposed to secondary (or long term) memory, are likely to bring negligible benefits (Roediger, 2008). To ensure that retrieval draws on secondary memory and is therefore sufficiently effortful, a learner can seek (or be given) feedback only after a delay. Indeed, it has been proposed more generally that there is such a thing as "desirable difficulty" in the learning of anything (Bjork & Kroll, 2015). Kornell et al. (2015, p. 291) have gone so far as to say that because learners profit least from retrieving information about which they are relatively sure, "retrieval success may be a sign that relatively little learning is occurring and that one should have waited longer before attempting to retrieve" (Kornell et al., 2015, p. 291). As to feedback, it should be stressed that it is particularly necessary that feedback be given after tests which expose learners to incorrect information, as recognition and multiple choice tests do (Roediger & Butler, 2011). If feedback is not given, then the expectation should be that rates of successful retrieval will be reasonably high.

Two types of tests known to engender the testing effect are tests of free recall and tests of cued recall (where a cue for retrieving an L2 word might be an L1 equivalent or the L2 word's first letter). Also effective are variants of cued recall in which learners produce an L2 word or phrase in response to a question or a gap in a context. Crucially, the testing effect can eventuate not just from formal classroom tests but from retrieval exercises in general, including retrieval activities with a game-like character. Thus, incorporating more testing practice into a syllabus or study plan does not mean that instruction or autonomous study must be conspicuously laborious and serious. A possible (and possibly culture-specific) obstacle to implementing a regime of markedly test-like learning events is suggested by reports that American learners, for instance, are likely to doubt that being tested is a good way to learn (Dunlosky et al., 2013; Karpicke & Roediger, 2008). Also, it is easy to imagine that young learners may wilt under a regime of retrieval practice unless a proportion of the tests are somehow made fun to do. Finally, alleged differences in personal learning styles do not constitute an impediment to widespread implementation of good learning practices such as retrieval practice (Arbuthnott & Krätzig, 2015; Pashler, McDaniel, Rohrer, & Bjork, 2008).

Levels of Processing (LOP) Theory and the Elaborative Processing of Lexical Items

The notion of deep, rich, or elaborative mental processing of, say, L2 vocabulary stems substantially from Levels of Processing Theory (LOP) (e.g., Craik, 2002; Craik & Lockhart, 1972; Craik & Tulving, 1975). Key ideas in LOP theory as set out by Craik and Tulving (1975) are that the durability of a memory trace is a positive function of degree of "semantic involvement" (i.e., engagement with meaning) (p. 268) and that memory performance depends on the elaborateness of the final encoding of lexical information.[5]

Semantic Elaboration in General and Image-Based Elaboration in Particular

With reference to a given lexical item, *semantic elaboration* is an umbrella term in LOP theory for mental operations resulting in a more detailed mental representation of the meaning of a given lexical meaning item. This may include the addition of neural-connections to memory traces for meanings of other lexical items. An important general type of semantic elaboration is the integration of the meaning of a newly or partly learned vocabulary item into the mental lexicon (e.g., Thompson, 1987). A specific case of semantic elaboration is mapping the meaning and form of an L2 target to the meaning and form of an L1 cognate.

An additional type of semantic elaboration is entailed by Dual Coding Theory (Paivio, 1986; Paivio & Desrochers, 1979; Paivio, Walsh, & Bons, 1994; see also Holcomb, Anderson, Kounios, & West, 1999; and, with respect to multiword expressions, Li, 2009). This theory holds that many items of vocabulary are encoded (or represented) in memory in one or both of two ways. One type of encoding is iconic in character and one is purely verbal in character. The former type of encoding supports lexical meanings that include images – visual and sensori-motoric ones, for example. Because imageability is highly correlated with concreteness (generally, $r \approx .84$), abstract vocabulary – unless it is quite emotive – may be encoded in memory with few if any associated images (Dellantonio, Mulatti, Pastore, & Job, 2014). It is well documented that imageable L2 words are comparatively easy to acquire in situations of intentional learning. Steinel, Hulstijn, and Steinel (2007) found that the same is true for L2 idioms. Dual Coding Theory suggests that encoding imageable words in both verbal and iconic channels rather than in just one channel, enhances learnability.

A number of researchers have attempted to confirm that learners' ability to learn and durably remember L2 expressions is enhanced by tasks intended to promote imagistic encoding. For example, Boers (2001), Boers, Demecheleer, and Eyckmans (2004), and Boers, Eyckmans, and Stengers (2007) have reported good results for an approach to learning L2 English figurative idioms which involves exploring or speculating about the domain of activity in which targeted idioms are, or were, used literally. A key rationale is that such reflection is likely to feature the generation of mental images. For additional discussion, see Boers and Lindstromberg (2008, 2009).

The (Elaborative) Processing of Lexical Forms

Although LOP theory recognizes that learners can process orthographic and phonological forms, past versions of the theory heavily prioritized meaning (i.e., semantic) processing. This probably accounts in part for the fact that L2 researchers have paid much more attention to (elaborative) meaning processing than to (elaborative) form processing. Let's consider a recent theory that takes a balanced view of these two types of processing along with a posited third type of processing, the processing of form-meaning mappings.

Barcroft's "Type of Processing – Resource Allocation" Model

Barcroft and colleagues (e.g., Barcroft, 2002, 2006, 2007, 2015; Barcroft, Sommers, and Sunderman, 2011) have presented persuasive evidence that LOP theory requires important qualifications with respect to L2 vocabulary learning (see also Roediger, 2008). To begin at the beginning, Craik and Tulving (1975) described a within-subjects experiment (their experiment number 4) which involved the free recall of L1 concrete nouns studied in a situation of intentional learning. Of the three experimental conditions, one called for processing of orthographic form (e.g., participants were asked whether a targeted word was shown in capital letters), one called for processing of phonological form (i.e., participants were asked whether a targeted word rhymes with a certain other word), and one called for processing of meaning. In the latter condition participants were asked to judge whether or not a targeted word fits thematically in a given gapped sentence. Subsequent free recall of words encountered in the meaning-processing condition was found to be superior to free recall of words encountered in the two form processing conditions. Since Craik and Tulving (1975) equated semantic processing with deep processing and processing of form with shallow (i.e., relatively superficial) processing, they concluded from the results of this experiment, and from similar ones, that semantic processing promotes word learning more effectively than processing of form does. Barcroft (e.g., 2015), however, has argued that the relative effectiveness of semantic processing and form processing (aka, structure processing) crucially depends on how much there is to be learned about a given L2 item. That is, with respect to a given learner, questions such as the following are germane: Does the item have both an unfamiliar form and an unfamiliar meaning, that is to say, a meaning which is not expressed by a lexeme in L1? Or is only the form of the item unfamiliar, because its meaning *is* known from L1? A key to the relevance of these and certain other questions is Barcroft's *resource depletion hypothesis*, which holds that there is a limit to the processing capacity available to a given learner in a given situation with respect to a lexical item encountered in input. So, for instance, a learner who is intensively processing meaning may have little or no capacity left over for the processing of form (and vice versa). This hypothesis is an element of Barcroft's Type of Processing – Resource Allocation (TOPRA) model, the gist of which is given by the following three statements. First, processing of form, processing of meaning, and processing of form-meaning mappings can each operate largely independently of each other. Second, "increases in one of these three types of processing . . . increases processing and learning for the type of processing in question, which is reflected in increased learning for the component of vocabulary learning in question" (2015, p. 90). However, "increases in one of these three types of processing . . . can decrease available processing resources for the other types of processing, which is reflected in the relative amount of learning associated with the different types of processing and learning counterparts in question" (p. 90).

One implication of the TOPRA model is that a task which focuses learners' attention on meaning can lead to comparatively good results in a test of recall (such as the test figuring in Craik and Tulving's experiment 4 referred to earlier) if, *but only if,* the learners already have good knowledge of the forms of the to-be-recalled items. (It should be noted that to-be-learned words in Craik and Tulving's experiment were common L1 nouns). If, on the other hand, learners do not already know the forms of the to-be-learned items to a substantial degree, then engaging in intensive processing of meanings will leave them with insufficient capacity to process the forms. These learners are likely to do worse in a test of recall than learners who have engaged in a task involving supposedly shallower processing of form. As may be evident, and as pointed out by Barcroft (2015), his TOPRA model is consistent with Morris, Bransford, and Franks's (1977) influential model of *transfer-appropriate learning*, which holds in essence that recollection will be best when the processes that take place during encoding match the processes that take place during retrieval.

For a better idea of what TOPRA means, let's consider aspects of a within-subjects study summarized in detail by Barcroft (2015). That researcher began by asking Anglophone learners of Spanish to try to learn 24 unfamiliar Spanish words that they were soon going to encounter. In the encounter phase itself, each word was matched with an illustrative picture. Eight words were encountered in a meaning-processing condition where the task was to give each word a pleasantness rating. Eight other words were encountered in a form processing condition where the task was to count the letters in each word. For the remaining eight words, participants were given no instruction beyond the common instruction that they should try to learn these words. The study phase was followed by two posttests of free recall and one posttest of cued recall. In the first of these tests, participants were asked to write down as many of the 24 to-be-learned Spanish words as they could remember. In the second, they were asked to write down all the English equivalents that they could remember. In the third, they were shown a picture corresponding to each Spanish word and asked to write down the Spanish words in question. On the first posttest, which probed participants' ability to recall the *forms* of targeted words, the average score for the words studied in the form processing condition exceeded the average score for the words studied in the meaning-processing condition. The results of the second test (which probed participants' ability to recall the *meanings* of targeted words) were the reverse of those for the first test. Apparently, and as predicted by the TOPRA model, participants who were encouraged to process meaning experienced reduced capacity to process form whereas participants who were encouraged to process form experienced reduced capacity to process meaning. Finally, the highest average scores on all three tests were for the eight words that participants were left to study however they wished. Barcroft's (2015) interpretation of this outcome is that neither of the specific processing tasks took account of the fact that participants were being asked to learn new forms and new form-meaning mappings all at the same time, with the result that both tasks depleted participants' capacity to encode the targeted words in an optimal manner. In another TOPRA-related within-subjects investigation, Barcroft (2003) investigated what happens when learners are called on to answer questions about the meanings of previously unfamiliar words that they are in the midst of learning. For 12 of the 24 targeted words, the learners' task was to consider questions about each word's meaning (e.g., *In what way can this object be used?*) whereas their task for the other 12 words was just to try to learn them somehow. Scores in an immediate and in a ten-minute delayed posttest of picture-to-target cued recall were lowest in the question condition, that is, the condition which encouraged focus on the *meanings* of the new L2 words. Even greater negative effects of asking learners to engage in semantic processing of novel L2 words have been observed in various studies in which the semantic processing task was to use each targeted word in a written sentence illustrating its meaning (for summaries and references, see Barcroft, 2015). The clear implication of such results is that a task that tends to induce a specific type of lexical processing can be productive or detrimental depending on circumstances (cf., Roediger, 2008). For instance, a task which is oriented toward meaning processing can help learners remember L2 forms that they have already acquired, but it can also sharply reduce learners' ability to remember word forms that are new to them. To state the obvious, this is important because a word whose form cannot be recalled is a word that cannot be spontaneously used in communication.

Finally, to touch on a matter of research methodology, recall that in the TOPRA-related experimental studies just summarized the baseline condition was defined by the instruction to learners that they should "do their best to learn the target words in question" (Barcroft, 2015, p. 77). Barcroft's rationale for having such a condition is that the effects of a task which promotes a specific type of lexical processing (e.g., semantic processing) should ideally be compared with a task that does not promote a specific type of processing. A possible disadvantage of having a just-do-your-best baseline condition is the difficulty of determining what strategies participating learners applied and what sort(s) of lexical processing they engaged in. It may therefore be argued that it is better to have at least one condition in which learners are set a comparison task that they are all likely to carry out in more or less the same way – a sensible proviso being, of course, that this task should have effects that can be estimated from prior research. So far as I know, the L2 research community has not reached a consensus about this issue.

A Case Study of Complexities Encountered in Research: The Keyword Method

Many streams of research have cast light on the effectiveness of types of tasks (methods, techniques, and so on) that play, or may play, a positive role in intentional L2 vocabulary learning. This section reviews one of these streams, the one comprising investigations of the keyword method.

For purposes of illustration, the keyword method seemed a good choice. First, use of this method is an extremely clear case of intentional L2 vocabulary learning. Second, the keyword method has figured in well over 100 published studies since it was introduced in the 1970s (e.g., Atkinson, 1975; Atkinson & Raugh, 1975; Ellis & Beaton, 1993; Sagarra & Alba, 2006; Shapiro & Waters, 2005) and in a number of unpublished theses and dissertations as well (e.g., Hauptmann, 2004). (For additional references, see Barcroft, 2015; Hauptmann, 2004; Nation, 2013; Wei, 2015; and www.victoria.ac.nz/lals/resources/vocrefs/vocref-20.) Third, consideration of the literature on the keyword method provides a background against which certain complications may be easier to discern.

In what seems to be the commonest version of the keyword (or linkword) method a researcher, teacher, or a learner chooses a familiar, and highly concrete L1 word, the keyword, as a mediator between a targeted L2 word and an L1 translation. For optimum recollection of form as well as meaning, the keyword should be phonologically similar to (part of) the L2 target. The next step is to think of an image which (1) is based on the meaning of the keyword and (2) involves both the L2 target and the L1 equivalent. Shapiro and Waters (2005) gave the example of English *steel* as an L1 keyword for learning L2 French *stylo* ("pen") and the mediatory image of a large pen made of a steel girder. Shapiro and Waters also described how, for hopefully enhanced mnemonic effect, this image can be played out mentally, like a movie clip.

Many results have indicated that use of the keyword method can result in impressive rates of receptive word learning. For example, Atkinson and Raugh (1975) found that the participants in their study learned 120 words in three days. The effectiveness of this method has been attributed to various combinations of the following partly overlapping factors: (1) elaborative imagistic mental processing of word meanings (e.g., Ellis and Beaton, 1993; Baddeley et al., 2009), (2) increased distinctiveness of the encoded information (Marschark & Surian, 1989), (3) integration of new knowledge with old knowledge (Thompson, 1987),

(4) provision of retrieval cues (Thompson, 1987), and (5) encouragement of effortful processing (Shapiro & Waters, 2005).

Notwithstanding the mountain of results already accumulated, the keyword method continues to be investigated by L2 researchers who are, for instance, interested in assessing its effectiveness compared to that of other methods of intentional vocabulary learning. Not all results are wholly positive. In particular, some reports have noted limitations with respect to type of learner. Campos, Amor, and González (2004) concluded from their results that the keyword method is most suited to learners with high imaging capacity. Wei (2015) concluded from her results and from results of five earlier studies that that the keyword method may not be worthwhile for "experienced and intellectually mature learners" (p. 60). An additional, and perhaps more serious concern is that when words are learned using the keyword method, access to their stored meanings is likely to be less direct and slower to negotiate than is so for words learned, say, by rote association of meanings and forms (Barcroft, Sommers, & Sunderman, 2011). In any case, effectiveness is not the only virtue that a method should have: Efficiency, practicality, versatility, and appeal to learners and teachers matter too. Taking such matters into consideration, Dunlosky et al. (2013) concluded that the keyword method is of "limited utility" because (1) it is not applicable to items of low imageability (also, the method seems inapplicable to MWEs [Boers & Lindstromberg, 2009]), (2) the time needed for training and for keyword generation can be better spent, and (3) it is not only insufficiently clear that the keyword method results in durable learning but there is even some evidence that it leads to accelerated forgetting. To elaborate about the last point, in many studies of the keyword method all targeted words were tested in two posttests of retrieval, one immediate and one delayed, and these tests were taken by all participants. In such a design, superior *delayed* posttest results in the keyword condition could be an artifact of experimental design because if more of the targeted words are retrieved in the keyword condition in the *immediate* posttest than are retrieved in the comparison condition(s), which is a typical outcome, then later retrieval of targeted items in the keyword condition would be likely to benefit disproportionally from retrieval practice. Having identified this as a potential problem, Wang, Thomas, and colleagues got around it by conducting a series of experiments in which all participants experienced the treatment to which they were randomly assigned, but only half of each treatment group took the immediate test (Wang & Thomas, 1995; Wang, Thomas, & Ouellette, 1992; Wang, Thomas, Inzana, & Primicerio, 1993). The delayed test was taken by the remaining participants in each treatment group. Each of these experiments included a condition in which the researchers provided the keywords (but participants were asked to think up their own image). There was also a comparison condition, which was either rote learning of a list of L2–L1 equivalents or study of L2 words in meaningful sentences; and some experiments included a third condition in which participants were asked to choose keywords on their own. For example, Wang et al. (1993) randomly assigned 89 participants to two groups and informed them of eventual testing: $n_{Words} = 24$ (L2 tagalog); 2 conditions × 2 test times. The immediate and delayed posttests were of two types: cued recall (cue = L2 word; response = L1 meaning) and matching L2 words with L1 equivalents. On the *immediate* posttest of cued recall, the mean scores of the keyword and rote learners were virtually identical ($\approx 79\%$ successes). By the time of a delayed posttest only two days later, the keyword learners had forgotten the meanings of nearly double the number of targeted words that the rote learners had. Relative performances on the delayed matching test were similar. Wang and Thomas (1995) replicated these findings using a comparison condition in which learners studied L2 targets presented in meaningful sentences (see also Thomas & Wang, 1996). One of the four experiments reported by Wang et al. (1992) had the standard design in which immediate and delayed posttests were taken by the same learners: Only in this case was the initial superiority of the keyword learners preserved in the delayed test. With respect to the steep forgetting curves they observed for the keyword learners in the three of their experiments that controlled for effects of retrieval practice on the immediate posttest, Wang et al. (1992) speculated that pre-experimental associations to keywords interfere with retrieval of the interactive images formed during the treatment to the extent that during the delayed test, even if learners recall their keywords and keyword images, it may be difficult for them to remember which of the multiple elements in the image went with the keyword.[6] Additionally, it is not clear that the keyword method results in any substantial processing of the *form* of a L2 target or even of its meaning since the method may well induce learners to devote too much attention to the L1 keyword (cf., Barcroft, 2015) and to the linking image. This could be a problem since, after all, the phonological form of a keyword is rarely identical to that of the L2 target, and the linking image is bound to include elements that have nothing to do with the meaning of the target. As might be expected, then, the wider literature on the keyword method is peppered with accounts of how learners and teachers have found it unappealing (e.g., Hauptmann, 2004; Hulstijn, 1997).[7]

Future Directions

A major aim of experimental research is theory development. Accordingly, experimental studies of intentional L2 vocabulary learning do not necessarily involve tasks that teachers and learners would regard as useful. This probably accounts for the rather large amount of attention that researchers have paid to the keyword method and to certain other time-consuming and generally problematic procedures, such as composing, and then writing out, meaningful sentences that use targeted expressions. Although theory development is desirable, it would be good if experimental studies nevertheless focused more often on tasks that are feasible and useful outside of an experimental context. The possibility of change in this direction may depend on prior refinement of contemporary theory. It seems to me, for example, that the TOPRA model – which has been a very beneficial spur to research – lacks detail in at least two regards. Specifically, it would be good to know how it is that mapping processing differs from simultaneous processing of form and meaning. As to the disadvantage of trying to carry out two types of processing at the same time, it can be asked how long one must wait after finishing one type of processing before beginning another. If wait-time can be very brief, then the resource depletion hypothesis may not be a formidable factor in task design. The relevance of these issues is exemplified by experimental studies of the form-focused practice of "word writing", that is, writing to-be-learned L2 words out by hand. While results of some studies indicate that this practice is not beneficial (e.g., Barcroft, 2006, 2007), results of other studies indicate the contrary. Specifically, Thomas & Dieter (1987); Candry, Elgort, Deconinck, & Eyckmans (2017); Elgort, Candry, Eyckmans, Boutorwick, & Brysbaert (2018); and Webb & Piasecki (2018) found statistically significant benefits of word writing in situations where form *and* meaning were processed. However, it may be necessary for learners to work at their own pace rather than under time pressure (Webb & Piasecki, 2018).

Finally, to consider intentional L2 vocabulary learning in a general way, there is a great deal of evidence that it can be highly fruitful to approach vocabulary learning in an organized manner with a readiness to invest time and effort. Engaging in retrieval practice is recommendable, especially if it includes plenty of tests of ability to recall spoken and written forms as well as meanings. It would be interesting to know whether cultural background is an important variable in how likely learners are to tackle vocabulary learning in the spirit just indicated.

Further Reading

Karpicke, J. (2017). Retrieval-based learning: A decade of progress. In J. Wixted (Ed.), *Cognitive psychology of memory, Vol. 2 of Learning and memory: A comprehensive reference* (J. Byrne, Series Ed.). https://doi.org/10.1016/B978-0-12-809324-5.21055-9

This recent major survey of evidence for the effectiveness of retrieval practice follows on from Roediger and Butler (2011), which I also recommend.

Kornell, N., Klein, P., & Rawson, K. (2015). Retrieval attempts enhance learning, but retrieval success (versus failure|) does not matter. *Journal of Experimental Psychology: Learning, Memory, and Cognition, 41*(1), 283–94.

Although written for specialists, this article provides a clear and detailed account of the place of retrieval in contemporary theory of learning and memory.

Laufer, B. (2005). Focus on Form in second language vocabulary acquisition. In S. Foster-Cohen (Ed.), *EUROSLA yearbook 5* (pp. 223–50). Amsterdam: John Benjamins.

This is a master class on thinking about learning vocabulary in another language.

Roediger, H. (2008). The relativity of remembering: Why the laws of memory vanished. *Annual Review of Psychology, 59*, 225–254.

Here Roediger explains why there are no known laws of learning and memory.

Related Topics

Incidental learning, retrieval practice, desirable difficulty, experimental design, levels of processing, (elaborative) processing of meaning, (elaborative) processing of form, dual processing, Type of Processing – Resource Allocation (TOPRA) model, keyword method

Notes

1 It appears that a sizeable minority of L2 research reports include no mention of whether learners were forewarned of tests or not.
2 In reading for this chapter I came across no empirical studies in which learners were asked to pre-specify their own items to target.
3 A useful reminder from Laufer (2005) is that the terms *focus on form* and *focus on forms* (which come to us from the literature of task-based learning) disguise the fact that both orientations concern meaning as well as form.
4 Note that the Involvement Load Hypothesis is not discussed in this chapter since it was conceived with incidental learning in mind. In any case, the construct of "search" is scarcely relevant in intentional learning.
5 For Baddeley et al. (2009) LOP is a hypothesis; for Roediger (2008) it is a frequently observed effect for which a theory is lacking.
6 The experimental design of Wang and Thomas seems to have been radically underused by subsequent L2 researchers with respect to interventions whose effects might be strong initially but might dissipate relatively quickly.
7 Baddeley et al. (2009) discuss strengths and limitations of some other word learning mnemonic techniques.

References

Arbuthnott, K., & Krätzig, G. (2015). Effective teaching: Sensory learning styles versus general memory processes. *Comprehensive Psychology, 4*, Article 2. https://doi.org/10.2466/06.IT.4.2

Atkinson, R. (1975). Mnemotechnics in second-language learning. *American Psychologist, 30*(8), 821–828. https://doi.org/10.1037/h0077029

Atkinson, R., & Raugh, M. (1975). An application of the mnemonic keyword method to the acquisition of Russian vocabulary. *Journal of Experimental Psychology: Human Learning and Memory, 1*(2), 126–133. https://doi.org/10.1037/0278-7393.1.2.126

Baddeley, A., Eysenck, M., & Anderson, M. (2009). *Memory.* Hove, UK: Psychology Press.

Barcroft, J. (2002). Semantic and structural elaboration in L2 lexical acquisition. *Language Learning, 52*(2), 323–363. https://doi.org/10.1111/0023-8333.00186

Barcroft, J. (2003). Effects of questions about word meaning during L2 Spanish lexical learning. *The Modern Language Journal, 87*(4), 546–561.

Barcroft, J. (2006). Can writing a new word detract from learning it? More negative effects of forced output during vocabulary learning. *Second Language Research, 22*(4), 487–497. https://doi.org/10.1191/0267658306sr276oa

Barcroft, J. (2007). Effects of word and fragment writing during L2 vocabulary learning. *Foreign Language Annals, 40*(4), 713–726. https://doi.org/10.1111/j.1944-9720.2007.tb02889.x

Barcroft, J. (2015). *Lexical input processing and vocabulary learning.* Amsterdam: John Benjamins.

Barcroft, J., Sommers, M., & Sunderman, B. (2011). Some costs of fooling mother nature: A priming study on the Keyword Method and the quality of developing L2 lexical representations. In P. Trofimovitch & K. McDonough (Eds.), *Applying priming methods to L2 learning, teaching, and research, part 1* (pp. 49–72). Amsterdam: John Benjamins.

Bjork, R. A., Dunlosky, J., & Kornell, N. (2013). Self-regulated learning: Beliefs, techniques, and illusions. *Annual Review of Psychology, 64*, 417–444. https://doi.org/10.1146/annurev-psych-113011–143823

Bjork, R. A., & Kroll, J. (2015). Desirable difficulties in vocabulary learning. *The American Journal of Psychology, 128*(2), 241–245. Retrieved from www.ncbi.nlm.nih.gov/pmc/articles/PMC4888598/

Boers, F. (2001). Remembering figurative idioms by hypothesising about their origin. *Prospect, 16*, 35–43. Retrieved from www.ameprc.mq.edu.au/docs/prospect_journal/volume_16_no_3/Prospect_16,3_Article_3.pdf

Boers, F., Demecheleer, M., & Eyckmans, J. (2004). Etymological elaboration as a strategy for learning figurative idioms. In P. Bogaards & B. Laufer (Eds.), *Vocabulary in a second language: Selection, acquisition and testing* (pp. 53–78). Amsterdam: John Benjamins.

Boers, F., Eyckmans, J., & Stengers, H. (2007). Presenting figurative idioms with a touch of etymology: More than mere mnemonics? *Language Teaching Research, 11*(1), 43–62. https://doi.org/10.1177/1362168806072460

Boers, F., & Lindstromberg, S. (2008). How cognitive linguistics can foster effective vocabulary teaching. In F. Boers & S. Lindstromberg (Eds.), *Cognitive linguistic approaches to teaching vocabulary and phraseology* (pp. 1–61). Berlin and New York, NY: Mouton de Gruyter.

Boers, F., & Lindstromberg, S. (2009). *Optimizing a lexical approach to instructed second language acquisition.* Basingstoke, UK: Palgrave Macmillan.

Campos, A., Amor, A., & González, M. (2004). The importance of the keyword-generation method in keyword mnemonics. *Experimental Psychology, 51*(2), 125–131. https://doi.org/10.1027/1618-3169.51.2.125

Candry, S., Elgort, I., Deconinck, J., & Eyckmans, J. (2017). Word writing vs. meaning inferencing in contextualized L2 vocabulary learning: Assessing the effect of different vocabulary learning strategies. *The Canadian Modern Language Review, 73*(3), 294–318. https://doi.org/10.3138/cmlr.3688

Craik, F. (2002). Levels of processing: Past, present . . . and future? *Memory, 10*(5/6), 305–318. https://doi.org/10.1080/09658210244000135

Craik, F., & Lockhart, R. (1972). Levels of processing: A framework for memory research. *Verbal Learning and Verbal Behavior, 11*(6), 671–684. https://doi.org/10.1016/S0022–5371(72)80001-X

Craik, F., & Tulving, E. (1975). Depth of processing and the retention of words in episodic memory. *Journal of Experimental Psychology: General, 104*(3), 268–294. https://doi.org/10.1037/0096-3445.104.3.268

De Groot, A., & Keijzer, R. (2000). What is hard to learn is easy to forget: The roles of words concreteness, cognate status, and word frequency in foreign-language vocabulary learning and forgetting. *Language Learning, 50*(1), 1–56. https://doi.org/10.1111/0023-8333.00110

Dellantonio, S., Mulatti, C., Pastore, L., & Job, R. (2014). Measuring inconsistencies can lead you forward: Imageability and the x-ception theory. *Frontiers of Psychology, 5*, 708. https://doi.org/10.3389/fpsyg.2014.00708

Dunlosky, J., Rawson, K., Marsh, E., Nathan, M., & Willingham, D. (2013). Improving students' learning with effective learning techniques: Promising directions from cognitive and educational psychology. *Psychological Science in the Public Interest, 14*(1), 4–58. https://doi.org/10.1177/1529100612453266.

Eagle, M., & Leiter, E. (1964). Recall and recognition in intentional and incidental learning. *Journal of Experimental Psychology, 68*(1), 58–63. https://doi.org/10.1037/h0044655.

Elgort, I. (2011). Deliberate learning and vocabulary acquisition in a second language. *Language Learning, 61*(2), 367–413. https://doi.org/10.1111/j.1467-9922.2010.00613.x

Elgort, I., Candry, S., Eyckmans, J., Boutorwick, T., & Brysbaert, M. (2018). Contextual word learning with form-focused and meaning-focused elaboration. *Applied Linguistics*. https://doi.org/10.1093/applin/amw029

Ellis, N., & Beaton, A. (1993). Factors affecting the learning of foreign language vocabulary: Imagery keyword mediators and phonological short-term memory. *Quarterly Journal of Experimental Psychology A, 46*(3), 522–558. https://doi.org/10.1080/14640749308401062

Ellis, R., Basturkmen, H., & Loewen, S. (2002). Doing focus on form. *System, 30*(4), 419–432. https://doi.org/10.1016/S0346-251X(02)00047-7

Hauptmann, J. (2004). *Effect of the integrated keyword method on vocabulary retention and motivation*. PhD dissertation, University of Leicester, Leicester, UK.

Holcomb, P., Anderson, J., Kounios, J., & West, C. (1999). Dual-coding, context-availability, and concreteness effects in sentence comprehension: An electrophysiological investigation. *Journal of Experimental Psychology: Learning, Memory, and Cognition, 25*(3), 721–742. https://doi.org/10.1037/0278-7393.25.3.721

Hulstijn, J. H. (1997). Mnemonic methods in foreign language learning: Theoretical considerations and pedagogical implications. In J. Coady & T. Huckin (Eds.), *Second language vocabulary acquisition: A rational for pedagogy* (pp. 203–224). Cambridge, UK: Cambridge University Press.

Hulstijn, J. H. (2001). Intentional and incidental second language vocabulary learning: A reappraisal of elaboration, rehearsal and automaticity. In P. Robinson (Ed.), *Cognition and second language instruction* (pp. 258–286). Cambridge, UK: Cambridge University Press.

Hulstijn, J. H. (2003). Incidental and intentional learning. In C. Doughty & M. Long (Eds.), *The handbook of second language acquisition* (pp. 349–381). Malden, MA: Blackwell Publishing.

Karpicke, J. (2017). Retrieval-based learning: A decade of progress. In J. Wixted (Ed.), *Cognitive psychology of memory, Vol. 2 of Learning and memory: A comprehensive reference* (J. Byrne, Series Ed.). https://doi.org/10.1016/B978-0-12-809324-5.21055-9

Karpicke, J., & Roediger, H. (2008). The critical importance of retrieval for learning. *Science, 319*(5865), 966–968. https://doi.org/10.1126/science.1152408

Kornell, N., Klein, P., & Rawson, K. (2015). Retrieval attempts enhance learning, but retrieval success (versus failure|) does not matter. *Journal of Experimental Psychology: Learning, Memory, and Cognition, 41*(1), 283–294. https://doi.org/10.1037/a0037850

Kuhnert, M.-T., Bialonski, S., Noennig, N., Mai, H., Hinrichs, H., & Lehnertz, K. (2013). Incidental and intentional learning of verbal episodic material differentially modifies functional brain networks. *PLOS One, 8*(11), e80273. https://doi.org/10.1371/journal.pone.0080273

Laufer, B. (2005). Focus on form in second language vocabulary acquisition. In S. Foster-Cohen (Ed.), *EUROSLA yearbook 5* (pp. 223–250). Amsterdam: John Benjamins.

Li, T. F. (2009). *Metaphor, image, and image schemas in second language pedagogy*. Köln: Lambert Academic Publishing.

Lindstromberg, S., & Eyckmans, J. (2019). The effect of frequency on learners' ability to recall the forms of deliberately learned L2 multiword expressions. *ITL – International Journal of Applied Linguistics*. Online 22 April. https://doi.org/10.1075/itl.18005.lin

Marschark, M., & Surian, L. (1989). Why does imagery improve memory? *European Journal of Cognitive Psychology, 1*(3), 251–263. https://doi.org/10.1080/09541448908403084

McLaughlin, B. (1965). "Intentional" and "incidental" learning in human instructions: The role of instructions to learn and motivation. *Psychological Bulletin, 63*(5), 359–376. https://doi.org/10.1037/h0021759

Morris, C., Bransford, J., & Franks, J. (1977). Levels of processing versus transfer appropriate processing. *Journal of Verbal Learning and Verbal Behavior, 16*(5), 519–533. https://doi.org/10.1016/S0022–5371(77)80016–9

Nation, I. S. P. (2013). *Learning vocabulary in another language* (3rd ed.). Cambridge, UK: Cambridge University Press.

Paivio, A. (1986). *Mental representations: A dual-coding approach.* Oxford, UK and New York, NY: Oxford University Press.

Paivio, A., & Desrochers, A. (1979). Effects of an imagery mnemonic on second language recall and comprehension. *Canadian Journal of Psychology, 33*(1), 17–28. https://doi.org/10.1037/h0081699

Paivio, A., Walsh, M., & Bons, T. (1994). Concreteness effects on memory: When and why? *Journal of Experimental Psychology: Learning, Memory, and Cognition, 20*(5), 1196–1204. https://doi.org/10.1037/0278-7393.20.5.1196

Pashler, H., McDaniel, M., Rohrer, D., & Bjork, R. (2008). Learning styles: Concepts and evidence. *Psychological Science in the Public Interest, 9*(3), 105–119. www.psychologicalscience.org/journals/pspi/PSPI_9_3.pdf

Postman, L. (1964). Short-term memory and incidental learning. In A. Melton (Ed.), *Categories of human learning* (pp. 145–209). New York, NY: Academic Press.

Roediger, H. (2008). The relativity of remembering: Why the laws of memory vanished. *Annual Review of Psychology, 59*, 225–254. https://doi.org/10.1146/annurev.psych.57.102904.190139

Roediger, H., & Butler, A. (2011). The critical role of retrieval practice in long-term retention. *Trends in Cognitive Science, 15*(1), 20–27. https://doi.org/10.1016/j.tics.2010.09.003

Sagarra, N., & Alba, M. (2006). The key is in the keyword: L2 vocabulary learning methods with beginning learners of Spanish. *Modern Language Journal, 90*(2), 228–243. https://doi.org/10.1111/j.1540-4781.2006.00394.x

Shapiro, A., & Waters, D. (2005). An investigation of the cognitive processes underlying the keyword method of foreign vocabulary learning. *Language Teaching Research, 9*(2), 129–146. https://doi.org/10.1191/1362168805lr151oa

Steinel, M., Hulstijn, J., & Steinel, W. (2007). Second language idiom learning in a paired-associate paradigm: Effects of direction of learning, direction of testing, idiom imageability, and idiom transparency. *Studies in Second Language Acquisition, 29*(3), 449–484. https://doi.org/10.1017/S0272263107070271

Thomas, M., & Dieter, J. (1987). The positive effects of writing practice on integration of foreign words in memory. *Journal of Educational Psychology, 79*(3), 249–253. https://doi.org/10.1037/0022-0663.79.3.249

Thomas, M., & Wang, A. (1996). Learning by the keyword mnemonic: Looking for long-term benefits. *Journal of Experimental Psychology: Applied, 2*(4), 330–342. http://dx.doi.org/10.1037/1076-898X.2.4.330

Thompson, I. (1987). Memory in language learning. In A. Wenden & J. Rubin (Eds.), *Learner strategies in language learning* (pp. 43–56). Englewood Cliffs, NJ: Prentice-Hall.

Wang, A., & Thomas, M. (1995). Effects of keywords on long-term retention: Help or hindrance? *Journal of Educational Psychology, 87*(3), 468–475. https://doi.org/10.1037/0022-0663.87.3.468

Wang, A., Thomas, M., Inzana, C., & Primicerio, L. (1993). Long-term retention under conditions of intentional learning and the keyword method. *Bulletin of the Psychonomic Society, 31*(6), 545–547. https://doi.org/10.3758/BF03337348

Wang, A., Thomas, M., & Ouellette, J. (1992). Keyword mnemonic and retention of second-language vocabulary words. *Journal of Educational Psychology, 84*(4), 520–528. https://doi.org/10.1037/0022-0663.84.4.520

Webb, S., & Piasecki, A. (2018). Re-examining the effects of word writing on vocabulary learning. *ITL – International Journal of Applied Linguistics, 169*(1), 72–94. https://doi.org/10.1075/itl.00007.web

Wei, Z. (2015). Does teaching mnemonics for vocabulary learning make a difference? Putting the keyword method and the word part technique to the test. *Language Teaching Research, 19*(1), 43–69. https://doi.org/10.1177/1362168814541734

17

Approaches to Learning Vocabulary Inside the Classroom

Jonathan Newton

Introduction

This chapter addresses the topic of how to teach and learn vocabulary effectively inside the classroom. Given the time constraints faced in most classroom learning contexts, this is a question of identifying instructional priorities from among a myriad of options. Fortunately, as discussed in the first half of this chapter, second language (L2) vocabulary research provides plenty of evidence on which to base decisions about instructional design for vocabulary learning. But, however strong the research evidence for particular vocabulary learning and teaching (henceforth, VLT) strategies, implementing them in real classrooms is seldom a straightforward process. Teaching decisions are always local and contingent. Thus, the second half of the chapter focuses on VLT research in real classroom contexts and on the mediating impact of teachers and learners on affordances for VLT.

Critical Issues and Topics

Classroom Vocabulary Learning: A Conundrum

The job of teaching and learning vocabulary inside the classroom faces a conundrum. On the one hand, the size of the vocabulary learning task is considerable. It is estimated that for learners to participate in conversational English, knowledge of the most frequent 3,000 word families is required (Webb & Rodgers, 2009), although as Schmitt and Schmitt (2014, p. 490) suggest, this may be too few words to enable full comprehension and enjoyment. For listening, van Zeeland and Schmitt (2012) found that to achieve a reasonable level of comprehension, 95% coverage of the vocabulary of informal spoken narratives was needed, and that this in turn also required a vocabulary of 2,000 to 3,000 words. Nation's (2006) analysis of a corpus of spoken texts suggested a higher figure of 6,000 to 7,000 words to attain 98% coverage. To read academic texts with some ease (i.e., again, 98% known words), learners will need a vocabulary size of around 8,000 to 9,000 words (Laufer & Ravenhorst-Kalovski, 2010). In addition to size, we need to also consider the depth of vocabulary knowledge required. Depth includes dimensions such as sensitivity to collocational frequency, register constraints on use (e.g., colloquial vs. formal uses), the range of meanings a word can convey, how a word is used in multiword units such as formulaic sequences and idioms, and so on (Nation, this volume; 2013). These are not issues to be taken lightly; vocabulary knowledge (both size and depth) has been shown to be a strong (if not the strongest) predictor of proficiency (Qian, 2002; Qian and Lin, this volume).

It is clear therefore that, given the scope of the vocabulary learning challenge, considerable investment in learning time is required to meet this challenge. And yet, and here is the conundrum, in many second language classrooms around the globe timetabled classroom hours for language learning fall well short of what is needed to achieve the required vocabulary learning. For example, a study by Webb and Chang (2012) found that EFL learners in Taiwan had between two and four hours of instruction per week. Consequently, they achieved vocabulary size gains per year ranging between 18 and 282 words. These figures are derived from scores on the Vocabulary Levels Test and so, given the extrapolation involved, need to be treated with some caution. However, even at the highest rate, it is clear that after five years of study, gains in vocabulary size were modest. As Gao and Ma (2011, p. 345) express it, "Students typically need to know words measured in thousands, not hundreds, but receive language instruction measured in months, not years".

Of course there are other contexts in which learners have much more exposure to taught second languages in their schooling. In many countries worldwide, English and/or other second languages are not just taught as subjects but are used as the language of instruction to teach other subjects in the curriculum. Naturally, in such contexts, students are exposed to many more hours of English in schooling, and their vocabulary size is likely to reflect this. But overall, the point stands; for many learners – and for the majority in foreign language contexts, the time available in the classroom to learn vocabulary falls short of what is required. What then can be done to maximize vocabulary learning opportunities inside the classroom in the context of limited classroom hours? Clearly, the answer will require some prioritization from among the many teaching and learning options available, and it is to the issue of setting priorities that we turn in the next section.

Priorities for VLT Inside the Classroom

An extensive research literature exists to guide instructional planning with respect to VLT, and no shortage of guidelines for teachers have been derived from it – see, for example, Barcroft (2013, 2015), Boers (2015), Laufer (2016), Nation (2008, 2013), Schmitt (2008), Siyanova-Chanturia and Webb (2016) and Webb and Nation (2017). In this section I have attempted to synthesize from this literature a set of six priorities for VLT. These are presented in Table 17.1 and discussed in more detail in following sections. The six priorities first address the issue of *what* lexical items to teach (priority 1) and then, as the main focus of the chapter, *how* to teach them (priorities 2–6).

Priorities 1 through 5 cover similar ground to Nation's (2008) list of the four jobs of the vocabulary teacher. These are (in descending order of importance): (1) *plan* what vocabulary is to be taught and how; (2) *guide* learners in the use of vocabulary learning strategies; (3) *assess* learners' vocabulary knowledge and size, and their progress towards learning goals; and (4) *teach* lexical items.[1] These priorities involve teachers and learners working together on the vocabulary learning challenge. As Schmitt (2008) notes, "students need the willingness to be active learners over a long period of time, for without this, they are unlikely to achieve any substantial vocabulary size, regardless of the quality of instruction" (p. 333). Elaborating on this point, Nation (2008) sees the three main jobs for the learner as (1)

Table 17.1 Priorities for vocabulary learning and teaching inside the classroom

---

Priority 1. Set vocabulary learning attainment targets
Learn lexical items which have been selected with reference to (1) learner needs and current vocabulary knowledge, (2) word frequency, and (3) relevance criteria. (See Read in Part IV and Vilkaitė-Lozdienė and Schmitt in Part I of this volume.)

Priority 2. Develop learners' vocabulary learning strategic competence
Provide opportunities to learn about and develop expertise in using vocabulary learning strategies. (See Gu in Part II of this volume.)

Priority 3. Audit, curate, and link vocabulary learning opportunities inside and outside the classroom
- Identify and co-curate (with learners) opportunities for VLT that link learning inside the classroom to learning beyond the classroom.
- Foster autonomous vocabulary learning.

Priority 4. Maximize vocabulary learning opportunities in classroom activities
Adopt a principled approach to incorporating VLT into classroom activities across the four skills and four strands in a program.

Priority 5. Assess progress
- Regularly assess progress towards vocabulary learning goals. (See Kremmel in Part III of this volume.)
- Use assessment to inform VLT decision-making.

Priority 6. Embrace technology-mediated vocabulary learning
With reference to evidence-based best practice, select and utilize technology to enhance vocabulary learning and teaching across the four strands in a program. (See Ballance and Cobb, and Meunier in Part II of this volume.)

---

putting language to real use; (2) deliberately learning lexical items; and (3) developing an autonomous orientation to vocabulary learning, including deciding which words to learn, and managing vocabulary learning beyond the classroom. We return to a focus on the learner later in this chapter.

The following sections elaborate on each of the VLT priorities presented in Table 17.1 with the aim of providing a broad conceptual framework for understanding vocabulary learning inside the classroom. The reader who wishes to pursue any of these topics in greater depth is encouraged to refer to the citations in Table 17.1 and to other chapters in this volume that address each priority area in detail.

Priority 1. Set Vocabulary Learning Attainment Targets

Careful planning is needed to ensure that learners spend time on lexical items that are relevant to their needs and that provide the best return for the effort invested in learning these items (Webb & Nation, 2017). Such planning is likely to involve four main steps. The first is a needs analysis in which information is gathered on the lexical component of learners' language learning needs and purpose for learning. Of course, in many classroom contexts the lexical items to be learned at each curriculum level are pre-set in the curriculum and/ or textbook. Here, needs analysis can focus on critically evaluating the alignment of prescribed vocabulary learning goals with learners' needs and with the frequency principle (see below).

A second step in needs analysis is diagnostic assessment of learners' current vocabulary knowledge, focusing on gathering information on vocabulary size and on what lexical items relevant to learning needs are known, at what depth, and where the main gaps in knowledge lie.

Pooling these two sets of information provides the starting point for a third step: setting attainment targets. The frequency principle (Nation, 2013) provides one source of guidance on how to set and sequence attainment targets. In simple terms, it states that higher frequency lexical items (both words and multiword phrases) have more utility and therefore should be learned first. On this basis, Nation (2013) argues that learners should spend time on high-frequency words, including high-frequency formulaic sequences such as idioms and phrasal verbs, but not spend time on learning low-frequency words unless they have particular utility.

Schmitt and Schmitt (2014) argue that the 3,000 most frequent word families justify inclusion within the set of high frequency vocabulary. Kremmel (2016) further proposes that for high-frequency vocabulary, the traditional 1,000-item frequency bands are too broad and that 500-item banks are more informative, especially for diagnostic purposes.

In a fourth planning step, the results of these analyses need to be mapped onto a program of study so that daily and weekly vocabulary learning goals can be set and monitored, either for each individual student, groups of students, or whole classes. Kremmel's proposal for smaller frequency bands is certain to make this job easier. (For more information on measuring vocabulary size, see the chapters in Part III, and the chapter by Read in Part IV of this volume.) Setting goals requires planning of how best to achieve these goals. This is the focus for instructional priorities 2 to 6, which follow.

Priority 2. Develop Learners' Vocabulary Learning Strategic Competence

Helping learners become more effective managers of their vocabulary learning is important for at least two reasons. First, it is clear that the teacher cannot teach all the lexical items learners need to learn. Second, even accounting for extensive language input outside the classroom, for the vast majority of language learners, too little time is available to rely on incidental learning as the main source of vocabulary growth (Schmitt, 2008). Strategy training provides the most efficient way to address both these limitations. It uses small amounts of classroom time to maximum effect by equipping learners to more effectively use time outside the classroom for vocabulary learning (Nation, 2008). Strategic learners are better able to make judicious decisions about which lexical items they will invest learning effort in, and what form that effort will take (for more information on vocabulary learning strategies, see Gu, this volume).

Logically, for learners to develop this expertise, they will first need to know *what* to learn. This involves the teacher collating and sharing information with learners about their vocabulary size along with information about the nature of vocabulary, including, in particular, the frequency principle. This may not be straightforward since many teachers are likely to have limited knowledge of vocabulary size and frequency-based principles of vocabulary learning (Schmitt, 2008).

A strategic orientation also involves reflexive awareness of one's self, including reflection on one's preferences, past learning experiences, beliefs about VLT, self-efficacy, and so on (Murray, Gao, & Lamb, 2011). Learners may also benefit from being made aware of the accelerated learning gains they can achieve through strategic and well-informed independent learning effort. Not least, learners need training in specific strategies such as guessing words in context (Webb & Sasao, 2013), learning words on word cards, and imaging strategies. Such training should be accompanied by guided opportunities to practice these strategies (Nation, 2013). As this brief list shows, strategy training involves three main types of strategies: cognitive, metacognitive, and affect strategies (Zhang & Li, 2011).

Let me illustrate this topic with reference to the strategy of guessing the meaning of unknown words. This strategy involves five steps: (1) identify the part of speech of the unknown word; (2) ask "What does what?" in the sentence (i.e., what is the subject of the sentence, what does the subject do, and to what/whom does it do it); (3) look for wider context and textual cues (for example referential chains, conjunctions); (4) make a guess; (5) check the guess with reference to the meaning of word parts (Nation, 2013). There has been some debate over the effectiveness of this strategy. For example, Bensoussan and Laufer (1984), claim that the strategy is counterproductive since, more often than not, it leads learners to guess incorrectly. However, Nation (2013), points out that the Bensoussan and Laufer study and others like it fail to take into account the learners' vocabulary size and the density of unknown words in surrounding text. These studies thereby set up conditions that make successful guessing unlikely. Further, Nation (ibid., p. 352) makes the point that, "it may be that training in guessing helps vocabulary learning simply because it encourages learners to give deliberate thoughtful attention to vocabulary items". So yes, if you want durable knowledge from one guessing attempt at a word regardless of text difficulty and a learner's vocabulary size, then guessing is not well supported by research. If, however, you more reasonably give credit for partial knowledge and consider vocabulary learning to be a cumulative process, then guessing – and by inference, training in guessing words in context – is well supported by research. Training is a particularly viable option for the guessing strategy because the sequence set of steps in the strategy require structured practice and guidance (Webb & Sasao, 2013).

The value of training in vocabulary learning strategies is well attested by research (see chapters by Gu, Nakata, and Sasao in this volume) and so deserves to be allocated classroom time.

Priority 3. Audit, Curate, and Link Vocabulary Learning Opportunities Inside and Outside the Classroom

As noted earlier, many L2 learners have too little time and opportunity for the extensive exposure to language input and meaningful language use needed if incidental encounters with vocabulary are to meet their vocabulary learning needs (Nation, 2013). Neither can this gap be filled by the limited time available in class for deliberate VLT (Schmitt, 2008). What is achievable within these limitations however is for teachers and learners to strategically manage the learning opportunities found in and beyond the classroom so as to build synergistic links between deliberate teaching, independent vocabulary study, and incidental learning. This requires the teacher, in collaboration with learners, to take responsibility for auditing and curating vocabulary learning opportunities rather than leaving them to chance. The need for teacher guidance is confirmed in a study by Ranta and Meckelborg (2013) who used learner diaries to track the extent to which young adult ESL learners in Canada used English beyond the classroom. Overall, they found that the learners made relatively light use of English outside of class. They concluded that:

> The relatively limited exposure to spoken English either through interaction or watching movies or TV for some of the participants is of particular concern since it is generally believed that L2 proficiency development requires both input and output opportunities.
> *(Ranta & Meckelborg, 2013, p. 25)*

This finding highlights how important it is for teachers to know what opportunities are available to learners beyond the classroom, and how well these opportunities are being taken up. A useful heuristic to help with auditing and curating these opportunities is found in the *four strands* framework developed by Nation (2007, 2008). Nation argues that for effective vocabulary learning, target vocabulary should be met in each of four strands: meaning-focused input, meaning-focused output, language-focused learning, and fluency. In *meaning-focused input*, the learner's primary attention is on the ideas and messages conveyed by the language and met in listening and reading (i.e., the receptive skills). In *meaning-focused output* (i.e., speaking and writing; the productive skills), the learners' attention is on conveying ideas and messages to another person. The *fluency* strand is made up of opportunities to develop fluent use of known language items. To complement these three meaning-focused strands, the fourth strand, *language-focused learning*, involves deliberate attention to learning language items, structures, and features. As Nation (2007) points out, these strands should be seen as long continuous sets of learning conditions that run through a whole language program.

The auditing job involves identifying vocabulary learning opportunities in each of the four strands, and identifying how these opportunities can be linked together across the strands. The curating job involves selecting and marshaling resources that provide for learning opportunities in each strand. This might involve, for example, providing resources for extensive reading for pleasure, setting extension tasks linked to classroom learning, and providing links to appropriate viewing/listening resources online. The massive expansion of free, accessible online materials for using and enriching vocabulary learning beyond the classroom makes the curator role more critical than ever.

Priority 4. Maximize Vocabulary Learning Opportunities in Classroom Activities

Teachers and researchers alike are interested in how vocabulary learning opportunities can be enriched in the many activities and tasks that constitute classroom teaching and learning. The pivotal question in this regard is:

> Which tasks, involving which ways of information processing, lead to better attainment of which types of vocabulary learning?

Three frameworks have been proposed to answer this question: the Involvement Load Hypothesis (ILH) (Laufer & Hulstijn, 2001), the Technique Feature Analysis (TFA) (Nation & Webb, 2011) and the Type of Processing – Resource Allocation (TOPRA) model (Barcroft, 2002). All of these frameworks seek to model the ways language learning activities in which learners encounter unfamiliar lexical items determine how these items are processed and the likelihood that they will be learned (see Laufer, this volume). Examples of activities which have been researched using these frameworks include reading comprehension activities, writing sentences to practice using new words, and written composition activities.

The first of these frameworks, the ILH, hypothesizes that the likelihood of lexical items met in an activity being learned is predicated on the degree to which three components – need, search, and evaluation – are present. Together, these three components make up the involvement load of the activity. "Need" refers to the extent to which learners need to know the meaning of a word; search to the nature of retrieval involved, including the effort involved in finding the meaning and whether retrieval is receptive or productive; and evaluation to the effort involved in matching the meaning that has been retrieved to the context. Each component has three levels: weak (0), moderate (1), or strong (2) allowing for activities to be coded for their involvement index on a scale of 0 to 6, with tasks rated higher on the scale claimed to be more effective for language learning. In general, research on the ILH has shown tasks with a higher involvement load to lead to better vocabulary learning outcomes, although results have been somewhat mixed across studies, and the differential gains for activities with higher compared to lower involvement loads have been modest (Keating, 2008; Kim, 2008).

Nation and Webb (2011) point out that the ILH fails to sufficiently account for the range of factors that determine how effective a technique will be for vocabulary learning. To address this gap, they developed a more elaborate framework called Technique Feature Analysis (TFA) which identifies five main features: motivation, noticing, retrieval, generation, and retention, and breaks each of these down into sets of sub-features. The TFA framework is presented in Table 17.2.

In the first study to empirically compare these two frameworks, Hu and Nassaji (2016) assigned 96 Taiwanese university students to four different task conditions, each of which they categorized based on ILH and TFA indexes and in which 14 unknown words appeared. The results of pretest and posttest comparisons of knowledge of the 14 words showed that the TFA was a significantly stronger predictor of learning than the ILH. Interestingly, the task which led to the best retention of words on the posttest was the one which included a productive dimension in which participants were required to reword sentences using the target words in an appropriate form and without changing meaning. Hu and Nassaji conclude

Table 17.2 Technique Feature Analysis

Motivation
- Is there a clear vocabulary learning goal?
- Does the activity motivate learning?
- Do the learners select the words?

Noticing
- Does the activity focus attention on the target words?
- Does the activity raise awareness of new vocabulary learning?
- Does the activity involve negotiation?

Retrieval
- Does the activity involve retrieval of the word?
- Is it productive retrieval?
- Is it recall?
- Are there multiple retrievals of each word?
- Is there spacing between retrievals?

Generation
- Does the activity involve generative use?
- Is it productive?
- Is there a marked change that involves the use of other words?

Retention
- Does the activity ensure successful linking of form and meaning?
- Does the activity involve instantiation?
- Does the activity involve imaging?
- Does the activity avoid interference?

Source: Adapted from Nation & Webb, 2011, p. 7

from this finding that the requirements to use a word generatively and to deliberately focus on form (Laufer, 2005) are key factors that contribute to better word learning (see Laufer in this volume for a contrasting evaluation of Hu and Nassaji, 2016). To date, no other studies of which I am aware have subjected the TFA to empirical testing.

The third framework, the TOPRA model (Barcroft, 2002, 2013), accounts for how different types of processing (i.e., semantic processing, form processing, and processing for mapping) lead to different kinds of learning. It has close parallels with the transfer-appropriate processing (TAP) model of memory (Goldstein, 2015), which posits that the way we process information determines the facets we will remember/get better at. Central to the TOPRA model is the problem of limited attentional capacity. That is, because attentional resources are necessarily finite, and because processing L2 input is cognitively demanding for learners, allocating attention to one facet of the input will necessarily reduce the resource available to attend to other aspects. For example, Barcroft (2004) found that when learners were required to write novel sentences using words they had just learned, their ability to recall these words was significantly poorer than for learners who did not do a productive task but instead did an activity that focused their attention on the form of the words. In a summary of the research findings relevant to TOPRA, Barcroft (2013) identifies five key implications for vocabulary learning:

1   Exposure to repeated occurrences of new words is beneficial for word learning.
2   Variability in aural aspects of spoken input (e.g., speaker style and speech rate) enhances learnability.
3   During the initial stages of learning lexical items, tasks that require semantic elaboration detract from learning.
4   Requiring learners to produce new words without recourse to meaning can be detrimental to word learning.
5   Word retrieval (i.e., productive retrieval) is beneficial for learning after the initial stage of form learning.

To sum up, all three models share the goal of establishing a principled basis on which to select and design learning activities in order to improve the effectiveness of L2 vocabulary learning in the classroom. However, three qualities of the TOPRA model distinguish it from the other two. First, it makes specific predictions about sequencing, namely that the processes of attending to form and establishing form-meaning mappings should precede opportunities for deeper semantic encoding. Second, it makes predications about the impact of *input* features on vocabulary learning. Third, it accounts for the multifaceted nature of vocabulary learning by distinguishing between three dimensions of word learning: memory for new words, the ability to create form-meaning mappings, and memory for known words.

Priority 5. Assess Progress

Formative assessment, or what is known as assessment *for* learning, is an integral part of effective learning and teaching (Hattie, 2012; Wiliam, 2011). It not only provides information on what has or hasn't been learned over the short term (i.e., daily or weekly), it is *part of the process of this learning*. As such, formative assessment stands in contrast to summative assessments such as standardized tests of achievement or proficiency (e.g., the VLT and VST), which typically take place outside of classroom learning and teaching.

For VLT, formative assessment involves regularly assessing learners' attainments and their progress towards vocabulary learning goals. Information on how well students are learning vocabulary and how effective the curriculum is in this area is an important guide for future decision-making by both teachers and learners. As Grabe and Stoller (2018, pp. 38–39) argue,

> the concept of assessment for learning . . . is one that all teachers should embrace as part of their ongoing efforts to improve students' learning. Assessment for learning focuses on students' performance "at the moment," most commonly through informal measures of progress. This form of assessment should result in teacher feedback that helps students:
>
> - become aware of their learning progress,
> - engage in self-assessment (i.e., self-reflection) to improve learning outcomes, and
> - work with the teacher and peers to improve their performance.

Despite a great deal of interest and research on assessing vocabulary knowledge and learning, little of this scholarship deals with formative assessment of short term vocabulary learning achievements. And yet for classroom teachers, this is likely to be a major concern. Recognizing this concern, Nation (2013) suggests that formative tests need to be easy to make and mark, and should fairly reflect what can be expected from a short learning time. Examples of test formats that meet these criteria are translation, matching, gap-filling, and true/false items (Nation, 2013, p. 521). Formative tests can also be used to guide strategy training. Sasao (2013) report on the development of a series of tests designed to guide and assess learners' facility with the guessing words in context strategy and with learning the form, meaning, and function of word parts (prefixes and suffixes) (see also Mizumoto, Sasao, and Webb, 2017; Sasao, this volume).

An important principle of formative vocabulary assessment is that the information it provides needs to be integrated into a feedback process so that today's assessment informs tomorrow's learning. This requires that learners understand the feedback they are given and apply it to their ongoing learning. It also requires that teachers work with students to develop (1) an appropriate disposition towards the feedback process, and (2) the skills to take on an effective agentive role in this process (i.e., knowing what the appropriate standards are, being able to compare one's learning to these standards, and knowing how to close the gap between the two (Sadler, 1989). Feedback processes such as these are valuable for helping learners develop a strategic disposition towards vocabulary learning. It is worth noting that feedback has been shown to be among the highest ranking of any single factor that influences learning (Hattie, 2009). It is not unreasonable to assume that feedback is also important for vocabulary learning.

Priority 6. Embrace Technology-Mediated Vocabulary Learning

More than any other single area of language learning, digital technologies have been developed to cater for vocabulary learning, which also happens to be one of the most extensively researched topics in relation to mobile-assisted language learning (Ma, 2017). The impressive range of digital resources available for vocabulary learning include corpora-based learning programs, lexical profiling programs, concordancers, online vocabulary tests, and mobile apps, to name a few. This raises the challenge for teachers and learners of how to select appropriate technologies from amongst the bewildering array of options available, and how to incorporate these technologies into classroom instruction.[2] Three starting points can help teachers address this challenge.

First, Nation's advice that target lexical items should be met across the four strands in a program (Nation, 2008) can be applied to technology. This involves checking that technology is being harnessed effectively in each of the strands, and especially that it is used for a balance of implicit and explicit vocabulary learning opportunities. For example, the digital resources available through the Extensive Reading Foundation[3] cater for the meaning-focused input and fluency strands; digital word cards[4] cater for the language-focused learning strand; and computer mediated communication (e.g., Skype, text chat, Twitter) caters for the meaning-focused output strand.

Second, Ma (2017, pp. 46–47) proposes that technology should be harnessed to help learners with four key stages of vocabulary learning: discovering new words, obtaining word meanings, mapping the word meanings with forms, and consolidating the words. She argues that, left to their own devices, learners will tend to use technology for the first two of these processes, i.e., using digital dictionaries, translation software, or article hyperlinks to find the meaning or pronunciation of words they encounter. But they are much less likely, unless guided by the teacher, to use technology for mapping meaning and form, and consolidating word meaning. To address this issue, Ma offers strategies such as encouraging learners to record words they look up using the record function in e-dictionaries, and then spending time reviewing these words. Alternatively, important lexical items can be added to a learner's inventory of digital word cards.

In presenting technology as a separate priority area I have perhaps run the risk of siloing it. But while technology *is* important enough to deserve being singled out in this way (Chapelle & Sauro, 2017; Ma, 2017), even more importantly, it warrants being an integral component of *every* aspect of VLT, and of each of the six priorities discussed in this section.

Future Directions: Accounting for Teachers and Learners

The question of how teachers make sense of VLT and what factors shape or constrain their decision-making has, to date, been under-researched. The messy reality of language classrooms in all their rich diversity calls for an approach which values the local and contingent over the generalizable. From this perspective, the question may be less one of what approaches to vocabulary learning should be adopted in the language classroom and more a question of how classroom factors shape affordances for VLT, or what effect classroom ecologies have on VLT. The answers to these questions offer a valuable bridge between the work of researchers and the daily VLT decision-making of learners and teachers.

Among the classroom factors that determine how VLT is realized in practice are the classroom setting, the teacher, the learners, the curriculum, materials and resources, and whatever language teaching methodologies are in play. A more nuanced, empirically based understanding of the relationship between these factors and VLT is likely to make a valuable contribution to the VLT research agenda. In this section, we focus on two of these factors: teachers and learners.

Teachers

At the risk of repeating a somewhat tired trope, the quality of teachers has been shown in a large body of educational research to be a key determinant of variation in student learning (Darling-Hammond, 2000; Hattie, 2012). In EFL contexts, in which learners may not have opportunities to use English or be exposed to rich English input beyond the classroom, the teacher's expertise and proficiency is an even more critical factor for vocabulary learning. Teachers bring to the classroom a wide range of experience, training, proficiency, commitment, and many other personality variables which impact on learning. Importantly, they may or may not be first language speakers of the target language, and may or not be bi- or multi-lingual, sharing or not, the language(s) of their learners. In the area of VL, a small study by Wode (1999) found that in the context of English immersion programs in German schools, the teachers' oral use of English appeared to be a not insignificant source of incidental vocabulary learning, that is, of lexical items that were not included in word lists or in teaching materials.

Teachers also bring to the classroom a variety of beliefs, attitudes, identity constructions, perceptual frames, and knowledge about VLT, all of which shape their decision-making and classroom practice (Borg, 2006; Darvin & Norton, 2015). Given the importance of teachers, and the large body of research on language teacher cognition, it is remarkable that, to date, so little of this research has addressed teacher cognition in relation to VLT. The research that is available has focused on what teachers know about the structure of the English lexicon, and the relationship between teachers' classroom vocabulary teaching practices and their beliefs about effective vocabulary teaching and the contextual factors which inform their decision-making. The following points summarize findings from a selection of studies that have investigated these topics.

1   The accuracy with which native-speaker English teachers were able to judge the frequency of low and high frequency words was no better than university graduates. Neither group was successful in judging the frequency of words in the middle frequency range (McCrostie, 2007).

2   In a survey of 201 ESL and EFL teachers, Nassaji (2012) found that the second most frequent priority for SLA research identified by the teachers was how to teach grammar and vocabulary effectively, although most of the teachers reported rarely reading research articles.

3   In a qualitative study of the vocabulary teaching practices of four university EFL teachers in two Chinese universities, Xie (2013) found the teachers drew on a very restricted range of vocabulary teaching strategies. They overwhelmingly chose a heavily transmission-oriented stance which involved presenting information in English first and then in Chinese about words, mostly in the form of explicit definitions without examples. In addition, they deliberately and explicitly taught every word they thought to be difficult.

4   In an interesting contrast to Xie's findings, Folse (2010) observed one week (25 hours) of classes in an intensive English program at a North American university. He found a low occurrence of episodes with an explicit vocabulary focus, and an especially low number of student initiated episodes. In the reading class, where he expected to see a stronger emphasis on vocabulary, vocabulary episodes were notably few and far between.

5   Coxhead (2011) used a questionnaire to identify the approach taken to the teaching of specialized vocabulary by 66 secondary school mainstream and ESOL teachers in New Zealand. A common impetus for teaching vocabulary as reported by the teachers was student initiated vocabulary enquiries. In other words, VLT was reactive rather than planned, and when it did occur, it was focused on defining or explaining single lexical items.

6   While the studies discussed earlier are typically small in scale and focus, Gao and Ma (2011) undertook a larger scale study of beliefs concerning vocabulary instruction

involving pre- and in-service teachers in Hong Kong and Mainland China. Using a questionnaire (Likert-scale and open-ended questions) and follow-up interviews, the research found general agreement among the four groups on the efficacy of learning through memorization and the value of contextual use. Responses to the open-ended questions also revealed general agreement on the need to explicitly teach lexical knowledge. However, the groups differed on questions of strategy use and how much emphasis should be placed on putting words to use as part of the learning process. Perhaps the most interesting finding from the study concerns the effect of the teachers' own language learning experiences on their beliefs. Teachers who as learners had experienced an excess of copying and dictation as a primary form of vocabulary learning showed a stronger preference for alternatives such as directly teaching word meaning.

Learners

How VLT is approached in the classroom will be determined to a large extent by not just who the learners are and their purpose for learning but by a raft of other learner variables, including how motivated they are to succeed, their beliefs about vocabulary learning, their educational background and previous L2 learning experiences, their willingness and capacity to engage with VL, by the other languages they bring with them to the classroom, and whether or not learners in a class share an L1.

As with the state of research on teacher factors, L2 vocabulary research on the learner variables and vocabulary learning is rare. This is despite the claim that acquisition of vocabulary is typically seen by learners as a major hurdle. As Meara (1980, p. 221), noted, "learners themselves readily admit that they experience considerable difficulty with vocabulary, and . . . most learners identify the acquisition of vocabulary as their greatest single source of problems". From a classroom perspective, this suggests that in addition to assessing learners' vocabulary size and learning goals, teachers need to develop a pedagogy that is responsive to the particular challenges learners face. To this end, more VLT research focused on learner perspectives is needed and has a valuable role to play. As Folse (2004, p. 10) so aptly argues:

> Perhaps the recent interest in second language vocabulary research will also mean a rethinking of the way we approach the teaching of vocabulary – including the necessity to teach vocabulary extensively – to our students. For too long, second language teaching has been dominated by an emphasis on communication, but accurate communication depends largely on an extensive knowledge of vocabulary. A good curriculum is based on student needs, and vocabulary is high on student priority lists. It is time to listen not only to the data from these studies but also to our students who are all too aware of their lack of L2 vocabulary knowledge.

Conclusions

Everything that goes on in the language classroom (or any other classroom for that matter) involves vocabulary. Words are so ubiquitous that vocabulary learning opportunities exist whether or not VLT is planned or deliberate (Wode, 1999). Assuming some level of perceptual processing has occurred, each encounter with a lexical item contributes, however incrementally, to the neural pathways associated with recognition, learning, and mental storage of that item (Ellis, 2012). However, in the absence of a planned and principled pedagogy for vocabulary expansion, much of this learning is likely to be haphazard, superficial and, consequently, inefficient, with learning gains easily lost. Indeed, as discussed earlier in this chapter, research suggests that certain approaches to teaching and learning vocabulary such as requiring learners to produce new words without reference to meaning can be detrimental to learning (Barcroft, 2004). There is good reason therefore to approach vocabulary teaching and learning in the classroom in a principled manner and with reference to empirical evidence, rather than assume it is taken care of through, for example, providing a language rich environment without deliberate planning for vocabulary growth. The aim of this chapter, as with this overall volume is to aid in this endeavor.

Further Reading

Webb, S., & Nation, I. S. P. (2017). *How vocabulary is learned*. Oxford, UK: Oxford University Press.

This is a highly practical book which addresses questions of direct relevance to classroom teaching, such as, how much classroom time should be spent teaching vocabulary, and what is the best way to group vocabulary for learning.

Barcroft, J. (2015). *Lexical input processing and vocabulary learning* (Vol. 43). New York, NY: John Benjamins.

This book provides a comprehensive account of research on lexical input processing and of Barcroft's TOPRA model. It is valuable both for its contribution to theoretical understanding of L2 vocabulary learning and for its implications for teaching and learning.

Ma, Q. (2017). Technologies for teaching and learning L2 vocabulary. In C. A. Chapelle & S. Sauro (Eds.), *The handbook of technology and second language teaching and learning* (pp. 45–61). Hoboken, NJ: John Wiley & Sons.

This is a practical and well-informed book chapter which discusses the range of technologies available for vocabulary teaching and learning.

Laufer, B. (2016). The Three "I" s of second language vocabulary learning. In E. Hinkel (Ed.), *Handbook of research in second language teaching and learning* (Vol. 3, pp. 343–354). New York, NY: Routledge.

This book chapter is a concise and highly informative discussion of instructional options for vocabulary learning and teaching.

Related Topics

Approaches to vocabulary learning outside the classroom, strategies for learning single-word items, evaluating exercises for vocabulary learning, key issues in teaching single-word items, key issues in teaching multiword items

Notes

1 The wording here is an adaption of Nation's terms of *Planning, Strategy Training, Testing*, and *Teaching* (2008, p. 1).
2 For a useful resource on digital teaching see https://thedigitalteacher.com/framework
3 http://erfoundation.org/wordpress/graded-readers/
4 E.g., https://quizlet.com/

References

Barcroft, J. (2002). Semantic and structural elaboration in L2 lexical acquisition. *Language Learning*, *52*(2), 323–363. https://doi.org/10.1111/0023-8333.00186
Barcroft, J. (2004). Effects of sentence writing in second language lexical acquisition. *Second Language Research*, *20*(4), 303–334. https://doi.org/10.1191=0267658304sr233oa

Barcroft, J. (2013). Input-based incremental vocabulary instruction for the L2 classroom. In J. W. Schwieter (Ed.), *Innovative research and practices in second language acquisition and bilingualism* (pp. 107–138). New York, NY: John Benjamins.

Barcroft, J. (2015). *Lexical input processing and vocabulary learning* (Vol. 43). New York, NY: John Benjamins.

Bensoussan, M., & Laufer, B. (1984). Lexical guessing in context in EFL reading comprehension. *Journal of Research in Reading, 7*(1), 15–32.

Boers, F. (2015). Words in second language learning and teaching. In J. R. Taylor (Ed.), *The Oxford handbook of the word* (pp. 1–17). Oxford: Oxford University Press.

Borg, S. (2006). *Teacher cognition and language education: Research and practice*. London, UK: Continuum.

Chapelle, C. A., & Sauro, S. (Eds.). (2017). *The Handbook of technology and second language teaching and learning*. Hoboken, NJ: John Wiley & Sons.

Coxhead, A. (2011). Exploring specialised vocabulary in secondary schools: What difference might subject, experience, year level, and school decile make. *TESOLANZ Journal, 19*, 37–52.

Darling-Hammond, L. (2000). Teacher quality and student achievement. *Education Policy Analysis Archives, 8*, 1. http://dx.doi.org/10.14507/epaa.v8n1.2000

Darvin, R., & Norton, B. (2015). Identity and a model of investment in applied linguistics. *Annual Review of Applied Linguistics, 35*, 36–56.

Ellis, N. (2012). Frequency-based accounts of second language acquisition. In S. Gass & A. Mackey (Eds.), *The Routledge handbook of second language acquisition* (pp. 193–210): New York, NY: Routledge.

Folse, K. S. (2004). Myths about teaching and learning second language vocabulary: What recent research says. *TESL Reporter, 37*(2), 1–13.

Folse, K. S. (2010). Is explicit vocabulary focus the reading teacher's job? *Reading in a Foreign Language, 22*(1), 139.

Gao, X., & Ma, Q. (2011). Vocabulary learning and teaching beliefs of pre-service and in-service teachers in Hong Kong and mainland China. *Language Awareness, 20*(4), 327–342. https://doi.org/10.1080/09658416.2011.579977

Goldstein, E. B. (2015). *Cognitive psychology: Connecting mind, research and everyday experience*. Stamford, CT: Cengage Learning.

Grabe, W., & Stoller, F. L. (2018). Building an effective reading curriculum: Guiding principles. In J. Newton, D. R. Ferris, C. C. M. Goh, & L. Vandergrift (Eds.), *Teaching English to second language learners in academic contexts* (pp. 28–47). New York: Routledge.

Hattie, J. (2009). The black box of tertiary assessment: An impending revolution. In L. H. Meyer, S. Davidson, H. Anderson, R. Fletcher, P. M. Johnston, & M. Rees (Eds.), *Tertiary assessment & higher education student outcomes: Policy, practice & research* (pp. 259–275). Wellington, New Zealand: Ako Aotearoa.

Hattie, J. (2012). *Visible learning for teachers: Maximizing impact on learning*. New York, NY: Routledge.

Hu, H.-c. M., & Nassaji, H. (2016). Effective vocabulary learning tasks: Involvement load hypothesis versus technique feature analysis. *System, 56*, 28–39.

Keating, G. D. (2008). Task effectiveness and word learning in a second language: The involvement load hypothesis on trial. *Language Teaching Research, 12*(3), 365–386. https://doi.org/10.1177/1362168808089922

Kim, Y. (2008). The role of task-induced involvement and learner proficiency in L2 vocabulary acquisition. *Language Learning, 58*(2), 285–325. https://doi.org/10.1111/j.1467-9922.2008.00442.x

Kremmel, B. (2016). Word families and frequency bands in vocabulary tests: Challenging conventions. *TESOL Quarterly, 50*(4), 976–987. https://doi.org/10.1002/tesq.329

Laufer, B. (2005). Focus on form in second language vocabulary learning. In S. H. Foster-Cohen, M. Garcia-Mayo, & J. Cenoz (Eds.), *EUROSLA yearbook* (Vol. 5, pp. 223–250). Philadelphia: John Benjamins.

Laufer, B. (2016). The Three "I" s of second language vocabulary learning. In E. Hinkel (Ed.), *Handbook of research in second language teaching and learning* (Vol. 3, pp. 343–354). New York, NY: Routledge.

Laufer, B., & Hulstijn, J. (2001). Incidental vocabulary acquisition in a second language: The construct of task-induced involvement. *Applied Linguistics, 22*(1), 1–26.

Laufer, B., & Ravenhorst-Kalovski, G. C. (2010). Lexical threshold revisited: Lexical text coverage, learners' vocabulary size and reading comprehension. *Reading in a Foreign Language, 22*(1), 15.

Ma, Q. (2017). Technologies for teaching and learning L2 vocabulary. In C. A. Chapelle & S. Sauro (Eds.), *The handbook of technology and second language teaching and learning* (pp. 45–61). Hoboken, NJ: John Wiley & Sons.

McCrostie, J. (2007). Investigating the accuracy of teachers' word frequency intuitions. *RELC Journal, 38*(1), 53–66. https://doi.org/10.1177/0033688206076158

Meara, P. (1980). Vocabulary acquisition: A neglected aspect of language learning. *Language Teaching, 13*(3–4), 221–246.

Mizumoto, A., Sasao, Y., & Webb, S. A. (2017). Developing and evaluating a computerized adaptive testing version of the Word Part Levels Test. *Language Testing*, 1–23. doi.org/10.1177/0265532217725776

Murray, G., Gao, X., & Lamb, T. (Eds.). (2011). *Identity, motivation and autonomy in language learning*. Bristol, UK: Multilingual Matters.

Nassaji, H. (2012). The relationship between SLA research and language pedagogy: Teachers' perspectives. *Language Teaching Research, 16*(3), 337–365. https://doi.org/10.1177/1362168812436903

Nation, I. S. P. (2006). How large a vocabulary is needed for reading and listening? *Canadian Modern Language Review, 63*(1), 59–82. https://doi.org/10.3138/cmlr.63.1.59

Nation, I. S. P. (2007). The four strands. *International Journal of Innovation in Language Learning and Teaching, 1*(1), 2–13. https://doi.org/10.2167/illt039.0

Nation, I. S. P. (2008). *Teaching vocabulary: Strategies and techniques*. Boston, MA: Heinle Cengage Learning.

Nation, I. S. P. (2013). *Learning vocabulary in another language*. Cambridge, UK: Cambridge University Press.

Nation, I. S. P., & Webb, S. (2011). *Researching and analyzing vocabulary*. Boston, MA: Heinle Cengage Learning.

Qian, D. D. (2002). Investigating the relationship between vocabulary knowledge and academic reading performance: An assessment perspective. *Language Learning, 52*(3), 513–536. https://doi.org/10.1111/1467-9922.00193

Ranta, L., & Meckelborg, A. (2013). How much exposure to English do international graduate students really get? Measuring language use in a naturalistic setting. *Canadian Modern Language Review, 69*(1), 1–33. https://doi.org/10.3138/cmlr.987

Sadler, D. R. (1989). Formative assessment and the design of instructional systems. *Instructional Science, 18*(2), 119–144. https://doi.org/10.1007/bf00117714

Sasao, Y. (2013). *Diagnostic tests of English vocabulary learning proficiency: Guessing from context and knowledge of word parts*. PhD thesis, Victoria University, Wellington, New Zealand.

Schmitt, N. (2008). Instructed second language vocabulary learning. *Language Teaching Research, 12*(3), 329–363. https://doi.org/10.1177/1362168808089921

Schmitt, N., & Schmitt, D. (2014). A reassessment of frequency and vocabulary size in L2 vocabulary teaching. *Language Teaching, 47*(4), 484–503.

Siyanova-Chanturia, A., & Webb, S. (2016). Teaching vocabulary in the EFL context. In W.A. Renandya & H. P. Widodo (Eds.), *English language teaching today: Building a closer link between theory and practice* (pp. 227–239). Switzerland: Springer International Publishing.

van Zeeland, H., & Schmitt, N. (2012). Lexical coverage in L1 and L2 listening comprehension: The same or different from reading comprehension? *Applied Linguistics, 34*(4), 457–479. https://doi.org/10.1093/applin/ams074

Webb, S., & Chang, A. C.-S. (2012). Second language vocabulary growth. *RELC Journal, 43*(1), 113–126. https://doi.org/10.1177/0033688212439367

Webb, S., & Nation, I. S. P. (2017). *How vocabulary is learned*. Oxford, UK: Oxford University Press.

Webb, S., & Rodgers, M. P. H. (2009). Vocabulary demands of television programs. *Language Learning, 59*(2), 335–366. https://doi.org/10.1111/j.1467-9922.2009.00509.x

Webb, S., & Sasao, Y. (2013). New directions in vocabulary testing. *RELC Journal, 44*(3), 263–277. https://doi.org/10.1177/0033688213500582

Wiliam, D. (2011). *Embedded formative assessment*. Bloomington, IN: Solution Tree Press.

Wode, H. (1999). Incidental vocabulary acquisition in the foreign language classroom. *Studies in Second Language Acquisition, 21*(2), 243–258.

Xie, X. (2013). Vocabulary explanation in English-major university classrooms in China. *ELT Journal, 67*(4), 435–445. https://doi.org/10.1093/elt/cct031

Zhang, B., & Li, C. (2011). Classification of L2 vocabulary learning strategies: Evidence from exploratory and confirmatory factor analyses. *RELC Journal, 42*(2), 141–154. https://doi.org/10.1177/0033688211405180

18

Strategies for Learning Vocabulary

Peter Yongqi Gu

Introduction

Vocabulary learning is a daunting task. There is a massive number of single words and multiword units to be learned in any language. This is especially true for English vocabulary that is growing by the day. The latest Oxford English Dictionary contains more than 600,000 words (*Oxford English Dictionary*, 2017). Most people know a fraction of these words only. Goulden, Nation, and Read (1990) estimated that "the average educated native speaker has a vocabulary of around 17,000 base words" (p. 376). Native-speaker children are exposed to vocabulary in use and "pick up" most useful words as they grow up. For learners of English as a second (ESL) or foreign language (EFL), however, deciding which words are most needed, where to access these words, and how to treat the learning of each of these words are very much strategic tasks. Although not specifically addressing vocabulary learning strategies (VLS) in the learning of any specific language, this article will use EFL/ESL vocabulary learning examples.

Strategic vocabulary learning is an intentional, dynamic and iterative process for the effective, efficient, and even enjoyable learning of vocabulary. It is normally triggered by a difficult or new vocabulary learning task. We first notice an item and then focus our attention on it. Next, we do a quick analysis of the learning task, of ourselves as learners and of the learning environment, and move on to form an attack plan. The plan is then executed, and we monitor its effectiveness along the way and evaluate its success in achieving the learning goal. Very often this evaluation will necessitate a re-analysis of the task and reconfiguration of strategies, turning it into a spiraling and complex problem-solving process.

To be specific, learners of vocabulary are faced with an array of questions. Strategic decisions in answering these questions will lead to various degrees of success in learning. Some of these questions include, among others:

Questions	Task type
• Which words do I need to learn?	Picking and choosing
• When and where can I find the words that I need?	Sources

(Continued)

(Continued)

• What are the task demands and difficulties in learning each vocabulary item?	Task analysis
• To what extent should I learn this item?	Learning aim
• How should I deal with the different types of vocabulary that I decide to learn?	Tactics
• Which tactic out of my bag of tricks is my best bet in learning this item?	Person analysis and strategy analysis
• What contextual resources or constraints are there for me to learn this item?	Context analysis

Strategic learning will help direct the learner to the most needed and crucially important vocabulary, as opposed to focusing on any words the student encounters, or studying words in alphabetical order in dictionaries and some vocabulary lists. It will also help the learner decide when and where to find and engage the needed vocabulary. Strategic vocabulary learning also means that the learner distinguishes among different types of vocabulary and allocates appropriate strategies for each type. Strategic learners monitor the degree of usefulness of the strategies they choose to use and flexibly change and coordinate the use of clusters of strategies until the task is completed to their satisfaction.

Every time a new, important, or difficult task is identified, strategic learners go through the choice, use, and evaluation of strategic learning cycles. In other words, the nature of the learning task is crucially important in determining what strategies are the most appropriate and most effective. In addition, what strategies are triggered is also dependent on who the learner is and what strategy repertoire is available. The need and effectiveness of a strategy are also influenced by contextual affordances and constraints.

Critical Issues and Topics

Strategies for Vocabulary Learning Tasks

The learning, teaching, assessment, and research of any topic are as good as our understanding of the construct in question. In other words, our conceptions of the target construct and the task involved in learning, teaching, assessing, and in researching the construct are crucially important. They determine what we pay attention to, how we do it, and also what we get at the end. As the saying goes, we reap what we sow. What is it that we sow in the learning of vocabulary then?

Vocabulary as a learning target and/or learning outcome can be seen in different ways; and each perspective of the vocabulary learning task will demand the use of different strategies. For example, if learners realize that some words are more frequently used than others, they would direct their strategic attention to the most frequent words, and those that fall within the appropriate frequency bands at their own proficiency level. When learners become aware that vocabulary knowledge can be viewed from different dimensions such as breadth, depth, automaticity, and appropriateness, they would understand the need for different strategies to tackle each dimension. Likewise, if learners aim for the receptive rather than productive knowledge of a word, they should know that these two types of vocabulary knowledge are best learned in different ways.

Strategies for Vocabulary Breadth, Depth, Automaticity, and Appropriateness

For learners, teachers, and researchers alike, vocabulary was traditionally understood as how many words one knows (size or breadth). We realized later that for each word we know, there are different shades and richness of meaning and various degrees of relatedness to other words (depth) (Richards, 1976). Only starting from the mid-1990s did researchers begin to see the importance of a "third dimension" (Meara, 1996) of vocabulary knowledge, i.e., automaticity of use. In addition, I would single out a fourth dimension of vocabulary knowledge as needing attention, appropriateness in use, because real competency in vocabulary would entail not only knowing enough items with a rich knowledge of them, and being able to use these items automatically when needed, but it also entails the ability to know when to use what with whom in what context. If the first two dimensions (size and depth) describe vocabulary as "knowledge", the next two dimensions (automaticity and appropriateness) describe vocabulary as "skill" and "use".

By far, the lion's share of attention on VLS has been on the expansion of vocabulary size. The widespread availability of vocabulary size tests, e.g., the Vocabulary Levels Test (VLT) (Nation, 1990; Schmitt, Schmitt, & Clapham, 2001; Webb, Sasao, & Ballance, 2017), Vocabulary Size Test (VST) (Coxhead, Nation, & Sim, 2015; Nation & Beglar, 2007), and the Yes/No Test (Meara & Buxton, 1987) has made it practical to observe the effects of VLS on vocabulary size (e.g., Gu & Johnson, 1996; Kojic-Sabo & Lightbown, 1999). Most studies on this research question take either a survey approach or an experimental approach. Survey studies normally make use of a questionnaire that covers a range of VLS and relate these strategies to a vocabulary size measure. With only very few strategies (e.g., visual repetition) that are negatively related to vocabulary size, most other strategies from initial handling of new words (e.g., guessing, dictionary use) to reinforcement (rehearsal, encoding) and productive use (activation) have been found to correlate positively to vocabulary size. The highest correlations in Gu and Johnson were 0.35 (self-initiation) and 0.31 (activation); while Kojic-Sabo and Lightbown obtained higher correlations (0.36 for review, 0.47 for dictionary use, and 0.61 for independence). In general, like in most other studies on language learning strategies, quantitative patterns reveal that the larger repertoire of strategies learners use, and the more often these strategies are used, the larger the vocabulary size.

In order to obtain a cause and effect relationship between VLS and vocabulary size, a number of studies have been conducted to train learners with a combination of vocabulary strategies. Mizumoto and Takeuchi (2009) examined the effectiveness of strategy instruction among a group of EFL learners at a Japanese university. A range of metacognitive and cognitive strategies for vocabulary learning were taught explicitly for a period of ten weeks. Their results showed that "strategy training was effective for both changing the repertoire of strategies used and improving their frequency of use" (p. 425). The study also showed that initial low strategy users benefited the most from the training, and that the learners were picking and choosing rather than taking in all strategies being trained. Some studies focused on the instruction of metacognitive strategies (Rasekh & Ranjbary, 2003), and some on specific cognitive strategies such as memory strategies (Atay & Ozbulgan, 2007) and guessing in context (Craigo, Ehri, & Hart, 2017). All strategy instruction studies showed effectiveness in improving the retention of vocabulary and in increasing the vocabulary size of the learners involved.

Strategies aiming directly at the learning of vocabulary depth have been studied. However, compared to those for vocabulary size, research on vocabulary depth strategies has barely scratched the surface. This is partly due to the relatively late interest in depth and partly due to the difficulty in measuring vocabulary depth precisely. For example, a widely used test of vocabulary depth is the Word Associates Test (WAT) (Read, 1993); and it doesn't cover many areas of depth (Read, 2000). Another known test that covers depth is the Vocabulary Knowledge Scale (Paribakht & Wesche, 1993; Wesche & Paribakht, 1996). But as a research tool, it lacks the focus and precision needed for research purposes (Bruton, 2009). Despite these difficulties, research and pedagogical efforts have been directly aimed at learning strategies for vocabulary depth in recent years. Zhang and Lu (2015) used Schmitt's (1997) questionnaire to elicit VLS, and asked the participants to complete two vocabulary breadth tests, i.e., Schmitt et al.'s (2001) version of the VLT for meaning recognition and a meaning recall test based on the same words in the VLT, plus Read's (2000) WAT as a depth test. Structural Equation Modeling indicated that strategies for learning the form of words and association strategies benefited both vocabulary breadth and depth. However, word list strategies negatively predicted both breadth and depth measures. Ranalli (2013a, 2013b) designed an innovative strategy instruction package for personalized training of dictionary strategies online. The online platform also included just-in-time information for "Deep Vocabulary Knowledge". Error identification and error correction tasks were performed as pretest and posttests. The results indicated that the online strategy instruction package was effective in improving both dictionary strategies and error identification and correction.

Practically no research can be found investigating how learners aim at improving the automaticity and appropriateness of their vocabulary. While the "skill" and "use" dimensions of vocabulary might not surface in the learner's awareness to warrant deliberate strategic learning, at least not as often as the breadth and depth "knowledge" dimensions, the lack of research on the strategic learning of these dimensions reveals researchers' lack of awareness as well.

Frequency Bands and Learning Strategies

Not all words are equally used. In fact, some words are used so often that they appear in virtually all texts and contexts; while some other words are rarely encountered, if at all. Nation (2001) distinguished four types of vocabulary: high-frequency vocabulary, academic vocabulary, technical vocabulary, and low-frequency vocabulary (see also chapters by Liu and Lei, Coxhead, Vilkaitė-Lozdienė and Schmitt in this volume). The first 2,000 most frequent word families account for about 85% of any text. Clearly these words are the most important words to be learned as early as possible, using whatever strategic resources. The most frequent words represent the core meaning system in any language, without which a functional working language, no matter how rudimentary, will be impossible to establish. Direct, intentional learning of form-meaning pairs making use of word cards or smartphone apps should be very efficient in the initial learning of these words. The nature of the high frequency category normally ensures multiple, context-based further encounters in natural language acquisition contexts. However, in input-poor environments where the classroom and the textbook constitute the major forms of input, deliberately looking for and adding opportunities to encounter these words would also be needed for the incidental acquisition of depth, automaticity, and contextual appropriateness.

Academic words are words often used across a range of academic disciplines. Coxhead's (2000) Academic Word List (AWL) contains only 570 of these words; and yet this small group of words constitutes about 8% to 10% of academic texts. Learners aiming to study beyond the secondary school level will find this list strategically useful. Like the high frequency list, it is highly cost-effective to allocate attentional resources to the learning of academic vocabulary. Again, direct and list learning would be a useful strategy for initial learning, followed by both deliberate and more natural exposures to these words in academic reading and listening exercises.

Technical vocabulary refers to the words closely related to a specific technical topic area such as chemistry, mathematics, engineering, or education. There are about 2,000 words in this category under each of these areas. These words cover up to 30% of technical texts depending on different subjects. They are a must for students of a particular field, and can be ignored by other language learners. Learners of technical words are normally learning the subject matter at the same time, and therefore are already functional users of the language. As such, direct list learning would be enough to quickly add the new words (mostly nouns and verbs) to their existing system to form the conceptual disciplinary background for further learning.

The low-frequency group, which broadly includes all remaining words, make up only about 5% of academic texts. If we remove mid-frequency vocabulary (the 4th to 9th 1,000 frequency bands) (Schmitt & Schmitt, 2014), the low-frequency group's coverage of texts would be so low that they become dispensable. Learners would not be making the best use of their time if considerable attention is paid to learn low-frequency words. The overwhelming majority of these words, if encountered in text, would be easily guessable through vocabulary guessing strategies (Gu, 2015). The most appropriate strategies for learning these words would be incidental learning, i.e., deliberately leaving the acquisition of these words to potential natural encounters, with the hope of picking them up with or without even the conscious awareness of the learner when enough repetitions occur.

It should be noted that no empirical research can be found as to what strategies learners naturally use for the learning of each type of vocabulary illustrated in this section. This lack of research again reflects the VLS researchers' lack of awareness of the importance of analyzing learning goals. Of course, a simple awareness of the statistical distribution of vocabulary by learners and teachers should not only trigger differentiated strategic treatment of vocabulary learning, but also empower learners to selectively allocate their learning resources for the most relevant kinds of vocabulary they need.

Strategies for Receptive and Productive Vocabulary

Vocabulary knowledge can be seen as either receptive (passive) or productive (active). Receptive knowledge represents the ability to recognize the form, meaning, and use of a vocabulary item, whereas productive knowledge enables the learner to use the item in the right form, meaning, and use (Nation, 2001). In natural language acquisition situations, most words are learned receptively through extensive exposure. Only a small proportion of words become productive. In other words, most scholars believe that there is a continuum and progression from receptive to productive vocabulary, and that the receptive vocabulary of any learner would be much larger than his or her productive vocabulary (Laufer & Paribakht, 1998). For example, the productive/receptive ratio for a group of 10th grader Israeli high school students was 89%, and that for the 11th graders was 73% (Laufer, 1998). Webb (2008) examined the vocabulary of a group of Japanese university EFL learners and played with two types of scoring methods (sensitive vs. strict). The ratio for the sensitive scoring method was 93% and that for strict scoring was 77%. The gap between productive and receptive vocabulary is relatively small at high-frequency levels, but becomes increasingly wider as the frequency level decreases (Laufer & Paribakht, 1998; Zhong & Hirsh, 2009).

Empirical research on receptive and productive vocabulary has mainly focused on vocabulary tests. Due to the possibility of a relatively finite vocabulary in English for sampling purposes, receptive vocabulary tests that require recognition and recall are relatively easy to design. The same cannot be said of productive vocabulary, although a number of fruitful attempts at measuring productive vocabulary have been explored. One such attempt is the lexical frequency profile (Laufer & Nation, 1995); another is Lex30 (Meara & Fitzpatrick, 2000).

Researchers have also explored the learning of receptive and productive vocabulary in recent years. Waring (1997) explored the learning of receptive vs. productive vocabulary by a group of Japanese learners of English, and concluded that receptive learning is easier than productive learning, in that productive learning takes more time and is retained less well than receptive learning. Waring also found that words learned receptively can become productive or vice versa. Likewise, Webb (2005) also found that both reading (receptive) and writing (productive) tasks led to multiple aspects of vocabulary knowledge, although, when time on task was not controlled, productive tasks were more effective than receptive tasks for all aspects of vocabulary knowledge measured.

Most studies on VLS have focused on receptive vocabulary. An explicit distinction is rarely made between strategies for receptive or productive vocabulary, and the overwhelming dependent variables in these studies are typically receptive vocabulary size measures. Two studies did look at the strategies related to both receptive and productive vocabulary. Fan (2000) examined the gap between the receptive and productive vocabulary knowledge among a group of first-year students at a university in Hong Kong. She also used a questionnaire to elicit VLS from these learners. Notably, Fan defined passive vocabulary in her study as the ability to recognize an item when presented, and active vocabulary as the ability to recall the target word when presented with some sort of stimuli. In this sense, the active vocabulary test in this study is similar to the "controlled production vocabulary levels test" (Laufer & Nation, 1999). Fan found that the ratio between active and passive vocabulary among different groups of students ranged from 81.3% to 53%, with an average ratio of 69.2%. Interestingly, the seven strategies found significantly correlated with the active vocabulary scores in this study were not actually aimed at the development of productive vocabulary. Gu (2010) studied the productive vocabulary of a group of Chinese ESL learners preparing for university study in Singapore, and correlated the strategies elicited in a questionnaire with measures of the lexical frequency profile in a composition. An interesting finding was the negative correlations between VLS and the proportion of the first 1,000 most frequent words found in the compositions. In other words, if the students used VLS more often, they would have used less of the first 1,000 words and more sophisticated words beyond the first 1,000 level. Beyond the 1,000-band level, the picture was much more complex.

It should be noted that despite recent interest in helping learners bridge the gap between receptive and productive vocabulary (Lee & Muncie, 2006; Yamamoto, 2011), VLS researchers have so far not paid explicit attention to the strategies for learning productive vocabulary. The most often seen taxonomies of VLS have either ignored these strategies (Schmitt, 1997) or paid cursory attention to them (Gu, 2013b). Given the importance of productive vocabulary and our knowledge of the divergent routes for the development of receptive and productive vocabularies, future research should examine how learners deal with the learning of productive vocabulary.

The way a learner perceives the vocabulary learning task not only influences what strategies will be chosen, but also whether strategic learning of vocabulary will become useful at all. For example, if a learner tries to increase her vocabulary size (breadth), there is a high probability that she will see the vocabulary learning task as mainly a memory task. Accordingly, her attention would probably be allocated to the addition of form-meaning pairs without due consideration for the depth of knowledge, the automaticity of use, and the appropriateness of using each word. As a consequence, the learner may be able to increase her vocabulary size successfully, but this does not mean that her language proficiency would be improved proportionally. This was borne out in Gu and Johnson (1996) where the strategies that were significantly correlated with vocabulary size did not always correlate highly with a general proficiency measure. In extreme situations, the fixated aim of "size" may even prevent the learner from succeeding in developing a functional level of competence that can be described as vocabulary in use.

Strategic Self-Regulation in Vocabulary Learning

Strategic learning of vocabulary is, by nature, a matter of human agency, and not just a matter of the learning task demanding different strategies. Learners themselves bring with them cultural and educational backgrounds that perceive certain types of strategies more favorably than others. Learners also differ along an array of individual difference factors such as motivation, personality, aptitude, and preferred learning styles. In other words, which strategies are used and how useful they become are very much not just a function of what tasks are being attended to and what strategies are needed, but also what strategies are available, preferred, and whether a learner proactively engages in the whole process at all (Gu, 2003b).

Learner factors in strategic vocabulary learning has always been a central concern. Over the years, empirical research has explored quantitative grouping of learners into types by examining their use of VLS (Ahmed, 1989; Gu & Johnson, 1996). There are also many insightful qualitative accounts of how cultural and individual difference factors combine to influence the choice, use, and effectiveness of VLS (Gu, 2003a; Parry, 1997; Sanaoui, 1995).

Ahmed (1989) used a think-aloud task supported by observations and interviews to elicit the VLS among 300 Sudanese learners of English. Cluster analysis of these strategies revealed three types of good learners and two types of underachieving learners. The good learners used more strategies more often; and were found to be clearly aware of what they could learn about new words. They chose when to ask teachers and peers for help and when to use the dictionary as a source of information. They knew the importance of learning words in context and were conscious of the relationship between new words and known words. The underachieving groups were not aware of what they could learn about new words; and did not show interest in learning new words in context. One group was characterized by a limited number of strategies. They overlooked or ignored unknown words, did not use the dictionary and did not use the L2 at all. The other group of underachievers used very few practice strategies, although some of them did take notes about the new word meanings.

Gu and Johnson's (1996) cluster analysis also revealed five types of learners based on the VLS these learners used. One small group of highly successful learners used context-based strategies almost exclusively and were labeled "readers". Another group of very successful learners actively used most of the strategies more often than others and were labeled "active strategy users". A mirror image of the active strategy users was a group of learners who used only the visual repetition strategy up to a medium level; and used all other strategies much less than other learners. This group was labeled "passive strategy users". This was a group who were probably not interested in learning, exerted minimum effort, and had much lower results in both vocabulary size and general English proficiency. Two other groups only differed between themselves in terms of the amount of effort they spent on encoding strategies. They were both medium-level strategy users and achieved medium-level learning results. It is interesting to note that the five groups of learners had been indistinguishable in terms of their English proficiency level at university entry. The dramatic differences in vocabulary size and general proficiency a year later when the study took place could well have been due to the different configurations of their VLS.

The importance of learner factors in strategic vocabulary learning is well documented in a number of case studies. For example, the two types of good learners and their strategic learning efforts in Gu and Johnson (1996) were illustrated in detail in Gu (2003a) in terms learning style differences. Earlier, Gu (1994) also showed striking contrasts between the strategic learning efforts of a successful learner and an unsuccessful learner in learning vocabulary.

It is interesting to note that most case studies have discovered different approaches or styles in vocabulary learning, e.g., holistic vs. analytic (Parry, 1991, 1997), structured vs. unstructured (Sanaoui, 1995), or fine-brush vs. free-hand (Gu, 2003a). These case studies were not able to conclude if any approach was better than any other approach. Sanaoui (1995) indicated that the structured approach was more effective than the unstructured approach. Parry (1997) advocated for flexibility because "both approaches are necessary but that neither is appropriate at all times" (p. 67).

Another way of examining learner-related factors in strategic learning is looking at the learner's self-regulation of motivation. Rather than focusing on the "skill" of self-regulated learning of vocabulary, this line of research has focused on the "will" side of self-regulation in vocabulary learning. Based on Kuhl's (1987) motivation theory of "action control", Tseng, Dörnyei, and Schmitt (2006) developed a "Self-Regulating Capacity in Vocabulary Learning" scale which included five "volition control strategies": commitment, metacognitive, satiation, emotion, and environment control. Essentially "volition control strategies" are meta-level strategies for controlling cognition (metacognitive), motivation, and emotion in making sure that desirable goals are achieved after the goals are set (Corno & Kanfer, 1993). They can, therefore, be seen as a type of learning strategies for the management of cognitive, motivational, and emotional tasks in vocabulary learning.

Learning Context and Vocabulary Learning Strategies

Learning vocabulary in different places and environments naturally means different affordances and constraints in terms of input frequency, modality, authenticity and output demands and opportunities, among other things. When faced with new or difficult learning tasks presented by varied contexts of learning, learners normally need to adjust their learning strategies in order to maximize opportunities and increase efficiency of the learning process. Commonly observed learning context differences include English as a Foreign Language (EFL) and English as a Second Language (ESL), L1 learning vs. the learning of English Language Learners (ELL) or the learning of English as an Additional Language (EAL). With rapid globalization, migration, and international moves and transitions being a common phenomenon of today's world, language learning strategies for study abroad and immersion or CLIL (Content and Language Integrated Learning) programs warrant serious attention. Likewise, vocabulary strategies for learning inside vs. outside classrooms, especially online learning environments, need to be studied as well.

When learners move from one learning context to another, the sudden change of input or output affordances may provide enough of an impetus to prompt the adoption of new

VLS. One typical scenario is the study abroad context, mostly a move from an EFL to an ESL learning environment. Gao (2003) interviewed 13 Chinese EFL learners' uses of VLS after they moved from mainland China to Britain. Three major changes in strategies were reported: (1) The participants became more selective in choosing which words to focus on. In particular, attention was paid mostly to words that were related to academic and social needs. (2) Dictionaries (which had been the primary source of meaning when they were in China) became a last resort that was used only for the discovery of meaning. Contextual guessing and occasionally asking for clarification became the primary strategies for meaning-making. (3) Consolidation of newly learned words which had been done mainly through rote repetitions before their arrival in the UK were now being done mainly through authentic language use in reading and writing. Out of the ten factors identified in the interviews as having influenced the changes in VLS, four factors were grouped under "learner factors" and the other six "contextual factors". The learner factors included changes in motivation and in beliefs about vocabulary learning, and improvement of language proficiency. For a couple of learners with prior experience of language use, they simply continued and reinforced what they used to do after they arrived in the UK. In a sense, even these "learner factors" were closely related to contextual factors. Understandably, the contextual factors included mostly affordances and needs such as input and output opportunities, academic needs, priorities, culture, and the use of technology.

The out-of-class language needs and task demands in a study abroad context were examined in Briggs' (2015) study of 241 adult English language learners residing in the UK. Twenty-eight statements were included in a questionnaire asking about out-of-class language contact. Exploratory factor analysis identified three major types of out-of-class language activities: (1) "interactive" activities included listening to and speaking English; (2) "literate" activities involved reading and writing; and (3) "narrative" activities mainly focused on comprehending or producing the narration of experiences. Notably, only a long stay group (16–20 weeks) achieved an overall gain in vocabulary size with a large effect size.

Wang (2015) went further and described how exactly two Chinese learners of English at foundation programs in the UK selected strategies to learn vocabulary and how they combined strategies into sequences or clusters to tackle vocabulary learning tasks. Some of these tasks and strategies might be appropriate for an in-class context; and some of them were more relevant to out-of-class contexts, such as learning at home to check out the details of word meanings in a dictionary after a class encounter, or talking to a shop assistant to find out if the guessed meaning of "cleansing lotion" was correct. This way, the learning of each vocabulary item was shown to be contextualized and situated. The dynamic process of vocabulary learning was seen in motion as the strategies were selected, combined, used, and evaluated.

Another contextual dimension for vocabulary learning is the difference between first language (L1) and second language (L2). Most research so far on VLS has focused on L2 contexts, partly due to the difficult nature of L2 vocabulary learning, and partly due to the common perception that L1 vocabulary develops easily. Task demands and learning context differences constitute the major differences between vocabulary learning in L1 and L2. Learning the vocabulary of a foreign language especially at an early stage is very much part of establishing the foreign language system as a working linguistic system. In L1 vocabulary learning contexts, on the other hand, children's vocabulary development is heavily dependent on the functioning language system that has already been established to a certain extent. It is also dependent on the widespread ease of exposure and to language use opportunities. Under such circumstances, the most natural strategies for vocabulary learning would focus on mapping new or existing concepts to new word forms. As such, strategies for incidental vocabulary learning that make full use of the existing linguistic functions become not only possible but also desired. Strategies for intentional learning, when needed, can afford to focus on mapping meaning to form. With multiple exposure opportunities, contextual nuances and depth of meaning will be gradually added.

There might be a Matthew effect for incidental acquisition of vocabulary, i.e., higher proficiency level students with a higher level of reading/listening ability acquire more vocabulary through reading and listening than their lower level counterparts (Penno, Wilkinson, & Moore, 2002). This means that those who need strategic incidental learning most may not be equipped with the right skills to do it. Contextual guessing and word learning has been a long-standing research issue (e.g., Ames, 1966; McKeown, 1985), although strategic vocabulary learning in general has remained in the side lines of L1 vocabulary research.

The issue of Matthew effect demands more attention in L1 vocabulary learning in view of the enormous "vocabulary gap" found in early childhood development and the "achievement gap" in later schooling between children of different socioeconomic status groups (Hart & Risley, 2003). In addition to the quantity and quality of exposure to words, there has to be other intervention efforts including "purposeful, strategic conversations" with children (Wasik & Hindman, 2015; Wasik & Iannone-Campbell, 2012), strategic selection of vocabulary (Biemiller, 2005), and the instruction of VLS (Carlo, August, & Snow, 2005). A related and equally pressing issue is the vocabulary and achievement gap between local children and a substantial number of immigrant children in schools (August, Carlo, Dressler, & Snow, 2005). Surprisingly, besides efforts on contextual guessing and other vocabulary intervention programs (Kelley, Lesaux, Kieffer, & Faller, 2010; Stahl & Fairbanks, 1986), empirical research on the strategic learning of vocabulary by ELLs or even L1 children remains nonexistent, or at best sporadic (Gu, 2013a).

Future Directions

Strategies for vocabulary learning are in widespread demand. Empirical studies on the topic abound. Nevertheless, a quick examination of research efforts reveals a surprisingly narrow focus. Most studies tend to view VLS as stable gimmicks that can be discovered and tallied, through a quick tool such as a questionnaire. Vocabulary is mostly seen as a collection of words in isolation; and frequently, vocabulary learning is measured by some sort of a vocabulary size measure that captures only the receptive recognition of form-meaning pairs.

Future research on VLS should go further than replications of strategy tally studies or reinventing the wheel by designing more questionnaires that capture the same construct (Gu, 2018b). One point to start at is the need to develop a much more sophisticated understanding of vocabulary. For example, seeing vocabulary as contextualized and dynamic competence that is situated in authentic language use requires strikingly different strategic treatment from seeing vocabulary as the recognition of form-meaning pairs, and learning as being able to recognize the same pairs in a week or two. Much more should also be done from a learner perspective to fully appreciate the skill, will, and co-construction of strategies and self- and co-regulation of vocabulary learning. Future research can also explicate the complex and dynamic nature of strategic learning. If we view VLS as moving pictures rather than static single shots, empirical studies should demand very different research methods which in turn should produce hitherto unseen insights. In addition, there should be more contextually responsive research. Wherever a spotlight is shone upon a socio-educational issue that involves vocabulary learning as a major problem, VLS researchers should be seen there taking up the challenge. For example, further VLS studies of L1 acquisition, ELL achievement, immersion, CLIL, or EMI (English as a medium of instruction) programs are warranted. Most importantly, VLS researchers should take practical usefulness as the target of their ultimate research objective, and make sure that their findings are understandable and useful for those who need their help.

In 2003, I summarized vocabulary acquisition research into ten points and presented my hopes for future research (Gu, 2003b, pp. 17–18). Although a lot has happened since then in vocabulary studies and in language learning strategies research, an overwhelming number of these observations remains the same today. In the following section, I will briefly highlight three foci that I see as absolutely necessary and urgent for future research on strategic vocabulary learning. These are vocabulary, strategic learning, and usefulness of research findings.

Focusing on Vocabulary

Task analysis is a defining feature of strategic behavior. It is a crucial first step of strategic learning. In addition to generic strategies for vocabulary learning, future research should aim to investigate the strategies required for learning different types of multiword units, and different types and components of knowledge of single words.

Applied linguists have long realized the importance of multiword units. The first of Rod Ellis's (2005) ten "principles of instructed language learning" highlights the need "to ensure that learners develop both a rich repertoire of formulaic expressions and a rule-based competence" (p. 210). Vocabulary experts' attention to multiword units has also lasted for at least two decades (Schmitt, 2004). It is surprising to see that research on VLS has not caught up with the development of the vocabulary construct.

Early research on VLS did point to the importance of multiword units. For example, the two good learners in Gu (2003a) both "consciously emphasized multiword units such as phrasal verbs and idiomatic expressions" (p. 96). Ding's (2007) successful learners also deliberately recited texts to learn collocations and sequences. Nevertheless, rarely has effort been directed to explicitly studying the strategic learning of multiword units. Studies on the teaching of multiword units are beginning to emerge. Eyckmans, Boers, and Lindstromberg (2016) compared two often suggested instruction strategies for the learning of lexical phrases, i.e., (1) contrastive analysis between L1 and L2 to check if the target L2 lexical phrase shares a similar lexical composition with its L1 counterpart; and (2) analysis of the lexical makeup of L2 phrases to draw learners' attention to phonological patterns such as alliteration or assonance. Their findings suggested that the first strategy did not work; while the second strategy of attending to alliteration was found to be useful for retention. More effort along these lines with an explicit focus on the strategies used for learning lexical chunks is urgently needed.

Continued research is also needed on the strategic learning of single words, although more effort should be directed to the learning of productive vocabulary, and on the strategic learning of the depth, automaticity and appropriateness dimensions of vocabulary knowledge. In addition, English for Specific Purposes (ESP) and English for Academic Purposes (EAP) have become more and more important. It will be very useful to examine the strategies best suited for the learning of discipline-specific "technical vocabulary" and discipline-general "academic vocabulary".

Focusing on Strategic Learning in Action

Strategies are verbs, not nouns. When we talk about learning strategies, what we are actually referring to are strategic actions. In fact, an ideal strategy involves at least the following procedures (Gu, 2012, pp. 336–337):

- Attending selectively to learning problems and tasks
- Analyzing the task at hand, analyzing the self as learner, and analyzing the learning context
- Making decisions and choices
- Executing plans
- Monitoring progress and modifying plans
- Evaluating results
- Coordinating an orchestrating strategic behavior

Furthermore, this process happens in spiraling cycles and can be modified based on the learner's on-the-spot judgment of its effectiveness in solving the learning problem or completing the learning task, contingent upon contextual demands at the same time.

This conception of learning strategies demands a much more situated and dynamic examination of VLS than the strategy tally approach that has been dominant. For example, when counting the presence or absence of a strategy, any of the above steps involved could go astray. Research tasks that help elicit and observe strategic learning in action will need to be explored. Some new research tools that document the complex and dynamic nature of strategy execution and growth are beginning to emerge (e.g., Dong, 2016). More effort could be directed towards uncovering the dynamics of each stage of a strategic event and determining how different configurations and coordination of the stages could influence the effectiveness of the strategy.

A related direction for future research is the study of multiple strategies in sync. This would involve looking at the simultaneous use of strategy clusters or strings. For example, metacognitive strategies can be deployed before (planning), during (monitoring), and after (evaluating) the completion of a learning task when a number of cognitive strategies can be used. This entails another complex and dynamic view of strategy choice and use, in which multiple strategies are being used consecutively, synchronously, or in a combined fashion and coordinated in sync. Wang (2015) showed how VLS were combined and coordinated for successful learning and how these changed over time before and after the learners' arrival in the UK. Cohen and Wang (2018) illustrated how the multiple functions of a single strategy could shift from moment to moment and how learners combined multiple strategies for a vocabulary learning task. Much more effort along similar lines should be invested before we could reach another level of understanding for the choice, use, coordination, and effectiveness of multiple strategies in use.

Focusing on Usefulness

For learners and teachers in language classrooms, VLS must be among the hottest perennial topics. Language learning strategies as a field of research also started with the practical aim of helping learners become more effective and efficient in their language learning. Nevertheless, it is frustrating to see that very few research findings on VLS find their way into the language classroom (Gu, 2018a). Part of the disconnect between research and practice must be blamed on the research community for not being consciously aware of our consuming audience, and therefore not making enough effort in communicating research findings to the learners and teachers in need. Despite the narrow focus of research, I have discussed in this chapter, decades of research on VLS have produced many insights into strategic vocabulary learning that deserve the cross-over from journal articles to the language classroom.

The research-to-practice pathway is, of course, a proverbial problem for educational research in general (Levin, 2004), and for the social sciences as well (Wittrock, 1991). Schneider (2014) analyzed the characteristics of "boundary-crossing scholarship" (p. 34) and summarized them into four simple characteristics: research ideas need to be visible, believable, practical, and sharable before they can "make the long leap from the ivory tower to the schoolhouse" (p. 31). Put against these criteria, it is not too hard to make VLS research findings believable. However, we do need extra effort to make our research practically useful and sharable, and to go beyond academia to reach out to learners and teachers in order to make our findings visible as well. Specifically, I believe action research that involves teachers adopting innovative ways of incorporating VLS training into their classrooms is warranted. As part of the innovation, formative assessment of VLS should be a link between language diagnosis and differentiated instruction that would help learners improve their use of VLS (Gu, 2017).

If we count Ahmed (1989) and his PhD study a year earlier as the first study exclusively focusing on VLS in second language acquisition, the topic has been explored for exactly three decades. During these last three decades, we have accomplished the task of exploring which naturally occurring VLS second language learners normally use, and determining how these strategies are related to the development of vocabulary size and general language proficiency. We have also discovered that the choice, use, and effectiveness of VLS are mediated by task, learner, and contextual factors, and that the configurations of factors and relationships are complex, dynamic, and situated. It is now high time to do less surface-level explorations and more in-depth examinations. It is also time to look beyond our own empirical studies and extend our practical help to the learners and teachers in classrooms who need to learn from our insights.

Further Reading

Gu, Y. (2003). Vocabulary learning in a second language: Person, task, context and strategies. *TESL-EJ*, *7*(2). Retrieved from http://tesl-ej.org/ej26/a4.html

This is a comprehensive review of research on vocabulary learning strategies. The review is based on a tetrahedral model of language learning strategies that sees VLS being influenced by learners, tasks, and learning contexts.

Nyikos, M., & Fan, M. (2007). A review of vocabulary learning strategies: Focus on language proficiency and learner voice. In A. D. Cohen & E. Macaro (Eds.), *Language learner strategies: 30 years of research and practice* (pp. 251–273). Oxford, UK: Oxford University Press.

This is another review of VLS research. It appears in an influential volume that reviews 30 years of research on various aspects of language learning strategies.

Related Topics

The different aspects of vocabulary knowledge, factors affecting the learning of single-word items, factors affecting the learning of multiword items, incidental vocabulary learning, deliberate vocabulary learning, approaches to learning vocabulary inside the classroom, learning words through flash cards and word cards, resources for learning single-word items, resources for learning multiword items

References

Ahmed, M. O. (1989). Vocabulary learning strategies. In P. Meara (Ed.), *Beyond words* (pp. 3–14). London, UK: British Association for Applied Linguistics, in association with Centre for Information on Language Teaching and Research.

Ames, W. S. (1966). The development of a classification scheme of contextual aids. *Reading Research Quarterly, 2*(1), 57–82. https://doi.org/10.2307/747039

Atay, D., & Ozbulgan, C. (2007). Memory strategy instruction, contextual learning and ESP vocabulary recall. *English for Specific Purposes, 26*(1), 39–51. https://doi.org/10.1016/j.esp.2006.01.002

August, D., Carlo, M., Dressler, C., & Snow, C. (2005). The critical role of vocabulary development for English language learners. *Learning Disabilities Research and Practice, 20*(1), 50–57.

Biemiller, A. (2005). Size and sequence in vocabulary development: Implications for choosing words for primary grade vocabulary instruction. In E. H. Hiebert & M. L. Kamil (Eds.), *Teaching and learning vocabulary: Bringing research to practice* (pp. 223–242). Mahwah, NJ: Routledge.

Briggs, J. G. (2015). Out-of-class language contact and vocabulary gain in a study abroad context. *System, 53*, 129–140. https://doi.org/10.1016/j.system.2015.07.007

Bruton, A. (2009). The vocabulary knowledge scale: A critical analysis. *Language Assessment Quarterly, 6*(4), 288–297. https://doi.org/10.1080/15434300902801909

Carlo, M. S., August, D., & Snow, C. E. (2005). Sustained vocabulary-learning strategy instruction for English-language learners. In E. H. Hiebert & M. L. Kamil (Eds.), *Teaching and learning vocabulary: Bringing research to practice* (pp. 137–153). Mahwah, NJ: Routledge.

Cohen, A. D., & Wang, I. K.-H. (2018). Fluctuation in the functions of language learner strategies. *System, 74*, 169–182. https://doi.org/10.1016/j.system.2018.03.011

Corno, L., & Kanfer, R. (1993). The role of volition in learning and performance. *Review of Research in Education, 19*(1), 301–341. https://doi.org/10.3102/0091732X019001301

Coxhead, A. (2000). A new academic word list. *TESOL Quarterly, 34*(2), 213–238.

Coxhead, A., Nation, I. S. P., & Sim, D. (2015). Measuring the vocabulary size of native speakers of English in New Zealand secondary schools. *New Zealand Journal of Educational Studies, 50*(1), 121–135. https://doi.org/10.1007/s40841-015-0002-3

Craigo, L., Ehri, L. C., & Hart, M. (2017). Teaching community college students strategies for learning unknown words as they read expository text. *Higher Learning Research Communications, 7*(1), 43–64. http://dx.doi.org/10.18870/hlrc.v7i1.350

Ding, Y. (2007). Text memorization and imitation: The practices of successful Chinese learners of English. *System, 35*(2), 271–280.

Dong, J. (2016). A dynamic systems theory approach to development of listening strategy use and listening performance. *System, 63*(Supplement C), 149–165. https://doi.org/10.1016/j.system.2016.10.004

Ellis, R. (2005). Principles of instructed language learning. *System, 33*(2), 209–224.

Eyckmans, J., Boers, F., & Lindstromberg, S. (2016). The impact of imposing processing strategies on L2 learners' deliberate study of lexical phrases. *System, 56*(Supplement C), 127–139. https://doi.org/10.1016/j.system.2015.12.001

Fan, M. Y. (2000). How big is the gap and how to narrow it? An investigation into the active and passive vocabulary knowledge of L2 learners. *RELC Journal, 31*(2), 105–119.

Gao, X. (2003). Changes in Chinese students' learner strategy use after arrival in the UK: A qualitative enquiry. In D. Palfreyman & R. C. Smith (Eds.), *Learner autonomy across cultures* (pp. 41–57). Hampshire, UK: Palgrave MacMillan.

Goulden, R., Nation, I. S. P., & Read, J. (1990). How large can a receptive vocabulary be? *Applied Linguistics, 11*(4), 341–363.

Gu, Y. (1994). Vocabulary learning strategies of good and poor Chinese EFL learners. In N. Bird, P. Falvey, A. B. M. Tsui, D. M. Allison, & A. McNeill (Eds.), *Language and learning* (pp. 376–401). Hong Kong: The Education Department.

Gu, Y. (2003a). Fine brush and freehand: The vocabulary learning art of two successful Chinese EFL learners. *TESOL Quarterly, 37*(1), 73–104.

Gu, Y. (2003b). Vocabulary learning in a second language: Person, task, context and strategies. *TESL-EJ, 7*(2). Retrieved from http://tesl-ej.org/ej26/a4.html

Gu, Y. (2010). Learning strategies for vocabulary development. *Reflections on English Language Teaching, 9*(2), 105–118.

Gu, Y. (2012). Learning strategies: Prototypical core and dimensions of variation. *Studies in Self-Access Learning Journal, 3*(4), 330–356.

Gu, Y. (2013a). Second language vocabulary. In J. Hattie & E. M. Anderman (Eds.), *International guide to student achievement* (pp. 307–309). New York, NY: Routledge.

Gu, Y. (2013b). Vocabulary learning strategies. In C. A. Chapelle (Ed.), *The encyclopedia of applied linguistics*. Chichester: Blackwell Publishing Ltd. https://doi.org/10.1002/9781405198431.wbeal1329

Gu, Y. (2015). Vocabulary guessing strategies. In C. A. Chapelle (Ed.), *The encyclopedia of applied linguistics* (pp. 1–7). Chichester: John Wiley & Sons, Inc. https://doi.org/10.1002/9781405198431.wbeal1469

Gu, Y. (2017). Formative assessment of language learning strategies. 英语学习（教师版）*English Language Learning (Teacher Edition), 2017*(9), 16–24.

Gu, Y. (2018a). Making language learning strategies research useful: Insights from China for the world. In R. L. Oxford & C. M. Amerstorfer (Eds.), *Language learning strategies and individual learner characteristics: Situating strategy use in diverse contexts* (pp. 143–163). New York, NY: Bloomsbury Academic.

Gu, Y. (2018b). Validation of an online questionnaire of vocabulary learning strategies for ESL learners. *Studies in Second Language Learning and Teaching, 8*(2), 325–350. https://doi.org/10.14746/ssllt.2018.8.2.7

Gu, Y., & Johnson, R. K. (1996). Vocabulary learning strategies and language learning outcomes. *Language Learning, 46*(4), 643–679.

Hart, B., & Risley, T. R. (2003). The early catastrophe: The 30 million word gap by age 3. *American Educator, Spring*, 4–9.

Kelley, J. G., Lesaux, N. K., Kieffer, M. J., & Faller, S. E. (2010). Effective academic vocabulary instruction in the urban middle school. *The Reading Teacher, 64*(1), 5–14. https://doi.org/10.1598/RT.64.1.1

Kojic-Sabo, I., & Lightbown, P. M. (1999). Students' approaches to vocabulary learning and their relationship to success. *The Modern Language Journal, 83*(ii), 176–192.

Kuhl, J. (1987). Action control: The maintenance of motivational states. In F. Halisch & J. Kuhl (Eds.), *Motivation, intention, and volition* (pp. 279–291). Berlin: Springer.

Laufer, B. (1998). The development of passive and active vocabulary in a second language: Same or different. *Applied Linguistics, 19*(2), 255–271.

Laufer, B., & Nation, I. S. P. (1995). Vocabulary size and use: Lexical richness in L2 written production. *Applied Linguistics, 16*(3), 307–322.

Laufer, B., & Nation, I. S. P. (1999). A vocabulary-size test of controlled productive ability. *Language Testing, 16*(1), 33–51.

Laufer, B., & Paribakht, T. S. (1998). The relationship between passive and active vocabularies: Effects of language learning context. *Language Learning, 48*(3), 365–391.

Lee, S. H., & Muncie, J. (2006). From receptive to productive: Improving ESL learners' use of vocabulary in a postreading composition task. *TESOL Quarterly, 40*(2), 295–320.

Levin, B. (2004). Making research matter more. *Education Policy Analysis Archives, 12*(56). http://dx.doi.org/10.14507/epaa.v12n56.2004

McKeown, M. G. (1985). The acquisition of word meaning from context by children of high and low ability. *Reading Research Quarterly, 20*(4), 482–496. https://doi.org/10.2307/747855

Meara, P. (1996). *The third dimension of vocabulary knowledge. AILA 96, the 11th World Congress of Applied Linguistics*, Jyväskylä, Finland.

Meara, P., & Buxton, B. (1987). An alternative to multiple choice vocabulary tests. *Language Testing, 4*(2), 142–154. https://doi.org/10.1177/026553228700400202

Meara, P., & Fitzpatrick, T. (2000). Lex30: An improved method of assessing productive vocabulary in an L2. *System, 28*(1), 19–30.

Mizumoto, A., & Takeuchi, O. (2009). Examining the effectiveness of explicit instruction of vocabulary learning strategies with Japanese EFL university students. *Language Teaching Research, 13*(4), 425–449.

Nation, I. S. P. (1990). *Teaching and learning vocabulary*. Boston, MA: Heinle & Heinle Publishers.

Nation, I. S. P. (2001). *Learning vocabulary in another language*. Cambridge, UK: Cambridge University Press.

Nation, I. S. P., & Beglar, D. (2007). A vocabulary size test. *The Language Teacher, 31*(7), 9–13.

Oxford English Dictionary. (2017). Oxford, UK: Oxford University Press.

Paribakht, T. S., & Wesche, M. B. (1993). Reading comprehension and second language development in a comprehension-based ESL program. *TESL Canada Journal, 11*(1), 09–29.

Parry, K. (1991). Building a vocabulary through academic reading. *TESOL Quarterly, 25*, 629–653.

Parry, K. (1997). Vocabulary and comprehension: Two portraits. In J. Coady & T. Huckin (Eds.), *Second language vocabulary acquisition: A rationale for pedagogy* (pp. 55–68). Cambridge, UK: Cambridge University Press.

Penno, J. F., Wilkinson, I. A. G., & Moore, D. W. (2002). Vocabulary acquisition from teacher explanation and repeated listening to stories: Do they overcome the Matthew effect? *Journal of Educational Psychology, 94*(1), 23–33. http://dx.doi.org/10.1037/0022-0663.94.1.23

Ranalli, J. (2013a). Designing online strategy instruction for teaching knowledge of English word patterns as a complex cognitive skill. *CALICO Journal, 30*(1), n/a. http://dx.doi.org/10.11139/cj.30.1.16-43

Ranalli, J. (2013b). Online strategy instruction for integrating dictionary skills and language awareness. *Language Learning & Technology, 17*(2), 75–99.

Rasekh, Z. E., & Ranjbary, R. (2003). Metacognitive strategy training for vocabulary learning. *TESL-EJ, 7*(2), A-5.

Read, J. (1993). The development of a new measure of L2 vocabulary knowledge. *Language Testing, 10*, 355–371.

Read, J. (2000). *Assessing vocabulary*. Cambridge, UK: Cambridge University Press.

Richards, J. C. (1976). The role of vocabulary teaching. *TESOL Quarterly, 10*, 77–89.

Sanaoui, R. (1995). Adult learners' approaches to learning vocabulary in second languages. *The Modern Language Journal, 79*, 15–28.

Schmitt, N. (1997). Vocabulary learning strategies. In N. Schmitt & M. McCarthy (Eds.), *Vocabulary: Description, acquisition and pedagogy* (pp. 199–227). Cambridge, UK: Cambridge University Press.

Schmitt, N. (Ed.). (2004). *Formulaic sequences: Acquisition, processing, and use*. Amsterdam and Philadelphia, PA: John Benjamins Publishing.

Schmitt, N., & Schmitt, D. (2014). A reassessment of frequency and vocabulary size in L2 vocabulary teaching. *Language Teaching, 47*(4), 484–503. https://doi.org/10.1017/S0261444812000018

Schmitt, N., Schmitt, D., & Clapham, C. (2001). Developing and exploring the behaviour of two new versions of the Vocabulary Levels Test. *Language Testing, 18*(1), 55–88.

Schneider, J. (2014). Closing the gap . . . between the university and schoolhouse. *Phi Delta Kappan, 96*(1), 30–35. https://doi.org/10.1177/0031721714547859

Stahl, S. A., & Fairbanks, M. M. (1986). The effects of vocabulary instruction: A model-based meta-analysis. *Review of Educational Research, 56*, 72–110.

Tseng, W.-T., Dörnyei, Z., & Schmitt, N. (2006). A new approach to assessing strategic learning: The case of self-regulation in vocabulary acquisition. *Applied Linguistics, 27*(1), 78–102.

Wang, K.-H. (Isobel). (2015). The use of dialogic strategy clusters for vocabulary learning by Chinese students in the UK. *System, 51*, 51–64. https://doi.org/10.1016/j.system.2015.04.004

Waring, R. (1997). A study of receptive and productive learning from word cards. *Studies in Foreign Languages and Literature, 21*, 94–114.

Wasik, B. A., & Hindman, A. H. (2015). Talk alone won't close the 30-million word gap. *Phi Delta Kappan, 96*(6), 50–54. https://doi.org/10.1177/0031721715575300

Wasik, B. A., & Iannone-Campbell, C. (2012). Developing vocabulary through purposeful, strategic conversations. *The Reading Teacher, 66*(4), 321–332. https://doi.org/10.1002/TRTR.01095

Webb, S. (2005). Receptive and productive vocabulary learning: The effects of reading and writing on word knowledge. *Studies in Second Language Acquisition, 27,* 33–52.

Webb, S. (2008). Receptive and productive vocabulary sizes of L2 learners. *Studies in Second Language Acquisition, 30,* 79–95.

Webb, S., Sasao, Y., & Ballance, O. (2017). The updated Vocabulary Levels Test. *ITL – International Journal of Applied Linguistics, 168*(1), 33–69. https://doi.org/10.1075/itl.168.1.02web

Wesche, M. B., & Paribakht, T. S. (1996). Assessing second language vocabulary knowledge: Depth versus breadth. *The Canadian Modern Language Review, 53*(1), 13–40.

Wittrock, B. (1991). Social knowledge and public policy: Eight models of interaction. In P. Wagner, C. H. Weiss, B. Wittrock, & H. Wollman (Eds.), *Social sciences and modern states* (pp. 333–354). Cambridge, UK: Cambridge University Press. http://dx.doi.org/10.1017/CBO9780511983993.015

Yamamoto, M. (2011). Bridging the gap between receptive and productive vocabulary size through extensive reading. *The Reading Matrix, 11*(3), 226–242.

Zhang, X., & Lu, X. (2015). The relationship between vocabulary learning strategies and breadth and depth of vocabulary knowledge. *The Modern Language Journal, 99*(4), 740–753. https://doi.org/10.1111/modl.12277

Zhong, H., & Hirsh, D. (2009). Vocabulary growth in an English as a foreign language context. *University of Sydney Papers in TESOL, 4,* 85–113.

19

Corpus-Based Word Lists in Second Language Vocabulary Research, Learning, and Teaching

Thi Ngoc Yen Dang

Introduction

Corpora are principled collections of naturally occurring spoken, written, or multimodal data which are stored in electronic format for quantitative and qualitative analysis. Data from large and representative corpora capture actual language use, and therefore, are reliable resources for list developers to identify the words that second language (L2) learners are likely to encounter in their future use of the target language. Given this benefit, corpora have been widely used to develop and validate word lists for L2 learners, and these lists have made valuable contributions to multiple aspects of L2 vocabulary learning and teaching. This chapter examines current research on corpus-based word lists for L2 learners of English. It begins with critical issues and topics in the area and then proposes some directions for future research.

Critical Issues and Topics

This section is organized into six subsections. The first subsection provides an overview of different kinds of corpus-based word lists. The next four subsections discuss critical issues drawn from the review: the unit of counting, corpus construction, selection criteria, and the reconceptualization of different vocabulary types. The last subsection looks at the application of corpus-based word lists in L2 vocabulary learning and teaching.

Overview of Corpus-Based Word Lists for L2 Learners

Word lists can be classified into lists of single-word items and multiword items. Depending on the learning purposes, each type can be further divided into general service lists and specialized word lists. General service lists focus on the lexical items that are useful for any learning purpose while specialized word lists draw learners' attention to items that are useful for academic or specific purposes. This section reviews lists of single words and multiword items in turn. Within each type, we will look at general service lists and then specialized word lists.

Lists of Single Words

General service words or high-frequency words (e.g., *know, good*) have been widely suggested as the crucial starting point of L2 vocabulary learning. They are small in number, but cover a large proportion of words in different text types. Thus, knowledge of these words may provide learners with a good chance to comprehend language. Given the importance of these words, a large number of general service lists have been developed. Most of them consist of 2,000 to 3,000 items. West's (1953) General Service List (GSL) is the oldest and most influential list. It has a long-established status and has had a huge impact on L2 vocabulary learning, teaching, and research. However, developed from texts written in the 1930s, the General Service List may not fully reflect current vocabulary. Subsequent studies have addressed this limitation in two ways. The first way is to develop totally new lists which can potentially replace the GSL: Nation's (2006) BNC2000, Nation's (2012) BNC/COCA2000, Browne's (2013) New General Service List, and Brezina and Gablasova's (2015) New General Service List. The second way is to compile a list with a more manageable size for a specific group of learners from items in existing general service lists: Dang and Webb's (2016a) Essential Word List.

Specialized word lists can be classified into three types: general academic word lists, discipline-specific word lists, and subject-specific word lists. In this chapter, a discipline refers to a broad group of academic subject areas. For example, academic subject areas such as mathematics and biology can be classified into one disciplinary group (hard sciences) while other subjects such as law and history can be put under another group (soft sciences). The degree of specificity becomes greater from general academic word lists, discipline-specific word lists, to subject-specific word lists.

General academic word lists are concerned with the shared vocabulary among different academic disciplines. They are useful in English for General Academic Purposes programs (see Coxhead, this volume). To date, Coxhead's (2000) Academic Word List (AWL) is the best-known corpus-based general academic word list. This list was developed with the aim to help L2 learners improve comprehension of academic written text, and has had a great impact on EAP learning and teaching. However, using West's GSL as the general service vocabulary baseline, the AWL contains a number of current general service words that the GSL fails to capture (Cobb, 2010; Dang & Webb, 2014). Two new lists have been created with the aim to replace the AWL – Gardner and Davies's (2014) Academic Vocabulary List and Browne, Culligan, and Phillips's (n.d.) New Academic Word List. Two others were also developed to supplement the AWL by focusing on academic spoken discourse – Nesi's (2002) Spoken Academic Word List and Dang, Coxhead, and Webb's (2017) Academic Spoken Word List.

The second type of specialized word list – discipline-specific word lists – narrows its focus on the words that occur across a specific discipline; that is, a group of academic subjects. These lists are suitable for English for Specific Academic Purposes programs. This group includes one written word list – Coxhead and Hirsh's (2007) EAP Science Word List – and two spoken word lists – Dang's (2018a) Hard Science Spoken Word List and Dang's (2018b) Soft Science Spoken Word List.

The third type of specialized word list – subject-specific word lists – have the narrowest focus, but have generated a growing interest from researchers. Subject-specific word lists are also commonly referred to as lists of technical vocabulary (see Liu and Lei in this volume). These lists are relevant to English for Specific Purposes (ESP) programs where all learners plan to study the same subject area (see Coxhead, this volume, for the definition of the term). They focus on the shared vocabulary in a particular subject area, such as agriculture (Martínez, Beck, & Panza, 2009), applied linguistics (Khani & Tazik, 2013; Vongpumivitch, Huang, & Chang, 2009), business (Konstantakis, 2007), chemistry (Valipouri & Nassaji, 2013), medicine (Hsu, 2013; Lei & Liu, 2016; Wang, Liang, & Ge, 2008), engineering (Hsu, 2014; Ward, 1999, 2009; Watson-Todd, 2017), nursing (Yang, 2015), or environmental science (Liu & Han, 2015). All of these word lists have been based on the language found in written texts.

Lists of Multiword Items

Compared with lists of single words, lists of multiword items are limited in number. Multiword items can refer to any kinds of continuous and discontinuous sequences of words, and how this broad term is interpreted varies from study to study (see Wood, this volume). Most general service lists of multiword items focus on phrasal verbs (Gardner & Davies, 2007; Garnier & Schmitt, 2015; Liu, 2011), collocations (Shin & Nation, 2008), or phrasal expressions (Martinez & Schmitt, 2012). Most specialized multiword lists are general academic word lists. Three of these general academic word lists were derived from written text (Ackerman & Chen, 2013; Byrd & Coxhead, 2010; Durrant, 2009), while the others focused on both spoken and written discourse (Biber, Conrad, & Cortes, 2004; Simpson-Vlach & Ellis, 2010). The focus of these lists also varies from lexical bundles (Biber et al., 2004; Byrd & Coxhead, 2010) to formulas (Simpson-Vlach & Ellis, 2010) to collocations (Ackerman & Chen, 2013; Durrant, 2009).

So far this chapter has briefly reviewed different kinds of word lists, the next sections discuss four critical issues in word list studies: the unit of counting, corpus construction, selection criteria, and the reconceptualization of different vocabulary types.

Unit of Counting

One core issue in word list studies is what should be counted as a word. Different ways of counting words can influence the results of these studies (Nation, 2016). Words can be seen either as single words or multiword items, and the way to count both of these constructs varies between studies.

Table 19.1 shows that four common units of counting in lists of single words are: type, lemma, flemma, and level 6 word family. The word type is the number of unrepeated word forms in a text. For example, the sentence, *Counting words is difficult but it is fun*, contains eight word forms but seven word types because the word form *is* is used twice. The lemma (*admire*) consists of a stem (*admire*) together with its inflected forms (*admires, admired, admiring*). Members of a lemma belong to the same word class. The flemma is similar to the lemma, but it does not distinguish parts of speech. For example, *form* (verb) and *form* (noun) are counted as two lemmas but only one flemma. The word family consists of a stem, together with its potential inflections and derivations that include affixes up to a certain level in Bauer and Nation's (1993) scale. This scale is a set of levels (levels 1–7) based on frequency, productivity, predictability, and regularity of affixes. A level 6 word family (*admire*) would include the stem (*admire*), and members derived from one or more affix up to level 6 (*admirable, admirably, admiration, admirer, admirers, admiringly*) (see Nation, 2016 for more details).

Together with the variation in the unit of counting of single words is the continual debate about the best unit for L2 learners. Nation (2016) points out that all of these units are, in fact,

Table 19.1 The unit of counting in different word lists

Kind of word lists	Unit of counting			
	Word type	Lemma	Flemma	Level 6 word family
General service lists	Essential Word List (Dang & Webb, 2016a)	New-General Service List (Brezina & Gablasova, 2015)	New General Service List (Browne, 2013), Essential Word List (Dang & Webb, 2016a)	General Service List (West, 1953), BNC2000 (Nation, 2006), BNC/COCA2000 (Nation, 2012)
General academic word lists	None	Academic Vocabulary List* (Gardner & Davies, 2014)	New Academic Word List (Browne et al., n.d.)	Academic Word List (Coxhead, 2000), Spoken Academic Word List (Nesi, 2002), Academic Spoken Word List** (Dang, Coxhead, & Webb, 2017)
Discipline-specific word lists	None	None	None	EAP Science Word List (Coxhead & Hirsh, 2007), Hard Science Spoken Word List** (Dang, 2018a), Soft Science Spoken Word List** (Dang, 2018b)
Subject-specific word lists	Applied Linguistics Academic Word List (Vongpumivitch et al., 2009)	New Medical Academic Word List (Lei & Liu, 2016)	None	Engineering Word List (Ward, 1999), Business Word List (Konstantakis, 2007), Medical Academic Word List (Wang et al., 2008), Agriculture Academic Word List (Martínez, Beck, & Panza, 2009), Applied Linguistics Academic Word List (Khani & Tazik, 2013), Medical Word List (Hsu, 2013), Chemistry Academic Word List (Valipouri & Nassaji, 2013), Engineering English Word List (Hsu, 2014), Environmental Academic Word List (Liu & Han, 2015), Nursing Academic List (Yang, 2015), Opaque engineering word list (Watson-Todd, 2017)

* The list is also available in the word family format.
** The list is also available in the flemma format.

different levels of word families in Bauer and Nation's (1993) scale. Word types should be considered as level 1 word families, lemmas as level 2 families, flemmas as level 2.5, while word families have typically been set at level 6. Therefore, a more accurate question should be which word family level is the most appropriate for a particular group of learners.

The level of word families should match the study purpose (Nation, 2016). Some important questions that need to be answered when determining the unit of counting are (1) who the target users of the list are, (2) whether the list will be used for receptive or productive purposes, and (3) whether the list examines technical words or nontechnical words. To find the answer to these questions, the learning burden should be taken into account. Learning burden is the amount of effort needed to acquire a word family at a certain level (Nation, 2013). The idea behind the concept of word families is that learners may be able to see that word forms with the same stems are related to each other, and therefore, may find it easier to recognize or learn an unknown word. For example, *unhappy* is morphologically related to *happy* rather than a totally unrelated word (*cringe*).

In terms of list users' characteristics, the unit of counting should match the characteristics of learners in a *particular* context. Most existing lists are at either end of Bauer and Nation's (1993) scale. Research has shown that (1) learners from a certain L1 background had difficulty seeing the relationship between stems and derived forms because their L1 does not have these characteristics (Ward, 2009), and (2) learner knowledge of affixes increases with their vocabulary level (Mochizuki & Aizawa, 2000; Schmitt & Meara, 1997; Schmitt & Zimmerman, 2002). These findings indicate that the most suitable level of counting will vary according to the characteristics of target list users such as their L1 background or their L2 proficiency. Consequently, a certain list may be relevant to a certain group of learners, but may be less applicable to others. In recognition of this need, several recent word lists (Dang, 2018a, 2018b; Dang, Coxhead, & Webb, 2017; Dang & Webb, 2016a; Gardner & Davies, 2014) chose one word family level as the primary unit of counting but also made the lists available in other units of counting so that the lists would be useful to a wide range of learners.

In terms of list purposes, if the list is used for productive purposes, level 1 word families (word types) (Durrant, 2014), level 2 word families (lemmas) (Nation, 2016), or level 2.5 word families (flemmas) are most suitable because knowledge of one word form does not mean that learners are able to use derivations of this word productively (Schmitt & Zimmerman, 2002). However, if the study investigates receptive use, word families at higher levels may be more appropriate (Nation, 2016). Learners with knowledge of the base word or one or two members of the word family may be able to recognize other members of the same word-family when reading or listening. If the study deals with subject-specific technical words, level 1 word families may be most suitable because not all members of a word family are technical words (Chung & Nation, 2004; Nation, 2016).

Let us take Dang and Webb (2016a) Essential Word List (EWL) as an example of how the unit of counting can be selected to match the study purpose. The level 2.5 word family (flemma) was chosen in favor of word families at higher levels for the EWL because it better suits the proficiency level of the target users – L2 beginners, who are still learning the first 1,000 words of English. Because vocabulary size and morphological knowledge are closely related, it is expected that these learners have very limited morphological knowledge, and may not be able to recognize most word family members at higher levels. The level 2.5 word family was chosen over the level 2 word family (lemma) because distinguishing parts of speech may overestimate the learning burden of very closely related items like *smile* (verb) and *smile* (noun). It may not be difficult to infer the meaning of *smile* (noun) in *She has a beautiful smile* if the meaning of *smile* (verb) is known.

Similar to single words, there is variation in the way to count multiword items. As shown in the overview, word list studies have examined multiword items from different perspectives: collocations, lexical bundles, phrasal expressions, phrasal verbs, and formulas. Because Wood (this volume) has discussed this issue in detail, this chapter only emphasizes that the variation in the way to interpret multiword items has raised the need for a clear definition of this term in each study. Importantly, a framework that systematically draws all units of counting of multiword items together like Bauer and Nation's (1993) word family scale for single words would be useful. Such framework would allow a high degree of consistency in comparing and interpreting results of word list studies.

Corpus Construction

The nature of corpora has a great impact on the quality of corpus-based word lists because word selection is primarily based on the information from corpora. This subsection examines the construction of the source corpora (to develop lists) and validating corpora (to validate lists) in turn.

With advances in technology, new lists have been created from larger corpora with the aim to replace existing lists. This, however, does not necessarily mean that these new lists are better if the corpora from which they were developed are not well-designed and clearly described. Source corpora should represent as closely as possible the kind of texts that their target users are likely to encounter often in their language use, and detailed descriptions of their composition should be available to users so that they can judge whether the lists developed from these corpora suit their needs. Biber (1993) provides comprehensive guidelines on how to achieve representativeness for corpora in terms of defining the target population, establishing sampling frames and methods, and evaluating the extent to which the final sample represents the full range of text type variation and linguistic variation. Nation (2016) points out that the construction of corpora for word list studies should carefully consider the content and the size of corpora, and the nature and size of the subcorpora. Unfortunately, while some corpora used to develop word lists satisfy these guidelines, others do not.

Let us take general service lists of single words as an example. These lists aim to capture the words that students are likely to encounter in a range of discourse types. Therefore, an ideal corpus to create a general service list should have equal proportions of spoken and written materials (Nation & Waring, 1997). However, as shown in Table 19.2, only Nation's (2012) BNC/COCA2000 satisfies this guideline. The BNC/COCA2000 corpus has a good balance between spoken (60%) and written materials (40%) while the corpora used to develop the other lists consist of mainly written materials (75.03%–99.92%). The superiority of the BNC/COCA2000 over the other lists is supported by studies (Dang, 2017; Dang & Webb, 2016b) which compared the five general service lists using lexical coverage, learner vocabulary knowledge, and teacher perceptions of word usefulness as criteria. They found that the BNC/COCA2000 is the most suitable for L2 learners from the perspectives of corpus linguistics, learners, and teachers.

Table 19.2 Corpora used to develop general service lists of single words

Word lists	Size (words)	Components	
		Written	Spoken
West's (1953) General Service List	5 million	100%	0%
Nation's (2006) BNC2000	100 million	90%	10%
Nation's (2012) BNC/COCA2000	10 million	40%	60%
Browne's (2013) NGSL	274 million	75.03%	24.97%
Brezina and Gablasova's (2015) New General Service List	12 billion	99.92%	0.08%

Another example is general academic word lists. The aim of these lists is to help learners from a wide range of academic disciplines to comprehend academic written/spoken English. Therefore, the corpora to develop these lists should represent materials from various academic disciplines that these students are likely to encounter frequently in their future study. Importantly, to ensure that the lists are not biased towards the vocabulary in a certain discipline or subject area, the number of subjects per discipline should be the same. So is the number of words per subject. However, as shown in Table 19.3, except for Coxhead (2000) and Dang et al. (2017), corpora used to develop general academic word lists were either unclearly described or unbalanced in terms of the number of subjects per discipline and the number of words per subject.

Apart from the corpora used to create word lists, the corpora used to validate the lists are also important. Testing word lists in independent corpora provides a valid assessment because the results of the validation are not biased towards the corpora from which the lists were derived (Nation & Webb, 2011). Ideally, the validating corpora should be around the same sizes as those used to develop the lists so that they can capture the vocabulary in the target language as well as the source corpus. Unfortunately, the validating stage is absent from most word list studies. Among those having the validation stage, the majority did not meet the mentioned guideline. They either validated word lists in corpora with smaller sizes than those from which the list was developed or did not test the list in corpora of the same or different genres. For example, of the five lists presented in Table 19.3, only Coxhead's (2000) AWL, Gardner and Davies's (2014) Academic Vocabulary List and Dang et al.'s

Table 19.3 Corpora used to develop general academic word lists

Word lists	Developing corpus						
	Components	Text types	Size	Subcorpus			
				Number of disciplines	Words/ discipline	Number of subjects/ discipline	Words/ subject
Coxhead (2000) AWL	100% written	University textbooks, articles, book chapters, laboratory manuals	3.5 million	4	875,000	7	125,000
Browne et al. (n.d.) NAWL	98.90% written 1.1% spoken	Journal articles, nonfictions, student essays, lectures, seminars	288 million	Unclear	Unclear	Unclear	Unclear
Nesi (2002) SAWL	100% spoken	Lectures, seminars	1.6 million	4	Around 400,000	10–19	2,038– 36,251
Gardner and Davies (2014) AVL	100% written	Journal articles, newspapers, magazines	120 million	Not applicable	Not applicable	9	8 to 22 million
Dang, Coxhead, and Webb (2017) ASWL	100% spoken	Lectures, seminar, labs, tutorials	13 million	4	3.5 million	6	500,000

(2017) Academic Spoken Word List were tested against independent academic and non-academic corpora. Only the validating corpora of the Academic Spoken Word List had a similar size as the corpus used to develop the list (13 million words). The other validating corpora were much smaller than the source corpora – 678,000 words compared to 3.5 million words (Academic Word List) and 16 million to 83 million words compared to 120 million words (Academic Vocabulary List).

Selection Criteria

The third issue to consider when evaluating corpus-based word list studies is the selection criteria. Most studies (e.g., Brezina & Gablasova, 2015; Byrd & Coxhead, 2010) rely solely on objective corpus-driven criteria. Common selection criteria in both lists of single words and multiword items are frequency, range, and dispersion. Frequency is the number of occurrences of a word or a multiword in the entire corpus. Range indicates the number of different texts or subcorpora that the word/multiword occurs in. Dispersion shows how evenly a word/multiword is distributed across different texts or subcorpora. The higher frequency, wider range, and more even distribution a word/multiword has, the more likely learners are to encounter it in their language use. Apart from frequency, range, and dispersion, some criteria are unique to the selection of single words or multiword items. Lexical coverage – the percentage of known words in a corpus – is a common criterion to select single words. The higher the lexical coverage a word provides, the greater value it may have to learners. N-grams, Mutual Information, *t*-scores, and log-likelihood are popular criteria to select multiword items. N-grams refer to the length of the word sequence while the other criteria indicate the extent to which the items in a certain sequence occur more frequently together than would be expected by chance.

Relying solely on objective corpus-driven criteria to select and validate word lists has two strengths (Nation, 2016). First, it results in a list that is replicable, which then allows the comparison of the list with other lists using different corpora or different criteria. Second, this approach makes it easier to divide the list into frequency-based sub-lists that can be set as short-term learning goals. However, lists developed from this approach will inevitably be affected by the nature of the corpus from which they were developed. Consequently, some items that may be useful for L2 learners may be absent from these lists because they do not meet the objective selection criteria of the corpus from which the items were derived.

Two approaches have been taken to address this limitation. The first approach is to use objective corpus-driven information as the main criterion in word selection but also use subjective criteria as a guide to adjust these objective criteria so that the lists are more suitable and useful for a particular group of learners. Let us take Dang et al.'s (2017) Academic Spoken Word List as an example. This list is aimed at L2 learners in English for General Academic Purposes programs who plan to study different academic disciplines and have different language proficiency levels. Range, frequency, and dispersion were used as the primary criteria to select items in this list. However, given the limited learning time and slow vocabulary growth rates of L2 learners compared to L1 children, different versions adopting different range, frequency, and dispersion cutoff points were compared. Four key considerations – (1) *size and coverage*, (2) *word families outside general high frequency word-families*, (3) *distribution across the four disciplinary subcorpora*, and (4) *adaptability to learners' levels* – were used as the guide to see which version would have the greatest pedagogical value. The first two criteria ensured that the Academic Spoken Word List contained a smaller number of items but provided higher lexical coverage than a general service list. These criteria were necessary because if the Academic Spoken Word List either had a larger size but provided less coverage than a general service list, or mainly consisted of general service words, it would not have much value for the target users. It would simply be more useful to learn with existing general service lists. The last two criteria were important because they made sure that the Academic Spoken Word List could benefit the target users irrespective of their academic disciplines and proficiency levels.

Another example is Shin and Nation's (2008) list of high-frequency collocations of spoken English. This list targets elementary learners of English whose vocabulary level is at the most frequent 1,000 words. Frequency of word sequences was used as the main criterion for selection. However, Shin and Nation also made some subjective judgments by only selecting collocations with node words that were content words and among the most frequent 1,000 words. This decision ensured that the selected collocations were meaningful units that would have value for teaching and deliberate learning. Thus, by learning items from the list, it would help strengthen and enrich knowledge of known words. Moreover, Shin and Nation only selected collocations that met a certain frequency threshold and expressed a complete meaning so that their list was a manageable size and useful for the users.

The second approach to selecting items is to use subjective criteria together with objective corpus-driven criteria in word list development and validation. Let us look at some examples of this approach. West (1953) used one objective corpus-driven criterion (frequency) as the primary criterion to select items for his GSL but also used other subjective criteria (ease of learning, necessity, cover, stylistic level, and emotional neutrality) so that the list was suitable for L2 learners. Similarly, range, frequency, and dispersion were the main criteria to select Nation's (2006) BNC2000 and Nation's (2012) BNC/COCA2000 words. However, items that did not meet the objective criteria but were considered useful for L2 learners such as informal spoken words (e.g., *ok*, *hello*), modern words (e.g., *internet*, *web*), survival words (e.g., *delicious*, *excuse*), numbers, weekdays, and months were also included so that these lists were suitable for L2 learning and teaching. Similarly, Ackerman and Chen (2013) used objective corpus-driven criteria (frequency, range, N-grams, MI, *t*-score, word classes) as the primary criteria to select items for their Academic Collocation List, and then used subjective criterion (experts' judgment) to filter items in the list.

Using corpus-driven information together with subjective criteria may lead to the development of word lists that better serve L2 learning and teaching purposes compared to solely relying on objective corpus-driven information to develop word lists. This claim is supported by Dang, Webb, and Coxhead's (under review) study, which examined the relationships between lexical coverage, L2 learner knowledge, and English language teacher perceptions of the usefulness of general service words. These researchers found that although these three factors were related, the relationships between lexical coverage and the other two factors were not as strong as that between learner vocabulary knowledge and teacher perceptions. This finding indicates that, although corpora can provide valuable information for word list construction, the use of subjective criteria from learners and teachers might be also be necessary to make corpus-based word lists more relevant to L2 learning and teaching purposes.

Reconceptualization of Different Kinds of Vocabulary

One issue that arises from the review of word list studies is the reconceptualization of different kinds of words. According to Nation (2001), words can be divided into different 1,000-item bands based on their frequency and range. Items at the first 1,000-word band are the most frequent and wide ranging words while those at the second 1,000-word band have lower frequency and narrower range. The further the 1,000-word bands are from the first 1,000-word band, the less frequent these bands are. Based on this, Nation (2001) categorized vocabulary into four types – high-frequency words, low-frequency words, academic words, and technical words. High-frequency words are those at the first and second 1,000-word bands. Academic words and technical words are considered as specialized vocabulary and have lower frequency compared to high-frequency words. Low-frequency words are those outside high-frequency words, academic words, and technical words. This traditional classification has been widely accepted, and has had a great influence on word list studies. However, recent research has questioned this classification regarding the boundary between high and low-frequency words, and between general and specialized words. Such questions have been reflected in word list studies.

Regarding the boundary between high- and low-frequency words, 2,000 items has been widely accepted as the number of high-frequency words. As a result, most general service lists (Brezina & Gablasova, 2015; Nation, 2006, Nation, 2012; West, 1953) have around this size. However, investigating the issue from different perspectives (frequency and incidental acquisition, frequency and use of graded readers, and lexicography and dictionary defining vocabulary), Schmitt and Schmitt (2014) suggest that this cutoff point should be expanded to 3,000 (1st–3rd 1,000) words, and items outside general high-frequency words should be divided into mid-frequency words (4th–9th 1,000) and low-frequency words (beyond 9th 1,000). Recognizing the limitation of Nation's (2001) classification, Nation (2013) then reconstructed his classification by adding the mid-frequency word level. Compared with the traditional classification, the classification of high-, mid-, and low-frequency words provides a more precise learning goal for L2 learners at different proficiency stages (see Vilkaitė-Lozdienė and Schmitt, this volume).

Regarding the boundary between general and specialized vocabulary, following Nation's (2001) classification, the most common approach towards developing specialized word lists (e.g., Browne et al., n.d.; Coxhead, 2000; Coxhead & Hirsh, 2007; Nesi, 2002) has been to consider academic and technical vocabulary as being outside of general service vocabulary, and therefore, general service words are not included in these lists. For example, Coxhead's (2000) Academic Word List does not include items from West's (1953) list. The strength of this approach is that it considers learners' existing knowledge of general vocabulary, and enables learners and teachers to avoid repeatedly learning and teaching known items. However, specialized word lists following this approach are inevitably affected by the nature of the general service lists on which they were built.

In recognition of this limitation, a more recent approach has been to consider specialized vocabulary as a separate kind of vocabulary that does not directly relate to general service vocabulary (e.g., Gardner & Davies, 2014; Lei & Liu, 2016; Ward, 1999, 2009). For instance, Gardner and Davies (2014) included in their Academic Vocabulary List all items that have wider range and higher frequency in academic text than non-academic text that meet the selection criteria even if they are included in existing general service lists. Specialized word lists following this approach cut across the high-, mid-, and low-frequency levels, and are not affected by the limitation related to existing general service lists. Yet, as learners' knowledge of general vocabulary is not considered in the list development, there may be a risk of repeatedly teaching and learning known items, which may result in inefficient learning and teaching time.

The third approach (Dang et al., 2017; Dang, 2018a, 2018b) expands on the two previous approaches. It views specialized vocabulary as a separate kind of vocabulary but also looks at it in relation to general vocabulary. Let us take Dang et al.'s (2017) Academic Spoken Word List as an example. Following the second approach, general service words were still included in the list if they met the selection criteria. Following the first approach, learners' knowledge of general vocabulary was also considered in the list development. However, instead of setting a fixed benchmark of the number of words these learners need to know before learning items from the list, the Academic Spoken Word List was divided into four levels according to Nation's (2012) BNC/COCA lists. Depending on their current level of general vocabulary, learners can skip certain levels of the Academic Spoken Word List. This approach proposes a systematic way to integrate specialized vocabulary and general vocabulary. On one hand, it reflects the blurred boundary between general and specialized vocabulary. On the other hand, it ensures that learners' knowledge of general vocabulary is taken into account.

Corpus-Based Word Lists in L2 Learning and Teaching

How to apply corpus-based word lists in L2 curriculum and instruction is a growing concern of current vocabulary research. While there is still a great deal of interest in replacing existing lists with new lists by making use of larger corpora and more powerful statistical measures, an interesting and meaningful move in corpus-based word list studies is to make existing lists more suitable to a particular learning and teaching context.

One trend is to create smaller lists that match the proficiency level of a particular group of learners. Ward's (2009) Basic Engineering English word list has only 299 items, but may allow its target users (low proficiency foundation engineering undergraduates in Thailand) to recognize around 16% of the words in their textbooks. Dang and Webb's (2016a) Essential Word List consists of the best 800 items (in terms of lexical coverage) from West's GSL, Nation's (2006) BNC2000, Nation's (2012) BNC/COCA2000, and Brezina and Gablasova's (2015) New General Service List. Knowledge of the Essential Word List headwords and lemmas may enable its target users (L2 beginners) to recognize 60% and 75% of the words in a wide range of spoken and written English texts, respectively.

The second trend is to make a list that is adaptable to learners' proficiency levels (Dang, 2018a, 2018b; Dang et al., 2017) or break a list into sub-lists with manageable size to fit in individual courses within a language program (Coxhead, 2000; Dang, 2018a, 2018b; Dang et al., 2017; Dang & Webb, 2016a). For instance, as discussed previously, Dang et al.'s Academic Spoken Word List is divided into four levels based on lists of general vocabulary, and learners can focus their attention on the Academic Spoken Word List levels that are relevant to their current level of general vocabulary. Each level is further divided into sub-lists with manageable sizes to allow easy incorporation of the list in language learning programs.

The third trend is to help learners achieve deeper knowledge of items in existing lists. Shin and Nation's (2008) collocation list allows L2 beginners to expand their knowledge of the most frequent 1,000 words from single words to multiword items. Garnier and Schmitt's (2015) PHaVE List supports learners to acquire the most frequent meanings of items in Liu's (2011) phrasal verb list.

Let us now look at the contributions of corpus-based word lists to different aspects of L2 vocabulary learning and teaching. The most obvious value of these lists can be seen in the area of setting learning goals. Different kinds of words in English do not occur with similar frequencies. Therefore, determining what and how many words need to be learned at different stages of language learning is extremely important. It ensures that learners can get the best return for their learning effort. Word lists provide course designers with a practical way to decide which words to focus on in a course. The new classification of vocabulary into three levels of high-, mid-, and low-frequency words provides more precise long-term learning goals for L2 learners, and better supports their continual vocabulary development. Similarly, the reconceptualization of specialized vocabulary provides EAP/ESP course designers with more flexibility when integrating different kinds of word lists into the curriculum to meet learners' target subject areas, language proficiency, and learning purposes (see Dang, 2018a for a model of selecting relevant word lists for different language programs).

The value of corpus-based word lists has not just been restricted to setting learning goals but also includes the development of vocabulary tests. Tests developed based on corpus-based word lists such as Vocabulary Levels Test (Nation, 1990, Schmitt, Schmitt, & Clapham, 2001; Webb, Sasao, & Ballance, 2017) and Vocabulary Size Test (Nation & Beglar, 2007) have been widely used to assist teachers in setting learning goals and monitoring learners' progress.

With respect to L2 learning and teaching, discussion of word lists is commonly associated with negative ideas of deliberate rote learning of words out of context. However, it is worth stressing that when effectively done with the right words, such learning can positively contribute to L2 vocabulary development (see Nakata, this volume). Well-designed word lists, therefore, are essential resources for effective deliberate learning. Importantly, presenting items that learners should learn in the format of word lists does not mean that these lists should be learned and taught solely through decontextualized methods (Coxhead, 2000; Nation, 2016). Deliberate learning should account for no more than 25% of the amount of time of a well-balanced vocabulary learning program (Nation, 2007, 2013; Webb & Nation, 2017). The remaining time should be equally spent in learning from meaning-focused input, meaning-focused output, and fluency development. Learning from meaning-focused input means that learners acquire new words through listening or reading activities while learning from meaning-focused output means that learners acquire new words through speaking and writing activities. Fluency development involves all four skills and does not aim to help students learn new words but to make them become more fluent at using known words. In all three cases, the main focus of attention is on meaning; that is, to understand the messages that are received or to produce meaningful messages. These strands are only effective if learners have sufficient vocabulary knowledge to make them truly meaning-focused. This means that for learning from meaning-focused input and output to happen, learners should already know at least 95% of the words in spoken materials (van Zeeland & Schmitt, 2013) and 98% of the words in written materials (Hu & Nation, 2000). The low proportion of words beyond learners' current vocabulary knowledge allows them to pay more attention to new words and learn them from contexts or with reference to dictionaries or glossaries. Similarly, materials for fluency development activities should involve no or very few unknown words so that learners can process and produce the known words at a fast speed. For these reasons, corpus-based word lists play a key role in the selection and development of learning materials for meaning-focused input, meaning-focused output, and fluency development activities. Using these lists together with vocabulary processing programs like RANGE (Heatley, Nation, & Coxhead, 2002), AntwordProfiler (Anthony, n.d), or Lextutor (Cobb, n.d) allows teachers to analyze vocabulary in the materials, and then adapt it so that these materials are relevant to learners' vocabulary levels (Webb & Nation, 2008).

Future Directions

There are two directions for future research on corpus-based word lists. The first direction is to focus more on some under-researched areas of corpus-based word lists, including mid-frequency vocabulary, spoken vocabulary, subject-specific vocabulary, and multiword units. The second direction is to bring more pedagogical value to corpus-based research on word lists. Most corpus-based word lists rely solely on objective corpus-driven criteria; therefore, future research should also include other sources of information such as teacher perceptions and learner vocabulary knowledge to support the information from corpora.

Further Reading

Dang, T. N. Y., Coxhead, A., & Webb, S. (2017). The academic spoken word list. Language Learning, 67(4), 959–997.

This article includes discussion of important issues in this chapter: unit of counting, corpus construction, selection criteria, and reconceptualization of general academic vocabulary.

Dang, T. N. Y., & Webb, S. (2016b). Evaluating lists of high-frequency words. *ITL – International Journal of Applied Linguistics, 167*(2), 132–158.

This article provides comprehensive discussion of high-frequency word lists and how to evaluate lists of different units of counting.

Nation, I. S. P. (2016). *Making and using word lists for language learning and testing.* Amsterdam: John Benjamins.

This book provides very detailed guidelines for making word lists for language teaching and testing. It covers important issues in word lists studies such as identifying the list purposes, deciding the unit of counting, constructing corpora, and criteria to select words.

Nation, I. S. P., & Webb, S. (2011). *Researching and analyzing vocabulary.* Boston: Heinle, Cengage Learning.

Chapter 8 of this book describes the basic steps of making word lists.

O'Keeffe, A., McCarthy, M., & Carter, R. (2007). *From corpus to classroom: Language use and language teaching.* Cambridge: Cambridge University Press.

Chapter 1 of this book explains the definition of corpora, basic steps of making a corpus, and the most common techniques of analyzing language in a corpus.

Related Topics

The different aspects of vocabulary knowledge, defining multiword items, high-, mid-, and low-frequency words, academic vocabulary, technical vocabulary

References

Ackermann, K., & Chen, Y.-H. (2013). Developing the Academic Collocation List (ACL) – A corpus-driven and expert-judged approach. *Journal of English for Academic Purposes, 12*(4), 235–247. https://doi.org/10.1016/j.jeap.2013.08.002

Anthony, L. (n.d.). *AntwordProfiler.* Retrieved from www.laurenceanthony.net/antwordprofiler_index.html

Bauer, L., & Nation, P. (1993). Word families. *International Journal of Lexicography, 6*(4), 253–279.

Biber, D. (1993). Representativeness in corpus design. *Literary and Linguistic Computing, 8*(4), 243–257.

Biber, D., Conrad, S., & Cortes, V. (2004). If you look at . . . : Lexical bundles in university teaching and textbooks. *Applied Linguistics, 25*(3), 371–405.

Brezina, V., & Gablasova, D. (2015). Is there a core general vocabulary? Introducing the New General Service List. *Applied Linguistics*, *36*(1), 1–22.

Browne, C. (2013). The New General Service List: Celebrating 60 years of vocabulary learning. *The Language Teacher*, *4*(37), 13–16.

Browne, C., Culligan, B., & Phillips, J. (n.d.). *A new academic word list.* Retrieved from www.newacademicwordlist.org/

Byrd, P., & Coxhead, A. (2010). On the other hand: Lexical bundles in academic writing and in the teaching of EAP. *University of Sydney Papers in TESOL*, *5*, 31–64.

Chung, T. M., & Nation, I. S. P. (2004). Identifying technical vocabulary. *System*, *32*(2), 251–263.

Cobb, T. (n.d.). *Lextutor.* Retrieved from www.lextutor.ca

Cobb, T. (2010). Learning about language and learners from computer programs. *Reading in a Foreign Language*, *22*(1), 181–200.

Coxhead, A. (2000). A new academic word list. *TESOL Quarterly*, *34*(2), 213–238.

Coxhead, A., & Hirsh, D. (2007). A pilot science-specific word list. *Revue Française de Linguistique Appliqueé*, *12*(2), 65–78.

Dang, T. N. Y. (2017). *Investigating vocabulary in academic spoken English: Corpora, teachers, and learners.* Unpublished PhD thesis, Victoria University, Wellington, New Zealand.

Dang, T. N. Y. (2018a). The hard science spoken word list. *ITL – International Journal of Applied Linguistics*, *169*(1), 44–71.

Dang, T. N. Y. (2018b). The nature of vocabulary in academic speech of hard and soft sciences, *English for Specific Purposes*, *51*, 69–83.

Dang, T. N. Y., Coxhead, A., & Webb, S. (2017). The academic spoken word list. *Language Learning*, *67*(4), 959–997.

Dang, T. N. Y., & Webb, S. (2014). The lexical profile of academic spoken English. *English for Specific Purposes*, *33*, 66–76.

Dang, T. N. Y., & Webb, S. (2016a). Making an essential word list. In I. S. P. Nation (Ed.), *Making and using word lists for language learning and testing* (pp. 153–167). Amsterdam: John Benjamins.

Dang, T. N. Y., & Webb, S. (2016b). Evaluating lists of high-frequency words. *ITL – International Journal of Applied Linguistics*, *167*(2), 132–158.

Dang, T. N. Y., Webb, S., & Coxhead, A. (under review). The relationships between lexical coverage, learner knowledge, and teacher perceptions of the usefulness of high-frequency words.

Durrant, P. (2009). Investigating the viability of a collocation list for students of English for academic purposes. *English for Specific Purposes*, *28*, 157–169.

Durrant, P. (2014). Discipline and level specificity in university students' written vocabulary. *Applied Linguistics*, *35*(3), 328–356.

Gardner, D., & Davies, M. (2007). Pointing out frequent phrasal verbs: A corpus-based analysis. *TESOL Quarterly*, *41*(2), 339–359.

Gardner, D., & Davies, M. (2014). A new academic vocabulary list. *Applied Linguistics*, *35*(3), 305–327.

Garnier, M., & Schmitt, N. (2015). The PHaVE List: A pedagogical list of phrasal verbs and their most frequent meaning senses. *Language Teaching Research*, *19*(6), 645–666.

Heatley, A., Nation, I. S. P., & Coxhead, A. (2002). *Range: A program for the analysis of vocabulary in texts.* Retrieved from www.vuw.ac.nz/lals/staff/paul-nation/nation.aspx

Hsu, W. (2013). Bridging the vocabulary gap for EFL medical undergraduates: The establishment of a medical word list. *Language Teaching Research*, *17*(4), 454–484.

Hsu, W. (2014). Measuring the vocabulary load of engineering textbooks for EFL undergraduates. *English for Specific Purposes*, *33*, 54–65.

Hu, M., & Nation, I. S. P. (2000). Vocabulary density and reading comprehension. *Reading in a Foreign Language*, *13*(1), 403–430.

Khani, R., & Tazik, K. (2013). Towards the development of an Academic Word List for applied linguistics research articles. *RELC Journal*, *44*(2), 209–232.

Konstantakis, N. (2007). Creating a business word list for teaching business English. *Elia*, *7*, 79–102.

Lei, L., & Liu, D. (2016). A new medical academic word list: A corpus-based study with enhanced methodology. *Journal of English for Academic Purposes, 22*, 42–53.

Liu, D. (2011). The most frequently used English phrasal verbs in American and British English: A multicorpus examination. *TESOL Quarterly, 45*(4), 661–688.

Liu, J., & Han, L. (2015). A corpus-based environmental academic word list building and its validity test. *English for Specific Purposes, 39*, 1–11.

Martínez, I. A., Beck, S. C., & Panza, C. B. (2009). Academic vocabulary in agriculture research articles: A corpus-based study. *English for Specific Purposes, 28*(3), 183–198.

Martinez, R., & Schmitt, N. (2012). A phrasal expressions list. *Applied Linguistics, 33*(3), 299–320.

Mochizuki, M., & Aizawa, K. (2000). An affix acquisition order for EFL learners: An exploratory study. *System, 28*(2), 291–304.

Nation, I. S. P. (1990). *Teaching and learning vocabulary*. New York, NY: Newbury House.

Nation, I. S. P. (2001). *Learning vocabulary in another language* (1st ed.). Cambridge, UK: Cambridge University Press.

Nation, I. S. P. (2006). How large a vocabulary is needed for reading and listening? *Canadian Modern Language Review, 63*(1), 59–82.

Nation, I. S. P. (2007). The four strands. *Innovation in Language Learning and Teaching, 1*(1), 1–12.

Nation, I. S. P. (2012). *The BNC/COCA word family lists*. Retrieved from www.victoria.ac.nz/lals/about/staff/paul-nation

Nation, I. S. P. (2013). *Learning vocabulary in another language* (2nd ed.). Cambridge, UK: Cambridge University Press.

Nation, I. S. P. (2016). *Making and using word lists for language learning and testing*. Amsterdam: John Benjamins.

Nation, I. S. P., & Beglar, D. (2007). A vocabulary size test. *The Language Teacher, 31*(7), 9–13.

Nation, I. S. P., & Waring, R. (1997). Vocabulary size, text coverage, and word lists. In N Schmitt & M. McCarthy (Eds.), *Vocabulary: Description, acquisition and pedagogy* (pp. 6–19). Cambridge, UK: Cambridge University Press.

Nation, I. S. P., & Webb, S. (2011). *Researching and analyzing vocabulary*. Boston, MA: Heinle, Cengage Learning.

Nesi, H. (2002). An English spoken academic word list. In A. Braasch & C. Povlsen (Eds.), *Proceedings of the Tenth EURALEX International Congress* (Vol. 1, pp. 351–358). Copenhagen, Denmark. Retrieved from www.euralex.org/elx_proceedings/Euralex2002/036_2002_V1_Hilary%20Nesi_An%20English%20Spoken%20Academic%20Wordlist.pdf

Schmitt, N., & Meara, P. (1997). Researching vocabulary through a word knowledge framework. *Studies in Second Language Acquisition, 19*(01), 17–36.

Schmitt, N., & Schmitt, D. (2014). A reassessment of frequency and vocabulary size in L2 vocabulary teaching. *Language Teaching, 47*(4), 484–503.

Schmitt, N., Schmitt, D., & Clapham, C. (2001). Developing and exploring the behaviour of two new versions of the Vocabulary Levels Test. *Language Testing, 18*(1), 55–88.

Schmitt, N., & Zimmerman, C. B. (2002). Derivative word forms: What do learners know? *TESOL Quarterly, 36*(2), 145–171.

Shin, D., & Nation, P. (2008). Beyond single words: The most frequent collocations in spoken English. *ELT Journal, 62*(4), 339–348.

Simpson-Vlach, R., & Ellis, N. C. (2010). An Academic Formulas List: New methods in phraseology research. *Applied Linguistics, 31*(4), 487–512.

Valipouri, L., & Nassaji, H. (2013). A corpus-based study of academic vocabulary in chemistry research articles. *Journal of English for Academic Purposes, 12*(4), 248–263.

van Zeeland, H., & Schmitt, N. (2013). Lexical coverage in L1 and L2 listening comprehension: The same or different from reading comprehension? *Applied Linguistics, 34*(4), 457–479.

Vongpumivitch, V., Huang, J., & Chang, Y.-C. (2009). Frequency analysis of the words in the Academic Word List (AWL) and non-AWL content words in applied linguistics research papers. *English for Specific Purposes, 28*(1), 33–41.

Wang, J., Liang, S., & Ge, G. (2008). Establishment of a medical academic word list. *English for Specific Purposes, 27*(4), 442–458.

Ward, J. (1999). How large a vocabulary do EAP engineering students need? *Reading in a Foreign Language, 12*(2), 309–323.

Ward, J. (2009). A basic engineering English word list for less proficient foundation engineering undergraduates. *English for Specific Purposes, 28*(3), 170–182.

Watson-Todd, R. (2017). An opaque engineering word list: Which words should a teacher focus on? *English for Specific Purposes, 45*, 31–39. https://doi.org/10.1016/j.esp.2016.08.003

Webb, S., & Nation, I. S. P. (2008). Evaluating the vocabulary load of written text. *TESOLANZ Journal, 16*, 1–10.

Webb, S., & Nation, I. S. P. (2017). *How vocabulary is learned*. Oxford, UK: Oxford University Press.

Webb, S., Sasao, Y., & Ballance, O. (2017). The updated Vocabulary Levels Test. *ITL – International Journal of Applied Linguistics, 168*(1), 34–70.

West, M. (1953). *A general service list of English words*. London, UK: Longman, Green.

Yang, M.-N. (2015). A nursing academic word list. *English for Specific Purposes, 37*, 27–38.

20

Learning Words With Flash Cards and Word Cards

Tatsuya Nakata

Introduction

Flash cards (sometimes referred to as word cards) are a set of cards where the second language (L2) word is written on one side and its meaning, usually in the form of a first language (L1) translation, L2 synonym, or definition, is written on the other. Flash card learning is a type of paired-associate learning, where target items are encountered in a decontextualized format, and learners are asked to connect the L2 word form and its meaning. Possibly due to its unfortunate associations with behaviorism, flash card learning is not necessarily popular among researchers and teachers. Existing studies, nonetheless, show that flash card learning is a common learning strategy. Wissman, Rawson, and Pyc (2012), for instance, surveyed 374 American undergraduate students and report that 67.6% of them study with flash cards. Similarly, Schmitt (1997) surveyed 600 Japanese learners of English and found that 51% of junior high school students and 29% of senior high school students use flash cards for learning English vocabulary. A number of flash card programs are also available as computer software, smartphone applications, or web-based applications (for a review, see Nakata, 2011).

Research also shows that flash card learning is not only common but also effective and efficient. Studies demonstrate that memory for paired-associates may persist over years if reviewed regularly (Bahrick, Bahrick, Bahrick, & Bahrick, 1993; Bahrick & Phelps, 1987). Although contextual vocabulary learning is often considered superior to paired-associate learning, research shows that paired-associate learning may be as effective as or more effective than vocabulary learning from context (Laufer & Shmueli, 1997; Prince, 1996; Webb, 2007). A recent review also found that despite the belief that memory of paired-associate learning decays quickly, it may be as effective as the keyword mnemonic in the long term (Dunlosky, Rawson, Marsh, Nathan, & Willingham, 2013). Flash card learning is also efficient because it allows learners to acquire a large number of lexical items in a relatively short time (Fitzpatrick, Al-Qarni, & Meara, 2008; Nation, 1980).

Studies also suggest that flash card learning improves L2 learners' ability to use the words in communication and is a useful learning activity. Elgort (2011), for instance, showed that flash card learning contributes to implicit as well as explicit vocabulary knowledge, thus resulting in not only the *learning* but also the *acquisition* of L2 vocabulary. Webb (2009a) also found that paired-associate learning improves learners' ability to use L2 words in both reading and writing. Although paired-associate learning is only an initial step towards mastering new vocabulary, most researchers agree that it should have a place in L2 vocabulary instruction. Hulstijn (2001) and Laufer (2005), for instance, point out that incidental vocabulary learning alone is insufficient and should be supplemented with word-focused activities such as paired-associate learning. Nation (2008) considers flash card learning to be one of the most effective vocabulary learning strategies, along with guessing from context, word part learning, and dictionary use. Nation and Webb (2011) analyzed 12 vocabulary learning activities using a framework called Technique Feature Analysis and concluded that flash card learning is the most effective. Of course, flash card learning is not without limitations and should only be a part of a well-balanced curriculum (Nation, 2013). At the same time, given the effectiveness, efficiency, and usefulness of flash card learning, this chapter reviews empirical studies on flash card learning and discusses principles for effective flash card learning. Note that where necessary, this chapter discusses not only studies on flash card learning but also studies on paired-associate learning in general. This is because we can expect the findings of paired-associate learning studies to be applicable to flash card learning.

Critical Issues and Topics

Effects of Retrieval on Flash Card Learning

Perhaps one of the most important principles for effective flash card learning is to use retrieval. Retrieval is defined as remembering information about previously encountered L2 words. For example, suppose English speakers are attempting to learn the Japanese word *inu* (dog). When learners translate *inu* into English, this requires them to recall its meaning (dog). Hence, this activity involves retrieval. When the Japanese word *inu* is presented together with its meaning (dog), however, learners do not need to recall any information about *inu*. This activity, therefore, does not include a retrieval component. Studies have shown that retrieval significantly increases L2 vocabulary learning (e.g., Barcroft, 2007; Karpicke & Roediger, 2008).

Karpicke and Roediger (2008), for instance, examined the effects of retrieval on L2 vocabulary learning. In their study, 40 American undergraduate students studied Swahili-English word pairs (e.g., *malkia – queen*) using flash card software. The treatment consisted of a series of study (presentation) and test (retrieval) episodes. In a study episode, participants were presented with a Swahili word together with its L1 (English) translation (e.g., *malkia – queen*). In a test episode, participants were presented with a Swahili word and asked to type in the corresponding L1 (English) translation (e.g., *malkia* = _____?). No correct response was provided as feedback after each test episode. Learning was measured by a one-week delayed posttest, where participants were asked to translate Swahili words into English. The posttest results showed that while increasing the number of study episodes had little effect on retention (33 → 36%), increasing the number of test episodes increased retention significantly (33 → 81%). Their findings suggest that it is the test episodes (retrievals), not study episodes, that determine retention.

One important question is whether the benefits of repeated retrieval are retained in the long term: Karpicke and Roediger (2008) did not administer a posttest after a delay greater than one week. In an L1 vocabulary study, Rohrer, Taylor, Pashler, Wixted, and Cepeda

(2005) showed that although practicing retrieval repeatedly facilitates learning in the short term, it is not necessarily beneficial in the long term. In Rohrer et al.'s study, 88 American undergraduate students studied low-frequency English words paired with higher frequency synonyms (e.g., *acrogen – fern*). The participants were divided into two groups: low and high. The low group practiced retrieval of each word pair (e.g., *acrogen* = _____ ?) five times, and the high group practiced retrieval ten times. While the high group fared significantly better than the low group on a one-week delayed posttest (low: 38%; high: 64%), no statistically significant difference existed between the two groups four weeks after the treatment (low: 18%; high: 22%). Rohrer et al.'s study indicates that the positive effects of repeated retrieval may disappear over time.

In order to test whether Rohrer et al.'s (2005) findings are also applicable to L2 vocabulary learning, Nakata (2017) attempted to assess the long-term effects of repeated retrieval. In his study, 98 Japanese college students studied 16 English-Japanese word pairs using flash card software. The participants were randomly assigned to one of the four retrieval frequency levels: one, three, five, and seven. Nakata found that five and seven retrievals were significantly more effective than one and three retrievals not only immediately and one week later, but also four weeks after the treatment. The results indicate that contrary to the findings of Rohrer et al. (2005), the advantage of repeated retrieval may be retained at least four weeks after learning. Repeated retrieval, however, inevitably increased the study time. For instance, while practicing retrieval of 16 target items once took only 6.48 minutes, practicing the same number of items seven times required 22.82 minutes. When the number of words learned per minute was calculated, Nakata found that single retrieval resulted in larger gains than repeated retrieval. The findings suggest that (1) if learners have enough time, increasing retrieval frequency is desirable, and (2) if learners do not have enough time, it may be efficient to practice retrieval only once.

Research also shows that the direction of retrieval (i.e., receptive vs. productive) affects learning. Productive retrieval is defined as remembering the L2 word corresponding to the meaning, while receptive retrieval is defined as remembering the meaning corresponding to the L2 word. For instance, when English speakers are asked to translate *dog* into Japanese, this involves productive retrieval. In contrast, when English speakers are asked to translate the Japanese word *inu* (dog) into English, this involves receptive retrieval. (Some researchers prefer to use the term *meaning recall* instead of receptive retrieval and *form recall* instead of productive retrieval.) Research shows that receptive retrieval is effective if learning is measured by a receptive test, whereas productive retrieval is effective if learning is measured by a productive test (e.g., Steinel, Hulstijn, & Steinel, 2007; Webb, 2009a, 2009b). The results are consistent with the transfer-appropriate processing framework (Morris, Bransford, & Franks, 1977), which states that learning is most optimal when the learning condition matches the testing condition. The findings suggest that if learning both productive and receptive lexical knowledge is the goal, learners should practice retrieval both productively and receptively. Research also shows that while receptive retrieval is not very effective for learning productive knowledge, productive retrieval results in a relatively large increase in receptive knowledge (e.g., Schneider, Healy, & Bourne, 2002; Steinel et al., 2007; Webb, 2009a). The findings suggest that if learners have to choose either receptive or productive retrieval for some reason (e.g., they do not have enough time to practice both directions), it may be useful to practice productive retrieval rather than receptive retrieval.

In addition to the dichotomy of receptive vs. productive, retrieval can also be categorized according to the dichotomy of recognition vs. recall. In recall, learners are required to generate a response, whereas in recognition, learners are required to select a correct response from options provided. For instance, when learners are asked to translate *dog* into Japanese, the treatment involves recall. In contrast, when learners are asked to choose the Japanese equivalent of *dog* from multiple-choice options, this involves recognition. The dichotomies of receptive vs. productive and recognition vs. recall result in the following four kinds of retrieval formats: receptive recognition, receptive recall, productive recognition, and productive recall (e.g., Laufer & Goldstein, 2004). One may wonder which of these four formats is the most effective for learning. Nakata (2016) found that the answer probably depends on how vocabulary knowledge is measured. His study showed that if learning was measured by a productive recall test, learning using productive recall was the most effective, which is consistent with the transfer-appropriate processing framework. However, learning using recognition was more desirable than learning using recall when measured by one of the following three tests: receptive recall, productive recognition, and receptive recognition. Recognition formats also required less study time than recall formats. Pedagogically, the findings suggest that (1) for learning the productive knowledge of orthography, productive recall should be used, and (2) when the productive knowledge of orthography is not the goal, recognition formats should be used.

Types of Information

One important decision that learners have to make in flash card learning is what kind of information to add to the flash cards. Because research shows that the use of L1 translations increases vocabulary learning (e.g., Laufer & Shmueli, 1997), it may be useful to provide the meaning in the form of L1 translations rather than L2 definitions or synonyms. Research also suggests that providing the core meaning of polysemous words facilitates the acquisition of multiple meanings of words (Morimoto & Loewen, 2007; Verspoor & Lowie, 2003). The core meaning refers to the most central, underlying meaning of a word. For instance, the word *draw* can be used in many senses, as in *draw a picture, draw a curtain, draw criticism, draw attention, draw a bath,* or *open a drawer*. Most dictionaries give different translations or definitions for each of these senses. For instance, in a typical English-Japanese dictionary, *draw* in *draw a picture* is translated into 描く, while *draw* in *draw a curtain* is translated into 引く. However, most senses of *draw* are related to its core meaning, which is to move or pull something. For instance, *draw a picture* involves making a line by moving a pen. *Draw attention* or *draw criticism* involves bringing (or moving) attention or criticism to somebody. A *drawer* is something you open by pulling. Providing the core meaning may be useful because it helps learners to understand how different meanings of a word are connected to each other.

Although flash card learning is often considered as a form of decontextualized learning, it is possible to add short contextual sentences to flash cards. Empirical studies, however, suggest that context has no or little effect on vocabulary learning (Laufer & Shmueli, 1997; Prince, 1996; Webb, 2007). It may also be useful to add some information that helps connect the form and meaning of L2 words such as the keyword (e.g., Ellis & Beaton, 1993; Hulstijn, 1997; Rodriguez & Sadoski, 2000) or word parts (Wei, 2015). The keyword refers to a word in the L1 that sounds like an L2 target word. For instance, when learning the French word *clef* (key), it may be useful to think of an English word that sounds like *clef* such as *cliff* and create a mental image that connects the two (e.g., a key is on top of a cliff; Dunlosky et al., 2013). Even if learners forget the meaning of *clef*, the keyword *cliff* and the mental image may help learners to retrieve its meaning. Adding information about word parts to flash cards is also useful because the knowledge of affixes and roots may help strengthen form-meaning connection. For instance, the English word *prospect* can be broken down into *pro* and *spect*, where *pro* means *forward* (as in *proceed* or *progress*) and *spect* means *to look* (as in *spectacle* or *spectator*). Knowing the meanings of *pro* and *spect* may help learners to remember the meaning of *prospect* (i.e., *prospect* is a looking forward, so it means *anticipation* or *expectation*; Wei, 2015). In computer-based flash cards, multimedia information such as images, videos, or audios can also be added to flash cards. Images and videos are useful because visual information helps illustrate the meaning of words (especially in the case of concrete nouns or verbs describing actions) and may facilitate learning (e.g., Carpenter & Olson, 2012). Adding audio recordings of L2 words may also be useful for acquiring their spoken form.

One caveat to be considered is that trying to teach or learn multiple aspects of unfamiliar words at once may lead to information overload and possibly have negative effects on learning. Barcroft (2002), for instance, found that when study time is limited (e.g., 12 seconds per target word), although paying attention to the word form (structural elaboration) facilitates the acquisition of knowledge of the word form, it inhibits the acquisition of knowledge of the meaning. Similarly, Barcroft showed that although paying attention to the meaning (semantic elaboration) facilitates the acquisition of meaning, it inhibits the acquisition of knowledge of the word form. These findings are known as the Type of Processing – Resource Allocation (TOPRA) model (Barcroft, 2002, 2015). Because the knowledge of form-meaning connection is considered the most important aspect, it is perhaps best to focus on linking meaning with form in the first encounter with unfamiliar words and try to acquire other aspects (e.g., spelling, collocations, constraints on use) only in later stages.

Effects of Practice Schedule

Even though flash card learning is a very effective vocabulary learning method, memory decays over time and needs to be reinforced. This raises the question of what kind of review schedule should be used to maximize long-term retention. The review schedule can be divided into massed learning and spaced learning. In massed learning, the same materials are studied multiple times sequentially (e.g., studying the Japanese word *inu* repeatedly in a row). In spaced learning, the same materials are studied multiple times after certain intervals (e.g., studying the Japanese word *inu* every week). Research shows that spaced learning increases L2 vocabulary learning more than massed learning (e.g., Nakata, 2015a). This finding is known as the spacing effect. Studies have also shown that the magnitude of the spacing effect tends to be large. Nakata (2015a), for instance, found that a spaced schedule increased learning by more than 100% compared to a massed schedule on a one-week delayed posttest (massed = 14%; spaced = 29%).

Since spaced learning is more effective than massed learning, one might wonder how retrieval opportunities should be distributed in order to maximize retention. Studies have demonstrated that longer lags between retrievals often facilitate long-term retention more than shorter lags (e.g., Karpicke & Bauernschmidt, 2011; Nakata & Webb, 2016a). For instance, practicing retrieval of a given item every week (lag of one week) facilitates retention more than practicing retrieval every day (lag of one day). This finding is referred to as the lag effect. While spaced learning is found to be more effective than massed learning irrespective of the retention interval, the lag effect is sometimes not observed depending on the retention interval. (The retention interval refers to an interval between the last encounter with a given item and the posttest. For instance, if the posttest is given ten days after the treatment, the retention interval is ten days.) Specifically, while long lags between retrievals are often effective when learning is measured at a long retention interval, short lags are sometimes effective when learning is measured at a short retention interval. This finding is referred to as the spacing-by-retention interval interaction (e.g., Nakata, 2015a; Nakata & Webb, 2016a). Research suggests that L2 vocabulary acquisition is influenced by the spacing effect, the lag effect, and the spacing-by-retention interval interaction (e.g., Bahrick et al., 1993; Nakata, 2015a; Nakata & Webb, 2016a).

In Nakata (2015a), for instance, 128 Japanese university students studied 20 English-Japanese word pairs using flash card software. The participants were randomly assigned to one of the following four spacings: massed-, short-, medium-, and long-spaced. The participants in the massed group practiced retrieval of a given English word three times in a row. The short-, medium-, and long-spaced groups used average spacing of approximately one, two, and six minutes, respectively (that is, participants in the long-spaced group practiced retrieval of a given target word approximately every six minutes). Nakata found that the massed group was the least effective among the four groups both immediately and one week after the treatment, supporting the spacing effect. Moreover, while the short-spaced group fared significantly better than the massed group immediately after learning, the advantage disappeared at a one-week retention interval. The medium- and long-spaced groups, in contrast, were significantly more effective than the massed group not only on the immediate but also on the one-week delayed posttest. The findings are consistent with the spacing-by-retention interval interaction, which states that the benefits of short lags disappear over time. Nakata and Webb (2016a, Experiment 2) also observed the positive effects of long lags for L2 vocabulary learning. They compared the effects of short and long spacing. Encounters of a given target item were separated by approximately 30 seconds and three minutes in the short- and long-spaced conditions, respectively. While the long-spaced group failed to outperform the short-spaced group immediately after the treatment (short = 58%; long = 62%), the long-spaced group fared significantly better than the short-spaced group at a one-week retention interval (short = 8%; long = 20%; Figure 20.1). These findings support the lag effect and spacing-by-retention interval interaction.

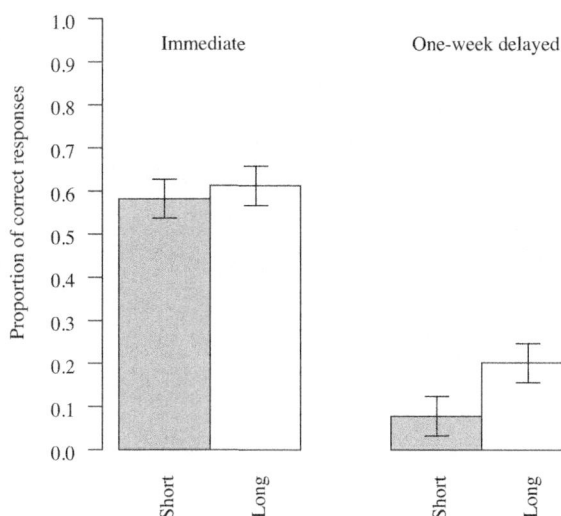

Figure 20.1 Proportion of correct responses on the immediate and one-week delayed posttests in Nakata and Webb (2016a, Experiment 2)

Note: The error bars indicate standard errors.

Source: Adapted from Nakata and Webb, 2016a, Experiment 2

One important finding related to spacing is that although long lags tend to induce more retrieval failures during the learning phase compared with no or short lags, long lags often lead to superior retention in the long term. For instance, in Nakata (2015a), although the spaced group produced significantly fewer correct responses during the learning phase than the massed group (massed = 89%; spaced = 21%), the results were reversed on the posttest conducted immediately after learning (massed = 32%; spaced = 52%). On the one-week delayed posttest, the spaced group's average score was more than twice as high as that of the massed group (massed = 14%; spaced = 29%; see Figure 20.2). Similarly, in Nakata and Webb (2016a, Experiment 2), although the short-spaced group produced more correct responses during the learning phase (short: 76%; long: 44%), the long-spaced group significantly outperformed the short-spaced group one week after the treatment (short: 8%; long: 20%). These findings are consistent with the desirable difficulty framework (Bjork, 1999), according to which a treatment that increases learning difficulty can be effective in the long term. Pedagogically, the findings suggest that teachers and learners should not be concerned too much about learning phase performance. Methodologically, the findings suggest that it may be inappropriate to equate learning phase performance with long-term retention (however, see Tinkham, 1993, 1997; Waring, 1997).

Another important finding related to spacing is that learners are often unaware that spacing increases learning. In Nakata and Suzuki (in press), for instance, 133 Japanese college students studied 48 English-Japanese word pairs using flash card software. Half of the participants were assigned to the short-spaced group, while the other half were assigned to the long-spaced group. Encounters of a given target item were separated by five and 40 trials on average in the short- and long-spaced groups, respectively. Learning was measured by a posttest conducted immediately after and one week after the treatment. Upon completion of the immediate posttest, learners in both groups were asked to predict how many target

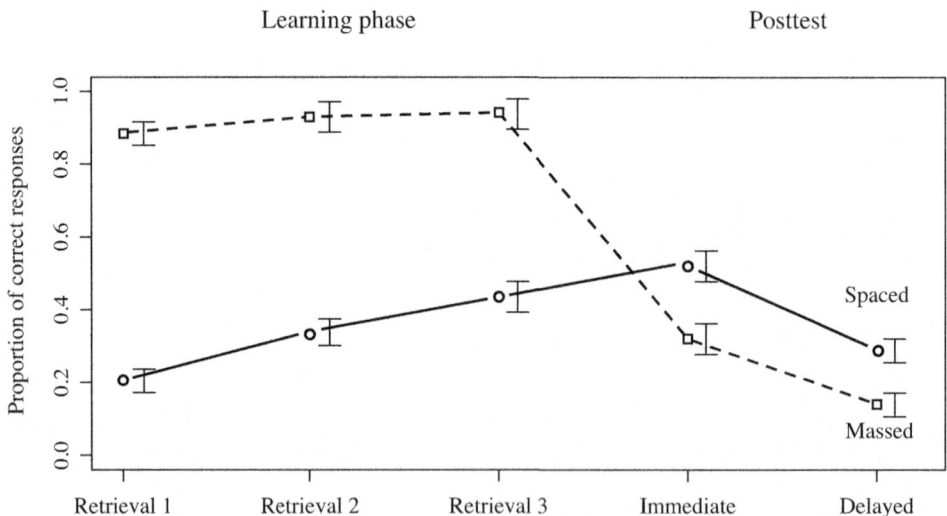

Figure 20.2 Learning phase and posttest performance in Nakata (2015a). The three data points on the left show the proportion of correct responses during the learning phase, and the two data points on the right show the proportion of correct responses on the posttests.

Note: The error bars indicate standard errors.

Source: Adapted from Nakata, 2015a

items out of 48 they might be able to recall in one week (judgments of learning). Although the long-spaced group significantly outperformed the short-spaced group on the one-week delayed posttest (short: 17%; long: 27%), the short-spaced group predicted that they would recall as many target words as the long-spaced group (short: 29%; long: 28%), overestimating retention (Figure 20.3). The findings are consistent with metacognition literature showing that learners are often unaware that spacing increases learning (e.g., Kornell, 2009; Wissman et al., 2012). The results support raising awareness of the value of spacing for vocabulary learning.

Spacing schedules can also be divided into expanding and equal spacing. Expanding spacing refers to a practice schedule where the lags between retrieval opportunities of a given word are increased in an expanding manner (e.g., two weeks, four weeks, six weeks). Equal spacing refers to a schedule where the lags between retrievals of a given word are fixed (e.g., four weeks, four weeks, four weeks). While many researchers claim that expanding spacing is the most optimal review schedule (e.g., Barcroft, 2015; Hulstijn, 2001; Nation & Webb, 2011), empirical evidence supporting the value of expanding spacing for L2 vocabulary learning is scant (Kang, Lindsey, Mozer, & Pashler, 2014; Karpicke & Bauernschmidt, 2011; Nakata, 2015a; Pyc & Rawson, 2007). Karpicke and Bauernschmidt (2011), for instance, did not find any significant difference between the effects of equal and expanding spaced conditions. In Nakata (2015a), 96 Japanese students studied 20 English-Japanese word pairs using flash card software. Half of the target items were studied under equal spaced conditions, while the other half were studied under expanding spaced conditions. Posttest results

Actual vs. predicted scores

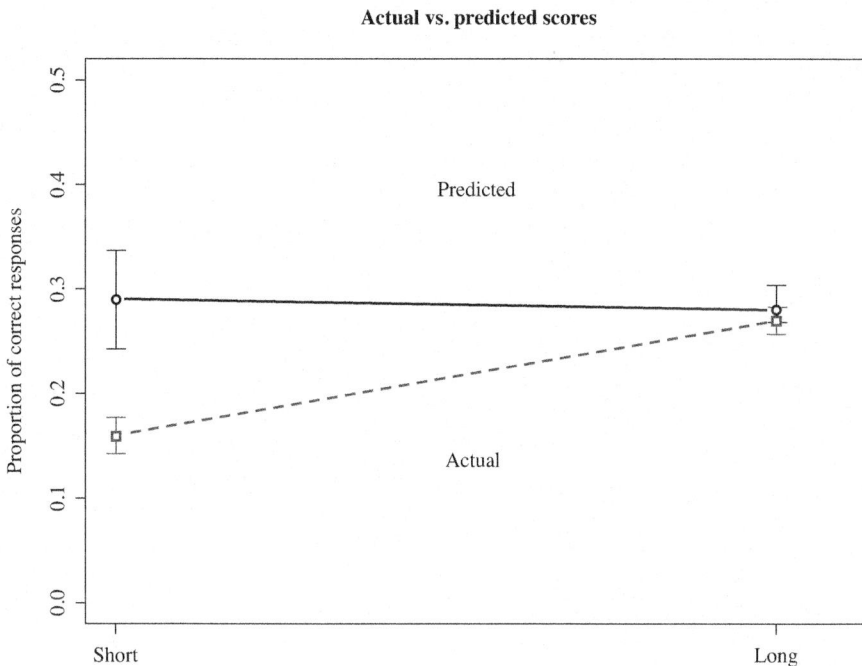

Figure 20.3   Actual vs. predicted scores on the one-week delayed posttest in Nakata and Suzuki (in press)

Note: The error bars indicate standard errors.

Source: Adapted from Nakata and Suzuki, in press

showed only limited, if any, superiority of expanding spacing over equal spacing. Overall, existing studies indicate that although introducing long lags between retrievals is critical for long-term retention, whether spacing is distributed in an equal or expanding manner is not as important (Karpicke & Bauernschmidt, 2011).

Another issue related to the review schedule is the effects of part and whole learning. Whole learning refers to a practice schedule where the target items are repeated as a whole. For example, when 100 words are studied in whole learning, 100 words are learned in sequence in one large deck of 100 items. Part learning, in contrast, refers to a practice schedule where the target items are repeated in smaller decks. In part learning, for instance, 100 words may be divided into five decks of 20 items and repeated in these smaller decks. Although part learning is often considered more effective than whole learning (e.g., Kornell, 2009; Wissman et al., 2012), research suggests that whole learning is actually more effective (Kornell, 2009). The results are possibly due to spacing. For instance, when 100 words are studied in whole learning, repetitions of a given target word are intervened by 99 other items. However, when 100 words are repeated in five decks of 20 items, repetitions of a given target word are intervened by only 19 other items. Whole learning, as a result, has a longer lag between repetitions (99 intervening items) than part learning (19 intervening items). Considering that a longer lag generally facilitates long-term retention more than a shorter lag (the lag effect), the advantage of whole learning in previous research may be due in part to differential lags rather than the part-whole distinction per se. This view is supported by Nakata and Webb (2016a), who compared the effects of part and whole learning while controlling spacing.

In Nakata and Webb (2016a), Japanese university students studied 20 English-Japanese word pairs using flash card software under part or whole learning conditions. Unlike previous studies, part and whole learning had equivalent lags between retrievals. Posttest results found no significant differences between the two conditions. In their Experiment 2, Nakata and Webb compared the effects of the following three treatments: (1) whole learning, (2) part learning with short lags, and (3) part learning with equivalent lags to whole learning. They found that (1) when part learning and whole learning have equivalent lags, there is no significant difference between the two schedules; (2) when part learning has shorter lags than whole learning, part learning is less effective than whole learning; and (3) part learning with longer lags is more effective than part learning with shorter lags. These results suggest that it is spacing, not the part-whole distinction, that affects learning.

Effects of Feedback

Another factor that is found to affect flash card learning is feedback. Feedback refers to the provision of the correct answer after retrieval. For instance, suppose learners were asked to translate *dog* into Japanese. If learners are provided with the correct answer (*inu*) after the retrieval attempt, the treatment involves feedback. Although retrieval without feedback can increase learning (e.g., Karpicke & Roediger, 2008), the provision of feedback enhances learning even more (e.g., Metcalfe & Kornell, 2007). One interesting issue regarding feedback is whether it should be provided immediately after the retrieval attempt (immediate feedback) or after a delay (delayed feedback). Some researchers argue that delayed feedback is more effective than immediate feedback because the former introduces longer lags between the retrieval attempt and feedback and according to the lag effect, longer lags often enhance learning more than shorter lags (e.g., Butler, Karpicke, & Roediger, 2007; Metcalfe, Kornell, & Finn, 2009).

Nakata (2015b), however, did not find any benefits of delaying feedback for L2 vocabulary learning. In his study, 98 Japanese university students studied 16 English-Japanese words pairs using flash card software. For half of the target items, the correct response was provided immediately after each retrieval attempt (immediate feedback). For the other half, the correct response was provided only after all 16 target items were practiced (delayed feedback). Nakata did not find any significant differences in immediate or delayed posttest scores between the two types of feedback. Considering that non-L2 vocabulary research has found benefits of delayed feedback (e.g., Butler et al., 2007; Metcalfe et al., 2009), it may be useful to further examine the effects of feedback timing on L2 vocabulary learning.

Effects of Interference

In flash card learning, some learners choose to study words that are semantically related to each other such as near-synonyms (e.g., *big, large*), antonyms (e.g., *hot, cold*), or coordinates (e.g., *cat, dog*). Researchers argue that presenting vocabulary in semantically related sets should be avoided because it decreases learning by causing interference (or cross-associations) among related words (e.g., Nation, 2000, 2013; Nation & Webb, 2011; Schmitt, 2010). However, empirical evidence is rather mixed regarding the effects of learning semantic sets. While some studies have shown the inhibitory effects of learning semantic sets (e.g., Tinkham, 1993, 1997; Waring, 1997), other studies have failed to do so (e.g., Hoshino, 2010; Ishii, 2015; Nakata & Suzuki, in press; Schneider et al., 2002). Ishii (2015), for instance, found that although physical similarity (e.g., *pencil, fishing pole, chopsticks*) inhibits learning, semantic similarity (e.g., *chicken, pig, giraffe*) may not. Nakata and Suzuki (in press) also compared the effects of learning semantically related and unrelated sets. One significant aspect of their study is that they ensured that the semantically related and unrelated sets were controlled for lexical variables that might affect learning other than semantic relatedness (e.g., word length, frequency, familiarity, imageability, pronounceability). Unlike some earlier research (e.g., Tinkham, 1993, 1997; Waring, 1997), they also gave a one-week delayed posttest to measure long-term retention. Nakata and Suzuki found that although semantic sets led to more cross-association errors than unrelated sets, no significant difference existed between the semantically related and unrelated sets in posttest scores. The results, together with those of other recent research (e.g., Hoshino, 2010; Ishii, 2015; Schneider et al., 2002), indicate that the negative effects of semantic sets might not be as robust as researchers have claimed.

Computer-Based Flash Cards

Recently, many flash card programs have become available as computer software, smartphone applications, or web-based applications (Nakata, 2011). Computer-based flash cards have several advantages over traditional paper-based flash cards. First, computer-based flash cards can help learners to implement principles of effective learning. Research suggests that many learners are unaware of principles for effective learning such as retrieval or spacing (e.g., Kornell, 2009; Nakata & Suzuki, in press; Wissman et al., 2012). Flash card software is useful because it can be programmed to ensure that learning follows principles for effective flash card learning. Second, computer-based flash cards can offer exercises that are hard to implement with paper-based flash cards. For instance, multiple-choice questions or exercises involving sounds (e.g., listening to the pronunciation of a word and typing the written form or its meaning) can be implemented relatively easily with computer-based flash cards. Third, flash card software can also keep record of learners' performance and determine the scheduling so that unfamiliar items are reviewed regularly after sufficient spacing (Nakata, 2011). Computers can also be programmed to manipulate not only scheduling but also retrieval formats. For instance, in earlier stages, flash card software can use relatively easy formats (e.g., multiple choice) and only in later stages introduce more challenging formats (e.g., recall of meaning or form). Gradually increasing difficulty is helpful according to the retrieval effort hypothesis, which states that difficult retrievals facilitate learning more than easy retrievals (Pyc & Rawson, 2009). Fourth, multimedia information, such as images, videos, and sounds, can be added to computer-based flash cards relatively easily. Fifth, some flash card programs facilitate flash card creation by supporting data entry. For instance, *Quizlet* (https://quizlet.com/), a popular web-based flash card program, automatically suggests the meanings and images corresponding to lexical items entered by users. It would also be helpful if flash card programs could automatically provide information such as the part of speech, pronunciation, collocations, contexts, frequency levels, inflected forms, derivations, or associations.

Limitations of Flash Card Learning

Although flash card learning is useful for vocabulary development, it is not without limitations. One limitation is that flash card learning typically focuses on initial form-meaning mapping and may not necessarily facilitate the learning of other aspects such as collocations, associations, or constraints on use (Nation, 2013). Another limitation is that it does not necessarily promote generative use. Generative use refers to a situation where learners encounter (at least partially) known words in new contexts (e.g., Joe, 1998). Imagine, for example, that a learner was first exposed to the English word *round* in the phrase "a round face". This learner might assume that the word *round* is an adjective that describes the shape of a concrete object. If this learner subsequently meets collocations such as *a round of drinks*, *a round of applause*, *a round number*, *a round dozen*, or *a round table*, s/he may be able to acquire a more precise understanding of this word. Flash card learning is not very effective in promoting generative use because target items are usually encountered without context or in a single context. Furthermore, flash card learning does not necessarily promote negotiation, instantiation, or imaging, all of which are found to facilitate vocabulary learning (Nakata & Webb, 2016b; Nation & Webb, 2011). Due to the aforementioned limitations, although flash card learning is one of the most effective vocabulary learning strategies, it should be supplemented with more meaning-focused activities, such as extensive reading, listening, or viewing.

Future Directions

Research on paired-associate learning dates back to the 19th century, and a number of studies have been conducted since. Nonetheless, there are still some issues related to flash card learning that warrant further investigation. First, considering that the duration of the treatment is relatively short in most existing studies, it is useful to conduct more longitudinal research on flash card learning. Second, because most existing studies on flash card learning define vocabulary acquisition as the ability to connect an L2 word with its meaning, research examining the effects of flash card learning on other aspects of vocabulary knowledge is warranted (for examples, see Webb, 2007, 2009a, 2009b). It will also be useful to examine the effects of flash card learning not only on explicit but also implicit vocabulary knowledge using priming (e.g., Elgort, 2011; Elgort & Piasecki, 2014) or event-related brain potential (Chun, Choi, & Kim, 2012).

One useful direction for future research may be to draw on findings from cognitive or educational psychology literature. Numerous studies have been conducted on paired-associate learning in not only the field of applied linguistics but also psychology. For instance, psychologists have examined the effects of a number of factors related to flash card learning such as spacing, retrieval, keyword mnemonics, and interference (for a review, see Dunlosky et al., 2013). Because most psychology studies have investigated the learning of materials other than L2 vocabulary, such as L1 vocabulary, some of the findings may not necessarily be applicable to L2 vocabulary learning. At the same time, they have nonetheless provided useful starting points for many L2 vocabulary studies (e.g., Barcroft, 2002, 2007; Nakata, 2015a, 2015b, 2016, 2017; Nakata & Webb, 2016a). It may be useful for applied linguists to empirically test the findings of the cognitive or educational psychology studies in the context of L2 vocabulary learning.

Another useful direction for future research is to examine whether different learners and lexical items benefit differently from flash card learning. In a grammar learning study, Suzuki and DeKeyser (2017) found that learners with different language aptitude (working memory capacity and language-analytic ability) benefit differently from massing and spacing. It would be useful to examine whether language learning aptitude affects flash card learning. For instance, do learners with higher working memory capacity benefit more from long spacing or whole learning? Another interesting issue is whether different lexical items benefit differently from flash card learning. Nakata and Suzuki (in press), for instance, found that although spacing facilitated the retention of both semantically related (e.g., *porcupine*, *raccoon*) and unrelated lexical sets (e.g., *berth*, *ointment*), semantically unrelated items benefited more from spacing. It would be useful to examine what kinds of words are particularly amenable to flash card learning. Since flash card learning is one of the most effective, efficient, and useful vocabulary learning strategies, future research on flash card learning is valuable for teachers, learners, and materials developers.

Further Reading

Nation, I. S. P. (2013). *Learning vocabulary in another language* (2nd ed.). Cambridge, UK: Cambridge University Press.

Chapter 11 of this book is devoted entirely to flash card learning. It surveys a number of important studies on flash card learning and discusses principles for effective flash card learning.

Nakata, T., & Webb, S. (2016b). Evaluating the effectiveness of vocabulary learning activities using Technique Feature Analysis. In B. Tomlinson (Ed.), *SLA research and materials development for language learning* (pp. 123–138). New York, NY: Routledge.

This book chapter analyzes three common vocabulary learning activities including flash card learning. The chapter discusses advantages and disadvantages of flash card learning and proposes how to optimize L2 vocabulary learning from flash cards.

Schmitt, N. (2010). *Researching vocabulary: A vocabulary research manual*. Basingstoke, UK: Palgrave Macmillan.

Although none of the chapters specifically addresses flash card learning, a number of issues related to flash card learning are discussed throughout the book. Part 3 of the book is particularly valuable for researchers planning to conduct experiments on flash card learning because it addresses a number of important considerations in designing experiments.

Barcroft, J. (2015). *Lexical input processing and vocabulary learning*. Amsterdam: John Benjamins.

This book discusses a number of key concepts, such as retrieval, spacing, interference, mnemonics, levels (depth) of processing, transfer-appropriate processing, and Type of Processing – Resource Allocation (TOPRA) model, which have implications for effective flash card learning.

Nakata, T. (2011). Computer-assisted second language vocabulary learning in a paired-associate paradigm: A critical investigation of flashcard software. *Computer Assisted Language Learning, 24*, 17–38.

This article proposes 17 criteria for evaluating computer-based flash card programs drawn from research on paired-associate learning. The article then analyzes nine freely or commercially available flash card software programs using these criteria.

Related Topics

Intentional L2 vocabulary learning, strategies for learning vocabulary resources for learning single-word items, evaluating exercises for learning vocabulary

References

Bahrick, H. P., Bahrick, L. E., Bahrick, A. S., & Bahrick, P. E. (1993). Maintenance of foreign language vocabulary and the spacing effect. *Psychological Science, 4*, 316–321. https://doi.org/10.1111/j.1467-9280.1993.tb00571.x

Bahrick, H. P., & Phelps, E. (1987). Retention of Spanish vocabulary over 8 years. *Journal of Experimental Psychology: Learning, Memory, & Cognition, 13*, 344–349. https://doi.org/10.1037/0278-7393.13.2.344

Barcroft, J. (2002). Semantic and structural elaboration in L2 lexical acquisition. *Language Learning, 52*, 323–363. https://doi.org/10.1111/0023-8333.00186

Barcroft, J. (2007). Effects of opportunities for word retrieval during second language vocabulary learning. *Language Learning, 57*, 35–56. https://doi.org/10.1111/j.1467-9922.2007.00398.x

Barcroft, J. (2015). *Lexical input processing and vocabulary learning*. Amsterdam, Netherlands: John Benjamins.

Bjork, R. A. (1999). Assessing our own competence: Heuristics and illusions. In D. Gopher & A. Koriat (Eds.), *Attention and performance XVII: Cognitive regulation of performance: Interaction of theory and application* (pp. 435–459). Cambridge, MA: MIT Press.

Butler, A. C., Karpicke, J. D., & Roediger, H. L. (2007). The effect of type and timing of feedback on learning from multiple-choice tests. *Journal of Experimental Psychology: Applied, 13*, 273–281. https://doi.org/10.1037/1076–898X.13.4.273

Carpenter, S. K., & Olson, K. M. (2012). Are pictures good for learning new vocabulary in a foreign language? Only if you think they are not. *Journal of Experimental Psychology: Learning, Memory, and Cognition, 38*, 92–101. https://doi.org/10.1037/a0024828

Chun, E., Choi, S., & Kim, J. (2012). The effect of extensive reading and paired-associate learning on long-term vocabulary retention: An event-related potential study. *Neuroscience Letters, 521*, 125–129. https://doi.org/10.1016/j.neulet.2012.05.069

Dunlosky, J., Rawson, K. A., Marsh, E. J., Nathan, M. J., & Willingham, D. T. (2013). Improving students' learning with effective learning techniques: Promising directions from cognitive and educational psychology. *Psychological Science in the Public Interest, 14*, 4–58. https://doi.org/10.1177/1529100612453266

Elgort, I. (2011). Deliberate learning and vocabulary acquisition in a second language. *Language Learning, 61*, 367–413. https://doi.org/10.1111/j.1467-9922.2010.00613.x

Elgort, I., & Piasecki, A. E. (2014). The effect of a bilingual learning mode on the establishment of lexical semantic representations in the L2. *Bilingualism: Language and Cognition, 17*, 572–588. https://doi.org/10.1017/S1366728913000588

Ellis, N. C., & Beaton, A. (1993). Psycholinguistic determinants of foreign-language vocabulary learning. *Language Learning, 43*, 559–617. https://doi.org/10.1111/j.1467-1770.1993.tb00627.x

Fitzpatrick, T., Al-Qarni, I., & Meara, P. (2008). Intensive vocabulary learning: A case study. *Language Learning Journal, 36*, 239–248. https://doi.org/10.1080/09571730802390759

Hoshino, Y. (2010). The categorical facilitation effects on L2 vocabulary learning in a classroom setting. *RELC Journal, 41*, 301–312. https://doi.org/10.1177/0033688210380558

Hulstijn, J. H. (1997). Mnemonic methods in foreign language vocabulary learning: Theoretical considerations and pedagogical implications. In J. Coady & T. Huckin (Eds.), *Second language vocabulary acquisition: A rationale for pedagogy* (pp. 203–224). Cambridge, UK: Cambridge University Press.

Hulstijn, J. H. (2001). Intentional and incidental second language vocabulary learning: A reappraisal of elaboration, rehearsal, and automaticity. In P. Robinson (Ed.), *Cognition and second language instruction* (pp. 258–286). Cambridge, UK: Cambridge University Press.

Ishii, T. (2015). Semantic connection or visual connection: Investigating the true source of confusion. *Language Teaching Research, 19*, 712–722. https://doi.org/10.1177/1362168814559799

Joe, A. (1998). What effects do text-based tasks promoting generation have on incidental vocabulary acquisition? *Applied Linguistics, 19*, 357–377. https://doi.org/10.1093/applin/19.3.357

Kang, S. H. K., Lindsey, R. V., Mozer, M. C., & Pashler, H. (2014). Retrieval practice over the long term: Should spacing be expanding or equal-interval? *Psychonomic Bulletin & Review, 21*, 1544–1550. https://doi.org/10.3758/s13423-014-0636-z

Karpicke, J. D., & Bauernschmidt, A. (2011). Spaced retrieval: Absolute spacing enhances learning regardless of relative spacing. *Journal of Experimental Psychology: Learning, Memory, and Cognition, 37*, 1250–1257. https://doi.org/10.1037/a0023436

Karpicke, J. D., & Roediger, H. L. (2008). The critical importance of retrieval for learning. *Science, 319*, 966–968. https://doi.org/10.1126/science.1152408

Kornell, N. (2009). Optimising learning using flashcards: Spacing is more effective than cramming. *Applied Cognitive Psychology, 23*, 1297–1317. https://doi.org/10.1002/acp.1537

Laufer, B. (2005). Focus on form in second language vocabulary learning. *EUROSLA Yearbook, 5*, 223–250. https://doi.org/10.1075/eurosla.5.11lau

Laufer, B., & Goldstein, Z. (2004). Testing vocabulary knowledge: Size, strength, and computer adaptiveness. *Language Learning, 54*, 399–436. https://doi.org/10.1111/j.0023-8333.2004.00260.x

Laufer, B., & Shmueli, K. (1997). Memorizing new words: Does teaching have anything to do with it? *RELC Journal, 28*, 89–108. https://doi.org/10.1177/003368829702800106

Metcalfe, J., & Kornell, N. (2007). Principles of cognitive science in education: The effects of generation, errors, and feedback. *Psychonomic Bulletin and Review, 14*, 225–229.

Metcalfe, J., Kornell, N., & Finn, B. (2009). Delayed versus immediate feedback in children's and adults' vocabulary learning. *Memory & Cognition, 37*, 1077–1087. https://doi.org/10.3758/MC.37.8.1077

Morimoto, S., & Loewen, S. (2007). A comparison of the effects of image-schema-based instruction and translation-based instruction on the acquisition of L2 polysemous words. *Language Teaching Research, 11*, 347–372.

Morris, C. D., Bransford, J. D., & Franks, J. J. (1977). Levels of processing versus transfer appropriate processing. *Journal of Verbal Learning and Verbal Behavior, 16*, 519–533. https://doi.org/10.1016/S0022-5371(77)80016-9

Nakata, T. (2011). Computer-assisted second language vocabulary learning in a paired-associate paradigm: A critical investigation of flashcard software. *Computer Assisted Language Learning, 24*, 17–38. https://doi.org/10.1080/09588221.2010.520675

Nakata, T. (2015a). Effects of expanding and equal spacing on second language vocabulary learning: Does gradually increasing spacing increase vocabulary learning? *Studies in Second Language Acquisition, 37*, 677–711. https://doi.org/10.1017/S0272263114000825

Nakata, T. (2015b). Effects of feedback timing on second language vocabulary learning: Does delaying feedback increase learning? *Language Teaching Research, 19*, 416–434. https://doi.org/10.1177/1362168814541721

Nakata, T. (2016). Effects of retrieval formats on second language vocabulary learning. *International Review of Applied Linguistics in Language Teaching, 54*, 257–289. https://doi.org/10.1515/iral-2015-0022

Nakata, T. (2017). Does repeated practice make perfect? The effects of within-session repeated retrieval on second language vocabulary learning. *Studies in Second Language Acquisition, 39*, 653–679. https://doi.org/10.1017/S0272263116000280

Nakata, T., & Suzuki, Y. (in press). Effects of massing and spacing on the learning of semantically related and unrelated words. *Studies in Second Language Acquisition.* https://doi.org/10.1017/S0272263118000219

Nakata, T., & Webb, S. (2016a). Does studying vocabulary in smaller sets increase learning? The effects of part and whole learning on second language vocabulary acquisition. *Studies in Second Language Acquisition, 38*, 523–552. https://doi.org/10.1017/S0272263115000236

Nakata, T., & Webb, S. (2016b). Evaluating the effectiveness of vocabulary learning activities using Technique Feature Analysis. In B. Tomlinson (Ed.), *SLA research and materials development for language learning* (pp. 123–138). New York, NY: Routledge.

Nation, I. S. P. (1980). Strategies for receptive vocabulary learning. *RELC Guidelines, 3*, 18–23.

Nation, I. S. P. (2000). Learning vocabulary in lexical sets: Dangers and guidelines. *TESOL Journal, 9*(2), 6–10.

Nation, I. S. P. (2008). *Teaching vocabulary: Strategies and techniques.* Boston, MA: Heinle Cengage Learning.

Nation, I. S. P. (2013). *Learning vocabulary in another language* (2nd ed.). Cambridge, UK: Cambridge University Press.

Nation, I. S. P., & Webb, S. (2011). *Researching and analyzing vocabulary.* Boston, MA: Heinle Cengage Learning.

Prince, P. (1996). Second language vocabulary learning: The role of context versus translations as a function of proficiency. *Modern Language Journal, 80*, 478–493. https://doi.org/10.1111/j.1540-4781.1996.tb05468.x

Pyc, M. A., & Rawson, K. A. (2007). Examining the efficiency of schedules of distributed retrieval practice. *Memory & Cognition, 35*, 1917–1927. https://doi.org/10.3758/BF03192925

Pyc, M. A., & Rawson, K. A. (2009). Testing the retrieval effort hypothesis: Does greater difficulty correctly recalling information lead to higher levels of memory? *Journal of Memory and Language, 60*, 437–447. https://doi.org/10.1016/j.jml.2009.01.004

Rodriguez, M., & Sadoski, M. (2000). Effects of rote, context, keyword, and context/keyword methods on retention of vocabulary in EFL classrooms. *Language Learning, 50*, 385–412. https://doi.org/10.1111/0023-8333.00121

Rohrer, D., Taylor, K. M., Pashler, H., Wixted, J. T., & Cepeda, N. J. (2005). The effect of overlearning on long-term retention. *Applied Cognitive Psychology, 19*, 361–374. https://doi.org/10.1002/acp.1083

Schmitt, N. (1997). Vocabulary learning strategies. In N. Schmitt & M. McCarthy (Eds.), *Vocabulary: Description, acquisition and pedagogy* (pp. 199–227). Cambridge, UK: Cambridge University Press.

Schmitt, N. (2010). *Researching vocabulary: A vocabulary research manual.* Basingstoke, UK: Palgrave Macmillan.

Schneider, V. I., Healy, A. F., & Bourne, L. E. (2002). What is learned under difficult conditions is hard to forget: Contextual interference effects in foreign vocabulary acquisition, retention, and transfer. *Journal of Memory and Language, 46*, 419–440. https://doi.org//10.1006/jmla.2001.2813

Steinel, M. P., Hulstijn, J. H., & Steinel, W. (2007). Second language idiom learning in a paired-associate paradigm: Effects of direction of learning, direction of testing, idiom imageability, and idiom transparency. *Studies in Second Language Acquisition, 29*, 449–484. https://doi.org/10.1017/S0272263107070271

Suzuki, Y., & DeKeyser, R. (2017). Exploratory research on second language practice distribution: An Aptitude × Treatment interaction. *Applied Psycholinguistics, 38*, 27–56. https://doi.org/10.1017/S0142716416000084

Tinkham, T. (1993). The effect of semantic clustering on the learning of second language vocabulary. *System, 21*, 371–380. https://doi.org/10.1191/026765897672376469

Tinkham, T. (1997). The effects of semantic and thematic clustering on the learning of second language vocabulary. *Second Language Research, 13*, 138–163. https://doi.org/10.1191/026765897672376469

Verspoor, M., & Lowie, W. (2003). Making sense of polysemous words. *Language Learning, 53*, 547–586.

Waring, R. (1997). The negative effects of learning words in semantic sets: A replication. *System, 25*, 261–274. https://doi.org/10.1016/S0346-251X(97)00013-4

Webb, S. (2007). Learning word pairs and glossed sentences: The effects of a single context on vocabulary knowledge. *Language Teaching Research, 11*, 63–81. https://doi.org/10.1177/1362168806072463

Webb, S. (2009a). The effects of pre-learning vocabulary on reading comprehension and writing. *Canadian Modern Language Review, 65*, 441–470. https://doi.org/10.1353/cml.0.0046

Webb, S. (2009b). The effects of receptive and productive learning of word pairs on vocabulary knowledge. *RELC Journal, 40*, 360–376. https://doi.org/10.1177/0033688209343854

Wei, Z. (2015). Does teaching mnemonics for vocabulary learning make a difference? Putting the keyword method and the word part technique to the test. *Language Teaching Research, 19*, 43–69. https://doi.org/10.1177/1362168814541734

Wissman, K. T., Rawson, K. A., & Pyc, M. A. (2012). How and when do students use flashcards? *Memory, 20*, 568–579. https://doi.org/10.1080/09658211.2012.687052

21

Resources for Learning Single-Word Items

Oliver Ballance and Tom Cobb

Introduction

This chapter begins with a discussion of critical issues in relation to two of the key terms in the title, *learning* and *single-word items*. First it discusses the status of single-word items and their implications for learning resources. Second it discusses vocabulary learning in relation to three different types of vocabulary knowledge. These components are then brought together in an overview of resources for learning single words. Finally, we suggest ways that teachers and learners can assess particular resources in terms of the type of learning targeted.

Critical Issues and Topics

Single-Word Items

The idea of a single-word vocabulary item may seem transparent, but for applied linguists working in vocabulary the problem of providing an exact definition of what to count as a word is well-established (Hanks, 2013; Kilgarriff, 2015; Nation, 2016; Wray, 2015). The problem is not only theoretical but has practical ramifications for language teachers. In brief, the concept of word is made problematic by inflected and derived forms of words (are *medicine* and *medicinal* the same word?); polysemy (do all the meanings of *get* add up to a single word?); homonyms, homographs, and homophones (is *bank* = *money* and *bank* = *river* one word or two?); variation in orthographic or phonological form (are *color* and *colour* the same word?); and ambiguity over the status of multiword lexical items that can be decomposed into smaller, single-word items (is *look into* = investigate two words or one?; see Wood, this volume). For teachers, the issue involves whether a multiword item can be taught without focusing on each one of its components (*rice krispies* without *rice* and *crisp*), or whether one of the meanings of a homoform can be taught apart from others (*bank* = *money* apart from *bank* = *river*), or to what degree comprehension of polysemes is generalizable (is *frosty reception* inferable from *frosty morning*?). Such issues are compounded by the common second language (L2) learners' assumption that words should present stable correspondences between particular forms and particular meanings, as they typically believe they do in their first languages (L1s). Unfortunately, on examination this assumption frequently fails to hold true, and a number of corpus linguists and lexicographers are now casting doubt on the status of the word as the primary carrier of linguistic meaning, or even a reliable unit of analysis (Hanks, 2013; Sinclair, 2010; Wray, 2015).

But while the discussion above implies an unmarked continuum between sub-word, single-word, and multiword vocabulary unit, this does not quite amount to a rejection of the word as a pedagogically useful unit. We propose that the idea of "word" as a discrete meaning-carrying item be retained on two conditions, first that not all single-word items will conform to this prototypical idea of the word, and second that the meaning of many words will be *fuzzy*, with their exact semantic import determined by both their semantic contexts and the other words they are used with (Hanks, 2013; Murphy, 2010; Wray, 2015). This position has much in common with the *monosemic* approach to word meaning proposed by Nation (2016) and Ruhl (1989). From this perspective, the vast majority of single-word items correspond to basic, underlying, unparaphrasable root-meanings, notwithstanding that communication requires their interpretation in both particular contexts of use and in relation to the other words they are used with. Empirical support for monosemism comes from Beretta, Fiorentino, and Poeppel (2005) who show that seemingly polysemous items are processed through computation from a single entry in the mental lexicon. That is, "look up", "look into", "good looking" and "have a look" are all processed via the underlying monoseme "look", such that there is one basic learning act behind the acquisition of at least recognition knowledge of these several manifestations.

The precise status of single words may be debatable, but the pedagogical value of placing a high importance on single-word learning is not. First, the vast majority of learners assume that words are the basic units of a language and the main thing to be learned. There is probably no reason to try and convince learners of the problems with this assumption; teachers are better advised to work with it. Second, despite the undoubted importance in any language of units other than single words, such as multiword units, research by Bogaards (2001) has shown that knowledge of the single words that make up such units strongly facilitates their acquisition, even when the multiword unit is metaphorical or idiomatic. Bogaards had two groups of learners process idiomatic multiword units, one of whom had previously learned the single-word meanings composing the units and one that had not. Those who knew the constituent words were significantly better able to comprehend and retain the multiword units (while incidentally the inverse was not the case). In other words, knowing *look* facilitates learning *look into*, lending support to both monoseme theory and the typical learners' attitude to learning single-word items.

Another important issue in learning single-word items is the extent to which cognate word-forms between the L1 and L2 allow single-word items to transfer fairly reliably between languages. Although learners rarely assume that multiword units such as *eye for an eye* or *look forward to* will have direct translations (Kellerman, 1986), virtually all learners view cognate word-forms, if available, as an essential bridge to creating the second lexicon. Many linguists, on the other hand, are skeptical of naïve transfer theories (e.g., Granger, 1993) in view of the likelihood of false friends in some of the pairings. However, the failure to recognize cognates is almost certainly a greater danger for learners than false friends (White & Horst, 2011). For instance, Ringbom (2007) notes that virtually all Swedes learn English successfully while most Finns struggle, the main difference between them being the degree of lexical similarity between their L1s and English, despite the usual number of false friends. Hence, teachers are probably best advised to exploit any available cognate forms, at least as a starting strategy. In relation to learning languages that share few cognate forms with the L1, the situation is more complex.

Swan (1997) argues that virtually all learners assume that single-word items in their L1 will have translation equivalents in their target language, and to a greater extent such an assumption provides another bridge to the second language (L2) lexicon. Not only learners, but also pedagogically oriented researchers such as Nation (2013) see L1 vocabulary knowledge as having the potential to reduce the learning burden of L2 vocabulary items. Clearly, however, when learners are confronted with vocabulary in use, they will encounter places where the L2 translation equivalent diverges in use from the L1 word-form, and the learners will need to adjust their L2 lexicons appropriately (Swan, 1997). Still, the most radical of these adjustments will not involve wholesale departure from the form-meaning link established via the translation equivalent, but rather the addition or removal of particular senses of a word, the other words that it is commonly used with (collocations), the grammatical patterns they typically occur in (colligation), the frequency with which they are used, or the contexts they are typically employed in, including such notions such as register, connotation and the semantic space a word occupies vis-à-vis other words within the same language (synonyms, antonyms, hypernyms, and hyponyms).

A final reason to learn single words is the generalizability of such knowledge. When a frequent, single word is learned it will be seen often and may help to unlock a good number of related meanings, but this cannot normally be said of multiword units. *Look* is used frequently both as a single word and in numerous multiword units, so knowledge of this word is highly valuable. For example, the core sense of the single-word item *look* contributes to the overall meaning of the multiword expression *look forward to*. However, although the multiword expression *look forward to* also carries with it the sense of *pleasurable anticipation*, this sense is not activated in otherwise comparable VB+forward items such as *think forward to*, *bring forward*, or especially *push (oneself) forward*. In this way, single-word items are more productive than multiword items, which tend to be one-offs. While single-word items frequently contribute their senses to the overall sense activated by larger multiword items, multiword items are rarely productive in this way. In fact, what productivity multiword items possess appears to depend on knowledge of single-word lexical sets that can be substituted for others within the structure – e.g., *pour/throw cold water on* something (see Hanks, 2013, for an in-depth discussion).

In sum, there are at least three important reasons to value the learning of single-word items and to be interested in the resources available for doing so. Learners expect to be learning single-word items; they expect their knowledge of single words to transfer between related languages; and knowledge of single words is highly productive compared to knowledge of multiword items. While the role of multiword items was undoubtedly neglected in many traditional linguistic analyses, recognizing their importance does not imply neglecting the value of single-word items.

Types of Vocabulary Learning

The materials available to teachers and learners for learning single-word items can be categorized in relation to the types of vocabulary learning they target. It is common in applied linguistics research to distinguish three types of vocabulary knowledge (cf. Henriksen, 1999): Type 1, knowledge of form-meaning relationships; Type 2, knowledge of how words are used in sentences and texts, including considerations of connotation, register, pragmatics, and collocational and colligational preferences and restrictions; and Type 3, the skill of accessing knowledge of single-word items quickly, with automatized access the ultimate goal (Meara, 1996; Schmitt, 2010; see also Nation, this volume, for a different perspective).

Traditionally, single-word learning mainly involves developing knowledge in a receptive context that relates to Types 1 and 3 – in other words, form-meaning links, with regard to both spoken and written form, and the speed or fluidity of accessing one from the other (meaning from form, and form from meaning). This framework allows us to be quite precise about whether a particular resource introduces or practices spoken word recognition, written word recognition, or how either of these links to meaning. It also allows us to temporarily set aside resources for interpretation and production of words in combination. In the early stages of language learning at least, the learner has enough to do in each of these three areas without mixing them together, despite the fact they will eventually come together in language use.

Examples of Resources for Single-Word Learning

This section discusses paper or computer-based word lists, dictionaries, flash cards, textbooks, written and audio texts, and some resources that are only computer based, focusing primarily on Type 1 and Type 3 learning, but suggesting implications for Type 2 learning where these are not fully separable.

Word Lists

The most common resource for anyone wishing to learn a set of words is almost certainly a simple word list, whether made by learners themselves or by someone else on their behalf. The obvious benefits of a word list are ease of construction, portability, equality of focus on each word, and decontextualization. The benefit of decontextualization is that all of the learner's attention is focused on learning the form-meaning link. In contrast, when words are encountered in context, the learner's attention may move from the form-meaning connection of the word to comprehension of other aspects of the sentence, which can reduce learning of the single word *per se* (Mondria & Wit-de Boer, 1991). Hence, word lists can be seen as facilitating Type 1 learning through decontextualization, although from the perspective of Type 2 learning decontextualization could also be seen as a drawback. Two further drawbacks of word lists just from the perspective of Type 1 learning are the fixed order of the words and the limitations of a written and non-audible representation.

Computer-based lists offer several additional benefits over paper lists. One is randomization, so that words need not be learned in a fixed order such that each primes the next. Another is potential completeness. If the list has been generated from a text or corpus, as is increasingly the case, every word of the text will be equally represented and none will get lost. Another is morphological grouping, which can be achieved through simple alphabetization of the words in a text or corpus (e.g., "cat" and "cats" will appear together), or through software that is able to groups words in relation to lists of word families, lemmas or the like. Another is utility grouping; if the words are ranked by frequency of occurrence in a text, then their importance for handling that text is made clear through the display of their frequencies, such as when software pitches list against texts or other learning resources (as in RANGE, Antprofiler, or Vocabprofile). Alternatively, if the words are ranked by range and frequency in a large reference corpus, then their importance in the language as a whole is clear. Indeed, list-building projects by West (1953; the General Service List, GSL, of 2,000 headwords), Nation (2006, the British National Corpus, BNC, list of 14,000 word families; and 2016, the BNC-Corpus of Contemporary American English, BNC-COCA, list of 20,000 word families), and many others are major contributions to the resource stock available for learning the single-word lexicon of English. These corpus-based lists combine the advantages of completeness, grouping, randomization, and utility, and Nation (2016) has set down guidelines for developing further word lists based on his own extensive experience. Such lists let us expand utility to a broader category, something like curriculum design, where whole programs of study can be sequenced in part or in whole according to the words that are needed at different stages of learning. This curriculum-design role can apply to a language as a whole (frequency lists) or specific parts of it (for example, Coxhead's, 2000, Academic Word List that supplements the GSL). Importantly, in their role as curriculum shapers, corpus-based word lists help us to identify which single-word items are of most value to learners (see also Dang, Liu and Lei, Vilkaitė-Lozdienė and Schmitt, and Coxhead's chapters in this volume).

Further affordances of computer-based word lists can no doubt be supplied by readers in their areas of interest, but a general affordance worth mentioning is linkability: the ease of linking computer word lists to other digital and non-digital resources. Text-to-speech (TTS) links, where a clicked word will produce its spoken form with reasonable accuracy, strongly reduces one negative affordance of traditional word lists, but the possibilities are endless (pictures, example sentences, L1 glosses, L2 glosses, and others). Pedagogy can even be incorporated into lists. Learners have often written little definitions beside, over, or under the items on their lists and found ways to fold and bend them to quiz themselves or each other, and computer technology can multiply this dimension.

Flash Cards

Another variant of learning from word lists is flash cards, or word cards, which can incorporate all the benefits of word lists but integrate further pedagogical advantages in relation to Type 3 learning. (See Nakata, this volume, for a fuller account of flash cards). Importantly, Elgort (2011) found that learning new words with paper word cards could create lasting word knowledge that could be accessed so quickly that it attained the psycholinguistic criteria of automaticity, and Krashen's (1989) criteria for "acquired learning", which is distinct from "learned learning". Hence, flash cards are an extremely important resource for learning single-word items.

It was mentioned in the context of word lists that learners often make a list of parallel glosses or synonyms and quiz themselves or each other by folding the paper in half – look at the word, produce the meaning, or vice versa, and check. This practice fosters both Type 1 and Type 3 learning because it involves form-meaning retrieval. The flash card basically focuses and formalizes this particular use of the word list. Flash cards divide a word list into a set of word cards each with a word on one side of the card and its meaning on the other, so that retrieval can be practiced.

An extensive body of psychological research has demonstrated that the practice of retrieving word information from memory, as compared to simply seeing the form and meaning together, leads to improved retention (for an overview, see Nation, 2013). Admittedly, retrieval of a word's meaning is practiced every time a word is encountered, but the extra advantage of flash cards is the option of reversing the sequence and retrieving the L2 word when cued by its meaning. Meaning-to-word retrieval is essentially what happens in production (we have a meaning in mind and we look for an L2 word to express it), and flash cards make it possible to engage extensively in this more complex lexical operation at a learning stage when production is limited. (This is also labeled "active recall practice" in Laufer & Goldstein's, 2004, framework.) It is important to practice retrieval in both directions because, as research by Webb (2009) has shown, word knowledge reflects the way that words were learned. Learning words only receptively (recalling or recognizing the meaning when presented with the form) may not develop all the knowledge necessary for productive use. Productive lexicons in an L2 are almost always some fraction of the size of their receptive counterparts (Laufer, 1998), but regular practice of productive retrieval (retrieving the L2 form of the word when presented with its meaning) may help reduce this difference.

Flash cards deploy all of the original benefits of word lists (completeness, decontextualization, presentational equality, etc.) and further facilitate randomization (cards can be shuffled, as words on a list cannot) and retrieval (either the word or the meaning is out of sight when the other is visible). In their turn, phone/computer flash cards deploy all the benefits of paper ones, improve on some of them (more perfect randomization, tighter record keeping) as well as introducing some new advantages. For example, many flash card apps allow meaning to be represented via multimedia clues like pictures or speech, and in addition have a quiz option (either in the productive direction, from meaning clue to a list of candidate words, or the receptive direction, from word to list of candidate definitions). When learners use the quiz option, they will get every word either right or wrong, which the app can record, and this allows the app to engage in some on-the-fly instructional design. With this information, the app can focus more on the words learners need to work on, potentially increasing the efficiency of the learning operation.

Another advantage of electronic flash cards is that when the dimension of timing is included, and a higher speed of retrieval is encouraged in a game or competitive setting, their value is intensified as a Type 3 learning resource. Single-word lexical access (or word recognition speed) has often been shown (first by Perfetti, 1985) to be the strongest predictor of L1 reading ability, sometimes in interaction with listening comprehension ability (Gough & Tunmer, 1986). Meara (1996) made the pioneering argument for bringing processing speed into L2 research on vocabulary, emphasizing the importance of word processing as a dimension of L2 lexical knowledge. Twenty years later, however, few studies in applied linguistics have looked at ways this type of knowledge could be pedagogically facilitated or created. Timed, record-keeping flash cards would appear to be an excellent candidate.

One study that has looked at the possibility of improving word recognition speed pedagogically is Cobb and Horst's (2011) study of the Nintendo game *My Word Coach*, which is a set of video games that are mainly variations of flash card learning. My Word Coach also includes timing and record keeping. Francophone learners of English who practiced retrieving both form and meaning with a focus on increasing their rate of retrievals, not only significantly improved their word recognition speed, but also their general ability in English on a series of broader measures including production.

Whether high-tech or paper, the flash card format can be adapted into a number of other game-like resources for building single-word fluency. The form side of a flash card can be used to play a game called Word Snap where learners draw cards from a stack of cards containing duplicates and quickly decide if they are the same or different. This simple game may help to develop receptive fluency for simple word-form recognition. Alternatively, the meaning side of a flash card can be replaced with other lexical information and learners can play Word Ping-Pong. This involves "batting" a word to an opponent who must return relevant lexical information such as a synonym, antonym, or a word in the same word class, as determined by a teacher. This not only gives practice in productive fluency, but can also extend flash card learning to Type 2 vocabulary knowledge.

Dictionaries

A dictionary is fundamentally a type of word list, a list of forms and associated meanings in the form of definitions or glosses. It is not, however, primarily intended as a resource for word learning; few learners will attempt to learn all the words serially in even a smallish dictionary.

Owing to its typical size, it is primarily a resource to reveal the meanings of words encountered elsewhere (e.g., in a text), or in the case of the bilingual dictionary, a resource for finding the L2 forms of words and their meanings. Many researchers view dictionaries as the most used resource by language learners (Nesi, 2014; Scholfield, 1997) and how they use them and to what effect are interesting issues that we do not know enough about. Consequently, despite occasional fears that definitions and glosses may lead to the development of superficial form-meaning connections (e.g., Cobb, 2012; Webb, 2007), a good deal of effort was invested in the 1980s and 90s into improving the quality of dictionaries for the purposes of L2 learners.

COBUILD (Sinclair, 1987) developed the "sentence definition" where, e.g., the everyday meaning of a word such as *drive* was defined not as "propel a four-wheeled vehicle forward in a controlled manner", in the classic genus and distinguishers format, but in a comprehensible, mini-scenario such as, "When you drive somewhere, you operate a car or other vehicle and control its movement and direction" (from COBUILD online, consulted May 10, 2019, at https://www.collinsdictionary.com/dictionary/english/drive).

Longman's *Learners Dictionary of Contemporary English* (LDOCE, 1987) wrote its definitions in a constrained defining vocabulary of 3,000 high-frequency words, whereby most look-up words would be defined in words more frequent than that word itself. Dictionaries of this type also provided explicit information of interest to learners rather than native speakers, such as extensive unpacking of different senses and plentiful grammatical information (exemplification, countability, frequency in speech and writing, register). Much of this information aims at supporting productive use of words in speaking or writing, thus pushing the resource towards Type 2 learning, with at least one variant of the genre designated as a "production dictionary" (the *Longman Language Activator*, 2005).

The effect of these learner dictionary modifications, however, remains unknown. Looking into these modifications was a narrow but important strand of applied linguistics research in the 1990s (e.g., Hulstijn, Hollander, & Greidanus, 1996; Knight, 1994) but since then it has fallen off. A search for "language learners use of dictionary features" on Google Scholar yields few studies more recent than those discussed in Nesi's (2014) timeline of research in this area which ends at 2012. Nesi concurs that this fall-off has occurred (personal communication, July 26, 2016) and offers two plausible reasons: "since e-dictionaries became more prevalent it is much more difficult to get a group of research participants together who are all using the same dictionary", and that "it is more difficult to find out exactly what dictionaries people are using (they often use portals or aggregators, where queries might be directed to one of a number of dictionaries)".

There are several reasons for the waning interest in dictionaries. One is that research findings on dictionary use (including Cobb, 2012), or glosses in general (Webb, 2007) suggest that because information in a gloss or definition is limited, it may result in superficial learning, and so learners may need further supplementation from exposure to language in use or other Type 2 focused resources to gain more comprehensive vocabulary knowledge. However, the potential benefits of dictionaries for Type 1 learning are considerable, and when added to those of mobile technologies, they are more so.

Willingness on the part of learners to use dictionaries is in itself a major feature of dictionaries. Lewis (1993, p. 25) attributes to Krashen the famous observation that, "When students travel, they don't carry grammar books, they carry dictionaries". Indeed a major affordance of dictionaries is their portability, and this has only increased with the widespread use of smartphones that include system-level look-up links to every word of the texts they contain. The user/learner is of course free to choose from several dictionaries on the smartphone and only some of the choices available will be learning-adapted dictionaries such as those mentioned earlier. In fact, often learners will choose bilingual dictionaries. A bilingual dictionary entry typically offers information in L1 about an L2 word. Nesi (2014) reports that the bilingual dictionary is the resource of preference for the vast majority of learners, despite the fact that monolingual dictionaries are generally believed to be superior because they do not encourage learners to believe in simplistic L1–L2 word equivalence and as mentioned have been extensively adapted to learner needs. However, one strand in the 1990s work with adaptations that received less research but was actually quite promising (as shown by Laufer & Hadar, 1997) was the bilingual*ized* dictionary, where some amount of L1 is used in the definition of the L2 word but also enough target-language exemplification and explanation to discourage simple L1–L2 word matching, and many of the smartphone dictionaries have extensively developed this feature. For example, the WordReference.com entry for *gum* bilingualized for French readers or learners is shown in in Figure 21.1. The English word

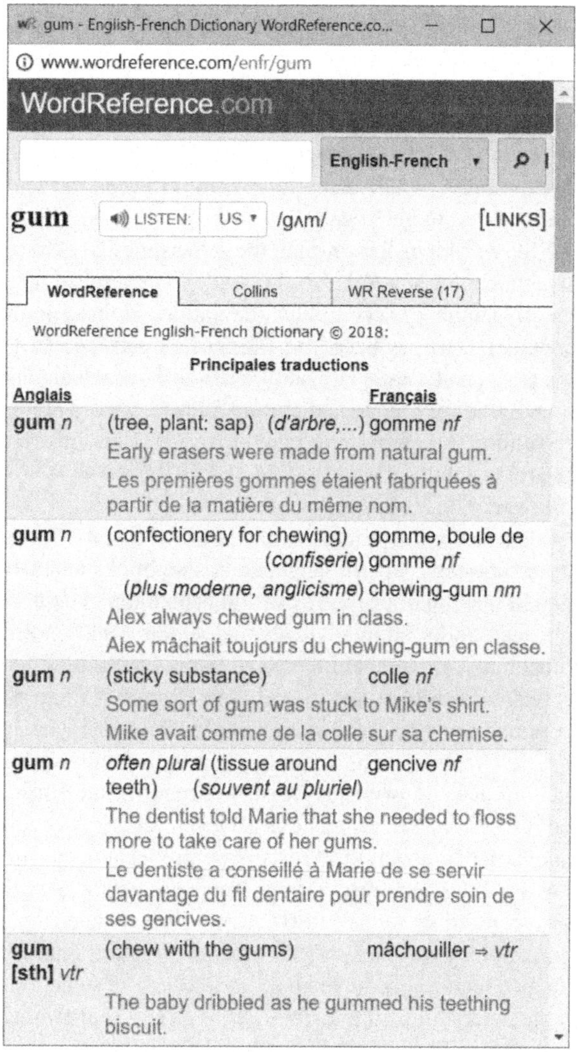

Figure 21.1   Bilingualized definition of *gum* for French readers from WordReference.com

gum is translated into several French equivalents (*gomme, gencive, colle*) and the distinctions between them explained in both English and French (*made from gum, for gluing*, etc.) such that a simplistic gum–*gomme* equivalence is unlikely to be established in the learner's inter-lexicon. Virtually all e-format dictionaries offer text-to-speech sound renditions of the word (*qua* single word) and many also offer Type 2 resources like an extensive listing of the multiword units the headword is involved in, with translation and exemplification.

This pick-up of research-indicated features by an agency of mass distribution, though probably unintentional, is nevertheless fortuitous and should be exploited. ESL and EFL instructors are well advised to encourage bilingual dictionary use early in the learning process, in line with suggestions made earlier, and then later give their learners the training and access information they will need to use a bilingualized and then monolingual dictionary.

Course Books

From a vocabulary learning perspective, there are two types of course books or textbooks. One is dedicated specifically to vocabulary learning; the other is a more general course book with a vocabulary element as one of its parts. Dedicated vocabulary expansion course books focus directly on word learning and might be called expanded word lists. The best known of these remains Barnard's (1972) four-workbook set of *Advanced English Vocabulary*, which was designed for three months of self-study in the aim of preparing learners for academic work in English, and included target vocabulary from West's GSL. Each volume put about 400 high-frequency GSL word families through the same set of five exercises (introduction, dictation, word study, encounter in a text, word completion exercise) in each unit. This type of treatment is eminently suitable for computer adaptation. In fact, Tom Cobb's *List_Learn* suite (http://lextutor.ca/list_learn) is based on Barnard's treatment. In List_Learn, several lists in addition to the GSL can be called up, and each word in each list is linked to a dictionary, a personal glossary-building routine, a dictation routine, a word recognition routine, and a meaning inference routine, all employing randomization. Barnard's pioneering work has been followed by several vocabulary book sets, including the multiple volumes of McCarthy and O'Dell's (1997 onward) *English Vocabulary In Use*.

The other type of course book is a multi-skills book with some focus on vocabulary. It should be noted that traditionally, not all language course books had a significant focus on vocabulary, but assumed that unknown words would be explained by a teacher or looked up in a dictionary. Most such works in the lexically aware post-1980s era however do claim a specific focus on vocabulary. Once again the word list is key to how vocabulary is treated in modern course books. Typically, novel lexical items from a reading passage or grammar exercise are pulled out and given focus in the form of a list, often with in-context glossing, thereby addressing Type 1 learning. These same words are often then met again later in the unit in either a matching activity or cloze passage related to the original reading passage for retrieval practice. Occasionally further lexical development is encouraged through the inclusion of morphology tables, semantic maps, or comprehension questions that require use of the target words, expanding such resources to Type 2 learning. Some course books also offer vocabulary strategy training, such as instruction on how to keep a vocabulary notebook or ways to devise mnemonics for hard-to-remember words. External (for example corpus based) word lists can also feature in course books as a source of selection for the vocabulary used and targeted in the book. For example, the *Collins COBUILD English Course* (Willis & Willis, 1988) focused on the 700 most frequent word families in Book 1 and a further 850 word families in Book 2. The benefit provided by word lists in this case was to assure exposure to the most used words of the language a sufficient number of times for learning to occur.

Texts

Texts in the target language other than course books are also potential resources for single-word learning (see Webb, this volume, on incidental vocabulary learning). Research has shown that while the Type 1 learning rate from reading an L2 text is quite slow (Horst, Cobb, & Meara, 1998), it is nonetheless possible for learners to acquire vocabulary simply from repeated encounters with a new word in comprehensible contexts (Webb & Chang, 2015) in L2 as in L1. In fact, the Type 1 learning rate from reading is quite slow in both L2 and L1, but in L1 the much larger amount of input means that L1 reading can play a greater role in the building of a lexicon, especially for the many words that appear mainly in text but rarely in speech. It is not clear whether reading can play the same role in L2 lexical development (Cobb, 2016), at least in the early stages of learning. Problems with lexical growth from L2 reading include the relatively infrequent appearance of all but the most common words (in the amount of text that learners are able to read); the dispersion of the encounters, such that words are forgotten by the time they are re-encountered; the lack of opportunities for using learned words after reading; and the general density of unknown words in texts written for native speakers. Some of these problems can be solved by having learners read graded readers, which are texts written within a controlled vocabulary. However, a problem with learning new words from reading that applies equally to graded and ungraded texts is the one raised earlier with regard to the benefits of decontextualization: when words are encountered in rich, meaningful contexts, the learner's attention can often be focused on larger linguistic units than just single words which can reduce the learning or even noticing of the single word (Mondria & Wit-de Boer, 1991).

We thus conclude that reading is not particularly rich in affordances for initial Type 1 single-word learning, for which word lists and flash cards are almost certainly faster and more efficient. However, initial word learning is not the whole of word learning, and reading has other advantages for lexical development. First, many of the weaknesses of list-based word learning can be addressed by subsequently meeting words in a variety of novel contexts, and so reading has value for developing Type 2 vocabulary knowledge. Second, reading can be used to build fluency and rapid access for words that learners already know (Type 3 learning). Nation (e.g., 2013) has argued that extensive reading of level appropriate texts should be used to increase fluency, and a study by Horst (2009) provides support for this claim. Horst found that extensive reading had a positive effect on lexical access. Third, in the later stages of learning, reading is almost certainly the only way to expand the lexicon into zones where commercially produced lists, flash cards, or textbooks are no longer of much use, especially since so much of any language's mid- to low-frequency lexicon appears primarily in text.

Audio texts are also a useful learning resource. However, they may suffer from the same drawbacks as written texts but perhaps in a more extreme form. The real-time process of listening (although this can be controlled with technology), as well as variations in pronunciation, present significant barriers to learning new L2 words (Stahl, 1990, offers evidence in L1 but few studies have investigated this issue in L2). Listening to audio texts, however, almost certainly affords fluency building for words once known. Conversation with native speakers or other learners, on the other hand, while possibly not a resource as traditionally understood, provide several benefits for single-word learning. In conversation, the other words in the context are normally known, and new words if important are typically focused on through emphasis, and ample opportunities exist for clarification and repetition (see Newton in this volume).

Teachers are well advised to encourage their learners to read and listen a good deal of level appropriate material, and provide them with opportunities and incentives to do so, but not to expect large amounts of new, Type 1 word learning to occur as a result, at least in the short term. Rather, the immediate vocabulary benefits of extensive reading and listening relate to consolidation of learning that has occurred using other resources, and gains in Type 2 and Type 3 knowledge.

Concordancers

Information technology to this point has been considered for what it can add to existing learning resources (e.g., randomization of word lists, timing and scoring of flash cards, sound renditions of dictionary words). It seems fair to say that the computational version of many of the resources we have looked at have effectively replaced the original in most learners' and teachers' thinking and have become the principal resource for vocabulary study (Ballance, 2018; Cobb, 2012). Few learners use paper word lists or flash cards any more. However, there also exist computational vocabulary learning resources that deserve discussion in their own right that only had remote precedents in the pre-computational era. One of these is a concordancer, a piece of software that taps into a text or corpus to generate all the examples that exist for any word or phrase. A concordancer thus presents a target single-word item in relation to other words in a context, and so it is primarily thought of as promoting Type 2 learning, but it also has value as a resource for Type 1 learning. Indeed single-word vocabulary learning is one of the principle and most successful uses concordancers were shown to have in Boulton and Cobb's (2017) meta-analysis of data-driven learning studies. Several studies showed that by working with multiple assembled examples of a word learners developed deep representations of word meaning.

Figure 21.2 is a concordance output for the word family *struggle* from Lextutor's English concordancer drawn from the typical school text *Call of the Wild*. The concordance shows various inflections of the item *struggle* being used in context, and reports the frequency of each. It can also report the words that typically come before and after it in the novel. Also, what cannot be seen is that the program invites several types of collocation search (for example, *struggle* with any form of *desperate* on either side).

An important Type 1 word-learning advantage that a concordance provides is the elimination of lexical dispersion. As mentioned in the discussion of learning words from texts, the time between occurrences of unknown words is a negative factor in learning from reading, but the concordance brings all the occurrences of a whole book into a single physical space and time frame. A related advantage is that a concordance creates an opportunity for constructing a complex meaning representation. It was mentioned earlier that while learners are entitled to start building their lexicons through L1 translation equivalents, this strategy will rarely suffice as learning proceeds.

Cobb (1997) showed that concordance lines are more comprehensible to learners than dictionary definitions and that the meanings inferred from multiple examples were more durable, flexible, and transferable to novel contexts than meanings inferred from single contexts or gleaned from bilingual dictionaries. A possible reason for this could be that by providing several examples, concordancers increase the potential that at least one or two examples will be comprehensible such that an informed inference can be made. Moreover,

Figure 21.2 Concordance for word family *struggle* from a typical school text

when several examples are partially comprehensible, it may be that some sense of a word's range of meanings becomes apparent. Another reason that concordance lines may lead to durable learning of form and meaning is that a concordancer appears to provide a kind of automatized simplification of the ambient contexts that words are being inferred from. Ballance and Coxhead (under review) found that the average lexical difficulty of the examples assembled by a concordancer is considerably lower than the average level of the corpus or texts it is drawn from, such that the technology enables learners to work with texts that are beyond their current vocabulary level. Technology can also amplify this useful feature of concordances. *Sketch Engine for Language Learning* (SKEL; at https://skell.sketchengine. co.uk/run.cgi/skell) uses algorithms to select the easiest example sentences in its corpus and present these at the top of the output (Kilgarriff, Marcowitz, Smith, & Thomas, 2015). Similarly, Lextutor's concordancer allows output to be sorted by average VP (or VocabProfile, i.e., frequency) of the words surrounding the keyword, with more comprehensible contexts at the top. Figure 21.3 shows examples of *diagnose* ranging from easy (averaging level 1 or most frequent 1,000 words) to difficult (level 4) from a corpus of Dr. House television scripts (available from www.springfieldspringfield.co.uk/ under a "fair use" agreement).

Thus for single-word learning of the Type 1 variety, the concordancer may function as a kind of reading assistant, making up for some of the drawbacks of natural text: the elimination of natural amounts of lexical dispersion and the provision of good conditions for inferring complex word meanings. It is thus natural that concordance programs have been teamed with texts through click-on interfaces. Of course, by providing ready access to concentrated exemplification, it can also provide a wealth of information about how a word is used, facilitating Type 2 learning via inductive analysis in a technique generally known as data-driven learning (see Boulton & Cobb, 2017 for more on this topic).

Concordance extract for *family* **DIAGNOSE** With <u>no associate</u> on EITHER side sorted wds **level** of key

```
001. ☐  way. Unless we know which ones are which, I can't DIAGNOSE you. I'll take any other tests or treatme [1.00]
002. ☐  conds later I was blind! How is that difficult to DIAGNOSE? Who the hell knows what else you guys do [1.00]
003. ☐  reatened to sue us is now heading home completely UNDIAGNOSED. He'll soon be on his way back. He's s [1.00]
004. ☐    lactulose. If this thing kills him before we can DIAGNOSE, it won't be fun anymore. Okay. You're go [1.00]
005. ☐  versation's gonna take twice as long. Yes. He was DIAGNOSED six months ago. He do a lot of cooking? [1.00]
101. ☐   is gonna cause neurological symptoms. - We can't DIAGNOSE that without a biopsy. - Yes, we can. We  [2.00]
102. ☐  No, no. Nothing. - Any relatives who've ever been DIAGNOSED with lupus? I don't even know what that  [2.00]
103. ☐  p a diagnosis. You don't seem that upset by it. I DIAGNOSED a guy with adenocarcinoma three months a [2.07]
104. ☐  and mental confusion. Ah, bad sushi is so hard to DIAGNOSE. You're being childish. Look, if his case [2.08]
119. ☐   bilirubin's off the charts. Even fetuses lie. We DIAGNOSED a lower urinary tract obstruction becaus [3.67]
121. ☐  be something to it? Cuddy feels guilty about not DIAGNOSING psittacosis any earlier? I think so. Th [4.15]
122. ☐  ad. It's just slow. Damaged his ulnar nerves. Was MISDIAGNOSED as carpal tunnel. Never trust doctors [4.17]
```

Figure 21.3 Concordance for word family *diagnose* with more comprehensible contexts first

Future Directions

To this point we have argued for the importance of single-word learning; situated this type of learning within three standard types of vocabulary knowledge (form-meaning relationships, ability to use words in context, and speed of access to both these types of knowledge) and argued that resources for single-word learning traditionally focus on the first and third of these. A number of what-to-use-when suggestions for language teachers seeking single-word learning resources for their students can be taken away from the foregoing discussion.

The first takeaway from this chapter is that we should be aware which of the three general types of vocabulary knowledge we are targeting, what resources can be expected to promote that knowledge, and which stage of the learning process the resource mainly applies to. Single-word resources for building form-meaning links will typically help learners amass receptive vocabulary knowledge initially, but are unlikely in themselves to do much for production. (We have all seen or been the teacher that introduces learners to a list of words and then sees them struggle to use the words in sentences.) Resources focused on knowledge of how words are used will help learners with aspects of production, like collocation and word order, but may assume form-meaning knowledge is already in place when it may not be. (We have all seen or been the teacher that introduces learners to grammar patterns composed of words they have never seen before.) Fluency resources will give practice in accessing form-meaning links but are unlikely to do much to create these links in the first place. (We have all seen or been the teacher that launches a fluency game such as Word Snap using words that learners have never seen.) Thinking about resources in terms of the three types framework can help us to be aware of the assumptions in our choices.

A complementary set of suggestions can be built from what was said earlier about the typical benefits of particular single-word resources. If laying an initial lexical base is the goal (as Meara 1995 convincingly argued that it should be), then some sort of list-based approach (e.g., L1–L2 flash cards) with the strong affordances of coverage and completeness are more suitable than reading or fluency building activities, which are better for other purposes. Similarly, instruction in the use of a concordancer as a means of deepening knowledge of L2 meanings would not be appropriate for this goal. On the other hand, for learners who already have basic form-meaning links for the most frequent (say 3,000) word families, resources that build fluency (reading), deepen word meanings (monolingual or bilingualized dictionary), or provide opportunities for contextual inference (reading or concordancer) are more appropriate than flash cards or word lists.

It should be remembered that any what-to-use-when suggestions are about proportions not absolutes. Learners should not be asked to study flash cards for six months before they are allowed to read a text. As Nation (2007) has convincingly argued, every language course at any level should have some representation from all "four strands". These are meaning focused input (reading, listening), meaning-focused output (speaking, writing), language-focused learning (grammar, vocabulary, multiword units), and fluency development (lexical access, reading speed, fluent production). The resources discussed in this chapter can be used for learning words in all strands. For example, flash cards might be used initially to develop receptive knowledge of form and meaning of 20 target words (language focused learning). This might be followed up by having students encountering these words in a written text (meaning-focused input) and then writing about what they have read (meaning-focused output). They could then do a fluency development activity such as playing Word Snap or doing a timed reading of a text recycling the same words.

Further Reading

Ballance, O. J. (2018). Technology to teach vocabulary. In J. I. Liontas (Ed.), *The TESOL encyclopedia of English language teaching*. Hoboken, NJ: Wiley.

This article has a main focus on how technology can support vocabulary study, whether it be the study of single-word items or multiword items. It explores the affordances of technology in relation to vocabulary learning mechanisms such as recall, noticing, and generative use.

Cobb, T. (2012). Technology and learning vocabulary. In C. A. Chapelle (Ed.), *The Encyclopedia of Applied Linguistics*. Hoboken, NJ: Wiley.

This article also discusses technology and vocabulary study, but it illustrates general vocabulary learning principles and the affordances of technology in relation to a particular suite of vocabulary learning resources: Compleat Lexical Tutor (www.lextutor.ca/).

Nation, I. S. P. (2013). *Learning Vocabulary in another Language* (2nd ed.). Cambridge, UK: Cambridge University Press.

This authoritative book length treatment of L2 vocabulary acquisition not only provides an insightful review of the main findings in the field but also provides summaries of many resources for learning single-word items as well as links to the resources.

Nesi, H. (2014). Dictionary use by English language learners. *Language Teaching*, *47*(1), 38–55.

Because of the status of dictionaries as a resource for learning single-word items, this summary of the main research findings on second language dictionary use highlights some fundamental pedagogical issues related to learning single-word items.

Related Topics

Factors affecting the learning of single-word items, learning single-word items vs. multiword items, strategies for learning single-word items, word lists, learning words through flash cards and word cards, evaluating exercises for learning vocabulary, key issues in teaching single-word items

References

Ballance, O. J. (2018). Technology to teach vocabulary. In J. I. Liontas (Ed.), *The TESOL encyclopedia of English language teaching*. Hoboken, NJ: Wiley. https://doi.org/10.1002/9781118784235.eelt0920

Ballance, O. J., & Coxhead, A. (under review). How much vocabulary is needed to use a concordance? *International Journal of Corpus Linguistics*.

Barnard, H. (1972). *Advanced English vocabulary* (4 vols.). Rowley, MA: Newbury House.

Beretta, A., Fiorentino, R., & Poeppel, D. (2005). The effects of homonymy and polysemy on lexical access: An MEG study. *Cognitive Brain Research*, *24*, 57–65.

Bogaards, P. (2001). Lexical units and the learning of foreign language vocabulary. *Studies in Second Language Acquisition, 23*(3), 321–343.

Boulton, A., & Cobb, T. (2017). Corpus use in language learning: A meta-analysis. *Language Learning, 67*(2), 348–393.

Cobb, T. (1997). Is there any measurable learning from hands-on concordancing? *System, 25*(3), 301–315.

Cobb, T. (2012). Technology and learning vocabulary. In C. A. Chapelle (Ed.), *The encyclopedia of applied linguistics*. Hoboken, NJ: Wiley.

Cobb, T. (2016). Numbers or numerology? A response to Nation (2014) & McQuillan (2016). *Reading in a Foreign Language, 28*(2), 299–304.

Cobb, T., & Horst, M. (2011). Does Word Coach coach words? *CALICO Journal, 28*(3), 639–661. https://doi.org/10.11139/cj.28.3.639–661

Coxhead, A. (2000). A new academic word list. *TESOL Quarterly, 34*(2), 213–238. https://doi.org/10.2307/3587951

Elgort, I. (2011). Deliberate learning and vocabulary acquisition in a second language. *Language Learning, 61*(2), 367–413.

Gough, P. B., & Tunmer, W. E. (1986). Decoding, reading, and reading disability. *Remedial & Special Education, 7*, 6–10.

Granger, S. (1993). Cognates: An aid or a barrier to successful L2 vocabulary development? *ITL – International Journal of Applied Linguistics, 99*(1), 43–56.

Hanks, P. (2013). *Lexical analysis: Norms and exploitations*. Cambridge, MA: MIT Press.

Henriksen, B. (1999). Three dimensions of vocabulary development. *Studies in Second Language Acquisition, 21*(2), 303–317. https://doi.org/10.1017/S0272263199002089

Horst, M. (2009). Developing definitional vocabulary knowledge and lexical access speed through extensive reading. In Z. Han & N. Anderson (Eds.), *Second language reading research and instruction: Crossing the boundaries* (pp. 40–63). Ann Arbor, MI: University of Michigan Press.

Horst, M., Cobb, T., & Meara, P. (1998). Beyond a Clockwork Orange: Acquiring second-language vocabulary through reading. *Reading in a Foreign Language, 11*, 207–223.

Hulstijn, J., Hollander, M., & Greidanus, T. (1996). Incidental vocabulary learning by advanced foreign language students: The influence of marginal glosses, dictionary use, and reoccurrence of unknown words. *Modern Language Journal, 80*(3), 327–339. https://doi.org/10.1111/j.1540-4781.1996.tb01614.x

Kellerman, E. (1986). An eye for an eye: Crosslinguistic constraints on the development of the L2 lexicon. In E. Kellerman & M. Sharwood-Smith (Eds.), *Cross-linguistic influences in second language acquisition*. Oxford, UK: Pergamon.

Kilgarriff, A. (2015). How many words are there? In J. R. Taylor (Ed.), *The Oxford handbook of the word* (pp. 29–36). Oxford, UK: Oxford University Press.

Kilgarriff, A., Marcowitz, F., Smith, S., & Thomas, J. (2015). Corpora and language learning with the Sketch Engine and SKELL. *Revue Française de Linguistique Appliquée, 20*(1), 61–80.

Knight, S. (1994). Dictionary use while reading: The effects on comprehension and vocabulary acquisition for students of different verbal abilities. *Modern Language Review, 78*(3), 285–299. https://doi.org/10.1111/j.1540-4781.1994.tb02043.

Krashen, S. D. (1989). We acquire vocabulary and spelling by reading: Additional evidence for the input hypothesis. *Modern Language Journal, 73*, 440–463.

Laufer, B. (1998). The development of passive and active vocabulary in a second language: Same or different? *Applied Linguistics, 19*, 255–271.

Laufer, B., & Goldstein, Z. (2004). Testing vocabulary knowledge: Size, strength, & computer adaptiveness. *Language Learning, 54*(3), 399–436.

Laufer, B., & Hadar, L. (1997). Assessing the effectiveness of monolingual, bilingual, and "bilingualised" dictionaries in the comprehension and production of new words. *Modern Language Journal, 81*(2), 189–196.

Lewis, M. (1993). *The lexical approach: The state of ELT and a way forward*. Hove, UK: Language Teaching Publications.

Longman dictionary of contemporary English. (1987). Harlow, UK: Pearson Education.

Longman language activator. (2005). Harlow, UK: Pearson Education.

McCarthy, M., & O'Dell, F. (1997). *English vocabulary in use: Upper intermediate.* Cambridge, UK: Cambridge University Press.

Meara, P. (1995). The importance of an early emphasis on L2 vocabulary. *The Language Teacher, 19*(2), 8–11.

Meara, P. (1996). The dimensions of lexical competence. In G. Brown, K. Malmkjaer, & J. Williams (Eds.), *Performance and competence in second language acquisition* (pp. 35–53). Cambridge, UK: Cambridge University Press.

Mondria, J. A., & Wit-de Boer, M. (1991). The effects of contextual richness on the guessability and retention of words in a foreign language. *Applied Linguistics, 12*(3), 249–267.

Murphy, M. L. (2010). *Lexical meaning.* Cambridge, UK: Cambridge University Press.

Nation, I. S. P. (2006). *The frequency ordered 1,000 word family lists based on the British National Corpus.* https://www.victoria.ac.nz/lals/about/staff/paul-nation#vocab-lists.

Nation, I. S. P. (2007). The four strands. *Innovation in Language Learning & Teaching, 1*(1), 1–12.

Nation, I. S. P. (2013). *Learning vocabulary in another Language* (2nd ed.). Cambridge, UK: Cambridge University Press.

Nation, I. S. P. (2016). *Making and using word lists for language learning and testing.* Amsterdam: John Benjamins.

Nesi, H. (2014). Dictionary use by English language learners. *Language Teaching, 47*(01), 38–55.

Perfetti, C. (1985). *Reading ability.* New York, NY: Basic Books.

Ringbom, H. (2007). The importance of cross-linguistic similarities. *JALT Journal, 31*(9), 3–7.

Ruhl, C. (1989). *On monosemy: A study in linguistic semantics.* Albany, NY: University of New York Press.

Schmitt, N. (2010). *Researching vocabulary: A vocabulary research manual.* Basingstoke, UK; New York, NY: Palgrave Macmillan.

Scholfield, P. (1997). Vocabulary reference works in foreign language learning. In N. Schmitt & M. McCarthy (Eds.), *Vocabulary: Description, acquisition & pedagogy* (pp. 279–302). Cambridge, UK: Cambridge University Press.

Sinclair, J. M. (2010). Defining the definiendum. In G.-M. De Schryver (Ed.), *A way with words: Recent advances in lexical theory and analysis* (pp. 37–47). Kampala, Uganda: Menha.

Sinclair, J. S. (1987). *Collins COBUILD English language dictionary.* London, UK: Harper Collins Publishers.

Stahl, S. (1990). *Learning meaning vocabulary through listening: A sixth-grade replication.* Paper presented at the Annual Meeting of the National Reading Conference, 40th, Miami, FL, November 27–December 1, 1990.

Swan, M. (1997). The influence of the mother tongue on second language vocabulary. In N. Schmitt & M. McCarthy (Eds.), *Vocabulary: Description, acquisition & pedagogy* (pp. 156–180). Cambridge, UK: Cambridge University Press.

Webb, S. (2007). Learning word pairs and glossed sentences: The effects of a single context on vocabulary knowledge. *Language Teaching Research, 11*(1), 63–81. https://doi.org/10.1177/1362168806072463

Webb, S. (2009). The effects of receptive and productive learning of word pairs on vocabulary knowledge. *RELC Journal, 40*(3), 360–376. https://doi.org/10.1177/0033688209343854

Webb, S., & Chang, A. C.-S. (2015). Second language vocabulary learning through extensive reading with audio support: How do frequency and distribution of occurrence affect learning? *Language Teaching Research, 19*(6), 667–686. https://doi.org/10.1177/1362168814559800

West, M. (1953). *A general service list of English words.* London, UK: Longman.

White, J., & Horst, J. (2011). Cognate awareness -raising in late childhood: Teachable and useful. *Language Awareness, 21*(1–2), 181–196. https://doi.org/10.1080/09658416.2011.639885

Willis, J., & Willis, D. (1988). *COBUILD English course* (3 vols.). London, UK: Collins.

Wray, A. (2015). Why are we so sure we know what a word is? In J. R. Taylor (Ed.), *The Oxford handbook of the word* (pp. 725–750). Oxford, UK: Oxford University Press.

22

Resources for Learning Multiword Items

Fanny Meunier

Introduction

Some of the preceding sections in the volume have addressed multiword items (MWI) from various angles: defining (types of) MWI (see Wood, this volume); factors affecting the learning of MWI (see Boers, this volume); learning single-word items vs. multiword items (see Pellicer-Sánchez, this volume); and processing single-word and multiword items (see Conklin, this volume). The present chapter specifically targets resources for learning MWI. However, before discussing such resources in more detail, I will briefly comment on the two views of "learning" that have been adopted to frame this section: the learning-for-use perspective (Edelson, 2001) and the Technological Pedagogical Content Knowledge (TPACK) model (Mishra & Koehler, 2006). It should be stressed that I have deliberately chosen to focus on learning in instructed settings as I consider teachers/instructors as key actors in presenting learners with useful resources to foster the acquisition and use of MWI. I would also like to add that while MWI is the preferred term throughout the volume, I may at times use the terms multiword units, phrasemes (phraseology), or formulae (formulaic language) as synonyms.

I have adopted the learning for use perspective, initially developed by Edelson in 2001, as it supports "the design of learning activities that achieve both content and process learning" (2001, p. 356). While Edelson's focus was on technology-supported science teaching, his approach can easily be applied to language learning and teaching. Learning-for-use rejects memorization, which often leads to "inert knowledge" that learners/users can often not retrieve when they most need it, and supports (the design of) learning activities aiming at both content and process learning. Inert knowledge was first referred to in 1929 by Whitehead, a late 19th to early 20th-century English mathematician and philosopher. He was one of the first proponents of the process philosophy school and explained that inert knowledge is information/facts/knowledge that someone can express but not use in real situations. Typical examples of inert knowledge in language learning would be recently studied vocabulary items available for a specific test but no longer accessible in a real communicative situation, or the correct explicit wording of a grammar rule which is later not applied in a context where it would clearly be required. The four key tenets of the learning-for-use model (Edelson, 2001, p. 357) are:

- Learning takes place through the construction and modification of knowledge structures.
- Knowledge construction is a goal-directed process that is guided by a combination of conscious and unconscious understanding of goals.
- The circumstances in which knowledge is constructed and subsequently used determine its accessibility for future use.
- Knowledge must be constructed in a form that supports use before it can be applied.

Such tenets very nicely tie in with current communicative and usage-based approaches to language learning in general, and to the learning of MWI in particular. Usage-based analyses of language (be it in corpus linguistics, cognitive linguistics, or psycholinguistics) have provided ample evidence of the highly formulaic nature of language. As stated by Ellis, Römer, and Brook O'Donnell (2016, p. 45) a number of psychological factors "conspire in the acquisition and use of any linguistic construction", both in first (L1) language acquisition or in the acquisition of additional languages (L2, L3, etc.). MWI are ubiquitous linguistic constructions and have been shown to be subjected to a number of interconnected determinants of learning that include (1) frequency effects; (2) categorization, meaning, and prototypes; (3) contingency (the association of forms and meanings); (4) salience; and (5) various forms of learning (implicit vs. explicit). See for instance Harris, Murphy, and Rehder (2008), Smith (2014), Ellis (2017) and Siyanova-Chanturia and Pellicer-Sánchez (2019) for lengthier explanations on such determinants of learning. Native speakers implicitly (unconsciously) acquire and use MWI thanks to the preceding cited determinants of learning. Non-native speakers, in contrast, while also being sensitive to statistical patterns of use, are subject to cross-linguistic influence interfering in the process. Adopting a foreign language learning perspective, Meunier (2012, p. 111) suggests:

- Language as a whole is highly conventional.
- Even when alternative combinations exist only one is usually preferred.
- Rules and formalisms are often of little help in the acquisition of such combinations, and may be considered to increase teaching and learning difficulty.

Frequency information, prototypes, and form-meaning mappings are less directly accessible to non-native speakers than to native speakers. This view, also shared by Liu, Liu, Yu, Li, and Wen (2014, p. 682), led the authors to state that "EFL learners heavily depend on technology for learning authentic English", precisely because technology can help learners access, among other things, frequency information or form-meaning mappings.

The second view of language that has been adopted in this part of the volume is the Technological Pedagogical Content Knowledge model. It is the second view on learning that will be used as a structuring device in this chapter. Mishra and Koehler's (2006) and Koehler and Mishra's (2008) Technological Pedagogical Content Knowledge model nicely complements the usage-based, learning-for-use model, and technological aspects mentioned in the previous paragraph. While the usage-based view concerns language as such and learning-for-use is more learner centered, the Technological Pedagogical Content Knowledge model can be said to be teacher oriented. As the use of technology can enhance foreign language teaching and learning, Liu et al. (2014, p. 683) argue that "EFL teachers need to 'technologize' their professional knowledge". In that respect, Koehler and Mishra's (2008) Technological

Pedagogical Content Knowledge model encompasses three main types of knowledge, as explained by Koehler et al. (2013, pp. 14–16) and summarized as follows:

- Content knowledge (CK) is the teachers' knowledge about the subject matter to be learned or taught. In an L2 learning context, it is the knowledge of the target language itself.
- Pedagogical knowledge (PK) is teachers' knowledge about the appropriate and up-to-date processes and practices or methods of teaching and learning (including the knowledge of overall educational purposes, values, and aims, the understanding of how students learn. For example, in L2 vocabulary learning this would involve knowledge of theoretical and applied perspectives on Second Language Acquisition, general classroom management skills, lesson planning capacities, and student assessment skills).
- Technological knowledge (TK), constantly in flux and going beyond traditional computer literacy, includes an in-depth understanding of information technology which enables the teacher not only to apply technology productively but also to be able to assess whether information technology can assist or impede the achievement of a learning goal.

These three types of knowledge can interact in dyadic or triadic ways. Technology and content knowledge (TCK) can for instance be strongly intertwined. Koehler et al. explain that "progress in fields as diverse as medicine, history, archeology, and physics have coincided with the development of new technologies that afford the representation and manipulation of data in new and fruitful ways" (2013, pp. 15–16). They list the discovery of X-rays in medicine or the technique of carbon-14 dating in archeology. Another typical dyadic interaction is that between technological and pedagogical Knowledge (TPK). This includes an understanding of "how teaching and learning can change when particular technologies are used in particular ways" (ibid). As will be explained in the next section, (learner) corpus research and its associated technologies and tools have been instrumental in L2 learning. They have directly contributed to technology and content knowledge by offering "a new way of thinking about language" (Leech, 1992, p. 106) but also to technology and pedagogical knowledge as the technological affordances of (learner) corpus research have made it possible to revisit the pedagogical approaches used in foreign language learning.

As for the all-encompassing triadic Technological Pedagogical Content Knowledge model, it is defined as "an understanding that emerges from interactions among content, pedagogy, and technology knowledge" (Koehler et al., 2013, p. 16). In the coming sections the focus will thus be on technological resources that can help language learners/users/teachers better understand SLA processes and access information such as frequency, form and meaning pairing, and "situated use" of MWI so as to enhance the construction and modification of language knowledge structures and foster subsequent use of MWI. Situated use (Norén & Linell, 2007, p. 390) entails that "(a) theory of meaning potentials assumes that parts of a word's meaning are evoked, activated or materialized, foregrounded or backgrounded, in different ways in the different contexts, in which it is exploited". Situated use is typically something that corpora can give plenty of access to, as will be explained in the next section.

Critical Issues and Topics

Technical and Content Knowledge: Identifying MWI – (Learner) Corpus Research as a Window on Situated Use

Viana, Zyngier, and Barnbrook (2011) explain that the partnership between the collection and analysis of corpora containing hundreds of millions of words enabled scholars "to expect answers to questions that it would have been impracticable to ask a generation ago" (Crystal, 2003, p. 447, in Viana et al., 2011, p. 133). This "corpus revolution", as Rundell and Stock (1992) call it, made it possible to describe "the way people actually use words when they communicate with one another" (Rundell, 2008, p. 23). The centrality of context, as postulated in situated language use (Norén & Linell, 2007, p. 390), has thus found a very concrete embodiment in corpus linguistics, and particularly so when it comes to MWI. In a terminological discussion of the notions of genres, registers, text types, domains, and styles, Lee (2001, p. 38) explains that "it is impossible to make many useful generalizations about 'the English language' or 'general English' since these are abstract constructions. Instead, it is far easier and theoretically more sound to talk about the language of different genres of text, or the language(s) used in different domains, or the different types of register available in a language, and so forth". Corpora (be they native or learner corpora) and corpus tools have played a particularly significant role in "the increased focus on phraseological research" (Oksefjell Ebeling & Hasselgård, 2015, p. 207) and it is now possible to (semi)-automatically retrieve MWI in all sorts of text types and genres. Those MWI include lexical bundles (e.g., Biber, Conrad, & Cortes, 2004), n-grams (e.g., Stubbs, 2009), collocations (e.g., Sinclair, 1991), collostructions (e.g., Stefanowitsch & Gries, 2003), or constructions of various levels and types (Ellis et al., 2016, p. 17) (see also Wood in this volume for more details on the different types of MWI).

Leaving aside what Granger (2009b, p. 63) calls the "terminological chaos that besets theoretical phraseological studies", it can be stated that corpus research has helped uncover target like MWI in native corpora while learner corpus research has helped "teachers identify the lexical, grammatical and discourse features that differentiate learners' production from the targeted norm" (Granger, 2009a, p. 19). Adopting a formulaic approach to L2 learning and teaching has been shown to be relevant for three main reasons (Meunier, 2012, p. 112): (1) formulaicity is ubiquitous in language; (2) formulaic language use has been shown to be a marker of proficiency in an L2; and (3) studies have demonstrated that L2 language learners find formulaicity particularly challenging as it is impossible for them to use the innate native intuition usually associated with formulaic language use.

Illustrations: Concrete Impact of (Learner) Corpus Research on the Production of Learning Materials of Various Types

Some publishers are now using corpus data to inform textbook writing. Meunier (2012) gives concrete examples of corpus-informed textbooks and discusses the advantages and limitations of such materials, with a specific focus on MWI. Some textbooks now include sections such as collocations, metaphors, idioms, phrasal verbs, frequent lexical chunks or communicative phrasemes in conversational English. Mishan and Timmis (2015) devote a whole chapter of their *Materials Development for TESOL* volume to corpus-informed materials for teaching vocabulary and grammar. They argue for the benefit of using corpora as resources. Farr (2015) also devotes a whole section of her book to corpus-based materials, discussing concepts, findings, and literature on the topic. Farr (2015) also proposes tasks to explore corpora (see for instance Task 3.9 on p. 41) and offers a list of corpus-based reference books, corpus-informed course books, and skills books in an appendix. Meyer (2017) explores what makes corpus-informed materials different and why teachers and learners should use them. In her blog post, she explains what a corpus is and how it can be helpful in answering questions like "What are the most frequent words and phrases in English?" or "How often do people use idiomatic expressions and why?" She also explains how the analysis of learner corpora can help teachers prioritize what to focus on in their teaching time. She not only stresses the fact that corpora lend themselves particularly well to the study of collocation (and gives concrete examples) but she also insists on the importance of developing learners' awareness and familiarity with MWI from the early stages of language acquisition onwards (for more details, see www.cambridge.org/elt/blog/2017/04/24/corpus-informed-materials/).

Besides textbooks, some online resources provide learners and teachers with information on MWI. Some of these resources are simply lists of collocations, as is the case of the academic collocation list available in .pdf or .xls formats at https://pearsonpte.com/wp-content/uploads/2014/07/AcademicCollocationList.pdf, which contains over 2,400 academic collocations. For instance the 2,241st most frequent combination is *(be) strongly correlated (with)*, 2,242nd is *strongly disagree*, and 2,243rd is *(be) strongly influenced (by)*.

As indicated on the website (https://pearsonpte.com/organizations/researchers/academic-collocation-list/), the academic collocation list contains the 2,469 most frequent and pedagogically relevant lexical collocations in written academic English and was compiled from the written curricular component of the Pearson International Corpus of Academic English (PICAE) comprising over 25 million words. The development involved four stages: a computational analysis of the corpus, the refinement of the data-driven list based on quantitative and qualitative parameters, an expert review, and finally a systematization of the results presented. Expert judgment was used to ensure pedagogical relevance and usability of the results (cross-disciplinary collocations were for instance favored). As explained by the authors of the list, it can help learners increase their collocational competence but can also support EAP teachers in their lesson planning.

While the .xls format of the list allows for filtering and sorting, such lists remain rather static in format and may not be ideal in a learning-for-use perspective. Other resources offer a more flexible approach. One such free resource is SkELL, which stands for Sketch Engine for Language Learning (see Baisa and Suchomel (2014) for a lengthier discussion of the tool). As indicated on the SkELL website (see www.sketchengine.co.uk/skell/), it is a simple tool for students and teachers of English that can be used to easily check how a particular phrase or a word is used by real speakers of English. Behind the user-friendly interface in which the user simply keys in a search word (see http://skell.sketchengine.co.uk/run.cgi/skell), the tool searches a corpus of more than one billion words in English (news, scientific papers, Wikipedia articles, fiction books, web pages, and blogs). If the user clicks on Wordsketch, a list of words which occur frequently together with the searched word appears, and those words are sorted into various categories. A Wordsketch output of a search for the keyword *food* (with context button on) will provide users with categories such as "verb with food as object" (as in *eat/cook/prepare/consume/grow* food), with "adjectives with food" (as in *food was delicious, food is plentiful, foods rich in . . .*), or with "nouns modified by food" (as in *food supply, food allergies, food poisoning, food processor*).

If the user wants more context, clicking on the desired word combination (e.g., *food allergies*) generates example sentences of the MWI selected found in corpora, as for instance:

- *The role of **food allergy** is controversial.*
- ***Food allergies** seem far less common in underdeveloped countries.*
- ***Food allergies** are another major health concern with genetically engineered foods.*

As the search engine uses fuzzy matching techniques and works with lemmatized, part-of-speech tagged, and partially parsed corpora, both singular and plural forms of *food allergy* are provided. If the *food + serve* MWI had been selected, the user would have been provided with examples of active and passive sentences with the verb in potentially different forms, such as in the following examples also extracted from SkELL:

- *An excellent restaurant **serving** traditional **food** and wine.*
- *The delicious food served wad a daily feast.*
- ***Food** is **served** in small baskets.*
- ***Food** was beautifully **served**.*

A tool like SkELL (with its rather intuitive interface) may be used by all types of learners while they are writing to help them find, for instance, frequent collocations (delicious, excellent, fantastic food). The word sketch tab gives a quick overview of frequent combinations. As for the examples tab, it offers up to 40 example sentences for each search, which allows slightly more advanced users to spot patterns of use. In the preceding examples, *food + serve* appears more often in passive constructions of the type *food is served* than in active constructions (*someone serves food*). Being able to spot patterns of use requires however, a slightly more complex competence needing at least some basic training (see the next section for a discussion of teacher-led DDL activities).

The SkELL interface is also available for languages other than English (at the time of writing, Russian and Czech). If (more advanced) users want to work on other languages, or use more complex search criteria they can use Sketch Engine, which is not freely available but which offers more options (see www.sketchengine.co.uk/), as it explores how language works by using complex algorithms to "analyse authentic texts of billions of words (text corpora) to identify instantly what is typical in language and what is rare, unusual or emerging usage. . . . [It] is used by linguists, lexicographers, translators, students and teachers . . . [and] contains 400 ready-to-use corpora in 90+ languages, each having a size of up to 20 billion words to provide a truly representative sample of language".

Another example of an online tool that allows users to highlight MWI in a text is IDIOM Search (see http://idiomsearch.lsti.ucl.ac.be/). The online interface allows users to test a new algorithm for extracting the most set phrases from a text ranging from simple collocations and proper nouns (named entities) to idioms and proverbs (for the scientific background of the IDIOM Search project, see Colson, 2016). The beta version is available for Chinese, French, Spanish, and English, and the corpora used for the extraction of phrases are web corpora of about 200 million tokens. The noise in the output is an estimated 10%, varying from one language to another. Users have to select their language, copy paste the text to analyze, and the results page displays the set phrases identified in the input text. Colors correspond to the degree of fixedness and range from light shading (partly fixed) to dark shading (very fixed) combined with information on frequency (see Figure 22.1). Two ratios are also provided: a PW ratio corresponding to the number of phrases divided by the number of tokens, and a PT ratio which corresponds to the percentage of word tokens that are in the shaded zones. For example, a PT ratio of 0.42 indicates that 58% of the words are not part of a set phrase. Figure 22.1 presents the result of the query for the first three paragraphs of *Alice in Wonderland* (by Lewis Carroll in 1865).

While SkELL can potentially be used by learners as a reference tool to find collocations while they are writing a text for instance, IDIOM Search is more of a diagnostic tool as it somehow assesses the idiomaticity of a text. A preliminary study (Meunier & Bulon, forthcoming) shows that IDIOM Search can be useful is assessing the phraseological competence of lower to upper intermediate learners of English and that the PT ratio provided can help

IDIOM Search Results

Alice was beginning to get very tired of sitting by her sister on the river bank, and of having nothing to do. Once or twice she looked into the book her sister was reading, but it had no pictures or conversations in it. "What is the use of a book without pictures or conversations?", thought Alice. So she was considering (as well as she could, because the hot day made her feel very sleepy and stupid), whether the pleasure of making a daisy chain would be worth the trouble of getting up and picking the daisies. Suddenly a white rabbit with pink eyes ran close by her. There was nothing so very remarkable in that, nor did Alice think it very much out of the way to hear the rabbit say to itself " Oh dear! Oh dear! I shall be too late! "(When she thought about it afterward, it occurred to her she ought to have wondered about this, but at that the time it all seemed quite natural). But when the rabbit actually took a watch out of its pocket, and looked at it, Alice realised she had never before seen a rabbit with either pocket, or a watch to take out of it. She ran across the field after the rabbit, and was just in time to see it pop down a large rabbit hole under the hedge.

PARTLY FIXED: 20 FIXED: 13 VERY FIXED: 6 TOTAL: 39 WORDS: 231 PW RATIO: 0.17 PT RATIO: 0.49

LEGEND

| | PARTLY FIXED AND FREQUENT: grammatical pattern, routine, collocation | | FIXED AND FREQUENT: formula, collocation, idiom | | VERY FIXED AND FREQUENT: idiom, compound term |
| | PARTLY FIXED AND NOT FREQUENT: collocation, formula | | FIXED AND NOT FREQUENT: collocation, idiom | | VERY FIXED AND NOT FREQUENT: idiom, compound term, proverb |

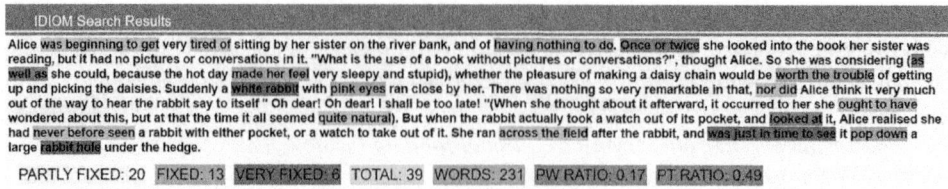

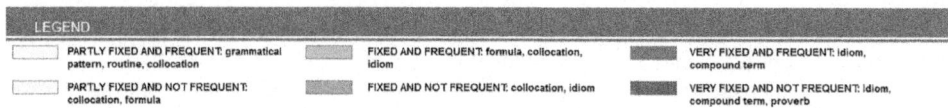

Figure 22.1   IDIOM Search results output

Source: Illustration reproduced with permission of J.P. Colson

discriminate between levels of proficiency (0.66 correlation, with a rise up to 0.87 when a few other complexity measures are added). Teachers and learners could for instance use IDIOM Search to get a first impression of the types and proportion of MWI in their texts, and compare them to similar text types produced by other learners or by native speakers with a view of using the information presented in the comparison to adapt or edit their text.

The examples just listed are only some of the available tools that illustrate how (Learner) Corpus Research ((L)CR) has led to a new perception and representation of language in general, and of MWI in particular. Such examples account for the teaching content knowledge part of the Technological Pedagogical Content Knowledge model of MWI. One drawback, however, is that such tools may sometimes be used in a way that may lead to inert knowledge (as mentioned in the first section of the chapter) as the focus may be on "content" learning – e.g., memorization of MWI for a particular test without a focus on having learners retrieve those MWI for when they need them productively at a later stage.

In the next two sections I will comment on activities that foster process learning and attend to the second and third tenets of learning-for-use, which involves activities promoting goal-directed processes that put learners in situations where knowledge is constructed, used, and made accessible for future use.

Technical and Pedagogical Knowledge: Data-Driven Learning

As a reminder, technical and pedagogical knowledge (TPK) refers to how teaching and learning can change when particular technologies are used in particular ways. Some technological affordances of (L)CR have made it possible to revisit the pedagogical approaches used in foreign language learning. They include, among others, data-driven learning (DDL) approaches and tools. The term data-driven learning was coined in Johns (1991) and mainly refers to the fact that learners and/or teachers can work with/manipulate/query/use corpus data for language awareness-raising tasks (see Chambers, 2010, for a detailed history of data-driven learning, Leńko-Szymańska & Boulton, 2015, Boulton, 2017, and Boulton & Cobb, 2017, for in-depth discussions and illustrations of the potential of data-driven learning in language learning).

Data-driven learning activities are essentially a new form of consciousness-raising tasks exploiting the affordances of corpus tools. The corpus provides the data from which learners discover patterns for themselves, and the tools (concordancers mainly) act as some sort of combined input flood and input enhancement providers; see concrete illustrations and screenshots in the next section. A concordancer lists all of the examples of a keyword from a corpus or text.

Teachers can also manipulate the concordances to scaffold the awareness-raising activities (sorting the word on the right of the initial search word to make typical collocations more salient), see Mishan and Timmis (2015, pp. 81–82) for a concrete illustration of a scaffolded DDL activity. In such cases, teachers act as facilitators/guides in providing a scaffolded approach to the analysis of the data. Mishan and Timmins (ibid., p. 81) state that data-driven learning "places responsibility on learners to discover patterns in the data presented". In addition, the authors note the similarities between data-driven learning and communicative language teaching as learners are seen as "active constructors" of knowledge instead of being passive recipients. The cognitive and analytical skills practiced and developed in data-driven learning activities offer more autonomy to learners and can (hopefully) become transferrable process skills. Readers interested in the impact of input flood on language proficiency are invited to read Mahvelati and Mukundan's (2012) study of the role of participants' cognitive style in collocational knowledge development. Another recommended article is Vyatkina's (2016) study of the effects of data-driven learning of German lexico-grammatical constructions by North American college students with intermediate foreign language proficiency (see also Further Reading section at the end of the chapter). It should also be added here that data-driven learning activities, while generally useful, also have drawbacks (such as the loss of a larger context) and may not be beneficial to all types of learners. For a lengthier discussion of the limitations and potential drawbacks of data-driven learning, see Mishan and Timmis (2015) and Boulton (2017).

Illustrations: Some Online Tools Fostering Process Learning Activities

Data-driven learning activities are not necessarily computer-based and "paper-based" data-driven learning activities have also been shown to be effective for learners (see Vyatkina, 2016 for examples of both paper- and computer-based activities). As the present chapter focuses on the Technological Pedagogical Content Knowledge model however, I will only include digital open educational resources (OERs) in the present section (for more information on OERs, see www.unesco.org/new/en/communication-and-information/access-to-knowledge/open-educational-resources/what-are-open-educational-resources-oers/). Dudeney, Hockly, and Pegrum (2013) list the three main types of factors affecting digital activity choice: pedagogical (students as language learners), personal (students as individuals), and digital (students as technology users). Pedagogical factors include, among other things, class context (native, second, or foreign language environment), language level (linguistic proficiency of the students) and language needs (particular language needs of the students). Personal factors are related to age, interests, and cultures of the students; and digital factors refer to students' attitudes towards digital technologies, their technological proficiency and confidence, their digital literacy levels, and the equipment and tools students (and teachers) have access to.

Masterman and Wild (2011), in turn, focus on the teacher's perspective and list factors that are critical in whether or not teachers use open educational resources. They include the relevance of content and fit to the lecturer's current purpose, and provenance and pedagogic intent as factors. Masterman and Wild also analyze the logistical factors that can account for teachers' willingness to work with OER, and these include among others: technical and implementation issues; a conceptualization of teaching as helping students to become active, independent learners; and readiness to learn (i.e., continuous professional development practice).

As can be seen from the two preceding paragraphs, a sustainable use of digital tools by both learners and teachers is far from being undemanding, especially if all the learner- and teacher-related factors have to be met simultaneously. The two tools that will be presented next have the potential to address learner- and teacher-related factors but the actual use that will be made of the tools – as well as their potential long-term benefits for learners – cannot be assessed or predicted once and for all. They will be very much related to specific contextual elements.

The first tool is the Word and Phrase Info tool, available at www.wordandphrase.info/analyzeText.asp. This tool allows users to enter any text and see useful information about words and phrases in the text. The information accessed is based on data from the Corpus of Contemporary American English (COCA). In addition to information at the single-word level (e.g., highlighting of all of the medium and lower-frequency words in the text, or of academic words) clicking on any word in the text gives access to a detailed word sketch with re-sortable concordance lines, and frequency of the word (overall, and by genre). The Word and Phrase Info tool allows for searches on selected phrases in the text (and provides related phrases in COCA). This resource is defined as a "collocational thesaurus" by its creator (Mark Davies). Figure 22.2a shows a screenshot of a sample of text analyzed by Word and Phrase. In the example selected, I clicked on the word *embedded* in the text and was provided by a list of concordances of the word in several text types.

As can be seen, *embed* is particularly frequent in academic English (when compared to spoken English for instance). In addition, a quick look at the concordances lines (only seven are visible in Figure 22.2a, but a total of 201 concordance lines were produced) shows that the preferred structure is a passive one, followed by *in* as a preposition (121 instances out of the 201 displayed) – see Figure 22.2b for a screenshot of the concordances and the ease of spotting frequent structures thanks to the colors and the pre-sorted concordance lines.

As for phrases, Davies also explains that clicking on the groups of words (e.g., *potent argument* in the text entered), will provide the user with alternate ways of expression (e.g., *powerful* or *convincing* argument), and will show the frequency of those phrases in COCA. This helps users find just the right phrase based on a huge collection of native English texts (see www.wordandphrase.info/analyzeText.asp).

The second tool is the Louvain English for Academic Purposes Dictionary (LEAD). Paquot (2012, p. 165) defines LEAD as "an integrated dictionary and corpus tool intended to help non-native speakers write academic texts in English". Corpus data in LEAD is meant to be customized "to users' needs in terms of discipline and mother tongue background". LEAD is both a dictionary and a writing-aid tool that when used successfully should contribute to

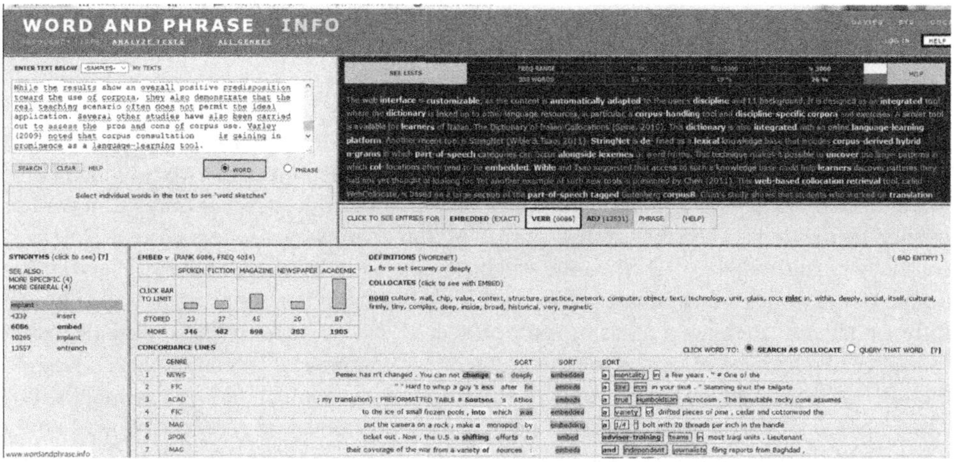

Figure 22.2a Screenshot from Word and Phrase Info (accessed January 7, 2018)

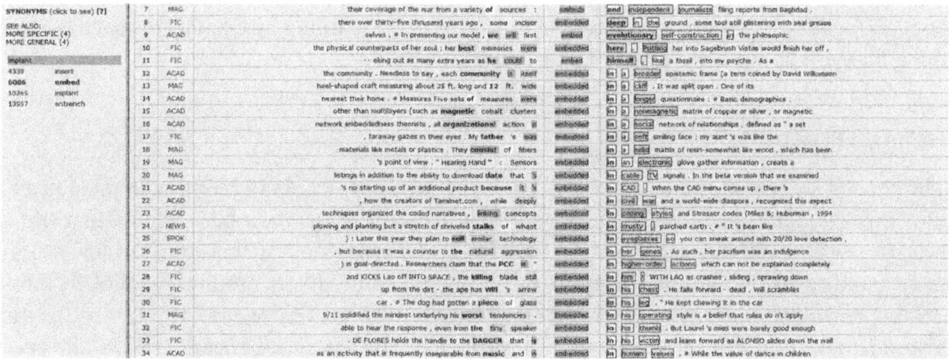

Figure 22.2b More examples of pre-sorted concordance lines

learning. LEAD offers options to search for English academic words and expressions (see Paquot, 2012, for illustrations and screenshots of the tool). It can be used to access:

- Definitions and examples of word use in context (preferred position in the sentence, typical collocations and recurrent phrases),
- Charts to help users remember salient features (e.g., frequency differences across genres),
- Warnings against frequent errors, and usage notes that compare learner and expert writing,
- Context-sensitive lexicographical treatment of phraseology, as corpora of expert and learner writing have been used in the compilation of the tool,
- Numerous exercises on various EAP language functions.

Interestingly, Granger and Paquot (2015) have recently conducted a needs analysis of users of LEAD. The results indicate that a large proportion of the users (80%) believe that they will use this tool for future assignment, thereby pointing towards one of the key tenets of learning-for-use: accessibility for future use. Students liked the hyperlinked discipline-specific examples. However, the direct access to a concordancer was not particularly well-rated by MA students, which constrasted with PhD students' appreciation of the concordancing p-facility.

Teachers' perceptions of online tools is also an important predictor of their future inclusion in the classroom. The assessment of a project aiming to foster teachers' uptake of OERs including natural language processing aspects (the TELL-OP project, see www.tellop.eu/ for more details) has revealed the importance of pre- and in-service teacher training in the use of such digital tools. The 169 teachers (spread in four cohorts over four countries: Belgium, Germany, Spain, and the UK) who followed the online module set up for the teacher training output of the project showed a lot of interest in the teaching opportunities provided by the different natural language processing tools presented. They explained that such tools would indeed enable learners to gain autonomy in their learning process (Meunier, 2017). Despite the interest expressed, however, some of the corpus tools and data-driven learning activities proposed generated tepid reactions on average, even though they scored slightly better among mobile-trained respondents and teachers working in a mobile-friendly environment (Meurice, 2018; Pérez-Paredes, Ordoñana Guillamón, & Aguado Jiménez, 2018). As is (still too) often the case in studies presenting tools and approaches for data-driven learning, the main focus is on training teachers in how to use specific tools. However, there is still not enough focus on what Koehler and Mishra (2005) call a learning by design approach, something that will be further discussed in the next section.

Future Directions

The second section of the chapter has, I hope, shown that access to MWI in situated use is now possible thanks to (L)CR and its multiple features. It has also been shown that some tools are more static and some are more dynamic; that some tools are better suited for assessment purposes (how phraseological is my text) and some others are more useful for productive tasks (what are the possible collocations for the specific word I want to use). It is also obvious from the various examples presented that not all tools can retrieve all types of MWI, and that each tool often uses its own terminology. For example, IDIOM Search (see Figure 22.1) uses very broad categories, whereas a tool like LEAD will provide users with more complex search options including specific parts-of-speech. While some users may regret the lack of terminological homogeneity, I do not necessarily find it problematic from a learning-for-use perspective. I would even go as far as saying that too strong a focus on meta-language (is this a communicative phraseme? is this a fixed or semi-fixed idiom? is this a phrasal verb or a prepositional verb?) obscures the value of tools and makes both teachers and learners shy away from data-driven learning that they find either too specific or too linguistically complex. This is particularly the case for instructors teaching learners with lower levels of proficiency. I see the overall added-value of each of the tools presented here as serving the cause of revealing the highly conventional nature of language to both teachers and learners and as key resources in understanding and accessing frequency information or form-meaning mappings in use. I also hope that researchers in (L)CR and natural language processing circles will go developing and refining such tools in the future.

With time and experience in pre- and in-service teacher training, I have also come to realize that advertising tools is just as important as explaining what they could actually do. While in the past I tended to present "corpus linguistics tools" to teachers, I now present them as "get your 24/7 native speaker assistant for free" (Meunier, Vincent, Suner, & Van de Vyver, 2016). Such a small verbal move has made a huge difference in how teachers approach the tools and their features, and I can recommend using similar analogies to help potential users to see the benefits of data-driven learning in pre- and in-service teacher training circles.

The importance of learner- and teacher-oriented pedagogical, personal and digital factors (Dudeney et al., 2013, and Masterman & Wild, 2011) that are critical in whether or not teachers use open educational resources should not be underestimated. The actual use that will be made of the exiting tools, their future developments, and their potential long-term benefits for learners will depend on the awareness of, attention to, and integration of such factors. As the Technological Pedagogical Content Knowledge model is the "understanding that emerges from interactions among content, pedagogy, and technology knowledge" (Koehler et al., 2013, p. 16), I second Koehler and Mishra's (2005) plea for a learning by design approach to the teaching and learning of MWI. This may be achieved by helping both teachers and learners develop "an understanding of the complex set of interrelationships between artifacts, users, tools, and practices" as it will promote a "flexible and situated understanding of technology" (Koehler & Mishra, 2005, p. 94).

I would like to finish this chapter by prompting teachers and learners alike to use existing Open Educational Resources to get to grips with MWI. One such example is a recently created SPOC (Small Private Online Course) from the University of Queensland (Australia) entitled "Improving Writing Through Corpora: Data-Driven Learning". This short (five-hour) course, created by Peter Crosthwaite (see https://edge.edx.org/courses/course-v1:UQx+SLATx+2018_S2/about), aims to provide its users with the tools, knowledge, and skills to improve their writing. While the course contains functions that are only available to UQ students (marking of tasks for instance), it is open to anyone who would like to know more about corpora and some freely available collocation tools. Despite the fact that each course will probably have its strengths and weaknesses and target more or less specific audiences, sharing good practices through open educational resources seems to be the right way to help promote Technological Pedagogical Content Knowledge.

Further Reading

Boulton, A., & Cobb, T. (2017). Corpus use in language learning: A meta-analysis. *Language Learning*, *67*(2), 348–393.

> This study uses systematic meta-analytic procedures to summarize findings from experimental and quasi-experimental investigations into the effectiveness of using the tools and techniques of corpus linguistics for second language learning or use. Sixty-four separate studies representing 88 unique samples are covered. Large overall effects for both control/experimental group comparisons and for pretest/posttest designs are reported. The authors also explain that while DDL research has improved over the period investigated, changes in practice and reporting are recommended.

Leńko-Szymańska A., & Boulton, A. (Eds.). (2015). *Multiple affordances of language corpora for data-driven learning*. Amsterdam: John Benjamins.

> This volume explores how corpus data can be used as part of the learning process. It provides research insights based in the classroom context and reports on several state-of-the-art projects around the world. It also addresses issues involving different types of corpora, for different learner profiles, and for different purposes.

Siyanova-Chanturia, A., & Pellicer-Sánchez, A. (2019). *Understanding Formulaic Language. A Second language acquisition perspective*. New York, NY and London, UK: Routledge.

> This brand new book offers a multifocal perspective on formulaic language from a second language acquisition perspective. It addresses cognitive, psycholinguistic, sociocultural, pragmatic, and pedagogical aspects. The six chapters of Part 3 of the book will be particularly relevant for readers with pedagogical interests.

Vyatkina, N. (2016). Data-driven learning of collocations: Learner performance, proficiency and perceptions. *Language Learning & Technology, 20*(3), 159–179.

This paper explores the effects of data-driven learning of German lexico-grammatical constructions and compares the effects of computer-based and paper-based activities in learners' immediate and delayed performance gains. It also explores changes in learners' proficiency and perceptions of data-driven learning. It is one of the rare studies focusing on a second language other than English, and it also combines the different outcome measures in a multilevel modeling design.

Related Topics

Classifying and identifying formulaic language, factors affecting the learning of multiword items, resources for learning single-word items, key issues in teaching multiword items

References

Baisa, V., & Suchomel, V. (2014). SkELL – Web interface for English language learning. In *Eighth workshop on recent advances in Slavonic natural language processing* (pp. 63–70). Brno: Tribun EU.

Biber, D., Conrad, S., & Cortes, V. (2004). If you look at . . . : Lexical bundles in university teaching and textbooks. *Applied Linguistics, 25*(3), 371–405.

Boulton, A. (2017). Data driven learning and language pedagogy. In S. Thorne & S. May (Eds.), *Language, education and technology. Encyclopedia of language and education*. New York, NY: Springer.

Boulton, A., & Cobb, T. (2017). Corpus use in language learning: A meta-analysis. *Language Learning, 67*(2), 348–393.

Chambers, A. (2010). What is data-driven learning. In A. O'Keeffe & M. McCarthy (Eds.), *The Routledge handbook of corpus linguistics* (pp. 345–358). London, UK: Routledge.

Colson, J.-P. (2016). Set phrases around globalization: An experiment in corpus-based computational phraseology. In F. Alonso Almeida, I. Ortega Barrera, E. Quintana Toledo, & M. E. Sánchez Cuervo (Eds.), *Input a word, analyze the world: Selected approaches to corpus linguistics* (pp. 141–152). Newcastle, UK: Cambridge Scholars Publishing.

Crystal, D. (2003). *The Cambridge Encyclopedia of the English language*. Cambridge: Cambridge University Press.

Dudeney, G., Hockly, N., & Pegrum, M. (2013). *Digital literacies*. Harlow, UK: Pearson.

Edelson, D. C. (2001). Learning-for-use: A framework for the design of technology-supported inquiry activities. *Journal of Research in Science Teaching, 38*(3), 355–385.

Ellis, N. C. (2017). Cognition, corpora, and computing: Triangulating research in usage-based language learning. *Language Learning, 67*(S1), 40–65.

Ellis, N. C., Römer, U., & Brook O'Donnell, M. (2016). *Usage-based approaches to language acquisition and processing: Cognitive and corpus investigations of construction grammar*. Hoboken, Wiley-Blackwell.

Farr, F. (2015). *Practice in TESOL*. Edinburgh, UK: Edinburgh University Press.

Granger, S. (2009a). The contribution of learner corpora to second language acquisition and foreign language teaching: A critical evaluation. In K. Aijmer (Ed.), *Corpora and language teaching* (pp. 13–32). Amsterdam: Benjamins.

Granger, S. (2009b). Commentary on part I: Learner corpora: A window onto the L2 phrasicon. In A. Barfield & H. Gyllstad (Eds.), *Researching collocations in another language: Multiple interpretations* (pp. 60–65). Basingstoke, UK: Palgrave Macmillan.

Granger, S., & Paquot, M. (2015). Electronic lexicography goes local: Design and structures of a needs-driven online academic writing aid. *Lexicographica – International Annual Review for Lexicography, 31*(1), 118–141.

Harris, H. D., Murphy, G. L., & Rehder, B. (2008). Prior knowledge and exemplar frequency. *Memory & Cognition, 36*(7), 1335–1350.

Johns, T. (1991). Should you be persuaded: Two samples of data-driven learning materials. *English Language Research Journal, 4,* 1–16.

Koehler, M. J., & Mishra, P. (2005). Teachers learning technology by design. *Journal of Computing in Teacher Education, 21*(3), 94–102.

Koehler, M. J., & Mishra, P. (2008). *Handbook of technological pedagogical content knowledge (TPCK) for educators.* New York, NY: Routledge.

Koehler, M. J., Mishra, P., & Cain, W. (2013). What is technological pedagogical content (TPACK)? *Journal of Education, 193,* 13–19.

Lee, D. (2001). Genres, registers, text types, domains, and styles: Clarifying the concepts and navigating a path through the BNC jungle. *Language Learning & Technology, 5*(3), 37–72.

Leech, G. (1992). Corpora and theories of linguistic performance. In Svartvik, J. (ed). *Directions in corpus linguistics.* Berlin: Mouton de Gruyter, 105–122.

Leńko-Szymańska, A. & Boulton, A. (Eds.). (2015). *Multiple affordances of language corpora for data-driven learning.* Amsterdam: Benjamins.

Liu, S., Liu, H., Yu, Y., Li, Y., & Wen, T. (2014). TPACK: A New Dimension to EFL Teachers' PCK. *Journal of Education and Human Development, 3*(2), 681–693.

Mahvelati, E., & Mukundan, J. (2012). The role of cognitive style in the collocational knowledge development of Iranian EFL learners through input flood treatment. *English Language Teaching, 5*(10), 182–194.

Masterman, L., & Wild, J. (2011). *OER impact study: Research report.* JISC Open Educational Resources Programme: Phase 2. [Online] University of Oxford. Retrieved January 28, 2018 from www.jisc. ac.uk/media/documents/programmes/elearning/oer/JISCOERImpactStudyResearchReportv1-0.pdf

Meunier, F. (2012). Formulaic language and language teaching. *Annual Review of Applied Linguistics, 32,* 111–129.

Meunier, F. (2017). Online training module for language professionals: Promoting the uptake of open educational NLP resources in language learning and teaching. *BAAHE 2017 Conference – Let's Inter-Act! Innovative Teaching Practices in English Studies,* Friday 1 December 2017, Louvain-la-Neuve, Université catholique de Louvain.

Meunier, F., & Bulon, A. (forthcoming). Using IDIOM Search to assess phraseological competence in learner writing.

Meunier, F., Vincent, A., Suner Munoz, F., & Van de Vyver, J. (2016). TICEs et apprentissage des langues modernes. *Journées de formation CECAFOC du 1 et 2 février 2016,* Louvain-la-Neuve: Université catholique de Louvain.

Meurice, A. (2018). *The TELLOP online training programme: An analysis of the trainees' perception of the French-speaking module.* MA dissertation, Université catholique de Louvain.

Meyer, D. (2017). *How are corpus-informed materials different?* [Online] Blog post published 24 April 2017. Retrieved January 28, 2018 from www.cambridge.org/elt/blog/2017/04/24/corpus-informed-materi]als/

Mishan, F., & Timmis, T. (2015). *Materials development for TESOL.* Edinburgh Textbooks in TESOL series. Edinburgh, UK: Edinburgh University Press,.

Mishra, P., & Koehler, M. J. (2006). Technological pedagogical content knowledge: A framework for teacher knowledge. *Teachers College Record, 108*(6), 1017–1054.

Norén, K., & Linell, P. (2007). Meaning potentials and the interaction between lexis and contexts: An empirical substantiation. *Pragmatics, 17*(3), 387–416.

Oksefjell Ebeling, S., & Hasselgård, H. (2015). Learner corpora and phraseology. In S. Granger, G. Gilquin, & F. Meunier (Eds.), *The Cambridge handbook of learner corpus research* (pp. 207–230). Cambridge, UK: Cambridge University Press.

Paquot, M. (2012). The LEAD dictionary-cum-writing aid: An integrated dictionary and corpus tool. In S. Granger & M. Paquot (Eds.), *Electronic lexicography* (pp. 163–185). Oxford, UK: Oxford University Press.

Pérez-Paredes, P. F., Ordoñana Guillamón, C., & Aguado Jiménez, P. (2018). Language teachers' perceptions on the use of OER language processing technologies in MALL. *Computer Assisted Language Learning*, 1–24.

Rundell, M. (2008). The corpus revolution revisited. *English Today, 24*, 23–27.

Rundell, M., & Stock, P. (1992). The corpus revolution. *English Today, 8*(4), 45–51.

Sinclair, J. (1991). *Corpus, concordance, collocation*. Oxford, UK: Oxford University Press.

Siyanova-Chanturia, A., & Pellicer-Sánchez, A. (2019). *Understanding formulaic language. A Second language acquisition perspective*. New York, NY and London, UK: Routledge.

Smith, J. D. (2014). Prototypes, exemplars, and the natural history of categorization. *Psychonomic Bulletin & Review, 21*(2), 312–331.

Stefanowitsch, A., & Gries, S. Th. (2003). Collostructions: Investigating the interaction of words and constructions. *International Journal of Corpus Linguistics, 8*(2), 209–243.

Stubbs, M. (2009). Technology and phraseology: With notes on the history of corpus Linguistics. In U. Römer & R. Schulze (Eds.), *Exploring the lexis–grammar interface* (pp. 15–31). Amsterdam: Benjamins.

Viana, V., Zyngier, S., & Barnbrook, G. (2011). *Perspectives on corpus linguistics*. Amsterdam: John Benjamins.

Vyatkina, N. (2016). Data-driven learning of collocations: Learner performance, proficiency, and perceptions. *Language Learning & Technology, 20*(3), 159–179.

Whitehead, A. N. (1929). *The aims of education and other essays*. New York, NY: The Free Press.

23

Evaluating Exercises for Learning Vocabulary

Batia Laufer

Introduction

Learners of their first language (L1) do not need to do vocabulary exercises in order to acquire large numbers of words and acquire them well. Most L1 vocabulary is believed to be learned from input to spoken and written language and not by vocabulary instruction (Nagy, Herman, & Anderson, 1985; Sternberg, 1987). This is true at least for a few thousand content words acquired during the first years of life. But second language (L2) learning, particularly in the classroom learning context, can hardly provide the learners with the kind of massive exposure to the foreign language that is necessary for "picking up" words. In primary, secondary, and tertiary education, the number of second language lessons is usually limited to two to five hours per week, and they are mainly devoted to language structure and the language skills – listening, writing, speaking, and reading – in schools, and to academic skills in colleges and universities. It is questionable, therefore, whether learners are free to engage with quantities of listening and reading input, inside or outside the classroom, quantities that will ensure numerous repetitions of words. Cobb (2007) computed, on the basis of corpus analysis, that most words beyond the 2,000 most frequent words will not be learned in a year or two even if we assume the largest plausible amounts of free reading. Nation (2014), however, calculated that in order to have 10 to 12 encounters with words at the fifth 1,000-word frequency in one year, learners will need to read a million words, which would take about 33 minutes of reading per day. Learners would need to read 3,000,000 words in order to have 10 to 12 encounters with words at the ninth 1,000-frequency level, which would involve 1 hour 40 minutes of reading per day. This is certainly a more optimistic outlook than Cobb's, but if encounters with new words are to result in learning, then learners should understand 98% of the texts they are reading. This means that, in addition to the regular teaching materials, learners should engage in extensive reading of graded readers that are suitable for learners whose vocabulary size is up to 3,000, 4,000, 6,000, and 8,000 word families. However, a practical question is whether learners, particularly in non-L2-speaking countries, can be expected to read large quantities of graded readers.

When opportunities for repeated exposures to new words are insufficient due to limited amounts of input, these words may go unnoticed, and, if noticed, their meanings may not be inferred. Moreover, even when words are noticed and inferred, many of them may be forgotten shortly after exposure (for a discussion of problems related to learning vocabulary-through-input, see Laufer, 2003; Laufer, 2005). Hence, if motivated L2 readers, let alone average students, do not meet new words frequently enough, they will benefit from an intervention by teachers and material writers in the form of word-focused instruction, or, in simple language, vocabulary exercises.[1] A vocabulary exercise is defined here as a response to a language prompt, a response that requires the understanding of the words on which the exercise focuses, with or without producing them. (The term "exercise" will be used interchangeably with "task" and "activity".) This definition encompasses both authentic communicative and artificial non-communicative exercises. An example of the former is looking up unknown words that appear in a text in a dictionary because they are necessary for understanding the subsequent comprehension questions. An example of the latter is filling in gaps in isolated unconnected sentences with words provided at the end of the exercise with or without their translations. In the two exercises, the learner has to respond by selecting the dictionary meaning that fits the text context, in the first exercise, and by selecting the appropriate target words to fill the blanks in the second exercise. The definition also encompasses exercises with new words whose function is to help learners remember these words as well as exercises for expansion and consolidation of the knowledge of already familiar words. The filling in gaps exercise can include words that have been learned for the first time, or words that were learned at an earlier stage, but are practiced again in a different text context.

There is a wealth of evidence showing that word-focused activities are beneficial for vocabulary learning. Any instructional technique, e.g., glosses, dictionary use, negotiation of meaning, sentence completion, sentence writing, computer assisted learning devices (hypertexts, concordances, online dictionaries) was usually found to be superior to the "word unfocused" condition in terms of the number of words retained after task completion (Agustin Llach, 2009; Ellis & He, 1999; Kim, 2006; Knight, 1994; Laufer, 2001; Paribakht & Wesche, 1997; Peters Hulstijn, Sercu, & Lutjeharms, 2009; Zimmerman, 1997, to mention just a few studies). Moreover, when one or two exercises focused on learning target words were compared with reading 18–21 occurrences of the same words in a text, it was the former condition that yielded much better results (Laufer & Rozovski-Roitblat, 2015).

Critical Issues and Topics

Having established that word-focused activities are effective, the obvious question is what makes some exercises more effective than others. The answer to this question can benefit materials designers who create vocabulary exercises in textbooks and workbooks and teachers who produce their own materials for particular students and particular course objectives. In trying to answer this question, I will not discuss what I consider to be nonobjective factors like learners' personal interest in words pertaining to a specific subject area, the overall motivation to learn a language, and age-dependent motivating activities, like labeling pictures for younger learners and doing crossword puzzles for older learners. These nonobjective factors are important, but as they differ in different groups of learners and in individuals, they may act favorably for some learners and adversely for other learners. Neither will I consider the task effectiveness in terms of the teaching time it requires. The investment of specific amounts of teaching time in vocabulary may differ from lesson to lesson and from course to course depending on the overall teaching and syllabus aims.

Instead, I will try to evaluate vocabulary exercises by objective criteria that specify what learners do with the words, or what task features are conducive to learning. I will examine three different theoretical frameworks that explain what makes some exercises more effective than other exercises. These are Involvement Load Hypothesis (Laufer & Hulstijn, 2001), Technique Feature Analysis (Nation & Webb, 2011), and TOPRA (Type of Processing – Resource Allocation) model (Barcroft, 2002). I will also briefly summarize some empirical studies that compare different types of exercises and test the predictions of the three theories vis-à-vis learning data. These studies examine the learning of new words. As I am not familiar with any theories and controlled studies on exercises that expand and consolidate existing word knowledge, I will suggest several criteria for designing and evaluating such exercises: "beyond basics", "a glimpse of a system", "differential learnability", and "activating receptive knowledge".

Involvement Load Hypothesis

One theoretical framework for evaluating exercises is the Involvement Load Hypothesis, which was proposed by Laufer and Hulstijn in 2001, as a first attempt to operationalize the concepts of "attention" and its related notions (e.g., degree of elaboration, cognitive effort, depth of processing) into concrete and measurable L2 vocabulary learning tasks. Laufer and Hulstijn postulate that retention of words is conditional upon three factors found in word practice: need, search, and evaluation. Taken together, these three factors combine into what Laufer and Hulstijn call *involvement*.

The *need* component is the motivational, noncognitive dimension of involvement based on a drive to comply with the task requirements, which can be either externally imposed or self-imposed. Two degrees of prominence were suggested for need: *moderate* and *strong*. Need is moderate when it is imposed by an external agent. An example is the need to use a word in a sentence that the teacher asked for. Need is strong when it is intrinsically motivated, for instance, by the decision to look up a word in an L1–L2 dictionary when writing a composition. *Search and evaluation* are the two cognitive dimensions of involvement, contingent upon allocating attention to form-meaning relationships (Schmidt, 2001). *Search* is the attempt to find the meaning of an unknown L2 word or trying to find the L2 word form expressing a concept (e.g., trying to find the L2 translation of an L1 word) by consulting a dictionary or another authority (e.g., a teacher). Originally, no distinction was made between moderate or strong search. However, in later discussions of the construct, such a distinction was suggested, whereby a *moderate* search would be a search for meaning of a given word and a *strong* search – a search for word form to express familiar meaning.[2]

Evaluation entails a comparison of a given word with other words, a specific meaning of a word with its other meanings, or comparing the word with other words in order to assess whether a word does or does not fit its context. For example, when a word looked up in a dictionary is a homonym (e.g., bank of a river, or bank as a financial institution), a decision has to be made about its meaning by comparing all its meanings against the specific context and choosing the one that fits best. Evaluation that entails recognizing differences between words (as in a fill-in task with words provided), or differences between several senses of a word in a given context, is referred to as *moderate*. Evaluation that requires a decision as to how additional words will combine with the new word in an original (as opposed to given) context is referred to as *strong* evaluation.

An authentic or a teacher designed learning task can induce any one, two, or all three of the components of involvement for each word: need, search, and evaluation. The combination of components with their degrees of prominence constitutes *involvement load*. Consider two tasks that vary in involvement load. In task one, the learner is asked to write original sentences with some new words and these words are translated or explained by the teacher. The task induces a moderate need (imposed by the teacher), no search (the words are glossed), and strong evaluation because the new words have to be used correctly (e.g., with suitable collocations) in a learner-generated context. If we want to describe the task in terms of an *involvement index*, where absence of a factor is marked as 0, a moderate presence of a factor as 1, and a strong presence as 2, then the involvement index of the task is 3 (1 + 0 + 2). In another task, the student has to read a text and to answer comprehension questions. New words, which are relevant to the questions, are glossed. The task will induce a moderate need to look at the glosses (moderate because it is imposed by the task), but it will induce neither search nor evaluation. Its involvement index is 1. Hence, the first task induces a greater involvement load than the second.

The Involvement Load Hypothesis (ILH) postulates that words which are processed with higher involvement load will be retained better than words which are processed with lower involvement load (when other word factors, such as phonological, morphological and semantic complexity of the word, learners' L2 proficiency and conceptual development are equal).

All three factors can be manipulated separately and in different combinations by researchers or teachers to create tasks with varying involvement loads. Therefore, as a research and evaluation paradigm, ILH offers multiple possibilities to explore the relationship between retention and various aspects of deep processing. There have now been several studies investigating the hypothesis directly or indirectly and mostly confirming its predictive value, completely or partially (Hulstijn & Laufer, 2001; Keating, 2008; Kim, 2006, 2008; Nassaji & Hu, 2012, Pichette, de Serres, & Lafontaine, 2012; Sun, 2017; Webb, 2005; Zou, 2017).

Here is an example of three tasks with different involvement loads: reading and comprehension exercise with glossed new words (need = 1, search = 0, evaluation = 0), reading and a fill in exercise with glossed new words (need = 1, search = 0, evaluation = 1), and composition writing where the new words (glossed) had to be used (need = 1, search = 0, evaluation = 2). The third task, which has the highest involvement load, is supposed to result in best retention rates of the practiced words, followed by the second task. The first task should yield the worst results. These were the results in Hulstijn and Laufer (2001), Keating (2008), and Kim (2008). Moreover, Kim (ibid.) compared two tasks with an identical involvement load, composition writing and sentence writing, and found that the results were similar, in line with the prediction of the Involvement Load Hypothesis. The results were the same for two L2 proficiencies.

The construct of involvement load was developed in the context of incidental second language vocabulary learning. Laufer and Hulstijn perceive "incidental" learning as learning from language input and from word-focused tasks, but without the learner's deliberate intention to commit words to memory. For example, tasks such as cloze activities, writing sentences, and matching exercises are all word-focused tasks that could be evaluated by involvement load, as long as there was no intention to commit the words to memory (operationalized as knowledge that learning will be followed by a test). In other words, incidental learning is not necessarily devoid of attention though it is devoid of learners' intention. The authors claim that when learning is intentional, it is impossible to know what strategies learners use when they commit words to memory. Therefore, it is impossible to determine the involvement load of intentional learning. (For an extensive discussion of incidental and intentional learning, see Hulstijn, 2001.[3]) Moreover, the IL framework has been suggested for tasks practicing new words/chunks of words, or new meanings only. Even though involving tasks are useful for recapitulating or consolidating prior knowledge, it is hard, if not impossible, to research task effectiveness empirically with familiar words as it will be necessary to show that the knowledge that is tested is not the result of prior learning.

Technique Feature Analysis

Another framework for evaluating task effectiveness is Technique Feature Analysis (Nation & Webb, 2011). Zou, Wang, Kwan, and Xie (2018) investigated the predictive ability of Technique Feature Analysis and found that it was successful in ranking the efficacy of different activities. Unlike ILH, this framework suggests five (rather than three in ILH) major criteria that are subdivided into 18 specific features. The presence of each feature is assigned a score of 1, absence = a score of 0. Thus the maximum score is 18. A more detailed framework like TFA is bound to results in a finer classification of tasks in terms of features that affect effectiveness. The list of features that determine task effectiveness is presented in the following table.

A checklist: Technique Feature Analysis

Criteria	Scores	
Motivation		
Is there a clear vocabulary learning goal?	0	1
Does the activity motivate learning?	0	1
Do the learners select the words?	0	1
Noticing		
Does the activity focus attention on the target words?	0	1
Does the activity raise awareness of new vocabulary learning?	0	1
Does the activity involve negotiation?	0	1
Retrieval		
Does the activity involve retrieval of the word?	0	1
Is it productive retrieval	0	1
Is it recall?	0	1
Are there multiple retrievals of each word?	0	1
Is there spacing between retrievals?	0	1
Generation		
Does the activity involve generative use?	0	1
Is it productive?	0	1
Is there a marked change that involves the use of other words?	0	1
Retention		
Does the activity ensure successful linking of form and meaning?	0	1
Does the activity involve instantiation?	0	1
Does the activity involve imaging?	0	1
Does the activity avoid interference?	0	1
Maximum score	18	

Source: Adapted from Nation & Webb, 2011, p. 7

"Motivation" is defined in terms of the goal the learners see in the task, pleasantness of activity, and personal decision on which words should be selected for learning. The score of the motivational components ranges from 0 to 3. Preparing word cards and learning from them is assigned a point on all three features.

"Noticing" is achieved by focusing attention on the target words, making the learner aware that there is something new to learn, and inducing negotiation about the word's meaning and use. Reading and filling in blanks with new words that are provided with glosses will satisfy the features of focus and new learning, but since glosses are provided, there is no negotiation of meaning. The composite score of the noticing features could range from 0 to 3.

The retrieval score is 1 if meaning is retrieved from given options. If it is recalled without options, another point is added. If the word itself is retrieved for a given meaning, an additional point is given for productive recall. Additionally, the "retrieval" criterion includes the number of retrievals (multiple retrievals receive one point) and spacing between them (the presence of spacing receives a point. Hence, the composite score for retrieval ranges from 0 to 5. The retrieval feature is present in tasks that practice already familiar or partly familiar words (we cannot retrieve the meaning or form of something we do not know). Filling in blanks with words given in a list without any explanations requires recalling the meaning. The retrieval feature is given two points (one for retrieval, one for recall). Learning from word cards in the receptive direction (looking at word form and retrieving its meaning) requires recall of meaning, multiple retrievals and some spacing between the retrievals. Hence, the composite retrieval score is 4 (retrieval, receptive recall, multiple retrievals, spacing). Whereas, learning from word cards in the productive direction would receive an additional point for recalling the word form.

The "generation" feature ranges from 0 (no generative use) to 3 depending on whether the word is seen in a new context (1), used in a new context (2) and used with "marked change that involves the use of other words" (3). For example, writing sentences with target words scores three (generative use, productive, change that involves the use of other words).

Retention is claimed to comprise four components, and the presence of each one is assigned one point: successful linking of form and meaning, which depends on a low chance of error of response; presence of instantiation, which involves seeing an instance of a word such as when the word is used in a meaningful situation; presence of imaging – deliberately imagining a visual representation related to the meaning of the word; and avoidance of interference. Interference refers to presenting new words that are related in meaning, e.g., synonyms, antonyms, co-hyponyms, or form, as in the case of base word and its derivations and words such as *accept-except*, *different-difficult*, and *firm-form* that have similar forms but different meanings. These words are often confused. Hence avoidance of interference receives one point. In total, retention can receive 4 points. As stated earlier, the maximum "task effectiveness score" is 18.

Here are some examples of exercises evaluated in terms of Technique Feature Analysis taken from Nation and Webb (ibid.). Exercises with higher ratings are supposed to be more effective than exercises with lower ratings.

Fill-in blanks (words provided)

Criteria	Scores
Motivation	
Is there a clear vocabulary learning goal?	1
Does the activity motivate learning?	1
Do the learners select the words?	0
Noticing	
Does the activity focus attention on the target words?	1
Does the activity raise awareness of new vocabulary learning?	1
Does the activity involve negotiation?	0
Retrieval	
Does the activity involve retrieval of the word?	1
Is it productive retrieval?	1
Is it recall?	0
Are there multiple retrievals of each word?	0
Is there spacing between retrievals?	0
Generation	
Does the activity involve generative use?	1
Is it productive?	0
Is there a marked change that involves the use of other words?	0
Retention	
Does the activity ensure successful linking of form and meaning	0
Does the activity involve instantiation?	0
Does the activity involve imaging?	0
Does the activity avoid interference?	1
Maximum score	8

As the activity involves retrieval, the words to be filled in are not new. Yet a point is given to "raising awareness of new vocabulary learning". Apparently, the teacher who assigns the task knows how much the learners know about the words and what new learning the fill-in task involves. As "avoid interference" is given one point, we can assume the target words and/or the distractors do not include similar words.

Reading words, choosing the definitions

Criteria	Scores
Motivation	
Is there a clear vocabulary learning goal?	1
Does the activity motivate learning?	1
Do the learners select the words?	0
Noticing	
Does the activity focus attention on the target words?	1
Does the activity raise awareness of new vocabulary learning?	1
Does the activity involve negotiation?	0

(Continued)

Criteria	Scores
Retrieval	
Does the activity involve retrieval of the word?	1
Is it productive retrieval?	0
Is it recall?	0
Are there multiple retrievals of each word?	0
Is there spacing between retrievals?	0
Generation	
Does the activity involve generative use?	0
Is it productive?	0
Is there a marked change that involves the use of other words?	0
Retention	
Does the activity ensure successful linking of form and meaning?	0
Does the activity involve instantiation?	0
Does the activity involve imaging?	0
Does the activity avoid interference?	1
Maximum score	6

Completing a word parts table

Criteria	Scores
Motivation	
Is there a clear vocabulary learning goal?	1
Does the activity motivate learning?	0
Do the learners select the words?	0
Noticing	
Does the activity focus attention on the target words?	1
Does the activity raise awareness of new vocabulary learning?	1
Does the activity involve negotiation?	0
Retrieval	
Does the activity involve retrieval of the word?	1
Is it productive retrieval?	1
Is it recall?	1
Are there multiple retrievals of each word?	1
Is there spacing between retrievals?	0
Generation	
Does the activity involve generative use?	1
Is it productive?	1
Is there a marked change that involves the use of other words?	0
Retention	
Does the activity ensure successful linking of form and meaning?	0
Does the activity involve instantiation?	0
Does the activity involve imaging?	0
Does the activity avoid interference?	0
Maximum score	9

As there is retrieval, presumably the words in the text are not new. As for the feature "awareness of new vocabulary learning", the explanation is as in the "fill-in" task. Since a 0 is given to successful linking of form and meaning, the authors assume there is a high possibility of error in the response.

A detailed description of a task in terms of its features should lead to a better understanding of which activities are more effective than others. The TFA seems to provide a better distinction between tasks than the IL does. To verify the predictions of a framework empirically, studies should compare tasks with different total feature scores to find out whether tasks with a higher score are more effective for learning words. Yet not all tasks can be easily compared. It is hard to compare a task where learners are required to commit words to memory, e.g., learning words from cards, or learning words using the keyword method, with a task where no such attempt is required, as in fill in blanks, true/false, sentence writing. When people try to commit words to memory, we have no control over the number of times they repeat the words, or the personal memorization strategies they may use. The number of retrievals can be considered an additional variable similar to a number of exposures. If we compare sentence writing with a word and filling the word in three blanks, as in Folse (2006), the difference may not result from the nature of the task, but from the number of exposures/retrievals/encounters with the new word. Since multiple exposures to words lead to better learning than single exposures, a task with multiple retrievals, e.g., keyword method may work better because of the number of retrievals, not because of other task features.

Similarly, it is hard to compare tasks where one task has the feature "new learning" and the other task does not. This is because knowledge of the target words prior to the comparison may not be the same for different words, or for different people. Doing research on partially or fully familiar words is problematic as it is not clear what constitutes old and new knowledge. For example, the degree of the "generation" feature depends on the novelty of context in which the target word is used. It is hard to decide whether the task induces small or marked changes if different words have been learned to a different degree by different people before the task. Even if we design multiple pretests in which we check different areas of word knowledge, this can hardly be done with a large number of words. As for the feature "does the activity motivate learning?", it is possible that different populations may consider different activities as motivating.

The TFA is feasible in teaching situations, where tasks are designed by teachers who know their learners, the materials in which words are taught, and the approximate vocabulary knowledge the learners have. In such a context, the teachers know what constitutes old and new learning, what is low and high generation based on small and marked contextual changes, and what tasks motivate their particular students. Therefore, the framework is useful for everyday teaching activities.

It would be interesting to see whether the two frameworks, ILH and TFA, grade task effectiveness in the same way. In other words are tasks that are rated as more effective than other tasks by IL also be rated as more effective by TFA? However, a comparison of tasks in terms of involvement load and Technique Feature Analysis is not simple at all. First, only incidental learning could be compared because Laufer and Hulstijn (2001) claim that they cannot control what the learners are doing when they deliberately memorize words. Indeed, deliberate word learning was shown to be quite successful, but possibly because of multiple repetitions and particular cognitive effort to memorize words (Elgort, 2011; Laufer, 2006; Qian, 1996). Second, IL was devised for new words only while TFA includes tasks that practice partially or fully known words. These differences restrict the possibilities of comparisons though do not eliminate them altogether.

To my knowledge, there are no sound comparisons of the two frameworks with regard to their predictability of task effectiveness. The papers I am familiar with that attempt to do this are, unfortunately flawed, both conceptually and methodologically. Therefore, the results of these studies cannot be considered valid[4].

TOPRA (Type of Processing – Resource Allocation)

The third theoretical framework for evaluating exercises is TOPRA (Type of Processing – Resource Allocation) suggested by Barcroft (2002). The idea behind the framework is that different types of processing affect distinct components of word knowledge, such as word form, word meaning, and form-meaning mapping. Semantic processing affects learning for semantic word properties, while form processing affects learning of word form. Barcroft also claims that since there is a competition for cognitive resources when learners try to learn several things, increased semantic processing will decrease learning of formal word properties because fewer processing resources remain available to process word form.

In several studies Barcroft (e.g., 2004, 2009) showed that semantic elaboration interferes with learning form-meaning connection. In one experiment (2004) learners of L2 Spanish were asked to learn 24 new words in two conditions. In one condition they viewed 12 cards with pictures and corresponding words in Spanish. Each word was presented for six seconds four times. In another condition, they viewed 12 other words for which they were asked to write original sentences. They were given 48 seconds for a sentence. The no-sentence condition produced better results than the sentence-writing condition for recalling the new words. In another experiment, learners saw the first set of 12 words only once, for 24 seconds each, and wrote sentences for the other 12 words, using 24 seconds per sentence. The results were better in the no-sentence condition. It is true that focusing on a picture with its corresponding word, once or four times, while trying to remember the word, requires more attention to the word itself than writing a sentence with the word in 24 or 48 seconds, which may not even leave time for committing the word to memory. The sentence seems to act as a distraction, or according to TOPRA a resource depleting device. In another experiment, Barcroft (2009) tested the effect of semantic elaboration on incidental and intentional learning. Learners read a text in English (L2) with target words translated into Spanish (L1) and were assigned to one of four conditions: (1) read the text for meaning only (incidental), (2) read for meaning and try to learn the translated words (intentional), (3) read for meaning and generate Spanish synonyms for the translated words (incidental + semantic), (4) read for meaning, try to learn the ten translated words, and generate Spanish synonyms for the translated words (intentional + semantic). The + synonym condition fared worse both in incidental and intentional conditions. The results were interpreted as support for the detrimental effect of semantic elaboration on learning new words. However, it should be noted that learners were required to generate Spanish (L1) synonyms for Spanish (L1) translations of the target words. Hence, the time and attention that should have been invested in L2 words was spent on finding L1 words for other L1 words. It is questionable, therefore, whether the + synonym condition was worse than – synonym condition because of semantic elaboration as such, or because the semantic elaboration might have occurred without focusing on the English target words. Similarly, tasks used in other studies that are claimed to induce semantic elaboration may not require much attention to the words to be learned. For example, when learners see a picture of an object with the corresponding word and are asked to think what this object can be used for, or how pleasant it is, they may do what is required by the task holding the image of the object in their minds, focusing on the corresponding L1 meaning, not L2 word.

It seems to me that in the teaching context, semantic elaboration is unlikely to involve focusing on word meaning without also focusing on word form when the elaboration is performed in L2. Let us look at Nation's (2001) classification of word knowledge components. Under the "meaning" component, Nation asks what meaning the word form signals (receptive knowledge), or what word form can be used to express the meaning (productive knowledge). Thus, we cannot claim that there is knowledge of an L2 word meaning without the knowledge of form. The learner may have the concept in his mind by virtue of L1 knowledge, but without the corresponding L2 form, there is no knowledge of the L2 word. Tests or exercises that ask learners to supply the meanings of given L2 words do not test meaning only, but always the relationship between form and meaning. A fill-in-the-blanks exercise where specific target words are placed in specific semantic contexts is an activity requiring semantic decision, or elaboration. But this decision is performed looking at word forms and the contexts in which they can occur. Another example is organizing a list of separate words into several groups so that the words in each group are related in meaning. This is a sematic task, but it cannot be completed without knowing which meaning is represented by which word form.

Knowledge of form is defined by Nation as knowing what the word sounds like, how the word is spelled, and what parts are recognizable in the word and needed to express the meaning. Even though it is possible to pronounce words without understanding them (children often sing songs in a foreign language without understanding all the words), I doubt whether sensible teaching would be satisfied with learners' ability to pronounce or spell strings of sounds and letters that are meaningless to them. Classroom tasks are unlikely to include practicing word form without any reference to meaning like counting letters in a word, as students were asked to do in Barcroft (2002). Even in a dictation of phrases or sentences, in order to reproduce what is dictated one requires some degree of understanding of what has been read.

The different positions regarding the value of semantically oriented tasks by TOPRA on the one hand and by the ILH and TFA on the other hand seem to result from a different view of classroom vocabulary tasks and subsequently of vocabulary knowledge tests. While the TOPRA model assumes that form and meaning can be learned and tested separately, and each type of learning depends on the processing demands of a task, the ILH and TFA do not separate learning form only and meaning only. Therefore, in experiments that examine the ILH, tests of word form require learners to recall or to recognize a word for a given meaning while tests of word meaning – to recall or recognize the meaning of a given word form. The TOPRA model contributes to our understanding of word learning in highlighting the phenomenon of *competition* in cognitive processing and showing experimentally the importance of focusing on words, or allocating processing resources, for successful learning. This can explain the effectiveness of intentional learning (in the sense of committing words to memory) as reflected in activities like learning from lists or cards and the effectiveness of activities where contextual environment is minimal (e.g., fill in blanks in sentences rather than fill in blanks in a text).

A note of caution is in order when doing or reading research that compares task effectiveness, whatever theoretical framework is used. A task assigned to learners should be appropriate for the learners' level. In many studies we do not know how "intermediate", "pre-intermediate", "advanced" learners were taught and how they function in a language. Assigning a sentence or composition writing task to learners who have difficulties with writing cannot be expected to be effective. For example, Hu and Nassaji's (2016) task performance results show that out of 14 sentences with target words, the average number of correct sentences was two. This means that the learners did not have the ability to complete the task.

There was no sense, therefore, in checking how effective such a task was for subsequent retention of the target words. Another problem is assigning an unrealistic "time-on-task" in the name of research validity. For example, Barcroft (2004) allowed 24 seconds for sentence writing and word learning for one set of words and the same time for looking at a picture with a word underneath for another set of words. It is questionable whether 24 seconds are enough to compose and write a meaningful sentence and to attempt to memorize the target word. Insufficient time on task means that the task is not completed and cannot be expected to affect learning, while excess time on task means that we do not know whether completing the task, or what was done after completing the task, contributed to learning. A fair comparison of tasks means that each task should be appropriate to the learners' level and should be given the time it takes to complete in real life.

Expansion and Consolidation Exercises

Two of the aforementioned frameworks, the IL and TOPRA, have been developed for evaluating the learning of new words only. TFA, on the other hand, is suitable for already familiar words (hence, the feature "retrieval" which is present when words have already been encountered), as well as new words. I define a newly learned word as a word that is presented and practiced in the first teaching session in which learners encounter it irrespective of the number of times it appears in a text, or in exercises. Most words are not taught or learned fully in the first teaching session. Therefore, expansion and consolidation exercises are necessary to add new knowledge to what has already been taught, and to prevent forgetting what has been learned. As I am not familiar with any framework that has been designed particularly for evaluating task effectiveness for already familiar words, I will suggest some guiding principles. I will refer to them as "beyond the basics", "a glimpse of a system", "differential treatment", and "activation of receptive knowledge".

Beyond the Basics

The first principle for effective exercises is "beyond the basics", that is adding knowledge which is beyond the basic level. Initial instruction typically includes the basic meaning of the word, its pronunciation, spelling, basic grammatical features, possibly a collocation in which the word was encountered. For example, the initial encounter with the word *provide* may be in the pattern V + Direct Object (The site *provided* some useful links to the material). Assuming this basic knowledge has been acquired, expansion exercises can include additional uses and constructions of *provide*: "providing something for someone" (the office provides useful information for students), "provide somebody with something" (the scholarship is designed to provide graduate students with money for research), and "provide for" (parents are expected to provide for their children). In addition, the noun *provision* can be added in an expansion exercise. Another example of the "beyond basics" principle is adding metaphorical meanings to some common nouns, e.g., *foot* (of a mountain), *leg* (of a table), *mouth* (of a river), *head* (of state, institution), *eye* (of a needle, potato). Yet another example is deepening word knowledge by demonstrating how it is different from words that are in the same semantic area. After the meaning of *fee* has been explained, and assuming the words *salary* and *payment* had been studied at some point, "the beyond the basics" principle will mean that the learner will be taught to distinguish between *fee*, *salary*, *payment*, as in Dr. H. charges a high ___ for his services (a. fee b. profit c. salary d. payment).

A Glimpse of a System

The second principle is what I suggest to call "a glimpse of a system". Even though vocabulary is an open set, it is not devoid of systematicity. The obvious case is word families. Even though different parts of speech of the same base words, e.g., *avoid, avoidable, avoidance, unavoidable* are different lemmas, or lexical items, the learning burden of adding derived words to the learner's vocabulary is not the same as adding lemmas that do not belong to the same word family, e.g., *avoid, abolish, respond*. In the case of a word family, the basic form and the basic meaning are related to one another. Furthermore, many affixes are regular in the sense that they add the same meaning to the base word. Exercises with derived words provide an opportunity to teach the morphological system. Once learners understand how some affixes change the meaning of the base word, they will understand a large number of new words without the need to be taught what they mean. For example, if they understand the meaning of the affixes in *unreadable* and *happiness*, they will probably transfer this understanding to *unbearable* and *emptiness*. There have been suggestions that knowledge of base words does not extend to knowledge of derived words (e.g., McLean, 2017), but studies that make such a claim and support it with data, do not provide information of whether and how the learners in the studies were taught morphology. I contend that the benefit of exercises with derived words is twofold. Learners add words to their lexicon without too much learning effort and acquire rules for understanding additional new words in the future.[5]

Another example of systematicity in vocabulary is a certain type of phrasal verbs where a particular particle modifies the meaning of the verbs in a similar way. One of the meanings of the particle *up* in phrasal verbs is completion, one meaning of *down* is reduction, one meaning of *on* is continuation. Expansion exercises can group phrasal verbs with the same particles and the same meaning modifications. Thus *drink up* can be grouped with *burn up, clean up, finish up, tear up, fill up*, and *mess up. Calm down* can be practiced with *narrow down, cool down, slow down*, and *quiet down; go on* – with *keep on, lead on, carry on, stay on*, and *move on*. Such groupings are not claimed to be the solution to learning phrasal verbs with their multitudes of meanings. However, awareness of a system can simplify the learning task and add additional units of meaning to the learner's lexicon.

Differential Treatment

The third principle for effective expansion and consolidation exercises is "differential treatment due to different learnability". Not all words are equally easy or difficult for learners. Languages borrow words from other languages albeit with phonological adaptations. These words are easy to learn and can be introduced in large numbers in the input without any special treatment in exercises. Difficult words, however, deserve special treatment. There are two major types of difficulty. The first one is interlingual, that is, results from relating the new L2 words to L1 words, which learners take to be equivalent in meaning. The second one is intralingual, which stems from relating the new words to already familiar words within the foreign language (for reviews and summaries, see Laufer, 1990; Laufer, 1997; Laufer & Nation, 2011; Swan, 1997). An example of interlingual difficulty is different lexicalization of concepts in different languages and the resulting lack of semantic overlap between L2 words and their L1 equivalents. For example, *song* and *poem* are represented by one word *shir* in Hebrew, since Hebrew does not distinguish between rhyming words with or without music. Similarly *evaluate/appreciate/estimate* are translated by one Hebrew word *leha'arich*. Each time learners speak or write in English, they have to make the choice between several variants that designate a concept represented by one lexical item in their L1. An effective exercise that consolidates the knowledge of one of the above options should also practice the other options that are bound to be confused due to interlingual difference. It is hard to design such exercises in classes with learners with different L1s. Intralingual difficulties, however, can be treated in any class.

Two examples of intralingual difficulties are synformy – similarity of form between different words – and multiplicity of meaning. Learners confuse pairs or groups of words that are similar in sound, script, and morphology. (For definitions and classifications of synformy see Laufer, 1988.) Some examples of synforms are *tired/tried, place/palace, person/ prison, plant/planet, conceal/cancel/counsel, industrious/industrial, exhausted/exhaustive, economic/economical*, and *sensible/sensitive/sensual*. After at least one of the words in a pair/group is known, or possibly both words were encountered, an exercise where learners have to distinguish between the synforms can prevent possible confusion.

The English words like *lie, abstract, bank, pupil*, and *plant* are homonyms, i.e., words with unrelated meanings. Learners may learn one meaning and not suspect that there is an additional unrelated meaning as well. An exercise that practices both meanings in different contexts raises awareness of this phenomenon.

Activation of Receptive Knowledge

The fourth principle required of effective exercises is activation of receptive knowledge, in other words adding the productive dimension of word knowledge. Productive vocabulary knowledge is more difficult to achieve and retain than receptive knowledge (Laufer, 1998). First, while the meaning of a word will often suffice to comprehend a message, additional features of knowledge are required to use a word, such as pronunciation or spelling, the specific grammatical features, collocations, and pragmatic characteristics. Second, since most basic content can be expressed with frequent vocabulary, less frequent words that are not used may be forgotten or become temporarily inaccessible. Hence, it is important to elicit already taught vocabulary that we want learners to use correctly and not to forget.

One option is to supply words and phrases and ask learners to rearrange them in such a way that they form a sentence, with or without adding connecting words. For example, to practice *convenient, inconvenient, abolish* learners should rearrange the following phrases: *be abolished, be created, convenient, inconvenient, waterfall, mountain, can*. The resulting sentence is: *An inconvenient mountain can be abolished and a convenient waterfall can be created.*

Another exercise that forces learners to use the target words is rewriting sentences or pieces of text with words/phrases that have to be replaced. For example, to elicit the words *immense, increase, effect, acceleration*, the following sentences can be provided with the phrases in italics to be replaced: There has been *a big growth* in the sense of human power. This is one *result* of the *speeding up* of scientific progress. The rewritten sentences are: There has been *an immense increase* in the sense of human power. This is one *effect* of the *acceleration* of scientific progress. An easier version of the exercise will have the target words in a word bank, or the first letter of the word underneath the word to be replaced. A more challenging version will have no options or clues.

Another useful exercise that elicits specific words and phrases is what I refer to as "controlled writing". When asking open-ended comprehension questions on a text, or assigning a short composition, keywords and phrases can be provided by the teacher. Learners will have to use them in their answers.

Finally, in monolingual classes translation can be practiced from L1 to L2. Sentences for translation should be kept simple and each one should focus on one or two specific lexical items that we want to elicit. In my experience, translation exercises have been very effective for producing words and phrases and for practicing interlingual contrasts that contribute to reducing some negative effects of cross linguistic influence (see Laufer & Girsai, 2008).

Future Directions

In this chapter I surveyed three theoretical frameworks that explain effectiveness of exercises. The Involvement Load Hypothesis and the Technique Features Analysis attempt to provide specific task characteristics that contribute to learning. The TOPRA model shows the importance of focused learning and allocating cognitive resources in learning tasks. Future research could refine these frameworks and seek evidence for their validity. Though the ILH was researched in quite a number of studies, the TFA was not. I would contend that this framework can best be studied in the context of familiar learners and familiar syllabi. In the case of some of the TFA features like motivating the learners, new learning, interference (which is related to new learning), form-meaning connection (which is related to chance of error, which, in turn may be dependent on learners' learning experience and knowledge), it is hard to decide whether they are or are not a part of the task characteristics when we experiment with unfamiliar populations.

For both the ILH and TFA it is interesting to find out which task features are more influential when tasks have an identical total rating. This would require comparisons of tasks with an identical total rating, but different distribution of features. For example, sentence writing has an IL of 3 when meanings of the words are provided by the teacher (+ need, – search ++ evaluation). Filling in blanks with words from a word bank, where the meanings have to be looked up in the dictionary, also has an IL of 3 (+ need, + search, + evaluation). A comparison of the effectiveness of these two tasks for word retention could show us whether the features "search" and "evaluation" are equally important. Finally, there is hardly any research on an increase of knowledge of words that are familiar to some degree. Additional studies could investigate what exercises can best contribute to such an increase. For example, in the case of L2 collocations that are different from L1, research could compare the effectiveness of an exercise of translation with an exercise of constructing original sentences with the collocations. A lot of foreign language learning occurs in the classroom. Research on the effectiveness of exercises can inform our understanding of vocabulary learning and is highly beneficial to the language teaching profession.

Further Reading

Hulstijn, J., & Laufer, B. (2001). Some empirical evidence for the involvement load hypothesis in vocabulary acquisition. *Language Learning, 51*, 539–558.
The paper summarizes the Involvement Load Hypothesis and shows how the hypothesis can be tested empirically.
Nation, I. S. P., & Webb, S. (2011). *Researching and analyzing vocabulary*. Boston, MA: Heinle Cengage Learning.

The book addresses a variety of issues in vocabulary learning and research, such as incidental and intentional vocabulary learning, including teaching techniques, making word lists, and assessing vocabulary.

Related Topics

Incidental and intentional learning, the effect of frequency of exposure on word memorization, acquisition from viewing and using computers

Notes

1 "Word-focused instruction" is the adaptation of form-focused instruction (FFI) to vocabulary (Laufer, 2005, 2010).
2 Nation and Webb (2011) suggested that "search" was similar to "retrieval" in the TFA framework. However, the two features are not the same. "Retrieval" refers to retrieving information from the mental lexicon and is, therefore, present in tasks that practice already familiar or partly familiar words (we cannot retrieve the meaning or form of something we do not know). "Search" for meaning or form is associated with new words, since the IL framework was designed for new words only.
3 "Incidental" does not mean "unfocused". Learning that occurs after word-focused exercises like writing sentences with target words, or filling them in given sentences is incidental if no conscious effort has been made to memorize the words.
4 For example, Hu and Nassaji (2016) discuss success in *task completion* in terms of IL and TFA, while these frameworks were designed to test *word retention as a result of a task* after its completion. Furthermore, the authors reassigned IL values to tasks based on learners' retention of words, but IL of a task depends on *task features*, not on learners' success. Otherwise, the same task would have a different IL and TFA rating for different learners. Both frameworks are independent of learners' results and have been misrepresented in the paper.
5 When learning to decompose words into morphemes, learners should be warned that some words look as if they were constructed of morphemes, but in fact they cannot be decomposed, e.g., *discourse, outline, nevertheless* (Laufer, 1989).

References

Agustin Llach, M. P. (2009). The effect of reading only, reading and comprehension, and sentence writing in lexical learning in a foreign language: Some preliminary results. *RESLA*, *22*, 9–33.

Barcroft, J. (2002). Semantic and structural elaboration in L2 lexical acquisition. *Language Learning*, *52*, 323–363.

Barcroft, J. (2004). Effects of sentence writing in second language lexical acquisition. *Second Language Research*, *20*, 303–334.

Barcroft, J. (2009). Effects of synonym generation on incidental and intentional L2 vocabulary learning. *TESOL Quarterly*, *43*, 79–103.

Cobb, T. (2007). Computing the vocabulary demands of L2 reading. *Language Learning and Technology*, *11*(3), 38–63.

Elgort, I. (2011). Deliberate learning and vocabulary acquisition in a second language. *Language Learning*, *61*, 367–413.

Ellis, R., & He, X. (1999). The roles of modified input and output in the incidental acquisition of word meanings. *Studies in Second Language Acquisition*, *21*, 285–301.

Folse, S. K. (2006). The effect of type of written exercise on L2 vocabulary retention. *TESOL Quarterly*, *40*, 273–293.

Hu, Hsueh-chao M., & Nassaji, H. (2016). Effective vocabulary learning tasks: Involvement Load Hypothesis versus Technique Feature Analysis. *System*, *56*, 28–39.

Hulstijn, J. H. (2001). Intentional and incidental second language vocabulary learning: A reappraisal of elaboration, rehearsal and automaticity. In P. Robinson (Ed.), *Cognition and second language instruction* (pp. 258–286). Cambridge, UK: Cambridge University Press.

Hulstijn, J. H., & Laufer, B. (2001). Some empirical evidence for the involvement load hypothesis in vocabulary acquisition. *Language Learning, 51*, 539–558.

Keating, G. (2008). Task effectiveness and word learning in a second language: The involvement load hypothesis on trial. *Language Teaching Research, 12*, 365–386.

Kim, Y. J. (2006). Effects of input elaboration on vocabulary acquisition through reading by Korean learners of English as a foreign language. *TESOL Quarterly, 40*, 341–370.

Kim, Y. J. (2008). The role of task-induced involvement and learner proficiency in L2 vocabulary acquisition. *Language Learning, 58*, 285–325.

Knight, S. (1994). Dictionary use while reading: The effects on comprehension and vocabulary acquisition for students of different verbal abilities. *The Modern Language Journal, 78*, 285–299.

Laufer, B. (1988). The concept of "synforms" (similar lexical forms) in L2 vocabulary acquisition. *Language and Education, 2*, 113–132.

Laufer, B. (1989). A factor of difficulty in vocabulary learning: Deceptive transparency. *AILA Review, 6*, 10–20.

Laufer, B. (1990). Words you know: How they affect the words you learn. In J. Fisiak (Ed.), *Further insights into contrastive linguistics* (pp. 573–593). Amsterdam: John Benjamins.

Laufer, B. (1997). What's in a word that makes it hard or easy? Intralexical factors affecting the difficulty of vocabulary acquisition. In N. Schmitt & M. McCarthy (Eds.), *Vocabulary description, acquisition and pedagogy* (pp. 140–155). Cambridge, UK: Cambridge University Press.

Laufer, B. (1998). The development of passive and active vocabulary in a second language: Same or different? *Applied Linguistics, 12*, 255–271.

Laufer, B. (2001). Reading, word-focused activities and incidental vocabulary acquisition in a second language. *Prospect, 16*, 44–54.

Laufer, B. (2003). Vocabulary acquisition in a second language: Do learners really acquire most vocabulary by reading? Some empirical evidence. *Canadian Modern Language Review, 59*, 567–587.

Laufer, B. (2005). Focus on form in second language vocabulary learning. In S. H. Foster-Cohen, M. Garcia-Mayo, & J. Cenoz (Eds.), *EUROSLA yearbook* (Vol. 5, pp. 223–250). Amsterdam: Benjamins.

Laufer, B. (2006). Comparing focus on form and focus on formS in second language vocabulary learning. *Canadian Modern Language Review, 63*, 149–166.

Laufer, B. (2010). Form focused instruction in second language vocabulary learning. In R. Chacón-Beltrán, C. Abello-Contesse, M. M. Torreblanca-López, & M. D. López-Jiménez (Eds.), *Further insights into non-native vocabulary teaching and learning* (pp. 15–27). Bristol, UK, Buffalo, NY and Toronto: Multilingual Matters.

Laufer, B., & Girsai, N. (2008). Form-focused instruction in second language vocabulary learning: A case for contrastive analysis and translation. *Applied Linguistics, 29*, 694–716.

Laufer, B., & Hulstijn, J. (2001). Incidental vocabulary acquisition in a second language: The construct of task-induced involvement. *Applied Linguistics, 22*, 1–26.

Laufer, B., & Nation, I. S. P. (2011). Vocabulary. In S. M. Gass & A. Mackey (Eds.), *The Routledge handbook of second language acquisition* (pp. 163–176). London, UK and New York, NY: Routledge.

Laufer, B., & Rozovski-Roitblat, B. (2015). Retention of new words: Quantity of encounters, quality of task, and degree of knowledge. *Language Teaching Research, 19*, 1–25.

McLean, S. (2017). Evidence for the adoption of the flemma as an appropriate word counting unit. *Applied Linguistics.* Advance online publication. http://dx.doi.org/10.1093/applin/amw050

Nagy, W., Herman, P., & Anderson, R. (1985). Learning words from context. *Reading Research Quarterly, 20*, 233–253.

Nassaji, H., & Hu, H. C. M. (2012). The relationship between task-induced involvement load and learning new words from context. *International Review of Applied Linguistics in Language Teaching, 50*, 69–86.

Nation, I. S. P. (2001). *Learning vocabulary in another language*. Cambridge, UK: Cambridge University Press.

Nation, I. S. P. (2014). How much input do you need to learn the most frequent 9,000 words? *Reading in a Foreign Language, 26*(2), 1–16.

Nation, I. S. P., & Webb, S. (2011). *Researching and analyzing vocabulary*. Boston, MA: Heinle Cengage Learning.

Paribakht, T. S., & Wesche, M. (1997). Vocabulary enhancement activities and reading for meaning in second language vocabulary acquisition. In J. Coady & T. Huckin (Eds.), *Second language vocabulary acquisition: A rationale for pedagogy* (pp. 20–34). Cambridge, UK: Cambridge University Press.

Peters, E., Hulstijn, J. H., Sercu, L., & Lutjeharms, M. (2009). Learning L2 German vocabulary through reading: The effect of three enhancement techniques compared. *Language Learning, 59*, 113–151.

Pichette, F. L., de Serres, L., & Lafontaine, M. (2012). Sentence reading and writing for second language vocabulary acquisition. *Applied Linguistics, 33*, 66–82.

Qian, D. D. (1996). ESL vocabulary acquisition: Contextualization and decontextualization. *Canadian Modern Language Review, 53*, 120–142.

Schmidt, R. (2001). Attention. In P. Robinson (Ed.), *Cognition and second language instruction* (pp. 3–32). Cambridge University Press.

Sternberg, R. J. (1987). Most vocabulary is learnt from context. In M. G. McKeown & M. E. Curtis (Eds.), *The nature of vocabulary acquisition* (pp. 89–105). Hillsdale, NJ: Erlbaum.

Sun, Chia-Ho. (2017). The value of picture-book reading-based collaborative output activities for vocabulary retention. *Language Teaching Research, 21*, 96–117.

Swan, M. (1997). The influence of the mother tongue on second language vocabulary acquisition and use. In N. Schmitt & M. McCarthy (Eds.), *Vocabulary description, acquisition and pedagogy* (pp. 156–180). Cambridge, UK: Cambridge University Press.

Webb, S. (2005). Receptive and productive vocabulary learning: The effects of reading and writing on word knowledge. *Studies in Second Language Acquisition, 27*, 33–52.

Zimmerman, C. B. (1997). Do reading and interactive vocabulary instruction make a difference? An empirical study. *TESOL Quarterly, 31*, 121–140.

Zou, D. (2017). Vocabulary acquisition through cloze exercises, sentence-writing and composition-writing: Extending the evaluation component of the involvement load hypothesis. *Language Teaching Research, 21*, 54–75.

Zou, D., Wang, F. L., Kwan, R., & Xie, H. (2018). Investigating the effectiveness of vocabulary learning tasks from the perspective of the technique feature analysis: The effects of pictorial annotations. In S. K. S. Cheung, J. Lam, K. C. Li, O. Au, W. W. K. Ma, & W. S. Ho (Eds.), *Technology in education: Innovative solutions and practices* (Vol. 843, pp. 3–15). Singapore: Springer Singapore.

Part III
Measuring Knowledge of Vocabulary

24
Measuring Depth of Vocabulary Knowledge

Akifumi Yanagisawa and Stuart Webb

Introduction

Vocabulary research tends to focus on knowledge of form-meaning connection. Studies investigating the effects of teaching interventions on vocabulary learning often test whether participants can provide first language (L1) translations or synonyms for second language (L2) target words, or whether they can select corresponding L1 translations or synonyms for target words from among several options. Studies measuring the vocabulary size or breadth of learners' knowledge also exclusively focus on whether test takers know the meanings of words. Measuring whether L2 learners know the meanings of L2 words is important without doubt; it may provide a better indication of whether learners can potentially understand words, compared to measuring other aspects of vocabulary knowledge such as spelling, pronunciation, and grammatical functions. However, the results of tests that only measure knowledge of the form-meaning connections of words may be misleading because vocabulary knowledge involves knowing many different things (e.g., derivations, collocations, associations) apart from form and meaning. Hence, how well words are known should also be considered.

Depth of vocabulary knowledge is typically defined as how well a word is known. Thus, measuring depth of vocabulary knowledge should tell us how well test takers know words. The importance of knowing vocabulary deeply is based mainly on two ideas: (1) L2 learners have to know different aspects of word knowledge in order to fulfill communicative tasks (i.e., reading, listening, writing, and speaking), and (2) advanced learners who can use vocabulary proficiently can demonstrate different aspects of knowledge of words. For example, knowledge of spelling is required for writing, knowledge of pronunciation is necessary for speaking, and knowledge of collocation is needed for both of these skills. Moreover, to use words appropriately, learners also have to know the contexts where specific words should and should not be used. Tests of vocabulary depth are thus of great value because they may signal the extent to which students have the knowledge to use vocabulary proficiently. Accordingly, measuring depth of knowledge is important for both educators and researchers. For educators, scores on depth measurements might indicate the extent to which L2 students have made progress in their vocabulary learning and the areas of vocabulary knowledge (e.g., spoken form of vocabulary as opposed to written form) that require further attention. For researchers, scores on depth measurements may reveal how vocabulary knowledge develops and is associated with learning a language.

There are now many studies that have investigated depth of vocabulary knowledge. These studies vary greatly in their conceptualization and measurement of vocabulary depth. This chapter provides an overview of how depth has been defined and investigated. Moreover, the chapter will discuss important topics related to measuring depth of vocabulary knowledge and look at questions such as: To what extent can depth of vocabulary knowledge be measured? Which aspects of vocabulary knowledge should be measured? Which words to measure?

Critical Issues and Topics

How Has Depth of Vocabulary Knowledge Been Defined?

Depth of knowledge is often contrasted with breadth (or size) of knowledge, which refers to the number of words that are known. One oft-cited definition is provided by Anderson and Freebody (1981):

> The first [vocabulary knowledge] may be called "breadth" of knowledge, by which we mean the number of words for which the person knows at least some of the significant aspects of meaning. . . . [There] is a second dimension of vocabulary knowledge, namely the quality or "depth" of understanding. We shall assume that, for most purposes, a person has a sufficiently deep understanding of a word if it conveys to him or her all of the distinctions that would be understood by an ordinary adult under normal circumstances.
>
> *(pp. 92–93)*

One important message from the conceptualization of depth by contrasting it with breadth is that in order to use the language competently, L2 learners need to not only know many words but also need to know each word deeply. It may be possible that some learners can provide the L1 translations for many L2 words by learning vocabulary with flash cards or word lists. In contrast, there may be other learners who do not know many words but have a deep understanding of words through engaging in different types of activities (e.g., extensive reading, writing activities, oral communication) that include a limited number of words (Schmitt, 2014).

Depth of vocabulary knowledge has been defined in many ways. For example, in Read (1993, p. 357), depth is described as "the quality of the learners' vocabulary knowledge". Wesche and Paribakht (1996, p. 13) defined depth "in terms of kinds of knowledge of specific words or in terms of degrees of such knowledge". Henriksen (1999) conceptualized depth of knowledge as one of the three dimensions of lexical competence:

1   Partial to precise knowledge
2   Depth of knowledge
3   Receptive to productive use ability

The first dimension, partial to precise knowledge, refers to the strength of word knowledge. Henriksen's description mainly focuses on the extent to which a word's meaning or form is known. As to the second dimension, depth refers to different aspects of vocabulary knowledge (e.g., various meanings of a word, associations among words, word class specification). She reports that to measure depth of knowledge, "researchers must ideally use a combination of test formats that tap [into] different aspects of knowledge" (p. 306). However, she discusses depth mainly in the context of network building, which is "the process of discovering the sense relations or intentional links between words – that is, fitting the words together in semantic networks" (p. 308). The third dimension, receptive to productive use ability, refers to the ability to understand and use a word. Henriksen suggests using various types of tests to measure each dimension of vocabulary knowledge.

Read (2004) noted that the term depth of knowledge has been used by many researchers in various ways. Read classified depth of knowledge into the following three components:

1   Precision of meaning
2   Comprehensive word knowledge
3   Network knowledge

The first and second categories, precision of meaning and comprehensive word knowledge, resemble the first and second dimensions of Henriksen's (1999) conceptualization of lexical competence. Precision of meaning refers to how well the meaning of a word is known. Comprehensive word knowledge refers to multiple aspects of word knowledge. Read listed aspects of vocabulary knowledge as semantic, orthographical, morphological, syntactic, collocational, and pragmatic characteristics. The last category, network knowledge, refers to the degree to which words are organized or linked with each other in one's mental lexicon.

In attempting to review earlier studies that focused on depth of knowledge in order to examine the relationship between depth and size (or breadth) of knowledge, Schmitt (2014) grouped depth of knowledge into seven conceptualizations: (1) receptive vs. productive mastery, (2) knowledge of multiple word knowledge components, (3) knowledge of polysemous meaning senses, (4) knowledge of derivative forms (word family members), (5) knowledge of collocation, (6) the ability to use lexical items fluently, and (7) the degree and kind of lexical organization.

As described earlier, depth of knowledge has been defined and conceptualized in many ways. Studies have adopted various conceptualizations of depth of knowledge, and accordingly, different conceptualizations require different approaches to measure depth of knowledge. The next section will look at how depth has been measured while referring to the corresponding conceptualizations of depth of knowledge described above.

How Has Depth of Vocabulary Knowledge Been Measured?

Ways to measure depth of knowledge can be categorized into three approaches: a developmental approach, a lexical network approach, and a components approach.

Developmental Approach

This approach operationalizes depth of vocabulary knowledge as developmental degree of word knowledge and considers that word knowledge develops from no knowledge to fully developed knowledge. Studies adopting the developmental approach use scales that indicate the developmental stage of vocabulary knowledge (Paribakht & Wesche, 1993; Schmitt & Zimmerman, 2002; Wesche & Paribakht, 1996). The most established and widely used test adopting this approach is the Vocabulary Knowledge Scale (VKS: Paribakht & Wesche, 1993; Wesche & Paribakht, 1996). The VKS is designed to capture the developmental stage of word knowledge ranging "from complete unfamiliarity, through recognition of the word and some idea of its meaning, to the ability to use the word with grammatical and semantic accuracy in a sentence" (Wesche & Paribakht, 1996, p. 29). VKS's five stages of word knowledge (Wesche and Paribakht call them categories) to measure depth are as follows:

I I don't remember having seen this word before.
II I have seen this word before, but I don't know what it means.
III I have seen this word before, and I *think* it means _____. (synonym or translation)
IV I *know* this word. It means _____. (synonym or translation)
V I can use this word in the sentence: _____. (If you do this section, please also do Section IV.)

Test takers are asked to select the category that best represents how well one knows each word, and if possible, demonstrate their knowledge of the word. Points are provided based on their performance in the categories; when test takers select category I, one point is awarded, and when they use a word in a sentence with grammatical accuracy and semantic appropriateness, five points are awarded.

Although the VKS has been widely used in the field of vocabulary research, its validity has been frequently questioned (e.g., Bruton, 2009; Nation & Webb, 2011; Read, 2000; Schmitt, 2010; Webb, 2012; see also Kremmel, this volume). Among many issues that have been pointed out, the main critiques relate to two assumptions. First, the VKS assumes that the degree of difficulty between each category of the scale is equally spaced. However, this assumption is not based on any research findings, and different degrees of difficulty may be involved in advancing from one category to the next. For example, development from category I (i.e., I don't remember having seen this word before) to category II (i.e., I have seen this word before, but I don't know what it means) could be more easily achieved compared to the development from category II to category III (i.e., I have seen this word before, and I *think* it means _____). Usually studies use the combined VKS scores of tested words for each test taker; however, because the degrees of difficulty across categories are probably not equally spaced, the combined test scores cannot be appropriately interpreted. Second, the VKS also assumes that vocabulary knowledge develops linearly from category I (i.e., no knowledge of word form) to category V (i.e., words are used with grammatical accuracy and semantical appropriateness). Although this assumption seems reasonable, one can use a word with grammatical accuracy without clearly understanding its meaning (McNeill, 1996). Hence, this linear developmental assumption may not always be accurate. Despite these problematic assumptions, studies usually combine the VKS test scores across different categories, which obscures what type of vocabulary knowledge the test scores represent.

Lexical Network Approach

This approach conceptualizes depth of vocabulary knowledge as a lexical network in L2 learners' mental lexicon, and research adopting this approach aims to inquire into the extent to which words are connected to each other (Henriksen, 1999; Meara, 1996, 2009; Meara & Wolter, 2004). This conceptualization corresponds to Read's (2004) third definition of depth of knowledge, network knowledge. L2 learners' lexical networks have been investigated mainly by free word-association tasks (e.g., Fitzpatrick, 2013 for a review) as well as other passive association recognition tasks (e.g., Meara, 2009; Meara & Wolter, 2004; Wilks & Meara, 2002). Free word-association tasks ask examinees to provide the first word that comes to mind when hearing or seeing each cue word. It is believed that "[a] spontaneous response will reflect the strongest, or most salient, or most automatic link from that cue word" (Fitzpatrick, 2013, p. 6193). Building on word-association research, Read (1993, 1998) made the Word Associates Format (WAF) that requires learners to identify words that are associated with the target words instead of producing them. The WAF is arguably the most frequently used test format for measuring depth of vocabulary knowledge. Researchers have used the WAF to measure depth of knowledge and investigate the relationships between depth and breadth of knowledge, and/or between depth and language proficiency (e.g., reading, listening) (e.g., Qian, 1999, 2002; Qian & Schedl, 2004; Stæhr, 2009; Zhang & Yang, 2016; see also Qian and Lin, this volume). The following is an example of the WAF described in Read (1998).

sudden

| beautiful | quick | surprising | thirsty | change | doctor | noise | school |

The WAF involves learners selecting four words out of eight choices that have either a paradigmatic (have a related meaning) or syntagmatic (appear together in context, i.e., collocate) relationship with the cue word. In this example, *quick* and *surprising* are the paradigmatic associations for *sudden*, while *change* and *noise* are the syntagmatic associations for *sudden*.

The advantage of the WAF is that it measures multiple aspects of vocabulary knowledge, synonymy, polysemy, and collocations. However, the WAF also has several limitations. First, test takers can sometimes select appropriate associates without knowing a target word (Read, 1993; Schmitt, Ng, & Garras, 2011). Second, researchers' use of the WAF varies from study to study in terms of the selection of cue words, association relationships, and test formats; therefore, research findings are not easily interpreted nor comparable across studies (see Zhang & Koda, 2017 for a recent review). Furthermore, studies administering the WAF tend to score the different associations as one variable, despite the WAF measuring different types of associations (i.e., paradigmatic and syntagmatic). This may limit the extent to which depth is revealed (Webb, 2012; Zhang & Koda, 2017). Lastly, because the WAF includes a focus on form-meaning connection, it might provide a rather narrow measurement of depth of vocabulary knowledge (Webb, 2012). For example, other dimensions of vocabulary knowledge, such as spelling, pronunciation, and grammatical functions, are also important for communicative tasks and would also be useful to measure.

Components Approach

This approach, also called the dimensions approach, conceptualizes depth of vocabulary knowledge by describing separate elements involved in knowing a word. This corresponds to Henriksen's (1999) definition of depth of knowledge and Read's (2004) second component of depth, comprehensive word knowledge. Among many others (e.g., Cronbach, 1942; Richards, 1976), Nation's (2013) description of vocabulary knowledge is the most comprehensive and widely cited classification of the different dimensions (Table 24.1).

Nation (2013) classified vocabulary knowledge into three components: form, meaning, and use. Each component is broken down into three aspects of knowledge. Each aspect

Table 24.1 Description of word knowledge

Form	Spoken	R	What does the word sound like?
		P	How is the word pronounced?
	Written	R	What does the word look like?
		P	How is the word written and spelled?
	Word parts	R	What parts are recognizable in this word?
		P	What word parts are needed to express the meaning?
Meaning	Form and meaning	R	What meaning does this word form signal?
		P	What word form can be used to express this meaning?
	Concept and referents	R	What is included in the concept?
		P	What items can the concept refer to?
	Associations	R	What other words does this make us think of?
		P	What other words could we use instead of this one?
Use	Grammatical functions	R	In what patterns does the word occur?
		P	In what patterns must we use this word?
	Collocations	R	What words or types of words occur with this one?
		P	What words or types of words must we use with this one?
	Constraints on use	R	Where, when, and how often would we expect to meet this word?
	(register, frequency . . .)	P	Where, when, and how often can we use this word?

Note: R = receptive knowledge, P = productive knowledge.

Source: Adapted from Nation (2013, p. 49)

is further broken down into receptive and productive knowledge. Receptive (or passive) knowledge is the knowledge that is required to comprehend words when encountered during reading or listening. Productive (or active) knowledge is what is required to use words for speaking or writing. Studies adopting this components approach have focused upon measuring one or several of these aspects of vocabulary knowledge.

In the components approach, it is very important to clearly distinguish *depth of knowledge* and *strength of knowledge* (Nation & Webb, 2011; Webb, 2012). Webb (2012, p. 3) defines strength of knowledge as "how well a single aspect is known". For example, the written form of a word (i.e., spelling) can be known to different degrees, from no knowledge to degrees of partial knowledge, which may include being able to identify the word when seeing it or being able to write the word with an inaccurate but identifiable spelling, to full knowledge, where one can quickly produce the complete and exact spelling of a word. In Laufer and her colleagues' studies (Laufer, Elder, Hill, & Congdon, 2004; Laufer & Goldstein, 2004), the term strength of knowledge is used to compare the different degrees of knowledge of form-meaning connections: receptive (or passive) recognition and recall, and productive (or active) recognition and recall. Strength of knowledge may also refer to fluency of word knowledge, i.e., how quickly one aspect of word knowledge can be accessed (see also Godfroid, this volume, for how different aspects of word knowledge can be measured with tacit-implicit, automatized explicit, or procedural methods). Strength of knowledge is thus one important indicator of the quality of word knowledge. However, strength and depth of knowledge should not be considered as equivalents. Because these two terms refer to two different qualities of word knowledge, treating them as one construct complicates the term depth and may reduce the generalizability of findings across studies. For example, Vermeer (2001) operationalized depth as how well the meanings of words are known when investigating the relationship between depth and breadth of knowledge. The results showed a strong correlation between the two. This led Vermeer to claim that depth and breadth are the same construct. However, as Nation and Webb (2011) and Schmitt (2014) point out, looking only at one aspect (in this case form-meaning connection) may not be enough to reveal comprehensive depth of vocabulary knowledge. Hence, it would be more meaningful to distinguish between the quality of one aspect of word knowledge from the quality of multiple aspects of word knowledge by referring to the former as *strength of knowledge* and the latter as *depth of knowledge.*

Studies using the components approach can be further divided into two groups, studies measuring multiple aspects of knowledge and studies focusing on one single aspect of word knowledge (e.g., collocation, derivatives). The former studies conceptualize depth of knowledge as the degree to which different components are known (or learned) while measuring the same set of words. For example, Schmitt (1998) tracked three advanced English learners' acquisition of 11 words over a year. He assessed the learner's strength of knowledge of spelling, associations, grammatical information, and polysemy for the words. The results showed that multiple aspects of vocabulary knowledge developed gradually. While knowledge of spelling was high from the beginning, learners rarely knew all of a tested word's multiple meanings or derivative forms. In a series of studies, Webb investigated the degree to which different learning conditions contributed to vocabulary depth by measuring five different components of knowledge: orthography, syntax, association, grammatical functions, and form-meaning connection (Webb, 2005, 2007a, 2007b, 2009a, 2009b). Each component was measured using receptive and productive tests (recognition and recall formats, respectively). For example, Webb (2007b) demonstrated that different aspects of word knowledge can be learned incidentally through reading. Furthermore, frequency of encounters influenced the development of different aspects of word knowledge differently.

One advantage of measuring multiple aspects of vocabulary knowledge is that test scores may be more meaningful. When using one test that measures multiple aspects of vocabulary knowledge together, it may not be clear what type of vocabulary knowledge the test score represents. Another advantage is that scores on different tests can be directly compared with each other because every test measures the same set of words. This allows researchers to examine how comprehensively different components of word knowledge are known and the hierarchical order of acquisition of various components of a word. However, measuring different components of knowledge does have some limitations. For example, measuring multiple aspects of vocabulary knowledge tends to take a long time (Nation & Webb, 2011; Schmitt, 1998), which increases the burden on both test takers and researchers. Accordingly, only small numbers of words are focused on in each individual study. Test results based on the measurement of a small number of words may not adequately describe L2 learners' comprehensive vocabulary knowledge (Meara & Wolter, 2004; Read, 2000; Schmitt, 2010).

The second group of studies that might be classified under the components approach have focused on providing a more accurate measurement of one aspect of knowledge rather than measuring several aspects. Quite frequently measurements focusing on vocabulary knowledge, such as collocations, word parts, and grammatical functions, have been referred to as depth tests even when measurement focused only on one aspect of word knowledge (e.g., Gyllstad, 2013; Henriksen, 1999; Milton, 2009; Schmitt, 2000, 2014).

For example, several tests have been developed to measure knowledge of collocations (Gyllstad, 2009; Nguyen & Webb, 2017; see also Gyllstad, this volume), and word parts (or derivatives) (Sasao & Webb, 2017; Schmitt & Zimmerman, 2002; see also Sasao, this volume). The following is an example of the collocation test format administered by Nguyen and Webb (2017).

1 **money**   a. check   b. drop   c. make   d. miss
2 **figure** a. central b. funny   c. happy   d. usual

In this example, test takers were asked to choose the most suitable verb (make) and adjective (central) that can be combined with noun prompt words. Nguyen and Webb sampled collocations from three frequency levels (1,000, 2000, and 3,000) when selecting target items.

Schmitt and Zimmerman's (2002) Test of English Derivatives taps into knowledge of different derivative forms within major word classes (i.e., noun, verb, adjective, and adverb). The following is one example. The words in parentheses are the answers.

1 **stimulate**

Noun	A massage is good _____.	(stimulation)
Verb	Massages can _____ tired muscles.	(stimulate)
Adjective	A massage has a _____ effect.	(stimulating)
Adverb	He massaged _____.	(X)

Test takers are to write the correct form of the cue word in each sentence. If there is more than one possible answer, test takers are to write only one, and if there is no form, to write X.

Tests measuring one specific aspect of vocabulary knowledge are helpful to reveal an L2 learner's strength of knowledge for a specific aspect. If a more common test of form-meaning connection, such as the Vocabulary Levels Test, is also administered then together they may provide some indication of depth. However, one limitation would be that because each test is developed separately, the test scores may not necessarily be comparative across different aspects. Focusing only on one aspect of word knowledge should also be considered a very narrow measurement of vocabulary depth. To overcome this limitation, Ishii and Schmitt (2009) proposed a principled approach to diagnosing vocabulary weakness by comparing student performance to the norm of their peers. In their study, Japanese EFL students' vocabulary size and knowledge of multiple meanings, derivatives, and lexical choice between near-synonyms were measured. Each student's scores on different vocabulary tests were presented in a radar chart, by which a student can easily understand the area of vocabulary knowledge that they should focus on. Ishii and Schmitt could successfully detect variations in different vocabulary measurements. It would also be beneficial for researchers to develop standardized tests, in which different aspects of word knowledge can be directly compared with each other.

Which Approach Should We Use to Measure Depth of Knowledge?

As described earlier, researchers have conceptualized depth in several ways and have used different approaches to measure the quality of L2 learners' vocabulary knowledge. In order to disentangle the definition of depth of vocabulary knowledge, it is beneficial to discuss which approach works best.

The first approach is the developmental approach, which examines depth of word knowledge by looking at the developmental stage of word knowledge. However, as seen in many criticisms of the VKS, combining different aspects of word knowledge in a single test may reduce the validity of the test by making it unclear which type of knowledge the test scores reflect. One might argue that the developmental approach can be used by focusing on one aspect of word knowledge and tracking its development (e.g., from no knowledge to full knowledge of the spelling of a given word). Although this is a useful measurement, it may be better treated as a measure of a single component rather than depth, unless it is measured together with other aspects of knowledge. It is also quite different from what many researchers consider as depth of knowledge. Instead, it might be best to consider it a measure of strength of knowledge (Nation & Webb, 2011; Webb, 2012).

Another approach is the lexical network approach, which examines the L2 learners' mental lexicon. Read's (1993, 1998) WAF has been used to indicate one's lexical network or knowledge of paradigmatic and syntagmatic connections among words. For example, synonyms, near-synonyms, and collocations are treated as an indication of one's depth of vocabulary knowledge. However, two main issues were pointed out. First, because the WAF combines scores of different types of word connections, it is not clear which aspects of vocabulary knowledge the test scores represent. Second, the degree of depth of knowledge that the WAF taps into is quite narrow and may not be sufficiently comprehensive to claim that the test reflects one's comprehensive lexical network or depth of knowledge. Although the WAF represents an important development in vocabulary testing, within the lexical network approach we might hope for the development of a test that taps into more aspects of vocabulary knowledge.

This leaves the components approach as the last plausible path. The advantage of the components approach is that each measurement has high construct validity (i.e., measuring the construct that a test is supposed to be addressing) because it focuses on each aspect of word knowledge separately. Because of this, test scores are more easily and clearly interpreted, compared to using one test that claims to be measuring depth of vocabulary knowledge. Additionally, each aspect can be investigated more deeply by using different levels of sensitivity to measure its strength of knowledge. It is also necessary to simultaneously measure different aspects of word knowledge in order to reveal a comprehensive picture of L2 learners' quality of vocabulary knowledge. Recent advancements in the use of statistical analysis in the vocabulary research field can also broaden research on depth of knowledge. For example, Structural Equation Modeling (SEM) allows us to examine multiple aspects of vocabulary knowledge in an integrated manner (Kieffer & Lesaux, 2012; Koizumi & In'nami, 2013; Tseng & Schmitt, 2008; Zhang, 2012). Mixed-effects statistical models enable us to examine the influence of the characteristics of words (e.g., cognate status, pronounceability) and the characteristics of examinees (e.g., proficiency, L1 background, learning contexts) on test performance simultaneously (e.g., Cunnings, 2012). In addition to the use of traditional approaches (e.g., statistical inference to compare mean differences, multiple regression analysis), advanced statistical analyses may further help us investigate the complicated relationships between proficiency and different aspects of vocabulary knowledge and between size, depth, and lexical development.

To What Extent Can Depth of Vocabulary Knowledge Be Measured?

It may not be realistic to provide a comprehensive measure of vocabulary depth. The reason behind this is that even when using a large battery of tests or an interview, we may only measure a fraction of knowledge of a word. Imagine a case in which we would like to measure knowledge of the word *make*. We could ask students to provide an L1 translation for *make*. However, *make* has multiple meanings. For example, *make dinner*, *make money*, *make a reservation*, and *make one's bed* refer to different actions. One can also express different meanings by combining *make* with other words, such as *I didn't make it to the train last night*, *make up your mind*, or *I could not make out what she was saying*. Furthermore, knowing the written form of *make* does not necessarily mean that one knows the spoken form, and vice versa. If we want to measure knowledge of collocation, there are a large number of useful words that co-occur with *make*, such as *sure, sense, difference, money, decision(s), feel, clear, easier, changes, happen, living*, and many more. However, it would be difficult to measure knowledge of more than a small number of collocations for a word. Similarly, if we want to measure knowledge of the derivations of *make*, then we would hope to reveal whether test takers know *makes, making, makings, made, maker, remake, remade, unmake*, and *unmade*. As this example of *make* illustrates, there is a great deal involved in knowing a word, and it may be very challenging to determine the extent to which everything is known about a word. Even in studies measuring multiple aspects of word knowledge, a fraction of a student's knowledge may be measured. One way to deal with this difficulty is to focus on the strength of knowledge regarding specific aspects of depth of knowledge in relation to the purpose of the study.

Which Aspects of Vocabulary Knowledge Should Be Measured?

In research and pedagogy, it is important to consider which aspects of vocabulary knowledge to measure. The aspects of vocabulary knowledge that are measured should be selected in relation to the teaching and learning purpose. If we are interested in the degree to which words are learned in different activities, the aspects that the activities contribute to should be measured. For example, crossword puzzles, matching activities, and multiple-choice questions typically contribute most to learning form-meaning connection and written form, so perhaps these two aspects might be measured. Meaning-focused reading and listening activities contribute to most aspects of knowledge and so may merit measuring knowledge of aspects such as grammatical functions, word parts, collocations, and form-meaning connection. Perhaps of most interest in activities that involve the use of words in speech and writing would be measuring knowledge of collocations and associations because these aspects are of particular importance in production. However, it would also be meaningful to measure spoken and written word form when comparing vocabulary learning from reading, reading while listening, and listening activities. For example, reading while listening activities might better facilitate learning of spoken word forms (e.g., pronunciation) in addition to written word forms.

Which Words to Measure?

Which target words to measure should be based on the purpose of the study. When trying to draw a comprehensive picture of L2 learners' vocabulary knowledge, it is probably helpful to measure knowledge of words at different frequency levels. Frequency is considered to be one of the most influential factors contributing to language acquisition (e.g., Ellis, 2002). More frequent words tend to be learned before less frequent words (e.g., Webb, Sasao, & Ballance, 2017). Additionally, learners may have deeper knowledge of words at higher frequency levels compared to those at lower frequency levels (Schmitt, 2014). For example, Nguyen and Webb (2017) found that Vietnamese EFL learners' receptive knowledge of collocations tended to develop according to the frequency of the individual words in the collocations; collocation knowledge increased as the frequency of the individual words comprising the collocations increased. However, to date, few attempts have been made to look at depth of knowledge of words at different frequency levels (Greidanus, Bogaards, van der Linden, Nienhuis, & de Wolf, 2004; Nguyen & Webb, 2017). Measuring words at different frequency levels would be beneficial because this may indicate (1) up to which frequency level learners have acquired a specific component of vocabulary knowledge, and (2) which frequency level learners should focus on to foster their depth of knowledge. Furthermore, longitudinally tracking multiple components of word knowledge at different frequency levels may show the developmental speed of each component of word knowledge, which in turn would help to reveal a more comprehensive picture of how vocabulary knowledge develops.

In studies examining how different aspects of word knowledge are developed through language learning (e.g., Pigada & Schmitt, 2006; Schmitt, 1998; Webb, 2005, 2007a, 2007b, 2009b), words that participants encounter during a learning condition are best suited to be tested. Target words can be the words that participants do not know, or words that are partially known; some components of word knowledge may be known while other components may not be known.

Future Directions

There are three key areas for further research on depth of vocabulary knowledge. The first is to examine how different components of depth relate to each other and to vocabulary size. Research demonstrates that different measures of depth of knowledge tend to correlate with each other (e.g., Ishii & Schmitt, 2009; Schmitt & Meara, 1997). Furthermore, studies tend to find a high correlation between tests measuring different components of depth and size tests that measure knowledge of the form-meaning link (e.g., Gyllstad, 2009; Qian, 1999; Tannenbaum, Torgesen, & Wagner, 2006; Vermeer, 2001). These findings may indicate that some aspects of vocabulary knowledge develop simultaneously while others develop at different rates. The high correlation between size and depth measurements indicates that there may be little value in measuring depth of knowledge (Milton, 2009; Schmitt, 2014). However, as mentioned in Schmitt's (2014) comprehensive review of earlier studies measuring both size and depth, the correlation between size and depth varies from study to study. Hence, it is still not clear how different aspects of vocabulary knowledge relate to each other. The size of the correlation may be dependent upon variables such as test format, participant differences, and study design. It may be worth conducting individual studies or meta-analyses to investigate when correlations between depth and size increase and/or decrease. Similarly, looking at the relationships between different aspects of word knowledge may reveal how closely they are related. However, it is also important to note that if measurements highly correlate with each other, those measures may merely be different tests measuring the same construct. On the other hand, lower correlations between different aspects of knowledge may signal constructs that researchers should not combine.

The second area where research is needed is examining how depth of knowledge contributes to language teaching. Researchers have emphasized the pedagogical importance of depth of vocabulary knowledge (e.g., Nation & Webb, 2011; Schmitt, 2014; Webb, 2012) suggesting that language learners should not only focus on learning form-meaning links but also try to learn multiple aspects of knowledge of a word in order to use it in a communicative context. However, few studies have focused on how measures of depth of vocabulary knowledge benefit language teaching. Ishii and Schmitt (2009) pointed out that there is little practical advice on how depth test scores can be interpreted for pedagogical purposes. They proposed a principled approach to diagnosing vocabulary weakness by comparing student performance to the norms of their peers. In order to increase the value of such an approach, it is also important to investigate to what extent each aspect of knowledge relates to students' actual use of words.

Two lines of research could conceivably deepen our understanding of the relationship between how well words are known and how well the words can be used. The first is to investigate how well scores on different depth of knowledge measurements explain students' language proficiency (i.e., reading, writing, listening, and speaking). Research has demonstrated that vocabulary size largely predicts learners' language abilities (e.g., Milton, 2010, see also Qian and Lin, this volume). Some researchers looked at the relationship between language ability and vocabulary knowledge by measuring both size and depth (Kieffer & Lesaux, 2012; Koizumi & In'nami, 2013; Qian, 1999, 2002; Qian & Schedl, 2004; Stæhr, 2009; Tannenbaum et al., 2006; Zhang & Yang, 2016). The findings show that depth and size tests tend to highly correlate with each other, and by and large depth and size tests provide similar predictive power of learners' proficiency. For example, Qian (1999) looked at the relationship between reading comprehension and size and depth of vocabulary knowledge. Depth of vocabulary knowledge was measured with Read's WAF. The results showed that depth added a further 11% to the prediction of reading comprehension over and above the prediction already provided by vocabulary size. Based on this, Qian concluded that not only size but also depth is an important aspect of vocabulary knowledge for predicting reading comprehension. On the other hand, Stæhr (2009) examined the relationships between vocabulary size, depth, and listening comprehension, and found that depth only added 2% to the prediction of listening comprehension on top of the prediction already made by size. The contribution of depth of knowledge may differ based on the component of depth measured and on the characteristics of the language ability measured. Zhang and Yang (2016) investigated learners of Chinese and found that vocabulary size was a more important predictor of comprehension of longer passages than depth of knowledge, while depth was a better predictor of comprehension of shorter passages. So far, a general agreement of whether depth (and depth components) uniquely contributes to the prediction of language ability over and above vocabulary size has not been reached, making further research warranted. Results from further research may indicate (1) which aspects of vocabulary knowledge are important to certain language abilities, and (2) which aspect of depth of knowledge teachers should measure to get an idea of how proficient students are in a specific language ability.

The second line of research on the pedagogical value of depth of knowledge would be to measure different aspects of vocabulary knowledge that are developed through completing different types of language activities. It is reasonable to assume that activities in which learners focus on form-meaning connection exclusively develop learners' knowledge of this aspect. Interestingly, two of Webb's (2007a, 2009b) studies investigating the effects of different types of learning activities provided counterintuitive results. Webb (2007a) investigated the effects of learning word pairs and learning from a single glossed sentence. The results indicated that the provision of context did not contribute to greater learning of different aspects of vocabulary knowledge. In Webb's (2009b) study, EFL students learned L2 vocabulary using word lists. A battery of ten tests measuring several aspects of vocabulary knowledge revealed that students can learn not only form-meaning connection but also collocation, grammatical functions, and associations to some extent just through linking L1 translations to target words. Therefore, it would be useful to further investigate which types of activities foster different aspects of vocabulary knowledge.

The last research area that requires more attention is the development of standardized tests that tap into each aspect of vocabulary knowledge. There are already many tests developed and recommended for measuring different aspects of vocabulary knowledge (e.g., Gyllstad's (2009) COLLEX and COLLMATCH tap into knowledge of collocation; Sasao and Webb's (2017) Word Part Levels Test measures knowledge of word parts). However, because existing measurements are developed independently, scores on the tests cannot be directly compared to each other. It would also be useful to develop a battery of tests designed to measure different aspects of vocabulary knowledge of words at different frequency bands (Milton & Hopkins, 2006; Nation & Webb, 2011; Nguyen & Webb, 2017). Nguyen and Webb (2017) measured collocational knowledge of words at the first three 1,000-word frequency levels, as well as single-word items at the same frequency levels. Milton and Hopkins (2006) measured students' knowledge of written and spoken form-meaning connection by using two different test formats (i.e., X-Lex & AuralLex). Similar methods can be applied to develop a set of vocabulary tests that measure other aspects of vocabulary knowledge such as derivational forms, semantic associations, and polysemy. The results of this test battery may reveal the quality of students' knowledge of words at different frequency levels. The test scores could also be directly compared to each other and could be interpreted much easier.

Further Reading

Webb, S. (2007b). The effects of repetition on vocabulary knowledge. *Applied Linguistics*, 28(1), 46–65.

This study investigated how encountering words in 1, 3, 7, and 10 sentences contributed to different aspects of vocabulary knowledge. The article described how different components of depth of vocabulary knowledge can be measured and interpreted.

Nation, I. S. P., & Webb, S. (2011). *Researching and analyzing vocabulary*. Boston, MA: Heinle.

The chapter on measuring depth of vocabulary knowledge describes the steps that researchers should take when measuring depth of knowledge. It also provides a practical guide to measuring depth of knowledge.

Schmitt, N. (2010). *Researching vocabulary: A vocabulary research manual*. New York, NY: Palgrave Macmillan.

The chapter on measuring vocabulary knowledge provides a review of previous studies focused on measuring depth of knowledge and discusses the advantages and issues related to different test formats.

Related Topics

Vocabulary assessment, vocabulary tests, quality of word knowledge, vocabulary size, lexical development, measuring vocabulary learning progress

References

Anderson, R. C., & Freebody, P. (1981). Vocabulary knowledge. In J. T. Guthrie (Ed.), *Comprehension and teaching: Research reviews* (pp. 77–117). Newark, DE: International Reading Association.

Bruton, A. (2009). The vocabulary knowledge scale: A critical analysis. *Language Assessment Quarterly*, 6(4), 288–297. https://doi.org/10.1080/15434300902801909

Cronbach, L. J. (1942). An analysis of techniques for diagnostic vocabulary testing. *The Journal of Educational Research*, 36(3), 206–217. https://doi.org/10.1080/00220671.1942.10881160

Cunnings, I. (2012). An overview of mixed-effects statistical models for second language researchers. *Second Language Research*, 28(3), 369–382. https://doi.org/10.1177/0267658312443651

Ellis, N. C. (2002). Frequency effects in language processing. *Studies in Second Language Acquisition*, 24(2), 143–188.

Fitzpatrick, T. (2013). Word associations. In C. A. Chapelle (Ed.), *The encyclopedia of applied linguistics* (pp. 6193–6199). Oxford, UK: Wiley-Blackwell. https://doi.org/10.1002/9781405198431.wbeal1283

Greidanus, T., Bogaards, P., van der Linden, E., Nienhuis, L., & de Wolf, T. (2004). 10. The construction and validation of a deep word knowledge test for advanced learners of French. In P. Bogaards & B. Laufer (Eds.), *Language learning & language teaching* (Vol. 10, pp. 191–208). Amsterdam: John Benjamins Publishing Company. https://doi.org/10.1075/lllt.10.14gre

Gyllstad, H. (2009). Designing and evaluating tests of receptive collocation knowledge: COLLEX and COLLMATCH. In A. Barfield & H. Gyllstad (Eds.), *Researching collocations in another language* (pp. 153–170). New York, NY: Palgrave Macmillan. https://doi.org/10.1057/9780230245327_12

Gyllstad, H. (2013). Looking at L2 vocabulary knowledge dimensions from an assessment perspective – challenges and potential solutions. In C. Bardel, C. Lindquist, & B. Laufer (Eds.), *L2 vocabulary acquisition, knowledge and use: New perspectives on assessment and corpus analysis* (pp. 11–28). Amsterdam: Eurosla.

Henriksen, B. (1999). Three dimensions of vocabulary development. *Studies in Second Language Acquisition, 21*(2), 303–317.

Ishii, T., & Schmitt, N. (2009). Developing an integrated diagnostic test of vocabulary size and depth. *RELC Journal, 40*(1), 5–22. https://doi.org/10.1177/0033688208101452

Kieffer, M. J., & Lesaux, N. K. (2012). Direct and indirect roles of morphological awareness in the English reading comprehension of native English, Spanish, Filipino, and Vietnamese speakers: Roles of morphological awareness. *Language Learning, 62*(4), 1170–1204. https://doi.org/10.1111/j.1467-9922.2012.00722.x

Koizumi, R., & In'nami, Y. (2013). Vocabulary knowledge and speaking proficiency among second language learners from novice to intermediate levels. *Journal of Language Teaching and Research, 4*(5), 900–913. https://doi.org/10.4304/jltr.4.5.900-913

Laufer, B., Elder, C., Hill, K., & Congdon, P. (2004). Size and strength: Do we need both to measure vocabulary knowledge? *Language Testing, 21*(2), 202–226. https://doi.org/10.1191/0265532204lt277oa

Laufer, B., & Goldstein, Z. (2004). Testing vocabulary knowledge: Size, strength, and computer adaptiveness. *Language Learning, 54*(3), 399–436.

McNeill, A. (1996). Vocabulary knowledge profiles: Evidence from Chinese-speaking ESL teachers. *Hong Kong Journal of Applied Linguistics, 1*, 39–63.

Meara, P. (1996). *The vocabulary knowledge framework. Vocabulary Acquisition Research Group Virtual Library.* Retrieved from www.lognostics.co.uk/vlibrary/meara1996c.pdf

Meara, P. (2009). *Connected words: Word associations and second language vocabulary acquisition* (Vol. 24). Amsterdam: John Benjamins Publishing Company. https://doi.org/10.1075/lllt.24

Meara, P., & Wolter, B. (2004). V_Links: Beyond vocabulary depth. In K. Haastrup & B. Henriksen (Eds.), *Angles on the English speaking world* (Vol. 4, pp. 85–96). Copenhagen, Denmark: Museum Tusculanum Press.

Milton, J. (2009). *Measuring second language vocabulary acquisition.* Bristol, UK: Multilingual Matters.

Milton, J. (2010). The development of vocabulary breadth across the CEFR levels. In I. Bartning, M. Martin & I. Vedder (Eds.), *Communicative proficiency and linguistic development: Intersections between SLA and language testing research* (pp. 211–232). Eurosla Monographs Series, 1. http://eurosla.org/monographs/EM01/EM01home.html.

Milton, J., & Hopkins, N. (2006). Comparing phonological and orthographic vocabulary size: Do vocabulary tests underestimate the knowledge of some learners? *Canadian Modern Language Review, 63*(1), 127–147. https://doi.org/10.3138/cmlr.63.1.127

Nation, I. S. P. (2013). *Learning vocabulary in another language* (2nd ed.). Cambridge, UK: Cambridge University Press.

Nation, I. S. P., & Webb, S. (2011). *Researching and analyzing vocabulary.* Boston, MA: Heinle.

Nguyen, T. M. H., & Webb, S. (2017). Examining second language receptive knowledge of collocation and factors that affect learning. *Language Teaching Research, 21*(3), 298–320. https://doi.org/10.1177/1362168816639619

Paribakht, T. S., & Wesche, M. B. (1993). Reading comprehension and second language development in a comprehension-based ESL program. *TESL Canada Journal, 11*(1), 9–29. https://doi.org/10.18806/tesl.v11i1.623

Pigada, M., & Schmitt, N. (2006). Vocabulary acquisition from extensive reading: A case study. *Reading in a Foreign Language, 18*(1), 1–28.

Qian, D. D. (1999). Assessing the roles of depth and breadth of vocabulary knowledge in reading comprehension. *Canadian Modern Language Review, 56*(2), 282–308. https://doi.org/10.3138/cmlr.56.2.282

Qian, D. D. (2002). Investigating the relationship between vocabulary knowledge and academic reading performance: An assessment perspective. *Language Learning, 52*(3), 513–536.

Qian, D. D., & Schedl, M. (2004). Evaluation of an in-depth vocabulary knowledge measure for assessing reading performance. *Language Testing, 21*(1), 28–52. https://doi.org/10.1191/0265532204lt273oa

Read, J. (1993). The development of a new measure of L2 vocabulary knowledge. *Language Testing, 10*(3), 355–371. https://doi.org/10.1177/026553229301000308

Read, J. (1998). Validating a test to measure depth of vocabulary knowledge. In A. Kunnan (Ed.), *Validation in language assessment* (pp. 41–60). Mahwah, NJ: Erlbaum.

Read, J. (2000). *Assessing vocabulary*. Cambridge, UK: Cambridge University Press.

Read, J. (2004). Plumbing the depths: How should the construct of vocabulary knowledge be defined? In P. Bogaards & B. Laufer (Eds.), *Vocabulary in a second language* (pp. 209–227). Amsterdam: John Benjamins.

Richards, J. C. (1976). The role of vocabulary teaching. *TESOL Quarterly, 10*(1), 77–89. https://doi.org/10.2307/3585941

Sasao, Y., & Webb, S. (2017). The Word Part Levels Test. *Language Teaching Research, 21*(1), 12–30. https://doi.org/10.1177/1362168815586083

Schmitt, N. (1998). Tracking the incremental acquisition of second language vocabulary: A longitudinal study. *Language Learning, 48*(2), 281–317. https://doi.org/10.1111/1467-9922.00042

Schmitt, N. (2000). *Vocabulary in language teaching*. Cambridge, UK and New York, NY: Cambridge University Press.

Schmitt, N. (2010). *Researching vocabulary: A vocabulary research manual*. Basingstoke, UK: Palgrave McMillan.

Schmitt, N. (2014). Size and depth of vocabulary knowledge: What the research shows. *Language Learning, 64*(4), 913–951. https://doi.org/10.1111/lang.12077

Schmitt, N., & Meara, P. (1997). Researching vocabulary through a word knowledge framework. *Studies in Second Language Acquisition, 19*(1). https://doi.org/10.1017/S0272263197001022

Schmitt, N., Ng, J. W. C., & Garras, J. (2011). The Word Associates Format: Validation evidence. *Language Testing, 28*(1), 105–126. https://doi.org/10.1177/0265532210373605

Schmitt, N., & Zimmerman, C. B. (2002). Derivative word forms: What do learners know? *TESOL Quarterly, 36*(2), 145–171. https://doi.org/10.2307/3588328

Stæhr, L. S. (2009). Vocabulary knowledge and advanced listening comprehension in English as a foreign language. *Studies in Second Language Acquisition, 31*(4), 577–607. https://doi.org/10.1017/S0272263109990039

Tannenbaum, K. R., Torgesen, J. K., & Wagner, R. K. (2006). Relationships between word knowledge and reading comprehension in third-grade children. *Scientific Studies of Reading, 10*(4), 381–398. https://doi.org/10.1207/s1532799xssr1004_3

Tseng, W.-T., & Schmitt, N. (2008). Toward a model of motivated vocabulary learning: A structural equation modeling approach. *Language Learning, 58*(2), 357–400. https://doi.org/10.1111/j.1467-9922.2008.00444.x

Vermeer, A. (2001). Breadth and depth of vocabulary in relation to L1/L2 acquisition and frequency of input. *Applied Psycholinguistics, 22*(2), 217–234. https://doi.org/10.1017/S0142716401002041

Webb, S. (2005). Receptive and productive vocabulary learning: The effects of reading and writing on word knowledge. *Studies in Second Language Acquisition, 27*(1), 33–52.

Webb, S. (2007a). Learning word pairs and glossed sentences: The effects of a single context on vocabulary knowledge. *Language Teaching Research, 11*(1), 63–81.

Webb, S. (2007b). The effects of repetition on vocabulary knowledge. *Applied Linguistics*, *28*(1), 46–65. https://doi.org/10.1093/applin/aml048

Webb, S. (2009a). The effects of pre-learning vocabulary on reading comprehension and writing. *Canadian Modern Language Review*, *65*(3), 441–470.

Webb, S. (2009b). The effects of receptive and productive learning of word pairs on vocabulary knowledge. *RELC Journal*, *40*(3), 360–376. https://doi.org/10.1177/0033688209343854

Webb, S. (2012). Depth of vocabulary knowledge. In C. A. Chapelle (Ed.), *The encyclopedia of applied linguistics* (pp. 1656–1663). Oxford, UK: Wiley-Blackwell. https://doi.org/10.1002/9781405198431.wbeal1325

Webb, S., Sasao, Y., & Ballance, O. (2017). The updated Vocabulary Levels Test. *ITL-International Journal of Applied Linguistics*, *168*(1), 33–69.

Wesche, M., & Paribakht, T. S. (1996). Assessing second language vocabulary knowledge: Depth versus breadth. *Canadian Modern Language Review*, *53*(1), 13–40.

Wilks, C., & Meara, P. (2002). Untangling word webs: Graph theory and the notion of density in second language word association networks. *Second Language Research*, *18*(4), 303–324. https://doi.org/10.1191/0267658302sr203oa

Zhang, D. (2012). Vocabulary and grammar knowledge in second language reading comprehension: A structural equation modeling study. *The Modern Language Journal*, *96*(4), 558–575. https://doi.org/10.1111/j.1540-4781.2012.01398.x

Zhang, D., & Koda, K. (2017). Assessing L2 vocabulary depth with word associates format tests: Issues, findings, and suggestions. *Asian-Pacific Journal of Second and Foreign Language Education*, *2*(1), 1–30. https://doi.org/10.1186/s40862-017-0024-0

Zhang, D., & Yang, X. (2016). Chinese L2 learners' depth of vocabulary knowledge and its role in reading comprehension. *Foreign Language Annals*, *49*(4), 699–715. https://doi.org/10.1111/flan.12225

25

Measuring Knowledge of Multiword Items

Henrik Gyllstad

Introduction

Besides single orthographic words (i.e., sequences of letters surrounded by spaces on each side), in most of the world's languages there are multiword items (MWIs). For example, in the case of English, there are also structures including but not restricted to idioms (*shoot the breeze*), collocations (*blissfully happy*), proverbs (*a watched pot never boils*), binomials *(wear and tear, part and parcel)*, compound nouns (with three spelling variants: concatenated: *boyfriend*, spaced: *blood pressure*, and hyphenated: *word-play*) (Kuperman & Bertram, 2013), and phrasal verbs (*play up*) (see Wood, this volume, for more examples and definitions). As a whole, these MWIs are very common (Erman & Warren, 2000; Pawley & Syder, 1983; Jackendoff, 1995), with Bolinger (1976, p. 1), among others, reminding us about the fact that "our language does not expect us to build everything starting with lumber, nails, and blueprint, but provides us with an incredibly large number of prefabs". In terms of terminology, Wray (2002) has illustrated how many labels have been used in the literature, among those "prefabs", to capture these MWIs and to research them. On the assumption, then, that MWIs abound in language and that efficient language use (comprehension and production) relies on individuals having knowledge of and access to a very large number of these, it is important that knowledge and use can be measured in valid and reliable ways.

Some scholars, such as (McNamara, 2000, p. 55) suggest that the term measurement refers to "the theoretical and empirical analysis of scores and score meaning" (McNamara, 2000, p. 55). As such, measurement can be seen to be the rather more technical side of assessment and testing, where scores are assigned and subjected to various statistical calculations. Other scholars, like Bachman and Palmer (2010, p. 19*f*) pragmatically argue that "measurement", "test", and "assessment" are best seen as terms referring to the same thing: collecting information. However, they add that the important thing for test developers is to clearly specify the conditions under which test takers' performance will be obtained and the procedures followed for recording this performance. Accordingly, in this chapter, "measurement", "assessment", and "testing" will be used interchangeably. The focus will be on measuring knowledge in a second (L2, L3, Ln) or foreign language.

Critical Issues and Topics

Prerequisites for Sound Measurement

Any measurement that lays claim to being a good measure of a specific type of knowledge needs to be valid and reliable. Measuring knowledge of MWIs is no different. Primarily, validity has to do with the notion that what we *intend* to measure or test is also what we in fact *do* measure (Fulcher, 2010). At the heart of any assessment enterprise is the "construct", i.e., that knowledge, skill, or behavior purported to be tested. We will return to this concept later.

It is not uncommon for researchers and test developers to discuss different types of validity, such as construct, content, and criterion validity, but ever since Messick's (1989) seminal work, validity is generally treated as a single concept but with a number of facets. It is important to note that validity is not technically a characteristic of a particular test but rather the inferences and interpretations made from the test scores and their use.

Reliability refers to the consistency of measures across different conditions in the measurement process (Bachman, 2004), and, moreover, whether there is cause for concern that additional construct-irrelevant factors also affect the measurement (Bachman, 1990). We always want to minimize the potential for error in our measurement, and if we can do that, then we will achieve a high level of reliability. A very commonly used analogy is that of a person weighing themselves. If I stand on a scale one day and weigh myself, and then do the same again ten minutes later, I expect the scale to show the same value again, of course on the assumption that I have not eaten or drunk a lot in between, and that I wear the same amount of clothes at both occasions. With respect to measuring knowledge of MWIs, if we for example designed a test to be a reliable measure of this construct, we would expect test takers to get the same or a very similar score if tested on two occasions, as long as no learning was assumed to have taken place in-between. Also, if many test takers who get a high total score on a test answer a question wrongly, and many test takers who get a low total score on the test answer that same question correctly, then it is likely that our measure of the construct will not be very reliable. Reliability can be measured in several ways, for example test-retest, parallel forms, split-half, and internal consistency (see Bachman, 2004, and Weir, 2005, for good accounts of these, and Fulcher, 2010, for calculation examples). There are also specific reliability measures to be used with criterion-referenced tests (see Bachman, 2004).

As was mentioned earlier, in any language measurement endeavor, a link needs to be made between an individual's performance and a specific type of language knowledge or skill (a construct). Bachman (1990, p. 40*f*) has suggested a procedure consisting of three steps to achieve this: (1) defining the construct theoretically, (2) defining the construct operationally, and (3) establishing procedures for quantifying observations. In the case of MWIs, we thus first need a theoretical definition. As an illustration, we could formulate a construct which is "receptive recognition knowledge of English proverbs" (e.g., proverbs like *when in Rome*, *every little helps*, and *better the devil you know*). Once such a definition is in place, we can start working with the population of items that supposedly can be linked to the construct and subsequently sample from this. This is when we operationalize the theoretical construct. This is a tall order, since we ideally want to base our population of items and sampling on some kind of model. Potentially, we could start by asking a sizeable group of native speakers for the proverbs they think are the most useful and frequently used in daily communication. Alternatively, we could specify that the proverbs should have a particular function in the language (in which case the theoretical construct may have to be adjusted). We could additionally ask them to rank them in bins by their relative frequency; for example, extremely frequent, highly frequent, moderately frequent, and frequent. We could then use a large native-speaker corpus to check things like raw frequency and see if we can validate the ranking. An additional check with a second native-speaker group is desirable. If in their judgment the items and their estimated relative frequency can be corroborated, we then have a sample of items. The final step is then to create procedures for measuring and quantifying our observation. For example, we could decide to use a receptive recognition task in which 30 frequent MWIs are presented together with ten distractors (nonexistent sequences of words for which we have evidence of their nonexistence) in a regular pencil-and-paper test format, in which test takers are asked to circle those that they know are frequent and conventional language sequences, or as an additional criterion those they know the meaning of. Our scoring procedures could then be based on a maximum score of 40 points, and we could award one point for each correctly circled proverb MWI, and also one point for each distractor that is left uncircled. Thus, an individual's score is the number of items answered correctly. It would also be possible to employ a correction formula for guessing (see Eyckmans (2004) and Huibregtse, Admiraal, and Meara (2002) for accounts of such formulas).

Different MWI Measurement Approaches

Traditional Test Items and Formats

When it comes to measuring knowledge of MWIs, the literature abounds with various test item formats or elicitation formats. A useful approach for classifying item formats for single-word vocabulary knowledge has been suggested by Laufer and Goldstein (2004). They distinguish between active and passive types of knowledge and also recognition and recall. This makes it possible to create a 2 × 2 matrix whereby four kinds of knowledge can be defined. Based on this work, Schmitt (2010) has argued that the use of terms like "active" and "passive" is somewhat unclear and should be avoided, and that the use of the terms "form" and "meaning" are more transparent and should be used instead. Figure 25.1 shows what Schmitt's take on Laufer and Goldstein's original 2 × 2 matrix would look like for MWIs rather than single-word items.

MWI knowledge aspect given as a prompt		MWI knowledge tested	MWI knowledge tested
MEANING:		FORM RECALL: (supply all or part of the L2 MWI)	FORM RECOGNITION: (select the L2 MWI from options)
example: (Swe. L1) *klen tröst*	→	example: (Eng. L2) *cold comfort*	example: (Eng. L2) a. *weak comfort* b. *feeble comfort* c. *cold comfort*
FORM:		MEANING RECALL: (supply definition/L1 translation)	MEANING RECOGNITION: (select definition/L1 translation from options)
example: (Eng. L2) *play with fire*	→	example: (Swe. L1) *leka med elden*	example: (Swe. L1) a. *spela med lågor* b. *skoja med elden* c. *leka med elden*

Figure 25.1 Matrix for deciding what type of MWI knowledge a test/elicitation item is tapping into
Source: Adapted from Schmitt, 2010, p. 86

In order to illustrate the use of the matrix in Figure 25.1, please consider the following item types taken from studies investigating MWI knowledge. In a study by Webb and Kagimoto (2011, p. 268), an L2 form recall item type is used to test L1 Japanese learners of English in terms of their collocation knowledge:

(1) 出世街道 _____

In (1) the L1 Japanese meaning for the English collocation "fast track" is provided and the test taker is asked provide the L2 form. In (2), we see an example of a use of form recognition items, taken from Gyllstad's COLLEX 3 test format (2007, p. 108). In this item, prompted by the provided L1 Swedish meaning prompt "be en bön" to the left, a test taker is required to select one of the two decontextualized L2 MWI forms provided by ticking the corresponding box to the right. The target MWI in this case is the English collocation *say a prayer*.

			a	b
(2) (be en bön)	a. say a prayer	b. tell a prayer		

In (3), we find an example of a meaning recall format. The item type is taken from a study by Webb, Newton, and Chang (2013, p. 104) investigating incidental learning of collocation.

(3) *meet demand* _____

The format requires test takers to supply the meaning of the L2 MWI by writing an L1 translation, which in the case of this particular study was Mandarin Chinese. Finally, in (4), we see an example of a meaning recognition format. The item is taken from McGavigan's (2009) study of Greek learners' knowledge of idioms. The test taker is expected to select the most appropriate choice out of the four options provided that best matches the meaning of the idiom, in this case *the silver lining*. Interestingly, the multiple-choice item format is the same as that used in the Vocabulary Size Test (Nation & Beglar, 2007) and also the PHRASE Test (Martinez, 2011).

(4) *11. the silver lining*
    A. a wedding present
    B. there is always good in bad situations
    C. hidden treasure
    D. something which is mysterious

Yet another item type used to measure productive knowledge of MWIs is exemplified in a study by Schmitt, Dörnyei, Adolphs, and Durow (2004). The study investigated the acquisition of MWIs through two- to three-month-long treatments of exposure to target MWIs in a presessional EAP course. The researchers created and used a productive test that was a type of cloze test. In each item (see (5) below), a range of academically based MWIs were embedded in multi-paragraph contexts with all or most of the content words in the target MWIs deleted. However, the initial letter(s) of each word was left as a form prompt. The meaning of the targeted phrase was provided next to the item in parentheses to ensure that the ability to produce the form of the MWI was measured, not comprehension of its meaning.

(5) A. The problem is that many people do not want the government to pay the banks. They feel that the banks caused their own problems by lending money too easily.

B. **I s**_____ **what you me**_____. Many special-   (I understand your argument)
ists told the banks that some countries had very
weak economies and could not repay the loans. **In**

sp_____ **of** this, the banks loaned the money   (doing something even though
anyway.   there is a good reason not to)

The item in (5), from Schmitt et al. (2004, p. 73), is reminiscent of Laufer and Nation's (1999) format used for controlled productive vocabulary (a test called the PVLT). Arguably, it has the advantage of being difficult to guess for the test taker if they do not know the target MWI (in this case *I see what you mean* and *in spite of*), while seemingly relatively easy to complete if the target MWI is known. According to Schmitt's matrix (adapted to MWIs) for what type of knowledge is tested (2010, p. 86) (see Figure 25.1), the item format would be classified as "form recall", and the test administrator can make the test harder by being strict when it comes to correct spelling of the missing words of the MWI. It should be noted that getting these items right does not necessarily mean that test takers are able to use (produce) these phrases in natural language communication (writing and speaking).

An additional attempt to measure knowledge of MWIs can be found in Schmitt, Grandage, and Adolphs (2004). The study was aimed at investigating the psycholinguistic validity of corpus-derived recurrent clusters, such as *as a matter of fact* and *in the same way as*. The authors compiled a list of 25 such items based on corpora and textbooks, and devised a method intended to show whether these items were stored holistically or not in native and non-native-speakers' mental lexicons (see Conklin, and Siyanova-Chanturia and Omidian, this volume). The measurement was done through a dictation task with oral responses, and the assumption was that if the stretches of dictation are long enough, short term working memory gets cognitively overloaded, and language users consequently have to rely on representations residing in long term memory to be able to repeat back the language stretches. Two examples of stretches used are given next in (6) and (7) (target items bold and underlined):

(6) I didn't answer, letting his voice drift over me ***in the same way as*** the snow drifted over the hills in the distance.

(7) ***To make a long story short***, I threw out his pack and drove off without him. I'll never pick up a hitchhiker again!

For the target phrase in (6), 14 native speakers (3 correctly and 11 partially incorrectly) (out of 30) and 15 non-native speakers (1 correctly and 14 partially incorrectly) (out of 45) produced this item. For the phrase in (7), 26 native speakers (23 correctly and 3 partially incorrectly) (out of 30) produced this item compared to 39 of the non-native speakers (9 correctly and 30 partially incorrectly) (out of 45). In terms of measurement, the authors engage in discussions on how these scores can be interpreted. Furthermore, potential variables affecting the performance are discussed, and correlations between item corpus frequency, length, and transparency of meaning, and native-speaker performance are reported (only transparency of meaning was significant). However, no analysis employing inferential statistics on target item position in the stretches was carried out. The authors conclude that measuring holistic storage this way is fraught with problems, and this is of course the case. But the study showcases innovative attempts at measuring MWI knowledge outside of a controlled lab setting.

Extant Tests Targeting MWI Types

One type of measurement of MWIs involves what can be seen as traditional tests, either as paper-and-pencil tests, or computerized ones. In the literature, there are a number of tests that have been given a proper name and that in most cases have been subjected to more or less extensive validation procedures. Examples of such tests are the Word Associates Test (WAT) (Read, 1993, 1998), the Association Vocabulary Test (Vives Boix, 1995), V_Links (Wolter, 2005), CONTRIX (Revier, 2009, 2014), COLLEX and COLLMATCH (Gyllstad, 2007, 2009), DISCO (Eyckmans, 2009), and The Phrasal Vocabulary Size Test (Martinez, 2011). Despite these efforts, it is clear that there is a lack of truly standardized tests of MWIs, and instead a number of tests exist that target subtypes of MWIs, such as idioms, collocations, phrasal verbs, and lexical bundles.

Of those listed here, WAT is the oldest and probably also the most well-known test of knowledge that is at least partially referable to MWIs. Originally, it was designed to be a test of depth of vocabulary knowledge (Read, 2004). In its most recent configuration (Read, 2000), the test consists of 40 items, in which a prompt adjective word is supplied together with eight potential associated words, four of them adjectives and four nouns (see Figure 25.2).

The test format is a receptive recognition format designed to target two knowledge types: meaning knowledge and collocation knowledge. A test taker is asked to choose those words, in total four, from the left-most box that are synonyms or near-synonyms of the prompt word, and those words from the right-most box that are collocates. The test is capable of providing reliable scores, with Read (1993) reporting reliability coefficients of around .90 using an Item Response Theory (IRT) Rasch analysis (for accessible and nontechnical accounts, see McNamara, 1996 and Knoch & McNamara, 2015), where reliability measures are not dependent on the particular sample of participants tested. The test is in effect a multiple-choice test, with eight choices to be made for each of the 40 items (i.e., 320 choices). Recent validation of the test and its scores (Schmitt, Ng, & Garras, 2011) has shown that finding a suitable scoring system is indeed challenging.

In a volume on L2 collocation research (Barfield & Gyllstad, 2009b), four tests of MWIs are presented. Three of them involve decontextualized test items, and one includes items

fast

drowsy	quick	revealing	hungry	car	nurse	Food	flower

Figure 25.2 An example test item in the format used in the Word Associates Test
Source: Adapted from Read, 2000, p. 184

with short sentence contexts. Gyllstad's (2007, 2009) two contributions – COLLEX and COLLMATCH – are both receptive recognition formats and aimed at tapping into test takers' knowledge of verb + NP collocations. Both tests are based on corpus analyses of frequent collocates of higher-frequency verbs, and Gyllstad used z-scores (similar to t-scores) from the BNC to inform selection of word combinations as being existing or non-attested in language use.

The COLLEX test (version 5) consists of 50 items of the kind shown in Figure 25.3. In each item, the test taker is asked to choose the option that is a conventional and frequently occurring word combination in the English language out of the three that are presented.

Based on a large-scale administration of the test ($N = 269$), Gyllstad reported on validity and reliability evidence by examining native-speaker group performance compared to non-native learner groups (L1 Swedish), and by comparing non-native-speaker groups of test takers of different overall proficiency levels. Using Classical Test Theory (CTT) approaches to item quality and test reliability (see Bachman, 2004), Gyllstad showed that a high level of internal consistency is attainable for COLLEX scores (Cronbach's alpha = .89).

Eyckmans's (2009) DISCO test is similar to COLLEX in that it is also a receptive recognition test comprising 50 items. In a DISCO item, test takers are asked to choose two options out of three that are deemed idiomatic verb + noun combinations (see Figure 25.4).

The items were constructed based on an initial selection of 40 high-frequency verbs, after which significant collocates were retrieved from the British National Corpus (BNC). Z-scores were used to identify suitable collocations, just like in Gyllstad's (2007, 2009) studies. However one difference with Eyckmans' items selection criteria is that she checked the phrasal frequency of her target items (in an additional corpus), and subsequently divided the items into three frequency bands. This is appealing as it implies modeling MWIs in a similar way to single words, in the sense that frequency is a strong predictor of phrase exposure and ease of acquisition on the part of learners. Using a computerized version of DISCO, Eyckmans tested a fairly small group of L1 Dutch learners of English ($N = 25$). A high level of reliability was observed for the scores (Cronbach's alpha = .90). An ANOVA showed that "frequency band" was a significant factor, and the author argued

	a	b	c
1. a. tell a prayer b. say a prayer c. speak a prayer			

Figure 25.3 An item from COLLEX

Source: From Gyllstad, 2007, p. 306

do time   pay tribute   run chores

Figure 25.4   An example test item in the format used in DISCO

Source: Adapted from Eyckmans, 2009, p. 146

1 have a say	2 lose sleep	3 do justice	4 draw a breath	5 turn a reason
☐ yes	☐ yes	☐ yes	☐ Yes	☐ yes
☐ no	☐ no	☐ no	☐ No	☐ no

Figure 25.5   Five example items from COLLMATCH

Source: From Gyllstad, 2007, p. 310

that DISCO was sensitive enough to pick up on differences in learners' developing collocational knowledge.

Gyllstad's (2007, 2009) COLLMATCH test (version 3) is a 100-item test also aimed at tapping into receptive recognition knowledge. In its earliest inception it started out as a grid format, but in its third version it is in effect a yes/no test. Test takers are asked to indicate for each item (see Figure 25.5 for five example items) whether the word combination exists in the English language. In order to counter overestimation of knowledge, 30 of the 100 items are pseudo-collocations, i.e., non-attested word combinations. For all items, irrespective of category, z-scores were retrieved from the BNC to ensure significance for the target collocations and conversely lack of significance for the pseudo-collocations. Thus, it would be possible to adjust scores for guessing if a suitable adjustment formula can be found (see Pellicer-Sánchez & Schmitt, 2012).

Gyllstad argued that COLLMATCH seems capable of yielding reliable scores (Cronbach's alpha = .89), and that there is evidence of construct validity as well as concurrent validity (correlation between COLLEX and COLLMATCH at $r = .86$).

The COLLEX, COLLMATCH, and DISCO tests are all formats that require test takers to process decontextualized MWIs, and to match these sequences to potential representations in their mental lexicons. If the test taker has a salient representation that matches the MWI in the test, then they should be able to select this with relative ease. If no matching representation can be activated, then the test taker is likely to draw on other strategies, some of them construct-relevant, such as accessing partial knowledge of component words, and estimating the probabilities of certain words to be combinable with others. Other strategies are arguably more construct-irrelevant (Messick, 1995) to a greater or lesser extent, such as blind guessing and using processes of elimination. On a related note, although expressing some praise for high-quality and innovative test development research, in a critical commentary on the preceding tests, Shillaw (2009) argues that COLLEX, DISCO, and COLLMATCH may tap into test takers' sensitivity to collocational potential rather than actual knowledge of collocations, and that all these tests are likely to require further validation.

Revier's (2009, 2014) CONTRIX is different in a number of ways from the three tests described so far. Firstly, CONTRIX is a 45-item test of verb + noun collocations. An example of a CONTRIX item is shown in Figure 25.6. The item consists of a short-sentence context with a gap where one suitable collocation fits. The test taker must choose from the three-column matrix on the right by selecting a verb, a determiner (or none), and a noun that constitutes a conventional MWI in English. In the example, the expected answer is *keep + a + diary*. Secondly, following semantic classification models (Howarth, 1996; Nesselhauf,

Even as a child, John decided to _____. As an adult, he really likes being able to read about his thoughts and other things that happened to him in his childhood.	push	a/an	secret
	keep	the	idea
	pull	–	diary

Figure 25.6   An example test item in the format used in CONTRIX

Source: Adapted from Revier, 2014, p. 89

2005) the test is aimed at testing MWIs belonging to three categories: transparent, semi-transparent, and nontransparent.

The items for CONTRIX were developed by searching for collocates for 15 high-frequency verbs and creating three test parts of 15 verb + noun collocations, thus in total 45 items. In each part, the same verb appeared but with different noun collocates (e.g., *play chess*, *play tricks*, and *play the field*).

Revier argues perhaps somewhat unconventionally that CONTRIX could be said to tap into "productive knowledge for test takers must not only create (i.e., produce) meaning by combining lexical constituents, but they must also grammatically encode the noun constituent for determination" (2009, p. 129). This is an interesting claim. If using the matrix adapted from Schmitt (2010) (see Figure 25.1), the format arguably taps into "form recognition", on the basis that the short-sentence context implicitly hints at a meaning, and the test taker should then find the combination of forms that best fits that implied meaning. However, one could also argue that test takers who are not sure which meaning is targeted in the prompt could look at the provided word forms, and based on a specific combination "recall" the meaning of that MWI. Revier's CONTRIX item format is thus an illustration of the fact that it is not always straightforward to clearly distinguish between form and meaning aspects of knowledge.

A final test format reviewed here, used to measure learners' knowledge of MWIs, can be found in Nguyen and Webb's (2017) receptive knowledge of collocation test. The test targets knowledge of 90 verb + noun and 90 adjective + noun items, and thus consists of a total of as many as 180 items. The items are pairings of words taken from the first thousand most frequent words of English (1K), the second thousand (2K), and the third thousand (3K). Thus, the selection of the target collocations was based on the frequency of the individual words that made up the collocations rather than their frequencies as whole collocations. This highlights the distinction between word-centered and holistic approaches to collocation (see Gyllstad, 2009, p. 169). The format is multiple-choice and two example items can be seen in Figure 25.7.

Much like the WAT, the format tests learners' ability to recognize which of the verb alternatives in 1 goes with the noun *friends*. Similarly, they need to choose the adjective in 2 that goes with the noun *car*. As opposed to the WAT, though, in each item, only one alternative is correct. In terms of measurement reliability, in a study with 100 Vietnamese learners of English, a Cronbach's Alpha of .77 was observed. With so many items, a higher alpha would be expected, but the authors note the rather homogeneous scores of the test takers, and we know that limited variance leads to lower reliability levels for internal consistency approaches to reliability. The learners' scores decreased as a function of decreased word frequency level, something which is expected and observed also for single-word knowledge.

| 1. friends | a. halt | b. check | c. make | d. feel |
| 2. car | a. fair | b. powerful | c. happy | d. sorry |

Figure 25.7 An example of two test items in the format used in Nguyen and Webb's (2017) collocation test (p. 308)

Analysis of Written/Spoken Texts (Manual and Automated Analyses of MWIs)

In addition to more traditional paper and pencil test formats for measuring knowledge of MWIs, one strand of research has focused on assessing the MWIs used in written and spoken production. This entails getting access to texts produced by learners (or/and native speakers) and using either manual procedures for identification of MWIs, or automated ones, or a combination of the two. Examples of such studies are Granger (1998), Howarth (1996, 1998), Erman and Warren (2000), Nesselhauf (2005), Siyanova and Schmitt (2008), Durrant and Schmitt (2009), Chen and Baker (2010), Forsberg (2010), and Laufer and Waldman (2011).

In studies that employ manual identification/measurement, it is of course essential that a clear set of criteria is used to guide this procedure. Erman and Warren (2000) is an oft-cited study worth taking a closer look at in this regard. The authors analyzed texts from a native-speaker spoken corpus, a native-speaker written corpus, and short extracts from a novel, and found that the average proportion of MWIs in texts (in their study called "prefabs") was observed at between 52% (written texts) and 59% (spoken texts). There is no bullet point list of criteria for identification of MWIs provided in the paper, but the following main criteria can be discerned upon scrutiny (pp. 31–34):

1   A prefab is a word combination of at least two orthographic words favored by native speakers even though alternatives exist that are not conventionalized.
2   There is restricted exchangeability as to the word components of the prefab.
3   Completely compositional word combinations are not seen as prefabs.

Even though many easily identifiable prefabs appear in texts (e.g., idioms, compounds, non-compositional collocations, prepositional and phrasal verbs), Erman and Warren emphasize that the identification of prefabs is difficult, depending in part on the fact that what one language user sees or uses as a prefab may not be seen or used as such by another language user. This is very much echoed by Read and Nation (2004, p. 25) who when discussing formulaic sequences argue that what is "holistic" varies from person to person, and even varies from time to time within a person. On a critical note, measurement-wise, only single raters seem to have been used in Erman and Warren's study, and thus no inter-rater reliability (IRR) was established. Best practice would dictate that at least a part of the data be subjected to ratings by at least two raters, using a coefficient for IRR. Commonly used IRR variants are Cohen's Kappa, Cronbach's Alpha, and Krippendorff's Alpha. Hayes and Krippendorff (2007) provide a good discussion of suitability of different coefficients for different types of data. Furthermore, a validity issue resides in the fact that the theoretical definition mentions prefabs favored by native speakers, whereas the material, does not seem to have been checked by or with native speakers.

Another example of a study using a set of criteria for identifying/measuring MWIs can be found in Wray and Namba (2003). Compared to that of Erman and Warren (2000), their approach is much more comprehensive and avoids the pitfall of seeing language sequences as a binary phenomenon of MWIs or not MWIs (in their case formulaic sequences) by using a gradient Likert scale of five steps. No less than 11 criteria are used. Two of the criteria are provided here.

By my judgment, part or all of the wordstring lacks semantic transparency.   [1 2 3 4 5]

By my judgment, the wordstring as a whole performs a function in communica-   [1 2 3 4 5]
tion or discourse other than, or in addition to, conveying the meaning of the words
themselves.

In many studies of written production, measurement of MWIs is aided by some kind of frequency criterion and word association measure. As an example, consider Durrant and Schmitt (2009), who analyzed a corpus of 96 NS and NNS texts, ranging in mean length between ~3,000 words and ~600 words. The MWI investigated was adjacent premodifier-noun word pairs. First, through manual extraction, 10,839 such MWIs were collected. Next, two frequency-based methods for determining collocation strength were applied. One of them entailed tallying the frequency of each MWI in the British National Corpus (BNC), and the other computing measures of collocational strength: t-score and Mutual Informa-tion (MI) score. Both are statistical measures based on taking the observed frequency of the MWI in a corpus and comparing it with the expected frequency by which it would be expected to appear by chance if looking at the frequencies of the component words. For a technical account of these and other types of word association measures, see Evert (2005), and for easy-to-follow calculation examples, see Schmitt (2010). Whereas the t-score gives us a measure of how confident we can be of there being an association, it has a bias in favor of high-frequency pairs (Evert, 2005, p. 84), e.g., *hard work*. MI scores, on the other hand, give us a measure of the strength of an association between two words. MI scores have been found to also have a bias but in this case towards word combinations consisting of relatively low-frequency words, but where the words appear rather exclusively with each other, e.g., *ultimate arbiter*. This applies even when the raw frequency of the word combination as a whole is low (Schmitt, 2010). By convention, t-scores of ≥ 2 and MI scores of ≥ 3 are seen as cutoffs for significant associations. Furthermore, because of the biases mentioned earlier, it is often recommended that MI scores be used in conjunction with a minimum raw frequency threshold (Stubbs, 1995), or in combination with t-scores.

Chen and Baker (2010) is an example of a study in which an automated frequency-driven approach to analyzing texts for MWIs was used. The authors retrieved lexical bundles from one L1 corpus of published academic texts and two L2 corpora of student academic writing, using the corpus tool WordSmith 4.0 (Scott, 2007). Frequency and distribution thresholds for determining four-word lexical bundles were set to ≥ 4 times (approximately 25 times per million words on average) and occurring in at least three texts, respectively. A distinction was also made between different types of bundles (types) and frequencies of bundles (tokens). The authors then relied on a structural classification of lexical bundles in the Longman Gram-mar of Spoken and Written English (Biber, Johansson, Leech, Conrad, and Finegan, 1999), by which 14 categories of lexical bundles are grouped in conversation and 12 categories in academic prose. The bundles from their search were classified and the results were then com-pared with the proportions of structural categories in the LSWE corpus.

Future Directions

Increasing Use of Psycholinguistic Techniques for MWI Measurement

Recently, we have seen an increase in the use of more psycholinguistically oriented techniques for MWI measurement. As this use is expected to increase in the future, a brief account is merited. Most of these techniques of measurement make use of processing time as an indirect indicator of how individuals cognitively master comprehension and production of MWIs, and how different types of MWIs are represented in their mental lexicons (see Conklin, Godfroid, this volume).

One type of measurement that has been used to investigate MWIs is the self-paced reading (SPR) task. The task requires participants to read language sequences (words or sentences) on a computer screen, and their reading times are measured in milliseconds (ms). The participant is asked to press a button once the displayed sentence or phrase has been read, and then a new sequence appears. The assumption for MWIs is that, at least for some types, e.g., idioms like *to flog a dead horse*, language users will read these more quickly on the basis that the idiom is represented as a holistic unit which allows for quicker processing compared to a similar language unit (control) like *to flog a dead cat*. An example of a study using the SPR technique is Conklin and Schmitt (2008). See also a study by Tremblay, Derwing, Libben, and Westbury (2011) investigating the effect of displaying target MWIs either word-by-word, phrase-by-phrase, or sentence-by-sentence.

Another useful technique for measuring MWIs is priming. In priming tasks, participants sitting in front of a computer screen are presented with a series of items, in which a word or wordstring is first shown (the prime) followed by another word (the target). If there is a relationship between the prime and the target (e.g., *say → prayer*) then the processing of the target is facilitated (processing measured in ms is quicker) compared to when there is no relationship between the prime and the target (e.g., *say → table*). It is widely believed that this priming of the target word happens thanks to a process called spreading activation (Collins & Loftus, 1975) by which words perceived to be related to the prime receive a residual level of activation prior to actual presentation. An example of a study using the priming technique is Wolter and Gyllstad (2011). These authors used a primed lexical decision task (LDT) to investigate participants' collocation knowledge. The participant's task was to identify whether or not the target string represented a real word in the specified language, by pressing a corresponding key on a keyboard. The time it took for them to respond was recorded as reaction time (RT). RT was faster for collocations (*say + prayer*) than for non MWIs (*do + prayer*), unrelated items functioning as baselines. Furthermore, RT was also faster for congruent items, i.e., collocations with word-for-word translations in terms of core meanings across Swedish and English, than for incongruent items, i.e., collocations for which word-for-word translations are not possible across the two languages. The sequence of presentation of an item is shown in Figure 25.8.

Eye tracking (ET) has presented itself as another useful technique for measuring knowledge, processing and representation of MWIs (see Conklin, Godfroid, this volume). ET is seen as a more ecologically valid technique compared to SPR. In ET experiments, participants' eye gaze is measured as they read material on a computer screen. In MWI experiments, target items are embedded as regions of interest and presented in displayed sentences, and the assumption is that fixation, fixation count, first pass reading time, and total reading time (in milliseconds) are indications of how well the participant "knows" the target and the nature of the target representation. An example study using ET is Siyanova-Chanturia, Conklin, and Schmitt (2011). These authors investigated and compared native and

Fixation point display		Prime word		Blank screen		Target word
***	⇨	PAY	⇨		⇨	ATTENTION
(250 ms)		(250 ms)		(50 ms)		(RT in ms)

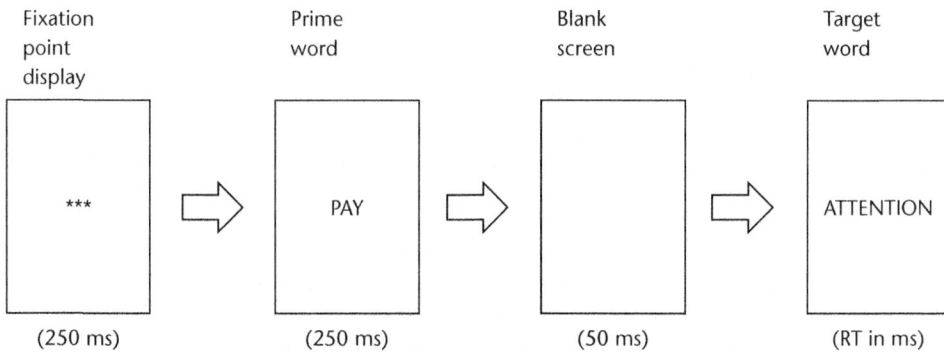

Figure 25.8 An example sequence of item presentation in a primed LDT

Source: Adapted from Wolter & Gyllstad, 2011

non-native-speaker processing of idiomatic MWIs, either as literal items (*at the end of the day = in the evening*), or as figurative (*at the end of the day = eventually*). Another study investigating idiom processing in native and non-native speakers through ET is Carrol, Conklin, and Gyllstad (2016). This study was focused on measuring the influence of the L1 on the processing of idioms in an L2. See also Conklin, Pellicer-Sanchez, and Carroll (2018) for a recent and accessible account of the use of ET in applied linguistics.

A final type of measurement technique for MWI measurement is Event-Related Potentials (ERP). ERP is a noninvasive, but rather technical, neurophysiological technique measuring brain function through recordings of electrical activity in the brain. So far, the technique has been scarcely but increasingly used for studies into MWIs. See Siyanova-Chanturia (2013) for a good overview of methods and findings relevant for MWI research.

With a View to the Future: The Construction of MWI Tests

In this subsection, a number of principles for designing tests of MWIs will be suggested (see also Gyllstad & Schmitt, 2018). It stands to reason that although many attempts have been made to create tests measuring knowledge of MWIs, capable of yielding valid and reliable scores, they all have limitations and are more or less in need of further validation. In the following, some key issues will be discussed as to how future tests can be developed.

Test Development and Use for Particular Purposes

Just like many tests of single-word vocabulary, it is not uncommon for MWI tests to be developed for generic use, without indications of what purposes, contexts, or test takers are the specific targets. Thus, there is a need to move away from a situation where one-size-fits-all tests prevail. The testing of MWIs must to a greater extent follow the lead of mainstream testing where tests are developed and validated for specific contexts and learners (Bachman & Palmer, 2010). In doing this, test developers should use standard validation procedures and concomitant statistical methods (see Bachman, 2004). In order to be clear on what tests are designed to measure, developers of MWI knowledge tests should aim at compiling some type of test manual accompanying the test in which the purpose and rationale of the test is provided, observed reliability (ideally sample-independent reliability), evidence of validity for intended test use, and also how to score the test and – importantly – how to interpret these scores.

Selecting What MWIs to Test

At the beginning of this chapter, as well as in other chapters of this volume, it has been argued that MWIs are very common in language. There are also many subtypes, all with their own characteristics in terms of varying length (*do sports* vs. *in a way* vs. *a watched pot never boils*), frequency (*blow the gaff* [*f* 5,340 in a Google Books search], *face the music* [*f* 225,000 in a Google Books search]), semantic transparency and compositionality (*by the end* vs. *by and large*), and function (discourse markers used to signpost text organization, e.g., *on the one hand*; idioms used to express meaning, e.g., *a green light* = "getting permission for something to start"). Furthermore, we know that some items can have both a literal and figurative meaning (*at the end of the day* [= late in the day, time-wise] vs. *at the end of the day* [= to give one's final opinion after considering all the possibilities]). Since this is the case, it is essential to have a precise definition of the MWI that is being measured in order to have a chance of obtaining a valid and representative sample.

Many specialized dictionaries exist that focus on various categories of MWIs and can be consulted when selecting suitable MWIs. These modern dictionaries are based on corpora, and they generally have a large number of items, e.g., the *Oxford Dictionary of English Idioms* (3rd edition) has ~6,000 items; the *Oxford Idioms Dictionary for Learners of English* (2nd edition, 2006) has ~10,000 items; the *Cambridge Idioms Dictionary* (2006, 2nd ed.) has ~7,000 items; *Oxford Phrasal Verbs Dictionary* (2006, 2nd edition) has ~7,000 items; *Collins COBUILD Phrasal Verbs Dictionary* (2012) has more than 4,000 items, and the *Oxford Collocations Dictionary for Students of English* (2009, 2nd ed.) has ~250,000 items. However, these numbers can be daunting for test developers, when it comes to deciding which MWIs to use. Another approach is to use some kind of frequency list. As an example, Liu (2011) created a condensed list of 150 phrasal verbs based on an initial list of 9,000 phrasal verbs from the British National Corpus. Other lists which provide frequent and pedagogically relevant items include the Pearson Academic Collocation List (2,469 items) (Ackermann & Chen, 2017), the PHRASE List (505 items; Martinez & Schmitt, 2012), the PHaVE List (Garnier & Schmitt, 2015), which covers information about the meaning senses of the most frequent 150 English phrasal verbs, and the Academic Formulas List (Simpson-Vlach & Ellis, 2010), which categorizes the identified formulas according to their function (see Dang, this volume).

As yet an alternative, test developers can use corpora to cull their own selection of MWIs. Mark Davies has made many excellent corpora available to test developers, teachers, and students. They are available online at https://corpus.byu.edu/, and include *The Corpus of Contemporary American English* (COCA) (Davies, 2008), *The British National Corpus* (BYU-BNC) (Davies, 2004), and *the Corpus of Global Web-Based English* (GloWbE) (Davies, 2013). The interface used for these corpora enables test developers to control many aspects of the search criteria for MWIs, such as lemmatized searches, search span, and what specific language structures are targeted. In addition, association measures such as Mutual Information (MI) and raw frequencies are presented.

Sampling

After having chosen an appropriate list or selection of MWIs, test developers have to decide on a suitable number of items to sample for the test. Different language skills require different numbers of items. For example, if testing grammar skills like the application of the simple present third person verb inflection (*–s*), a fairly limited number of items provide a good indication of knowledge of the construct. This is because with the construct being measured is generalizable knowledge about a rule or a system. However, MWIs are not rule-based in that sense, and even though frequency is a strong predictor of knowledge of MWIs (but not the only one, as variables like salience and semantic transparency can also have a strong effect (e.g., Wolter & Gyllstad, 2013; Gyllstad & Wolter, 2016), just like for single words, we cannot strictly expect that learners' knowledge of one phrasal verb or binomial implies knowledge of another. Ideally, if we know the underlying population of items, we can draw a (random, stratified) sample from that population, test it and then extrapolate to the complete population. This works relatively well if we use a frequency-based model of MWIs. The obvious question is of course what sampling rate can yield valid test scores (see Beglar, 2010; Gyllstad, Vilkaitė, and Schmitt, 2015 for discussions on this). We clearly need to strike a balance between a higher number of items, as this provides better and more valid test information, and a smaller number of items, as this leads to a shorter and more practical test. We have seen that MWI tests developed so far have featured anything from 40 items (WAT), 45 items (CONTRIX), 50 items (DISCO and COLLEX), to 100 items (COLLMATCH). However, for a majority of these, it is not at all clear how scores from these tests relate to the underlying population of items for the specified constructs. Evidently, future tests need to pay closer attention to this issue.

Further Reading

Bachman, L. F., & Palmer, A. (2010). *Language assessment in practice*. Oxford, UK: Oxford University Press.

This monograph explains in detail not only how an assessment can be designed but also how an assessment use argument can be employed to justify the way in which the assessment is used.

Nation, I. S. P. (2013). *Learning vocabulary in another language*. Cambridge, UK: Cambridge University Press.

This book is the second edition of one of the more influential handbooks on vocabulary to date. Chapter 12 (Finding and Learning Multiword Units) describes the nature of MWIs and their learning, and Chapter 13 (Testing Vocabulary Knowledge and Use), even though focusing primarily on single-word vocabulary, provides clear guidelines for important factors to consider for testing, also applicable to MWIs.

Bachman, L. F. (2004). *Statistical analyses for language assessment*. Cambridge, UK: Cambridge University Press.

On the whole, this book provides a comprehensive account of various statistical concepts and analyses relevant for language assessment and testing. For some more advanced topics, it provides an overview which can serve as a point of departure towards more specialized accounts elsewhere. There is also a companion workbook for those wanting to learn and deepen their knowledge of the material in the main book.

Related Topics

Classifying and identifying formulaic language, factors affecting the learning of multiword items, measuring vocabulary learning progress, sensitive measures of vocabulary knowledge and processing, expanding Nation's framework, key issues in researching multiword items

References

Ackermann, K., & Chen, Y.-H. *Academic collocation list*. Retrieved June 28, 2017 from http://pearsonpte.com/research/academic-collocation-list/.

Bachman, L. (1990). *Fundamental considerations in language testing*. Oxford, UK: Oxford University Press.

Bachman, L. (2004). *Statistical analyses for language assessment*. Cambridge, UK: Cambridge University press.

Bachman, L., & Palmer, A. (2010). *Language assessment in practice*. Oxford, UK: Oxford University Press.

Barfield, A., & Gyllstad, H. (2009a). Introduction: Researching L2 collocation knowledge and development. In A. Barfield & H. Gyllstad (Eds.), *Researching collocations in another language: Multiple interpretations* (pp. 1–18). New York, NY: Palgrave Macmillan.

Barfield, A., & Gyllstad, H. (Eds.). (2009b). *Researching collocations in another language – Multiple interpretations*. Basingstoke, UK: Palgrave Macmillan.

Beglar, D. (2010). A Rasch-based validation of the Vocabulary Size Test. *Language Testing, 27*(1), 101–118.

Biber, D., Johansson, S., Leech, G., Conrad, S., & Finegan, E. (1999). *Longman grammar of spoken and written English*. Harlow, UK: Longman.

Bolinger, D. (1976). Meaning and memory. *Forum Linguisticum, 1*, 1–14.

Carrol, G., Conklin, K., & Gyllstad, H. (2016). Found in translation: The influence of the L1 on the reading of idioms in a L2. *Studies in Second Language Acquisition, 38*(3), 403–443.

Chen, Y.-H., & Baker, P. (2010). Lexical bundles in L1 and L2 academic writing. *Language Learning & Technology, 14*(2), 30–49.

Collins, A. M., & Loftus, E. F. (1975). A spreading-activation theory of semantic processing. *Psychological Review, 82*(6), 407–428.

Conklin, K., Pellicer-Sanchez, A., & Carroll, G. (2018). *Eye-tracking: A guide for applied linguistics research*. Cambridge, UK: Cambridge University Press.

Conklin, K., & Schmitt, N. (2008). Formulaic sequences: Are they processed more quickly than non-formulaic language by native and non-native speakers. *Applied Linguistics, 29*(1), 72–89.

Davies, M. (2004–). *BYU-BNC*. (Based on the British National Corpus from Oxford University Press). Retrieved from https://corpus.byu.edu/bnc/.

Davies, M. (2008–). *The Corpus of Contemporary American English (COCA): 560 million words, 1990-present*. Retrieved from https://corpus.byu.edu/coca/.

Davies, M. (2013). *Corpus of Global Web-based English: 1.9 billion words from speakers in 20 countries (GloWbE)*. Retrieved from https://corpus.byu.edu/glowbe/.

Durrant, P., & Schmitt, N. (2009). To what extent do native and non-native writers make use of collocations? *IRAL International Review of Applied Linguistics in Language Teaching, 47*(2), 157–177.

Erman, B., & Warren, B. (2000). The idiom principle and the open choice principle. *Text – Interdisciplinary Journal for the Study of Discourse, 20*(1), 29–62.

Evert, S. (2005). *The statistics of word cooccurrences: Word pairs and collocations*. Unpublished PhD dissertation, University of Stuttgart. Retrieved from https://elib.uni-stuttgart.de/handle/11682/2573

Eyckmans, J. (2004). *Measuring receptive vocabulary size: Reliability and validity of the Yes/No Vocabulary Test for French-speaking learners of Dutch*. Utrecht: LOT.

Eyckmans, J. (2009). Toward an assessment of learners' receptive and productive syntagmatic knowledge. In A. Barfield & H. Gyllstad (Eds.), *Researching collocations in another language: Multiple interpretations* (pp. 139–152). New York, NY: Palgrave Macmillan.

Forsberg, F. (2010). Using conventional sequences in L2 French. *International Review of Applied Linguistics, 48*(1), 25–50.

Fulcher, G. (2010). *Practical language testing*. London, UK: Hodder Education.

Garnier, M., & Schmitt, N. (2015). The PHaVE List: A pedagogical list of phrasal verbs and their most frequent meaning senses. *Language Teaching Research, 19*(6), 645–666.

Granger, S. (1998). Prefabricated patterns in advanced EFL writing: Collocations and formulae. In A. P. Cowie (Ed.), *Phraseology: Theory, analysis and applications* (pp. 145–160). Oxford, UK: Clarendon Press.

Gyllstad, H. (2007). *Testing English collocations*. Unpublished PhD thesis, Lund University, Lund. Retrieved from https://lup.lub.lu.se/search/publication/599011

Gyllstad, H. (2009). Designing and evaluating tests of receptive collocation knowledge: COLLEX and COLLMATCH. In A. Barfield & H. Gyllstad (Eds.), *Researching collocations in another language*: *Multiple interpretations* (pp. 153–170). New York, NY: Palgrave Macmillan.

Gyllstad, H., & Schmitt, N. (2018). Testing formulaic language. In A. Siyanova-Chanturia & A. Pellicer-Sánchez (Eds.), *Understanding formulaic language*: *A second language acquisition perspective* (pp. 174–191). London, UK: Routledge.

Gyllstad, H., Vilkaitė, L., & Schmitt, N. (2015). Assessing vocabulary size through multiple-choice formats: Issues with guessing and sampling rates. *ITL International Journal of Applied Linguistics*, *166*(2), 276–303.

Gyllstad, H., & Wolter, B. (2016). Collocational processing in light of the phraseological continuum model: Does semantic transparency matter? *Language Learning*, *66*(2), 296–323.

Hayes, A. F., & Krippendorff, K. (2007). Answering the call for a standard reliability measure for coding data. *Communication Methods and Measures*, *1*(1), 77–89.

Howarth, P. (1996). *Phraseology in English academic writing*: *Some implications for language learning and dictionary making*. Lexicographica Series Maior 75. Tübingen: Max Niemeyer.

Howarth, P. (1998). Phraseology and second language proficiency. *Applied Linguistics*, *19*(1), 24–44.

Huibregtse, I., Admiraal, W., & Meara, P. (2002). Scores on a yes-no vocabulary test: Correction for guessing and response style. *Language Testing*, *19*(3), 227–245.

Jackendoff, R. (1995). The boundaries of the lexicon. In M. Everaert, E. van der Linden, A. Schenk, & R. Schreuder (Eds.), *Idioms: Structural and psychological perspectives* (pp. 133–166). Hillsdale, NJ: Erlbaum.

Knoch, U., & McNamara, T. (2015). Rasch analysis. In L. Plonsky (Ed.), *Advancing quantitative methods in second language research* (pp. 275–304). New York, NY: Routledge.

Kuperman, V., & Bertram, R. (2013). Moving spaces: Spelling alternation in English noun-noun compounds. *Language and Cognitive Processes*, *28*(7), 939–966.

Laufer, B., & Goldstein, Z. (2004). Testing vocabulary knowledge: Size, strength, and computer adaptiveness. *Language Learning*, *54*(3), 399–436.

Laufer, B., & Nation, I. S. P. (1999). A vocabulary-size test of controlled productive ability. *Language Testing*, *16*(1), 33–51.

Laufer, B., & Waldman, T. (2011). Verb-noun collocations in second language writing: A corpus analysis of learners' English. *Language Learning*, *61*(2), 647–672.

Liu, D. (2011). The most frequently used English phrasal verbs in American and British English: A multicorpus examination. *TESOL Quarterly*, *45*(4), 661–688.

Martinez, R. (2011, September). *Putting a test of multiword expressions to a test*. Presentation given at the IATEFL Testing, Evaluation and Assessment SIG, University of Innsbruck, Austria.

Martinez, R., & Schmitt, N. (2012). A phrasal expressions list. *Applied Linguistics*, *33*(3), 299–320.

McGavigan, P. (2009). *The acquisition of fixed idioms in Greek learners of English as a foreign language*. Unpublished PhD dissertation, University of Wales, Swansea.

McNamara, T. (1996). *Measuring second language performance*. London, UK: Longman.

McNamara, T. (2000). *Language testing*. Oxford, UK: Oxford University Press.

Messick, S. (1989). Validity. In R. L. Linn (Ed.), *Educational measurement* (pp. 13–103). New York, NY: Macmillan.

Messick, S. (1995). Validity of psychological assessment. *American Psychologist*, *50*(9), 741–749.

Nation, I. S. P., & Beglar, D. (2007). A vocabulary size test. *The Language Teacher*, *31*(7), 9–13.

Nesselhauf, N. (2005). *Collocations in a learner corpus*. Amsterdam: John Benjamins.

Nguyen, T. M. H., & Webb, S. (2017). Examining second language receptive knowledge of collocation and factors that affect learning. *Language Teaching Research*, *21*(3), 298–320.

Pawley, A., & Syder, F. H. (1983). Two puzzles for linguistic theory: Nativelike selection and nativelike fluency. In J. C. Richards & R. W. Schmidt (Eds.), *Language and communication* (pp. 191–225). London, UK: Longman.

Pellicer-Sánchez, A., & Schmitt, N. (2012). Scoring Yes–No vocabulary tests: Reaction time vs. nonword approaches. *Language Testing*, *29*(4), 489–509.

Read, J. (1993). The development of a new measure of L2 vocabulary knowledge. *Language Testing*, *10*(3), 355–371.

Read, J. (1998). Validating a test to measure depth of vocabulary knowledge. In A. Kunnan (Ed.), *Validation in language assessment* (pp. 41–60). Mahwah, NJ: Lawrence Erlbaum.

Read, J. (2000). *Assessing vocabulary*. Cambridge, UK: Cambridge University Press.

Read, J. (2004). Plumbing the depths: How should the construct of vocabulary knowledge be defined? In P. Bogaards & B. Laufer (Eds.), *Vocabulary in a second language*: *Selection, acquisition, and testing* (pp. 209–227). Amsterdam: John Benjamins.

Read, J., & Nation, I. S. P. (2004). Measurement of formulaic sequences. In N. Schmitt (Ed.), *Formulaic sequences*: *Acquisition, processing, and use* (pp. 23–35). Amsterdam: John Benjamins.

Revier, R. L. (2009). Evaluating a new test of whole English collocations. In A. Barfield & H. Gyllstad (Eds.), *Researching collocations in another language*: *Multiple interpretations* (pp. 125–138). New York, NY: Palgrave Macmillan.

Revier, R. L. (2014). *Testing knowledge of whole English collocations available for use in written production*: *Developing tests for use with intermediate and advanced Danish learners*. Unpublished PhD thesis, Aarhus University, Aarhus.

Schmitt, N. (2010). *Researching vocabulary: A vocabulary research manual*. Basingstoke, UK: Palgrave Macmillan.

Schmitt, N., Dörnyei, Z., Adolphs, S., & Durow, V. (2004). Knowledge and acquisition of formulaic sequences: A longitudinal study. In N. Schmitt (Ed.), *Formulaic sequences*: *Acquisition, processing, and use* (pp. 55–86). Amsterdam: John Benjamins.

Schmitt, N., Grandage, S., & Adolphs, S. (2004). Are corpus-derived recurrent clusters psycholinguistically valid? In N. Schmitt (Ed.), *Formulaic sequences*: *Acquisition, processing, and use* (pp. 127–151). Amsterdam: John Benjamins.

Schmitt, N., Ng, J. W. C., & Garras, J. (2011). The word associates format: Validation evidence. *Language Testing*, *28*(1), 105–126.

Scott, M. (2007). *Oxford WordSmith tools* (Version 4.0) [Computer software]. Oxford, UK: Oxford University Press.

Shillaw, J. (2009). Commentary on Part III: Developing and validating tests of L2 collocation knowledge. In A. Barfield & H. Gyllstad (Eds.), *Researching collocations in another language: Multiple interpretations* (pp. 171–177). New York, NY: Palgrave Macmillan.

Simpson-Vlach, R., & Ellis, N. C. (2010). An Academic Formulas List: New methods in phraseology research. *Applied Linguistics*, *31*(4), 487–512.

Siyanova-Chanturia, A. (2013). Eye-tracking and ERPs in multi-word expression research: A state-of-the-art review of the method and findings. *The Mental Lexicon*, *8*(2), 245–268.

Siyanova-Chanturia, A., Conklin, K., & Schmitt, N. (2011). Adding more fuel to the fire: An eye-tracking study of idiom processing by native and non-native speakers. *Second Language Research*, *27*(2), 251–272.

Siyanova-Chanturia, A., & Schmitt, N. (2008). L2 learner production and processing of collocation: A multi-study perspective. *Canadian Modern Language Review*, *64*(3), 429–458.

Stubbs, M. (1995). Collocations and semantic profiles: On the cause of the trouble with quantitative studies. *Functions of Language*, *2*(1), 23–55.

Tremblay, A., Derwing, B., Libben, G., & Westbury, C. (2011). Processing advantages of lexical bundles: Evidence from self-paced reading and sentence recall tasks. *Language Learning*, *61*(2), 569–613.

Vives Boix, G. (1995). *The development of a measure of lexical organisation: The Association Vocabulary Test*. Unpublished PhD thesis, University of Wales, Swansea.

Webb, S., & Kagimoto, E. (2011). Learning collocations: Do the number of collocates, position of the node word, and synonymy affect learning? *Applied Linguistics*, *32*(3), 259–276.

Webb, S., Newton, J., & Chang, A. (2013). Incidental learning of collocation. *Language Learning*, *63*(1), 91–120.

Weir, C. (2005). *Language testing and validation*. Basingstoke, UK: Palgrave Macmillan.

Wolter, B. (2005). *V_Links: A new approach to assessing depth of word knowledge*. Unpublished PhD thesis, University of Wales, Swansea.

Wolter, B., & Gyllstad, H. (2011). Collocational links in the L2 mental lexicon and the influence of L1 intralexical knowledge. *Applied Linguistics, 32*(4), 430–449.

Wolter, B., & Gyllstad, H. (2013). Frequency of input and L2 collocational processing: A comparison of congruent and incongruent collocations. *Studies in Second Language Acquisition, 35*(3), 451–482.

Wray, A. (2002). *Formulaic language and the lexicon*. Cambridge, UK: Cambridge University Press.

Wray, A., & Namba, K. (2003). Use of formulaic language by a Japanese-English bilingual child: A practical approach to data analysis. *Japan Journal for Multilingualism and Multiculturalism, 9*(1), 24–51.

26

Measuring Vocabulary Learning Progress

Benjamin Kremmel

Introduction

Measuring vocabulary learning gains is a key aspect of language teaching as well as of multiple research studies on language learning. In pedagogy, vocabulary tests are often used to check lexical learning progress summatively at the end of one or several instructional units. The purpose of such tests is to check how much of the taught vocabulary has been acquired by language learners, and thus indirectly to check the quality of the instruction, or inform future learning activities. In research, vocabulary gains are often measured to investigate the effectiveness of a particular teaching or learning method. Numerous studies have thereby looked at various aspects of vocabulary acquisition. Studies have been conducted to examine incidental vocabulary learning, from written input through extensive or narrow reading (e.g., Barcroft, 2009; Fraser, 1999; Horst, 2005; Horst, Cobb, & Meara, 1998; Hwang & Nation, 1989; Paribakht & Wesche, 1993; Pellicer-Sánchez, 2016; Pellicer-Sánchez & Schmitt, 2010; Pigada & Schmitt, 2006; Rott, 1999; Saragi, Nation, & Meister, 1978; Waring & Takaki, 2003; Webb & Chang, 2015), as well as from oral or audio-visual input through listening to conversations, lectures, radio, or stories (e.g., Elley, 1989; Vidal, 2003, 2011; van Zeeland & Schmitt, 2013), or viewing films and television (Montero Perez, Peters, Clarebout, & Desmet, 2014; Webb, 2015), or even a mixture of modalities (e.g., Brown, Waring, & Donkaewbua, 2008; Pellicer-Sánchez et al., 2018). Other studies have probed differences between incidental and intentional vocabulary learning, and have compared which approach leads to greater vocabulary learning progress (e.g., Min, 2008). A strand of research similar to this has investigated the effectiveness of different vocabulary teaching and learning activities or enhancement techniques in vocabulary learning (Bauer & Nation, 1993; Beaton, Gruneberg, & Ellis, 1995; Ellis & He, 1999; Hulstijn, 1992; Hulstijn & Trompetter, 1998; Hulstijn, Hollander, & Greidanus, 1996; Joe, 1998; Knight, 1994; Laufer, 2000; Newton, 1995; Paribakht & Wesche, 1997; Watanabe, 1997). Comparing measured vocabulary learning progress has also been employed to research the beneficence of various learning conditions, such as elaboration effects (e.g., Ellis & He, 1999), repetition effects (e.g., Horst et al., 1998; Webb, 2007a; Webb & Chang, 2012; Webb, Newton, & Chang, 2013), the effects of spaced rehearsal (Nakata, 2015), or study conditions (Nakata & Webb, 2016), among many more. While most of these studies have focused on vocabulary learning gains in the form-meaning link knowledge dimension, i.e., how effective various approaches were for acquiring the meaning of an L2 form, a number of researchers have also investigated the learning of other word knowledge aspects, such as collocations (e.g., Boers, Demecheleer, Coxhead, & Webb, 2014; Boers, Demecheleer, & Eyckmans, 2004; Laufer & Girsai, 2008; Lindstromberg & Boers, 2008; Webb & Kagimoto, 2009, 2011; Webb et al., 2013).

The measurement of vocabulary gains is therefore probably the most common type of measurement, both in language classrooms as well as in vocabulary research studies. Any intervention study will have to provide robust measurement to demonstrate whether a particular treatment was or was not effective. However, this also seems one of the most challenging types of measurement as there are a number of critical issues that require careful consideration. This chapter will discuss three of these in the following section.

Critical Issues and Topics

Study Design

In research, examining vocabulary gains often takes the form of intervention studies. Such studies involve one or more experimental treatments of one or more groups of learners and measurements of vocabulary knowledge before and after this intervention. The measurement of vocabulary gains implicitly presupposes some kind of baseline that indicates the vocabulary knowledge before any type of learning would occur. This baseline is often referred to as the pretest. The pretest determines the level of knowledge before the treatment and is crucial to know how much room for learning there is for the learners and which vocabulary items (and which word knowledge aspects of these) are already known by the learners.

The intervention or treatment may then take various forms. Depending on whether incidental or intentional vocabulary learning is to be studied, the treatment can range from giving students reading, listening or viewing materials, to having them work through a number of tasks or exercises, or providing them with a particular method of instruction. Often, this also involves some kind of comparison, so that two or more groups of learners receive different treatments, or that one or more groups receive a treatment (i.e., experimental groups) and one group does not (i.e., control group). Ideally, we should make sure that these different groups are as similar as possible in terms of their background variables, proficiency, and, most importantly, their vocabulary knowledge in terms of the target knowledge to be investigated, which is again indicated by the scores on the pretest. One way to ensure this is to assign learners at random to one of the examined groups. This, however, is often challenging when working with intact school classes. If the learner groups differ considerably in their pretest scores, then this should be accounted for when analyzing and interpreting the posttest scores.

After the intervention, there needs to be some type of posttest to identify the vocabulary gains. This test needs to be identical to the one administered prior to the treatment. Only through this comparison of knowledge in the pretest vs. posttest can we know how much or what about the vocabulary items has or has not been learned. If a different test is used as a posttest than was used as a pretest, we cannot be certain that any difference in scores from the two administrations are, in fact, due to vocabulary learning from the intervention or input, and not due to the nature of the different tests.

There are two different types of posttests. An immediate posttest is administered at the end of an intervention and measures the immediate gains of the treatment. A delayed posttest may be administered several days or weeks after the immediate posttest or treatment. A delayed posttest is generally employed when we are interested in longer-term retention of vocabulary gains. Researchers have to decide whether they want to administer either an immediate or a delayed posttest, or both. Only using an immediate posttest in a research design, however, often results in an overestimation of the vocabulary learning that has actually taken place (Waring & Takaki, 2003). Rott (1999) has rightly criticized the lack of a delayed posttest as a measurement of long-term learning effects as one of the key shortcomings of much research on incidental word learning from reading, among other factors, such as failure to employ control groups and using measuring instruments that lack the necessary sensitivity to pick up on incremental changes in word knowledge.

Posttests will usually show an effect immediately after the treatment, but robust learning may not be found after some time has passed. Schmitt (2010) therefore argues for the need for a delayed posttest in vocabulary learning studies. He states that the information gleaned from immediate posttests is limited because it disregards the fact that learning is "always liable to attrition" (Schmitt, 2010, p. 155) and only gives a snapshot view of vocabulary knowledge when we know the learning process is incremental, dynamic, and nonlinear. This leads to limited generalizability of immediate posttest scores. In addition, Schmitt (2010) states that initial practice will almost always be more effective than later or additional practice, where returns will be diminishing. Using only an immediate posttest would therefore again be overestimating practice effects and thus durable learning. In other words, while an immediate posttest gives an indication of the effectiveness of the treatment, only a delayed posttest should be interpreted as an indication of learning (Schmitt, 2010).

Nation and Webb (2011) outline some further crucial points to consider when conducting intervention studies with pretests and posttests. First, all tests need not only be identical but also need to be administered identically. Moreover, researchers need to be aware that a pretest may already prime test takers to certain learning, which may confound results. For instance, in a study on incidental vocabulary learning, a pretest may alert learners to pay more attention to the lexical items from the pretest and thereby bias findings. Nation and Webb (2011) suggest that this could be avoided by using filler or distracter items both in the test as well as the intervention, i.e., including items in the test that will not appear in the experiment and vice versa, so that learners will not be unduly influenced by the pretest. Researchers also need to be aware of the fact that the testing event itself constitutes exposure and a learning event. Pretests and posttests "involve motivated deliberate attention to the tested words" (Nation & Webb, 2011, p. 277), which may result in learning. Control groups who only take the pretest and posttest, or splitting the experimental groups to have them take either the immediate or the delayed or both posttests, could again be a solution to account for testing effects (Avila & Sadoski, 1996). This, however, is sometimes unfeasible given limited sample sizes. Further, researchers are often unable to control whether any deliberate (or even incidental) learning of participants takes place between an immediate and a delayed posttest. Particularly with small groups of test takers, only a few learners engaging in deliberate learning may affect the outcomes considerably (Nation & Webb, 2011). On the other hand, a delayed posttest may enable an investigation of exactly such intervening variables that may influence retention (Nation & Webb, 2011).

The ideal research design for measuring vocabulary gains after one particular treatment may therefore look as shown in Table 26.1.

A control group takes all tests but does not receive any treatment. Two experimental groups receive the same treatment, but one of them only sits the pretest and the delayed

Table 26.1 Model research design for investigating vocabulary learning progress after a treatment

Group	Pretest	Treatment	Immediate posttest	Delayed posttest
Control	Yes	No	Yes	Yes
Experimental I	Yes	Yes	Yes	Yes
Experimental II	Yes	Yes	No	Yes

Table 26.2 Model research design for investigating vocabulary learning progress through different treatments

Group	Pretest	Treatment A	Treatment B	Immediate posttest	Delayed posttest
Control	Yes	No	No	Yes	Yes
Experimental I	Yes	Yes	No	Yes	Yes
Experimental II	Yes	Yes	No	No	Yes
Experimental III	Yes	No	Yes	Yes	Yes
Experimental IV	Yes	No	Yes	No	Yes

posttest, while the other group completes all tests. This then allows for singling out the effect of the treatment as well as the effect of the immediate posttest.

With a comparison of different treatments, this design would technically inflate to involving five different groups (see Table 26.2). This is often impractical, so researchers may revert to only using two experimental groups (e.g., Experimental I and III).

When measuring vocabulary gains in classroom situations, teachers often only have one experimental group and no control group. This usually suffices for small-scale interest of assessing the achievement of learners but does not allow for comparisons to other (or no) interventions. Any inferences about students' learning still requires the basic pretest and posttest design.

A further key issue in implementing this design is the timing of the delayed posttest. There is no standardized recommendation for how delayed a delayed posttest should be. The interval between the end of the treatment and the delayed posttest usually spans between one to two weeks, sometimes even extending to four weeks or several months. Schmitt (2010), for example, recommends a span of three weeks and no less than one week. However, the span is often based on a theoretical convention rather than an empirically motivated rationale. Nation and Webb (2011) thus rightly caution that the strength of the treatment effect and the sensitivity of the measurement instrument need to be considered when deciding on the delayed posttest interval. They recommend that the interval should be determined based on the context and purpose, depending on how long one would "want and expect learners to retain their knowledge of the word gained from the treatment" (Nation & Webb, 2011, p. 280). For instance, in a classroom-based study, this interval might be determined by looking at when the learners would be likely to encounter the learned word again, which would often mean a minimum interval of at least two to three days between the immediate and the delayed posttest as this would be a typical interval between two lessons. Other researchers have stated that a two week interval would be more appropriate as teaching materials or graded readers typically do not repeat new words sooner than that (Nation & Wang, 1999). Research has shown that sleep consolidation may also have some effect in this and needs to be taken into account when deciding on the delay. It has been found that sleep sometimes even increases the scores on a posttest that is only delayed by one day (Davis, Di Betta, Macdonald, & Gaskell, 2008; Dumay & Gaskell, 2007; Gaskell & Dumay, 2003). The appropriate delay for any particular measurement will therefore have to be decided in consideration of such context-dependent variables.

There are a few exceptions to the design outlined earlier that would still allow measuring vocabulary learning progress. One such exception is when the immediate posttest is treated as another form of pretest, as is sometimes done in vocabulary attrition research. In attrition studies, researchers will often want to take as a starting point the time when all words were demonstrated as known on some test. This may involve repeated measurements with immediate posttests after learning activities to determine at what point all lexical items were known and thus the attrition process may set in. Repeated immediate posttests thereby also allow investigating how much learning effort might have gone into mastering a particular item; the more immediate posttests required to show that an item is learned, the more difficult that item is to learn. The ultimate immediate posttest trial could be treated as a starting point and thus a pretest before other delayed posttests – with no treatments in between – will be administered.

Another such exception is when non-words are used in a study instead of real words. Since it is fair to assume that participants in the intervention study will not be familiar with words that the researcher made up, no pretest will be necessary to establish the nonexistent previous knowledge of the target words. While such a design may have the disadvantage of not having much real-life practical use for participants and may potentially be lacking in ecological validity, it is a very effective way to eliminate any priming effects that may occur through the use of a pretest. However, since the non-words are often mapped onto meanings of real words, and researchers may not control for knowledge of those in the participants' L1 or L2, there may also be some bias in findings of such studies. However, Webb (2007b) states that the use of non-words, or disguised forms of low-frequency words, has advantages because it is often difficult to find target words that no participant has any prior knowledge of. It seems unclear, though, whether this problem does not also hold for the low-frequency words or concepts that form the basis of the disguised forms. He further states that non-words or disguised form's lack of requiring a pretest is beneficial because pretests are not typically sensitive enough to pick up prior partial knowledge of items. In any case, this non-word approach has been successfully employed in a number of studies (Pellicer-Sánchez, 2016; Webb, 2007b).

Another approach that circumvents the use of formal pretests and posttests is sometimes found in psycholinguistic studies of incidental learning. In studies such as that by Pellicer-Sánchez (2016), initial reading times of new words may be compared to the reading times of those words after repeated exposure. In such designs, the initial reading time might be considered the pretest, and the final reading time the immediate posttest, while the repeated exposures would represent a treatment of sorts leading to an improvement in processing time and thus an indication of vocabulary learning gains. In most designs, however, vocabulary learning gains are measured more explicitly with the use of formal tests. The next section will problematize some issues with such tests.

Instruments

Much like there is no standard period of delay for posttests, there is also no standard instrument to measure vocabulary gains. The choice of test, or rather test format, usually depends on what aspect of word knowledge learning is intended to be captured. While in most cases, measuring vocabulary learning will be taken to mean measuring the number of words for which a previously unknown meaning has been acquired, it is possible to conceive of interventions that focus on other aspects of word knowledge, such as pronunciation or spelling, in which case a specific test or test format would need to be used to assess these knowledge aspects before and after the learning period. Nation and Webb (2011) recommend using several measures of vocabulary knowledge in any case, as there may be incidental learning of various (even unintended) word knowledge aspects taking place during a treatment. Even for the same word knowledge aspect, it might be advisable to use several different tests or test formats. For instance, a battery of recall and recognition tests may be used for just the form-meaning link knowledge aspect to determine the strength of the learning. This is particularly important as one instrument alone is often not sensitive enough to detect minimal changes in the incremental learning of vocabulary knowledge aspects. Particularly standardized vocabulary tests, such as the Vocabulary Levels Test (Schmitt, Schmitt, & Clapham, 2001), the Vocabulary Size Test (Nation & Beglar, 2007), or the updated Vocabulary Levels Test (Webb, Sasao, & Ballance, 2017), are not designed or intended to be used for pretest and posttest designs with short-term interventions. These measures of vocabulary breadth are not fine-grained enough to pick up small changes in vocabulary size, even when supposedly parallel versions of the tests are used. While general vocabulary size is unlikely to increase noticeably over short periods of instruction, the test formats they employ, i.e., Multiple Choice and Multiple Matching for form or meaning recognition, may still be feasible when targeting specific words that are focused on in the treatment. The choice of test format will mainly depend on the degree of sensitivity useful for investigating the gains. One format that is often credited for being more sensitive to vocabulary learning gains than other formats is the Vocabulary Knowledge Scale (VKS) (Wesche & Paribakht, 1996).

Vocabulary Knowledge Scale (VKS)

The VKS was designed to track small incremental changes in vocabulary knowledge as it follows a developmental approach to vocabulary measurement (Paribakht & Wesche, 1997). In its original version, it asks learners to indicate their degree of word knowledge on a five-point elicitation scale ranging from "I don't remember having seen this word before" to "I can use this word in a sentence" (Paribakht & Wesche, 1993).

I   I don't remember having seen this word before.
II I have seen this word before, but I don't know what it means.
III I have seen this word before, and I think it means _____ (synonym or translation).
IV I know this word it means _____ (synonym or translation).
V   I can use this word in a sentence: _____ (write a sentence).

The scale can thereby be employed for every L2 target word, and learners, after seeing the decontextualized target, have to report the stage of mastery for each target. Stages III, IV, and V are complemented by a request to provide a synonym, L1 translation, or sentence. The original authors thereby claim that the VKS combines "self-report and performance items" (Paribakht & Wesche, 1997). The scale is popular for intervention study designs because it takes into account the partial and incremental process of word knowledge and combines assessing the form-meaning link as well as some aspects of depth of word knowledge. While Laufer and Goldstein (2004) argue that the VKS is an indirect test of word meaning rather than a test of vocabulary depth, it is often classified as the latter.

The VKS surpasses ordinary self-report scales in that the higher stages of the scale require not only a self-assessment but also demonstration of that self-asserted knowledge. The major problem, however, with the VKS, as with all other developmental approaches to vocabulary measurement, is that we do not know enough about the incremental acquisition of vocabulary knowledge in order to decide on the best scale to measure it (Schmitt, 2010). Even Wesche and Paribakht (1996) acknowledge the "lack of theoretical consensus about the nature and course of development of L2 vocabulary knowledge" (p. 32) and therefore the arbitrariness of the VKS. Neither the number of levels or stages nor the actual stages are grounded in a sufficient amount of empirical research to design a measurement scale which would allow for highly valid claims. Also, Schmitt (2010) argues that the scale might not be unidimensional in that it involves a "constellation of lexical knowledge" (p. 220) at the different stages, mixing receptive and productive elements in an unprincipled way and offering various degrees of contextualization. Schmitt (2010) further echoes Read's (2000) critique that the intervals between the five stages might not be equidistant. Stewart, Batty, and Bovee (2012) explored the psychometric dimensionality of the VKS empirically and found a weak multidimensionality and unclear construct distinctions. The close difficulty proximity of some knowledge levels, they argue, impedes the results' interpretability and the VKS' usefulness as a diagnostic measure for educators.

In terms of demonstration of knowledge, produced sentences at the highest level, presumably showing the highest degree of mastery, bear a number of scoring issues as acceptable and even sophisticated sentences could be produced by candidates that do not sufficiently demonstrate knowledge of the target word (McNeill, 1996; Schmitt, 2010). The VKS does not come with adequate scoring rubrics and guidelines that would minimize marker subjectivity at this stage (Bruton, 2009). Bruton (2009) also argues that the VKS precludes L2 form recall and that in cases of homographs it is not clear for the candidate which core meaning is actually targeted. Schmitt and Zimmerman's (2002) simplified variation of the VKS, which comprises four rather than five stages, unfortunately suffers from the same limitations in principle.

Despite this, the VKS has frequently been used as a research tool (e.g., Bruton, 2009; de la Fuente, 2002; Horst, Cobb, & Nicolae, 2005; Paribakht & Wesche, 1997; Paribakht, 2005; Pulido, 2004; Rott, Williams, & Cameron, 2002; Wesche & Paribakht, 2009). Golonka et al. (2015) even claim that the VKS is "the most widely used scale for measuring vocabulary depth" (p. 25). Despite its operationalization of some valid assumptions, however, its merit for measuring vocabulary learning gains is still contested. While it may be useful as a supplementary instrument for classroom teachers, particularly for capturing initial stages in word learning (Schmitt, 2010), Wesche and Paribakht (1996) themselves admit that the VKS "is not suitable for testing large numbers of students in its present form" (p. 33).

Given that available, standardized tests will rarely fit the purpose of any individual scenario in which we are interested in the vocabulary gains of learners, the majority of studies investigating vocabulary growth have designed bespoke measures for their respective purposes. While this in itself is not problematic, few of these research endeavors have concerned themselves with the need for validating such new, custom-made measurement tools. This seems potentially troublesome as any new test or any change to a vocabulary test would ideally require robust information on the functioning of its items before it is being used in research, so that findings can be interpreted with confidence. However, it is often not feasible to subject new instruments to the extensive piloting and test validation procedures that would be necessary. In that case, the reporting of descriptive statistics from the actual administrations is arguably the bare minimum to demonstrate trustworthiness of the measurement instruments and thus the yielded results.

Target Word Selection

In light of most measurement tools being custom-made, another key consideration when measuring vocabulary learning progress is that of target word selection. When assessing learning gains in classroom settings, this selection will be driven by the syllabus or course book, i.e., the words that are supposed to be useful for students to learn and have their knowledge assessed on. In research scenarios, careful attention needs to be paid to choosing words that participants will not know at the time of the pretest. Studies measuring vocabulary learning gains need to allow for maximum learning possibilities at the outset. As mentioned before, non-words have been used to preempt potential existing knowledge of words before learning or teaching interventions in research settings. This ensures that no items are known before the intervention. However, aside from the issues raised already in the preceding section, there are also ethical issues to having candidates learn or study non-words that will not be of use to them outside the research setting.

Related to this is also the number of words that are selected for the pretest and posttest measurement. Fewer target words in both the intervention and the tests allow for more focused instruction or learning and potentially larger gains to be demonstrated. However, more target words could hypothetically give more learning opportunities, and also allow for more progress. Moreover, in incidental learning studies, filler items in the tests that are not the focus of the intervention may need to be considered, so as to mask which items will be targeted in the intervention. Practical considerations such as testing duration and participant fatigue also have to be weighed up when it comes to the item selection. For example, it may be possible to measure one word knowledge aspect of many words, or several word knowledge aspects for fewer vocabulary items. However, it may be challenging to measure several aspects of word knowledge for many words. Therefore, the limited number of words that most vocabulary learning intervention studies employ as their sample size, does indeed often make it challenging to generalize from findings to greater theoretical or pedagogical implications.

Future Directions

Three key issues seem to warrant particular attention by researchers in this area in the future. The first is the need for validating instruments thoroughly for making any substantial claims. Measurement instrument design or selection require deliberation and demonstration that any tool is assessing what is intended to be assessed validly and reliably to generate meaningful claims. To address this, one suggestion would be to encourage more collaboration between SLA vocabulary researchers and language testers, or for vocabulary researchers to engage more with measurement issues and the literature of the field of language testing (Kremmel & Pellicer-Sánchez, forthcoming). Ideally the field of vocabulary learning research would follow the model of Révész' study (2012), which – albeit not a study on vocabulary learning – has been pointed out as exemplary in demonstrating validity evidence for research instruments within an SLA paper. Within her paper on the role of working memory and recasts on learning as measured by different instruments such as a grammaticality judgment task (GJT), a written picture description task, and two oral production tasks, she included "several analyses that could be considered validation evidence" (Purpura, Brown, & Schoonen, 2015, p.

42) for her outcome measurement instruments. Even though it was not systematically framed in an established validation approach, Révész provided different kinds of evidence that could be linked to different aspects or claims of current validation frameworks, demonstrating the soundness and validity of her claims based on results. For instance, she administered her tasks to different L1 groups to provide domain description evidence and ensure that the "tasks generated approximately the same number of obligatory contexts for the target form [past progressive], and that the use of the target construction was natural in each task" (2012, p. 106). She also examined the functionality of the developmental rating scale in detail using Multi-Facet Rasch Measurement (MFRM), which – in validation terms – contributed to her evaluation claims based on her instruments. Generalizability claims were supported in her study by, among other things, having a substantial portion of the data rated by two raters and providing a high inter-rater agreement value. Révész also investigated the model fit of her data in MFRM and found "expectedly high correlations between the productive skills and moderate correlations with the GJT, suggesting a meaningful relationship between knowledge of the past progressive (grammatical knowledge) and the ability to use this form in productive language use contexts (grammatical ability)" (Purpura et al., 2015, p. 53). This added backing that would support her explanation claims in an argument-based validation model. She also examined whether the type of outcome measure influenced the learning of the past progressive (the feature in focus in her study) when recasts were employed, so that the measurement of learning would not have to rely on one source of measurement or information only. Emulating Révész' study, therefore, there are numerous pieces of validation evidence about the tests and measurement instruments employed in a particular study that could and should be provided within papers on language (including vocabulary) learning. Adopting this approach is also what Purpura et al. (2015) suggest, alongside several other guidelines to improve the quality of quantitative SLA (vocabulary) research. Their recommendation to look to language test validation research and models as well as their checklist on measurement issues to consider (e.g., using a sufficient number of good quality test items, reporting descriptive statistics, appropriate reliability estimates, as well as details of how codings and raw scores were generated, checking assumptions and analyzing items thoroughly, describing the construct(s) in question, and selecting/designing appropriate measures to assess the construct(s) in focus) are important and overdue pointers for the future of the field.

The second key area for the future of research on vocabulary learning progress and its measurement is the issue of replication. The replicability of results is closely connected to the description of methodologies and measurement tools. If the latter is lacking, then it will be very difficult to replicate studies, which is direly needed in vocabulary learning research. This is particularly relevant, as recent research syntheses and meta-analyses have yielded that the reporting practices in the field are in need of improvement, even for the most basic information on the functioning of instruments or other key methodological aspects (e.g., Elgort, 2018; Huang, Eslami, & Willson, 2012). Most studies that have measured vocabulary learning progress have been one-offs, and have yet to be replicated robustly with controlled modifications of selected key variables, such as the L1 of participants, or participants' proficiency levels. Sharing study data and materials openly on platforms such as the IRIS depository (Marsden, Mackey, & Plonsky, 2016) in the spirit of open scientific practices could be key to this endeavor.

A third area of particular interest in the future has already been opened up through technological advances. Online measures, such as eye tracking, are being increasingly used in SLA vocabulary research, and will allow us to investigate or measure not just the product of vocabulary learning progress, or regress for that matter, but shed light on the process and cognitive factors influencing the outcome of vocabulary learning in increasing detail. They will also allow to exert much more control in learning experiments and will likely create exciting new avenues for the measurement of vocabulary learning progress.

Further Reading

Rott, S. (1999). The effect of exposure frequency on intermediate language learners' incidental vocabulary acquisition through reading. *Studies in Second Language Acquisition, 21*, 589–619.

Rott's study offers a model approach of a research design that aims at measuring vocabulary learning progress, and offers a useful critique of previous studies on incidental vocabulary learning from reading.

Nation, I. S. P., & Webb, S. (2011). *Researching vocabulary*. Boston, MA: Heinle-Cengage ELT.

Nation and Webb's research handbook is a helpful practical guide for setting up measurements of vocabulary learning gains and discusses several considerations that need to be taken into account when designing an intervention study with pretests and posttests.

Purpura, J. E., Brown, J. D., & Schoonen, R. (2015). Improving the validity of quantitative measures in applied linguistics research. *Language Learning, 65*(S1), 37–75.

This paper by three key figures in SLA research and language assessment highlights the need for SLA researchers to look to language testing literature for support in validating their instruments. Since most SLA researchers interested in vocabulary learning engage in some form of measurement of language ability or knowledge, this is a useful overview of why it is essential that claims are based on validly and reliably operationalized variables in tests, instruments, and scores. It includes an exemplification of such an approach applied and a valuable checklist for practical measurement issues to consider in doing quantitative research.

Related Topics

Vocabulary assessment, vocabulary tests, vocabulary learning, research designs, research methodology, validation

References

Avila, E., & Sadoski, M. (1996). Exploring new applications of the keyword method to acquire English vocabulary. *Language Learning, 46*(3), 379–395.

Barcroft, J. (2009). Effects of synonym generation on incidental and intentional L2 vocabulary learning during reading. *TESOL Quarterly, 43*, 79–103.

Bauer, L., & Nation, I. S. P. (1993). Word families. *International Journal of Lexicography, 6*(4), 253–279.

Beaton, A., Gruneberg, M., & Ellis, N. (1995). Retention of foreign vocabulary using the keyword method: A ten-year follow-up. *Second Language Research, 11*, 112–120.

Boers, F., Demecheleer, M., Coxhead, A., & Webb, S. (2014). Gauging the effectiveness of exercises on verb-noun collocations. *Language Teaching Research, 18*(1), 50–70.

Boers, F., Demecheleer, M., & Eyckmans, J. (2004). Etymological elaboration as a strategy for learning figurative idioms. In P. Bogaards & B. Laufer (Eds.), *Vocabulary in a second language: Selection, acquisition and testing* (pp. 53–78). Amsterdam: John Benjamins.

Brown, R., Waring, R., & Donkaewbua, S. (2008). Incidental vocabulary acquisition from reading, reading-while-listening, and listening. *Reading in a Foreign Language, 20*, 136–163.

Bruton, A. (2009). The Vocabulary Knowledge Scale: A critical analysis. *Language Assessment Quarterly, 6*(4), 288–297.

Davis, M. H., Di Betta, A. M., Macdonald, M. J. E., & Gaskell, M. G. (2008). Learning and consolidation of novel spoken words. *Journal of Cognitive Neuroscience, 21*(4), 803–820.

de la Fuente, M. J. (2002). Negotiation and oral acquisition of vocabulary. *Studies in Second Language Acquisition, 24*, 81–112.

Dumay, N., & Gaskell, M. G. (2007). Sleep-associated changes in the mental representation of spoken words. *Psychological Science, 18*, 35–39.

Elgort, I. (2018). Technology-mediated second language vocabulary development: A review of trends in research methodology. *CALICO Journal, 35*(1), 1–29.

Elley, W. B. (1989). Vocabulary acquisition from listening to stories. *Reading Research Quarterly, 24*(2), 174–187.

Ellis, R., & He, X. (1999). The roles of modified input and output in the incidental acquisition of word meanings. *Studies in Second Language Acquisition, 21*, 285–301.

Fraser, C. A. (1999). Lexical processing strategy use and vocabulary learning through reading. *Studies in Second Language Acquisition, 21*, 225–241.

Gaskell, M. G., & Dumay, N. (2003). Lexical competition and the acquisition of novel words. *Cognition, 89*, 105–132.

Golonka, E., Bowles, A., Silbert, N., Kramasz, D., Blake, C., & Buckwalter, T. (2015). The role of context and cognitive effort in vocabulary learning: A study of intermediate-level learners of Arabic. *Modern Language Journal, 99*(1), 19–39.

Horst, M. (2005). Learning L2 vocabulary through extensive reading: A measurement study. *Canadian Modern Language Review, 61*, 355–382.

Horst, M., Cobb, T., & Meara, P. (1998). Beyond a Clockwork Orange: Acquiring second language vocabulary through reading. *Reading in a Foreign Language, 11*, 207–223.

Horst, M., Cobb, T., & Nicolae, I. (2005). Expanding academic vocabulary with an interactive on-line database. *Language Learning and Technology, 9*(2), 99–110.

Huang, S.-F., Eslami, Z., & Willson, V. (2012). The effects of task involvement load on L2 incidental vocabulary: A meta-analytic study. *Modern Language Journal, 96*(4), 544–557.

Hulstijn, J. H. (1992). Retention of inferred and given word meanings: Experiments in incidental word learning. In P. J. L. Arnaud & H. Béjoint (Eds.), *Vocabulary and applied linguistics* (pp. 113–125). London, UK: Macmillan.

Hulstijn, J. H., Hollander, M., & Greidanus, T. (1996). Incidental vocabulary learning by advanced foreign language students: The influence of marginal glosses, dictionary use and reoccurrence of unknown words. *Modern Language Journal, 80*(3), 327–339.

Hulstijn, J. H., & Trompetter, P. (1998). Incidental learning of second language vocabulary in computer-assisted reading and writing tasks. In D. Albrechtsen, B. Henriksen, I. M. Mees & E. Poulsen (Eds.), *Perspectives on foreign and second language pedagogy: Essays presented to Kirsten Haastrup on the occasion of her sixtieth birthday* (pp. 191–200). Odense: Odense University Press.

Hwang, K., & Nation, I. S. P. (1989). Reducing the vocabulary load and encouraging vocabulary learning through reading newspapers. *Reading in a Foreign Language, 6*, 323–335.

Joe, A. (1998). What effects do text-based tasks promoting generation have on incidental vocabulary acquisition? *Applied Linguistics, 19*, 357–377.

Knight, S. (1994). Dictionary, the tool of last resort effects on comprehension and vocabulary acquisition for students of different verbal abilities. *Modern Language Journal, 78*, 285–298.

Kremmel, B., & Pellicer-Sánchez, A. (forthcoming). Measuring vocabulary development. In P. Winke & T. Brunfaut (Eds.), *The Routledge handbook of SLA and language testing*. New York, NY: Routledge.

Laufer, B. (2000). Electronic dictionaries and incidental vocabulary acquisition. Does technology make a difference? In U. Heid, S. Evert, E. Lehmann, & C. Rohrer (Eds.), *EURALEX* (pp. 849–854). Stuttgart: Stuttgart University.

Laufer, B., & Girsai, N. (2008). Form-focused instruction in second language vocabulary learning: A case for contrastive analysis and translation. *Applied Linguistics, 29*, 694–716.

Laufer, B., & Goldstein, Z. (2004). Testing vocabulary knowledge: Size, strength, and computer adaptiveness. *Language Learning, 54*(3), 399–436.

Lindstromberg, S., & Boers, F. (2008). The mnemonic effect of noticing alliteration in lexical chunks. *Applied Linguistics, 29*, 200–222.

Marsden, E., Mackey, A., & Plonsky, L. (2016). The IRIS Repository: Advancing research practice and methodology. In A. Mackey & E. Marsden (Eds.), *Advancing methodology and practice: The IRIS repository of instruments for research into second languages* (pp. 1–21). New York, NY: Routledge.

McNeill, A. (1996). Vocabulary knowledge profiles: Evidence from Chinese-speaking ESL teachers. *Hong Kong Journal of Applied Linguistics, 1*, 39–63.

Min, H.-T. (2008). EFL vocabulary acquisition and retention: Reading plus vocabulary enhancement activities and narrow reading. *Language Learning, 58*(1), 73–115.

Montero Perez, M., Peters, E., Clarebout, G., & Desmet, P. (2014). Effects of captioning on video comprehension and incidental vocabulary learning. *Language Learning and Technology, 18*(1), 118–141.

Nakata, T. (2015). Effects of expanding and equal spacing on second language vocabulary learning: Does gradually increasing spacing increase vocabulary learning? *Studies in Second Language Acquisition, 37*(4), 677–711.

Nakata, T., & Webb, S. (2016). Does studying vocabulary in smaller sets increase learning?: The effects of part and whole learning on second language vocabulary acquisition. *Studies in Second Language Acquisition, 38*(3), 523–552.

Nation, I. S. P., & Beglar, D. (2007). A vocabulary size test. *The Language Teacher, 31*(7), 9–13.

Nation, I. S. P., & Wang, K. (1999). Graded readers and vocabulary. *Reading in a Foreign Language, 12*(2), 355–380.

Nation, I. S. P., & Webb, S. (2011). *Researching vocabulary*. Boston, MA: Heinle-Cengage ELT.

Newton, J. (1995). Task-based interaction and incidental vocabulary learning: A case study. *Second Language Research, 11*, 159–177.

Paribakht, T. S. (2005). The influence of L1 lexicalization of L2 lexical inferencing: A study of Farsi-speaking EFL learners. *Language Learning, 55*(4), 701–748.

Paribakht, T. S., & Wesche, M. B. (1993). The relationship between reading comprehension and second language development in a comprehension-based ESL program. *TESL Canada Journal, 11*(1), 68–83.

Paribakht, T. S., & Wesche, M. B. (1997). Vocabulary enhancement activities and reading for meaning in second language vocabulary acquisition. In J. Coady & T. Huckin (Eds.), *Second language vocabulary acquisition* (pp. 174–200). Cambridge, UK: Cambridge University Press.

Pellicer-Sánchez, A. (2016). Incidental L2 vocabulary acquisition from and while reading: An eye-tracking study. *Studies in Second Language Acquisition, 38*(1), 97–130.

Pellicer-Sánchez, A., & Schmitt, N. (2010). Incidental vocabulary acquisition from an authentic novel: Do things fall apart? *Reading in a Foreign Language, 22*, 31–55.

Pellicer-Sánchez, A., Tragant, E., Conklin, K., Rodgers, M., Llanes, A., & Serrano, R. (2018). *L2 reading and reading-while-listening in multimodal learning conditions: An eye-tracking study*. ELT Research Papers.

Pigada, M., & Schmitt, N. (2006). Vocabulary acquisition from extensive reading: A case study. *Reading in a Foreign Language, 18*, 1–28.

Pulido, D. (2004). The effect of cultural familiarity on incidental vocabulary acquisition through reading. *The Reading Matrix, 4*(2), 20–53.

Purpura, J. E., Brown, J. D., & Schoonen, R. (2015). Improving the validity of quantitative measures in applied linguistics research. *Language Learning, 65*(S1), 37–75.

Read, J. (2000). *Assessing vocabulary*. Cambridge, UK: Cambridge University Press.

Révész, A. (2012). Working memory and the observed effectiveness of recasts on different L2 outcome measures. *Language Learning, 62*(1), 93–132.

Rott, S. (1999). The effect of exposure frequency on intermediate language learners' incidental vocabulary acquisition through reading. *Studies in Second Language Acquisition, 21*, 589–619.

Rott, S., Williams, J., & Cameron, R. (2002). The effect of multiple-choice L1 glosses and input-output cycles on lexical acquisition and retention. *Language Teaching Research, 6*, 183–222.

Saragi, T., Nation, P., & Meister, F. (1978). Vocabulary learning and reading. *System, 6*, 72–78.

Schmitt, N. (2010). *Researching vocabulary: A vocabulary research manual*. Basingstoke, UK: Palgrave Macmillan.

Schmitt, N., Schmitt, D., & Clapham, C. (2001). Developing and exploring the behaviour of two new versions of the Vocabulary Levels Test. *Language Testing, 18*(1), 55–88. https://doi.org/10.1177/026553220101800103

Schmitt, N., & Zimmerman, C. B. (2002). Derivative word forms: What do learners know? *TESOL Quarterly, 36*(2), 145–171. https://doi.org/10.2307/3588328

Stewart, J., Batty, A. O., & Bovee, N. (2012). Comparing multidimensional and continuum models of vocabulary acquisition: An empirical examination of the Vocabulary Knowledge Scale. *TESOL Quarterly, 46*(4), 695–721.

van Zeeland, H., & Schmitt, N. (2013). Incidental vocabulary acquisition through L2 listening: A dimensions approach. *System, 41*, 609–624.

Vidal, K. (2003). Academic listening: A source of vocabulary acquisition? *Applied Linguistics, 24*(1), 56–86.

Vidal, K. (2011). A comparison of the effects of reading and listening on incidental vocabulary acquisition. *Language Learning, 61*(1), 219–258.

Waring, R., & Takaki, M. (2003). At what rate do learners learn and retain new vocabulary from reading a graded reader? *Reading in a Foreign Language, 15*, 130–163.

Watanabe, Y. (1997). Input, intake, and retention: Effects of increased processing on incidental learning of foreign language vocabulary. *Studies in Second Language Acquisition, 19*, 287–308.

Webb, S. (2007a). The effects of repetition on vocabulary knowledge. *Applied Linguistics, 28*(1), 46–65.

Webb, S. (2007b). Learning word pairs and glossed sentences: The effects of a single context on vocabulary learning. *Language Teaching Research, 11*, 63–81.

Webb, S. (2015). Extensive viewing: Language learning through watching television. In D. Nunan & J. C. Richards (Eds.), *Language learning beyond the classroom* (pp. 159–168). New York, NY: Routledge.

Webb, S., & Chang, A. (2012). Vocabulary learning through assisted and unassisted repeated reading. *Canadian Modern Language Review, 68*(3), 267–290.

Webb, S., & Chang, A. (2015). Second language vocabulary learning through extensive reading: How does frequency and distribution of occurrence affect learning? *Language Teaching Research, 19*(6), 667–686.

Webb, S., & Kagimoto, E. (2009). The effects of vocabulary learning on collocation and meaning. *TESOL Quarterly, 43*, 55–77.

Webb, S., & Kagimoto, E. (2011). Learning collocation: Do the number of collocates, position of the node word, and synonymy affect learning. *Applied Linguistics, 32*, 259–276.

Webb, S., Newton, J., & Chang, A. (2013). Incidental learning of collocation. *Language Learning, 63*(1), 91–120.

Webb, S., Sasao, Y., & Ballance, O. (2017). The updated Vocabulary Levels Test: Developing and validating two new forms of the VLT. *ITL – International Journal of Applied Linguistics, 168*(1), 34–70.

Wesche, M. B., & Paribakht, T. S. (1996). Assessing second language vocabulary knowledge: Depth vs. breadth. *Canadian Modern Language Review, 53*(1), 13–40.

Wesche, M. B., & Paribakht, T. S. (2009). *Lexical inferencing in a first and second language: Cross-linguistic dimensions.* Clevedon, UK: Multilingual Matters.

27

Measuring the Ability to Learn Words

Yosuke Sasao

Introduction

A number of attempts have been made to create and validate vocabulary tests. Established vocabulary tests include the Vocabulary Levels Test (Beglar & Hunt, 1999; Nation, 1983, 1990; Schmitt, Schmitt, & Clapham, 2001; Webb, Sasao, & Ballance, 2017), the Vocabulary Size Test (Beglar, 2010; Nation & Beglar, 2007), the Word Associates Test (Read, 1993, 1998; Schmitt, Ng, & Garras, 2011), the Eurocentres Vocabulary Size Test (Meara & Buxton, 1987; Meara & Jones, 1988), the Vocabulary Knowledge Scale (Wesche & Paribakht, 1996), CATSS (Laufer, Elder, Hill, & Congdon, 2004; Laufer & Goldstein, 2004), Lex 30 (Fitzpatrick & Clenton, 2010; Meara & Fitzpatrick, 2000), and the Integrated Diagnostic Test of Vocabulary Size and Depth (Ishii & Schmitt, 2009).

These tests are of great value because they reveal a learner's current level of vocabulary knowledge. The test results may indicate how many words or which aspect of a word need to be learned to achieve a particular goal. A pretest and posttest design may be used to assess vocabulary growth over a period of time, or as the result of a particular teaching/learning method. However, existing vocabulary tests do not aim at indicating how learners can become efficient in vocabulary learning. There is a dearth of research on developing and validating tests that will help reveal learners' ability to learn words and provide them with diagnostic information on how they can improve their vocabulary learning strategies. There is a need for new diagnostic tests measuring vocabulary learning ability; that is, how efficiently words can be learned.

This chapter discusses the notion of vocabulary learning ability (VLA) and gives a brief description of two tests measuring VLA; namely, the Word Part Levels Test and the Guessing from Context Test.

Critical Issues and Topics

What Is Vocabulary Learning Ability?

Vocabulary learning ability (VLA) is the ability necessary to facilitate L2 vocabulary learning. It determines how efficiently words are learned and predicts the rate of vocabulary growth. VLA refers to how well a learner can actually *use* vocabulary learning strategies such as guessing from context, direct learning of vocabulary, word part knowledge, and dictionary use. This is different from how well a learner *knows* vocabulary learning strategies. The distinction between use and knowledge is important, because teachers often have difficulty spending sufficient time on vocabulary instruction within limited class hours, and thus a learner may not be able to use the strategies effectively even if they are known explicitly (Nation, 2013, p. 518).

VLA may be taken as one of the learner factors that affect vocabulary learning (e.g., individual learner differences in knowledge, effort, strategies), because different learners are assumed to have different levels of VLA. VLA is different from other learner factors because it is teachable. Thus, research on VLA will be readily applicable to teaching in normal classroom settings. In contrast, L1 knowledge, including cognates and loanwords, may be hard to teach for instructors with different L1 backgrounds from their students. Other individual differences such as personality, learning styles, and motivation may also affect vocabulary learning, but they are also hard to teach.

One major VLA component is the skill of guessing the meanings of unknown words from context. Although correctly guessed words may not always lead to learning, being skillful at guessing is likely to contribute to vocabulary growth because it allows better text comprehension and a larger amount of input processing (Perfetti, 2010; Pulido & Hambrick, 2008). In addition, instruction seems to have a positive effect on the development of the guessing skill (Fukkink & de Glopper, 1998; Kuhn & Stahl, 1998; Walters, 2004). The effectiveness of instruction may vary according to proficiency level. Walters (2006) found that less proficient learners benefited most from general strategy instruction (presenting a general rule for guessing followed by practice), while more advanced learners benefited most from context instruction (making learners aware of specific types of context clues).

Another important VLA component is deliberate word-pair learning, or learning from word cards, which may be seen as a complementary activity to incidental vocabulary learning. Intentional learning enables learners to focus on particular words that meet their needs and to control how often the words are encountered so that they may be effectively stored in memory. Research shows that deliberate, decontextualized vocabulary learning may lead to implicit knowledge which is required for normal language use (Elgort, 2007), and it may also result in gains in knowledge of more than form-meaning connections including grammatical functions and associations (Webb, 2009). Deliberate word-pair learning may be facilitated by flash card software, because it may help control for intervals of repetition, learning modes (productive vs. receptive, and recall vs. recognition), and the sequencing of items (Nakata, 2011).

There is also plenty of research evidence that shows the positive effects of dictionary use on vocabulary learning (Chun & Plass, 1996; Hill & Laufer, 2003; Hulstijn, Hollander, & Greidanus, 1996; Knight, 1994; Laufer & Hill, 2000; Luppescu & Day, 1993; Peters, 2007). However, some learners may have difficulty locating the appropriate meaning of a word that is looked up in a dictionary. Tono (1988) examined the skill of dictionary use by Japanese university students with a low to intermediate level of proficiency by measuring multiple aspects of dictionary use, including pronunciation, spelling, part of speech, meaning, reference speed, derivatives, synonyms, usage, and social background. The results showed that the participants were successful in deriving the appropriate meaning of 67% to 71% of the words that were looked up in a dictionary. The results also showed that the participants performed better for some aspects of dictionary use (e.g., success rate of finding inflected forms = 78%) than others (e.g., success rate of finding derivatives = 46%). Fraser (1999) examined eight Francophone university students' strategies for dealing with unknown words while reading, and found that the participants were successful in deriving the appropriate meaning of 78% of the words that were looked up in a dictionary. These studies indicate that there is still room for improving learners' skill of dictionary use.

In addition to these skills (guessing from context, deliberate word-pair learning, and dictionary use), increasing some types of knowledge may also contribute to more effective vocabulary learning. Word part knowledge plays an important role in facilitating vocabulary learning. First, knowledge of word parts can help learners infer the meaning of an unknown word that is derived from an already known word within the same word family. For example, the meaning of *unlucky* may be transferred easily from knowledge of the word *lucky* when a learner knows the prefix *un-* and sees the relationship between these two words. Second, corpus-based research (Nagy & Anderson, 1984) shows that a morphologically basic word has an average of 1.57 to 3.22 derivatives depending on the definition of a derivative, and lower-frequency words tend to have a larger number of semantically transparent derivatives. Third, empirical studies with L2 learners of English have shown that knowledge of word parts moderately or strongly correlates with vocabulary size (Ishii & Schmitt, 2009; Mochizuki & Aizawa, 2000; Qian, 1999; Schmitt & Meara, 1997). Fourth, Wei (2015) found that the use of word part knowledge was more effective in word retention than the keyword method for Chinese learners of English. Finally, Schmitt and Zimmerman (2002) found that learners might not acquire word part knowledge automatically through exposure, arguing that word parts need to be learned explicitly, especially for productive use. This indicates that using word part knowledge helps expand vocabulary knowledge, and there is a need for helping learners gain knowledge of word parts.

Phonological knowledge may also facilitate vocabulary learning. Research findings indicate that while totally unfamiliar words are largely dependent on phonological short-term memory, for learners with larger vocabulary sizes existing long-term lexical knowledge becomes more important in vocabulary learning than short-term memory (Ellis & Sinclair, 1996; Gathercole & Baddeley, 1989; Masoura & Gathercole, 1999; Papagno, Valentine, & Baddeley, 1991; Service, 1992). Gathercole (1995) found that English-like nonsense words (e.g., *defermication*) were easier for L1 English children to remember than non-English-like words (e.g., *perplisteronk*). Further analysis showed that short-term memory (as measured by tests of digit span and one- and three-syllable span) was more closely related to non-word repetition accuracy for the non-English-like than for the English-like words. Cheung (1996), in a study with Hong Kong 7th graders learning English, found that phonological short-term memory as measured by non-word repetition was related to vocabulary acquisition only for those with a small English vocabulary size. Masoura and Gathercole (2005) found that Greek children's speed of learning English words in a paired-associate learning task was strongly affected by their current English vocabulary knowledge. They argued that learners with considerable familiarity with the L2 benefit from the use of existing knowledge representations. Gathercole, Service, Hitch, Adams, and Martin (1999) argue that long-term memory has an impact on short-term memory, because it can help to reconstruct words at the point of retrieval by constraining possible sequences of sounds with reference to phonotactic regularity.

Another type of knowledge that may contribute to effective vocabulary learning is knowledge of phonics: the relationships between spelling and pronunciation. Research (e.g., Bradley & Huxford, 1994; Rosenthal & Ehri, 2008) has shown that orthographic and phonological knowledge is strongly related to each other. While the English language uses phonograms, there seems to be a complex relationship between the English sounds and the spellings that they represent. However, knowledge of phonics seems to facilitate vocabulary learning.

Abbott (2000) showed that the English sound-letter relationships were highly predictable (75% or greater generalization reliability), indicating the effectiveness of phonic knowledge in vocabulary learning. Bruck, Treiman, Caravolas, Genesee, and Cassar (1998) found that children with phonics instruction produced more accurate word spellings than children without phonics instruction when asked to learn and spell a list of words; in addition, children with phonics instruction produced more conventional and phonologically acceptable patterns for the spellings of nonsense words. Similar results were obtained by Roberts and Meiring (2006).

To sum up, VLA refers to the ability to increase vocabulary learning and may include at least six types of knowledge and skills:

1   Guessing from context,
2   Learning from word cards,
3   Dictionary use,
4   Knowledge of word parts,
5   Knowledge of a sound system, and
6   Knowledge of sound-spelling relationships.

As an initial attempt to make VLA tests, this chapter focuses on guessing from context and knowledge of word parts. The skill of guessing from context plays a critical role in vocabulary learning. It may be a major source of vocabulary learning through reading and listening for both L1 (Jenkins, Stein, & Wysocki, 1984; Nagy, Anderson, & Herman, 1987; Nagy, Herman, & Anderson, 1985; Shu, Anderson, & Zhang, 1995) and L2 acquisition (Brown, Waring, & Donkaewbua, 2008; Day, Omura, & Hiramatsu, 1991; Dupuy & Krashen, 1993; Horst, Cobb, & Meara, 1998; Hulstijn, 1992; Pitts, White, & Krashen, 1989; Waring & Takaki, 2003). For L2 acquisition, the guessing skill may become more important for mid- and low-frequency words, because teachers may have little time to deal with the large number of unknown words in the classroom, and so students may need to learn these words on their own while reading or listening to the texts that are of interest to them. In addition, guessing from context is the most frequent and preferred strategy when learners deal with unknown words in context (Cooper, 1999; Fraser, 1999; Paribakht & Wesche, 1999). However, the success rate for deriving the appropriate meanings of words encountered in context is low: 12% to 33% in one study (Parry, 1991) and 25.6% in another (44.2% if partially correct guesses were allowed) (Nassaji, 2003). Taken together, improving the skill of guessing has the potential to facilitate vocabulary learning through reading or listening, because learners rely on the guessing strategy most frequently when dealing with unknown words in context and good guessers may be more likely to find opportunities to derive the appropriate meanings of unknown words and learn them.

Knowledge of word parts also contributes to vocabulary learning. Research (Anglin, 1993; Goulden, Nation, & Read, 1990; Nagy & Anderson, 1984) shows that about half of English words are morphologically complex. In addition, word part knowledge may help learners check whether an unknown word has been successfully guessed from context; in other words, integration of information from context and word parts helps to make guessing more successful (Mori, 2002; Mori & Nagy, 1999; Nagy & Anderson, 1984; Nation, 2001). Word meanings may not easily be determined by a single source of information, because contextual clues are not always sufficient for deriving the meanings of unknown words (Beck, McKeown, & McCaslin, 1983; Schatz & Baldwin, 1986) and word part analysis is sometimes misleading (e.g., *bother* is not *both* + *–er*) (Bensoussan & Laufer, 1984).

Why Is It Important to Measure VLA?

Very few attempts have been made to develop and validate tests measuring how efficiently words can be learned. Existing vocabulary tests aim to measure how many words are known (e.g., the Vocabulary Levels Test; Nation, 1983, 1990) or how well a word is known (e.g., the Word Associates Test; Read, 1993, 1998). These tests, however, do not indicate how learners can improve their ability to learn vocabulary. This makes it difficult to provide learners with diagnostic information on what is needed to become more efficient in vocabulary learning. A lack of tests measuring VLA indicates a need for new approaches to vocabulary assessment. These tests may provide learners with specific information on how to improve their VLA.

VLA tests will benefit teachers because they may diagnose their students' vocabulary learning weaknesses and provide information that can be used to improve their learning skills. The tests will reveal which types of knowledge and strategies specifically need to be learned in order to become more proficient in vocabulary learning. Since teachers have limited time to deal with low-frequency words in class, it is important to help students become more efficient in vocabulary learning strategies so that they can effectively learn these words on their own.

VLA tests may also help to determine a critical threshold after which vocabulary learning becomes significantly easier. An investigation into the relationship between learners' performance on VLA tests and their vocabulary size may indicate a general tendency that a learner with a particular vocabulary size has a particular level of VLA. If the goal of vocabulary learning were set at developing a vocabulary size of 8,000 words, which might be necessary to achieve the 98% coverage of written text (Laufer & Ravenhorst-Kalovski, 2010; Nation, 2006), then the VLA level of learners with a vocabulary size of 8,000 words might be taken as the threshold levels for efficient vocabulary learning.

VLA tests may also contribute to a better understanding of L2 vocabulary learning. Earlier studies have investigated the relationship between learners' existing knowledge/strategies and vocabulary learning; for example, existing phonological knowledge was found to relate to vocabulary learning (e.g., Hulme, Maughan, & Brown, 1991) and existing word part knowledge also has a positive relationship with learning words (e.g., Schmitt & Meara, 1997). However, few attempts have been made to collectively approach the notion of VLA; that is, previous research has focused only on specific areas of learning proficiency and VLA remains to be synthesized from a theoretical and practical perspective. VLA tests may be useful in approaching this issue empirically and may shed new light on the theory of L2 vocabulary acquisition.

How Can VLA Be Measured?

The purpose of VLA tests is to diagnose a learner's aptitude for learning words. A diagnostic test should identify specific areas of strengths and weaknesses in language ability and provide detailed and prompt feedback to teachers and learners (Alderson, 2005; Alderson, Clapham, & Wall, 1995; Bachman, 1990; Bachman & Palmer, 1996). To this end, VLA tests will have the following features in common:

- The tests consist of multiple components specified in content specifications. Examining different aspects of an individual VLA separately has at least two advantages over measuring a single aspect. First, by isolating and measuring different aspects of knowledge and skills necessary to learn word effectively, a test can provide learners with more precise information about their strengths and weaknesses. Teachers may then be able to offer a more effective vocabulary teaching program that caters to their students' needs. Second, it raises awareness of VLA for both teachers and students. Teaching VLA may be challenging especially for native speakers because they have rarely learned the skills necessary to learn words explicitly.

- The tests are easy to complete and grade so that clear feedback can be given soon after administration of the test to students. Immediate feedback is desirable because learners may still remember the reasons for their responses if they receive the feedback soon after completing the test. This may allow them to make use of the feedback in order to develop their knowledge and skills (Alderson, 2005).

Based on these criteria, the Word Part Levels Test (WPLT) and the Guessing from Context Test (GCT) were created. Both tests have three sections each measuring different aspects of an individual VLA, and are written in multiple-choice format. The tests are freely available at http://ysasaojp.info/.

The Word Part Levels Test (WPLT)

The WPLT aims to measure knowledge of English affixes and provide diagnostic information on a learner's gaps in affix knowledge to facilitate current and future vocabulary learning. The test consists of three sections each measuring different components of receptive affix knowledge: form, meaning, and use (Bauer & Nation, 1993; Nation, 2001; Tyler & Nagy, 1989). The form section measures the ability to recognize the written form of an affix (e.g., *non–* and *–ful* are affixes while *kno–* and *–ack* are not). Here are two example items of the form section.

1   (1)   non–   (2)   kno–   (3)   spo–   (4)   orn–

2   (1)   –rse   (2)   –ack   (3)   –ful   (4)   –uin

For the meaning section, test takers must choose the closest meaning of the target affix (e.g., the meanings of the affixes *dis–* and *–ist* are "not" and "person", respectively). For each item, two example words containing the target affix are provided. Here are two example items of the meaning section.

3   dis– (disbelieve; dissimilar)   4   –ist (specialist; artist)
    (1)   not   (1)   against
    (2)   person   (2)   person
    (3)   new   (3)   two
    (4)   main   (4)   not

The use section measures knowledge of the function of an affix (e.g., *en–* has the function of making a verb, while *–ness* has the function of making a noun). For each item, two example words containing the target affix are provided. Each item had a fixed set of four options: noun, verb, adjective, and adverb. Here are two example items of the use section.

5   en– (<u>en</u>sure; <u>en</u>able)
    (1)   noun
    (2)   verb
    (3)   adjective
    (4)   adverb

6   –ness (aware<u>ness</u>; ill<u>ness</u>)
    (1)   noun
    (2)   verb
    (3)   adjective
    (4)   adverb

The WPLT includes a total of 118 affixes (42 prefixes and 76 suffixes) which appear in more than one word in the most frequent 10,000 word families in the British National Corpus (BNC) word lists developed by Nation (2004) (available at www.victoria.ac.nz/lals/staff/paul-nation.aspx). Rasch analysis was used to determine the item difficulty levels of the affixes according to the responses of 1,348 learners and categorize the affixes into three different levels (beginner, intermediate, and advanced). There are 40, 39, and 39 affixes in the beginner, intermediate, and advanced levels, respectively. The WPLT has three difficulty levels rather than a single comprehensive form, because (1) it allows teachers to choose a test at an appropriate level for their students; (2) it provides teachers and students with a manageable number of word parts for a course; and (3) it proposes the effective order of learning affixes (see Sasao & Webb, 2017, for a detailed explanation about the test development procedure).

The Guessing From Context Test (GCT)

The purpose of the GCT is to measure the ability to guess the meanings of unknown words from context. The GCT has two equivalent versions each with 20 items. Each item in the GCT has a 50-to-60-word passage and three questions to examine three different steps in guessing from context (Figure 27.1). The three question types are part of

---

[Passage]

    Cats have a good nose for food. Many cats smell food and then (1) <u>walk away without even trying it</u>. Like a wine **candintock** (2) <u>who only has to smell the wine to know how good it is,</u> (3) <u>a cat can learn all it wants to know without actually eating the food.</u>

[Question 1] Choose the part of speech of the bold, underlined word.

    (1) Noun   (2) Verb   (3) Adjective   (4) Adverb

[Question 2] Choose the word or phrase that helps you to work out the meaning of the bold, underlined word.

    (1) walk away without even trying it

    (2) who only has to smell the wine to know how good it is

    (3) a cat can learn all it wants to know without actually eating the food

[Question 3] Guess the meaning of the bold, underlined word.

    (1) consumer

    (2) specialist

    (3) seller

Figure 27.1   Example items of the GCT

speech, contextual clue, and meaning. These three aspects of the guessing from context strategy were based on Clarke and Nation's (1980) guessing procedure which is perhaps the best-known version of the guessing strategy. Using three different types of questions to measure three different components of the strategy make it possible to provide specific information about where a learner's strengths and weaknesses lie. The part of speech question examines the ability to identify the part of speech of the target word. Every item had the following four options: noun, verb, adjective, and adverb. The contextual clue question measures the ability to find a discourse clue which can be used to help a learner guess the meaning of the unknown word. Each passage has one contextual clue, and the different types of clues were identified in earlier research (e.g., Ames, 1966). The meaning question measures the ability to derive the meaning of the unknown word. The correct answer is the option that best fits to the context and the meaning of the original word. The two distractors are of the same part of speech as the correct answer but contain irrelevant or lack important meaning (see Sasao & Webb, 2018 for a detailed explanation about the test development procedure).

How Can Feedback Be Provided to Learners?

Diagnostic feedback needs to be easy to understand and clearly reveal a learner's strengths and weaknesses in the VLA. For easier interpretation of the scores, the percentage of correctly answered items for each section may be expressed in a bar graph because the information is intuitively interpretable. Figure 27.2 illustrates an example score report to a learner who took the GCT and got 90%, 50%, and 50% for the part of speech, contextual clue, and meaning sections, respectively. This indicates that while this learner demonstrated good knowledge of part of speech, his weakness lies in finding contextual clues and deriving the meaning based on that information; thus, this learner should focus on the learning of contextual clues to potentially improve the guessing skill. (For a proposal of the level classification of the guessing skill, see Sasao & Webb, 2018.)

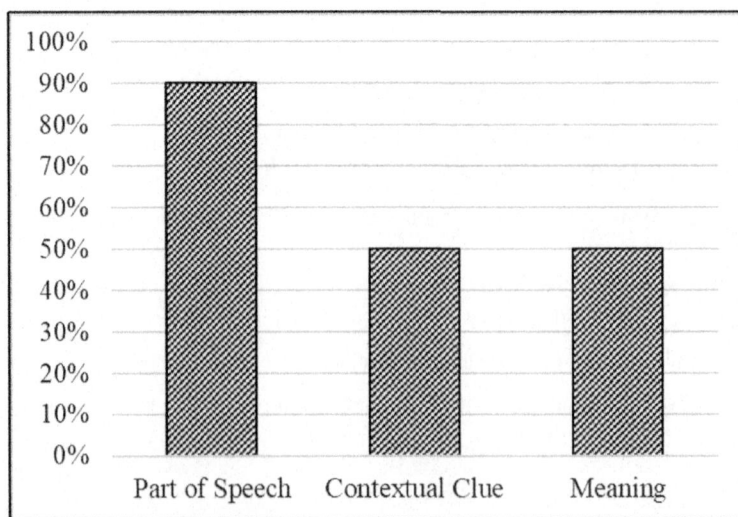

Figure 27.2 Example score report (WPLT)

Future Directions

The GCT and the WPLT make a number of future studies of VLA possible. First, the effects of teaching may be investigated with the GCT and the WPLT. Previous studies on the guessing skill (Fukkink & de Glopper, 1998; Kuhn & Stahl, 1998; Walters, 2006) generally indicate that teaching may result in improvement of the guessing skill but are not consistent with the relative efficacy of teaching methods. One of the reasons for this inconsistency is that only one aspect of guessing (deriving the meaning of an unknown word) was measured. The GCT measures three aspects of the guessing skill, and thus may determine effective teaching methods to a particular aspect of the guessing skill. For example, teaching a variety of contextual clues might be effective because learners may increase discourse knowledge which contributes to the improvement of the guessing skill. Teaching a general strategy (Bruton & Samuda, 1981; Clarke & Nation, 1980; Williams, 1985) might also be effective because learners may become aware that integrating grammar information (part of speech of an unknown word) and discourse information (contextual clues) is important. Cloze exercises might also be effective because they provide learners with the opportunity to do a lot of guessing, but might be effective only when learners know the majority of words in the context so that the target words may be guessable. Research looking at different approaches to improving guessing might indicate the best approaches to improving this specific VLA. Moreover, research might also make it possible to identify where learners find difficulty and choose the appropriate teaching method that is most effective to improve their weaknesses.

The development of the WPLT will also make it possible to investigate the effects of teaching on word part knowledge. Research with L1 children (e.g., Baumann et al., 2002) indicates that teaching has a positive effect on the improvement of word part knowledge; however, little is known about L2 learners. Using the WPLT in a pretest, intervention, post-test quasi-experimental design may contribute to determining the relative efficacy of teaching methods. Different approaches to learning affixes might be compared to determine which is most effective. For example, knowledge of affix form and meaning might effectively be gained by providing some example words with a particular affix rather than simply providing the relationships between affix form and meaning because affixes do not exist on their own. Knowledge of affix use might be effectively gained when learners encounter sentences that include a word with a particular affix rather than encountering only an example word that includes the affix.

Second, future research may also investigate the interrelationships among vocabulary size, word part knowledge, and guessing from context. This will reveal the combined effect of the guessing skill and word part knowledge on vocabulary size. It has been claimed that both the guessing skill and word part knowledge play an important role in vocabulary learning (e.g., Nation, 2013), but little is known about the extent to which these two VLA components contribute to vocabulary size. This may be effectively investigated using the WPLT and the GCT.

Third, creating tests measuring other aspects of VLA such as the skill of dictionary use and phonological knowledge may be useful both for research and education. Future research may indicate the relative efficacy of some aspects of VLA over others. This may be different according to learners' proficiency level, L1 background, age, gender, learning style, and so on. Having a variety of VLA tests may be useful to teachers because this will help them determine which components of VLA they should deal with in class and offer a more effective teaching program.

Finally, web-based VLA tests may be useful to develop (Alderson, 2005; Hughes, 1989). Currently, the GCT and the WPLT are available only in a paper-based format, but web-based tests will allow learners to take the tests anytime and anywhere if they have access to the internet. They can receive immediate feedback on their scores when they finish the tests. Preferably, when the tests are completed the scores are automatically calculated and are reported to learners using a bar graph which clearly indicates their strengths and weaknesses. Online tests might also have the function of recording the response time for each item so that teachers could identify learners who took the tests without thinking carefully (too short response time) or those who relied on external resources such as a dictionary (too long response time). A recent study (Mizumoto, Sasao, & Webb, 2019) involved the development and evaluation of a computerized adaptive testing (CAT) version of the WPLT and found that the CAT-WPLT produced the same or greater reliability estimates than the original WPLT with a smaller number of items. This indicates that CAT provides an effective and efficient way of diagnosing learners' VLA, and future research may develop and evaluate the tests of other components of VLA using the CAT system.

Further Reading

Webb, S., & Nation, I. S. P. (2017). *How vocabulary is learned*. Oxford, UK: Oxford University Press.

Chapter 7 of this book proposes ways in which students may become more effective autonomous learners of vocabulary.

Webb, S. A., & Sasao, Y. (2013). New directions in vocabulary testing. *RELC Journal, 44*(3), 263–277.

This paper discusses some of the gaps in vocabulary assessment and the importance of making new vocabulary tests to fill these gaps.

Related Topics

Computer adaptive testing, deliberate vocabulary learning, incidental vocabulary learning, language assessment, vocabulary learning strategies

References

Abbott, M. (2000). Identifying reliable generalizations for spelling words: The importance of multi-level analysis. *The Elementary School Journal, 101*(2), 233–245.

Alderson, J. C. (2005). *Diagnosing foreign language proficiency: The interface between learning and assessment*. London, UK: Continuum.

Alderson, J. C., Clapham, C. M., & Wall, D. (1995). *Language test construction and evaluation*. Cambridge, UK: Cambridge University Press.

Ames, W. S. (1966). The development of a classification scheme of contextual aids. *Reading Research Quarterly, 2*(1), 57–82.

Anglin, J. M. (1993). Vocabulary development: A morphological analysis. *Monographs of the Society for Research in Child Development Serial No. 238, 58*(10).

Bachman, L. F. (1990). *Fundamental considerations in language testing*. Oxford, UK: Oxford University Press.

Bachman, L. F., & Palmer, A. (1996). *Language testing in practice: Designing and developing useful language tests*. Oxford, UK: Oxford University Press.

Bauer, L., & Nation, I. S. P. (1993). Word families. *International Journal of Lexicography, 6*(4), 253–279.

Baumann, J. F., Edwards, E. C., Font, G., Tereshinski, C. A., Kame'enui, E. J., & Olejnik, S. (2002). Teaching morphemic and contextual analysis to fifth-grade students. *Reading Research Quarterly, 37*(2), 150–176.

Beck, I. L., McKeown, M. G., & McCaslin, E. S. (1983). Vocabulary development: All contexts are not created equal. *Elementary School Journal, 83*(3), 177–181.

Beglar, D. (2010). A Rasch-based validation of the Vocabulary Size Test. *Language Testing, 27*(1), 101–118.

Beglar, D., & Hunt, A. (1999). Revising and validating the 2000 word level and the university word level vocabulary tests. *Language Testing, 16*(2), 131–162.

Bensoussan, M., & Laufer, B. (1984). Lexical guessing in context in EFL reading comprehension. *Journal of Research in Reading, 7*(1), 15–32.

Bradley, L., & Huxford, L. (1994). Organising sound and letter patterns for spelling. In G. D. A. Brown & N. C. Ellis (Eds.), *The handbook of spelling: Theory, process and intervention* (pp. 425–439). Chichester, UK: John Wiley & Sons.

Brown, R., Waring, R., & Donkaewbua, S. (2008). Incidental vocabulary acquisition from reading, reading-while-listening, and listening to stories. *Reading in a Foreign Language, 20*(2), 136–163.

Bruck, M., Treiman, R., Caravolas, M., Genesee, F., & Cassar, M. (1998). Spelling skills of children in whole language and phonics classrooms. *Applied Psycholinguistics, 19*(4), 669–684.

Bruton, A., & Samuda, V. (1981). Guessing words. *Modern English Teacher, 8*(3), 18–21.

Cheung, H. (1996). Nonword span as a unique predictor of second-language vocabulary learning. *Developmental Psychology, 32*(5), 867–873.

Chun, D. M., & Plass, J. L. (1996). Effects of multimedia annotations on vocabulary acquisition. *Modern Language Journal, 80*(2), 183–198.

Clarke, D. F., & Nation, I. S. P. (1980). Guessing the meanings of words from context: Strategy and techniques. *System, 8*(3), 211–220.

Cooper, T. C. (1999). Processing of idioms by L2 learners of English. *TESOL Quarterly, 33*(2), 233–262.

Day, R. R., Omura, C., & Hiramatsu, M. (1991). Incidental EFL vocabulary learning and reading. *Reading in a Foreign Language, 7*(2), 541–551.

Dupuy, B., & Krashen, S. D. (1993). Incidental vocabulary acquisition in French as a foreign language. *Applied Language Learning, 4*(1&2), 55–63.

Elgort, I. (2007). *The role of intentional decontextualised learning in second language vocabulary acquisition: Evidence from primed lexical decision tasks with advanced bilinguals.* Unpublished doctoral dissertation, Victoria University, Wellington, New Zealand.

Ellis, N. C., & Sinclair, S. G. (1996). Working memory in the acquisition of vocabulary and syntax: Putting language in good order. *Quarterly Journal of Experimental Psychology, 49A*(1), 234–250.

Fitzpatrick, T., & Clenton, J. (2010). The challenge of validation: Assessing the performance of a test of productive vocabulary. *Language Testing, 27*(4), 537–554.

Fraser, C. A. (1999). Lexical processing strategy use and vocabulary learning through reading. *Studies in Second Language Acquisition, 21*(2), 225–241.

Fukkink, R. G., & de Glopper, K. (1998). Effects of instruction in deriving word meaning from context: A meta-analysis. *Review of Educational Research, 68*(4), 450–469.

Gathercole, S. E. (1995). Is nonword repetition a test of phonological memory or long-term knowledge? It all depends on the nonwords. *Memory and Cognition, 23*(1), 83–94.

Gathercole, S. E., & Baddeley, A. D. (1989). Evaluation of the role of phonological STM in the development of vocabulary in children: A longitudinal study. *Journal of Memory and Language, 28,* 200–213.

Gathercole, S. E., Service, E., Hitch, G. J., Adams, A. M., & Martin, A. J. (1999). Phonological short-term memory and vocabulary development: Further evidence on the nature of the relationship. *Applied Cognitive Psychology, 13*(1), 65–77.

Goulden, R., Nation, I. S. P., & Read, J. (1990). How large can a receptive vocabulary be? *Applied Linguistics, 11*(4), 341–363.

Hill, M., & Laufer, B. (2003). Type of task, time-on-task and electronic dictionaries in incidental vocabulary acquisition. *IRAL, 41,* 87–106.

Horst, M., Cobb, T., & Meara, P. (1998). Beyond a Clockwork Orange: Acquiring second language vocabulary through reading. *Reading in a Foreign Language, 11*(2), 207–223.

Hughes, A. (1989). *Testing for language teachers*. Cambridge, UK: Cambridge University Press.

Hulme, C., Maughan, S., & Brown, G. D. A. (1991). Memory for familiar and unfamiliar words: Evidence for a long-term memory contribution to short-term memory span. *Journal of Memory and Language*, *30*, 685–701.

Hulstijn, J. H. (1992). Retention of inferred and given word meanings: Experiments in incidental vocabulary learning. In P. J. L. Arnaud & H. Bejoint (Eds.), *Vocabulary and applied linguistics* (pp. 113–125). London, UK: Macmillan.

Hulstijn, J. H., Hollander, M., & Greidanus, T. (1996). Incidental vocabulary learning by advanced foreign language students: The influence of marginal glosses, dictionary use, and reoccurrence of unknown words. *Modern Language Journal*, *80*(3), 327–339.

Ishii, T., & Schmitt, N. (2009). Developing an integrated diagnostic test of vocabulary size and depth. *RELC Journal*, *40*(1), 5–22.

Jenkins, J. R., Stein, M. L., & Wysocki, K. (1984). Learning vocabulary through reading. *American Educational Research Journal*, *21*(4), 767–787.

Knight, S. M. (1994). Dictionary use while reading: The effects on comprehension and vocabulary acquisition for students of different verbal abilities. *Modern Language Journal*, *78*(3), 285–299.

Kuhn, M. R., & Stahl, S. A. (1998). Teaching children to learn word meanings from context. *Journal of Literacy Research*, *30*(1), 119–138.

Laufer, B., Elder, C., Hill, K., & Congdon, P. (2004). Size and strength: Do we need both to measure vocabulary knowledge? *Language Testing*, *21*(2), 202–226.

Laufer, B., & Goldstein, Z. (2004). Testing vocabulary knowledge: Size, strength, and computer adaptiveness. *Language Learning*, *54*(3), 399–436.

Laufer, B., & Hill, M. (2000). What lexical information do L2 learners select in a CALL dictionary and how does it affect word retention? *Language Learning and Technology*, *3*(2), 58–76.

Laufer, B., & Ravenhorst-Kalovski, G. C. (2010). Lexical threshold revisited: Lexical text coverage, learners' vocabulary size and reading comprehension. *Reading in a Foreign Language*, *22*(1), 15–30.

Luppescu, S., & Day, R. R. (1993). Reading, dictionaries and vocabulary learning. *Language Learning*, *43*(2), 263–287.

Masoura, E. V., & Gathercole, S. E. (1999). Phonological short-term memory and foreign language learning. *International Journal of Psychology*, *34*(5/6), 383–388.

Masoura, E. V., & Gathercole, S. E. (2005). Contrasting contributions of phonological short-term memory and long-term knowledge to vocabulary learning in a foreign language. *Memory*, *13*(3/4), 422–429.

Meara, P., & Buxton, B. (1987). An alternative to multiple choice vocabulary tests. *Language Testing*, *4*(2), 142–151.

Meara, P., & Fitzpatrick, T. (2000). Lex30: An improved method of assessing productive vocabulary in L2. *System*, *28*(1), 19–30.

Meara, P., & Jones, G. (1988). Vocabulary size as a placement indicator. In P. Grunwell (Ed.), *Applied linguistics in society* (pp. 80–87). London, UK: CILT.

Mizumoto, A., Sasao, Y., & Webb, S. A. (2019). Developing and evaluating a computerized adaptive testing version of the Word Part Levels Test. *Language Testing*, *36*(1), 101–123.

Mochizuki, M., & Aizawa, K. (2000). An affix acquisition order for EFL learners: An exploratory study. *System*, *28*(2), 291–304.

Mori, Y. (2002). Individual differences in the integration of information from context and word parts in interpreting unknown kanji words. *Applied Psycholinguistics*, *23*(3), 375–397.

Mori, Y., & Nagy, W. (1999). Integration of information from context and word elements in interpreting novel kanji compounds. *Reading Research Quarterly*, *34*(1), 80–101.

Nagy, W. E., & Anderson, R. C. (1984). How many words are there in printed school English? *Reading Research Quarterly*, *19*(3), 304–330.

Nagy, W. E., Anderson, R. C., & Herman, P. A. (1987). Learning word meanings from context during normal reading. *American Educational Research Journal*, *24*(2), 237–270.

Nagy, W. E., Herman, P., & Anderson, R. C. (1985). Learning words from context. *Reading Research Quarterly, 20*(2), 233–253.

Nakata, T. (2011). Computer-assisted second language vocabulary learning in a paired-associate paradigm: A critical investigation of flashcard software. *Computer Assisted Language Learning, 24*(1), 17–38.

Nassaji, H. (2003). L2 vocabulary learning from context: Strategies, knowledge sources, and their relationship with success in L2 lexical inferencing. *TESOL Quarterly, 37*(4), 645–670.

Nation, I. S. P. (1983). Testing and teaching vocabulary. *Guidelines, 5*(1), 12–25.

Nation, I. S. P. (1990). *Teaching and learning vocabulary.* Rowley, MA: Newbury House.

Nation, I. S. P. (2001). *Learning vocabulary in another language.* Cambridge, UK: Cambridge University Press.

Nation, I. S. P. (2004). A study of the most frequent word families in the British National Corpus. In P. Bogaards & B. Laufer (Eds.), *Vocabulary in a second language: Selection, acquisition, and testing* (pp. 3–13). Amsterdam: John Benjamins.

Nation, I. S. P. (2006). How large a vocabulary is needed for reading and listening? *Canadian Modern Language Review, 63*(1), 59–82.

Nation, I. S. P. (2013). *Learning vocabulary in another language* (2nd ed.). Cambridge, UK: Cambridge University Press.

Nation, I. S. P., & Beglar, D. (2007). A vocabulary size test. *The Language Teacher, 31*(7), 9–13.

Papagno, C., Valentine, T., & Baddeley, A. (1991). Phonological short-term memory and foreign-language vocabulary learning. *Journal of Memory and Language, 30*, 331–347.

Paribakht, T. S., & Wesche, M. (1999). Reading and "incidental" L2 vocabulary acquisition: An introspective study of lexical inferencing. *Studies in Second Language Acquisition, 21*(2), 195–224.

Parry, K. (1991). Building a vocabulary through academic reading. *TESOL Quarterly, 25*(4), 629–653.

Perfetti, C. (2010). Decoding, vocabulary, and comprehension: The golden triangle of reading skill. In M. G. McKeown & L. Kucan (Eds.), *Bringing reading research to life.* New York, NY: Guilford.

Peters, E. (2007). Manipulating L2 learners' online dictionary use and its effect on L2 word retention. *Language Learning and Technology, 11*(2), 36–58.

Pitts, M., White, H., & Krashen, S. (1989). Acquiring second language vocabulary through reading: A replication of the Clockwork Orange study using second language acquirers. *Reading in a Foreign Language, 5*(2), 271–275.

Pulido, D., & Hambrick, D. Z. (2008). The *virtuous* circle: Modeling individual differences in L2 reading and vocabulary development. *Reading in a Foreign Language, 20*(2), 164–190.

Qian, D. (1999). Assessing the roles of depth and breadth of vocabulary knowledge in reading comprehension. *Canadian Modern Language Review, 56*(2), 282–307.

Read, J. (1993). The development of a new measure of L2 vocabulary knowledge. *Language Testing, 10*(3), 355–371.

Read, J. (1998). Validating a test to measure depth of vocabulary knowledge. In A. J. Kunnan (Ed.), *Validation in language assessment* (pp. 41–60). Mahwah, NJ: Lawrence Erlbaum Associates.

Roberts, T. A., & Meiring, A. (2006). Teaching phonics in the context of children's literature or spelling: Influences on first-grade reading, spelling and writing and fifth-grade comprehension. *Journal of Educational Psychology, 98*(4), 690–713.

Rosenthal, J., & Ehri, L. C. (2008). The mnemonic value of orthography for vocabulary learning. *Journal of Educational Psychology, 100*(1), 173–191.

Sasao, Y., & Webb, S. (2017). The Word Part Levels Test. *Language Teaching Research, 21*(1), 12–30.

Sasao, Y., & Webb, S. (2018). The guessing from context test. *ITL – International Journal of Applied Linguistics, 169*(1), 115–141.

Schatz, E. K., & Baldwin, R. S. (1986). Context clues are unreliable predictors of word meaning. *Reading Research Quarterly, 21*(4), 439–453.

Schmitt, N., & Meara, P. (1997). Researching vocabulary through a word knowledge framework: Word associations and verbal suffixes. *Studies in Second Language Acquisition, 19*(1), 17–36.

Schmitt, N., Ng, J. W. C., & Garras, J. (2011). The word associates format: Validation evidence. *Language Testing, 28*(1), 105–126.

Schmitt, N., Schmitt, D., & Clapham, C. (2001). Developing and exploring the behaviour of two new versions of the Vocabulary Levels Test. *Language Testing, 18*(1), 55–88.

Schmitt, N., & Zimmerman, C. B. (2002). Derivative word forms: What do learners know? *TESOL Quarterly, 36*(2), 145–171.

Service, E. (1992). Phonology, working memory, and foreign language learning. *Quarterly Journal of Experimental Psychology, 45A*(1), 21–50.

Shu, H., Anderson, R. C., & Zhang, Z. (1995). Incidental learning of word meanings while reading: A Chinese and American cross-cultural study. *Reading Research Quarterly, 30*(1), 76–95.

Tono, Y. (1988). Assessment of EFL learners' dictionary using skills. *JACET Bulletin, 19*, 103–126.

Tyler, A., & Nagy, W. (1989). The acquisition of English derivational morphology. *Journal of Memory and Language, 28*(6), 649–667.

Walters, J. (2004). Teaching the use of context to infer meaning: A longitudinal survey of L1 and L2 vocabulary research. *Language Teaching, 37*, 243–252.

Walters, J. (2006). Methods of teaching inferring meaning from context. *RELC Journal, 37*(2), 176–190.

Waring, R., & Takaki, M. (2003). At what rate do learners learn and retain new vocabulary from reading a graded reader? *Reading in a Foreign Language, 15*(2), 130–163.

Webb, S. (2009). The effects of receptive and productive learning of word pairs on vocabulary knowledge. *RELC Journal, 40*(3), 360–376.

Webb, S., Sasao, Y., & Ballance, O. (2017). The updated Vocabulary Levels Test: Developing and validating two new forms of the VLT. *ITL – International Journal of Applied Linguistics, 168*(1), 34–70.

Wei, Z. (2015). Does teaching mnemonics for vocabulary learning make a difference? Putting the keyword method and the word part technique to the test. *Language Teaching Research, 19*(1), 43–69.

Wesche, M., & Paribakht, T. S. (1996). Assessing second language vocabulary knowledge: Depth versus breadth. *Canadian Modern Language Review, 53*(1), 13–40.

Williams, R. (1985). Teaching vocabulary recognition strategies in ESP reading. *ESP Journal, 4*(2), 121–131.

28

Sensitive Measures of Vocabulary Knowledge and Processing

Expanding Nation's Framework[1]

Aline Godfroid

Introduction: Real-Time Measurement of Vocabulary Knowledge and Processing

Vocabulary is a key building block of language. As such, measuring vocabulary knowledge in an accurate manner provides crucial information regarding, for example, a learner's progress towards becoming an expert user of the target language. In studying and measuring vocabulary knowledge, researchers need to consider two inextricably related issues: firstly, *how* they are measuring vocabulary knowledge, and secondly, *what* knowledge they are measuring. Traditionally, the field of vocabulary research and teaching has relied on offline measures of vocabulary knowledge, such as multiple choice, translation, fill-in-the-blank, and matching tests. Offline tests are a convenient way of measuring vocabulary knowledge because they provide information about learners' ability to recognize or retrieve the form or meaning of a word, often with no time restrictions (hence the name *offline*). More recently, offline measures are increasingly being used in conjunction with a qualitatively different type of measure, known as online measure. Online measures typically involve measuring learners' lexical knowledge during language processing (hence the name *online*) when there are real time restrictions.

A daily-life analogy of online and offline measurements would be a case of watching football (or soccer). One could watch a match live (i.e., in real time) in the stadium or on TV. In that case, one would view the detailed happenings of the match as they unfold, such as how a particular player scores a goal, and who has a great shot but misses. In other words, the real-time watching allows the viewer to know the dynamics of the match, similarly to researchers investigating language processing using online measures. In contrast, researchers using offline measures are primarily interested in the overall outcomes or products of vocabulary knowledge and perhaps less in the fine-grained details of the process (or at least, their instruments do not provide this information). In our analogy, this would be someone simply scanning the headlines of the sports section of a newspaper in order to know the result of the football match, and perhaps the standing of a given team in the league after the weekend.

Measuring vocabulary knowledge is an integral part of studying vocabulary. Whether the goal is to compare different teaching methods, or track vocabulary growth over time, researchers or teachers need to have a measure of their students' vocabulary knowledge. Most commonly this measure will be a paper-and-pencil or computer-based test that involves word recognition (e.g., multiple choice, matching) or recall or retrieval (e.g., translation, fill-in-the-blank). Therefore, much of what we know about the learning and teaching of vocabulary in another language derives from offline measures of vocabulary knowledge. These tests measure explicit-declarative word knowledge, because learners could declare their vocabulary knowledge out loud (e.g., *To drive is to use a car*) if they were asked to. Given the predominance of offline measures in vocabulary research and teaching, it is perhaps no surprise that Nation's (2013) framework of vocabulary knowledge, which is the most comprehensive framework of vocabulary knowledge in second language (L2) studies to date, is also geared heavily towards explicit-declarative knowledge (see Table 28.1). That is, although Nation's framework greatly broadened the scope of *what* vocabulary knowledge entails, the default approach to *how* vocabulary knowledge is measured is still very much offline and declarative. Here, I aim to expand and explore the *how* dimension, so teachers and researchers may opt for more diverse and comprehensive measures of vocabulary knowledge in their work.

Offline measures of vocabulary knowledge are not without limitations. Most of all, these tests are separate or divorced from actual language performance. Recognizing or being able to recall a word's meaning or form on a paper-based test is not the same as recognizing or recalling the word during interaction with another speaker. Actual language usage is often characterized by a certain amount of time pressure, which makes the task of word recognition or retrieval more demanding. Language users must access their lexical knowledge rapidly so they can focus their efforts on larger meaning units. This requirement of quick lexical access

Table 28.1 Nation's (2013) framework of vocabulary knowledge

Aspects of vocabulary knowledge		Receptive/ productive	What does it means to master this aspect?
Form	Spoken	R	What does the word sound like?
		P	How is the word pronounced?
	Written	R	What does the word look like?
		P	How is the word written and spelled?
	Word parts	R	What parts are recognizable in this word?
		P	What word parts are needed to express the meaning?
Meaning	Form and meaning	R	What meaning does this word form signal?
		P	What word form can be used to express this meaning?
	Concept and referents	R	What is included in the concept?
		P	What items can the concept refer to?
	Association	R	What other words does this make us think of?
		P	What other words could we use instead of this one?
Use	Grammatical functions	R	In what patterns does the word occur?
		P	In what patterns must we use this word?
	Collocations	R	What words or types of words occur with this one?
		P	What words or types of words must we use with this one?
	Constraints on use	R	Where, when, and how often would we expect to meet this word?
		P	Where, when, and how often can we use this word?

could also partly explain why listening, where learners have little control over the speed of the incoming speech stream, is claimed to be the most difficult foreign language skill to acquire (e.g., Vandergrift & Goh, 2012). To capture these aspects of vocabulary knowledge-in-action more fully, researchers can measure not only learners' explicit-declarative knowledge, but also their automatized explicit, procedural, or implicit knowledge of vocabulary; that is, how easily people can retrieve words from their mental dictionaries and how well the words are connected in their minds. Thanks to the advance of technology, new methods and techniques have made it possible to ask and answer new questions about the non-declarative aspects of vocabulary knowledge. The finer distinctions between these different knowledge types (i.e., automatic knowledge, procedural knowledge, tacit-implicit knowledge) are still being sorted out in the literature. In reviewing different methodologies, I will therefore adopt the same terminology as the authors of primary studies have used, bypassing subtle theoretical distinctions that may exist between the different knowledge types. The overarching idea is that there is a type of non-declarative knowledge of vocabulary – which researchers variously refer to as automatic knowledge, procedural knowledge, or tacit-implicit knowledge – that can be assessed by online measurements.

Online measures are often about how long it takes a participant to do something. Consequently, most online measures used in the field of Second Language Acquisition (SLA) offer some kind of reaction time data. The processes that are studied with these reaction time measures tend to be very fast, in the order of tenths and hundredths of a second, and therefore their length is normally measured in milliseconds (msec). For example, the average time it takes to retrieve the meaning of a word is one-fourth of a second, or 250 msec (e.g., Inhoff & Rayner, 1986). Consequently, the fine-grained details offered by online measurements can reveal the dynamics of language processing as in watching a football match live. Furthermore, these online measures add a new dimension to our understanding of vocabulary knowledge, by illuminating *how well* learners can access their knowledge of different aspects of a word. In the following overview, I will therefore link the different methodologies back to Nation's (2013) framework and, in so doing, expand it by adding a whole new dimension (see Table 28.2 later in the chapter). As such, this chapter does not only serve as an introduction to new methods and techniques which could tap into a learner's implicit, automatized explicit, or procedural vocabulary knowledge; it also invites readers and researchers to see new meanings of vocabulary knowledge. This could potentially inform a more usage-focused teaching practice and, I hope, inspire more research that examines the lexical iceberg in full – that is, both conscious knowledge (the tip) and unconscious knowledge (the part underwater).

In the second section of the chapter, I will review three key online methodologies in the context of vocabulary knowledge and processing. These methodologies are, first, general reaction time measures in, for example, a lexical decision task, where the participant decides whether a letter string (or a spoken item) forms a word or not; second, the coefficient of variability, a measure derived from reaction times; and, third, eye-movement registration or eye tracking, which tracks the eyes' dwell times in different locations. For each method, the discussion will start with introducing how it works and what type of information researchers can obtain from it, followed by a general overview of vocabulary studies that have used the methodology. A couple of representative studies will be highlighted and reviewed. In the third section of the chapter, I present an extension of Nation's framework and provide directions for future research to measure new dimensions of vocabulary knowledge. Interested readers will be pointed to some further reading and related topics in the fourth section.

Critical Issues and Topics

Measures from psychology have found their way into L2 vocabulary research in the form of various reaction time methodologies and, to some extent, neurocognitive measures. These sensitive measures of vocabulary knowledge generally fall into two categories (also see Leow, 2015):

1   Measures of vocabulary knowledge *as a product* capture how well words or phrases are known.
2   Measures of vocabulary learning and knowledge *as a process* capture the incremental learning of vocabulary over time, as L2 learners are engaged in processing new words or phrases.

Online product measures supplement traditional, offline measures and are often used to shed new light onto well-established, well-studied research questions. The best-known example is the primed lexical decision task. Another prototypical example of an online processing measure is eye tracking (Conklin, Pellicer-Sánchez, & Carrol, 2018; Godfroid, 2019a), the filming of participants' eye movements, although eye tracking can also be used to study the product or outcome, rather than the process, of vocabulary acquisition (Godfroid, 2019b). The introduction of eye tracking in L2 vocabulary research has been an important source of innovation in the field, making it possible to study new questions in a detailed and fine-grained manner (Godfroid & Winke, 2015).

Priming Tasks and Other Reaction Time Tasks

How It Works

Primed lexical decision tasks are lexical decision tasks with an additional priming component. For the lexical decision part, participants are asked to judge whether a string of letters or a sound sequence forms a real word in a given language. This is the lexical decision. For instance, CAT is a word in English, and therefore requires a yes response, but CAX is a non-word that requires a no response. Participants are asked to hit the "yes" or "no" key on a response box or a keyboard as quickly and accurately as possible when they see or hear a stimulus (called the *target*). Of interest are their reaction times for correct yes responses, because these reflect the participants' knowledge of the target language (the non-words are not a part of the target language and are, therefore, less informative). Reaction times are recorded on a computer running special software, such as E-Prime (Psychology Software Tools Inc., 2012), DMDX (Forster & Forster, 2003), PsychoPy (Peirce, 2007), Inquisit (Inquisit 5.0.9, 2017), or SuperLab (Cedrus Corporation, 2017).

Lexical decision tasks afford a measure of speed of lexical access (the retrieval of a word's form or meaning). The assumption is that to judge a word correctly as a word, participants must access the form in their mental lexicon, much like looking up a word in a dictionary. Whether this requires looking up a word's meaning or whether lexical decisions could be purely form based remains a matter of debate. Favoring a form-based explanation, Grainger, Dufau, Montant, Ziegler, and Fagot (2012) showed, in an article published in *Science*, that even baboons can be trained to do lexical decision tasks! For this reason, some researchers prefer semantic categorization tasks to lexical decision tasks (Lim & Godfroid, 2015; Phillips, Segalowitz, O'Brien, & Yamasak, 2004; Segalowitz & de Almeida, 2002; Segalowitz &

Frenkiel-Fishman, 2005). Semantic categorization tasks are similar to lexical decisions, except all the items are real words (there are no non-words). A participant's task is to judge whether the word is a member of a predetermined semantic category or not. For instance, if participants are asked to judge whether or not a word refers to a living being, BOY should elicit a yes response and BOOK a no response.

Responding yes or no to word and non-word stimuli is the lexical decision part; now what about the priming component? In a primed lexical decision task, a prime appears shortly before the target word. For instance, the prime *dog* may precede the target CAT (*dog* → CAT), potentially leading to faster response times to CAT because *dog* and *cat* are semantically related. This is known as *positive priming* or *facilitation*. The opposite, *negative priming* or *inhibition*, also exists and will result in slower reaction times. By manipulating the relationship between the prime and the target, researchers can probe whether a word is a part of someone's mental lexicon (whether it has its own *lexical entry*) and, if so, how well connected the word is to others. There are orthographic priming experiments, phonological priming experiments, semantic priming experiments, and others (see examples below). Priming experiments are thus quite useful to address a range of questions about the mental lexicon, conceptualized here as a giant interconnected network of words and phrases (e.g., Meara, 2009).

Furthermore, researchers can vary the interval between the prime and target, so participants may be more or less likely to perceive the prime consciously. In *unmasked* priming, participants can see both the prime and the target. In *masked* priming, the prime is flashed only briefly on the screen so most participants remain unaware of it (they report seeing only a flicker). The masked priming technique allows researchers to study connections in the mental lexicon outside of participants' awareness; that is, with masked priming, researchers can explore parts of the lexical iceberg that are deeply buried under water.

Priming and Reaction Time Research in L2 Vocabulary Studies

Priming research has been gaining popularity among L2 vocabulary researchers, who are now also using the technique to study the effects of vocabulary instruction on word knowledge (for other applications, see Carrol & Conklin, 2014; Frenck-Mestre & Prince, 1997; Wolter & Gyllstad, 2011). To my knowledge, Elgort (2011) introduced priming into L2 vocabulary teaching research, in an oft-cited study on the effectiveness of deliberate word learning from word cards. In the study, 48 advanced L2 English learners were presented with 48 English pseudowords in the lab (e.g., *prolley*, defined as "a large strong beam, often of steel or iron, forming a main supporting element in a framework of buildings or bridges", p. 409). They were given a set of word cards to study for a week, before returning to take part in three priming experiments. On average, the participants had spent four hours studying the words at home when they returned for the main experiments. In three priming experiments, Elgort measured both representational and functional aspects of vocabulary knowledge. To do so, she compared participants' responses to the newly learned pseudowords vs. (1) real, low-frequency words (established in the lexicon) and (2) non-words (not established in the lexicon). The goal was to investigate whether pseudowords would behave similarly to the real words or the non-words in the priming experiments. In all three experiments, the pseudowords patterned with the real, low-frequency words; that is, they elicited priming effects when the real words did and no priming effects when the real words did not either. This suggested L2 participants had created formal-lexical representations of the newly learned pseudowords in their lexicons (form priming, Experiments 1 and 2) and begun to integrate the pseudowords semantically (semantic priming, Experiment 3). These findings, along with Elgort's findings for the coefficient of variability (reportd below) showed that deliberate learning activities, such as learning from flash cards, can generate word knowledge that can be used online, in real time, and thus potentially in spontaneous communication. Interestingly, in a follow-up study with a similar group of L2 English participants, Elgort and Warren (2014) did not find robust priming effects for pseudowords that learners encountered between 6 and 88 times (median: 12 times) when reading multiple chapters from a nonfiction book for pleasure. This may suggest, then, that the massive amounts of word repetition and focused practice that are typical of deliberate vocabulary learning are difficult to match in more naturalistic tasks.

Amount of exposure may also be a factor in Sonbul and Schmitt's (2013) results for the teaching and learning of medical collocations. In this study, adult native and advanced non-native English speakers learned 15 medical collocations using a combination of input flood (collocations embedded in a story context), input flood with input enhancement (collocations in red and boldface), and decontextualized presentation (no story context). Participants learned five collocations in each condition and each collocation occurred three times during training. After the learning phase, the participants completed two measures of explicit collocational knowledge (form recall and form recognition) and a novel measure of implicit knowledge, called automatic collocation priming. The rationale behind the priming test was that if participants had gained implicit knowledge of the medical collocations (e.g., *vanishing lung*), the first word (e.g., *vanishing*) would prime the second word (e.g., *lung*), causing participants to respond faster to LUNG in *vanishing* → LUNG than in the matched control pair *decaying* → LUNG (*decaying lung* is not a medical collocation). Although participants demonstrated significant explicit knowledge of the newly taught collocations on the immediate and delayed posttests, neither native nor non-native speakers showed a significant priming effect. This finding differed from Elgort (2011), who used 48 single words (English pseudowords), form priming and semantic priming, and several hours of decontextualized study over a one-week time period as instruction. Sonbul and Schmitt (2013) argued their results showed "a clear dissociation between explicit and implicit lexical knowledge" (p. 151).

Paciorek and Williams (2015a) also focused on the acquisition of collocational knowledge, but different from all other researchers, they adopted a pure reaction time methodology. In Experiment 2, Paciorek and Williams trained native and non-native English speakers on four novel verbs embedded in 20 verb phrases each. Participants were informed that two of the verbs (*powter* and *mouten*) meant "increase" and the other two (*gouble* and *conell*) meant "decrease". Critically, they were not told that one verb in each pair only took abstract collocates (e.g., *powter* "increase" *the significance*) and the other required concrete collocates (e.g., *mouten* "increase" *the calcium*). This hidden regularity was the object for learning in the study. The participants saw verb phrases word-by-word and were tasked to decide whether the collocate in each verb phrase had a positive, negative, or neutral connotation and whether the verb in the phrase meant "increase" or "decrease". Results showed that in trials where the semantic preferences of the verb were violated (e.g., *powter the calcium*), native speakers made slower increase-decrease decisions. The non-native speakers did not slow down. Because none of the participants commented on the role of concreteness in the collocations, Paciorek and Williams argued native speakers had learned the collocational information implicitly; that is, unintentionally and without being aware of it (for further evidence, see Paciorek & Williams, 2015b).

Taken together, these four studies demonstrate how priming experiments and reaction time tasks can be used to measure aspects of implicit vocabulary knowledge, which are normally hidden below water. In particular, these methods can reveal whether or not a learner has established a lexical entry for new words (form priming), acquired the meaning of a word and integrated it into a larger semantic network (semantic priming), and learned patterns of co-occurrence (collocation priming, reaction times to semantic-violation trials). All examples used visual priming, but auditory and cross-modal priming are also available (see "Future Directions"). Similarly, cross-linguistic priming (Carrol & Conklin, 2014; Wolter & Gyllstad, 2011) could be used to address additional research questions about the L1-L2 relationship. The key contribution of all these methods is that they can probe the unconscious (tacit-implicit) dimensions of vocabulary knowledge, which might not be assessed using traditional vocabulary tests, such as the Vocabulary Knowledge Scale, the Vocabulary Size Test, the Vocabulary Levels Test, the yes/no test, and many other examples.

Coefficient of Variability

How It Works

The coefficient of variability, or CV_{RT}, is a measure that can be calculated for any type of task (lexical decision, semantic judgment, eye tracking) that produces reaction times as an outcome measure (for sample tasks, see the previous section and next section). Computation of CV_{RT} is straightforward: $CV_{RT} = \dfrac{SD_{RT}}{M_{RT}}$; in other words, CV_{RT} is the standard deviation of all of an individual's reaction times divided by his or her mean reaction time (Segalowitz & Segalowitz, 1993). The resulting value provides a measure of processing stability. Processing stability is one of three hallmarks of automaticity of knowledge (for reviews, see Lim & Godfroid, 2015; Segalowitz, 2010; Segalowitz & Hulstijn, 2005); that is, knowledge that can be retrieved rapidly and with little conscious effort.

Smaller CV_{RT} values are generally better; however, they are specific to the task at hand. This means CV_{RT} must be compared for different individuals doing the same task or for the same individual repeating a task at different time points. A smaller CV_{RT} value suggests that someone can perform the same task (e.g., lexical decision) with roughly the same speed over and over again, assumedly because it takes them little effort or controlled attention to do so. The knowledge they use is predominantly automatic, much like experienced drivers can execute many of the actions involved in driving a car without conscious thought. The distinction between controlled and automatic processing is central to skill acquisition theory (for a review, see DeKeyser, 2015). The idea is that, across a range of different tasks, linguistic and otherwise, controlled processes tend to be slow, effortful, and variable, whereas automatic processes are fast, effortless, and reliable. A decrease in CV_{RT} suggests a qualitative change in underlying processes: from more controlled to more automatic.

Use of CV_{RT} in L2 Vocabulary Studies

Applications of CV_{RT} in L2 vocabulary studies are diverse. Researchers have used CV_{RT} (1) as a pretest/posttest measure of lexical fluency or automaticity coupled with vocabulary training or instruction (Akamatsu, 2008; Elgort, 2011; Fukkink, Hulstijn, & Simis, 2005; Segalowitz, Segalowitz, & Wood, 1998; Segalowitz, Watson, & Segalowitz, 1995), (2) as an individual difference measure (Elgort & Warren, 2014; Segalowitz & Freed, 2004), and most recently (3) as a measure of novel word learning (Solovyeva & DeKeyser, 2018). These different approaches attest to researchers' ongoing experimentation with what CV_{RT} means and how it can be used to enrich our understanding of L2 vocabulary acquisition.

Following the introduction of CV_{RT} into L2 research (Segalowitz & Segalowitz, 1993), Segalowitz and his colleagues focused on measuring the effects of instruction or exposure on lexical fluency (Segalowitz et al., 1995; Segalowitz et al., 1998). The idea was later taken up in training studies with middle school EFL learners in the Netherlands (Fukkink et al., 2005), college-level EFL learners in Japan (Akamatsu, 2008) and a deliberate learning study with adult ESL learners in New Zealand (Elgort, 2011). A representative study of this kind is Segalowitz, Segalowitz and Wood (1998). The researchers tracked Canadian-English-speaking university students over two semesters of French instruction. The students took part in multiple French lexical decision tasks over the year, for which their RTs and CV_{RTs} were calculated. Segalowitz and colleagues identified two subgroups within the Year 1 students: those with comparatively slow and those with comparatively fast word recognition skills at the outset of the study. Differences in processing speed (RTs) correlated with differences in automaticity (CV_{RT}) in the comparatively fast group only. This suggested it is only at more advanced levels that students differ among themselves in terms of processing efficiency. At lower levels, students may well differ in terms of what they know of the language only (Segalowitz et al., 1998, p. 63). Importantly, both subgroups showed improvements in automaticity over the year, suggesting that incidental exposure to words in a year-long French course results in significant automaticity gains.

Taking a somewhat different approach, Elgort and Warren (2014) studied how individual differences in lexical proficiency (as well as many other variables) might influence gains in vocabulary from reading several chapters from a nonfiction book. The authors measured two dimensions of lexical proficiency: explicit lexical knowledge, using the Vocabulary Size Test (Nation & Beglar, 2007), and implicit lexical knowledge, using CV_{RT} derived from an English lexical decision task performed prior to the reading. Results showed that learners with more automatized lexical processing skills (lower CV_{RT} values) picked up more word meanings from the text. A learner's vocabulary size, on the other hand, enhanced the benefits of repeated exposure: those with larger vocabularies benefited more from seeing a word repeatedly in the text, as shown in their higher test scores. These results show that CV_{RT} and the Vocabulary Size Test were related, yet distinct measures of lexical proficiency, which contributed to vocabulary learning in different ways.

Although the use of CV_{RT} has spread and now also includes sentence processing research (Hulstijn, Van Gelderen, & Schoonen, 2009; Lim & Godfroid, 2015), it is unlikely that applications of CV_{RT} will end here. Solovyeva and DeKeyser (2018) reported data to suggest that *increases* in CV_{RT} may also be informative, specifically in the *early* stages of word learning. The authors administered a primed lexical decision task before and after deliberate study of 40 Swahili-English word pairs. They found an increase in CV_{RT} on the second lexical decision task (after word learning) even though mean RTs went down. This response signature – faster, but less stable performance – is not consistent with automatization, where speed and automaticity are expected to go together (Segalowitz, 2010). Rather, the authors argued that the CV_{RT} increase may reflect learners adding new knowledge to their lexicons. The idea is that as new information is added to memory, it cannot yet be called upon reliably and will thus give rise to variable performance and a large CV_{RT}. If Solovyeva and DeKeyser's results can be replicated by other researchers, future use of CV_{RT} may well cover the whole learning spectrum: from adding new information to memory (CV_{RT} increase), to simple speed up of retrieval of existing knowledge (no change in CV_{RT}), to automatization of well-established, highly practiced routines (CV_{RT} decrease).

Eye Tracking

How It Works

Eye-movement recordings can offer a window into participants' cognition because in complex tasks such as reading, watching a video, or listening to a picture-based story, there is a link between what a participant looks at and what he or she is currently processing. This phenomenon is termed the *eye-mind link* (Just & Carpenter, 1980; Reichle, Pollatsek, & Rayner, 2006). It is the reason eye-movement recordings have found their way into many areas of research, including aviation and driving, human expertise in chess and medical diagnosis, problem solving, scene perception, as well as gaming and consumer research. Researchers believe that by filming and analyzing their participants' eye movements, they can learn something about the cognitive mechanisms that are at play in these various domains.

In the majority of eye-tracking studies with language, the participants perform a language-related task on a computer. The eye tracker records participants' looks to the screen. Language researchers are primarily interested in two types of eye behavior, namely fixations and saccades. *Fixations* are periods (typically measured in msec) during which a participant's eyes pause in a specific location (e.g., on a word on the screen). Fixations tell us something about the where and when of eye movements. Per the eye-mind link, *where* a participant is currently looking is an indication of what the participant is currently processing, although the relationship is by no means perfect. In contrast, *when* a participant moves their eyes determines the duration of the fixation. Importantly, eye fixation durations are susceptible to linguistic influences, such as how easy or difficult it is for a participant to process a word (for reviews, see Rayner, 1998, 2009). Processing difficulty, therefore, often gives rise to longer and more fixations in the same area.

The movements that occur in between two fixations are called *saccades*, after the French word for "twist" or "jerk" (Wade & Tatler, 2005). Indeed, with peak velocities of 600°/s to 1000°/s (Wright & Ward, 2008), saccades are the fastest displacements of which the human body is capable (Holmqvist et al., 2011). Saccades bring the eyes from one location to the next to provide the brain with fresh, quality visual input. In reading, saccades to an earlier part of the text (i.e., right to left eye movements in English) are called *regressions*. Regressions during reading are another sign the participant may be experiencing processing difficulty. Saccades are also interesting in the context of multimodal input (e.g., captioned video or spoken text plus images). In these cases, how often participants visit the different elements on the screen may signal their relative importance or salience and reveal to what extent participants are attempting to integrate multiple sources of information during processing.

Eye-Tracking Research in L2 Vocabulary Studies

Eye tracking has been adopted in many areas of SLA, including vocabulary studies (for a synthetic review, see Godfroid, 2019a). For one, researchers use eye tracking to document, in fine detail, the real-time process of learning words from reading (Elgort, Brysbaert, Stevens, & Van Assche, 2018; Godfroid, Boers, & Housen, 2013; Godfroid et al., 2018; Mohamed, 2018; Pellicer-Sánchez, 2015), watching captioned video (e.g., Montero Perez, Peters, & Desmet, 2015), or looking-while-listening to short stories read aloud (Kohlstedt & Mani, 2018). Additionally, researchers use eye tracking to study the processing and representation of multiword sequences such as idioms (e.g., *spill the beans*) and collocations (e.g., *a fatal mistake*). The focus here is on how multiword units are represented in L2 speakers' lexicon, specifically whether these sequences show stronger internal connections, and are therefore processed more easily than random word combinations are (Carrol & Conklin, 2017; Carrol, Conklin, & Gyllstad, 2016; Siyanova-Chanturia, Conklin, & Schmitt, 2011; Sonbul, 2015; Yi, Lu, & Ma, 2017). Finally, eye tracking has also played an important role in demonstrating that words from a bilingual's two languages are jointly activated, even when the task requires use of a single language only (e.g., Balling, 2013). Research on the bilingual lexicon can advance our understanding of bilingual cognition, which carries clear societal implications (see Kroll & Bialystok, 2013), but is further removed from L2 vocabulary learning and instruction. Therefore, in the remainder of this section we will focus on what eye-tracking research has revealed about vocabulary learning and the representation of multiword sequences in L2 speakers' mind.

In one of the first learning studies with eye tracking, Godfroid et al. (2013) recorded the eye gaze as a measure of learner attention in the context of incidental L2 vocabulary acquisition (for a similar study on grammar, see Godfroid & Uggen, 2013). In the study, L1 Dutch – advanced L2 English speakers read short texts (about 100 words each) embedded with English-like pseudowords, which served as targets for word learning. The authors found that the length of time (total eye gaze duration) readers spent on the target words related positively to their performance on a surprise vocabulary posttest: learners who looked longer at individual target words during reading had a better chance of recognizing them on the test. This was important because it suggested that incidental vocabulary learning (understood as learning from a meaning-focused task) is in a fundamental sense not incidental (also see Gass, 1999; Paribakht & Wesche, 1999): those who spend more attention to language form – in this case, novel words – are more likely to learn. In subsequent studies, vocabulary researchers have progressively moved towards the use of longer reading materials, including short stories (Pellicer-Sánchez, 2015), graded readers (Mohamed, 2018), five chapters from a novel (Godfroid et al., 2018), or a general-academic textbook (Elgort et al., 2018). Studies with longer readings have found both L1 and L2 readers become faster as they encounter the same target words repeatedly in the text (Elgort et al., 2018; Godfroid et al., 2018; Mohamed, 2018; Pellicer-Sánchez, 2015). This speed up may reflect a type of implicit or procedural learning, different from what is measured by traditional vocabulary posttests (Elgort et al., 2018; Godfroid et al., 2018). Another noteworthy finding is that prolonged attention (longer looks) may be especially important for the acquisition of word meaning (Godfroid et al., 2018; Montero Perez et al., 2015; Pellicer-Sánchez, 2015) relative to the acquisition of word form (but see Mohamed, 2018).

A second major strand of eye-tracking research concerns the processing and representation of formulaic language. It is well known that formulaic language brings cognitive and communicative advantages (Wray, 2002, 2008) by lowering the processing burden on language users. This is because language users can essentially pull up a whole string of words from their lexicon to express an idea (compare *bang for the buck*, which is one multiword unit, with *value for one's efforts*, which is four lexical units). This advantage presupposes, however, that language users have deeply entrenched knowledge of fixed and semi-fixed expressions in the language (Boers & Lindstromberg, 2012), an assumption that is not to be taken for granted in the case of lower-input L2 speakers.

To study the status of formulaic language for L2 learners, Carrol and Conklin (2017) examined L1 Chinese – intermediate L2 English students' processing of idioms presented in short English sentence contexts (see also Carrol et al., 2016, for a similar study with Swedish and English). There were two kinds of idioms in the study: English idioms (e.g., *spill the beans*) and translated Chinese idioms, such as *draw a snake and add feet* (画蛇添足), which means "to ruin something by adding unnecessary detail" in Chinese (Carrol & Conklin, 2017, p. 300). Like previous researchers, Carrol and Conklin observed an idiom advantage in L1 processing: English native speakers read *beans* in *spill the beans* (i.e., an idiom, meaning "reveal a secret") faster than *chips* in *spill the chips* (a literal phrase). The Chinese speakers did not show this effect for English idioms, but quite interestingly, they did for the translated Chinese idioms (an effect the authors explained in terms of cross-linguistic priming). When taken together with previous studies (Carrol et al., 2016; Siyanova-Chanturia et al., 2011), these results suggest that real-time advantages for L2-specific formulaic language may only emerge at advanced proficiency levels. Simply knowing the meaning of an L2 idiom (as is often the case at intermediate proficiency levels) does not guarantee that the idiom will be processed more easily during authentic language tasks.

Future Directions: How Can We Measure Knowledge of Form, Meaning, and Use in Real Time?

The goal of this chapter has been to introduce three sensitive measures of vocabulary knowledge and processing: (1) lexical decision, priming, and other reaction time tasks; (2) the coefficient of variability; and (3) eye tracking. A recurring theme is that these newer temporal measures assess different dimensions of vocabulary knowledge compared to more traditional vocabulary tests. As a result, the time is now ripe to revisit Nation's seminal framework of vocabulary knowledge and consider how these newer methods could contribute to a fuller understanding of what it means to know a word (see Table 28.2). Doing so can help advance the field of vocabulary studies theoretically. Expanding Nation's framework also carries practical implications, because it might raise awareness of whether different types of input and instruction are effective in moving learners along a path towards fluent language use.

As with any type of assessment, real-time measures are not without limitations. One area that is currently underdeveloped is the use of real-time measures to gauge productive aspects of vocabulary knowledge. Although picture naming or word reading tasks are two sample production tasks that can supply reaction time data (e.g., Ellis, Simpson-Vlach, & Maynard, 2008), their use in L2 vocabulary research is still fairly limited. Given small changes in task instructions and materials, however, picture or word naming tasks (and indeed many other behavioral tasks) with reaction time measurement could tap into most dimensions of productive vocabulary knowledge. As such, the limit is the creativity of researchers, who are free to experiment with and build new tasks to suit their research needs. In the following, I revisit Nation's framework with an aim to elaborate on how different aspects of word knowledge can be assessed in real time.

Assessing Form

Primed and unprimed lexical decision tasks can add new layers of understanding to traditional measures of form knowledge, such as dictation, yes/no tests, or reading aloud. To date, primed and unprimed lexical decision tasks have predominantly been used with visual stimuli; however, auditory and cross-modal priming and reaction time experiments also exist, so that this family of tasks lends itself to measuring both spoken and written form. Another type of priming, called morphological priming (e.g., walkable → WALK), would be suited to assess knowledge of word parts (for a recent review, see Clahsen & Veríssimo, 2016).

One advantage of priming and related techniques is that they afford a relatively pure measure of formal-lexical knowledge, with little to no interference from knowledge of word

Table 28.2 Expanding on Nation's framework with different measures of vocabulary knowledge

Aspects of vocabulary knowledge		Receptive/ productive	What does it mean to master this aspect?	Example of offline measures	Example of online measures	Fluency of use
Form	Spoken	R	What does the word sound like? Does the learner have a formal-lexical representation (spoken form) of the new word in memory?	Auditory yes/no tests	Auditory lexical decision tasks; auditory priming	Automaticity
		P	How is the word pronounced? How rapidly can the learner produce word forms?	Reading aloud exercises	Naming tasks	
	Written	R	What does the word look like? Does the learner have a formal-lexical representation (written form) of the new word in memory?	Proofreading exercises (identifying spelling errors)	Visual lexical decision tasks; form priming; masked repetition priming	
		P	How is the word written and spelled? How rapidly can the learner produce word forms?	Dictation exercises	Written naming (typing) tasks	
	Word parts	R	What parts are recognizable in this word? Does the learner use morphological information to recognize a word?	Word segmentation tasks	Morphological priming	
		P	What word parts are needed to express the meaning? Does the learner put together word parts to produce complex words?	Generating word derivations		
Meaning	Form and meaning	R	What meaning does this word form signal? How rapidly can the meaning of the word be accessed in the lexicon?	Meaning recognition/recall; translation tasks	Lexical decision tasks; semantic categorization tasks; eye tracking	
		P	What word form can be used to express this meaning? How rapidly can the word form for a given meaning be retrieved from the lexicon?	Translation tasks	Naming tasks	
	Concepts and referents	R	What is included in the concept? How rapidly can the learner access the concept and referents of the word?	Picture-based vocabulary tests	Visual world eye-tracking paradigm	
		P	What items can the concept refer to? How rapidly can the learner produce a word form for a given concept?		Naming tasks	

					Automaticity
Use	Association	R	What other words does this make us think of? Has the new word been integrated into an existing semantic network in memory?	Word Associates Test	Semantic priming
		P	What other words could we use instead of this one? How rapidly can the leaner produce word associations?	Synonyms tests	Naming tasks
	Grammatical functions	R	In what patterns does the word occur? Is the learner sensitive to ungrammatical uses of words?	Grammaticality judgment tasks	Grammaticality judgment tasks with online measures (self-paced reading, eye tracking, or event-related potentials)
		P	In what patterns must we use this word? Can the learner use the word correctly in real-time conversation?	Guided, untimed writing or speaking tasks (e.g., picture description)	Free, real-time writing or speaking tasks (e.g., story retelling)
	Collocations	R	What words or types of words occur with this one? Do collocations and idioms enjoy a special status in L2 learners' lexicons? How are L2 idioms and L1 idioms in the lexicon related?	Collocation matching tasks	Collocation priming; crosslinguistic priming; eye tracking
		P	What words or types of words must we use with this one? Do collocations and idioms enjoy a special status in L2 learners' lexicons?	Fill-in-the-blank exercises	Naming tasks
	Constraints on use	R	Where, when, and how often would we expect to meet this word? Is the learner sensitive to how often words occur and co-occur in the language		Lexical decision tasks; eye tracking
		P	Where, when, and how often can we use this word? Does the learner use words appropriately in context?	Guided, untimed writing or speaking tasks (e.g., picture description)	Free, real-time writing or speaking tasks (e.g., story retelling)

meaning. For instance, in Elgort's (2011) form priming experiment, participants had to make a decision on a familiar English word, which was primed by the newly learned target word with a similar form (e.g., prolley → TROLLEY). For form priming to occur, learners needed to have added *prolley* to their lexicon (i.e., created a new lexical entry for *prolley*), but beyond that no semantic knowledge of *prolley* was required.

Form knowledge is also central to eye-tracking research on incidental vocabulary acquisition from reading long texts. These studies have consistently shown that L1 and L2 readers gradually speed up their reading as they encounter a new word repeatedly in the text (Elgort et al., 2018; Godfroid et al., 2018, Mohamed, 2018; Pellicer-Sánchez, 2015). This indicates a growing familiarity with the word form and, presumably, less effort to integrate the new word into the surrounding sentence context. What is interesting is that these substantial gains in reading fluency do not necessarily coincide with similar gains in offline word knowledge or, for that matter, other measures of online word knowledge. For instance, Elgort et al. (2018) found that L2 English readers slowed down again (indicative of non-fluent reading) when they encountered target words in new (unsupportive) sentence contexts. This suggested that their participants could not apply their knowledge of word meaning to new contexts yet, even though they had become more fluent reading the words in familiar (supportive) contexts. That vocabulary learning proceeds incrementally was also central to Godfroid et al.'s (2018) findings. The authors found that gains in reading speed followed an S-shaped learning curve, meaning every encounter with the unknown words helped readers build up vocabulary knowledge, but some repetitions led to higher gains than others.

Assessing Meaning

Similar to measures of word form, online measures of word meaning include the unprimed and primed lexical decision task, but in this case semantic rather than form priming is used (Elgort, 2011; Elgort & Warren, 2014). New in this area is the semantic categorization task, a variant of the lexical decision task that has been developed specifically so that participants retrieve the meaning of a word (Lim & Godfroid, 2015; Phillips et al., 2004; Segalowitz & de Almeida, 2002; Segalowitz & Frenkiel-Fishman, 2005). Compared with offline measures such as translation and meaning recognition, online measures provide a more indirect measure of word meaning that is able to capture partial word knowledge. In a semantic categorization task, for instance, the participant may be able to respond "yes" that a *badger* is a living being (correct yes response) without knowing what kind of animal it is. The same answer (i.e., *badger = an animal*) on a meaning recall test might receive a partial score or no credit depending on the teacher's or researcher's scoring rubric. The semantic categorization task therefore can measure breadth of knowledge and, if a reaction time component is included, it can also measure lexical fluency or automaticity (e.g., Lim & Godfroid, 2015; Segalowitz & de Almeida, 2002).

Other online measures of word meaning come from eye tracking, primarily from the visual world paradigm, where spoken words in context are presented alongside their possible referents on the screen (see Dussias, Valdés Kroff, & Gerfen, 2014, and Godfroid, 2019a, for L2-specific reviews). For instance, in a recent visual world study Kohlstedt and Mani (2018) found that L1 and L2 speakers can make use of the discourse context to infer the meaning of new (pseudo) words in a short story. They found participants looked at target pictures on the screen that represented the new nouns (e.g., a picture of a cane, representing a German pseudoword for "cane") before the nouns had occurred in the spoken story, based on semantic associations with other nouns in the story (e.g., *Opa*, "grandpa"). Bolger and Zapata (2011), using a variant of visual-world eye tracking, uncovered subtle semantic interference effects in the retrieval of word meaning, which occurred after participants had studied new vocabulary in semantically related sets.

In reading research, eye movements reflect the fluency with which participants can access a new word in context, but the data do not speak to the question of acquisition of meaning directly. This is why researchers have triangulated their eye-movement data with offline meaning recognition and meaning recall tests (Godfroid et al., 2018; Mohamed, 2018; Montero Perez et al., 2015; Pellicer-Sánchez, 2015) or other online measures of word meaning (Elgort et al., 2018). For both listening and reading, therefore, eye-movement recordings can offer insight into learners' knowledge of word form and meaning. For word meaning, recording eye movements can reveal developmental trajectories or learning curves, bring semantic relationships to light, and probe how robust the knowledge is that learners have acquired.

Assessing Use

Assessing word use oftentimes involves gathering writing and/or speaking samples with a view to identifying errors and classifying and describing them. Of the different types of errors, lexical errors are especially difficult to code reliably (e.g., Polio, 1997; Polio & Shea, 2014), in part because of uncertainty as to "whether or not a native speaker would produce the word or structure in the context" (Polio & Shea, 2014, p. 20). With technology, researchers have turned to corpora to help compare and contrast how learners and native speakers use a particular word structure. For example, Altenberg and Granger (2001) compared two learner corpus databases (one of French learners of English and one of Swedish learners of English) against a native English speaker corpus to investigate the use of MAKE in writing. The authors found that learners have difficulty in mastering native-like use of this highly frequent verb. Importantly, in this type of research the distinction between vocabulary and grammar is often blurred, as particular lexical items tend to call for particular syntactic constructions.

Another area that blurs the distinction between grammar and vocabulary is collocations and idioms. Also using corpus data, Yi and his colleagues (2017) identified how native Chinese speakers tend to combine monosyllabic adverbs. For example, some combinations as a whole are more common (e.g., 仍不, literally "still did not"), while some are grammatical but not so common (e.g., 仍没, literally "still had not"). With this information, the researchers were able to test learners of Chinese to see if they had acquired this knowledge of word co-occurrence (i.e., these statistical properties of Chinese adverbials) using eye tracking. Eye-movement data from reading showed that the L2 speakers were as sensitive as the L1 speakers to the statistical properties of Chinese adverbials (for similar findings for English, see Sonbul, 2015). This was an important finding because it suggests that L2 learners may draw on the same general learning mechanisms (statistical learning) as L1 speakers do. Yi et al.'s and Sonbul's eye-tracking research complements the collocation and idiom priming literature (e.g., Carrol & Conklin, 2017; Sonbul & Schmitt, 2013; Wolter & Gyllstad, 2011). Researchers, then, have a number of options to choose from when the goal is to gain a real-time perspective on language users' knowledge of word patterns.

For constraints on word use, offline grammaticality judgment tasks and proofreading exercises to spot ungrammatical forms can reveal learners' receptive knowledge, while guided production (e.g., picture description) can tap into the productive aspects of word usage. A nice feature is that these tasks can be extended with an online component to bring the temporal factor into the assessment. For instance, in my own collaborative work, I have replicated the grammaticality judgment tasks from R. Ellis' influential study (Ellis, 2005) but with the addition of eye tracking (Godfroid et al., 2015). Eye tracking is valuable here because it affords insight into how L1 and L2 speakers process grammaticality judgments under different testing conditions (e.g., timed and untimed grammaticality judgments). Because the sentence grammaticality depended crucially on the individual lexical items used in some of the structures (i.e., verb complements, indefinite article, dative alternation, and ergative verbs), this was partially a test of word usage, in addition to grammar. Godfroid and colleagues found that when L2 participants were asked to make grammaticality judgments under time pressure, they were more likely to read the sentence straight through, without making any regressions. They argued that the drop in regressions signaled a reduction in controlled processing that marks the retrieval (successful or not) of explicit-declarative knowledge (Ellis, 2005). Adding time pressure to a grammaticality judgment test may thus make it more difficult for L2 speakers to access their explicit-declarative knowledge base. More generally, eye-tracking research with lexical/grammatical violations can tell us about L1 and L2 speakers' knowledge of word use when they have little time for conscious reflection, mimicking how a lot of real-time language exchanges take place.

Assessing Automaticity

The previous sections have highlighted how different reaction time methodologies and eye tracking can enrich teachers' and researchers' understanding of what it means to know a word. The icing on the cake is that all of these measures can also yield a CV_{RT} value for each study participant, as long as there are multiple observations for each person. Once researchers have obtained reaction time data, they basically get the CV_{RT} measure for free.

CV_{RT} provides a measure of automaticity of lexical knowledge, which cuts across the three primary dimensions of word knowledge (i.e., form, meaning, use). Researchers can assess how automatically a learner can retrieve formal-lexical information, how easily they can map the form to meaning, and how consistently they react to word pattern violations. This is why automaticity spans all rows in Table 28.2. It is a crucial component of lexical competence that underpins all aspects of vocabulary knowledge. Automatic lexical knowledge is also essential for skilled language use more generally, because fast, automatic retrieval of words is at the basis of listening and reading comprehension (Grabe & Stoller, 2013; Vandergrift & Goh, 2012) and speaking and writing fluency (Segalowitz, 2010; Galbraith, 2009). Thus, CV_{RT} has a place both in and outside of the language laboratory, as it can document growth in classroom learning and study abroad contexts (Akamatsu, 2008; Fukkink et al., 2005; Segalowitz & Freed, 2004; Segalowitz et al., 1998; Serafini, 2013).

Concluding Remarks

Nation's seminal framework (Nation, 2013), which dates back to his 1990 book, raised awareness of the need for researchers and teachers to espouse a broader view of vocabulary learning than creating new form-meaning links. The impact of his ideas is shown in the fact that there are now numerous tasks available that tap into the form and usage dimensions of lexical knowledge. Indeed, there is no doubt that the field of L2 vocabulary studies has seen tremendous growth over the last 30 years. In this chapter, I have argued that such development could be propelled even further if researchers focused not only on lexical knowledge (in all its dimensions) but also on the command speakers have over that knowledge – that is, measure both the tip of the iceberg and the submerged part. This question is commonly framed in terms of tacit-implicit, automatized explicit, or procedural knowledge, which is to be contrasted with explicit-declarative knowledge, the object of most offline vocabulary tests. Three sensitive measures – reaction times in primed and unprimed lexical decision tasks, eye tracking, and CV_{RT} – all lend themselves to studying these hidden dimensions of vocabulary knowledge. Many studies reviewed in this chapter show that researchers have successfully triangulated these online measures with offline tests to gain a more complete understanding of vocabulary learning and knowledge. Indeed, online methods and offline methods can go together in research. As reaction time and eye-tracking methodologies become increasingly accessible, the use and impact of these measures is likely to continue to rise in the coming years (Sanz, Morales-Front, Zalbidea, & Zárate-Sández, 2015). Vocabulary researchers are invited to adopt an online mindset and secure a front-row seat for the game by observing vocabulary learning and use as they are happening.

Further Reading

Conklin, K., Pellicer-Sánchez, A., & Carrol, G. (2018). *Eye-tracking: A guide for applied linguistics research.* Cambridge, UK: Cambridge University Press.

This book provides an overview of eye-tracking research in applied linguistics, including reading, listening, corpus linguistics, and translation research. Exemplary studies in each subdomain are used to introduce basic methodological facts and practical considerations in eye tracking. Research on vocabulary learning and use is well represented in the book.

Godfroid, A. (2019). *Eye tracking in second language acquisition and bilingualism: A research synthesis and methodological guide.* New York: Routledge.

This book provides foundational knowledge about eye tracking for language researchers. It provides a synthetic review of existing eye-tracking research in L2 and bilingual reading, listening, speaking, and multimodal language processing. It also provides a systematic treatment of topics in the design, execution, and analysis of eye-tracking research. Research on vocabulary learning and use is well represented in the book.

Jiang, N. (2013). *Conducting reaction time research in second language studies.* New York, NY: Routledge.

This accessible guide to reaction time research details the steps for collecting accurate reaction time data and includes a tutorial for DMDX, a piece of experimental software. The chapters on lexical and phonological tasks as well as that on semantic tasks are most relevant to measuring vocabulary knowledge.

Segalowitz, N. (2010). *Cognitive bases of second language fluency.* New York, NY: Routledge.

This book represents the culmination of Segalowitz's empirical work on automatization and CV_{RT} up until 2010. The book also has a comprehensive review of empirical work on speech production, automaticity, and lexical access, all of which are germane to the discussion of online measures of vocabulary.

Related Topics

Different aspects of vocabulary knowledge, learning single-word and multiword items, processing single-word and multiword items, measuring knowledge of single-word items, measuring knowledge of multiword items, measuring vocabulary learning progress, incidental vocabulary learning, deliberate vocabulary learning, developing fluency with words

Note

1 This chapter benefited a great deal from the skilled assistance and thoughtful input of Bronson Hui, a PhD candidate in second language studies at Michigan State University.

References

Akamatsu, N. (2008). The effects of training on automatization of word recognition in English as a foreign language. *Applied Psycholinguistics, 29*(2), 175–193.

Altenberg, B., & Granger, S. (2001). The grammatical and lexical patterning of MAKE in native and non-native student writing. *Applied Linguistics, 22*(2), 173–195.

Balling, L. W. (2013). Reading authentic texts: What counts as cognate? *Bilingualism: Language and Cognition, 16*(3), 637–653.

Boers, F., & Lindstromberg, S. (2012). Experimental and intervention studies on formulaic sequences in a second language. *Annual Review of Applied Linguistics, 32*, 83–110.

Bolger, P., & Zapata, G. (2011). Semantic categories and context in L2 vocabulary learning. *Language Learning, 61*(2), 614–646.

Carrol, G., & Conklin, K. (2014). Getting your wires crossed: Evidence for fast processing of L1 idioms in an L2. *Bilingualism: Language and Cognition, 17*(4), 784–797.

Carrol, G., & Conklin, K. (2017). Cross language lexical priming extends to formulaic units: Evidence from eye-tracking suggests that this idea "has legs". *Bilingualism: Language and Cognition, 20*(2), 299–317.

Carrol, G., Conklin, K., & Gyllstad, H. (2016). Found in translation. *Studies in Second Language Acquisition, 38*(3), 403–443.

Cedrus Corporation [SuperLab 5]. (2017). www.cedrus.com/superlab/.

Clahsen, H., & Veríssimo, J. (2016). Investigating grammatical processing in bilinguals: The case of morphological priming. *Linguistic Approaches to Bilingualism, 6*(5), 685–698.

Conklin, K., Pellicer-Sánchez, A., & Carrol, G. (2018). *Eye-tracking: A guide for applied linguistics research.* Cambridge, UK: Cambridge University Press.

DeKeyser, R. (2015). Skill acquisition theory. In B. Van Patten & J. Williams (Eds.), *Theories in second language acquisition: An introduction* (pp. 94–112). New York, NY: Routledge.

Dussias, P. E., Valdés Kroff, J., & Gerfen, C. (2014). Visual world eye-tracking. In J. Jegerski & B. Van Patten (Eds.), *Research methods in second language psycholinguistics* (pp. 93–124). New York, NY: Routledge.

Elgort, I. (2011). Deliberate learning and vocabulary acquisition in a second language. *Language Learning, 61*(2), 367–413.

Elgort, I., Brysbaert, M., Stevens, M., & Van Assche, E. (2018). Contextual word learning during reading in a second language: An eye-movement study. *Studies in Second Language Acquisition, 40*(2), 341–366.

Elgort, I., & Warren, P. (2014). L2 vocabulary learning from reading: Explicit and tacit lexical knowledge and the role of learner and item variables. *Language Learning, 64*(2), 365–414.

Ellis, N. C., Simpson-Vlach, R., & Maynard, C. (2008). Formulaic language in native and second language speakers: Psycholinguistics, corpus linguistics, and TESOL. *TESOL Quarterly, 42*(3), 375–396.

Ellis, R. (2005). Measuring implicit and explicit knowledge of a second language: A psychometric study. *Studies in Second Language Acquisition, 27*(2), 141–172.

Forster, K. I., & Forster, J. C. (2003). DMDX: A Windows display program with millisecond accuracy. *Behavior Research Methods, 35*(1), 116–124.

Frenck-Mestre, C., & Prince, P. (1997). Second language autonomy. *Journal of Memory and Language, 37*(4), 481–501.

Fukkink, R. G., Hulstijn, J., & Simis, A. (2005). Does training in second-language word recognition skills affect reading comprehension? An experimental study. *The Modern Language Journal, 89*(1), 54–75.

Galbraith, D. (2009). Cognitive models of writing. *German as a Foreign Language, 2–3*, 7–22.

Gass, S. (1999). Discussion: Incidental vocabulary learning. *Studies in Second Language Acquisition, 21*(2), 319–333.

Godfroid, A. (2019a). *Eye tracking in second language acquisition and bilingualism: A research synthesis and methodological guide.* New York: Routledge.

Godfroid, A. (2019b). Investigating instructed second language acquisition using L2 learners' eye-tracking data. In R. P. Leow (Ed.), *The Routledge handbook of second language research in classroom learning* (pp. 44–57). New York: Routledge.

Godfroid, A., Ahn, J., Choi, I., Ballard, L., Cui, Y., Johnston, S., . . . Yoon, H. J. (2018). Incidental vocabulary learning in a natural reading context: An eye-tracking study. *Bilingualism: Language and Cognition, 21*(3), 563–584.

Godfroid, A., Boers, F., & Housen, A. (2013). An eye for words: Gauging the role of attention in incidental L2 vocabulary acquisition by means of eye-tracking. *Studies in Second Language Acquisition, 35*(3), 483–517.

Godfroid, A., Loewen, S., Jung, S., Park, J. H., Gass, S., & Ellis, R. (2015). Timed and untimed grammaticality judgments measure distinct types of knowledge: Evidence from eye-movement patterns. *Studies in Second Language Acquisition, 37*(2), 269–297.

Godfroid, A., & Uggen, M. S. (2013). Attention to irregular verbs by beginning learners of German: An eye-movement study. *Studies in Second Language Acquisition, 35*(2), 291–322.

Godfroid, A., & Winke, P. (2015). Investigating implicit and explicit processing using L2 learners' eye-movement data. In P. Rebuschat (Ed.), *Implicit and explicit learning of languages* (pp. 73–90). Philadelphia, PA: John Benjamins Publishing Company.

Grabe, W. P., & Stoller, F. L. (2013). *Teaching and researching: Reading*. New York, NY: Routledge.

Grainger, J., Dufau, S., Montant, M., Ziegler, J. C., & Fagot, J. (2012). Orthographic processing in baboons (*papio papio*). *Science, 336*(6078), 245–248.

Holmqvist, K., Nyström, M., Andersson, R., Dewhurst, R., Jarodzka, H., & Van de Weijer, J. (2011). *Eye tracking: A comprehensive guide to methods and measures*. Oxford, UK: Oxford University Press.

Hulstijn, J. H., Van Gelderen, A., & Schoonen, R. (2009). Automatization in second language acquisition: What does the coefficient of variation tell us? *Applied Psycholinguistics, 30*(4), 555–582.

Inhoff, A. W., & Rayner, K. (1986). Parafoveal word processing during eye fixations in reading: Effects of word frequency. *Perception and Psychophysics, 40*(6), 431–439.

Inquisit 5.0.9 [Computer software]. (2017). Retrieved from www.millisecond.com.

Just, M. A., & Carpenter, P. A. (1980). A theory of reading: From eye fixations to comprehension. *Psychological Review, 87*(4), 329.

Kohlstedt, T., & Mani, N. (2018). The influence of increasing discourse context on L1 and L2 spoken language processing. *Bilingualism: Language and Cognition, 21*(1), 121–136.

Kroll, J. F., & Bialystok, E. (2013). Understanding the consequences of bilingualism for language processing and cognition. *Journal of Cognitive Psychology, 25*(5), 497–514.

Leow, R. P. (2015). *Explicit learning in the L2 classroom: A student-centered approach*. New York, NY: Routledge.

Lim, H., & Godfroid, A. (2015). Automatization in second language sentence processing: A partial, conceptual replication of Hulstijn, Van Gelderen, and Schoonen's 2009 study. *Applied Psycholinguistics, 36*(5), 1247–1282.

Meara, P. (2009). *Connected words: Word associations and second language vocabulary acquisition* (Vol. 24). Philadelphia, PA: John Benjamins Publishing Company.

Mohamed, A. A. (2018). Exposure frequency in L2 reading: An eye-movement perspective of incidental vocabulary learning. *Studies in Second Language Acquisition, 40*(2), 269–293.

Montero Perez, M., Peters, E., & Desmet, P. (2015). Enhancing vocabulary learning through captioned video: An eye-tracking study. *The Modern Language Journal, 99*(2), 308–328.

Nation, I. S. P. (1990). *Teaching and learning vocabulary*. New York, NY: Newbury House.

Nation, I. S. P. (2013). *Learning vocabulary in another language*. Cambridge, UK: Cambridge University Press.

Nation, I. S. P., & Beglar, D. (2007). A vocabulary size test. *The Language Teacher, 31*(7), 9–13.

Paciorek, A., & Williams, J. N. (2015a). Implicit learning of semantic preferences of verbs. *Studies in Second Language Acquisition, 37*(2), 359–382.

Paciorek, A., & Williams, J. N. (2015b). Semantic generalization in implicit language learning. *Journal of Experimental Psychology: Learning, Memory, and Cognition, 41*(4), 989–1002.

Paribakht, T. S., & Wesche, M. (1999). Reading and "incidental" L2 vocabulary acquisition. *Studies in Second Language Acquisition, 21*(2), 195–224.

Peirce, J. W. (2007). PsychoPy – psychophysics software in Python. *Journal of Neuroscience Methods, 162*(1), 8–13.

Pellicer-Sánchez, A. (2015). Developing automaticity and speed of lexical access: The effects of incidental and explicit teaching approaches. *Journal of Spanish Language Teaching, 2*(2), 126–139.

Phillips, N. A., Segalowitz, N., O'Brien, I., & Yamasaki, N. (2004). Semantic priming in a first and second language: Evidence from reaction time variability and event-related brain potentials. *Journal of Neurolinguistics, 17*(2), 237–262.

Polio, C. (1997). Measures of linguistic accuracy in second language writing research. *Language Learning, 47*(1), 101–143.

Polio, C., & Shea, M. C. (2014). An investigation into current measures of linguistic accuracy in second language writing research. *Journal of Second Language Writing, 26*, 10–27.

Psychology Software Tools, Inc. [E-Prime 2.0]. (2012). Retrieved from www.pstnet.com.

Rayner, K. (1998). Eye movements in reading and information processing: 20 years of research. *Psychological Bulletin, 124*(3), 372.

Rayner, K. (2009). Eye movements and attention in reading, scene perception, and visual search. *The Quarterly Journal of Experimental Psychology, 62*(8), 1457–1506.

Reichle, E. D., Pollatsek, A., & Rayner, K. (2006). E–Z Reader: A cognitive-control, serial-attention model of eye-movement behavior during reading. *Cognitive Systems Research, 7*(1), 4–22.

Sanz, C., Morales-Front, A., Zalbidea, J., & Zárate-Sández, G. (2015). Always in motion the future is: Doctoral students' use of technology for SLA research. In R. Leow, L. Cerezo, & M. Baralt (Eds.), *A psycholinguistic approach to technology and language learning* (pp. 49–68). Berlin: De Gruyter Mouton.

Segalowitz, N. (2010). *Cognitive bases of second language fluency.* New York, NY: Routledge.

Segalowitz, N., & De Almeida, R. G. (2002). Conceptual representation of verbs in bilinguals: Semantic field effects and a second-language performance paradox. *Brain and Language, 81*(1), 517–531.

Segalowitz, N., & Freed, B. (2004). Context, contact, and cognition in oral fluency acquisition: Learning Spanish in at home and study abroad contexts. *Studies in Second Language Acquisition, 26*(2), 173–199.

Segalowitz, N., & Frenkiel-Fishman, S. (2005). Attention control and ability level in a complex cognitive skill: Attention shifting and second-language proficiency. *Memory and Cognition, 33*(4), 644–653.

Segalowitz, N., & Hulstijn, J. (2005). Automaticity in bilingualism and second language learning. In J. F. Kroll & A. De Groot (Eds.), *Handbook of bilingualism: Psycholinguistic approaches* (pp. 371–388). New York, NY: Oxford University Press.

Segalowitz, N., & Segalowitz, S. (1993). Skilled performance, practice, and the differentiation of speed-up from automatization effects: Evidence from second language word recognition. *Applied Psycholinguistics, 14*(3), 369–385.

Segalowitz, N., Watson, V., & Segalowitz, S. (1995). Vocabulary skill: Single-case assessment of automaticity of word recognition in a timed lexical decision task. *Second Language Research, 11*(2), 121–136.

Segalowitz, S., Segalowitz, N., & Wood, A. (1998). Assessing the development of automaticity in second language word recognition. *Applied Psycholinguistics, 19*(1), 53–67.

Serafini, E. J. (2013). *Cognitive and psychosocial factors in the long-term development of implicit and explicit second language knowledge in adult learners of Spanish at increasing proficiency.* Unpublished doctoral dissertation, Georgetown University, Washington, DC.

Siyanova-Chanturia, A., Conklin, K., & Schmitt, N. (2011). Adding more fuel to the fire: An eye-tracking study of idiom processing by native and non-native speakers. *Second Language Research, 27*(2), 251–272.

Solovyeva, K., & DeKeyser, R. (2018). Response time variability signatures of novel word learning. *Studies in Second Language Acquisition, 40*(1), 225–239.

Sonbul, S. (2015). Fatal mistake, awful mistake, or extreme mistake? Frequency effects on off-line/on-line collocational processing. *Bilingualism: Language and Cognition, 18*(3), 419–437.

Sonbul, S., & Schmitt, N. (2013). Explicit and implicit lexical knowledge: Acquisition of collocations under different input conditions. *Language Learning, 63*(1), 121–159.

Vandergrift, L., & Goh, C. C. (2012). *Teaching and learning second language listening: Metacognition in action.* New York, NY: Routledge.

Wade, N., & Tatler, B. W. (2005). *The moving tablet of the eye: The origins of modern eye movement research.* Oxford, UK: Oxford University Press.

Wolter, B., & Gyllstad, H. (2011). Collocational links in the L2 mental lexicon and the influence of L1 intralexical knowledge. *Applied Linguistics, 32*(4), 430–449.

Wray, A. (2002). *Formulaic language and the lexicon.* Cambridge, UK: Cambridge University Press.

Wray, A. (2008). *Formulaic language: Pushing the boundaries.* Oxford, UK: Oxford University Press.

Wright, R. D., & Ward, L. M. (2008). *Orienting of attention.* New York, NY: Oxford University Press.

Yi, W., Lu, S., & Ma, G. (2017). Frequency, contingency and online processing of multiword sequences: An eye-tracking study. *Second Language Research, 33*(4), 519–549.

29

Measuring Lexical Richness

Kristopher Kyle

Introduction

Indices of lexical richness are used to analyze characteristics of lexical use in written and spoken responses. The term lexical richness was introduced by Yule (1944) to refer to the number of words in a particular author's vocabulary (as evidenced by the words used in their published works). Although Yule had a particular method of calculation in mind, subsequent researchers have used the term to refer to a number of different constructs, such as the propositional density of the words in a text (lexical density; Halliday, 1985; Linnarud, 1986; Lu, 2012; Ure, 1971), the diversity or variation of words in a text (lexical diversity; Malvern, Richards, Chipere, & Durán, 2004; McCarthy & Jarvis, 2007), and/or the proportion of difficult words in a text (lexical sophistication; Kyle & Crossley, 2015; Laufer & Nation, 1995; Meara, 2005). What connects the aforementioned constructs is the goal for which they are generally used, which is (broadly speaking) to measure productive lexical proficiency.

This chapter represents a critical introduction to a number of methods for measuring lexical richness (density, diversity, and sophistication). Key theoretical and practical issues are introduced, and a sample text produced by an L2 writer is used to demonstrate how each index of lexical richness is calculated. Additionally, a number of freely available text analysis tools for the measurement of lexical richness are introduced.

Critical Issues and Topics

Preliminary Vocabulary

Before discussing the various aspects of lexical richness, it is important to define some key terms related to how lexical items can be defined, as the chosen definitions can seriously impact the results of a study.

Types and Tokens

The number of *tokens* in a text refers to the number of running words in a text. For example, the sample text in Table 29.1 comprises 73 tokens. The number of *types* in a text refers to

Table 29.1 Sample text in three formats: original, tokenized, and typed

Original text	How do you feel if you enter a restaurant full of smoke? I want to escape from it as soon as possible. So in my opinion, smoking should be completely banned at all the restaurants in the country. As we all know, restaurant is a public place where people go there for enjoying meals. If someone there smokes, the environment is polluted. Can you enjoy a meal at a place full of smoke?
Tokens = 73	how do you feel if you enter a restaurant full of smoke i want to escape from it as soon as possible so in my opinion smoking should be completely banned at all the restaurants in the country as we all know, restaurant is a public place where people go there for enjoying meals if someone there smokes, the environment is polluted can you enjoy a meal at a place full of smoke
Word types = 54 type (frequency)	a (4), as (3), the (3), you (3), all (2), at (2), full (2), if (2), in (2), is (2), of (2), place (2), restaurant (2), smoke (2), there (2), banned (1), be (1), can (1), completely (1), country (1), do (1), enjoy (1), enjoying (1), enter (1), environment (1), escape (1), feel (1), for (1), from (1), go (1), how (1), i (1), it (1), know (1), meal (1), meals (1), my (1), opinion (1), people (1), polluted (1), possible (1), public (1), restaurants (1), should (1), smokes (1), smoking (1), so (1), someone (1), soon (1), to (1), want (1), we (1), where (1)

Note: Text from the International Corpus Network of Asian Learners of English (Ishikawa, 2011).

the number of *unique* words in a text. The sample text in Table 29.1 includes 54 word types. It should be noted that the operational definition of a lexical item will affect type counts in most cases (see Table 29.1).

Words, Lemmas, Flemmas, and Families

When calculating indices of lexical richness, it is important to consider the operational definition of a lexical item. Such a definition should reflect the presumed lexical knowledge of the writers/speakers. In most cases, lexical items are preliminarily identified as strings of letters separated by white space, end punctuation, hyphens, or commas. From there, lexical items can be grouped (or not) in a number of ways. The most common operational definitions of lexical items are included later in the chapter. The consequences of these choices will be illustrated with regard to type counts and reference corpus frequency counts in reference to the sample sentences in Table 29.2.

When lexical items are operationally defined as **words**, each distinct word form is treated as a separate unit. For example, each of the inflected and derived forms of the word *smoke* (e.g., *smoke, smoker, smoking*, etc.) would be treated as a distinct word. Defining lexical items as words creates an implicit presumption that writers/speakers have little to no knowledge of derivational or inflectional morphology. While the former may be true of a wide range of L2 users, the latter is likely only true for very low proficiency L2 users (i.e., true beginners).

A **lemma** is a group of words that share both semantics and part of speech. Thus, all inflected forms of a word are treated as members of the same lemma form (e.g., all inflections of the verb *to smoke*, including *smoke, smokes, smoked*, and *smoking* are members of the same lemma). In Table 29.2 we see that the type counts for lemmas differ slightly from the word type counts. In the lemmatized version of the text, both *be* and *is* are counted as the same form (the lemma "be"). Similarly, the singular *restaurant* and plural *restaurants* are

Table 29.2 Words, lemmas, and families in the example text

Word types = 53 type (frequency)	a (4), as (3), the (3), you (3), all (2), at (2), full (2), if (2), in (2), is (2), of (2), place (2), restaurant (2), smoke (2), there (2), banned (1), be (1), can (1), completely (1), country (1), do (1), enjoy (1), enjoying (1), enter (1), environment (1), escape (1), feel (1), for (1), from (1), go (1), how (1), i (1), it (1), know (1), meal (1), meals (1), my (1), opinion (1), people (1), polluted (1), possible (1), public (1), restaurants (1), should (1), smokes (1), smoking (1), so (1), someone (1), soon (1), to (1), want (1), we (1), where (1)
Lemma types = 48 type (frequency)	a (4), as (3), be (3), restaurant (3), the (3), you (3), all (2), at (2), enjoy (2), full (2), i (2), if (2), in (2), meal (2), of (2), place (2), smoke_noun (2), there (2), ban (1), can (1), completely (1), country (1), do (1), enter (1), environment (1), escape (1), feel (1), for (1), from (1), go (1), how (1), it (1), know (1), opinion (1), people (1), polluted (1), possible (1), public (1), should (1), smoke_verb (1), smoking_noun (1), so (1), someone (1), soon (1), to (1), want (1), we (1), where (1)
Family types = 46 type (frequency)	a (4), smoke (4), as (3), be (3), restaurant (3), the (3), you (3), all (2), at (2), enjoy (2), full (2), i (2), if (2), in (2), meal (2), of (2), place (2), there (2), ban (1), can (1), complete (1), country (1), do (1), enter (1), environment (1), escape (1), feel (1), for (1), from (1), go (1), how (1), it (1), know (1), opinion (1), people (1), pollute (1), possible (1), public (1), should (1), so (1), some (1), soon (1), to (1), want (1), we (1), where (1)

Note: Text from ICNALE corpus, W_CHN_SMK_022_A2_0.txt; families defined as per the revised BNC_COCA lists available on www.laurenceanthony.net.

counted as the same form (the lemma *restaurant*). Although these frequency differences are relatively few in our small sample, they can have a much larger effect over an entire corpus (particularly for verb frequencies). The use of lemmas indicates an implicit presumption that learners have a working knowledge of the verb and noun inflection system. As noted earlier, this is likely true for all but the lowest proficiency L2 users.

A slight variation of the lemma is the **flemma** (Nation, 2016; Pinchbeck, 2014, 2017), which includes all inflected forms of a words and their homographs (i.e., while lemmas are sensitive to part of speech, flemmas are not). In a flemmatized version of the sample text, the noun *smoke* and the verb *smoke* would both be represented as the same flemma *smoke*. Based on a strict definition, the noun *smoking* would also be counted as part of the flemma *smoke*. A practical advantage to the use of flemmas is that flemmatization of learner texts can be done without the use of a part of speech tagger, and in fact many tools that purport to lemmatize texts actually flemmatize them.

A word **family** (Nation, 2001) includes all inflected forms of a word and most of its derived forms. Most studies include derived forms up to and including Level 6 on Bauer and Nation's (1993) word family hierarchy. In Table 29.2, we see that the three lemmas related to the base form of *smoke* (the noun *smoke*, the noun *smoking*, and the verb *smoke*) are all counted as a single family, raising the frequency count to four instances. The use of families indicates an implicit presumption that learners have working knowledge of the inflection and derivation systems of a language. Although this may be a reasonable presumption for advanced L2 users and particularly in receptive modes (Nation & Webb, 2011; Webb, 2010) it may not be appropriate for lower proficiency L2 users and for productive modes (McLean, 2018; Schmitt, 2010).

Function and Content Words

Distinction between content words and function words is made in the calculation of a number of indices related to lexical richness. *Function* words refer to closed-class, grammatical words such as articles and prepositions (among many others). *Content* words refer to open-class, lexical words, including nouns, adjectives, most verbs, and some adverbs (Engber, 1995; Lu, 2012; Quirk, Greenbaum, Leech, & Svartik, 1985). Lexical verbs tend to be counted as content words, while copular verbs (i.e., *to be*) and auxiliary verbs (e.g., modals and auxiliary uses of *to be*, *to have*, and *to do*) tend to be counted as function words. Content adverbs tend to include those with adjectival bases (e.g., adverbs that end in *–ly* such as *basically* and *slowly*) while all other adverbs tend to be counted as function words (c.f., O'Loughlin, 1995). Table 29.3 includes a list of content and function lemma types that occur in the sample sentences.

Measuring Lexical Density

Of the three aspects of lexical richness that are outlined in the literature, lexical density is likely the one that is employed least often in productive L2 vocabulary research. Indices of lexical density compare the number of content words to the number of total words in a text. In doing so, lexical density provides a measure of the density of information in a text (Ure, 1971; Halliday, 1985). As we can see from Table 29.1 and Table 29.3, our sample text has 73 tokens, of which 31 are content words. Lexical density for our text is therefore calculated as:

$$lexical\ density = \frac{number\ of\ content\ words}{number\ of\ total\ words} = \frac{31}{73} = 0.425$$

Research has indicated that lexical density is a useful metric for distinguishing between spoken and written modes (Ure, 1971) and more specifically between performances on tasks that are more or less interactive (O'Loughlin, 1995; Shohamy, 1994). These studies indicated that less interactive tasks (including writing tasks) tend to have higher lexical density than more interactive ones (such as interviews). A number of studies have also attempted to use lexical density to model writing and speaking proficiency (Engber, 1995; Hyltenstam, 1988; Linnarud, 1986; Lu, 2012; Nihalani, 1981). Although two studies (Linnarud, 1986; Engber, 1995) demonstrated a small effect between lexical density and writing proficiency, no study that I am aware of has reported a significant relationship between the two. This

Table 29.3 Content and function lemmas that occur in the sample sentences

Content lemmas 31 tokens 24 types	restaurant (3), enjoy (2), full (2), meal (2), place (2), smoke_noun (2), ban (1), completely (1), country (1), enter (1), environment (1), escape (1), feel (1), go (1), know (1), opinion (1), people (1), polluted (1), possible (1), public (1), smoke_verb (1), smoking_noun (1), someone (1), want (1)
Function lemmas 42 tokens 24 types	a (4), as (3), be (3), the (3), you (3), all (2), at (2), i (2), if (2), in (2), of (2), there (2), can (1), do (1), for (1), from (1), how (1), it (1), should (1), so (1), soon (1), to (1), we (1), where (1)

preliminarily suggests that while lexical density may be appropriate for some purposes (e.g., distinguishing modes or registers), it may not be appropriate for measuring productive lexical proficiency.

Measuring Lexical Diversity

Lexical diversity indices are used to measure the variety of lexical items in a text, which is presumed to reflect the extent of the lexical knowledge of the writer of that text. Because more proficient speakers and writers have more lexical items at their disposal, they are able to use a wide variety of lexical items to accomplish a task, while less proficient speakers and writers will tend to repeat a smaller number of lexical items (e.g., Read, 2000). The most basic way to calculate lexical diversity is the simple type-token ratio (TTR; i.e., the number of types in a text divided by the number of tokens in a text). While some measures such as TTR are relatively straightforward, there are at least three key issues that must be addressed when measuring lexical diversity. First, a researcher must decide whether to analyze lemmas, words, or some other unit (e.g., word families, multiword units, etc.). Second, it must be decided whether all lexical items will be considered, only content lexical items, or only particular parts of speech (e.g., verbs or nouns). The third issue relates to the choice of a diversity index. TTR is consistently and strongly correlated with text length, wherein longer text samples tend to include less diversity (e.g., Linnarud, 1986; McCarthy & Jarvis, 2007). A number of lexical diversity measures have been proposed that attempt to disambiguate text length and diversity scores using statistical transformations and other, more complex methods. However, subsequent research has indicated that many of these, such as Root TTR (also referred to as Guiraud's index; Guiraud, 1960), are strongly correlated with text length (McCarthy & Jarvis, 2007). Next, the simple iteration of TTR is described for reference, followed by a number of indices that have been shown to be relatively independent of text length.

Simple Type-Token Ratio

The simple type-token ratio (TTR) was first proposed by Johnson (1944), and has been used in a number of studies to measure the diversity of words in a text (e.g., Laufer, 1991). TTR is calculated as the number of unique words (types) in a text divided by the number of running words (tokens) in a text: $TTR = \dfrac{ntypes}{ntokens}$. TTR can be calculated with raw words or lemmas, and can also be confined to all words, content words, or particular parts of speech such as verbs (Harley & King, 1989) or nouns (McClure, 1991). In our sample text (see Table 29.1), there are 48 lemma types and 73 tokens, resulting in $TTR = \dfrac{48}{73} = .658$. Although I have not found any studies that have done so, it is also possible to calculate TTR with word families. Although TTR is a well-known measure that has been used in some studies (e.g., Laufer, 1991), it is often avoided due to its well-documented negative relationship with text length (e.g., Johnson, 1944; McCarthy & Jarvis, 2007; 2010). Some studies have controlled for length by using a fixed number of words (e.g., the first 50 words) from a text (Grant & Ginther, 2000; Jarvis, Grant, Bikowski, & Ferris, 2003). However, alternatives such as Root TTR, MTLD, and D (see below) are much more commonly employed in the literature.

Maas' Index

Maas' index (Maas, 1972) is a transformation of type-token ratios that attempts to fit the TTR value to a logarithmic curve. This is calculated as: $Maas' index = \dfrac{Log(ntokens) - Log(ntypes)}{Log(ntokens)^2}$.

In the sample text, $Maas' index = \dfrac{Log(73) - Log(48)}{Log(73)^2} = \dfrac{1.863 - 1.681}{3.472} = .052$. As the ratio of types to tokens increases, Maas' index values decrease. McCarthy & Jarvis (2007, 2010) indicate that Maas' index is relatively independent from text length for spoken genres ($r = .320$) and particularly for written genres ($r = .120$). I am currently not aware of any study that has used Maas' index to investigate the relationship between lexical diversity and L2 proficiency, and this may be an area for future investigation.

Moving Average Type-Token Ratio

Moving average type-token ratio (MATTR) is a variant of simple TTR that controls for text length (Covington & McFall, 2010) by taking the average TTR value for all overlapping segments of the text of a specified length (e.g., 50 words). For example, in a 300-word text, the TTR value is calculated for words 1 through 50 in the text, then for words 2 through 51, then for words 3 through 52, and so on, until all of the words have been considered. While more difficult to calculate by hand than simple TTR or Guiraud's index, MATTR is still conceptually straightforward (and easy to interpret), is independent of text length (Covington & McFall, 2010), and is easy to automate. To calculate MATTR in the sample text, we first calculate TTR for the first 50-word segment, which begins with the word *how* and ends with the word *go* (TTR = .780). We then calculate TTR for the next 50-word segment, which begins with the word *do* and ends with the word *there* (TTR = .780), and then for all remaining segments. In total, the sample text includes 24 overlapping 50-word segments that have a mean TTR value of MATTR = .769.

A related variant is the mean segment type-token ratio (MSTTR) wherein the text is divided into non-overlapping segments of n words (e.g., 50 words) and TTR is calculated for each chunk and then averaged across chunks (Engber, 1995; Johnson, 1944). For example, a 250-word text would be divided into five chunks (words 1–50, 51–100, 101–150, 151–200, and 201–250). One problem with MSTTR is that a set of texts are rarely divisible by the same segment length, leaving wasted data. For example, in our example text, only the first 50 words would be used, and the final 23 words would be ignored.

Measure of Textual Lexical Diversity

The measure of textual lexical diversity (MTLD) measures lexical diversity by calculating the average number of words in a text it takes to reach a predetermined TTR value at which TTR is assumed to be stable. McCarthy and Jarvis (2010) analyzed a large corpus of written narrative and expository texts and found that TTR values tended to stabilize at a value of .720. McCarthy and Jarvis (2010) calculated MTLD using successive, non-overlapping text segments of at least ten words (which are referred to as factors). Any leftover segments (i.e., the end of a text) were counted as partial factors. Texts with higher MTLD values can be considered more lexically diverse (because it takes more words on average for TTR values to fall below .720). In the sample text, for example, it takes 67 words for the TTR value to fall below .720. MTLD can also be measured using a moving windows approach and partial factors can be avoided by using the beginning of the text to finish calculating the final factor.

Research has indicated that MTLD is relatively independent of text length (McCarthy & Jarvis, 2010), even for texts as short as 100 words in length (Koizumi & In'nami, 2012). Research investigating the relationship between language proficiency and MTLD scores has indicated a positive relationship between the two. Crossley, Salsbury, and McNamara (2009), for example, found that L2 speakers produced oral samples with higher MTLD values during one-year of study in an intensive English program. A number of other studies have also used MTLD to measure writing quality and lexical proficiency (e.g., Crossley, Salsbury, McNamara, & Jarvis, 2011; Guo, Crossley, & McNamara, 2013). However, these studies also used the index D (see next section), which was more strongly associated with quality/proficiency, and the results for MTLD were not reported.

D

The diversity index D (Malvern et al., 2004; Malvern & Richards, 1997; McCarthy & Jarvis, 2007) is an index with an interesting history. Malvern et al. (2004) conceptualized D as a curve fitting index wherein random samples from 35 to 50 words in length are taken from a text. TTR values for each segment are then used to create an empirical curve, which is then fit to a theoretical curve using a coefficient referred to as D (this is referred to as vocD; see Malvern et al., 2004, for more information). McCarthy and Jarvis (2007), however, found that vocD was essentially an approximation of the sum of probabilities that the words occurring in text would be included in a random sample from the text (in their data, the two indices were correlated at $r = .971$). They proposed the index HD-D, which uses the hypergeometric distribution to determine the probability of a particular word in a text occurring at least once in a random sample of a particular length (in this case, the length is 42 words – an approximate mean value between Malvern et al.'s 35 and 50). HD-D represents the sum of the probabilities that each type in a text will occur in a 42-word sample at least once. Texts with lower HD-D values can be considered to be more diverse than those with higher values. HD-D values can also be converted to the same scale as TTR by multiplying the probability of occurrence of each type by 1/sample size (McCarthy and Jarvis refer to this conversion as average TTR or ATTR). In the sample text, for example, the probability that the word *a*, which occurs four times in the sample will occur at least once in a random sample of 42 words (of our 73-word text) is .971 (i.e., there is a 97.1% chance that *a* would occur at least once). See Table 29.4 for a summary of the HD-D calculation for the sample text.

Table 29.4 HD-D calculation summary for sample text

Word frequency	Probability word will occur in 42-word sample	Words in sample text with frequency	Sum of probabilities
4	.971	1	.023
3	.923	5	.110
2	.823	12	.235
1	.575	30	.411
			HD-D = 32.712
			ATTR = .789

McCarthy and Jarvis (2007) found that vocD (and by extrapolation, HD-D) was relatively independent of text length in written (r = .190) and spoken (r = .350) genres. No studies that I am aware of have used HD-D to measure productive L2 proficiency, likely because until recently no freely available text processing software calculated the measure. VocD, which has been implemented in multiple tools, however, has been used in a number of studies to measure L2 productive proficiency. Guo et al. (2013), for example, found a positive relationship (r = .415) between vocD and holistic TOEFL independent writing scores. Crossley, Salsbury, and McNamara (2012) also found a positive relationship (r = .583) between vocD and written lexical proficiency scores.

Other Approaches

Another issue with prototypical indices of lexical diversity is that they treat all words equally. The sentence *This is my car and I like it*, for example, earns the same diversity score (TTR = 1.0) as the sentence *This exquisite vehicle is a veritable engineering marvel*, despite the fact that the former sentence arguably represents a higher level of lexical proficiency. At least two methods can be used to address this issue. One approach, proposed by Daller, Van Hout, and Treffers-Daller (2003) is to calculate lexical diversity indices that use the number of "advanced" types in the text instead of the total type count.

Daller et al. (2003) propose Advanced TTR $\left(\dfrac{number\ of\ \text{``advanced''}\ types}{total\ number\ of\ tokens} \right)$ and Advanced Guiraud $\left( \dfrac{number\ of\ \text{``advanced''}\ types}{\sqrt{total\ number\ of\ tokens}} \right)$. As with TTR and Root TTR, however, these indices will be strongly correlated with text length (Kojima & Yamashita, 2014) and are thus not particularly attractive options. A second method is to use a multivariate approach to the measurement of lexical richness by using both indices of diversity and indices of sophistication (Jarvis, 2013) in multivariate statistical models (e.g., multiple regression). The suitability of such an approach depends on the theoretical and empirical characteristics of the indices used in such a model.

Measuring Lexical Sophistication

Lexical sophistication is often referred to quite specifically as the "number of low frequency words that are appropriate to the topic and style of writing" (Read, 2000, p. 200). This definition highlights the importance that reference-corpus frequency has played in defining the construct. Frequency has been shown to be a reliable predictor of lexical proficiency in a number of studies (Guo et al., 2013; Laufer & Nation, 1995; Kyle & Crossley, 2015). However, a broader definition of lexical sophistication refers to the relative difficulty of learning and/or using a lexical item (e.g., Bulté & Housen, 2012; Kyle, Crossley, & Berger, 2018). This broader definition includes frequency as an important factor in learning (e.g., what makes a word "difficult" or "advanced"), but also recognizes that features beyond frequency (e.g., saliency and contextual distinctiveness among others) affect the learnability of a lexical item (see Ellis, 2002). Research that either implicitly or explicitly follows this latter definition has indicated that the most robust results are obtained using a multivariate approach (e.g., Crossley et al., 2011; Kyle & Crossley, 2015). A number of factors that affect perceptions of sophistication are outlined later in the chapter.

Frequency

Frequency is likely the most widely used method of measuring lexical sophistication. Generally speaking, frequency is measured by comparing the lexical items in a written or spoken text with their frequency in a reference corpus. Lexical items that occur less frequently in the reference corpus tend to be considered more sophisticated (Laufer & Nation, 1995; Guo et al., 2013; Kyle & Crossley, 2015). Spoken and written texts that include higher proportions of less frequent words are considered to be more sophisticated than those that contain higher proportions of more frequent words. As with indices of lexical diversity, decisions must be made with regard to the definition of a lexical item (words, lemmas, families, etc.) and the types of words considered (all words, content words, function words). Additionally, the reference corpus that is used to derive frequency counts is particularly important. A mismatch between reference corpus and target text type (e.g., using a corpus of sitcom subtitles to measure sophistication in academic texts) may result in misleading outcomes. A number of methods have been derived to measure frequency in texts. The most common of these are described next.

Lexical Frequency Profile

The lexical frequency profile (LFP; Laufer, 1994; Laufer & Nation, 1995) method of calculating frequency was one of the earliest approaches to measuring frequency in learner texts. The LFP method divides words in a reference corpus into frequency bands and then calculates the percentage of words in the target text that occur in each band. The LFP method considers word families to be a lexical unit, and all words in a text are analyzed. The original LFP was based on West's (1953) General Service List, though more recent versions include lists based on the British National Corpus (BNC Consortium, 2007) and the Corpus of Contemporary American English (COCA; Davies, 2010). Originally, LFPs distinguished between words that were among the 1,000 most frequent (1K) words, the second most frequent 1,000 words (2K), words that occurred in an early academic word list (Xue & Nation, 1984), and words that occurred in none of the preceding lists (off-list words). After the development of the Academic Word List (AWL; Coxhead, 2000), the academic word portion of LFPs were calculated using the updated list. More recent versions also allow for more fine-grained analyses (e.g., 100-word bands; Cobb, 2017). Table 29.5 shows the percentage of the sample text that are in the 1K, 2K, and AWL lists.

Table 29.5 Lexical frequency profile for the sample text

List	Percent coverage	Cumulative coverage	Family headwords
1K	83.56	83.56	a (4), as (3), be (3), the (3), you (3), all (2), at (2), enjoy (2), full (2), i (2), if (2), in (2), of (2), place (2), there (2), can (1), complete (1), country (1), do (1), enter (1), escape (1), feel (1), for (1), from (1), go (1), how (1), it (1), know (1), opinion (1), people (1), possible (1), public (1), should (1), so (1), some (1), soon (1), to (1), want (1), we (1), where (1)
2K	12.33	95.89	meal (2), restaurant (3), smoke (4)
AWL	1.37	97.26	environment (1)
Off list	2.74	100.00	ban (1), pollute (1)

LFPs have been used in a number of studies to measure lexical sophistication in student writing (Crossley, Cobb, & McNamara, 2013; Laufer, 1994; Laufer & Nation, 1995). These studies have indicated that more proficient L2 users tend to use fewer 1K words than less proficient L2 users. Although the results of an LFP analysis are easy to interpret (and nice visualization of the results is available when using VocabProfile), they have some limitations.

First, LFPs result in a number of related scores instead of a single score, which can be statistically unwieldy. The researcher has to choose which band (or collection of bands; Laufer, 1995) is appropriate for distinguishing between the proficiency levels represented in a particular sample. Second, LFPs are large-grained, meaning that the difference between the 1,000th most frequent word and the 1,001st most frequent word is considered the same as the difference between the most frequent word and the 2,000th most frequent word. This suggests that small gains in vocabulary use are likely to be obscured. Despite these potential limitations, LFPs have been used in a number of studies to model productive lexical proficiency.

P_Lex and S

P-Lex (Meara & Bell, 2001) and S (Kojima & Yamashita, 2014) are broadly based on LFPs, but result in a single score instead of a series of scores making the statistical analyses between frequency and speaking or writing proficiency (broadly construed) much more straightforward. Because both P-Lex and S are based on LFPs, word families are used as the lexical unit, and both content items and function items in a text are included in the analysis. P-Lex is calculated by first dividing a text into 10-item segments. Then, the number of advanced words in each segment (defined as words that are not among the 1K list, are not proper nouns, and are not numbers) is counted. The proportion of segments that include no advanced words, one advanced word, two advanced words and so on is calculated. The resulting data is then fit to a Poisson distribution (i.e., a distribution that is skewed to the left) using lambda. Texts with a low lambda score will have a steeper curve (i.e., will include fewer advanced words) and therefore be considered less sophisticated than those with a higher lambda score. To calculate lambda, our sample text is divided into seven segments. Five of these segments include one advanced word, while two of the segments include two advanced words. Our sample text earns a lambda score of 1.285 (see Figure 29.1 for a visualization of these results).

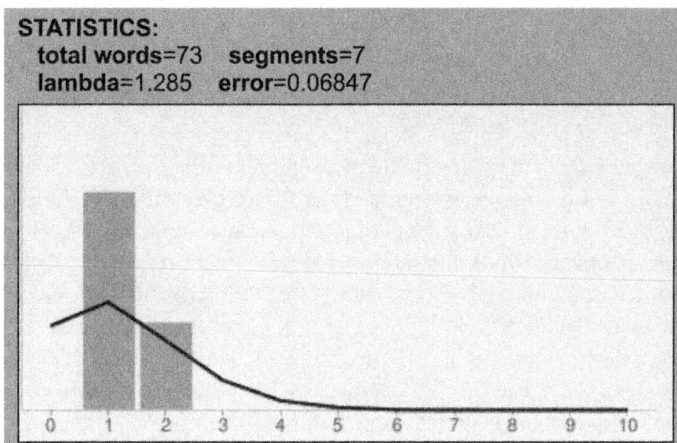

Figure 29.1 Text segments containing *n* advanced words

One potential weakness of P_Lex is the binary distinction that is made between basic words and advanced words, and thus a word that is the 1,001st most frequent word is considered to be as advanced as the 5,000th most frequent word. This may work well for distinguishing between low- and high-proficiency learners, but may not be appropriate for distinguishing between higher proficiency learners.

The S procedure, which was proposed by Kojima and Yamashita (2014), potentially improves upon P_Lex by considering finer-grained frequency bands. The index S is calculated by determining the cumulative text coverage of six 500-word frequency bands (1–500, 501–1,000, 1,001–1,500, 1,501–2,000, 2,001–2,500, and 2,501–3,000) in successive, overlapping 50-word segments in a text. The coverage rate is then fit to a theoretical curve, and S represents the point at which cumulative coverage would hit 100%. An S-value of 2,555, for example, would suggest that all words used in a text would be covered using the 2,555 most frequent word families. Higher S values suggest that, on average, writers and speakers are using less-frequent words. According to the S calculator on Kojima's website, the sample text earns an S score of 2978.42, suggesting that the writer of our sample text has a productive vocabulary of approximately 3,000 words. One limitation of S is that there is currently no available tool that can calculate the measure for more than one text at a time. If such a tool becomes available, S may be an attractive option for the calculation of frequency scores.

Mean Frequency

Another method of calculating frequency scores is to calculate the average frequency score for either all lexical items, content lexical items, or function lexical items in a text. Two advantages to using mean frequency scores as opposed to band scores is that they provide a single score (which eases further statistical analyses) and they are fine-grained (i.e., precise differences in word frequencies are maintained). Often, content frequency is differentiated from function frequency because function items tend to be of particularly high frequency. Some variants of mean frequency scores include logarithmically transformed frequency scores and mean rank frequency scores. Table 29.6 includes mean frequency scores for content flemmas and function flemmas in our sample text.

Mean frequency scores (particularly for content words) have demonstrated a fairly consistent negative relationship with writing and speaking proficiency scores, wherein performances perceived to be of higher quality tend to have lower mean frequency values (e.g., Guo et al., 2013; Kyle & Crossley, 2015; Kyle et al., 2018).

Measuring Lexical Sophistication: Beyond Frequency

While frequency has been a mainstay in the measurement of lexical sophistication for some time (e.g., Laufer, 1994; Laufer & Nation, 1995), related research in psychology (e.g., Brysbaert, Warriner, & Kuperman, 2014; Kuperman, Stadthagen-Gonzalez, & Brysbaert, 2012; Paivio, Yuille, & Madigan, 1968) and language development (Crossley, Kyle, & Salsbury, 2016; Ellis, 2006; MacWhinney, 2008) has suggested that frequency does not fully account for what makes a word more difficult to learn or use. Other lexical features such as saliency (e.g., concreteness), entrenchment (e.g., lexical access), and contextual distinctiveness (e.g., range), among many others, can be used in concert with frequency to more accurately model the sophistication of a particular lexical item. Further, a number of studies (Crossley et al., 2012; Guo et al., 2013; Kim, Crossley, & Kyle, 2018; Kyle & Crossley, 2015) have indicated the importance of measuring lexical sophistication using multivariate methods and as

Table 29.6 Frequencies per million words in the sample text based on the magazine section of COCA

Content flemma	Frequency	Function flemma	Frequency
go (1)	1,820.769	the (3)	53,641.466
people (1)	1,403.408	be (3)	32,439.882
know (1)	1,298.598	a (4)	28,259.271
want (1)	1,004.511	of (2)	25,782.247
place (2)	710.293	to (1)	24,925.015
feel (1)	669.088	in (2)	18,141.039
country (1)	454.233	for (1)	9,082.281
public (1)	349.851	you (3)	8,826.562
full (2)	222.047	i (2)	8,445.369
possible (1)	211.787	it (1)	8,260.920
someone (1)	204.881	as (3)	6,145.724
enjoy (2)	159.310	we (1)	5,480.012
enter (1)	129.806	at (2)	4,945.371
environment (1)	112.475	do (1)	4,751.696
restaurant (3)	103.513	from (1)	4,282.254
meal (2)	97.882	can (1)	3,012.655
completely (1)	94.473	if (2)	2,361.667
escape (1)	62.121	all (2)	2,299.371
opinion (1)	57.249	so (1)	2,043.916
smoke (3)	53.917	there (2)	1,960.505
ban (1)	40.963	how (1)	1,226.569
smoking (1)	27.778	where (1)	936.540
polluted (1)	4.553	should (1)	714.043
		soon (1)	196.677
Mean frequency (types)	404.066		10,756.710
Mean frequency (tokens)	469.474		25,374.237

Note: Counts are based on the downloadable version of COCA that includes texts from 1990 to 2012. Because the frequency counts are based on flemmas, the reported frequency of *smoke* includes counts for nouns, adjectives, and verbs.

a multidimensional construct. A non-exhaustive list of indices of lexical sophistication are included later, including word recognition norms, psycholinguistic word information, and contextual distinctiveness. Further description of indices and descriptions of a wider range of indices can be found in Kyle et al. (2018).

Psycholinguistic Word Information

Psycholinguistic word information indices measure word characteristics beyond frequency. These norms refer to individuals' perceptions of each characteristic for a particular word based on behavioral studies (i.e., surveys). One commonly used index is concreteness, which refers to how abstract the concept denoted by a word is and may be linked to the concept of saliency (Crossley et al., 2016). More concrete words are theorized to be easier to learn (Paivio, 1971; Schwanenflugel, Harnishfeger, & Stowe, 1988), and accordingly texts that on average include less concrete words tend to earn higher proficiency scores (e.g., Kyle et al., 2018). Other related psycholinguistic word information indices include familiarity, imageability, meaningfulness, and age of acquisition (Coltheart, 1981; Kyle et al., 2018; McNamara, Crossley, & McCarthy, 2010). Table 29.7 includes concreteness scores collected by Brysbaert et al. (2014)

Table 29.7 Average concreteness score for words in the sample text

Content flemma	Concreteness	Function flemma	Concreteness
smoke (3)	4.96	the (3)	1.43
restaurant (3)	4.89	be (3)	1.85
people (1)	4.82	a (4)	1.46
meal (2)	4.62	of (2)	1.67
smoking (1)	4.32	to (1)	1.55
country (1)	4.17	in (2)	3
environment (1)	3.74	for (1)	1.63
someone (1)	3.71	you (3)	4.11
full (2)	3.59	i (2)	3.93
place (2)	3.48	it (1)	2.81
escape (1)	3.34	as (3)	1.33
polluted (1)	3.34	we (1)	3.08
go (1)	3.15	at (2)	2.07
enter (1)	3.12	do (1)	2.46
public (1)	2.57	from (1)	1.84
ban (1)	2.37	can (1)	4.55
enjoy (2)	2.29	if (2)	1.19
feel (1)	2.28	all (2)	2.27
completely (1)	2.18	so (1)	1.42
want (1)	1.93	there (2)	2.2
opinion (1)	1.93	how (1)	1.35
know (1)	1.68	where (1)	1.66
possible (1)	1.56	should (1)	1.53
		soon (1)	1.79
Mean concreteness score (types)	3.219		2.174
Mean concreteness score (tokens)	4.683		3.764

Source: Based onBrysbaert et al., 2014

for each flemma in the sample text. Flemmas such as *smoke, restaurant*, and *people* are highly concrete, while flemmas such as *possible* and *know* are much less concrete.

Word Recognition Norms

Word recognition norms, such as lexical decision latencies, measure how quickly an individual can access a word. In a lexical decision task, individuals are presented with a string of characters (e.g., letters) and must decide whether that string is a word or not in the target language (e.g., English). Words that can be identified as part of the target language more quickly are suggested to be more entrenched in an individual's memory, and would therefore be considered less sophisticated than words that can be identified less quickly. Table 29.8 includes average lexical decision times (measured in milliseconds) for the words in the sample text based on data collected by Balota et al. (2007). Words such as *people, escape*, and *know* are accessed quickly (in approximately .5 seconds), while words such as *banned, polluted*, and *environment* are accessed more slowly (up to .8 second for the latter). Although

Table 29.8 Average lexical decision time (in milliseconds) for words in the sample text

Content word	Lexical decision time	Function word	Lexical decision time
people (1)	540.85	to (1)	551.27
escape (1)	546.38	so (1)	555.56
know (1)	549.71	there (2)	556.39
meal (1)	562.89	do (1)	558
restaurants (1)	568.97	we (1)	561.34
enter (1)	576.53	it (1)	566.85
enjoy (1)	582.29	soon (1)	585.28
place (2)	588.84	is (2)	588.85
feel (1)	593.65	my (1)	590.16
want (1)	596.21	all (2)	592.33
full (2)	597.63	for (1)	596.19
go (1)	597.69	can (1)	596.41
smoking (1)	607.32	be (1)	598.42
restaurant (2)	608.61	how (1)	599.37
smoke (2)	609	the (3)	600.19
public (1)	611.16	from (1)	607.85
possible (1)	623.06	should (1)	607.91
opinion (1)	623.69	you (3)	615.21
country (1)	633.18	in (2)	617.97
enjoying (1)	639.58	of (2)	620.42
completely (1)	640.97	i (1)	631.28
someone (1)	641.15	where (1)	635.06
smokes (1)	663.64	at (2)	651.8
banned (1)	733.69	as (3)	653.09
meals (1)	733.69	if (2)	658.3
polluted (1)	792.19	a (4)	798.92
environment (1)	816.82		
Mean lexical decision time (types)	625.16		607.48
Mean lexical decision time (tokens)	714.20		1008.24

Note: Balota et al. report lexical decision times for words (not lemmas or families).

word recognition norms have only recently begun to be used in the measurement of lexical sophistication, preliminary results are promising (see, e.g., Berger, Crossley, & Kyle, 2019).

Contextual Distinctiveness

Indices of contextual distinctiveness measure the degree to which a word is used in restricted context or is used in a wide variety of contexts. Words that are used in a wider variety of contexts are more likely to be encountered frequently, and therefore on average will be learned earlier/more easily than more specialized words. Contextual distinctiveness is measured using a number of methods. The most straightforward is range, which is calculated as the number of texts in a corpus a particular word occurs in, and is often reported as a percentage. For example, *the* occurs in 99.85% of texts in the magazine section of COCA while *smoke* occurs in only 5.67% of the texts. Another more statistically advanced corpus method is called

SemD (Hoffman, Ralph, & Rogers, 2013), which determines the number of contexts a word will occur in based on latent semantic analysis (Landauer, Foltz, & Laham, 1998). Words such as *possible* earn higher SemD values than words such as *polluted*, suggesting *possible* will occur in more contexts than *polluted*. A third method measures the number of words a particular lexical item is associated with based on free word association tasks, wherein participants are given a particular lexical item and are asked to list as many words as they can that are associated with that item (e.g., Kiss, Armstrong, Milroy, & Piper, 1973; Nelson, McEvoy, & Schreiber, 2004). Lexical items that elicit more associated words (and words that are elicited more often by other words) are less contextually distinct than those that elicit (or are elicited by) fewer. For example, Nelson et al. (2004) report that words such as *people* were elicited by 154 other words, while *smoking* was only elicited by six other words. Table 29.9 includes

Table 29.9 Number of associated words for each word in the sample text

	Use USF		
Content word	Contextual diversity	Function word	Contextual diversity
people (1)	154	do (1)	48
go (1)	70	can (1)	36
country (1)	65	in (2)	21
place (2)	62	to (1)	17
smoke (2)	44	all (2)	15
know (1)	38	you (3)	15
want (1)	33	there (2)	14
opinion (1)	29	be (1)	13
full (2)	28	how (1)	12
restaurant (2)	23	soon (1)	8
meal (1)	21	is (2)	8
feel (1)	21	it (1)	7
environment (1)	13	where (1)	7
escape (1)	12	a (4)	7
enjoy (1)	12	for (1)	6
enter (1)	11	from (1)	6
someone (1)	7	of (2)	6
smoking (1)	6	the (3)	5
public (1)	6	i (1)	4
possible (1)	5	so (1)	3
banned (1)	n/a	my (1)	3
completely (1)	n/a	should (1)	2
enjoying (1)	n/a	if (2)	2
meals (1)	n/a	as (3)	1
polluted (1)	n/a	at (2)	n/a
restaurants (1)	n/a	we (1)	n/a
smokes (1)	n/a		
Mean contextual diversity (types)	33.00		11.08
Mean contextual diversity (tokens)	40.85		16.46

Source: Based on Nelson et al., 2004

elicitation counts for each of the words in the sample text based on Nelson et al. Indices of contextual distinctiveness have been found to be predictive of both written (Kyle & Crossley, 2015) and spoken (Berger, Crossley, & Kyle, 2017) lexical proficiency.

Other Approaches

The indices outlined earlier represent only a small subset of the lexical characteristics that can be measured. Lexical features such as polysemy, hypernymy, and word neighbor indices can all provide further insights into the construct of lexical sophistication (Crossley et al., 2009; Guo et al., 2013; Kyle et al., 2018). One particularly important feature of lexical sophistication that was not discussed earlier and is beyond the scope of this chapter is collocation. As noted by many scholars, one important aspect of productive vocabulary knowledge is knowing which words tend to be used together (Nation, 2001; Nation & Webb, 2011; Sinclair, 1991). Accordingly, a number of studies have demonstrated a strong, positive relationship between the use of associated lexical items and proficient productive lexical use (Bestgen & Granger, 2014; Kyle & Crossley, 2015).

Tools for Automatically Measuring Lexical Richness

One benefit to the measurement of lexical richness is that there are many freely available resources available that calculate various indices of lexical richness. When choosing a tool for the measurement of lexical richness, there are at least four important considerations. The first, most obvious consideration is that the tool calculates the index/indices that you are interested in. Second, with an increasing amount of learner data available (i.e., learner corpora), a convenient feature is batch processing (i.e., the ability to process multiple texts at once). Third, transparency in the calculation of various measures is important. Some tools are black boxes that produce numbers from texts, but no one except the tool developers have the ability to determine whether one's particular texts are being processed properly. A fourth, more minor issue is data security. Sensitive/privileged data should likely not be processed over an unsecure web interface. Six groups of tools are described below with regard to (1) the indices measured, (2) the convenience of using the tool, and (3) transparency.

CLAN

CLAN is a text analysis program developed by Brian MacWhinney to analyze child language development data (MacWhinney & Snow, 1990). CLAN is available on both Windows and Apple operating systems and can be freely downloaded from https://childes. talkbank.org. CLAN calculates a wide range of measures for texts that adhere to CHILDES format (an automatic text converter is available through CLAN), which was designed to record interactions between children and their caretakers. With regard to the measurement of lexical richness, CLAN is likely most useful for its ability to calculate the lexical diversity index vocD. CLAN allows for batch processing and also provides some diagnostic output. CLAN is particularly useful for calculating complexity measures in interaction data, and while it can be used to calculate lexical richness indices, other tools may be easier to use. If for some reason a researcher needs to calculate vocD (as opposed to different instantiations of D such as HD-D), however, CLAN is the best tool for the job.

Kristopher Kyle

Coh-Metrix

Coh-metrix (Graesser, McNamara, Louwerse, & Cai, 2004; McNamara, Graesser, McCarthy, & Cai, 2014) has been used in a large number of studies by the research team that developed it. Coh-metrix calculates a wide range of indices related to lexical diversity (e.g., TTR for content words, MTLD, and vocD) and sophistication (e.g., psycholinguistic word information and mean frequency scores). The version of the tool that is available to users outside of the research team (www.cohmetrix.com) only allows for a single text to be processed at a time, which limits its usefulness for all but the smallest datasets. The online version of Coh-metrix also provides no diagnostic output, which also limits its attractiveness.

Lexical Complexity Analyzer

The lexical complexity analyzer (LCA; Lu, 2012) calculates one index of lexical density, 19 indices related to lexical diversity, and five band-based indices related to lexical sophistication. LCA is available in two versions. The first is a freely available Python script that works on Apple and Linux operating systems and is accessed via the command line (this requires a very small amount of computer literacy). With a small amount of programming knowledge, one can manipulate the script to provide any diagnostic information desired. This version can be downloaded from Xiaofe Lu's website (www.personal.psu.edu/xxl13). The second version, which is accessed via an online interface requires no programming knowledge and can batch process up to 200 texts at a time (see Haiyang Ai's website: http://aihaiyang.com/software/lca/). The only potential downside to the lexical complexity analyzer is that it does not calculate any of the lexical diversity indices suggested in this chapter (Maas' index, MATTR, MTLD, or HD-D). However, LCA does include a wide range of indices that have been commonly used in the field of applied linguistics.

P_Lex and S

At the time of writing, P_Lex (Meara & Bell, 2001) is only freely available as an online tool that can be accessed on Paul Meara's webpage (www.lognostics.co.uk). Texts can only be processed in single-file mode, limiting its usefulness for large-scale analyses. It does, however, provide a great deal of information regarding how the index is calculated for each text, which makes it particularly transparent. The related measure S (Kojima & Yamashita, 2014) can also only be calculated in single-file mode on Masumi Kojima's website (www.kojima-vlab.org). Although a number of curve fit diagnostics are reported, no other diagnostic output is provided.

Range, AntWordProfiler, and VocabProfile

Lexical frequency profiles (LFPs) can be generated for word families (with types or tokens) using Range (Heatley & Nation, 1994), which is available on Paul Nation's website, or AntWordProfiler (Anthony, 2014), which is available on Laurence Anthony's website (www.laurenceanthony.net). Range works on Windows machines only, but AntWordProfiler is available for both Windows and Apple operating systems. Both Range and AntWordProfiler allow for batch processing and provide a great deal of diagnostic output. Even more diagnostic output can be provided for single texts using VocabProfile (Cobb, 2018), which can be accessed at www.lextutor.ca/. The only downside to Range and AntWordProfiler is the format of the output. The output for each text is provided as a table (with intervening text

470

between the tables), which requires a fair amount of cleaning before any statistical analyses can be conducted.

TAALED and TAALES

The Tool for the Automatic Analysis of Lexical Diversity (TAALED) and the related Tool for the Automatic Analysis of Lexical Sophistication (TAALES; Kyle & Crossley, 2015; Kyle et al., 2018) together calculate the widest range of lexical richness indices of any freely available tool. These tools are available on Kristopher Kyle and Scott Crossley's website (www.linguisti-canalysistools.org). TAALED calculates lexical density for types and tokens, and eight distinct indices of lexical diversity, including Maas' index, MATTR, MTLD, and HD-D. TAALES calculates over 500 indices related to lexical sophistication including mean word frequency for a variety of reference corpora (for all words, content words, and function words), psycholinguistic word information, word recognition norms, contextual distinctiveness, polysemy, hypernymy, and n-gram association strength (among many others). Both TAALED and TAALES are available for Windows and Apple operating systems and allow for batch processing. Both TAALED and TAALES provide optional detailed diagnostic information for post-hoc analyses such as individual index scores for each word in a text. Additionally, TAALES 3.0, which will be released in late 2019 will also calculate LFPs, lambda (as per P_Lex), and S.

Future Directions

Lexical Diversity

As noted, indices of lexical diversity are widely used to model lexical richness (and, by extrapolation, productive lexical proficiency). However, care must be taken when selecting an index to use, as many commonly used indices are strongly correlated with text length and should be avoided. Preliminarily, the preceding four indices described favorably (Maas' index, MATTR, MTLD, and HD-D) appear to be attractive options in light of their relative independence of text length (e.g., McCarthy & Jarvis, 2007, 2010). At least two issues, however, warrant exploration. First, most studies that have investigated the impact of length (e.g., McCarthy & Jarvis, 2007, 2010) have used text segments from fairly long text (i.e., 2,000 words) to do so. L2 texts that are commonly analyzed in vocabulary studies tend to be much shorter (e.g., between 100 and 500 words), which may affect the relationship between these indices and text length. Koizumi and In'nami (2012), for example, found that only MLTD was relatively stable for texts between 110 and 200 words. However, their sample was fairly small (n = 38) and only represented one genre and mode, making this is a particularly rich area for future research. Second, as alluded to earlier, lexical diversity is most often measured as a univariate construct. However, Jarvis (2013) outlines a number of ways in which diversity can be conceptualized as a multivariate construct that includes a number of distinct aspects. A full treatment of Jarvis' ideas is beyond the scope of this chapter, but make an excellent starting point for those interested in further investigating the construct.

Lexical Sophistication

Given the number of available indices, the calculation of lexical sophistication can be quite complicated. For some purposes, the use of straightforward and univariate indices such as a variation of the LFP or mean frequency scores may be appropriate. However, both theoretical perspectives and empirical studies suggest that frequency is not the only determinant in the ease/difficulty of learning and using a word. This suggests that to obtain a fuller understanding of the sophistication of lexical items in a L2 user-produced text, multiple measurements are necessary. There are at least two directions that can be taken to move the field forward with regard to the measurement of lexical sophistication. First, unlike indices of lexical diversity, indices of lexical sophistication have not been subject to widescale, rigorous testing of length dependence, length stability, or reliability (though see Kojima & Yamashita, 2014). This is an important aspect of future research. Second, indices of lexical sophistication need to be tested in a variety of contexts to determine the degree to which these are stable across registers and modes.

Conclusion

This chapter has provided an overview of indices used to measure lexical richness, including those related to lexical density, lexical diversity, and lexical sophistication. The calculation of some of these indices has been outlined, with accompanying examples, and a number of critiques and suggestions have been made. Additionally, a number of freely available tools have been described, and each has benefits and drawbacks that each researcher must weigh. It should be clearly stated that no single index (or set of indices) is the best way to measure lexical richness in every context. For each study, researchers must make informed decisions about the benefits and drawbacks of each index (or set of indices). It is hoped that this chapter has provided the first steps in enabling such an informed choice.

Further Reading

Jarvis, S. (2013). Capturing the diversity in lexical diversity. *Language Learning, 63*(s1), 87–106.

> This article provides a critical examination of the construct of lexical diversity and introduces a multivariate approach for its measurement.

Kyle, K., Crossley, S. A., & Berger, C. M. (2018). The tool for the automatic analysis of lexical sophistication (TAALES): Version 2.0. *Behavior Research Methods, 50*(3), 1030–1046.

> This article introduces a wide range of indices related to lexical sophistication. At time of writing, it represents the most up-to-date description of newly developed indices. Importantly, it includes two validation studies that indicate the relationship between these indices and ratings of written lexical proficiency and writing quality.

Read, J. (2000). *Assessing vocabulary*. Cambridge, UK: Cambridge University Press.

> This widely cited book provides an excellent introduction to the construct of lexical richness and its measurement.

Related Topics

The relationship between vocabulary knowledge and proficiency, factors affecting the learning of single-word items, factors affecting the learning of multiword items, key issues in measuring vocabulary knowledge, key issues in researching single-word items, key issues in researching multiword items

References

Anthony, L. (2014). *AntWordProfiler* (Version 1.4. 1) [Computer Software]. Tokyo, Japan: Waseda University.

Balota, D. A., Yap, M. J., Hutchison, K. A., Cortese, M. J., Kessler, B., Loftis, B., . . . Treiman, R. (2007). The English lexicon project. *Behavior Research Methods*, *39*(3), 445–459. https://doi.org/10.3758/BF03193014

Bauer, L., & Nation, I. S. P. (1993). Word families. *International Journal of Lexicography*, *6*(4), 253–279.

Berger, C. M., Crossley, S. A., & Kyle, K. (2017). Using novel word context measures to predict human ratings of lexical proficiency. *Journal of Educational Technology & Society*, *20*(2), 201–212.

Berger, C. M., Crossley, S. A., & Kyle, K. (2019). Using Native-Speaker Psycholinguistic Norms to Predict Lexical Proficiency and Development in Second Language Production. *Applied Linguistics*, *40*(1), 22–42.

Bestgen, Y., & Granger, S. (2014). Quantifying the development of phraseological competence in L2 English writing: An automated approach. *Journal of Second Language Writing*, *26*, 28–41. https://doi.org/10.1016/j.jslw.2014.09.004

BNC Consortium. (2007). *The British National Corpus, version 3*. BNC Consortium. Retrieved from www.natcorp.ox.ac.uk/

Brysbaert, M., Warriner, A. B., & Kuperman, V. (2014). Concreteness ratings for 40 thousand generally known English word lemmas. *Behavior Research Methods*, *46*(3), 904–911.

Bulté, B., & Housen, A. (2012). Defining and operationalising L2 complexity. In A. Housen, F. Kuiken, & F. Vedder (Eds.), *Dimensions of L2 performance and proficiency: complexity, accuracy, and fluency in SLA*. Amsterdam: John Benjamins.

Cobb, T. (2017, March). *Broad v. narrow band lexical frequency profiling*. Presented at the American Association for Applied Linguistics, Portland. Retrieved from www.lextutor.ca/vp/comp/vocab@aaal.pdf

Cobb, T. (2018). *Web VocabProfile*. http://www.lextutor.ca/vp/

Coltheart, M. (1981). The MRC psycholinguistic database. *The Quarterly Journal of Experimental Psychology*, *33*(4), 497–505.

Covington, M. A., & McFall, J. D. (2010). Cutting the Gordian knot: The moving-average type – token ratio (MATTR). *Journal of Quantitative Linguistics*, *17*(2), 94–100.

Coxhead, A. (2000). A new academic word list. *TESOL Quarterly*, *34*(2), 213–238.

Crossley, S. A., Cobb, T., & McNamara, D. S. (2013). Comparing count-based and band-based indices of word frequency: Implications for active vocabulary research and pedagogical applications. *System*, *41*(4), 965–981. https://doi.org/10.1016/j.system.2013.08.002

Crossley, S. A., Kyle, K., & Salsbury, T. (2016). A usage-based investigation of L2 lexical acquisition: The role of input and output. *The Modern Language Journal*, *100*(3), 702–715.

Crossley, S. A., Salsbury, T., & McNamara, D. S. (2009). Measuring L2 lexical growth using hypernymic relationships. *Language Learning*, *59*(2), 307–334.

Crossley, S. A., Salsbury, T., & McNamara, D. S. (2012). Predicting the proficiency level of language learners using lexical indices. *Language Testing*, *29*(2), 243–263. https://doi.org/10.1177/0265532211419331

Crossley, S. A., Salsbury, T., McNamara, D. S., & Jarvis, S. (2011). Predicting lexical proficiency in language learner texts using computational indices. *Language Testing*, *28*(4), 561–580. https://doi.org/10.1177/0265532210378031

Daller, H., Van Hout, R., & Treffers-Daller, J. (2003). Lexical richness in the spontaneous speech of bilinguals. *Applied Linguistics*, *24*(2), 197–222.

Davies, M. (2010). The corpus of contemporary American English as the first reliable monitor corpus of English. *Literary and Linguistic Computing*, *25*(4), 447–464. https://doi.org/10.1093/llc/fqq018

Ellis, N. C. (2002). Frequency effects in language processing. *Studies in Second Language Acquisition*, *24*(2), 143–188.

Ellis, N. C. (2006). Selective attention and transfer phenomena in L2 acquisition: Contingency, cue competition, salience, interference, overshadowing, blocking, and perceptual learning. *Applied Linguistics*, *27*(2), 164–194.

Engber, C. A. (1995). The relationship of lexical proficiency to the quality of ESL compositions. *Journal of Second Language Writing*, *4*(2), 139–155. https://doi.org/10.1016/1060-3743(95)90004-7

Graesser, A. C., McNamara, D. S., Louwerse, M. M., & Cai, Z. (2004). Coh-Metrix: Analysis of text on cohesion and language. *Behavior Research Methods, Instruments, & Computers, 36*(2), 193–202. https://doi.org/10.3758/BF03195564

Grant, L., & Ginther, A. (2000). Using computer-tagged linguistic features to describe L2 writing differences. *Journal of Second Language Writing, 9*(2), 123–145.

Guiraud, P. (1960). *Problèmes et méthodes de la statistique linguistique.* Paris: Presses universitaires de France.

Guo, L., Crossley, S. A., & McNamara, D. S. (2013). Predicting human judgments of essay quality in both integrated and independent second language writing samples: A comparison study. *Assessing Writing, 18*(3), 218–238.

Halliday, M. A. (1985). *Spoken and written language.* Melbourne: Deakin University Press.

Harley, B., & King, M. L. (1989). Verb lexis in the written compositions of young L2 learners. *Studies in Second Language Acquisition, 11*(4), 415–439.

Heatley, A., & Nation, I. S. P. (1994). *Range.* Victoria University of Wellington, NZ. [Computer Program]. Retrieved from http://www.vuw.ac.nz/lals/

Hoffman, P., Ralph, M. A. L., & Rogers, T. T. (2013). Semantic diversity: A measure of semantic ambiguity based on variability in the contextual usage of words. *Behavior Research Methods, 45*(3), 718–730.

Hyltenstam, K. (1988). Lexical characteristics of near-native second-language learners of Swedish. *Journal of Multilingual & Multicultural Development, 9*(1–2), 67–84.

Ishikawa, S. (2011). A new horizon in learner corpus studies: The aim of the ICNALE project. *Corpora and Language Technologies in Teaching, Learning and Research,* 3–11.

Jarvis, S. (2013). Capturing the diversity in lexical diversity. *Language Learning, 63*(s1), 87–106.

Jarvis, S., Grant, L., Bikowski, D., & Ferris, D. (2003). Exploring multiple profiles of highly rated learner compositions. *Journal of Second Language Writing, 12*(4), 377–403. https://doi.org/10.1016/j.jslw.2003.09.001

Johnson, W. (1944). Studies in language behavior: I. A program of research. *Psychological Monographs, 56,* 1–15.

Kyle, K., Crossley, S. A., & Berger, C. (2018). The tool for the analysis of lexical sophistication (TAALES): Version 2.0. *Behavior Research Methods 50*(3), 1030–1046. https://doi.org/10.3758/s13428-017-0924-4

Kim, M., Crossley, S. A., & Kyle, K. (2018). Lexical sophistication as a multidimensional phenomenon: Relations to second language lexical proficiency, development, and writing quality. *The Modern Language Journal 102*(1), 120–141.

Kiss, G. R., Armstrong, C., Milroy, R., & Piper, J. (1973). An associative thesaurus of English and its computer analysis. *The Computer and Literary Studies,* 153–165.

Koizumi, R., & In'nami, Y. (2012). Effects of text length on lexical diversity measures: Using short texts with less than 200 tokens. *System, 40*(4), 554–564.

Kojima, M., & Yamashita, J. (2014). Reliability of lexical richness measures based on word lists in short second language productions. *System, 42,* 23–33.

Kuperman, V., Stadthagen-Gonzalez, H., & Brysbaert, M. (2012). Age-of-acquisition ratings for 30,000 English words. *Behavior Research Methods, 44*(4), 978–990.

Kyle, K., & Crossley, S. A. (2015). Automatically Assessing Lexical Sophistication: Indices, Tools, Findings, and Application. *TESOL Quarterly, 49*(4), 757–786. https://doi.org/10.1002/tesq.194

Kyle, K., Crossley, S. A., & Berger, C. M. (2018). The tool for the automatic analysis of lexical sophistication (TAALES): Version 2.0. *Behavior Research Methods, 50*(3),1030–1046.

Landauer, T. K., Foltz, P. W., & Laham, D. (1998). An introduction to latent semantic analysis. *Discourse Processes, 25*(2–3), 259–284.

Laufer, B. (1991). The development of L2 lexis in the expression of the advanced learner. *The Modern Language Journal, 75*(4), 440–448.

Laufer, B. (1994). The lexical profile of second language writing: Does it change over time? *RELC Journal, 25*(2), 21–33.

Laufer, B., & Nation, I. S. P. (1995). Vocabulary size and use: Lexical richness in L2 written production. *Applied Linguistics*, *16*(3), 307–322. https://doi.org/10.1093/applin/16.3.307

Linnarud, M. (1986). *Lexis in composition: A performance analysis of Swedish learners' written English*. Lund: CWK Gleerup.

Lu, X. (2012). The relationship of lexical richness to the quality of ESL learners' oral narratives. *The Modern Language Journal*, *96*(2), 190–208.

Maas, H. D. (1972). Zusammenhang zwischen Wortschatzumfang und Länge eines Textes. *Zeitschrift für Literaturwissenschaft und Linguistik*, *8*, 73–79.

MacWhinney, B. (2008). A unified model. In P. Robinson & N. Ellis (Eds.), *Handbook of cognitive linguistics and second language acquisition* (pp. 341–371). New York, NY: Routledge.

MacWhinney, B., & Snow, C. (1990). The child language data exchange system: An update. *Journal of Child Language*, *17*(2), 457–472.

Malvern, D. D., & Richards, B. J. (1997). A new measure of lexical diversity. *British Studies in Applied Linguistics*, *12*, 58–71.

Malvern, D. D., Richards, B. J., Chipere, N., & Durán, P. (2004). *Lexical diversity and language development: Quantification and assessment*. Houndsmill, UK: Palgrave Macmillan.

McCarthy, P. M., & Jarvis, S. (2007). vocd: A theoretical and empirical evaluation. *Language Testing*, *24*(4), 459–488.

McCarthy, P. M., & Jarvis, S. (2010). MTLD, vocd-D, and HD-D: A validation study of sophisticated approaches to lexical diversity assessment. *Behavior Research Methods*, *42*(2), 381–392. https://doi.org/10.3758/BRM.42.2.381

McClure, E. (1991). A comparison of lexical strategies in L1 and L2 written English narratives. *Pragmatics and Language Learning*, *2*, 141–154.

McLean, S. (2018). Evidence for the adoption of the flemma as an appropriate word counting unit. *Applied Linguistics*, *39*(6), 823–845. https://doi.org/10.1093/applin/amw050

McNamara, D. S., Crossley, S. A., & McCarthy, P. M. (2010). Linguistic features of writing quality. *Written Communication*, *27*(1), 57–86.

McNamara, D. S., Graesser, A. C., McCarthy, P. M., & Cai, Z. (2014). *Automated evaluation of text and discourse with Coh-Metrix*. Cambridge, UK: Cambridge University Press.

Meara, P. (2005). Lexical frequency profiles: A Monte Carlo analysis. *Applied Linguistics*, *26*(1), 32–47.

Meara, P., & Bell, H. (2001). P_Lex: A simple and effective way of describing the lexical characteristics of short L2 texts. *Prospect*, *3*, 5–19.

Nation, I. S. P. (2001). *Learning vocabulary in another language*. Cambridge, UK: Cambridge University Press.

Nation, I. S. P. (2016). *Making and using word lists for language learning and testing*. Amsterdam: John Benjamins Publishing Company.

Nation, I. S. P., & Webb, S. A. (2011). *Researching and analyzing vocabulary*. Heinle, Cengage Learning.

Nelson, D. L., McEvoy, C. L., & Schreiber, T. A. (2004). The University of South Florida free association, rhyme, and word fragment norms. *Behavior Research Methods, Instruments, & Computers*, *36*(3), 402–407.

Nihalani, N. K. (1981). The quest for the L2 index of development. *RELC Journal*, *12*(2), 50–56.

O'Loughlin, K. (1995). Lexical density in candidate output on direct and semi-direct versions of an oral proficiency test. *Language Testing*, *12*(2), 217–237.

Paivio, A. (1971). *Imagery and verbal processes*. New York, NY: Holt, Rinehart, and Winston.

Paivio, A., Yuille, J. C., & Madigan, S. A. (1968). Concreteness, imagery, and meaningfulness values for 925 nouns. *Journal of Experimental Psychology*, *76*(1p2), 1–1.

Pinchbeck, G. G. (2014, March). *Lexical frequency profiling of a large sample of Canadian high school diploma exam expository writing: L1 and L2 academic English*. Roundtable presented at the American Association for Applied Linguistics Annual Conference, Portland, OR. Retrieved from https://app.box.com/s/2772oofxkg6jyzmd3l7j

Pinchbeck, G. G. (2017). *Vocabulary use in academic-track high-school English literature diploma exam essay writing and its relationship to academic achievement.* Unpublished Ph.D. thesis, University of Calgary, UK.

Quirk, R., Greenbaum, S., Leech, G., & Svartik, J. (1985). *A comprehensive grammar of the English language.* London, UK and New York, NY: Longman.

Read, J. (2000). *Assessing vocabulary.* Cambridge, UK: Cambridge University Press.

Schmitt, N. (2010). *Researching vocabulary: A vocabulary research manual.* Basingstoke, UK: Palgrave McMillan.

Schwanenflugel, P. J., Harnishfeger, K. K., & Stowe, R. W. (1988). Context availability and lexical decisions for abstract and concrete words. *Journal of Memory and Language, 27*(5), 499–520.

Shohamy, E. (1994). The validity of direct versus semi-direct oral tests. *Language Testing, 11*(2), 99–123.

Sinclair, J. (1991). *Corpus, concordance, collocation.* Oxford, UK: Oxford University Press.

Ure, J. (1971). Lexical density and register differentiation. *Applications of Linguistics,* 443–452.

Webb, S. (2010). A corpus driven study of the potential for vocabulary learning through watching movies. *International Journal of Corpus Linguistics, 15*(4), 497–519.

West, M. (1953). *A general service list of English words: With semantic frequencies and a supplementary word-list for the writing of popular science and technology.* London: Longmans, Green and Co.

Xue, G., & Nation, I. S. P. (1984). A university word list. *Language Learning and Communication, 3*(2), 215–229.

Yule, C. U. (1944). *The statistical study of literary vocabulary.* Cambridge, UK: Cambridge University Press.

Part IV

Key Issues in Teaching, Researching, and Measuring Vocabulary

30

Key Issues in Teaching Single Words

Joe Barcroft

Introduction

Teaching single words typically refers to presenting individual or isolated words while providing learners with some means of access to their meaning. It is a type of instruction that may or may not involve engaging learners in concurrent tasks while the target items are being presented. Examples of teaching single words include when an instructor shows pictures of target words and pronounces each target word one by one, when word-picture or translation pairs are presented on a screen or on flash cards, and when someone provides the name of an item for a learner when the item is encountered in the immediate environment (e.g., learner: *What is that called?*; native speaker: *railing*). Although vocabulary teaching of this nature is only one of the many options available to instructors (and other interlocutors) for facilitating vocabulary learning, it is one that can be useful in some contexts. It can be considered as an option, for example, in the following contexts: when a learner needs to know a given set of novel words in order to complete a communicative act, to complete a specific task, or to understand some aspect of content being studied, such as a historical event, a biological process, or some piece of information related to linguistics.

Critical Issues and Topics

Among the many issues faced by language instructors are the following: (1) Under what circumstances should I teach single words? (2) What are the most effective techniques for teaching single words? Answering these questions will be the primary focus of what follows.

Types of Vocabulary Learning

To begin, any discussion of teaching single words should be couched within the larger context of the many possible types of vocabulary learning in which a learner can engage. These can be divided along two main fronts: (1) the extent to which vocabulary is learned incidentally as opposed to intentionally, and (2) the extent to which vocabulary is learned as individual items as opposed to being learned with other words and other linguistic structures, such as those that reflect the morphology, syntax, semantics, pragmatics, and sociocultural properties of any given language. More specifically, one can distinguish between (1) incidental vs. intentional vocabulary, on the one hand, and (2) isolated vs. integrated vocabulary learning, on the other. Before appraising the extent to which these two sets of distinctions might be viewed as two continua, let us consider some definitions and prototypical examples of the incidental-intentional and isolated-integrated distinctions.

Incidental vs. Intentional

Incidental vocabulary learning refers to when learners pick up vocabulary – words, lexical phrases, or both – without intending to do so, such as when a learner reads a passage for meaning and learns a new word or two without noticing that learning has occurred. Another example would be when a learner is focused on buying a series of items in a store and in the process of doing so manages to learn several new words for items without having paid attention to the process of learning these words. *Intentional vocabulary learning*, on the other hand, refers to when a learner intentionally learns one or more words or lexical phrases. Examples of intentional vocabulary learning include studying a series of target words and expressions for a pre-announced vocabulary quiz, looking up any new word or phrase that appears in a reading with the predetermined purpose of intentionally learning the items, or asking a native speaker the names of specific words or phrases and then consciously attempting to commit these items to memory (see also Lindstromberg, this volume).

Isolated vs. Integrated

Isolated vocabulary learning refers to when words or lexical phrases are learned in absence of or nearly in the absence of other words, lexical phrases, and other linguistic structures and information. One example of isolated vocabulary learning is learning the word for "apple" in another language – *manzana* in Spanish, *tagar* in Basque, *poma* in Catalán, *xocotl* in Nahuatl, *bilasáana* in Navajo, and so forth – by viewing a picture of an apple and hearing the word pronounced out loud or seeing a written version of the word. Learning the same word by using a translation pair, such as by showing cards or slides with *apple = manana* written on them or by saying the pair out loud in the spoken mode, would be another example of isolated vocabulary learning of this nature. In addition, isolated vocabulary learning need not be limited to single words only. One could use word-picture or translation pairs to learn any type of multiword lexical phrase as well, such as picture or translation-based and spoken or written versions of *on the one hand = por una parte* (*for one part*) and *It is raining cats and dogs = Llueve a cántaros* (*It is raining pitchers*). What is critical is that both the single-word version (isolated word learning) and the lexical-phrase version (isolated learning of lexical phrases or formulaic language) always appear as isolated items for this type of learning; they do not appear in the context of other words, phrases, or other linguistic structures, as would be the case with input that goes beyond the single vocabulary item in question. What is more is that isolated vocabulary learning can also occur in incidental contexts of learning. Consider the example provided earlier of learning new words while shopping. In such a context, a learner may be exposed to new words or lexicalized multiword phrases such as *lettuce, butter, soap, detergent, aluminum foil*, or *ice cream* as isolated lexical items on signs in the immediate environment and may pick up one or more of these terms without consciously intending to do so. This type of vocabulary leaning is isolated albeit incidental in nature.

Integrated vocabulary learning, in contrast, involves learning new words or phrases in the presence of other words, phrases, other linguistic structures or features, or any combination of these. It typically involves language *input*, or samples of a target language, that go beyond single words or phrases. It can involve sentence-level input, such as when the word *apple* (*manzana, tagar, poma, xocotl, bilasáana* . . .) is learned by hearing the sentence *I think these light-green Granny Smith apples are my favorite fruit*. Sentence-level input of this nature not only provides opportunities to ascertain the meaning of "apple" and to connect it to the word-form *apple* (whatever its form may be in any given language) but also provides opportunities to acquire language-specific meanings, uses, and collocational properties of the word. In this particular sentence-level example, the learner is exposed to *Granny Smith* as one type of apple, a connection between the word *green* and *apple*, and an example of the plural form of *apple*, illustrating a bit of how English morphology works for this word. The more that learners are exposed to information of this nature in the input that goes beyond single lexical items, the more opportunities they have to acquire, incrementally, a more complete range of the meanings, uses, and collocational properties of vocabulary. With regard to language-specific meanings of words in particular, note that the challenge of learning the *polysemy* (multiple but typically related meanings) and the *homonymy* (different unrelated meanings) of words and phrases can be a daunting task. For example, having learned the English word *soap* as an isolated noncount noun in reference to washing will not prevent the confusion that a learner might face at a later point in time when exposed to a sentence such as *You know, I pretty much always watch my soaps from 1 to 3*.

Incidental-Intentional and Isolated-Integrated as Continua

While these definitions and examples are helpful in understanding clear-cut distinctions between incidental vs. intentional vocabulary learning and isolated vs. integrated vocabulary learning, both sets of distinctions can be viewed as continua with *incidental* and *intentional* being endpoints in one case and *isolated* and *integrated* being endpoints in the other. Early research on second language vocabulary learning focused substantially on the distinction between incidental and intentional vocabulary learning (see, for example, books by Coady & Huckin, 1997; Schmitt & McCarthy, 1997), including questions about how much of each type of learning might be needed or most effective, and the view of incidental vs. intentional vocabulary learning as a continuum was part of the discussion (Coady, 1997; Gass, 1987). As with the intentional-incidental distinction, the distinction between isolated vs. integrated vocabulary learning can also be viewed as a continuum. In this case, one endpoint on the continuum represents vocabulary learning that is fully or largely isolated in nature, and the other endpoint represents vocabulary learning that is fully or largely integrated in nature.

Critically, the *isolated-integrated* distinction and its corresponding continuum are applicable regardless of whether a word or phrase is learned intentionally or incidentally. For example, the word *butter* can be learned as an isolated item intentionally based on a word-picture pair a learner is studying for a vocabulary quiz or it can be learned incidentally as an isolated item incident when a learner wants to buy butter in a supermarket, encounters the written form of the word in isolation on a sign, and picks up the word without intentionally trying to learn the word. In this latter case, if the learner encounters the butter in the supermarket and stops to make a conscious attempt to remember the word, perhaps repeating the word "butter, butter, butter" mentally, then this type of learning becomes less incidental and more intentional in nature, but it still remains isolated in nature. The more that the learner encounters the word *butter* along with other words and phrases, however, the less isolated and the more integrated this example becomes. The learner might encounter *salted butter* or *unsalted butter* as input, for example, or a supermarket employee might say to the learner:

You can find the butter along with all of the other dairy products we offer on the shelves at the very back of the store. These latter examples constitute less isolated and more integrated opportunities for vocabulary learning. As such, they also demonstrate how the *isolated-integrated* distinction in vocabulary learning can also be viewed as a continuum.

An I-Squared *Classification System for Vocabulary Learning*

Considering that both the *intentional-incidental* and *isolated-integrated* distinctions can be viewed as continua, the combination of these two continua on two axes can provide a classification system for numerous distinct types of vocabulary learning, all of which vary in degree according to the extent to which they are intentional, incidental, isolated, and integrated in nature. The classification system presented in Figure 30.1, dubbed *I-squared*, was designed and is being proposed here for this purpose. Using this classification system, points A, B, C, and D in the figure represent, respectively, cases of purely intentional and isolated (A), incidental and isolated (B), intentional and integrated (C), and incidental and integrated (D) types of vocabulary learning. The numbers in the figure depict levels at which different types of vocabulary learning can be classified ("most" meaning 100% to the extent to which this level is possible): point A = 1:1 (most intentional, most isolated); point B = 9:1 (most incidental; most isolated); point C = 1:9 (most intentional, most integrated); and point D = 9:9 (most incidental; most integrated).

What would constitute examples of distinct types of vocabulary learning following this classification system? An example of A would be intentionally studying word-picture pairs in preparation for a vocabulary quiz. An example of B would be learning the word for a grocery item without intending to do so when the word appears on one or more occasions in isolation (such as on a sign) in the input. An example of C would be intentionally learning a series of words or phrases while also intentionally trying to learn a series of language-specific meanings and uses of the words or phrases in question by purposefully attending to phrase-level, sentence-level, or discourse-level input. An example of D would be when a learner picks up a new word or phrase without intentionally trying to do so while listening to extended discourse (or reading an extended text) that happens to be rich in information about multiple meanings, uses, and collocational properties of the new words or phrases in question.

Using the same classification system, point E in Figure 30.1 would refer to any example of vocabulary learning at a level of 5:5 (the middle position on the 1-to-9 scale), which should correspond to 50% intentional, 50% incidental, 50% isolated, and 50% integrated. What might be a good example of vocabulary learning at this level? Any answer to this question is bound to be debatable given the challenge of quantifying degrees of intentional vs. incidental vocabulary learning as well as degrees of isolated vs. integrated vocabulary learning on the other. Nevertheless, consider the following possible example for point E as one possibility: a learner living in a country where the target language is spoken rents an apartment and is presented with a series of rules that tenants need to follow. Before reading the list, the person makes the following mental note just before reading the list: "I really should try to learn and remember as many of the new terms in these rules as I can". The learner then reads the list, focusing primarily on the meaning of each sentence, and looks up the meaning of some but not all of the novel words in this input, and "halfway" makes a conscious effort to learn some (but not all) of the words in the list of rules. The type of input provided by the list of rules is about "halfway" useful when it comes to exemplifying language-specific meanings, uses, and collocational properties of the novel words in question. The sentences are fairly short, but the information about meanings, uses, and collocations is helpful at what might

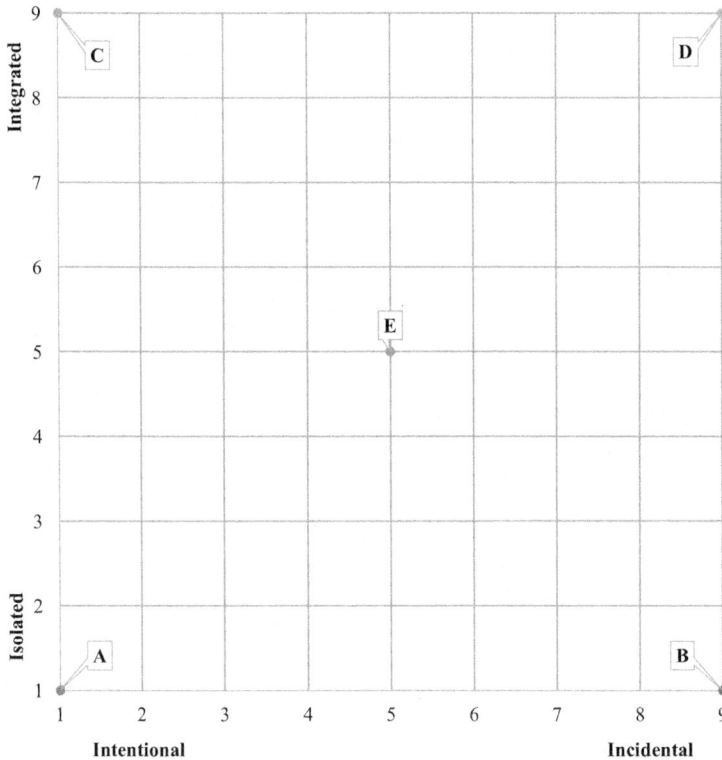

Figure 30.1   I-squared classification system for different types of vocabulary learning (with both intentional-incidental and isolated-integrated continua)

be considered an "average" (50%) level for the novel vocabulary in question. This example of vocabulary learning might be considered a good example of the 5:5 level following the classification system depicted in Figure 30.1.

What Is Common to All Types of Vocabulary Learning?

Before discussing advantages and disadvantages of teaching single words as one of many options for vocabulary instruction, it is useful to point out a critical element that is common to all four of the types of vocabulary learning represented by the endpoints of the two continua in Figure 30.1 (points A, B, C, and D) and common to point E at the 5:5 level as well as any other point that could be added. What all of these types of vocabulary learning have in common is that they all begin with input. Without input, vocabulary learning does not happen, and language acquisition in general does not happen. Remembering that vocabulary learning starts with input, regardless of how intentional or isolated it may be, is a critical point for language instructors to remember.

Imagine, for example, that a language instructor decides to ask students to complete a series of "vocabulary-focused" activities that require them to identify sets of words that do and do not constitute viable collocations in a language, providing phrases to students such as *crystal clear* and *shattered glass* as correct examples and **quartz clear* and **burst glass* as incorrect examples. Activities such as this raise the following questions: How could any student possibly do this activity correctly if they have not been exposed to *crystal clear* and *shattered glass* previously in the input, and most likely, on more than one occasion? Is it problematic to present incorrect collocations such as **quartz clear* and **burst glass* to students as part of the activity? Will students process the incorrect examples as real input, especially if they have not learned the correct versions? Input-related questions such as these need to be considered when it comes to providing effective vocabulary instruction, regardless of the particular type or context of vocabulary learning at hand.

Advantages and Disadvantages of Intentionally Learning Single Words in Isolation

As the preceding discussion should help to clarify, learning single words in isolation need not always imply intentional learning. It is possible to learn single words incidentally when the correct circumstances arise. Cases of isolated and incidental single-word learning (Level 9:1 in the *I-squared* classification system) afford learners with the advantage of being able to focus on a single word at a time, however uncommon full-fledged cases of this type of learning may be. This being noted, let us consider cases of intentional learning of single words in isolation (Level 1:1 in the *I-squared* classification system), which commonly involve the presentation of word-picture pairs or translation pairs as a learner intentionally tries to learn each target word that is presented. What are the advantages and disadvantages of this type of vocabulary learning?

Advantages

One notable advantage of intentional learning of single words in isolation concerns its high degree of transparency for mapping between word form and word meaning. Single-word learning in isolation typically provides the learner with one word form and a clear depiction or translation of its meaning. If the word can be represented visually in an unambiguous fashion, as in the case of concrete nouns such as *apple*, *chair*, or *squirrel*, a simple picture or photo of the word referent usually can suffice. One of the interesting features about learning single words in this manner is how it can be viewed as a microcosm of language learning in general. As with all language learning in general, learning individual words in isolation involves processing a new linguistic form as input, attaining access to the meaning of the form, and then creating a mental mapping between the form and meaning.

For single words whose meaning cannot be depicted clearly as concrete nouns using pictures or photos, translations may provide learners with unambiguous access to word meaning. However, involving first language (L1) translations of target second language (L2) words may slow, at least arguably, development of the type of *conceptual mediation* (direct connections between word forms and their meanings) that is typical of fluent advanced L2 learner-users (see Kroll & Sunderman, 2003, for more on development from *lexical mediation*, which involves connections through L1, toward conceptual mediation as learners increase in L2 proficiency over time). Providing sentence-level definitions to clarify meanings of single words does not constitute another option for clarifying meanings of target words during "single-word learning in isolation" per se because definitions, by their nature, involve integration of other words and phrases that are related to the target word in question, situating this type of learning somewhere else than 1:1 in the *I-squared* classification system, perhaps at 1:3 or even higher on the *isolated-integrated* axis.

Another advantage of intentional learning of single words is that it allows a learner, instructor, language program director, or any combination of these three to plan for vocabulary learning in a more concrete and concise manner than do other types of vocabulary learning, such as those that rely on incidental learning. With intentional learning of single words, one can easily select target words on the basis of their relative frequency in a language, ensuring exposure to and potential learning of different pivotal thresholds of word knowledge that have been focused on in the vocabulary research literature. For example, target thresholds of the 2,000 or 3,000 most frequent words in a language can be considered (see Dang, this volume; Nation & Waring, 1997; Nation, 2016; Vilkaitė-Lozdienė and Schmitt, this volume, for more on frequency and levels of language coverage). Single-word learning also can be used to focus on words that are essential for beginning language learning (see Dang & Webb, 2016), as well as words that can be selected on the basis of their relationship to a special field, such as medicine or business (see Liu and Lei, this volume), or a particular source of input, such as a book or a movie, that a learner is going to be reading or listening to while viewing.

Disadvantages

Perhaps the most critical disadvantage of learning single words in isolation is how this type of learning does not provide learners the language-specific meanings, uses, and collocational properties of words a learner needs to really *know* a word. Knowing a word involves not only learning the word form, its meaning, and a mapping between the two. It involves learning an array of other types of knowledge and development of other types of abilities (see Nation, this volume), including the following.

1   Knowing multiple denotative meanings of the word, such as how *back* can mean both a part of the body and "to support".
2   Knowing connotative meanings of the word, such as how *fresh* or *unpolluted* could be used to describe the same air, but *fresh* is more positive in nature.
3   Knowing the collocational properties of the word, such as in the case of *soft pillow* instead of **malleable pillow*.
4   Knowing lexicalized formulaic expressions in which the word is used, such as *around the corner* and *to be cornered* for the word *corner*.
5   Knowing idiomatic expressions in which the word appears, such as *once in a blue moon* for the words *blue* and *moon*.
6   Knowing morphosyntactic properties and syntactic projections of the word, such as how the verb *put* requires an object and a place (e.g., *put the book on the table*).
7   Being able to utilize all of the preceding knowledge in a fluent manner for both comprehension and production of language, such as when a learner of English is able to say *They wrapped the cake in aluminum foil* in a fluent manner without hesitating to produce any of the individual words or word combinations, such as aluminum foil, or when a learner of Spanish is able to write *¡Mira cómo nada ese ornitorrinco!* "Look how that platypus is swimming!" without stalling to produce the word *ornitorrinco* while maintaining the appropriate sentence structure in which this word appears

Single-word learning in isolation does not provide learners with what they need to develop all of these types of knowledge and abilities because, by definition, it involves word-level input only, which provides only one level of information about the word form and its meaning. Certainly, multiple meanings of a single word could also be taught using word-level input only, but it is sentence-level and discourse-level input that are needed to move forward on all seven of the fronts listed above as they develop and refine language-specific lexicose-mantic space for words gradually over time.

Another disadvantage of learning single words in isolation is that some words, by their nature, do not lend themselves well to this type of learning. Words that are difficult to depict in pictures and photos in transparent manner (e.g., *redundant, clarity, frankly*) can be translated for single-word learning, but extensive use of translation-based learning may limit learners in their development of the type of knowledge they need for fluent use of target words. For some target words, even the option of translation can fall short. Consider the challenges of teaching an English word such as *base* in isolation. Which meaning of the word should be taught first? A military *base*? *Base* as in *base*ball and other sports? *Base* as in the foundation of a structure? One could attempt to teach all of these meanings one by one without involving other words or sentence-level input, but why attempt to do so in this manner? After all, what learners need is to be exposed to different word combinations (phrases) with *base* and sentence-level input that includes *base* in order to develop appropriate English lexicosemantic space for this word.

Finally, another disadvantage of single-word learning in isolation is the extent to which this type of learning may *not* transfer to fluent use of the words in question in more natural communicative use of language. By definition, learning single words in isolation does not provide learners with the type of data that they need in order to be able to integrate these words fully among other words within their developing mental lexicon and overall develop-ing linguistic system for any given language. Even if a word does lend itself well to being learned as a single item, teaching it that way and learning in that way does not provide all of the information that learners need to be able to incorporate the word mentally in a manner that allows them to be able to use the word in a wholly fluent manner. Why not? Because single-word learning is limited when it comes to gaining the types of knowledge and abilities listed earlier in 1 to 7 and because fluent language use involves these types of knowledge and abilities, single-word learning in isolation does not provide all that is needed. This point does not negate, however, that learners may transfer knowledge of L1 words to corresponding L2 words as means of gaining abilities such as those listed in 1 to 7 when it is possible to do so (see Webb, 2007, for evidence of this type of transfer). The point also does not negate how deliberate learning of words can lead to substantially automatic processing of the words in question (see Elgort, 2011, for a study on learning of pseudowords that addressed this issue).

What Works Best?

Having discussed a few of the advantages and some major disadvantages of learning single words in isolation, let us now reflect upon different methods or techniques for teaching and learning words in this manner. Assuming that certain words are going to be taught and learned as isolated items, what are the most effective methods or techniques for teaching and learn-ing them? As reflected in theory and research on lexical input processing (lex-IP), two major options are available to us: (1) structuring input in ways that can lead to *input-based effects* on word learning and (2) engaging learners in tasks that can lead to *task-based effects* on word learning (see Barcroft, 2015, on how these two types of effects have informed lex-IP theory and research). This section argues that three clear ways of improving single-word learning are (1) increasing the number of times that target words appear in the input; (2) providing learners with opportunities to attempt to retrieve target words on their own, and (3) presenting target words using input that is enhanced in ways that have been demonstrated to be effective. Addi-tionally, possibly on certain occasions but while exercising caution, mnemonic techniques such as the Keyword Method might also be used to facilitate memory for challenging novel word forms. Note that increased repetition and enhanced input are input-based manipulations designed to elicit positive input-based effects whereas providing retrieval opportunities is a task-related effect designed to elicit positive task-based effects on word learning. The use of mnemonic techniques, depending on their nature, can involve either or both input- and task-based manipulations with the goal of facilitating particular aspects of word learning.

Increased Repetition

One basic provision that can improve single-word learning in isolation, or any type of vocabulary learning, is increased repetition of the target vocabulary. The well-documented memorial benefit of increasing the number of exposures to an item has a long history in research on human memory for a variety of different types of stimuli (see Greene, 1992). In the area of L2 vocabulary in particular, a longitudinal study by Bahrick, Bahrick, Bahrick, and Bahrick (1993) confirmed the benefits of increased repetition on intentional L2 vocabulary learning over long periods of time while also comparing the impact of different times of (re)study: intervals of 14, 28, and 56 days. The study assessed learning rates after one, two, three, and five years of study and revealed that longer intervals led to lower learning rates over shorter periods of time but higher learning rates over longer periods of time. Other studies on incidental L2 vocabulary learning have also confirmed that increasing the number of times that target words appear in a text augments learning of the words in question (Hulstijn, Hollander & Greidanus, 1996; Rott, 1999).

Opportunities for Retrieval

Another provision that can increase single-word learning and other types of vocabulary learning is providing learners with opportunities to retrieve target vocabulary items on their own after they have been exposed to them as input. Roediger and Guynn (1996, p. 197) defined retrieval as "accessing stored information". In the case of vocabulary learning, the stored information in question can be a target word that a learner has previously encountered. As with increased repetition, the benefits of providing retrieval opportunities also has a long history in research on human memory. Myers (1914), for example, provided a first demonstration of the benefits of retrieval and the *testing effect*, which makes reference to the learning benefits of periodic testing. Slamecka and Graf (1978) also demonstrated retrieval-oriented memorial benefits in support of what they referred to as the *generation effect*, that is, the memorial benefits that arise when we are provided with opportunities to generate target items on our own. Clearly, in order to *generate* an item, either partially or fully, one must be able to *retrieve* the item, either partially or fully, as well.

With regard to L2 word learning, several studies have demonstrated the benefits of providing learners with opportunities to retrieve target words. Royer (1973) demonstrated that index-card based learning of English-Turkish word pairs was higher for participants who attempted to retrieve target words during study as compared to participants who were not provided with opportunities to do so. In another study, McNamara and Healy (1995, Experiment 2) found that participants who studied target L2 words while attempting to generate them outperformed those who read target words only as they studied them. The retention rate for the generate group was .756 as compared to .658 for the read group. Consistent with both of these studies, Barcroft (2007) assessed the effects of providing English-speaking L2 learners of Spanish with opportunities for retrieval of target words as compared to a study-only condition in a classroom-based context. The results of the within-participants study, which exposed all participants to both learning conditions, revealed that vocabulary learning was higher in the retrieval-oriented condition as measured by posttests administered immediately, two days later, and one week later. The combined findings of all three of these studies strongly favor providing L2 learners with retrieval opportunities during L2 vocabulary learning.

Enhanced Aural Input

Another means of improving single-word learning of vocabulary is to enhance aural input in ways that have been found to be effective. Intriguingly, De Groot (2006) found that playing classical music in the background during L2 learning facilitated L2 word learning. In other studies, Barcroft and Sommers (2005) and Sommers and Barcroft (2007) demonstrated substantially improved learning of the spoken forms of L2 words when target words were presented using multiple talkers instead of a single talker, multiple speaking styles instead of one speaking style, and multiple speaking rates instead of one speaking rate. These findings, which confirm the benefits of acoustic variability based on sources such as these (talker, speaking style, and speaking rate), can easily be incorporated in both online and classroom-based language instruction in order to improve single-word learning considerably. The benefits observed between no talker variability and high talker variability, for example, corresponded to an increase in single-word learning from 38% to 64%.

Mnemonics Anyone? – Um, Maybe

Mnemonics are techniques designed to facilitate or increase memory for different types of items that one may want to remember and recall. For vocabulary learning, one mnemonic technique that has received substantial attention over the years is the Keyword Method (Atkinson & Raugh, 1975), which involves recoding a novel word form into a known word form (or known word forms) and creating a mental picture that connects the known forms. In order to learn the Spanish word *silla* "chair", for example, one could recode this Spanish word as the English words *See ya!* and create a mental image of a chair saying *See ya!* as someone who was sitting on it gets up to walk away. As such, this mnemonic involves a bit of both input-based manipulation (to the extent that recoding of novel word forms constitutes an input-based manipulation) and a task-based manipulation (to the extent that creating a mental image connecting the recoded form to the meaning of the original novel form constitutes a task-based manipulation).

In their seminal study in this area, Atkinson and Raugh (1975) demonstrated higher learning rates of L2 Russian words for a group who used the Keyword Method as compared to the performance of an unconstrained control group. Since this first study on the Keyword Method, many other studies, such as those by Ellis and Beaton (1993) and Sagarra and Alba (2006), have also demonstrated benefits of the Keyword Method over selected other competing methods of studying vocabulary. In light of mounting evidence in favor of the Keyword Method, researchers such as Hulstijn (1997) called for increased use of the Keyword Method in L2 instruction.

Other studies, however, have found that the Keyword Method does not always lead to higher amounts of word learning when compared to competing methods such as certain types of rote rehearsal (Barcroft, Sommers, & Sunderman, 2011; Kole, 2007; van Hell & Mahn, 1997), and critically, studies also have provided convincing evidence that the Keyword Method can lead to the development of qualitatively different lexicosemantic representations when compared to other more "naturalistic" types of word learning, such as word-picture based learning of single words. Barcroft et al. (2011) (see also Kole, 2007), found, for example, that not only did the Keyword Method not lead to significantly higher rates of L2 Spanish vocabulary learning when compared to repeated rehearsal as a competing technique, it also led to the development of qualitatively different lexicosemantic representations that maintained the odd associations needed to recode the novel L2 forms into known L1 forms (such as those created when imagining a *goat* riding in a *cab* for the Spanish word *cabra* "goat"). These representations, when accessed using masked priming, yielded patterns that were different from those produced by words that had been learned without the Keyword Method. Based on these and other earlier findings (Kole, 2007; van Hell & Mahn, 1997), Barcroft, Sommers, and Sunderman argued against the use of the Keyword Method as a means of teaching a large amount of vocabulary in a language in which one wishes to become proficient. Instead, they favored a more limited use of the Keyword Method in situations when a novel word form that a person encounters is particularly challenging, such as if someone wants to remember certain words or phrases in an unfamiliar language during a trip.

While demonstrations of the qualitative costs of using the Keyword Method beg caution with regard to using the Keyword Method extensively for L2 vocabulary learning, other techniques for recoding novel L2 forms into more familiar forms can differ when it comes to the qualitative costs they might pose to developing lexicosemantic representations. In one study, for example, Kida (2010) found that having Japanese-speaking learners of L2 English rewrite novel word forms that appeared in a text in Japanese script led to increased learning of those words, especially when compared to having them complete a semantically oriented pleasantness-ratings task. Recoding the novel English word forms into more familiar forms by using Japanese script is a mnemonic technique that differs substantially from the Keyword Method, raising several questions. What are the qualitative costs of recoding novel L2 word forms into different native scripts? Might these costs be less than the costs of recoding novel L2 words via the Keyword Method? If so, perhaps the technique examined by Kida is a more viable mnemonic than the Keyword Method when it comes to the overall goal of increasing L2 word learning.

Three Recommendations From a Lexical Input Processing Perspective

In addition to recommendations to increase exposures, to provide retrieval opportunities, and to enhance the input in which target words appear in effective ways, three other general recommendations can be made when it comes to teaching and learning single words. These three recommendations, which are informed by and consistent with a lexical input processing (lex-IP) approach to vocabulary (Barcroft, 2012, 2015), are to be *input-first*, *processing-specific*, and *incremental but persistent* when teaching L2 words. Each of these three recommendations is discussed briefly below.

Be Input-First

It is important to remember that all language learning begins with input, including vocabulary learning. Naturally, the input provided needs to be meaning-oriented in order for learners to make the type of form-meaning connections that are necessary for vocabulary learning and language learning in general. It is also critical to remember not to overburden learners with tasks during the early stages of word learning, including tasks that involve forced output of a parroting nature without access to meaning, because that can potentially decrease rates of single-word learning.

Be Processing-Specific

It is also important to avoid engaging learners in tasks that can detract from learning desirable aspects of vocabulary knowledge, such as word form and collocation. Semantically elaborative tasks such as sentence writing have been found to decrease L2 single-word learning substantially, and even more so when the L2 forms are more novel in nature, such as when English speakers attempt to learn single words in L2 Korean as compared to when they attempt to learn single words in L2 French (Wong & Pyun, 2012). For additional information and research on how semantically elaborative tasks can decrease word form learning and how the predictions of the Type of Processing – Resource Allocation (TOPRA) model informs our understanding of vocabulary learning and instructional practices related to vocabulary learning, see a book on lex-IP by Barcroft (2015).

Be Incremental and Persistent

Perhaps the most understated and challenging principle of the input-based incremental (IBI) approach to vocabulary instruction is Principle 8, which is to promote learning L2-specific meanings and usage of vocabulary over time. When it comes to all of the language-specific meanings and usage of words that a language learner/user needs, it is important to recognize the incremental nature of this process while also being persistent. What is needed is to expose learners to rich sources of meaningful input well beyond single words; input that exemplifies and provides the data that learners need to develop this type of knowledge gradually over time.

Beyond Teaching Single Words

While this chapter focuses on teaching and learning single words, in no way it is it intended to advocate this type of vocabulary teaching and learning, except for on a limited basis. It is critical not to over-rely on teaching single words in isolation. Vocabulary needs to be taught within larger contexts of meaning-oriented language instruction, including communicative, task-based, and content-focused varieties thereof, and it needs to be taught using input that goes well beyond the level of single words, including sentence-level and discourse-level input and activities that engage learners to process lexically oriented input at these other levels.

Future Directions

Research on single-word learning is intriguing by nature because it is the place at which form meets meaning at a very basic level. As such, it offers a vision of what is essential to language learning while exploring the effects of a variety of possible input-based and task-based manipulations. To date, research suggests that increased exposures to words and some types of input enhancement increase rates of single-word learning, as does providing learners with opportunities for target word retrieval. Future research can continue to explore other input-related variables and concurrent tasks during single-word learning to explore how we can add to the growing list of ways to teach and learn words effectively. Some topics that can be explored in future research include, for example, (1) studies on new ways of enhancing single words in input; (2) studies that examine previously untested predictions of the TOPRA model regarding the impact of different types of semantically, structurally, and mapping-oriented tasks; and (3) studies on the effectiveness of teaching multiple meanings of target words in the context of learning single words in isolation. The findings of new research in these and other areas that involve single-word learning will continue to provide new insights as to how best to teach single words while improving our understanding of vocabulary learning in general.

Further Reading

Barcroft, J. (2012). *Input-based incremental vocabulary instruction.* Alexandria, VA: TESOL International Association.

This book presents input-based incremental (IBI) vocabulary instruction, an evidence-based approach to vocabulary instruction that can be seamlessly integrated within different varieties of meaning-oriented (communicative, task-based, content-based) instruction. Key principles of the IBI approach are grounded in theory and research in lexical input processing.

Greene, R. L. (1992). *Human memory. Paradigms and paradoxes.* Hinsdale, NJ: Lawrence Erlbaum.

This book reviews research on the effects of a variety of variables on human memory. Many of these variables, such as those related to repletion, also have implications for learning single words in isolation.

Nation, I. S. P. (2013). *Learning vocabulary in another language.* Cambridge, UK: Cambridge University Press.

The second edition of this book summarizes and discusses a wide range of issues related to second language vocabulary learning, including topics that are pertinent to learning single words in isolation, such as making use of word frequency when selecting target words.

Related Topics

Factors affecting the learning of single-word items, learning single-word items vs. multiword items, processing single-word and multiword items, strategies for learning single-word items

References

Atkinson, R. C., & Raugh, M. R. (1975). An application of the mnemonic keyword method to the acquisition of a Russian vocabulary. *Journal of Experimental Psychology: Human Learning and Memory, 104,* 126–133.

Bahrick, H. P., Bahrick, L. E., Bahrick, A. S., & Bahrick, P. E. (1993). Maintenance of foreign language vocabulary and the spacing effect. *Psychological Science, 4,* 316–321.

Barcroft, J. (2007). Effects of opportunities for word retrieval during second language vocabulary learning. *Language Learning, 57,* 35–56.

Barcroft, J. (2012). *Input-based incremental vocabulary instruction.* Alexandria, VA: TESOL International Association.

Barcroft, J. (2015). *Lexical input processing and vocabulary learning.* Amsterdam and Philadelphia, PA: John Benjamins.

Barcroft, J., & Sommers, M. S. (2005). Effects of acoustic variability on second language vocabulary learning. *Studies in Second Language Acquisition, 27,* 387–414.

Barcroft, J., Sommers, M., & Sunderman, G. (2011). Some costs of fooling Mother Nature: A priming study on the keyword method and the quality of developing L2 lexical representation. In P. Trofimovic & K. McDonough (Eds.), *Applying priming research to L2 learning and teaching: Insights from psycholinguistics* (pp. 49–72). Amsterdam: John Benjamins.

Coady, J. (1997). L2 vocabulary acquisition: A synthesis of research. In J. Coady & T. Huckin (Eds.), *Second language vocabulary acquisition* (pp. 273–290). Amsterdam: John Benjamins.

Coady, J., & Huckin, T. (1997). *Second language vocabulary acquisition: A rationale for pedagogy.* Cambridge, UK: Cambridge University Press.

Dang, T. N. Y., & Webb, S. (2016). Making an essential word list for beginners. In I. S. P. Nation (Ed.), *Making and using word lists for language learning and testing* (pp. 153–167, 188–195). Amsterdam: John Benjamins.

De Groot, A. M. B. (2006). Effects of stimulus characteristics and background music on foreign language vocabulary learning and forgetting. *Language Learning, 56,* 463–506.

Elgort, I. (2011). Deliberate learning and vocabulary acquisition in a second language. *Language Learning, 61*, 367–413.

Ellis, N., & Beaton, A. (1993). Factors affecting the learning of foreign language vocabulary: Imagery keyword mediators and phonological short-term memory. *Quarterly Journal of Experimental Psychology, 46A*, 533–558.

Gass, S. (1987). Introduction. *Studies in Second Language Acquisition, 9*(2), 129–132.

Greene, R. L. (1992). *Human memory. Paradigms and paradoxes*. Hinsdale, NJ: Lawrence Erlbaum.

Hulstijn, J. (1997). Mnemonic methods in foreign language vocabulary learning: Theoretical considerations and pedagogical implications. In J. Coady & T. Huckin (Eds.), *Second language vocabulary acquisition* (pp. 203–224). Melbourne: Cambridge University Press.

Hulstijn, J. H., Hollander, M., & Greidanus, T. (1996). Incidental vocabulary learning by advanced foreign language students: The influence of marginal glosses, dictionary use, and recurrence of unknown words. *Modern Language Journal, 80*, 327–339.

Kida, S. (2010, March). *The role of quality and quantity of vocabulary processing in incidental L2 vocabulary acquisition through reading*. Paper presented on March 7, 2010 at the Annual Conference of the American Association of Applied Linguistics in Atlanta, GA.

Kole, J. A. (2007). *The retrieval process in mediated learning: Using priming effects to test the direct access and covert mediation models*. Doctoral dissertation, University of Colorado, Boulder, CO.

Kroll, J. F., & Sunderman, G. (2003). Cognitive processes in second language learners and bilinguals: The development of lexical and conceptual representations. In C. Doughty & M. Long (Eds.), *Handbook of second language acquisition* (pp. 104–129). Cambridge, MA: Blackwell.

McNamara, D. S., & Healy, A. F. (1995). A generation advantage for multiplication skill training and nonword vocabulary acquisition. In A. F. Healy & L. E. Bourne, Jr. (Eds.), *Learning and memory of knowledge and skills: Durability and specificity* (pp. 132–169). Thousand Oaks, CA: Sage.

Myers, G. C. (1914). Recall in relation to retention. *Journal of Educational Psychology, 5*, 119–130.

Nation, I. S. P. (2016). *Making and using word lists for language learning and testing*. Amsterdam: John Benjamins.

Nation, I. S. P., & Waring. (1997). Vocabulary size, text coverage and word lists. In N. Schmitt & M. McCarthy (Eds.), *Vocabulary: Description, acquisition and pedagogy* (pp. 238–254). Amsterdam: John Benjamins.

Roediger, H. L., & Guynn, M. J. (1996). Retrieval processes. In E. L. Bjork & R. A. Bjork (Eds.), *Memory* (pp. 197–236). San Diego, CA: Academic Press.

Rott, S. (1999). The effect of exposure frequency on intermediate language learners' incidental vocabulary acquisition and retention through reading. *Studies in Second Language Acquisition, 21*(4), 589–619.

Royer, J. M. (1973). Memory effects for test-like events during acquisition of foreign language vocabulary. *Psychological Reports, 32*, 195–198.

Sagarra, N., & Alba, M. (2006). The key is in the keyword: L2 vocabulary learning methods with beginning learners of Spanish. *Modern Language Journal, 90*, 228–243.

Schmitt, N., & McCarthy, M. (Eds.). (1997). *Vocabulary: Description, acquisition, and pedagogy*. Cambridge, UK: Cambridge University Press.

Slamecka, N. J., & Graf, P. (1978). The generation effect: Delineation of a phenomenon. *Journal of Experimental Psychology, 4*, 6, 592–604.

Sommers, M., & Barcroft, J. (2007). An integrated account of the effects of acoustic variability in L1 and L2: Evidence from amplitude, fundamental frequency, and speaking rate variability. *Applied Psycholinguistics, 28*, 231–249.

van Hell, J. G., & Mahn, A. C. (1997). Keyword mnemonics versus rote rehearsal: Learning concrete and abstract foreign words by experienced and inexperienced learners. *Language Learning, 47*(3), 507–546.

Webb, S. (2007). The effects of synonymy on second-language vocabulary learning. *Reading in a Foreign Language, 19*, 120–136.

Wong, W., & Pyun, D. O. (2012). The effects of sentence writing on L2 French and Korean lexical retention. *The Canadian Modern Language Review, 68*, 164–189.

31
Key Issues in Teaching Multiword Items

Brent Wolter

Introduction

Despite the widespread belief that multiword items (MWIs) are pervasive (e.g., Nattinger & DeCarrico, 1992; Erman & Warren, 2000) and important for fluency and general proficiency in an L2 (Schmitt, 2004; Wray, 2000, 2002), they are often neglected in language curricula. There are several possible reasons for this. One is simply inertia. In some parts of the world the preferred L2 pedagogy still places a strong emphasis on grammar with little attention paid to vocabulary beyond single words. Nonetheless, there are likely other reasons that are more practical and less ideological and traditional. One is a lack of consistency in terminology describing MWIs, which makes them difficult for teachers and learners to fully grasp. Wray (2000, p. 465), for example, lists nearly 50 terms that have been used in the research literature to describe MWIs. Naturally, this variability in terminology makes it difficult for someone perusing the research literature to gain a solid understanding of the various types of MWIs and what differentiates them. As Wray (2008, p. 93) has suggested, "you cannot reliably identify something unless you can define it", and MWIs have managed to evade consistent definition for quite some time (see also Wood, this volume).

To some extent, this lack of precision probably arises from confusion regarding what could be called structural vs. semantic labels for MWIs. Idioms, for example, are typically considered MWIs, and for good reason; they are typically composed of multiple words linked to a single idea or meaning (Sprenger, Levelt, & Kempen, 2006). Nonetheless, it is their opaque semantic qualities, rather than their structural qualities, that make them of theoretical interest and define them as idioms. There are relatively few structural restrictions on idioms, and as such they can take many forms such as verb phrases (e.g., *to twist someone's arm*) noun phrases (e.g., *the big cheese*), prepositional phrases (e.g., *between a rock and a hard place*), etc.

Other MWIs, however, tend to be defined not by their semantic qualities but by their structural qualities. What typically makes a phrasal verb an MWI is not its degree of transparency, but rather its structural qualities as a verb followed by an adverbial particle or (sometimes) preposition. This observation notwithstanding, phrasal verbs are still often highly idiomatic in nature (e.g., *put up* [*with someone/something*] or *stick up* [*for someone*]). Similar claims can be made in respect to other MWIs like binomials and trinomials. Many binomials will be fully transparent (e.g., *black and white* or *bride and groom*), while many trinomials will be idiomatic (e.g., *hook, line, and sinker* or *lock, stock, and barrel*).

Perhaps further complicating the situation is the fact that some researchers have approached formulaicity, which is conceptually (and practically) closely associated with MWIs, from more of a psychological perspective. Wray's influential work in this area (e.g., Wray, 2002; 2008) is based on her definition of a formulaic sequence as "a sequence, continuous or discontinuous, of words or other meaning elements, which is, or appears to be, prefabricated: that is, stored and retrieved whole from memory at the time of use, rather than being subject to generation or analysis by the language grammar" (2000, p. 465). This definition circumvents issues regarding distinctions in structure and semantics entirely, and instead focuses on psychological aspects.

Obviously, there are no overt attempts to be deceptive or subversive amongst researchers working in these areas. Terms are being applied in a principled manner, and there is no reason why a phrasal verb, for example, cannot be simultaneously defined in terms of its structure and its degree of transparency (or possibly even its qualities as a psychologically unified sequence). Nonetheless, it stands to reason that the tendency to place MWIs into a single, overarching category that (at least partially) disregards qualitative differences amongst the different types of MWIs sometimes causes unnecessary confusion. Once the distinctions become a little clearer, we can start to see why labels for different MWIs are so often used in inconsistent and/or overlapping ways. For example, Liu's (2003) list of the most frequent idioms in spoken American English shares a number of items with Shin and Nation's (2007) list of the most frequent spoken collocations in British English, including expressions like *in fact*, *as far as*, and *as well*. In contrast, the online Cambridge Dictionary labels *in fact* as a discourse marker, and *as far as* and *as well* simply as adverbs. In reality, none of these labels are wrong; the authors have just approached the same structures from different theoretical and/or historical perspectives.

Nonetheless, this leaves practitioners (both teachers and materials developers) in the unenviable position of trying to sort out and explain to learners what constitutes a particular type of MWI and what distinguishes it from other similar patterns. One possible solution to this problem is simply to approach MWIs from a statistical perspective with the aid of corpora. This allows practitioners to compile lists of the most frequent MWIs in language while disregarding the sometimes tricky distinctions between types of MWIs and their associated ambiguities. From a teaching/learning perspective, however, this approach offers limited help. This is because it ignores important distinctions in types of MWIs (no matter how imprecise these distinctions sometimes are), and in doing so dismisses distinguishing aspects of MWIs that can be very helpful from a pedagogical perspective. Mastering phrasal verbs, for example, also means mastering the movement aspect of the adverbial particle, which is sometimes optional but in other cases mandatory (see later in the chapter). With collocations, on the other hand, mastery requires not only the issue of movement, but also an understanding that languages tend to prefer certain combinations of words to express a given idea, even if other configurations are grammatically possible and seem equally plausible. Furthermore, it involves understanding that "correctness" is a variable concept when applied to collocations. That is, while some word combinations are clearly preferred and others are clearly non-preferred, many others will lie between these extremes such that they might seem possible or acceptable to native speakers, even if they are unlikely or uncommon. It is for these reasons that it seems reasonable to retain these distinctions with an eye on the fact that different MWIs will display different qualities that often lead to a unique set of challenges for learners trying to master them.

Critical Issues and Topics

In this section, I will take a closer look at three types of MWIs that seem essential for L2 learners to achieve even modest levels of mastery in English. I will start with phrasal verbs and collocations before moving on to considering idioms. My perspective on these MWIs will be pedagogical. Under this broad framework, however, I will start by considering what aspects of these MWIs are problematic for learners before moving on to some practical considerations regarding how they might be managed for curricular purposes and taught in the classroom. I will start by considering what are likely the most common and problematic MWIs for learners, specifically phrasal verbs.

Phrasal Verbs

Although phrasal verbs are pervasive in both spoken and written English, they are also some of the most difficult for L2 learners to master. Gardner and Davies (2007, p. 339), for example, assert that phrasal verbs are "one of the most notoriously challenging aspects of English language instruction". There are likely a number of reasons for this. One is the fact that phrasal verbs are, almost without exception, massively polysemous. Furthermore, many of these meanings will vary in respect to their degree of transparency. The phrasal verb *make out*, for example, can be interpreted in at least five ways, as demonstrated in the following examples extracted from the Corpus of Contemporary American English (COCA: Davies, 2008–).

Example 1

1a *I could **make out** a faint murmur.*
1b *If you're expected to **make out** with a guy on the first date, then it can be creepy.*
1c *And to think he had the nerve to break up with me and **make out** like it was my fault.*
1d *Mr. Snow and other executives like him **made out** like bandits.*
1e *How'd you **make out** at the track, dear?*

This is only one such instance; however, most phrasal verbs demonstrate highly polysemous tendencies. For example, in a corpus-based investigation of phrasal verbs using the British National Corpus, Gardner and Davies (2007) reported that the 100 most frequent verb + adverbial particle constructions had an average of 5.6 different meanings. Naturally, this level of polysemy means that even if a learner masters one meaning of a phrasal verb their knowledge may not serve them well in other contexts.

Related to this are issues related to the aforementioned lack of transparency for many of the meaning senses of phrasal verbs. White (2012) observed that there are no fewer than 21 different definitions for the phrasal verb *go on* listed in *The American Heritage Dictionary of Phrasal Verbs* (see also Garnier & Schmitt, 2015). Although some of these multiple definitions will be related semantically (see Ravin & Leacock, 2000), others will not. White (2012, p. 420) draws on the examples of *go on* meaning to start (*he just went on Vicodin*) and *go on* referring to turning a particular age (*she's going on 40*). Although it could be argued that both usages refer to beginning something, White (2012, p. 420) notes that "the relationship between beginning to take medication and turning a particular age is not obvious".

There are also syntactic qualities of phrasal verbs that make them challenging. One is that adverbial particles in many phrasal verbs often closely resemble prepositions, and as such learners might confuse them as marking the start of a prepositional phrase. This becomes most problematic when movement is involved, since particles can be placed after the object of the phrasal verb (a regularly mandatory movement when the object is a personal pronoun), while such movement is naturally not possible for prepositions in prepositional phrases. This phenomenon can be seen in Examples 2 (particle) and 3 (preposition).

Example 2

2a   *I picked up my brother.*
2b   *I picked my brother up.*
2c   *I picked up him.**
2d   *I picked him up.*

Example 3

3a   *I picked on my brother.*
3b   *I picked my brother on.**
3c   *I picked on him.*
3d   *I picked him on.**

(Note: the asterisk symbol (*) indicates an incorrect expression or formulation.)

Other qualities of phrasal verbs that make them challenging are the fact that their use can vary according to register (Liu, 2011) and their ubiquity (Celce-Murcia & Larsen-Freeman, 1999). In respect to ubiquity, Gardner and Davies (2007), estimate that learners will encounter one phrasal verb for every 150 English words they encounter.

Clearly then, the task faced by L2 learners and L2 teachers in respect to phrasal verbs is formidable. Nonetheless, there are some steps that can make the learning/teaching process for phrasal verbs considerably more manageable. A first crucial step is to reduce the learning load presented by phrasal verbs by lowering the number of items that need to be learned and taught, a task that can be aided by the use of corpora. Gardner and Davies (2007) observed that the 100-million-word British National Corpus contained a total of 518,923 instances of phrasal verb usage. However, they observed that more than one half of these occurrences consisted of "20 lexical verbs combine[d] with eight adverbial particles" (p. 339). Furthermore, they noted that about one-half of these instances could be accounted for by 100 specific phrasal verbs. In respect to the issue of polysemy discussed earlier, Gardner and Davies' (2007) analysis revealed that these 100 phrasal verbs had 559 potential meanings. These are still sizeable numbers, but clearly within the range of what could reasonably be learned.

In an attempt to better understand potential effects of register on phrasal verb use, Liu (2011) revisited the issue of phrasal verbs using Gardner and Davies' list, as well as an earlier corpus-based list compiled by Biber, Johansson, Leech, Conrad, and Finegan (1999). His investigation was supplemented through the use of four dictionaries of phrasal verbs. Liu observed that phrasal verb usage was significantly higher (per million words) in COCA's spoken and fiction subcorpora than in the magazine, newspaper, and academic subcorpora. Perhaps unsurprisingly, usage was significantly lowest in the academic subcorpus. Liu also generated a list of the 150 most common phrasal verbs. Although his list resembled Gardner and Davies' (2007) list and Biber et al.'s (1999) list to a large extent, it also included additional useful information from a pedagogical perspective that highlighted the main findings of his investigation (like the dispersal ratings across corpora, for instance).

A more recent attempt to refine Liu's list was taken up by Garnier and Schmitt (2015). Like their predecessors, Garnier and Schmitt recognized the potentially overwhelming learning burden posed by phrasal verbs and the need to identify essential phrasal verbs for pedagogical purposes. However, Garnier and Schmitt's work makes a unique contribution by also considering the thorny issue of polysemy which, as mentioned earlier, presents one of the biggest challenges related to phrasal verbs. Garnier and Schmitt state their goal as reducing "the total number of meaning senses to be acquired down to a manageable number based on frequency criteria" (2015, p. 652). To achieve this, they drew on a number of sources, including collocational dictionaries, COCA, and human judgments. The result of their efforts was the Phrasal Verb Pedagogical (PHaVE) list. The list not only catalogs the 150 most frequent phrasal verbs, but also provides definitions for the most common meaning senses along with the percentage of usages covered by these definitions. By disregarding meaning senses that were comparatively low in frequency, Garnier and Schmitt managed to reduce the total number of senses for all 150 items down to 288, which is clearly much more manageable than 559 senses identified by Gardner and Davies (2007).

Naturally, finding ways to reduce the learning burden can help a good deal with phrasal verbs. Nonetheless, even once this has been achieved, learners are still faced with the other difficulties outlined earlier. Gardner and Davies' (2007) investigation provided some potential solutions. From their corpus investigations, Gardner and Davies observed that the words like *out*, *up*, *down*, and *back* were usually used as adverbial particles while words like *in*, *under*, *by*, and *across* were almost always used as prepositions. This sort of information can also be imparted to learners so that they can at least make more informed assumptions regarding the likelihood of a phrasal verb vs. a verb followed by a prepositional phrase.

As far as classroom-based approaches are concerned, there have been a handful of attempts at evaluating the effectiveness of different techniques for teaching phrasal verbs. However, they have met with modest success. Nassaji and Tian (2010) investigated the effectiveness of two task types in two learning conditions on the acquisition of phrasal verbs. The tasks involved a cloze activity in which participants provided a missing phrasal verb and an editing activity in which participants identified a misused phrasal verb and corrected it. As for the conditions, Nassaji and Tian (2010) compared completion of the tasks both individually and collaboratively. The results showed better completion of the task in the collaborative condition, but no differences in respect to acquisition (as measured by a posttest). Nonetheless, they did report significant gains in knowledge for the editing task over the cloze task, a finding the authors attribute to a "higher degree of negotiation and scaffolding generated by the editing task" (pp. 412–413).

Another attempt to test the effectiveness of teaching techniques on the acquisition of phrasal verbs was reported by White (2012). Drawing on ideas from cognitive linguistics and sociocultural theory, White's approach was to have participants focus on the "spatial sense" of the particles in phrasal verbs and to connect this sense "to the opaque or idiomatic meaning" of phrasal verbs (p. 425). Using a highly inductive approach, ESL students were asked to identify, define, and create drawings depicting a set of phrasal verbs. These drawings were then shared with other students in the hope that they might promote acquisition and retention of the phrasal verbs. Statistical analyses performed on a pretest-posttest task showed a significant improvement for items that were evaluated in both testing sessions (specifically eight phrasal verbs ending with either the particle *up* or *out*), but no significant gains were reported for items for all 16 items used in the treatment. This indicates that there may have been a learning effect for the items that appeared on both tests, but that the teaching method as a whole did not significantly improve learning of phrasal verbs.

Given the lack of comparative teaching techniques in both these studies, and the lack of convincing results, it is difficult to conclude that either approach was particularly effective at teaching phrasal verbs. All we can reasonably conclude from these studies is that learners gained some knowledge of phrasal verbs through focused study, but it may have been the amount of study, rather than the type of study, that impacted learning. Nonetheless, given their importance and prominence in spoken English, it would seem prudent to include phrasal verbs with reference to the lists just described.

Collocations

As with multiword units in general, the term collocation has been subject to variation based in part on what theoretical perspective one takes (Barfield & Gyllstad, 2009). On the one hand, there is the approach that has developed since the advent of corpus linguistics in the early 1980s. This approach (e.g., Sinclair, 1991) relies on statistical measures of co-occurrence to define collocations. The operative notion underlying this approach is if a particular word co-occurs with another word (or set of words) much more frequently than we would expect given that word's overall frequency, then it should be viewed as a significant collocation. The other view centralizes semantic issues in arriving at a definition of collocation. This view is associated with the phraseological study of collocations (e.g., Howarth, 1998). In this tradition, for a set of words to be considered a "true" collocation, one of the words needs to be used in an at least a slightly figurative sense. Thus, despite its common co-occurrence, a word combination like *pay (the) bills* would be considered a so-called free combination rather than a collocation, since both words are being used in their literal, core sense. A combination like *pay attention*, on the other hand, would be considered a collocation since *pay* is used in a figurative rather than a literal sense.

Where both camps agree, however, is in respect to the fact that although languages often provide a number of potential ways a particular formulation could be expressed, only a small subset of these will be seen as acceptable by native speakers of a particular language. In English, for instance, words like *heavy* and *hard* are frequently used to describe the intensity of rain, while *strong* and *powerful* are not. When it comes to *wind* or *winds*, however, *heavy*, *strong*, and *powerful* are commonly used, while *hard* is not. To some extent, this may be related to the semantic properties of the individual words, since it could be argued that collocational knowledge is in many ways an extension of semantic knowledge (e.g., Jarvis & Pavlenko, 2007, p. 74). Nonetheless, L2 learners will often not be aware of the finer semantic distinctions between near-synonyms, and as such collocational combinations may seem more or less random from their perspective. Compounding this situation is the likelihood that learners often import semantic information from L1 words to L2 words, meaning their L2 lexical entries for certain words often do not align well with native speakers' entries for the same words (e.g., Jiang, 2000). One result of this is that learners often produce L1-like collocations in the L2 (Wolter & Song, under review). Where there is overlap between L1 and L2 collocational patterns, this will likely not cause any issues. When there is a mismatch between the L1 and the L2, however, at best the L2 speaker's collocational choices will mark them as sounding non-native like. At worst, it could lead to misunderstandings and miscommunication.

This situation is further compounded by the fact that because learners can often rely on word-based knowledge for comprehending collocations on a receptive level, they might not recognize a particular collocation as a standardized way of expressing a particular concept or idea. As Wray (2002) explains:

> The adult language learner, on encountering major catastrophe, would break it down into a word meaning "big" and a word meaning "disaster" and store the words separately, without any information about the fact that they went together. When the need arose in the future to express the idea again, they would have no memory of major catastrophe as the pairing originally encountered, and any pairing of words with the right meaning would seem equally plausible.

(p. 209)

Although subsequent studies have indicated that L2 learners are capable of recognizing common collocations in a manner that at least resembles holistic storage of collocations (e.g., Durrant & Schmitt, 2010), the fact remains that this compositional aspect of collocations can make them less salient to learners, which in turn may inhibit their acquisition. In short, learners often fail to recognize collocations as regularly occurring, routinized expressions, and while this may have minimal impact on them when using language receptively, it will have an effect in productive settings.

Indeed, research has indicated that productive collocation errors are common amongst L2 learners, even higher proficiency speakers, and that a key source of these errors is L1 interference. This was observed by Nesselhauf (2003) and Zhou (2016), both of whom investigated the causes of errors in L2 productive collocations. Nesselhauf, investigating the productive collocations of advanced learners of L2 English with L1 German, observed that nearly half of all the English collocational errors could be traced back to the influence of German. Similarly Zhou, focusing exclusively on the productive use of the verb *have* by L1 Chinese learners of English, concluded that the learners "employed a literal translation strategy and borrowed L1 equivalence of a collocation in the production of L2" (2016, p. 49). Similar findings were reported by Altenberg (2001) who looked at the productive use of the English word *make* among advanced L1 speakers of both French and Swedish, and Wolter and Song (under review) who looked at the productive collocations of L1 speakers of Chinese for ten high-frequency English verbs.

In addition to potential problems caused by L1–L2 interference, another aspect of collocations that makes them challenging to L2 learners is their pervasiveness. This quality of collocations is similar to phrasal verbs. But whereas phrasal verbs tend to feature most prominently in spoken and fictional genres, collocations are found in abundance across all registers. As noted in the *Oxford Collocations Dictionary*, "Collocation runs through the whole of the English language. No piece of natural spoken or written English is totally free of collocation" (p. v). Nonetheless, it appears that some collocations feature much more prominently in certain registers than others, while other collocations can have different interpretations based on the register in which it is situated. McCarthy, O'Keeffe, and Walsh (2010) make this point in reference to the English collocation *going forward*. They argue that in general settings, this collocation can be interpreted rather literally as an indication of movement through space. In business settings, however, they state that it is used to mean something akin to *from this point on*. Thus, collocations also seem sometimes to have an element of polysemy that is linked to register. Both of these qualities, specifically pervasiveness and variability across registers, also make collocations challenging to learners.

As with phrasal verbs, there have been attempts to identify the most common collocations for pedagogical purposes, such as Shin and Nation's (2008) corpus-based list mentioned earlier. Such lists can provide teachers and learners with a good starting place. Nonetheless, it is hard to imagine a situation in which a reasonably comprehensive, but still manageable, list of collocations could be generated. In addition to pervasiveness, one difficulty in generating such a list is the inherent flexibility of collocations. Whereas phrasal verbs behave more or less like single words, and as such a combination of a verb plus an adverbial particle either is or is not a phrasal verb, collocations typically vary in respect to their acceptability. That is, while some collocations will be viewed as definitely acceptable and others as definitely unacceptable, others will exist in a gray area where the collocation may be possible but unlikely. Compounding this situation is the fact that proficient language users will sometimes intentionally use nonstandard or entirely unique collocations in an attempt to create new perspectives on subjects. This, in turn, can create a poetic effect which can clearly be seen in many great works of poetry. One example is the final four lines of William Butler Yeats' well-known poem "The Second Coming":

> That twenty centuries of stony sleep
> Were vexed to nightmare by a rocking cradle,
> And what rough beast, its hour come round at last,
> Slouches towards Bethlehem to be born?

This short passage contains a number of nonstandard collocations such as *stony sleep*, *vexed to nightmare*, *rough beast*, and *slouch toward [some location]*. Yet they serve to mark Yeats as one who has achieved great mastery of the English language rather than a person who is struggling to sound native-like. This situation with collocations, then, creates something of a double standard for L2 speakers, since their nonstandard use of collocations will often be viewed as an indication of lack of knowledge of collocational patterns rather than an expression of creativity. It is therefore important for teachers to allow for some level of creativity for collocations in settings where nonstandard uses might be warranted.

Nonetheless, there will still certainly be a number of situations in which L2 speakers generate nonstandard or even unacceptable collocations not out of attempts at creativity, but out of lack of knowledge. So it is perhaps not surprising that a number of researchers have endeavored to learn more about what leads to learning standard L2 collocations. One technique that has frequently been endorsed is simply raising learners' awareness of collocations as a common and integral aspect of language, and asking them to attend to collocations in their language input. Lewis (1993), for example, has suggested that teachers can encourage learners to "chunk" texts by identifying multiword units such as strong collocations, a view that was later echoed by Nation (2001). Unfortunately, however, the empirical evidence suggests that this approach has only marginal impact on acquisition and retention of formulaic language, including collocations (e.g., Boers, Eyckmans, Kappel, Stengers, &

Demecheleer, 2006; Jones & Haywood, 2004). One solution that has been proposed is some form of typological enhancement (e.g., bold lettering, underlining, etc.). This approach has indicated that learners do notice enhanced collocations better than unenhanced collocations (e.g., Bishop, 2004; Peters, 2012), but as Boers and Lindstromberg (2012) point out, these studies involved some methodological aspects that limit the extent to which strong conclusions can be drawn.

The incidental learning technique that seems to have shown the most promise is one that exposes learners to the same collocations repeatedly. In one recent study, Pellicer-Sánchez (2017) found significant positive gains in knowledge for learners who were incidentally exposed to collocations (consisting of adjective-pseudoword constructions) either four or eight times in a self-constructed 2,309-word text. However, no significant difference was reported for the four-exposure vs. the eight-exposure group, indicating that the additional exposures had a negligible effect on learning. This finding partially overlaps with findings reported in Webb, Newton, and Chang (2013), who investigated the effectiveness of learning collocations through reading a text coupled with listening. These researchers exposed participants to collocations 1, 5, 10, or 15 times. They found significant gains in receptive knowledge of collocations that aligned with number of exposures for all four groups. Specifically, they reported gains of 27%, 33%, 55%, and 76% for the four exposure conditions, respectively. Perhaps not surprisingly, however, receptive gains considerably surpassed productive gains at all exposure levels. Other studies (e.g., Szudarski, 2012; Szudarski & Carter, 2014) have reported more modest gains through purely incidental exposure and enhanced incidental exposure (i.e., collocations presented with textual enhancement). Nonetheless the research as a whole suggests that repetition of exposure can improve collocational learning. In this respect, as Pellicer-Sánchez (2017) points out, incidental learning of collocations seems akin to incidental learning of individual words.

Other researchers have looked at the efficacy of various explicit forms of teaching collocation. Perhaps unsurprisingly, most studies have found that learners do show gains in collocational knowledge from explicit instruction. However, there are some factors that seem to increase (or lessen) the effectiveness of such instruction. Laufer and Girsai (2008), for example, investigated the learning of collocations in three conditions: meaning-focused instruction, form-focused instruction, and contrastive analysis and translation. They reported significantly higher gains, both immediate and delayed, for the contrastive analysis and translation group. They attributed these findings to the hypotheses of "noticing", "pushed-output", and "task-induced involvement". In terms of repetition in explicit learning, Peters (2014), found better and more durable gains in collocational knowledge for learners who took part in activities that had a greater number or repetitions. However, she noted that single words were retained better than collocations, indicating that single words were still easier to learn. In contrast to these positive findings regarding explicit learning, Boers, Demecheleer, Coxhead, and Webb (2014) tested the effectiveness of three matching exercises for verb-noun collocations. They reported minimal gains in knowledge, and suggested that matching exercises might even be detrimental due to learners developing memory traces for false connections. Overall, the research indicates that explicit learning can be effective, but some approaches are more effective than others.

Aside from types of instruction, there seem to be qualities of collocations themselves that tend to make them easier or more difficult to learn. One quality that has been shown time and again to affect learning is congruency vs. incongruency (see Peters, 2014).

Congruency describes a situation in which the collocation has an equivalent form in the learner's L1 (e.g., *strong wind* for an L1 Japanese learner who has the same word-for-word collocation of *tsuyoi kaze* in Japanese). Incongruency occurs when there is no direct, word-for-word translation in the L1 (e.g., *high wind(s)*, which would translate into the infelicitous *takaii kaze* in Japanese). In fact, research investigating L2 processing of congruent vs. incongruent collocations has shown a consistent advantage for congruent collocations, even amongst high-proficiency learners (e.g., Wolter & Gyllstad, 2011, 2013; Wolter & Yamashita, 2017), indicating that this phenomenon might have a psychological basis. In addition to congruency, Webb and Kagimoto (2011) reported that collocations for node words with a higher number of collocates were easier to learn than collocations for node words with fewer collocates. Synonymy, however, had the opposite effect; it was harder to learn synonymous collocations together than it was to learn unrelated collocations. Finally, Peters (2016) reported that adjective-noun collocations were easier to learn than verb-noun collocations.

Unfortunately, the research to date has focused mostly on receptive learning, with productive knowledge of collocations being tested far less frequently. Furthermore, when productive knowledge is tested, it tends to be assessed in rather restricted tasks, such as supplying one word of a two-word collocation in a fill-in-the-gap type exercise. While these sorts of restrictions are helpful from an empirical standpoint, they also limit our understanding of how learners approach collocations in more authentic, productive scenarios. Perhaps ironically, a key to understanding how learners formulate productive collocations might involve stepping away from a focus on collocations as MWIs, and instead focusing our attention on the semantic properties of the node words in collocations. As noted previously, research into L2 vocabulary acquisition has indicated that learners regularly transfer semantic and conceptual information from L1 words to their L2 lexical entries (Jiang, 2000; Jarvis & Pavlenko, 2010). When there is a very close match in semantics between an L1 word and its (so-called) L2 equivalent, this sort of transfer poses no major problems. However, this is frequently not the case, and in many cases there will be misalignment between L2 words and their common translations in the L2. Wolter (2006) for example, mentioned how Japanese-English dictionaries frequently provide a definition of *narrow* to the Japanese word *semai* and a definition of *wide* to the Japanese word *hiroi*. Nonetheless, these pairs of words are far from equivalent. *Semai* means not only *narrow*, but also *small or crowded* (e.g., with many things) in general. A similar pattern exists for *hiroi* which can be used to refer not only to wide things, but large things in general. Nonetheless, learners are often unaware of such discrepancies, and as such L1 Japanese speakers of L2 English have a tendency to produce collocations such as *narrow room* in English when *small room* would in fact be more appropriate (see also Wolter, Yamashita, & Leung, in preparation).

From a teaching and learning perspective, these results indicate that it might be useful (when possible) for teachers to point out differences in meaning between L1 words and their typical L2 translations in the hope that learners will be able to modify their understanding of the L2 words and ultimately produce more native-like collocations. This view is echoed by Liu (2010), who advocates having students, with the help of corpora, overtly focus their attention on why one keyword is chosen in place of seemingly plausible alternatives (e.g., *make a mistake* vs. *take* or *do a mistake*). He argues that this sort of activity not only helps learners understand which collocations are preferred in their L2, but also helps them to refine their understanding of the component words.

Overall, the research to date indicates that there are several factors that might influence the learning (and learnability) of collocations in an L2. However, simply asking learners to "chunk" or pay attention to longer stretches of language, such as collocations, might not be particularly effective. Instead, it seems the best approach is one that uses either carefully structured incidental reading activities, explicit instruction, or perhaps a combination of the two. If incidental approaches are used, then textual enhancement combined with repetition might be the most effective. If a teacher opts for a more explicit approach, then care should be taken to design activities that are going to be effective and, obviously, avoid activities, such as matching exercises, that might in fact be detrimental through the false input they provide. As far as productive training is concerned, our knowledge of this still lags behind what we know about receptive training. Nonetheless, it appears that focusing on semantic distinctions between L1 and L2 words, or various potential L2 words, may provide a useful method. One advantage of this is it has the potential to influence the range of collocations for a particular node word, which would likely be more efficient than teaching and learning collocations one at a time.

Idioms

As noted previously, idiomaticity is a quality that affects language at all grain sizes. Indeed, some researchers (e.g., Cooper, 1998) believe that even common metaphorical extensions of single words classify these words as idioms (e.g., the verb *weigh* in the expression *weigh a decision*). Wherever one chooses to draw the line between idiomatic and non-idiomatic, however, most researchers in this area would agree that there are qualities of idioms that distinguish them from other MWIs, and as such they deserve classification, recognition, and analysis as a separate category. Furthermore, most (if not all) researchers would agree that idioms display variations in two key ways: degree of idiomaticity and level of fixedness.

To account for variations in idiomaticity, several researchers have proposed frameworks for classifying idioms (and sometimes other MWIs) according to variations in semantic opacity. Howarth (1998), for example, described a continuum that classified MWIs into four categories: free combinations, collocations, figurative idioms, and pure idioms (see preceding for Howarth's distinction between free combinations and collocations). Figurative idioms are expressions that have both a literal and figurative expression (e.g., *under the microscope*), while pure idioms are expressions that are purely figurative and have no obvious literal interpretation (e.g., *under the weather*). Similar categorizations for idioms were proposed by Fernando (1996, p. 32) who used the terms "literal", "semiliteral", and "pure".

At first glance, these distinctions may seem more important for lexicographers and semanticists than for teachers and materials developers. However, there are clearly pedagogical implications as well. If one takes an extremely conservative approach in defining idioms, as has historically been the case in Chomskyan (1965) approaches to language, then pure idioms, and possibly some figurative/semiliteral idioms, would be the only truly idiomatic expressions. And as these are comparatively rare, and often not entirely necessary for effective expression, one might conclude that they should be reserved for upper intermediate and advanced learners of English as an L2 (to use one such idiom, *the icing on the cake*). However, if a more moderate (and probably more grounded) view is taken, then it soon becomes apparent that idioms need to be learned from a fairly early stage in L2 development.

The learning challenges posed by idioms are obvious and in line with challenges posed by the other MWIs reviewed in this chapter thus far. The first concern is dealing with opacity and the fact that many learners will have been trained to use a so-called words and rules approach in deciphering language. This renders interpretation of many idioms challenging, particularly when the context is insufficient in promoting successful inference. In many cases, then, idioms will have to be learned as separate lexical items with a fairly unique meaning assigned to them. Of course, many idioms will have a more literal equivalent expression, which will express more or less the same meaning. So learning idioms also involves learning how they are different in nuance from their literal equivalent, as well as potential register restrictions that may vary from idiom to idiom. Some idioms will be mostly used in informal registers while others will find their way into a number of different registers. Another similarity with idioms (and the other MWIs addressed here) is in respect to uncovering which idioms are essential for learners and which can be left to later in their learning experience. Jackendoff (1997) estimated that there are no fewer than 25,000 idioms in the English language, which clearly represents an unobtainable goal for most L2 learners (and perhaps native speakers). Furthermore, Liu (2003) points out that there are often considerable regional differences in idiom use, no doubt due in no small part to the fact that idiomatic expressions are tightly connected with the cultures that spawn them (e.g., the number of baseball-related idioms in American English), which makes a fully universal approach difficult to realize. Indeed, perhaps more than any other aspect of language, idioms are highly representative of and deeply ingrained in the culture(s) in which they are used.

In addition to opacity, number, and the cultural aspects, another potential problem area for idioms is their propensity to vary in terms of fixedness. As is well documented (e.g., Moon, 1998) some idioms are entirely fixed expressions with no room for lexical variation. Idiomatic expressions like *kick the bucket, under the weather, shooting fish in a barrel*, and *between a rock and a hard place* are seemingly not open to lexical variation, and failure to recognize this will, for most native speakers, instantly flag a person as a non-native speaker (e.g., **punt the bucket* or **between a stone and a hard place*). Others, however, allow for greater flexibility. Based on a corpus analysis, Moon (1998) estimated that around 40% of idioms and fixed expressions in English allowed for some form of variation. Nonetheless, these variations can also sometimes be limited, as in *beat/flog a dead horse*, or *up/raise the ante/stakes*, which have slots that usually vary in one of two ways. Other idioms that show greater variability include *have (one's) cake and eat it too*, which is amenable to all possessive pronouns.

Idioms in L2 learning/teaching contexts have been extensively researched for quite some time. Unsurprisingly, a first step is to reduce the number of idioms to a more manageable number. Many major publishers have dictionaries of idioms, but these are still extensive, and as such only provide partial relief to the sizeable learning burden. It is with this in mind that some researchers have endeavored to create more manageable corpus-based lists that learners and teachers can reference for pedagogical purposes. One such list is Liu's (2003) aforementioned collection of the 100 most frequent idioms in spoken American English. Although this approach provides an excellent starting point, it is no doubt insufficient beyond the most basic levels of proficiency.

Other strategies that have been proposed include using a word-based approach for high frequency words that appear to be rather "idiom prone" McCarthy et al. (2010, p. 66).

These include body parts like the hands, feet, and eyes that work their way into a wide range of idioms. In their *Idioms in Use* course book series, McCarthy and O'Dell (2002) group many idioms according to themes to help learners recognize (and presumably remember) sets of related expressions. These groupings include idioms based on sailing, war and conflict, games and sports, science and technology, etc. Approaching idioms in this way may help learners come to grips with not only the large range of idiomatic expressions, but also some of the historical and circumstantial conditions that gave rise to these idioms.

Others have called for a rather comprehensive approach to teaching L2 idioms. Both Liu (2008) and Liontas (2015) suggest that idioms are best learned through approaches that draw heavily on contextualized presentation coupled with a deeper understanding of the target language culture that gave rise to the idioms. Both also advocate an approach that provides structured presentation of idioms, yet encourages consciousness-raising and other discovery-based activities. The goal in both cases, it seems, is getting learners to develop autonomic skills that will allow them to recognize idioms without explicit instruction, internalize them, and finally be able to deploy them effectively in their own language use. Liontas (2015, p. 623) refers to this final stage as "idiomatic competence", which he defines as "the ability to understand and use idioms appropriately and accurately in a variety of sociocultural contexts, in a manner similar to native speakers, and with the least amount of mental effort". Although such approaches may very well represent the best way to obtain a native-like understanding of idioms, they are likely not practical in many teaching/learning scenarios. This may especially be the case in EFL settings where there is limited exposure to input in the target language and likely even less exposure to the target language culture. (Indeed, Liontas (2015, p. 627) himself suggests that the "development of idiomatic competence is an arduous and cumbersome process that extends over many years".)

Nonetheless there are some aspects of these approaches that seem relevant to all learners. One such factor is the role of context. In a recent study focusing on L1 English speakers learning L2 Korean, Türker (2016a) investigated the influence of context on three types of idioms: (1) idioms with the same form and the same meaning (e.g., *to catch one's eye*, which has the same composition and same meaning in Korean), (2) idioms with the same form but a different meaning (e.g., *to have a heart*, which has the same composition in Korean but means to be willing to do something, rather than to have compassion or kindness as it does in English), and (3) idioms that had no formal equivalent in the learners' L1. She found that the benefits of linguistic similarity in idiom learning were greatly lessened when sufficient contexts were provided. This finding resonates with Cooper's (1999) observation that learners tended to rely more heavily on contextual cues (28% of the time) than L1-based assumptions (5% of the time) when trying to determine the meaning of idioms in an L2.

Türker's (2016a) and Cooper's (1999) findings underscore the oftentimes complex interaction between the L1 and the L2 when it comes to idiom learning. Though it has been shown in some studies that idiomatic congruency (i.e., having the same idiom in one's L1) can play a facilitative role for L2 idiom learning (e.g., Irujo, 1986; Laufer, 2000; Türker, 2016b), learners have also shown a reluctance to apply L1-based assumptions too liberally. Laufer (2000), for example, found greater avoidance for idioms with partial form similarity (e.g., the English idiom *miss the boat* and its Hebrew equivalent *miss the train*) than idioms which had either exact translations in both English and Hebrew *or* idioms which were entirely formally distinct in the L1 and the L2 (e.g., English *to take someone for a ride* vs. Hebrew *to work on someone*). This tendency to avoid excessive reliance on the L1 when attempting to decipher L2 idioms is likely conditioned, at least in part, by a learner's psychotypology (i.e., a learner's perceptions about the transferability of L1 forms to the L2, regardless of the accuracy of these assumptions). Most learners have perceptions about idiomaticity in their own language, which in turn makes them reluctant to assume similarity between idioms in the L1 and the L2. This was demonstrated by Kellerman (1979) who asked L1 Dutch learners of L2 English to judge the acceptability of number of English translations for Dutch sentences. All sentences included the Dutch word *breken* and its English translation of *break*, and all sentences were possible in both languages. Nonetheless, Kellerman found that the participants showed a strong reluctance to assume transferability for sentences that used non-core (i.e., more idiomatic) instances of *breken/ break* (e.g., *the underground resistance was broken*; *some workers have broken the strike*; *his voice broke when he was 13*). It is worth noting, however, that learners and teachers may not always have the same perspectives on semantic transparency and subsequent transferability. Boers and Webb (2015), for example, found that there was often considerable disagreement between teachers and advanced learners regarding which expressions they considered to be transparent vs. opaque. This suggests that teachers should make a point of consulting students before investing a good deal of time and energy to the study of idioms.

Overall, then, it seems that from a teaching and learning perspective, approaches which present idioms in highly contextualized materials are likely to be more effective than those that rely on isolated presentation. Nonetheless, other factors have been shown to influence learners' tendency to remember L2 idioms. One such factor is phonological redundancy built into many English idiomatic expressions. Eyckmans and Lindstromberg (2017) found that idioms with repetition of sounds (both in the form of alliteration and assonance) were learned better than idioms with no such repetition (see also Boers, Lindstromberg, & Eyckmans, 2013; Boers, Lindstromberg, & Webb, 2014). However, this was only the case if the learners were made aware of sound repetitions during the treatment phase of the study; no such finding was reported for a control group who received no awareness training or attention direction. Given the observation that English idioms tend to incorporate alliteration and assonance more than we would expect by chance (Eyckmans & Lindstromberg, 2017), it seems prudent for practitioners to take advantage of this to lessen the challenging task of learning a wide array of idioms.

Future Directions

One thing that should be evident from this chapter is the fact that practitioners would benefit from more uniformity in respect to the terminology used to describe the various MWIs. However, any attempts to simplify terminology in a way that ultimately obscures the important distinctions between different types of MWIs should be avoided. In the end, it might be best to start with structural qualities of different MWIs (e.g., phrasal verbs, collocations, etc.), then consider the relative frequency, flexibility, and idiomaticity of these. In respect to idiomaticity in particular, it would appear to be useful to disentangle the label "idiom" from the more general principle of "idiomaticity", as these seem to be related but separate phenomena.

In respect to actual teaching practices, there are now a number of published works identifying aspects of MWIs that seem to affect acquisition. However, these remain disjointed in many respects. Ultimately it would be useful to try to gain a better understanding of how the different elements underpinning acquisition of MWIs can be woven into an integrated tapestry. Ideally this needs to take into account distinctions in MWIs, task type, environmental factors, and individual differences in learners (e.g., L1, psychotypological beliefs, cultural difference, etc.). Devising such a unified, holistic understanding of MWI acquisition is obviously no small task, but it represents a reasonable goal. Perhaps in the short term, researchers should endeavor to at least incorporate multiple factors into their research designs to observe how these interact, such as in Laufer's (2000) and Türker's (2016a) studies on idioms.

Further Reading

Liu, D. (2008). *Idioms: Description, comprehension, acquisition, and pedagogy.* New York, NY: Routledge.

This book takes a comprehensive and integrated look at idioms and considers three aspects: (1) definition and use, (2) comprehension and processing, and (3) acquisition and pedagogy. One particular strength of this text is the close integration between theory and practice.

McCarthy, M., O'Keeffe, A., & Walsh, S. (2010). *Vocabulary matrix.* Delhi: Cengage Learning.

This book represents a very practical guide to issues related to learning and teaching vocabulary, with a strong emphasis on MWIs.

Wray, A. (2002). *Formulaic language and the lexicon.* Cambridge, UK: Cambridge University Press.

This book played a major role in bringing MWIs to the fore in second language vocabulary research. Though many of the claims have been hotly contested, it still presents an ambitious attempt to explain how differences in L1 and L2 might lead to differentiated learning of MWIs.

Related Topics

Defining multiword items, types of multiword items, factors affecting the learning of multiword items, resources for learning multiword items, measuring knowledge of multiword items

References

Altenberg, B. G. (2001). The grammatical and lexical patterning of MAKE in native and non-native student writing. *Applied Linguistics*, 173–195.

Barfield, A., & Gyllstad, H. (2009). Introduction: Researching L2 collocation knowledge and development. In A. Barfield & H. Gyllstad (Eds.), *Researching collocations in another language: Multiple interpretations* (pp. 1–18). Basingstoke, UK: Palgrave Macmillan.

Biber, D., Johansson, S., Leech, G., Conrad, S., & Finegan, E. (1999). *Longman grammar of spoken and written English.* London, UK: Longman.

Bishop, H. (2004). The effect of typographic salience on the look up and comprehension of unknown formulaic sequences. In *Formulaic sequences: Acquisition, processing and use* (pp. 227–247). Basingstoke, UK: Palgrave Macmillan.

Boers, F., Demecheleer, M., Coxhead, A., & Webb, S. (2014). Gauging the effects of exercises on verb–noun collocations. *Language Teaching Research, 18*, 54–74.

Boers, F., Eyckmans, J., Kappel, J., Stengers, H., & Demecheleer, M. (2006). Formulaic sequences and perceived oral proficiency: Putting a lexical approach to the test. *Language Teaching Research, 10*, 245–261.

Boers, F., & Lindstromberg, S. (2012). Experimental and intervention studies on formulaic sequences in a second language. *Annual Review of Applied Linguistics, 32*, 83–110.

Boers, F., Lindstromberg, S., & Eyckmans, J. (2013). Is alliteration mnemonic without awareness-raising? *Language Awareness*, *23*(4), 291–303.

Boers, F., Lindstromberg, S., & Webb, S. (2014). Further evidence of the comparative memorability of alliterative expressions in second language learning. *RELC Journal*, *45*, 85–99.

Boers, F., & Webb, S. (2015). Gauging the semantic transparency of idioms: Do natives and learners see eye to eye? In R. R. Heredia (Ed.), *Bilingual figurative language processing* (pp. 368–392). Cambridge, UK: Cambridge University Press.

Celce-Murcia, M., & Larsen-Freeman, D. (1999). *The grammar book: An ESL/EFL teacher's course* (2nd ed.). Boston, MA: Heinle/Cengage.

Chomsky, N. (1965). *Aspects of the theory of syntax*. Cambridge, MA: MIT Press.

Cooper, T. C. (1998). Teaching idioms. *Foreign Language Annals*, *31*, 255–266.

Cooper, T. C. (1999). Processing of idioms by L2 learners of English. *TESOL Quarterly*, *33*, 233–262.

Davies, M. (2008–). *The Corpus of Contemporary American English (COCA): 560 million words, 1990-present*. Retrieved from https://corpus.byu.edu/coca/.

Durrant, P., & Schmitt, N. (2010). Adult learners' retention of collocations from exposure. *Second Language Research*, *26*, 163–188.

Erman, B., & Warren, B. (2000). The idiom principle and the open choice principle. *Text*, *20*, 29–62.

Eyckmans, J., & Lindstromberg, S. (2017). The power of sound in L2 idiom learning. *Language Teaching Research*, *21*, 341–361.

Fernando, C. (1996). *Idioms and idiomaticity*. Oxford, UK: Oxford University Press.

Gardner, D., & Davies, M. (2007). Pointing out frequent phrasal verbs: A corpus-based analysis. *TESOL Quarterly*, *41*, 339–359.

Garnier, M., & Schmitt, N. (2015). The PHaVE List: A pedagogical list of phrasal verbs and their most frequent meaning senses. *Language Teaching Research*, *19*, 645–666.

Howarth, P. (1998). Phraseology and second language proficiency. *Applied Linguistics*, *19*, 24–44.

Irujo, S. (1986). A piece of cake: Learning and teaching idioms. *ELT Journal*, *40*, 236–242.

Jackendoff, R. (1997). *The architecture of the language faculty*. Cambridge, MA: MIT Press.

Jarvis, S., & Pavlenko, A. (2010). *Crosslinguistic influence in language and cognition*. New York, NY: Routledge.

Jiang, N. (2000). Lexical representation and development in a second language. *Applied Linguistics*, *21*, 47–77.

Jones, M., & Haywood, S. (2004). Facilitating the acquisition of formulaic sequences: An exploratory study. In N. Schmitt (Ed.), *Formulaic sequences* (pp. 269–300). Amsterdam: John Benjamins.

Kellerman, E. (1979). Transfer and non-transfer: Where are we now? *Studies in Second Language Acquisition*, 37–57.

Laufer, B. (2000). Avoidance of idioms in a second language: The effect of L1–L2 degree of similarity. *Studia Linguistica*, *54*, 186–196.

Laufer, B., & Girsai, N. (2008). Form-focused instruction in second language vocabulary learning: A case for contrastive analysis. *Applied Linguistics*, *29*, 694–716.

Lewis, M. (1993). *The Lexical Approach*. Hove, UK: LTP.

Liontas, J. I. (2015). Developing idiomatic competence in the ESOL classroom: A pragmatic account. *TESOL Journal*, 621–658.

Liu, D. (2003). The most frequently used spoken American English idioms: A corpus analysis and its implications. *TESOL Quarterly*, *37*, 671–700.

Liu, D. (2008). *Idioms: Description, comprehension, acquisition, and pedagogy*. New York, NY: Routledge.

Liu, D. (2010). Going beyond patterns: Involving cognitive analysis in the learning of collocations. *TESOL Quarterly*, *44*, 4–30.

Liu, D. (2011). The most frequently used English phrasal verbs in American and British English: A multicorpus analysis. *TESOL Quarterly*, *45*, 661–688.

McCarthy, M., & O'Dell, F. (2002). *English idioms in use*. Cambridge, UK: Cambridge University Press.

McCarthy, M., O'Keeffe, A., & Walsh, S. (2010). *Vocabulary matrix*. Delhi: Cengage Learning.

Moon, R. (1998). *Fixed expressions and idioms in English*. Oxford, UK: Clarendon Press.

Nassaji, H., & Tian, J. (2010). Collaborative and individual output tasks and their effects on learning English phrasal verbs. *Language Teaching Research, 14*, 397–419.

Nation, I. S. P. (2001). *Learning vocabulary in another language*. Cambridge, UK: Cambridge University Press.

Nattinger, J., & DeCarrico, J. (1992). *Lexical phrases and language teaching*. Oxford, UK: Oxford University Press.

Nesselhauf, N. (2003). The use of collocations by advanced learners of English and some implications for teaching. *Applied Linguistics, 24*, 223–242.

Pellicer-Sánchez, A. (2017). Learning L2 Collocations Incidentally from Reading. *Language Teaching Research, 21*, 381–402.

Peters, E. (2012). Learning German formulaic sequences: The effect of two attention-drawing techniques. *Language Learning Journal, 40*, 65–79.

Peters, E. (2014). The effects of repetition and time of posttest administration on EFL learners' form recall of single words and collocations. *Language Teaching Research, 18*, 75–94.

Peters, E. (2016). The learning burden of collocations: The role of interlexical and intralexical factors. *Language Teaching Research, 20*, 113–138.

Ravin, Y., & Leacock, C. (2000). Polysemy: An overview. In Y. Ravin & C. Leacock (Eds.), *Polysemy: Theoretical and computational approaches* (pp. 1–29). Oxford, UK: Oxford University Press.

Schmitt. (2004). *Formulaic sequences: Acquisition, processing and use*. Amsterdam: Benjamins.

Shin, D., & Nation, I. S. P. (2007). Beyond single words: The most frequent collocations in spoken English. *ELT Journal, 62*, 339–348.

Sinclair, J. (1991). *Corpus, concordance, collocation*. Oxford, UK: Oxford University Press.

Sprenger, A., Levelt, W., & Kempen, G. (2006). Lexical access during the production of idiomatic phrases. *Journal of Memory and Language, 54*, 161–184.

Szudarski, P. (2012). Effects of meaning- and formed-focused instruction on the acquisition of verb-noun collocations. *Journal of Second Language Teaching and Research, 1*, 3–37.

Szudarski, P., & Carter, R. (2014). The role of input flood and input enhancement in EFL learners' acquisition of collocations. *International Journal of Applied Linguistics, 26*, 245–265.

Türker, E. (2016a). Idiom acquisition by second language learners: The influence of cross-linguistic similarity and context. *The Language Learning Journal*, 1–12.

Türker, E. (2016b). The role of L1 conceptual knowledge and frequency in the acquisition of L2 metaphorical expressions. *Second Language Research, 32*, 25–48.

Webb, S., & Kagimoto, E. (2011). Learning collocations: Do the number of collocates, position of the node word, and synonymy affect learning? *Applied Linguistics, 32*, 259–276.

Webb, S., Newton, J., & Chang, A. (2013). Incidental learning of collocation. *Language Learning, 63*, 91–210.

White, B. (2012). A conceptual approach to the instruction of phrasal verbs. *The Modern Language Journal, 96*, 419–439.

Wolter, B. (2006). Lexical network structures and L2 vocabulary acquisition: The role of L1 lexical/conceptual knowledge. *Applied Linguistics, 27*, 741–747.

Wolter, B., & Gyllstad, H. (2011). Collocational links in the L2 mental lexicon and the influence of L1 intralexical knowledge. *Applied Linguistics, 32*, 430–449.

Wolter, B., & Gyllstad, H. (2013). Frequency of input and L2 collocational processing. *Studies in Second Language Acquisition, 35*, 451–482.

Wolter, B., & Song, L. (under review). Productive collocations in the L2: The effects of L1 collocational overlap, concreteness, meaning senses, and collocational frequency.

Wolter, B., & Yamashita, J. (2017). Word frequency, collocational frequency, L1 congruency, and proficiency in L2 collocational processing: What accounts for L2 performance? *Studies in Second Language Acquisition*, 1–22.

Wolter, B., Yamashita, J., & Leung, C. Y. (in preparation). Conceptual transfer and conceptual restructuring in adjectives of space: Evidence from eye-tracking.

Wray, A. (2000). Formulaic sequences in second language teaching: Principle and practice. *Applied Linguistics*, 463–489.

Wray, A. (2002). *Formulaic language and the lexicon*. Cambridge, UK: Cambridge University Press.

Wray, A. (2008). *Formulaic language: Pushing the boundaries*. Oxford, UK: Oxford University Press.

Zhou, X. (2016). A corpus-based study on high frequency verb collocations in the case of "HAVE". *International Forum of Teaching and Studies*, *12*, 42–50.

32

Single, but Not Unrelated

Key Issues in Researching Single-Word Items

Tessa Spätgens and Rob Schoonen

Introduction

See cow. This is what is preserved of the stimulus sentence *I can see a cow* that is repeated by a two-year-old child in an experiment by Brown and Frase (Brown, 1973, p. 76), illustrating telegraphic speech. When we have limited resources, because of developmental constraints, or length limitations in old-fashioned telegrams or modern tweets, we resort to content words and mostly nouns and verbs as the main carriers of meaning. In studying language acquisition, we want to know how many words a language learner knows and can use, how these words are stored in and retrieved from the mental lexicon, and how often the language learner has encountered or will encounter the word in the everyday language environment.

Words, as part of linguistic systems, and lexical knowledge, as part of language users' language proficiency, play an essential role in language use and language learning. Investigating this role requires language researchers to take careful account of the words they use in their research materials and the way they investigate the lexical skills of language users and language learners. The contributions in this handbook underline that lexis and lexical knowledge are not as simple as is sometimes suggested. In this chapter we will focus on a few of the considerations researchers have to make in designing and conducting their research on single-word items. When we refer to the language user in general terms, this includes (L1 and L2) language learners. In this chapter, we confine ourselves to the features and processing of content words, that is nouns, verbs, adjectives, and adverbs, and ignore the processing of function words. The divide between these two categories, content and function words, can be somewhat fuzzy, but these discussions fall outside of the scope of this chapter.

Our discussion of issues in researching single-word items firstly focuses on the many word characteristics that play a role in lexical processing, and therefore should ideally be considered when conducting any type of vocabulary-oriented research. However, as stated in the title, while this chapter focuses on single words (contrary to collocations and other multiword expressions), these single words derive their meaning and usability to a large extent from the connections they have with other words, and their level of interconnectedness: in this chapter they are single, but not unrelated. Therefore, in the second part of this chapter, we will zoom in on tasks that can be used to target a special feature of knowledge of single-word items, namely, their place in the language user's semantic network.

Critical Issues and Topics: Form and Meaning Characteristics

Theoretical Issues

Including single-word items in stimulus materials or tests of one's research may initially seem quite straightforward. However, this impression is highly misleading. Content words in texts, stimulus sentences or vocabulary tests seldom represent unidimensional form-meaning combinations. A closer look at words as single linguistic units, and at the use of words in language interaction shows that words and word use are highly multidimensional or, in other words, have many facets that need to be taken into account when designing lexically oriented studies. Language users are sensitive to these word characteristics in processing lexical information, and therefore it is essential that researchers are aware of their possible effects. These characteristics or features not only relate to the form of the word, be it the acoustic or visual form, but also its meaning and its use. Multilingual language users find themselves in an even more complicated situation, because form, meaning and use of words in the different languages might interfere with each other, at all levels.

In this section we will introduce a number of word characteristics that may affect word processing and thus results of lexically oriented research. For practical reasons, we distinguish between characteristics relating to use, form and meaning, but obviously these facets are highly interconnected, as becomes evident when one takes into account derivational morphology of words. Our goal is to bring a number of important word characteristics to the readers' attention, which may either facilitate or inhibit smooth word processing, and which are sometimes mediated by other factors, such as language modality. Some characteristics are inherent to the word form or meaning, such as morphological complexity (cf. "intra-lexical factors"; Laufer, 1997) and others are induced by the use of the word or the language user, such as word frequency and cognate status of words in a multilingual's lexicon, respectively. Where possible, we will provide information on available databases targeting the various characteristics that are discussed. Our discussion of these issues is by no means comprehensive, but the reader will find additional sources in the other chapters of the book, or in Schmitt's vocabulary research manual (Schmitt, 2010; see Further Reading).

Use, Form and Meaning Characteristics in Research

Word Use Characteristics

Word use characteristics play a prominent role in the processing of lexical items in everyday language use, but also, or especially, in the assessment of receptive lexical skills or verbal fluency in research. For words that we have frequently heard or seen before, it will be relatively easy to process the form and to comprehend the meaning. This makes word frequency an important feature in language processing and thus in lexical research. In most cases it needs to be taken into account when designing lexical materials for empirical studies (cf. Baayen, 2001; Balota, Yap, & Cortese, 2006; Breland, 1996). Word frequencies in spoken and in written language are strongly correlated, and researchers, often for practical reasons, use written word frequencies in their studies as these are more widely available. However, it will be more accurate to distinguish between the two types of word frequency and to choose the one that fits one's research goals best. See, among others, Baayen, Feldman, & Schreuder (2006) for differential effects of spoken language and written language frequencies – as a written-to-spoken frequency ratio – on lexical decision and word naming latencies. At the same time, they showed that, – across modality – spoken word frequency can be predictive of latencies in visual word recognition, with highly frequent spoken words leading to shorter latencies in both visual word recognition and naming. Remarkably, words that are far more frequent in written language than in spoken language showed longer latencies in both tasks (Baayen et al., 2006). An interesting alternative to written and spoken word frequencies is presented in work by Brysbaert, who studied the quality of a corpus based on subtitles. He showed that the frequencies based on subtitles are in many respects superior to frequencies based on other corpora, such as Kučera and Francis's (1967) classical corpus of "present-day" American-English, CELEX (Baayen, Piepenbrock, & Van Rijn, 1993), and others (see Brysbaert & New, 2009). Word frequencies derived from subtitles are now available for a range of languages including American English, British English, Chinese, Dutch, German, Greek, Polish, and Spanish (see http://crr.ugent.be/programs-data/subtitle-frequencies).

Including word frequencies in one's studies as they can be derived from large corpora serves at least two purposes. One is that infrequent words are expected to be more difficult and less well known than frequent words. This kind of information will predict item difficulty in, for example, the development of (adaptive) lexical knowledge tests (Breland, 1996). Breland (1996) found values of .70 and higher for the correlations between word difficulty and standard frequency indices from multiple corpora. Many vocabulary size tests are organized according to frequency bands from which the words in the corpora are sampled, such as Nation's Vocabulary Size Test (Nation & Beglar, 2007; Coxhead, Nation, & Sim, 2014) or Nation's more diagnostic Vocabulary Levels Test and its successors (Nation, 1983; Schmitt, Schmitt, & Clapham, 2001; Webb, Sasao, & Ballance, 2017). A second purpose for including word frequencies in one's research is that these frequencies are considered to approximate the exposure an individual has had to the respective words. Frequent previous encounters and thus processing of a word most likely facilitates its processing upon new encounters, which may affect results in psycholinguistically oriented studies that use, for example, processing speed as measured by reaction times. These kinds of studies depend on subtle differences in reaction times between conditions, and poor control of word frequencies in the research design may confound research results. The extent to which word frequencies can be considered a valid approximation of an individual's exposure to the words very much depends on the match between the source materials of the corpus from which the frequencies were derived and the individual's acquaintance with such language materials. Obviously, word frequencies derived from a corpus of academic books will not be highly suitable for studies on language processing by primary school children. On the other hand, in many cases it will be difficult to find appropriate corpora for one's research goals (see however, Anthony, this volume, for a list of available corpora). Furthermore, in using corpora, the absolute frequency may not be the only relevant parameter to consider: words can be highly frequent in certain text types or topical domains but virtually nonexistent in others. To account for this imbalance, the dispersion of words across subcorpora could provide valuable additional information (Gries, 2010). Using word frequencies presupposes a clear distinction between the units that count as a word. However, this might not always be that simple. Do we want to count the frequency of specific form-meaning pairings, or just word form frequencies. For instance, the noun *work* as in *The work was done* will have a certain frequency, so will the verb *work* as in *We worked very hard*. The form *work* will have the combined frequency. In this example the part of speech, verb or noun, makes the difference, as the two word meanings are strongly related. This is very different in homonyms, such as *husky* referring to a type of dog and *husky* meaning hoarse. It will depend on the specific research questions whether we want to combine the two word frequencies or whether we are concerned about just one of them, especially in cases where there is a dominant, frequently used word meaning and a non-dominant, infrequently used one.

A final consideration regarding frequency concerns not just the frequency of the word as a whole, but of parts of the word, as encountered in written language. In studies on reading, highly frequent words may be easily processed because of the visual regularity of the letter pattern. The frequency of letter patterns can be a factor in speed of word recognition, and therefore the positional bigram frequency is often used as an index of the expected visual familiarity of the word. To calculate this measure, words are split up in all their bigrams (e.g., *mo-ot-th-he-er* for *mother*) and the frequency of the bigram at that particular position in a word is computed. For example, the bigram *mo* at the initial two positions in six-letter words has a frequency of 1,721, whereas its frequency would be 7 for the final two positions (Solso & Juel, 1980, using Kučera & Francis, 1967). The bigram frequencies can be summed and averaged according to word length (Ellis & Beaton, 1993). Assuming that language users are especially sensitive to unexpected patterns, researchers may want to include the lowest bigram frequency of a word as a special index in their analyses (Lemhöfer et al., 2008). This latter kind of index may also capture syllable boundaries in multisyllabic words, as bigrams surrounding a syllable boundary often show a relatively low bigram frequency (Balota et al., 2006). For example, a comparison of the bigram frequencies of *nt* as in *pint* vs. *tn* as in *fitness* in a Google corpus (Lydell, 2015) are very different: (rounded) 29.359×10^9 and 0.282×10^9, respectively.

Word Form Characteristics

The word form is the first to be encountered in listening or reading, and a main word form feature is word length. Longer words generally take longer to process. This is obvious in spoken language where words are produced and processed linearly in time. The more phonemes or syllables a word consists of, the more time it is likely to take to be processed, if all else remains the same. However, language users do not always need to hear the full sound string for adequate word identification. For instance, the English word /trespass/ will usually be identified at the /p/, because no other English word that has the same initial sounds, /tresp/, concurs with /trespass/ (Marslen-Wilson, 1987). At this so-called recognition point or uniqueness point, the word can be identified and selected, and the initially concurrent words can be inhibited; they are no longer competing as candidates for recognition (see the Cohort model, Marslen-Wilson, 1987). In written language, similar word length effects can be expected, although reading is not necessarily linear. Our eyes jump across the text lines, as is known from eye-tracking studies, and in a single fixation, multiple graphemes can be processed. The span of a fixation may thus cover full words, and this suggests that in a visual word recognition task one single fixation may be enough to recognize words of different lengths. This is in line with a study by Juhasz and Rayner (2003), in which participants read target words in a sentence and it was found that word length did not affect first fixation duration, nor fixation duration for words fixated *only once*. However, the likelihood of refixating on a word increased with its length, as did total fixation time, which includes backtracking and refixations of the word. These findings suggest that longer words require refixations in order to be processed properly, which implies that word length is a factor to take into account in both visual and aural word recognition. This conclusion is restricted to language perception, i.e., word recognition. The production of words as in naming follows an incremental process which can start almost immediately, irrespective of the length of the word to be produced. In an experimental study of naming action pictures, Shao, Roelofs, and Meyer (2014) found only a weak correlation between naming latency and word length. One can imagine that the naming latency is largely determined by the interpretation of the picture and the lexical word selection, as a speaker can start naming based on the partial representation of the word form, for example the initial syllable (Shao et al., 2014).

A word form characteristic that partially interacts with word length, is a word's morphological derivation. Some basic word forms reoccur in language in various derived forms and these derivations usually make the words longer, but in a structured way that will be familiar to the language user – though not necessarily to the second language learner. Moreover, the appearance of the base word in different derived forms could add to the word frequency of (at least) that part of the word. For example, *use* can be recognized in *usage*, *usable*, *usability*, *user*, and so on. These words belong to the family of *use*, and words with many of such family members are likely to be processed more easily. Family size of a word can be defined as the number of derivations and compounds of the base word involved; words with large families are associated with shorter response latencies in lexical decision tasks (Schreuder & Baayen, 1997; Lemhöfer et al., 2008), and this effect seems to exist independent of the cumulative frequency of the family members, that is a word's family size was a better predictor of the lexical decision reaction time than the cumulative frequency of these family members. However, the family size effect did not show in a progressive demasking task, which taps into the early stages of perceptual word recognition, suggesting that the family size effect occurs at a later stage in visual processing of words (Schreuder & Baayen, 1997).

That various words, i.e., family members, can influence the recognition and processing of a particular single target word, underscores that single words are not processed in isolation. These kinds of effects are not only shown in the family size effect, but also in the so-called neighborhood size effect. Whereas family members are linguistically related through derivation or compounding, neighbors are close to each other at a more superficial level, that is, by virtue of their visual or auditory similarities. Characteristics of the neighborhood also impact the recognition of target words. Neighborhood size or density refers to the number of words that differ orthographically in just one grapheme from the target word, preserving letter position (Grainger, O'Regan, Jacobs, & Segui, 1989), or to the size of the set of words that differ minimally in sound from the target word (Vitevitch & Luce, 2016). A large neighborhood implies that there are many competitors that need to be excluded for unique word identification. And it is not just the number of competitors that we should be concerned about, but also their relative word frequencies. A target word with a highly frequent neighbor will take more time and effort to be recognized (Grainger et al., 1989). Conversely, in word production the opposite seems to happen. Words with sparse neighborhoods are produced more slowly and less accurately, suggesting that activation spreads back and forth, thus reinforcing the production of the word form selected to match the intended lemma. Sparse neighborhoods provide little reinforcement (Vitevitch & Luce, 2016). The effects of neighborhood size are mediated by neighborhood spread, that is the distribution across the word of the replaceable graphemes or phonemes that form the neighborhood. For example, three letter word *peg* can have a grapheme replacement at all three positions: *beg*, *pig*, and *pen*, and thus has a P-metric of 3; for *hen* no replacement of the medial grapheme is possible, only at the initial and final position (*den* and *hem*, respectively) and thus its P-metric is 2 (Vitevitch, 2007). Vitevitch found – among other things – that in an auditory lexical decision task words with metric P = 2 were recognized more quickly than those with metric P = 3.

Word Meaning Characteristics

Characteristics of lexical meaning may affect the processing of words as well, especially when these characteristics are not represented in the word form per se. Transparent compounds (*travel agency*) and derivations (*friendliness*) may be long and less frequent, but the constituting parts may still be processed relatively easily, and thus the multi-morphemic word may not cause serious problems to the language learner. Still, some mono-morphemic words have features that make them harder to process than others. One such feature is abstractness or lack of concreteness. Abstract words (e.g., *virtue* and *regret*) are, generally speaking, harder to learn than concrete words (e.g., *needle* and *pirate*) in paired-associate learning tasks (cf. De Groot, 2006; De Groot & Keijzer, 2000). The differences are assumed to be related to differences in mental representations of concrete and abstract words; concrete words are supposed to have at least a visual and a verbal representation, whereas abstract words may only have a verbal one (De Groot, 2006). The dimension of concrete to abstract is highly correlated with the related dimension of imageability, with some scholars using one for the other. Balota et al. (2006) define concrete words as words that can be the object of a sense verb, such as *touch*, *see*, and *hear*, which would make *music* a concrete word; they also state that imageability usually is operationalized by gathering the subjective ratings of participants. Due to the high correlations between the two dimensions, researchers often do not make a distinction between them (Balota et al., 2006; De Groot & Keijzer, 2000). Effects of abstractness or imageability have been shown in lexical decision and naming tasks (Balota et al., 2006). In recent years, databases with concreteness and imageability ratings have become available for research purposes, such as Schock et al.'s (2012) imageability estimates for 3,000 disyllabic words, and Cortese and Fugett's (2004) imageability ratings for 3,000 monosyllabic words. Brysbaert and colleagues collected concreteness ratings for 40,000 words, including some two-word expressions (Brysbaert, Warriner, & Kuperman, 2014). Concreteness and frequency can coincide, but also go in opposite directions. A relatively frequent word such as *although* belonged to the least concrete words, whereas a less frequent words such as *walrus* was among the most concrete words.

Matters get more complicated, when the relationship between lexical form and meaning is not one-to-one, but one-to-multiple as is often the case in natural languages. This feature is captured in meaningfulness, which often quite literally refers to the number of meanings a word represents. Meaningfulness of stimulus words can be assessed straightforwardly as the number of entries in a dictionary (Balota et al., 2006), but more advanced approaches are used by, among others, Baayen and colleagues (2006). They counted the number of synsets a word is listed in; synsets being a set of semantically related words according to Wordnet (Miller, Beckwith, Fellbaum, Gross, & Miller, 1990). Words with high meaningfulness ratings show a facilitatory effect in lexical decisions and naming, but when semantic decision-making gets involved in the response, as is the case in semantic categorization or semantic relatedness judgment, "meaningful" words show inhibitory effects, probably indicating that the different meanings are in competition (Balota et al., 2006).

Interlanguage Effects

As mentioned earlier, in research on multilingual language users, features of words in the different languages interact with each other. This concerns form as well as meaning features. Language learners may benefit from similarities between languages, for example because of a common ancestor of the languages involved, such as Greek and Latin for many western languages. Dutch *medicijn*, coming from Latin (*res*) *medicina*, will not cause much problems for English, German, French, or Spanish learners of Dutch, as the translation in their first language is *medicine, Medizin, médecine, medicina*, respectively, whereas the Dutch synonym with a partial Gothic origin *geneesmiddel* will be much harder to recognize and to learn. These forms of overlap are helpful to the language learner, but can also lead to unexpected and maybe unwanted effects in psycholinguistic experiments. Both cognates – words that are similar both in form and meaning across two languages – and "false friends" – which are similar in form but misleadingly not in meaning (e.g., French/English: *attendre/attend* and *plus/plus*) – influence the processing of words in a target language. In a multilingual language learning setting, both the target word and its translation equivalent bring their characteristics to the table (cf., Dijkstra, Timmermans, & Schriefers, 2000). As a consequence, word frequency or family size in one language may affect processing speed of words in the other (Van Heuven, Dijkstra, & Grainger, 1998).

Word Use, Form and Meaning Characteristics: Concluding Remarks

Whether one wants to investigate effects of the aforementioned word features on language acquisition or language processing, or whether one wants to control for them or not, largely depends on the research context, research design, and resources. In most lexically oriented studies, it is important to pay careful attention to these characteristics in the compilation of the testing materials. An important distinction may be whether the research is geared towards auditory or visual recognition or towards semantic classification or interpretation. In the former case, form characteristics may be more important to control for, and in the latter meaning features may play a larger (additional) role. In the next section, we will zoom in on another characteristic of individual words, namely the position they occupy in the semantic network, connected to other words via various semantic relations.

Critical Issues and Topics: Connections in a Semantic Network

Theoretical Issues

Even when focusing on single words, it is important to note that knowledge of such items is never isolated: all words are connected in the mental lexicon through various types of semantic, phonological, and orthographic ties. These links form part of our knowledge of individual lexical items, which is a topic of interest in its own right: Which types of ties are prominent? In what order do they develop? How do they affect language use? In this section, we will focus on semantic links specifically, as they form part of individual words' meanings. We will discuss the different types of semantic ties that exist within the semantic network and various tasks used to measure knowledge and activation of these links.

Importance of Semantic Relations: Language Acquisition and Processing

When studying single-word items, what is the relevance of the semantic ties they hold with other words? Firstly, as with all other vocabulary knowledge, the semantic networks surrounding words need to be acquired. Researchers may therefore be interested in how the network develops and which relations are important throughout acquisition. For example, a developmental path from a focus on context-dependent knowledge, i.e., contextual semantic relations such as *squirrel – forest*, to the gradual abstraction towards more context-independent knowledge, i.e., categorical relations such as *squirrel – animal*, has been identified for L1 children (cf. Nelson, 2007, inter alia).

Secondly, many studies have shown that the processing of single-word items is affected by the processing of other items within their networks. During language use, the activation of individual words encountered in discourse spreads through the network to related words, which may then be accessed more quickly for comprehension and production during the immediately following discourse. This effect of spreading activation (Collins & Loftus, 1975) can be studied by means of semantic priming tasks which may take on various forms (McNamara, 2005).

Finally, the degree to which network knowledge of lexical items is developed may in turn affect other language skills. For example, a number of studies have found that there is a relation between reading comprehension and various measures of semantic network quality (cf. Betjemann & Keenan, 2008; Swart et al., 2017; Tannenbaum, Torgesen, & Wagner, 2006).

Types of Relations

The semantic network has been studied extensively and a multitude of relations that may exist between words in the network have been identified. Although many different classifications have been offered, most are centered around a dichotomy that distinguishes relations based on shared intrinsic characteristics, on the one hand, and concepts related through context, on the other hand. Table 32.1 provides examples and the most commonly used overarching terms. Typically, concepts considered to be related through shared characteristics include category relations such as sub-, super-, and coordination, and often also synonyms, antonyms, and part-whole relations. Contextual relations may include a wide variety of connections, for example between objects and their locations, typical events at which they occur, and instruments that may be used to manipulate them. Finally, the dichotomy may also be conceptualized as a continuum from context-independent relations to context-dependent relations, where some types of connections may be more in the middle of the scale, such as intrinsic characteristics or behaviors of objects, animals, or people.

In addition to these semantic classifications of word relations, there are two other important types of relations distinguished in the literature, which may or may not overlap with the semantic types discussed previously. Most notably, associative relationships are those identified through large-scale studies of people's word association responses. An example of a highly common associative stimulus – response pair is *blood – red*. Associative links may also include form-based connections, but these are typically far less common than meaning-based associations (De Deyne & Storms, 2008). Secondly, words may be related through collocation, i.e., common co-occurrence in speech and text (or in the outside world), such as *pencil – paper* (example from COCA, Davies, 2008). All three types of relations (semantic, associative, and collocation) may overlap, as is the case in the word pair *salt – pepper*.

Table 32.1 Schematic representation of various classification systems and their correspondence

The **paradigmatic/syntagmatic distinction** (i.e., Cruse, 2000): a syntactically defined categorization system	The **thematic/taxonomic distinction** (i.e., Estes, Golonka, & Jones, 2011): an object-focused categorization system	The **context-independent to context-dependent continuum** (from Spätgens & Schoonen, submitted; based on De Deyne & Storms, 2008; Cremer, Dingshoff, de Beer, & Schoonen, 2011): a semantically focused categorization system
Paradigmatic (between words of the same syntactic category): including coordinates, superordinates, subordinates, partonyms, and synonyms	**Taxonomic** (hierarchically related objects sharing many features): coordinates, superordinates, subordinates	**Taxonomic** (category relations) including coordinates, superordinates, subordinates, and synonyms
Syntagmatic (between words of a different syntactic category): typically, syntagmatic relations are not specifically defined other than by the difference in syntactic category	**Thematic** (concepts playing complementary roles in the same event), including relations that are spatial: *jungle – bird*; temporal: *summer – holiday*; causal: *wind – erosion*; functional: *fork – knife*; possessive: *police – badge*; and productive: *cow – milk*	**Feature** (necessary or prototypical characteristics), including physical characteristics: *banana – yellow*; internal characteristics: *snail – slow*; behavior: *dog – bark*; functions: *cot – sleep*; and partonyms **Situational** (concepts related through possible contexts), including co-occurrence: *princess – hat*; contexts: *ocean – rocks*; actions: *bakery – choose*; context-dependent attributes: *car – blue* **Subjective** (dependent on personal context), including emotion/evaluation: *cheese – eew*; personal: *hair dresser – my mother*

Context-independent ⟶ *Context-dependent*

Note: Overlap between the classification systems is not always complete, since definitions are not similarly detailed.

However, they may also exist separately, such as the pair *dolphin – elephant*, which are both mammals and therefore semantically related, but which are neither associates nor collocates.

Operationalizing the Semantic Network

In this section, we will discuss a number of methodologies commonly used to study the semantic network, and the types of results these methodologies yield.

Free Word Association Tasks

As was discussed earlier, word association studies provide us with information on commonly linked word pairs based on people's spontaneous responses. At the individual level however, word associations can also be used to uncover speakers' preferences for certain types of semantic links. The basics of the procedure are very simple: participants are provided with a stimulus word and asked to respond with the first word, or first few words, that come to mind. The task can be performed either orally or in writing.

Traditionally, only a single response is required in most word association studies. However, eliciting multiple responses appears to be more compatible with the fact that any given word likely has many different connections to other words in an individual's mental lexicon. Furthermore, recent research by De Deyne and Storms (2008) has shown that different response patterns occur when three responses are elicited. For example, they demonstrated that secondary and tertiary responses were less likely to be taxonomically related to their stimuli than first responses. Therefore, eliciting multiple responses appears to provide a more comprehensive view of a word's semantic network and of individuals' associative behavior.

Similar to the different types of classifications of semantic relations in general, there are many different coding schemes that have been used to classify word association responses, and these will of course affect the conclusions that can be drawn. Most early studies used a word class-based definition of the syntagmatic/paradigmatic distinction (see Table 32.1). A number of recent studies have provided more detailed classification schemes, defining not only specific context-independent relations but also context-dependent relations and sometimes form-related types (Cremer et al., 2011; De Deyne & Storms, 2008; Fitzpatrick, 2006; Spätgens & Schoonen, submitted). The choice for a specific coding scheme will of course affect the potential outcomes of any word association study: using a classification system that is detailed enough to distinguish the categories relevant to the research questions is therefore vital.

Besides the semantic classification of stimulus-response pairs, researchers have also used databases as a reference point to weigh participants' associations against (Fitzpatrick, Playfoot, Wray, & Wright, 2013; Swart et al., 2017; Zareva & Wolter, 2012). In this way, the degree of similarity between, for example, an L1 child's or an L2 adult's associative behavior can be compared to that of L1 adults, to study and compare the development of the semantic network in these groups.

In sum, the relatively spontaneous word association task can provide us with a qualitative mapping of individual language users' semantic networks, their potential preferences for certain kinds of semantic relations, and the way they compare to other groups of language users in this regard. Due to the spontaneous nature of the task however, it is difficult to use it as an assessment of semantic knowledge. Rather, it expresses the preferences or relative ease of access to certain kinds of semantic relations that language users may exhibit.

Tasks Assessing Declarative Knowledge of Semantic Relations

Various tools aimed at the assessment of knowledge of semantic relations have been developed, focusing on the ability to identify relations. In these tasks, participants are required to select semantically related words, distinguishing them from unrelated or differently related distractor words. For example, the Deep Vocabulary Knowledge (DVK) task developed by Qian (2002) based on the word associates format by Read (1993) requires participants to select synonyms and collocates for adjective stimuli. Similarly, a standardized task for knowledge of word relations is the CELF Word Classes subtest (Semel, Wiig, & Secord, 2003), which has been normed for children from 5 to 18 years of age. In this task, participants are required to select two related words from sets of three or four words. Semantic relations between these words include many different types, such as functional relations, contextual relations, and coordination, meaning that the task is suited for testing general knowledge, but not for targeting specific semantic relations or assessing the ability to distinguish them from other types of semantic relations.

The latter option has been explored by Schoonen and Verhallen (2008), who based their test on the finding that context-independent semantic knowledge develops later than context-dependent semantic knowledge. In their Word Association Task (WAT), developed in Dutch for children between 9 and 12 years of age, participants are required to select three target words that are context-independently related to a stimulus, with three unrelated or context-dependently related distractor words. Here then, not only the awareness of a semantic relation is tested, but also the ability to distinguish relations that hold true independent of context (i.e., *dog – poodle*) from context relations (*dog – jump*).

These tasks provide a measure of declarative knowledge of semantic relations, which can target knowledge of certain types of relations in a more principled way, with the potential of eliciting knowledge that is available but not accessed in the more spontaneous free association task.

Categorization Tasks

Differences in preferences for types of semantic organization can be tested using categorization tasks, in which participants are presented with a set of words or pictures and required to select the items that are related to a target. The set typically contains items that bear different types of semantic relations to the target, resulting in a measure of preference for different types of semantic relations.

For example, Mirman and Graziano (2012) tested adults (mean age 66) in a task which first presented a target picture (e.g., *finger*) followed by a thematically related (*ring*) and a taxonomically related picture (*thumb*) and required participants to choose the picture that "goes best" with a target picture. They found that most of their participants did not have a consistent preference for either type of semantic relation, but that participants who did show a taxonomic preference, also showed more competition of taxonomic items in a spoken word recognition task, as indicated by their fixations of taxonomic distractors within the array of visual response options. Conversely, Lin and Murphy (2001) did find many of their young adult participants exhibited consistent taxonomic or thematic preferences in a similar task using words instead of pictures, with a majority (62%) preferring thematic relations. This may be an indication of differences in organization preferences across the different age groups, but the use of different stimuli (pictures vs. words) may also play a role.

In contrast to tasks forcing participants to distinguish a certain type of semantic relation from unrelated or differently related word pairs, the categorization task allows for a more spontaneous measure of semantic preference, similar to word association tasks. However, by juxtaposing specific semantic relations, these preferences can be studied in a more principled and controlled fashion. An important methodological consideration in these types of tasks is the relationship strength between the target and the different answer options. A pretest establishing this strength is therefore a necessity and may be done using rating studies. For example, Mirman and Graziano (2012) asked a separate group of participants to indicate which two words in their triad stimuli belonged to the same category or were likely to occur in the same situation or scene, for taxonomic and thematic ratings, respectively.

Category Generation

In category generation tasks, knowledge of semantic relations within specific domains is targeted. Participants are asked to produce as many items as possible to fit a certain category, such as "tools", "animals" or "occupations". It can also be seen as a guided, instead of free, association task. Again, a normed and standardized version of such a task is available in the CELF test battery, namely the Word Association subtest (Semel et al., 2003). By setting a time limit (60s in the case of the CELF-WA subtest, but for example only 10s in a study by Tannenbaum et al., 2006), the response can be speeded, meaning that a measure of semantic fluency can be derived. Scores on this type of task have been found to be associated with reading comprehension skill (Nation & Snowling, 1998; Tannenbaum et al., 2006).

Different types of categories may be used to assess different types of semantic knowledge. Peña, Bedore, and Zlatic-Giunta (2002), for example, compared fluency in taxonomic categories such as "animals" with so-called slot-filler categories, such as "animals one would find at a farm". The latter type of category is supported by co-occurrence in experience, meaning that it is more context-dependent than purely taxonomic categories. Peña et al. studied bilingual children's ability to generate items within each of these types of categories in both of their languages and at different ages. They found that the bilinguals produced similar numbers of items across categories in each of their languages, but that older children produced more taxonomic items than slot-filler items, compared to a younger age group which produced similar numbers of concepts in each category.

The category generation task is thus an example of a guided production task that measures the fluency of access and availability of certain types of semantic relations, essentially by constraining the word association task. Careful definition of goal categories can allow for detailed comparisons of various semantic domains.

Semantic Priming

Online measures of the spreading activation that is occurring in individuals' semantic networks during language use are also available, in the form of a range of different types of semantic priming tasks. In these tasks, participants are traditionally presented with single-word stimuli and required to provide a response, which is timed. By including related and unrelated prime – target pairs in the stimulus lists, for example *animal – dog* and *bicycle – dog*, the effect of relatedness on response time can be measured. If participants are faster to respond to targets preceded by related primes compared to targets preceded by unrelated primes, a priming effect is present. Provided the experiment is set up to elicit automatic rather than strategic processing, the effect is considered to be due to spreading activation within the semantic network (cf., McNamara, 2005). In addition to single-word studies, the principle of semantic priming can be extended to the sentence level, for example by measuring reading times to related words in sentences using self-paced reading or eye tracking (Camblin, Gordon, & Swaab, 2007). Finally, some studies include neurological measures such as EEG (Landi & Perfetti, 2007) or fMRI (Sachs et al., 2008) to study the neural correlates of different types of semantic effects.

In all, an extensive number of studies have been conducted, demonstrating priming effects for many types of context-independent and context-dependent relations both with and without the presence of an associative relation. Many excellent reviews on different types of priming effects are available, for example on differences between associative, categorical, and thematic relations (Jones & Estes, 2012), semantic priming with and without association (Lucas, 2000), and priming effects in discourse (Ledoux, Camblin, Swaab, & Gordon, 2006).

Semantic priming studies thus allow for the study of a range of semantic relations and their effects in both the aural and written modality, with single words and in (short) discourse contexts. Careful construction of both the related and unrelated word pairs is crucial to allow for a fair comparison, which involves controlling for a wide range of factors, such as word frequency, length, and phonological similarities, as discussed earlier. Some authors perform norming studies to ensure the relationship strength between different conditions is similar, especially when comparing different types of semantic relations (Hare, Jones, Thomson, Kelly, & McRae, 2009; Spätgens & Schoonen, 2018). Depending on the goal of the study, the semantic relation in focus may also need to be carefully disentangled from potential associative relations. English word association data are currently available from various sources, e.g., the Edinburgh Associative Thesaurus (Kiss, Armstrong, Milroy, & Piper, 1973), the University of South Florida association norms (Nelson, McEvoy, & Schreiber, 2004) and notably, from the multiple association task used in the Small World of Words project (De Deyne & Storms, 2008; English data available from De Deyne via https://ppw.kuleuven.be/apps/concat/simon/?datasets). McNamara (2005) provides an excellent reference work for the many methodological considerations in priming studies. An important note here is that researchers have found that although priming effects are generally very robust at the group level, they may be less reliable within individuals. Especially when automatic processing is tapped, test-retest reliability may be low within participants, suggesting that such priming effects may be relatively unstable (Stolz, Besner, & Carr, 2005; Yap, Hutchison, & Tan, 2016).

Operationalizing the Semantic Network: Concluding Remarks

In sum, a host of tasks exist that can be used to measure semantic knowledge, each with their own specific characteristics and targeting knowledge of semantic relations in more or less guided ways, assessing both active and passive knowledge, both online and offline. Previous studies have shown that the semantic network evolves during language development, both in the L1 and the L2, and that differences in network structure and knowledge of semantic relations are associated with other aspects of language proficiency.

Future Directions

It will be obvious that word knowledge is multifaceted and that our language processing is affected by all these facets to a smaller or larger extent. It is virtually impossible to count with all these facets at the same time. In that respect we should conclude that each word is unique, in its form, its meaning, frequency, associations, and spot in the semantic network.

Nevertheless, we should strive for reasonable comparability when we select word stimuli for the different conditions in our lexical (training) experiments. Therefore, it is necessary that we continue our investigations into the relevant facets of single-word items and how they are interrelated and affect language processing, both language understanding and language production. Here we have focused on single-word items, but these cannot be completely isolated from their linguistic contexts, that is, the multiple word phrases they occur in, such as collocations and idiomatic expressions. These lines of research should be integrated.

Furthermore, most of the research reviewed discusses the effects of word characteristics at the participant group level, often young adults or language learning children. However, it is important to take this a step further to the level of the individual language user. How does an individual's preference for certain semantic relations affect his or her reading fluency? Or, how does one's sensitivity to priming relate to one's listening skills? Is a dense semantic network beneficial to fluent language production? These kinds of questions have so far only been scarcely touched upon. But then, addressing these questions requires a very good understanding of what facets of single (and multiple) word expressions need to be taken into account. Fortunately, more and more information comes available about the facets that really matter in lexical and semantic tasks, and also more corpora and lexical databases are compiled and made available for research purposes. It only takes a few clicks to find out that Brown's two-year-old's *cow* has a word frequency of 25.51 per million and occurs in 8.68% of the more than 8,000 subtitled films (cf. Brysbaert & New, 2009) and *milk* is its strongest associate.

Further Reading

Schmitt, N. (2010). *Researching vocabulary: A vocabulary research manual*. Houndmills, Basingstoke Hampshire, UK: Palgrave Macmillan.

Schmitt provides an extensive manual for vocabulary research, including many references to resources.

Balota, D. A., Yap, M. J., & Cortese, M. J. (2006). Visual word recognition: The journey from features to meaning (a travel update). In M. J. Traxler & M. A. Gernsbacher (Eds.), *Handbook of psycholinguistics* (2nd ed., pp. 285–375). Boston, MA: Elsevier.

Balota et al. conducted detailed research of factors involved in (visual) word recognition. They provide definitions and operationalizations of those factors. See also Lemhöfer et al. (2008) for another study on this topic.

McNamara, T. (2005). *Semantic priming: Perspectives from memory and word recognition*. New York, NY and Hove, UK: Psychology Press.

McNamara is an excellent introduction to (general) issues concerning semantic priming. More specific reviews of priming research can be found in Jones & Estes (2012), Lucas (2000), and Ledoux et al. (2006).

Related Topics

Different aspects of vocabulary knowledge, the mental lexicon, vocabulary and proficiency, processing single-word and multiword items, measuring depth of vocabulary knowledge, sensitive measures of vocabulary knowledge, key issues in measuring vocabulary knowledge, resources for researching vocabulary

References

Baayen, H. (2001). *Word frequency distributions*. Dordrecht, Boston, MA and London, UK: Kluwer Academic Publishers.

Baayen, R. H., Feldman, L. B., & Schreuder, R. (2006). Morphological influences on the recognition of monosyllabic monomorphemic words. *Journal of Memory and Language, 55*(2), 290–313.

Baayen, R. H., Piepenbrock, R., & Van Rijn, H. (1993). *The CELEX lexical database* (CDROM). University of Pennsylvania, Philadelphia, PA: Linguistic Data Consortium.

Balota, D. A., Yap, M. J., & Cortese, M. J. (2006). Visual word recognition: The journey from features to meaning (a travel update). In M. J. Traxler & M. A. Gernsbacher (Eds.), *Handbook of psycholinguistics* (2nd ed., pp. 285–375). Boston, MA: Elsevier.

Betjemann, R. S., & Keenan, J. M. (2008). Phonological and semantic priming in children with reading disability. *Child Development, 79*(4), 1086–1102.

Breland, H. M. (1996). Word frequency and word difficulty: A comparison of counts in four corpora. *Psychological Science, 7*(2), 96–99. https://doi.org/10.1111/j.1467-9280.1996.tb00336.x

Brown, R. (1973). *A first language. The early stages*. Cambridge, MA: Harvard University Press.

Brysbaert, M., & New, B. (2009). Moving beyond Kučera and Francis: A critical evaluation of current word frequency norms and the introduction of a new and improved word frequency measure for American English. *Behavior Research Methods, 41*(4), 977–990. https://doi.org/10.3758/BRM.41.4.977

Brysbaert, M., Warriner, A. B., & Kuperman, V. (2014). Concreteness ratings for 40 thousand generally known English word lemmas. *Behavior Research Methods, 46*(3), 904–911. https://doi.org/10.3758/s13428-013-0403-5

Camblin, C. C., Gordon, P. C., & Swaab, T. Y. (2007). The interplay of discourse congruence and lexical association during sentence processing: Evidence from ERPs and eye tracking. *Journal of Memory and Language, 56*(1), 103–128.

Collins, A. M., & Loftus, E. F. (1975). A spreading-activation theory of semantic processing. *Psychological Review, 82*(6), 407–428.

Cortese, M. J., & Fugett, A. (2004). Imageability ratings for 3,000 monosyllabic words. *Behavior Research Methods, Instruments, & Computers, 36*(3), 384–387. https://doi.org/10.3758/BF03195585.

Coxhead, A., Nation, I. S. P., & Sim, D. (2014). Creating and trialling six forms of the Vocabulary Size Test. *The TESOLANZ Journal, 22*, 13–27.

Cremer, M., Dingshoff, D., de Beer, M., & Schoonen, R. (2011). Do word associations assess word knowledge? A comparison of L1 and L2, child and adult word associations. *International Journal of Bilingualism, 15*(2), 187–204.

Cruse, D. A. (2000). *Meaning in language: An introduction to semantics and pragmatics*. Oxford/New York: Oxford University Press.

Davies, M. (2008). *The Corpus of Contemporary American English (COCA): 560 million words, 1990-present*. Retrieved from https://corpus.byu.edu/coca/.

De Deyne, S., & Storms, G. (2008). Word associations: Network and semantic properties. *Behavior Research Methods, 40*(1), 213–231.

De Groot, A. M. B. (2006). Effects of stimulus characteristics and background music on foreign language vocabulary learning and forgetting. *Language Learning, 56*(3), 463–506.

De Groot, A. M. B., & Keijzer, R. (2000). What is hard to learn is easy to forget: The roles of word concreteness, cognate status, and word frequency in foreign-language vocabulary learning and forgetting. *Language Learning, 50*(1), 1–56.

Dijkstra, T., Timmermans, M., & Schriefers, H. (2000). On being blinded by your other language: Effects of task demands on interlingual homograph recognition. *Journal of Memory and Language, 42*(4), 445–464. https://doi.org/10.1006/jmla.1999.2697.

Ellis, N. C., & Beaton, A. (1993). Psycholinguistic determinants of foreign language vocabulary learning. *Language Learning, 43*(4), 559–617.

Estes, Z., Golonka, S., & Jones, L. L. (2011). Thematic thinking: The apprehension and consequences of thematic relations. *Psychology of Learning and Motivation, 54*, 249–294.

Fitzpatrick, T. (2006). Habits and rabbits: Word associations and the L2 lexicon. *EUROSLA Yearbook, 6*(1), 121–145. https://doi.org/10.1075/eurosla.6.09fit.

Fitzpatrick, T., Playfoot, D., Wray, A., & Wright, M. J. (2013). Establishing the reliability of word association data for investigating individual and group differences. *Applied Linguistics, 36*(1), 23–50.

Grainger, J., O'Regan, J. K., Jacobs, A. M., & Segui, J. (1989). On the role of competing word units in visual word recognition: The neighborhood frequency effect. *Perception & Psychophysics, 45*(3), 189–195.

Gries, S. Th. (2010). Dispersions and adjusted frequencies in corpora: Further explorations. In S.Th. Gries, S. Wulf and M. Davies (Eds.), *Corpus-linguistic applications: Current studies, new directions* (pp. 197–212). Leiden, The Netherlands: Brill/Rodopi. https://doi.org/10.1163/9789042028012_014

Hare, M., Jones, M., Thomson, C., Kelly, S., & McRae, K. (2009). Activating event knowledge. *Cognition, 111*(2), 151–167.

Jones, L. L., & Estes, Z. (2012). Lexical priming: Associative, semantic and thematic influences on word recognition. In J. S. Adelman (Ed.), *Visual word recognition* (Vol. 2, pp. 44–72). Hove, UK: Psychology Press.

Juhasz, B. J., & Rayner, K. (2003). Investigating the effects of a set of intercorrelated variables on eye fixation durations in reading. *Journal of Experimental Psychology: Learning, Memory, and Cognition, 29*(6), 1312–1318.

Kiss, G. R., Armstrong, C., Milroy, R., & Piper, J. (1973). An associative thesaurus of English and its computer analysis. In A. Aitken, R. Bailey, & N. Hamilton-Smith (Eds.), *The computer and literacy studies* (pp. 153–165). Edinburgh, UK: University Press.

Kučera, H., & Francis, W. N. (1967). *Computational analysis of present-day American English.* Dartmouth Publishing Group.

Landi, N., & Perfetti, C. A. (2007). An electrophysiological investigation of semantic and phonological processing in skilled and less-skilled comprehenders. *Brain and Language, 102*(1), 30–45.

Laufer, B. (1997). What's in a word that makes it hard or easy? Intralexical factors affecting the difficulty of vocabulary acquisition. In N. Schmitt & M. McCarthey (Eds.), *Vocabulary: Description, acquisition and pedagogy* (pp. 141–155). Cambridge, UK: Cambridge University Press.

Ledoux, K., Camblin, C. C., Swaab, T. Y., & Gordon, P. C. (2006). Reading words in discourse: The modulation of lexical priming effects by message-level context. *Behavioral and Cognitive Neuroscience Reviews, 5*(3), 107–127.

Lemhöfer, K., Dijkstra, T., Schriefers, H., Baayen, H., Grainger, J., & Zwitserlood, P. (2008). Native language influences on word recognition in a second language: A megastudy. *Journal of Experimental Psychology: Learning, Memory, and Cognition, 34*(1), 12–31.

Lin, E. L., & Murphy, G. (2001). Thematic relations in adults' concepts. *Journal of Experimental Psychology: General, 130*(1), 3–28.

Lucas, M. (2000). Semantic priming without association: A meta-analytic review. *Psychonomic Bulletin & Review, 7*(4), 618–630.

Lydell, S. (2015). *Bigrams-to-pairs.js.* Retrieved March 29, 2018 from https://gist.github.com/lydell/c439049abac2c9226e53

Marslen-Wilson, W. D. (1987). Functional parallelism in spoken word-recognition. *Cognition, 25*(1–2), 71–102.

McNamara, T. (2005). *Semantic priming: Perspectives from memory and word recognition.* New York, NY and Hove, UK: Psychology Press.

Miller, G. A., Beckwith, R., Fellbaum, C., Gross, D., & Miller, K. J. (1990). Introduction to WordNet: An on-line lexical database. *International Journal of Lexicography, 3*(4), 235–244.

Mirman, D., & Graziano, K. M. (2012). Individual differences in the strength of taxonomic versus thematic relations. *Journal of Experimental Psychology: General, 141*(4), 601–609.

Nation, I. S. P. (1983). Testing and teaching vocabulary. *Guidelines, 5*(1), 12–25.

Nation, I. S. P., & Beglar, D. (2007). A Vocabulary Size Test. *The Language Teacher, 31*(7), 9–13.

Nation, K., & Snowling, M. J. (1998). Semantic processing and the development of word-recognition skills: Evidence from children with reading comprehension difficulties. *Journal of Memory and Language, 39*(1), 85–101.

Nelson, D. L., McEvoy, C. L., & Schreiber, T. A. (2004). The University of South Florida free association, rhyme, and word fragment norms. *Behavior Research Methods, Instruments, & Computers, 36*(3), 402–407.

Nelson, K. (2007). *Young minds in social worlds: Experience, meaning, and memory.* Cambridge, MA and London, UK: Harvard University Press.

Peña, E. D., Bedore, L. M., & Zlatic-Giunta, R. (2002). Category-generation performance of bilingual children: The influence of condition, category, and language. *Journal of Speech, Language, and Hearing Research, 45*(5), 938–947.

Qian, D. D. (2002). Investigating the relationship between vocabulary knowledge and academic reading performance: An assessment perspective. *Language Learning, 52*(3), 513–536.

Read, J. (1993). The development of a new measure of L2 vocabulary knowledge. *Language Testing, 10*(3), 355–371.

Sachs, O., Weis, S., Zellagui, N., Huber, W., Zvyagintsev, M., Mathiak, K., & Kircher, T. (2008). Automatic processing of semantic relations in fMRI: Neural activation during semantic priming of taxonomic and thematic categories. *Brain Research, 1218,* 194–205.

Schmitt, N. (2010). *Researching vocabulary : A vocabulary research manual.* Houndmills, Basingstoke Hampshire, UK: Palgrave Macmillan.

Schmitt, N., Schmitt, D., & Clapham, C. (2001). Developing and exploring the behaviour of two new versions of the Vocabulary Levels Test. *Language Testing, 18*(1), 55–88.

Schock, J., Cortese, M. J., & Khanna, M. M. (2012). Imageability estimates for 3,000 disyllabic words. *Behavior Research Methods, 44*(2), 374–379.

Schoonen, R., & Verhallen, M. (2008). The assessment of deep word knowledge in young first and second language learners. *Language Testing, 25*(2), 211–236.

Schreuder, R., & Baayen, R. H. (1997). How complex simplex words can be. *Journal of Memory and Language, 37*(1), 118–139.

Semel, E., Wiig, E. H., & Secord, W. A. (2003). *Clinical evaluation of language fundamentals* (4th ed. (CELF-4)). Toronto, Canada: The Psychological Corporation/A Harcourt Assessment Company.

Shao, Z., Roelofs, A., & Meyer, A. S. (2014). Predicting naming latencies for action pictures: Dutch norms. *Behavior Research Methods, 46*(1), 274–283. https://doi.org/10.3758/s13428-013-0358-6

Solso, R. L., & Juel, C. L. (1980). Positional frequency and versatility of bigrams for two-through nine-letter English words. *Behavior Research Methods & Instrumentation, 12*(3), 297–343.

Spätgens, T., & Schoonen, R. (2018). The semantic network, lexical access, and reading comprehension in monolingual and bilingual children: An individual differences study. *Applied Psycholinguistics, 39*(1), 225–256.

Spätgens, T., & Schoonen, R. (submitted). The structure of developing semantic networks: Evidence from single and multiple word associations in monolingual and bilingual readers. Manuscript submitted for publication.

Stolz, J., Besner, D., & Carr, T. (2005). Implications of measures of reliability for theories of priming: Activity in semantic memory is inherently noisy and uncoordinated. *Visual Cognition, 12*(2), 284–336.

Swart, N. M., Muijselaar, M. M., Steenbeek-Planting, E. G., Droop, M., de Jong, P. F., & Verhoeven, L. (2017). Differential lexical predictors of reading comprehension in fourth graders. *Reading and Writing, 30*(3), 489–507.

Tannenbaum, K. R., Torgesen, J. K., & Wagner, R. K. (2006). Relationships between word knowledge and reading comprehension in third-grade children. *Scientific Studies of Reading, 10*(4), 381–398.

Van Heuven, W. J. B., Dijkstra, T., & Grainger, J. (1998). Orthographic neighborhood effects in bilingual word recognition. *Journal of Memory and Language, 39*(3), 458–483.

Vitevitch, M. S. (2007). The spread of the phonological neighborhood influences spoken word recognition. *Memory and Cognition, 35*(1), 166–175.

Vitevitch, M. S., & Luce, P. A. (2016). Phonological neighborhood effects in spoken word perception and production. *Annual Review of Linguistics, 2*(1), 75–94.

Webb, S., Sasao, Y., & Ballance, O. (2017). The updated Vocabulary Levels Test: Developing and validating two new forms of the VLT. *ITL – International Journal of Applied Linguistics, 168*(1), 33–369.

Yap, M. J., Hutchison, K., & Tan, L. C. (2016). Individual differences in semantic priming performance: Insights from the semantic priming project. In M. N. Jones (Ed.), *Big data in cognitive science* (pp. 203–226). New York, NY: Psychology Press.

Zareva, A., & Wolter, B. (2012). The "promise" of three methods of word association analysis to L2 lexical research. *Second Language Research, 28*(1), 41–67.

33

Key Issues in Researching Multiword Items

Anna Siyanova-Chanturia and Taha Omidian

Introduction

Recent years have seen an unprecedented interest in multiword items as a linguistic, psycholinguistic, cognitive, and pedagogical phenomenon. They have firmly established themselves as a cornerstone of vocabulary research (see special issues dedicated to learning, processing, and using wordstrings in *Annual Review of Applied Linguistics*, 2012, Vol. 32; *Language Teaching Research*, 2017, Vol. 21:3; *The Mental Lexicon*, 2014, Vol. 9:3; *Topics in Cognitive Science*, Vol. 9:3). Yet some of the issues associated with researching multiword items (MWIs), their definition(s), approaches to their identification, and their properties and characteristics are still poorly understood, under-researched, or even disregarded. The present chapter will center on some of the key issues in researching strings above the word level. Specifically, it will focus on the need and the ways to define MWIs and approaches to studying them. It will also look at the properties of multiword speech that have figured prominently in the literature. In addition, directions and pathways for future research will be outlined. While we attempt to cover a variety of issues and topics that are central to MWI investigation, this review is, of course, selective.

Identifying the key issues in MWI inquiry is no trivial task. Not only do these ubiquitous strings of language vary in a multitude of ways, they have also been researched from a plethora of rather distinct perspectives. Some of the prominent strands of MWI research have included first (L1) and second language (L2) discourse/learner corpus research (Granger, 1998; Howarth, 1998; Nesselhauf, 2005); L1 acquisition (Clark, 1993; Peters, 1983); L2 acquisition (Schmidt, 1983; Vihman, 1982); online processing (Arnon & Snider, 2010; Bannard & Matthews, 2008; Siyanova-Chanturia, Conklin, & van Heuven, 2011; Siyanova-Chanturia & Janssen, 2018); L2 pedagogy (Boers & Lindstromberg, 2008; Meunier, 2012; Wood, 2002); academic discourse (Biber, Conrad, & Cortes, 2004; Hyland, 2008; Durrant & Mathews-Aydinli, 2011); prosody, fluency, and intonation (Lin, 2012, 2018; Van Lancker-Sidtis, 2003; Wood, 2004); pragmatics (Bardovi-Harlig, 2009; Bell, 2012); computational and corpus linguistics (Evert, 2009; Manning & Schutze, 1999), and others. Understandably, each of these strands will have its own key issues and topics in the examination of MWIs, which may be vastly different from those in another field. Despite this heterogeneity, however, some common aspects that are likely to be of interest to researchers across the various lines of MWI inquiry can be identified.

Critical Issues and Topics

Defining and Identifying Multiword Items

While the issue of terminology is dealt with in detail elsewhere (Wood, this volume), an important distinction should be made between two commonly used umbrella terms: *formulaic language* and *multiword items/expressions*. The two are often assumed to refer to the same concept and used interchangeably. Yet, for research purposes, in particular, it is important to make an informed decision as to which umbrella term, and consequently the broad underlying phenomenon, is of interest. In this chapter, we use the term *multiword items* because our primary focus is on strings of language that are, by definition, longer than a single word. In contrast, formulaic language embraces multiword as well as single-word items, such as expletives and exclamations (*darn, wow*), conversational speech formulas (*yeah, hello*), and other formulaic items at the (single) word level (Van Lancker-Sidtis & Rallon, 2004; Wray, 2002). This distinction is important, for example, in clinical observations involving individuals with language disorders (aphasia, right hemisphere damage, Alzheimer's disease and Parkinson's disease) where one's ability to produce and comprehend formulaic speech – of any size, length and complexity – is compared with the ability to deal with novel, propositional speech (Bridges & Van Lancker-Sidtis, 2013; Van Lancker-Sidtis, Choi, Alken, & Sidtis, 2015). The focus of the present chapter is thus on the key issues in researching multiword sequences, adjacent and not, but necessarily spanning two or more words.

A distinct but related issue pertains to choosing an approach to identifying MWIs. Although various approaches have figured in the literature, two in particular have been popular. As noted in Siyanova-Chanturia (2015a), some researchers have relied on language speakers' intuitions (at times, their own) about "prefabricated" or "formulaic" strings of words vs. novel word combinations (Foster, 2001), or free vs. restricted combinations (Howarth, 1998; Nesselhauf, 2005). This approach can be referred to as a qualitative or "phraseological" approach to defining and identifying MWIs. Very loosely, the term phraseology can be defined as "the study of the structure, meaning and use of word combinations" (Cowie, 1994, p. 3168). The focus of this approach is mainly on distinguishing compositional phrases from non-compositional ones with an emphasis on certain semantic criteria, as well as intuitive judgments to determine the degree to which the meaning of an MWI can be inferred from its constituent parts. What lies at the heart of this approach is its reliance on rather impressionistic evidence for the definition and identification of MWIs.

A different approach altogether has been a quantitative, "frequency-based" one in which intuitions and native-speaker judgments play no role (Durrant & Schmitt, 2009). The frequency-based tradition defines an MWI as "the relationship a lexical item has with items that appear with greater than random probability in its (textual) context" (Hoey, 1991, p. 7). Two or more words can be considered an MWI if they are found together more often than the frequencies of their constituents would predict (Jones & Sinclair, 1974; Manning & Schutze, 1999; also see Hoey, 2005; Sinclair, 2004; Stubbs, 1995). By utilizing large text corpora and various statistical metrics, such as frequency and measures of association strengths (e.g., mutual information, t-score), proponents of the frequency-based tradition have developed different methodologies to study the use of MWIs in natural language. Two general approaches have emerged from this tradition: "corpus-based" and "corpus-driven"

(Tognini-Bonelli, 2001). In the corpus-based approach, corpus evidence is used to analyze different patterns of use for a set of pre-defined sequences. This approach relies heavily on theoretical presumptions regarding the semantic and syntactic properties of MWIs and uses corpus analysis as an evidential tool to validate these pre-established conceptions (Erman & Warren, 2000; Moon, 1998; Nattinger & DeCarrico, 1992). The corpus-driven approach, however, is more inductive in nature, in the sense that sequences emerge from the corpus analysis with little theoretical assumptions guiding their identification (Biber, 2009). In this approach, it is the emerged linguistic patterns that form the foundation of a linguistic theory, and not vice versa.

Neither the more qualitative (intuition-based), nor the more quantitative (frequency-based) approach is perfect; both have their strengths as well as their limitations. For example, while adopting a frequency-based approach can provide us with a systematic description of commonly used linguistic features in a corpus, the extent to which the identified features are the preferred way of expressing the intended meaning in a given context requires a qualitative investigation (Wray, 2002). On the contrary, relying solely on qualitative techniques and intuitive judgments runs the risk of overlooking rather non-salient MWIs (lexical bundles) whose characteristics are more amenable to empirical and frequency-based approaches than intuitive ones (Biber et al., 1999; Durrant & Schmitt, 2009). Because of the clearly complementary nature of these approaches, the two have recently started to be combined (Chen & Baker, 2010; Durrant, 2017; Garnier & Schmitt, 2015; Omidian, Shahriari, & Siyanova-Chanturia, 2018; Simpson-Vlach & Ellis, 2010). For instance, Durrant (2017) adopted a quantitative approach to explore disciplinary variations in the use of lexical bundles. He used the data elicited from this approach as the basis for a qualitative analysis of the identified bundles and their distinctive discourse functions which marked the differences between disciplines.

Whether one approach or a combination of two is adopted, what is critical is to explicitly define MWIs under investigation and, correspondingly, state the approach(es) to identifying them, as these factors will have implications for how the target MWIs will be treated and researched, and how the findings may (or may not) be comparable across relevant studies in the field. These considerations are important in the context of any study focusing on MWIs, irrespective of the methodology adopted, ranging from questionnaire-, test- and corpora-based studies to psycholinguistic explorations, employing reaction times and eye movements.

Properties of Multiword Items

MWIs are extremely heterogeneous and multifarious in nature. They come in various shapes and sizes, vary along all sorts of continua, and are anything but easy to define and classify (see Wood, this volume). In this section, we will cover some of the common aspects of MWIs that have figured in the literature. It is important to understand these properties as they will determine how certain MWIs may or may not be researched, and whether some kinds of MWIs might be more suitable than others for the research question at hand.

Frequency

Frequency is one of the most prominent statistical properties of multiword speech. Language users generally prioritize those sequences that are frequently used in their speech community. Scholars have argued that the frequency with which lexical phrases occur in language determines their degree of prominence among language users (Ellis, 2002;

also see Conklin, this volume). With this understanding, many studies have considered frequency of occurrence as the ultimate arbiter of MWI usefulness. Indeed, it seems reasonable to link frequency of a phrase to its usefulness. However, it is important to note that there are numerous instances of useful MWIs, which are extremely infrequent in even the largest corpora (*in for a penny, in for a pound*). As Wray (2002) argues, such sequences are commonly used only in the context in which their communicative function is warranted. In other words, the communicative function of a sequence plays an important role in its prominence and usefulness in different contexts. For example, the lexical bundle *one of the most* performs a basic function in the language, which is the reason why this sequence is highly frequent in virtually all types of language use (Biber et al., 2004). On the contrary, the function of an expression such as *dish the dirt* is strongly associated with "gossiping", which renders the sequence useful and frequent only in that particular context. As Simpson-Vlach and Ellis (2010) point out, many instances of high-frequency word combinations (*that there is a*) lack distinctive functions or meanings, which questions their value for pedagogical purposes. This issue was addressed by Durrant and Mathews-Aydınlı (2011), who adopted a "function-first" approach in which the corpus under analysis was annotated for various communicative functions, and formulas were then identified as the recurrent linguistic units associated with each function. The authors argued that frequency of occurrence is an insufficient guide to recognizing the communicative functions associated with an MWI.

In addition, frequency in itself does not provide much information regarding the formulaic status of an MWI. In essence, the argument pertains to the assumption that the frequency of a phrase is a function of its formulaicity (Herbst, 2011; Widdowson, 1990). Schmitt, Grandage, and Adolphs (2004) investigated the formulaic status of highly recurrent clusters (extracted from different corpora) by presenting them to participants in a psycholinguistic task. The authors found that the holistic storage of the target sequences varied among participants and frequency alone was insufficient for drawing conclusions regarding the formulaicity of sequences. Schmitt et al. (2004) concluded that "it is unwise to take recurrence of clusters in a corpus as evidence that those clusters are also stored as formulaic sequences in the mind" (p. 147). Similar concerns have been voiced by Ellis (2012) who also stressed the inherent inadequacy of frequency in providing an accurate account of formulaicity. It is thus important to point out that drawing any psycholinguistic conclusions regarding the degree of formulaicity of a phrase solely on the grounds of frequency is indirect and subject to scrutiny (Durrant, 2008; Durrant & Mathews-Aydınlı, 2011; Siyanova-Chanturia, 2015b). As argued by Durrant and Siyanova-Chanturia (2015, pp. 74–75), "it is especially important that we avoid the temptation of automatically ascribing all patterns found in the corpus to features of mind without further interrogation".

Familiarity and Predictability

As noted earlier, frequency is often viewed as a key characteristic of MWIs, defining how these strings of language are acquired, processed, and used in an L1 and L2 (see Boers, this volume; Conklin, this volume). A related but distinct aspect of MWIs is familiarity. It seems sensible to propose that frequency should strongly correlate with familiarity. The more frequent a phrase is, the more likely it is to be familiar to a language user, and subsequently become encoded in their mental lexicon. However, familiarity and frequency are distinct and may be more or less important for various kinds of MWIs. There are sequences which are formulaic and familiar to the linguistic community but are, nevertheless, extremely infrequent.

For example, the expressions *never too late to mend* and *everything but the kitchen sink* are no doubt familiar to any native speaker of English; yet, they are rather infrequent, with the latter appearing just twice in the British National Corpus (BNC) and the former not being attested at all. Thus, very infrequent MWIs, like certain idioms and proverbs, may still be thought of and treated as highly conventional and formulaic (Hallin & Van Lancker-Sidtis, 2017; Moon, 1998; Reuterskiöld & Van Lancker-Sidtis, 2013). Recently, Hallin and Van Lancker-Sidtis (2017) investigated the prosodic characteristics of familiar infrequent Swedish proverbs spoken by a group of adults and children. In order to confirm the familiarity of the target proverbs, participants were asked to indicate, in a questionnaire, whether or not they had heard or used the target proverbs. The authors found that, although the included proverbs were extremely infrequent (0–0.3 occurrences per million words in a reference corpus), they had been either used or heard by all adult participants and the majority of children. The analyses of the prosodic characteristics revealed that the proverbs, despite their low frequency of occurrence, were spoken significantly faster and with less stressed tonal patterns than matched control sentences, a pattern of results similar to that reported in the studies with highly frequent MWIs (Bybee & Scheibman, 1999; Gregory, Raymond, Bell, Fosler-Lussier, & Jurafsky, 1999; Jurafsky, Bell, Gregory, & Raymond, 2001). This observation indicates that familiarity, irrespective of frequency, plays an important role in how MWIs are processed and used in speech.

One consequence of being a highly familiar string of language is that the sequence becomes uniquely recognizable, or predictable. That is, upon reading the initial constituent(s) of an idiom (*a piece . . .*), a saying (*early bird . . .*), or a collocation (*excruciating . . .*), a proficient speaker is very likely to complete the phrase correctly with *of cake, catches the worm*, and *pain*, respectively. Thus, the final constituent(s) of an MWI can be said to be almost redundant, in that they are uniquely anticipated prior to the reader reaching them. This feature of MWIs has, in particular, been interrogated in psycholinguistic (Siyanova-Chanturia et al., 2011; Underwood, Schmitt, & Galpin, 2004) and neurolinguistic studies (Molinaro & Carreiras, 2010; Vespignani, Canal, Molinaro, Fonda, & Cacciari, 2010). The latter suggest that distinct neural mechanisms may be involved in the processing of predictable phrasal information, where Word n is uniquely expected based on the reading of Word n-1. In a study looking at the comprehension of Italian idioms, Vespignani et al. (2010) put forward the notion of categorical template matching – a mechanism that operates specifically for multiword sequences and which is linked to the activation of a template believed to be stored in the semantic memory. This proposition is supported by probabilistic models of language, according to which information about the co-occurrence of single words (the fact that *bride* frequently appears next to *groom* to form a familiar binomial *bride and groom*) is represented in language users' mind (Gregory et al., 1999; McDonald & Shillcock, 2003). In line with these models, the brain draws on large amounts of statistical information to estimate the probability of Word n following Word n-1 during language comprehension.

Fixedness and Compositionality

It is often assumed that multiword speech is fixed or semi-fixed (Moon, 1998; Schmitt, 2004; Wray, 2002). That is, while novel propositional speech is characterized by full syntactic flexibility, multiword speech is, by and large, rather fixed. Indeed, many MWIs are rigid, such that no changes are permitted without the phrase losing its original meaning (*kith and kin, by and large, first and foremost*). Other MWIs, however, allow some degree of variation, such as adjectival modification (*make a good impression*), quantification (*pull a few strings*), passivization (*beans were spilled*), pluralization (*red herring[s]*), and so on. In such cases, the expression – when modified – does not lose its original meaning or the MWI status.

Idioms and their internal structure have, in particular, received attention in the literature. Researchers have proposed that, despite their fixedness, idiomatic expressions undergo analyses not unlike those of propositional speech, and have argued against the "wordlike" nature of idioms. For example, decompositional analyses have been reported in the processing of L1 idioms (Konopka & Bock, 2009; Peterson, Burgess, Dell, & Eberhard, 2001; Snider & Arnon, 2012; Sprenger, Levelt, & Kempen, 2006). In Sprenger et al. (2006), idioms and non-idioms were successfully primed by one of the constituent words, suggesting that during the planning of an idiom, individual components are accessed separately. It was further found that idioms' literal word meanings were active during the production of idioms. These findings, as well as those of related studied by Konopka and Bock (2009), Peterson et al. (2001), Snider and Arnon (2012), and others in part support the compositional nature of idioms.

Thus, as with other properties, MWIs vary along a continuum of fixedness, with some items being rather fixed (*by and large*) and others being modifiable (*spill the beans → beans were spilled*). What existing evidence also alludes to is that even those MWIs that have traditionally been considered rather fixed – such as idioms – possess internal structure and undergo – at least to some extent – regular decompositional analyses.

The preceding considerations are important because they demonstrate that definitions depending solely on the linguistic aspects of MWIs may not provide a clear picture of their processing and status in the mind. Therefore, it is important for studies focusing on MWIs to avoid drawing psycholinguistic conclusions on the basis of linguistic evidence garnered from text (see Durrant & Siyanova-Chanturia, 2015 for a discussion).

Adjacency

Much of the research on MWIs in the field of applied linguistics has overlooked the effect of adjacency on the acquisition, processing and use of these units. Researchers in the neighboring fields such as cognitive science and psycholinguistics, however, have extensively studied the role of this phenomenon. This line of research has largely focused on the learnability and processing of adjacent (contiguous) and nonadjacent (separated by one or more intervening elements) linguistic units at both word and phrase levels (Gomez, 2002; Misyak, Christiansen, & Tomblin, 2009; Newport & Aslin, 2004). The findings reported in these studies point to an important role of adjacency in language. For example, Cleeremans and McClelland (1991) and Misyak et al. (2009) found that sensitivity to nonadjacent and longer-distance strings required more exposure than adjacent ones. Similar differences were reported by Gomez (2002) and Newport and Aslin (2004) who found a higher degree of learnability for adjacent sequences compared to their nonadjacent counterparts.

These studies, however, were largely conducted on lexical items in an artificial language, as the primary purpose of this line of research was to shed light on the capabilities of the human brain in acquiring and processing a language. Few studies have so far looked at adjacent vs. nonadjacent sequences in a natural language. In a corpus-based study, Cheng, Greaves, and Warren (2006) investigated the collocational patterns that may exist between two or more words, using the ConcGram software. The authors found that the majority of the collocational patterns identified by the software were noncontiguous, which was taken to argue that "searches which focus on contiguous collocations present an incomplete picture of the word associations that exist" (p. 431). This issue is acknowledged by Durrant (2009), who points out that the majority of the studies on collocation have exclusively focused on adjacent MWIs, namely *lexical bundles*, and have overlooked those with nonadjacent constituents.

More recently, MWI adjacency has been explored in a series of psycholinguistic experiments (Vilkaitė, 2016; Vilkaitė & Schmitt, 2017). For example, Vilkaitė (2016) and Vilkaitė and Schmitt (2017) used eye movements to compare the reading of adjacent (*achieve status*) and nonadjacent collocations (*achieve a more secure status*) vs. their respective controls (*ignore status*, *ignore a more secure status*) in native and non-native speakers of English. Both adjacent and nonadjacent MWIs were read faster than their controls by native speakers (Vilkaitė, 2016). Although the evidence is still rather scarce, we can argue that frequent sequences, irrespective of adjacency, enjoy a processing advantage compared to lower frequency controls. Vilkaitė and Schmitt (2017), however, found that while non-native speakers read adjacent MWIs faster than their controls, they exhibited almost no processing advantage for nonadjacent MWIs relative to their controls. These findings suggest that adjacency may differently affect MWI processing in a more and less proficient language. It is therefore important to take into account the role of adjacency in the acquisition, processing, and use of MWIs when researching these units.

Polysemy

Meaning variation has long been of interest to semanticists in the context of single words (Ravin & Leacock, 2000). More recently, the existence of polysemes has been documented in the context of strings longer than a word, such as MWIs (Gardner & Davies, 2007; Garnier & Schmitt, 2015; Liu, 2011; Macis & Schmitt, 2017). For example, Macis and Schmitt (2017) found that a large number of collocations in their study was polysemous, carrying both literal and figurative meanings. In an earlier study, Gardner and Davies (2007) reported that each of the phrasal verbs included in their list (a list of the most frequent English phrasal verbs) had 5.6 meaning senses on average. This led the authors to conclude that researchers "should continue to explore ways of identifying, tagging, and preserving the meaning senses of multiword items" (p. 355).

The polysemic nature of MWIs can complicate matters for researchers. For instance, Macis and Schmitt (2017) observed that the figurative meaning of a polysemous collocation such as *big nose* is exclusive to the world of wine tasting. This indicates that recognizing the multiplicity of meanings associated with certain MWIs relies heavily on understanding their intricate associations with the context in which they commonly occur. As argued by Sinclair (2004), studying linguistic items and their meanings in isolation would only add to their ambiguity. Another challenging aspect of researching polysemous sequences is that the meaning senses they impart may not remain the same across different varieties of English and registers. A case in point is Liu (2011) who found that a number of phrasal verbs on his list had certain meaning senses that were unique to American English and were completely absent in such sources as the BNC. Liu also noted that there is a significant difference between the semantic distribution of phrasal verbs such as *make up* in spoken and academic registers.

Such complications have led researchers to recognize the need to raise awareness of the importance of integrating the semantic analysis of MWIs with their identification (Durrant & Mathews-Aydınlı, 2011; Gardner & Davies, 2007; Garnier & Schmitt, 2015; Liu, 2011; Wray, 2002). However, while this proposition appears to enrich the research into MWIs, the greatest challenge that researchers face is how to account for the variant meanings of a polysemous sequence. Gardner and Davies (2007) used WordNet (Miller, 2003) to identify different meaning senses of the phrasal verbs on their list. While such electronic resources as WordNet (ibid.) and VIEW (Davies, 2005) have the potential to take account of various meaning senses of a sequence, relying solely on these databases has certain limitations. These limitations are acknowledged by Garnier and Schmitt (2015), who note the inadequacy of lexical databases in providing an accurate account of the meaning senses of highly polysemous phrasal verbs.

Another source of information that can be used for researching polysemous strings is dictionaries. On the surface, due to their relative inclusiveness, dictionaries may seem to provide reliable information about polysemous words or phrases. However, as pointed out by a number of researchers, the information included in dictionaries is limited in that it provides no insight regarding the typicality and usefulness of the listed meanings (Gardner & Davies, 2007; Garnier & Schmitt, 2015; Liu, 2011). Garnier and Schmitt (2015) demonstrated that the vast majority of occurrences of phrasal verbs can be covered by only a limited number of their senses. This indicates that, akin to words, MWIs have certain prototypical senses that are far more conventional and common than others. The absence of such information in dictionaries renders invisible the prominence of certain polysemes. This brings us to corpus analysis as the most systematic way of identifying frequent patterns of language use. The analysis of language corpora can be useful in capturing the commonality of linguistic items and informing the researcher about the patterns of their usage in the language. However, corpus data alone are not sensitive to possible semantic variations of a linguistic form, thereby requiring the researcher to manually examine different entries associated with each meaning sense. This can prove challenging since frequent MWIs may have several meaning senses dispersed over hundreds, if not thousands, of concordance lines. This discussion leads to the conclusion that, perhaps, the best treatment of polysemy would be to employ an amalgam of the methods available.

Semantic Prosody

Finally, we turn our attention to what is arguably one of the most under-researched aspects of MWIs: semantic prosody. Brought to light for the first time by Sinclair (1987), semantic prosody refers to the affective meaning of a word or phrase, established through its semantic association with a set of collocates (Louw, 1993). According to Louw (2000), the primary function of semantic prosody is to disclose the attitudinal orientations of the speaker/writer towards a certain pragmatic situation. Sinclair (2004) observed that MWIs such as *naked eye* and *true feelings* were semantically associated with notions of "difficulty" and "reluctance/ inability", respectively. In Sinclair's view, such prosodies are the pragmatic functions of the node item and its surrounding context. In fact, as opposed to some researchers who view semantic prosody as a property of the node item (Partington, 2004), Sinclair believes that such meanings are beyond the normal semantic values of the core unit and belong to a larger "unit of meaning" (the core and its collocates).

Semantic prosody has been a major finding of corpus analysis. It has been argued that, as a functional/pragmatic concept, semantic prosody is unlikely to be detected by intuition or unaided human observation, and so corpus analysis is the only promising way forward in researching semantic prosody (Louw, 1993; Partington, 2004; Sinclair, 2004; Stubbs, 1996). However, it is important to note that, as mentioned earlier, corpus data can only identify the most frequent patterns of language use, and thus evaluative judgments regarding the semantic associations between the identified patterns should be made by the researcher. This can prove difficult as recognizing the semantic prosody of certain words or word sequences is not as straightforward as it may appear. For instance, Cheng, Greaves, Sinclair, and Warren (2008) investigated the semantic prosody of different collocational patterns generated by two frequently co-occurring words (referred to as *congrams*): *play/role*. The authors examined modifiers that commonly occurred between these two words (*important, key, major,* and so on) to determine the shared semantic profile of the whole unit of meaning. It was found that the collocational patterns containing the two words *play/role* were semantically associated with the concept of accomplishing "weighty/meaningful" tasks. However, the authors also noticed instances such as "who played only a cameo role" which were not, on the surface, in line with the identified affective meaning. This observation indicates that inferring the semantic prosody of linguistic units from corpus data is no trivial task and warrants a great deal of attention. As Dilt and Newman (2006) point out, this appears to be a common issue among studies on semantic prosody as "the researcher is required to make evaluative judgments in the absence of a set of principled criteria to guide the evaluation" (p. 233). Stewart (2010, p. 134) takes a step further to argue that the traditional link between corpus analysis and semantic prosody should be reconsidered, as the interpretive strategies adopted by analysts to infer semantic associations from corpus data may significantly differ from one researcher to another.

In addition, it has also been shown that the semantic prosody of a lexical item is sensitive to the genre or register in which it occurs (Hunston, 2007; Partington, 2004; Stewart, 2010). This issue was pointed out by Tribble (2000), who argued that "words in certain genres may establish local semantic prosodies which only occur in these genres, or analogues of these genres" (p. 86). For example, Stewart (2010) noted that while the sequence *rigor mortis set in* is generally considered to express a negative attitudinal meaning, it may not communicate the same prosody in scientific registers. This links up with the argument that the attitudinal meaning of a lexical item may not be transferable from one context to another (Whitsitt, 2005). Thus, any generalizations regarding the affective meaning of a word or phrase based solely on evidence garnered from a given genre or register can be tentative at best. These considerations are particularly important for areas of research focusing on the pedagogical aspects of MWIs. In fact, the implied corollary here is that teaching materials targeted at raising learners' awareness of MWIs should take into account the association between context and meaning at more abstract levels such as semantic prosody.

Future Directions

The bulk of evidence reviewed in this chapter point to the many and varied challenges involved in the investigation of MWIs and the combinatory nature of words. As we argued, these challenges introduce key research issues that warrant further examination. This section will recapitulate some of these issues and will outline suggestions for future research.

One area that has received surprisingly little attention is multiword speech that is not contiguous. The vast majority of the studies to date have looked at adjacent MWIs. Yet, as Vilkaite (2016) notes, many noncontiguous strings are as frequent as adjacent combinations. We still know little about the use of nonadjacent MWIs in L1 and L2 speech and writing, as well as the mechanisms involved in the processing of such items. Although the studies by Vilkaite (2016) and Vilkaite and Schmitt (2017) have been valuable contributions to this poorly researched area, they centered on one kind of MWIs (verb + noun collocations) and have looked at native and highly proficient non-native speakers of English. Future research should look at other kinds of nonadjacent MWIs and explore the role of L2 proficiency in the acquisition, processing, and use of nonadjacent items. Further, while it is clear that such items are ubiquitous in natural language, just how frequent they really are in various corpora (expert, L1 and L2, speech, and writing) remains to be addressed in future research. Finally, another – related – area ripe for future investigations is the way in which some MWIs, such as idioms and proverbs, might be modified (by means of insertion, passivization, pluralization, etc.) and the degree to which speakers of various proficiencies are tolerant to such modifications, as measured by offline (tests, questionnaires) and online measures (reaction times, eye movements).

As was noted earlier, semantic prosody is another aspect of multiword speech that has received little attention. Critically, the majority of the studies in this area have focused on the semantic prosody of single words. This is surprising as the unit of language that initially directed our attention to this phenomenon was the phrasal verb *set in* (see Sinclair, 1987). There are several reasons to consider the investigation of semantic prosody for MWIs. First, there are certain kinds of MWIs that appear to be commonly used to refer to unpleasant states of affairs, but they have also been attested in contexts with positive pragmatic effects (*break out* in *peace had broken out*). For example, Stewart (2010) points out that while the phrasal verb *break out* is conventionally used in unfavorable contexts (*the violence broke out*), it can impart positive prosodies when used ironically (*peace finally broke out between the two kingdoms*; also see Louw, 1993). Secondly, non-salient MWIs, such as lexical bundles, are intuitively considered to have neutral affective meanings in discourse. However, Cortes and Hardy (2013) found that, even in an impersonal genre such as the research article, certain lexical bundles were used mostly in positive contexts (*one of the most*). This indicates that the affective meaning of MWIs is an implicit aspect of these units that requires further investigation. Finally, as was noted earlier, the semantic prosodies of linguistic units appear to vary across different registers and genres. It remains to be seen whether the semantic prosodies of different kinds of MWIs are also sensitive to the register or genre in which they are commonly used.

A related issue that future research should attend to is polysemy. Even though several studies have consistently pointed out the importance of researching polysemes for pedagogical purposes (Gardner & Davies, 2007; Garnier & Schmitt, 2015, 2016; Liu, 2011; Macis & Schmitt, 2017), research in this area is still scarce. Garnier and Schmitt (2015) is the first study to systematically investigate various meaning senses of one type of MWI (phrasal verbs) and compile a list of the most frequent polysemes of these units in the language. Studies of this sort can further raise awareness about the multiplicity of meanings associated with certain kinds of MWIs and help both teachers and learners navigate the challenges posed by polysemous sequences.

MWIs are by definition highly familiar, conventional strings of language. However, not all MWIs are frequent. In fact, some are extremely infrequent such that they are not attested even in some of the biggest corpora. To the best of our knowledge, the relationship between frequency and familiarity and their respective influence on how MWIs are treated by a language user has not been investigated in detail. Researchers have traditionally looked at the role of frequency in MWI use and processing, where responses to higher frequency items are compared with response to lower frequency ones. However, some research suggests that high familiarity may have facilitative effects (in language processing) not unlike those ascribed to high frequency of occurrence (Hallin & Van Lancker-Sidtis, 2017). That is, highly familiar but infrequent items may be treated similar to frequent MWIs. It would thus be interesting to look at a range of MWIs varying in frequency and familiarity rankings to be able to tease these effects apart and look at their respective roles in language acquisition, processing, and use.

Finally, from a methodological standpoint, new ways of MWI identification, both quali-tative and quantitative, can be fruitfully combined (for an example, see Ellis, Simpson-Vlach, & Maynard, 2008), and more powerful ways of data presentation and analysis explored. For example, as Arnon and Snider (2010) note, in the research looking at the role of phrasal frequency in MWI learning and processing, a continuous measure of frequency, rather than a binary one (high vs. low), is a better predictor of the dependent variable under investigation. It is further recommended that researchers use more advanced statisti-cal approaches to data analysis, such as regression analyses and mixed-effects modeling (Baayen, Davidson, & Bates, 2008; Cunnings, 2012), rather than the more commonly used in applied linguistics ANOVAs and t-tests and their non-parametric equivalents. One of the advantages of mixed-effects modeling is the possibility to take into account the effects that unfold during the course of an experimental procedure (such as effects of learning) and to consider a range of relevant covariates (Baayen et al., 2008). Corpus studies can too benefit from more rigorous statistical approaches. For example, Gries and Deshors (2014) propose adopting regression analyses to explore variation and systematic deviations between L1 (baseline) and L2 (learner) corpora. It is argued that such analyses allow for "an unprecedented degree of granularity" and are important for the field of learner corpus research (and applied linguistics) to evolve and advance (Gries & Deshors, 2014, p. 109). A similar argument is put forward by Gries (2015) who suggests using multifactorial regres-sion modeling, rather than the more conventional chi-square or log-likelihood, in which a dependent variable is predicted on the basis of independent variables using a regression equation (Gries, 2015, p. 161).

In conclusion, looking at MWIs and their multifarious nature, it seems virtually impos-sible to embark upon the study of these units without taking stock of the issues related to their definition, identification, and properties. This chapter has attempted to highlight some of these issues and describe the complexities involved in addressing them. It is hoped that by shedding light on the key aspects of MWIs, researchers will be able to make an informed decision as to what aspects of this linguistic phenomenon should be prioritized for research, and how to navigate the complexities that can potentially limit or change the course of the study at hand.

Further Reading

Durrant, P., & Mathews-Aydinli, J. (2011). A function-first approach to identifying formulaic language in academic writing. *English for Specific Purposes 30*(1), 58–72.

This corpus-based study investigates the use of MWIs and their communicative functions in essays produced by novice writers and published research articles in matched subject areas. This paper is interesting in that it explores the differences between the two corpora using a "top-down" approach in which function is prioritized over frequency. The implications of this study are important as they offer valuable insights into the connection between MWIs and the communicative function they commonly perform.

Durrant, P., & Siyanova-Chanturia, A. (2015). Learner corpora and psycholinguistic research. In S. Granger, G. Gilquin, & F. Meunier (Eds.), *Cambridge handbook of learner corpus research* (pp. 57–77). Cambridge, UK: Cambridge University Press.

The chapter reviews the ways in which psycholinguistics and learner (as well as native-speaker) corpora have interacted in recent years. The evidence of such interdisciplinary interactions is criti-cally evaluated, with a specific focus on corpus data as evidence for psycholinguistic hypotheses about language acquisition and use, and fruitful ways of integrating corpora and experimental research.

Garnier, M., & Schmitt, N. (2015). The PHaVE List: A pedagogical list of phrasal verbs and their most frequent meaning senses. *Language Teaching Research, 19*(6), 645–666.

This paper investigates various meaning senses of highly frequent phrasal verbs. The authors use a combination of qualitative and quantitative analyses to compile a pedagogical list of phrasal verbs and their highly frequent meaning senses in the English language. This study is important as it attempts to address the pedagogical shortcomings of previous research on phrasal verbs by focusing on the polysemic nature of these units.

Hunston, S. (2007). Semantic prosody revisited. *International Journal of Corpus Linguistics, 12*(2), 249–268.

This review paper raises important questions with regard to the notion of semantic prosody and how this phenomenon has been defined in the literature. Hunston's work is enlightening in that it pins down the areas of disagreement that exist among scholars regarding the identification of semantic prosody and how corpus evidence should be interpreted when researching this phenomenon.

Related Topics

Aspects of vocabulary knowledge, defining multiword items, the mental lexicon, factors affecting multiword items, learning multiword items, processing multiword items, knowledge of multiword items, issues in researching single-word items

References

Arnon, I., & Snider, N. (2010). More than words: Frequency effects for multiword phrases. *Journal of Memory and Language, 62*(1), 67–82.

Baayen, R. H., Davidson, D. J., & Bates, D. M. (2008). Mixed-effects modeling with crossed random effects for subjects and items. *Journal of Memory and Language, 59*(4), 390–412.

Bannard, C., & Matthews, D. (2008). Stored word sequences in language learning: The effect of familiarity on children's repetition of four-word combinations. *Psychological Science, 19*(3), 241–248.

Bardovi-Harlig, K. (2009). Conventional expressions as a pragmalinguistic resource: Recognition and production of conventional expressions in L2 pragmatics. *Language Learning, 59*(4), 755–795.

Bell, N. (2012). Formulaic language, creativity, and language play in a second language. *Annual Review of Applied Linguistics, 32*, 189–205.

Biber, D. (2009). A corpus-driven approach to formulaic language in English. *International Journal of Corpus Linguistics, 14*(3), 275–311.

Biber, D., Conrad, S., & Cortes, V. (2004). If you look at . . . : Lexical bundles in university teaching and textbooks. *Applied Linguistics, 25*(3), 371–405.

Biber, D., Johansson, S., Leech, G., Conrad, S., Finegan, E., & Quirk, R. (1999). *Longman grammar of spoken and written English*. Harlow, UK: Longman.

Boers, F., & Lindstromberg, S. (2008). From empirical findings to pedagogical practice. In F. Boers & S. Lindstromberg (Eds.), *Cognitive linguistic approaches to teaching vocabulary and phraseology* (pp. 375–393). Berlin: Mouton de Gruyter.

Bridges, K. A., & Van Lancker-Sidtis, D. (2013). Formulaic language in Alzheimer's disease. *Aphasiology, 27*(7), 799–810.

Bybee, J., & Scheibman, J. (1999). The effect of usage on degrees of constituency: The reduction of don't in English. *Linguistics, 37*(4), 575–596.

Chen, Y. H., & Baker, P. (2010). Lexical bundles in L1 and L2 academic writing. *Language Learning and Technology, 14*(2), 30–49.

Cheng, W., Greaves, C., Sinclair, J. M., & Warren, M. (2008). Uncovering the extent of the phraseological tendency: Towards a systematic analysis of concgrams. *Applied Linguistics, 30*(2), 236–252.

Cheng, W., Greaves, C., & Warren, M. (2006). From n-gram to skipgram to concgram. *International Journal of Corpus Linguistics, 11*(4), 411–433.

Clark, E. V. (1993). *The lexicon in acquisition*. Cambridge, UK: Cambridge University Press.

Cleeremans, A., & McClelland, J. L. (1991). Learning the structure of event sequences. *Journal of Experimental Psychology: General, 120*(3), 235–253.

Cortes, V., & Hardy, D. (2013). Analysing the semantic prosody and semantic preference of lexical bundles. In D. Belcher & G. Nelson (Eds.), *Critical and corpus-based approaches to intercultural rhetoric* (pp. 180–201). Ann Arbor, MI: University of Michigan Press.

Cowie, A. P. (1994). Phraseology. In R. E. Asher (Ed.), *The encyclopedia of language and linguistics* (pp. 3168–3171). Oxford, UK: Oxford University Press.

Cunnings, I. (2012). An overview of mixed-effects statistical models for second language researchers. *Second Language Research, 28*(3), 369–382.

Davies, M. (2005). *VIEW: Variations in English words and phrases* (An online interface with the British National Corpus: World Edition). Provo, UT: Brigham Young University. Retrieved from http://view.byu.edu/

Dilts, P., & Newman, J. (2006). A note on quantifying "good" and "bad" prosodies'. *Corpus Linguistics and Linguistic Theory, 2*(2), 233–242.

Durrant, P. (2008). *High frequency collocations and second language learning*. PhD dissertation, University of Nottingham, Nottingham.

Durrant, P. (2009). Investigating the viability of a collocation list for students of English for academic purposes. *English for Specific Purposes, 28*(3), 157–169.

Durrant, P. (2017). Lexical bundles and disciplinary variation in university students' writing: Mapping the territories. *Applied Linguistics, 38*(2), 165–193.

Durrant, P., & Mathews-Aydınlı, J. (2011). A function-first approach to identifying formulaic language in academic writing. *English for Specific Purposes, 30*(1), 58–72.

Durrant, P., & Schmitt, N. (2009). To what extent do native and non-native writers make use of collocations?. *International Review of Applied Linguistics in Language Teaching, 47*(2), 157–177.

Durrant, P., & Siyanova-Chanturia, A. (2015). Learner corpora and psycholinguistics. In S. Granger, G. Gilquin, & F. Meunier (Eds.), *The Cambridge handbook of learner corpus research* (pp. 57–77). Cambridge, UK: Cambridge University Press.

Ellis, N. C. (2002). Frequency effects in language processing: A review with implications for theories of implicit and explicit language acquisition. *Studies in Second Language Acquisition, 24*(2), 143–188.

Ellis, N. C. (2012). Formulaic language and second language acquisition: Zipf and the phrasal teddy bear. *Annual Review of Applied Linguistics, 32*, 17–44.

Ellis, N. C., Simpson-Vlach, R., & Maynard, C. (2008). Formulaic language in native and second language speakers: Psycholinguistics, corpus linguistics, and TESOL. *TESOL Quarterly, 42*(3), 375–396.

Erman, B., & Warren, B. (2000). The idiom principle and the open choice principle. *Text, 20*(1), 29–62.

Evert, S. (2009). Corpora and collocations. In A. Lüdeling & M. Kytö (Eds.), *Corpus linguistics: An international handbook* (Vol. 2, pp. 1212–1248). Berlin and New York, NY: Mouton de Gruyter.Foster, P. (2001). Rules and routines: A consideration of their role in the task-based language production of native and non-native speakers. In M. Bygate, P. Skehan, & M. Swain (Eds.), *Researching pedagogic tasks: Second language learning, teaching, and testing* (pp. 75–94). Harlow, UK: Longman.

Gardner, D., & Davies, M. (2007). Pointing out frequent phrasal verbs: A corpus-based analysis. *TESOL Quarterly 41*(2) 339–359.

Garnier, M., & Schmitt, N. (2015). The PHaVE List: A pedagogical list of phrasal verbs and their most frequent meaning senses. *Language Teaching Research, 19*(6), 645–666.

Garnier, M., & Schmitt, N. (2016). Picking up polysemous phrasal verbs: How many do learners know and what facilitates this knowledge? *System, 59*, 29–44.

Gomez, R. L. (2002). Variability and detection of invariant structure. *Psychological Science, 13*(5), 431–436.

Granger, S. (1998). Prefabricated patterns in advanced EFL writing: Collocations and formulae. In A. P. Cowie (Ed.), *Phraseology: Theory, analysis, and applications* (pp. 79–100). Oxford, UK: Oxford University Press.

Gregory, M., Raymond, W., Bell, A., Fosler-Lussier, E., & Jurafsky, D. (1999). The effects of collocational strength and contextual predictability in lexical production. *Chicago Linguistic Society, 35*, 151–166.

Gries, S. Th. (2015). Statistics for learner corpus research. In S. Granger, G. Gilquin, & F. Meunier (Eds.), *The Cambridge handbook of learner corpus research* (pp. 159–181). Cambridge, UK: Cambridge University Press.

Gries, S. Th., & Deshors, S. C. (2014). Using regressions to explore deviations between corpus data and a standard/target: Two suggestions. *Corpora, 9*(1), 109–136.

Hallin, A. E., & Van Lancker-Sidtis, D. (2017). A closer look at formulaic language: Prosodic characteristics of Swedish proverbs. *Applied Linguistics, 38*(1), 68–89.

Herbst, T. (2011). Choosing sandy beaches – collocations, probabemes and the idiom principle. In T. Herbst, S. Faulhaber, & P. Uhrig (Eds.), *The phraseological view of language: A tribute to John Sinclair* (pp. 27–57). Berlin: De Gruyter Mouton.

Hoey, M. (1991). *Patterns of lexis in text.* Oxford, UK: Oxford University Press.

Hoey, M. (2005). *Lexical priming: A new theory of words and language.* London, UK: Routledge.

Howarth, P. (1998). The phraseology of learners' academic writing. In A. Cowie (Ed.), *Phraseology: Theory, analysis and applications* (pp. 161–186). Oxford, UK: Oxford University Press.

Hunston, S. (2007). Semantic prosody revisited. *International Journal of Corpus Linguistics, 12*(2), 249–268.

Hyland, K. (2008). As can be seen: Lexical bundles and disciplinary variation. *English for Specific Purposes, 27*(1), 4–21.

Jones, S., & Sinclair, J. M. (1974). English lexical collocations. A study in computational linguistics. *Cahiers de Lexicologie, 24*, 15–61.

Jurafsky, D., Bell, A., Gregory, M., & Raymond, W. D. (2001). Probabilistic relations between words: Evidence from reduction in lexical production. In J. Bybee & P. Hopper (Eds.), *Frequency and the emergence of linguistic structure* (pp. 229–254). Amsterdam: Benjamins.

Konopka, A., & Bock, K. (2009). Lexical or syntactic control of sentence formulation? Structural generalizations from idiom production. *Cognitive Psychology, 58*(1), 68–101.

Lin, P. M. S. (2012). Sound evidence: The missing piece of the jigsaw in formulaic language research. *Applied Linguistics, 33*(3), 342–347.

Lin, P. M. S. (2018). *The prosody of formulaic sequences: A corpus and discourse approach.* New York, NY: Bloomsbury.

Liu, D. (2011). The most frequently used English phrasal verbs in American and British English: A multi corpus examination. *TESOL Quarterly, 45*(4), 661–688.

Louw, B. (1993). Irony in the text or insincerity in the writer? The diagnostic potential of semantic prosodies. In M. Baker, G. Francis, & E. Tognini-Bonelli (Eds.), *Text and technology: In honour of John Sinclair* (pp. 157–175). Amsterdam: John Benjamins.

Louw, B. (2000). Contextual prosodic theory: Bringing semantic prosodies to life. In C. Heffer & H. Saunston (Eds.), *Words in context: In honour of John Sinclair* (pp. 48–94). Birmingham, UK: ELR.

Macis, M., & Schmitt, N. (2017). Not just "small potatoes": Knowledge of the idiomatic meanings of collocations. *Language Teaching Research, 21*(3), 321–340.

Manning, C., & Schutze, H. (1999). *Foundations of statistical natural language processing.* Cambridge, MA: MIT Press.

McDonald, S. A., & Shillcock, R. C. (2003). Low-level predictive inference in reading: The influence of transitional probabilities on eye movements. *Vision Research, 43*(16), 1735–1751.

Meunier, F. (2012). Formulaic language and language teaching. *Annual Review of Applied Linguistics, 32*, 111–129.

Miller, G. (2003). *WordNet* (Version 2.0) [software]. Retrieved from http://www.cogsci.princeton.edu/~wn/obtain.shtml

Misyak, J. B., Christiansen, M. H., & Tomblin, J. B. (2009). Statistical learning of nonadjacencies predicts on-line processing of long-distance dependencies in natural language. In N. A. Taatgen & H. van Rijn (Eds.), *Proceedings of the 31st annual conference of the Cognitive Science Society, 2009* (pp. 177–182). Austin, TX: Cognitive Science Society.

Molinaro, N., & Carreiras, M. (2010). Electrophysiological evidence of interaction between contextual expectation and semantic integration during the processing of collocations. *Biological Psychology*, *83*(3), 176–190.

Moon, R. (1998). *Fixed expressions and idioms in English: A corpus-based approach*. Oxford, UK: Clarendon Press.

Nattinger, J. R., & DeCarrico, J. S. (1992). *Lexical phrases and language teaching*. Oxford, UK: Oxford University Press.

Nesselhauf, N. (2005). *Collocations in a learner corpus*. Amsterdam: John Benjamins.

Newport, E., & Aslin, R. N. (2004). Learning at a distance I: Statistical learning of non-adjacent dependencies. *Cognitive Psychology*, *48*(2), 127–162.

Omidian, T., Shahriari, H., & Siyanova-Chanturia, A. (2018). A cross-disciplinary investigation of multi-word expressions in the moves of research article abstracts. *Journal of English for Academic Purposes*, *36*, 1–14.

Partington, A. (2004). Utterly content in each other's company: Semantic prosody and semantic preference. *International Journal of Corpus Linguistics*, *9*(1), 131–156.

Peters, A. M. (1983). *The units of language acquisition*. Cambridge, UK: Cambridge University Press.

Peterson, R., Burgess, C., Dell, G., & Eberhard, K. (2001). Disassociation between syntactic and semantic processing during idiom comprehension. *Journal of Experimental Psychology: Learning, Memory, and Cognition*, *27*(5), 1223–1237.

Ravin, Y., & Leacock, C. (Eds.). (2000). *Polysemy: Theoretical and computational approaches*. Oxford, UK: Oxford University Press.

Reuterskiöld, C., & Van Lancker-Sidtis, D. (2013). Retention of idioms following one-time exposure. *Child Language Teaching and Therapy*, *29*(2), 219–231.

Schmidt, R. W. (1983). Interaction, acculturation, and the acquisition of communicative competence: A case study of an adult. In N. Wolfson & E. Judd (Eds.), *Sociolinguistics and language acquisition* (pp. 137–174). Rowley, MA: Newbury House.

Schmitt, N. (Ed.). (2004). *Formulaic sequences*. Amsterdam: John Benjamins.

Schmitt, N., Grandage, S., & Adolphs, S. (2004). Are corpus-derived recurrent clusters psycholinguistically valid? In N. Schmitt (Ed.), *Formulaic sequences* (pp. 127–151). Amsterdam: John Benjamins.

Simpson-Vlach, R., & Ellis, N. C. (2010). An academic formulas list: New methods in phraseology research. *Applied Linguistics*, *31*(4), 487–512.

Sinclair, J. H. (1987). *Looking up*. London, UK and Glasgow, UK: Collins.

Sinclair, J. H. (2004). *Trust the text: Language, corpus and discourse*. London, UK and New York, NY: Routledge.

Siyanova-Chanturia, A. (2015a). Collocation in beginner learner writing: A longitudinal study. *System*, *53*, 148–160.

Siyanova-Chanturia, A. (2015b). On the "holistic" nature of formulaic language. *Corpus Linguistics and Linguistic Theory*, *11*(2), 285–301.

Siyanova-Chanturia, A., Conklin, K., & Schmitt, N. (2011). Adding more fuel to the fire: An eye-tracking study of idiom processing by native and nonnative speakers. *Second Language Research*, *27*(2), 251–272.

Siyanova-Chanturia, A., Conklin, K., & van Heuven, W. (2011). Seeing a phrase "time and again" matters: The role of phrasal frequency in the processing of multiword sequences. *Journal of Experimental Psychology: Language, Memory, and Cognition*, *37*(3), 776–784.

Siyanova-Chanturia, A., & Janssen, N. (2018). Production of familiar phrases: Frequency effects in native speakers and second language learners. *Journal of Experimental Psychology: Learning, Memory, and Cognition*. Advance online publication. http://dx.doi.org/10.1037/xlm0000562

Snider, N., & Arnon, I. (2012). A unified lexicon and grammar? Compositional and non-compositional phrases in the lexicon. In S. Gries & D. Divjak (Eds.), *Frequency effects in language* (pp. 127–163). Berlin: Mouton de Gruyter.

Sprenger, S., Levelt, W., & Kempen, G. (2006). Lexical access during the production of idiomatic phrases. *Journal of Memory and Language*, *54*, 161–184.

Stewart, D. (2010). *Semantic prosody: A critical evaluation*. New York: Routledge.

Stubbs, M. (1995). Collocations and semantic profiles: On the cause of the trouble with quantitative studies. *Functions of Language*, *2*(1), 23–55.

Stubbs, M. (1996). *Text and corpus analysis: Computer-assisted studies of language and culture*. Oxford, UK: Blackwell.

Tognini-Bonelli, E. (2001). *Corpus linguistics at work*. Amsterdam: John Benjamins.

Tribble, C. (2000). Genres, keywords, teaching: Towards a pedagogic account of the language of project proposals. In L. Burnard & A. McEnery (Eds.), *Rethinking language pedagogy from a corpus perspective* (pp. 75–90). Frankfurt: Peter Lang.

Underwood, G., Schmitt, N., & Galpin, A. (2004). The eyes have it: An eye-movement study into the processing of formulaic sequences. In N. Schmitt (Ed.), *Formulaic sequences* (pp. 153–172). Amsterdam: John Benjamins.

Van Lancker-Sidtis, D. (2003). Auditory recognition of idioms by native and nonnative speakers of English: It takes one to know one. *Applied Psycholinguistics*, *24*(1), 45–57.

Van Lancker-Sidtis, D., Choi, J., Alken, A., & Sidtis, J. J. (2015). Formulaic language in Parkinson's Disease and Alzheimer's Disease: Complementary effects of subcortical and cortical dysfunction. *Journal of Speech, Language, and Hearing Research*, *58*(5), 1493–1507.

Van Lancker-Sidtis, D., & Rallon, G. (2004). Tracking the incidence of formulaic expressions in everyday speech: Methods for classification and verification. *Language & Communication*, *24*(3), 207–240.

Vespignani, F., Canal, P., Molinaro, N., Fonda, S., & Cacciari, C. (2010). Predictive mechanisms in idiom comprehension. *Journal of Cognitive Neuroscience*, *22*(8), 1682–1700.

Vihman, M. M. (1982). Formulas in first and second language acquisition. In L. Obler & L. Menn (Eds.), *Exceptional language and linguistics* (pp. 261–284). New York, NY: Academic Press.

Vilkaitė, L. (2016). Are nonadjacent collocations processed faster?. *Journal of Experimental Psychology: Learning, Memory, and Cognition*, *42*(10), 1632–1642.

Vilkaitė, L., & Schmitt, N. (2017). Reading collocations in an L2: Do collocation processing benefits extend to non-adjacent collocations? *Applied Linguistics*, 1–27.

Whitsitt, S. (2005). A critique of the concept of semantic prosody. *International Journal of Corpus Linguistics*, *10*(3), 283–305.

Widdowson, H. G. (1990). *Aspects of language teaching*. Oxford, UK: Oxford University Press.

Wood, D. (2002). Formulaic language acquisition and production: Implications for teaching. *TESL Canada Journal*, *20*(1), 01–15.

Wood, D. (2004). An empirical investigation into the facilitating role of automatized lexical phrases in second language fluency development. *Journal of Language and Learning*, *2*(1), 27–50.

Wray, A. (2002). *Formulaic language and the lexicon*. Cambridge, UK: Cambridge University Press.

34

Key Issues in Measuring Vocabulary Knowledge

John Read

Introduction

This chapter focuses on some ongoing issues in designing and administering instruments to measure the vocabulary knowledge of second language learners. As such it is intended to complement the other chapters in this volume which deal with more specific aspects of vocabulary assessment. The work discussed here is concerned primarily with knowledge of individual words rather than, say, competence with multiword lexical units or the ability to use vocabulary for communicative purposes.

There has been a strong tendency in L2 vocabulary studies for certain tests to become recognized as standard measures for a variety of uses. For many years Nation's Vocabulary Levels Test (VLT), first in the original form (Nation, 1983) and then in its revised version (Schmitt, Schmitt, & Clapham, 2001), was widely seen as the best way to assess vocabulary size, or breadth of vocabulary knowledge – even though it was not designed to give an overall estimate of the total number of words known. This limitation was rectified to some extent by the development of the Vocabulary Size Test (VST) (Nation & Beglar, 2007), which sampled systematically across a range of word frequency levels and was shown to have very good measurement qualities, at least when it was administered to Japanese learners with different degrees of proficiency in English (Beglar, 2010). To a more limited extent, a series of tests developed by Meara and his associates based on the Yes/No test format (Meara & Jones, 1988; Meara & Miralpeix, 2016) have performed a similar, though less prominent role.

The same situation applies to measures of depth of vocabulary knowledge. As Schmitt (2014) notes, studies of depth have most often employed tests based on Read's (1993, 1998) word associates format, which assesses the ability to match words related in various ways that are assumed to reflect the organization of the mental lexicon. Another popular instrument is the Vocabulary Knowledge Scale (VKS) (Wesche & Paribakht, 1996), which requires learners to rate their knowledge of a set of target words and provide some confirming evidence if they do claim to know a word.

However, the attention given to this small number of high-profile instruments can obscure two points: one is that there are various purposes for setting out to assess learners' vocabulary knowledge; and the other is that there is a wider range of test formats available than just these few. Thus, first it is useful to clarify what the purposes for measuring vocabulary knowledge are: why do we want or need to use vocabulary tests and other forms of assessment?

Purposes of Assessment

One goal, broadly stated, is to measure vocabulary size, which is also referred to as breadth of vocabulary knowledge. Tests like the VLT and VST have been designed to sample words across a wide range of frequency levels, and the number of correct answers to the test items is used to estimate the learner's vocabulary size. A true size test like the VST sets out to obtain a measure of all the words that someone knows, which is conceptually challenging if not impossible – except perhaps in situations where a learner's exposure to the second language is restricted to the classroom and the textbook. The sampling frame for size tests will always be limited by the scope and representativeness of the corpora from which the word frequency data are derived. In addition to that, learners with relatively limited vocabulary knowledge may get frustrated and engage in blind guessing if the test contains a lot of unknown lower frequency words which they are required to work through just for the sake of finding the odd one that they do know. The alternative is a test like the VLT, which focuses on the range of frequency levels where the words which learners know – or *need* to know – are most likely to be found. Thus, Nation (2016) makes a generic distinction between a size test and a levels test, the latter having the more modest goal of establishing how many of the 3,000 or 5,000 most frequent words are known, rather than estimating total size.

But, to come back to purpose, why do we want to measure vocabulary size, in either an absolute or relative sense? Some distinct assessment purposes can be identified:

- To obtain a broad measure of proficiency in the language for diagnostic purposes, as in DIALANG, the web-based diagnostic assessment system (Alderson, 2005)
- To place students in classes in a language school (Harrington & Carey, 2009)
- To evaluate the adequacy of learners' vocabulary knowledge for specific communicative purposes such as reading academic texts (Schmitt, Jiang, & Grabe, 2011)

However, it is often not clear which of these purposes is being addressed in research studies on vocabulary breadth tests – a point I will return to in the section on validation.

Given the prominence of tests like the VLT and the VST, the goal of measuring vocabulary size tends to dominate the L2 vocabulary literature, but it is important to identify other purposes of measuring vocabulary knowledge, which may not necessarily be mutually exclusive.

- To measure the outcomes of a period of vocabulary learning. This may be quite brief, as in the results of an experiment to investigate, say, the effects of presenting a set of words in particular contexts or groupings within a single study session in a controlled environment; or it may be an extended period of study in a more naturalistic classroom setting. In this case, the testing will normally focus on the specific vocabulary items that the students were supposed to study. Particularly in the case of a controlled experiment, there may be pretesting as well as posttesting (see Kremmel, this volume).
- To measure specific vocabulary learning skills. So far there have been few published reports of such instruments, apart from ones used in specific studies, such as Schmitt and Zimmerman's (2002) Test of English Derivatives (TED). This research gap has been recently addressed more systematically by Sasao (Sasao & Webb, 2017, 2018)

with the development of his Word Part Levels Test and Guessing from Context Test (see Sasao, this volume).

• To gain a better understanding of the mental lexicon and of vocabulary learning processes. Paul Meara and his students and colleagues at Swansea have developed multiple tools for this purpose (Meara & Miralpeix, 2016) to investigate quite an array of research questions (Fitzpatrick & Barfield, 2009).

There are other purposes, such as to assess the ability of learners to use vocabulary productively in speech and writing, and to evaluate the contribution of vocabulary knowledge to the performance of communicative tasks, which go beyond the scope of this chapter (see Kyle, this volume). For further discussion of assessment purposes, see the section on validation in this chapter, and also Nation (2013, Chapter 13).

Critical Issues and Topics

Choice of Test Formats

In terms of test design there appear to be a limited number of item formats available to measure vocabulary knowledge. As in other areas of educational assessment, the predominant mode of delivery has been a group-administered, paper-based test in which the stimulus material is presented – and the learners respond – in written form. The advent of computer-based testing has opened up new opportunities: for learners to take tests individually, and at remote locations; for tests to be individualized to a learner's ability level, using computer-adaptive procedures; for reaction times and other elements of response behavior to be recorded; and for the results to be scored and analyzed automatically. However, the basic item types tend to remain the same. Although the sophisticated technology available to the major test publishers has the potential to offer a wider range of assessment formats, most smaller scale computerized tests rely on low-tech authoring software such as that available through learning management systems like Blackboard, Canvas and Moodle, with their restricted number of item types, which are largely the same as those used in most paper-based tests. These item types lend themselves well to conventional means of measuring vocabulary knowledge.

Let us review those standard item types. First, it is useful to distinguish between selected-response items, where the learners select a response from two or more options given, and constructed-response ones, where the learners write their own response in the form of a word, a phrase, a sentence, and so on.

This distinction fits neatly with the traditional division in vocabulary studies between receptive and productive vocabulary knowledge, although I much prefer the terms recognition and recall, for reasons I have given elsewhere (Read, 2000, pp. 155–156). Thus, selected-response items require the learners to show that they can recognize the correct meaning or form of a given target word, whereas constructed-response items set the more demanding task of being able to recall the meaning or form.

Selected-Response Items (Recognition Knowledge)

The multiple-choice format continues to be the classic way to measure recognition knowledge. It has gained new prominence through its use in the original Vocabulary Size Test (Nation, 2012; Nation & Beglar, 2007; Beglar, 2010) and the various versions derived from it. In this case, the format is employed to assess meaning recognition: the test takers select which of four options best represents the meaning of the target word presented in a short, non-defining sentence in the stem of the item:

circle: Make a <circle>.

    a   rough picture
    b   space with nothing in it
    c   round shape
    d   large hole

Multiple-choice items can also be used to measure form recognition, as in this example from an experiment by Webb (2007) to test knowledge of how to spell the pseudoword *denent*:

    1.   (a) denant   (b) danant   (c) danent   (d) denent

A second widely used format for meaning recognition is a matching task. The canonical example of an instrument of this kind is the Vocabulary Levels Test (Schmitt et al., 2001), where learners are presented with sets of three definitions and six words, and need to match each definition with the word it refers to. The same format has been retained in the updated computer-based Vocabulary Levels Test (Webb, Sasao, & Balance, 2017). In these tests the words in each set belong to the same part of speech but are quite different in meaning, so that the test provides what Nation (2013, pp. 536–537) calls a "sensitive" measure of vocabulary knowledge, in that it does not require the test takers to distinguish between semantically related words. The format could also be used in less sensitive tests to assess the ability of more advanced learners to make such distinctions.

Of course, in a sense all selected-response test items involve matching of some kind (including the multiple-choice format), but the label is conventionally applied to the type of test just described, where there are clusters of target words and definitions. Another variation on the matching theme is represented by the word associates format (Read, 1993) where the test takers select words that are semantically related to a given target word, as in this example:

team
| alternative | chalk | ear | group |
| orbit | scientists | sport | together |

The intended responses in this case are *group, scientists, sport,* and *together.* This again can be seen as a sensitive test, where the distractor words are not related to the target item. A less sensitive version of the format is this adaptation for primary school students in the Netherlands (Schoonen & Verhallen, 2008):

	fruit		monkey
nice		**banana**	(to) slip
	peel		yellow

Although all six associates have a connection to the target word, *fruit, peel,* and *yellow* are judged to constitute a more sophisticated definition of what the word *banana* means.

The matching principle has also been applied to tests of collocational knowledge, assessing the ability of learners to recognize the correct combination of words, as well as what the multiword unit means, as in this sample from Revier's (2009) CONTRIX format:

The quickest way to win a friend's trust is to show that you are able to _____	tell	a/an	joke
	take	the	secret
	keep	– – – –	truth

In short, then, items based on matching require learners to demonstrate their vocabulary knowledge by identifying connections between words and their meanings, or between words and other words – all of which are provided as an integral part of the test format.

A third type of selected-response item is found in the Yes/No test, which presents the test takers with a series of words and simply asks them to report whether they know the meaning of each one or not. Thus, it can be regarded as a kind of self-assessment task, which provides only indirect evidence of the validity of the test takers' responses by including a proportion of non-words (also called pseudowords) so that individuals' scores can be adjusted downwards if they respond Yes to one or more of the non-words.

A big issue, though, is the opportunity for test takers to guess answers from the options provided, as discussed further later. This forms part of the rationale for the alternative approach of requiring them to supply their own answers to the test items.

Constructed-Response Items (Recall Knowledge)

The essence of a constructed-response test item is that the test takers are prompted to recall the meaning or form of a target vocabulary item. In the simplest case, they are given a list of L2 words and must supply an expression of the meaning of each one: an L2 definition or synonym or an L1 equivalent. With some framing the same kind of item can be employed to elicit various other aspects of word knowledge: a word's part of speech (*undertake*: verb), a derived form (*receive → reception*), or a collocate (*to make + a decision*). A more demanding task is for the learners to produce a whole sentence containing each target word. Since it is also difficult to mark, this type of task is not normally included in formal, large-scale tests.

Thus, a more common type of constructed-response item involves completing a gap in a sentence. The idea is that the sentence is written to create a context which allows the test takers to infer what the missing word is (and where appropriate, what its grammatical form should be), as in these examples:

He worked in this office for a _____ of four years. [period]
Many houses were completely _____ in the earthquake. [destroyed]

It is often the case that more than one word can fill the gap. In a classroom progress test, the teacher may choose to accept only a word which the learners have recently studied. Another way to signal the *intended* answer is to supply the first letter of the word. One well-known test in this format, Laufer and Nation's (1995) Productive Levels Test, goes further than that. Since the test was intended to be the "productive" counterpart to the original Vocabulary Levels Test (Nation, 1983), the authors chose to supply up to six or seven initial letters in order to ensure that only the target words in the VLT were elicited, so that such items in effect involve more recognition than recall. This highlights the point that constructed-response items are inherently less controlled, and may be more difficult to score, than selected-response items.

One test which combines the two types of item is the Computer Adaptive Test of Size and Strength (CATSS) (Laufer & Goldstein, 2004). It is based on two distinctions:

- Supplying the form for a given concept vs. supplying the meaning for a given form, and
- Recall vs. recognition (of form or meaning) (Laufer, Elder, Hill, & Congdon, 2004, p. 206).

This gives rise to four "degrees of knowledge", each with a corresponding type of test item. Using Rasch analysis, Laufer et al. (2004) showed that the two types of recognition knowledge (of form and of meaning), which were both tested in the CATSS by means of multiple-choice items, were quite easy, whereas recall knowledge of meaning was significantly more challenging, and recall knowledge of form was most difficult of all. The results confirmed the general expectation that constructed-response items are more demanding for learners than selected-response items, and as a general rule vocabulary tests employ one of these types of item, rather than combining them in the way that the CATSS does.

Role of L1 and Bilingual Testing

Another issue is the role of the learners' first language in vocabulary testing. There is the obvious consideration of whether the intended population of test takers share a first language, in which case their own language represents an obvious resource for communicating the meaning of L2 vocabulary, whether it be through recognition or recall. This applies, for instance, to learners of English in Japan, learners of Japanese in Brazil, or learners of Spanish in New Zealand – although the use of L1 may be constrained if the teacher is not fluent in the students' language. On the other hand, the influential English vocabulary tests in the international literature have grown out of educational contexts in English-speaking countries where learners from different language backgrounds study together in the same class or school and where the teacher may not speak any of their languages. In those situations a monolingual test in English is often seen as the only practicable option.

To discuss the appropriate roles of L1 in the second language classroom more broadly is beyond the scope of this chapter. It is a matter of ongoing debate within both the mainstream literature on language teaching methodology (see, e.g., Du, 2016; Turnbull & Dailey-O'Cain, 2009), and the more recent work on translanguaging in bilingual and multilingual classrooms (Cenoz & Gorter, 2015; Garcia & Li, 2013). Within these diverse contexts appropriate forms of vocabulary assessment will find their place.

Research on L2 vocabulary testing has paid comparatively little attention to the L1 vs. L2 question until recently. Some researchers in Japan (e.g., Stubbe, 2015) have noted that one practical argument in favor of using the Yes/No format rather than a translation (L2 to L1) task for testing word knowledge is that it is time-consuming to mark manually the variety of L1 equivalents that the learners produce in the latter task. On the other hand, Schmitt (2010) argues that an individual face-to-face interview is "[p]erhaps the best way of determining 'true' underlying knowledge" of vocabulary (p. 182) and, in research studies he has co-authored (Gyllstad, Vilkaitė, & Schmitt, 2015; Schmitt, Ng, & Garras, 2011), at least some of the interviews have been conducted in the learners' L1.

Starting in the 1990s Paul Nation encouraged the development of bilingual versions of the Vocabulary Levels Test, with the definitions translated into various L1s, and made them available on his website. The argument was that the bilingual version of the test was a purer measure of L2 word knowledge because it reduced the reading load involved in comprehending the definitions (Nation, 2001, p. 351). However, there was no published work to evaluate any of the bilingual versions. This has changed with the advent of the Vocabulary Size Test (VST). Not only are there bilingual versions in various Asian languages (Mandarin, Japanese, Korean, Thai, Gujarati, Tamil), but also several validation studies have been published, for the Vietnamese (Nguyen & Nation, 2011), Persian (Karami, 2012), Russian (Elgort, 2013), and Mandarin (Zhao & Ji, 2016) versions. Both Nguyen and Nation (2011) and Karami (2012) found that their bilingual versions significantly distinguished between university student learners at three levels of proficiency, and there was a broad (though inconsistent) pattern of declining scores from the high frequency to lower frequency sections of the test. Zhao and Ji (2016) obtained similar results using Rasch analysis for a reduced 80-item version of the Mandarin test, covering the first 8,000 frequency levels.

In her study with intermediate-level Russian learners, Elgort (2013) was able to compare the performance of the two versions of the test. Each learner took 70 bilingual items and 70 monolingual ones. Although the difference in mean scores was not great (32.97 vs. 29.61 respectively), the items with Russian options were significantly easier than the monolingual items (with a large effect size). Further analysis showed that learners with lower scores overall gained more benefit from the bilingual options, as compared to higher scoring learners.

The Effects of Cognates

A related issue, arising particularly from Elgort's work, is the role of cognates and loanwords in test performance. Researchers have long been aware of the effects of cognates when the L1 and L2 have been related European languages. In his study of the Vocabulary Levels Test, Read (1988) noted that some Spanish-speaking students did not follow the general pattern of progressively lower scores at lower word frequency levels because of their knowledge of cognates at those levels. Similar results have come out of research with francophone students in Canada. Meara, Lightbown, and Halter (1994) found that a group of these students scored significantly higher on a Yes/No test of English vocabulary in which half the target words were French-English cognates than one in which cognates were excluded. In a larger-scale study of university placement test results, Cobb (2000) showed that the relatively high scores gained by francophone students on the 2,000-word level of the VLT masked a lack of knowledge of high-frequency words of Anglo-Saxon (or Germanic) origin. The students scored noticeably higher on items where the target word and its definition had cognates in French.

Returning to Elgort's (2013) research on the VST with Russian learners, one of her findings was that 34% of the target words in the test had Russian cognates, which was significantly higher than the estimated 27% of cognates in the language as a whole. Since responses to cognate target words were significantly more accurate, this suggested that the test may have overestimated the students' vocabulary size by as much as 1,000 word families. Thus, one further advantage of a version of the test designed for students with a particular L1 is that the proportion of cognate words can in principle be controlled, whereas it is a confounding variable when the monolingual VST is administered to learners from different language backgrounds.

The influence of English as a global language in the modern world means that many non-European languages, which have no genetic relationship to English, have expanded their lexicon by borrowing words from English. As has often been observed, this is a particularly salient feature of modern Japanese vocabulary (Daulton, 2008). Although linguistically cognates and loanwords have different origins, their potential for either facilitating L2 vocabulary acquisition or causing confusion through "false friends" is similar, with the result that the two terms tend to be used interchangeably in the current L2 literature.

In an L2 to L1 translation task for Japanese learners, Jordan (2012) found that beyond very familiar vocabulary at the 1,000-word frequency level noncognates were significantly more difficult to translate than cognates. Similar results emerged from a study by Laufer and McLean (2016) involving students in Japan and Israel who took the new Computer Adaptive Test of Size and Strength (CATSS). A version of the test which included loanwords in the respective L1s of the learners was easier than one which excluded such words, at least for the items in the test which required active or passive recall rather than just recognition of the words. In addition, the positive effect of loanwords on the test scores was more evident for lower proficiency learners than those with advanced vocabulary knowledge. In a recent study in Israel using the same test, Laufer and Levitsky-Aviad (2018) largely confirmed the results of the Laufer and McLean study. They found very little difference between a version with an uncontrolled number of loanwords and one with a proportionate number, but the actual numbers were small: six vs. three.

Thus, there is some evidence that the presence of cognates or loanwords as target items in a vocabulary test can affect the test takers' performance, especially for elementary and intermediate-level learners. This is not to say that such words should be omitted, but their possible influence should be taken into account, particularly in tests of vocabulary size administered to students with a single first language. If the proportion of loanwords is not controlled, it may lead to overestimates or underestimates of the number of words that the learners know within the word frequency range covered by the test.

Guessing and Confidence

With any kind of selected-response test format there is the potential for test takers to increase their score by guessing, without knowing what the correct answer should be to some or more of the items. It is important to distinguish between blind (or "wild") guessing and that based on some relevant knowledge. Traditionally, formulas to correct for guessing have been applied to various types of educational tests to discourage test takers from guessing blindly; however, measurement experts (e.g., Ebel & Frisbie, 1986, pp. 215–218) have tended to question their validity and effectiveness.

In vocabulary assessment, Nation (2001, 2013) has consistently argued that students should be encouraged to draw on partial knowledge of vocabulary items, even if they are not sure of what the correct answer is. However, in his research on the word associates format, Read (1993, 1998) observed that some learners were unwilling to guess unless they were confident about an answer and thus were more conservative in their responding behavior than others were. This has been a significant focus of the research on the Yes/No format, and a number of scoring formulas have been devised to adjust the final scores according to the number of false alarms (Yes responses to non-words) (Huibregtse, Admiraal, & Meara, 2002; Mochida & Harrington, 2006).

In the first instance, if guessing is an issue, it is desirable to include a statement in the instructions about whether it is acceptable to guess answers, and certainly there should be a warning if a penalty is to be imposed on incorrect responses. In a Yes/No test it is possible to add a "not sure" response category, with such answers being treated as No for scoring purposes. The V_YesNo test uses Yes and Next as its two response buttons (Meara & Miralpeix, 2016), presumably to encourage test takers to move on to the next item if they are not sure whether they know the currently displayed word. However, regardless of what is stated in test instructions, it is also important to investigate further ways in which to communicate the nature of the task to the test takers.

Jeffrey Stewart and his colleagues in Japan have conducted a series of studies on the effects of guessing in selected vocabulary tests. Stewart and White (2011) used elementary probability theory and multiple simulations to calculate the likelihood that guessing inflates the scores on a selected-response test like the VLT. The results showed that, if test takers are assumed to know up to 60% of the target L2 vocabulary, their VLT scores will be boosted nearly 17% by guessing. At higher levels of vocabulary knowledge, the effect is diminished by ceiling effects. The authors argue that constructed-response items will yield more accurate estimates of vocabulary size. Subsequently, Stewart (2014) published a similar critique of the VST, making the case that the probability of guessing correctly without knowing the target word is even higher with four-option multiple-choice items. He points out that Rasch analysis – as used by Beglar (2010) in his influential validation study of the VST – cannot detect systematic patterns of guessing in a whole test taker population, as distinct from the inconsistent patterns of individual test takers. Using the three-parameter logistic model instead of Rasch to analyze a large set of VST scores, McLean, Kramer, and Stewart (2015) found that a large proportion of the variance in scores for lower frequency words was attributable to guessing rather than actual knowledge of the words.

Research on the Vocabulary Size Test (VST) has investigated the effects of adding a fifth "I don't know" (IDK) option to each of the multiple-choice items. Zhang (2013) compared the original VST with a modified version containing this option. A meaning recall task, which required the test takers to give the meaning of each word in L1 or L2, was used to help identify whether they had at least some partial knowledge of the target word in responding to each VST item or were apparently guessing blindly. The IDK option significantly reduced both types of guesses, especially when it was accompanied by an explicit warning of a penalty for wrong guesses. The penalty warning in particular had the effect of discouraging learners from guessing on the basis of partial knowledge. However, this study did not take into account the fact that test takers select the IDK option to varying degrees. Using computer simulations, Stoeckel, Bennett, and McLean (2016) demonstrated that variable use of the IDK option was an extraneous factor which could significantly affect the validity of VST scores.

Selected-response test formats will continue to have a major role in measuring vocabulary knowledge because of their practical advantages, especially in large-scale tests. This means that we need to keep investigating the effects of guessing on test performance among particular populations of learners and to evaluate the effectiveness of the various strategies to discourage blind guessing while at the same time encouraging learners to demonstrate partial knowledge of the target vocabulary items.

Validation of Tests

A recurring issue with tests of vocabulary knowledge is how to validate them. There is a long tradition of using some kind of criterion measure of vocabulary knowledge, especially with selective-response tests. As we have seen, in small-scale studies it is possible to conduct individual interviews with learners to elicit what they "really" know about the target words and also to obtain retrospective verbal accounts of the strategies they employed in producing answers to the test items (see, e.g., Gyllstad et al., 2015; Read, 1993; Schmitt et al., 2011). On a larger scale, another popular criterion for validating tests based on selected-response formats is to use a written constructed-response task which requires the learners to provide their own synonym, definition, or L1 equivalent for each target word (see, e.g., Mochida & Harrington, 2006; Zhang, 2013). Going beyond single criterion measures, the study of the VLT by Schmitt et al. (2001) represented a kind of high-water mark in terms of the range of evidence assembled to validate the test as a profile of the test takers' vocabulary knowledge.

An alternative approach was adopted by Beglar (2010) for the validation of the original Vocabulary Size Test (see also McLean, Kramer, & Beglar, 2015). This approach draws primarily on Rasch analysis to generate evidence for the various components of an enhanced version of Messick's influential framework for test validity. It is true that well-designed vocabulary tests typically have high reliability and other positive measurement qualities which are reflected in the Rasch statistics. However, the approach has been criticized as the basis for justifying estimates of vocabulary size derived from VST scores (Gyllstad et al., 2015; Stewart, 2014) because it is not sensitive to systematic guessing behavior among the test takers.

Another weakness in the validation of vocabulary tests goes back to the introductory comments at the beginning of the chapter about the dominance of a small number of tests which have been promoted as one-size-fits-all instruments for use with learners worldwide. This is changing in the case of the VST, with the appearance of multiple versions of the test, including various bilingual versions, and debate over whether learners should take the whole test or just the items representing the higher frequency vocabulary they are likely to know. In addition, research on tests using the Yes/No format have shown rather different response behaviors by test takers in different parts of the world. Thus, it is desirable to see test validation as an ongoing process of justifying the use of tests and test formats in particular linguistic and educational contexts.

Modern test validity theory also requires that tests should be validated for specific purposes. In numerous studies of vocabulary tests, it is not very clear what purpose they are designed to serve. Among the studies reviewed in this chapter, several instruments have been designed for placement purposes (Fountain & Nation, 2000; Harrington & Carey, 2009; Meara & Jones, 1988). The original VLT (Nation, 1983) was presented as a diagnostic tool for teachers in the classroom. In the research by Harrington and his colleagues with the Timed Yes/No test (see below) in Australia and Oman, the purpose of the test is clearly stated and an appropriate external criterion measure (IELTS scores, grade point averages) was chosen. On the other hand, in discussing the validation of the VST, Beglar (2010) claims a whole range of uses for the test, from monitoring learner progress in the classroom through the achievement of curriculum objectives to understanding "the impact of educational reform on vocabulary growth" (p. 210). Although it could well be that a robust instrument like the VST can be used in all these different ways, its value for each of these purposes should be empirically evaluated.

Future Directions

Oral Vocabulary

The great preponderance of research on assessing vocabulary knowledge focuses on words in their written form, in keeping with the traditional relationship between vocabulary studies and research on reading in both L1 and L2. Perhaps it also reflects the fact that vocabulary study is popular in foreign language learning environments where there is limited exposure to the spoken language.

One early initiative to assess knowledge of spoken vocabulary was the graded dictation test developed by Fountain in the 1970s (Fountain & Nation, 2000). The dictation text was carefully constructed to incorporate words from progressively lower frequency levels. Although test takers write the whole text, only the target words are scored. A small-scale validation study showed a correlation of .78 with the (written) Vocabulary Levels Test, but there was no independent measure of the learners' ability to understand the individual words in their spoken form.

Other aural vocabulary tests have used the Yes/No format, presenting the target words in isolation. James Milton and his colleagues created AuralLex as an oral version of the written X-Lex test to investigate the development of what they refer to as phonological and orthographic vocabulary size. Milton and Hopkins (2006) observed that, after the initial period of language learning, orthographic word knowledge tended to outstrip phonological knowledge, particularly among advanced learners. This pattern was more marked among Greek-speaking learners than Arabic speakers, whose vocabulary size in both modes of input was relatively low. From a follow-up study, Milton and Riordan (2006) concluded that growth in phonological vocabulary among Arabic speakers was constrained by inefficient reading strategies transferred from L1. More recently, Milton, Wade, & Hopkins (2010) correlated scores on the two vocabulary tests with IELTS band scores. The correlations with the overall IELTS scores were quite substantial: .68 for X-Lex and .55 for AuralLex. As might have been expected, X-Lex had a stronger relationship with the IELTS reading and writing bands, whereas AuralLex correlated well with the listening and speaking scores.

McLean et al. (2015) created a Listening Vocabulary Levels Test, using the multiple-choice item format of the VST but covering only the first 5,000 words of English plus the Academic Word List. The stem of each item was spoken in English, with the response options written in Japanese to minimize the reading load. The scores on the 150-item test were moderately correlated (r = .54) with Parts 1 and 2 of the TOEIC listening test. In validating the test, the researchers employed the same Rasch-based framework adopted for Beglar's (2010) evaluation of the original VST, along with retrospective evidence from face-to-face interviews with a sample of the test takers. This qualitative evidence showed that blind guessing appeared to play only a small role in the learners' response behavior.

Thus, as with research on spoken vocabulary generally, there is a great deal of scope for further development of suitable tools for measuring knowledge of words in their oral form. The nature of speech makes it more challenging to hear and comprehend spoken words, especially if they are presented out of context, as words commonly are in their written form. This leads to the further question of whether words that learners can identify in isolation can be comprehended in a discourse context as well. In her research, van Zeeland (2013) found a substantial gap in aural word knowledge in and out of context. It also remains to be seen to what extent tests of spoken vocabulary knowledge can simply be adaptations of existing written tests.

Speed of Access

It seems obvious that one characteristic of fluent language use is rapid access to the mental lexicon, so that the user can perform communicative tasks in real time without consciously searching for the necessary vocabulary. However, until recently vocabulary tests have focused on accuracy of response to the test items, without taking into account how quickly the test taker responds. In this regard L2 vocabulary researchers have approached the investigation of word knowledge quite differently from psycholinguists, for whom reaction time (RT) measures have been a routine tool for many years (see Godfroid, this volume).

An early initiative to incorporate speed of response into an L2 vocabulary test was Laufer and Nation's (2001) study of a computer-based version of the Vocabulary Levels Test. There was significant variation in response times among learners at different levels of proficiency. The researchers also identified an apparent lag in performance whereby the learners responded faster to words at a particular frequency level only after they had demonstrated a good knowledge of that level in terms of accuracy.

Subsequent investigations of response fluency have almost all involved computer-based Yes/No vocabulary tests. Harrington (2006) sought to bridge the gap between the psycholinguistic and SLA perspectives, not only by applying reaction time measures in a Yes/No test but also introducing Segalowitz's (2010) coefficient of variation (CV) as a measure of how automatically participants responded to the stimulus words. Harrington administered a Yes/No test to participants at three proficiency levels: intermediate ESL, advanced ESL, and English as L1. After correction for guessing, the accuracy scores showed consistent increases across the proficiency levels and conversely both the mean reaction time and the mean CV decreased from the intermediate learners through to the native speakers. On the other hand, in a study with a somewhat similar design Miralpeix and Meara (2014) found very little relationship between vocabulary size and either reaction time or CV among students studying English at the University of Barcelona.

More promising evidence of the value of reaction times to evaluate Yes/No test performance was found by Pellicer-Sánchez and Schmitt (2012) in two linked studies. Their basic question was whether RT values could be an alternative to non-words for adjusting Yes/No scores for overestimation of knowledge. The analysis revealed that the participants responded significantly faster when a Yes response was accurate (as confirmed by a subsequent interview) than when it was inaccurate, and the researchers calculated a threshold reaction time to distinguish the two types of response. This proved to be a better basis for measuring knowledge of the target words than the standard approach of including non-words and then applying a correction formula. However the participants were highly proficient English users who produced few if any false alarms overall, so it remains to be seen whether these findings can be generalized to less proficient learners with more variable performance on a Y/N test.

The other main relevant research is a series of studies undertaken by Harrington and his associates in various educational contexts, using what they now call the Timed Yes/No test (TYN). In these investigations both accuracy and response speed have been measured. Harrington and Carey (2009) explored the value of a TYN test as a placement measure in a language school in Australia. The TYN results were comparable to those of the existing school placement test, although the reaction times were a little less effective at discriminating proficiency levels in the school program.

Since then, Harrington and Roche have conducted several studies (e.g., Harrington & Roche, 2014; Roche, Harrington, Sinha, & Denman, 2016) with students at higher education institutions in Oman, where English has been adopted as the medium of instruction. The studies have looked at the TYN as a measure of readiness for undergraduate study both before and after admission to a degree program. Generally speaking, the correlations between the TYN results and criterion measures have been quite modest, usually less than .40. Despite the efforts of the researchers to inform the test takers about the nature of the TYN task, the students have persistently responded Yes to non-words. According to the researchers, the students' lack of motivation to perform well in a low-stakes test situation was one factor influencing the results. Incidentally, the role of motivation in vocabulary test performance was highlighted by Nation (2007), and there is a substantial body of research on the topic in the educational measurement literature (Wise & Smith, 2016).

Drawing on the Oman studies and numerous others, Harrington (2018) has proposed the construct of lexical facility, which is defined conceptually as "the capacity to recognize words quickly" as a key component of fluent text comprehension, and operationally as a composite measure of accuracy, mean reaction time, and coefficient of variation (CV). He argues that the combination of accuracy and speed is a more sensitive measure of second language vocabulary competence, and more particularly academic language proficiency, than the accuracy scores produced by conventional vocabulary tests. The TYN has its limitations, as Harrington freely acknowledges, but this line of research may stimulate the development of other measures which take account of learners' ability to access their vocabulary knowledge fluently.

Oral vocabulary and speed of access are two dimensions among several that are the focus of the current vibrant upsurge in research on vocabulary testing, as the other chapters in this section of the volume amply demonstrate.

Further Reading

Read, J. (2000). *Assessing vocabulary*. Cambridge, UK: Cambridge University Press.

> This was the first comprehensive account of the assessment of second language vocabulary knowledge.

Milton, J. (2009). *Measuring second language vocabulary acquisition*. Bristol, UK: Multilingual Matters.

> This volume draws together research findings by the author along with his colleagues and doctoral students at Swansea University in the UK.

Schmitt, N. (2010). *Researching vocabulary: A vocabulary research manual*. Basingstoke, UK: Palgrave Macmillan.

Nation, I. S. P., & Webb, S. (2011). *Researching and analysing vocabulary*. Boston, MA: Heinle Cengage Learning.

> These two manuals on conducting various types of vocabulary research include extensive discussion and advice on measurement issues.

Read, J. (2013). Research timeline: Second language vocabulary assessment. *Language Teaching*, *46*(1), 41–52.

> This article presents an annotated bibliography of key developments in L2 vocabulary assessment from the 1980s to the present.

Related Topics

L1 and L2 vocabulary size and growth, measuring depth of vocabulary knowledge, measuring knowledge of multiword items, measuring vocabulary learning progress, measuring the ability to learn words, sensitive measures of vocabulary knowledge and processing, measuring lexical richness

References

Alderson, J. C. (2005). *Diagnosing foreign language proficiency*. London, UK: Continuum.

Beglar, D. (2010). A Rasch-based validation of the Vocabulary Size Test. *Language Testing*, *27*(1), 101–118.

Cenoz, J., & Gorter, D. (Eds.). (2015). *Multilingual education: Between language learning and translanguaging*. Cambridge, UK: Cambridge University Press.

Cobb, T. (2000). One size fits all? Francophone learners and English vocabulary tests. *Canadian Modern Language Review, 57*(2), 295–324.

Daulton, F. E. (2008). *Japan's built-in lexicon of English-based loanwords*. Clevedon, UK: Multilingual Matters.

Du, Y. (2016). *The use of first and second language in Chinese university EFL classrooms*. Singapore: Springer.

Ebel, R. L., & Frisbie, D. A. (1986). *Essentials of educational measurement* (4th ed.). Englewood Cliffs, NJ: Prentice-Hall.

Elgort, I. (2013). Effects of L1 definitions and cognate status of test items on the Vocabulary Size Test. *Language Testing, 30*(2), 253–272.

Fitzpatrick, T., & Barfield, A. (Eds.). (2009). *Lexical processing in second language learners Papers and Perspectives in honour of Paul Meara*. Bristol, UK: Multilingual Matters.

Fountain, R., & Nation, I. S. P. (2000). A vocabulary-based graded dictation test. *RELC Journal, 31*(2), 29–44.

Garcia, O., & Li, W. (2013). *Translanguaging: Language, bilingualism and education*. Basingstoke, UK: Palgrave Macmillan.

Gyllstad, H., Vilkaitė, L., & Schmitt, N. (2015). Assessing vocabulary size through multiple-choice formats: Issues with guessing and sampling rates. *ITL International Journal of Applied Linguistics, 166*(2), 276–303.

Harrington, M. (2006). The lexical decision task as a measure of L2 lexical proficiency. *EUROSLA Yearbook, 6*, 147–168.

Harrington, M. (2018). *Lexical facility: Size, recognition speed and consistency as dimensions of second language vocabulary knowledge*. Basingstoke, UK: Palgrave Macmillan.

Harrington, M., & Carey, M. (2009). The on-line yes/no test as a placement tool. *System, 37*(4), 614–626.

Harrington, M., & Roche, T. (2014). Post-enrolment language assessment for identifying at-risk students in in English-as-a-Lingua-Franca university settings. *Journal of English for Academic Purposes, 15*(1), 37–47.

Huibregtse, I., Admiraal, W., & Meara, P. (2002). Scores on a yes-no test: Correction for guessing and response style. *Language Testing, 19*, 227–245.

Jordan, E. (2012). Cognates in vocabulary size testing – A distorting influence? *Language Testing in Asia, 2*(3), 5–17.

Karami, H. (2012). The development and validation of a bilingual version of the Vocabulary Size Test. *RELC Journal, 43*(1), 53–67.

Laufer, B., Elder, C., Hill, K., & Congdon, P. (2004). Size and strength: Do we need both to measure vocabulary? *Language Testing, 21*(2), 202–226.

Laufer, B., & Goldstein, Z. (2004). Testing vocabulary knowledge: Size, strength and computer adaptiveness. *Language Learning, 54*(3), 399–436.

Laufer, B., & Levitsky-Aviad, T. (2018). Loanword proportion in vocabulary size tests: Does it make a difference? *ITL – International Journal of Applied Linguistics, 169*(1), 94–114.

Laufer, B., & McLean, S. (2016). Loanwords and Vocabulary Size Test scores: A case of different estimates for different L1 learners. *Language Assessment Quarterly, 13*(3), 202–217.

Laufer, B., & Nation, I. S. P. (1995). Vocabulary size and use: Lexical richness in L2 written production. *Applied Linguistics, 16*, 307–322.

Laufer, B., & Nation, I. S. P. (2001). Passive vocabulary size and the speed of meaning recognition: Are they related? *EUROSLA Yearbook, 1*, 7–28.

McLean, S., Kramer, B., & Beglar, D. (2015). The creation and validation of a listening vocabulary levels test. *Language Teaching Research, 19*(6), 741–760.

McLean, S., Kramer, B., & Stewart, J. (2015). An empirical examination of the effect of guessing on Vocabulary Size Test scores. *Vocabulary Learning and Instruction, 4*(1), 26–35.

Meara, P., & Jones, G. (1988). Vocabulary size as placement indicator. In P. Grunwell (Ed.), *Applied linguistics in society* (pp. 80–87). London, UK: CILT.

Meara, P., Lightbown, P., & Halter, R. (1994). The effect of cognates on the applicability of YES/NO vocabulary tests. *Canadian Modern Language Review, 50*(2), 296–311.

Meara, P., & Miralpeix, I. (2016). *Tools for researching vocabulary*. Bristol, UK: Multilingual Matters.

Milton, J., & Hopkins, N. (2006). Comparing phonological and orthographic size: Do vocabulary tests underestimate the knowledge of some learners? *Canadian Modern Language Review, 63*(2), 127–147.

Milton, J., & Riordan, O. (2006). Level and script effects in the phonological and orthographic size of Arabic and Farsi speakers. In P. Davidson, C. Coombe, D. Lloyd, & D. Palfreyman (Eds.), *Teaching and learning vocabulary in another language* (pp. 122–133). Dubai: TESOL Arabia.

Milton, J., Wade, J., & Hopkins, N. (2010). Aural word recognition and oral competence in a foreign language. In R. Chacón-Beltrán, C. Abello-Contesse, M. Torreblanca-López, & M. D. López-Jiménez (Eds.), *Further insights into nonnative vocabulary teaching and learning* (pp. 83–97). Bristol, UK: Multilingual Matters.

Miralpeix, I., & Meara, P. (2014). Knowledge of the written form. In J. Milton & T. Fitzpatrick (Eds.), *Dimensions of vocabulary knowledge* (pp. 30–44). Basingstoke, UK: Palgrave Macmillan.

Mochida, A., & Harrington, M. (2006). The Yes/No test as a measure of receptive vocabulary knowledge. *Language Testing, 23*(1), 73–98.

Nation, I. S. P. (1983). Testing and teaching vocabulary. *Guidelines, 5*, 12–25.

Nation, I. S. P. (2001). *Learning vocabulary in another language*. Cambridge, UK: Cambridge University Press.

Nation, I. S. P. (2007). Fundamental issues in modelling and assessing vocabulary knowledge. In H. Daller, J. Milton & J. Treffers-Daller (Eds.), *Modelling and assessing vocabulary knowledge* (pp. 35–43). Cambridge, UK: Cambridge University Press.

Nation, I. S. P. (2012). *The Vocabulary Levels Test*. Unpublished paper. Retrieved June 30, 2017 from: www.victoria.ac.nz/lals/about/staff/publications/paul-nation/Vocabulary-Size-Test-information-and-specifications.pdf

Nation, I. S. P. (2013). *Learning vocabulary in another language* (2nd ed.). Cambridge, UK: Cambridge University Press.

Nation, I. S. P. (2016). *Making and using word lists for language learning and testing*. Amsterdam: John Benjamins.

Nation, I. S. P., & Beglar, D. (2007). A vocabulary size test. *The Language Teacher, 31*(7), 9–13.

Nguyen, L. T. C., & Nation, I. S. P. (2011). A bilingual vocabulary size test of English for Vietnamese learners. *RELC Journal, 42*(1), 86–99.

Pellicer-Sánchez, A., & Schmitt, N. (2012). Scoring Yes/No vocabulary tests: Reaction time vs. nonword approaches. *Language Testing, 29*(4), 489–509.

Read, J. (1988). Measuring the vocabulary knowledge of second language learners. *RELC Journal, 19*(1), 12–25.

Read, J. (1993). The development of a new measure of L2 vocabulary knowledge. *Language Testing, 10*(3), 355–371.

Read, J. (1998). Validating a test to measure depth of vocabulary knowledge. In A. Kunnan (Ed.), *Validation in language assessment* (pp. 41–60). Mahwah, NJ: Erlbaum.

Read, J. (2000). *Assessing vocabulary*. Cambridge, UK: Cambridge University Press.

Revier, R. L. (2009). Evaluating a new test of *whole* English collocations. In A. Barfield & H. Gyllstad (Eds.), *Researching collocations in another language* (pp. 125–138). Basingstoke, UK: Palgrave Macmillan.

Roche, T., Harrington, M., Sinha, Y., & Denman, C. (2016). Vocabulary recognition skill as a screening tool in English-as-a-Lingua-Franca university settings. In J. Read (Ed.), *Post-admission language assessment of university students* (pp. 159–178). Cham, Switzerland: Springer.

Sasao, Y., & Webb, S. (2017). The Word Part Levels Test. *Language Teaching Research, 21*(1), 12–30.

Sasao, Y., & Webb, S. (2018). The guessing from context test. *ITL – International Journal of Applied Linguistics, 169*(1), 115–141.

Schmitt, N. (2010). *Researching vocabulary: A vocabulary research manual*. Basingstoke, UK: Palgrave Macmillan.

Schmitt, N. (2014). Size and depth of vocabulary knowledge: What the research shows. *Language Learning, 64*(4), 913–951.

Schmitt, N., Jiang, X., & Grabe, W. (2011). The percentage of words known in a text and reading comprehension. *Modern Language Journal, 95*(1), 26–43.

Schmitt, N., Ng, J. W. C., & Garras, J. (2011). The Word Associates Format: Validation evidence. *Language Testing, 28*(1), 105–126.

Schmitt, N., Schmitt, D., & Clapham, C. (2001). Developing and exploring the behaviour of two new versions of the Vocabulary Levels Test. *Language Testing, 18*(1), 55–88.

Schmitt, N., & Zimmerman, C. B. (2002). Derivative word forms: What do learners know? *TESOL Quarterly, 36*(2), 145–171.

Schoonen, R., & Verhallen, M. (2008). The assessment of deep word knowledge in young first and second language learners. *Language Testing, 25*(2), 211–236.

Segalowitz, N. (2010). *Cognitive bases of second language fluency*. New York, NY: Routledge.

Stewart, J. (2014). Do multiple-choice options inflate estimates of vocabulary size on the VST? *Language Assessment Quarterly, 11*(3), 271–282.

Stewart, J., & White, D. A. (2011). Estimating guessing effects on the Vocabulary Levels Test for differing degrees of word knowledge. *TESOL Quarterly, 45*(2), 370–380.

Stoeckel, T., Bennett, P., & McLean, S. (2016). Is "I don't know" a viable answer choice on the Vocabulary Size Test? *TESOL Quarterly, 50*(4), 965–975.

Stubbe, R. (2015). Replacing translation tests with Yes/No tests. *Vocabulary Learning and Instruction, 4*(2), 38–48.

Turnbull, M., & Dailey-O'Cain, J. (Eds.). (2009). *First language use in second and foreign language learning*. Bristol, UK: Multilingual Matters.

van Zeeland, H. (2013). L2 vocabulary knowledge in and out of context: Is it the same for reading and listening? *Australian Review of Applied Linguistics, 36*(1), 52–70.

Webb, S. (2007). The effects of repetition on vocabulary knowledge. *Applied Linguistics, 28*(1), 46–65.

Webb, S., Sasao, Y., & Balance, O. (2017). The updated Vocabulary Levels Test: Developing and validating two new forms of the VLT. *ITL – International Journal of Applied Linguistics, 168*(1), 33–69.

Wesche, M. B., & Paribakht, T. S. (1996). Assessing second language vocabulary knowledge: Depth vs. breadth. *Canadian Modern Language Review, 53*(1), 13–39.

Wise, S. L., & Smith, L. F. (2016). The validity of assessment when students don't give good effort. In G. T. L. Brown & L. R. Harris (Eds.), *Handbook of human and social conditions in assessment* (pp. 204–220). New York, NY: Routledge.

Zhang, X. (2013). The "I don't know" option in the Vocabulary Size Test. *TESOL Quarterly, 47*(4), 790–811.

Zhao, P., & Ji, X. (2016). Validation of the Mandarin version of the Vocabulary Size Test. *RELC Journal, 49*(3), 308–321. https://doi.org/10.1177/0033688216639761

35

Resources for Researching Vocabulary

Laurence Anthony

Introduction

Research on vocabulary has seen an enormous growth since the early 1990s, leading to new monographs, chapters, research journals, and conferences dedicated to the topic. No doubt this trend is partially spurred by the pioneering work of researchers such as Graham Kennedy, Batia Laufer, Mike McCarthy, Paul Meara, Paul Nation, John Read, Stuart Webb, and numerous others. However, two other factors have almost certainly contributed to this growth in vocabulary research. One is the increasing availability of large, easily-accessible general and discipline-specific corpus resources that can serve as primary data sources for research studies. The other is the increasing availability of powerful and easy-to-use desktop and online software tools. These resources allow vocabulary researchers to quickly collect primary corpus data and analyze that data at the word and multiword level. They also allow researchers to create new vocabulary resources in the form of ranked lists of vocabulary items. Finally, they allow researchers to quantitatively analyze vocabulary size, growth and usage patterns, develop vocabulary knowledge and complexity measures, and develop methods that can facilitate the teaching and learning of vocabulary in the classroom.

Although corpus resources and software tools play an essential role in many vocabulary research projects, researchers can often brush over their details in order to give more focus to the results of an analysis. Subsequently, it can sometimes be unclear what resources were used and for what purpose. Also, even when the resources are described, the researcher may neglect to explain the rationale for their selection over other resources with a similar purpose.

In this chapter, I will attempt to address these issues by discussing four distinct categories of resources that cover the broad spectrum of resources available to vocabulary researchers: (1) corpus resources that can serve as primary data for vocabulary research; (2) software tools that allow researchers to build primary data sources; (3) word lists that can serve as secondary data for vocabulary research; and (4) software tools that allow researchers to probe primary and secondary data sources in order to reveal new insights on the nature of vocabulary. Rather than attempt to provide a comprehensive list of resources in each of these categories (one that would almost certainly go out of date rather quickly), I will focus instead on the types of resources that are available in each of these categories and explain their defining characteristics. I will also describe more generally what the different resources in each category do, explain why they are useful, define their target audiences, and discuss their strengths and limitations. In order to contextualize the discussion, I will showcase a few of the more commonly used and cited resources in each category. Then, at the end of the chapter, I will discuss some of the current directions we see in vocabulary research and discuss possible future directions for vocabulary software tool and resource development.

Critical Issues and Topics

Corpus Resources as Primary Data for Vocabulary Research

At the heart of many studies aiming to understand the nature of vocabulary in different disciplines and contexts is a corpus (plural "corpora") of naturally occurring spoken or written texts which is designed to be a representative of the target language variety (see Biber, Conrad, & Reppen, 1998; McEnery & Wilson, 2001). In the past, creating such corpora was a complicated and time-consuming process. However, now, an increasing number of readily accessible corpora provide vocabulary researchers with access to huge amounts of raw language data. Schmitt (2010, p. 307) describes the importance of corpus resources in vocabulary research as follows:

> It is hard to imagine any area of vocabulary research into acquisition, processing, pedagogy, or assessment where the insights available from corpus analysis would not be valuable. In fact, it is probably not too extreme to say that most sound vocabulary research will have some corpus element.

Indeed, we can see the strong connection between vocabulary research and corpus developments by looking at citation counts for published research that include the search terms "vocabulary" and/or "corpus". As an example, Figure 35.1 shows citation counts for the two terms in the *Scopus*[1] abstract and citation database (www.scopus.com), where the two terms have a very strong correlation ($r = .9834$, $p < 0.00001$).

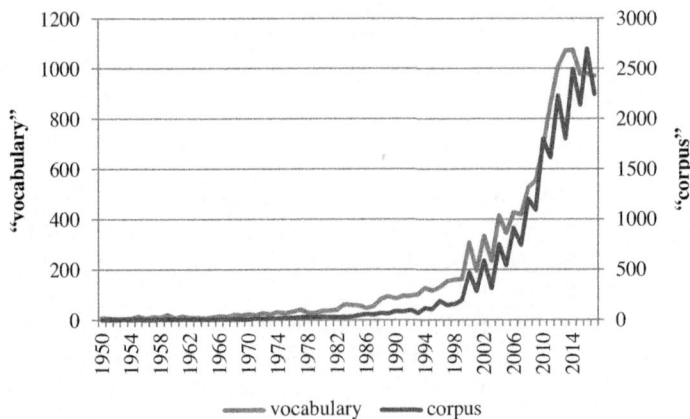

Figure 35.1   Citation counts for the search terms "vocabulary" and "corpus"
Source: Scopus, 2018

Table 35.1 Common vocabulary research aims

- Compare vocabulary knowledge of native and non-native speakers
- Consider how language functions similarly or differently in spoken and written contexts
- Describe vocabulary in terms of suffixes, affixes, and other vocabulary parts
- Establish the general importance of individual vocabulary items through a quantitative measure (e.g., relative frequency, dispersion, or a combination of the two)
- Identify associations between vocabulary items
- Identify categories of vocabulary (e.g., general, academic, technical vocabulary)
- Identify characteristic features of language in specialized disciplines
- Integrate vocabulary into teaching and learning methodologies
- Track the growth in the size and depth of vocabulary knowledge for different aged groups in a target population
- Understand the connections between vocabulary knowledge and other aspects of language proficiency, e.g., in reading, writing, listening, and speaking
- Understand the nature/construct of vocabulary through vocabulary forms, meanings, and uses

---

Corpora serve a number of important purposes in vocabulary research, being used as primary data sources when researchers want to achieve one or more of the aims listed in Table 35.1.

In order to decide which corpus resource will be most suitable for a particular research aim, it is important to understand the characteristic features of different corpora and be able to categorize them accordingly. In the following section, these features will be explained using some of the most commonly used corpora in the field as examples.

Characteristic Features of Corpus Resources

Corpora can be usefully categorized in terms of the language variety that the corpus attempts to model, the language user(s) represented in that model, the design of the corpus, and the way in which the corpus is stored and accessed. The characteristics features of corpora are summarized in Table 35.2.

The first defining characteristic of a corpus is the language variety it attempts to model. Many corpora are designed to model written language and are thus comprised of electronically stored written texts. However, it is also possible for a corpus to model spoken language through the inclusion of electronically stored transcripts of spoken language. Other corpora are based on a set of multimodal elements (e.g., text, sound, images) and attempt to model all facets of a communicative event. Some of the largest corpora to date have been designed to model general language (i.e., language used in a broad range of contexts, across various genres, by speakers of different genders and social groups). Others are designed to model a specific language variety, such as the language of a specific genre (e.g., newspaper articles), discipline (e.g., the language of mathematics), or speaker group (e.g., non-native speakers of English). Naturally, these corpora tend to be smaller, but there are some modern specialized corpora that are huge in comparison to early general language corpora (see, e.g., the *PERC* corpus[2] of professional English). Corpora can also model language at specific times (synchronic corpora) or over a period of time (diachronic corpora). Finally, corpora can be formed from monolingual language data (e.g., English newspapers) or multilingual data (e.g., newspapers in English and German).

Many corpora are modeled on the language of native or near-native (proficient) users with a matured language skill. Synchronic corpora of this type are frequently used as reference

Table 35.2 Summary of characteristic features of corpus resources

Language variety		
Written	vs.	Spoken (or multimodal)
General-purpose	vs.	Specific-purpose
Synchronic	vs.	Diachronic
Monolingual	vs.	Multilingual
Language user		
Native/proficient user	vs.	Learner
Matured language	vs.	Developmental/interlanguage
Corpus design		
"Small"	vs.	"Large"
Comparable	vs.	Parallel
Raw	vs.	Annotated
Static	vs.	Dynamic
Complete	vs.	Sampled from population
Corpus storage and access		
Direct access	vs.	Indirect access
Offline	vs.	Online
Publicly available	vs.	In-house (restricted use)
Freely available	vs.	License/fee requirements

sources for comparative studies (e.g., the British National Corpus[3]). On the other hand, diachronic corpora of native or near-native (proficient) speech can offer insights on first-language development as well as social/cultural change. For examples of research on first language development using the *CHILDES* corpus[4] of child language, see https://talkbank.org/info/usage/childesbib.pdf. For an example of diachronic corpora in the analysis of social/cultural change see Partington (2010).

A further factor that characterizes different corpora is the design. Depending on the language variety and user group that a corpus is intended to model, as well as its purpose and target user group, it can be designed to be "large" (e.g., several hundred million words) or "small" (e.g., several hundred thousand words). A corpus can also be specifically designed to make comparisons easy. Comparable corpora, for example, contain subcorpora that are designed according to the same criteria (e.g., size, population, subject area, time period) allowing general patterns of language usage to be compared even though the content of the subcorpora might be quite different. Parallel corpora, on the other hand, contain subcorpora with matching content that is aligned in some way. The most common parallel corpus is one formed of a particular language variety and its associated direct translations aligned at the word, sentence, or paragraph level. Again, this construction allows the subcorpora to be directly compared, but it also provides translators with a "translation memory" system so that they can check how they and others translated material in the past, and improve translations in the future (Hu, 2016).

As part of the design, many corpora store language variety samples in a "raw" text form. For written and spoken corpora, this usually means plain text files containing the contents of the written documents or the spoken transcripts. However, we also find corpora that are designed to store "annotated" versions of the original samples. In some cases, these can be "raw" texts with additional word-level Part-of-Speech (POS) annotations. In other cases, we can find more elaborate annotations included, for example, information of the target context, the speakers' biographic information, and the syntactic structures used in the texts. If the number of samples stored in the corpus is fixed, the corpus is considered to be static. If, however, samples are added to the corpus as they become available or over time, the corpus is considered to be dynamic (sometimes referred to as a "monitor" corpus). One other aspect of design is the question of whether the samples comprise the complete set of instances of a language variety or a sample from the population of possible instances. Most corpora contain a sample of texts but in some special cases, corpora can represent the complete set of instances, as illustrated by corpora of literature classics (e.g., the Shakespeare Corpus[5]).

One final defining characteristic of corpora is the way that they are stored and accessed. Some corpora are custom-built by the researcher for a particular research project and thus can be stored on a local computer or a network server and accessed directly. Similarly, many corpora that are built by third parties and released for public or private use can be downloaded in their entirety and stored and accessed in a similar way. The importance of direct access to such corpora cannot be understated as it enables the researcher to critique the design structure, investigate language at both the micro- and macro-level, as well as analyze the data with their preferred corpus analysis tool. Many corpora, however, are stored on a remote server and can only be indirectly accessed through an online web interface. This setup offers several advantages over local systems. For example, remote servers can store and offer access to very large, multi-million or multi-billion word corpora that would not feasibly fit on a personal computer or would require an expensive local server to host. The backend database architectures for these systems can also be optimized for the hosted corpora providing excellent search time performance. In addition, the interfaces to these systems can be optimized for the target audience allowing for interesting and useful ways to visualize the results. However, the systems also tend to restrict access to the corpus data (often for copyright reasons), and thus provide only a limited view of target texts or a restricting number of hits and searches. This setup also restricts the ability of researchers to critique the design structure of the corpus, investigate language at the macro-level, or analyze the data with their preferred corpus analysis tool. One related factor is whether or not the corpus can be downloaded or accessed freely or if the researcher must instead agree to license restrictions and/or pay a usage fee.

Examples of Resources From Different Corpus Categories

Each of the categories of corpora shown in Table 35.1 is represented by an ever-growing set of resources. Most of these can be easily found by simply performing an internet search with the appropriate terms, e.g., "spoken corpus of newspaper English". Also, lists of corpus resources can be found at an increasing number of sites dedicated to corpus resources, including (as of June 2018):

- http://martinweisser.org/corpora_site/CBLLinks.html
- http://courses.washington.edu/englhtml/engl560/corplingresources.htm
- https://linguistics.stanford.edu/resources/corpora/corpus-inventory
- www.helsinki.fi/varieng/CoRD/corpora/index.html
- www.unc.edu/~jlsmith/lex-corp.html

A review of vocabulary literature reveals that some corpus resources are especially prominent in the field. These are summarized in Table 35.3 with a brief synopsis of their defining features and a definitive research publication describing their design and potential uses.

Table 35.3 Prominent corpora used in vocabulary research

British National Corpus (BNC)	Access location
	• www.natcorp.ox.ac.uk
	Features
	Language variety: spoken + written, general + specific purpose, synchronic, monolingual
	Language user: native/proficient user, matured
	Corpus form and design: 100 m words, raw + annotated, static, sampled from population
	Corpus access: direct + indirect, offline + online (public/free)
	Research publication
	Aston, G. and Burnard, L. (1998). *The* BNC *handbook: exploring the* British National Corpus *with SARA*. Edinburgh: Edinburgh University Press.
Open American National Corpus (OANC)	Access location
	• www.anc.org/
	Features
	Language variety: spoken + written, general + specific purpose, synchronic, monolingual
	Language user: native/proficient user, matured
	Corpus form and design: 15 m words, raw + annotated, static, sampled from population
	Corpus access: direct + indirect, offline + online (public/free)
	Research publication
	Ide, N. (2008). The American National Corpus: then, now, and tomorrow. In M. Haugh, K. Burridge, J. Mulder & P. Peters (Eds.), *Selected proceedings of the 2008 HCSNet Workshop on Designing the Australian National Corpus: Mustering Languages, Cascadilla Proceedings Project*. Sommerville, MA.
Corpus of Contemporary American English (COCA)	Access location
	• http://corpus.byu.edu/coca/
	Features
	Language variety: spoken + written, general + specific purpose, diachronic, monolingual
	Language user: native/proficient user, matured
	Corpus form and design: 560 m words (as of 2018), raw + annotated, dynamic, sampled from population
	Corpus access: direct + indirect, offline (restricted/fee) + online (restricted/ semi-commercial)
	Research publication
	Davies, M. (2010). The Corpus of Contemporary American English as the first reliable monitor corpus of English. *Literary and Linguistic Computing, 25*(4), 447–464.
British Academic Spoken English (BASE) corpus	Access location
	• https://warwick.ac.uk/fac/soc/al/research/collections/base/
	• www.coventry.ac.uk/research/research-directories/current-projects/2015/ british-academic-spoken-english-corpus-base/
	Features
	Language variety: spoken, specific-purpose synchronic, monolingual
	Language user: native/proficient user, matured
	Corpus form and design: 1.6 m words, raw + annotated, static, sampled from population
	Corpus access: direct + indirect, offline + online (public/free)

British Academic Written English (BAWE) corpus	Research publication
	Thompson, P., & Nesi, H. (2001). The British Academic Spoken English (BASE) Corpus Project. *Language Teaching Research, 5*(3), 263–264.
	Access location
	• https://warwick.ac.uk/fac/soc/al/research/collections/bawe/
	• www.coventry.ac.uk/research/research-directories/current-projects/2015/british-academic-written-english-corpus-bawe/
	Features
	Language variety: written, specific-purpose synchronic, monolingual
	Language user: native/proficient user, matured
	Corpus form and design: 6.5 m words, raw + annotated, static, sampled from population
	Corpus access: direct + indirect, offline (public/free) + online (restricted/free)
	Research publication
	Alsop, S., & Nesi, H. (2001). Issues in the development of the British Academic Written English (BAWE) corpus. *Corpora, 4*(1), 71–83.
The Lancaster-Oslo/Bergen Corpus (LOB Corpus) + The Freiburg–LOB Corpus of British English (F-LOB)	Access location
	• www.helsinki.fi/varieng/CoRD/corpora/LOB/ www.helsinki.fi/varieng/CoRD/corpora/FLOB/
	Features
	Language variety: written, general + specific purpose, synchronic, monolingual
	Language user: native/proficient user, matured
	Corpus form and design: 1 m words, raw + annotated, static, sampled from population (LOB: sampled 1961; F-LOB: sampled 1991–1996)
	Corpus access: direct + indirect, offline + online (public/free)
	Research publication
	Johansson, S., Leech, G. N., & Goodluck, H. (1978). Manual of information to accompany the Lancaster-Oslo/Bergen Corpus of British English, for use with digital computer. Department of English, University of Oslo. Available online at: http://clu.uni.no/icame/lob/lob-dir.htm.
The Standard Corpus of Present-Day Edited American English (the Brown Corpus) + The Freiburg-Brown Corpus of American English (Frown)	Access location
	• www.helsinki.fi/varieng/CoRD/corpora/BROWN/
	• www.helsinki.fi/varieng/CoRD/corpora/FROWN/
	Features
	Language variety: written, general + specific purpose, synchronic, monolingual
	Language user: native/proficient user, matured
	Corpus form and design: 1 m words, raw + annotated, static, sampled from population (Brown: sampled 1961; F-LOB: sampled 1992–1996)
	Corpus access: direct + indirect, offline + online (public/free)
	Research publication
	Francis, W. N., & Kučera, H. (1964). Manual of Information to accompany A Standard Corpus of Present-Day Edited American English, for use with Digital Computers. Providence, Rhode Island: Department of Linguistics, Brown University. Revised 1971. Revised and amplified 1979. Available online at: http://icame.uib.no/brown/bcm.html.

(Continued)

Table 35.3 (Continued)

Michigan Corpus of Upper-Level Student Papers (MICUSP)	Access location • http://micusp.elicorpora.info/ Features **Language variety**: written, specific purpose, synchronic, monolingual **Language user**: learner, developmental **Corpus form and design**: 2.5 m words, annotated, static, sampled from population **Corpus access**: indirect, online (public/free) Research publication Römer, U., & O'Donnell, M. B. (2011). From student hard drive to web corpus (part 1): the design, compilation and genre classification of the Michigan Corpus of Upper-level Student Papers (MICUSP). *Corpora, 6*(2), 159–177.
Michigan Corpus of Academic Spoken English (MICASE)	Access location • https://quod.lib.umich.edu/m/micase/ Features **Language variety**: spoken, specific purpose, synchronic, monolingual **Language user**: native/proficient + learner, matured + developmental **Corpus form and design**: 1.8 m words, annotated, static, sampled from population **Corpus access**: direct + indirect, offline + online (public/free) Research publication Simpson-Vlach, R. C., & Leicher, S. (2006). *The MICASE handbook: A resource for users of the Michigan corpus of academic spoken English*. University of Michigan Press.
International Corpus of Learner English	Access location • https://uclouvain.be/en/research-institutes/ilc/cecl/icle.html Features **Language variety**: written, specific purpose (essays), synchronic, multilingual **Language user**: learner, developmental **Corpus form and design**: 200,000 words (per language), annotated, static, sampled from population **Corpus access**: direct + indirect, offline + online (public/fee) Research publication Granger S. (2008). Learner corpora. In A. Lüdeling & M. Kytö (Eds.) *Handbook on Corpus Linguistics*. Mouton de Gruyter.
Cambridge English Corpus (CEC)	Access location (in house only) • Details at: www.cambridge.org/about-us/what-we-do/cambridge-english-corpus Features **Language variety**: spoken + written, general + specific purpose, diachronic, monolingual **Language user**: details unpublished **Corpus form and design**: details unpublished **Corpus access**: in house only Research publication: None available

Longman Corpus Network	Access location (in house only) • details at: www.pearsonlongman.com/dictionaries/corpus/ Features **Language variety**: spoken + written, general + specific purpose, diachronic, monolingual **Language user**: details unpublished **Corpus form and design**: 179 m words (including 5 m words spoken, 100 m words written, 10 m words learner data), dynamic, diachronic **Corpus access**: in house only Research publication: Brief mention in Schmitt, N. (2010). *Researching vocabulary: A vocabulary research manual.* Springer.

Software Tools for Building Primary Corpus Data Sources

Some vocabulary research questions necessitate the creation of a completely new primary data source. For example, the researcher may be interested in profiling the vocabulary of native speakers of an under-researched minority language or the use of a dominant language by both native and non-native speakers in a narrow, highly specialized context. To facilitate the creation of such primary data sources, software tools that are able to convert existing data sources into a form suitable for corpus analysis are commonly used. Several of these are described in the following section

File Conversion Tools

Standard PC/Mac software tools are able to convert proprietary data formats into plain text formats that can then be used by vocabulary analysis tools and profiling tools (to be described later). As an example, Microsoft Office Word, Libre Office, and other "Office" tools can open and convert files created in various word processing tools (e.g., .doc/.docx files) into plain .txt files via the Save menu. In the same way, Adobe Acrobat, Foxit Reader, and similar tools can open and convert Portable Document Format (.pdf) files into plain .txt files. As these tools are usually found on every PC/Mac, they are essentially ubiquitous and intuitive to use. One downside to these tools is that by default they are only able to convert a single file at a time making the conversion of an entire corpus of data a potentially lengthy process. Although it is possible for tools to convert multiple files as a batch process, the setup can be complex (e.g., requiring the installation of macros in the case of Microsoft Office or creating an automated task within Adobe Acrobat). Another downside in the case of PDF to text conversion is that the conversion is inherently "noisy", with the plain text version of the files sometimes containing misaligned sentences (resulting from column data in the PDF) as well as including headers and footers from the original file. One way to deal with this noise is with an additional tool in the form of a good text editor with batch level search-and-replace functions (e.g., Notepad++[6] on Windows and TextWrangler[7] on Mac). An internet search will also reveal that there are numerous dedicated data cleaning tools, such as OpenRefine,[8] which can be helpful. However, most dedicated cleaning tools are designed to handle data in a tabular (spreadsheet) format.

Dedicated tools to batch convert multiple file formats into .txt files also exist. One easy-to-use, freeware, multiplatform (Win/Mac/Linux) tool in this category is AntFile-Converter[9] (see Figure 35.2). AntFileConverter is able to batch convert .docx and .pdf files through a drag-and-drop interface, with the resulting converted files appearing in a sub-folder where the original files were stored. This makes it ideal for vocabulary researchers without a technical background who want to quickly create a corpus, based for example, on research papers downloaded as PDF files from the internet, or learner essays created in-class on Microsoft Word. However, it cannot convert the older .doc file format of Microsoft Word or deal with the problem of noise when converting PDF files, limiting its use in some cases.

It should be noted that many online tools claim to do a similar job as AntFileConverter, but care should be taken when using them as it is not always clear how the developer will use the uploaded data. Similarly, many other freeware offline tools exist that can convert files. Again, however, care needs to be taken to ensure that they do not contain malware such as viruses, which can be a common hazard when downloading and installing utility programs of this kind.

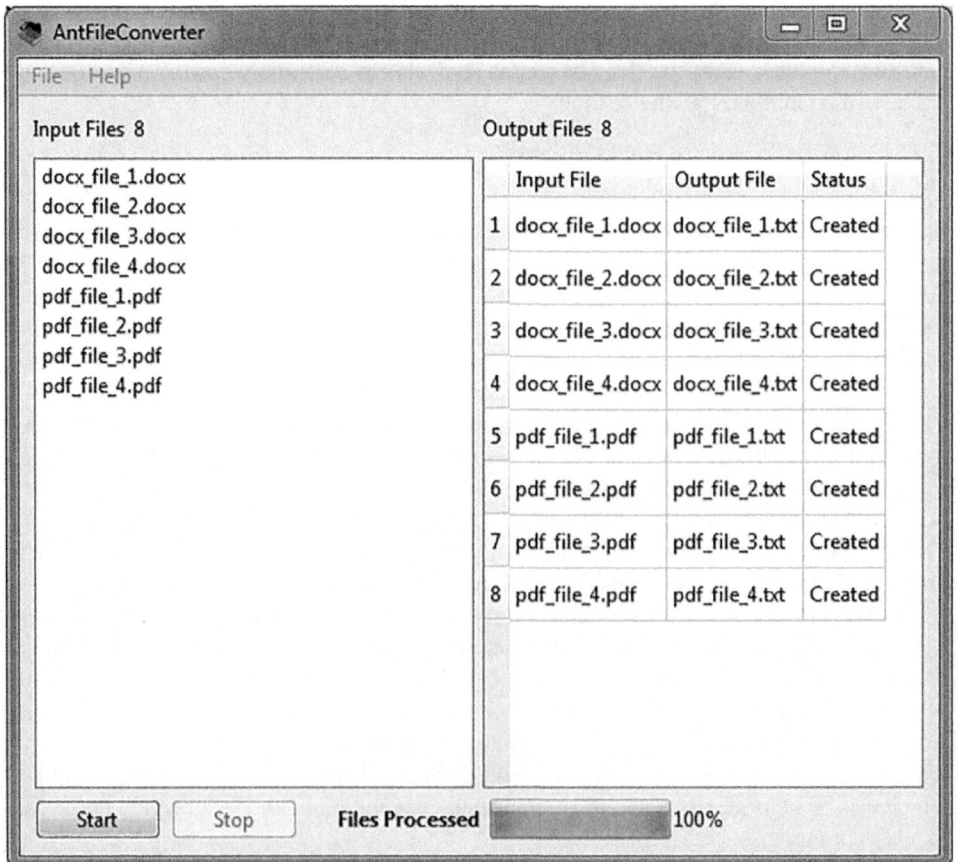

Figure 35.2   Screenshot of AntFileConverter converting PDF/docx files to plain text (.txt)

Web-Scraping Tools

A common approach to collect huge amounts of target language data is to "scrape" it directly from websites and other internet sources using dedicated web-scraping tools (Fairon, Naets, Kilgariff, & de Schryver, 2007). To use these tools, it is usually necessary to supply a set of "seed" search terms that are used by the web-scraping tool to collect relevant web pages (in the same way a standard search engine produces hits in the browser). Next, the tool searches through these pages for links to additional web pages. Once a complete set of links is created, the tool proceeds to download each webpage, extract the text data from a webpage, and store the new data in a folder. Figure 35.3 shows a screenshot of the interface to one of the most popular tools for creating corpora through web-scraping called BootCaT.[10]

Corpora that are created using web-scrapers are often described as "quick-and-dirty" (Nesselhauf, 2007), as they can contain unrelated webpage data, duplicate pages, and a host of other noise, such as headers, footers, links, and advertisements. The results can be greatly improved through a process of data "cleaning" (e.g., deleting duplicates) and some tools attempt to do this automatically. Some web-scraping tools (including BootCaT) will attempt to automatically remove some of this noise, but again, a good text editor or dedicated data cleaning tool can be extremely useful to help with this process.

The AntCorGen Corpus Creation Tool

One interesting software tool that offers an alternative to creating corpora through potentially "noisy" file conversion or web-scraping is AntCorGen[11] (see Figure 35.4). This freeware, multiplatform tool is designed to create "clean" discipline-specific research article corpora by directly

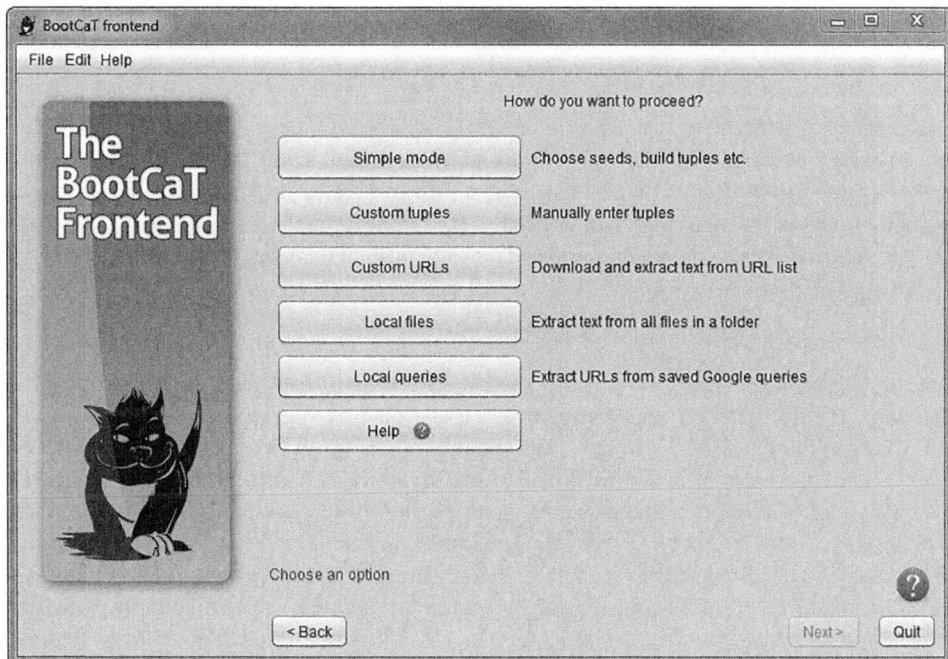

Figure 35.3   Screenshot of the BootCaT Frontend tool for web-scraping corpus data

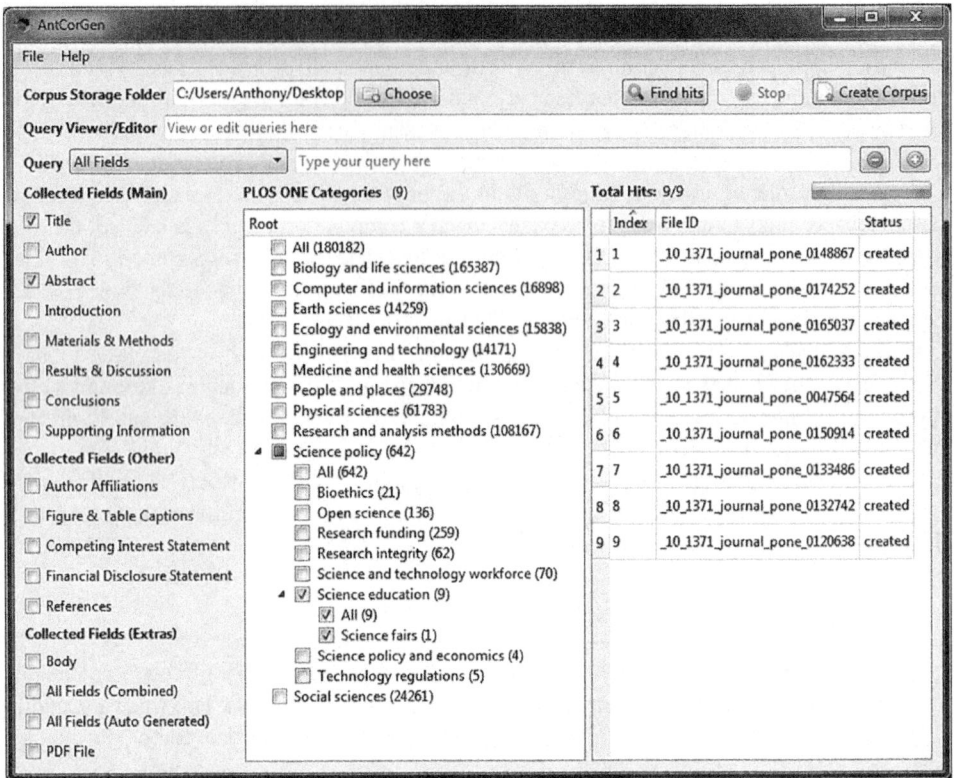

Figure 35.4 Screenshot of AntCorGen in the process of collecting data from the *PLOS One* open access scientific journal

communicating with the database behind the *PLOS One*[12] open access scientific journal. The language data obtained via AntCorGen is not only completely clean, but it can also be automatically saved to folders that match the section of the original article (e.g., title, introduction, method, results, discussion) from where it came. This allows for very refined analyses of vocabulary at the discourse level without the need for time-consuming manual annotation of the data.

The FireAnt Social Media Data Collection and Analysis Tool

Recent interest in the language of social media (e.g., Twitter, Facebook, Instagram) has led to a slew of new software tools that can collect and analyze this type of data. One way to collect social media data is through commercial collection services such as DataSift[13] or Gnip[14]. These services offer access to historical data as well as "fire-hose" collection methods, which allow all available data from a source to be collected in real time. However, the costs involved tend to favor those working in companies and large, well-funded academic institutions. One alternative to commercial tools is the freeware, multiplatform (Win, Mac, Linux) FireAnt tool.[15] This tool is designed to collect Twitter social media on particular topics or posted by individual users. It can also clean and filter the collected data in terms of topic or user and output the data in a form that can be used by traditional corpus analysis toolkits (described later in this chapter). FireAnt can also be used to carry out preliminary

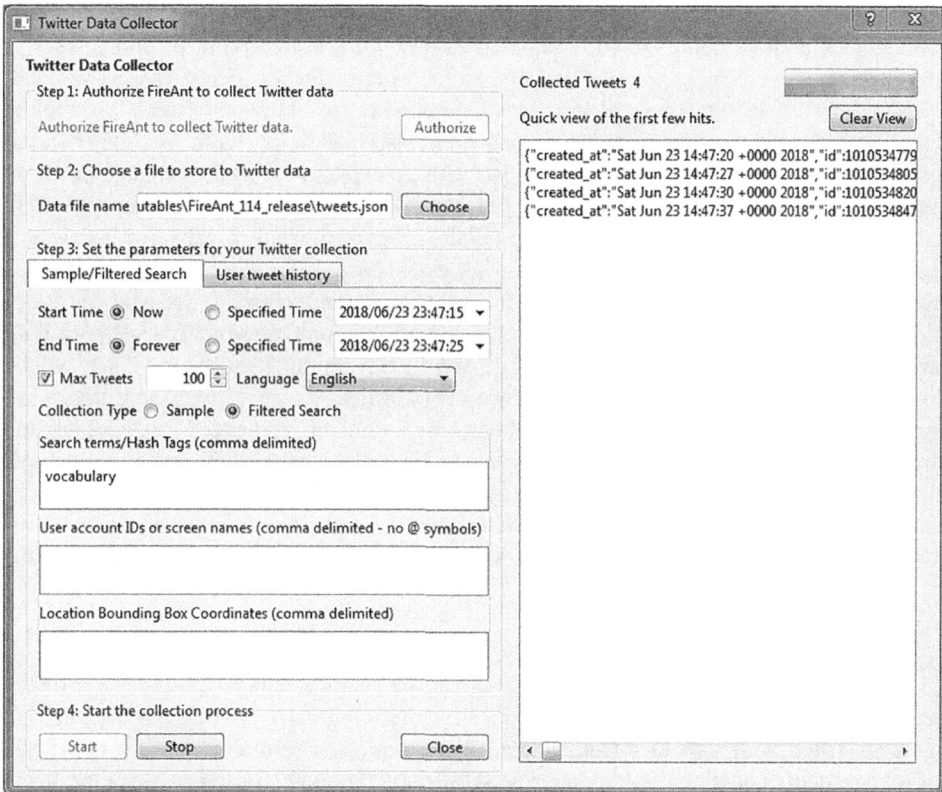

Figure 35.5 Screenshot of FireAnt in the processing of collecting data from Twitter under the search term "vocabulary"

analysis on the data and generate time-series plots, geo-positional maps, and network graphs that visualize social media language activity. However, it currently is not able to collect other social media data although it can analyze such data if loaded into the software. Figure 35.5 shows FireAnt during the collection of Twitter "tweets" related to the topic of "vocabulary".

Word Lists Serving as Secondary Data for Vocabulary Research

Raw language data in the form of a corpus may lie at the heart of many vocabulary research studies. However, an equally important resource for many vocabulary researchers is the secondary data that emerges from an analysis of vocabulary in a large-scale general or specific-language corpus. This secondary data is made available for use by researchers (and also teachers and learners) in the form of ranked lists of single-words, multiword items, as well as headwords and their associated lemma forms (see Francis & Kučera, 1982), flemma forms (see McLean, 2017), or word-family members (see Bauer & Nation, 1993) that appear in the original primary data source.

In practice, most word lists are both automatically and manually processed in numerous ways to make them more useful. Raw lists may be cleaned of "noisy" words that result from the data collection process. They may also be filtered to remove low frequency words or appended with words that happen to not appear in the target corpus but are relevant for research or pedagogic purposes. Unfortunately, most descriptions of these secondary data sources lack enough details to fully understand how they were produced. Some descriptions even neglect to fully describe the primary data source from which they were derived.

Word lists derived from general and specialized corpora are commonly used by vocabulary researchers as a reference standard when analyzing target language. Word lists may be used individually or in combination with other lists that are explicitly related or created based on similar assumptions, e.g., the Academic Word List of Coxhead (2000) serving as a supplement to the General Service List (GSL) of West (1953). One use for individual word lists is as a replacement for a full-text reference corpus when calculating "keywords" from a target corpus (see Bondi & Scott, 2010), especially when the full-text reference corpus is not available due to copyright or other reasons. One of the most common uses for multiple word lists is for profiling target texts to establish a quantitative measure of difficulty. In this case, the word lists will be divided into a series of "levels" based on a measure of difficulty such as frequency, dispersion, "range", or a combination of these. If the coverage of words in the "easy" levels is high, the target texts can be assumed to have a low difficulty level. Conversely, if the coverage of words in the "easy" levels is low and the target texts have a higher percentage of "difficult" level or "out-of-level" words, they can be deemed to be more difficult (for a discussion of vocabulary coverage, see Dang, this volume; Nation, 2001; Vilkaitė-Lozdienė and Schmitt, this volume).

Characteristic Features of Word Lists

As with primary corpus resources, word lists can be usefully categorized in terms of the language variety and user(s) represented in the underlying corpus. They can also be categorized in terms of unit of counting (e.g., word, lemma, flemma, multiword item), the number of items contained, the number of sub-levels, the method used to order the items (e.g., alphabetical, frequency, range, frequency/range), the format and availability (e.g., free or commercial), and perhaps most importantly, the purpose of the list and its intended audience (Nation, 2016). The characteristic features or word lists are summarized in Table 35.4.

Table 35.4 Summary of characteristic features of word lists

Language variety of underlying corpus
Written (e.g., research articles), spoken (e.g., conversation)
General purpose, specific-purpose (e.g., academic, workplace)
Synchronic (e.g., 2018), diachronic (e.g., 1900s–2000s)
Monolingual (e.g., English), multilingual (e.g., English and French)
Language users represented in underlying corpus
Learner (beginner), learner (intermediate), learner (advanced), near-native, native
Unit of counting
E.g., word, lemma, flemma, multiword item
Number of items and sub-levels
E.g., ten 1,000-item sub-levels
Method of ordering
E.g., random, alphabetical, frequency, range/dispersion
Format and availability
E.g., Microsoft Excel spreadsheet (free download), plain text file (paid license)
Purpose and target audience
E.g., language learning (university students), text profiling (vocabulary researchers)

Examples of Resources From Different Word List Categories

As was discussed in the section describing corpus resources, an ever-growing number of word lists is becoming available to vocabulary researchers. Many of these can be easily found through an internet search (e.g., "general English word list"), but some of the lists returned will be created ad hoc and designed as language learning resources for use by learners. As a result, it can be useful to refer directly to sites dedicated to corpus and vocabulary research that catalog commonly used research oriented word lists, such as the following (as of June 2018):

- http://martinweisser.org/corpora_site/CBLLinks.html (word lists are included in the category of "software")
- www.vocabulary.com/lists/

A review of vocabulary literature reveals that a rather select set of word lists dominate much of the current work. The word lists associated with English vocabulary research are summarized in Table 35.5 with a brief synopsis of their defining features and a definitive research publication describing their design and potential uses (if available).

Table 35.5 Prominent word lists used in (English) vocabulary research

General Service List (GSL)	Access location
	• http://jbauman.com/aboutgsl.html
	Features
	Unit of counting: word family
	Number of items and sub-levels: 2,284 headwords (one level)
	Method of ordering: (loosely) frequency-based
	Relevant research publication
	West, M. (1953). *A General Service List of English words*. London, UK: Longman.
Academic Word List (AWL)	Access location
	• www.victoria.ac.nz/lals/resources/academicwordlist
	Features
	Unit of counting: word family
	Number of items and sub-levels: 570 headwords (10 sub-levels)
	Method of ordering: frequency-based
	Relevant research publication
	Coxhead, A. (2000). A new Academic Word List. *TESOL Quarterly, 34*(2): 213–238.
The New General Service List	Access location
	• https://academic.oup.com/applij/article/36/1/1/226623#supplementary-data
	Features
	Unit of counting: lemma
	Number of items and sub-levels: 2,122 headwords (1 level)
	Method of ordering: frequency-based
	Relevant research publication
	Brezina, V., & Gablasova, D. (2015). Is there a core general vocabulary? Introducing the New General Service list, *Applied Linguistics, 36*(1:1), 1–22.

(Continued)

Table 35.5 (Continued)

Academic Vocabulary List (AVL)	Access location • www.academicvocabulary.info/
	Features
	Unit of counting: lemma
	Number of items and sub-levels: 3,000 headwords (1 level)
	Method of ordering: frequency-based
	Relevant research publication
	Gardner, D., & Davies, M. (2013). A new academic vocabulary list. *Applied Linguistics, 35*(3), 305–327.
Academic Formulas List (AFL)	Access location • www.eapfoundation.com/vocab/academic/afl/
	Features
	Unit of counting: multiword unit
	Number of items and sub-levels: 607 items (1 level)
	Method of ordering: formula teaching worth (FTW)
	Relevant research publication
	Simpson-Vlach, R., & Ellis, N. C. (2010). An academic formulas list: New methods in phraseology research. *Applied linguistics, 31*(4), 487–512.
The Academic Spoken Word List	Access location • https://osf.io/gwk45/
	Features
	Unit of counting: flemma
	Number of items and sub-levels: 1,741 items (4 levels)
	Method of ordering: frequency
	Relevant research publication
	Dang, T. N. Y., Coxhead, A., & Webb, S. (2017). The Academic Spoken Word List. *Language Learning, 67*(4), 959–997.
The Essential Word List	Access location • www.edu.uwo.ca/faculty-profiles/stuart-webb.html
	Features
	Unit of counting: flemma
	Number of items and sub-levels: 800 items (13 level + 1 function words level)
	Method of ordering: frequency
	Relevant research publication
	Dang, T. N. Y., & Webb, S. (2016). Making an essential word list for beginners. In I. S. P. Nation, *Making and using word lists for language learning and testing* (pp. 153–167, 188–195). Amsterdam: John Benjamins.

Software Tools for Probing Primary and Secondary Data Sources to Reveal New Insights on the Nature of Vocabulary

Much vocabulary research is concerned with achieving one or more of the aims listed in Table 35.1. To carry out such research, two types of software are used throughout the field. The first type is a vocabulary profiling tool. This takes one or more ready-built word list and applies it to a target corpus, measuring the frequency of occurrence and dispersion of items, counting items that are absent from the lists, and a host of other statistical measures. Through this process it is possible to establish the general importance of individual items, identify categories of vocabulary (e.g., general, academic, technical vocabulary), identify characteristic features of language in specialized disciplines, and quantitatively measure the complexity of target texts through using coverage as a metric.

The second type of software tool commonly used by vocabulary researchers is a corpus analysis toolkit. Corpus analysis toolkits offer a range of functions that can probe texts at the micro level (suffixes, affixes, words, phrases) and macro level (paragraphs, sections, complete texts) providing information about word/phrase associations, the connections between form, meaning, and usage, and the ways that language functions in spoken and written contexts. They can also be used to compare the vocabulary knowledge of native and non-native speakers and track the growth in the size and depth of vocabulary knowledge across different target groups, helping researchers to see the connections between vocabulary knowledge and other aspects of language proficiency (e.g., in reading, writing, listening, and speaking), and providing insights on how to integrate vocabulary into teaching and learning methodologies.

Currently, a surprisingly limited number of vocabulary profiling tools and corpus analysis toolkits are used widely in the vocabulary research community. These will be discussed in the following section.

Vocabulary Profiling Tools

One of the earliest and still commonly used vocabulary profiling tools is the freeware, Windows-based RANGE program[16] (see Figure 35.6). This tool provides a simple way to profile English texts against one or more word lists, with one version including the General Service List (GSL) and Academic Word List (AWL), another version including frequency derived lists from the British National Corpus (BNC), and another version including frequency derived lists from a combination of the BNC and Corpus of Contemporary American English (COCA). Performing a RANGE analysis of target texts requires simply loading

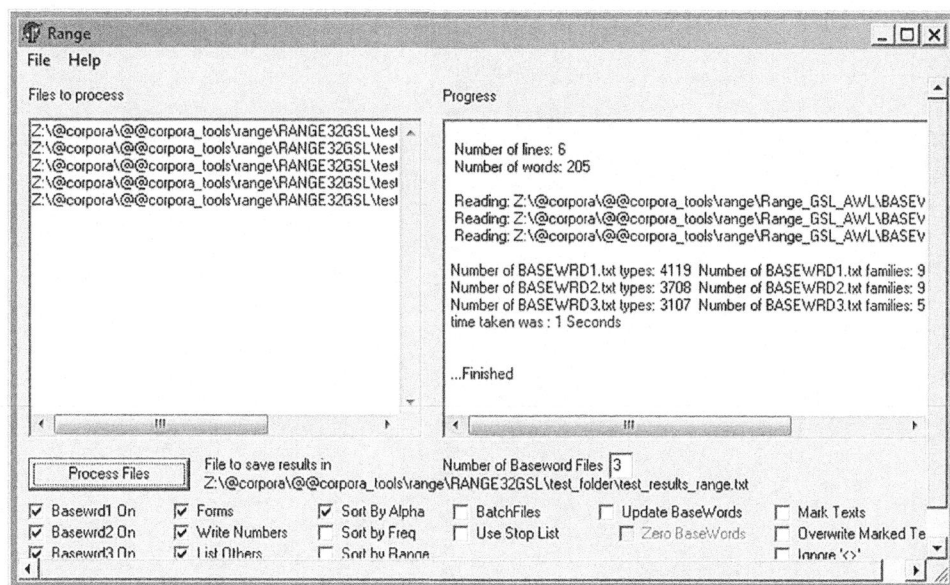

Figure 35.6 Screenshot of RANGE in the processing of five textbook chapters

plain text versions into the software, choosing a suitable file to save the results, and clicking the "Process Files" button to start the analysis. As RANGE is a very simple tool, researchers with even a very limited experience with computers will find it easy to use. On the other hand, the simplicity of RANGE can also be one of its downsides, as it is rather inflexible in terms of the word lists it accepts and the profile statistics it can produce. In addition, RANGE produces results in a format that does not lend itself well for further processing (e.g., in a spreadsheet program such as Microsoft Excel).

A more modern alternative to RANGE with numerous extra features is the AntWordProfiler tool[17] (see Figure 35.7). This freeware is a generic multiplatform (Win, Mac, Linux) tool that can profile target texts of any language with any number of word lists. The default tool includes the General Service List (GSL) and Academic Word List (AWL) to allow it to serve as a drop in replacement for RANGE. Moreover, numerous other word lists are provided directly on the tool website. The tool can be operated in an almost identical way to RANGE with the user only needing to load in a target corpus before pressing "Start". Results can be generated in an identical format to that of RANGE as well as in a tab-separated values (TSV) format that allows them to be copied directly into a spreadsheet program for further analysis. Importantly, AntWordProfiler can also provide a visual profile of individual texts from a target corpus with words from different levels highlighted in a variety of colors and the coverage values from the different levels shown numerically and

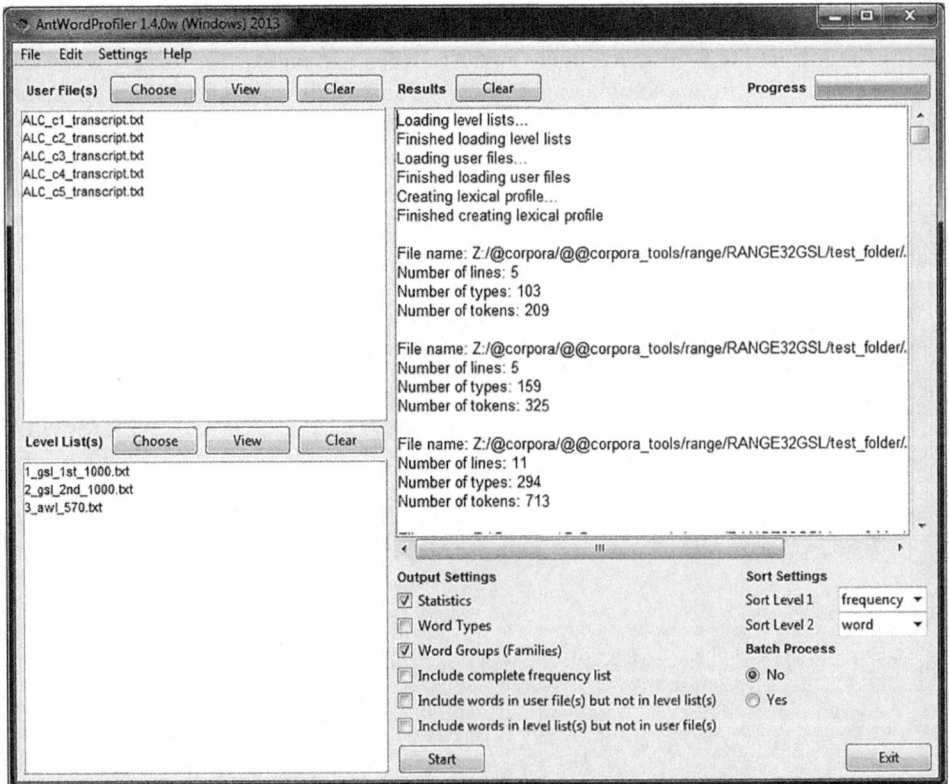

Figure 35.7 Screenshot of AntWordProfiler in the processing of five textbook chapters

User File: (ALC_c1_transcript.txt)

Chapter 1

Napoleon was a French soldier who became emperor of France. He was born in 1769 on the island of Corsica. When he was only ten years old, his father sent him to military school in France. Napoleon was not a very good student in most of his classes, but he excelled in mathematics and in military science. When he was sixteen years old, he joined the French army. In that year he began the military career that brought him fame, power, riches, and, finally, defeat. Napoleon became a general in the French army at the young age of 24. Several years later he became emperor of the French Empire.

Napoleon was many things. He was, first of all, a brilliant military leader. His soldiers were ready to die for him. As a result, Napoleon won many, many military victories. At one time he controlled most of Europe, but many countries, including England, Russia, and Austria fought fiercely against Napoleon. His defeat---his end---came when he decided to attack Russia. In this military campaign against Russia, he lost most of his army.

The great French conqueror died alone---deserted by his family and his friends---in 1821. He died in 1821, alone and deserted. Napoleon was only 51 years old when he died.

Token Coverage %
86.1

Level Coverage (%)
Level 1 80.9
Level 2 1.4
Level 3 3.8
Level 0 13.9

Total Hits 1
Hit Position 0
Local Freq 0

Prev Next

Save Options
⦿ None
○ Add Level Index Tags

Level List Words   Non-Level List Words   Save   Close

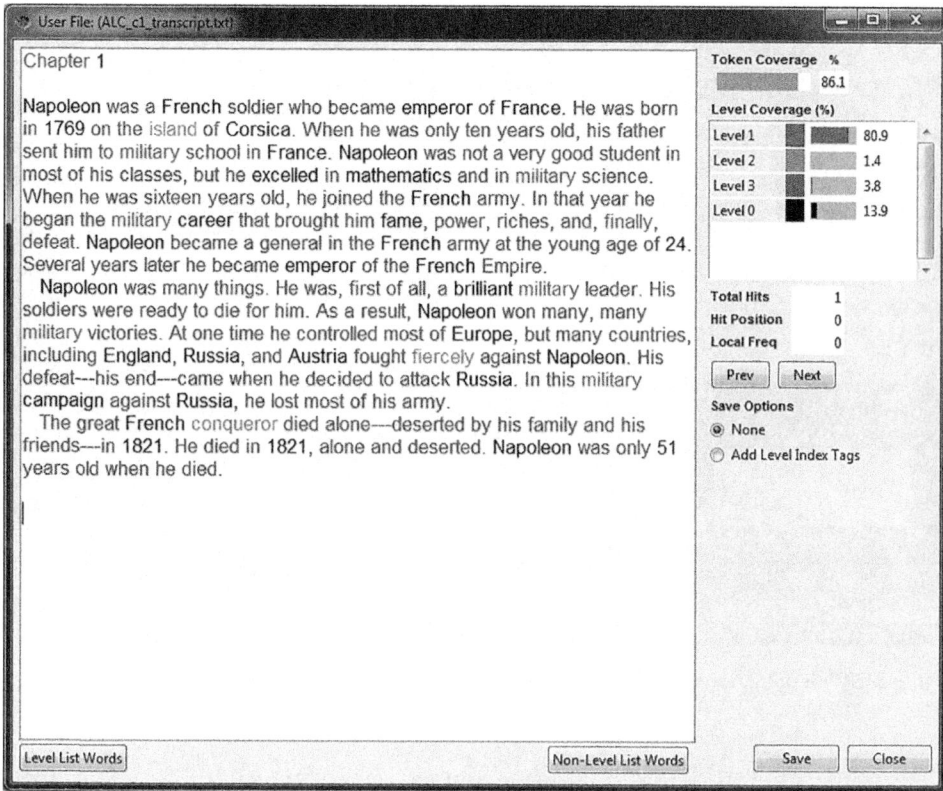

Figure 35.8 Screenshot of AntWordProfiler highlighting word levels in a single target corpus

as a bar chart (see Figure 35.8). This feature allows individual texts to be quickly compared. The same tool can also be used in an edit mode whereby vocabulary items at a particular level can be deleted or replaced in order to adjust the vocabulary load. Applications of this feature have already been seen in numerous vocabulary projects including the creation of mid-frequency readers for use in language teaching (Nation & Anthony, 2013). Although AntWordProfiler offers many advantages over RANGE, the additional flexibility of the tool can also be seen as a downside as the many options can sometimes be overwhelming to inexperienced users of computer software.

Numerous online tools are also able to profile texts. One commonly used tool in this category is Coh-Metrix,[18] which provides a simple interface to various word-, sentence-, paragraph-, and text-level statistics. Another popular tool is the Compleat Web VP tool, which is included as part of the Compleat Lexical Tutor[19] web application (see Figure 35.9). Although the interface to Compleat Web VP is rather complex, numerous research studies that cite it provide strong evidence of its value to the field. It should be noted, however, that most online profiling tools (including the Compleat Web VP tool) are limited in terms of the number of files they can process, the statistics they produce, and the output format of the results they generate. As a result, they are more generally geared towards pedagogic applications, such as profiling a small number of target texts for use in the classroom.

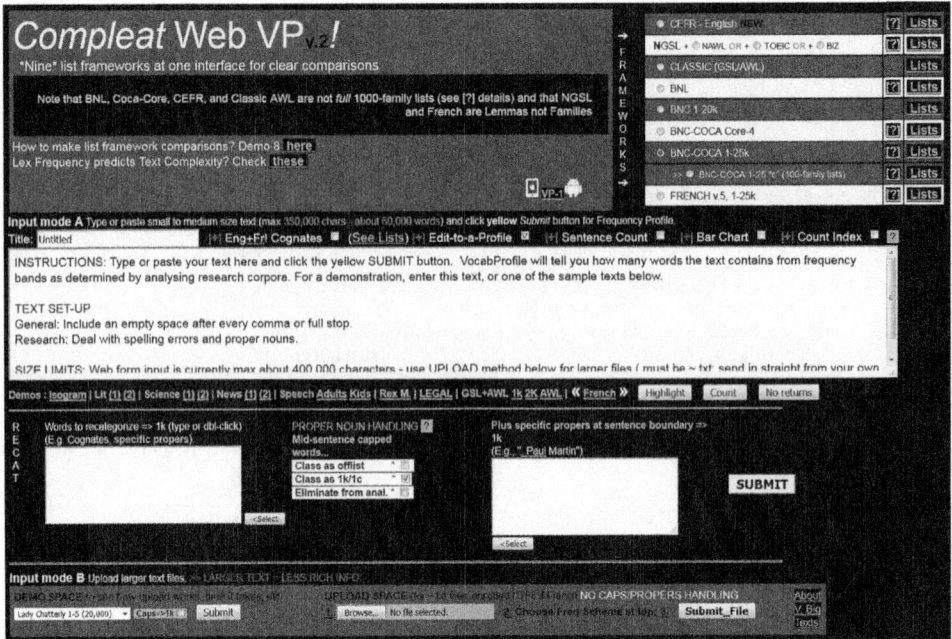

Figure 35.9 Screenshot of the Compleat Web VP tool for online vocabulary profiling

Online Corpus Analysis Toolkits

Corpus analysis toolkits can be divided into two distinct types. Online toolkits provide access to one or more ready-built corpora that may not be available through other means due to copyright and other restrictions. They also have a number of other strengths but also several weaknesses when it comes to performing vocabulary research. These are listed in Table 35.6.

One of the most widely used online corpus analysis toolkits is the corpus.byu.edu[20] (see Figure 35.10). The corpus.byu.edu tool offers access to large general English corpora, such as the Corpus of Contemporary American English (COCA), the Wikipedia Corpus, and the TIME Magazine Corpus. It provides access to historic corpora, including the Early English Books Online corpus, and the Hansard corpus, as well as monitor corpus, such as the News on the Web (NOW) corpus, which is updated daily. The system also contains numerous non-English corpora.

The search tools offered by corpus.byu.edu are relatively limited in number. The primary tools are word frequency searches, Key-Word-In-Context (KWIC) searches, collocate searches, and a collocate comparison tool. If the corpus contains historic data, it is also possible to display a chart showing the frequencies of search terms across time periods. It should be noted that the corpus.byu.edu will restrict users to a limited number of searches each day. Also, after 15 to 20 initial searches, the system will start to frequently request the user to complete a registration form. After registration, the number of daily searches will continue to be restricted unless the user pays a monthly or yearly fee. The system can thus be considered a form of commercial software.

Another popular online corpus analysis toolkit is Sketch Engine[21] (see Figure 35.11). The Sketch Engine tool is a commercial corpus analysis platform that adopts a standard

Table 35.6 Strengths and weaknesses of online corpus analysis toolkits

Strengths of many online tools:
- Direct access to corpora that may be inaccessible by any other means (e.g., due to copyright and other restrictions)
- Simple management of target corpora
- Cross-platform software compatibility (due to access via a standard internet browser)
- Fast processing (as a result of a well-designed corpus database architecture)
- Search functions that can be tailored towards the idiosyncrasies of embedded corpora and the metadata and annotation systems that they use

Weaknesses in many online tools:
- Inconvenient setup procedures (requiring registration and log in)
- A limited set of corpora that can be analyzed
- Limited (or restricted) access to the raw corpus data
- A limited number of analytical tools
- Poor support for exporting the results of analysis

corpus.byu.edu

home   corpora   users   related resources   my account   upgrade   help

Created by Mark Davies, BYU. **Overview**, search types, looking at variation, corpus-based resources, **updates**.

The most widely used online corpora -- more than 130,000 distinct researchers, teachers, and students each month.

English	# words	language/dialect	time period	compare
iWeb: The Intelligent Web-based Corpus **NEW!**	14 billion	US/CA/UK/IE/AU/NZ	2017	Info (PDF)
News on the Web (NOW)	6.0 **billion+**	20 countries / Web	2010-yesterday	
Global Web-Based English (GloWbE)	1.9 **billion**	20 countries / Web	2012-13	
Wikipedia Corpus	1.9 **billion**	English	-2014	Info
Hansard Corpus	1.6 **billion**	British (parliament)	1803-2005	Info
Early English Books Online	755 million	British	1470s-1690s	
Corpus of Contemporary American English (COCA)	560 **million**	American	1990-2017	★ ★ ★ ★ ★
Corpus of Historical American English (COHA)	400 million	American	1810-2009	★ ★
Corpus of US Supreme Court Opinions	130 million	American (law)	1790s-present	
TIME Magazine Corpus	100 million	American	1923-2006	
Corpus of American Soap Operas	100 million	American	2001-2012	★
British National Corpus (BYU-BNC)*	100 million	British	1980s-1993	★ ★
Strathy Corpus (Canada)	50 million	Canadian	1970s-2000s	
CORE Corpus	50 million	Web registers	-2014	
Other languages				
Corpus del Español (see also...)	2.1 billion	Spanish	1200s-1900s	★
Corpus do Português (see also...)	1.1 billion	Portuguese	1300s-1900s	
N-grams				
Google Books: American English	155 billion	American	1500s-2000s	★
Google Books: British English	34 billion	British	1500s-2000s	
Google Books: Spanish	45 billion	Spanish	1500s-2000s	

Figure 35.10a   Screenshots of the corpus.byu.edu online corpus analysis toolkit. Main interface to corpus.byu.edu

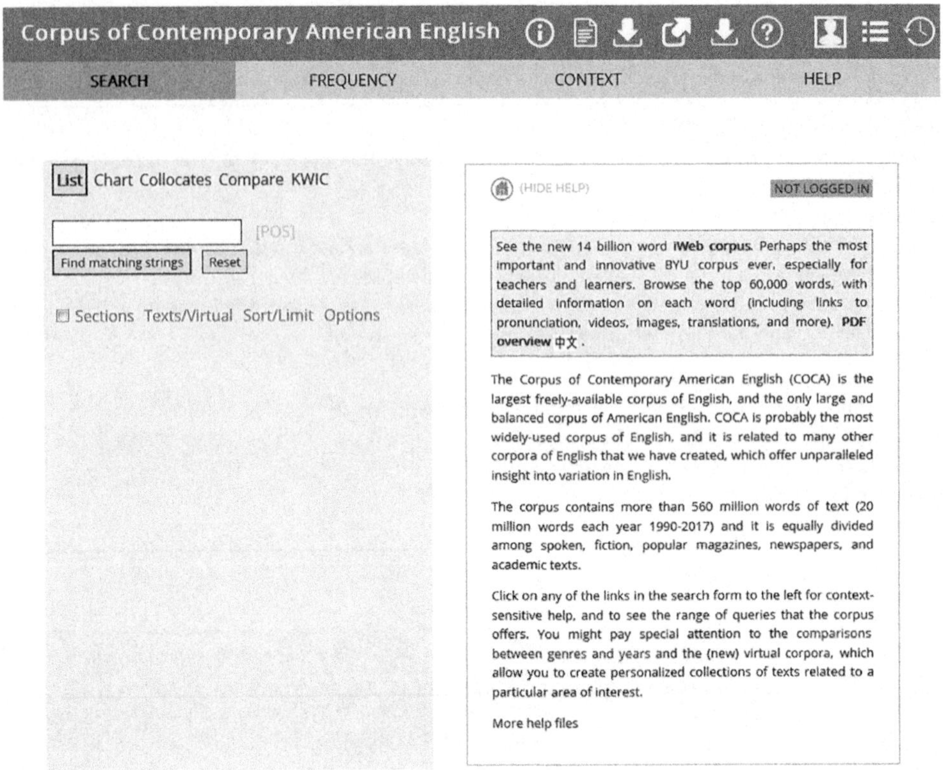

SEARCH   FREQUENCY   CONTEXT   HELP

List Chart Collocates Compare KWIC

[POS]

Find matching strings   Reset

Sections Texts/Virtual Sort/Limit Options

(HIDE HELP)   NOT LOGGED IN

See the new 14 billion word **iWeb corpus**. Perhaps the most important and innovative BYU corpus ever, especially for teachers and learners. Browse the top 60,000 words, with detailed information on each word (including links to pronunciation, videos, images, translations, and more). **PDF overview** 中文 .

The Corpus of Contemporary American English (COCA) is the largest freely-available corpus of English, and the only large and balanced corpus of American English. COCA is probably the most widely-used corpus of English, and it is related to many other corpora of English that we have created, which offer unparalleled insight into variation in English.

The corpus contains more than 560 million words of text (20 million words each year 1990-2017) and it is equally divided among spoken, fiction, popular magazines, newspapers, and academic texts.

Click on any of the links in the search form to the left for context-sensitive help, and to see the range of queries that the corpus offers. You might pay special attention to the comparisons between genres and years and the (new) virtual corpora, which allow you to create personalized collections of texts related to a particular area of interest.

More help files

Figure 35.10b   Main interface to the Corpus of Contemporary American English (COCA) sub-corpus of corpus.byu.edu

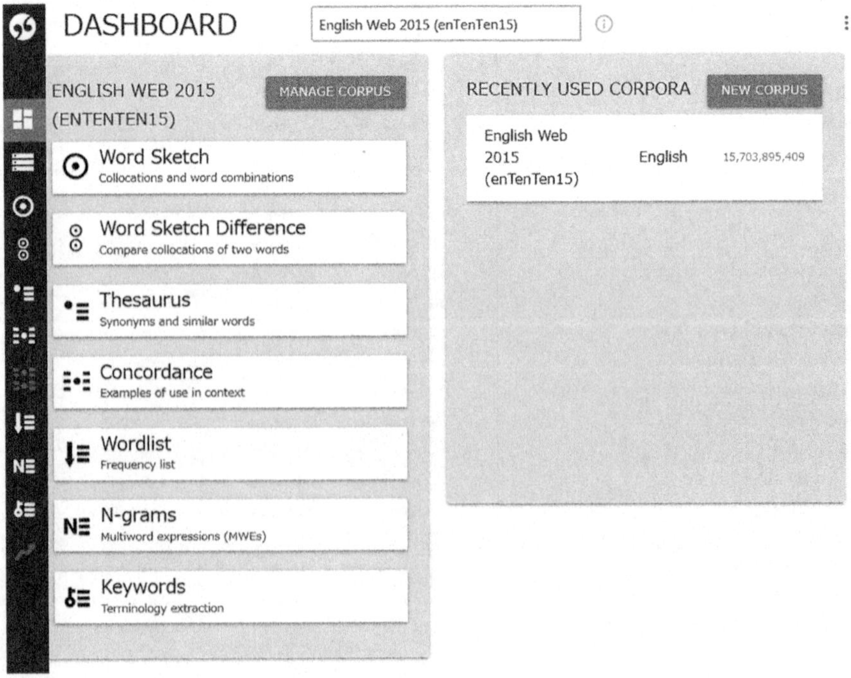

DASHBOARD   English Web 2015 (enTenTen15)

ENGLISH WEB 2015   MANAGE CORPUS   RECENTLY USED CORPORA   NEW CORPUS
(ENTENTEN15)

English Web 2015
(enTenTen15)   English   15,703,895,409

Word Sketch
Collocations and word combinations

Word Sketch Difference
Compare collocations of two words

Thesaurus
Synonyms and similar words

Concordance
Examples of use in context

Wordlist
Frequency list

N-grams
Multiword expressions (MWEs)

Keywords
Terminology extraction

Figure 35.11a   Screenshots of the Sketch Engine online corpus analysis toolkit. Main interface to Sketch Engine

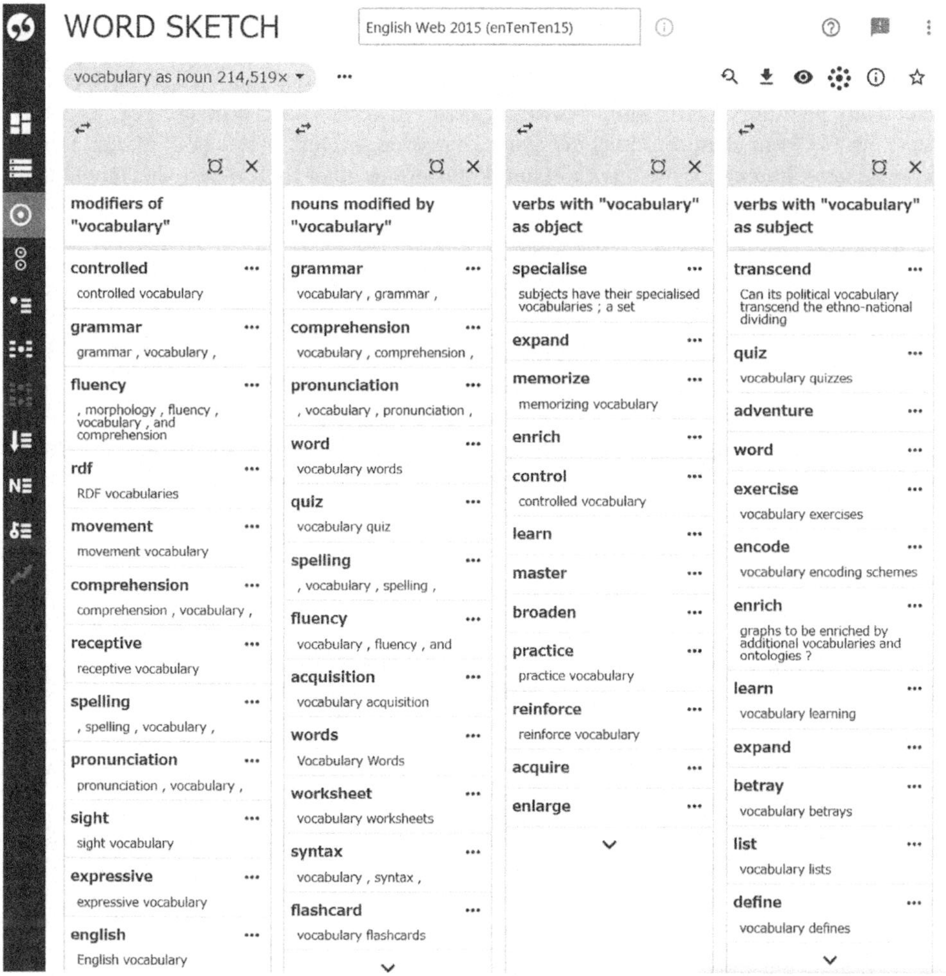

Figure 35.11b A "Word Sketch" result for the search term "vocabulary" in Sketch Engine

registration and license fee payment approach. The company hosts many hundreds if not thousands of corpora, with English corpora alone numbering over 60. While the majority of corpora in Sketch Engine require a payment to access, it does also offer a limited number of freely available corpora, some of which have been developed by university research groups using public funds and are hosted on the platform. Users are also able to upload a limited amount of their own data to Sketch Engine, allowing for the possibility of creating custom corpora.

Sketch Engine includes many equivalent tools to those offered by corpus.byu.edu. It also includes a number of additional tools with the "Word Sketch" tool being one of the most useful from a vocabulary research perspective. Word sketches are one-page summaries of the grammatical and collocational behavior of a search word. They enable a user to discover important features of a word without needing to carefully analyze numerous Key-Word-In-Context (KWIC) results. As an example, Figure 35.11b shows a Word Sketch for the word "vocabulary". Another useful tool in Sketch Engine is the "Word Sketch Difference" tool, which allows researchers to quickly see how various collocates relate more strongly or weakly to words with similar meanings (e.g., "clever" and "intelligent"). As Sketch Engine is a commercial tool, it does not limit the number of searches that a user can perform. Also, many institutions have site licenses for the tool meaning it can be used by individual researchers without charge. On the downside, however, the full, raw data of Sketch Engine corpora cannot be viewed directly or exported for use in other tools unless they are already released to the public.

Offline Corpus Analysis Toolkits

Offline corpus analysis toolkits provide users with a rich set of analysis tools with no restrictions on the number of searches performed or the corpora that can be analyzed, with the only condition being that they have been made available for open use by the corpus creators. Offline corpus analysis tools have a number of other strengths but also several weaknesses when it comes to performing vocabulary research. These are listed in Table 35.7.

WordSmith Tools[22] is a very popular commercial offline corpus analysis toolkit that runs on Windows systems (see Figure 35.12a). The software offers a rich set of analytical tools built around Key-Word-In-Context (KWIC) searches and their associated dispersion plots, collocations, and fix-string patterns, as well as word and keyword frequency counts, and concgrams (Cheng, Greaves, Sinclair, & Warren, 2008). All tools are explained in the detailed documentation provided with the tool.

Once a ready-built corpus has been loaded into WordSmith Tools, the full range of analysis tools become available. As an example, Figure 35.12b shows the results of a KWIC analysis of the word "many" in a corpus of textbook reading passages. Figure 35.12 also illustrates that the results of WordSmith Tools are highly detailed making the tool a good choice for vocabulary researchers who are looking for detailed statistical counts. However, one weakness of this tool is that it can sometimes be complicated to use, requiring many operations before the desired results are generated. Also, the detailed results produced by the tool can be considered by some to be difficult to interpret. The tool is also more geared towards the analysis of English language texts due to the way it handles file encodings and the definition of word tokens.

Table 35.7 Strengths and weaknesses of offline corpus analysis toolkits

Strengths of offline tools:
- Unrestricted access to open access corpora
- Cross-platform software compatibility (depending on the tool)
- Unlimited access to the raw corpus data
- A rich set of analytical tools
- Good support for exporting the results of analysis

Weaknesses of many offline tools:
- Complex management of corpora (stored on local storage media)
- Slower processing than high-end commercial tools that use advanced database storage systems
- Restricted corpora (e.g., as a result of copyright issues) cannot be used
- Limited searches based on metadata and annotations used in target corpora
- Complex setup procedures (e.g., downloading and installing the software)

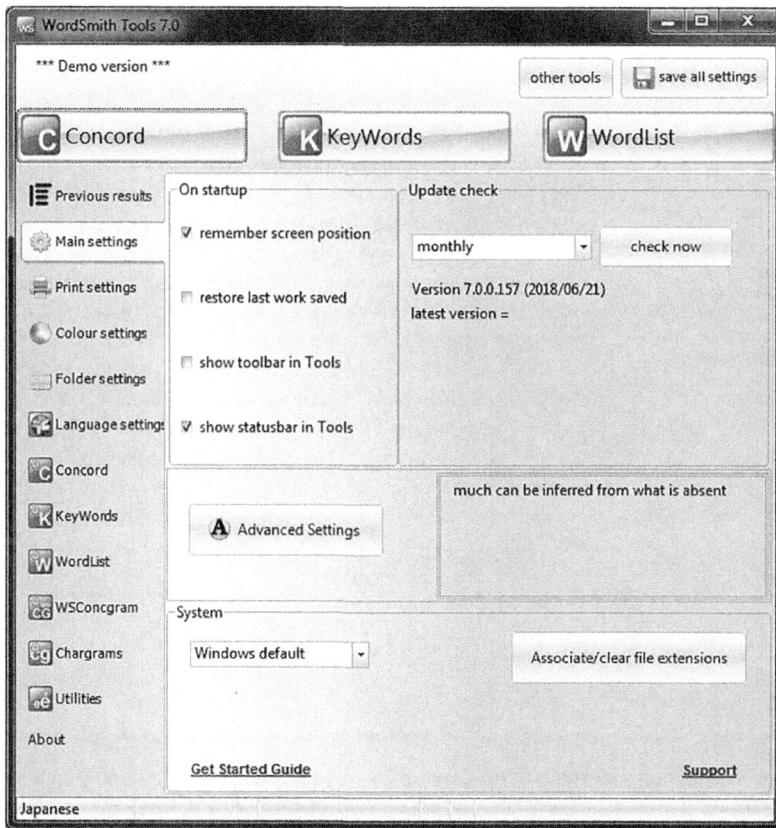

(a)

(b)

Figure 35.12 Screenshots of the WordSmith Tools offline corpus analysis toolkit. (a) Main interface to WordSmith Tools. (b) A Key-Word-In-Context (KWIC) result for the search term "many" in WordSmith Tools using a small corpus of textbook reading passages.

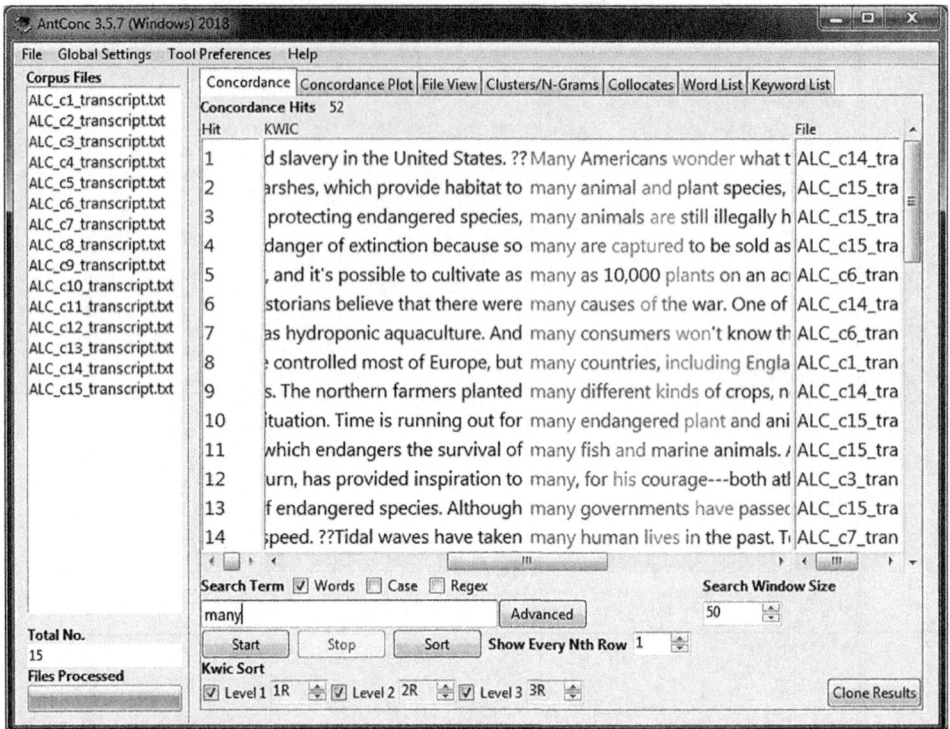

Figure 35.13 The main interface of AntConc showing a Key-Word-In-Context (KWIC) result for the search term "many" using a small corpus of textbook reading passages

AntConc[23] is a very popular freeware, multiplatform (Win, Mac, Linux), offline corpus analysis toolkit (see Figure 35.13). It offers a similar set of analytical tools to WordSmith Tools (with the exception of the concgram tool) and is designed from the outset to work smoothly with almost all languages of the world assuming they are written from left to right. This includes all European languages as well as Asian languages such as Chinese, Japanese, and Korean. AntConc also offers a cleaner, more intuitive interface that allows for rapid generation and interpretation of results. As with WordSmith Tools, all tools included in the software are explained in the detailed documentation provided with the tool. The developer also explains all the tools in a series of online YouTube tutorial videos (www.laurencean-thony.net/software/antconc/).

TAALES (Tool for the Automatic Analysis of Lexical Sophistication)[24] is another very useful offline lexical profiling tool. It provides 400 lexical sophistication indices, including coverage measures based on range and frequency similar to those of RANGE and AntWordProfiler, n-gram related measures, as well as psycholinguistic measures, such as familiarity, concreteness, imageability, and meaningfulness. Although TAALES provides no tools to visualize the results it produces, it does produce a simple .csv formatted table of the results that can then be processed using a spreadsheet program, such as Excel, a statistics package, such as SPSS,[25] or perhaps with a programming language such as Python[26] or R. Figure 35.14 shows the main screen of TAALES.

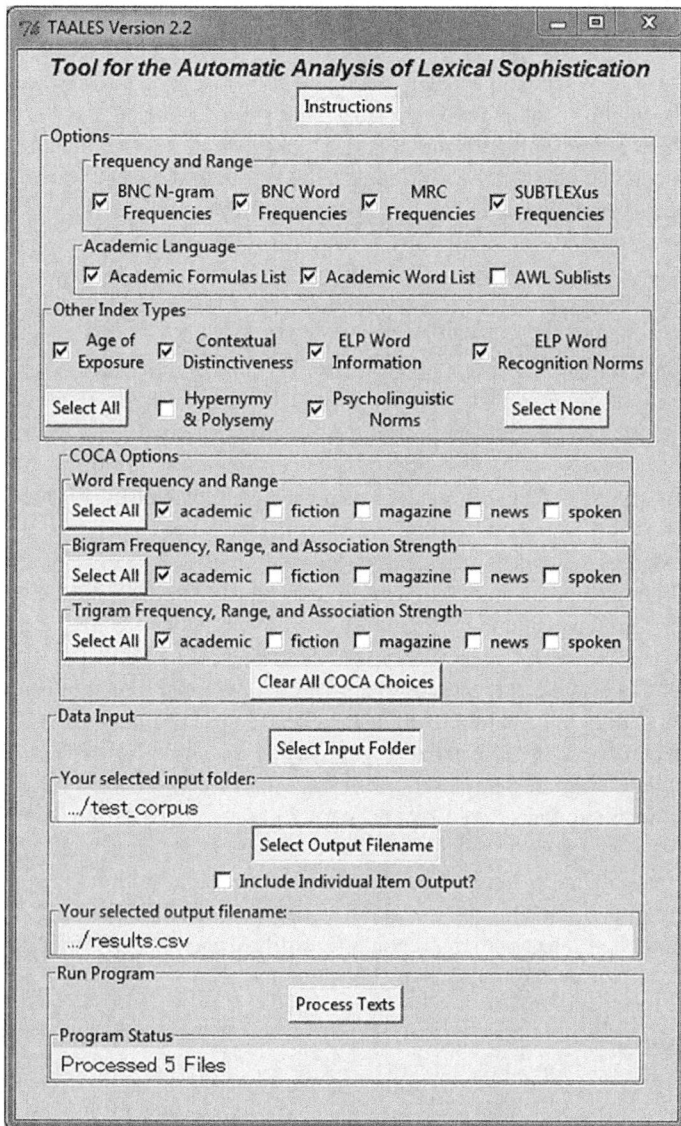

Figure 35.14 The main interface of TAALES

Future Directions

The current trend in vocabulary research is to use ready-built software tools and pre-compiled word lists to analyze existing and new primary corpus sources. As this chapter has shown, there is a wealth of such resources that can help researchers carry out interesting and valuable studies. On the other hand, as researchers become more adept at computer programming, using scripting languages such as Python and R,[27] there is a strong likelihood that the field will follow the path of corpus linguistics research and see the introduction of more custom-built tools and resources that are created to address specific research questions. Already we can see evidence of this trend in the reporting of results together with rigorous statistical analysis that necessitate the use of statistical packages, such as SPSS or R scripts. One related trend that, again, is already emerging in the field of corpus linguistics is for language researchers to collaborate more closely with software engineers and statisticians. These collaborations can lead not only to new and interesting research findings, but also new vocabulary tools and resources that can then be stored in language data and tool repositories, such as Clarin.[28]

A further common trend in vocabulary research is to analyze vocabulary in the form of isolated units, lemmas, and flemmas, with multiword items receiving little or no attention in much vocabulary research. This is a somewhat bizarre trend when the "idiom" principle (Erman, 2007; Erman & Warren, 2000; Sinclair, 2004) has been well documented and is used as a founding principle in much of mainstream corpus research. No doubt the tendency to relegate multiword items in an analysis is partially due to the lack of ready-built lists of multiword items and vocabulary profiling tools that can work with them. Fortunately, vocabulary tool developers have recently turned their attention to multiword items. As an example, AntGram[29] was recently released as a modern replacement for the powerful but dated kfNgram tool,[30] allowing researchers to generate positional-frame (p-frame) lists, which are contiguous sequences of words of varying length containing one or more open slots. As AntGram and other tools that can process multiword items become more widely known, there is a growing likelihood that multiword items will become the target of a new wave of vocabulary research.

One final set of vocabulary resources that is likely to see significant improvement in the coming years are tools to visualize relationships between vocabulary items. Currently, the majority of vocabulary studies visualize vocabulary relationships in the form of static lists (e.g., frequency lists, n-gram lists, collocate lists), with FireAnt being a notable exception. However, a growing number of web-based JavaScript data visualization frameworks allow for interesting presentations of data in the form of time-series plots, network graphs, and a host of other visualization forms. Some of these are listed at https://sonalake.com/latest/popular-open-source-javascript-frameworks-for-data-visualisation/. If these visualization tools can be integrated into popular vocabulary profiling and analysis tools, a new trend in the presentation of vocabulary research can be anticipated.

Further Reading

Godwin-Jones, R. (2010). Emerging technologies from memory palaces to spacing algorithms: Approaches to second-language vocabulary learning. *Language Learning & Technology*, *14*(2), 4–11.

Godwin-Jones' research article looks at various tools available in the early 2010s that facilitate vocabulary learning through mnemonics, spaced repetition, and electronic flash cards. The article is accompanied by links to 45 tools available at the time.

Anthony, L. (2013). A critical look at software tools in corpus linguistics. *Linguistic Research*, *30*(2), 141–161.

Anthony's research article takes a critical look at the development of traditional corpus tools and suggests ways in which future tools might be developed through a teamwork approach involving both applied linguists and computer scientists.

Meara, L., & Miralpeix, I. (2016). *Tools for researching vocabulary*. Bristol: Multilingual Matters.

Meara and Miralpeix's book on tools for researching vocabulary provides a detailed explanation of various easy-to-use, freeware tools developed by the authors that allow researchers to investigate lexical variation, sophistication, originality, as well as measure vocabulary size and growth. It also provides examples of how these tools can be used in research projects.

Related Topics

Corpus linguistics for vocabulary, programming for linguists, psycholinguistic approaches to vocabulary, vocabulary testing

Notes

1 *Scopus*. Accessed at: www.scopus.com
2 *PERC*. Accessed at: http://scn.jkn21.com/~percinfo/
3 *British National Corpus* (*BNC*). Accessed at: www.natcorp.ox.ac.uk/
4 *CHILDES* corpus. Accessed at: https://childes.talkbank.org/
5 *Shakespeare Corpus*. Accessed at: http://lexically.net/wordsmith/support/shakespeare.html
6 *Notepad++*. Accessed at: https://notepad-plus-plus.org/
7 *TextWrangler*. Accessed at: www.barebones.com/products/textwrangler/
8 *OpenRefine*. Accessed at: http://openrefine.org/
9 *AntFileConverter*. Accessed at: www.laurenceanthony.net/software/antfileconverter/
10 *BootCaT*. Accessed at: http://bootcat.sslmit.unibo.it/
11 *AntCorGen*. Accessed at: www.laurenceanthony.net/software/antcorgen/
12 *PLOS One*. Accessed at: http://journals.plos.org/plosone/
13 *DataSift*. Accessed at: https://datasift.com/
14 *Gnip*. Accessed at: http://support.gnip.com/
15 *FireAnt*. Accessed at: www.laurenceanthony.net/software/fireant/
16 *RANGE*. Accessed at: www.victoria.ac.nz/lals/resources/range
17 *AntWordProfiler*. Accessed at: www.laurenceanthony.net/software/antwordprofiler/
18 *Coh-Metrix*. Accessed at: http://tool.cohmetrix.com/
19 *Compleat Lexical Tutor*. Accessed at: www.lextutor.ca/
20 *corpus.byu.edu*. Accessed at: https://corpus.byu.edu/
21 *Sketch Engine*. Accessed at: www.sketchengine.eu/
22 *WordSmith Tools*. Accessed at: www.lexically.net/wordsmith/
23 *AntConc*. Accessed at: www.laurenceanthony.net/software/antconc/
24 *TAALES (Tool for the Automatic Analysis of Lexical Sophistication)*. Accessed at: www.linguisticanalysistools.org/taales.html/
25 *SPSS*. Accessed at: www.ibm.com/analytics/spss-statistics-software
26 *Python*. Accessed at: www.python.org/
27 R. Accessed at: www.r-project.org/
28 *CLARIN* (Common Language Resources and Technology Infrastructure). Accessed at: www.clarin.eu/
29 *AntGram*. Accessed at: www.laurenceanthony.net/software/antgram/
30 *kfNgram*. Accessed at: www.kwicfinder.com/*kfNgram*/kfNgramHelp.html

References

Bauer, L., & Nation, I. S. P. (1993). Word families. *International Journal of Lexicography, 6*(4), 253–279.

Biber, D., Conrad, S., & Reppen, R. (1998). *Corpus linguistics: Investigating language structure and use*. Cambridge, UK: Cambridge University Press.

Bondi, M., & Scott, M. (Eds.). (2010). *Keyness in texts*. Amsterdam: John Benjamins Publishing.

Cheng, W., Greaves, C., Sinclair, J. M., & Warren, M. (2008). Uncovering the extent of the phraseological tendency: Towards a systematic analysis of concgrams. *Applied Linguistics, 30*(2), 236–252.

Coxhead, A. (2000). A new academic word list. *TESOL Quarterly, 34*(2), 213–238.

Erman, B. (2007). Cognitive processes as evidence of the idiom principle. *International Journal of Corpus Linguistics, 12*(1), 25–53.

Erman, B., & Warren, B. (2000). The idiom principle and the open choice principle. *Text-Interdisciplinary Journal for the Study of Discourse, 20*(1), 29–62.

Fairon, C., Naets, H. Kilgariff, A., & de Schryver, G-M (2007). *Building and exploring web corpora (WAC3–2007): Proceedings of the 3rd Web as Corpus Workshop, Incorporating Cleaneval*. Belgique: Presses Universitaires De Louvain.

Francis, W., & Kučera, H. (1982). *Frequency analysis of English usage*. Boston, MA: Houghton Mifflin Company.

Hu, K. (2016). *Introducing corpus-based translation studies*. New York, NY: Springer.

McEnery, A. M., & Wilson, A. (2001). *Corpus linguistics: An introduction*. Edinburgh, UK: Edinburgh University Press.

McLean, S. (2017). Evidence for the adoption of the flemma as an appropriate word counting unit. *Applied Linguistics*. https://doi.org/10.1093/applin/amw050.

Nation, I. S. P. (2001). *Learning vocabulary in another language*. Cambridge, UK: Cambridge University Press.

Nation, I. S. P. (2016). Making word lists. In *The Vocab@Tokyo 2016 Handbook* (p. 34). Retrieved from http://vli-journal.org/wp/vocab-at-tokyo-handbook-2016/

Nation, I. S. P., & Anthony, L. (2013). Mid-frequency readers. *Journal of Extensive Reading, 1*(1), 5–16.

Nesselhauf, N. (2007). Diachronic analysis with the internet? Will and shall in ARCHER and in a corpus of e-texts from the web. *Language and Computers, 59*, 287–305.

Partington, A. (2010). Modern Diachronic Corpus-Assisted Discourse Studies (MD-CADS) on UK newspapers: An overview of the project. *Corpora, 5*(2), 83–108.

Schmitt, N. (2010). *Researching vocabulary: A vocabulary research manual*. New York, NY: Palgrave Macmillan.

Sinclair, J. (2004). The search for units of meaning. In J. Sinclair (Ed.), *Trust the text* (pp. 34–58). London, UK: Routledge.

West, M. (1953). *A general service list of English words*. London, UK: Longman, Green.

Index

Note: Page numbers in *italic* indicate a figure and page numbers in **bold** indicate a table on the corresponding page.

ability to learn 244, 419–428
Academic Keyword List (AKL) 101
Academic Vocabulary List (AVL) 99–101, **102**; and corpus-based word lists 289, **291**, 294–295, **294**, 297; and researching vocabulary **576**
academic word lists 24, 98–107, 113–114, 117, 194, **196–198**; and corpus-based word lists 289–290, **291**, 294–297, **294**; and learning single-word items 324, 334; and measuring lexical richness 462; and measuring vocabulary knowledge 555; and researching vocabulary 574, **575–576**, 577–578; and strategies for learning vocabulary 274, 284
Admiraal, W. 389
Adolphs, S. 37, 74, 390–391, 532
advanced words *463*, 463–464
Alali, F. 162, 164, 166
Altenberg, B. 447, 339
AntConc 7, 586, *586*
AntCorGen 571–572, *572*
AntFileConverter 570, *570*
Anthony, Laurence 7
AntWordProfiler 7, 72, 299, 470–471; and researching vocabulary *578*, 578–579, *579*, 586
assessment 3–4, 102–106, **257**, 257–258, 262–263, 387–388; and computer modeling 200–201; and researching multiword items 545–552; and researching single-word items 520–521
associated words 392, 468, **468**

Ballance, Oliver 92, 331
Barcroft, Joe 3–4; and aspects of vocabulary knowledge 25; and exercises for learning vocabulary 256, 262, 308, 360–362; and intentional vocabulary learning 242, 245–247; and S. Rott 128; and teaching single words 487–490

Beaton, A. 128–129, 488
Bečka, J. 113, 117
Biber, D. 36, 102–107, 393, 496–497
bilingualism *327*
bilingual lexicon 53–55, 57, 61, 442
bilingual testing 550–551
Boers, Frank 1, 3, 19, 121; and intentional vocabulary learning 244; and learning multiword items 146, 148, 150; and learning single words vs. multiword items 160; and learning vocabulary inside the classroom 256; and strategies for learning vocabulary 281; and teaching multiword items 501, 506
BootCaT Frontend 571, *571*
Brown corpus 89, *89*, **567**
Browne, C. 99, 101, 289, 297
Byrd, P. 102–104

Carter, Ron 104, 148, 165, 191
Choi, S. 148, 167
CLAN 469
Clapham, C. 106, 195
classification systems 482–484, **519**, 520
Cobb, Tom 3, 127, 201, 209, 325, 351, 551
COBUILD 36, 118, 198, 326, 328, 400
Coh-Metrix 9, 470
COLLEX 383, 390, 392–394, *393*, 401
COLLMATCH 383, 392–394, *394*, 401
collocation 6–7, 20–22, 26–32, 72–75, 102–103; and corpus-based word lists 290–292, 296–298; and exercises for learning vocabulary 362–365; and incidental vocabulary learning 228–235; and learning multiword items 143–146, 152–153, 339–347; and learning single-word items 330–332; and learning single words vs. multiword items 161–168; and measuring depth of vocabulary knowledge 371–383; and measuring knowledge of multiword items 390–400; and processing 176–179, 183–184;

Printed in Great Britain
by Amazon